NEGIMA!

OMNIBUS 5

Ken Akamatsu

TRANSLATED BY
Toshifumi Yoshida

ADAPTED BY
T. Ledoux & Ikoi Hiroe

LETTERING AND RETOUCH BY
Steve Palmer

A Kodansha Comics Trade Paperback Original.

Published in the United States by Kodansha Comics, an imprint of Kodansha USA Publishing, LLC, New York.

Publication rights for this English edition arranged through Kodansha Ltd., Tokyo.

First published in Japan in 2006 by Kodansha Ltd., Tokyo, as *Maho sensei Negima!* volumes 13, 14 and 15.

ISBN 978-1-61262-068-8

Printed in the United States of America.

www.kodanshacomics.com

9 8 7 6 5 4 3 2

Translator: Toshifumi Yoshida
Adaptor: T. Ledoux and Ikoi Hiroe
Lettering: Steve Palmer

CONTENTS

魔法先生

ネギま!

MAGISTER NEGI MAGI

13

赤松 健

Ken Akamatsu

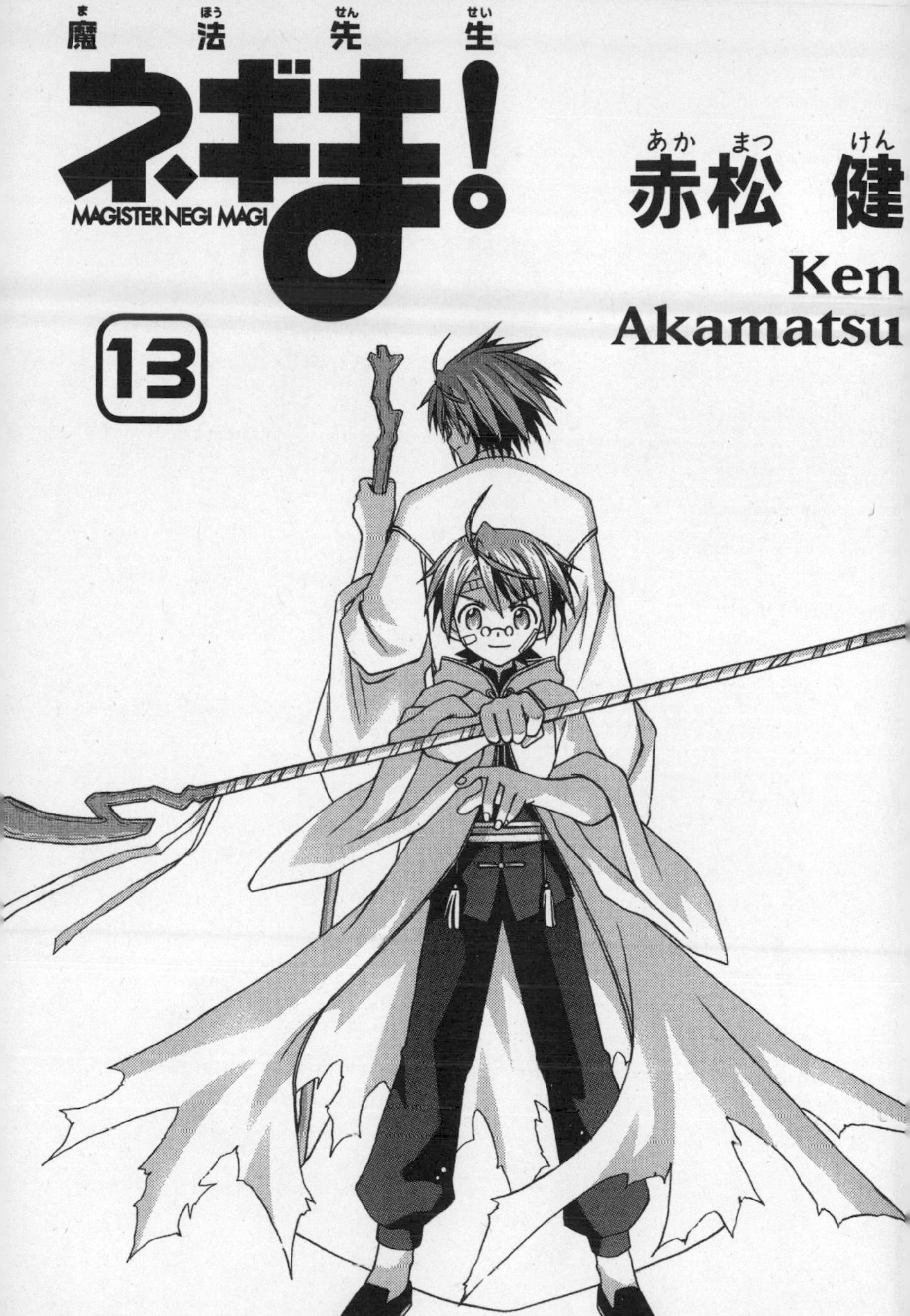

Contents

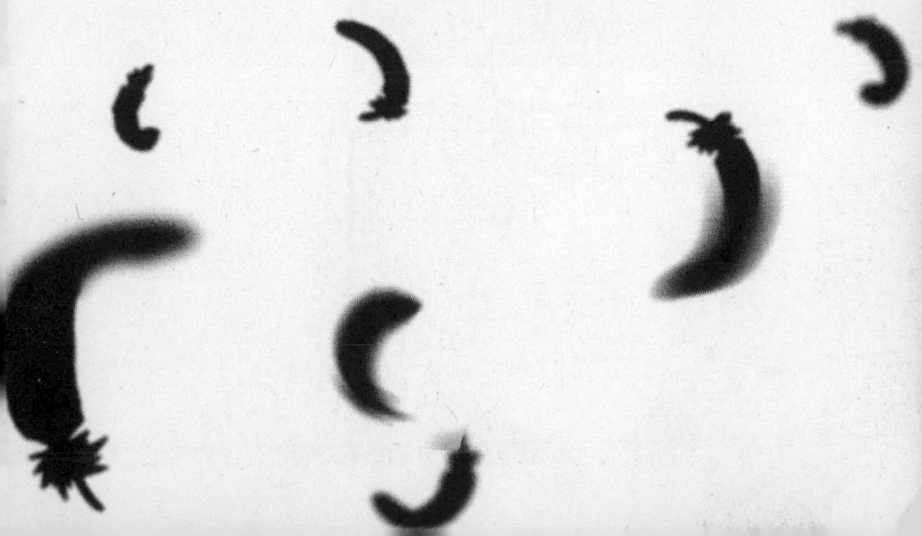

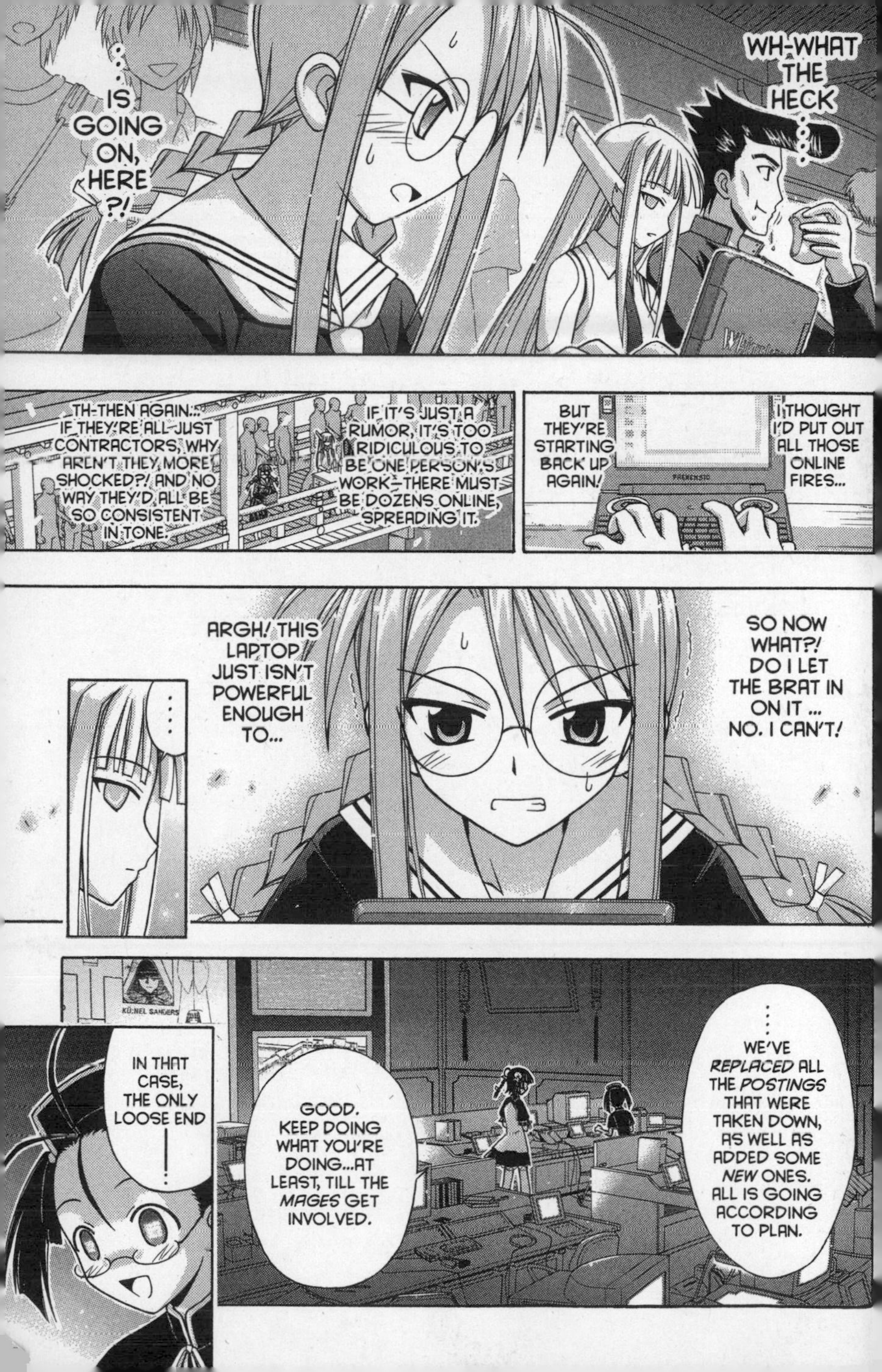
WH-WHAT THE HECK...
...IS GOING ON, HERE?!
I THOUGHT I'D PUT OUT ALL THOSE ONLINE FIRES...
BUT THEY'RE STARTING BACK UP AGAIN!
IF IT'S JUST A RUMOR, IT'S TOO RIDICULOUS TO BE ONE PERSON'S WORK–THERE MUST BE DOZENS ONLINE, SPREADING IT.
TH-THEN AGAIN... IF THEY'RE ALL JUST CONTRACTORS, WHY AREN'T THEY MORE SHOCKED?! AND NO WAY THEY'D ALL BE SO CONSISTENT IN TONE.
SO NOW WHAT?! DO I LET THE BRAT IN ON IT ... NO. I CAN'T!
ARGH! THIS LAPTOP JUST ISN'T POWERFUL ENOUGH TO...
....
...WE'VE *REPLACED* ALL THE *POSTINGS* THAT WERE TAKEN DOWN, AS WELL AS ADDED SOME *NEW* ONES. ALL IS GOING ACCORDING TO PLAN.
GOOD. KEEP DOING WHAT YOU'RE DOING...AT LEAST, TILL THE *MAGES* GET INVOLVED.
IN THAT CASE, THE ONLY LOOSE END —!

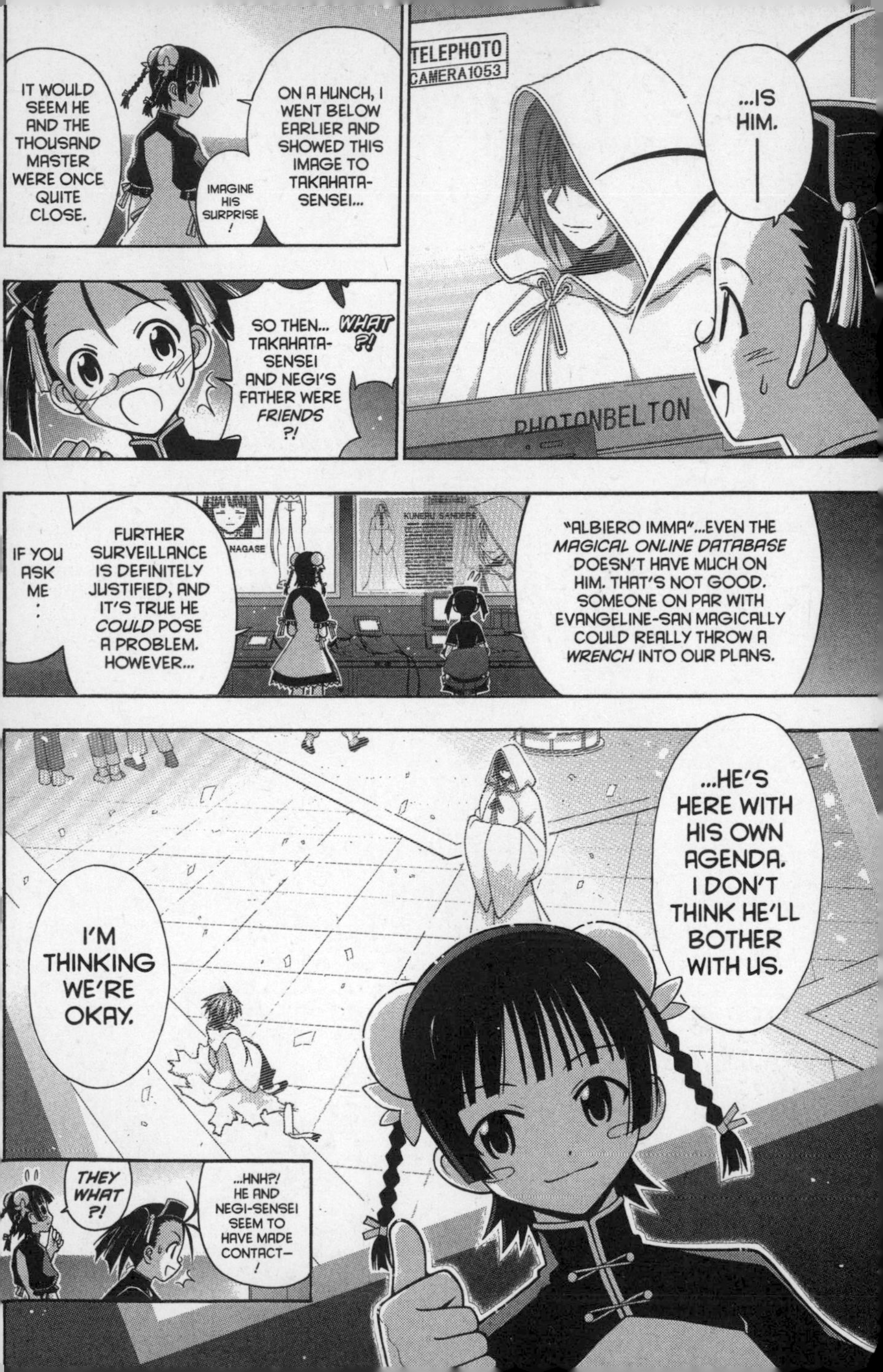
TELEPHOTO
CAMERA1053
...IS HIM.
PHOTONBELTON
ON A HUNCH, I WENT BELOW EARLIER AND SHOWED THIS IMAGE TO TAKAHATA-SENSEI...
IMAGINE HIS SURPRISE!
IT WOULD SEEM HE AND THE THOUSAND MASTER WERE ONCE QUITE CLOSE.
WHAT?!
SO THEN... TAKAHATA-SENSEI AND NEGI'S FATHER WERE *FRIENDS*?!
"ALBIERO IMMA"...EVEN THE *MAGICAL ONLINE DATABASE* DOESN'T HAVE MUCH ON HIM. THAT'S NOT GOOD. SOMEONE ON PAR WITH EVANGELINE-SAN MAGICALLY COULD REALLY THROW A *WRENCH* INTO OUR PLANS.
NAGASE
FURTHER SURVEILLANCE IS DEFINITELY JUSTIFIED, AND IT'S TRUE HE *COULD* POSE A PROBLEM. HOWEVER...
IF YOU ASK ME:
...HE'S HERE WITH HIS OWN AGENDA. I DON'T THINK HE'LL BOTHER WITH US.
I'M THINKING WE'RE OKAY.
...HNH?! HE AND NEGI-SENSEI SEEM TO HAVE MADE CONTACT—!
THEY WHAT?!

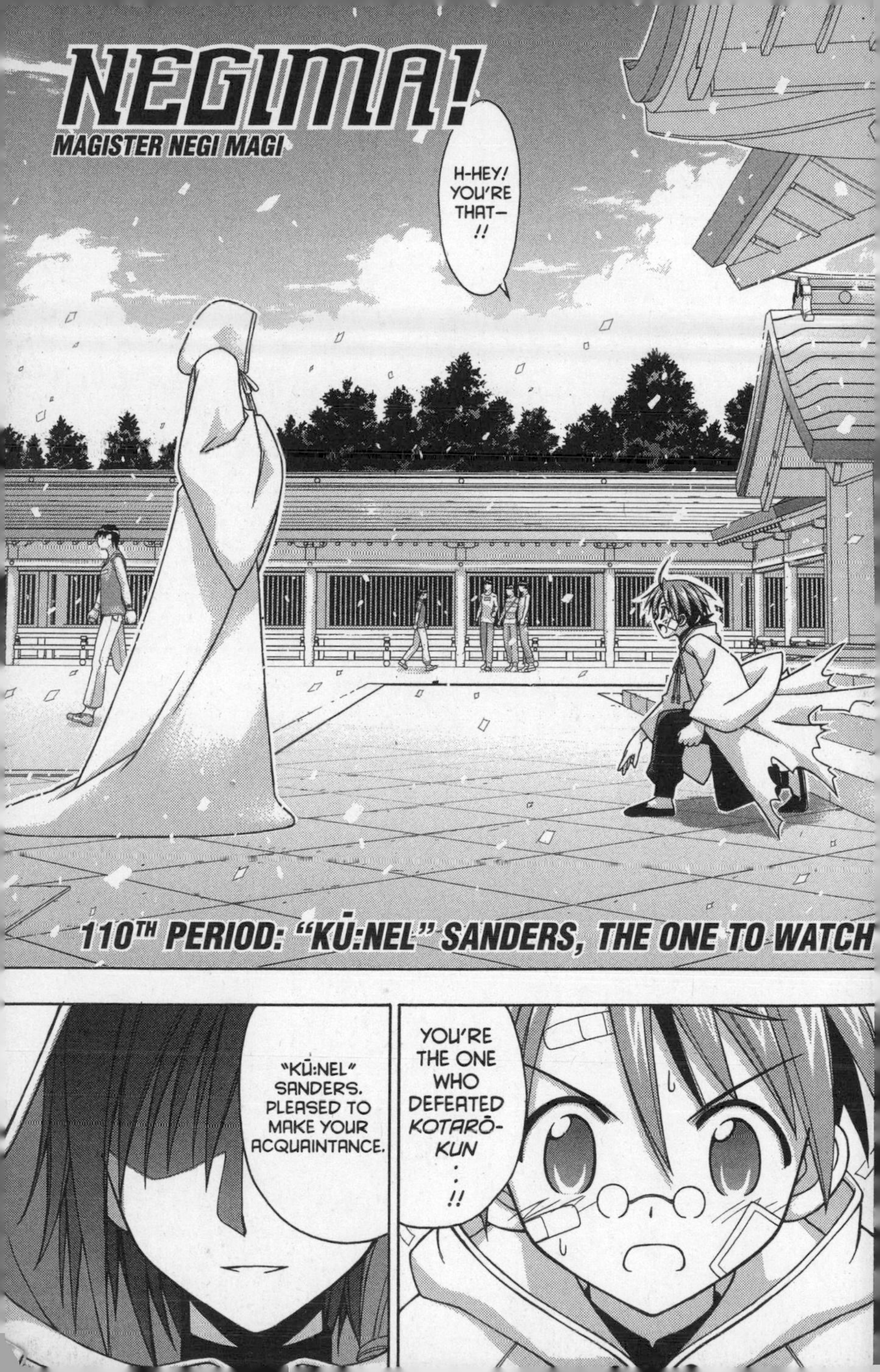
NEGIMA!
MAGISTER NEGI MAGI
H-HEY! YOU'RE THAT— !!
110TH PERIOD: "KŪ:NEL" SANDERS, THE ONE TO WATCH
YOU'RE THE ONE WHO DEFEATED KOTARŌ-KUN . . !!
"KŪ:NEL" SANDERS. PLEASED TO MAKE YOUR ACQUAINTANCE.

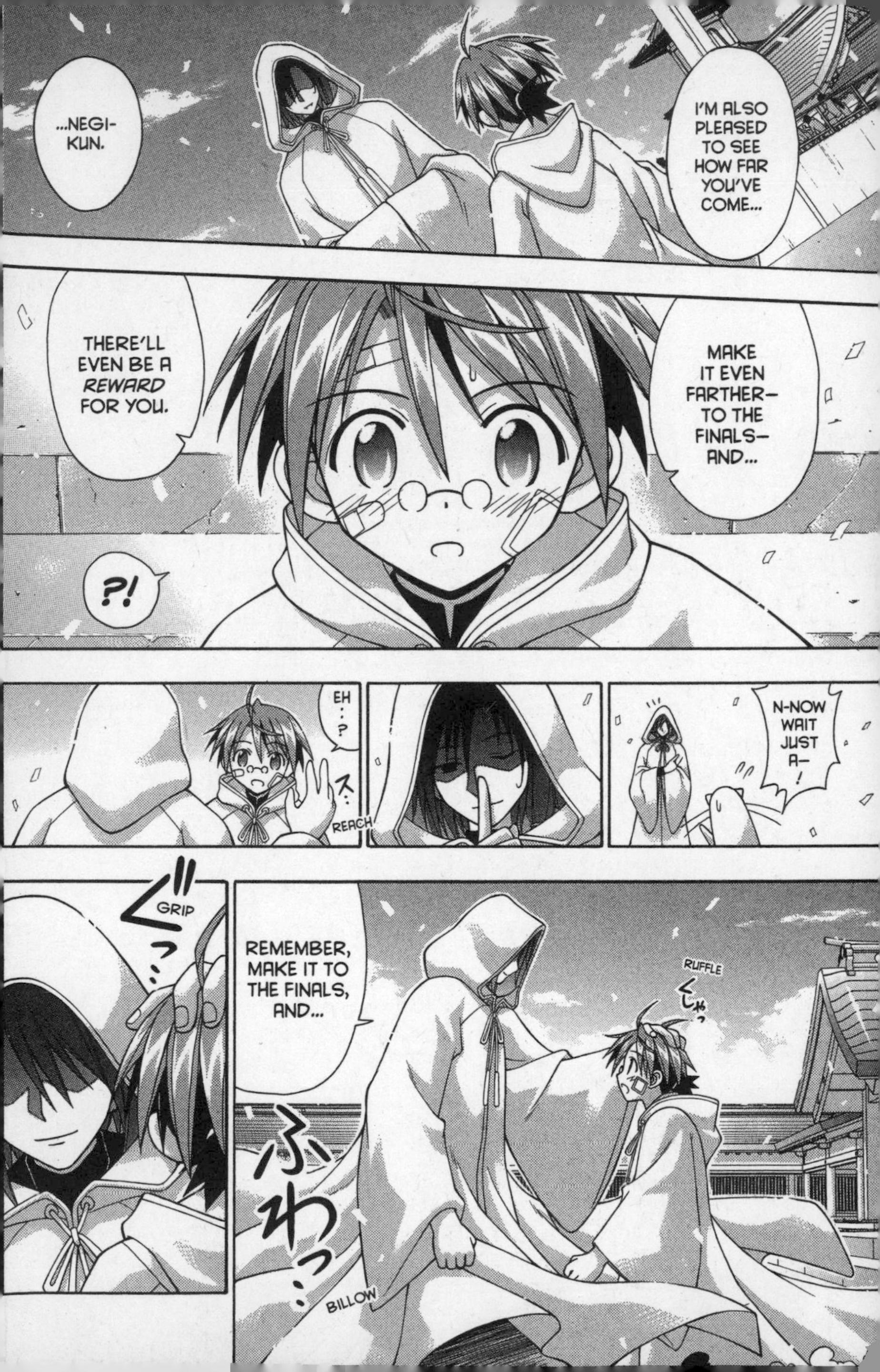
I'M ALSO PLEASED TO SEE HOW FAR YOU'VE COME...
...NEGI-KUN.
MAKE IT EVEN FARTHER— TO THE FINALS— AND...
THERE'LL EVEN BE A *REWARD* FOR YOU.
?!
N-NOW WAIT JUST A—!
EH...?
REACH
REMEMBER, MAKE IT TO THE FINALS, AND...
RUFFLE
BILLOW
GRIP

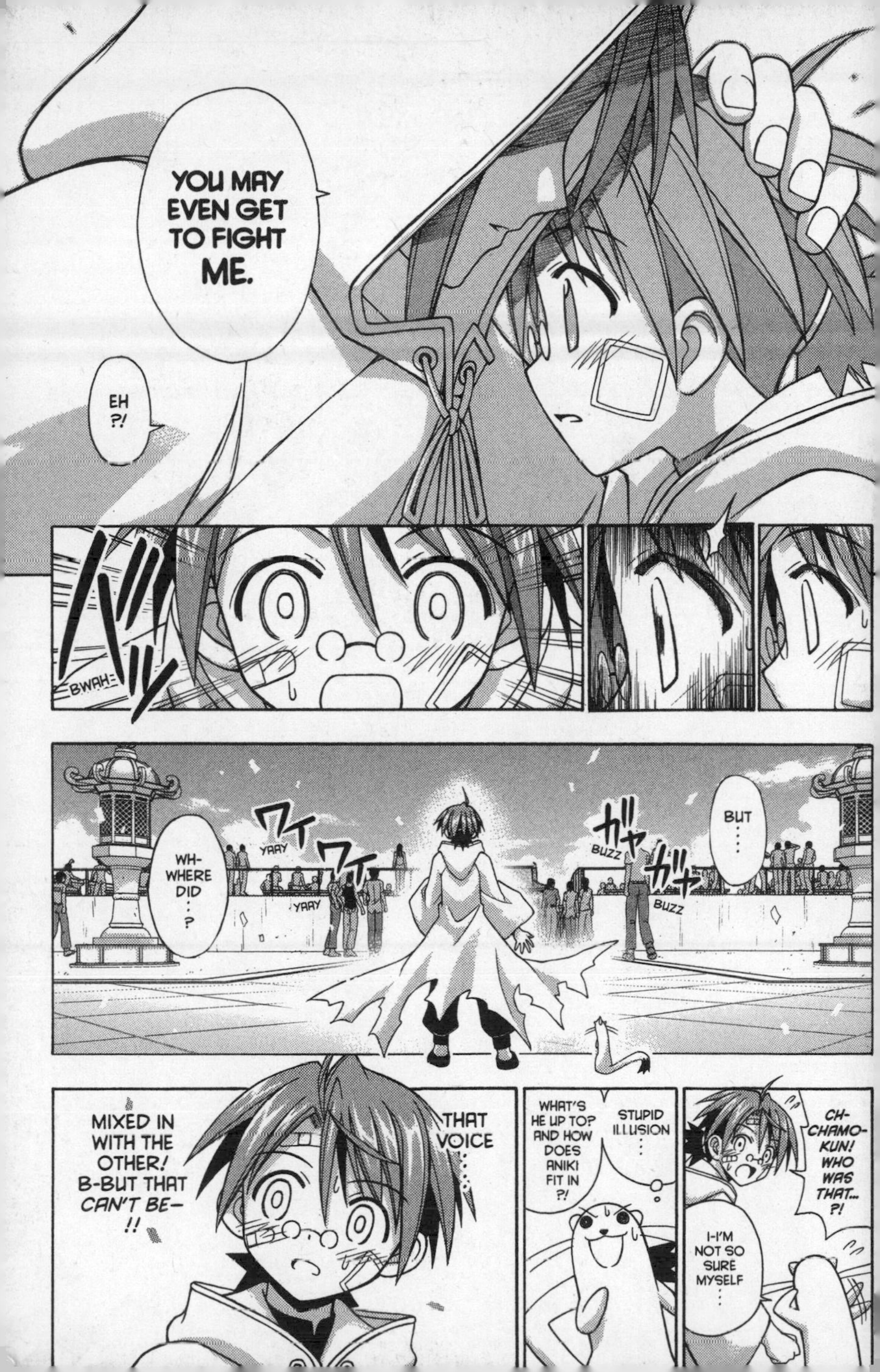
YOU MAY EVEN GET TO FIGHT ME.
EH ?!
BWAH
BUT....
BUZZ
BUZZ
YAAY
YAAY
WH- WHERE DID...?
CH- CHAMO- KUN! WHO WAS THAT...?!
I-I'M NOT SO SURE MYSELF...
STUPID ILLUSION...
WHAT'S HE UP TO? AND HOW DOES ANIKI FIT IN ?!
THAT VOICE....
MIXED IN WITH THE OTHER! B-BUT THAT CAN'T BE— !!

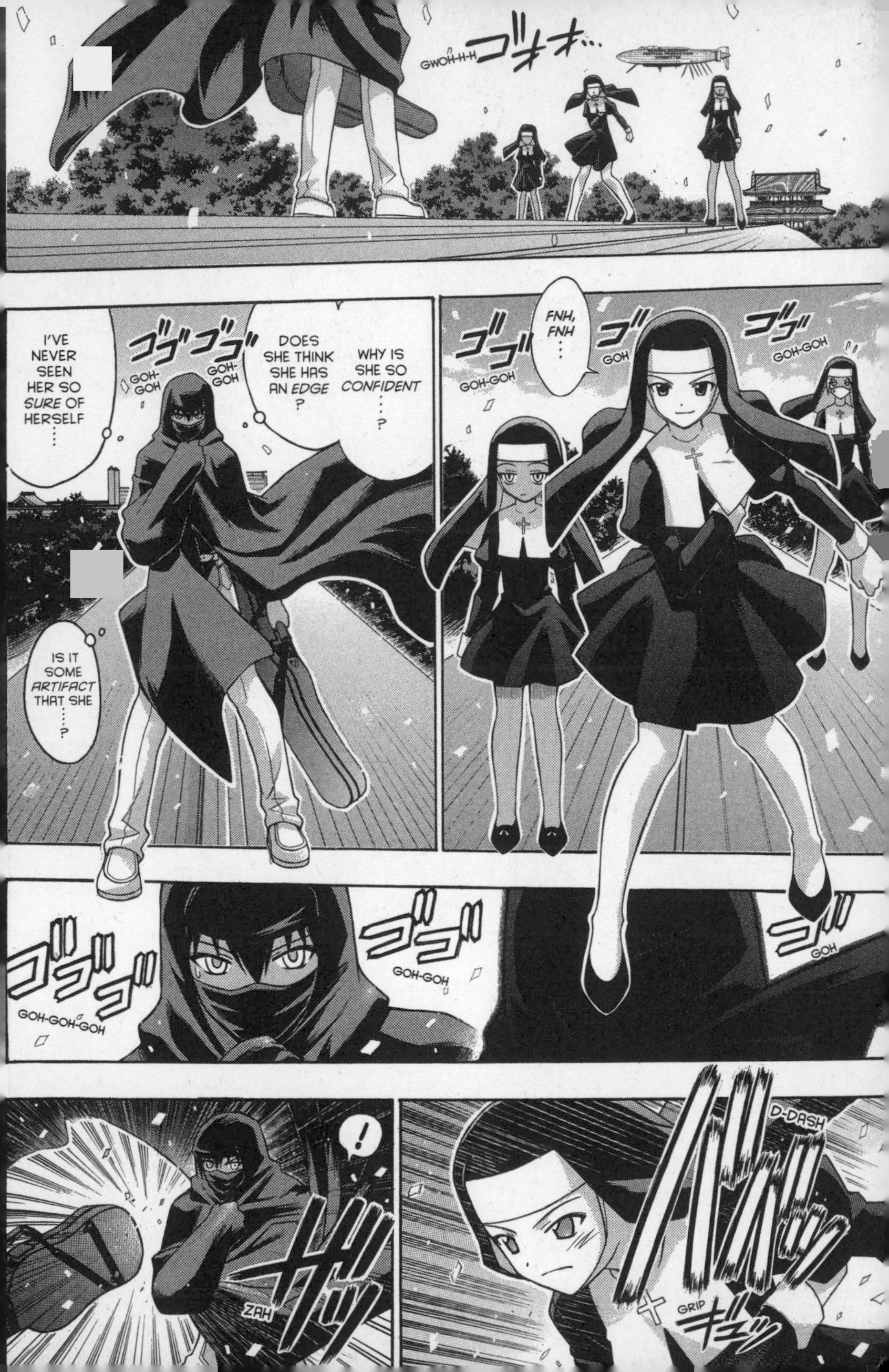
GWOH-H-H
FNH, FNH . . .
GOH
GOH-GOH
GOH-GOH
WHY IS SHE SO CONFIDENT . . . ?
DOES SHE THINK SHE HAS AN EDGE?
I'VE NEVER SEEN HER SO SURE OF HERSELF . . .
GOH-GOH
GOH-GOH
IS IT SOME ARTIFACT THAT SHE . . . ?
GOH
GOH-GOH
GOH-GOH-GOH
D-DASH
GRIP
!
ZAH

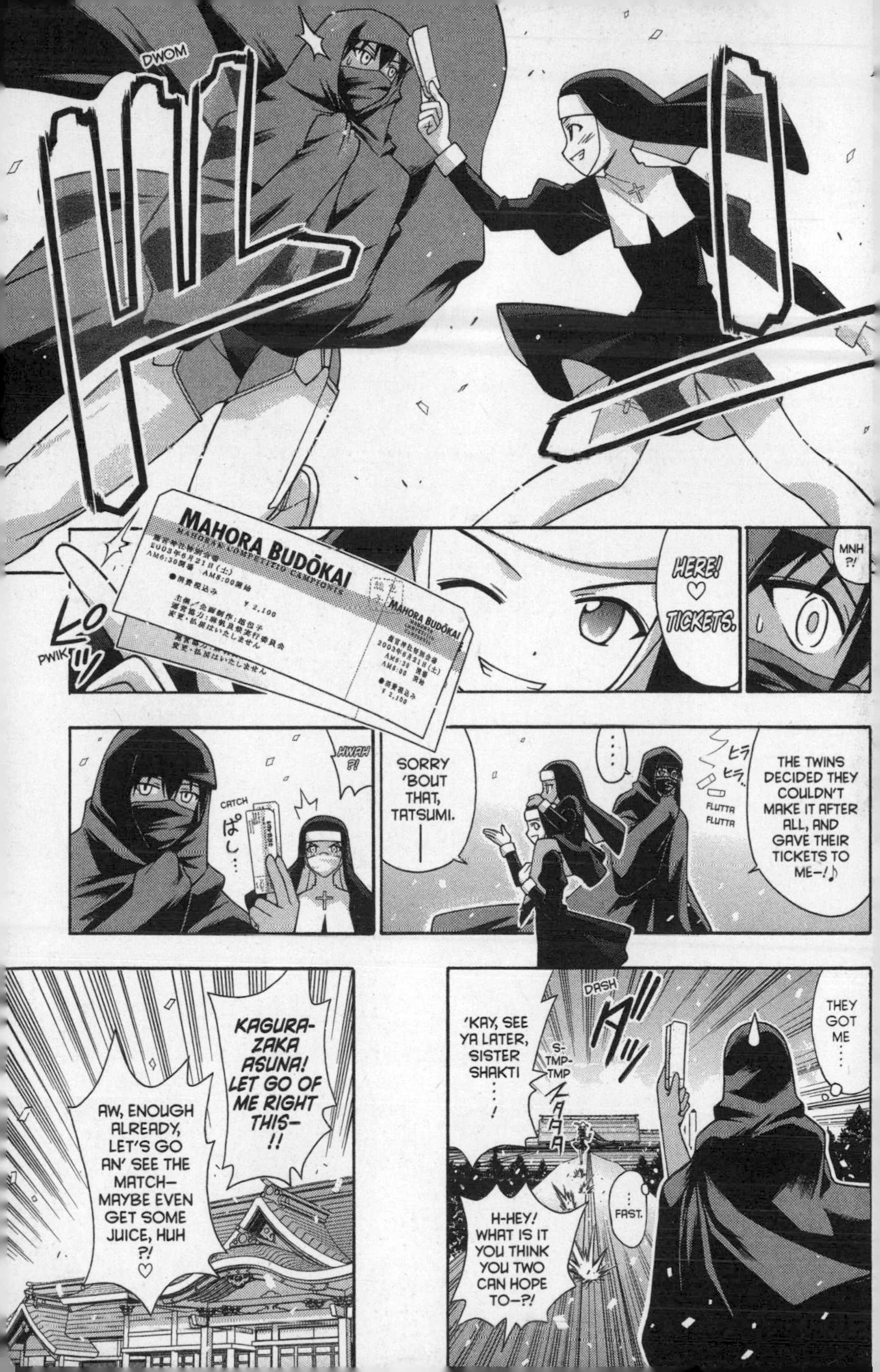
DWOM
MNH ?!
HERE! ♡ TICKETS.
MAHORA BUDŌKAI
MAHORA BUDŌKAI
PWIK
THE TWINS DECIDED THEY COULDN'T MAKE IT AFTER ALL, AND GAVE THEIR TICKETS TO ME—!♪
FLUTTA FLUTTA
....
SORRY 'BOUT THAT, TATSUMI.
HWAH ?!
CATCH
ぱし…
THEY GOT ME .....
DASH
'KAY, SEE YA LATER, SISTER SHAKTI ....!
S-TMP-TMP
...FAST.
H-HEY! WHAT IS IT YOU THINK YOU TWO CAN HOPE TO—?!
KAGURA-ZAKA ASUNA! LET GO OF ME RIGHT THIS—!!
AW, ENOUGH ALREADY, LET'S GO AN' SEE THE MATCH— MAYBE EVEN GET SOME JUICE, HUH ?! ♡

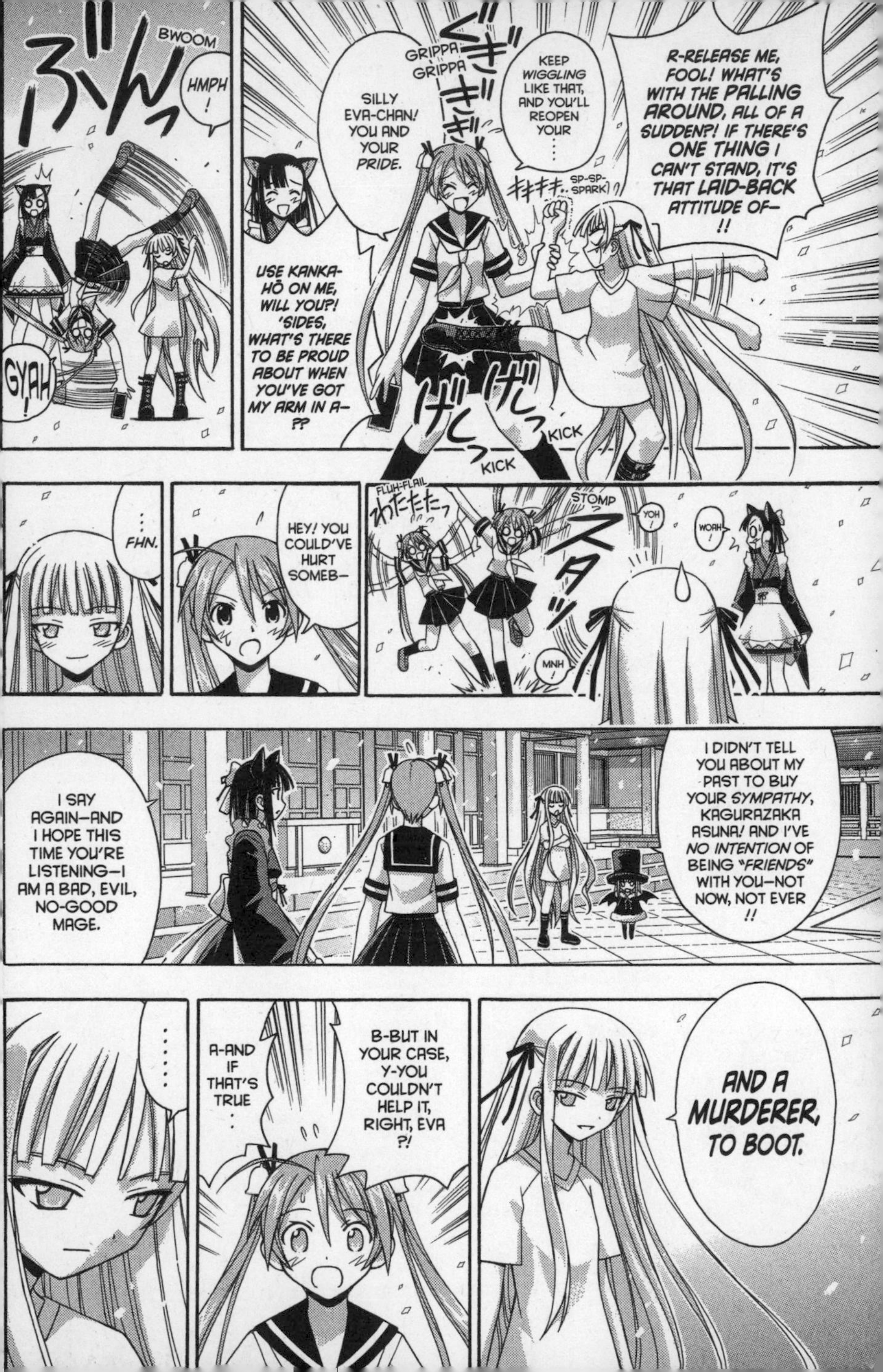

R-RELEASE ME, FOOL! WHAT'S WITH THE PALLING AROUND, ALL OF A SUDDEN?! IF THERE'S ONE THING I CAN'T STAND, IT'S THAT LAID-BACK ATTITUDE OF— !!
KEEP WIGGLING LIKE THAT, AND YOU'LL REOPEN YOUR ......
ぐぎぎぎ
GRIPPA GRIPPA
SILLY EVA-CHAN! YOU AND YOUR PRIDE.
キキキキ
SP-SP-SPARK
USE KANKA-HŌ ON ME, WILL YOU?! 'SIDES, WHAT'S THERE TO BE PROUD ABOUT WHEN YOU'VE GOT MY ARM IN A— ?!
げしっ げしっ
KICK
KICK
ぶんっ
BWOOM
HMPH!
GYAH!
STOMP
スタッ
YOH!
WOAH!
MNH!
わたたたっ
FLUH-FLAIL
HEY! YOU COULD'VE HURT SOMEB—
... FHN.
I DIDN'T TELL YOU ABOUT MY PAST TO BUY YOUR SYMPATHY, KAGURAZAKA ASUNA! AND I'VE NO INTENTION OF BEING "FRIENDS" WITH YOU—NOT NOW, NOT EVER !!
I SAY AGAIN—AND I HOPE THIS TIME YOU'RE LISTENING—I AM A BAD, EVIL, NO-GOOD MAGE.
AND A MURDERER, TO BOOT.
B-BUT IN YOUR CASE, Y-YOU COULDN'T HELP IT, RIGHT, EVA ?!
A-AND IF THAT'S TRUE ...
......

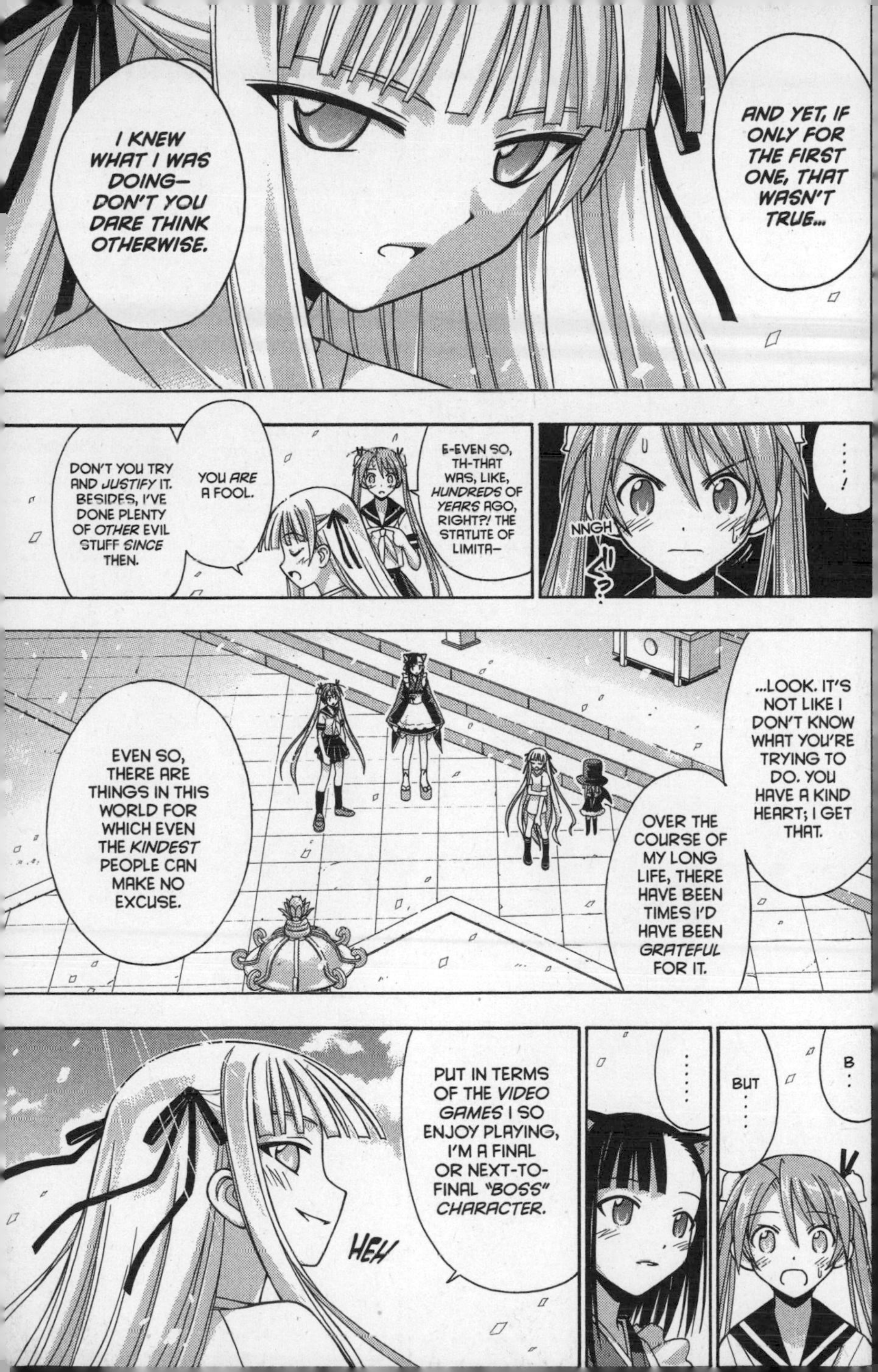
AND YET, IF ONLY FOR THE FIRST ONE, THAT WASN'T TRUE...
I KNEW WHAT I WAS DOING— DON'T YOU DARE THINK OTHERWISE.
...!
NNGH
E-EVEN SO, TH-THAT WAS, LIKE, HUNDREDS OF YEARS AGO, RIGHT?! THE STATUTE OF LIMITA—
YOU ARE A FOOL.
DON'T YOU TRY AND JUSTIFY IT. BESIDES, I'VE DONE PLENTY OF OTHER EVIL STUFF SINCE THEN.
...LOOK. IT'S NOT LIKE I DON'T KNOW WHAT YOU'RE TRYING TO DO. YOU HAVE A KIND HEART; I GET THAT.
OVER THE COURSE OF MY LONG LIFE, THERE HAVE BEEN TIMES I'D HAVE BEEN GRATEFUL FOR IT.
EVEN SO, THERE ARE THINGS IN THIS WORLD FOR WHICH EVEN THE KINDEST PEOPLE CAN MAKE NO EXCUSE.
B...
BUT......
......
PUT IN TERMS OF THE VIDEO GAMES I SO ENJOY PLAYING, I'M A FINAL OR NEXT-TO-FINAL "BOSS" CHARACTER.
HEH

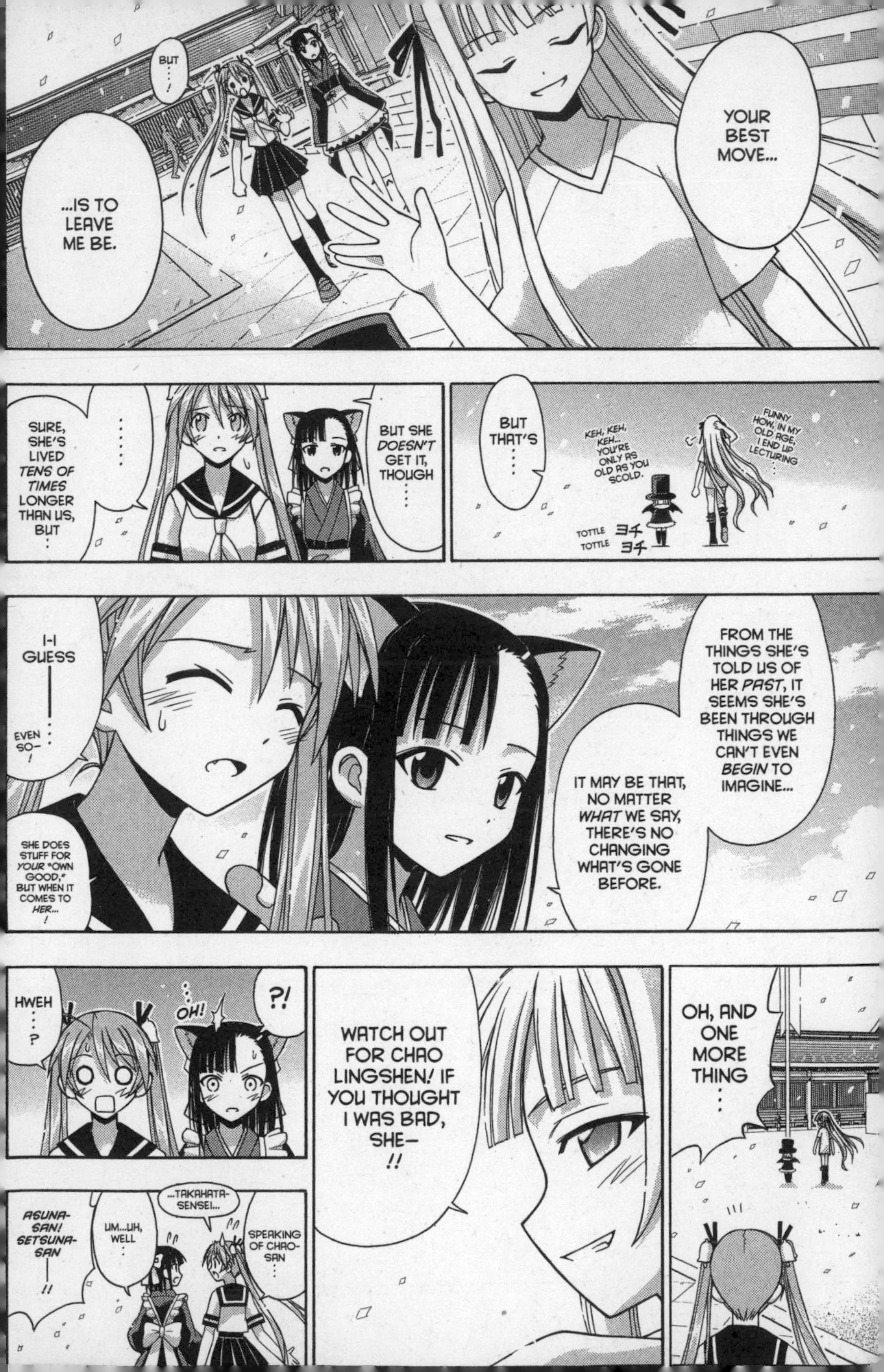
YOUR BEST MOVE...
...IS TO LEAVE ME BE.
BUT...!
FUNNY HOW, IN MY OLD AGE, I END UP LECTURING...
KEH, KEH, KEH... YOU'RE ONLY AS OLD AS YOU SCOLD.
TOTTLE ヨチ TOTTLE ヨチ
BUT THAT'S....
BUT SHE *DOESN'T* GET IT, THOUGH....
......
SURE, SHE'S LIVED *TENS OF TIMES* LONGER THAN US, BUT...
FROM THE THINGS SHE'S TOLD US OF HER *PAST*, IT SEEMS SHE'S BEEN THROUGH THINGS WE CAN'T EVEN *BEGIN* TO IMAGINE...
IT MAY BE THAT, NO MATTER *WHAT* WE SAY, THERE'S NO CHANGING WHAT'S GONE BEFORE.
I-I GUESS——...
EVEN SO—!
SHE DOES STUFF FOR *YOUR* "OWN GOOD," BUT WHEN IT COMES TO *HER*...!
OH, AND ONE MORE THING...
WATCH OUT FOR CHAO LINGSHEN! IF YOU THOUGHT I WAS BAD, SHE—!!
?!
...OH!
HWEH...?
SPEAKING OF CHAO-SAN...
...TAKAHATA-SENSEI...
UM...UH, WELL...
ASUNA-SAN! SETSUNA-SAN——!!

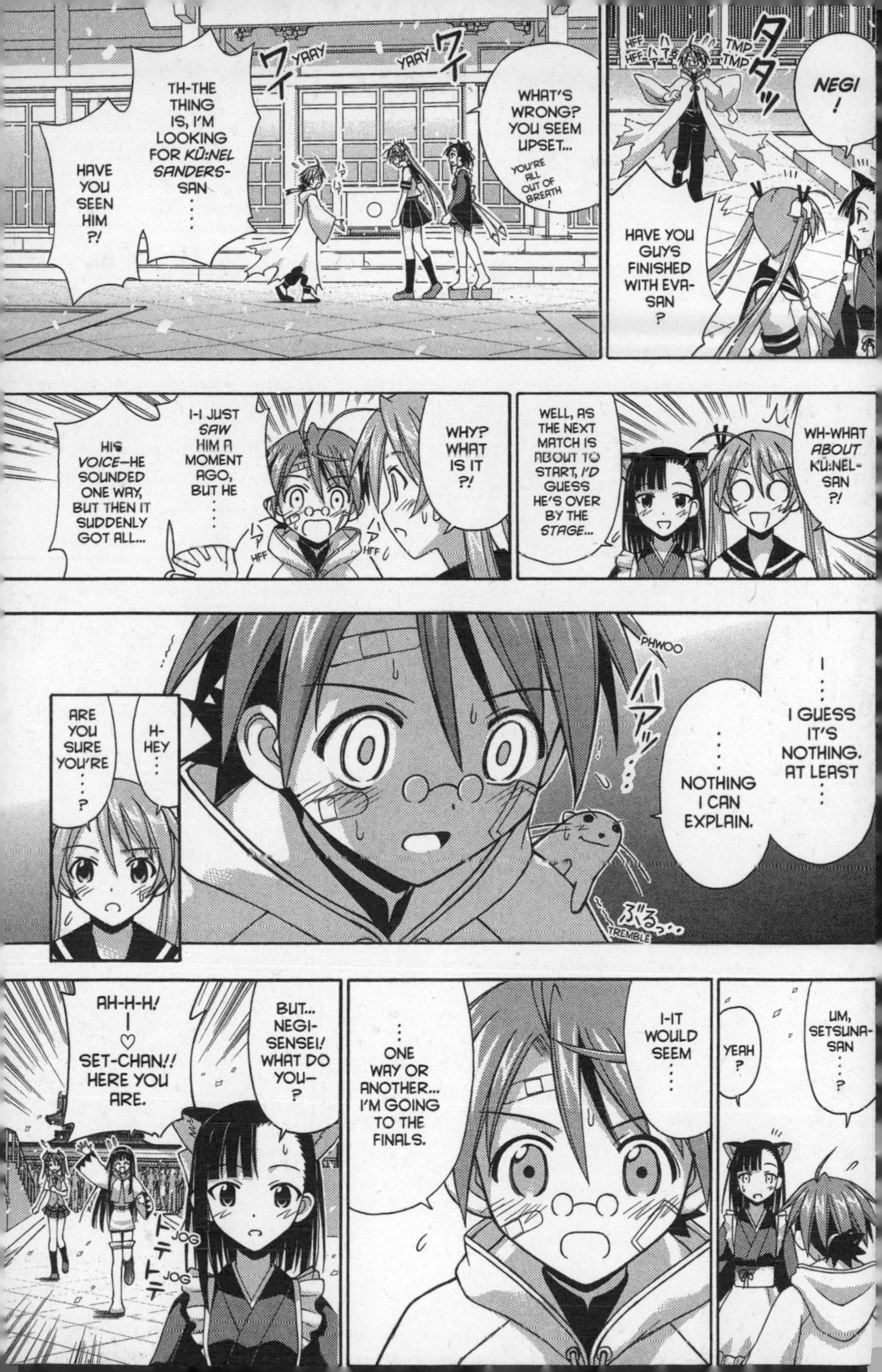
NEGI!
TMP TMP
HFF HFF
HAVE YOU GUYS FINISHED WITH EVA-SAN?
WHAT'S WRONG? YOU SEEM UPSET...
YOU'RE ALL OUT OF BREATH!
YAAY
YAAY
TH-THE THING IS, I'M LOOKING FOR KŪ:NEL SANDERS-SAN...
HAVE YOU SEEN HIM?!
WH-WHAT ABOUT KŪ:NEL-SAN?!
WELL, AS THE NEXT MATCH IS ABOUT TO START, I'D GUESS HE'S OVER BY THE STAGE...
WHY? WHAT IS IT?!
HFF HFF
I-I JUST SAW HIM A MOMENT AGO, BUT HE...
HIS VOICE—HE SOUNDED ONE WAY, BUT THEN IT SUDDENLY GOT ALL...
I... I GUESS IT'S NOTHING. AT LEAST...
...NOTHING I CAN EXPLAIN.
PHWOO
TREMBLE
H-HEY...
ARE YOU SURE YOU'RE...?
UM, SETSUNA-SAN...?
YEAH?
I-IT WOULD SEEM...
...ONE WAY OR ANOTHER... I'M GOING TO THE FINALS.
BUT... NEGI-SENSEI! WHAT DO YOU—?
AH-H-H! I ♡ SET-CHAN!! HERE YOU ARE.
JOG
JOG

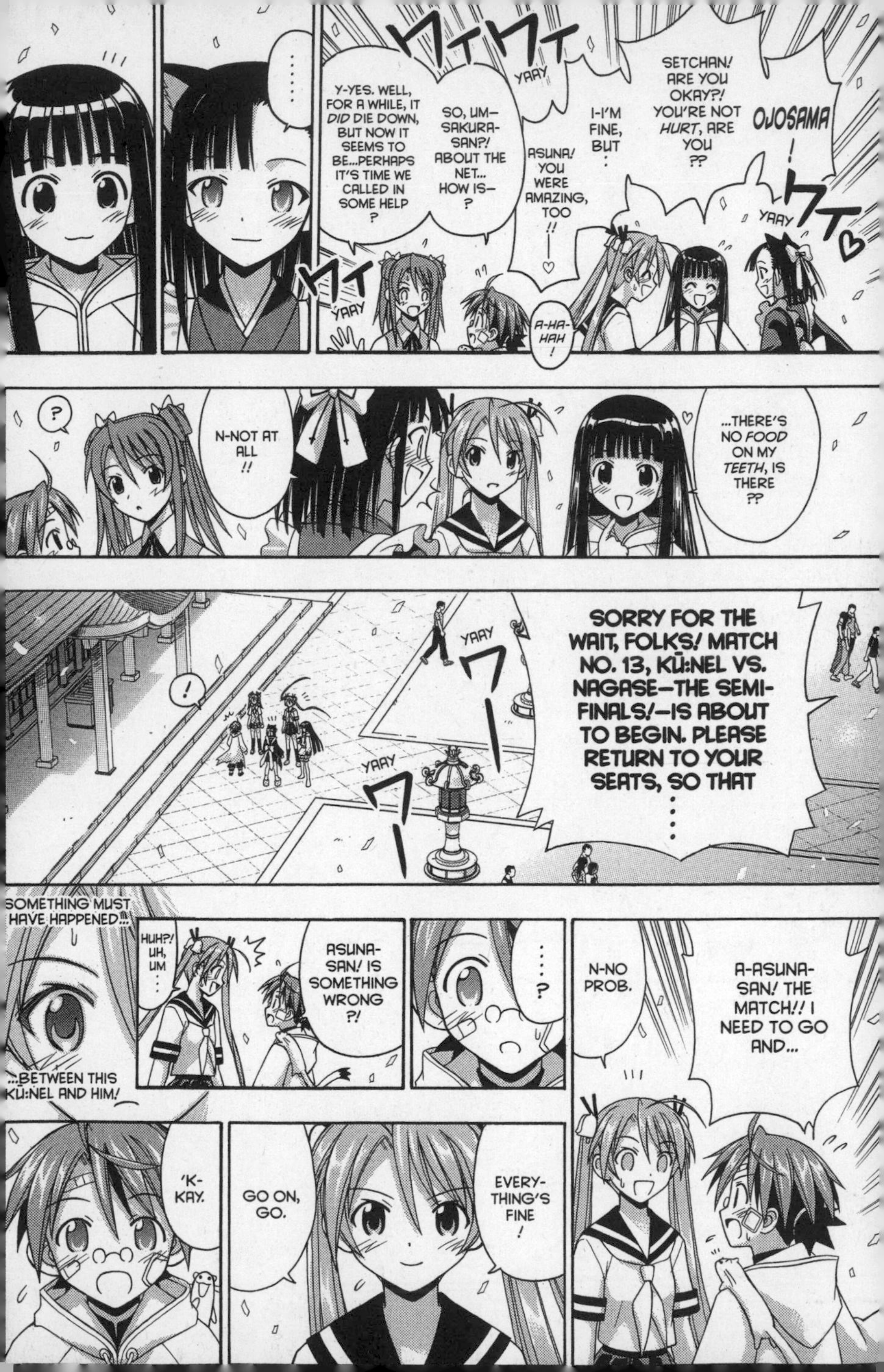
SETCHAN! ARE YOU OKAY?! YOU'RE NOT HURT, ARE YOU ??
OJOSAMA !
YAAY
I-I'M FINE, BUT :
ASUNA! YOU WERE AMAZING, TOO !!
YAAY
SO, UM— SAKURA-SAN?! ABOUT THE NET... HOW IS— ?
Y-YES. WELL, FOR A WHILE, IT DID DIE DOWN, BUT NOW IT SEEMS TO BE...PERHAPS IT'S TIME WE CALLED IN SOME HELP ?
A-HA-HAH !
YAAY
......
...THERE'S NO FOOD ON MY TEETH, IS THERE ??
N-NOT AT ALL !!
?
SORRY FOR THE WAIT, FOLKS! MATCH NO. 13, KŪ:NEL VS. NAGASE—THE SEMI-FINALS!—IS ABOUT TO BEGIN. PLEASE RETURN TO YOUR SEATS, SO THAT ...
YAAY
YAAY
!
A-ASUNA-SAN! THE MATCH!! I NEED TO GO AND...
N-NO PROB.
...?
ASUNA-SAN! IS SOMETHING WRONG ?!
HUH?! UH, UM ...
SOMETHING MUST HAVE HAPPENED...
...BETWEEN THIS KŪ:NEL AND HIM!
EVERY-THING'S FINE !
GO ON, GO.
'K-KAY.

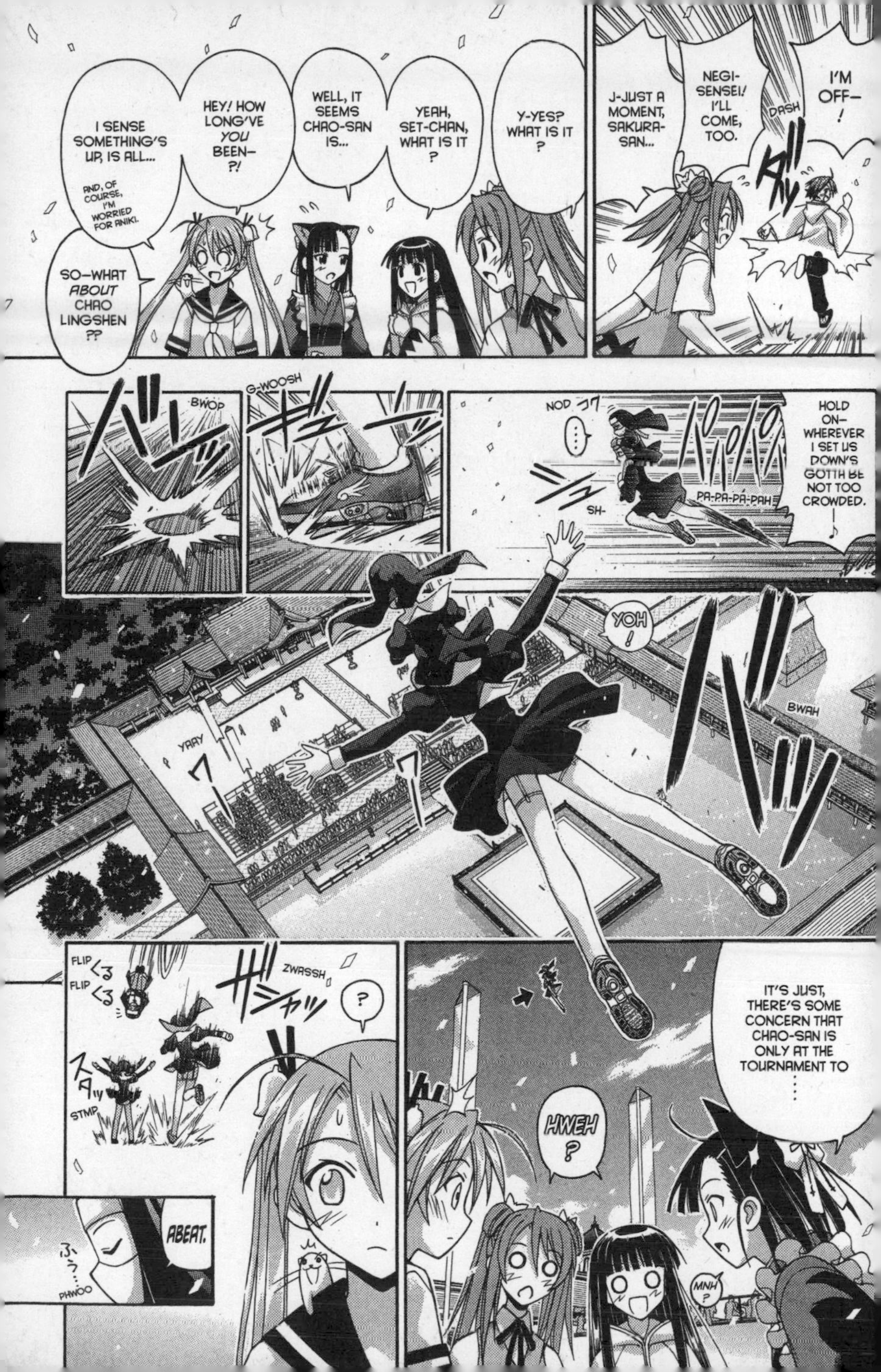
I'M OFF—!
DASH
NEGI-SENSEI! I'LL COME, TOO.
J-JUST A MOMENT, SAKURA-SAN...
Y-YES? WHAT IS IT?
YEAH, SET-CHAN, WHAT IS IT?
WELL, IT SEEMS CHAO-SAN IS...
HEY! HOW LONG'VE YOU BEEN—?!
I SENSE SOMETHING'S UP, IS ALL...
AND, OF COURSE, I'M WORRIED FOR ANIKI.
SO—WHAT ABOUT CHAO LINGSHEN??
HOLD ON— WHEREVER I SET US DOWN'S GOTTA BE NOT TOO CROWDED.
NOD
...
PA-PA-PA-PAH
SH-
G-WOOSH
BWOP
YOH!
BWAH
YAAY
IT'S JUST, THERE'S SOME CONCERN THAT CHAO-SAN IS ONLY AT THE TOURNAMENT TO ....
HWEH?
MNH?
ZWASSH
?
FLIP くる
FLIP くる
STMP
ABEAT.
ふう… PHWOO

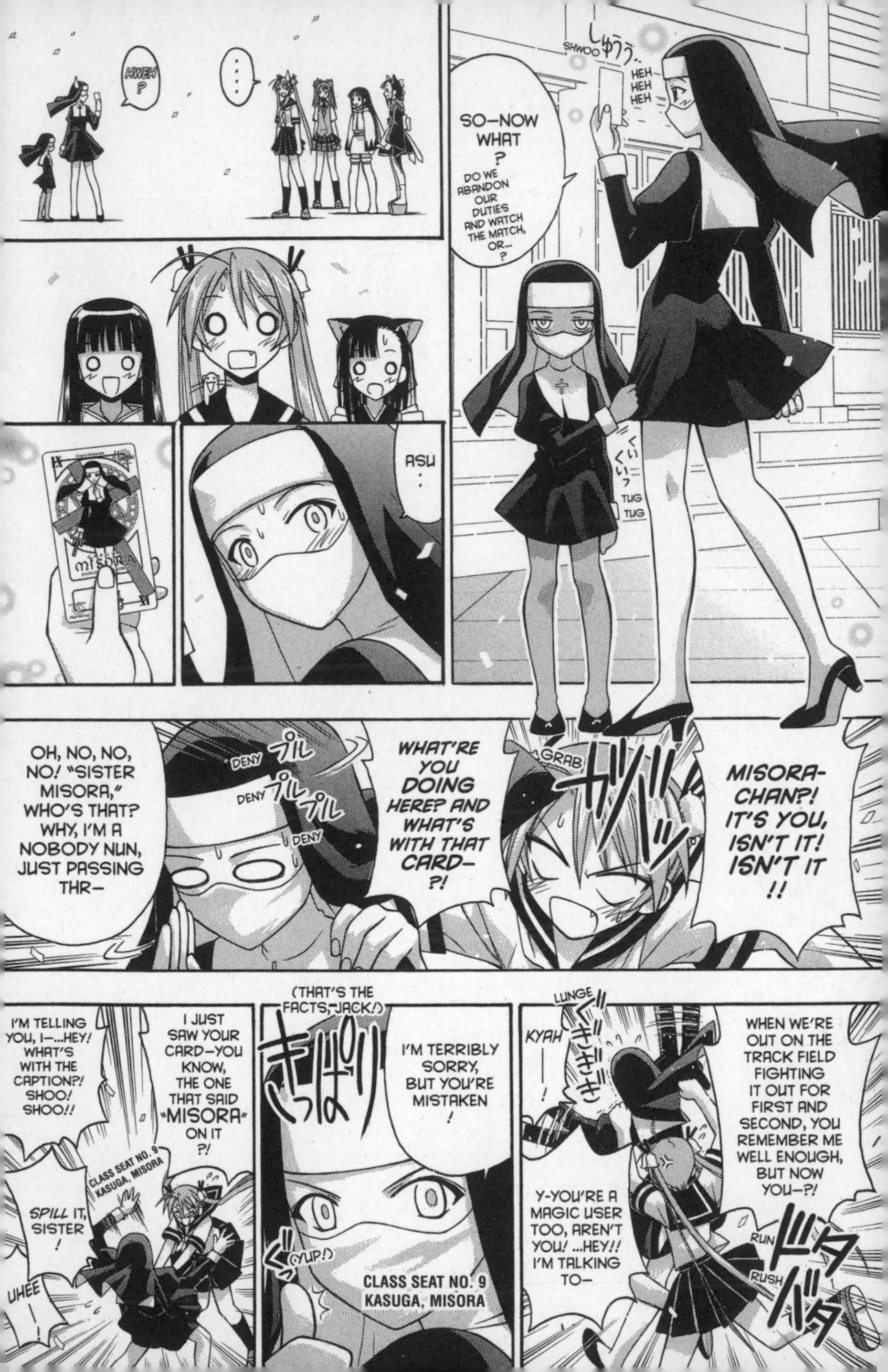
SHWOO しゅうう..
HEH HEH HEH
SO—NOW WHAT? DO WE ABANDON OUR DUTIES AND WATCH THE MATCH, OR...?
くいくいっ TUG TUG
HWEH?
. . . .
ASU . .
misora
MISORA-CHAN?! IT'S YOU, ISN'T IT! ISN'T IT!!
GRAB ガッ
WHAT'RE YOU DOING HERE? AND WHAT'S WITH THAT CARD—?!
DENY プル
DENY プルプル
DENY
OH, NO, NO, NO! "SISTER MISORA," WHO'S THAT? WHY, I'M A NOBODY NUN, JUST PASSING THR—
WHEN WE'RE OUT ON THE TRACK FIELD FIGHTING IT OUT FOR FIRST AND SECOND, YOU REMEMBER ME WELL ENOUGH, BUT NOW YOU—?!
LUNGE ぐぎぎぎ
KYAH!
Y-YOU'RE A MAGIC USER TOO, AREN'T YOU! ...HEY!! I'M TALKING TO—
RUN ドタ
RUSH バタ
(THAT'S THE FACTS, JACK!) きっぱり
I'M TERRIBLY SORRY, BUT YOU'RE MISTAKEN!
くっ (YUP!)
CLASS SEAT NO. 9 KASUGA, MISORA
I JUST SAW YOUR CARD—YOU KNOW, THE ONE THAT SAID "MISORA" ON IT?!
I'M TELLING YOU, I—...HEY! WHAT'S WITH THE CAPTION?! SHOO! SHOO!!
CLASS SEAT NO. 9 KASUGA, MISORA
SPILL IT, SISTER!
UHEE

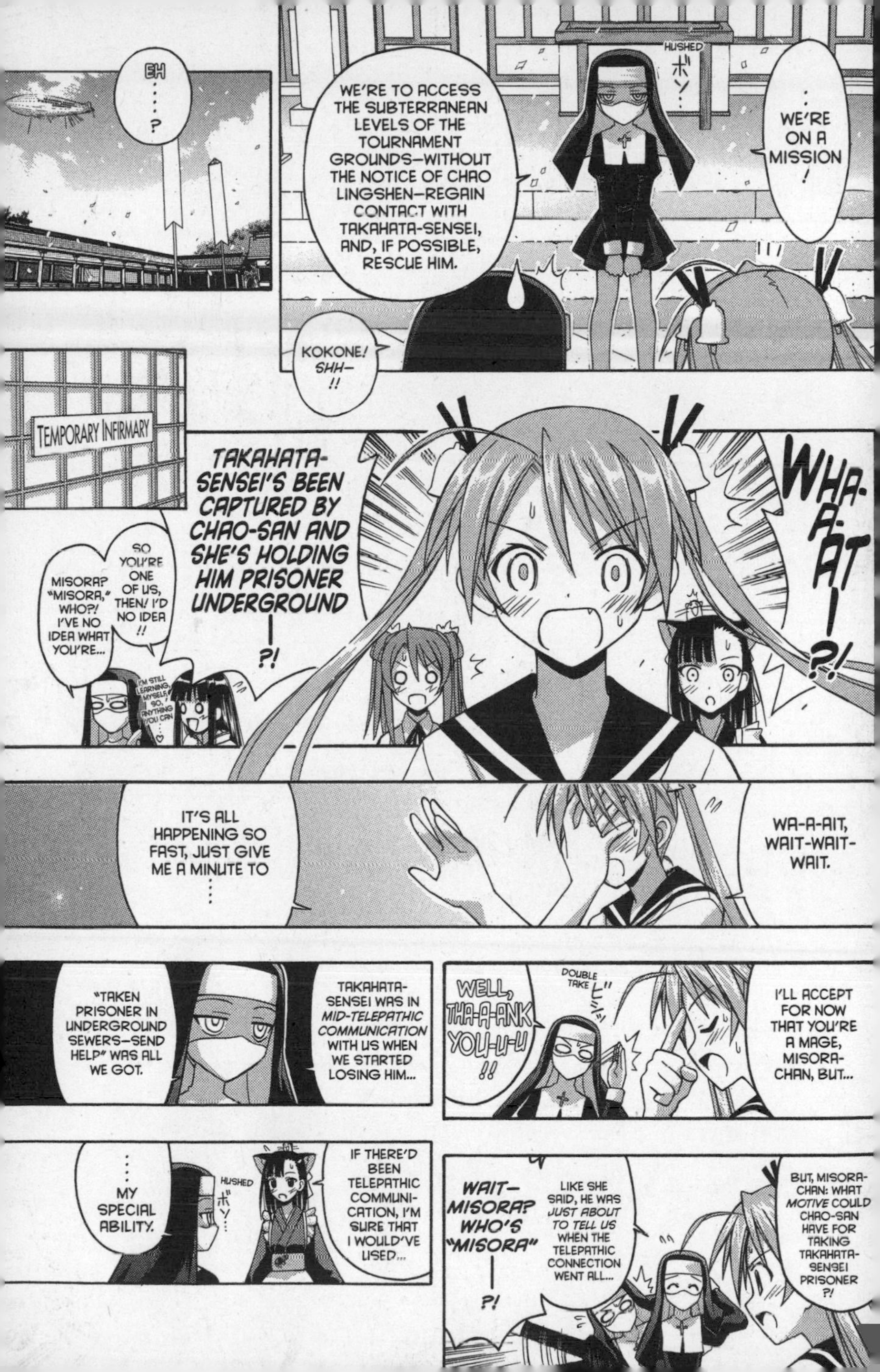

...WE'RE ON A MISSION!
HUSHED ボソ...
WE'RE TO ACCESS THE SUBTERRANEAN LEVELS OF THE TOURNAMENT GROUNDS—WITHOUT THE NOTICE OF CHAO LINGSHEN—REGAIN CONTACT WITH TAKAHATA-SENSEI, AND, IF POSSIBLE, RESCUE HIM.
KOKONE! SHH—!!
EH....?
WHA-A-AT!?!
TAKAHATA-SENSEI'S BEEN CAPTURED BY CHAO-SAN AND SHE'S HOLDING HIM PRISONER UNDERGROUND—?!
TEMPORARY INFIRMARY
SO YOU'RE ONE OF US, THEN! I'D NO IDEA!!
MISORA? "MISORA," WHO?! I'VE NO IDEA WHAT YOU'RE...
I'M STILL LEARNING, MYSELF, SO, ANYTHING YOU CAN...♡
WA-A-AIT, WAIT-WAIT-WAIT.
IT'S ALL HAPPENING SO FAST, JUST GIVE ME A MINUTE TO....
I'LL ACCEPT FOR NOW THAT YOU'RE A MAGE, MISORA-CHAN, BUT...
DOUBLE TAKE ビ"
WELL, THA-A-ANK YOU-U-U!!
TAKAHATA-SENSEI WAS IN MID-TELEPATHIC COMMUNICATION WITH US WHEN WE STARTED LOSING HIM...
"TAKEN PRISONER IN UNDERGROUND SEWERS—SEND HELP" WAS ALL WE GOT.
BUT, MISORA-CHAN: WHAT MOTIVE COULD CHAO-SAN HAVE FOR TAKING TAKAHATA-SENSEI PRISONER?!
LIKE SHE SAID, HE WAS JUST ABOUT TO TELL US WHEN THE TELEPATHIC CONNECTION WENT ALL...
WAIT—MISORA? WHO'S "MISORA"—?!
IF THERE'D BEEN TELEPATHIC COMMUNICATION, I'M SURE THAT I WOULD'VE USED...
HUSHED ボソ...
....MY SPECIAL ABILITY.

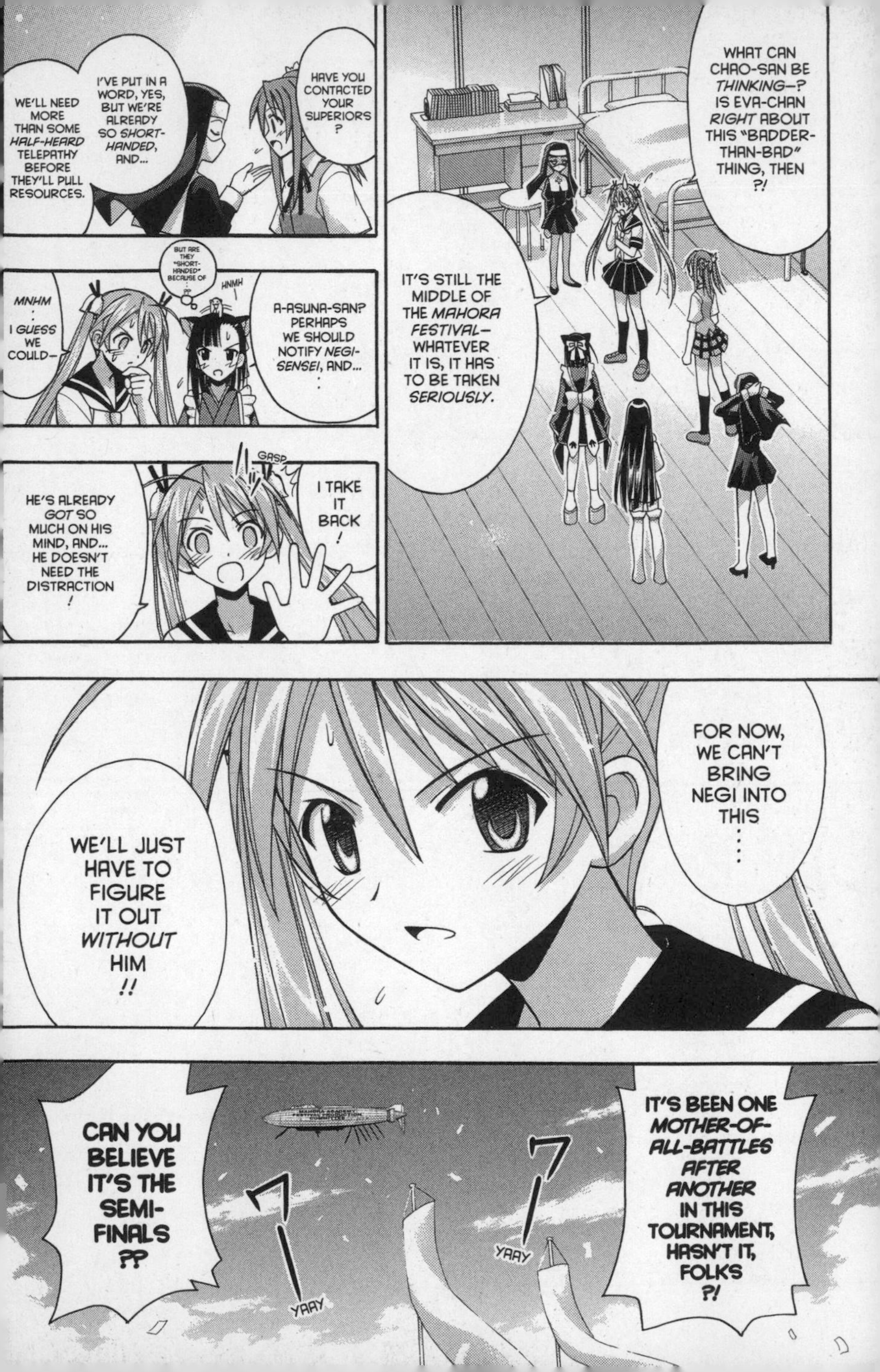
WHAT CAN CHAO-SAN BE *THINKING*—? IS EVA-CHAN *RIGHT* ABOUT THIS "BADDER-THAN-BAD" THING, THEN ?!
IT'S STILL THE MIDDLE OF THE *MAHORA FESTIVAL*—WHATEVER IT IS, IT HAS TO BE TAKEN *SERIOUSLY*.
HAVE YOU CONTACTED YOUR SUPERIORS ?
I'VE PUT IN A WORD, YES, BUT WE'RE ALREADY SO *SHORT-HANDED*, AND...
WE'LL NEED MORE THAN SOME *HALF-HEARD* TELEPATHY BEFORE THEY'LL PULL RESOURCES.
A-ASUNA-SAN? PERHAPS WE SHOULD NOTIFY *NEGI-SENSEI*, AND... :
HNMH
BUT ARE THEY "SHORT-HANDED" BECAUSE OF : ??
MNHM : I *GUESS* WE COULD—
I TAKE IT BACK !
GASP
HE'S ALREADY *GOT* SO MUCH ON HIS MIND, AND... HE DOESN'T NEED THE DISTRACTION !
FOR NOW, WE CAN'T BRING NEGI INTO THIS ....
WE'LL JUST HAVE TO FIGURE IT OUT *WITHOUT* HIM !!
IT'S BEEN ONE *MOTHER-OF-ALL-BATTLES AFTER ANOTHER* IN THIS TOURNAMENT, HASN'T IT, FOLKS ?!
YAAY
YAAY
CAN YOU BELIEVE IT'S THE SEMI-FINALS ??

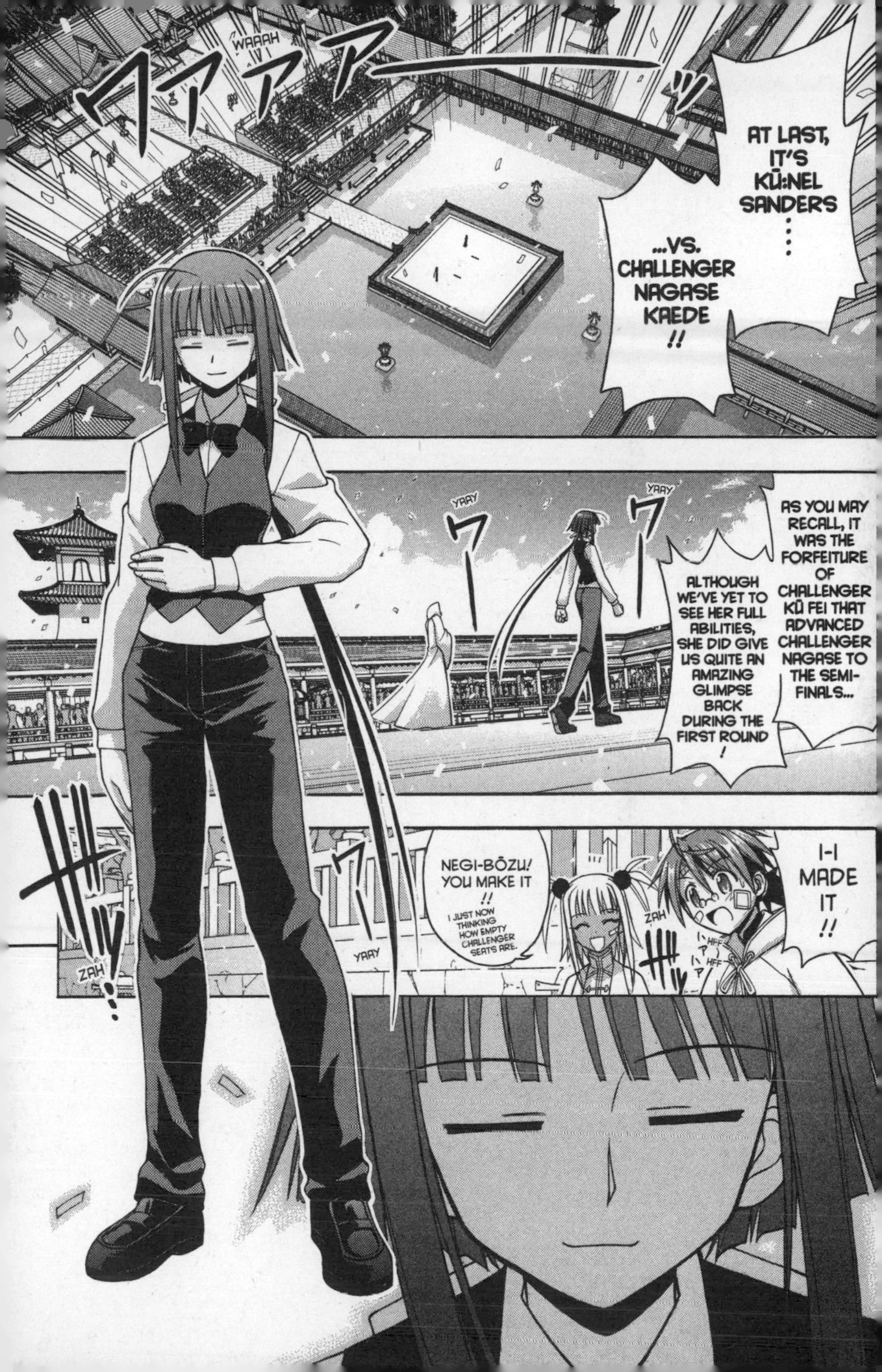
WAAAH
AT LAST, IT'S KŪ:NEL SANDERS ....
...VS. CHALLENGER NAGASE KAEDE !!
YAAY
YAAY
AS YOU MAY RECALL, IT WAS THE FORFEITURE OF CHALLENGER KŪ FEI THAT ADVANCED CHALLENGER NAGASE TO THE SEMI-FINALS...
ALTHOUGH WE'VE YET TO SEE HER FULL ABILITIES, SHE DID GIVE US QUITE AN AMAZING GLIMPSE BACK DURING THE FIRST ROUND !
I-I MADE IT !!
HFF HFF
ZAH
NEGI-BŌZU! YOU MAKE IT !!
I JUST NOW THINKING HOW EMPTY CHALLENGER SEATS ARE.
YAAY
ZAH

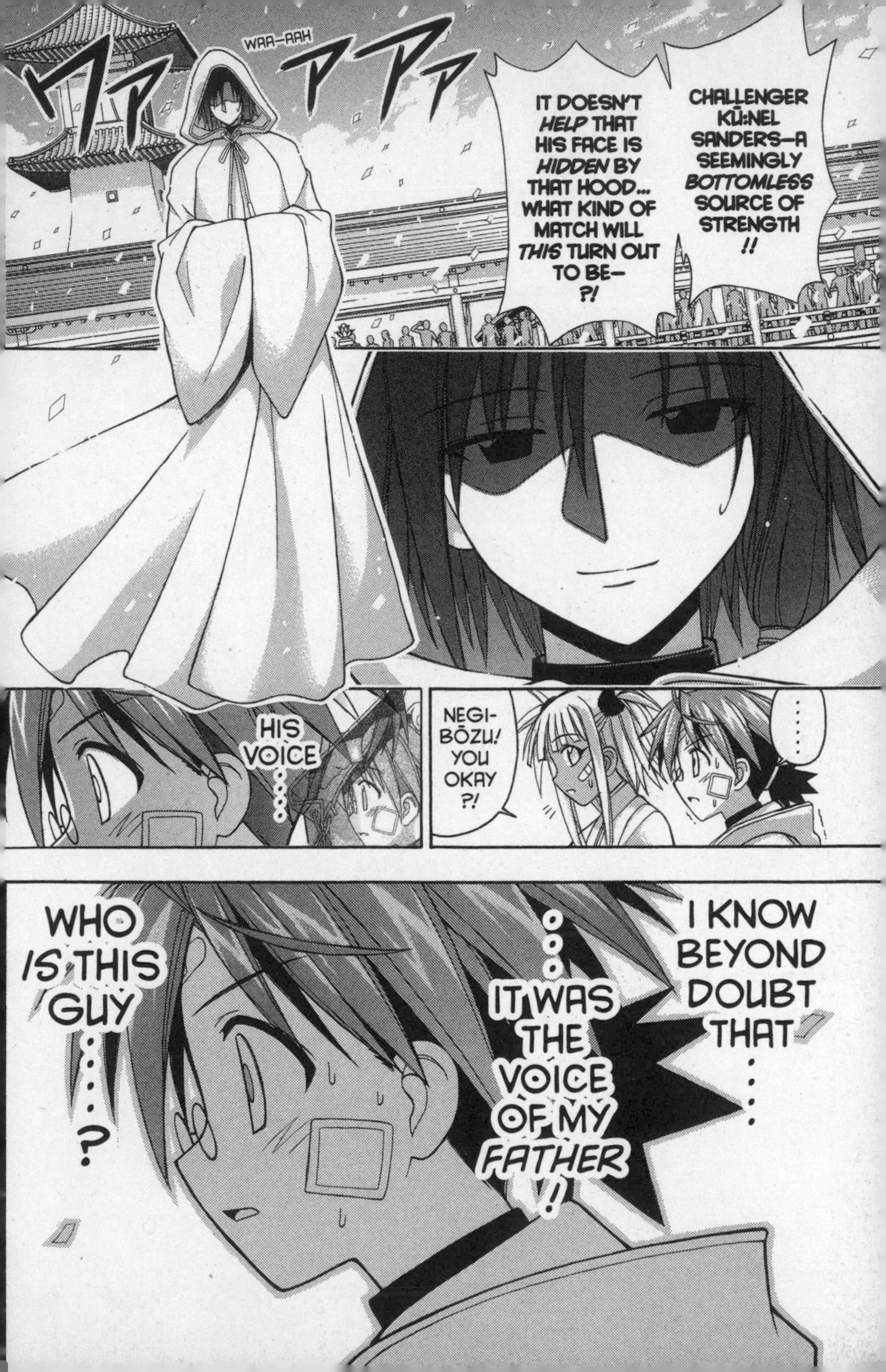
CHALLENGER KŪ:NEL SANDERS—A SEEMINGLY *BOTTOMLESS* SOURCE OF STRENGTH!!
IT DOESN'T *HELP* THAT HIS FACE IS *HIDDEN* BY THAT HOOD... WHAT KIND OF MATCH WILL *THIS* TURN OUT TO BE—?!
WAA—AAH
......
NEGI-BŌZU! YOU OKAY?!
HIS VOICE....
I KNOW BEYOND DOUBT THAT....
...IT WAS THE VOICE OF MY *FATHER*!
WHO IS THIS GUY....?

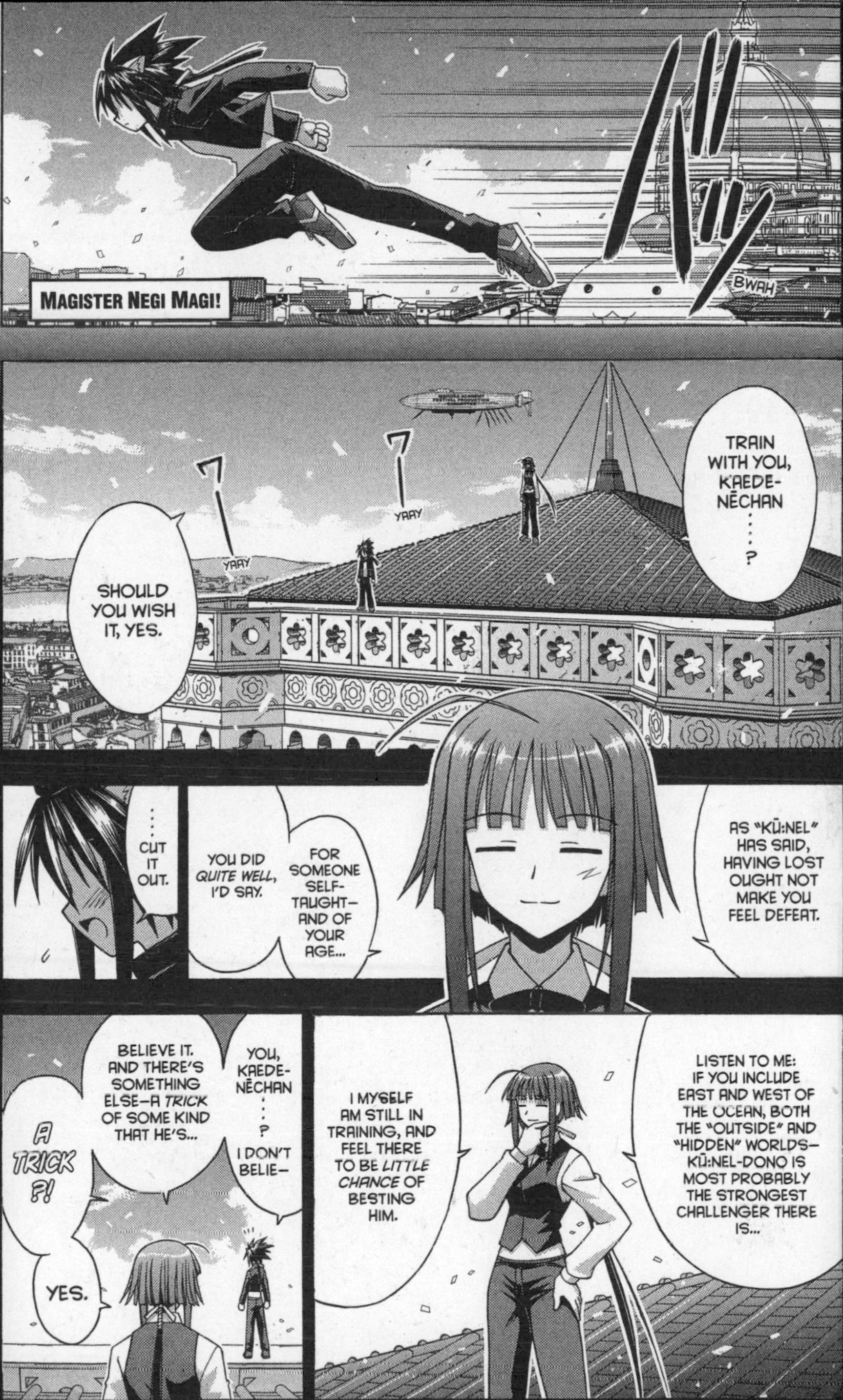
BWAH
MAGISTER NEGI MAGI!
TRAIN WITH YOU, KAEDE-NĒCHAN . . . . ?
YAAY
YAAY
SHOULD YOU WISH IT, YES.
AS "KŪ:NEL" HAS SAID, HAVING LOST OUGHT NOT MAKE YOU FEEL DEFEAT.
FOR SOMEONE SELF-TAUGHT—AND OF YOUR AGE...
YOU DID *QUITE WELL*, I'D SAY.
. . . . CUT IT OUT.
LISTEN TO ME: IF YOU INCLUDE EAST AND WEST OF THE OCEAN, BOTH THE "OUTSIDE" AND "HIDDEN" WORLDS—KŪ:NEL-DONO IS MOST PROBABLY THE STRONGEST CHALLENGER THERE IS...
I MYSELF AM STILL IN TRAINING, AND FEEL THERE TO BE *LITTLE CHANCE* OF BESTING HIM.
YOU, KAEDE-NĒCHAN . . . ?
I DON'T BELIE—
BELIEVE IT. AND THERE'S SOMETHING ELSE—A *TRICK* OF SOME KIND THAT HE'S...
A TRICK ?!
YES.

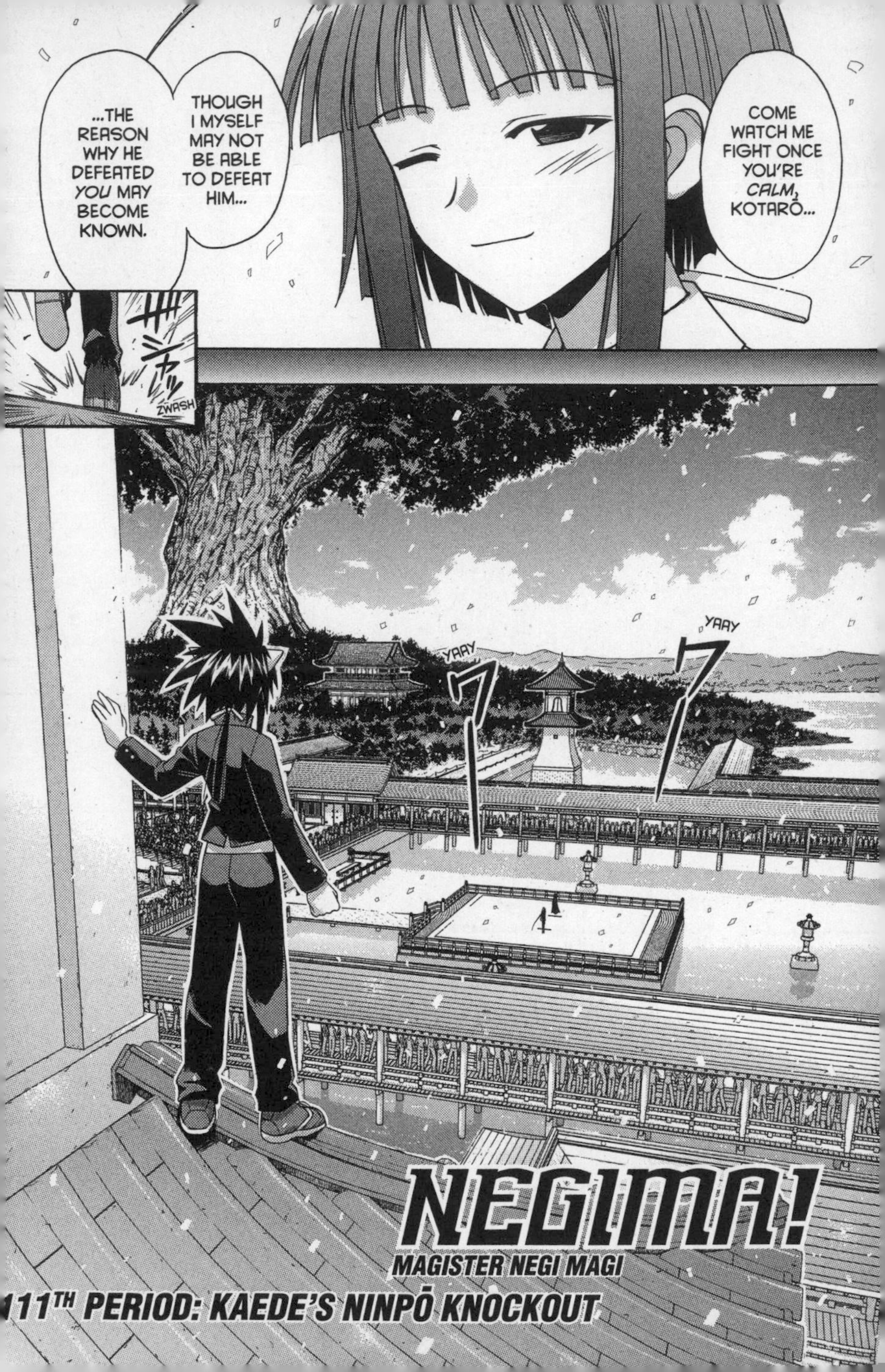
COME WATCH ME FIGHT ONCE YOU'RE *CALM*, KOTARŌ...
THOUGH I MYSELF MAY NOT BE ABLE TO DEFEAT HIM...
...THE REASON WHY HE DEFEATED *YOU* MAY BECOME KNOWN.
ZWASH
YAAY
YAAY
NEGIMA!
MAGISTER NEGI MAGI
111TH PERIOD: KAEDE'S NINPŌ KNOCKOUT

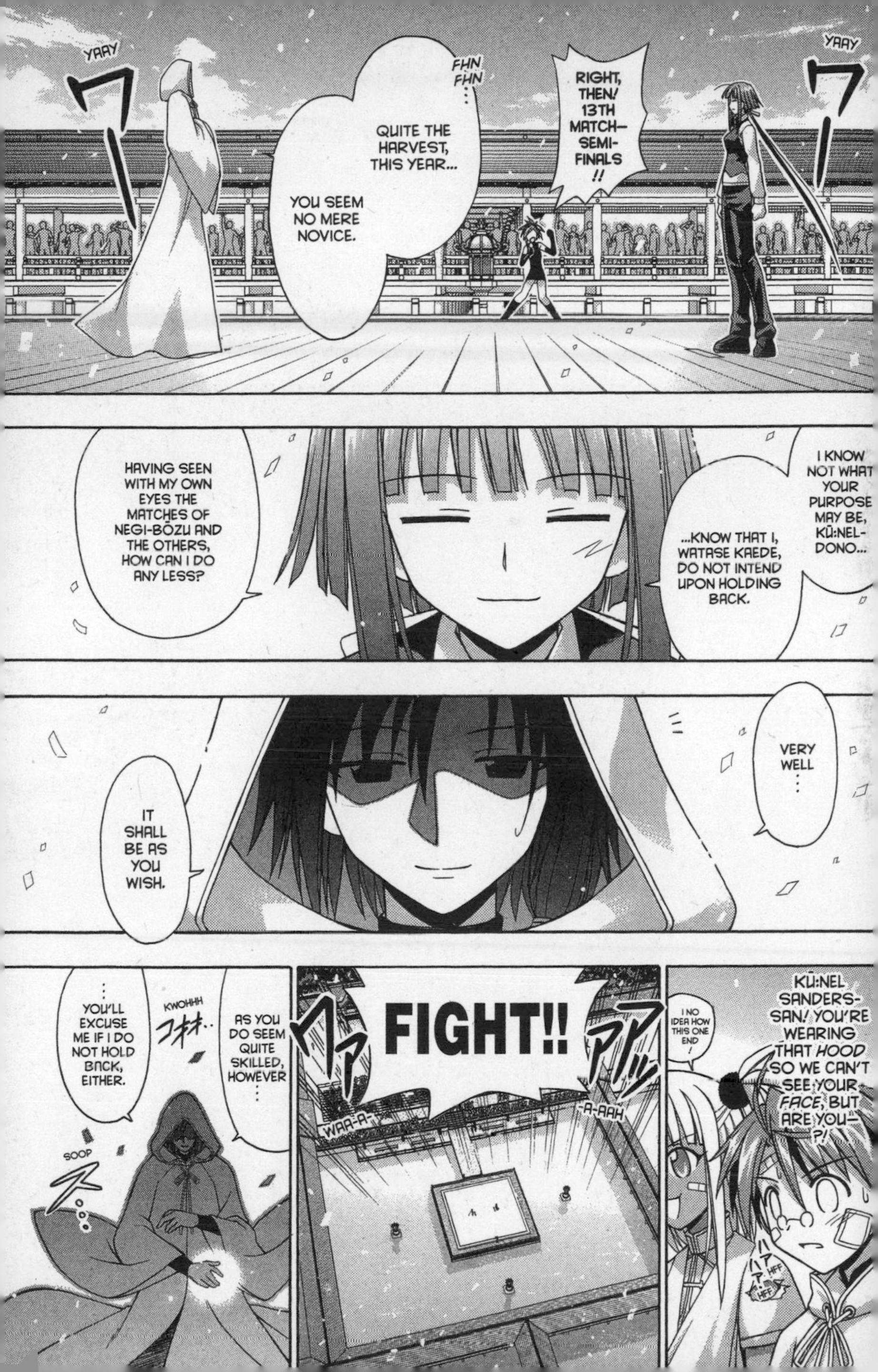
YAAY
ワー
RIGHT, THEN! 13TH MATCH—SEMI-FINALS !!
FHN FHN...
QUITE THE HARVEST, THIS YEAR...
YOU SEEM NO MERE NOVICE.
YAAY
ワー
I KNOW NOT WHAT YOUR PURPOSE MAY BE, KŪ:NEL-DONO...
...KNOW THAT I, WATASE KAEDE, DO NOT INTEND UPON HOLDING BACK.
HAVING SEEN WITH MY OWN EYES THE MATCHES OF NEGI-BŌZU AND THE OTHERS, HOW CAN I DO ANY LESS?
VERY WELL...
IT SHALL BE AS YOU WISH.
KŪ:NEL SANDERS-SAN! YOU'RE WEARING THAT HOOD SO WE CAN'T SEE YOUR FACE, BUT ARE YOU—?!
I NO IDEA HOW THIS ONE END !
ハァハァ
HFF HFF
アア
-A-AAH
FIGHT!!
ワア
WAA-A-
AS YOU DO SEEM QUITE SKILLED, HOWEVER...
KWOHHH
コオオ..
...YOU'LL EXCUSE ME IF I DO NOT HOLD BACK, EITHER.
SOOP
ス

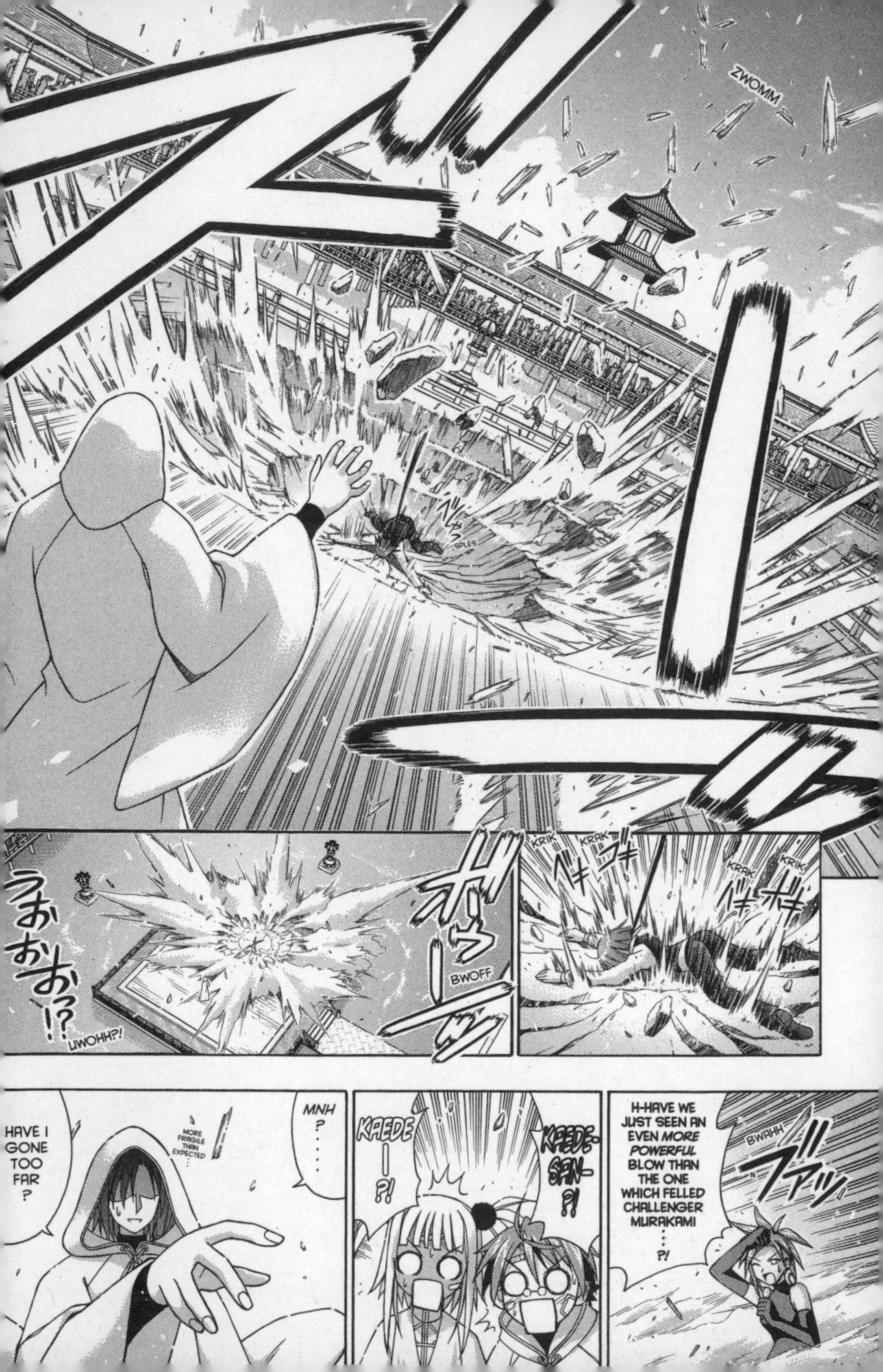
ZWOMM
SPLES
KRIK
KRAK
KRAK
KRIK
BWOFF
うおおおっ!?
UWOHH?!
H-HAVE WE JUST SEEN AN EVEN *MORE POWERFUL* BLOW THAN THE ONE WHICH FELLED CHALLENGER MURAKAMI ....?!
BWAHH
KAEDE-SAN--?!
KAEDE--?!
MNH? ....
HAVE I GONE TOO FAR?
MORE FRAGILE THAN EXPECTED...

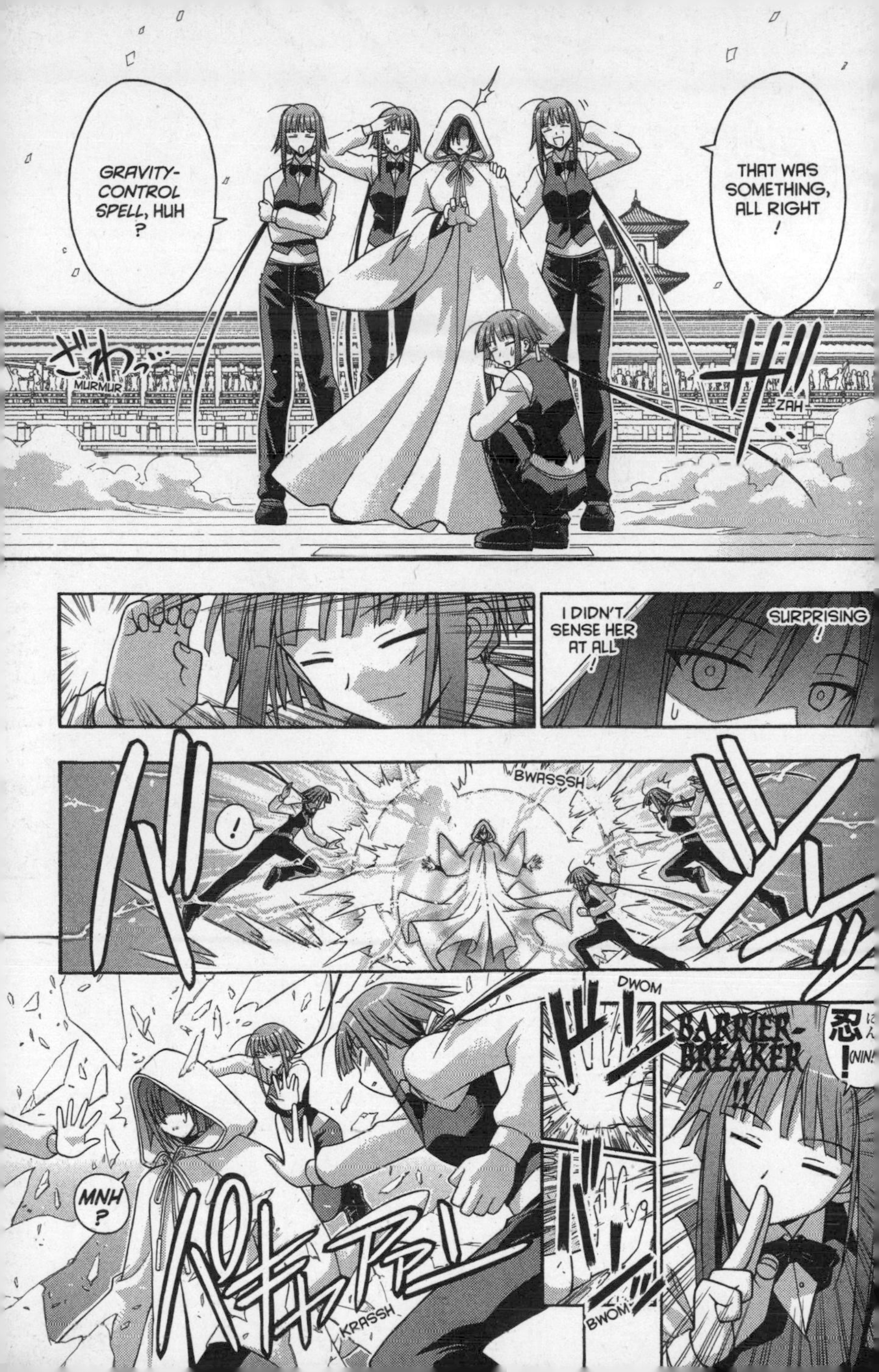
THAT WAS SOMETHING, ALL RIGHT!
ZAH
GRAVITY-CONTROL SPELL, HUH?
ざわっ
MURMUR
SURPRISING!
I DIDN'T SENSE HER AT ALL!
BWASSSH
!
忍!
(NIN!)
BARRIER-BREAKER!!
DWOM
BWOM
MNH?
KRASSH

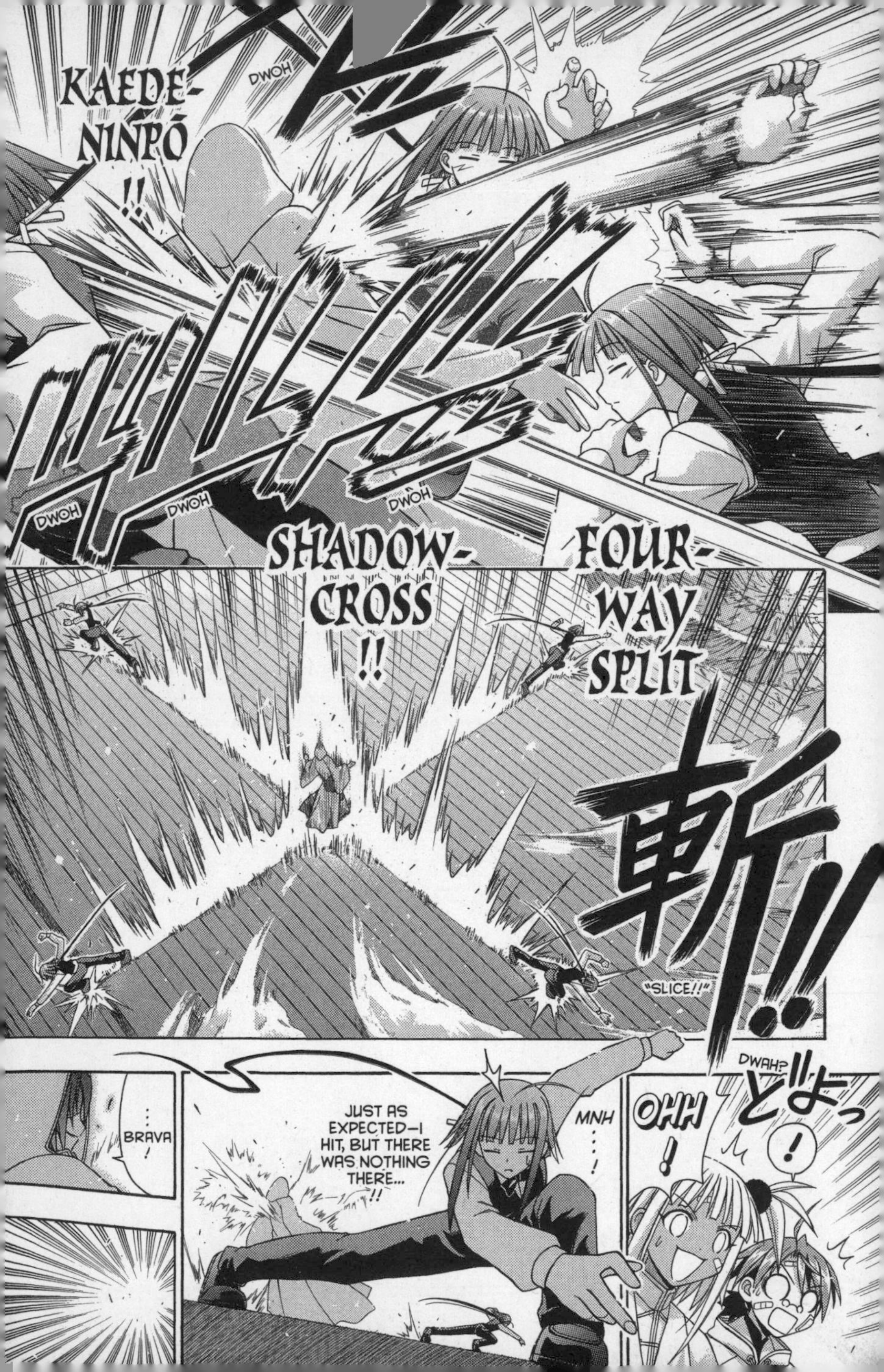
KAEDE-NINPŌ!!
DWOH
DWOH
DWOH
DWOH
FOUR-WAY SPLIT
SHADOW-CROSS!!
斬!!
"SLICE!!"
DWAH?!
どよっ
!
OHH!
MNH...!
JUST AS EXPECTED—I HIT, BUT THERE WAS NOTHING THERE...!!
...BRAVA!

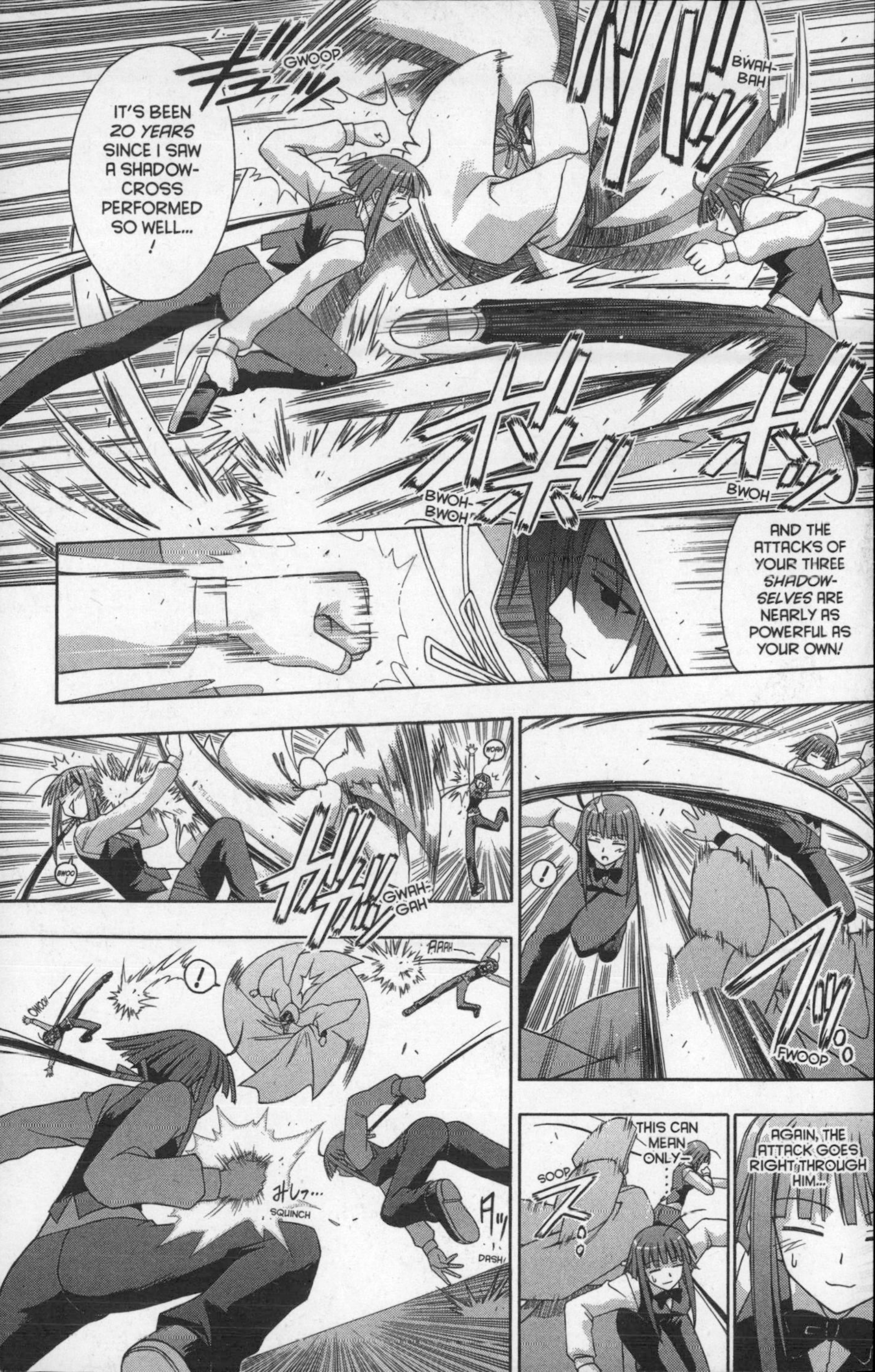
BWAH-BAH
GWOOP
IT'S BEEN *20 YEARS* SINCE I SAW A SHADOW-CROSS PERFORMED SO WELL...!
BWOH
BWOH-BWOH
AND THE ATTACKS OF YOUR THREE *SHADOW-SELVES* ARE NEARLY AS POWERFUL AS YOUR OWN!
!
FWOOP
WOAH
BWOO!
GWAH-GAH
AGAIN, THE ATTACK GOES RIGHT THROUGH HIM...
THIS CAN MEAN ONLY—
SOOP
DASH!
AAAH
!
SQUINCH

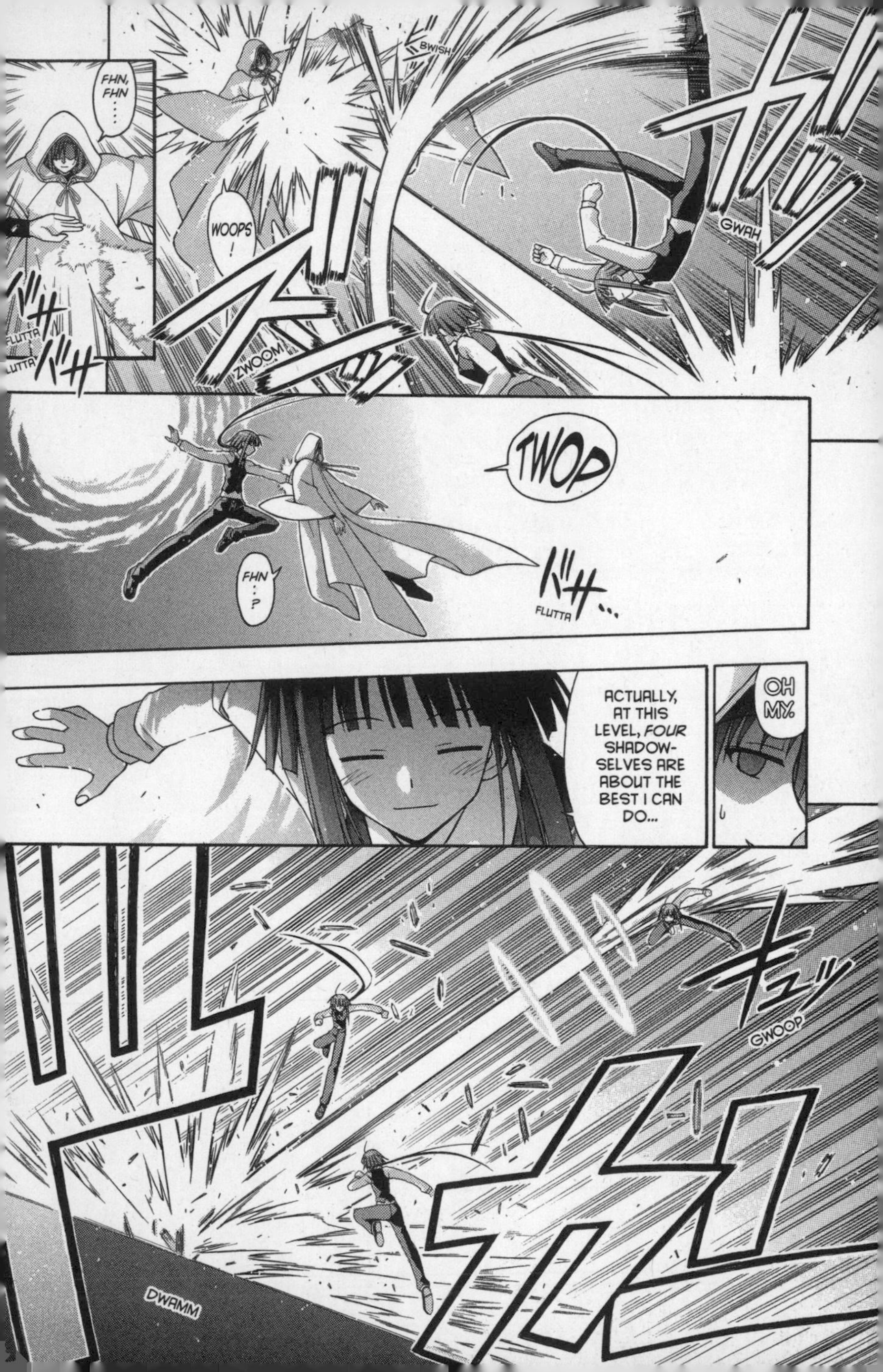
BWISH
GWAH
WOOPS!
ZWOOM
FHN, FHN......
FLUTTA
FLUTTA
TWOP
FLUTTA...
FHN..?
OH MY.
ACTUALLY, AT THIS LEVEL, *FOUR* SHADOW-SELVES ARE ABOUT THE BEST I CAN DO...
GWOOP
DWAMM

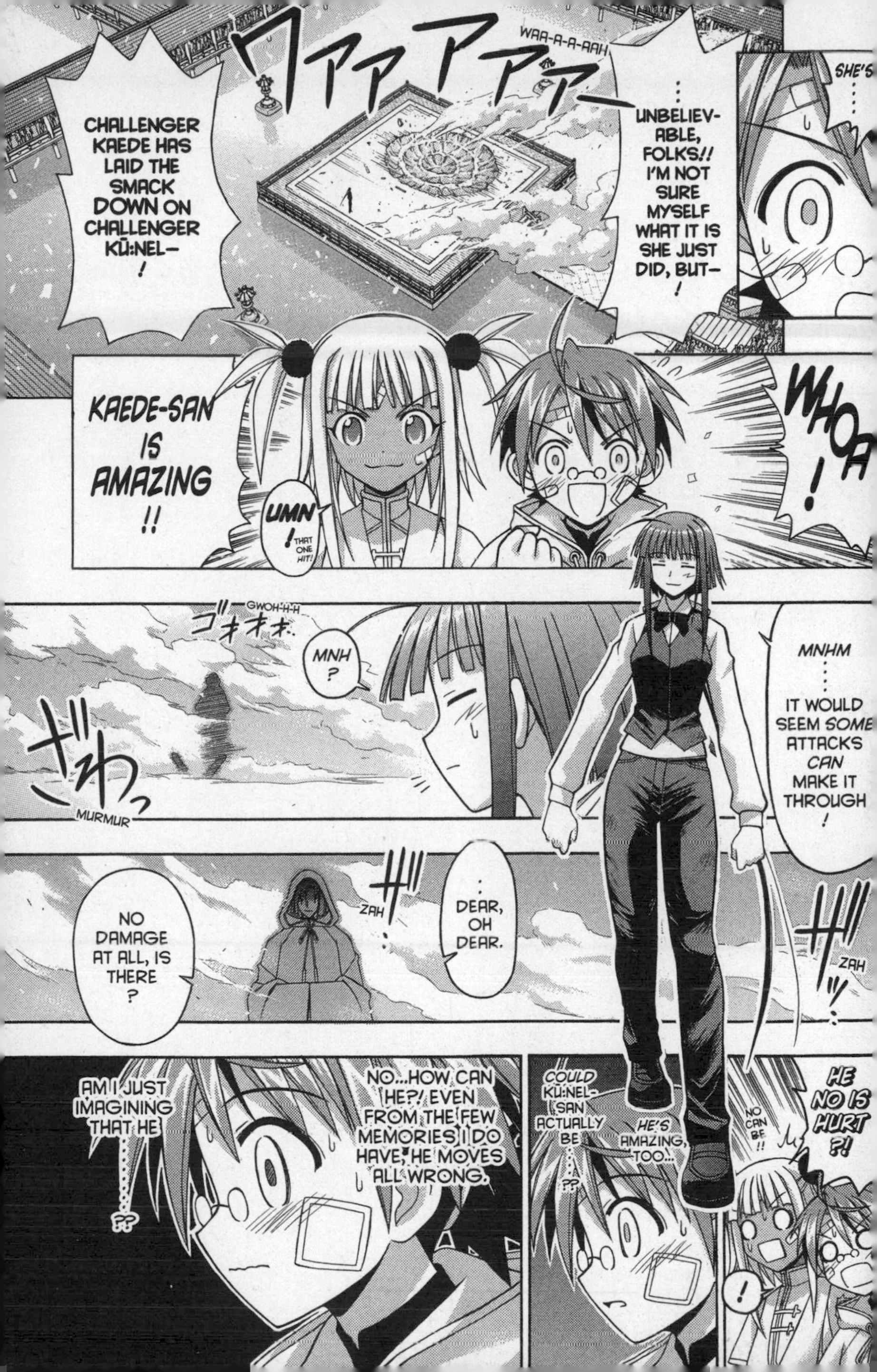
SHE'S......
WAA-A-A-AAH
...UNBELIEVABLE, FOLKS!! I'M NOT SURE MYSELF WHAT IT IS SHE JUST DID, BUT-!
CHALLENGER KAEDE HAS LAID THE SMACK DOWN ON CHALLENGER KŪ:NEL-!
WHOA!
UMN! THAT ONE HIT!
KAEDE-SAN IS AMAZING!!
MNHM... IT WOULD SEEM SOME ATTACKS CAN MAKE IT THROUGH!
MNH?
GWOH-H-H
MURMUR
ZAH
...DEAR, OH DEAR.
ZAH
NO DAMAGE AT ALL, IS THERE?
HE NO IS HURT?!
NO CAN BE!!
HE'S AMAZING, TOO...
COULD KŪ:NEL-SAN ACTUALLY BE...??
NO...HOW CAN HE?! EVEN FROM THE FEW MEMORIES I DO HAVE, HE MOVES ALL WRONG.
AM I JUST IMAGINING THAT HE......??

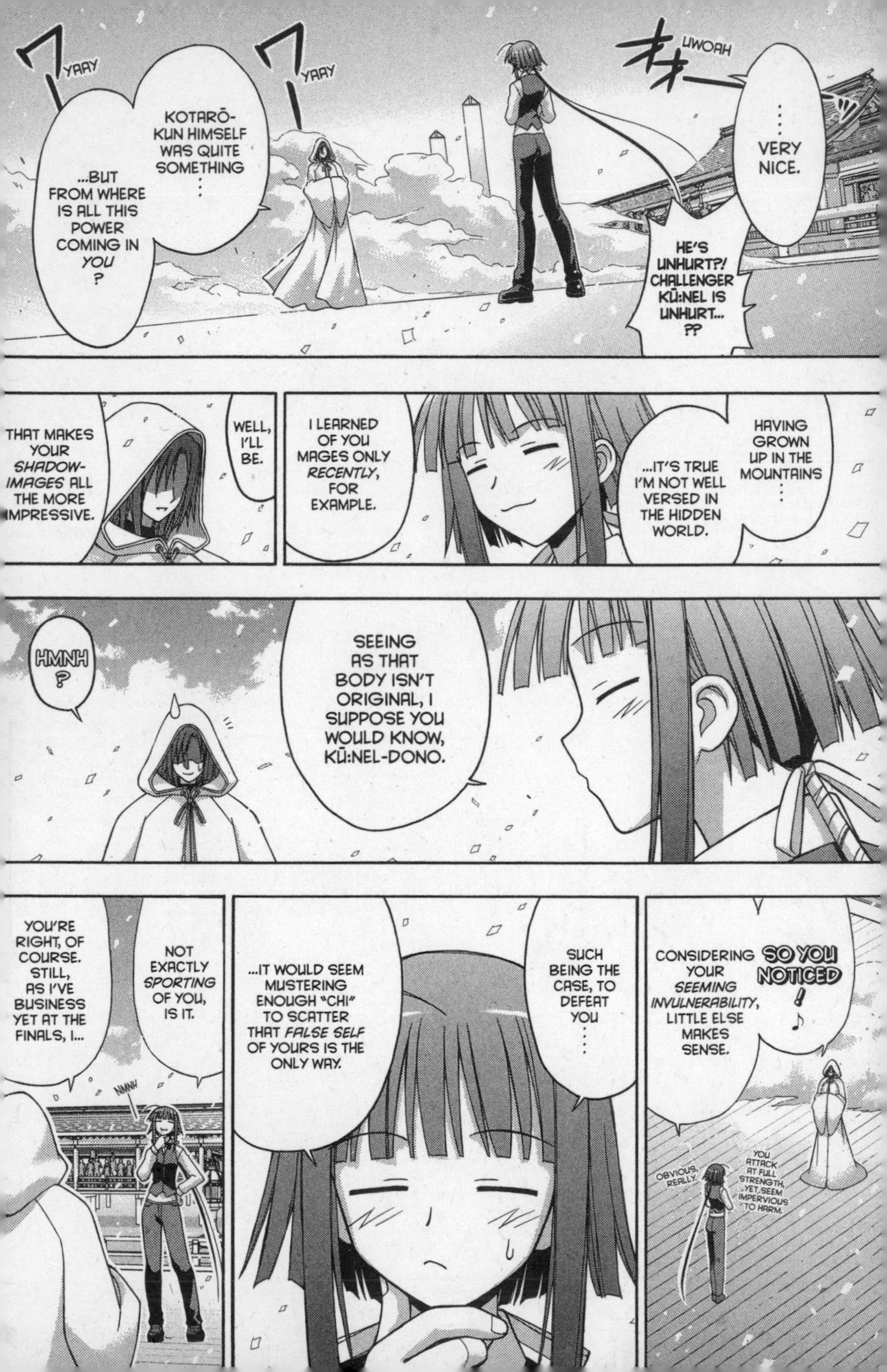
UWOAH
...VERY NICE.
HE'S UNHURT?! CHALLENGER KŪ:NEL IS UNHURT...??
YAAY
KOTARŌ-KUN HIMSELF WAS QUITE SOMETHING...
...BUT FROM WHERE IS ALL THIS POWER COMING IN *YOU*?
YAAY
HAVING GROWN UP IN THE MOUNTAINS...
...IT'S TRUE I'M NOT WELL VERSED IN THE HIDDEN WORLD.
I LEARNED OF YOU MAGES ONLY *RECENTLY*, FOR EXAMPLE.
WELL, I'LL BE.
THAT MAKES YOUR *SHADOW-IMAGES* ALL THE MORE IMPRESSIVE.
SEEING AS THAT BODY ISN'T ORIGINAL, I SUPPOSE YOU WOULD KNOW, KŪ:NEL-DONO.
HMNH?
SO YOU NOTICED! ♪
CONSIDERING YOUR *SEEMING INVULNERABILITY*, LITTLE ELSE MAKES SENSE.
YOU ATTACK AT FULL STRENGTH, YET SEEM IMPERVIOUS TO HARM.
OBVIOUS, REALLY.
SUCH BEING THE CASE, TO DEFEAT YOU...
...IT WOULD SEEM MUSTERING ENOUGH "CHI" TO SCATTER THAT *FALSE SELF* OF YOURS IS THE ONLY WAY.
NOT EXACTLY *SPORTING* OF YOU, IS IT.
YOU'RE RIGHT, OF COURSE. STILL, AS I'VE BUSINESS YET AT THE FINALS, I...
NMNH

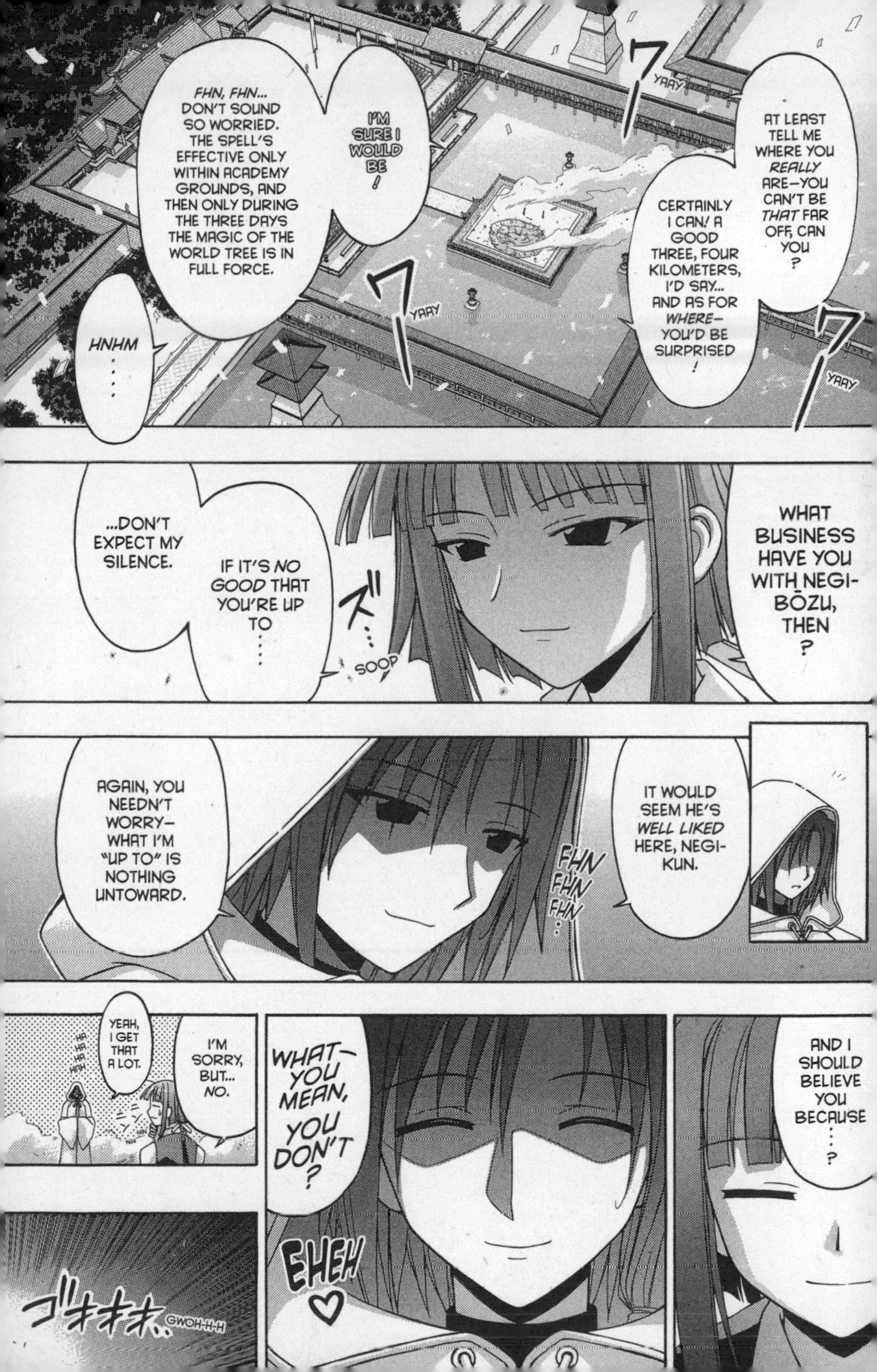
AT LEAST TELL ME WHERE YOU *REALLY* ARE—YOU CAN'T BE *THAT* FAR OFF, CAN YOU?
YAAY
CERTAINLY I CAN! A GOOD THREE, FOUR KILOMETERS, I'D SAY... AND AS FOR *WHERE*— YOU'D BE SURPRISED!
YAAY
I'M SURE I WOULD BE!
FHN, FHN... DON'T SOUND SO WORRIED. THE SPELL'S EFFECTIVE ONLY WITHIN ACADEMY GROUNDS, AND THEN ONLY DURING THE THREE DAYS THE MAGIC OF THE WORLD TREE IS IN FULL FORCE.
YAAY
HNHM....
WHAT BUSINESS HAVE YOU WITH NEGI-BŌZU, THEN?
IF IT'S *NO GOOD* THAT YOU'RE UP TO....
...DON'T EXPECT MY SILENCE.
SOOP
IT WOULD SEEM HE'S *WELL LIKED* HERE, NEGI-KUN.
FHN FHN FHN...
AGAIN, YOU NEEDN'T WORRY— WHAT I'M "UP TO" IS NOTHING UNTOWARD.
AND I SHOULD BELIEVE YOU BECAUSE...?
WHAT— YOU MEAN, YOU DON'T?
EHEH ♥
I'M SORRY, BUT... NO.
YEAH, I GET THAT A LOT.
HA HA HA HAH
GWOH-H-H

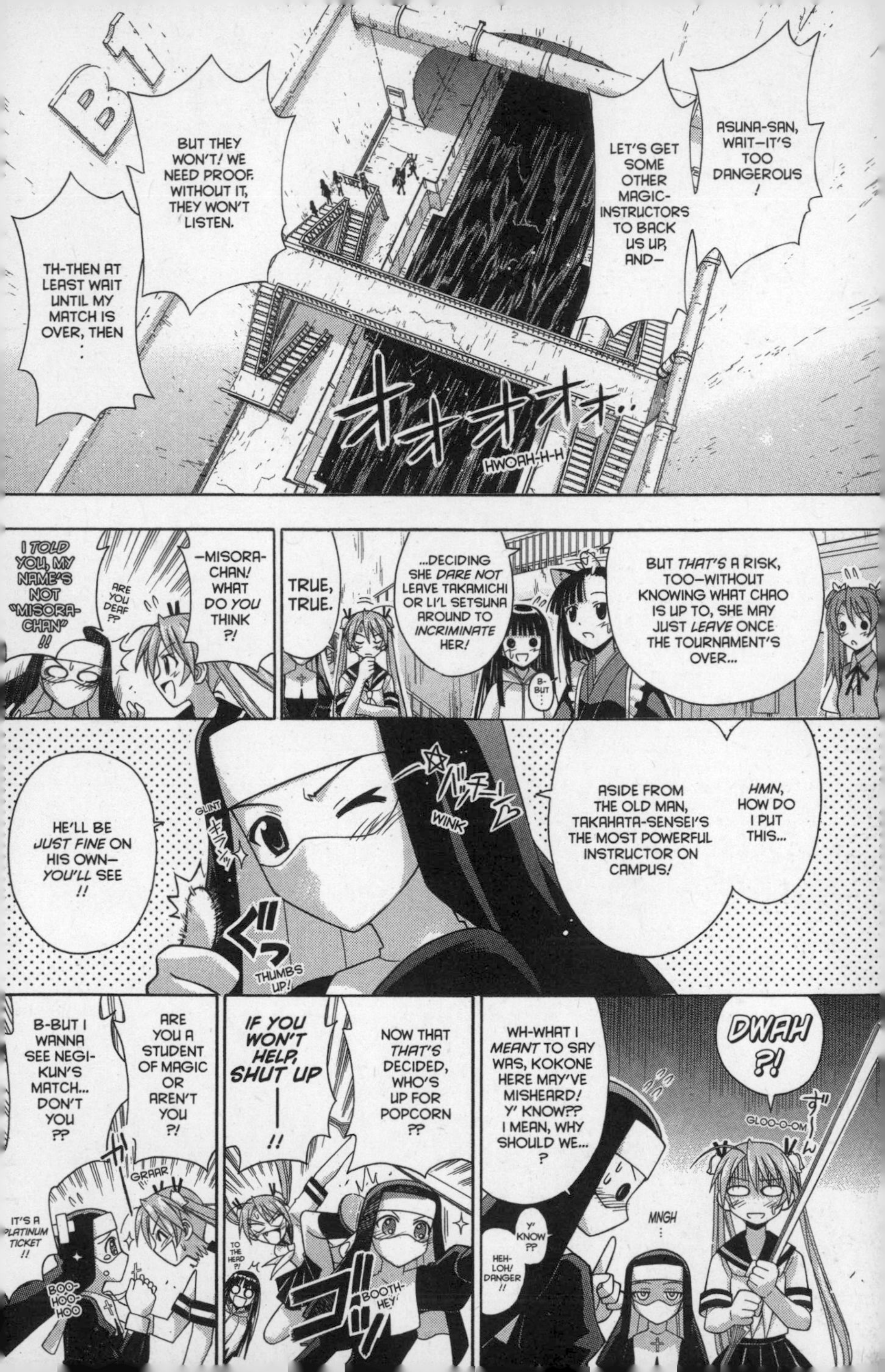
ASUNA-SAN, WAIT—IT'S TOO DANGEROUS!
LET'S GET SOME OTHER MAGIC-INSTRUCTORS TO BACK US UP, AND—
BUT THEY WON'T! WE NEED PROOF. WITHOUT IT, THEY WON'T LISTEN.
TH-THEN AT LEAST WAIT UNTIL MY MATCH IS OVER, THEN:
HWOAH-H-H
BUT THAT'S A RISK, TOO—WITHOUT KNOWING WHAT CHAO IS UP TO, SHE MAY JUST LEAVE ONCE THE TOURNAMENT'S OVER...
B-BUT...
...DECIDING SHE DARE NOT LEAVE TAKAMICHI OR LI'L SETSUNA AROUND TO INCRIMINATE HER!
TRUE, TRUE.
—MISORA-CHAN! WHAT DO YOU THINK?!
ARE YOU DEAF??
I TOLD YOU, MY NAME'S NOT "MISORA-CHAN"!!
HMN, HOW DO I PUT THIS...
ASIDE FROM THE OLD MAN, TAKAHATA-SENSEI'S THE MOST POWERFUL INSTRUCTOR ON CAMPUS!
WINK
GLINT
HE'LL BE JUST FINE ON HIS OWN—YOU'LL SEE!!
THUMBS UP!
DWAH?!
GLOO-O-OM
WH-WHAT I MEANT TO SAY WAS, KOKONE HERE MAY'VE MISHEARD! Y' KNOW?? I MEAN, WHY SHOULD WE...?
MNGH...
Y' KNOW??
HEH-LOH! DANGER!!
NOW THAT THAT'S DECIDED, WHO'S UP FOR POPCORN??
IF YOU WON'T HELP, SHUT UP—!!
TO THE HEAD?!
BOOTH-HEY
ARE YOU A STUDENT OF MAGIC OR AREN'T YOU?!
B-BUT I WANNA SEE NEGI-KUN'S MATCH... DON'T YOU??
GRAAR
IT'S A PLATINUM TICKET!!
BOO-HOO-HOO

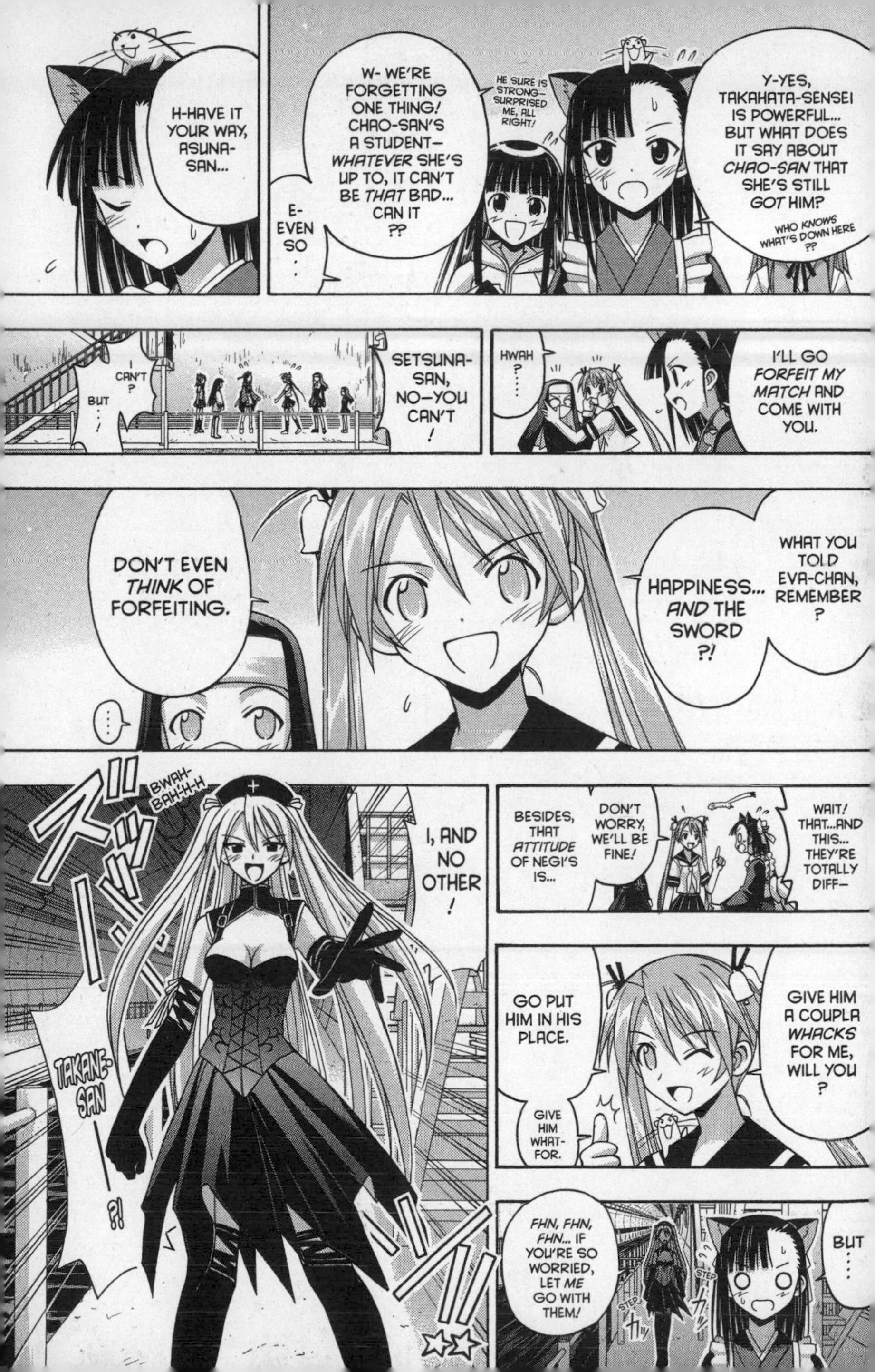
Y-YES, TAKAHATA-SENSEI IS POWERFUL... BUT WHAT DOES IT SAY ABOUT CHAO-SAN THAT SHE'S STILL GOT HIM?
WHO KNOWS WHAT'S DOWN HERE ??
HE SURE IS STRONG—SURPRISED ME, ALL RIGHT!
W- WE'RE FORGETTING ONE THING! CHAO-SAN'S A STUDENT—WHATEVER SHE'S UP TO, IT CAN'T BE THAT BAD... CAN IT ??
E-EVEN SO ..
H-HAVE IT YOUR WAY, ASUNA-SAN...
I'LL GO FORFEIT MY MATCH AND COME WITH YOU.
HWAH ?.....
SETSUNA-SAN, NO—YOU CAN'T !
I CAN'T ?
BUT . . !
WHAT YOU TOLD EVA-CHAN, REMEMBER ?
HAPPINESS... AND THE SWORD ?!
DON'T EVEN THINK OF FORFEITING.
.....
WAIT! THAT...AND THIS... THEY'RE TOTALLY DIFF—
DON'T WORRY, WE'LL BE FINE!
BESIDES, THAT ATTITUDE OF NEGI'S IS...
GIVE HIM A COUPLA WHACKS FOR ME, WILL YOU ?
GO PUT HIM IN HIS PLACE.
GIVE HIM WHAT-FOR.
BUT ....
STEP
STEP
FHN, FHN, FHN... IF YOU'RE SO WORRIED, LET ME GO WITH THEM!
I, AND NO OTHER !
BWAH-BAH-H-H
TAKANE-SAN— ?!

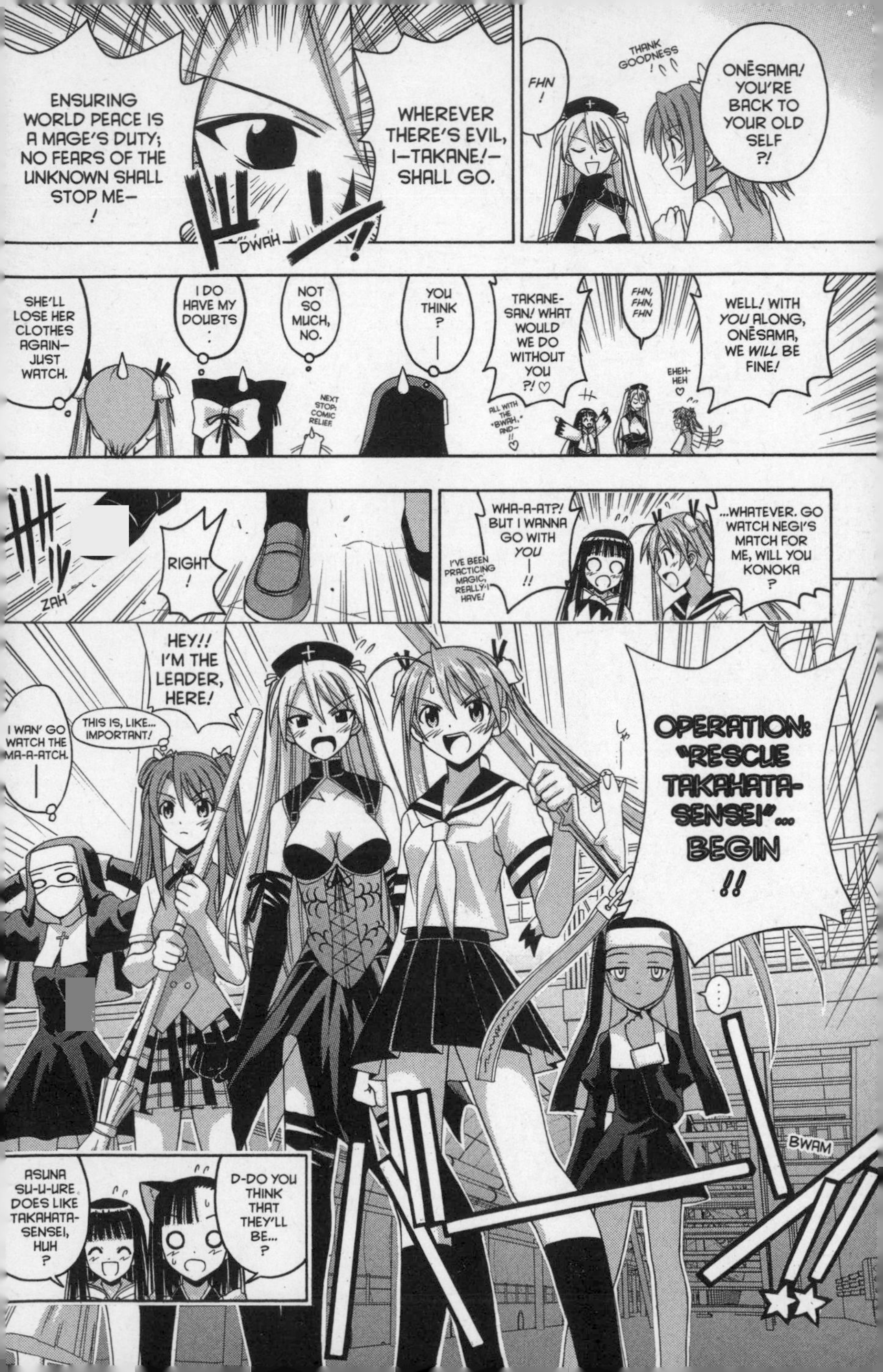
ONĒSAMA! YOU'RE BACK TO YOUR OLD SELF?!
THANK GOODNESS!
FHN!
WHEREVER THERE'S EVIL, I—TAKANE!—SHALL GO.
ENSURING WORLD PEACE IS A MAGE'S DUTY; NO FEARS OF THE UNKNOWN SHALL STOP ME—!
DWAH
WELL! WITH YOU ALONG, ONĒSAMA, WE WILL BE FINE!
EHEH-HEH
FHN, FHN, FHN
TAKANE-SAN! WHAT WOULD WE DO WITHOUT YOU?!♡
ALL WITH THE "BWAH," AND—!!♡
YOU THINK?
NEXT STOP: COMIC RELIEF.
NOT SO MUCH, NO.
I DO HAVE MY DOUBTS.
SHE'LL LOSE HER CLOTHES AGAIN—JUST WATCH.
...WHATEVER. GO WATCH NEGI'S MATCH FOR ME, WILL YOU KONOKA?
WHA-A-AT?! BUT I WANNA GO WITH YOU!!
I'VE BEEN PRACTICING MAGIC, REALLY I HAVE!
RIGHT!
ZAH
OPERATION: "RESCUE TAKAHATA-SENSEI"... BEGIN!!
HEY!! I'M THE LEADER, HERE!
THIS IS, LIKE... IMPORTANT!
I WAN' GO WATCH THE MA-A-ATCH.
...
BWAM
D-DO YOU THINK THAT THEY'LL BE...?
ASUNA SU-U-URE DOES LIKE TAKAHATA-SENSEI, HUH?

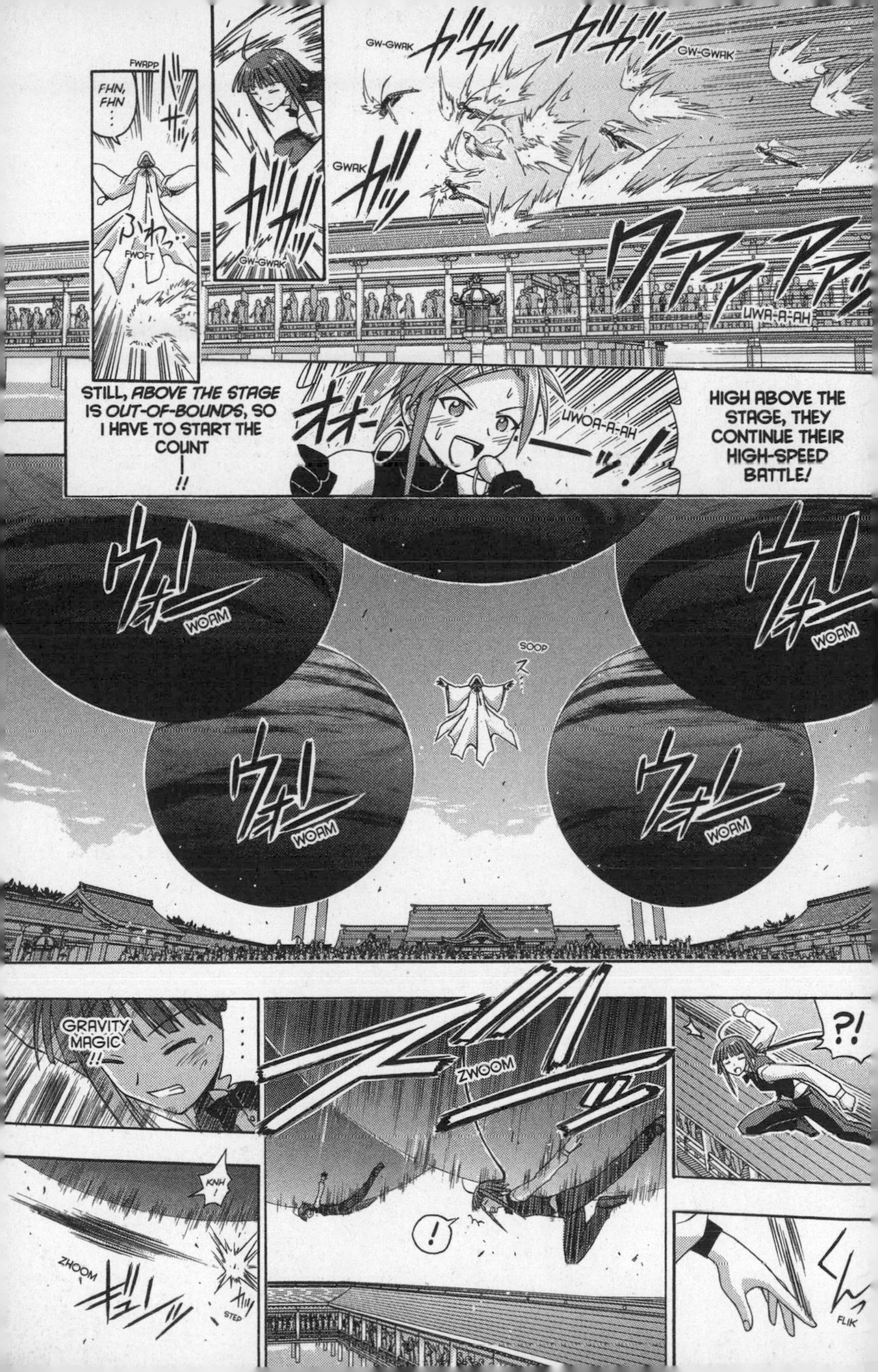
GW-GWAK
GW-GWAK
GWAK
UWA-A-AH
GW-GWAK
FWAPP
FHN, FHN...
FWOFT
HIGH ABOVE THE STAGE, THEY CONTINUE THEIR HIGH-SPEED BATTLE!
UWOA-A-AH
STILL, ABOVE THE STAGE IS OUT-OF-BOUNDS, SO I HAVE TO START THE COUNT—!!
WOAM
WOAM
SOOP
WOAM
WOAM
?!
ZWOOM
...
GRAVITY MAGIC!!
FLIK
!
KNH!
ZHOOM
STEP

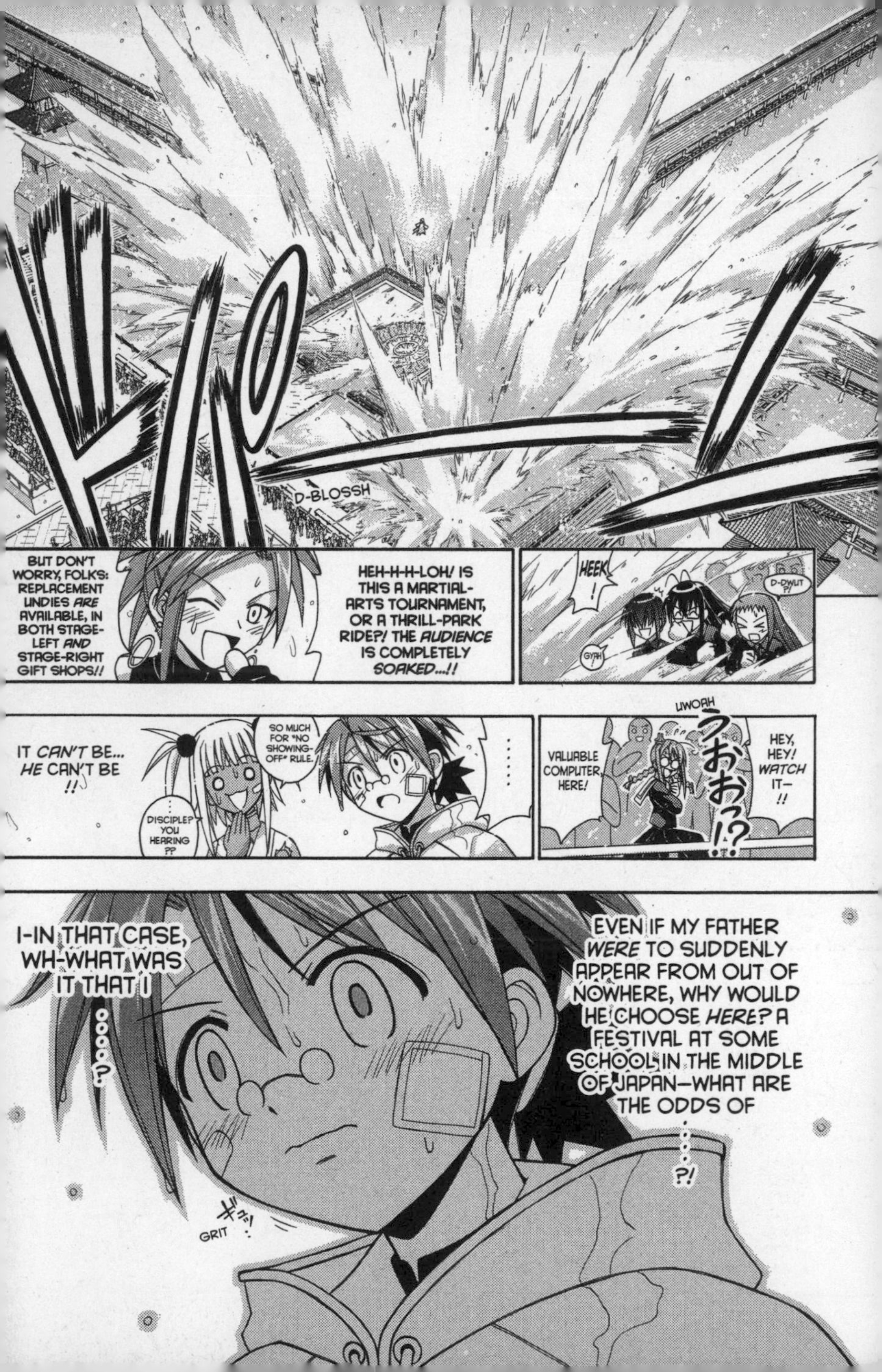
D-BLOSSH
HEEK!
D-DWUT?!
GYAH
HEH-H-H-LOH! IS THIS A MARTIAL-ARTS TOURNAMENT, OR A THRILL-PARK RIDE?! THE AUDIENCE IS COMPLETELY SOAKED...!!
BUT DON'T WORRY, FOLKS: REPLACEMENT UNDIES ARE AVAILABLE, IN BOTH STAGE-LEFT AND STAGE-RIGHT GIFT SHOPS!!
HEY, HEY! WATCH IT—!!
うおおっ!?
UWOAH
VALUABLE COMPUTER HERE!
......
SO MUCH FOR "NO SHOWING-OFF" RULE.
IT CAN'T BE... HE CAN'T BE!!
...DISCIPLE? YOU HEARING??
EVEN IF MY FATHER WERE TO SUDDENLY APPEAR FROM OUT OF NOWHERE, WHY WOULD HE CHOOSE HERE? A FESTIVAL AT SOME SCHOOL IN THE MIDDLE OF JAPAN—WHAT ARE THE ODDS OF ....?!
I-IN THAT CASE, WH-WHAT WAS IT THAT I ooooo?
GRIT

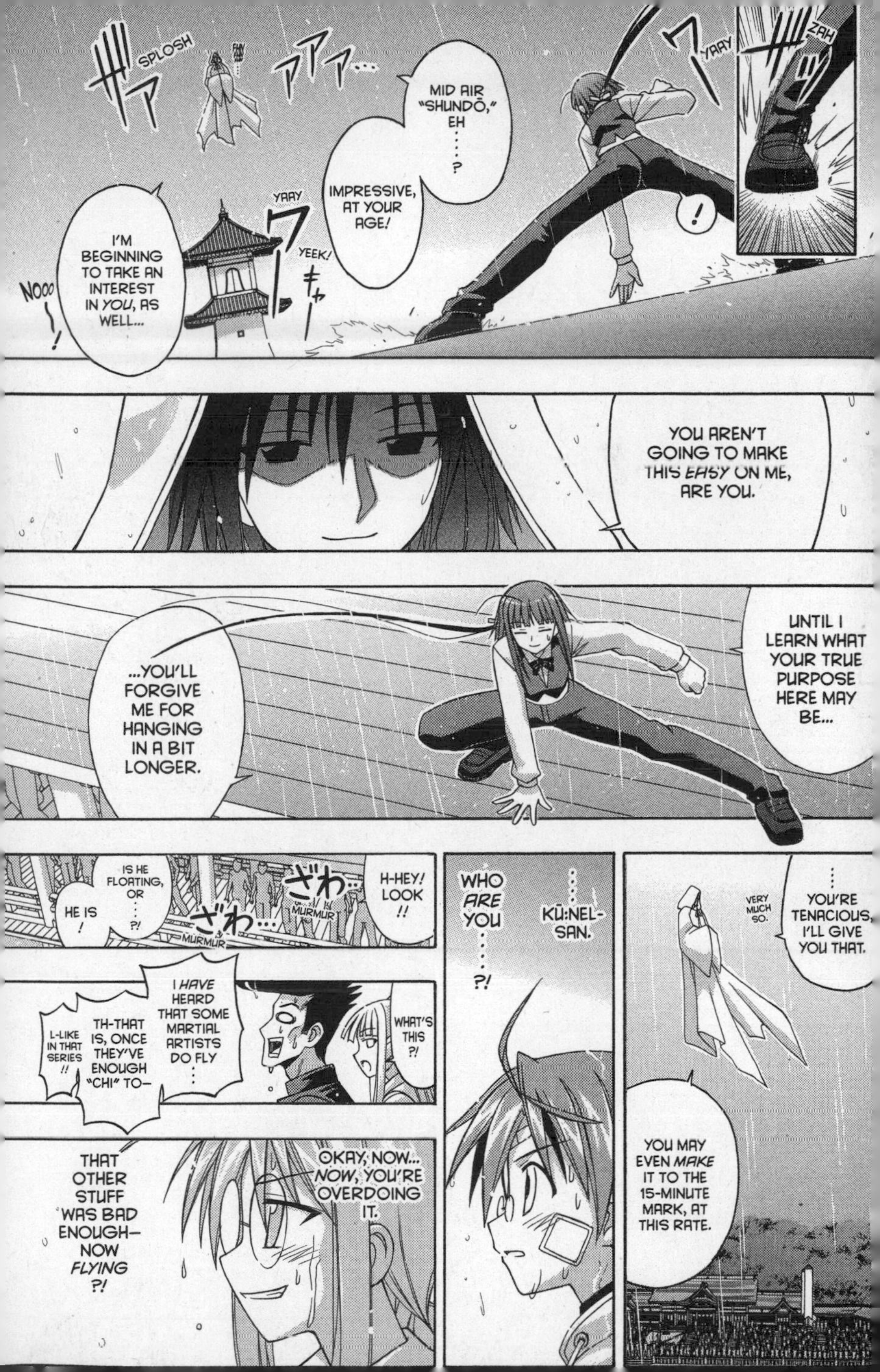

ZAH
ザッ
YAAY
ワ
!
MID AIR "SHUNDŌ," EH .....?
IMPRESSIVE, AT YOUR AGE!
アア...
SPLOSH
ザァ
YAAY
ワー
YEEK!
キャー
I'M BEGINNING TO TAKE AN INTEREST IN *YOU*, AS WELL...
NOOO~!
YOU AREN'T GOING TO MAKE THIS *EASY* ON ME, ARE YOU.
UNTIL I LEARN WHAT YOUR TRUE PURPOSE HERE MAY BE...
...YOU'LL FORGIVE ME FOR HANGING IN A BIT LONGER.
...YOU'RE TENACIOUS, I'LL GIVE YOU THAT.
VERY MUCH SO.
YOU MAY EVEN *MAKE* IT TO THE 15-MINUTE MARK, AT THIS RATE.
.....KŪ:NEL-SAN.
WHO *ARE* YOU.....?!
H-HEY! LOOK!!
ざわ...
MURMUR
ざわ...
MURMUR
IS HE FLOATING, OR ...?!
HE IS!
WHAT'S THIS?!
I *HAVE* HEARD THAT SOME MARTIAL ARTISTS DO FLY...
TH-THAT IS, ONCE THEY'VE ENOUGH "CHI" TO—
L-LIKE IN THAT SERIES!!
OKAY, NOW... *NOW*, YOU'RE OVERDOING IT.
THAT OTHER STUFF WAS BAD ENOUGH—NOW *FLYING*?!

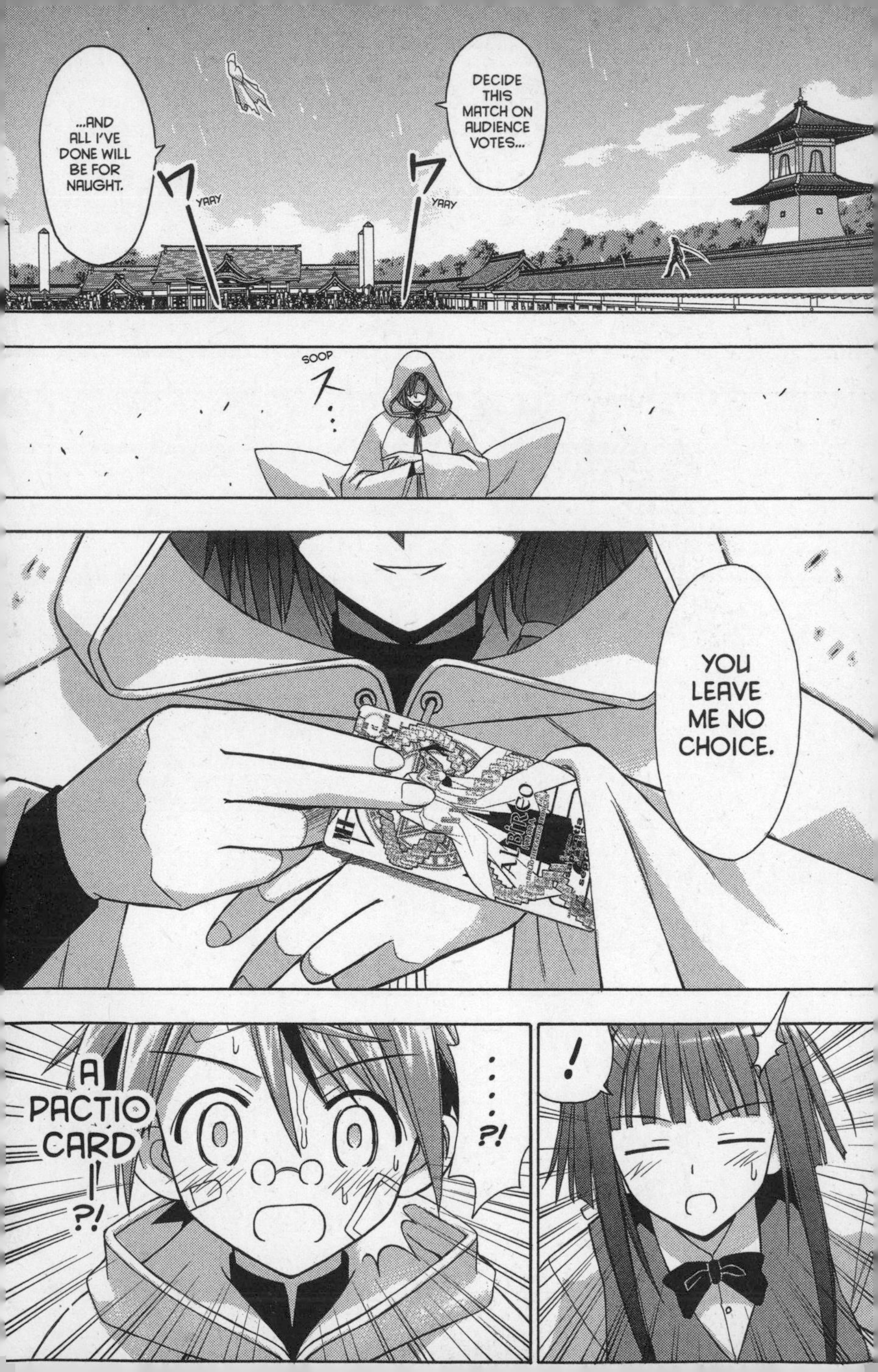
DECIDE THIS MATCH ON AUDIENCE VOTES...
YAAY
...AND ALL I'VE DONE WILL BE FOR NAUGHT.
YAAY
SOOP
YOU LEAVE ME NO CHOICE.
!
...?!
A PACTIO CARD!?!

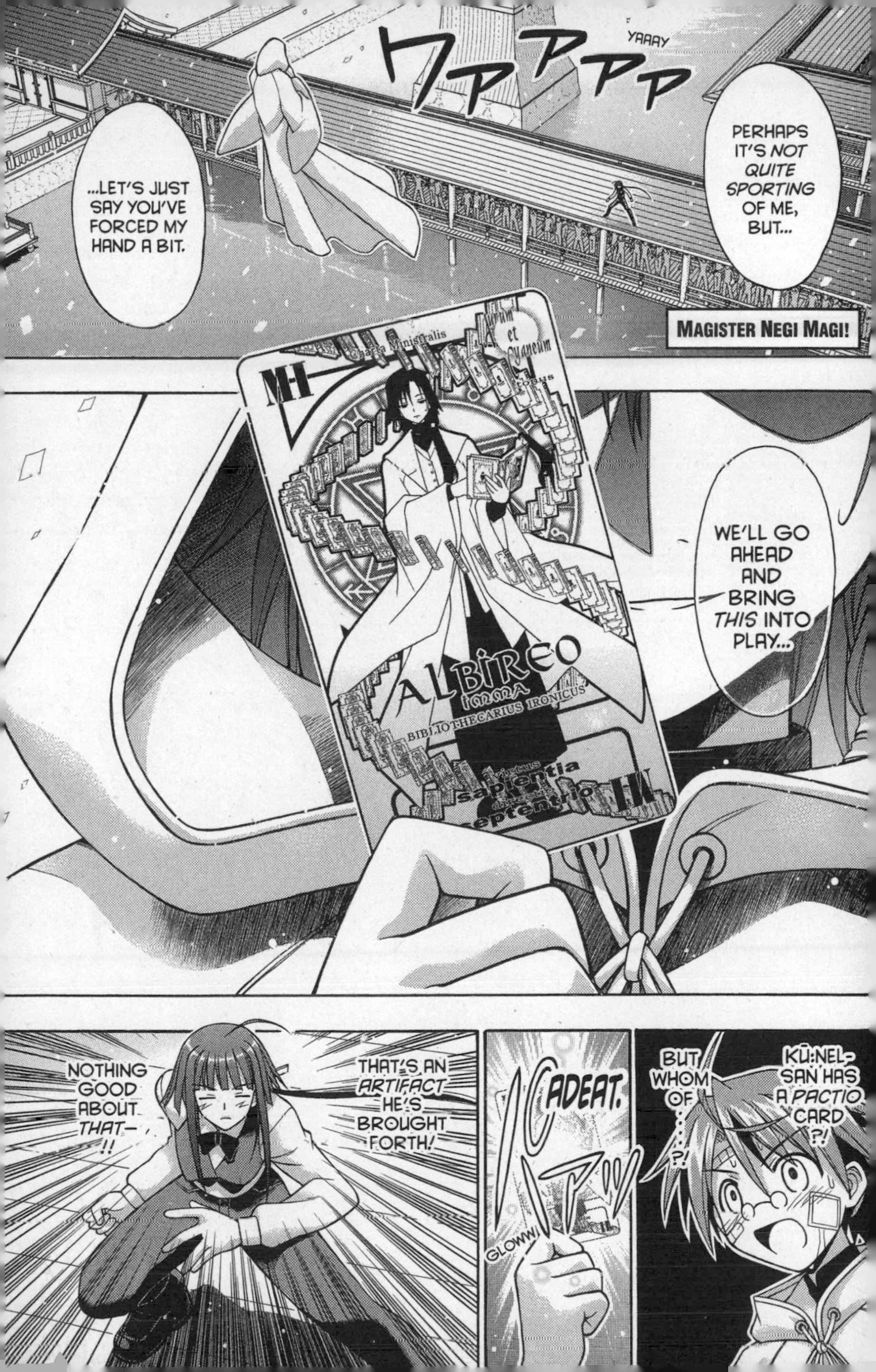
PERHAPS IT'S *NOT QUITE* SPORTING OF ME, BUT...
YAAAY
...LET'S JUST SAY YOU'VE FORCED MY HAND A BIT.
MAGISTER NEGI MAGI!
WE'LL GO AHEAD AND BRING *THIS* INTO PLAY...
ALBIREO
BIBLIOTHECARIUS IRONICUS
sapientia
septentrio
KŪ:NEL-SAN HAS A *PACTIO* CARD?!
BUT WHOM OF...?!
ADEAT.
GLOWW
THAT'S AN *ARTIFACT* HE'S BROUGHT FORTH!
NOTHING GOOD ABOUT *THAT*—!!

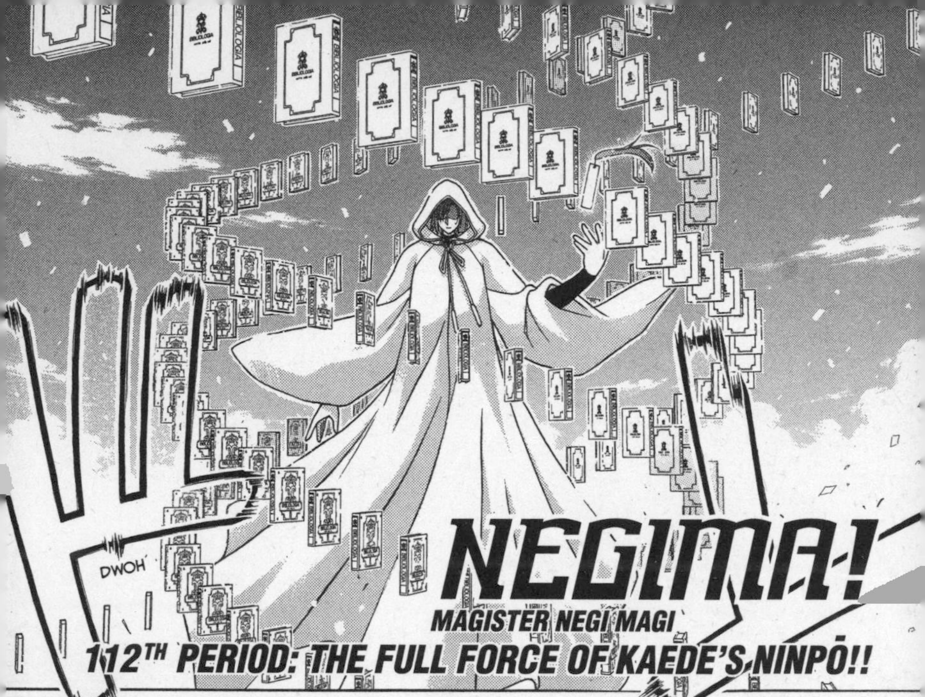
NEGIMA!
MAGISTER NEGI MAGI
112TH PERIOD: THE FULL FORCE OF KAEDE'S NINPŌ!!
DWOH

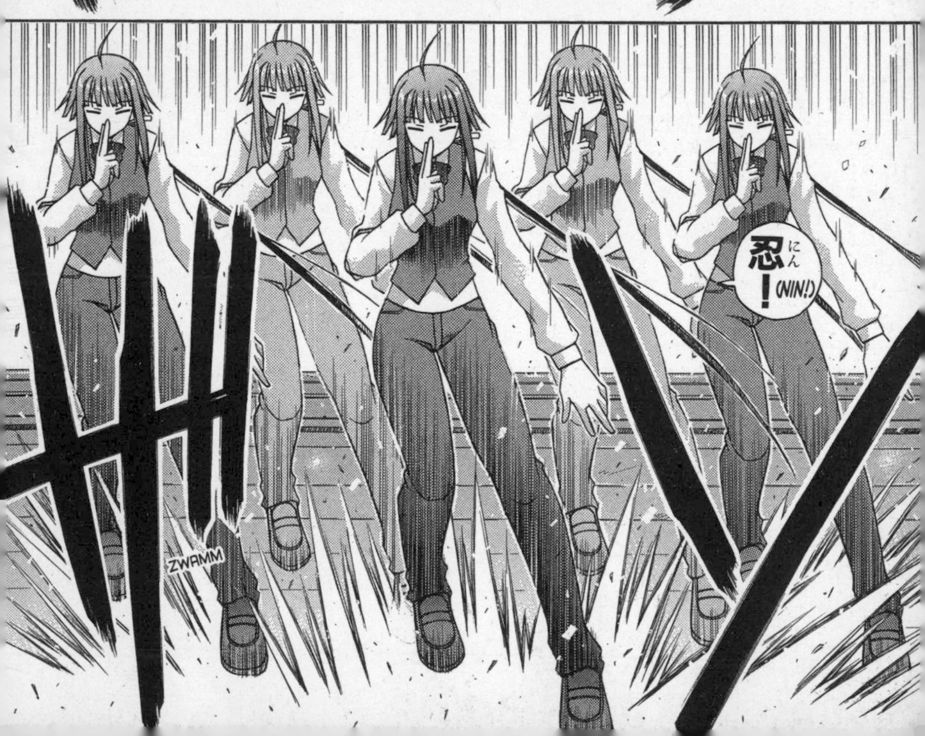
忍(にん)！ (NIN!)
ZWAMM

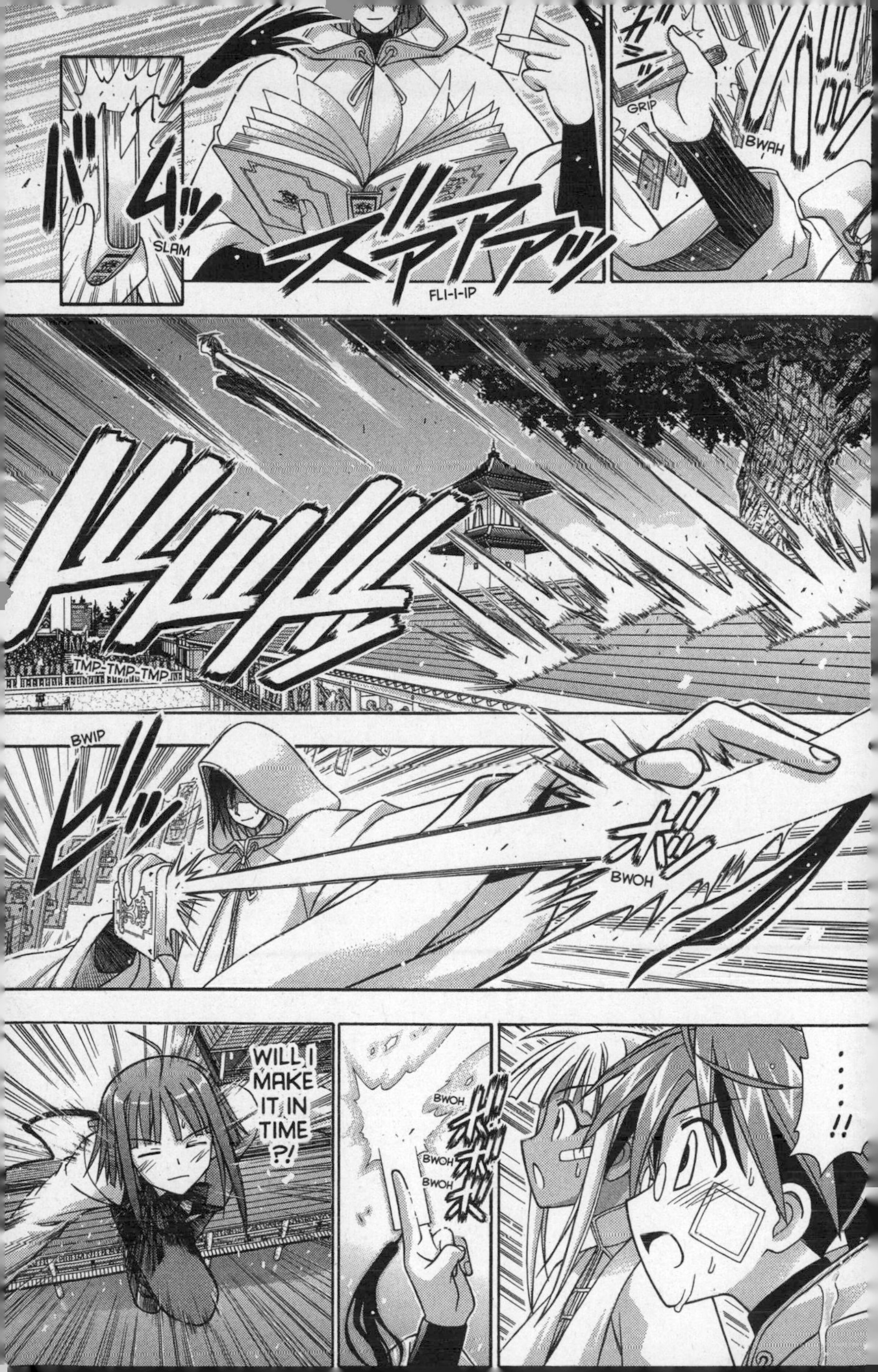
GRIP
BWAH
FLI-I-IP
SLAM
TMP-TMP-TMP
BWIP
BWOH
...!!
BWOH
BWOH
BWOH
WILL I MAKE IT IN TIME?!

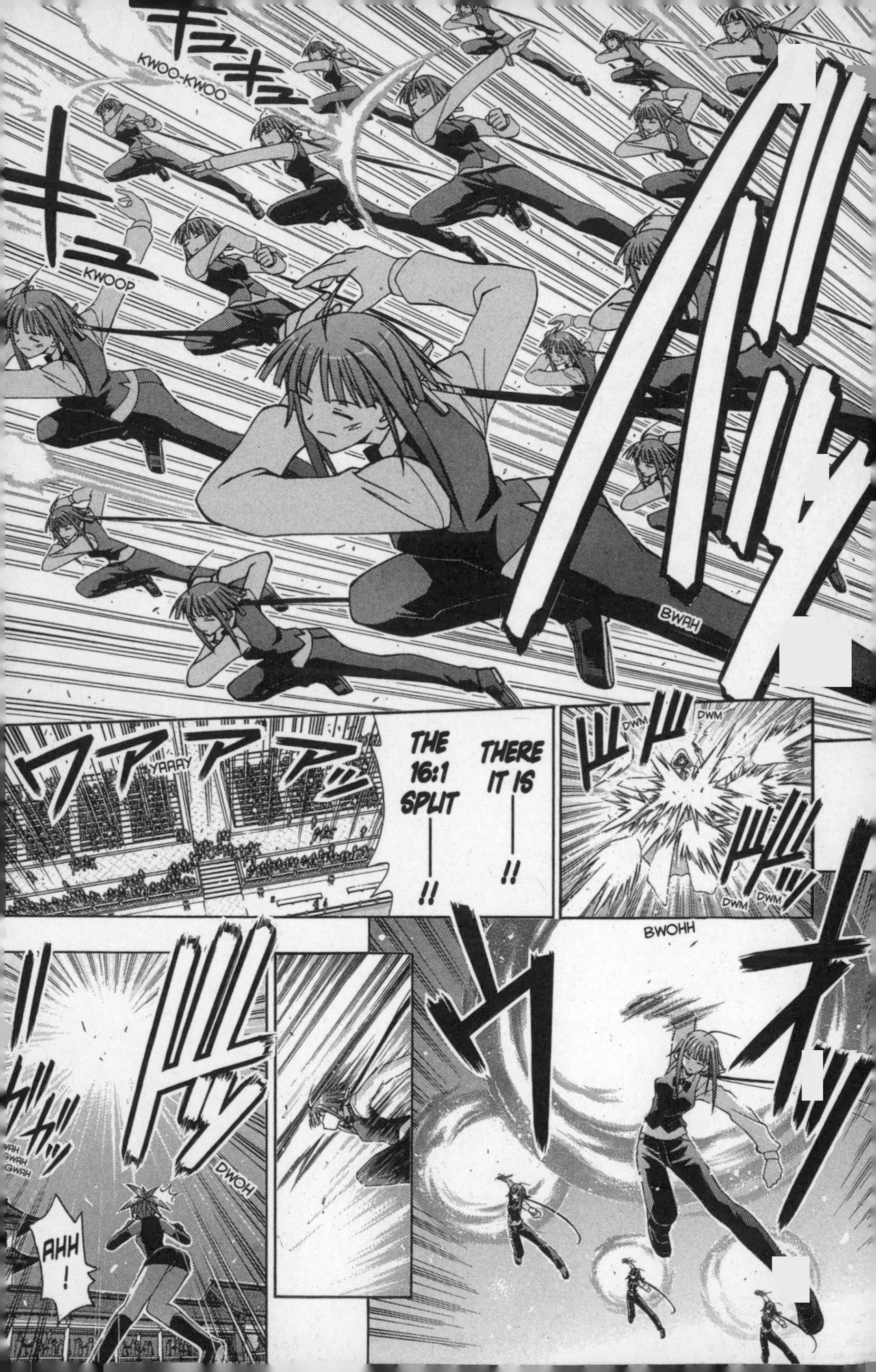
KWOO-KWOO
KWOOP
BWAH
DWM
DWM
DWM
DWM
THERE IT IS——!!
THE 16:1 SPLIT——!!
YAAAY
BWOHH
DWOH
GWAH
GWAH
AHH!

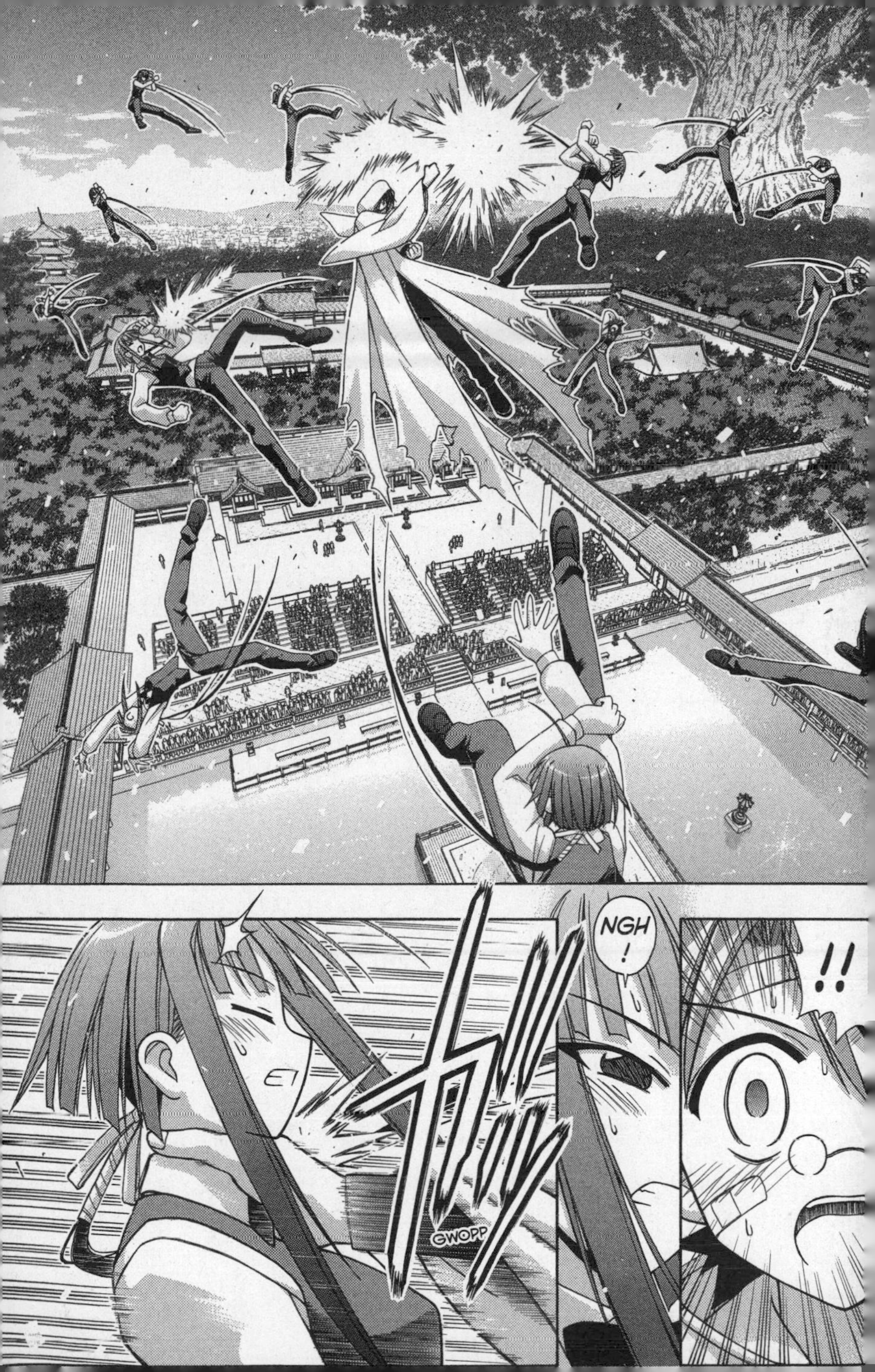
!!
NGH
!
GWOPP

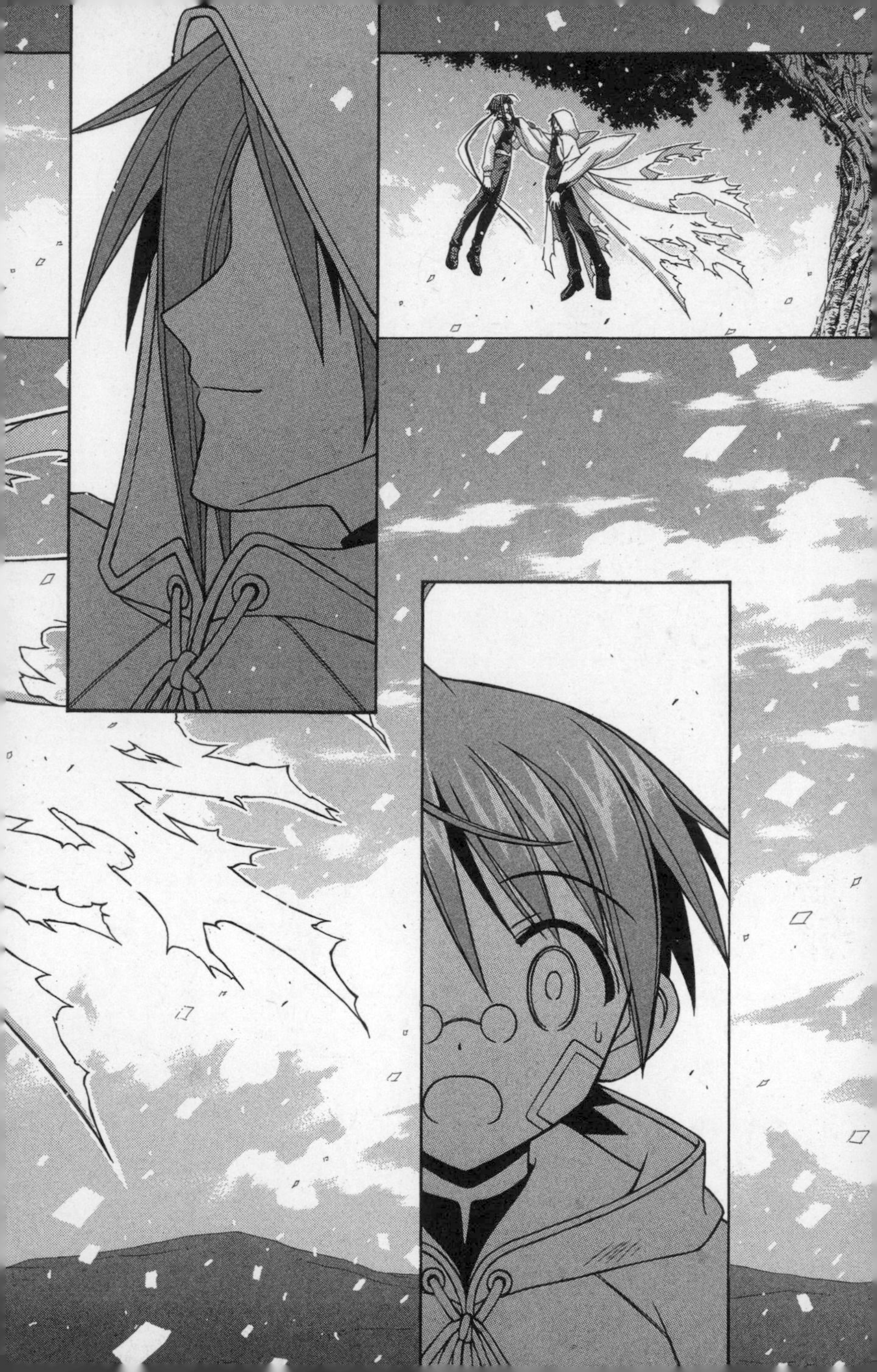

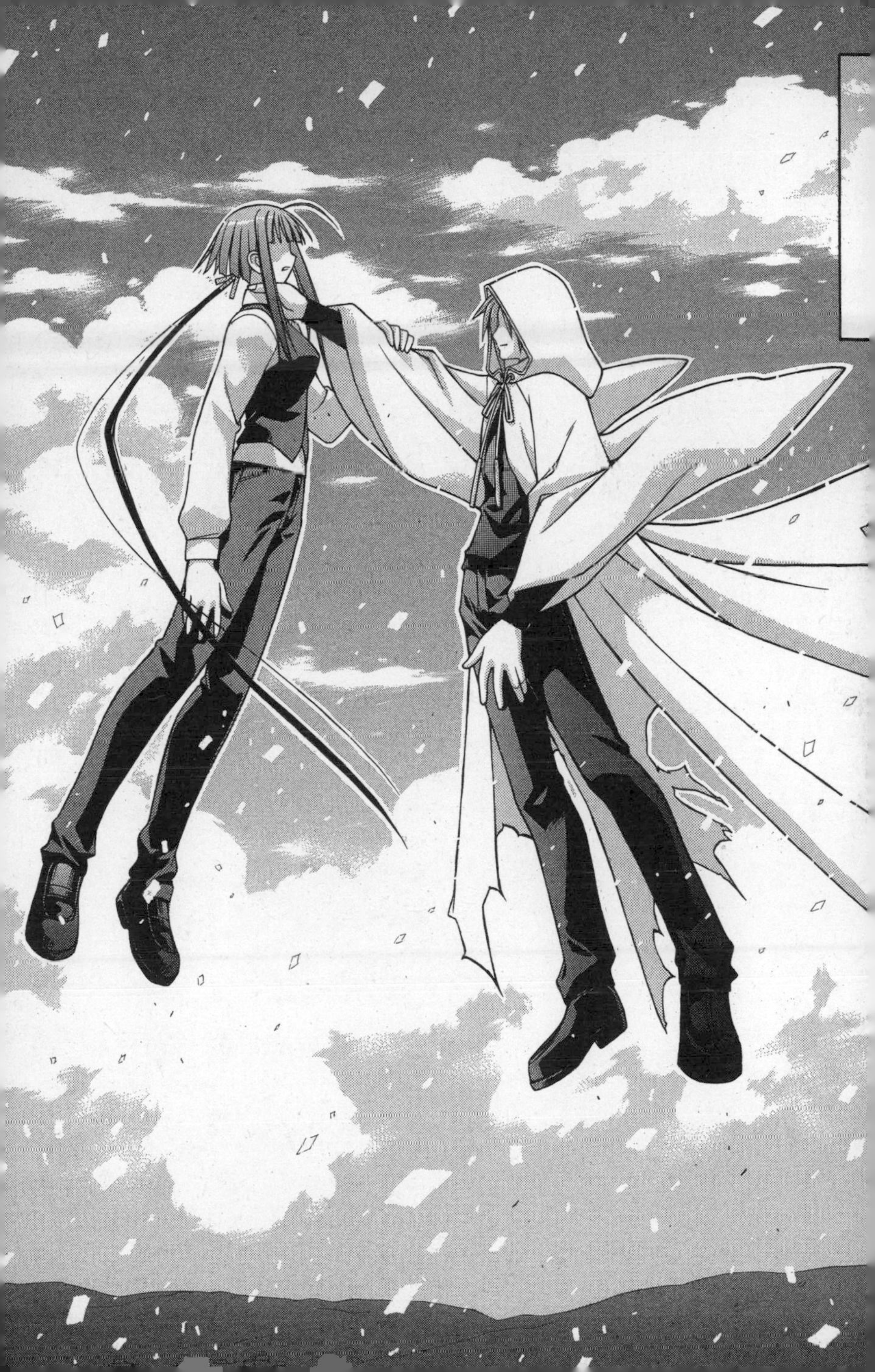

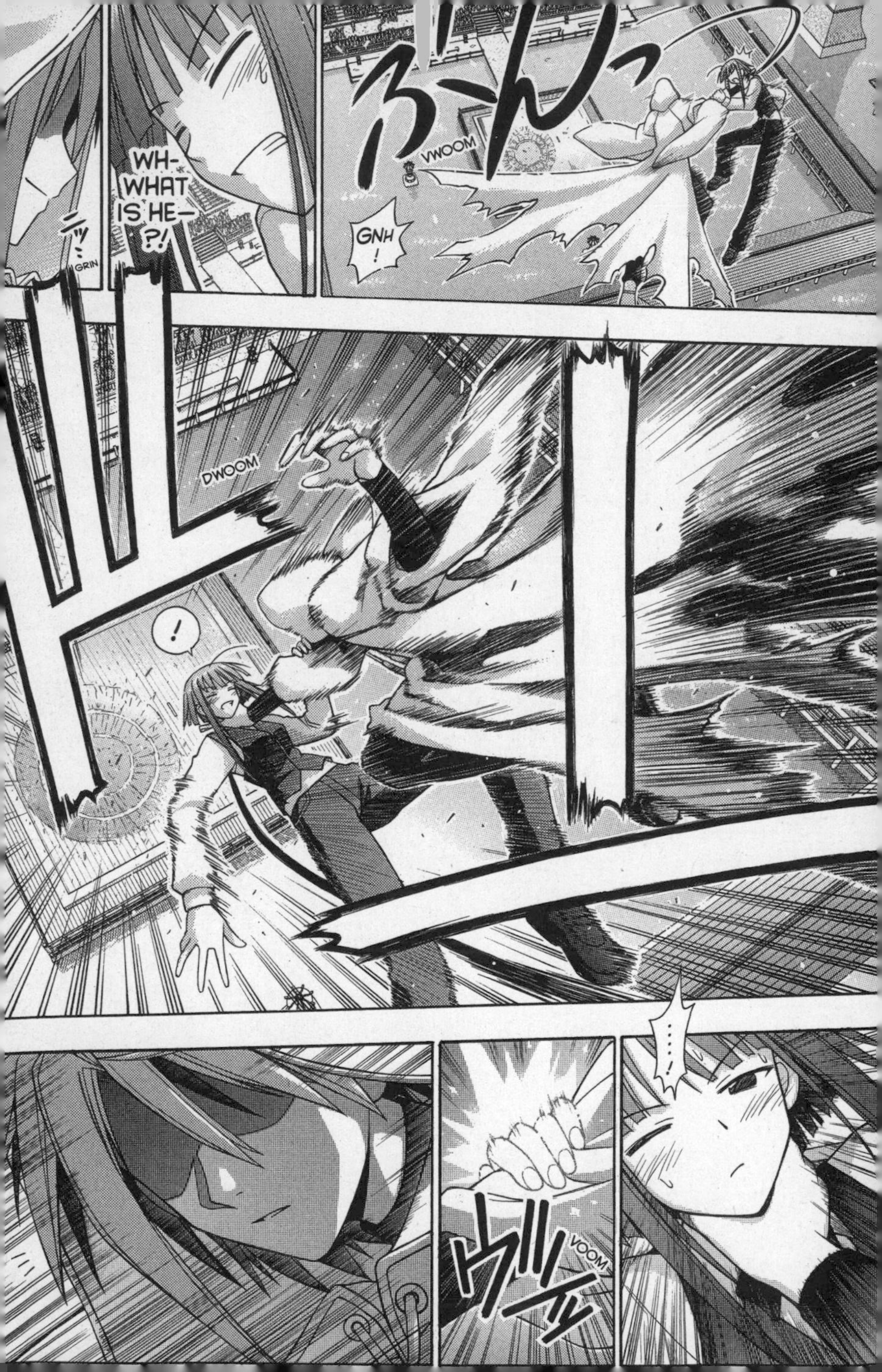

ぶんっ
VWOOM
GNH!
WH-WHAT IS HE—?!
ニッ…
GRIN
DWOOM
!
…!
VOOM

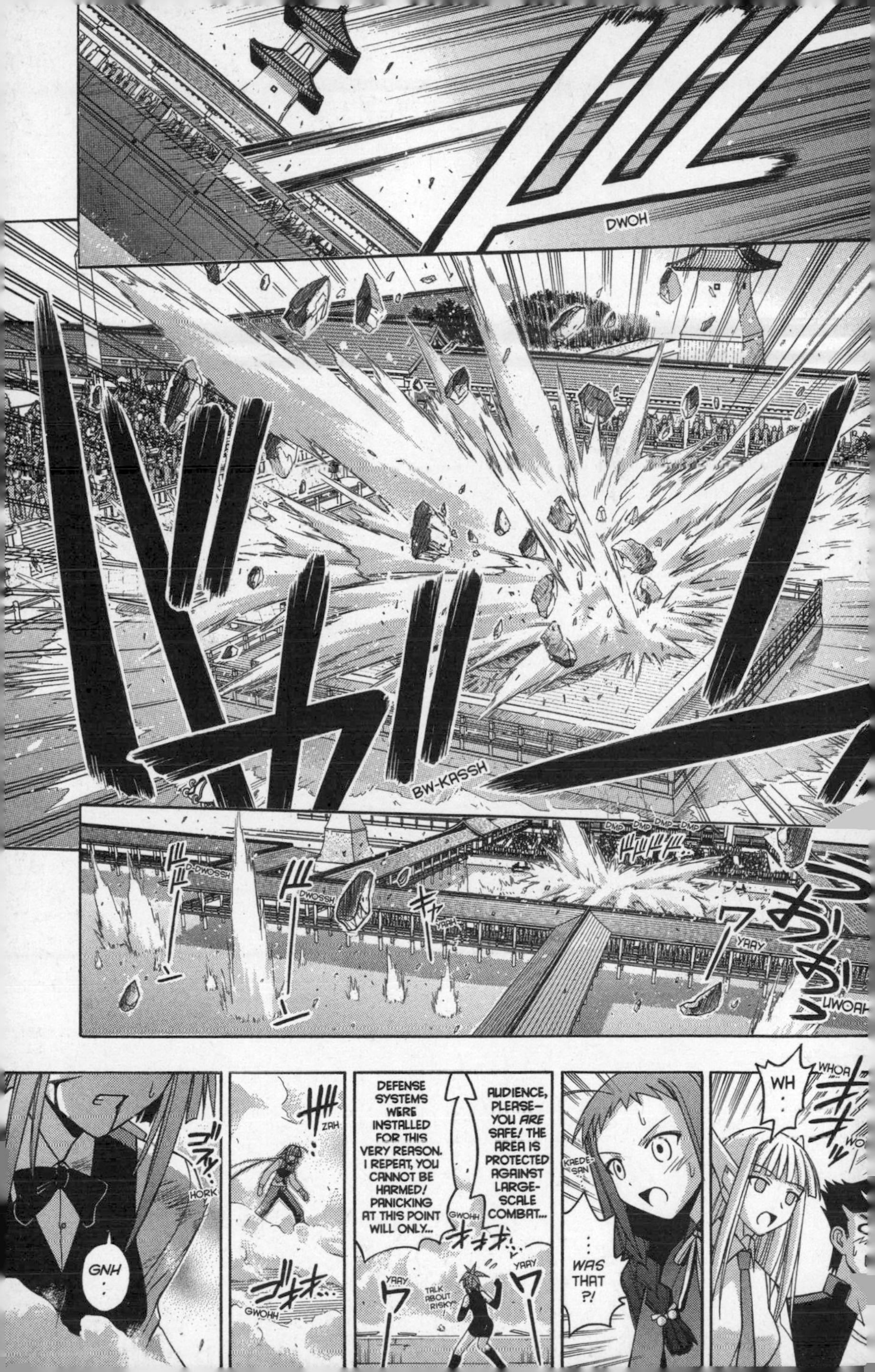
DWOH
BW-KASSH
UWOAH
YAAY
DMP DMP DMP DMP
YAAH
DWOSSH
D-DWOSSH
WH...
WHOA...
WO...
KAEDE-SAN...
...WAS THAT?!
AUDIENCE, PLEASE— YOU *ARE* SAFE! THE AREA IS PROTECTED AGAINST LARGE-SCALE COMBAT...
DEFENSE SYSTEMS WERE INSTALLED FOR THIS VERY REASON. I REPEAT, YOU CANNOT BE HARMED! PANICKING AT THIS POINT WILL ONLY...
GWOHH
YAAY
TALK ABOUT RISKY!
YAAY
ZAH
GWOHH
HORK
GNH...

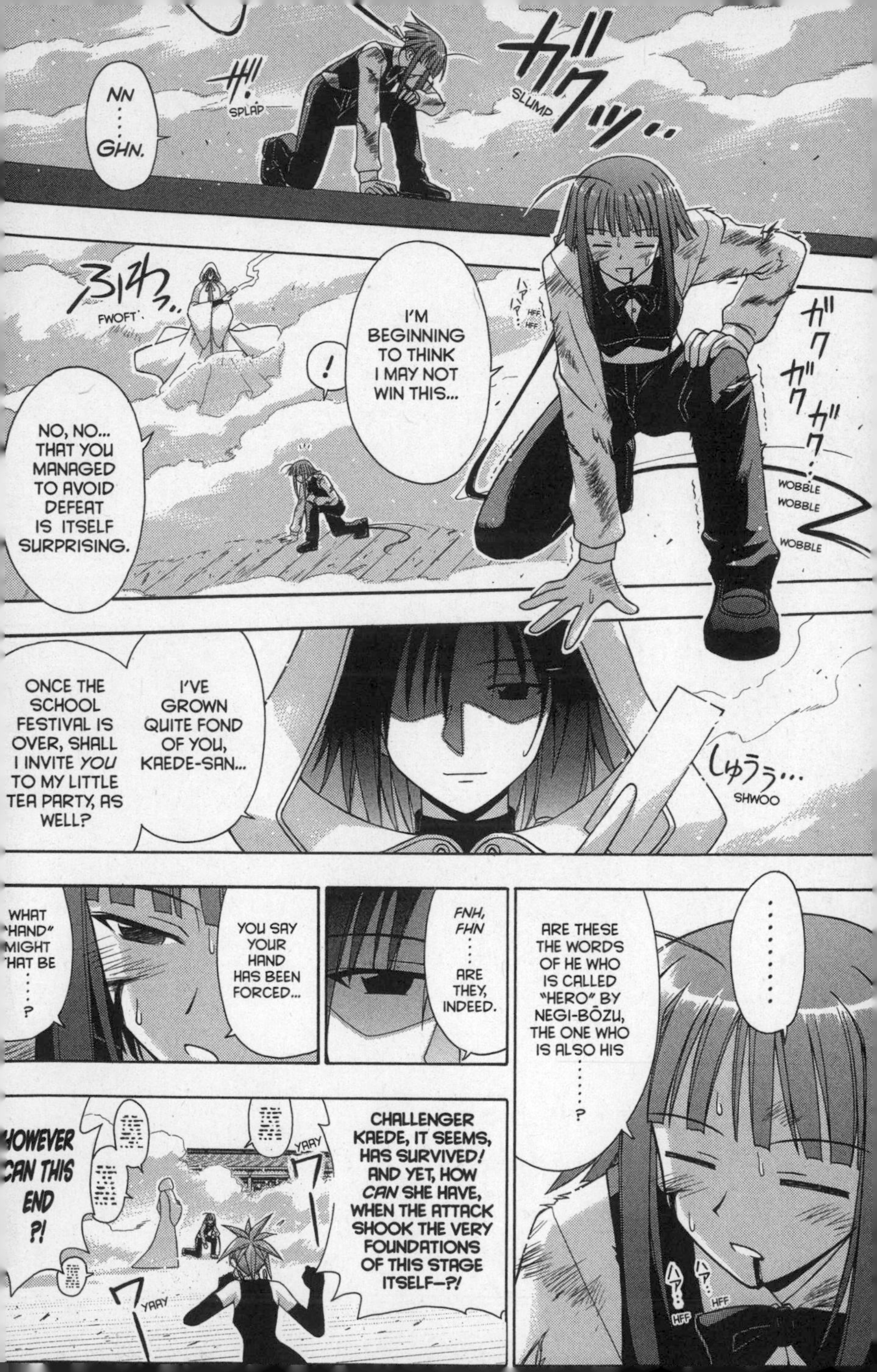
SLUMP
SPLAP
NN... GHN.
WOBBLE WOBBLE WOBBLE
HFF HFF
I'M BEGINNING TO THINK I MAY NOT WIN THIS...
!
FWOFT
NO, NO... THAT YOU MANAGED TO AVOID DEFEAT IS ITSELF SURPRISING.
SHWOO
I'VE GROWN QUITE FOND OF YOU, KAEDE-SAN...
ONCE THE SCHOOL FESTIVAL IS OVER, SHALL I INVITE *YOU* TO MY LITTLE TEA PARTY, AS WELL?
......
ARE THESE THE WORDS OF HE WHO IS CALLED "HERO" BY NEGI-BŌZU, THE ONE WHO IS ALSO HIS ......?
HFF HFF
FNH, FHN... ARE THEY, INDEED.
YOU SAY YOUR HAND HAS BEEN FORCED...
WHAT "HAND" MIGHT THAT BE ......?
CHALLENGER KAEDE, IT SEEMS, HAS SURVIVED! AND YET, HOW *CAN* SHE HAVE, WHEN THE ATTACK SHOOK THE VERY FOUNDATIONS OF THIS STAGE ITSELF—?!
YAAY
YAAY
HOWEVER CAN THIS END ?!

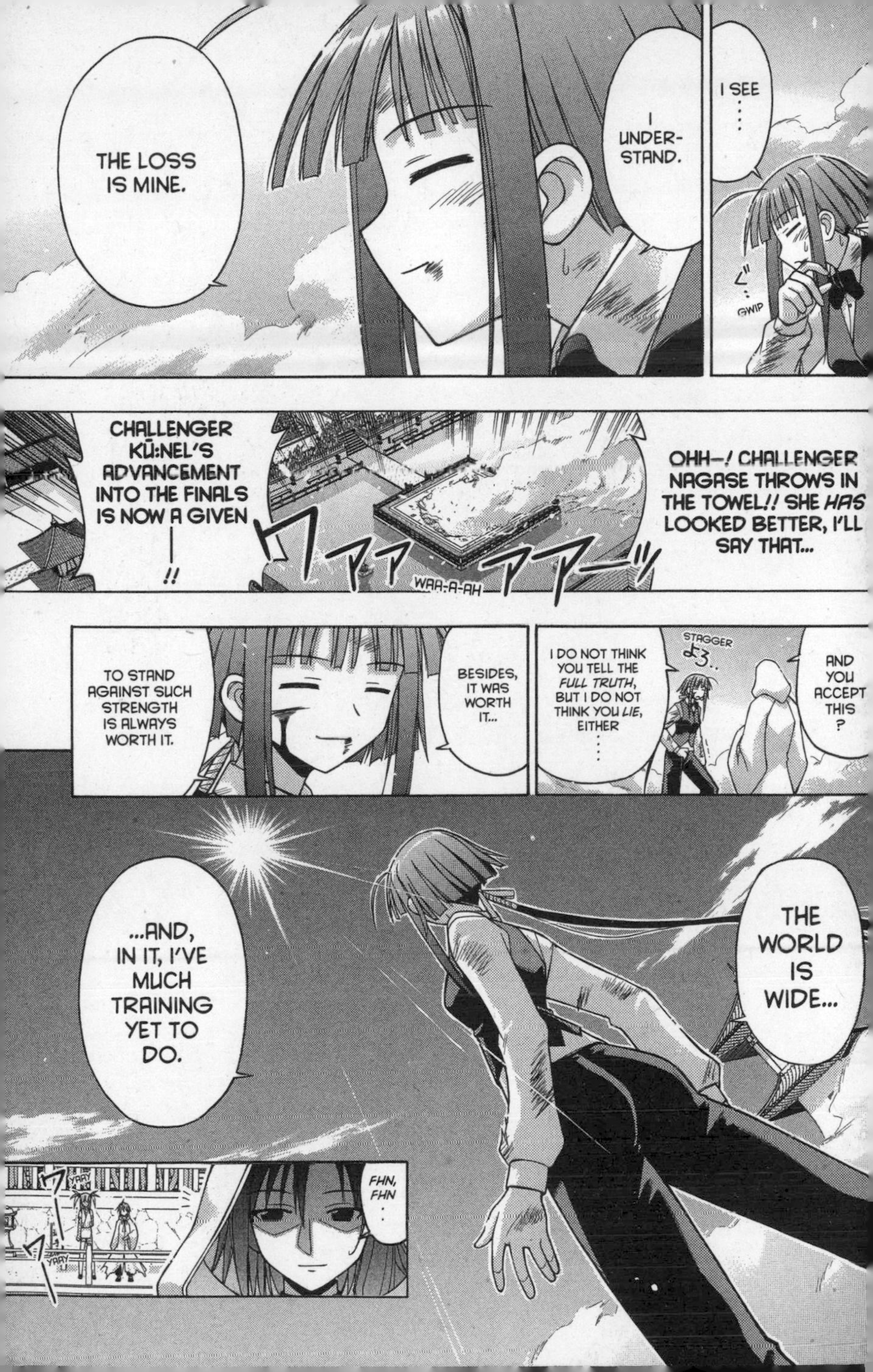
I SEE....
ぐ
GWIP
I UNDER-STAND.
THE LOSS IS MINE.
OHH-! CHALLENGER NAGASE THROWS IN THE TOWEL!! SHE *HAS* LOOKED BETTER, I'LL SAY THAT...
ワァァ アアーッ
WAA-A-AH
CHALLENGER KŪ:NEL'S ADVANCEMENT INTO THE FINALS IS NOW A GIVEN —!!
AND YOU ACCEPT THIS?
STAGGER
よろ..
I DO NOT THINK YOU TELL THE *FULL TRUTH*, BUT I DO NOT THINK YOU *LIE*, EITHER....
BESIDES, IT WAS WORTH IT...
TO STAND AGAINST SUCH STRENGTH IS ALWAYS WORTH IT.
THE WORLD IS WIDE...
...AND, IN IT, I'VE MUCH TRAINING YET TO DO.
FHN, FHN...
YAAY
YAAY

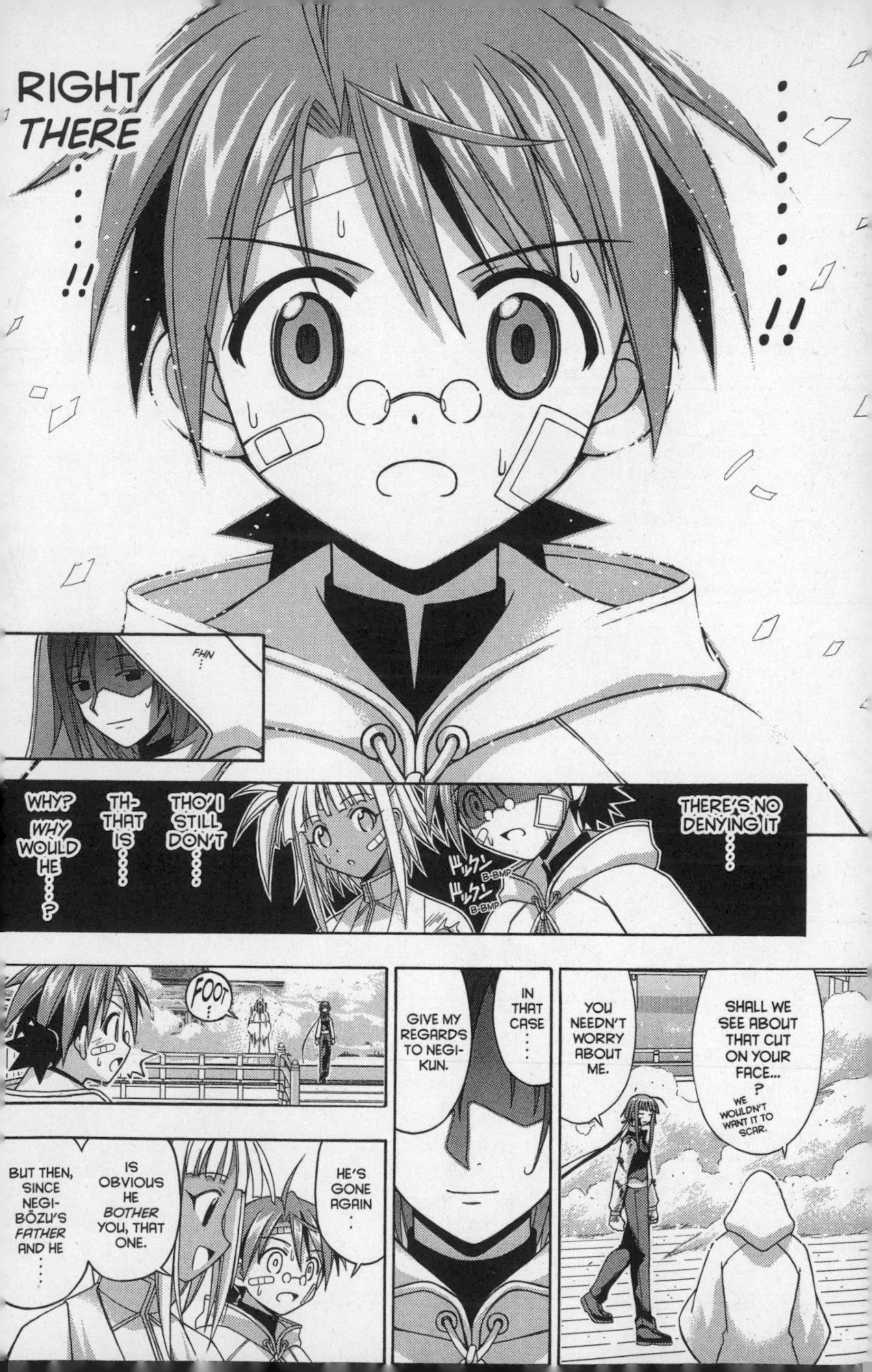

.........!!
RIGHT THERE ...!!
FHN...
THERE'S NO DENYING IT....
B-BMP
B-BMP
THO' I STILL DON'T....
TH-THAT IS....
WHY? *WHY* WOULD HE...?
SHALL WE SEE ABOUT THAT CUT ON YOUR FACE...?
WE WOULDN'T WANT IT TO SCAR.
YOU NEEDN'T WORRY ABOUT ME.
IN THAT CASE....
GIVE MY REGARDS TO NEGI-KUN.
FOOT...
HE'S GONE AGAIN..
IS OBVIOUS HE *BOTHER* YOU, THAT ONE.
BUT THEN, SINCE NEGI-BŌZU'S *FATHER* AND HE....

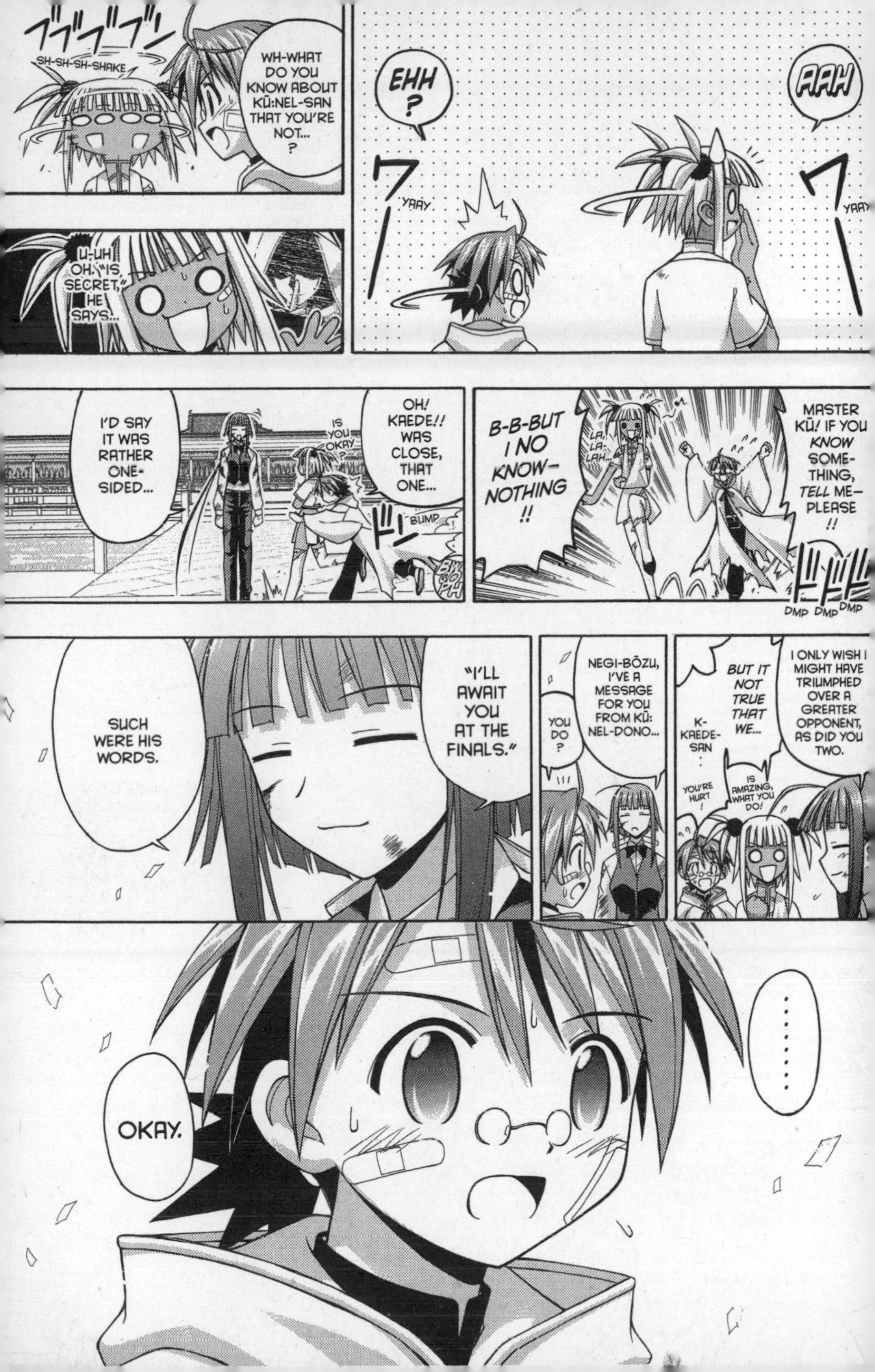
AAH
YAAY
EHH ?
YAAY
WH-WHAT DO YOU KNOW ABOUT KŪ:NEL-SAN THAT YOU'RE NOT... ?
SH-SH-SH-SHAKE
U-UH OH, "IS SECRET," HE SAYS...
MASTER KŪ! IF YOU KNOW SOME-THING, TELL ME-PLEASE !!
B-B-BUT I NO KNOW-NOTHING !!
LA, LA, LAH...
DMP DMP DMP
OH! KAEDE!! WAS CLOSE, THAT ONE...
IS YOU OKAY ?
BUMP
I'D SAY IT WAS RATHER ONE-SIDED...
I ONLY WISH I MIGHT HAVE TRIUMPHED OVER A GREATER OPPONENT, AS DID YOU TWO.
BUT IT NOT TRUE THAT WE...
K-KAEDE-SAN :
IS AMAZING, WHAT YOU DO!
YOU'RE HURT !
NEGI-BŌZU, I'VE A MESSAGE FOR YOU FROM KŪ: NEL-DONO...
YOU DO ?
"I'LL AWAIT YOU AT THE FINALS."
SUCH WERE HIS WORDS.
......
OKAY.

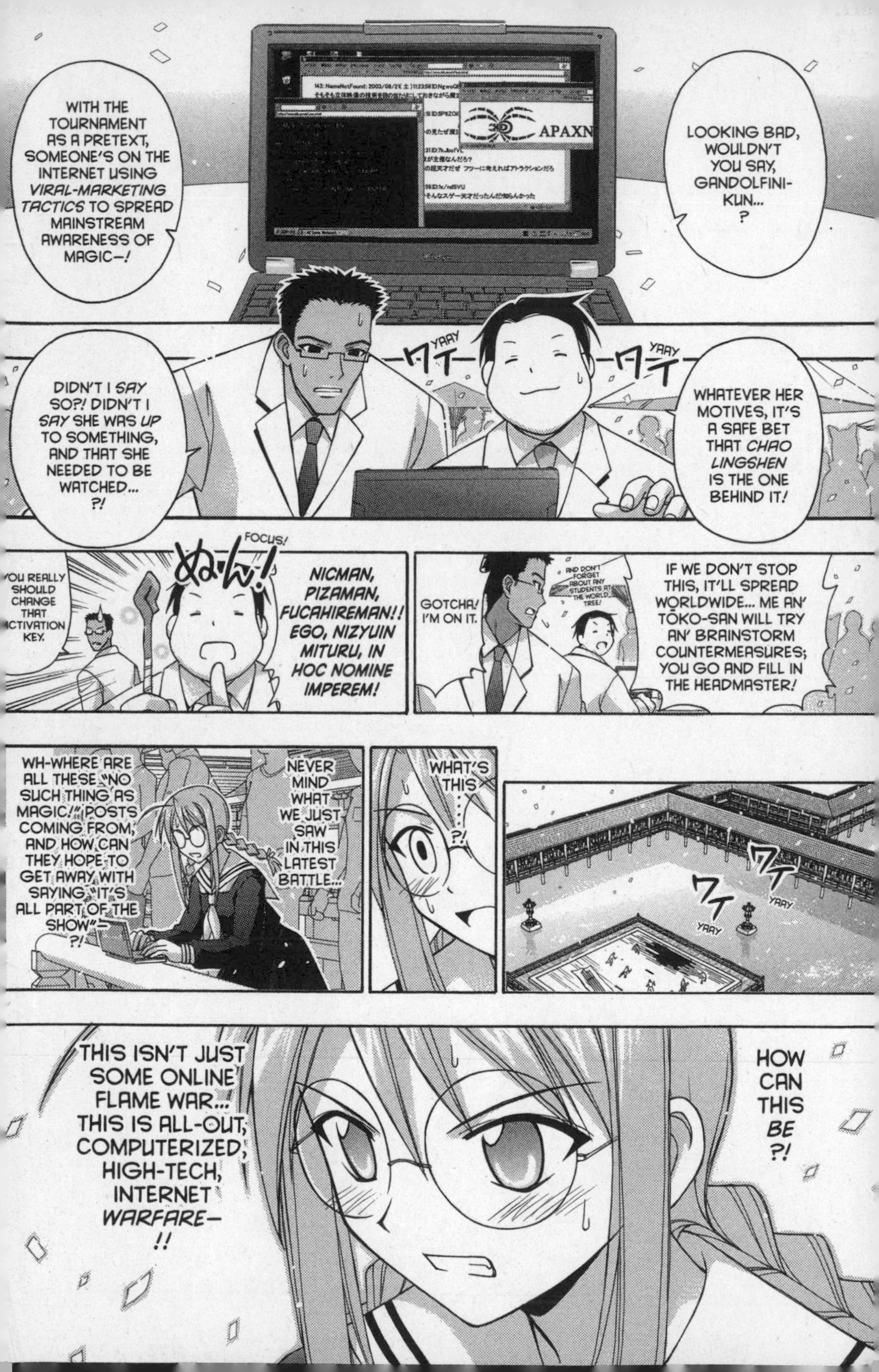
LOOKING BAD, WOULDN'T YOU SAY, GANDOLFINI-KUN...?
WITH THE TOURNAMENT AS A PRETEXT, SOMEONE'S ON THE INTERNET USING *VIRAL-MARKETING TACTICS* TO SPREAD MAINSTREAM AWARENESS OF MAGIC—!
APAXN
WHATEVER HER MOTIVES, IT'S A SAFE BET THAT *CHAO LINGSHEN* IS THE ONE BEHIND IT!
ワイ YAAY
ワイ YAAY
DIDN'T I *SAY* SO?! DIDN'T I *SAY* SHE WAS *UP* TO SOMETHING, AND THAT SHE NEEDED TO BE WATCHED...?!
IF WE DON'T STOP THIS, IT'LL SPREAD WORLDWIDE... ME AN' TŌKO-SAN WILL TRY AN' BRAINSTORM COUNTERMEASURES; YOU GO AND FILL IN THE HEADMASTER!
AND DON'T FORGET ABOUT ANY STUDENTS AT THE WORLD TREE!
GOTCHA! I'M ON IT.
NICMAN, PIZAMAN, FUCAHIREMAN!! EGO, NIZYUIN MITURU, IN HOC NOMINE IMPEREM!
ぬん! FOCUS!
OU REALLY SHOULD CHANGE THAT CTIVATION KEY.
ワイ YAAY
ワイ YAAY
WHAT'S THIS...?!
NEVER MIND WHAT WE JUST SAW IN THIS LATEST BATTLE...
WH-WHERE ARE ALL THESE "NO SUCH THING AS MAGIC!" POSTS COMING FROM, AND HOW CAN THEY HOPE TO GET AWAY WITH SAYING "IT'S ALL PART OF THE SHOW"—?!
HOW CAN THIS *BE*?!
THIS ISN'T JUST SOME ONLINE FLAME WAR... THIS IS ALL-OUT, COMPUTERIZED, HIGH-TECH, INTERNET *WARFARE*—!!

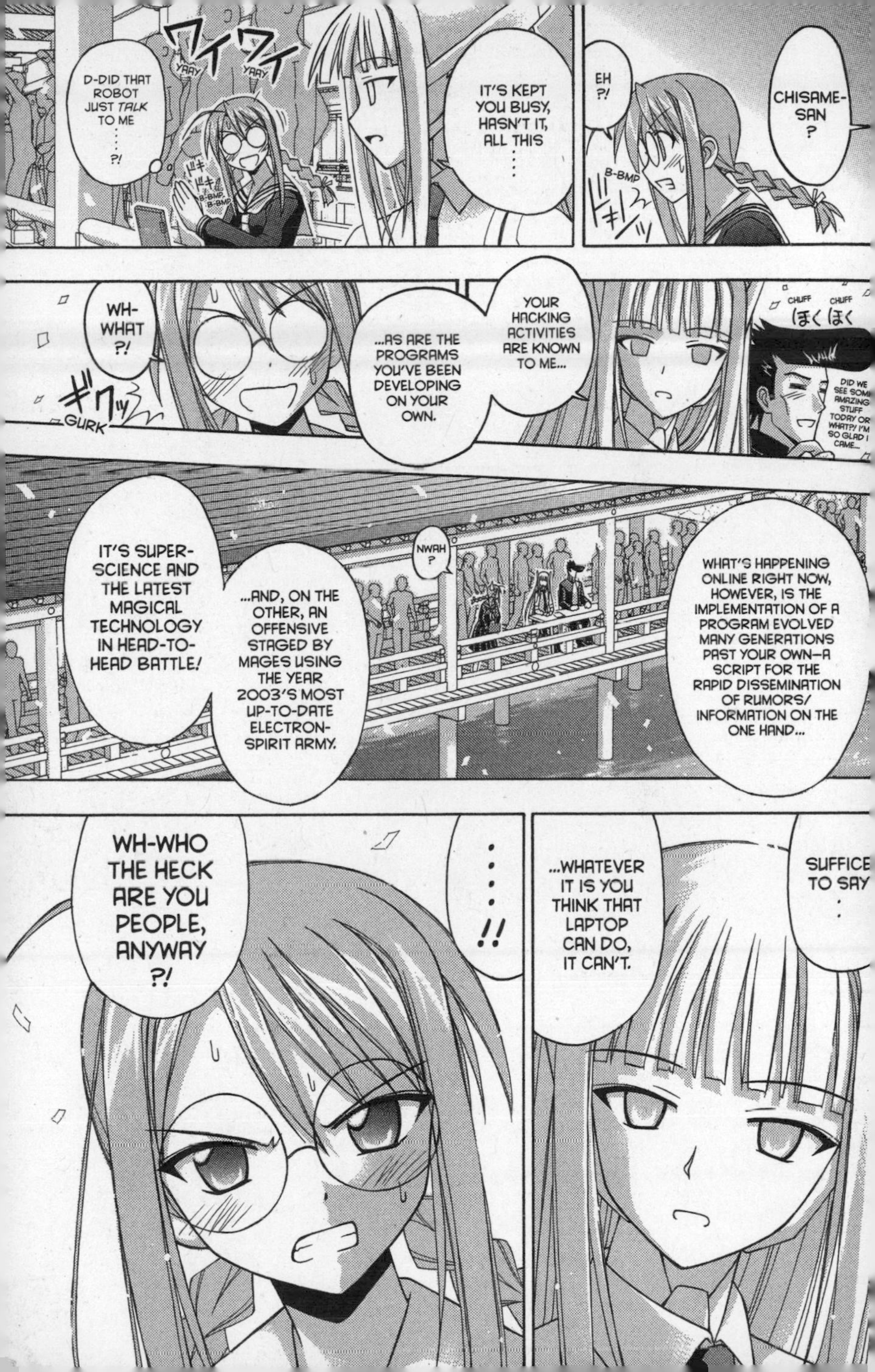
CHISAME-SAN ?
EH ?!
B-BMP
ドキンッ
IT'S KEPT YOU BUSY, HASN'T IT, ALL THIS ......
ワイワイ
YAAY YAAY
ドキドキ B-BMP, B-BMP
D-DID THAT ROBOT JUST *TALK* TO ME ...... ?!
ほくほく CHUFF CHUFF
DID WE SEE SOM AMAZING STUFF TODAY OR WHAT?! I'M SO GLAD I CAME...
YOUR HACKING ACTIVITIES ARE KNOWN TO ME...
...AS ARE THE PROGRAMS YOU'VE BEEN DEVELOPING ON YOUR OWN.
WH- WHAT ?!
ギクッ GURK
WHAT'S HAPPENING ONLINE RIGHT NOW, HOWEVER, IS THE IMPLEMENTATION OF A PROGRAM EVOLVED MANY GENERATIONS PAST YOUR OWN—A SCRIPT FOR THE RAPID DISSEMINATION OF RUMORS/ INFORMATION ON THE ONE HAND...
NWAH ?
...AND, ON THE OTHER, AN OFFENSIVE STAGED BY MAGES USING THE YEAR 2003'S MOST UP-TO-DATE ELECTRON-SPIRIT ARMY.
IT'S SUPER-SCIENCE AND THE LATEST MAGICAL TECHNOLOGY IN HEAD-TO-HEAD BATTLE!
SUFFICE TO SAY :
...WHATEVER IT IS YOU THINK THAT LAPTOP CAN DO, IT CAN'T.
......!!
WH-WHO THE HECK ARE YOU PEOPLE, ANYWAY ?!

LEXICON MAGICUM NEGIMARIUM

—*Negima!* Volume 13—
[111th thru 112th Periods]

■虚空瞬動

:OKŪ SHUNDŌ

Variation of the previously discussed "*shundō*" technique which enables the user o "kick off" in midair. (For more on *shundō*, please Kotarō's explanation in *Negima!* 'ol. 11, 92nd Period.)

An extremely useful variant in that it allows much quicker movement than the ·ase *shundō* technique, the *kokū shundō* is an especially effective avoidance tactic gainst rapid physical attacks and magical spells with an area of effect. However, s Takahata-sensei points out in Vol. 11's 97th Period, the greatest weakness of the *hundō* technique is that, once it is initiated, the user cannot change direction... hereby allowing an opponent to predict the user's destination and making the user n easy target.

Although the base *shundō* does have this weakness, it should also be pointed out hat it only applies when both feet are planted on the ground—not when initiating the *okū shundō*, for example, from midair. That being said, even the *kokū shundō* is not o great as to allow the user to fly...or so it is believed.

舞○術?

'U○JUTSU?

In Vol. 13 of the Japanese literary classic *Konjaku Monogatari-shū*, there is a tale f a man living in Nosa (currently, the northern area of Ishikawa Prefecture) named aoshu who mastered the Sendō—often referred to as "Taoist Magic." According to the ale, a determined-enough martial-arts master can achieve the ability to fly through ie air at will. In this volume of *Negima!*, although ringside commentator Gōtokuji aoru claims that he's never heard of anyone being able to train enough to fly by "*ki*" ower alone, the idea of it as a concept certainly exists in much of the imagery found ı the literatures of East Asian cultures.

■「ニクマン・ピザマン・フカヒレマン」

'IKUMAN, PIZAMAN, FUKAHIREMAN

ıicman pizaman fucahireman)

Magic-activation key of Nijūin-*sensei*. The issue of how appropriate it may or ıay not be aside, the fact that he's given some thought to his key's poetic meter must ırely speak well of his dedication to becoming a "proper" teacher of magic.

■「我、弐集院光の名に於て命ず」

エゴ・ニジュウイン・ミトゥル・イン・ホーク・ノミネー・インペレム

:go, Nizyuin Mituru, in hoc nomine imperem)

Spells cast using the caster's name are often high level, embodying some sort of ɔntract with a spiritual being enfolded within. For example, even though her name ıay not, in this case, be part of the spell itself, Evangeline's ultimate spell ΚΟΣΜΙΚΗ ΚΑΤΣΑΤΡΟΦΗ" is similar in that it can be inferred from the ıcantation that she has made a contract with a spiritual being.

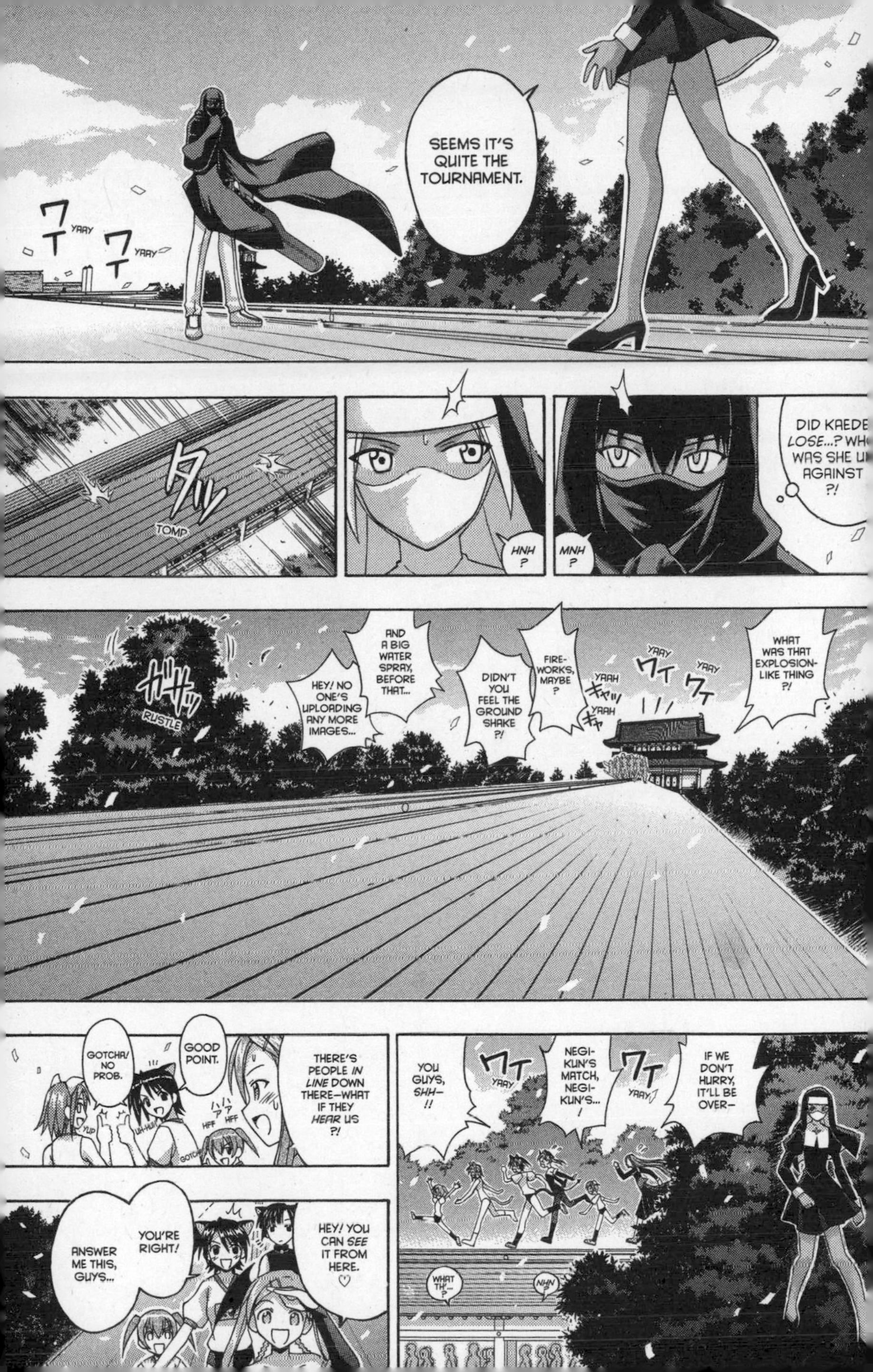
SEEMS IT'S QUITE THE TOURNAMENT.
YAAY
YAAY
DID KAEDE LOSE...? WHO WAS SHE UP AGAINST ?!
MNH ?
HNH ?
TOMP
WHAT WAS THAT EXPLOSION-LIKE THING ?!
YAAY
YAAY
YAAH
YAAH
FIRE-WORKS, MAYBE ?
DIDN'T YOU FEEL THE GROUND SHAKE ?!
AND A BIG WATER SPRAY, BEFORE THAT...
HEY! NO ONE'S UPLOADING ANY MORE IMAGES...
RUSTLE
IF WE DON'T HURRY, IT'LL BE OVER—
YAAY
NEGI-KUN'S MATCH, NEGI-KUN'S...!
YAAY
YOU GUYS, *SHH*—!!
NHN ?
WHAT TH'... ?
THERE'S PEOPLE *IN LINE* DOWN THERE—WHAT IF THEY *HEAR* US ?!
GOOD POINT.
GOTCHA! NO PROB.
HFF HFF
UH-HUH
YUP
GOTCHA
HEY! YOU CAN *SEE* IT FROM HERE. ♡
YOU'RE RIGHT!
ANSWER ME THIS, GUYS...

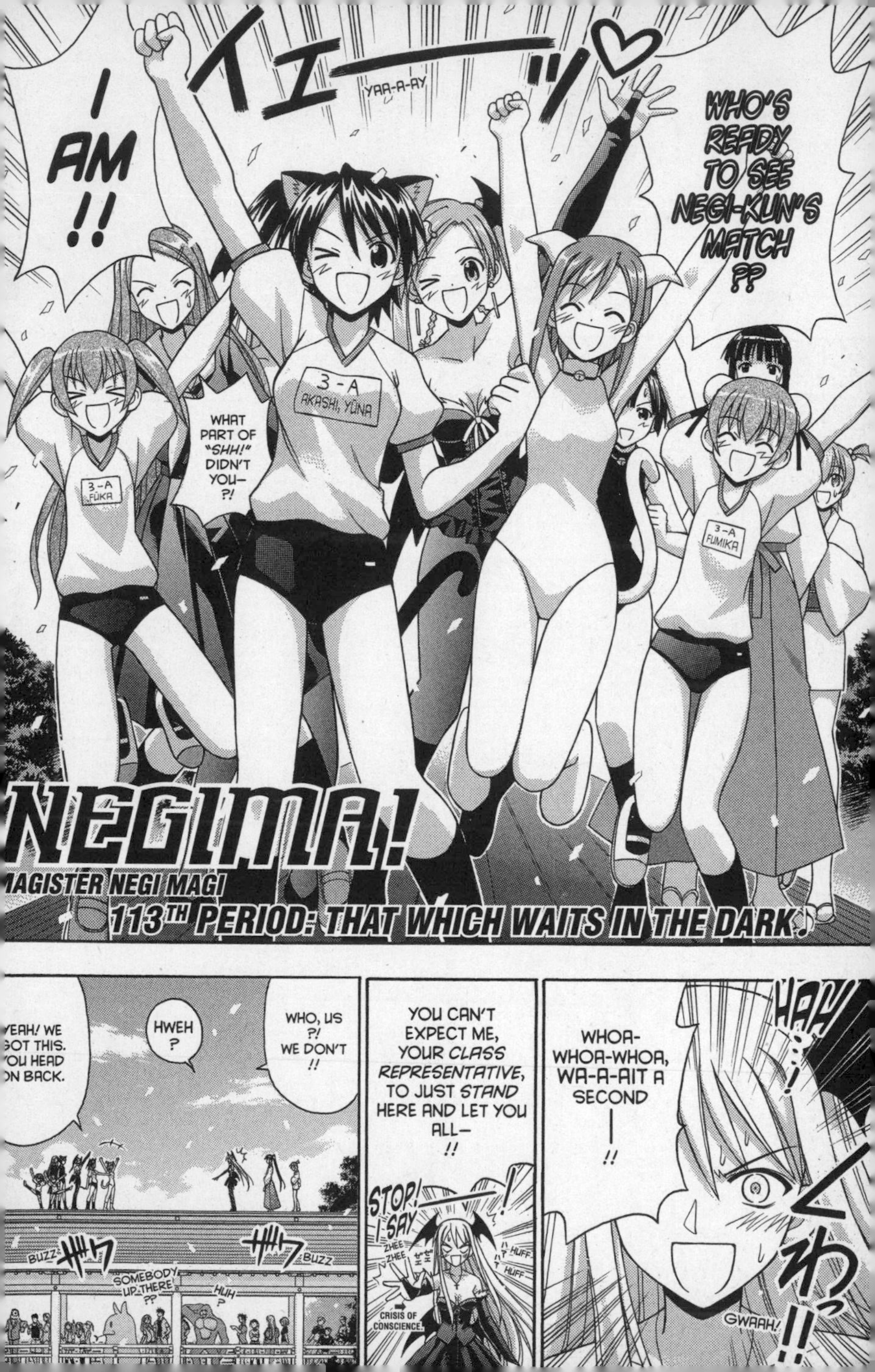
WHO'S READY TO SEE NEGI-KUN'S MATCH ??
イエーーーッ♡
YAA-A-AY
I AM !!
WHAT PART OF "SHH!" DIDN'T YOU—?!
3-A AKASHI, YŪNA
3-A FŪKA
3-A FUMIKA
NEGIMA!
MAGISTER NEGI MAGI
113TH PERIOD: THAT WHICH WAITS IN THE DARK♪
HAH…!
WHOA-WHOA-WHOA, WA-A-AIT A SECOND—!!
わっ
GWAAH!!
YOU CAN'T EXPECT ME, YOUR CLASS REPRESENTATIVE, TO JUST STAND HERE AND LET YOU ALL—!!
STOP! I SAY—!
ZHEE ZHEE
HUFF HUFF
CRISIS OF CONSCIENCE
WHO, US ?! WE DON'T !!
HWEH ?
YEAH! WE GOT THIS. YOU HEAD ON BACK.
BUZZ
BUZZ
SOMEBODY UP THERE ??
HUH ?

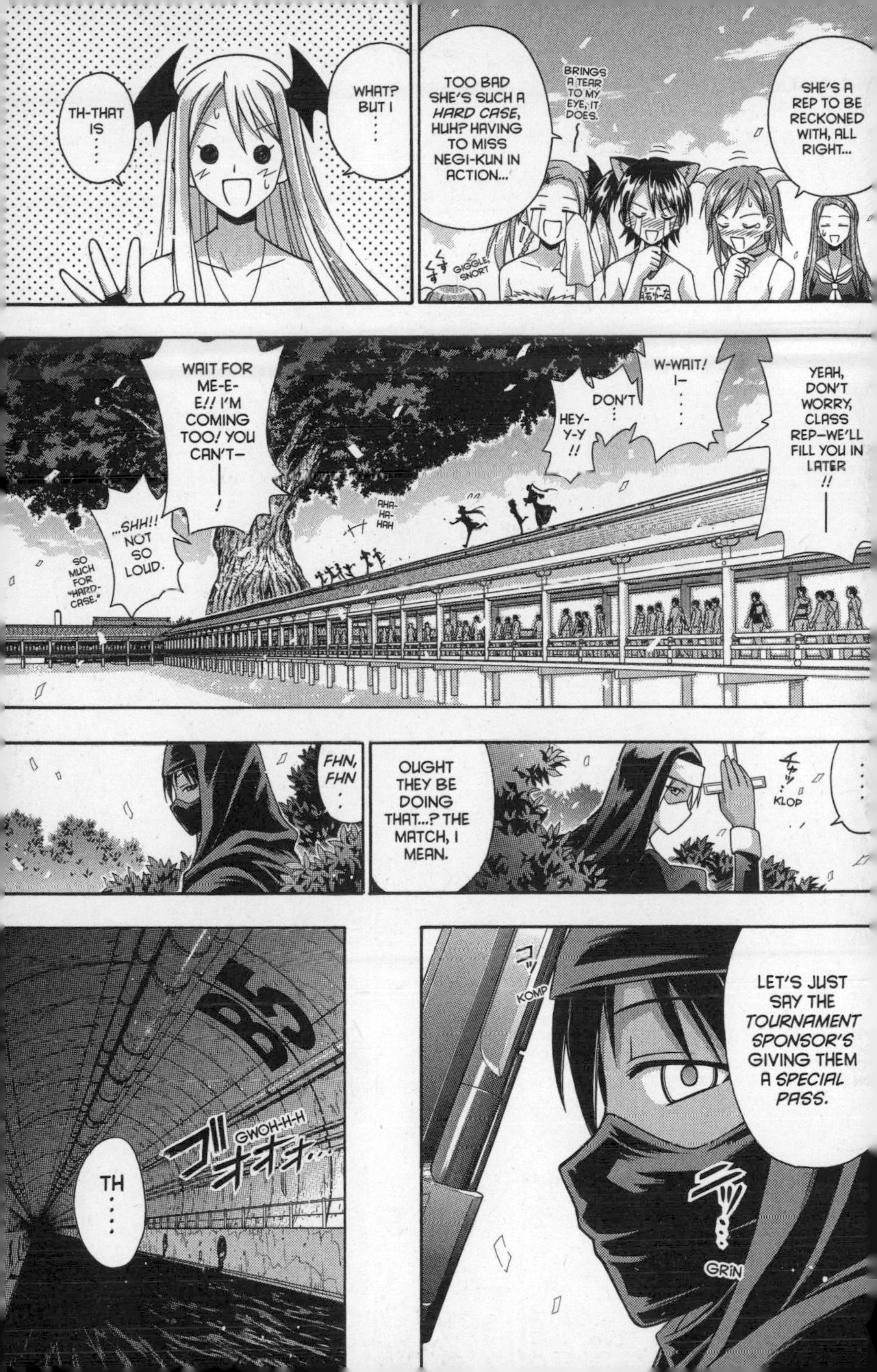
SHE'S A REP TO BE RECKONED WITH, ALL RIGHT...
BRINGS A TEAR TO MY EYE, IT DOES.
TOO BAD SHE'S SUCH A HARD CASE, HUH? HAVING TO MISS NEGI-KUN IN ACTION...
GIGGLE, SNORT
WHAT? BUT I ...
TH-THAT IS ......
YEAH, DON'T WORRY, CLASS REP—WE'LL FILL YOU IN LATER!!
W-WAIT! I— ...
DON'T ...
HEY-Y-Y!!
AHA-HA-HAH
WAIT FOR ME-E-E!! I'M COMING TOO! YOU CAN'T— !
...SHH!! NOT SO LOUD.
SO MUCH FOR "HARD-CASE."
...
KLOP
OUGHT THEY BE DOING THAT...? THE MATCH, I MEAN.
FHN, FHN ...
KOMP
LET'S JUST SAY THE TOURNAMENT SPONSOR'S GIVING THEM A SPECIAL PASS.
GRIN
GWOH-H-H
TH....

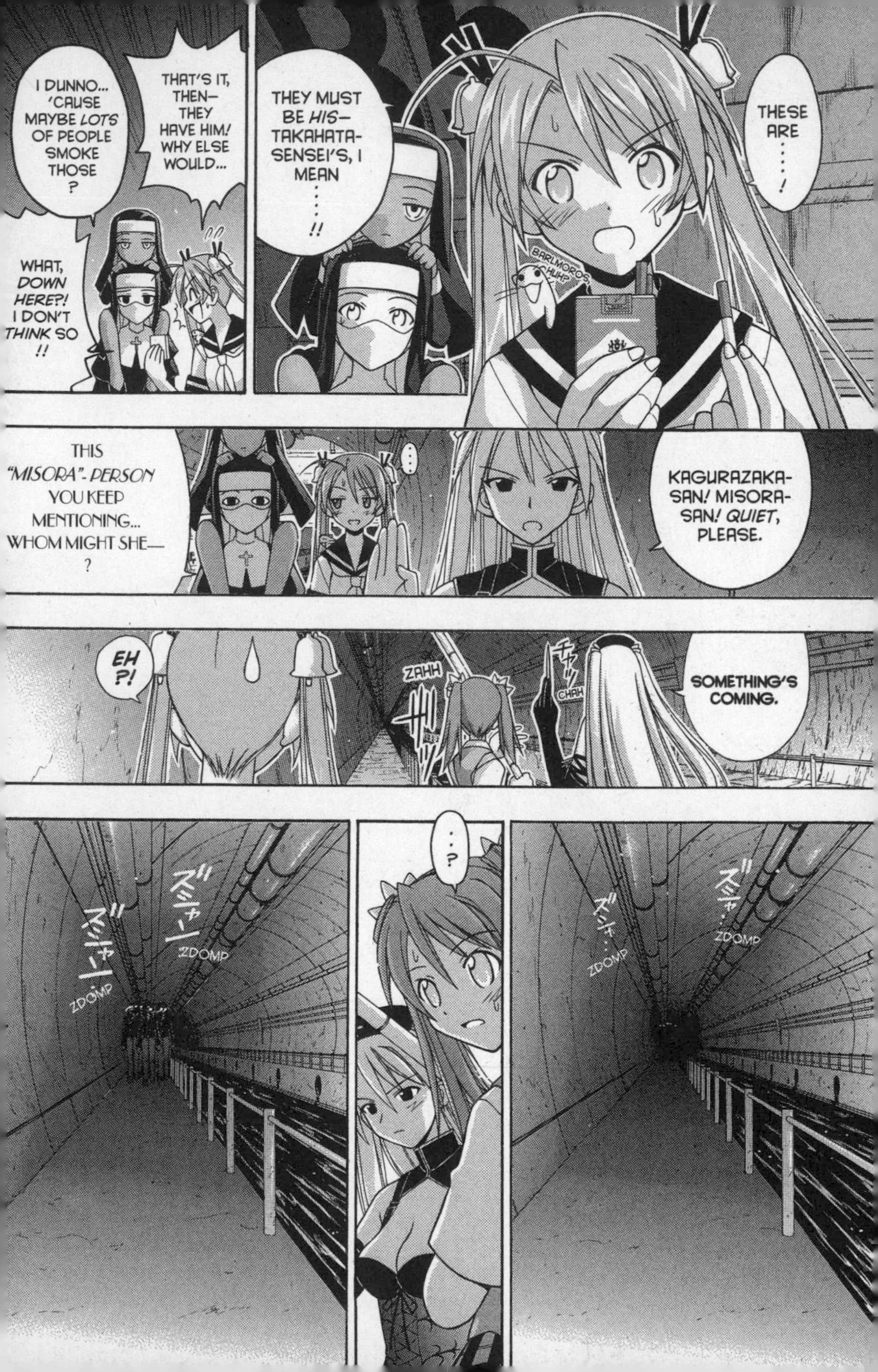
THESE ARE....!
BARLMOROS, CHUP
THEY MUST BE HIS— TAKAHATA-SENSEI'S, I MEAN....!!
THAT'S IT, THEN— THEY HAVE HIM! WHY ELSE WOULD...
I DUNNO... 'CAUSE MAYBE LOTS OF PEOPLE SMOKE THOSE?
WHAT, DOWN HERE?! I DON'T THINK SO!!
KAGURAZAKA-SAN! MISORA-SAN! QUIET, PLEASE.
...
THIS "MISORA"-PERSON YOU KEEP MENTIONING... WHOM MIGHT SHE—?
SOMETHING'S COMING.
CHAK
ZAHH
EH?!
ZDOMP
ZDOMP
...?
ZDOMP
ZDOMP

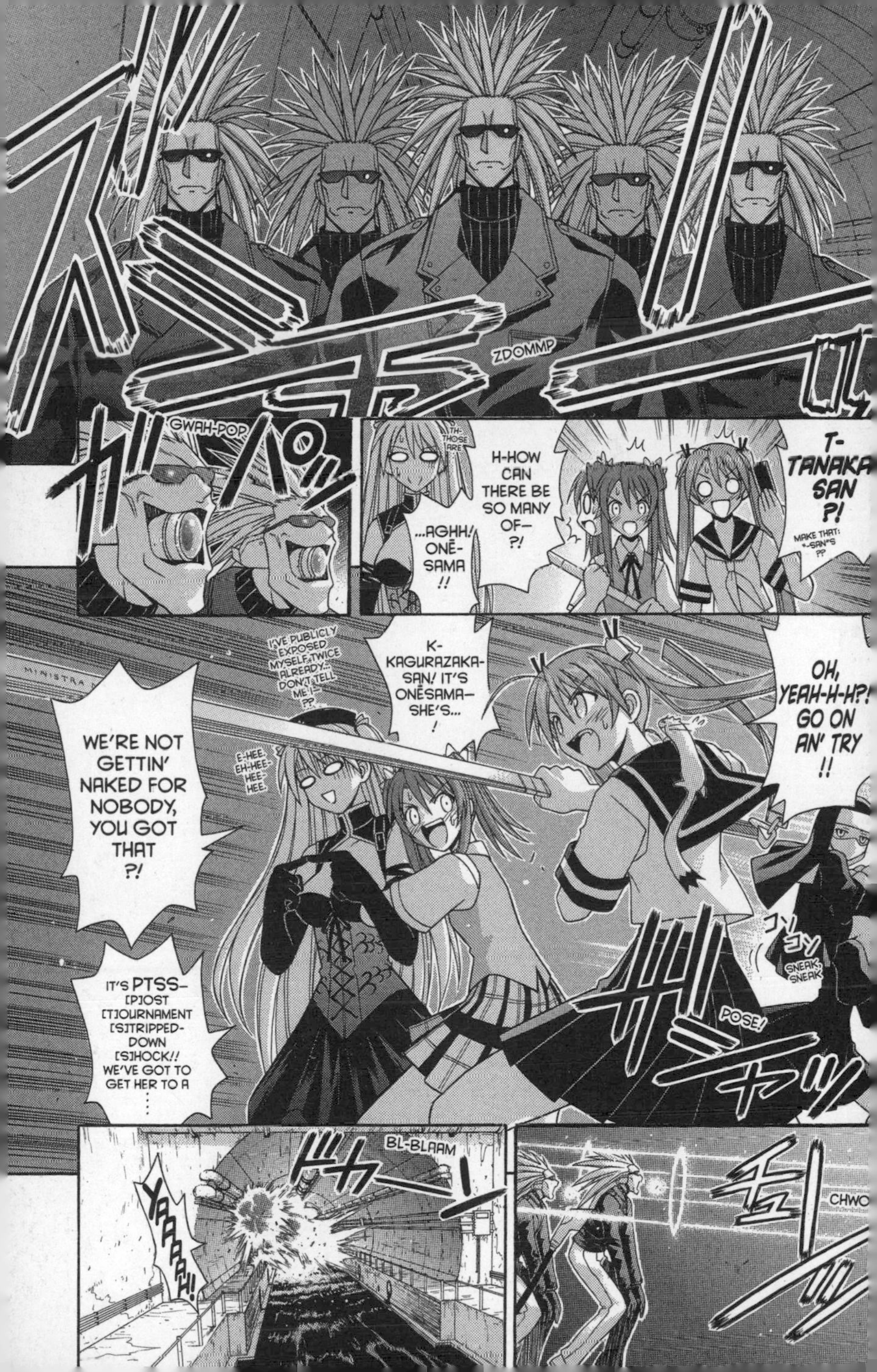
ZDOMMP
T-TANAKA SAN?!
MAKE THAT: "-SAN"S ??
H-HOW CAN THERE BE SO MANY OF—?!
TH-THOSE ARE
...AGHH! ONĒ-SAMA!!
GWAH-POP
OH, YEAH-H-H?! GO ON AN' TRY!!
K-KAGURAZAKA-SAN! IT'S ONĒSAMA—SHE'S...!
I'VE PUBLICLY EXPOSED MYSELF TWICE ALREADY... DON'T TELL ME I—??
E-HEE. EH-HEE-HEE-HEE.
WE'RE NOT GETTIN' NAKED FOR NOBODY, YOU GOT THAT?!
SNEAK, SNEAK
POSE!
IT'S PTSS—[P]OST [T]OURNAMENT [S]TRIPPED-DOWN [S]HOCK!! WE'VE GOT TO GET HER TO A ......
CHWO
BL-BLAAM
YAAAAAH!!

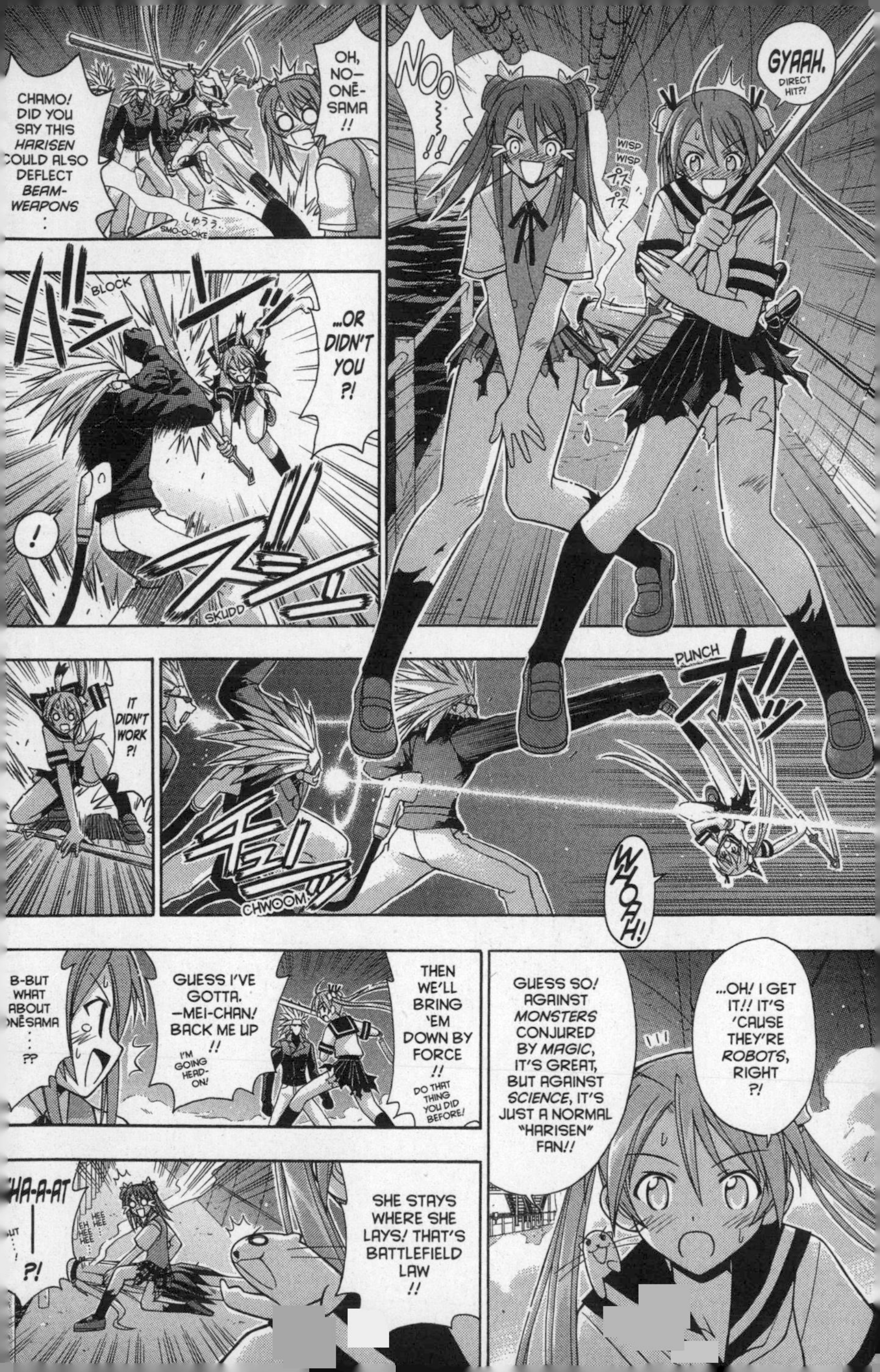
GYAAH, DIRECT HIT?!
NOO~~!!
WISP WISP
OH, NO— ONĒ-SAMA!!
CHAMO! DID YOU SAY THIS HARISEN COULD ALSO DEFLECT BEAM-WEAPONS :
しゅうう SMO-O-OKE
BLOCK
...OR DIDN'T YOU?!
!
SKUDD
PUNCH
WHOAH!
CHWOOM
IT DIDN'T WORK?!
...OH! I GET IT!! IT'S 'CAUSE THEY'RE ROBOTS, RIGHT?!
GUESS SO! AGAINST MONSTERS CONJURED BY MAGIC, IT'S GREAT, BUT AGAINST SCIENCE, IT'S JUST A NORMAL "HARISEN" FAN!!
THEN WE'LL BRING 'EM DOWN BY FORCE!!
DO THAT THING YOU DID BEFORE!
GUESS I'VE GOTTA. —MEI-CHAN! BACK ME UP!!
I'M GOING HEAD-ON!
B-BUT WHAT ABOUT NĒSAMA ...??
SHE STAYS WHERE SHE LAYS! THAT'S BATTLEFIELD LAW!!
HEE HEE HEE
EH HEE HEE
HA-A-AT—?!

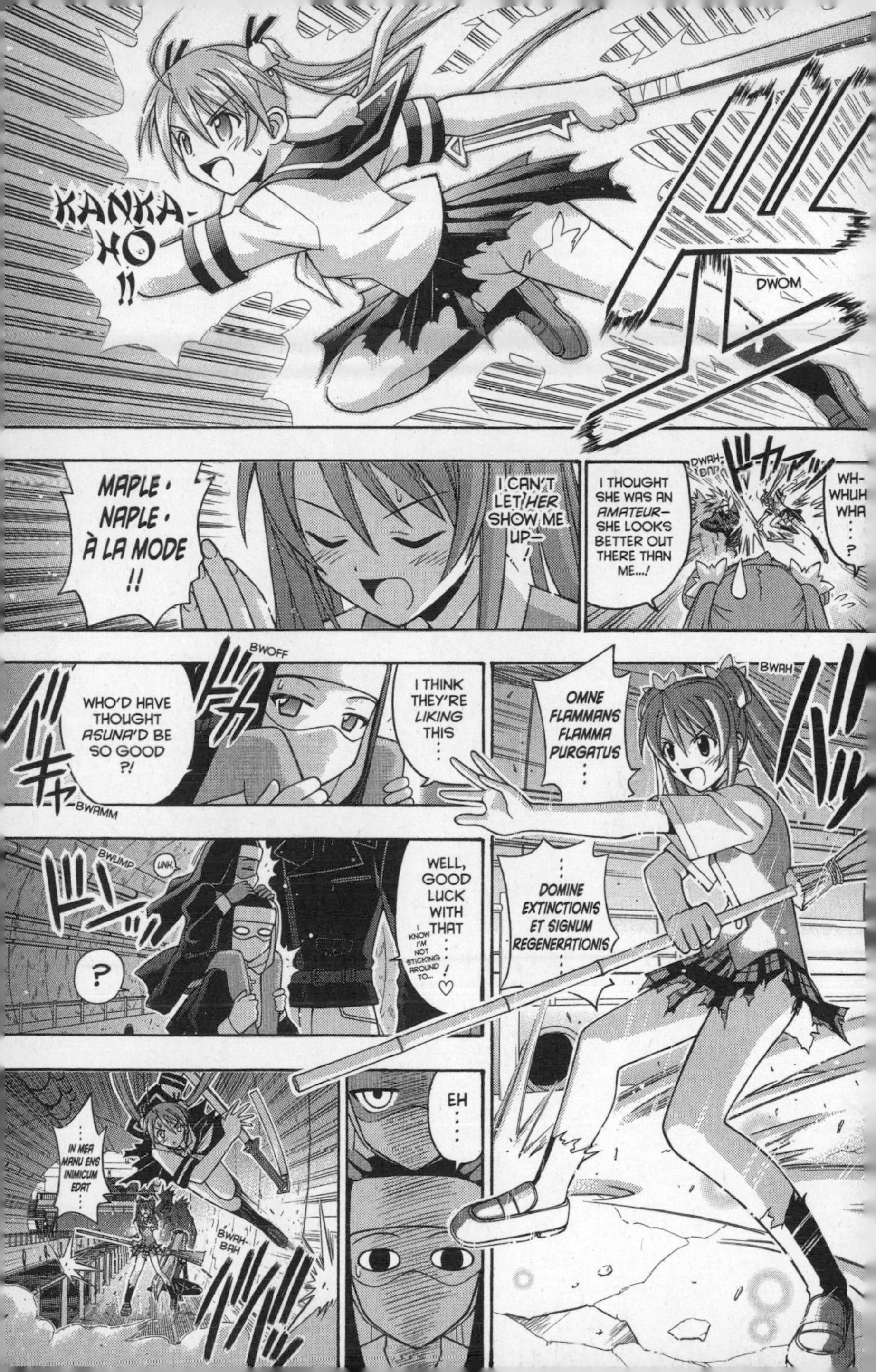
KANKA-HŌ !!
DWOM
WH-WHUH WHA...?
DWAH-BAP
I THOUGHT SHE WAS AN AMATEUR— SHE LOOKS BETTER OUT THERE THAN ME...!
I CAN'T LET HER SHOW ME UP—!
MAPLE · NAPLE · À LA MODE !!
BWAH
OMNE FLAMMANS FLAMMA PURGATUS...
...DOMINE EXTINCTIONIS ET SIGNUM REGENERATIONIS...
I THINK THEY'RE LIKING THIS...
BWOFF
WHO'D HAVE THOUGHT ASUNA'D BE SO GOOD?!
BWAMM
WELL, GOOD LUCK WITH THAT...!
I KNOW I'M NOT STICKING AROUND TO...♡
UNH.
BWLUMP
?
EH.....
...IN MEA MANU ENS INIMICUM EDAT...
BWAH-BAH

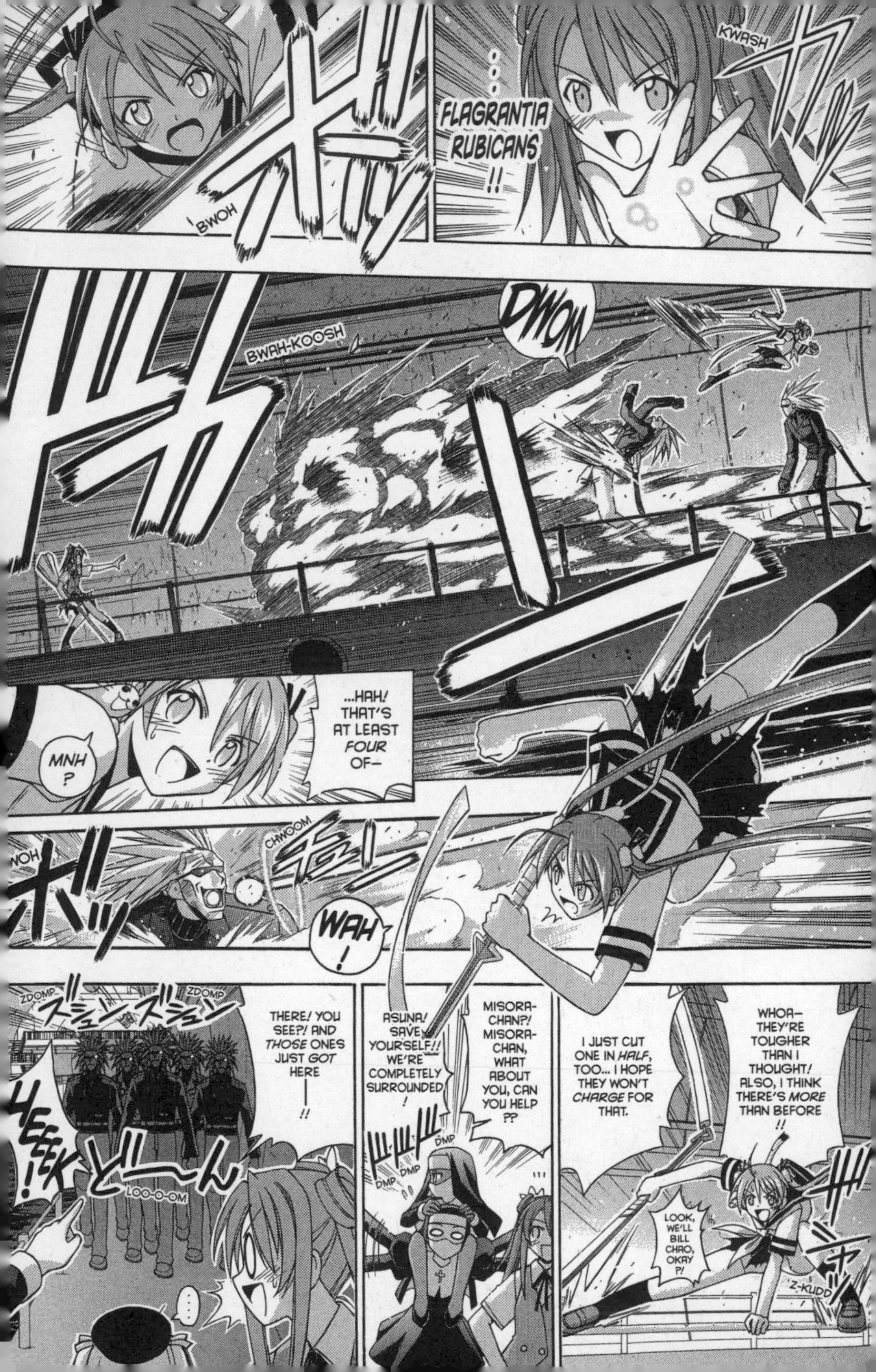
KWASH
...
FLAGRANTIA RUBICANS !!
BWOH
DWOM
BWAH-KOOSH
...HAH! THAT'S AT LEAST *FOUR* OF—
MNH ?
CHWOOM
WAH !
WOH
WHOA— THEY'RE TOUGHER THAN I THOUGHT! ALSO, I THINK THERE'S *MORE* THAN BEFORE !!
I JUST CUT ONE IN *HALF*, TOO... I HOPE THEY WON'T *CHARGE* FOR THAT.
LOOK, WE'LL BILL CHAO, OKAY ?!
Z-KUDD
MISORA-CHAN?! MISORA-CHAN, WHAT ABOUT YOU, CAN YOU HELP ??
ASUNA! SAVE YOURSELF!! WE'RE COMPLETELY SURROUNDED !
DMP
DMP
DMP
ZDOMP
ZDOMP
THERE! YOU SEE?! AND *THOSE* ONES JUST *GOT* HERE —!!
HEEEEK!
LOO-O-OM
...

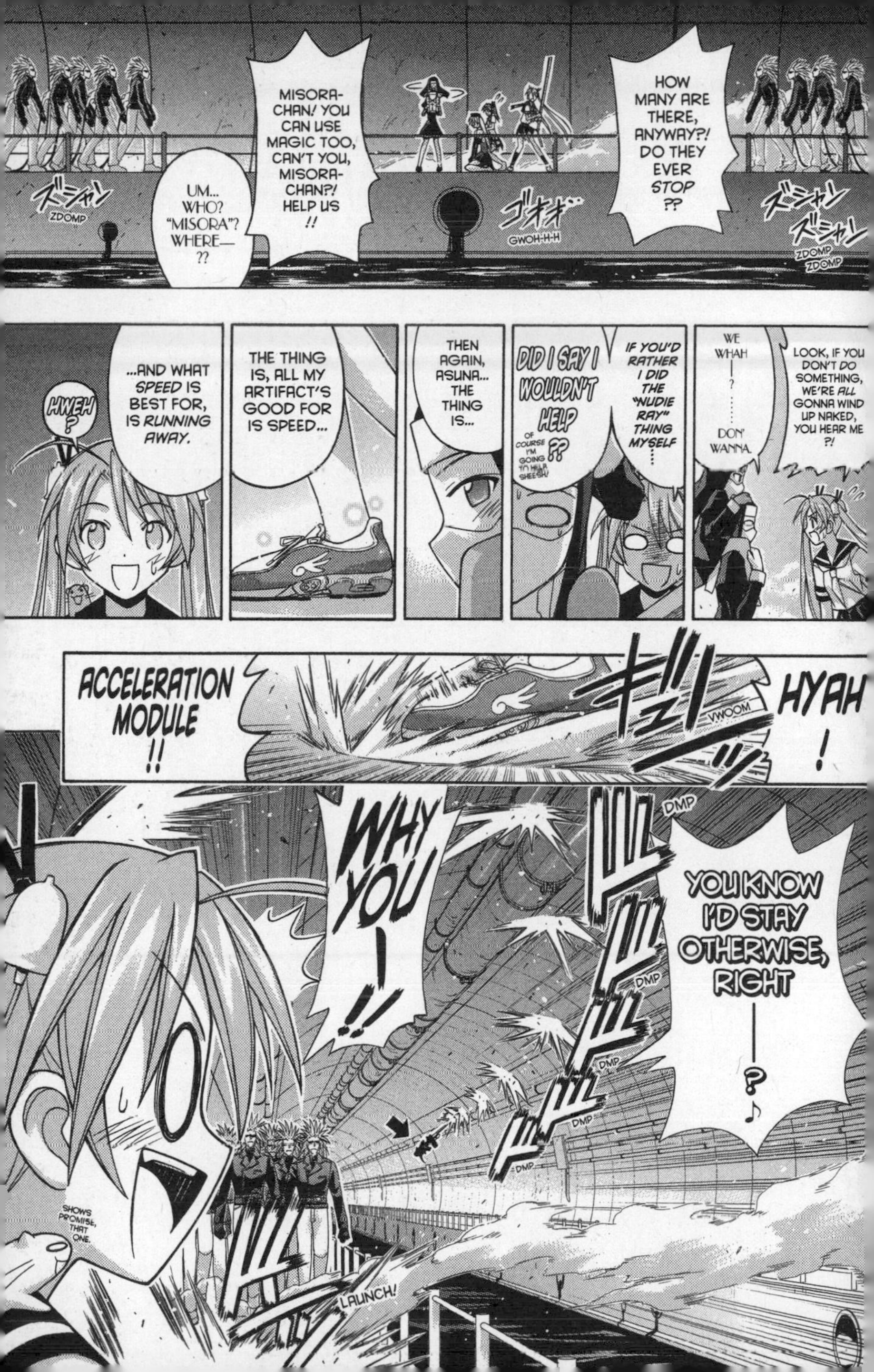
HOW MANY ARE THERE, ANYWAY?! DO THEY EVER STOP ??
ZDOMP ZDOMP
GWOH-H-H
MISORA-CHAN! YOU CAN USE MAGIC TOO, CAN'T YOU, MISORA-CHAN?! HELP US !!
UM... WHO? "MISORA"? WHERE— ??
ZDOMP
LOOK, IF YOU DON'T DO SOMETHING, WE'RE ALL GONNA WIND UP NAKED, YOU HEAR ME ?!
WE WHAH —? ...... DON' WANNA.
IF YOU'D RATHER I DID THE "NUDIE RAY" THING MYSELF......
DID I SAY I WOULDN'T HELP ??
OF COURSE I'M GOING TO HELP. SHEESH!
THEN AGAIN, ASUNA... THE THING IS...
THE THING IS, ALL MY ARTIFACT'S GOOD FOR IS SPEED...
...AND WHAT SPEED IS BEST FOR, IS RUNNING AWAY.
HWEH ?
HYAH !
VWOOM
ACCELERATION MODULE !!
YOU KNOW I'D STAY OTHERWISE, RIGHT —? ♪
DMP
DMP
DMP
DMP
DMP
WHY YOU — !!
SHOWS PROMISE, THAT ONE.
LAUNCH!

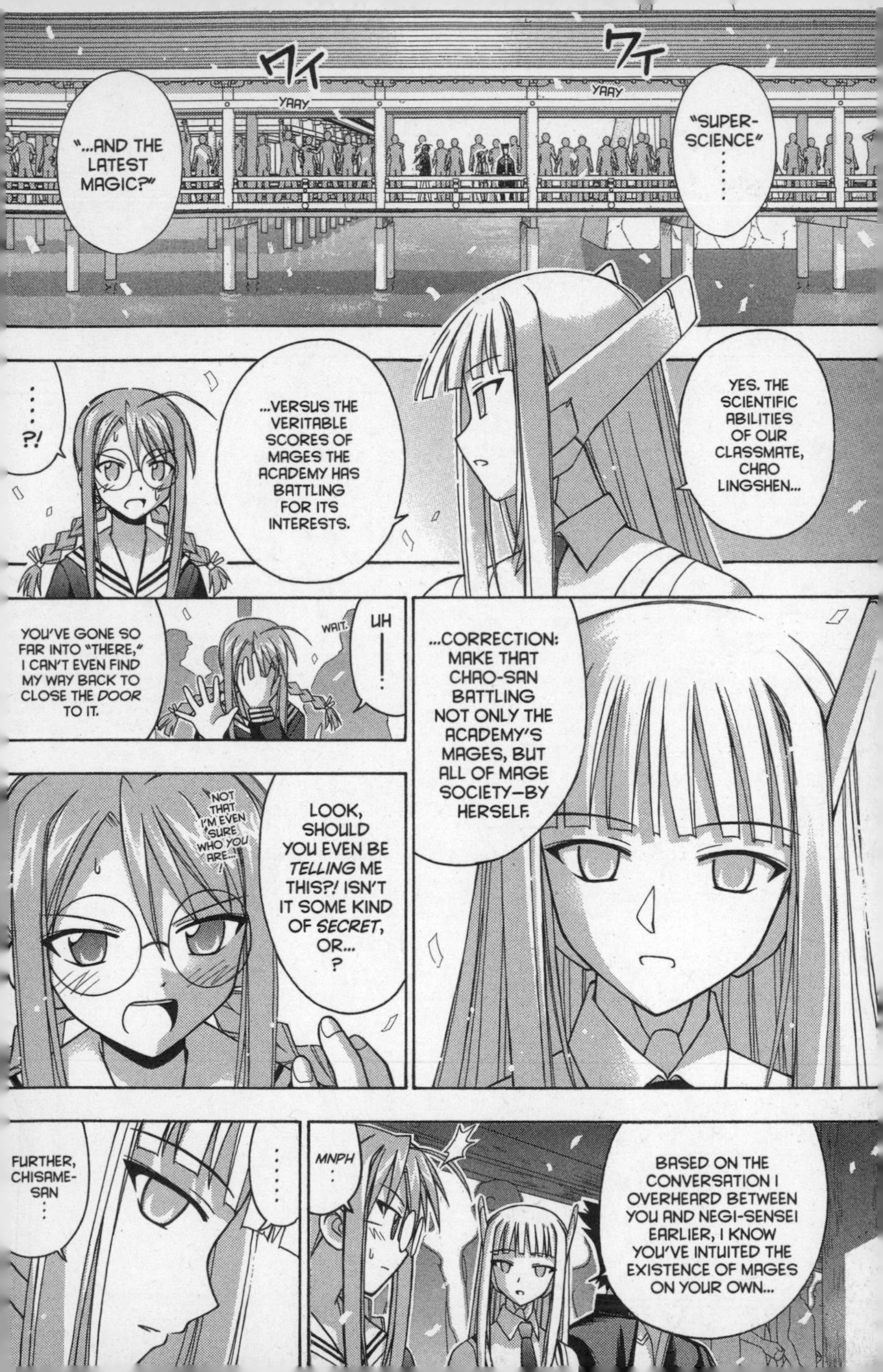
ワイ
YAAY
"SUPER-SCIENCE"
......
ワイ
YAAY
"...AND THE LATEST MAGIC?"
YES. THE SCIENTIFIC ABILITIES OF OUR CLASSMATE, CHAO LINGSHEN...
...VERSUS THE VERITABLE SCORES OF MAGES THE ACADEMY HAS BATTLING FOR ITS INTERESTS.
....?!
...CORRECTION: MAKE THAT CHAO-SAN BATTLING NOT ONLY THE ACADEMY'S MAGES, BUT ALL OF MAGE SOCIETY—BY HERSELF.
UH—!!
WAIT.
YOU'VE GONE SO FAR INTO "THERE," I CAN'T EVEN FIND MY WAY BACK TO CLOSE THE *DOOR* TO IT.
LOOK, SHOULD YOU EVEN BE *TELLING* ME THIS?! ISN'T IT SOME KIND OF *SECRET*, OR...?
NOT THAT I'M EVEN SURE WHO *YOU* ARE...!
BASED ON THE CONVERSATION I OVERHEARD BETWEEN YOU AND NEGI-SENSEI EARLIER, I KNOW YOU'VE INTUITED THE EXISTENCE OF MAGES ON YOUR OWN...
MNPH...
......
FURTHER, CHISAME-SAN...

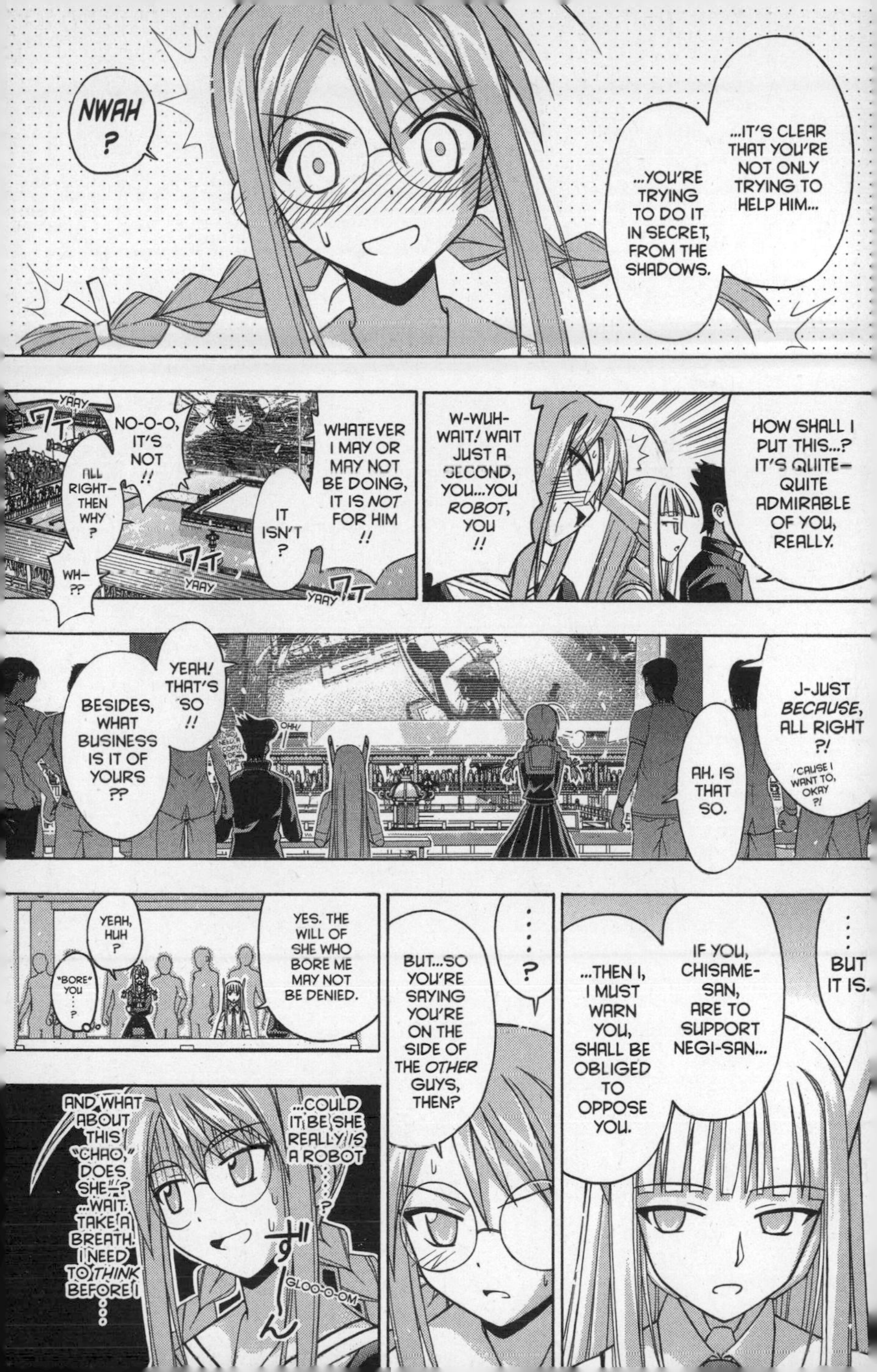
...IT'S CLEAR THAT YOU'RE NOT ONLY TRYING TO HELP HIM...
...YOU'RE TRYING TO DO IT IN SECRET, FROM THE SHADOWS.
NWAH ?
HOW SHALL I PUT THIS...? IT'S QUITE— QUITE ADMIRABLE OF YOU, REALLY.
W-WUH-WAIT! WAIT JUST A SECOND, YOU...YOU *ROBOT*, YOU !!
WHATEVER I MAY OR MAY NOT BE DOING, IT IS *NOT* FOR HIM !!
IT ISN'T ?
NO-O-O, IT'S NOT !!
ALL RIGHT— THEN WHY ?
WH— ??
YAAY
YAAY
YAAY
J-JUST *BECAUSE*, ALL RIGHT ?!
'CAUSE I WANT TO, OKAY ?!
AH. IS THAT SO.
YEAH! THAT'S SO !!
BESIDES, WHAT BUSINESS IS IT OF YOURS ??
OHH!
.... BUT IT IS.
IF YOU, CHISAME-SAN, ARE TO SUPPORT NEGI-SAN...
...THEN I, I MUST WARN YOU, SHALL BE OBLIGED TO OPPOSE YOU.
....?
BUT...SO YOU'RE SAYING YOU'RE ON THE SIDE OF THE *OTHER* GUYS, THEN?
YES. THE WILL OF SHE WHO BORE ME MAY NOT BE DENIED.
YEAH, HUH ?
"BORE" YOU ...?
...COULD IT BE SHE REALLY *IS* A ROBOT ...?
AND WHAT ABOUT THIS "CHAO," DOES SHE...? ...WAIT. TAKE A BREATH. I NEED TO *THINK* BEFORE I ....
GLOO-O-OM

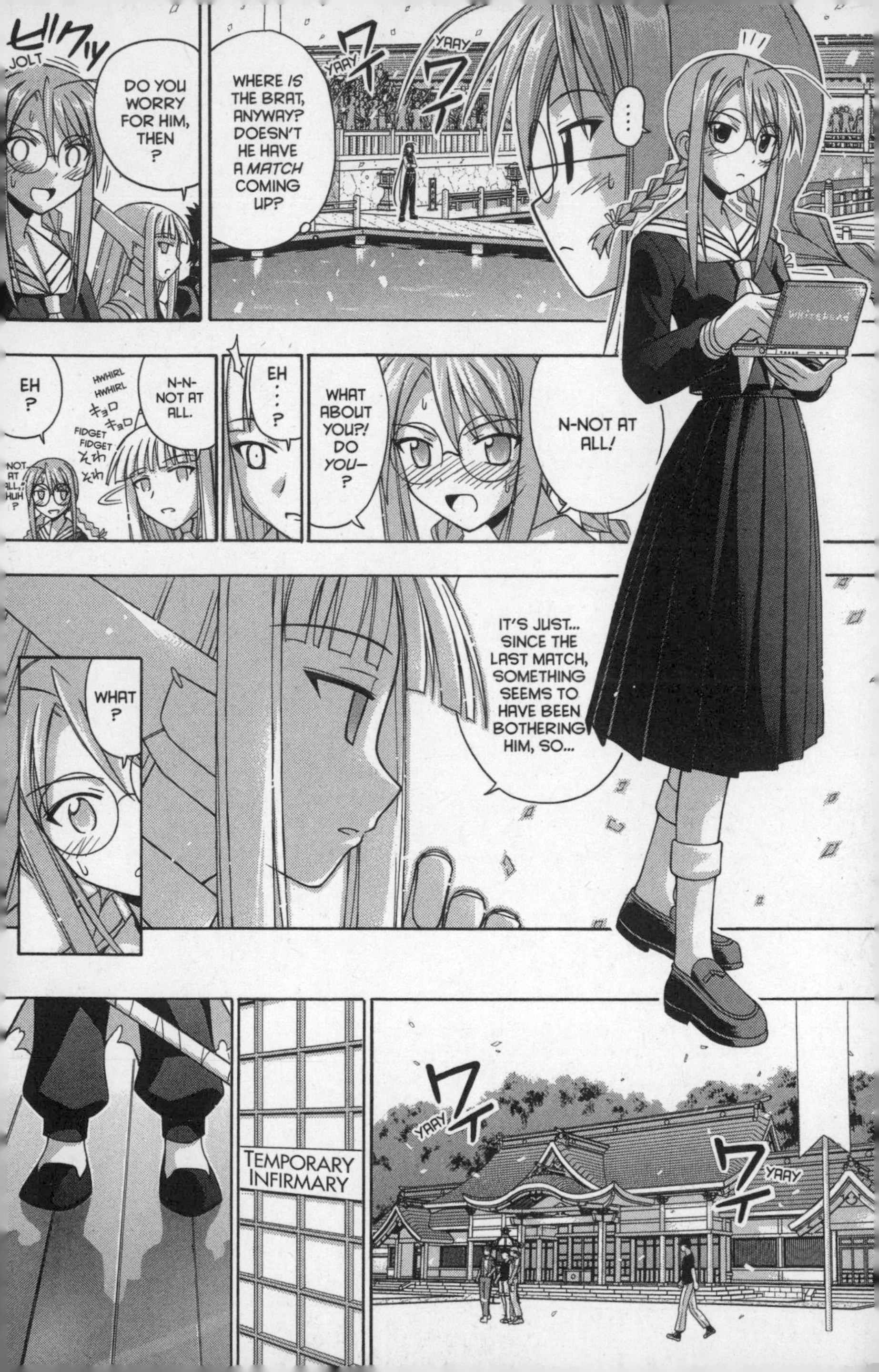
YAAY ワイ
YAAY ワイ
...
WHERE IS THE BRAT, ANYWAY? DOESN'T HE HAVE A MATCH COMING UP?
DO YOU WORRY FOR HIM, THEN ?
ビクッ JOLT
N-NOT AT ALL!
WHAT ABOUT YOU?! DO YOU— ?
EH... ?
N-N-NOT AT ALL.
HWHIRL HWHIRL キョロキョロ
FIDGET FIDGET そわそわ
EH ?
NOT AT ALL, HUH ?
IT'S JUST... SINCE THE LAST MATCH, SOMETHING SEEMS TO HAVE BEEN BOTHERING HIM, SO...
WHAT ?
YAAY ワイ
YAAY ワイ
TEMPORARY INFIRMARY

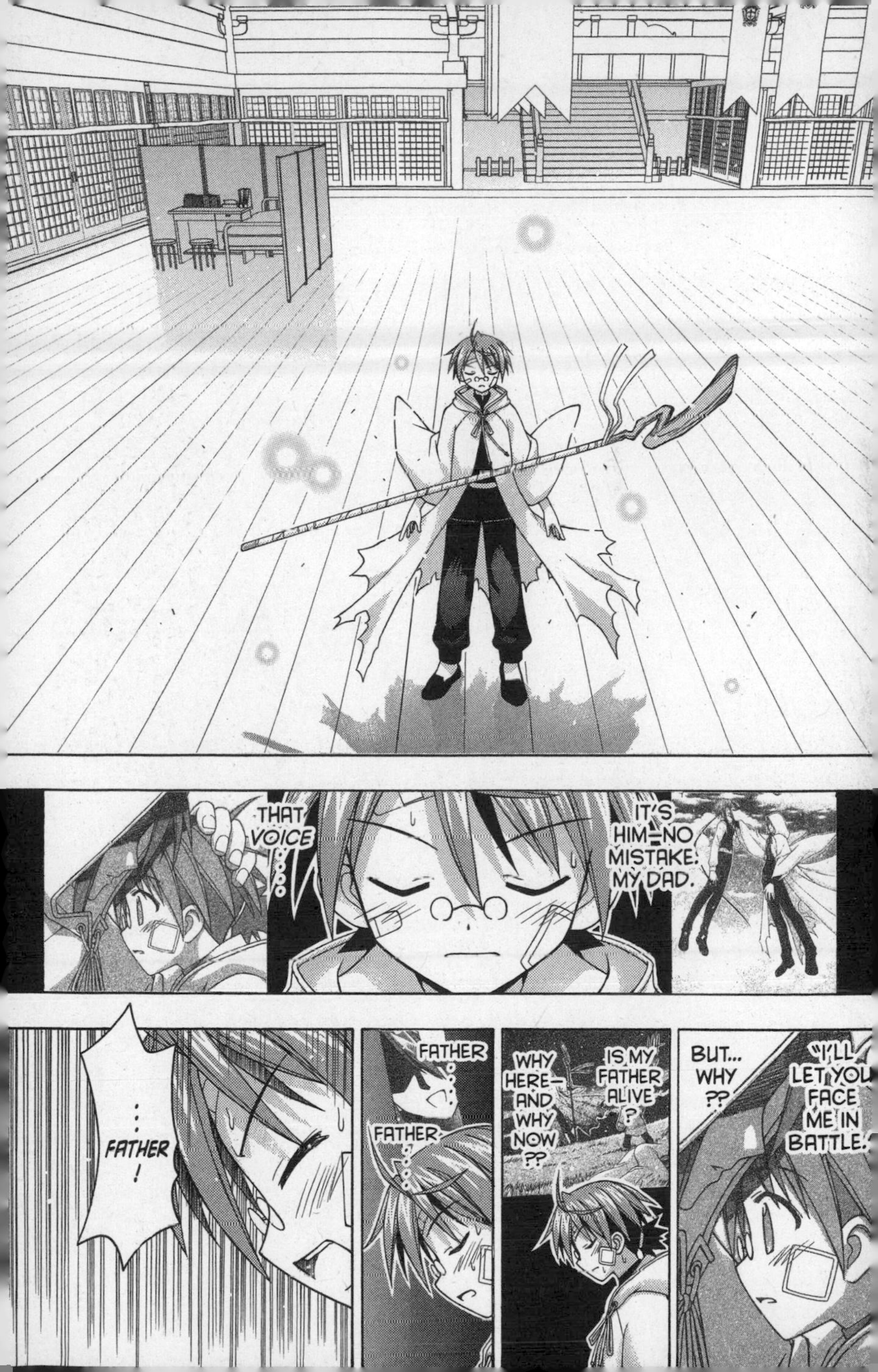
IT'S HIM—NO MISTAKE. MY DAD.
THAT VOICE...
"I'LL LET YOU FACE ME IN BATTLE."
BUT... WHY ??
IS MY FATHER ALIVE ?
WHY HERE—AND WHY NOW ??
FATHER...
FATHER...
...FATHER !

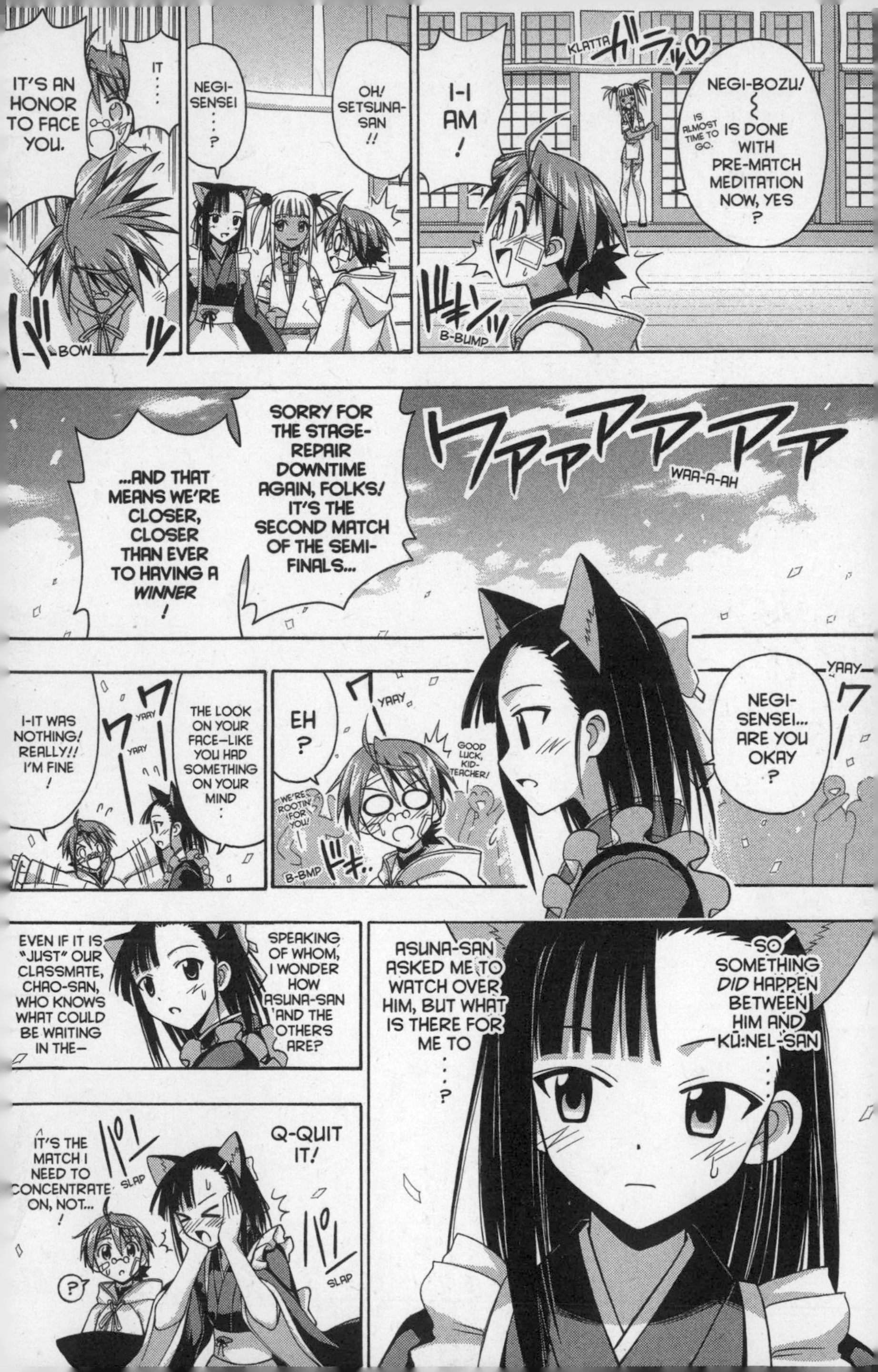
KLATTA
NEGI-BOZU! IS DONE WITH PRE-MATCH MEDITATION NOW, YES?
IS ALMOST TIME TO GO.
I-I AM!
B-BUMP
OH! SETSUNA-SAN!!
NEGI-SENSEI....?
IT....
IT'S AN HONOR TO FACE YOU.
BOW
WAA-A-AH
SORRY FOR THE STAGE-REPAIR DOWNTIME AGAIN, FOLKS! IT'S THE SECOND MATCH OF THE SEMI-FINALS...
...AND THAT MEANS WE'RE CLOSER, CLOSER THAN EVER TO HAVING A WINNER!
YAAY
NEGI-SENSEI... ARE YOU OKAY?
YAAY
EH?
GOOD LUCK, KID-TEACHER!
WE'RE ROOTIN' FOR YOU!
B-BMP
YAAY
YAAY
THE LOOK ON YOUR FACE—LIKE YOU HAD SOMETHING ON YOUR MIND...
I-IT WAS NOTHING! REALLY!! I'M FINE!
—SO SOMETHING DID HAPPEN BETWEEN HIM AND KŪ:NEL-SAN...
ASUNA-SAN ASKED ME TO WATCH OVER HIM, BUT WHAT IS THERE FOR ME TO ...?
SPEAKING OF WHOM, I WONDER HOW ASUNA-SAN AND THE OTHERS ARE?
EVEN IF IT IS "JUST" OUR CLASSMATE, CHAO-SAN, WHO KNOWS WHAT COULD BE WAITING IN THE—
Q-QUIT IT!
SLAP
SLAP
IT'S THE MATCH I NEED TO CONCENTRATE ON, NOT...!
?

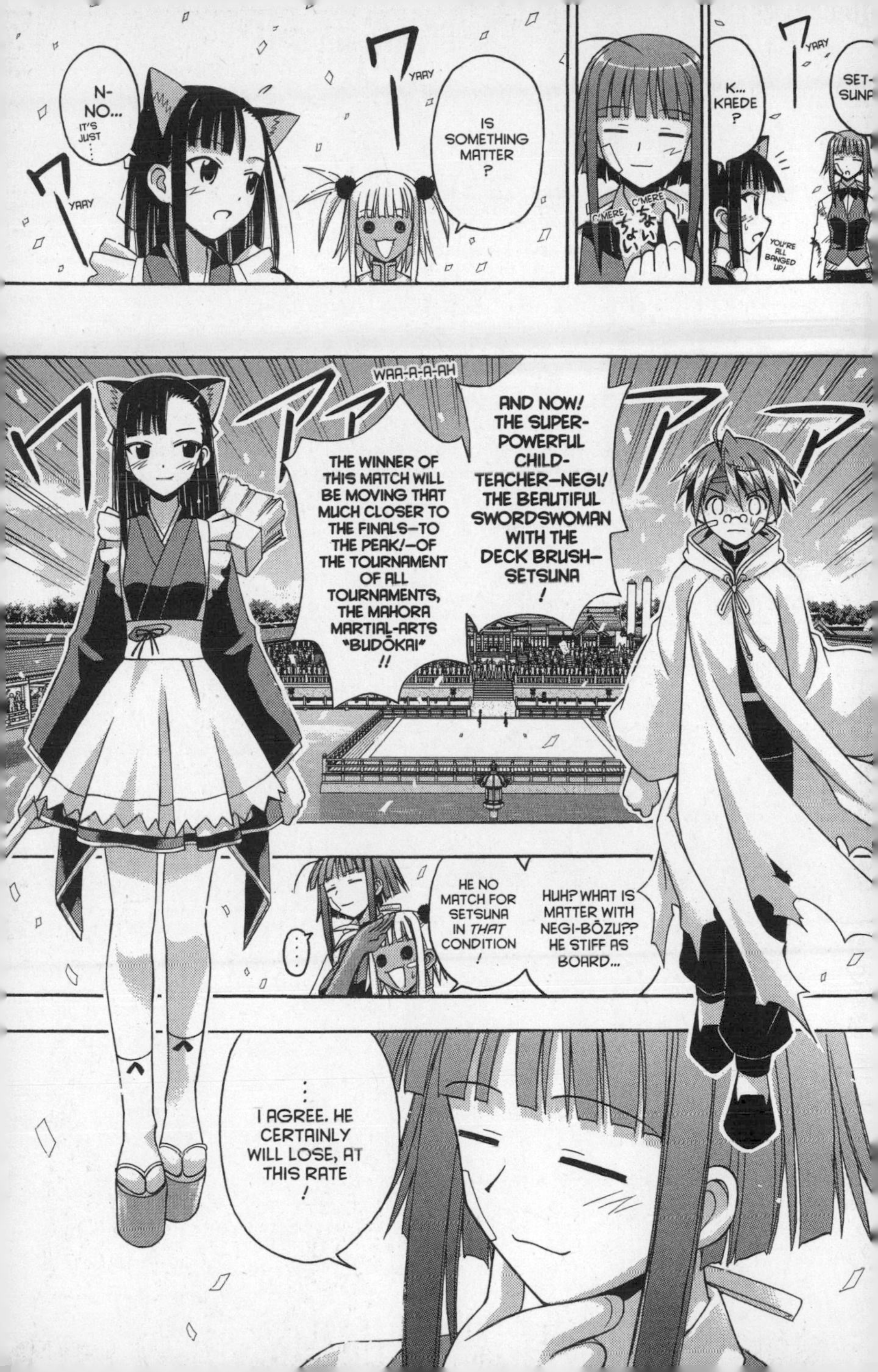
SET-SUNA
YARY
K... KAEDE?
YOU'RE ALL BANGED UP!
C'MERE C'MERE
ちょい ちょい
YARY
IS SOMETHING MATTER?
N-NO... IT'S JUST ...
YARY
AND NOW! THE SUPER-POWERFUL CHILD-TEACHER—NEGI! THE BEAUTIFUL SWORDSWOMAN WITH THE DECK BRUSH—SETSUNA!
WAA-A-A-AH
THE WINNER OF THIS MATCH WILL BE MOVING THAT MUCH CLOSER TO THE FINALS—TO THE PEAK!—OF THE TOURNAMENT OF ALL TOURNAMENTS, THE MAHORA MARTIAL-ARTS "BUDŌKAI"!!
HUH? WHAT IS MATTER WITH NEGI-BŌZU?? HE STIFF AS BOARD...
HE NO MATCH FOR SETSUNA IN *THAT* CONDITION!
...
... I AGREE. HE CERTAINLY WILL LOSE, AT THIS RATE!

LEXICON MAGICUM NEGIMARIUM

—*Negima!* Volume 13—

[113th Period]

■「メイプル・ネイプル・アラモード」

maple naple à la mode)

Magic-activation key of Mahora Academy Girls' Junior High second-year student ;akura Mei.

「ものみな焼き尽くす浄化の炎、破壊の主にして再生の徴よ、我が手に宿りて、敵を食らえ。『紅き焔』」

オムネ・フランマンス・フランマ・プルガートゥス・ドミネー・エクスティンクティオーニス・エト・シグヌム・レゲネラティオーニス・イン・メ

omne flammans flamma purgatus, domine extinctionis et signum regenerationis, in mea manu ens inimicum edat, FLAGRANTIA RUBICANS)

Spell that creates an extremely hot fire to burn its intended target. "In mea manu ens inimicum edat," the latter part of the incantation, is the same spell—Fulguration Albicans—used by Negi in Vol. 5, 41st Period, suggesting that both spells are of equal level.

As Aristotle wrote in his *Metaphysics*,

> Substance is thought to belong most obviously to bodies; and so we say that not only animals and plants and their parts are substances, but also natural bodies such as fire and water and earth and everything of the sort, and all things that are either parts of these or composed of these (either of parts or of the whole bodies), e.g. the physical universe and its parts, stars and moon and sun. But whether these alone are substances, or there are also others, or only some of these, or others as well, or none of these but only some other things, are substances, must be considered. Some think the limits of body, i.e. surface, line, point and unit, are substances, and more so than body or the solid (Book 7, Part 2).

In the the Old World, elements like fire—such as water, earth, air, and so forth—were thought to be on the same level as a substance. According to this belief, magical fire is not like fire (as we know), and is capable of unleashing light and heat without either fuel or oxygen. Therefore, this magic can be used underwater, or even in a vacuum.

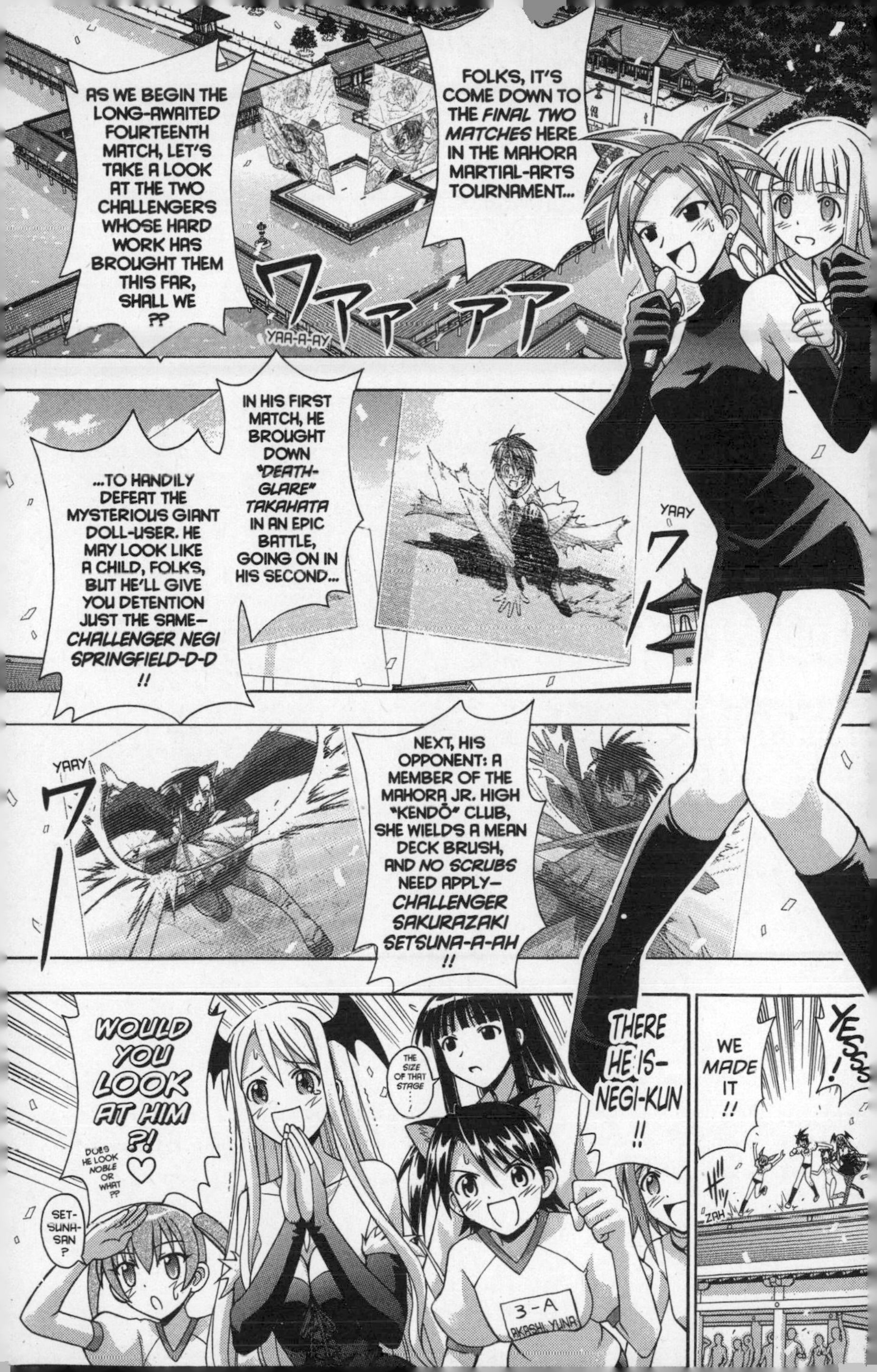
FOLKS, IT'S COME DOWN TO THE *FINAL TWO MATCHES* HERE IN THE MAHORA MARTIAL-ARTS TOURNAMENT...
AS WE BEGIN THE LONG-AWAITED FOURTEENTH MATCH, LET'S TAKE A LOOK AT THE TWO CHALLENGERS WHOSE HARD WORK HAS BROUGHT THEM THIS FAR, SHALL WE ??
ワァァ アア
YAA-A-AY
ワ
YAAY
IN HIS FIRST MATCH, HE BROUGHT DOWN *"DEATH-GLARE" TAKAHATA* IN AN EPIC BATTLE, GOING ON IN HIS SECOND...
...TO HANDILY DEFEAT THE MYSTERIOUS GIANT DOLL-USER. HE MAY LOOK LIKE A CHILD, FOLKS, BUT HE'LL GIVE YOU DETENTION JUST THE SAME— *CHALLENGER NEGI SPRINGFIELD-D-D* !!
NEXT, HIS OPPONENT: A MEMBER OF THE MAHORA JR. HIGH "KENDŌ" CLUB, SHE WIELDS A MEAN DECK BRUSH, AND *NO SCRUBS* NEED APPLY— *CHALLENGER SAKURAZAKI SETSUNA-A-AH* !!
ワ
YAAY
YESSS!
WE MADE IT !!
ZAH
THERE HE IS- NEGI-KUN !!
THE *SIZE* OF THAT *STAGE* ...!
WOULD YOU LOOK AT HIM ?! ♥
DOES HE LOOK *NOBLE* OR WHAT ??
SET-SUNA-SAN ?
3-A AKASHI YUNA

114TH PERIOD: IF YOU ALL ARE HERE, THEN SO AM I

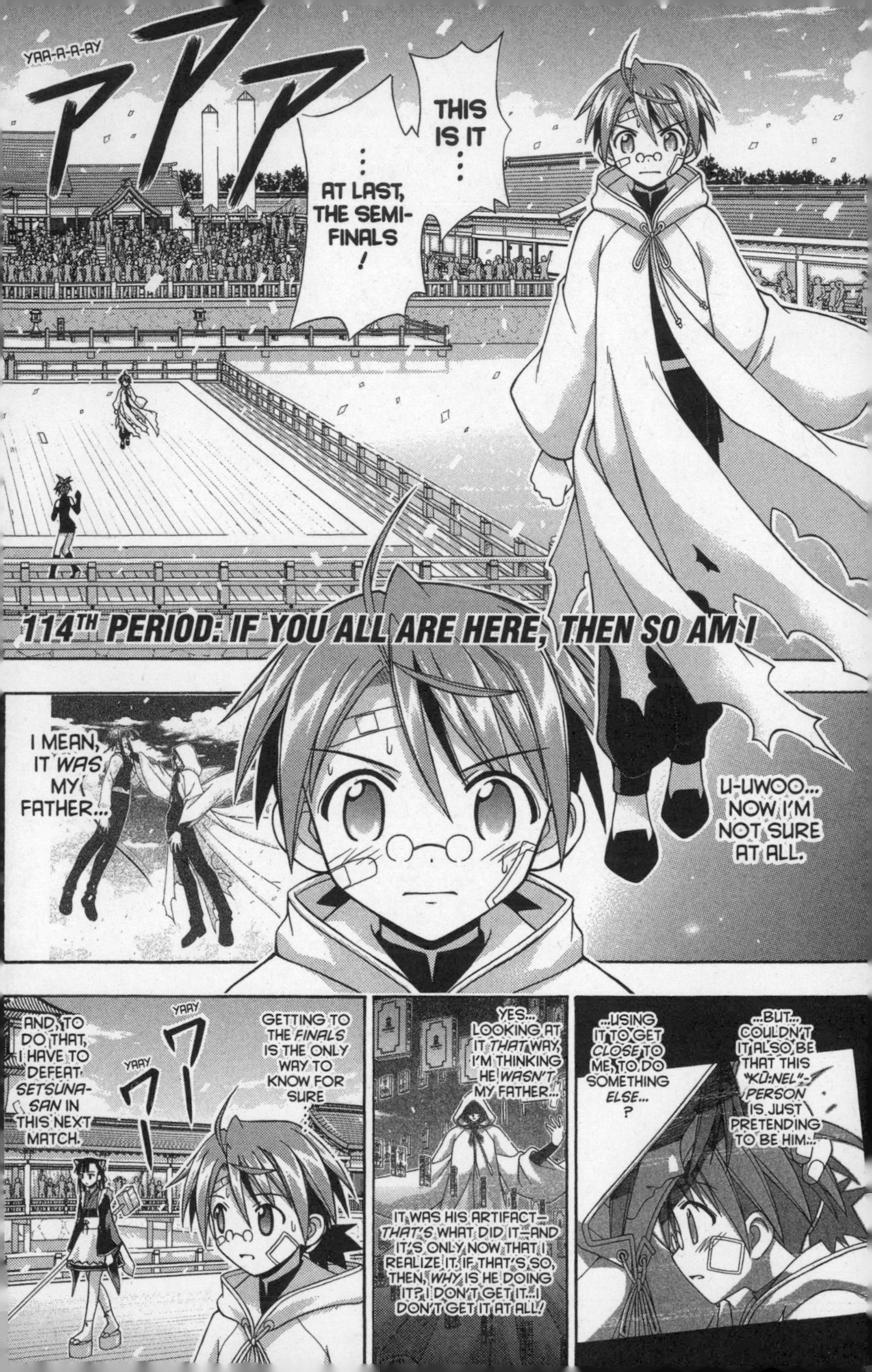
YAA-A-A-AY
THIS IS IT...
...AT LAST, THE SEMI-FINALS!
U-UWOO... NOW I'M NOT SURE AT ALL.
I MEAN, IT *WAS* MY FATHER...
...BUT... COULDN'T IT ALSO BE THAT THIS "KU:NEL"-PERSON IS JUST PRETENDING TO BE HIM...
...USING IT TO GET *CLOSE* TO ME, TO DO SOMETHING *ELSE*...?
YES... LOOKING AT IT *THAT* WAY, I'M THINKING HE *WASN'T* MY FATHER...
IT WAS HIS ARTIFACT—*THAT'S* WHAT DID IT—AND IT'S ONLY NOW THAT I REALIZE IT. IF THAT'S SO, THEN, *WHY* IS HE DOING IT? I DON'T GET IT... I DON'T GET IT AT ALL!
GETTING TO THE *FINALS* IS THE ONLY WAY TO KNOW FOR SURE
YAAY
YAAY
AND, TO DO THAT, I HAVE TO DEFEAT *SETSUNA-SAN* IN THIS NEXT MATCH.

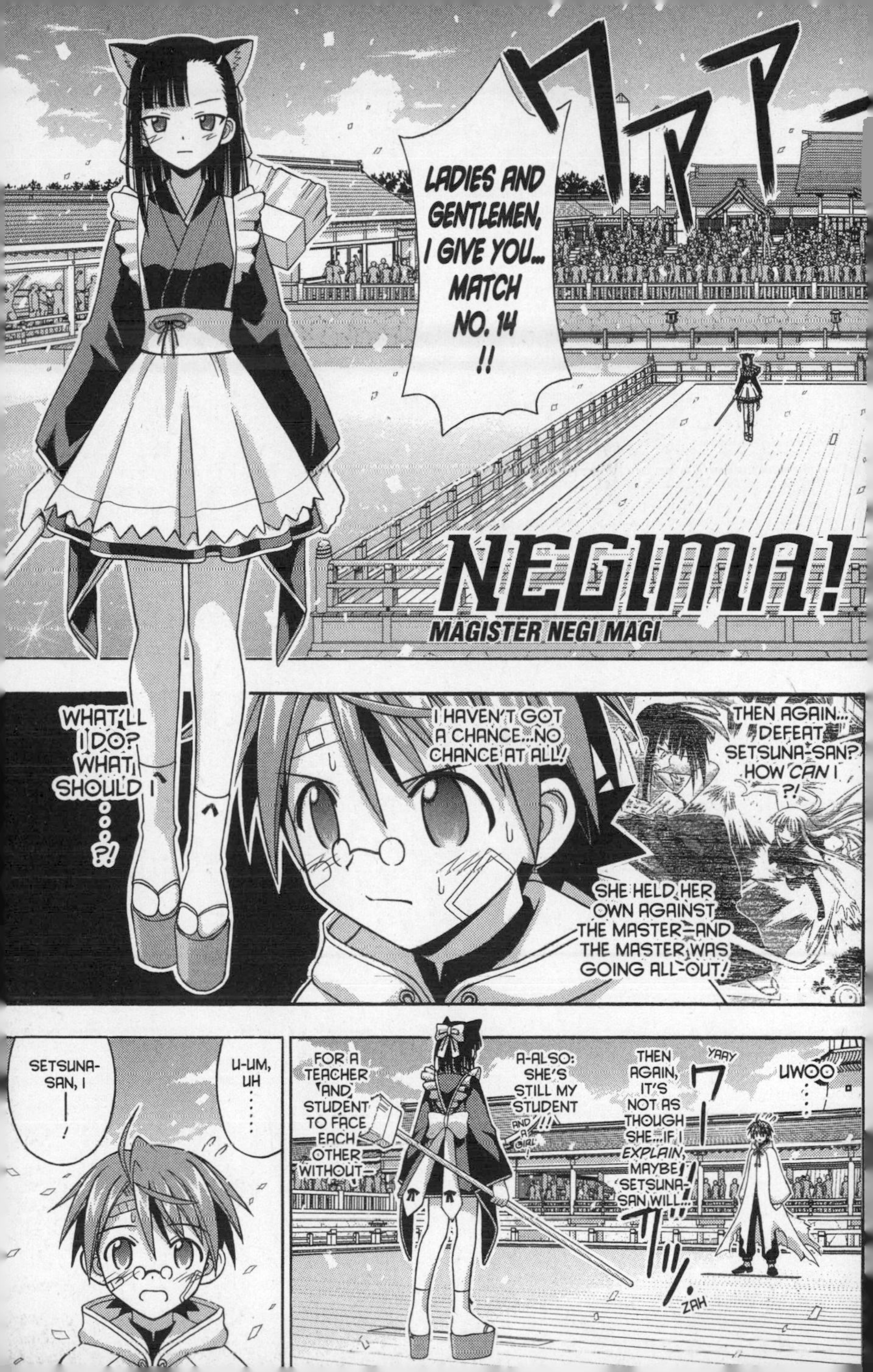
LADIES AND GENTLEMEN, I GIVE YOU... MATCH NO. 14 !!
NEGIMA!
MAGISTER NEGI MAGI
THEN AGAIN... DEFEAT SETSUNA-SAN? HOW CAN I ?!
SHE HELD HER OWN AGAINST THE MASTER—AND THE MASTER WAS GOING ALL-OUT!
I HAVEN'T GOT A CHANCE...NO CHANCE AT ALL!
WHAT'LL I DO? WHAT SHOULD I ....?!
UWOO...
YAAY
THEN AGAIN, IT'S NOT AS THOUGH SHE...IF I EXPLAIN, MAYBE SETSUNA-SAN WILL...
A-ALSO: SHE'S STILL MY STUDENT !!
AND A GIRL!
FOR A TEACHER AND STUDENT TO FACE EACH OTHER WITHOUT—
ZAH
U-UM, UH......
SETSUNA-SAN, I —!

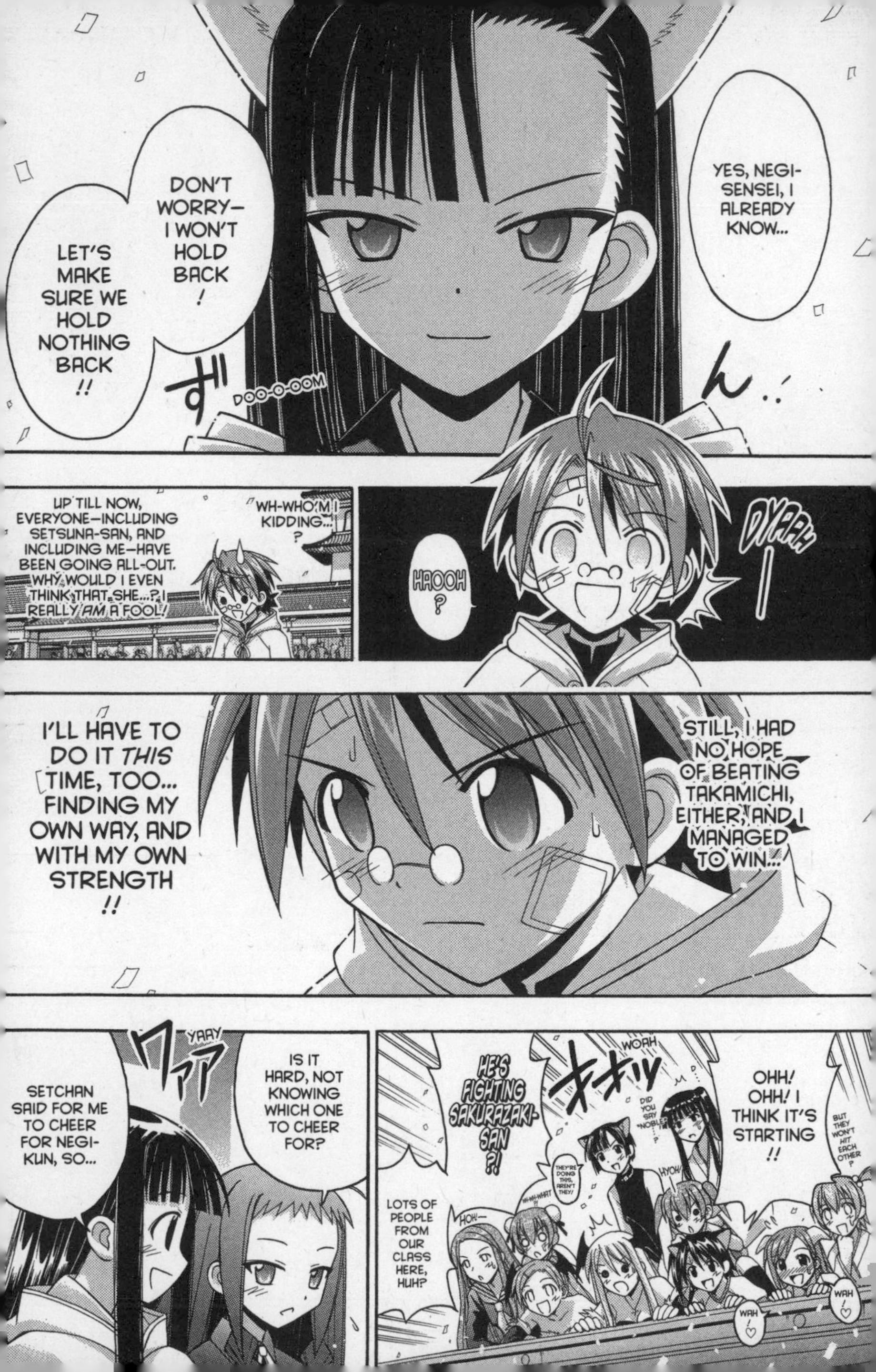
YES, NEGI-SENSEI, I ALREADY KNOW...
ん..
DON'T WORRY—I WON'T HOLD BACK!
LET'S MAKE SURE WE HOLD NOTHING BACK!!
ず
DOO-O-OOM
DYAAH!
HAOOH?
WH-WHO'M I KIDDING...?
UP TILL NOW, EVERYONE—INCLUDING SETSUNA-SAN, AND INCLUDING ME—HAVE BEEN GOING ALL-OUT. WHY WOULD I EVEN THINK THAT SHE...? I REALLY *AM* A FOOL!
STILL, I HAD NO HOPE OF BEATING TAKAMICHI, EITHER, AND I MANAGED TO WIN...
I'LL HAVE TO DO IT *THIS* TIME, TOO... FINDING MY OWN WAY, AND WITH MY OWN STRENGTH!!
OHH! OHH! I THINK IT'S STARTING!!
BUT THEY WON'T HIT EACH OTHER?
WOAH
オオッ
D...
DID YOU SAY "NOBLE"...?
HE'S FIGHTING SAKURAZAKI-SAN?!
HYOH!
THEY'RE DOING THIS, AREN'T THEY!
WH-WH-WHAT?!
LOTS OF PEOPLE FROM OUR CLASS HERE, HUH?
HOH—
WAH!♡
WAH!♡
IS IT HARD, NOT KNOWING WHICH ONE TO CHEER FOR?
YAAY
ワァア
SETCHAN SAID FOR ME TO CHEER FOR NEGI-KUN, SO...

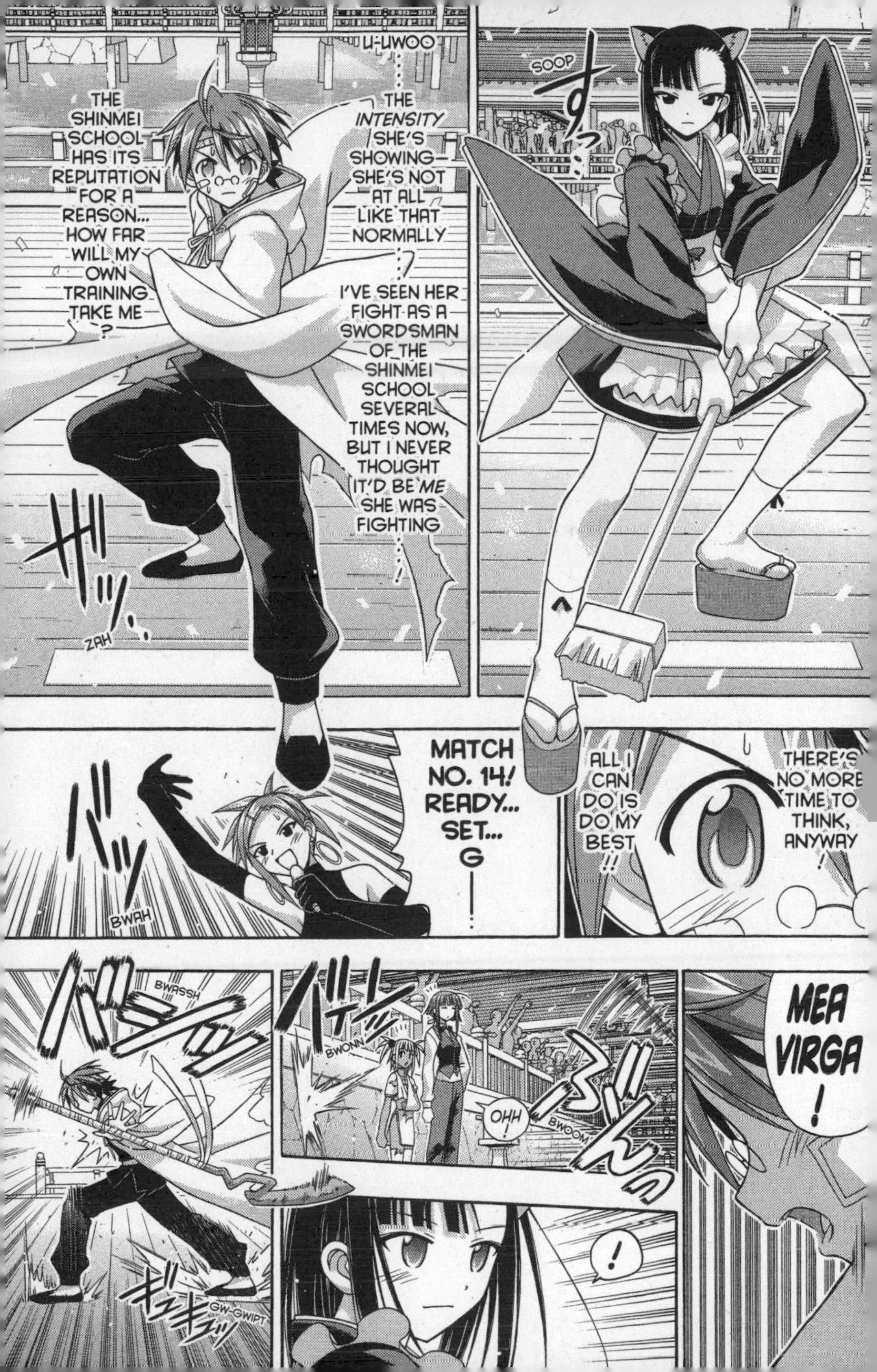
SOOP
U-UWOO...
THE INTENSITY SHE'S SHOWING—SHE'S NOT AT ALL LIKE THAT NORMALLY...?
I'VE SEEN HER FIGHT AS A SWORDSMAN OF THE SHINMEI SCHOOL SEVERAL TIMES NOW, BUT I NEVER THOUGHT IT'D BE ME SHE WAS FIGHTING...!
THE SHINMEI SCHOOL HAS ITS REPUTATION FOR A REASON... HOW FAR WILL MY OWN TRAINING TAKE ME?
ZAH
THERE'S NO MORE TIME TO THINK, ANYWAY!
ALL I CAN DO IS DO MY BEST!!
MATCH NO. 14! READY... SET... G—...!
BWAH
MEA VIRGA!
BWONN
OHH!
BWOOM
BWASSH
GW-GWIPT
!

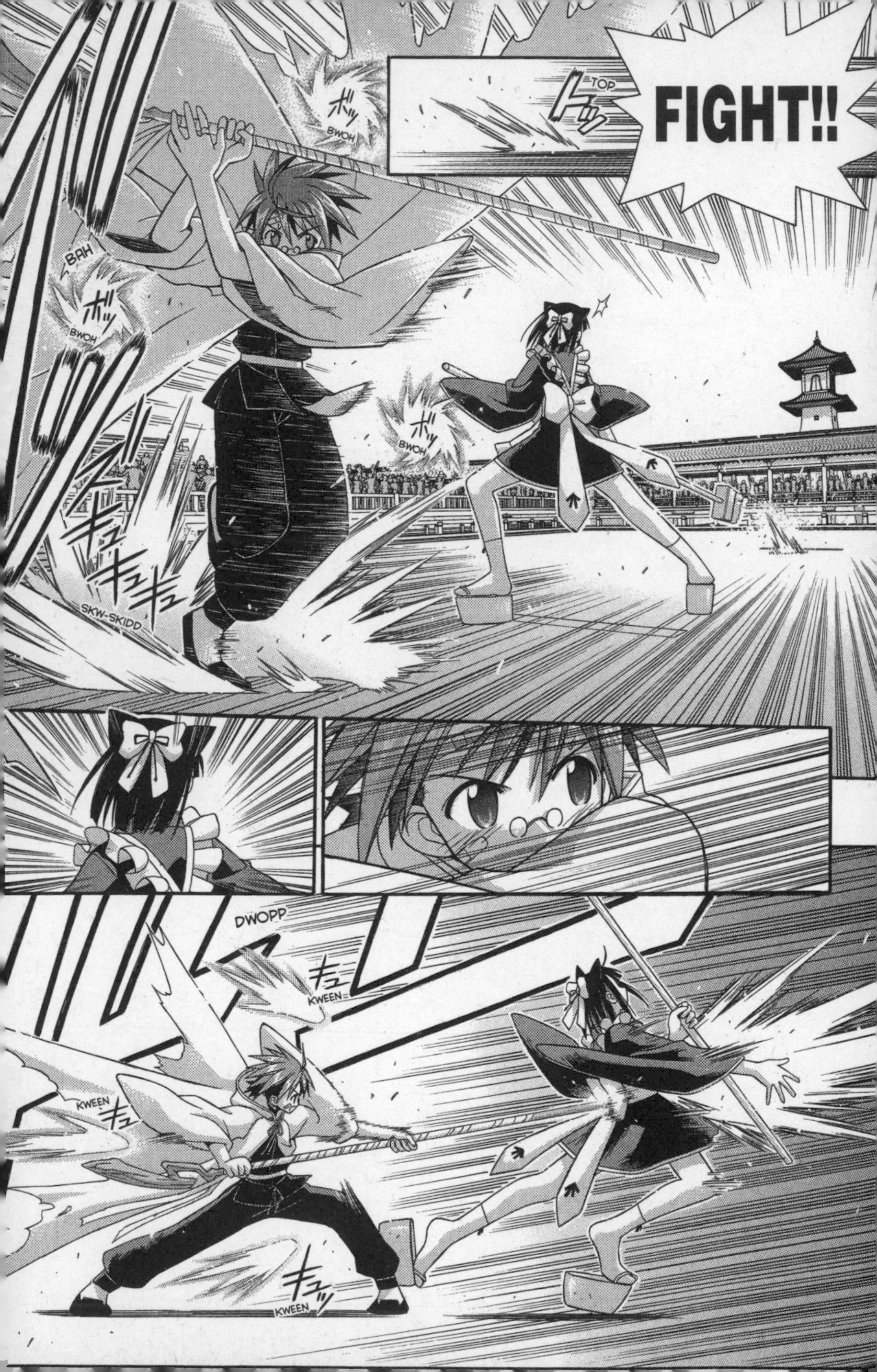
FIGHT!!
トッ
TOP
ボッ
BWOH
BAH
ボッ
BWOH
ボッ
BWOH
SKW-SKIDD
DWOPP
キュ
KWEEN
キュ
KWEEN
キュッ
KWEEN

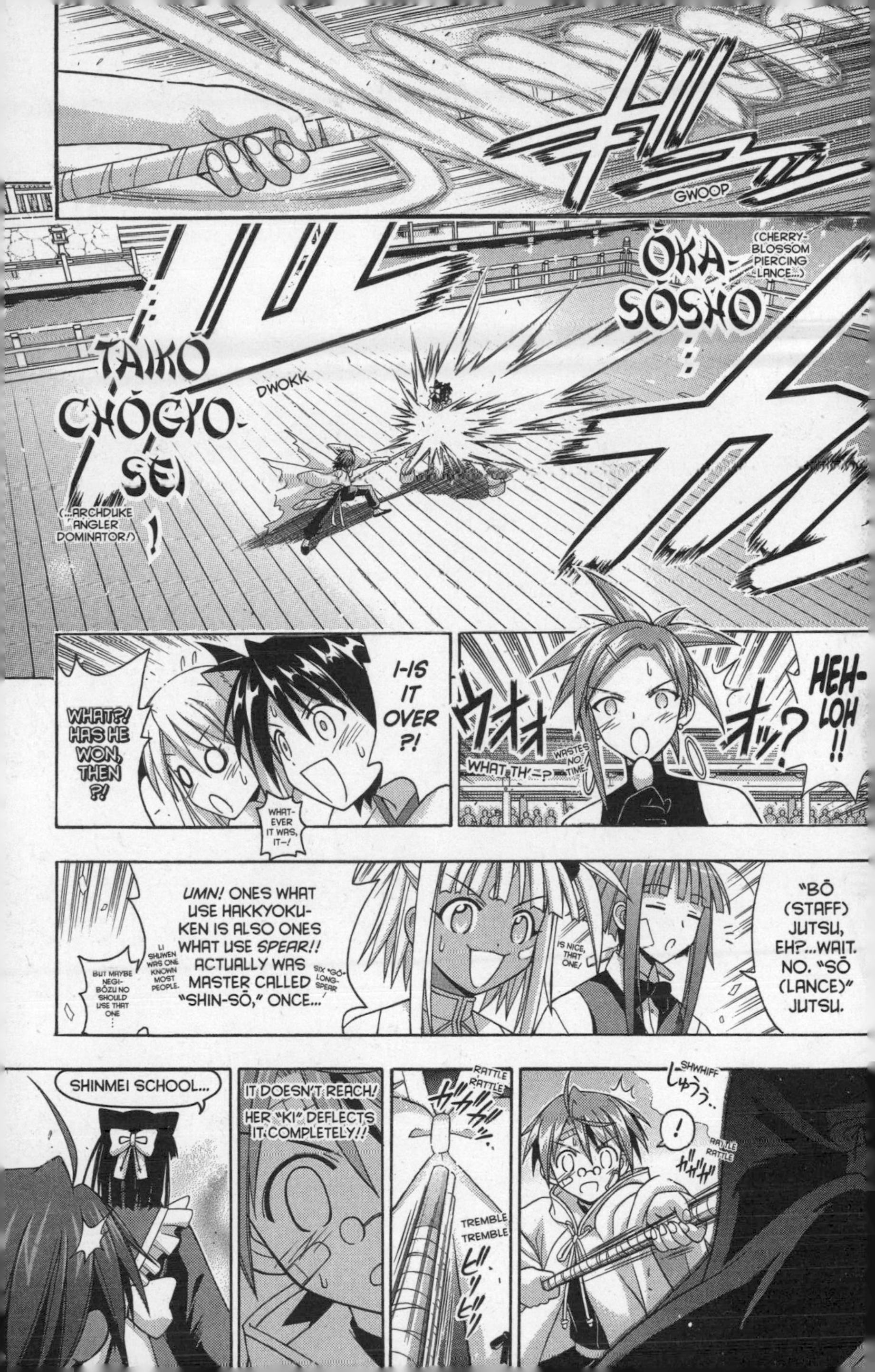
GWOOP
(CHERRY-BLOSSOM PIERCING LANCE...)
ŌKA SŌSHO
TAIKŌ CHŌGYO-SEI!
(...ARCHDUKE ANGLER DOMINATOR!)
DWOKK
HEH-LOH!!
WASTES NO TIME.
WHAT TH'--?
I-IS IT OVER?!
WHAT?! HAS HE WON, THEN?!
WHAT-EVER IT WAS, IT--!
"BŌ (STAFF) JUTSU, EH?...WAIT. NO. "SŌ (LANCE)" JUTSU.
IS NICE, THAT ONE!
UMN! ONES WHAT USE HAKKYOKUKEN IS ALSO ONES WHAT USE SPEAR!! ACTUALLY WAS MASTER CALLED "SHIN-SŌ," ONCE...
SIX "GŌ" LONG-SPEAR
LI SHUWEN WAS ONE KNOWN MOST PEOPLE.
BUT MAYBE NEGI-BŌZU NO SHOULD USE THAT ONE...
SHWHIFF
!
RATTLE RATTLE
TREMBLE TREMBLE
RATTLE RATTLE
IT DOESN'T REACH!
HER "KI" DEFLECTS IT COMPLETELY!!
SHINMEI SCHOOL...

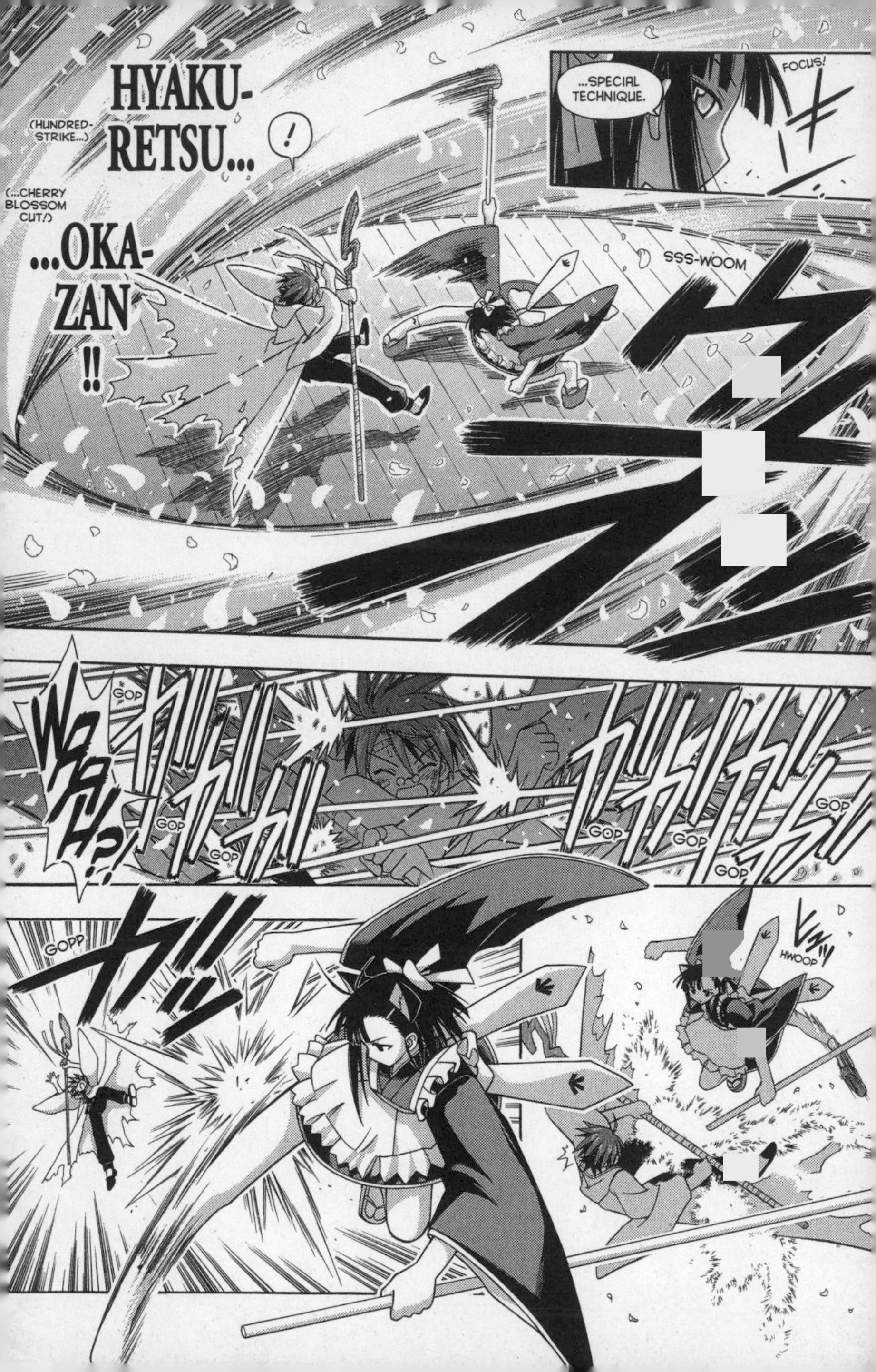
FOCUS!
...SPECIAL TECHNIQUE.
!
HYAKU-RETSU...
(HUNDRED-STRIKE...)
SSS-WOOM
...OKA-ZAN!!
(...CHERRY BLOSSOM CUT!)
GOP
GOP
GOP
GOP
GOP
GOP
GOP
WOAAH?!
HWOOP
GOPP

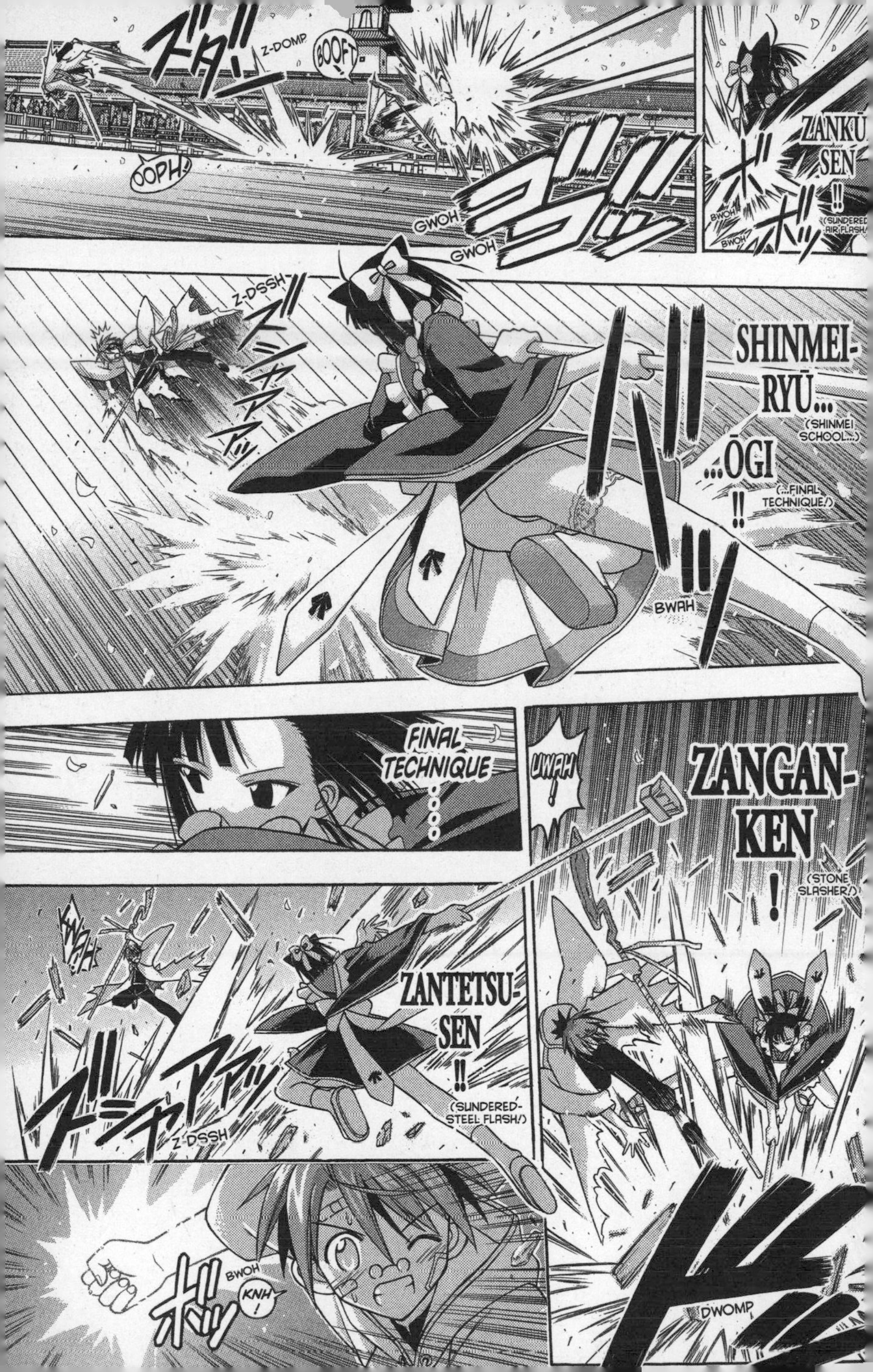
ZANKŪ SEN!!
(SUNDERED AIR FLASH!)
BWOH
BWOH
GWOH
GWOH
BOOFT
Z-DOMP
OOPH!
SHINMEI-RYŪ...
(SHINMEI SCHOOL...)
...ŌGI!!
(...FINAL TECHNIQUE!)
BWAH
Z-DSSH
ZANGAN-KEN!
(STONE SLASHER!)
UWAH!
FINAL TECHNIQUE....
ZANTETSU-SEN!!
(SUNDERED-STEEL FLASH!)
Z-DSSH
DWOMP
BWOH
KNH!

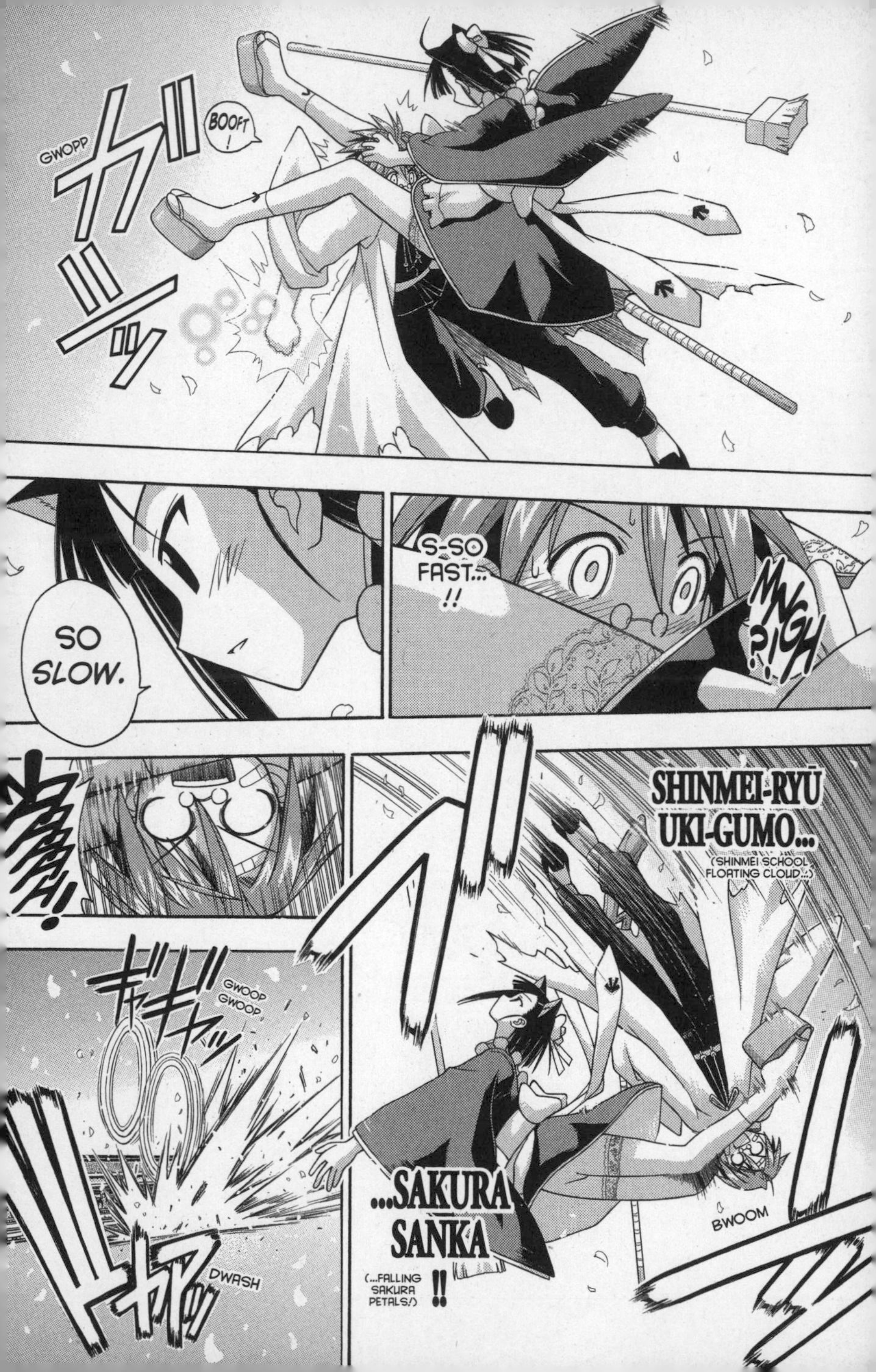
GWOPP
BOOFT!
S-SO FAST...!!
MNGH?!!
SO SLOW.
SHINMEI-RYŪ UKI-GUMO...
(SHINMEI SCHOOL FLOATING CLOUD...)
...SAKURA SANKA!!
(...FALLING SAKURA PETALS!)
BWOOM
GWOOP GWOOP
DWASH

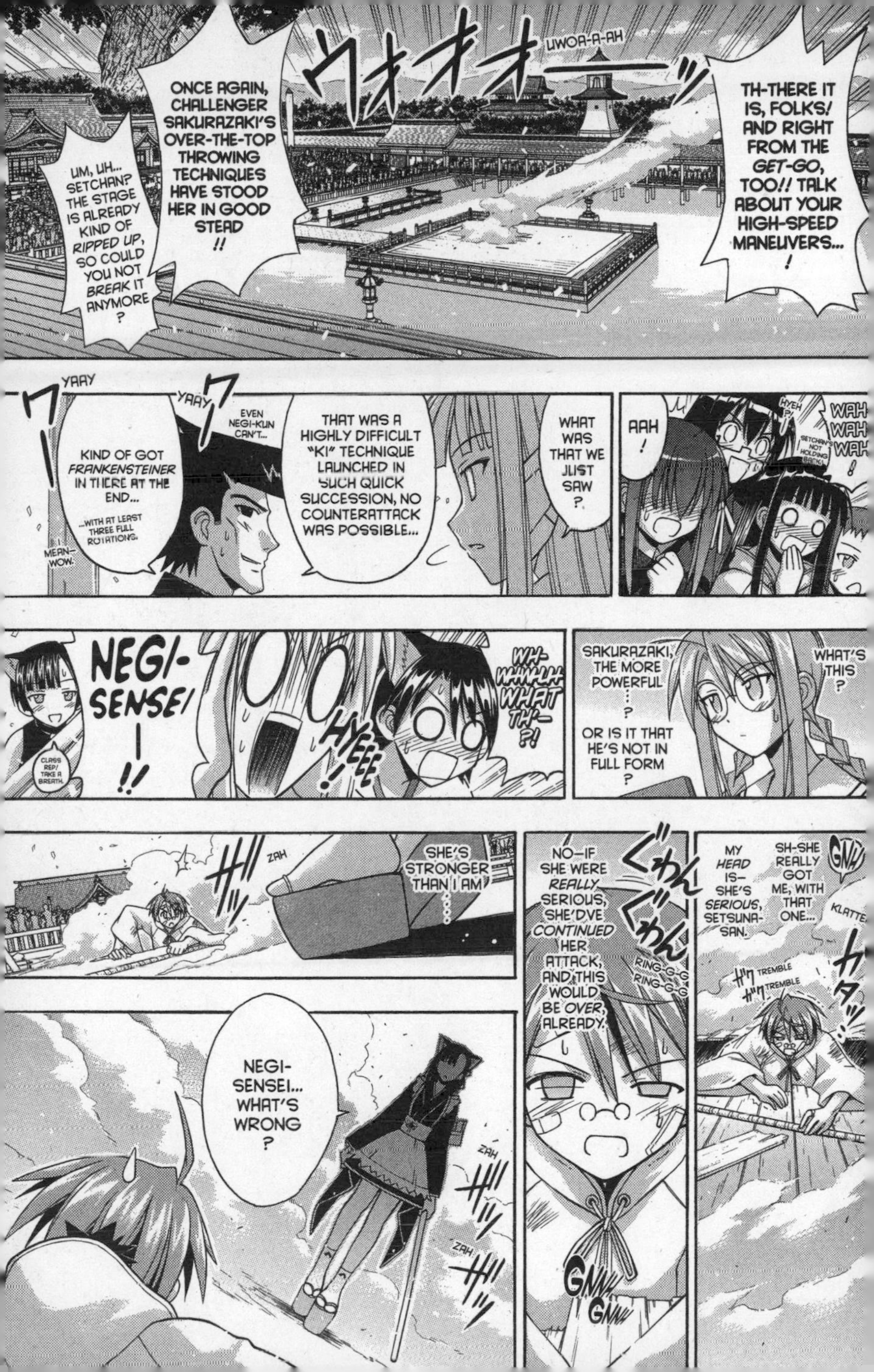
TH-THERE IT IS, FOLKS! AND RIGHT FROM THE GET-GO, TOO!! TALK ABOUT YOUR HIGH-SPEED MANEUVERS...!
ウォオオオーーッ
UWOA-A-AH
ONCE AGAIN, CHALLENGER SAKURAZAKI'S OVER-THE-TOP THROWING TECHNIQUES HAVE STOOD HER IN GOOD STEAD!!
UM, UH... SETCHAN? THE STAGE IS ALREADY KIND OF RIPPED UP, SO COULD YOU NOT BREAK IT ANYMORE?
WAH WAH WAH!
HYEH?!
SETCHAN'S NOT HOLDING BACK!
AAH!
WHAT WAS THAT WE JUST SAW?
THAT WAS A HIGHLY DIFFICULT "KI" TECHNIQUE LAUNCHED IN SUCH QUICK SUCCESSION, NO COUNTERATTACK WAS POSSIBLE...
EVEN NEGI-KUN CAN'T...
ワー
YAAY
ワー
YAAY
KIND OF GOT FRANKENSTEINER IN THERE AT THE END...
...WITH AT LEAST THREE FULL ROTATIONS.
I MEAN- WOW.
WHAT'S THIS?
SAKURAZAKI, THE MORE POWERFUL...?
OR IS IT THAT HE'S NOT IN FULL FORM?
WH-WHWUH WHAT TH-?!
HYEEE!
NEGI-SENSEI!!
CLASS REP! TAKE A BREATH.
SH-SHE REALLY GOT ME, WITH THAT ONE...
GNH
MY HEAD IS— SHE'S SERIOUS, SETSUNA-SAN.
ガタッ
KLATTE
TREMBLE TREMBLE
ぐわん ぐわん
NO—IF SHE WERE REALLY SERIOUS, SHE'DVE CONTINUED HER ATTACK, AND THIS WOULD BE OVER ALREADY.
RING-G-G RING-G-G
GNH GNH
SHE'S STRONGER THAN I AM...
ZAH
NEGI-SENSEI... WHAT'S WRONG?
ZAH
ZAH

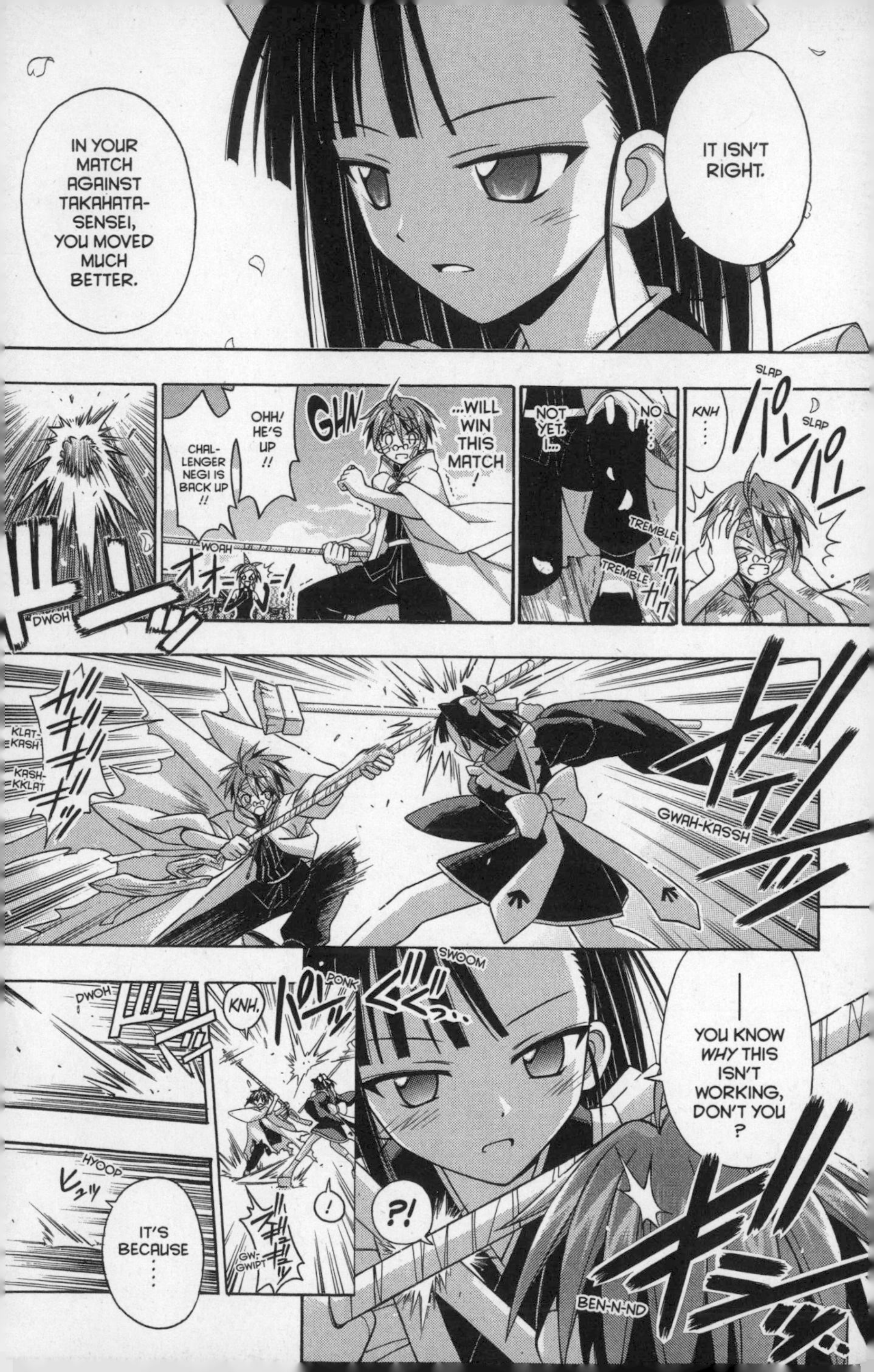
IT ISN'T RIGHT.
IN YOUR MATCH AGAINST TAKAHATA-SENSEI, YOU MOVED MUCH BETTER.
SLAP
SLAP
KNH ...
NO ......
NOT YET. I...
TREMBLE
TREMBLE
...WILL WIN THIS MATCH !
GHN
OHH! HE'S UP !!
CHAL-LENGER NEGI IS BACK UP !!
WOAH
DWOH
GWAH-KASSH
KLAT-KASH
KASH-KKLAT
YOU KNOW *WHY* THIS ISN'T WORKING, DON'T YOU ?
SWOOM
?!
BEN-N-ND
PONK
KNH.
!
GW-GWIPT
DWOH
HYOOP
IT'S BECAUSE ....

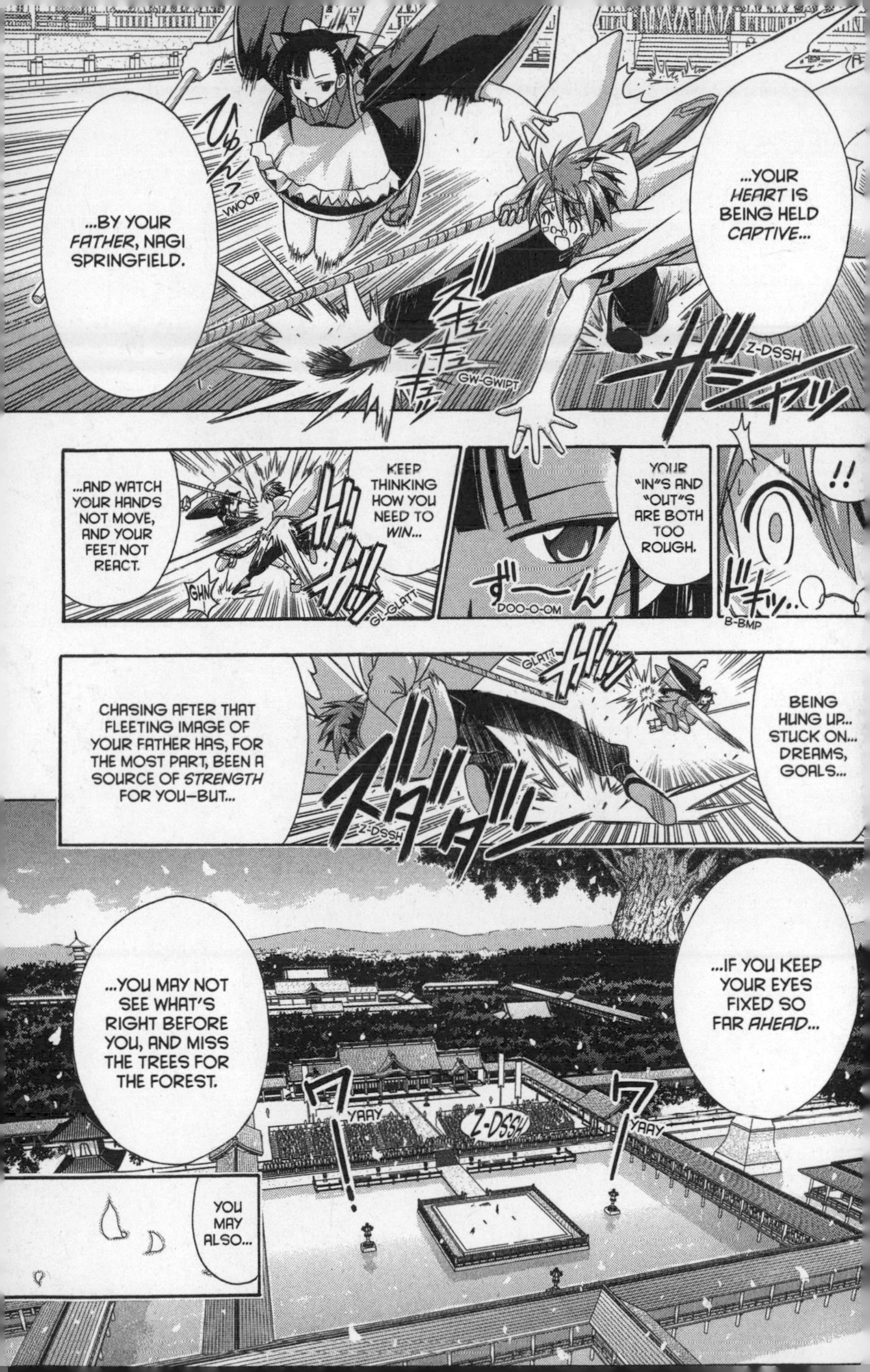
...YOUR HEART IS BEING HELD CAPTIVE...
VWOOP
...BY YOUR FATHER, NAGI SPRINGFIELD.
Z-DSSH
GW-GWIPT
!!
B-BMP
YOUR "IN"S AND "OUT"S ARE BOTH TOO ROUGH.
DOO-O-OM
KEEP THINKING HOW YOU NEED TO WIN...
...AND WATCH YOUR HANDS NOT MOVE, AND YOUR FEET NOT REACT.
GHN
GL-GLATT
BEING HUNG UP... STUCK ON... DREAMS, GOALS...
GLATT
CHASING AFTER THAT FLEETING IMAGE OF YOUR FATHER HAS, FOR THE MOST PART, BEEN A SOURCE OF STRENGTH FOR YOU—BUT...
Z-DSSH
...IF YOU KEEP YOUR EYES FIXED SO FAR AHEAD...
YAAY
Z-DSSH
YAAY
...YOU MAY NOT SEE WHAT'S RIGHT BEFORE YOU, AND MISS THE TREES FOR THE FOREST.
YOU MAY ALSO...

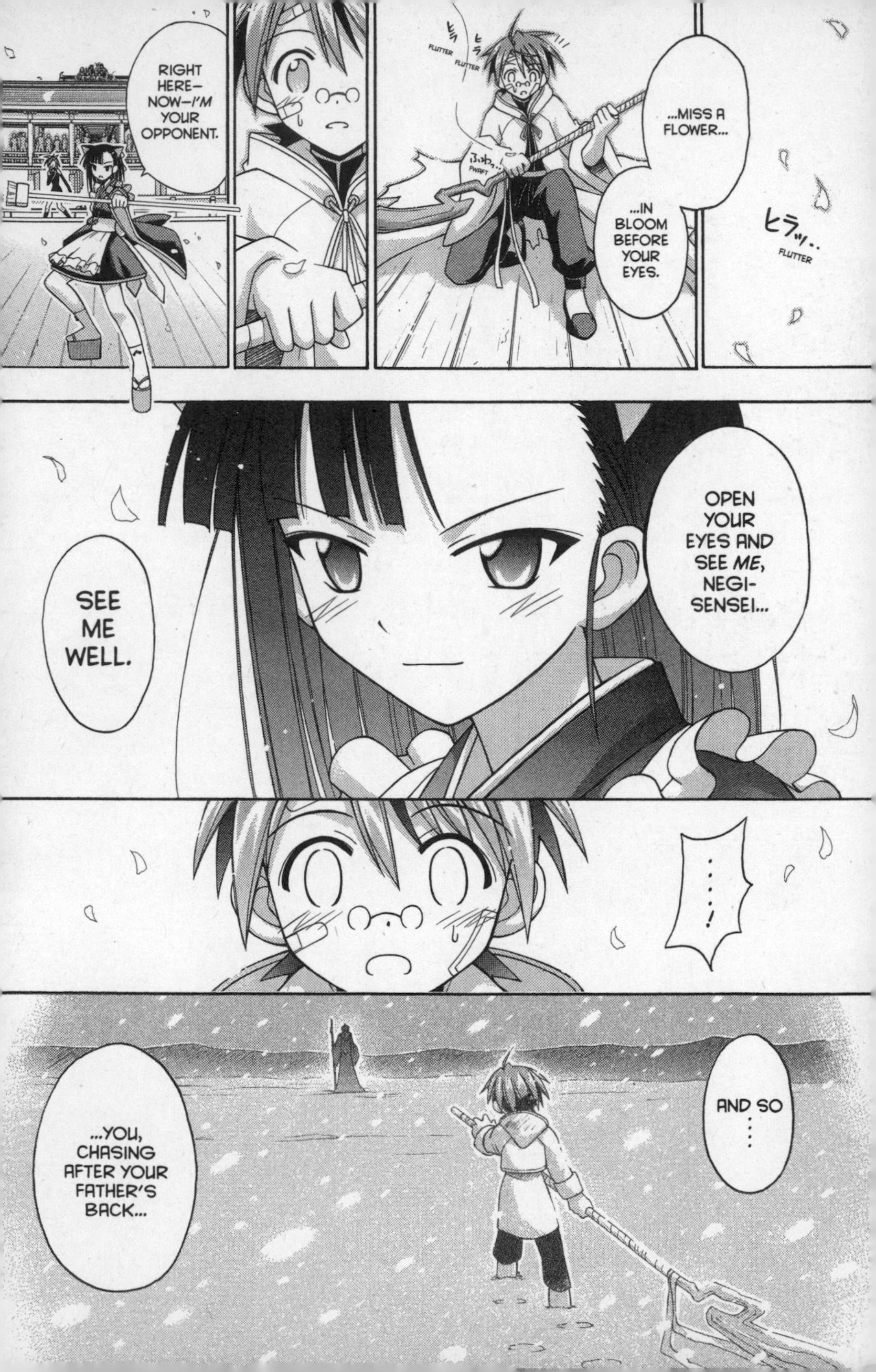
ヒラッ..
FLUTTER
...MISS A FLOWER...
...IN BLOOM BEFORE YOUR EYES.
ヒラ ヒラ
FLUTTER FLUTTER
ふゎ...
PWAFT
RIGHT HERE—NOW—*I'M* YOUR OPPONENT.
OPEN YOUR EYES AND SEE *ME*, NEGI-SENSEI...
SEE ME WELL.
......!
AND SO....
...YOU, CHASING AFTER YOUR FATHER'S BACK...

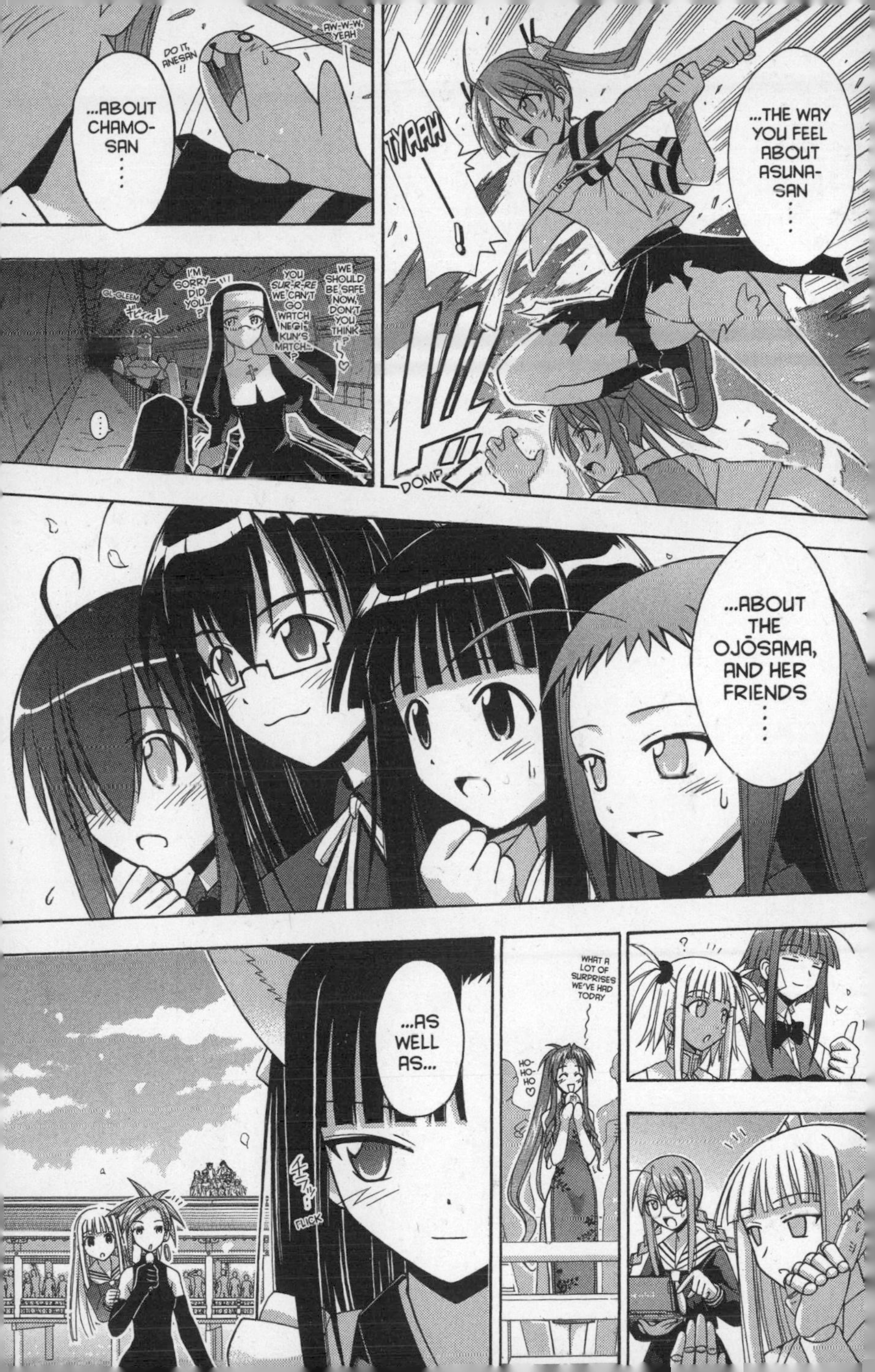

...THE WAY YOU FEEL ABOUT ASUNA-SAN ....
TYAAAH —!
DOMP
AW-W-W, YEAH
DO IT, ANESAN !!
...ABOUT CHAMO-SAN ....
WE SHOULD BE SAFE NOW, DON'T YOU THINK? ♡
YOU SUR-R-RE WE CAN'T GO WATCH NEGI-KUN'S MATCH...?
I'M SORRY— DID YOU...?
GL-GLEEM
...
...ABOUT THE OJŌSAMA, AND HER FRIENDS ....
WHAT A LOT OF SURPRISES WE'VE HAD TODAY ~
HO-HO-HO ♡
...AS WELL AS...
FLICK

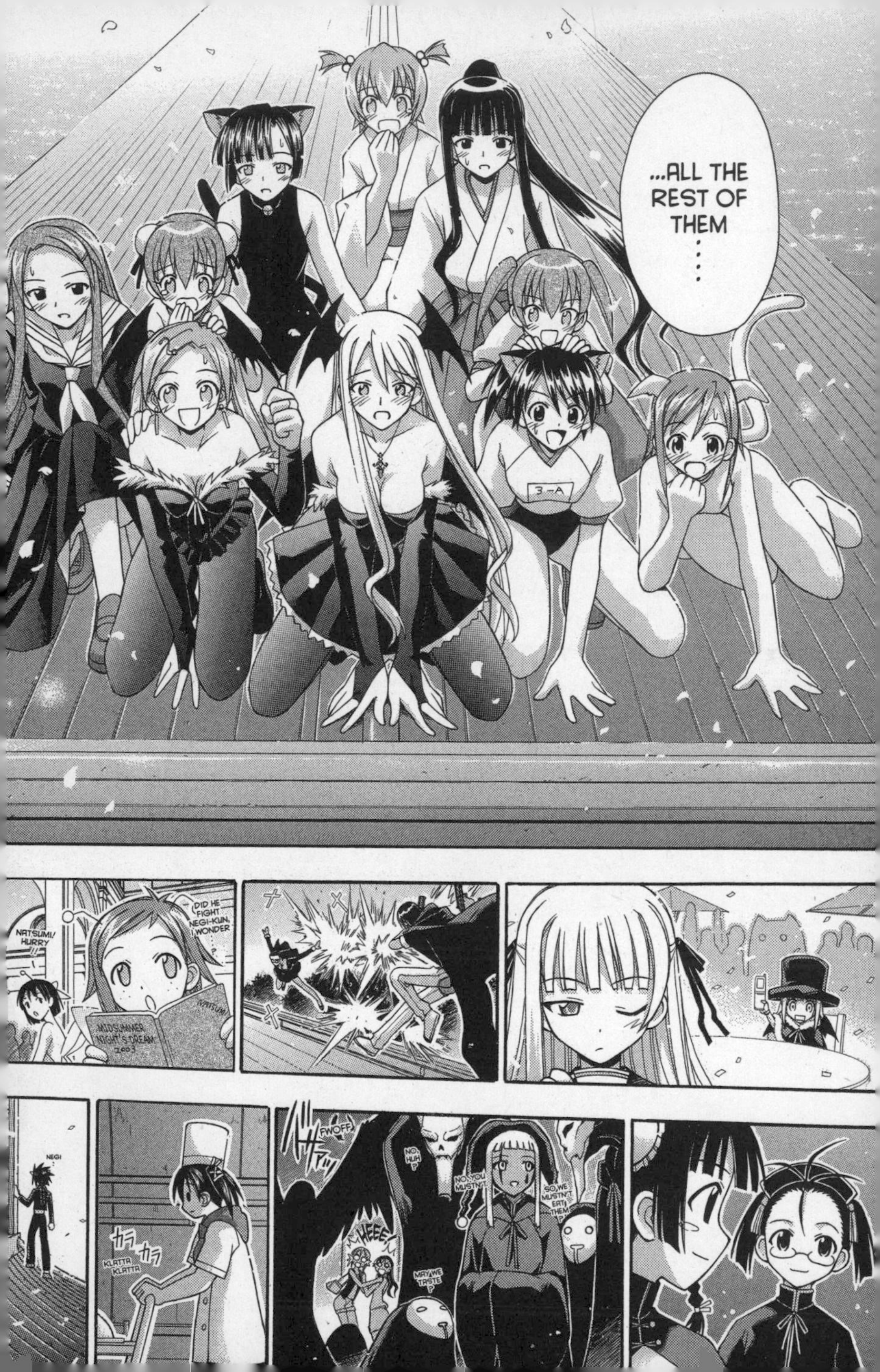

...ALL THE REST OF THEM ....
3-A
DID HE FIGHT NEGI-KUN, I WONDER...?
NATSUMI! HURRY!!
MIDSUMMER NIGHT'S DREAM 2003
NATSUMI
SO, WE MUSTN'T EAT THEM?
NO, YOU MUSTN'T.
NO, HUH?
MAY WE TASTE?
HEEE!
FWOFF
カラ カラ
KLATTA KLATTA
NEGI...

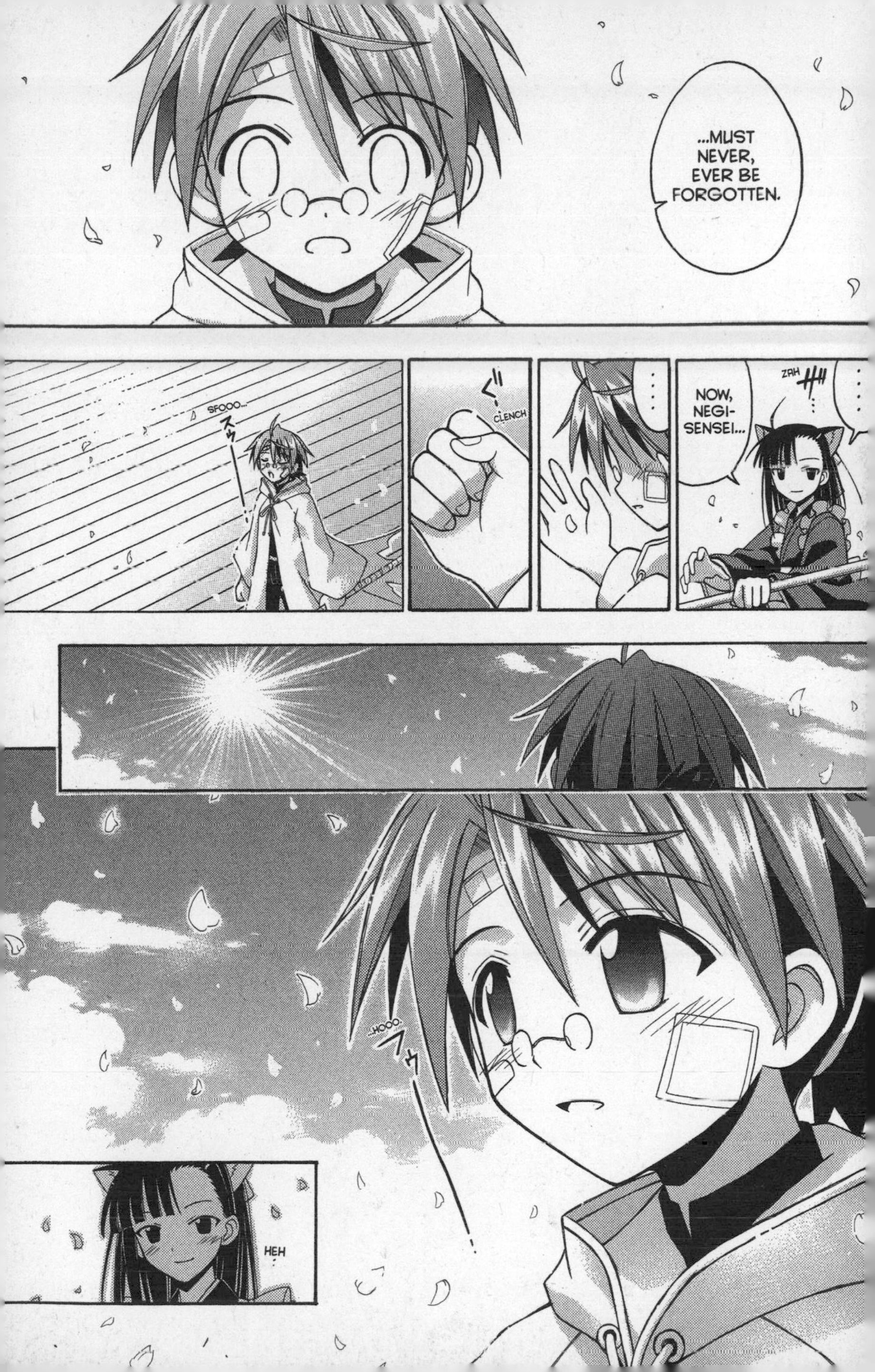
...MUST NEVER, EVER BE FORGOTTEN.
ZAH
...
NOW, NEGI-SENSEI...
...
CLENCH
SFOOO...
...HOOO
HEH

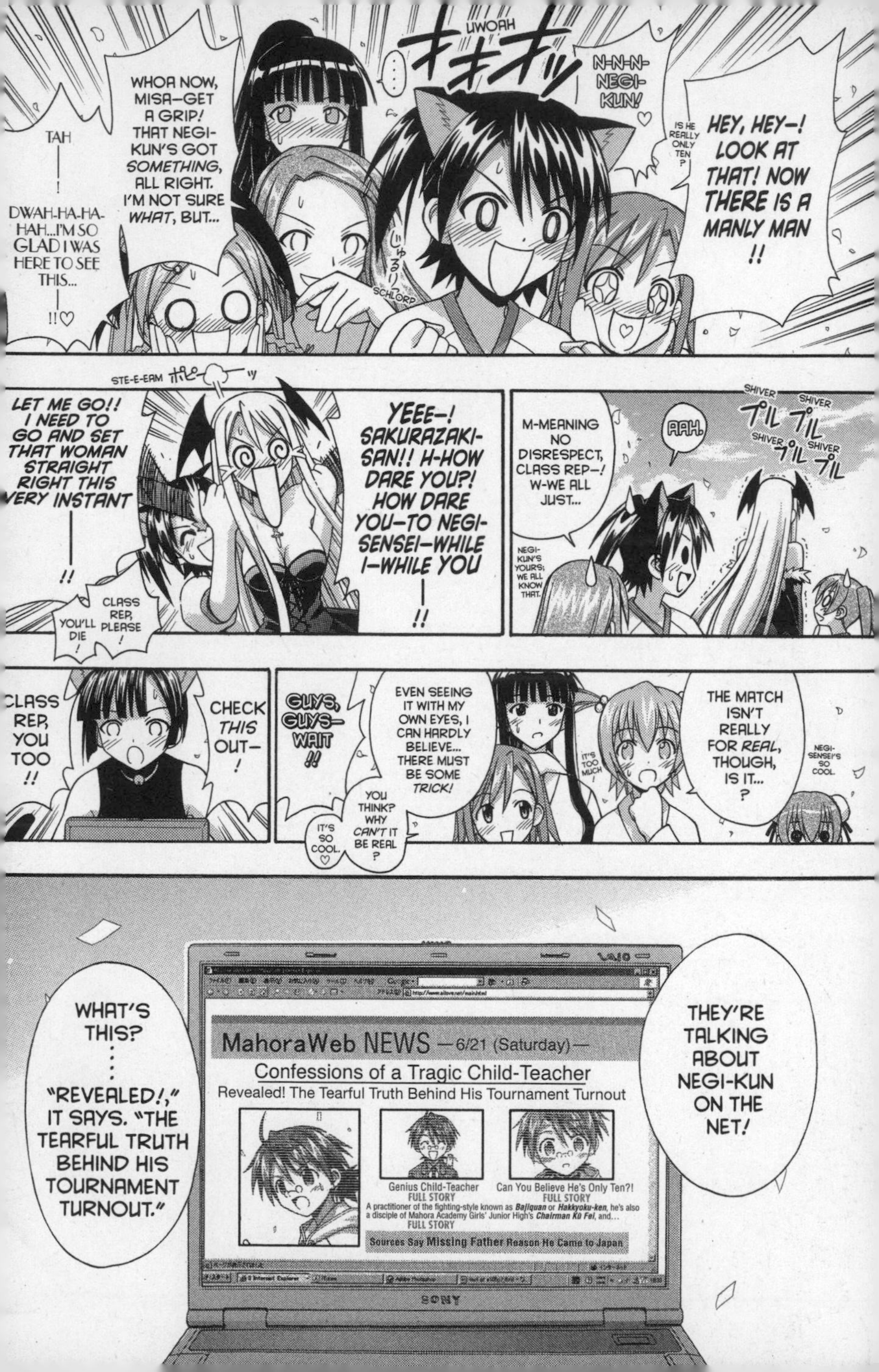
HEY, HEY—! LOOK AT THAT! NOW THERE IS A MANLY MAN !!
IS HE REALLY ONLY TEN?
N-N-N-NEGI-KUN! ♡
UWOAH
...
WHOA NOW, MISA—GET A GRIP! THAT NEGI-KUN'S GOT SOMETHING, ALL RIGHT. I'M NOT SURE WHAT, BUT...
TAH—! DWAH-HA-HA-HAH...I'M SO GLAD I WAS HERE TO SEE THIS—!!♡
SCHLORP
SHIVER SHIVER SHIVER SHIVER
AAH.
M-MEANING NO DISRESPECT, CLASS REP—! W-WE ALL JUST...
NEGI-KUN'S YOURS; WE ALL KNOW THAT.
STE-E-EAM
YEEE—! SAKURAZAKI-SAN!! H-HOW DARE YOU?! HOW DARE YOU—TO NEGI-SENSEI—WHILE I—WHILE YOU—!!
LET ME GO!! I NEED TO GO AND SET THAT WOMAN STRAIGHT RIGHT THIS VERY INSTANT—!!
CLASS REP, PLEASE!
YOU'LL DIE!
NEGI-SENSEI'S SO COOL.
THE MATCH ISN'T REALLY FOR REAL, THOUGH, IS IT...?
IT'S TOO MUCH
EVEN SEEING IT WITH MY OWN EYES, I CAN HARDLY BELIEVE... THERE MUST BE SOME TRICK!
GUYS, GUYS—WAIT!!
YOU THINK? WHY CAN'T IT BE REAL?
IT'S SO COOL. ♡
CHECK THIS OUT—!
CLASS REP, YOU TOO!!
THEY'RE TALKING ABOUT NEGI-KUN ON THE NET!
WHAT'S THIS? ... "REVEALED!," IT SAYS. "THE TEARFUL TRUTH BEHIND HIS TOURNAMENT TURNOUT."
MahoraWeb NEWS —6/21 (Saturday)—
Confessions of a Tragic Child-Teacher
Revealed! The Tearful Truth Behind His Tournament Turnout
Genius Child-Teacher
FULL STORY
Can You Believe He's Only Ten?!
FULL STORY
A practitioner of the fighting-style known as Bajiquan or Hakkyoku-ken, he's also a disciple of Mahora Academy Girls' Junior High's Chairman Ku Fei, and...
FULL STORY
Sources Say Missing Father Reason He Came to Japan
SONY

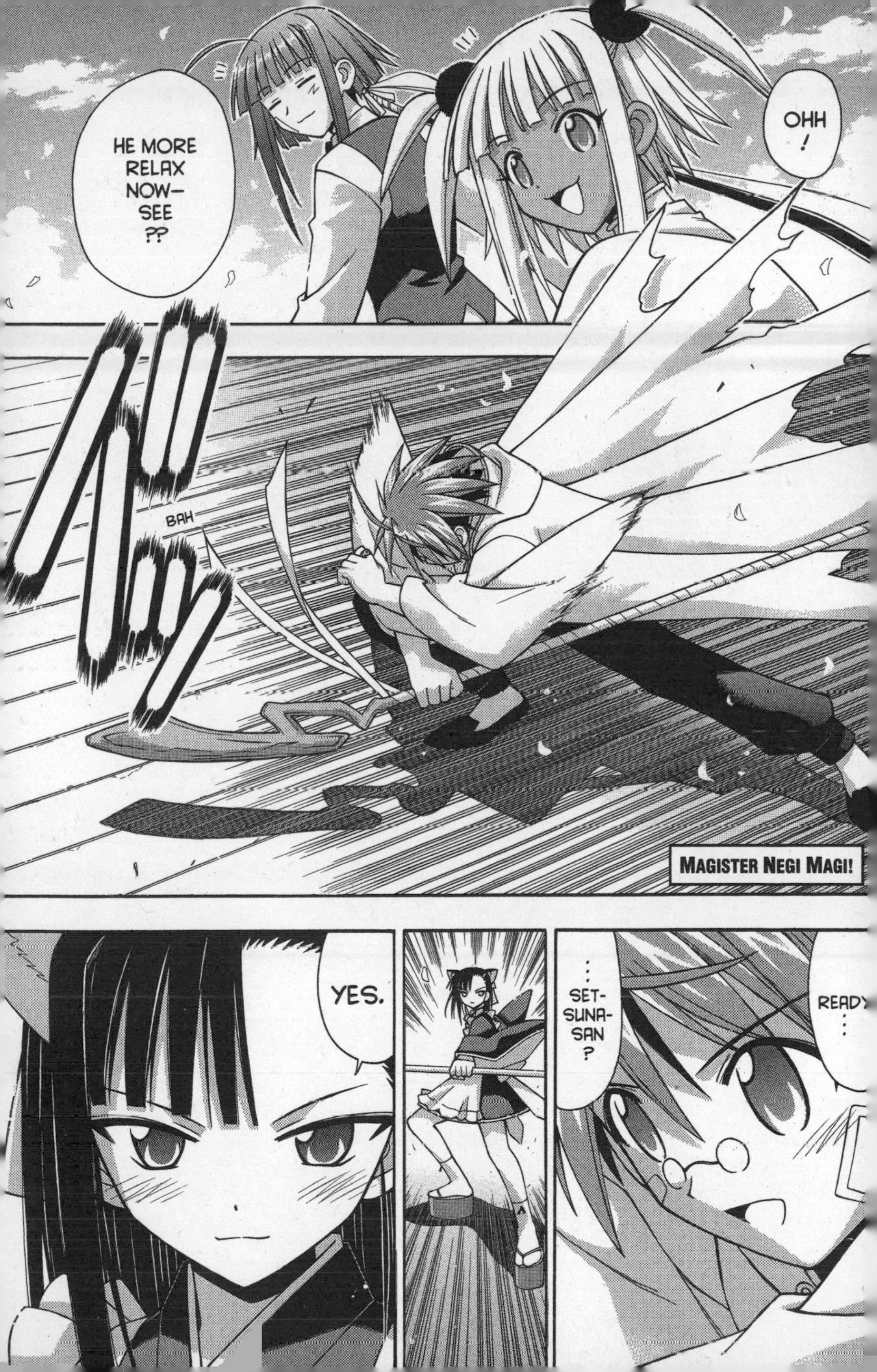
OHH!
HE MORE RELAX NOW—SEE ??
BAH
MAGISTER NEGI MAGI!
READY...
...SET-SUNA-SAN?
YES.

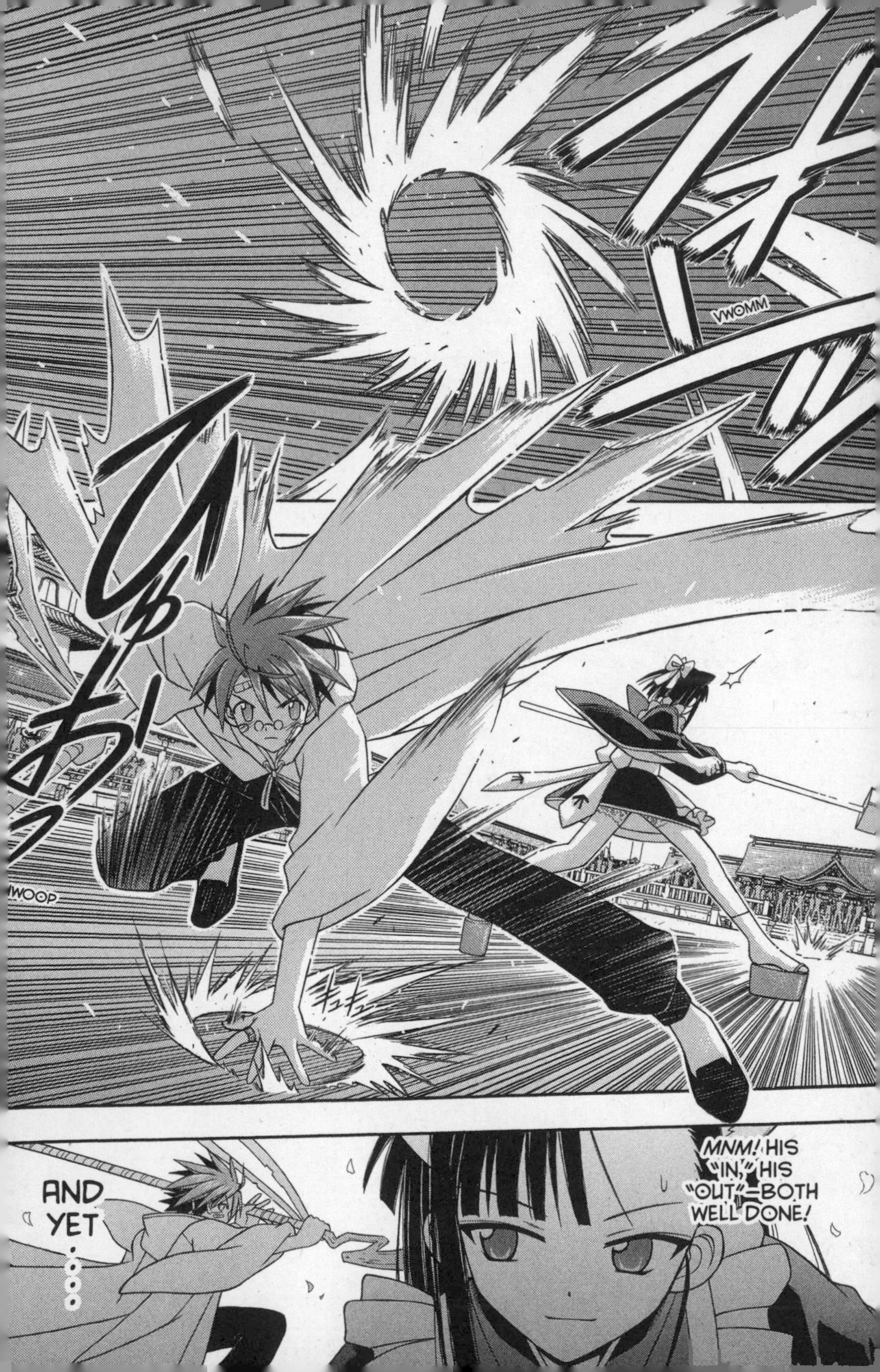
VWOMM
WOOP
MNM! HIS "IN," HIS "OUT"—BOTH WELL DONE!
AND YET......

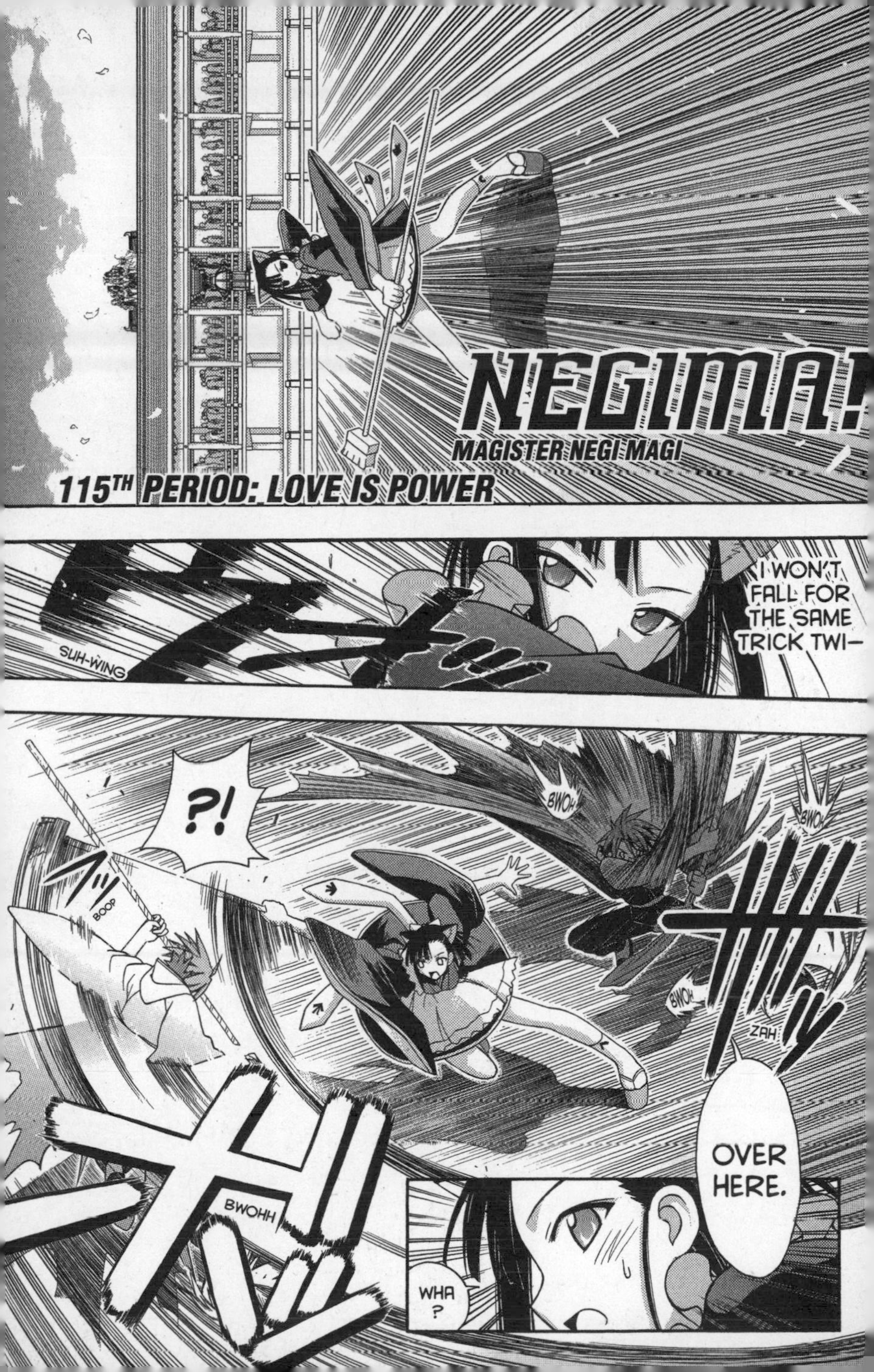
NEGIMA!
MAGISTER NEGI MAGI
115TH PERIOD: LOVE IS POWER
I WON'T FALL FOR THE SAME TRICK TWI—
SUH-WING
BWOH
BWOH
?!
BOOP
BWOH
ZAH
OVER HERE.
BWOHH
WHA ?

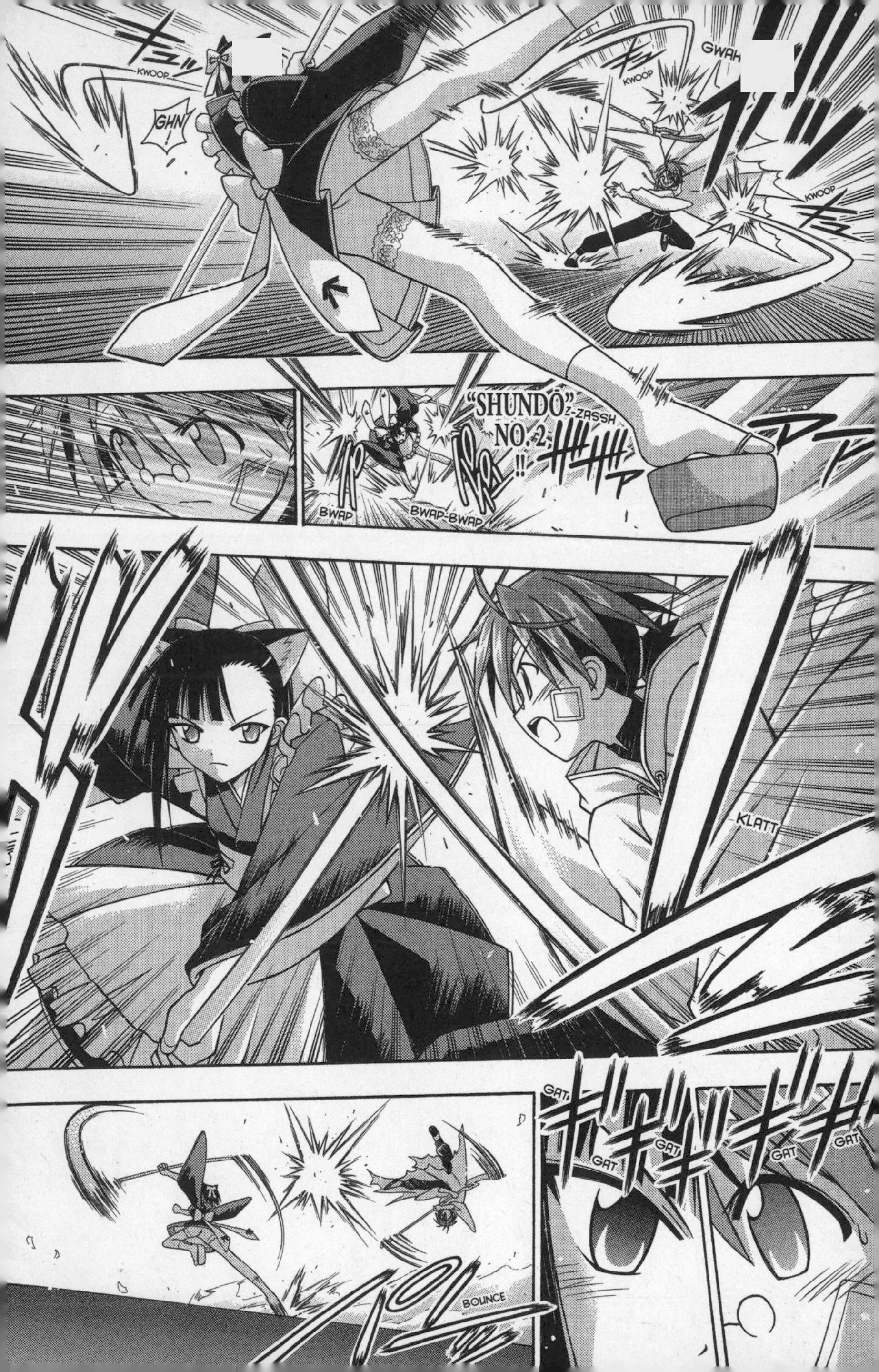
GWAH
KWOOP
KWOOP
KWOOP
GHN!
"SHUNDŌ" NO. 2!!
Z-ZASSH
BWAP-BWAP
BWAP
KLATT
GAT
GAT
GAT
GAT
GAT
BOUNCE

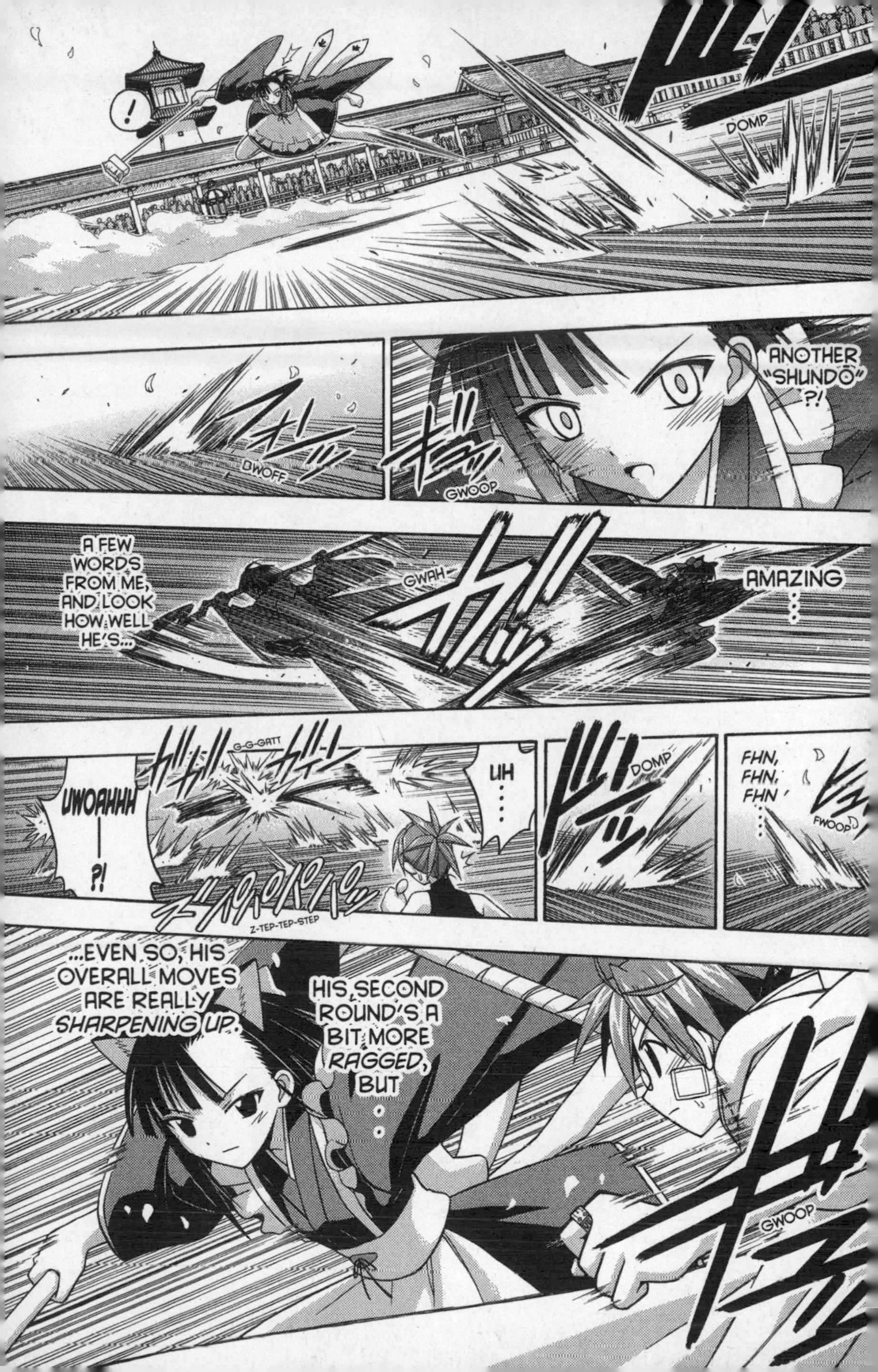

!
DOMP
ANOTHER "SHUNDŌ" ?!
GWOOP
DWOFF
AMAZING ...
GWAH
A FEW WORDS FROM ME, AND LOOK HOW WELL HE'S...
FHN, FHN, FHN ...
FWOOP
DOMP
UH ...
G-G-GATT
UWOAHHH —?!
Z-TEP-TEP-STEP
HIS SECOND ROUND'S A BIT MORE *RAGGED*, BUT
...EVEN SO, HIS OVERALL MOVES ARE REALLY *SHARPENING UP*.
GWOOP

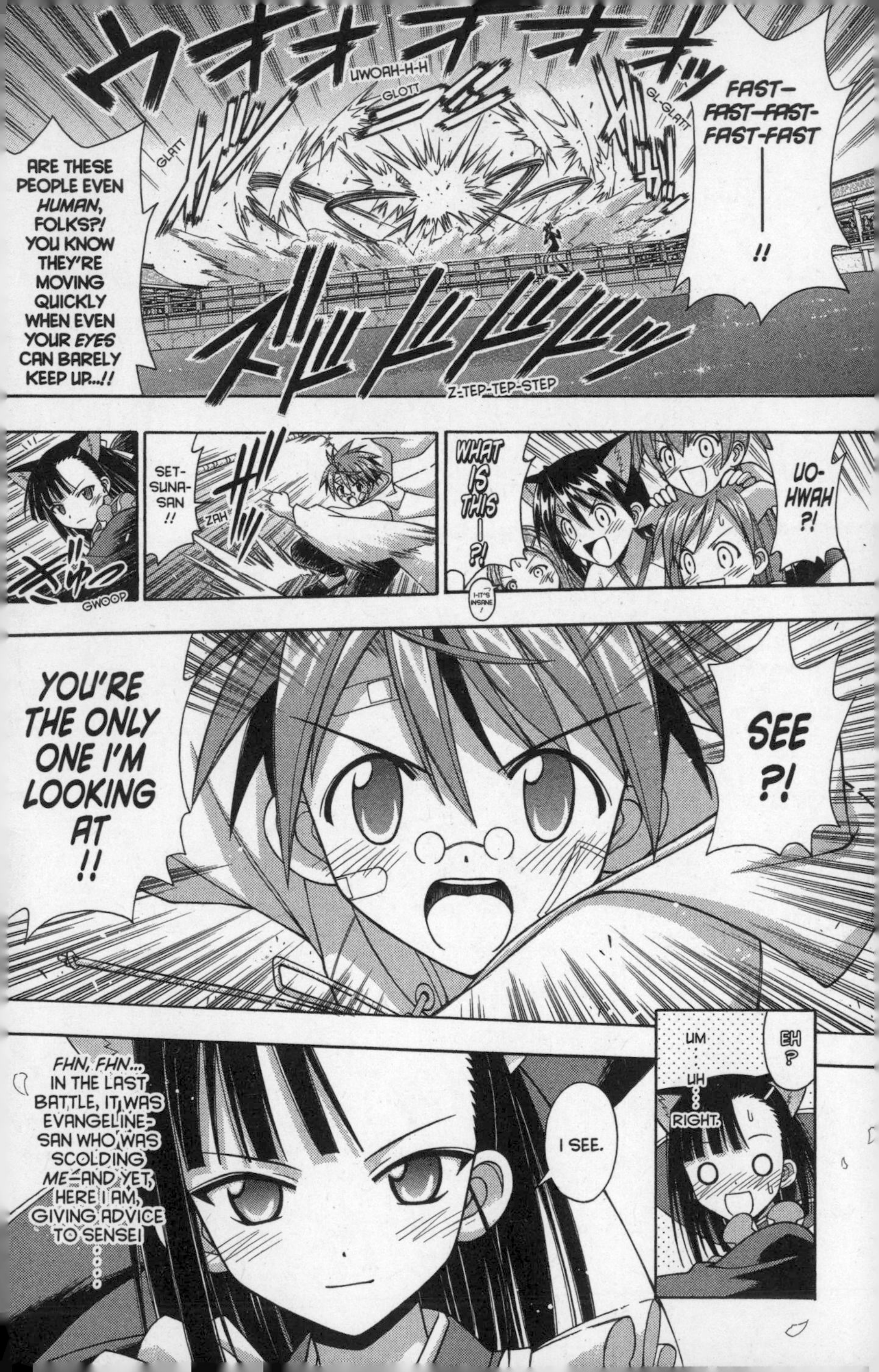
FAST-FAST-FAST-FAST-FAST —— !!
GL-GLATT
GLOTT
UWOAH-H-H
GLATT
ARE THESE PEOPLE EVEN HUMAN, FOLKS?! YOU KNOW THEY'RE MOVING QUICKLY WHEN EVEN YOUR EYES CAN BARELY KEEP UP...!!
Z-TEP-TEP-STEP
UO-HWAH ?!
WHAT IS THIS —?!
IT'S INSANE!
SET-SUNA-SAN !!
ZAH
GWOOP
SEE ?!
YOU'RE THE ONLY ONE I'M LOOKING AT !!
EH ?
UM... UH... RIGHT.
I SEE.
FHN, FHN... IN THE LAST BATTLE, IT WAS EVANGELINE-SAN WHO WAS SCOLDING ME—AND YET, HERE I AM, GIVING ADVICE TO SENSEI.....

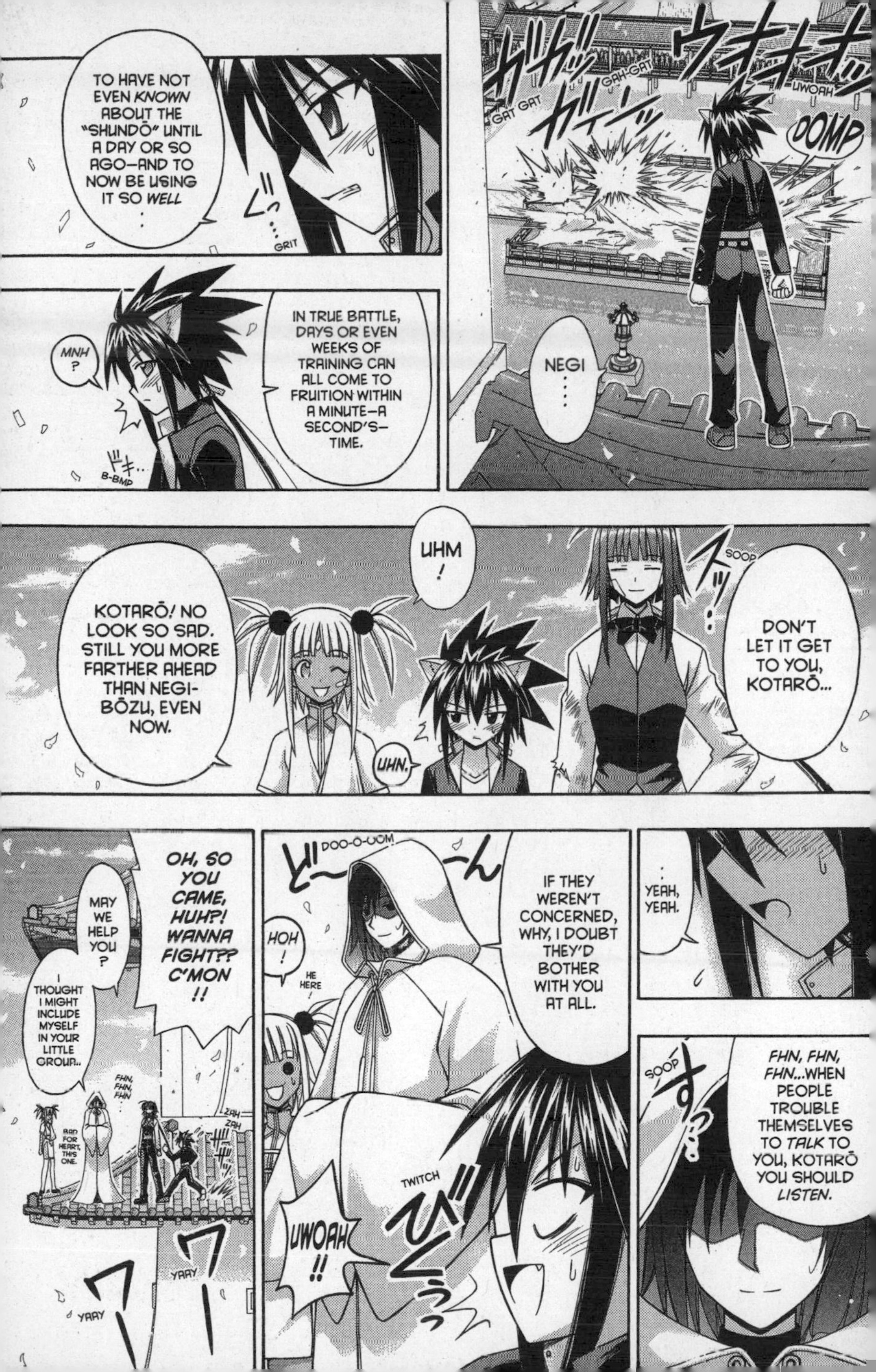
ガガッ
GAT GAT
ガィーッ
GAH-GAT
ウオォオッ
UWOAH
DOMP
NEGI....
TO HAVE NOT EVEN KNOWN ABOUT THE "SHUNDŌ" UNTIL A DAY OR SO AGO—AND TO NOW BE USING IT SO WELL
GRIT
IN TRUE BATTLE, DAYS OR EVEN WEEKS OF TRAINING CAN ALL COME TO FRUITION WITHIN A MINUTE—A SECOND'S—TIME.
MNH?
B-BMP
SOOP
DON'T LET IT GET TO YOU, KOTARŌ...
UHM!
KOTARŌ! NO LOOK SO SAD. STILL YOU MORE FARTHER AHEAD THAN NEGI-BŌZU, EVEN NOW.
UHN.
YEAH, YEAH.
SOOP
FHN, FHN, FHN...WHEN PEOPLE TROUBLE THEMSELVES TO TALK TO YOU, KOTARŌ YOU SHOULD LISTEN.
IF THEY WEREN'T CONCERNED, WHY, I DOUBT THEY'D BOTHER WITH YOU AT ALL.
TWITCH
UWOAH!!
DOO-O-OOM
HOH!
HE HERE!
OH, SO YOU CAME, HUH?! WANNA FIGHT?? C'MON!!
MAY WE HELP YOU?
I THOUGHT I MIGHT INCLUDE MYSELF IN YOUR LITTLE GROUP..
FHN, FHN, FHN
ZAH ZAH
BAD FOR HEART, THIS ONE.
YRAY
YRAY

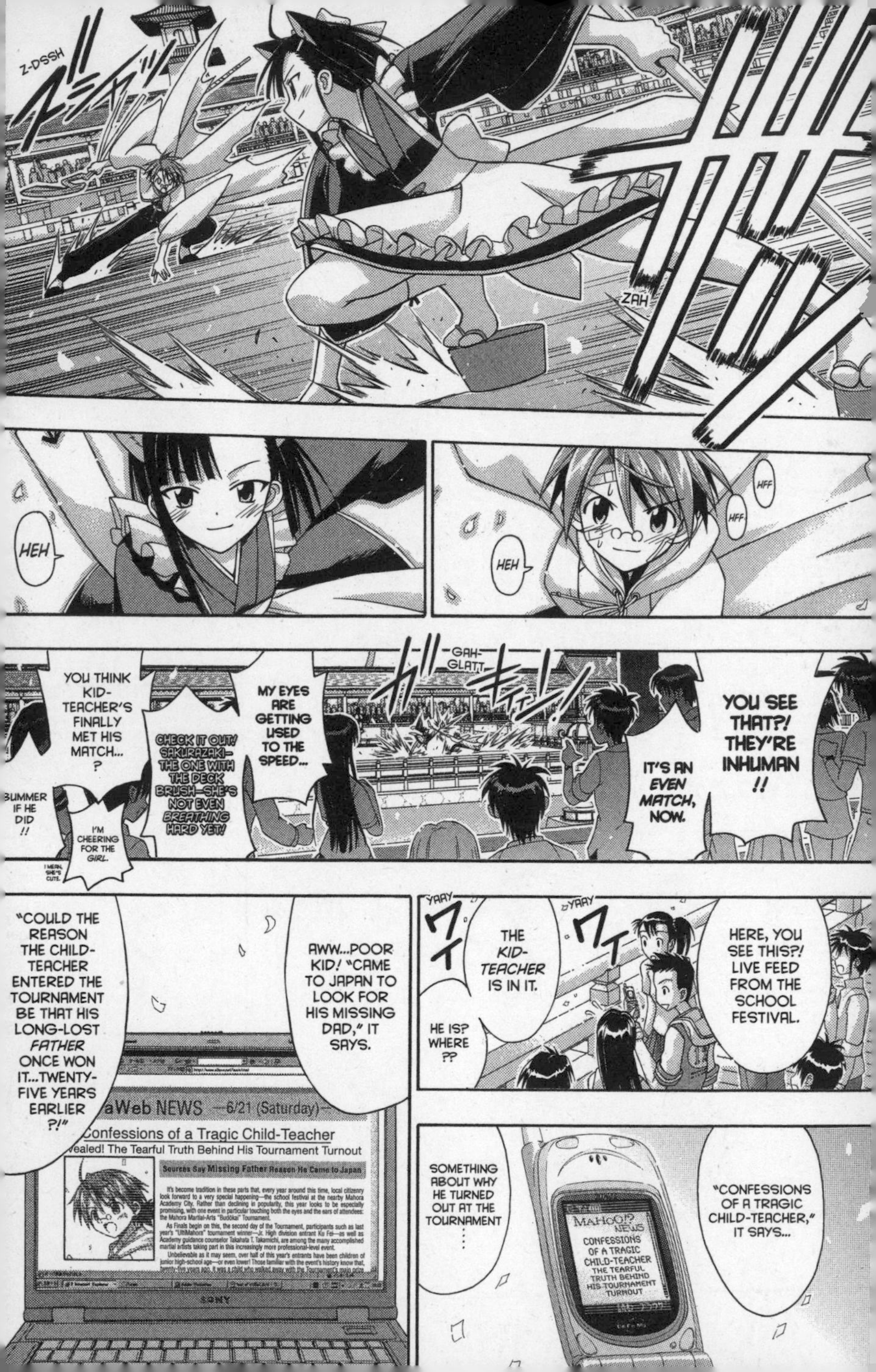
ZAH
Z-DSSH
HFF
HFF
HEH
HEH
YOU SEE THAT?! THEY'RE INHUMAN!!
IT'S AN EVEN MATCH, NOW.
GAH-GLATT
MY EYES ARE GETTING USED TO THE SPEED...
CHECK IT OUT! SAKURAZAKI—THE ONE WITH THE DECK BRUSH—SHE'S NOT EVEN BREATHING HARD YET!
YOU THINK KID-TEACHER'S FINALLY MET HIS MATCH...?
BUMMER IF HE DID!!
I'M CHEERING FOR THE GIRL.
I MEAN, SHE'S CUTE.
HERE, YOU SEE THIS?! LIVE FEED FROM THE SCHOOL FESTIVAL.
YAAY
THE KID-TEACHER IS IN IT.
YAAY
HE IS? WHERE??
"CONFESSIONS OF A TRAGIC CHILD-TEACHER," IT SAYS...
MAHOO!? NEWS
CONFESSIONS OF A TRAGIC CHILD-TEACHER THE TEARFUL TRUTH BEHIND HIS TOURNAMENT TURNOUT
SOMETHING ABOUT WHY HE TURNED OUT AT THE TOURNAMENT...
AWW...POOR KID! "CAME TO JAPAN TO LOOK FOR HIS MISSING DAD," IT SAYS.
"COULD THE REASON THE CHILD-TEACHER ENTERED THE TOURNAMENT BE THAT HIS LONG-LOST FATHER ONCE WON IT...TWENTY-FIVE YEARS EARLIER?!"
aWeb NEWS —6/21 (Saturday)—
Confessions of a Tragic Child-Teacher
vealed! The Tearful Truth Behind His Tournament Turnout
Sources Say Missing Father Reason He Came to Japan
It's become tradition in these parts that, every year around this time, local citizenry look forward to a very special happening—the school festival at the nearby Mahora Academy City. Rather than declining in popularity, this year looks to be especially promising, with one event in particular touching both the eyes and the ears of attendees: the Mahora Martial-Arts "Budōkai" Tournament.
As Finals begin on this, the second day of the Tournament, participants such as last year's "UltiMahora" tournament winner—Jr. High division entrant Ku Fei—as well as Academy guidance counselor Takahata T. Takamichi, are among the many accomplished martial artists taking part in this increasingly more professional-level event.
Unbelievable as it may seem, over half of this year's entrants have been children of junior high-school age—or even lower! Those familiar with the event's history know that,
SONY

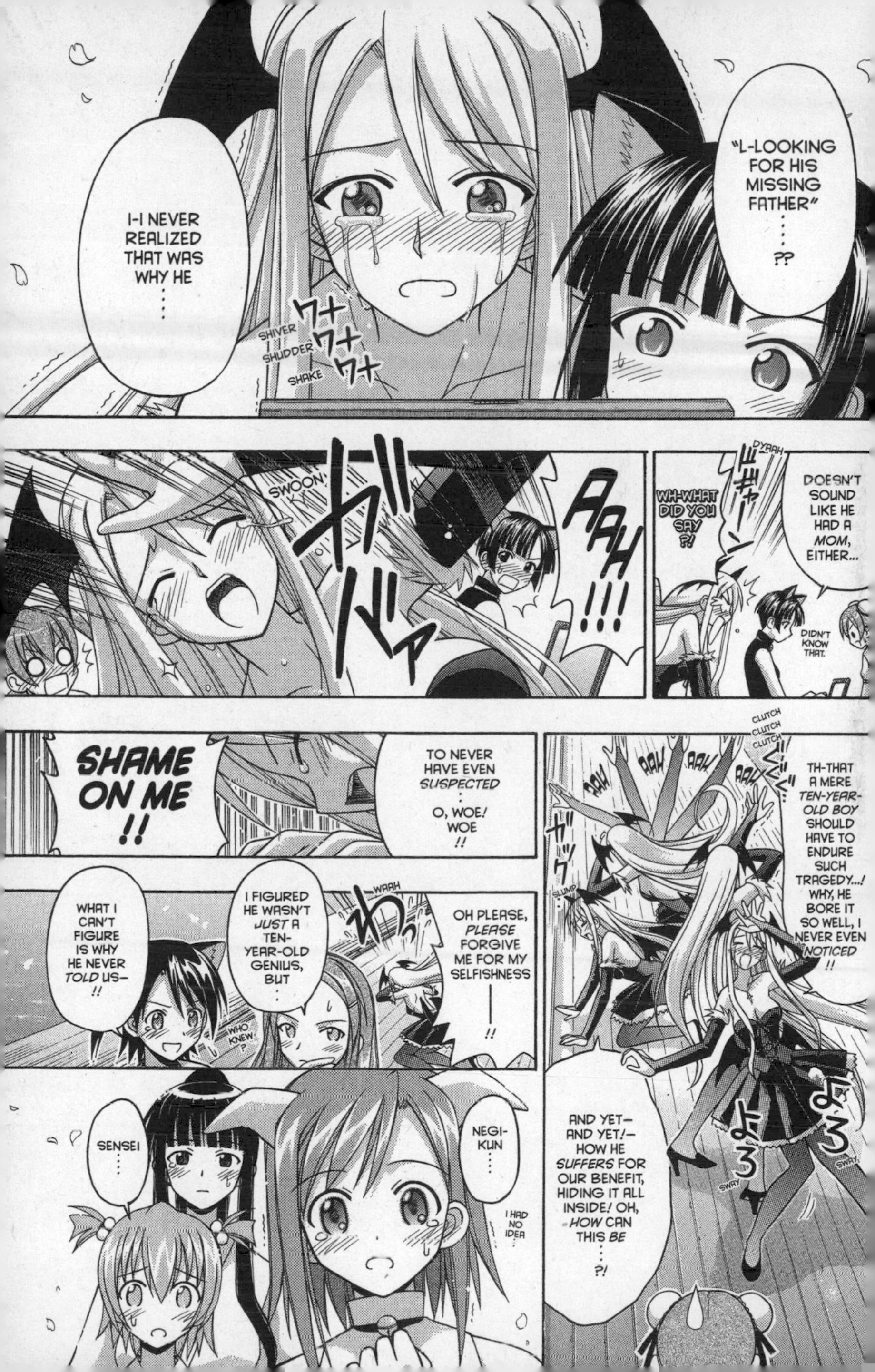
"L-LOOKING FOR HIS MISSING FATHER" ....??
I-I NEVER REALIZED THAT WAS WHY HE ...
SHIVER
SHUDDER
SHAKE
DOESN'T SOUND LIKE HE HAD A MOM, EITHER...
DYAAH
WH-WHAT DID YOU SAY?!
DIDN'T KNOW THAT.
AAH!!!
SWOON
CLUTCH CLUTCH CLUTCH
TH-THAT A MERE TEN-YEAR-OLD BOY SHOULD HAVE TO ENDURE SUCH TRAGEDY...! WHY, HE BORE IT SO WELL, I NEVER EVEN NOTICED!!
AAH AAH AAH AAH
SLUMP
AND YET— AND YET!— HOW HE SUFFERS FOR OUR BENEFIT, HIDING IT ALL INSIDE! OH, HOW CAN THIS BE...?!
SWAY
SWAY
TO NEVER HAVE EVEN SUSPECTED: O, WOE! WOE!!
SHAME ON ME!!
OH PLEASE, PLEASE FORGIVE ME FOR MY SELFISHNESS——!!
WAAH
I FIGURED HE WASN'T JUST A TEN-YEAR-OLD GENIUS, BUT...
WHO KNEW?
WHAT I CAN'T FIGURE IS WHY HE NEVER TOLD US—!!
NEGI-KUN...
I HAD NO IDEA
SENSEI...

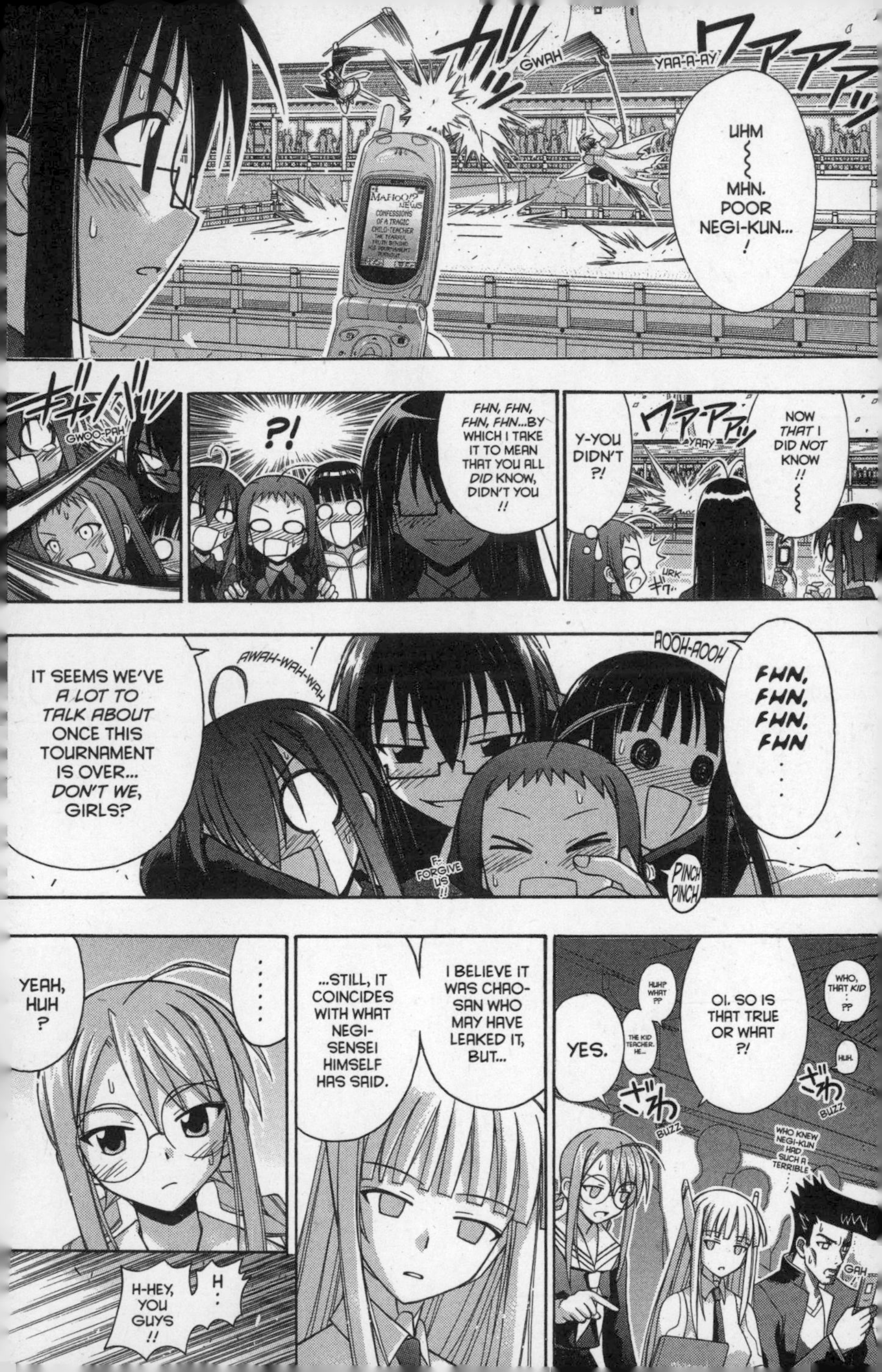
YAA-A-AY
UHM ~ MHN. POOR NEGI-KUN...!
GWAH
MAHOO!? NEWS
CONFESSIONS OF A TRAGIC CHILD-TEACHER
NOW THAT I DID NOT KNOW!! ~
YRAY
Y-YOU DIDN'T ?!
URK
FHN, FHN, FHN, FHN...BY WHICH I TAKE IT TO MEAN THAT YOU ALL DID KNOW, DIDN'T YOU !!
?!
GWOO-PAH
AOOH-AOOH
FHN, FHN, FHN, FHN ...
PINCH PINCH
F-FORGIVE US!!
AWAH-WAH-WAH
IT SEEMS WE'VE A LOT TO TALK ABOUT ONCE THIS TOURNAMENT IS OVER... DON'T WE, GIRLS?
WHO, THAT KID :?
OI. SO IS THAT TRUE OR WHAT ?!
HUHP WHAT ??
THE KID TEACHER. HE...
HUH.
BUZZ
YES.
BUZZ
WHO KNEW NEGI-KUN HAD SUCH A TERRIBLE...
GAH
I BELIEVE IT WAS CHAO-SAN WHO MAY HAVE LEAKED IT, BUT...
...STILL, IT COINCIDES WITH WHAT NEGI-SENSEI HIMSELF HAS SAID.
......
YEAH, HUH ?
H...
H-HEY, YOU GUYS !!

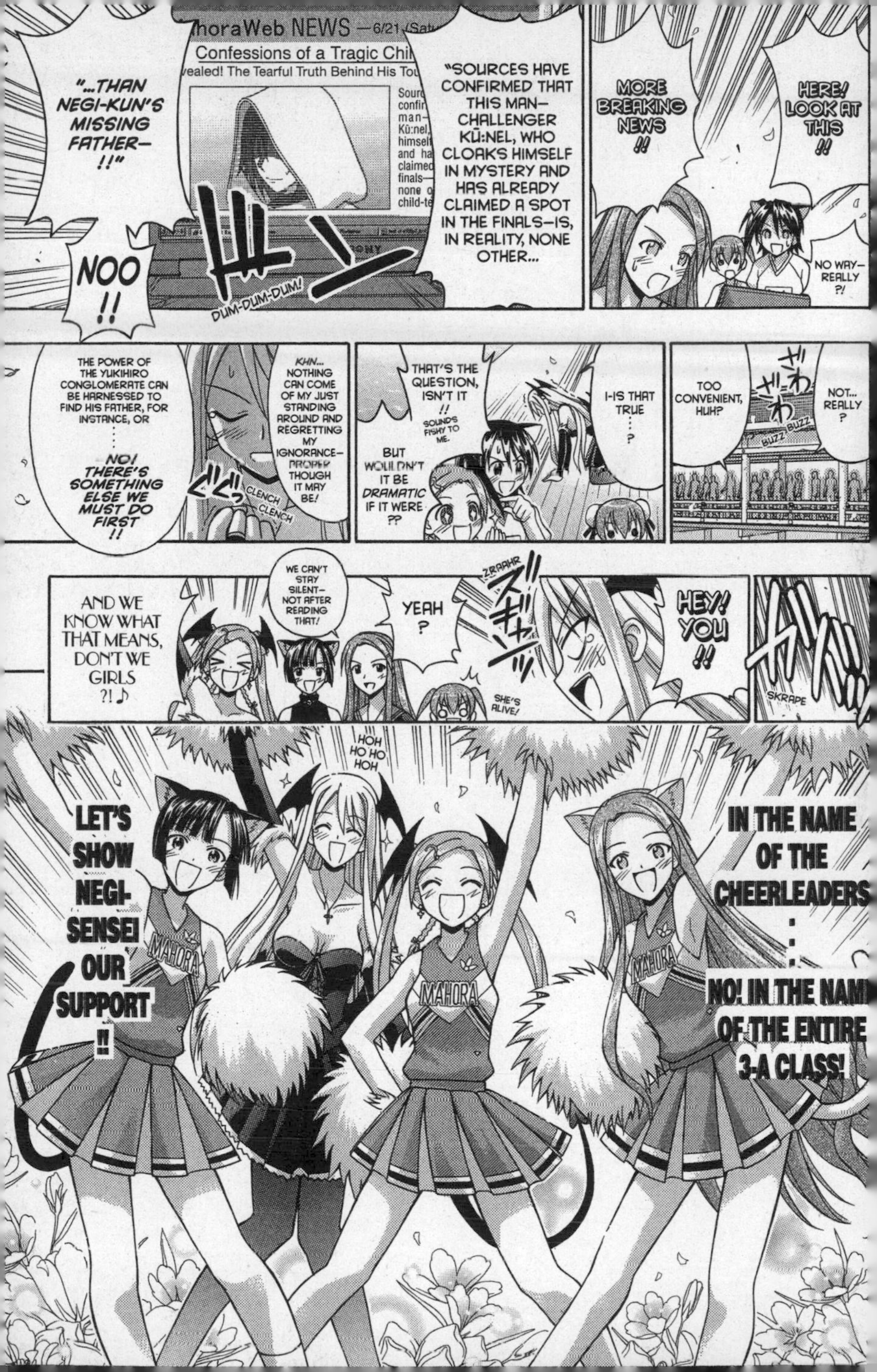
HERE! LOOK AT THIS!!
MORE BREAKING NEWS!!
NO WAY—REALLY?!
"SOURCES HAVE CONFIRMED THAT THIS MAN—CHALLENGER KŪ:NEL, WHO CLOAKS HIMSELF IN MYSTERY AND HAS ALREADY CLAIMED A SPOT IN THE FINALS—IS, IN REALITY, NONE OTHER...
horaWeb NEWS —6/21 (Sat
Confessions of a Tragic Chil
vealed! The Tearful Truth Behind His Tou
"...THAN NEGI-KUN'S MISSING FATHER—!!"
NOO!!
DUM-DUM-DUM!
NOT... REALLY?
TOO CONVENIENT, HUH?
ざわ ざわ
BUZZ BUZZ
I-IS THAT TRUE...?
THAT'S THE QUESTION, ISN'T IT!!
SOUNDS FISHY TO ME.
BUT WOULDN'T IT BE DRAMATIC IF IT WERE??
KHN... NOTHING CAN COME OF MY JUST STANDING AROUND AND REGRETTING MY IGNORANCE—PROPER THOUGH IT MAY BE!
THE POWER OF THE YUKIHIRO CONGLOMERATE CAN BE HARNESSED TO FIND HIS FATHER, FOR INSTANCE, OR
......
NO! THERE'S SOMETHING ELSE WE MUST DO FIRST!!
CLENCH CLENCH
SKRAPE
HEY! YOU!!
ZRAAHR
SHE'S ALIVE!
YEAH?
WE CAN'T STAY SILENT—NOT AFTER READING THAT!
AND WE KNOW WHAT THAT MEANS, DON'T WE GIRLS?! ♪
IN THE NAME OF THE CHEERLEADERS...
NO! IN THE NAME OF THE ENTIRE 3-A CLASS!
HOH HO HO HOH
LET'S SHOW NEGI-SENSEI OUR SUPPORT!!

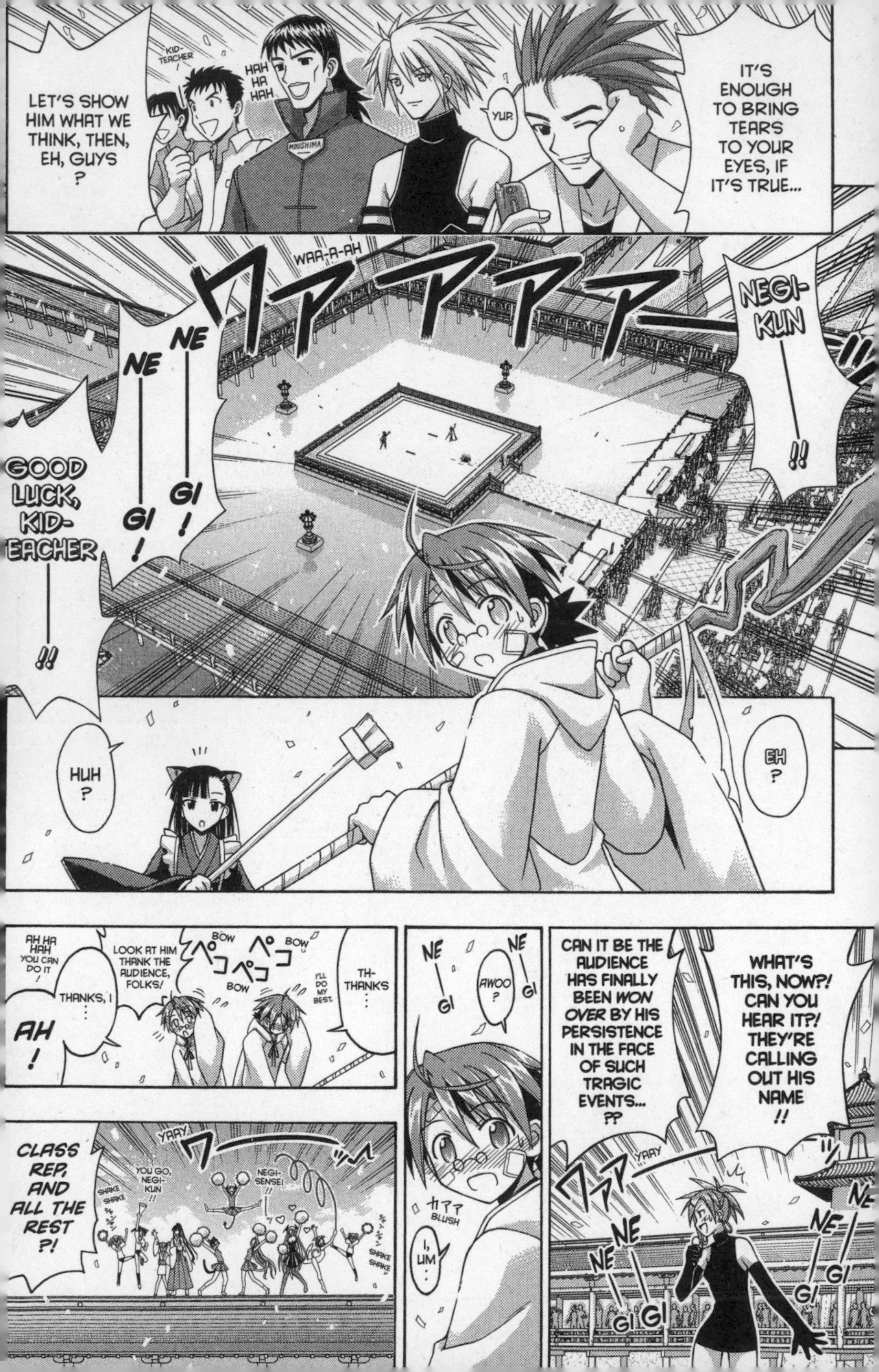
IT'S ENOUGH TO BRING TEARS TO YOUR EYES, IF IT'S TRUE...
YUP.
HAH HA HAH
KID-TEACHER!
LET'S SHOW HIM WHAT WE THINK, THEN, EH, GUYS?
NEGI-KUN!!
WAA-A-AH
NE-GI!
NE-GI!
GOOD LUCK, KID-TEACHER!!
EH?
HUH?
WHAT'S THIS, NOW?! CAN YOU HEAR IT?! THEY'RE CALLING OUT HIS NAME!!
YAAY
NE-GI NE-GI NE-GI NE-GI
CAN IT BE THE AUDIENCE HAS FINALLY BEEN *WON OVER* BY HIS PERSISTENCE IN THE FACE OF SUCH TRAGIC EVENTS...??
NE-GI
AWOO?
NE-GI
BLUSH
I, UM...
TH-THANKS...
I'LL DO MY BEST.
BOW BOW BOW
LOOK AT HIM THANK THE AUDIENCE, FOLKS!
AH HA HAH YOU CAN DO IT!
THANKS, I...
AH!
YAAY
NEGI-SENSEI!!
YOU GO, NEGI-KUN!!
SHAKE SHAKE
SHAKE SHAKE
CLASS REP, AND ALL THE REST?!

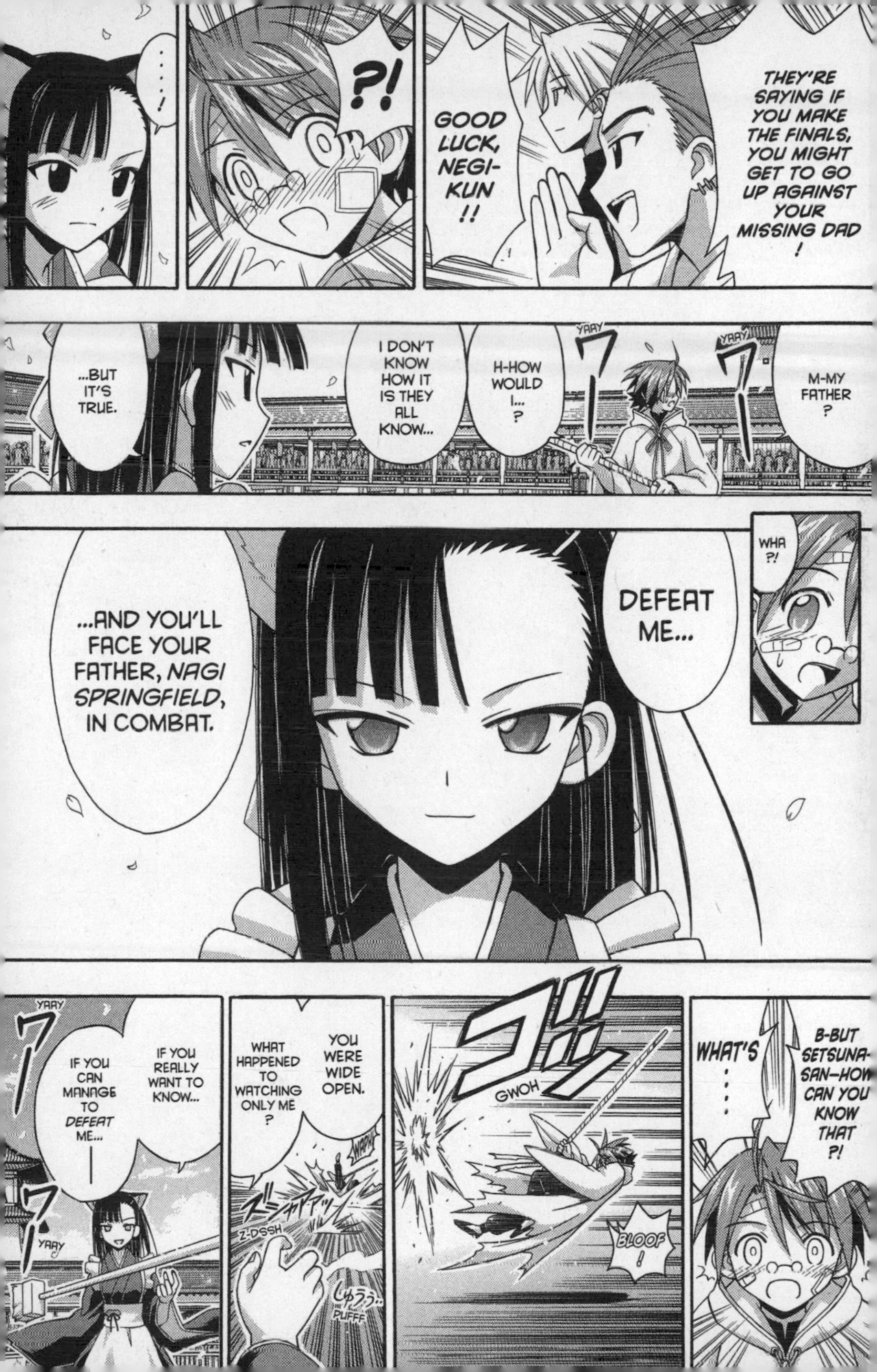
THEY'RE SAYING IF YOU MAKE THE FINALS, YOU MIGHT GET TO GO UP AGAINST YOUR MISSING DAD!
GOOD LUCK, NEGI-KUN!!
?!
...!
M-MY FATHER?
YAAY
YAAY
H-HOW WOULD I...?
I DON'T KNOW HOW IT IS THEY ALL KNOW...
...BUT IT'S TRUE.
WHA?!
DEFEAT ME...
...AND YOU'LL FACE YOUR FATHER, *NAGI SPRINGFIELD*, IN COMBAT.
B-BUT SETSUNA-SAN—HOW CAN YOU KNOW THAT?!
WHAT'S...
GWOH
BLOOF!
YOU WERE WIDE OPEN.
WHAT HAPPENED TO WATCHING ONLY ME?
WAAH!
Z-DSSH
PUFFF
IF YOU REALLY WANT TO KNOW...
IF YOU CAN MANAGE TO *DEFEAT* ME...
YAAY
YAAY

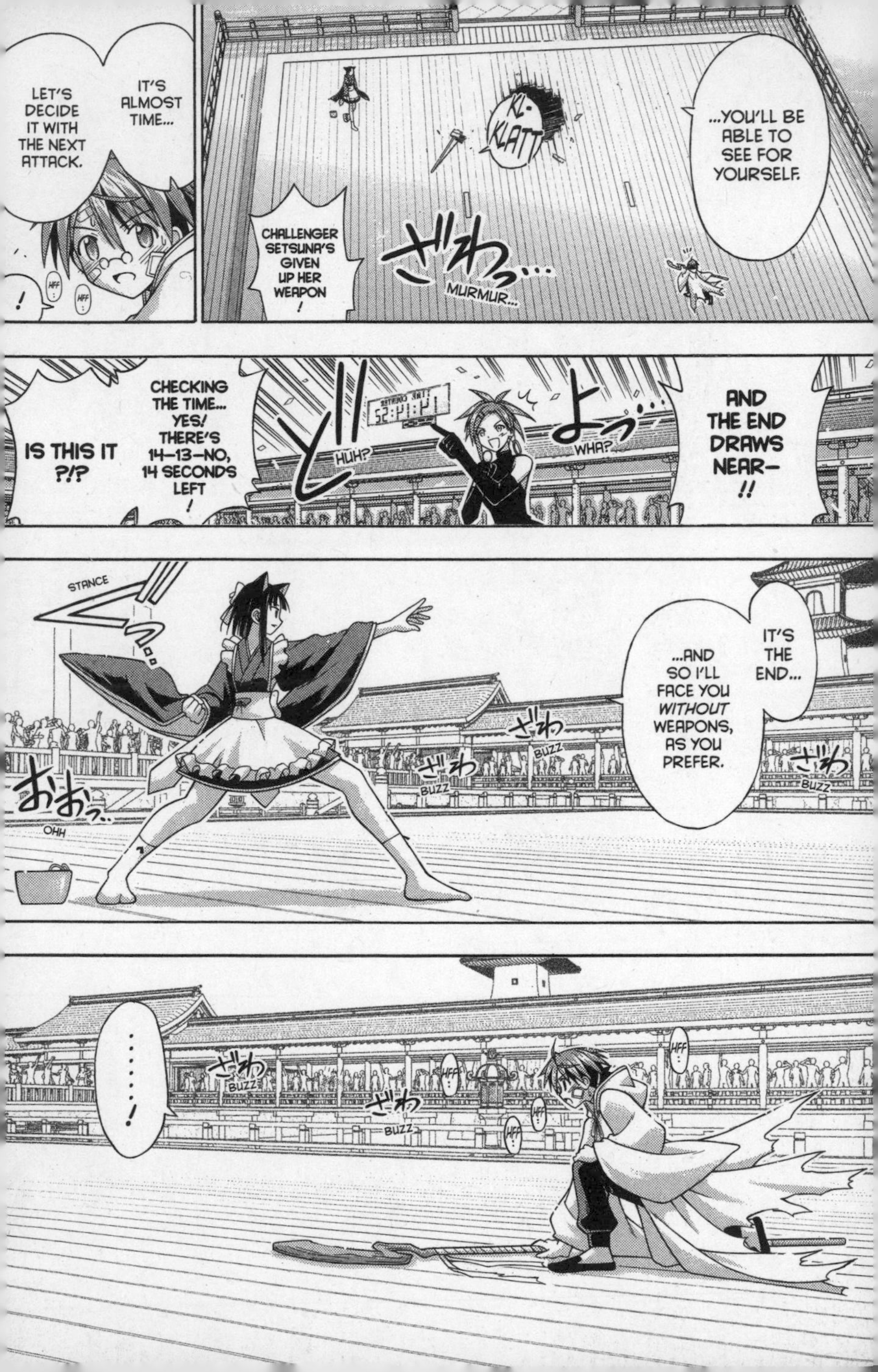
...YOU'LL BE ABLE TO SEE FOR YOURSELF.
KL-KLATT
ざわっ...
MURMUR...
CHALLENGER SETSUNA'S GIVEN UP HER WEAPON!
IT'S ALMOST TIME...
LET'S DECIDE IT WITH THE NEXT ATTACK.
HFF
HFF
!
AND THE END DRAWS NEAR—!!
WHA?
HUH?
CHECKING THE TIME... YES! THERE'S 14–13—NO, 14 SECONDS LEFT!
IS THIS IT?!?
IT'S THE END...
...AND SO I'LL FACE YOU *WITHOUT* WEAPONS, AS YOU PREFER.
ざわ
BUZZ
ざわ
BUZZ
ざわ
BUZZ
STANCE
おおっ...
OHH
HFF
HFF
HFF
HFF
ざわ
BUZZ
ざわ
BUZZ
......!

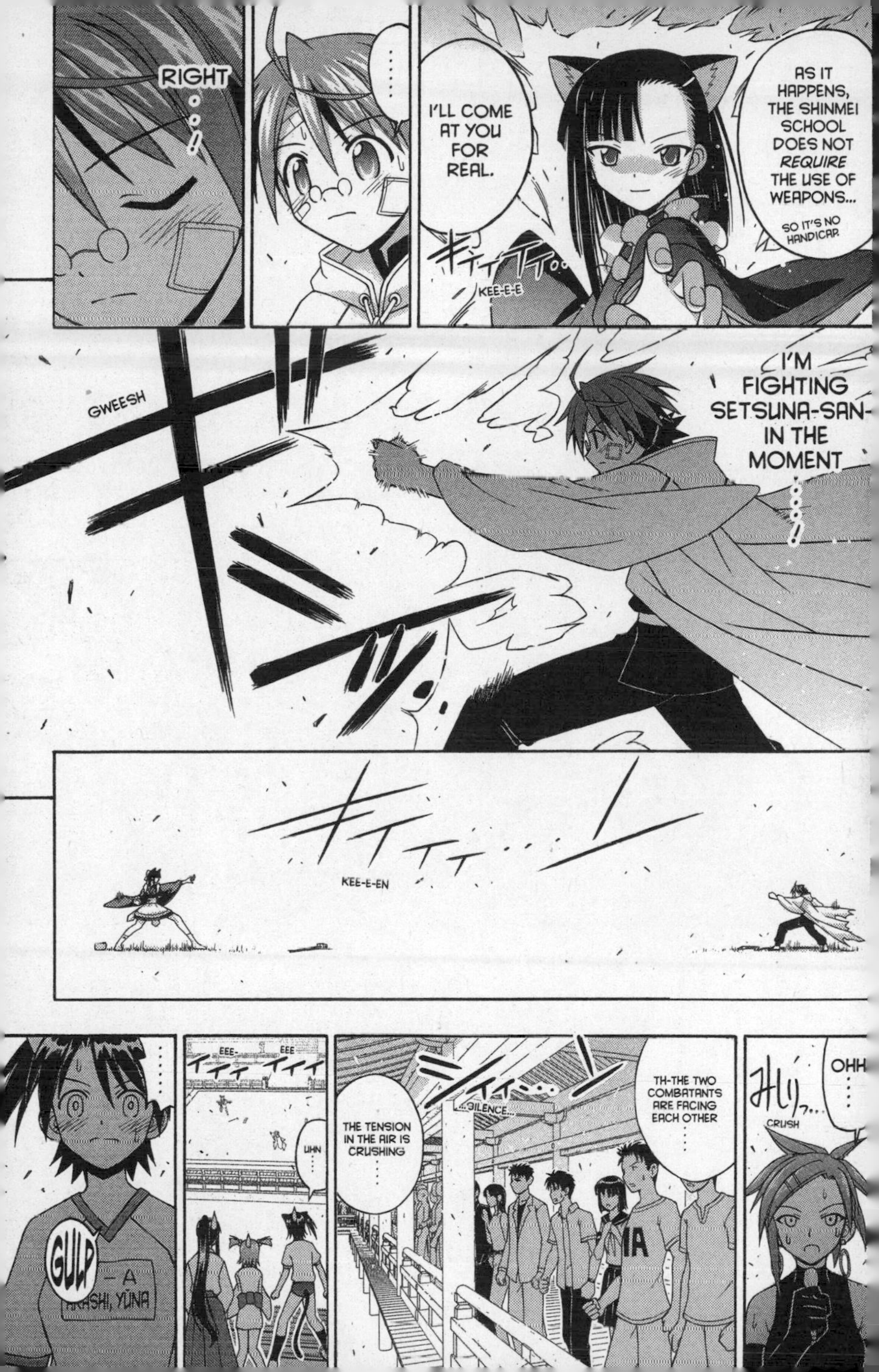
AS IT HAPPENS, THE SHINMEI SCHOOL DOES NOT *REQUIRE* THE USE OF WEAPONS...
SO IT'S NO HANDICAP.
I'LL COME AT YOU FOR REAL.
KEE-E-E
......
RIGHT...!
I'M FIGHTING SETSUNA-SAN-IN THE MOMENT...!
GWEESH
KEE-E-EN
OHH......
CRUSH
TH-THE TWO COMBATANTS ARE FACING EACH OTHER......
...SILENCE...
THE TENSION IN THE AIR IS CRUSHING......
UHN
EEE-
EEE
......
GULP
- A
AKASHI, YŪNA

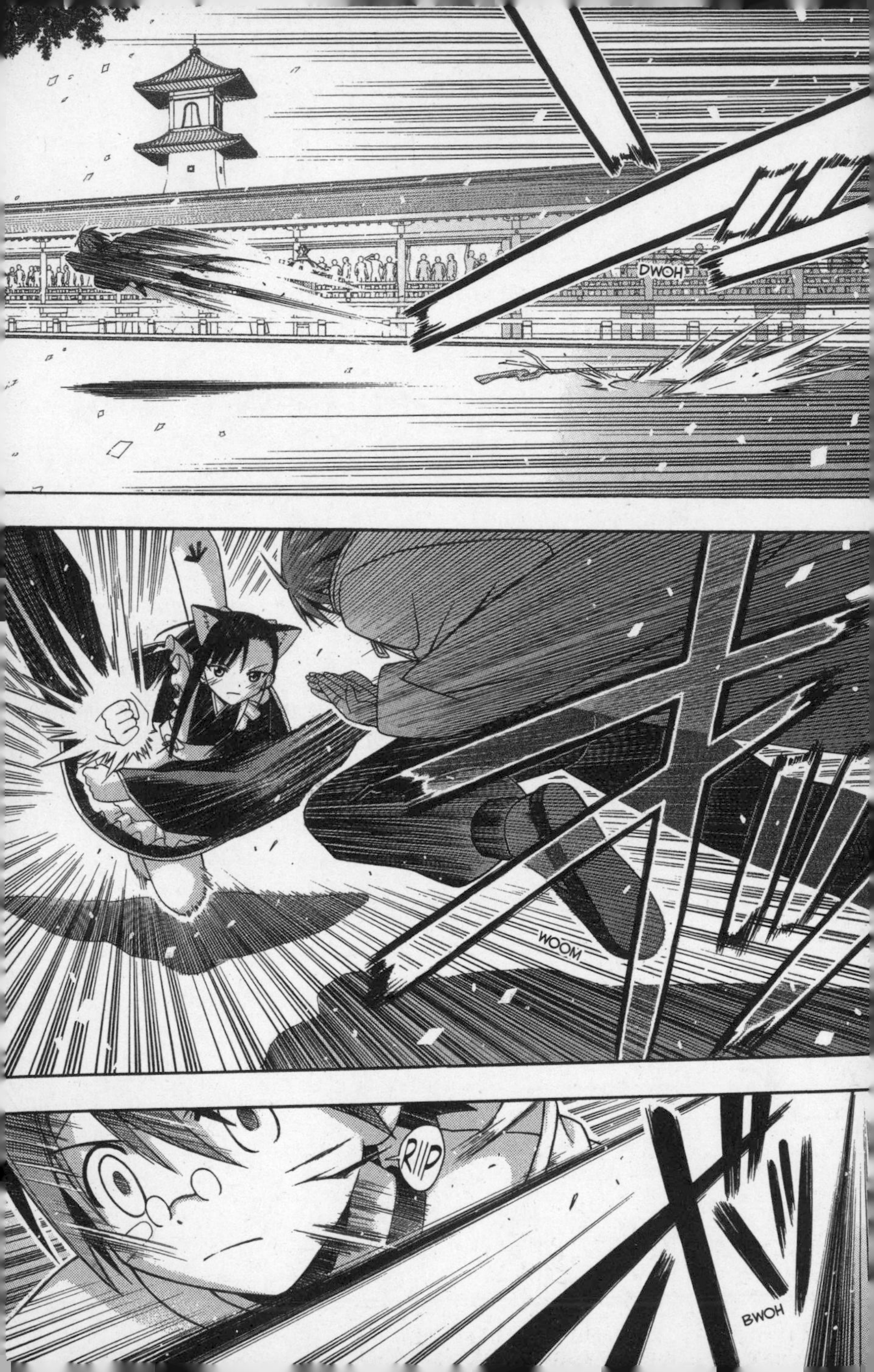
DWOH
WOOM
RIIP
BWOH

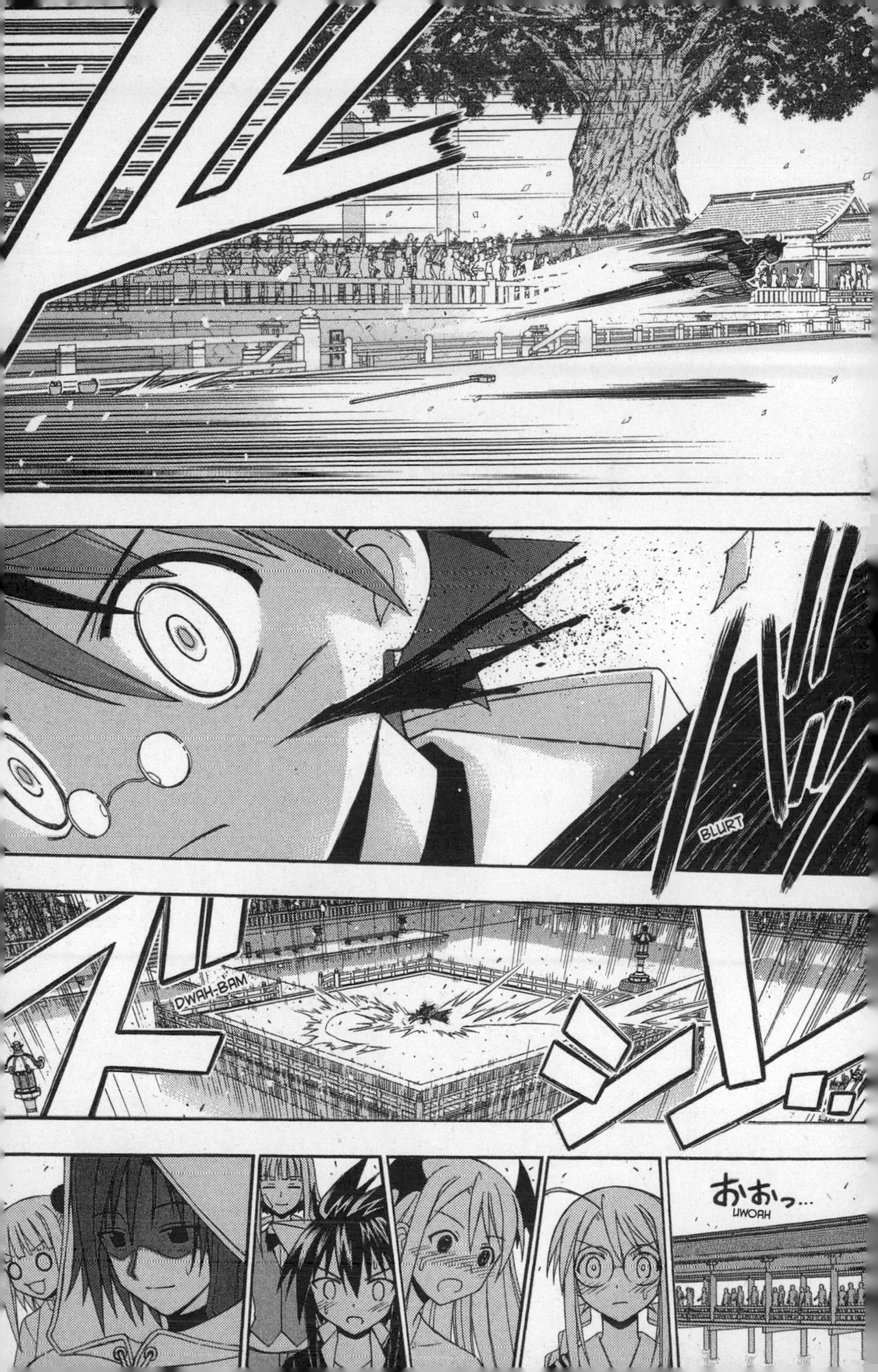
BLURT
DWAH-BAM
おおっ…
UWOAH

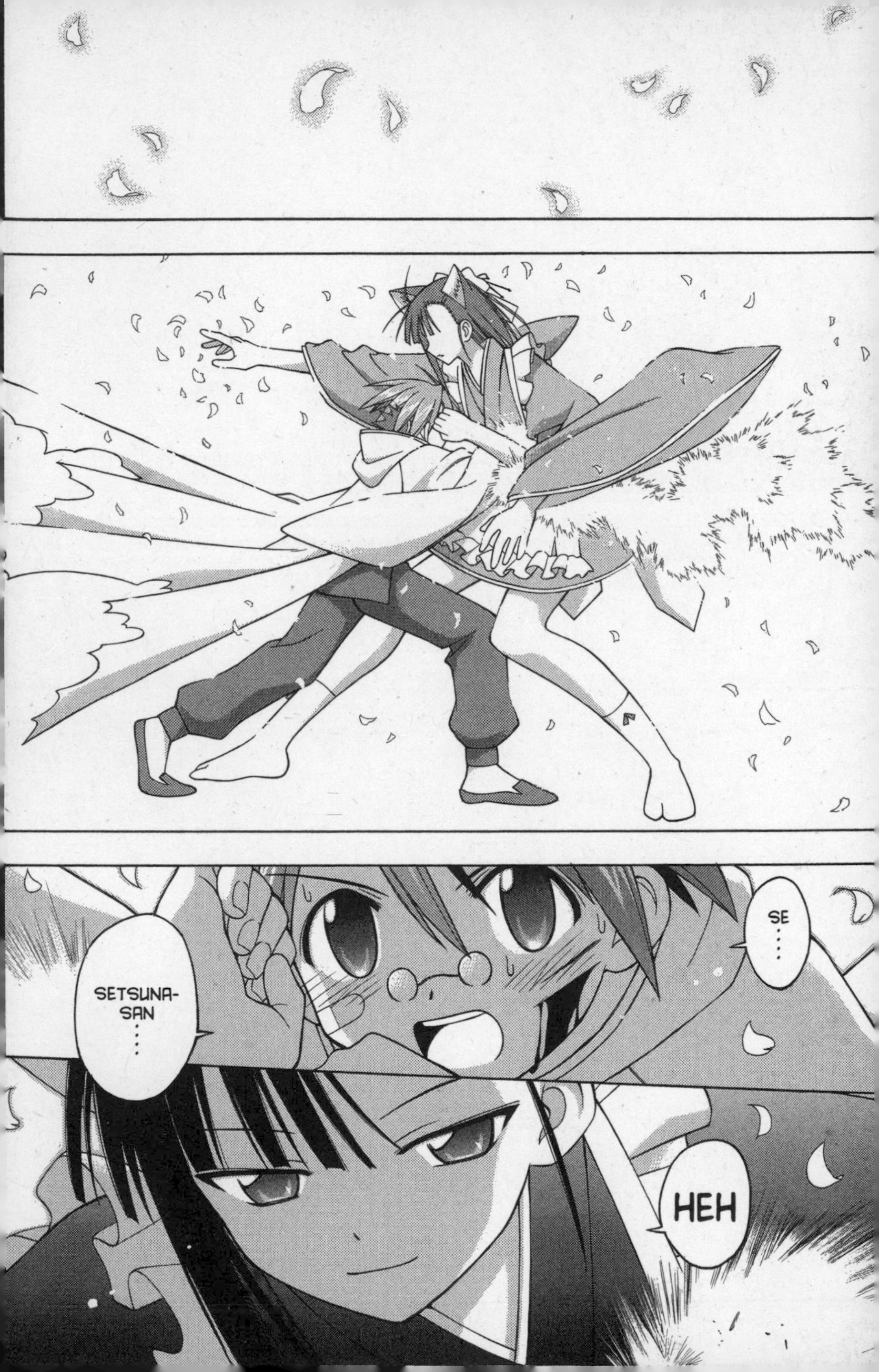
SE......
SETSUNA-SAN......
HEH

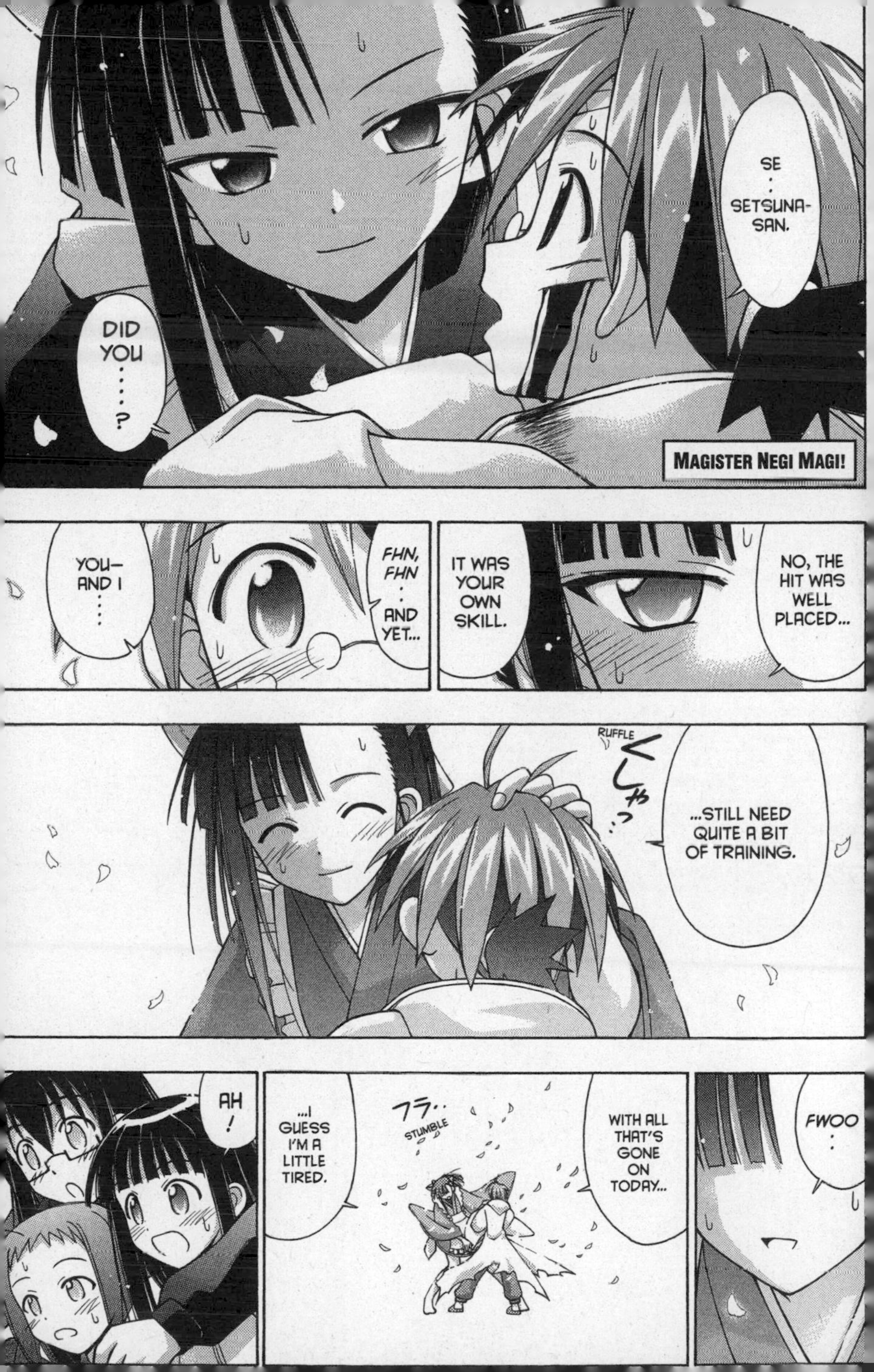
SE . . SETSUNA-SAN.
DID YOU .....?
MAGISTER NEGI MAGI!
NO, THE HIT WAS WELL PLACED...
IT WAS YOUR OWN SKILL.
FHN, FHN . . AND YET...
YOU— AND I ....
RUFFLE
くしゃっ
...STILL NEED QUITE A BIT OF TRAINING.
FWOO :
WITH ALL THAT'S GONE ON TODAY...
フラ‥
STUMBLE
...I GUESS I'M A LITTLE TIRED.
AH!

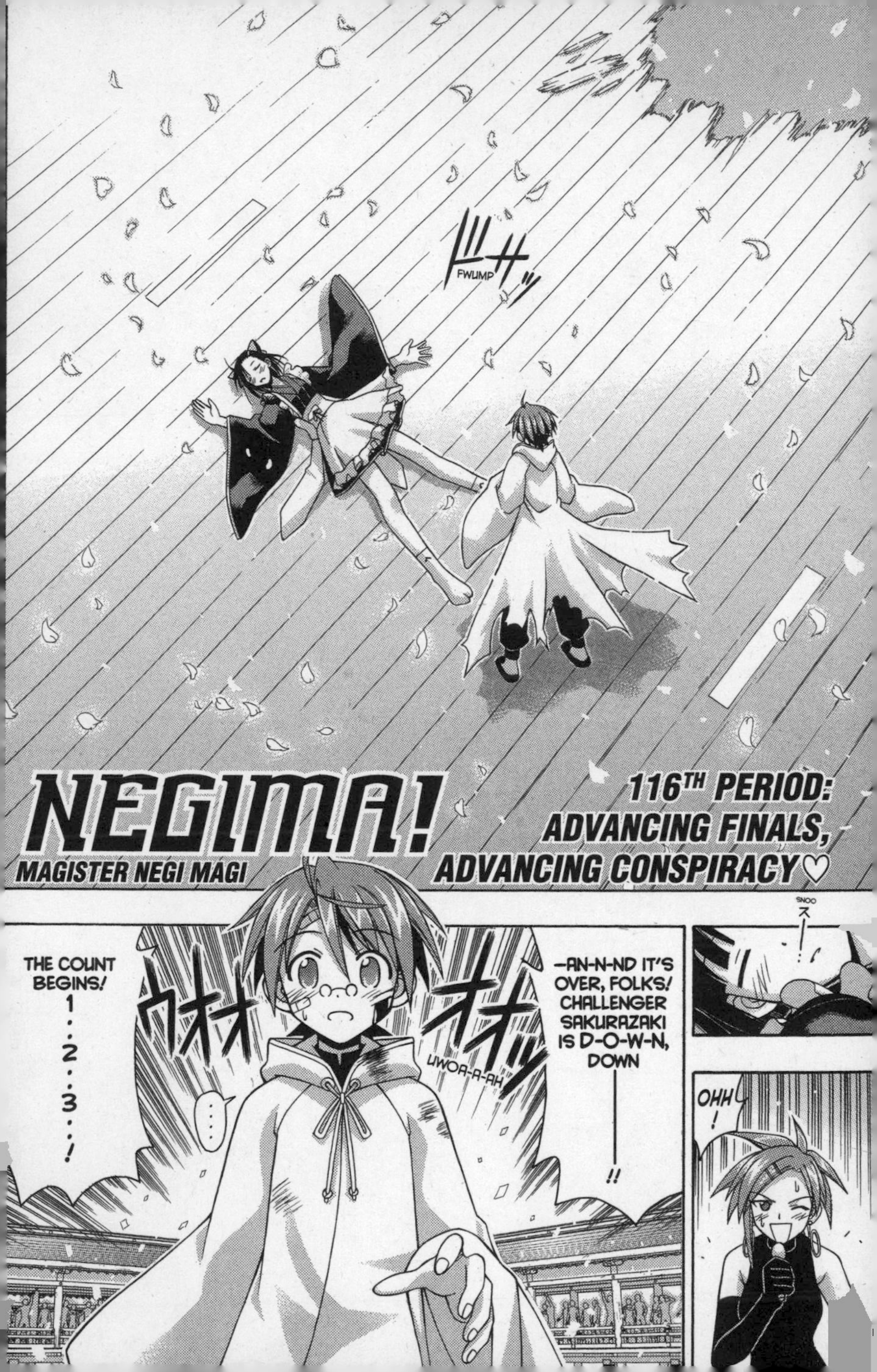
ドサッ
FWUMP
NEGIMA!
MAGISTER NEGI MAGI
116TH PERIOD: ADVANCING FINALS, ADVANCING CONSPIRACY♡
スー
SNOO
OHH!
—AN-N-ND IT'S OVER, FOLKS! CHALLENGER SAKURAZAKI IS D-O-W-N, DOWN——!!
ウオオオオッ
UWOA-A-AH
...
THE COUNT BEGINS! 1...2...3...!

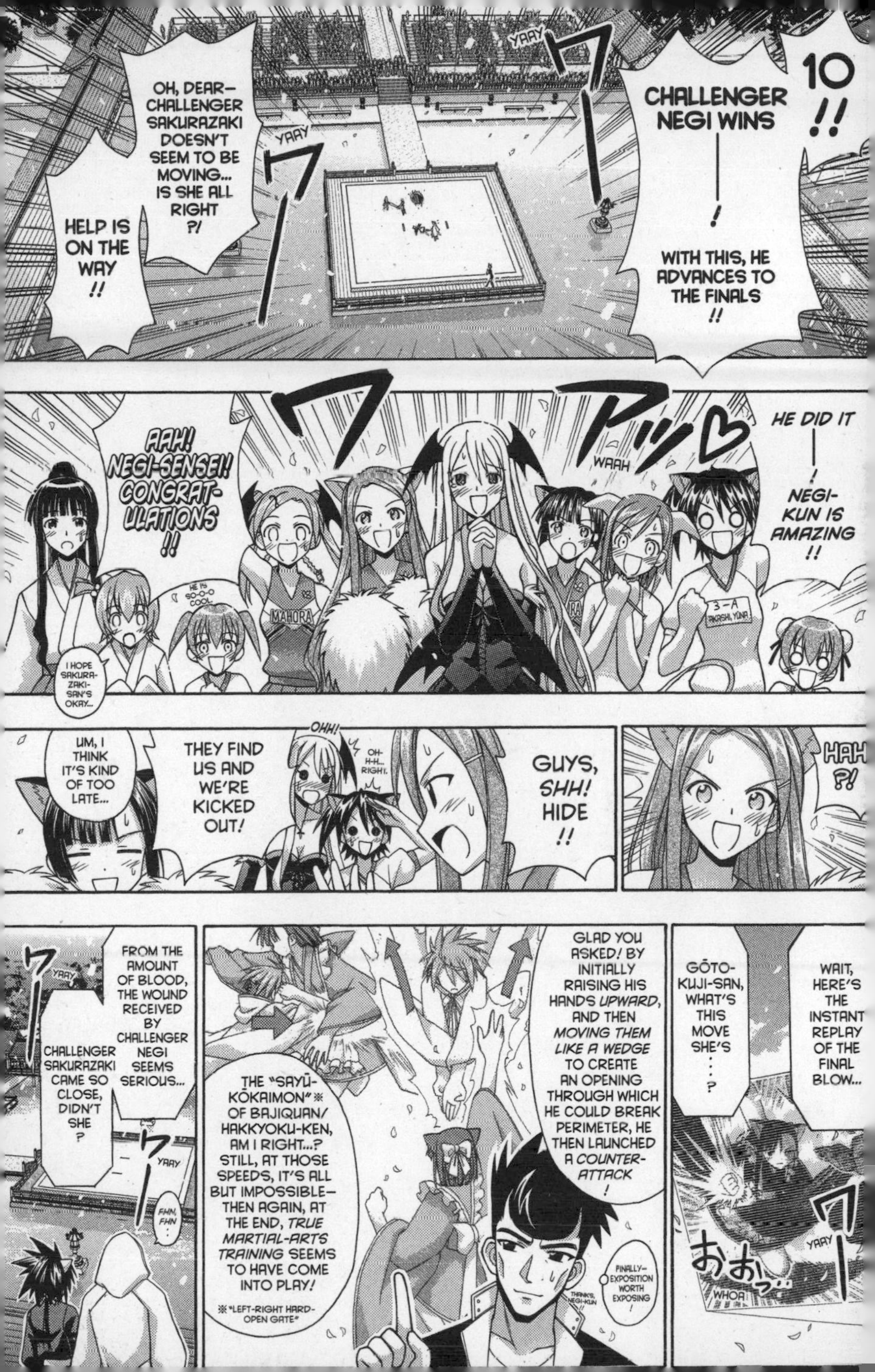
10 !!
CHALLENGER NEGI WINS —— ! WITH THIS, HE ADVANCES TO THE FINALS !!
YAAY
YAAY
OH, DEAR— CHALLENGER SAKURAZAKI DOESN'T SEEM TO BE MOVING... IS SHE ALL RIGHT ?!
HELP IS ON THE WAY !!
HE DID IT —— ! NEGI-KUN IS AMAZING !!
WAAH
AAH! NEGI-SENSEI! CONGRATULATIONS !!
HE IS SO-O-O COOL
I HOPE SAKURAZAKI-SAN'S OKAY...
HAH ?!
GUYS, SHH! HIDE !!
OHH!
OH-H-H... RIGHT.
THEY FIND US AND WE'RE KICKED OUT!
UM, I THINK IT'S KIND OF TOO LATE...
WAIT, HERE'S THE INSTANT REPLAY OF THE FINAL BLOW...
GŌTO-KUJI-SAN, WHAT'S THIS MOVE SHE'S ...?
YAAY
WHOA
GLAD YOU ASKED! BY INITIALLY RAISING HIS HANDS UPWARD, AND THEN MOVING THEM LIKE A WEDGE TO CREATE AN OPENING THROUGH WHICH HE COULD BREAK PERIMETER, HE THEN LAUNCHED A COUNTER-ATTACK !
THE "SAYŪ-KŌKAIMON"※ OF BAJIQUAN/HAKKYOKU-KEN, AM I RIGHT...? STILL, AT THOSE SPEEDS, IT'S ALL BUT IMPOSSIBLE— THEN AGAIN, AT THE END, TRUE MARTIAL-ARTS TRAINING SEEMS TO HAVE COME INTO PLAY!
FINALLY— EXPOSITION WORTH EXPOSING !
THANKS, NEGI-KUN !!
※"LEFT-RIGHT HARD-OPEN GATE"
FROM THE AMOUNT OF BLOOD, THE WOUND RECEIVED BY CHALLENGER NEGI SEEMS SERIOUS...
CHALLENGER SAKURAZAKI CAME SO CLOSE, DIDN'T SHE ?
YAAY
YAAY
FHN, FHN ...

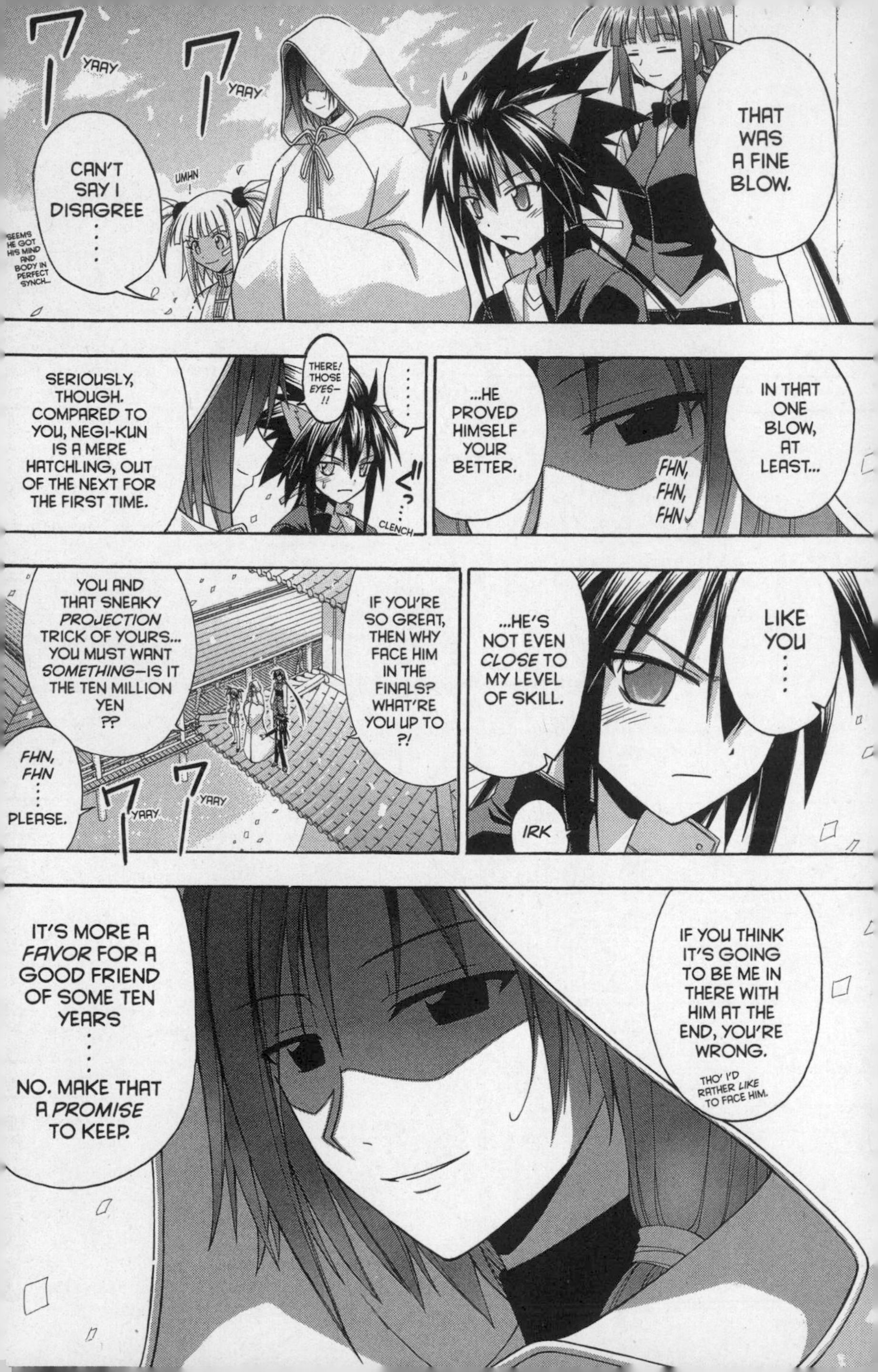
THAT WAS A FINE BLOW.
YAAY
YAAY
CAN'T SAY I DISAGREE . . .
UMHN!
SEEMS HE GOT HIS MIND AND BODY IN PERFECT SYNCH...
IN THAT ONE BLOW, AT LEAST...
...HE PROVED HIMSELF YOUR BETTER.
FHN, FHN, FHN
......
THERE! THOSE *EYES*—!!
SERIOUSLY, THOUGH. COMPARED TO YOU, NEGI-KUN IS A MERE HATCHLING, OUT OF THE NEXT FOR THE FIRST TIME.
CLENCH
LIKE YOU . . .
...HE'S NOT EVEN *CLOSE* TO MY LEVEL OF SKILL.
IRK
IF YOU'RE SO GREAT, THEN WHY FACE HIM IN THE FINALS? WHAT'RE YOU UP TO ?!
YOU AND THAT SNEAKY *PROJECTION* TRICK OF YOURS... YOU MUST WANT *SOMETHING*—IS IT THE TEN MILLION YEN ??
FHN, FHN . . . PLEASE.
YAAY
YAAY
IF YOU THINK IT'S GOING TO BE ME IN THERE WITH HIM AT THE END, YOU'RE WRONG.
THO' I'D RATHER *LIKE* TO FACE HIM.
IT'S MORE A *FAVOR* FOR A GOOD FRIEND OF SOME TEN YEARS . . .
NO. MAKE THAT A *PROMISE* TO KEEP.

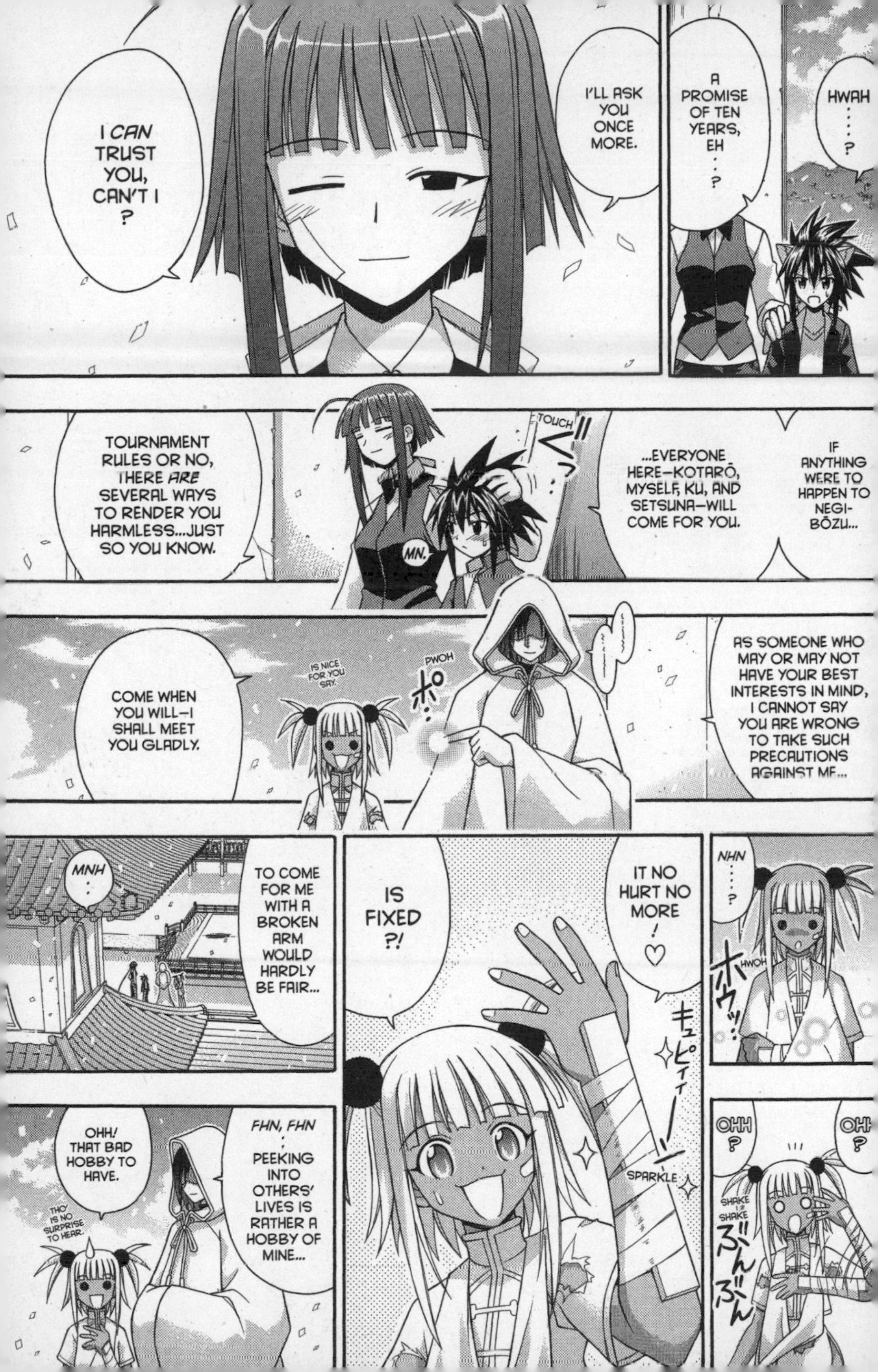
HWAH ...?
A PROMISE OF TEN YEARS, EH ...?
I'LL ASK YOU ONCE MORE.
I *CAN* TRUST YOU, CAN'T I ?
IF ANYTHING WERE TO HAPPEN TO NEGI-BŌZU...
...EVERYONE HERE—KOTARŌ, MYSELF, KU, AND SETSUNA—WILL COME FOR YOU.
TOUCH
MN.
TOURNAMENT RULES OR NO, THERE *ARE* SEVERAL WAYS TO RENDER YOU HARMLESS...JUST SO YOU KNOW.
AS SOMEONE WHO MAY OR MAY NOT HAVE YOUR BEST INTERESTS IN MIND, I CANNOT SAY YOU ARE WRONG TO TAKE SUCH PRECAUTIONS AGAINST ME...
PWOH
ポ
IS NICE FOR YOU SAY.
COME WHEN YOU WILL—I SHALL MEET YOU GLADLY.
NHN ...?
HWOH
ホウッ
OHH ?
OH!?
SHAKE SHAKE
ぶんぶん
IT NO HURT NO MORE! ♥
IS FIXED ?!
SPARKLE
TO COME FOR ME WITH A BROKEN ARM WOULD HARDLY BE FAIR...
MNH ...
FHN, FHN:
PEEKING INTO OTHERS' LIVES IS RATHER A HOBBY OF MINE...
OHH! THAT BAD HOBBY TO HAVE.
THO' IS NO SURPRISE TO HEAR.

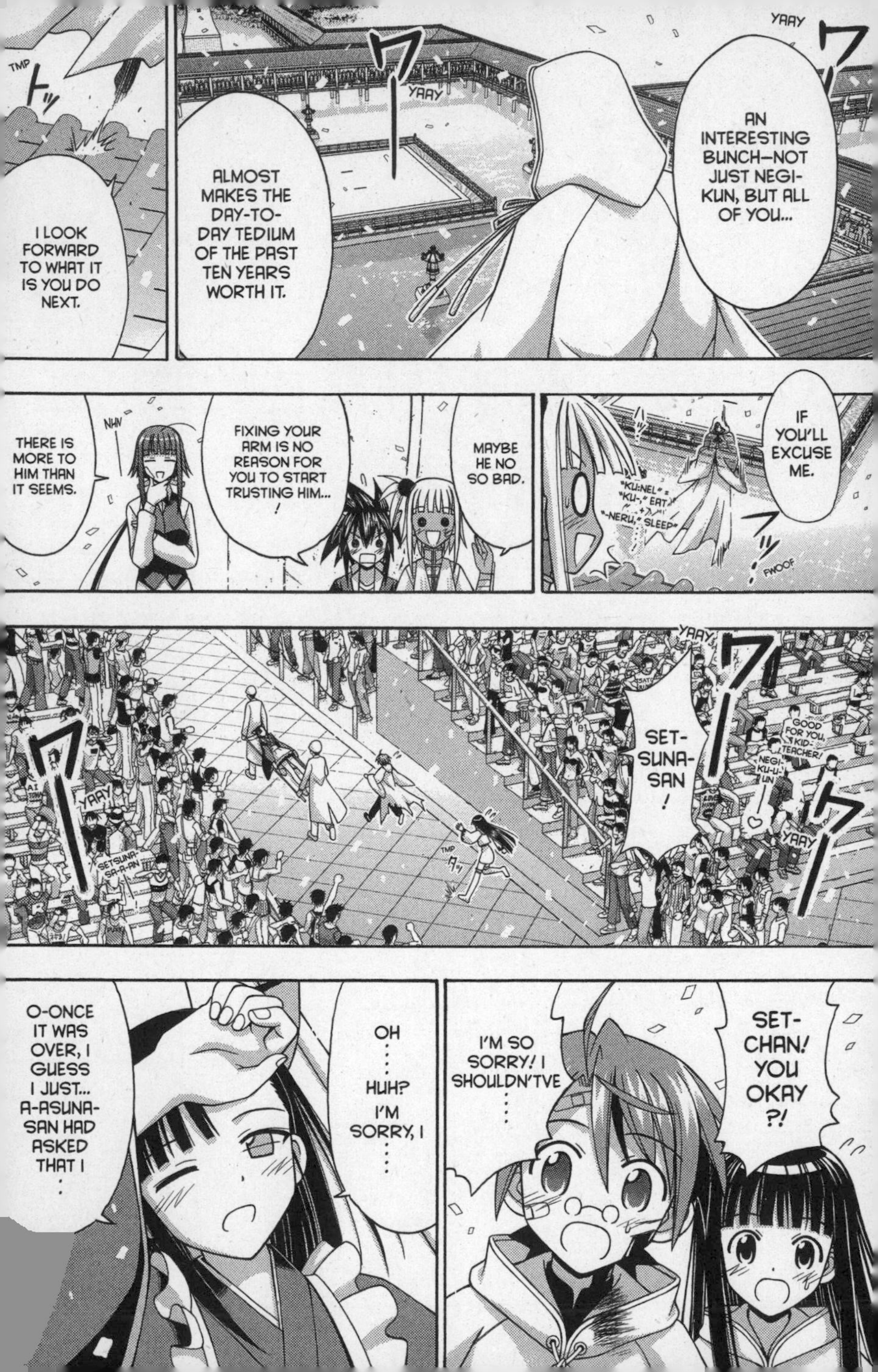
YAAY
AN INTERESTING BUNCH—NOT JUST NEGI-KUN, BUT ALL OF YOU...
YAAY
ALMOST MAKES THE DAY-TO-DAY TEDIUM OF THE PAST TEN YEARS WORTH IT.
TMP
I LOOK FORWARD TO WHAT IT IS YOU DO NEXT.
IF YOU'LL EXCUSE ME.
"KU:NEL" = "KU-," EAT + "-NERU," SLEEP
FWOOF
MAYBE HE NO SO BAD.
FIXING YOUR ARM IS NO REASON FOR YOU TO START TRUSTING HIM...!
NHN
THERE IS MORE TO HIM THAN IT SEEMS.
YAAY
GOOD FOR YOU, KID-TEACHER!
NEGI-KU-U-UN!
SET-SUNA-SAN!
YAAY
TMP
SETSUNA-SA-A-AN
YAAY
SET-CHAN! YOU OKAY?!
I'M SO SORRY! I SHOULDN'TVE...
OH... HUH? I'M SORRY, I...
O-ONCE IT WAS OVER, I GUESS I JUST... A-ASUNA-SAN HAD ASKED THAT I...

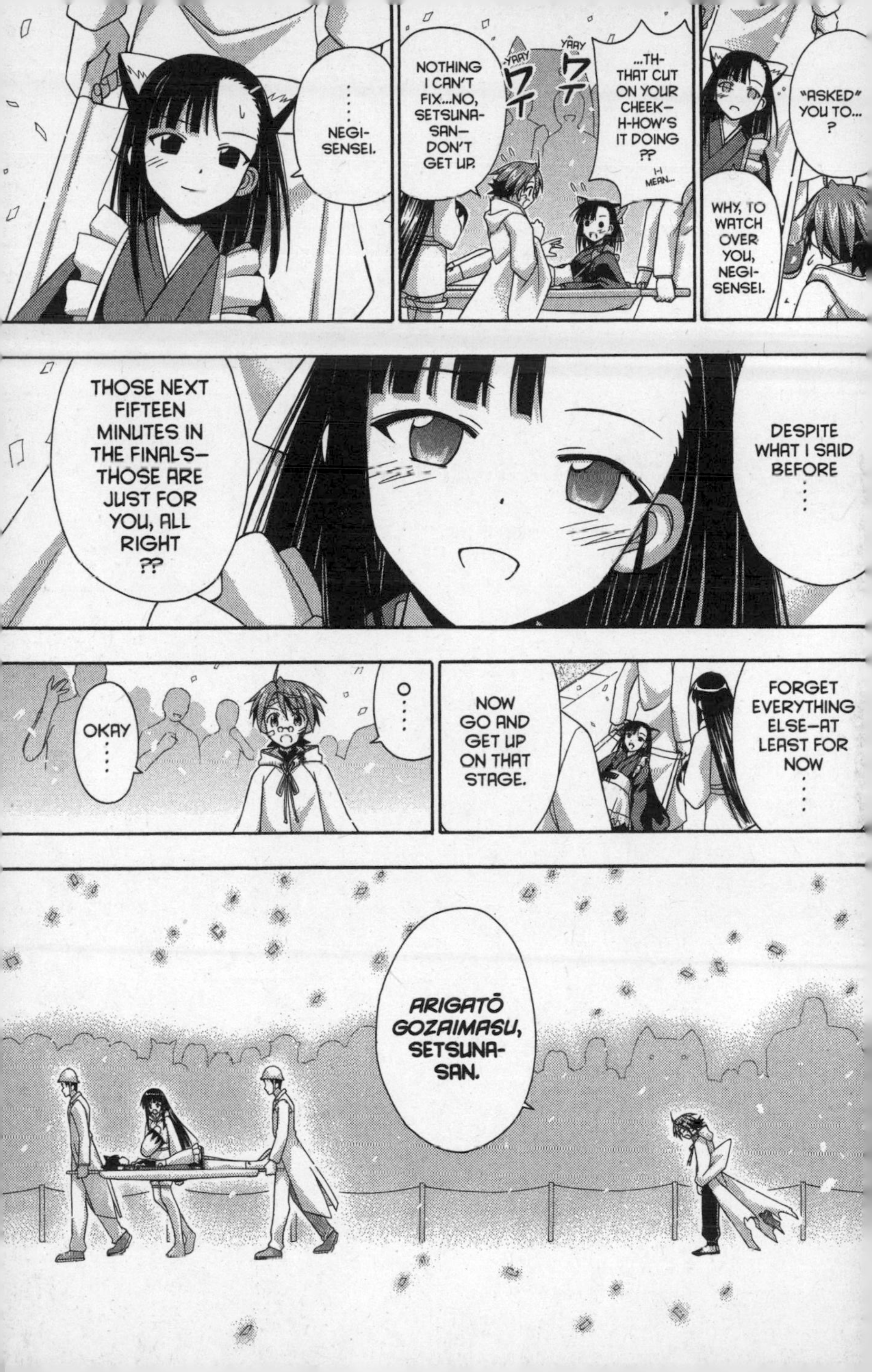
"ASKED" YOU TO...?
WHY, TO WATCH OVER YOU, NEGI-SENSEI.
...TH-THAT CUT ON YOUR CHEEK—H-HOW'S IT DOING ??
I-I MEAN...
YAAY ワイ
YAAY ワイ
NOTHING I CAN'T FIX...NO, SETSUNA-SAN—DON'T GET UP.
...NEGI-SENSEI.
DESPITE WHAT I SAID BEFORE...
THOSE NEXT FIFTEEN MINUTES IN THE FINALS—THOSE ARE JUST FOR YOU, ALL RIGHT ??
FORGET EVERYTHING ELSE—AT LEAST FOR NOW...
NOW GO AND GET UP ON THAT STAGE.
O...
OKAY...
ARIGATŌ GOZAIMASU, SETSUNA-SAN.

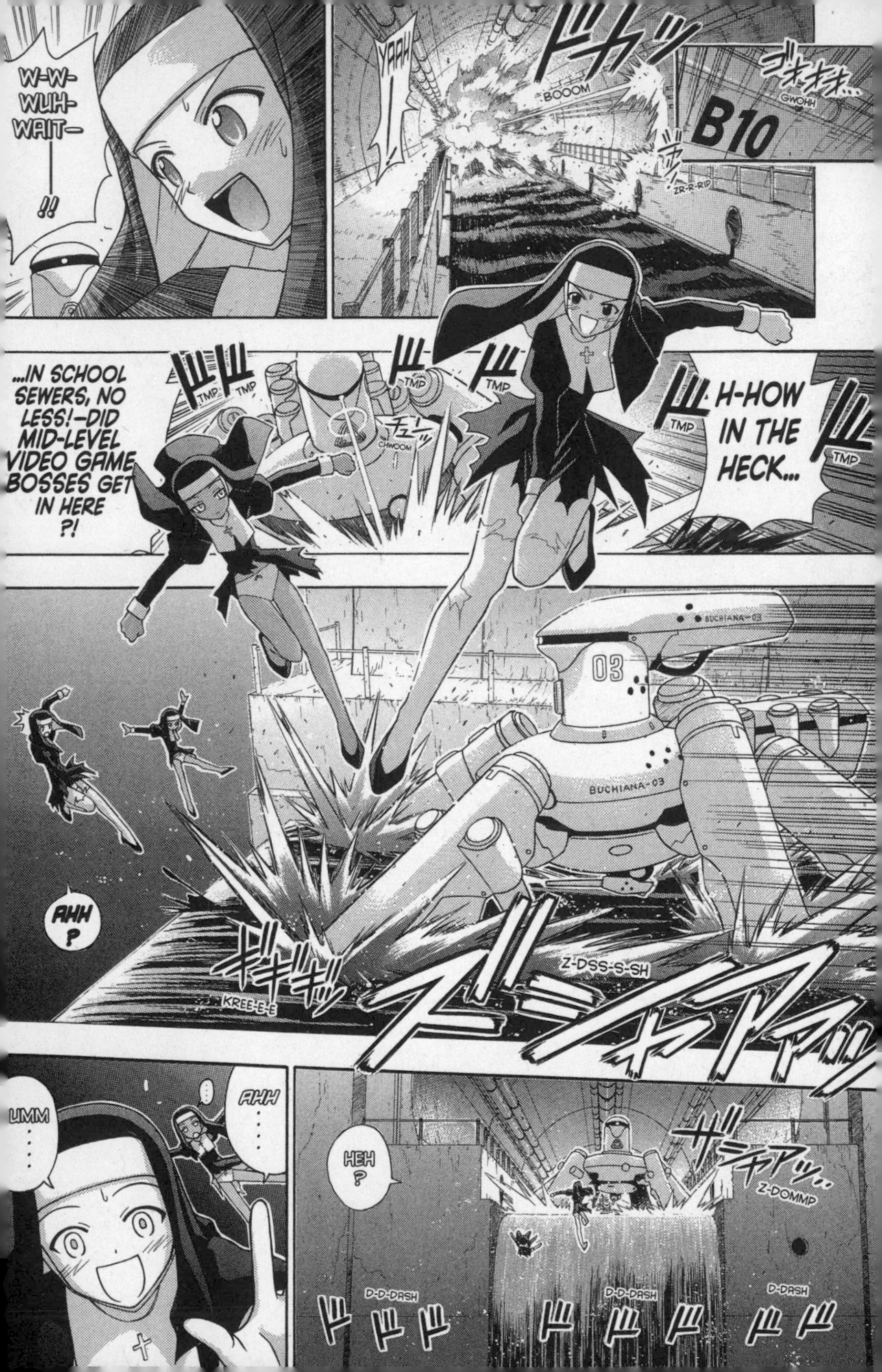
BOOOM
YAAH!
GWOHH
B10
ZR-R-RIP
W-W-WUH-WAIT—!!
TMP
TMP
H-HOW IN THE HECK...
TMP
TMP
TMP
TMP
CHWOOM
...IN SCHOOL SEWERS, NO LESS!—DID MID-LEVEL VIDEO GAME BOSSES GET IN HERE?!
BUCHIANA-03
03
BUCHIANA-03
AHH?
Z-DSS-S-SH
KREE-E-E
Z-DOMMP
HEH?
D-DASH
D-D-DASH
D-D-DASH
AHH....
...
UMM....

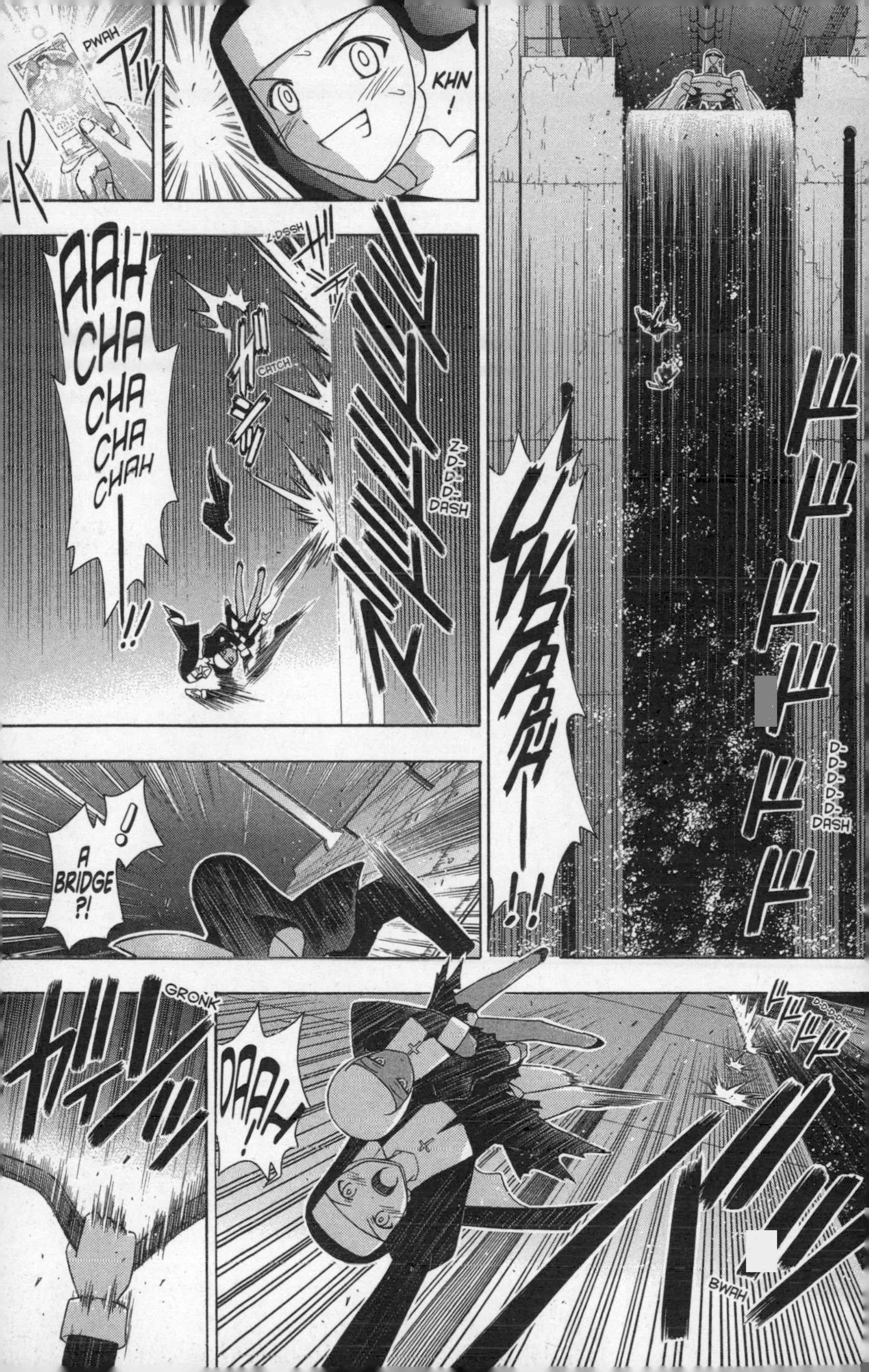
D-D-D-D-D-DASH
KHN!
PWAH
Z-D-D-D-D-DASH
Z-DSSH
CATCH
AAH CHA CHA CHA CHAH—!!
!
A BRIDGE?!
D-D-D-DASH
BWAH
DAAH!
GRONK

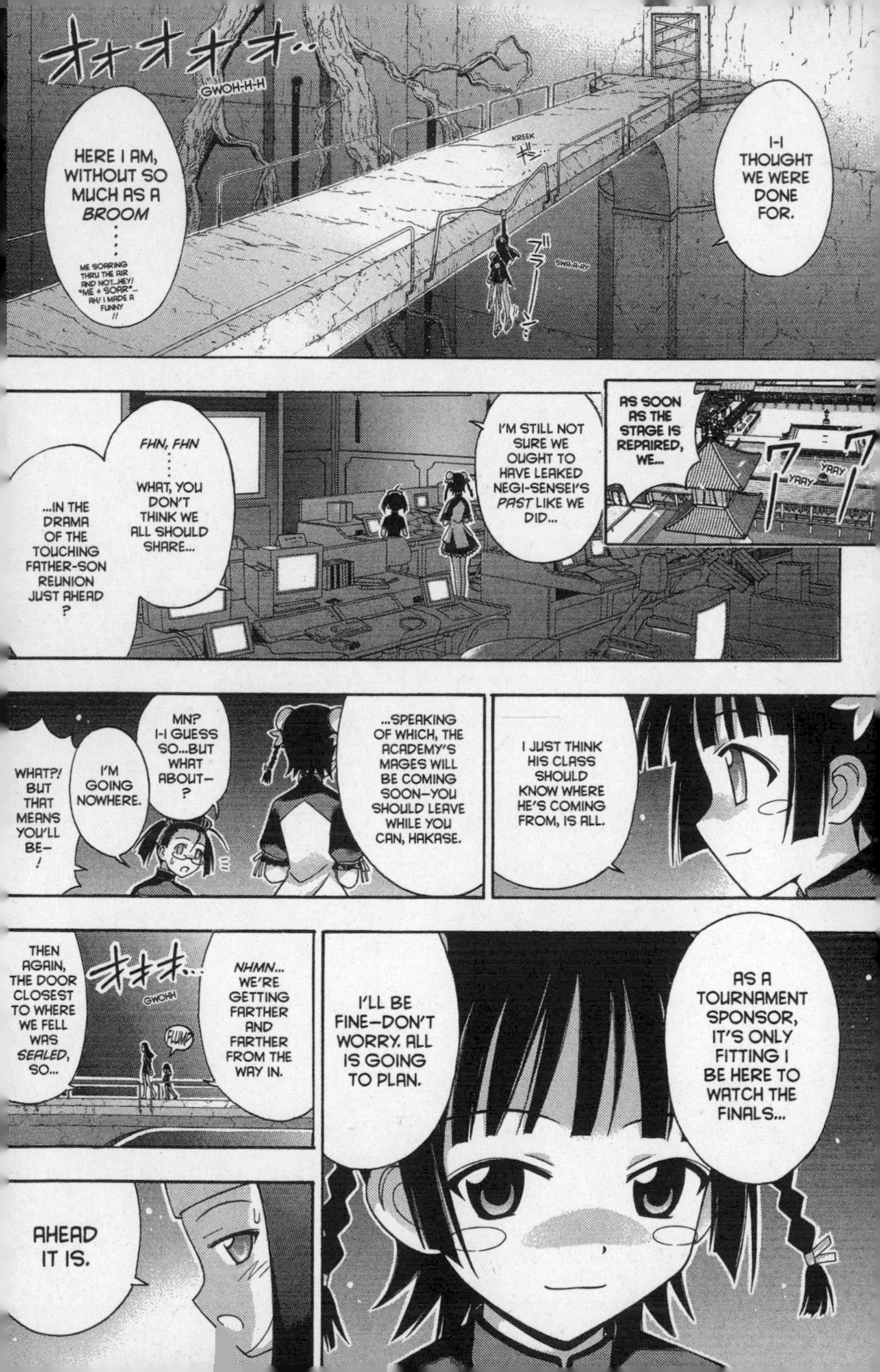
I-I THOUGHT WE WERE DONE FOR.
KREEK
SWA-A-AY
GWOH-H-H
HERE I AM, WITHOUT SO MUCH AS A *BROOM* ....
ME SOARING THRU THE AIR AND NOT...HEY! "ME + SOAR"-- AH! I MADE A FUNNY !!
AS SOON AS THE STAGE IS REPAIRED, WE...
YAAY
YAAY
I'M STILL NOT SURE WE OUGHT TO HAVE LEAKED NEGI-SENSEI'S *PAST* LIKE WE DID...
FHN, FHN ... WHAT, YOU DON'T THINK WE ALL SHOULD SHARE...
...IN THE DRAMA OF THE TOUCHING FATHER-SON REUNION JUST AHEAD ?
I JUST THINK HIS CLASS SHOULD KNOW WHERE HE'S COMING FROM, IS ALL.
...SPEAKING OF WHICH, THE ACADEMY'S MAGES WILL BE COMING SOON—YOU SHOULD LEAVE WHILE YOU CAN, HAKASE.
MN? I-I GUESS SO...BUT WHAT ABOUT— ?
I'M GOING NOWHERE.
WHAT?! BUT THAT MEANS YOU'LL BE— !
AS A TOURNAMENT SPONSOR, IT'S ONLY FITTING I BE HERE TO WATCH THE FINALS...
I'LL BE FINE—DON'T WORRY. ALL IS GOING TO PLAN.
NHMN... WE'RE GETTING FARTHER AND FARTHER FROM THE WAY IN.
GWOHH
FLUMP
THEN AGAIN, THE DOOR CLOSEST TO WHERE WE FELL WAS *SEALED*, SO...
AHEAD IT IS.

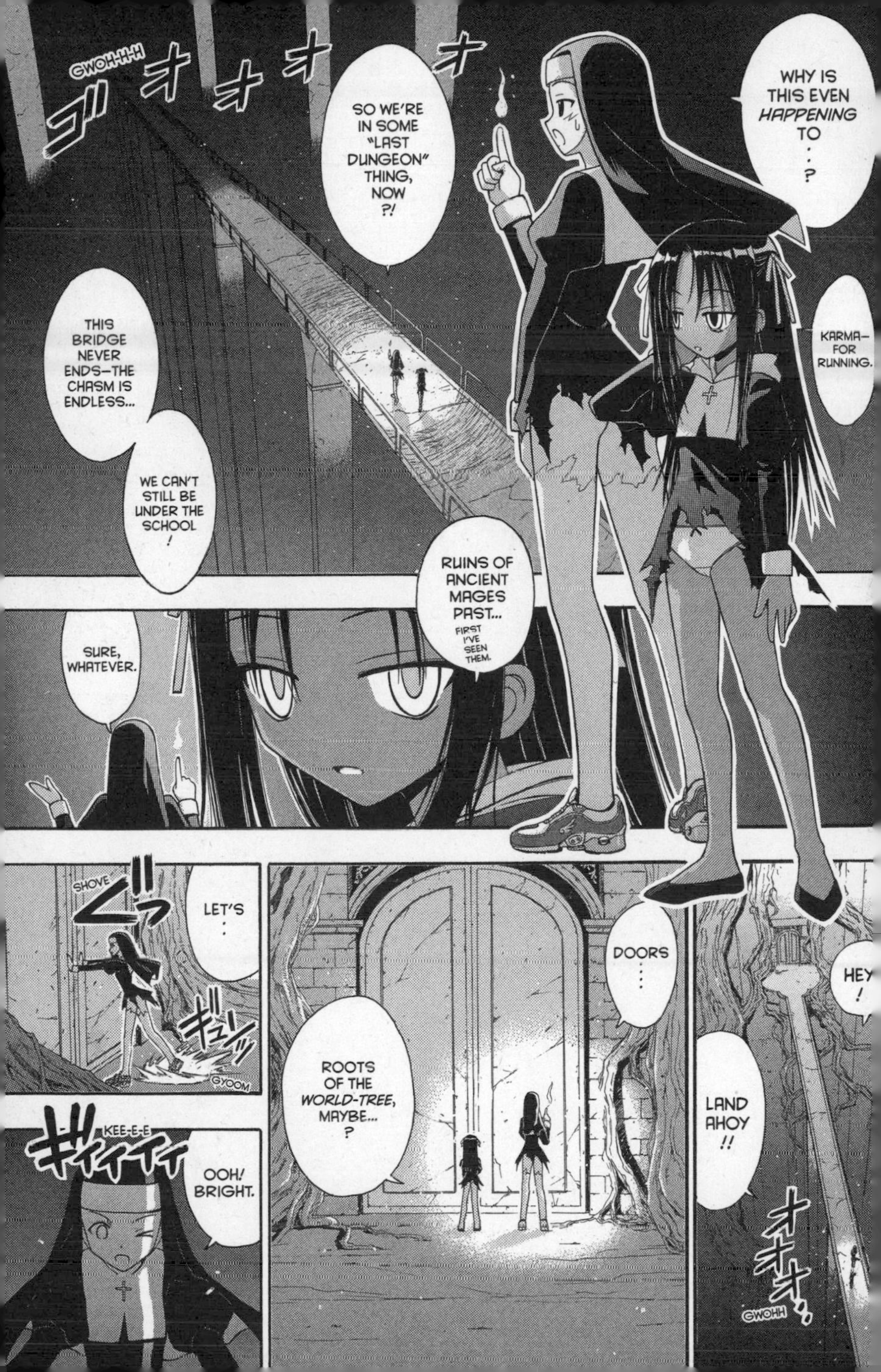
WHY IS THIS EVEN *HAPPENING* TO . . . ?
SO WE'RE IN SOME "LAST DUNGEON" THING, NOW ?!
GWOH-H-H
KARMA—FOR RUNNING.
THIS BRIDGE NEVER ENDS—THE CHASM IS ENDLESS...
WE CAN'T STILL BE UNDER THE SCHOOL !
RUINS OF ANCIENT MAGES PAST...
FIRST I'VE SEEN THEM.
SURE, WHATEVER.
HEY !
LAND AHOY !!
GWOHH
DOORS . . . .
ROOTS OF THE *WORLD-TREE*, MAYBE... ?
SHOVE
LET'S .
GYOOM
KEE-E-E
OOH! BRIGHT.

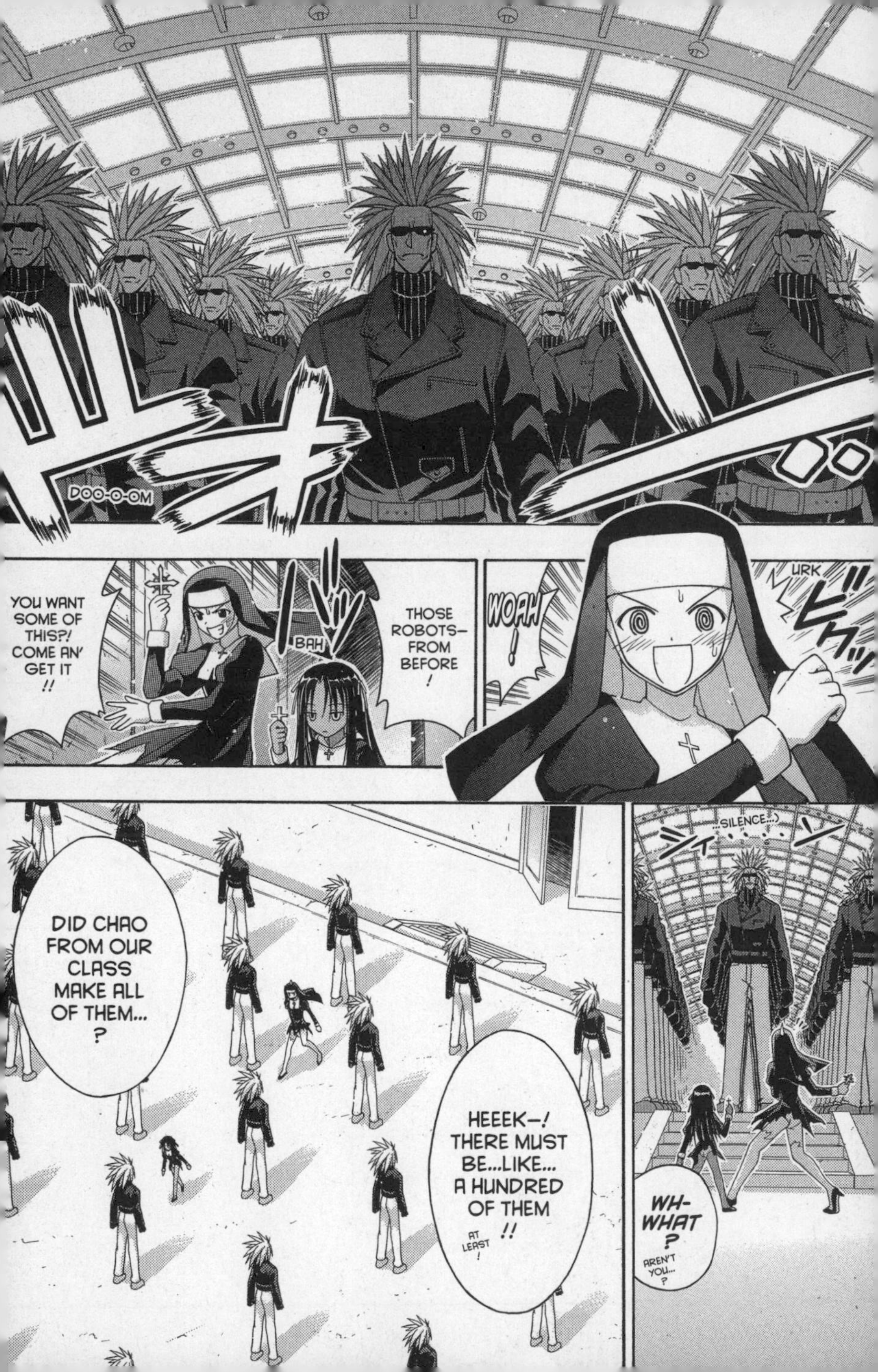
DOO-O-OM
URK
WOAH!
THOSE ROBOTS—FROM BEFORE!
BAH
YOU WANT SOME OF THIS?! COME AN' GET IT!!
...SILENCE...)
WH-WHAT?
AREN'T YOU...?
DID CHAO FROM OUR CLASS MAKE ALL OF THEM...?
HEEEK—! THERE MUST BE...LIKE... A HUNDRED OF THEM!!
AT LEAST!

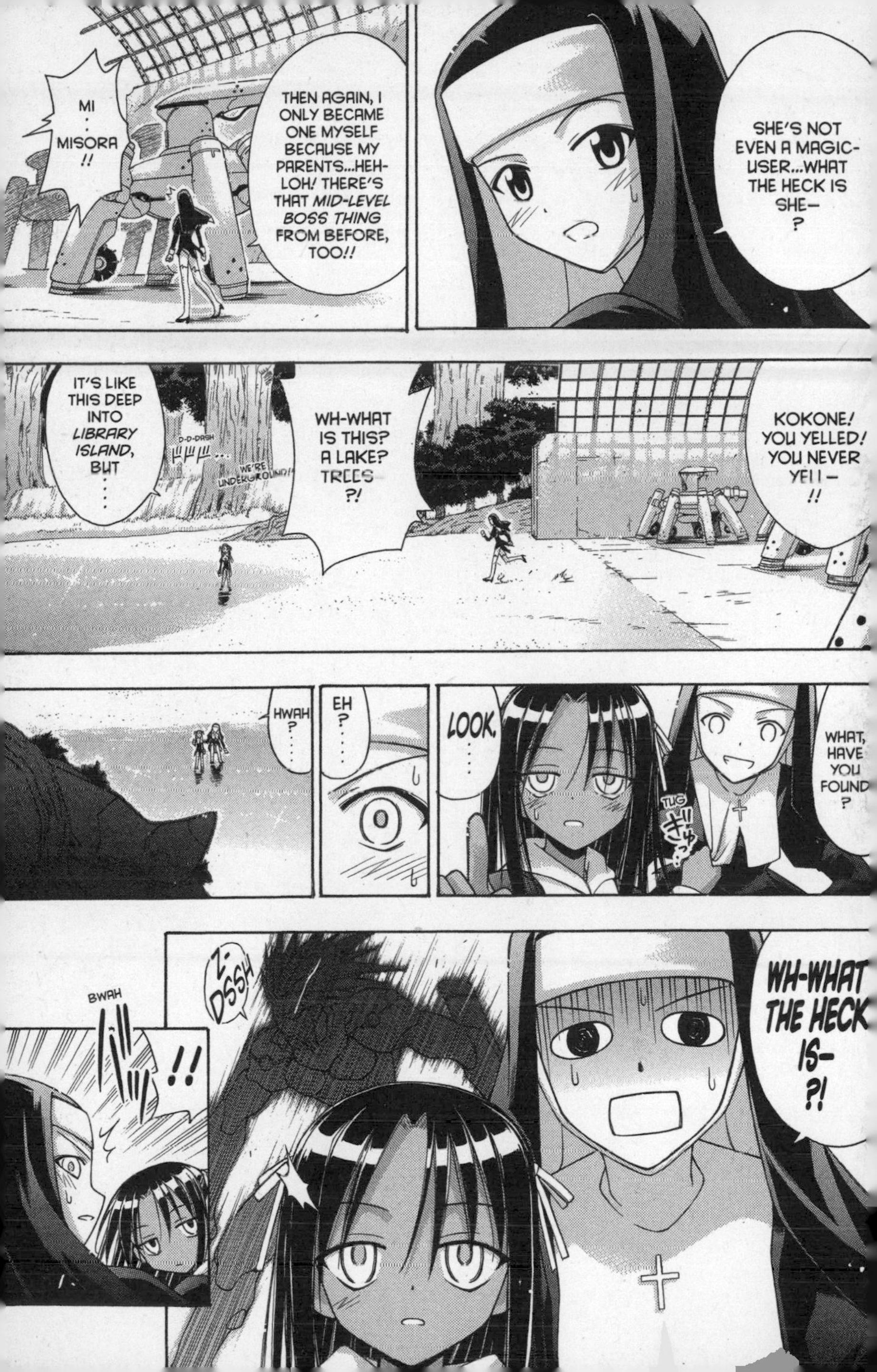
SHE'S NOT EVEN A MAGIC-USER...WHAT THE HECK IS SHE—?
THEN AGAIN, I ONLY BECAME ONE MYSELF BECAUSE MY PARENTS...HEH-LOH! THERE'S THAT MID-LEVEL BOSS THING FROM BEFORE, TOO!!
MI... MISORA!!
KOKONE! YOU YELLED! YOU NEVER YELL—!!
WH-WHAT IS THIS? A LAKE? TREES?!
WE'RE UNDERGROUND!!
D-D-DASH
IT'S LIKE THIS DEEP INTO LIBRARY ISLAND, BUT.....
WHAT, HAVE YOU FOUND?
TUG
LOOK.....
EH?.....
HWAH?.....
WH-WHAT THE HECK IS—?!
Z-DSSH
!!
BWAH

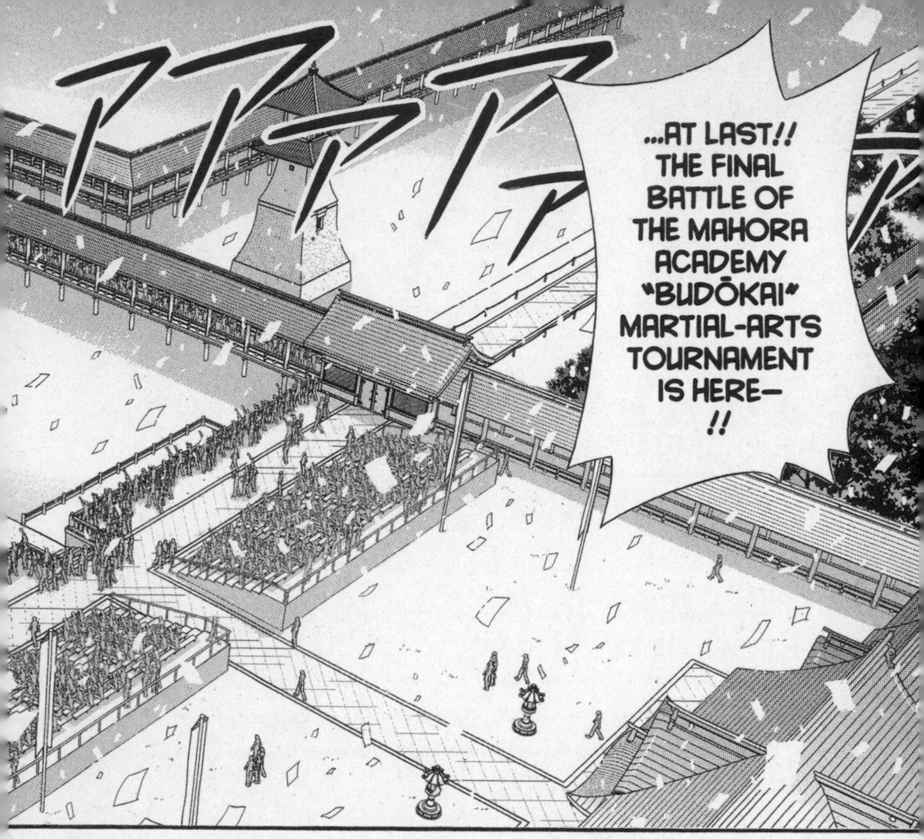
...AT LAST!! THE FINAL BATTLE OF THE MAHORA ACADEMY "BUDŌKAI" MARTIAL-ARTS TOURNAMENT IS HERE— !!

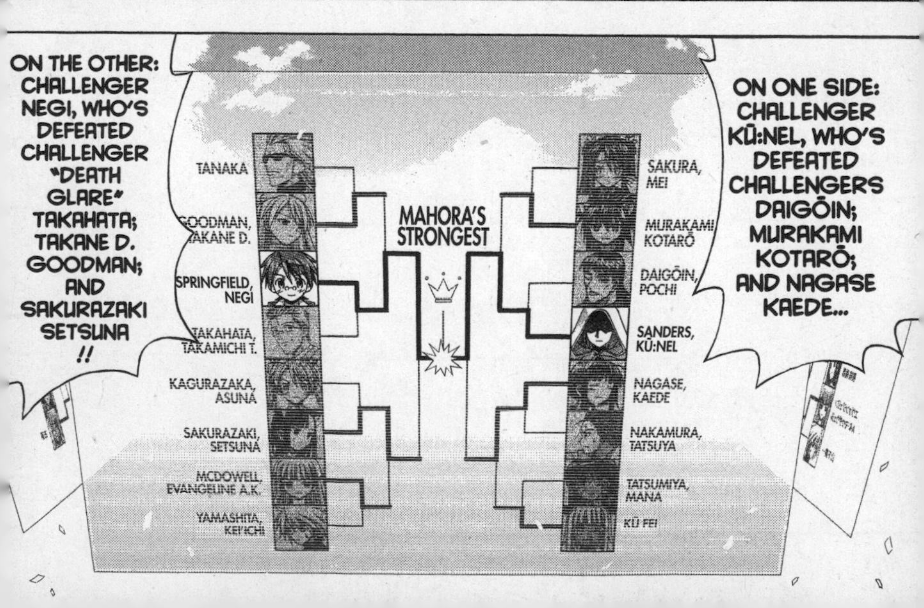
ON ONE SIDE: CHALLENGER KŪ:NEL, WHO'S DEFEATED CHALLENGERS DAIGŌIN; MURAKAMI KOTARŌ; AND NAGASE KAEDE...
MAHORA'S STRONGEST
SAKURA, MEI
MURAKAMI KOTARŌ
DAIGŌIN, POCHI
SANDERS, KŪ:NEL
NAGASE, KAEDE
NAKAMURA, TATSUYA
TATSUMIYA, MANA
KŪ FEI
TANAKA
GOODMAN, AKANE D.
SPRINGFIELD, NEGI
TAKAHATA, TAKAMICHI T.
KAGURAZAKA, ASUNA
SAKURAZAKI, SETSUNA
MCDOWELL, EVANGELINE A.K.
YAMASHITA, KEI'ICHI
ON THE OTHER: CHALLENGER NEGI, WHO'S DEFEATED CHALLENGER "DEATH GLARE" TAKAHATA; TAKANE D. GOODMAN; AND SAKURAZAKI SETSUNA !!

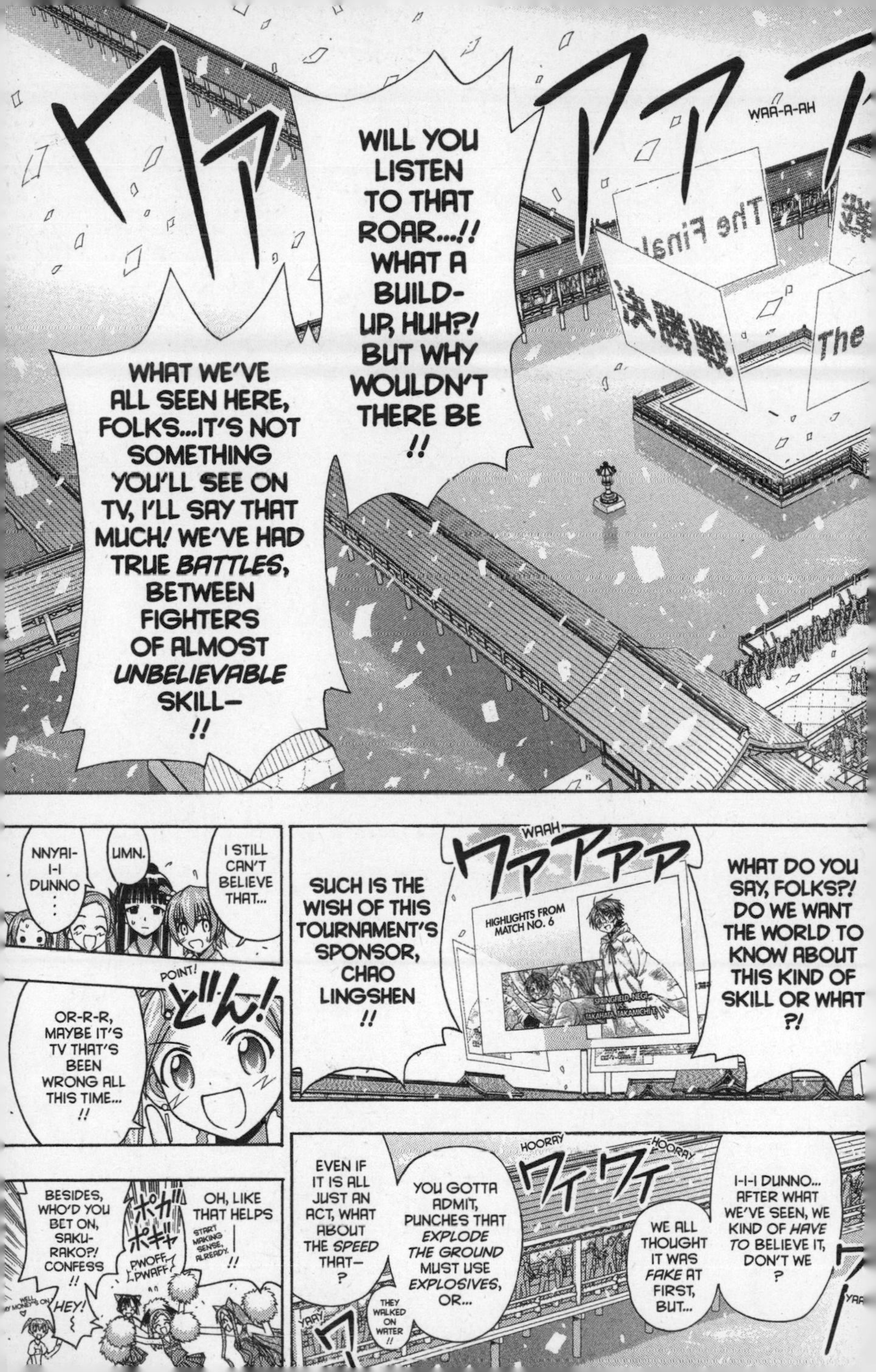
WAA-A-AH
WILL YOU LISTEN TO THAT ROAR...!! WHAT A BUILD-UP, HUH?! BUT WHY WOULDN'T THERE BE!!
WHAT WE'VE ALL SEEN HERE, FOLKS...IT'S NOT SOMETHING YOU'LL SEE ON TV, I'LL SAY THAT MUCH! WE'VE HAD TRUE *BATTLES*, BETWEEN FIGHTERS OF ALMOST *UNBELIEVABLE* SKILL—!!
決勝戦
WHAT DO YOU SAY, FOLKS?! DO WE WANT THE WORLD TO KNOW ABOUT THIS KIND OF SKILL OR WHAT?!
WAAH
HIGHLIGHTS FROM MATCH NO. 6
SUCH IS THE WISH OF THIS TOURNAMENT'S SPONSOR, CHAO LINGSHEN!!
I STILL CAN'T BELIEVE THAT...
UMN.
NNYAI-I-I DUNNO...
POINT!
OR-R-R, MAYBE IT'S TV THAT'S BEEN WRONG ALL THIS TIME...!!
HOORAY
HOORAY
I-I-I DUNNO... AFTER WHAT WE'VE SEEN, WE KIND OF *HAVE TO* BELIEVE IT, DON'T WE
WE ALL THOUGHT IT WAS *FAKE* AT FIRST, BUT...
YOU GOTTA ADMIT, PUNCHES THAT *EXPLODE THE GROUND* MUST USE *EXPLOSIVES*, OR...
EVEN IF IT IS ALL JUST AN ACT, WHAT ABOUT THE *SPEED* THAT—?
THEY WALKED ON WATER!!
OH, LIKE THAT HELPS
START MAKING SENSE, ALREADY.!!
PWOFF PWAFF
BESIDES, WHO'D YOU BET ON, SAKURAKO?! CONFESS!!
HEY!

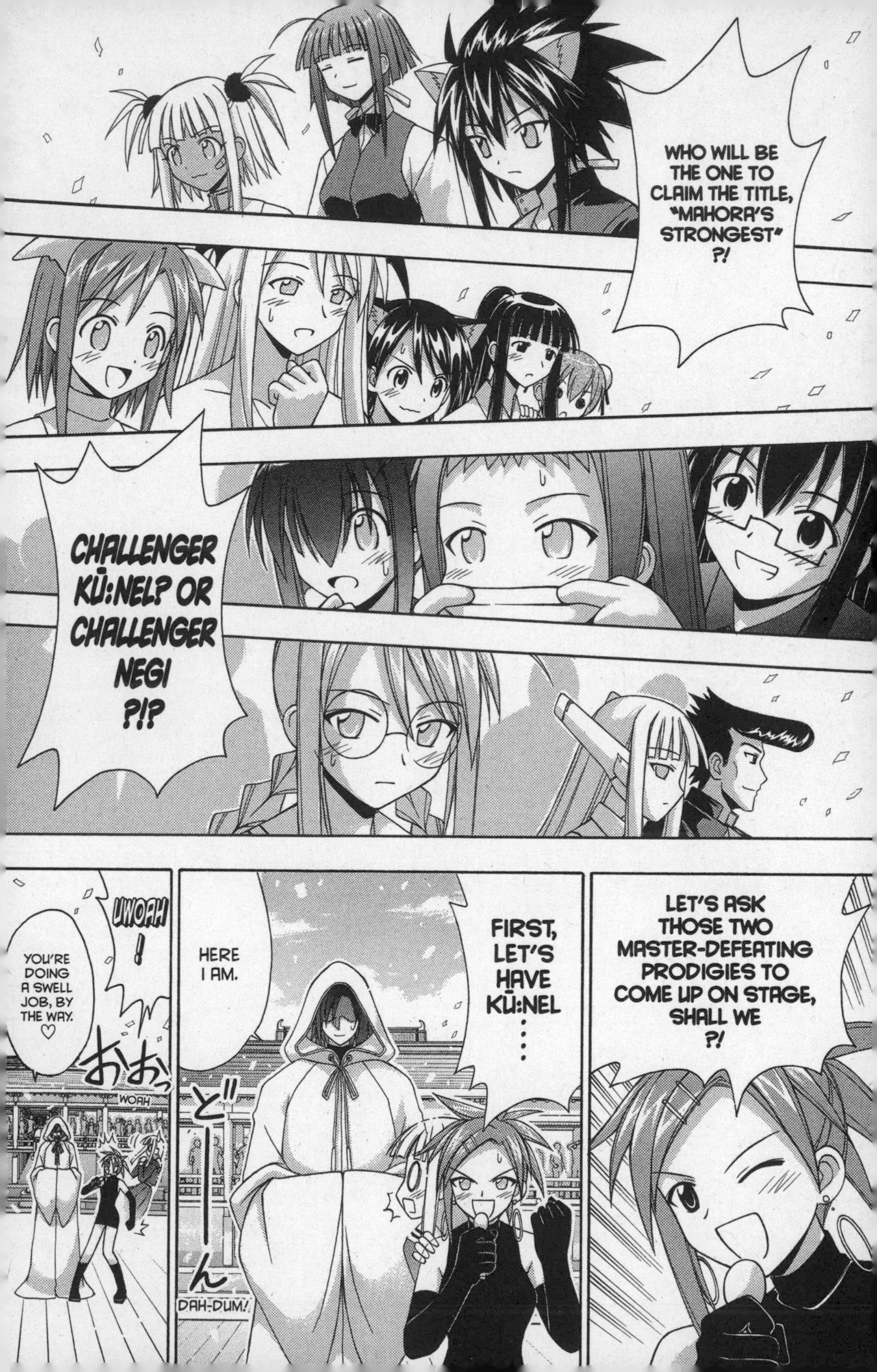

WHO WILL BE THE ONE TO CLAIM THE TITLE, "MAHORA'S STRONGEST" ?!
CHALLENGER KŪ:NEL? OR CHALLENGER NEGI ?!?
LET'S ASK THOSE TWO MASTER-DEFEATING PRODIGIES TO COME UP ON STAGE, SHALL WE ?!
FIRST, LET'S HAVE KŪ:NEL ....
HERE I AM.
ど〜ん
DAH-DUM!
UWOAH !
YOU'RE DOING A SWELL JOB, BY THE WAY. ♡
おおっ
WOAH

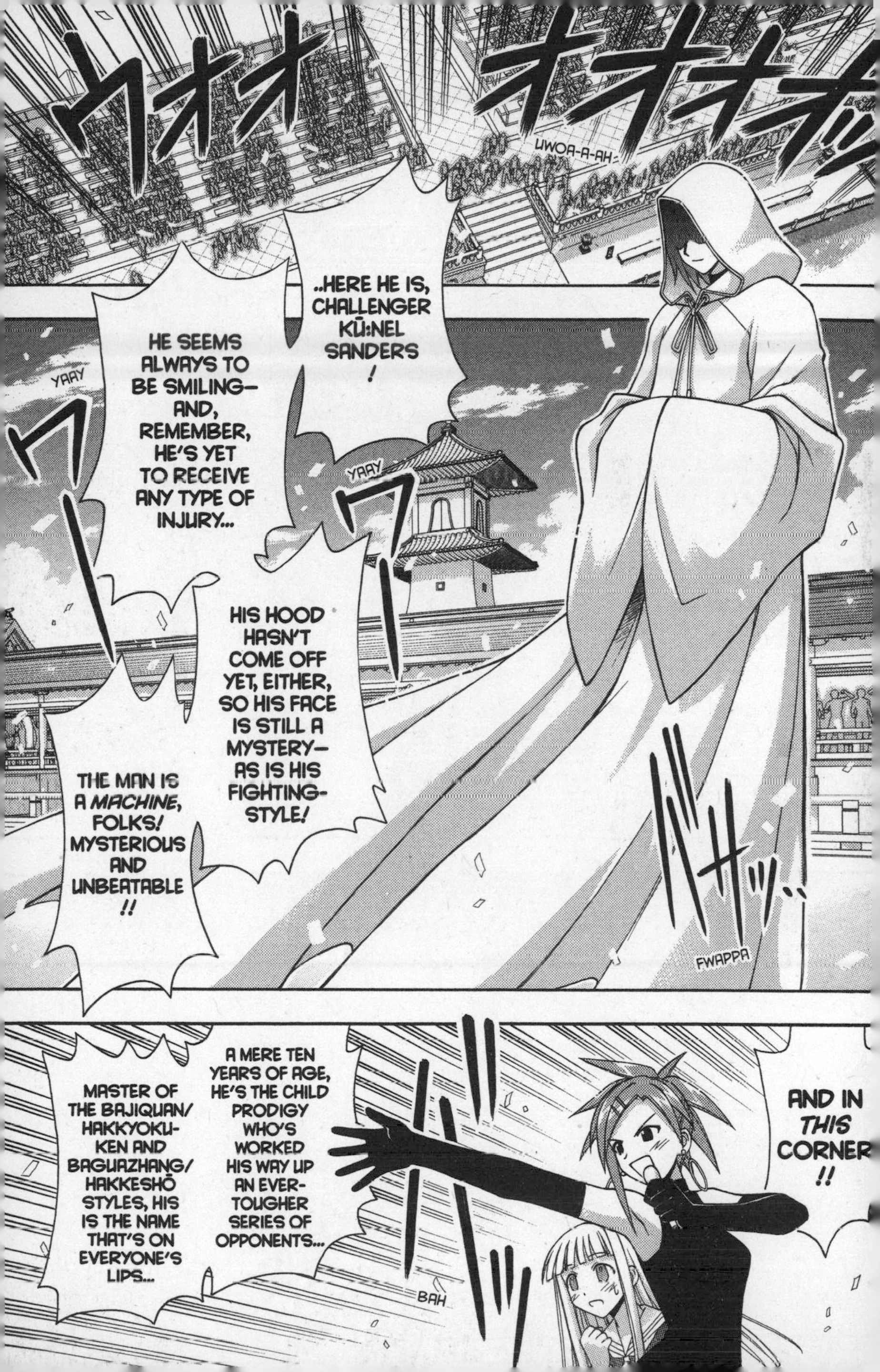
UWOA-A-AH
..HERE HE IS, CHALLENGER KŪ:NEL SANDERS!
FWAPPA
YAAY
HIS HOOD HASN'T COME OFF YET, EITHER, SO HIS FACE IS STILL A MYSTERY— AS IS HIS FIGHTING-STYLE!
YAAY
HE SEEMS ALWAYS TO BE SMILING— AND, REMEMBER, HE'S YET TO RECEIVE ANY TYPE OF INJURY...
THE MAN IS A *MACHINE*, FOLKS! MYSTERIOUS AND UNBEATABLE!!
AND IN *THIS* CORNER!!
A MERE TEN YEARS OF AGE, HE'S THE CHILD PRODIGY WHO'S WORKED HIS WAY UP AN EVER-TOUGHER SERIES OF OPPONENTS...
MASTER OF THE BAJIQUAN/HAKKYOKU-KEN AND BAGUAZHANG/HAKKESHŌ STYLES, HIS IS THE NAME THAT'S ON EVERYONE'S LIPS...
BAH

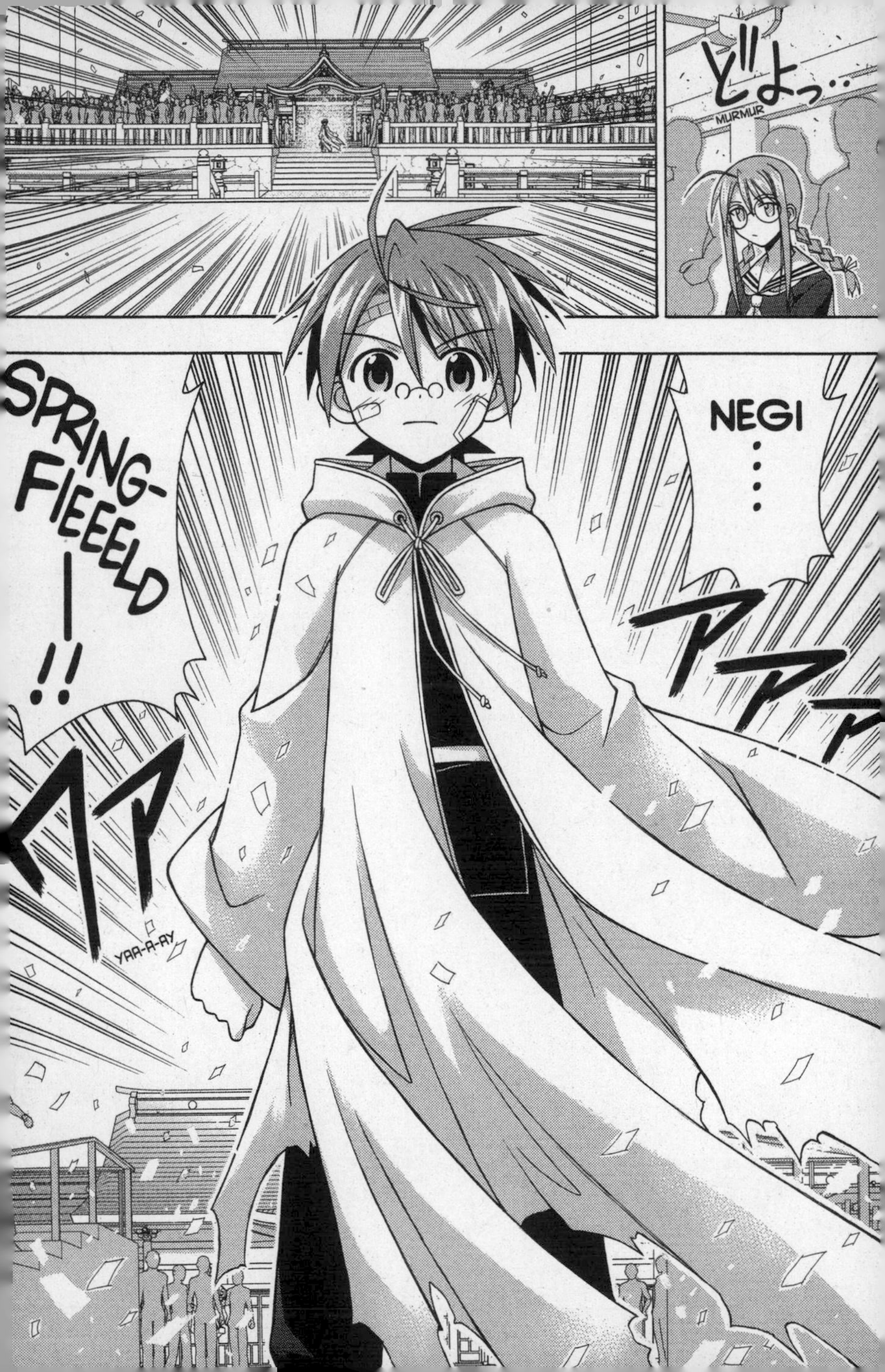
どよっ…
MURMUR
NEGI
…
アアァ
SPRING-FIEEELD—!!
ワア
YAA-A-AY

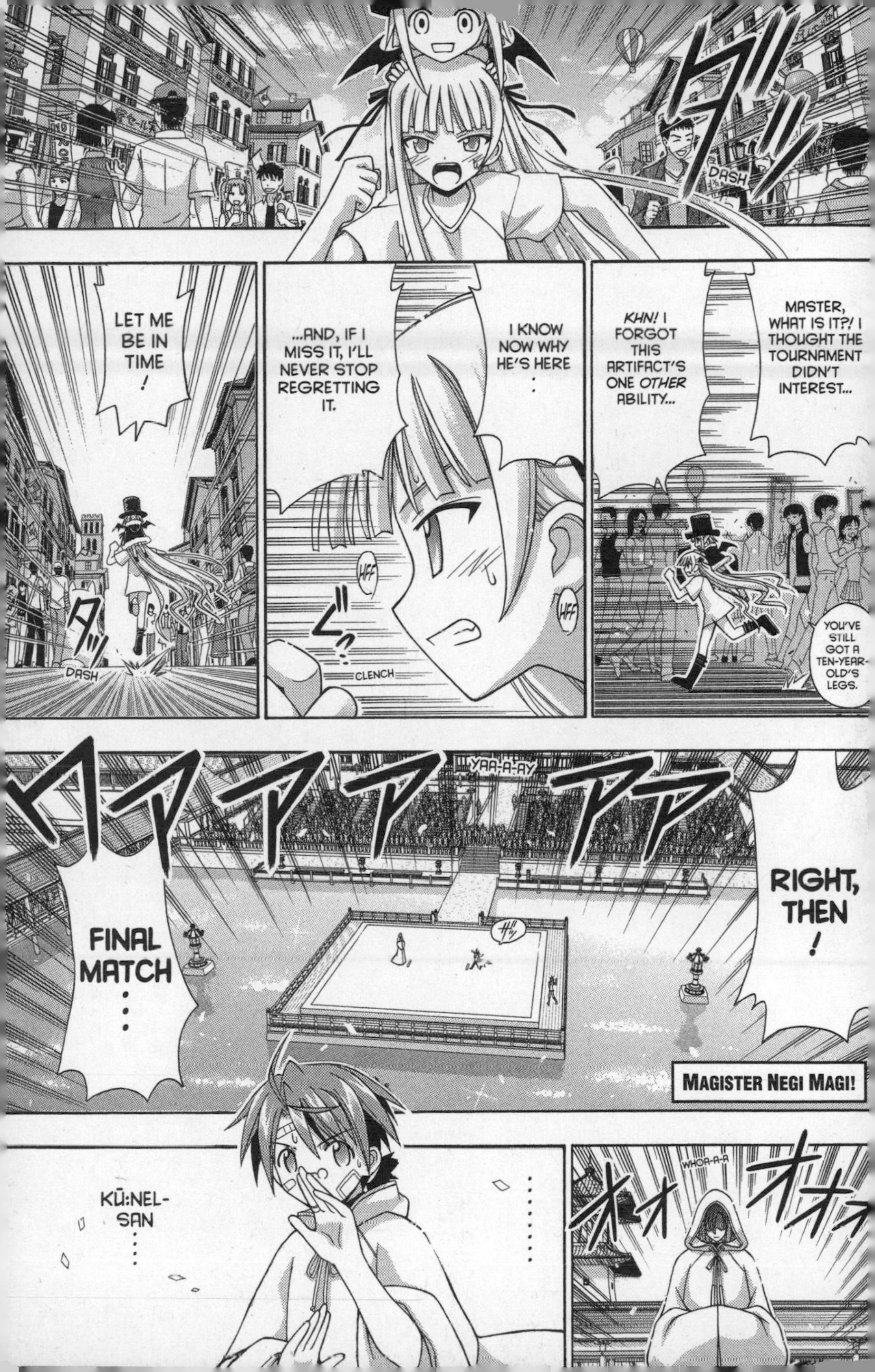
DASH
MASTER, WHAT IS IT?! I THOUGHT THE TOURNAMENT DIDN'T INTEREST...
KHN! I FORGOT THIS ARTIFACT'S ONE *OTHER* ABILITY...
YOU'VE STILL GOT A TEN-YEAR-OLD'S LEGS.
I KNOW NOW WHY HE'S HERE
...AND, IF I MISS IT, I'LL NEVER STOP REGRETTING IT.
HFF
HFF
CLENCH
LET ME BE IN TIME !
DASH
YAA-A-AY
RIGHT, THEN !
FINAL MATCH ...
MAGISTER NEGI MAGI!
WHOA-A-A
......
KŪ:NEL-SAN ...

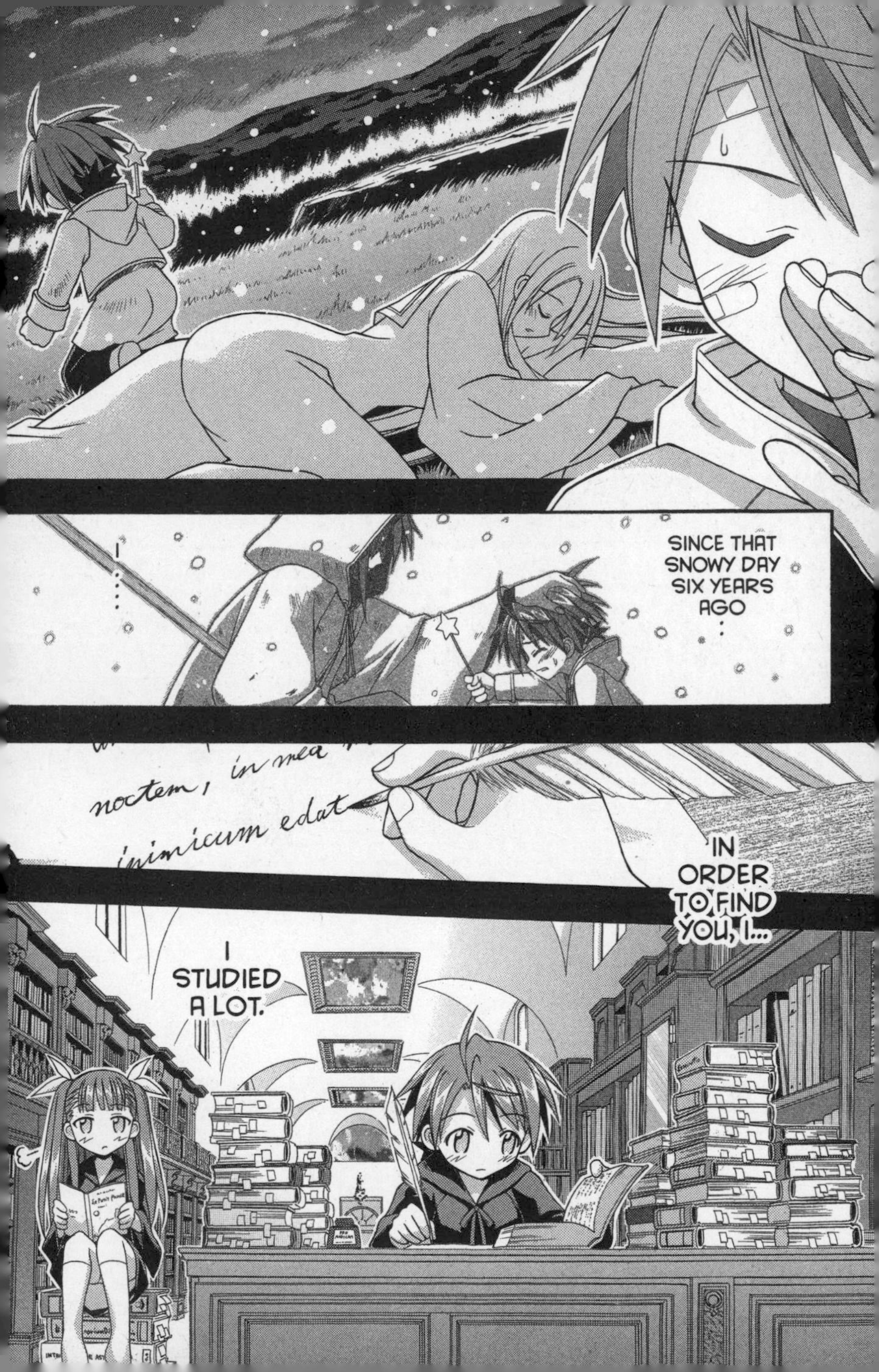
SINCE THAT SNOWY DAY SIX YEARS AGO...
I......
noctem, in mea
inimicum edat
IN ORDER TO FIND YOU, I...
I STUDIED A LOT.

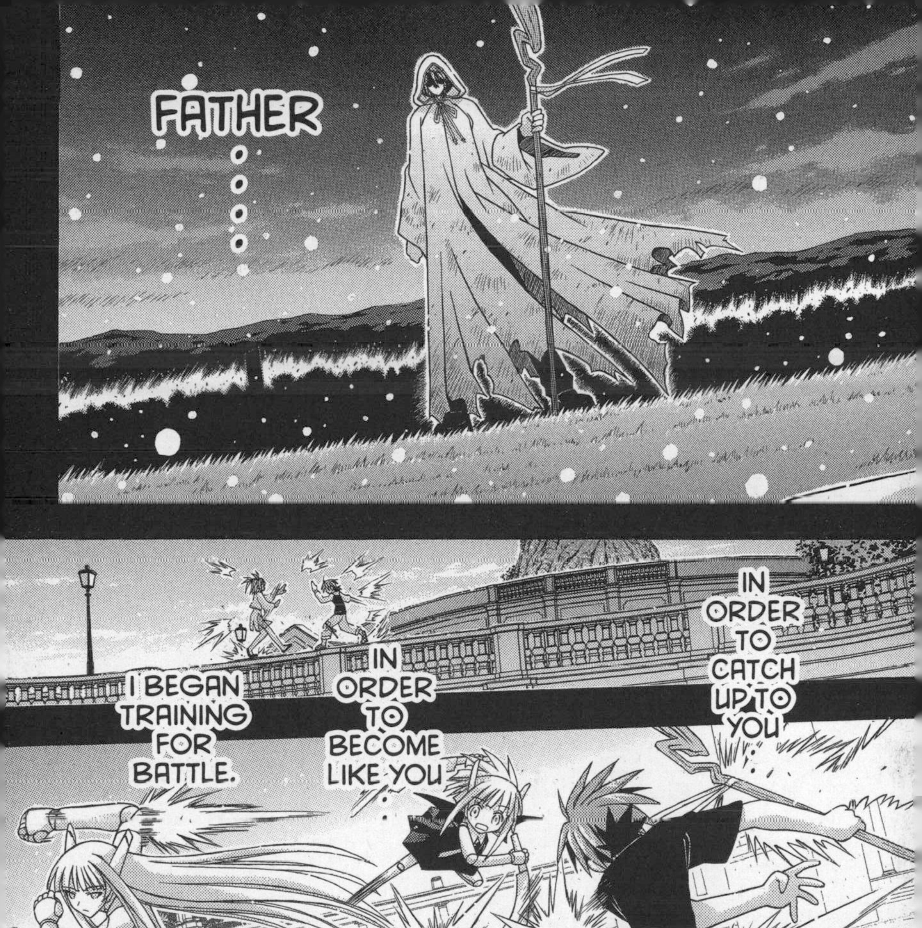
FATHER.....
IN ORDER TO CATCH UP TO YOU...
IN ORDER TO BECOME LIKE YOU...
I BEGAN TRAINING FOR BATTLE.
I MAY EVEN ALLOW YOU...
...TO FIGHT YOUR FATHER, NAGI SPRINGFIELD.
FATHER...
WILL I REALLY SEE YOU, TODAY?

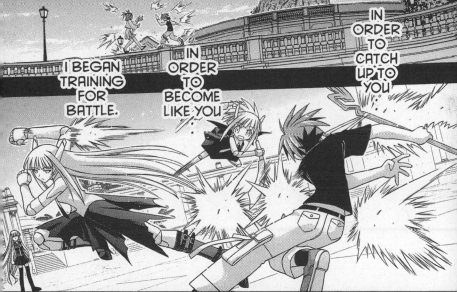

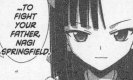

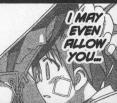

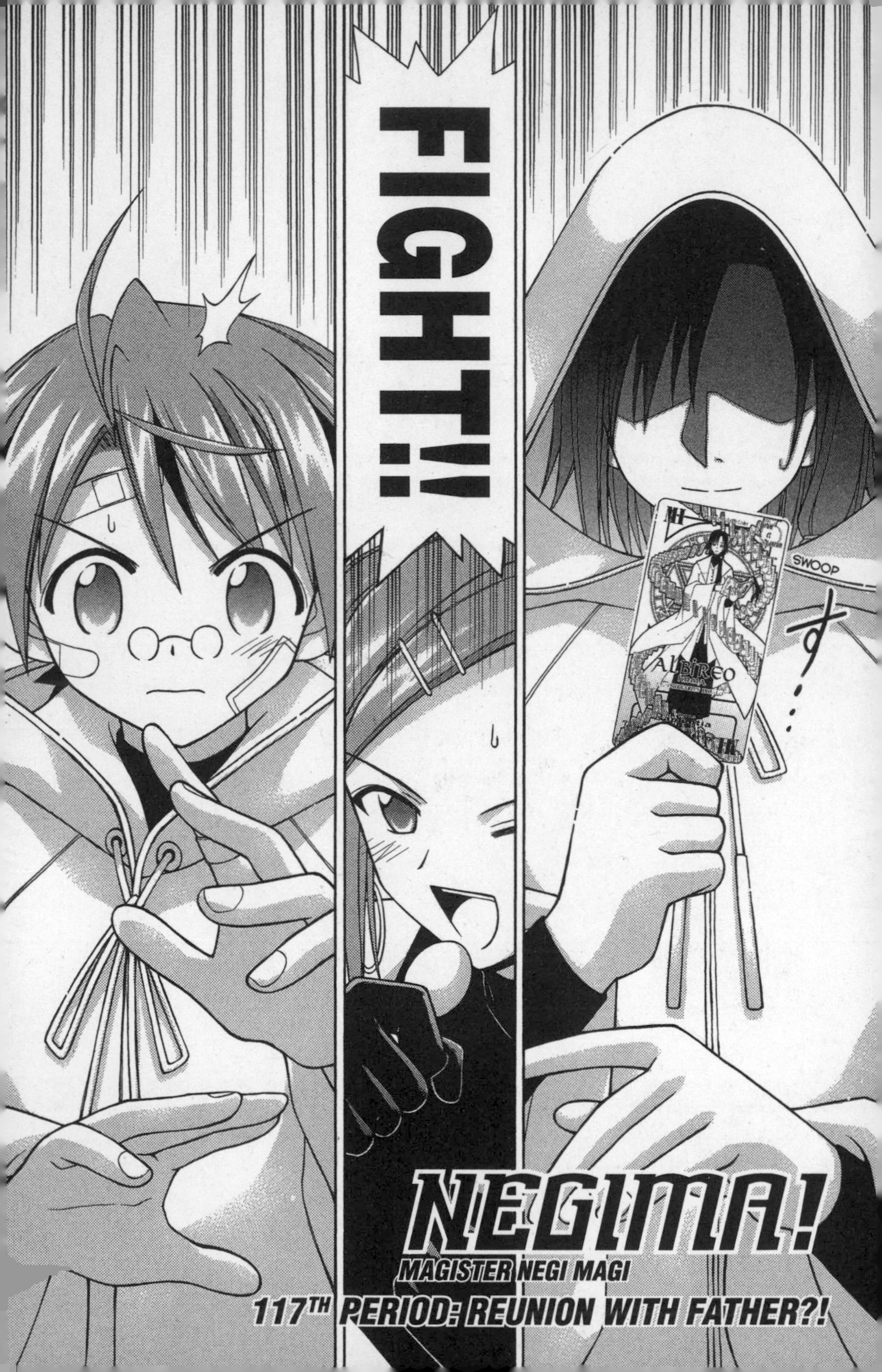
SWOOP
す…
FIGHT!!
NEGIMA!
MAGISTER NEGI MAGI
117TH PERIOD: REUNION WITH FATHER?!

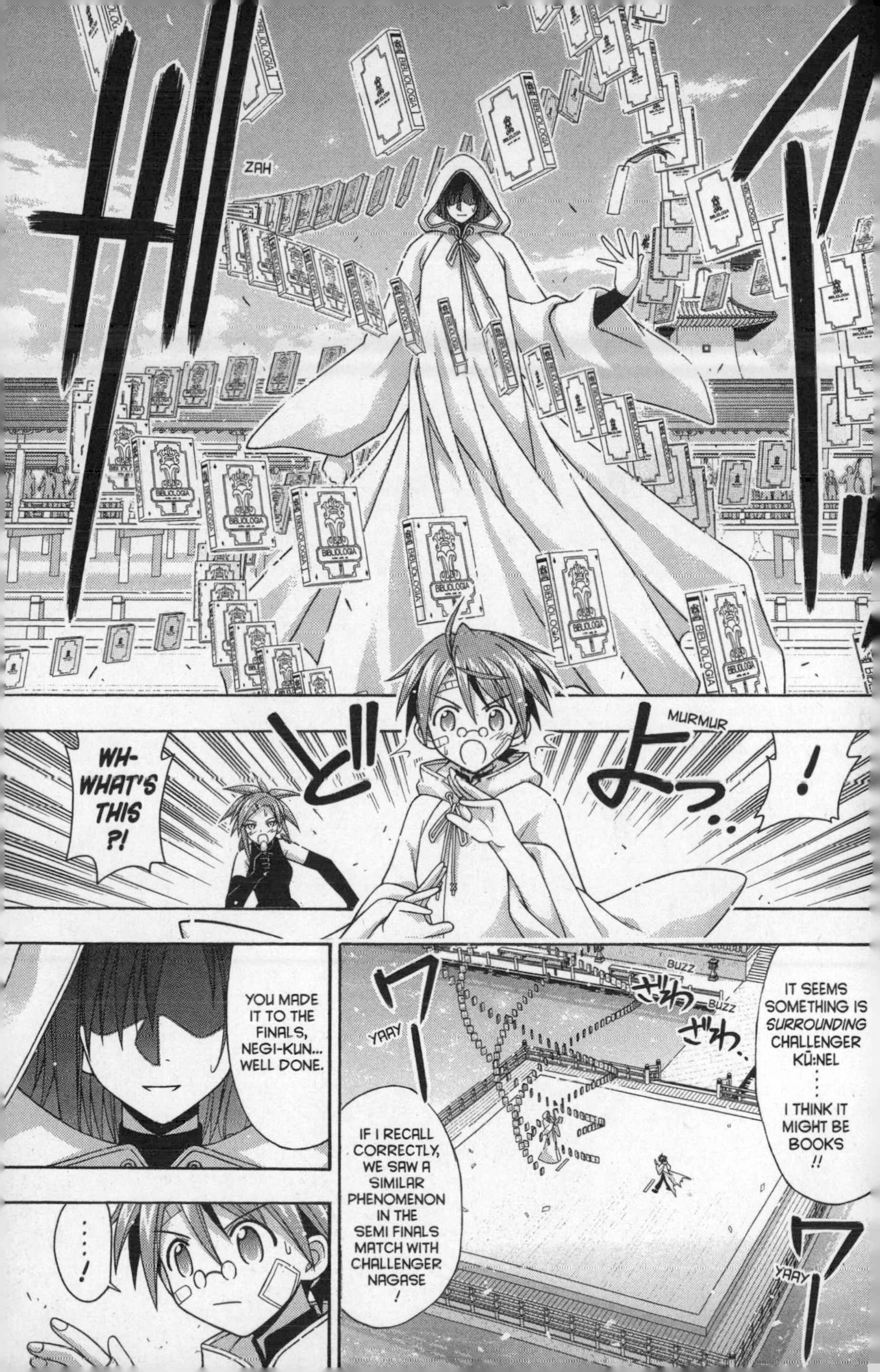

ZAH
MURMUR
どよっ..!
WH- WHAT'S THIS ?!
IT SEEMS SOMETHING IS *SURROUNDING* CHALLENGER KŪ:NEL
.....
I THINK IT MIGHT BE BOOKS !!
BUZZ
ざわ
BUZZ
ざわ..
YAAY
ワー
YAAY
ワー
IF I RECALL CORRECTLY, WE SAW A SIMILAR PHENOMENON IN THE SEMI FINALS MATCH WITH CHALLENGER NAGASE !
YOU MADE IT TO THE FINALS, NEGI-KUN... WELL DONE.
....!

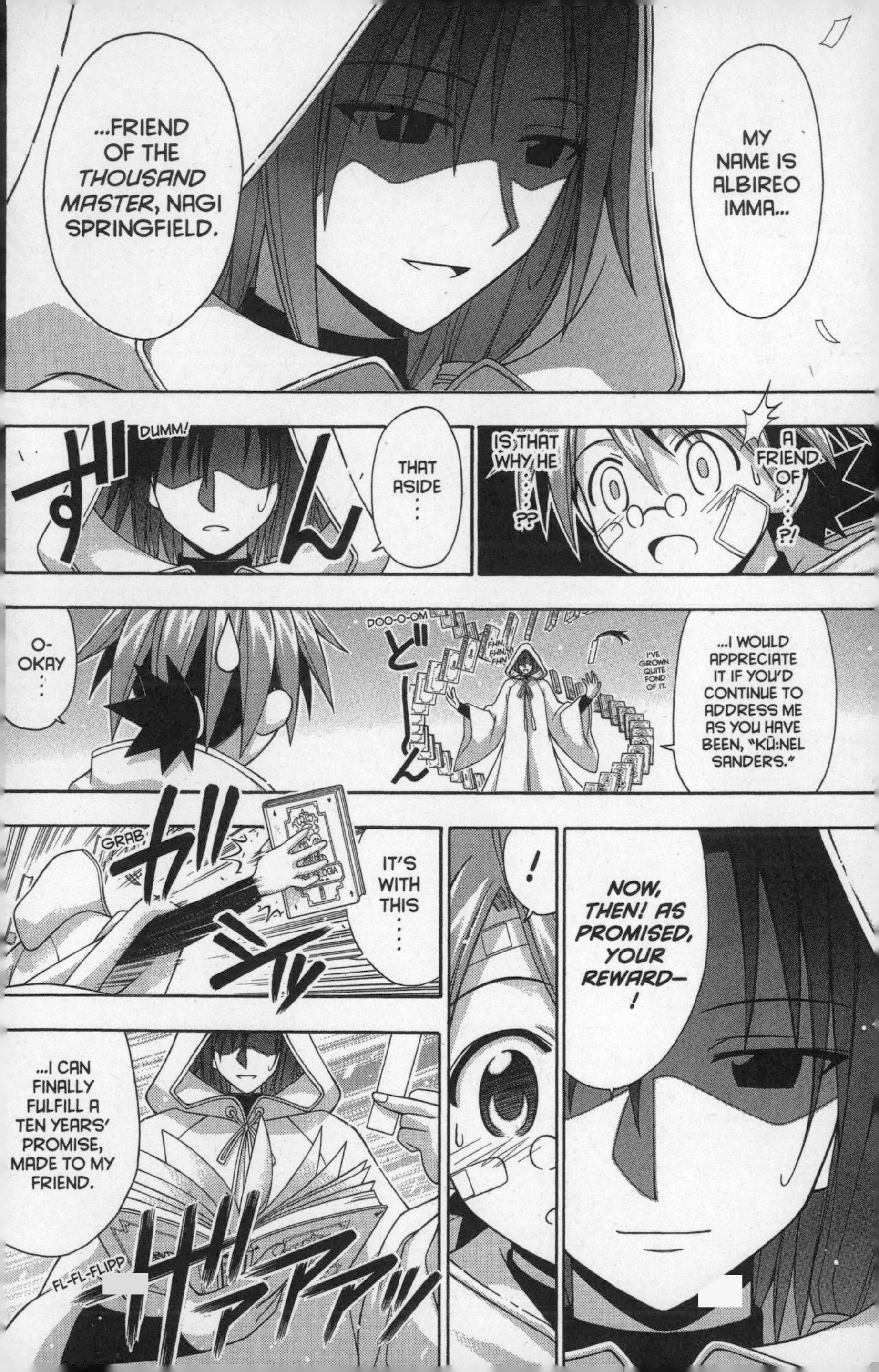
MY NAME IS ALBIREO IMMA...
...FRIEND OF THE *THOUSAND MASTER*, NAGI SPRINGFIELD.
A FRIEND OF...?!
IS THAT WHY HE ??
THAT ASIDE...
DUMM!
...I WOULD APPRECIATE IT IF YOU'D CONTINUE TO ADDRESS ME AS YOU HAVE BEEN, "KŪ:NEL SANDERS."
I'VE GROWN QUITE FOND OF IT.
FHN FHN FHN
DOO-O-OM
O-OKAY...
NOW, THEN! AS PROMISED, YOUR REWARD—!
!
IT'S WITH THIS...
GRAB
...I CAN FINALLY FULFILL A TEN YEARS' PROMISE, MADE TO MY FRIEND.
FL-FL-FLIPP

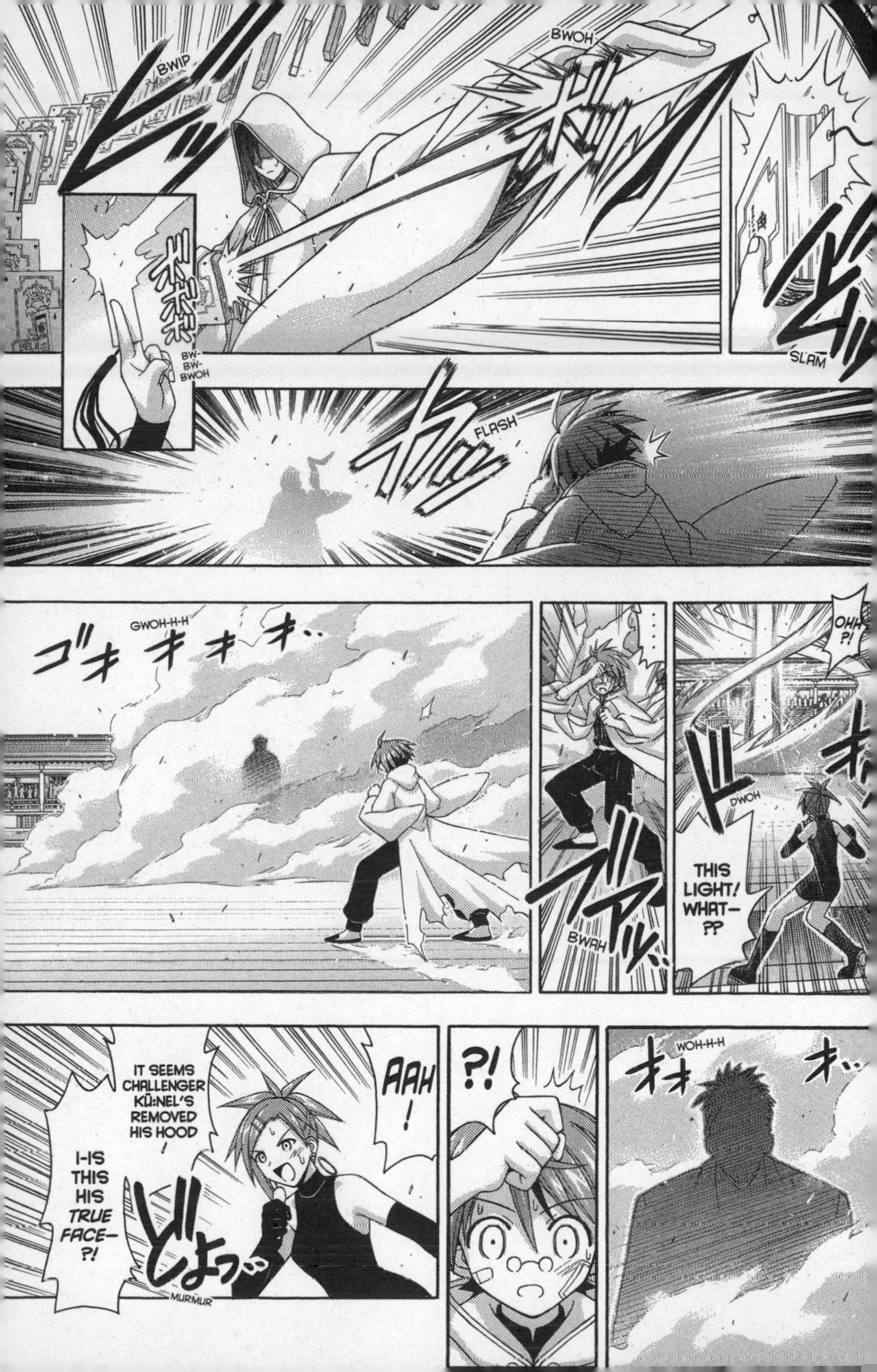
SLAM
BWOH
BWIP
BW-BW-BWOH
FLASH
OHH?!
DWOH
THIS LIGHT! WHAT—??
BWAH
GWOH-H-H
WOH-H-H
?!
AAH!
IT SEEMS CHALLENGER KŪ:NEL'S REMOVED HIS HOOD!
I-IS THIS HIS TRUE FACE—?!
MURMUR

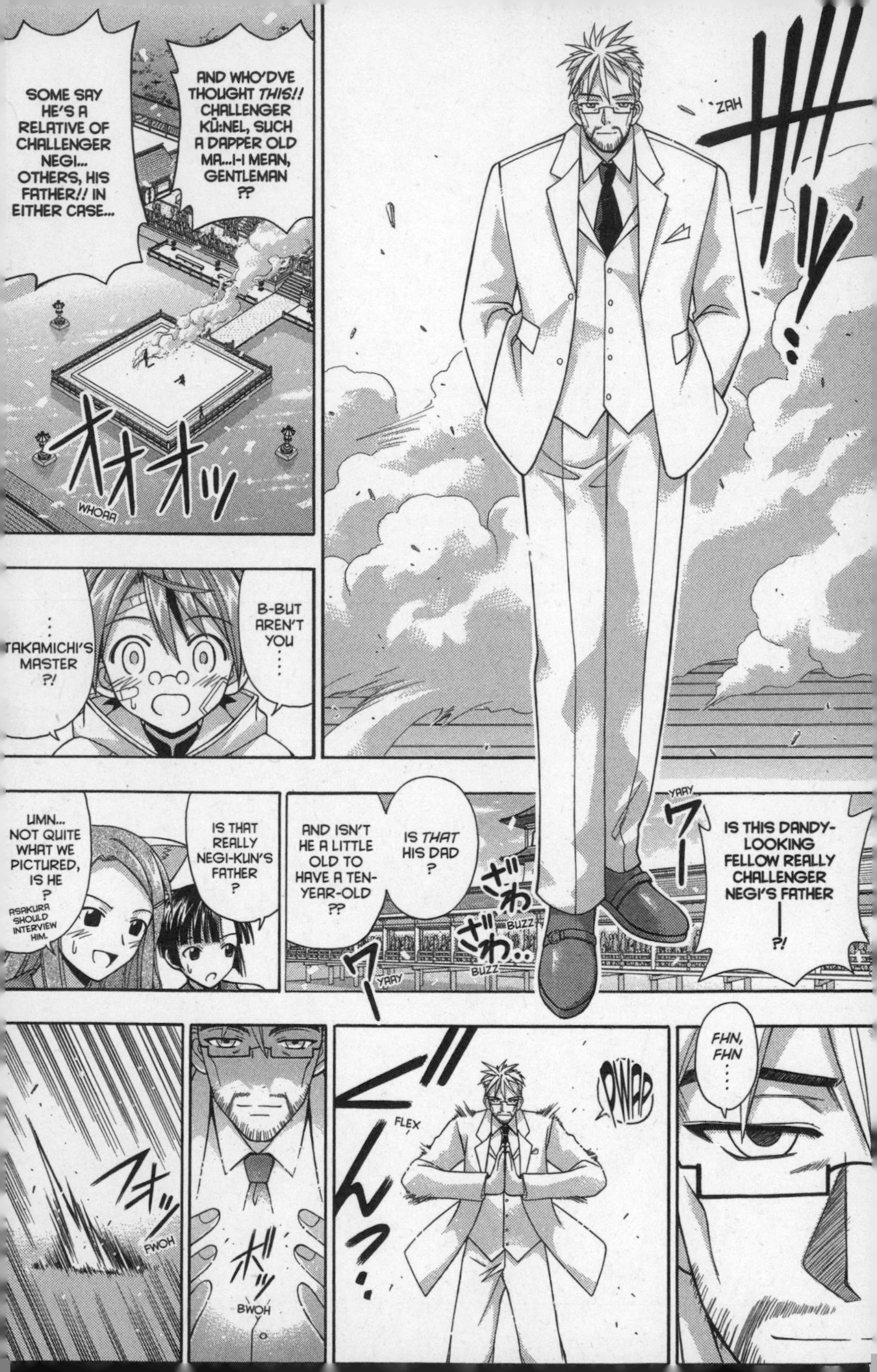

ZAH
AND WHO'D'VE THOUGHT *THIS!!* CHALLENGER KŪ:NEL, SUCH A DAPPER OLD MA...I-I MEAN, GENTLEMAN ??
SOME SAY HE'S A RELATIVE OF CHALLENGER NEGI... OTHERS, HIS FATHER!! IN EITHER CASE...
WHOAA
B-BUT AREN'T YOU ....
... TAKAMICHI'S MASTER ?!
IS THIS DANDY-LOOKING FELLOW REALLY CHALLENGER NEGI'S FATHER — ?!
YAAY
IS *THAT* HIS DAD ?
AND ISN'T HE A LITTLE OLD TO HAVE A TEN-YEAR-OLD ??
BUZZ
BUZZ
YAAY
IS THAT REALLY NEGI-KUN'S FATHER ?
UMN... NOT QUITE WHAT WE PICTURED, IS HE ?
ASAKURA SHOULD INTERVIEW HIM.
FHN, FHN ....
DWAP
FLEX
BWOH
FWOH

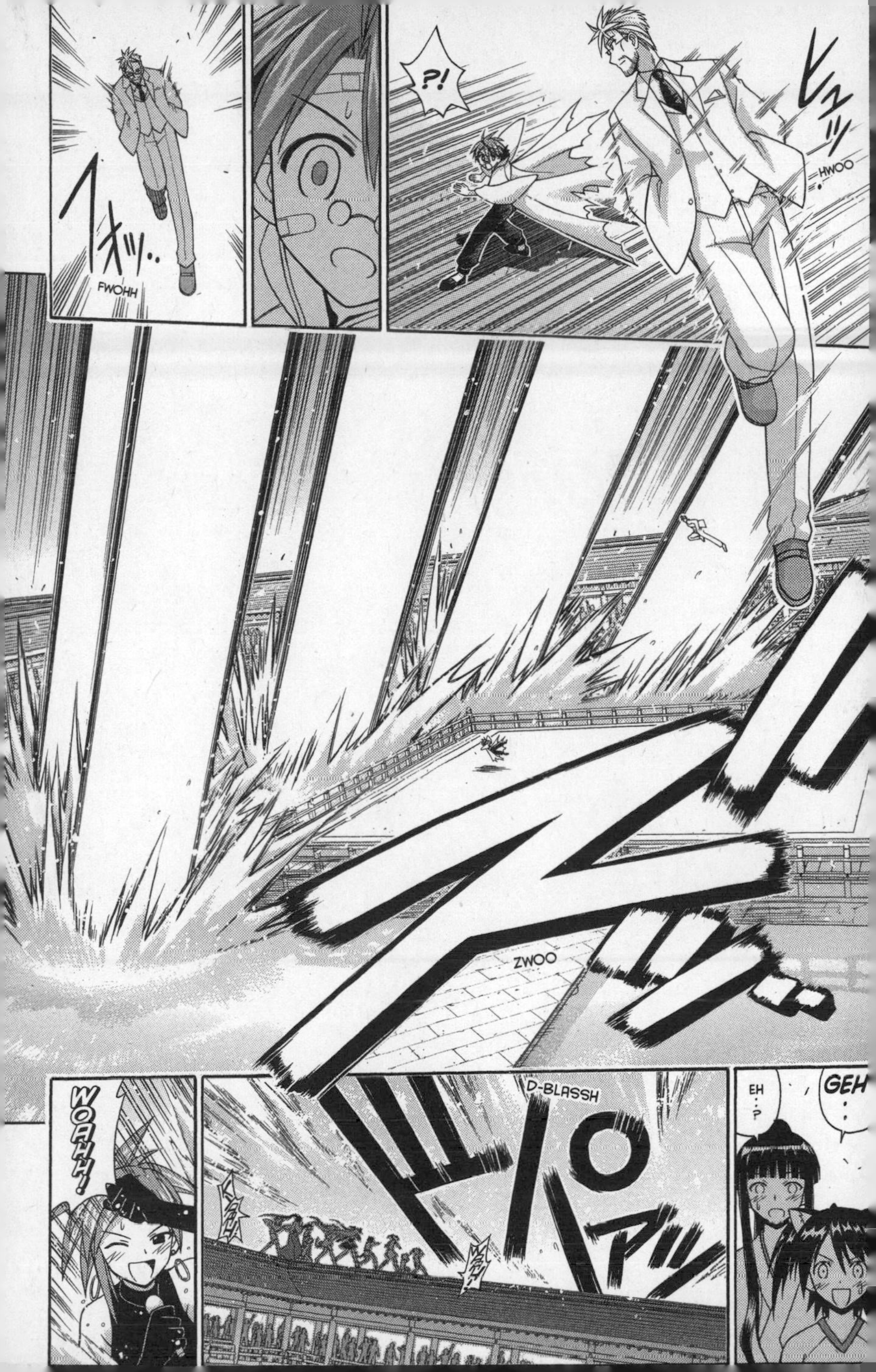
?!
HWOO
FWOHH
ZWOO
GEH...
EH...?
D-BLASSH
WOAHHH!

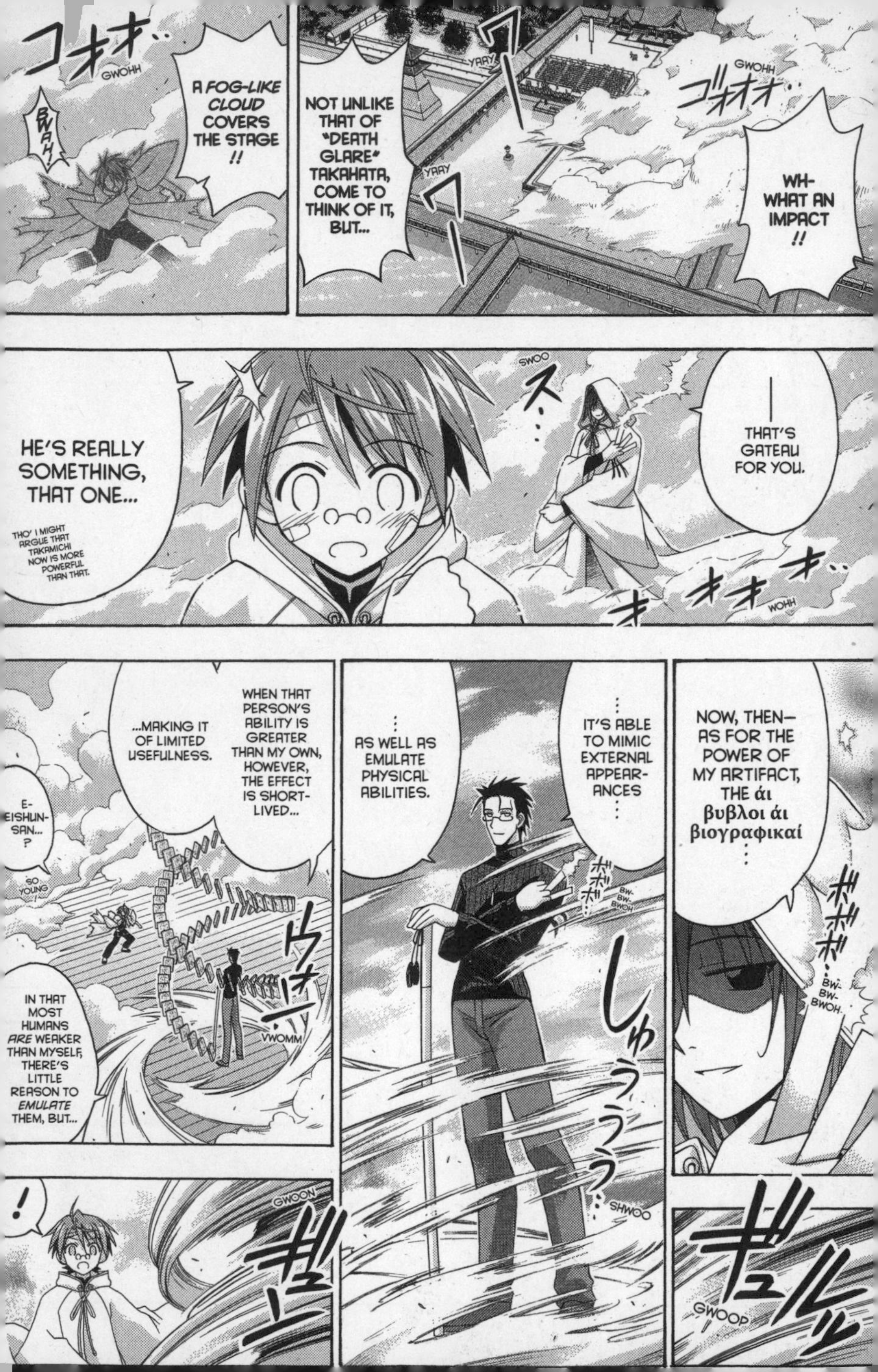
GWOHH
WH-WHAT AN IMPACT!!
YAAY
YAAY
NOT UNLIKE THAT OF "DEATH GLARE" TAKAHATA, COME TO THINK OF IT, BUT...
A FOG-LIKE CLOUD COVERS THE STAGE!!
GWOHH
BWAH!
THAT'S GATEAU FOR YOU.
SWOO
WOHH
HE'S REALLY SOMETHING, THAT ONE...
THO' I MIGHT ARGUE THAT TAKAMICHI NOW IS MORE POWERFUL THAN THAT.
NOW, THEN—AS FOR THE POWER OF MY ARTIFACT, THE άι βυβλοι άι βιογραφικαί...
BW-BW-BWOH.
...IT'S ABLE TO MIMIC EXTERNAL APPEARANCES...
...AS WELL AS EMULATE PHYSICAL ABILITIES.
BW-BW-BWOH
SHWOO
WHEN THAT PERSON'S ABILITY IS GREATER THAN MY OWN, HOWEVER, THE EFFECT IS SHORT-LIVED...
...MAKING IT OF LIMITED USEFULNESS.
E-EISHUN-SAN...?
SO YOUNG!
VWOMM
IN THAT MOST HUMANS ARE WEAKER THAN MYSELF, THERE'S LITTLE REASON TO EMULATE THEM, BUT...
GWOOP
GWOON
!

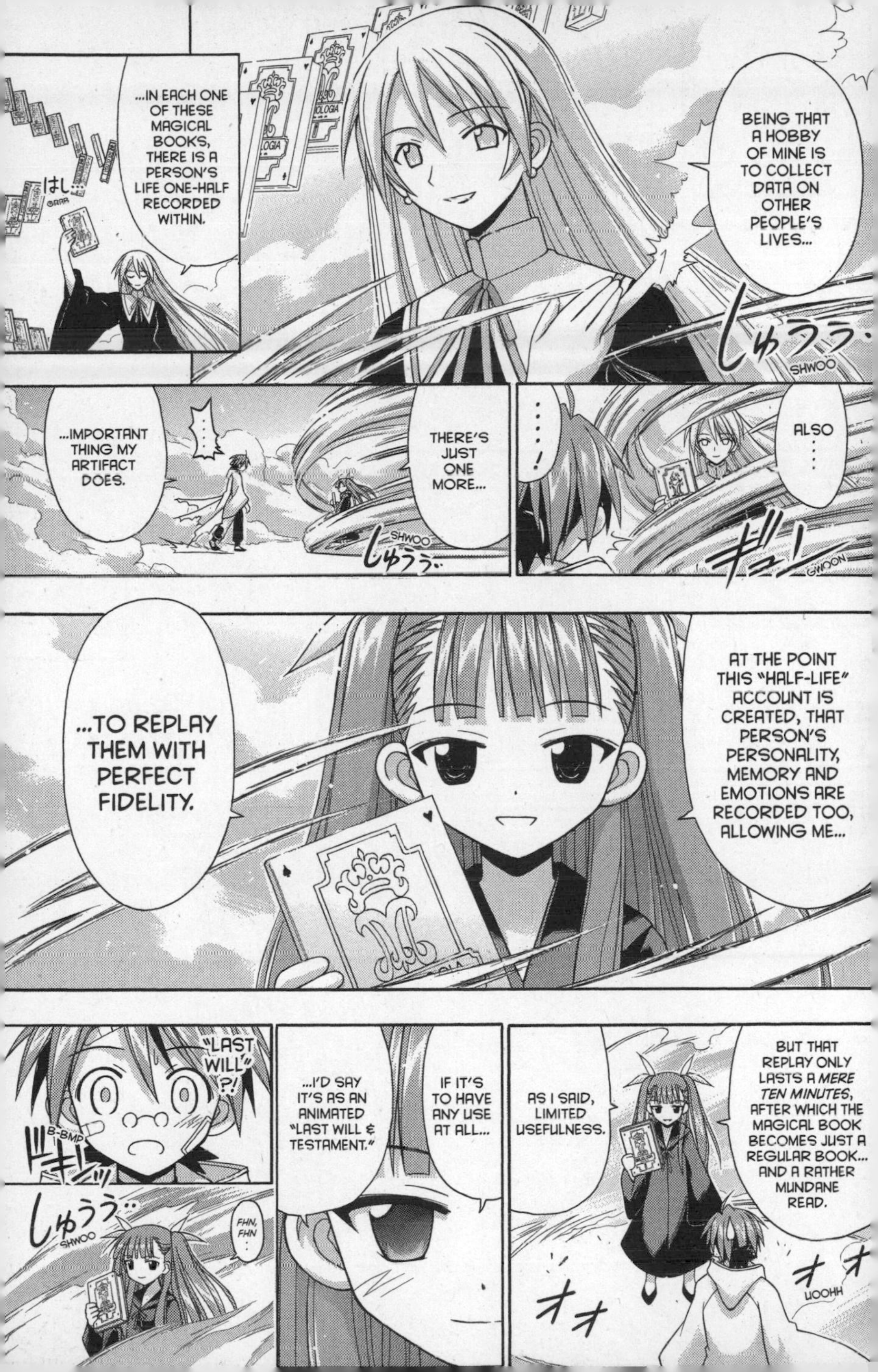
BEING THAT A HOBBY OF MINE IS TO COLLECT DATA ON OTHER PEOPLE'S LIVES...
SHWOO
...IN EACH ONE OF THESE MAGICAL BOOKS, THERE IS A PERSON'S LIFE ONE-HALF RECORDED WITHIN.
はし… GRAB
ALSO...
...!
GWOON
THERE'S JUST ONE MORE...
SHWOO
...IMPORTANT THING MY ARTIFACT DOES.
...!
AT THE POINT THIS "HALF-LIFE" ACCOUNT IS CREATED, THAT PERSON'S PERSONALITY, MEMORY AND EMOTIONS ARE RECORDED TOO, ALLOWING ME...
...TO REPLAY THEM WITH PERFECT FIDELITY.
BUT THAT REPLAY ONLY LASTS A *MERE TEN MINUTES*, AFTER WHICH THE MAGICAL BOOK BECOMES JUST A REGULAR BOOK... AND A RATHER MUNDANE READ.
AS I SAID, LIMITED USEFULNESS.
UOOHH
IF IT'S TO HAVE ANY USE AT ALL...
...I'D SAY IT'S AS AN ANIMATED "LAST WILL & TESTAMENT."
"LAST WILL"?!
B-BMP
SHWOO
FHN, FHN...

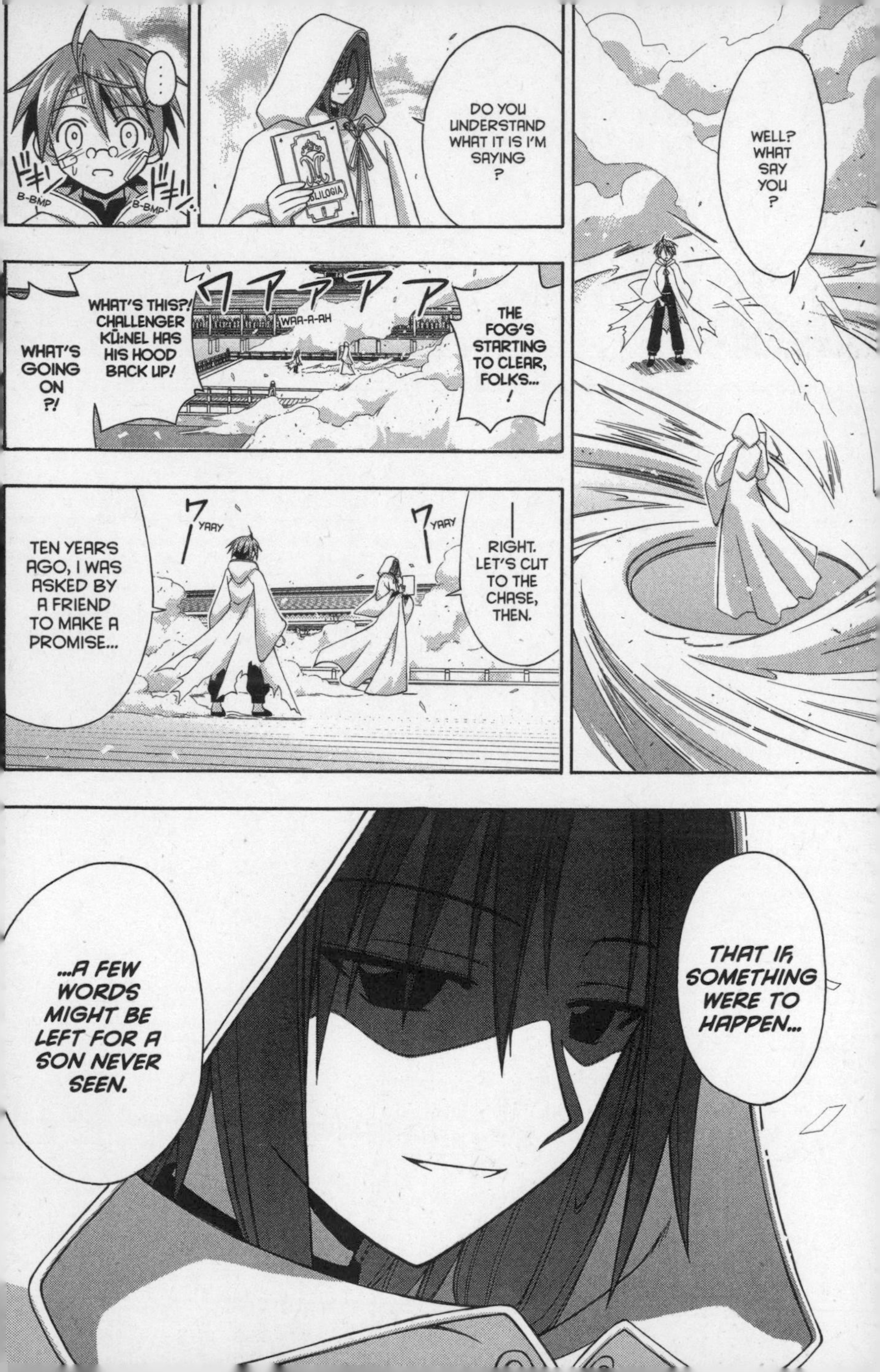
WELL? WHAT SAY YOU?
DO YOU UNDERSTAND WHAT IT IS I'M SAYING?
...
B-BMP
B-BMP
THE FOG'S STARTING TO CLEAR, FOLKS...!
WAA-A-AH
WHAT'S THIS?! CHALLENGER KŪ:NEL HAS HIS HOOD BACK UP!
WHAT'S GOING ON?!
RIGHT. LET'S CUT TO THE CHASE, THEN.
YAAY
YAAY
TEN YEARS AGO, I WAS ASKED BY A FRIEND TO MAKE A PROMISE...
THAT IF, SOMETHING WERE TO HAPPEN...
...A FEW WORDS MIGHT BE LEFT FOR A SON NEVER SEEN.

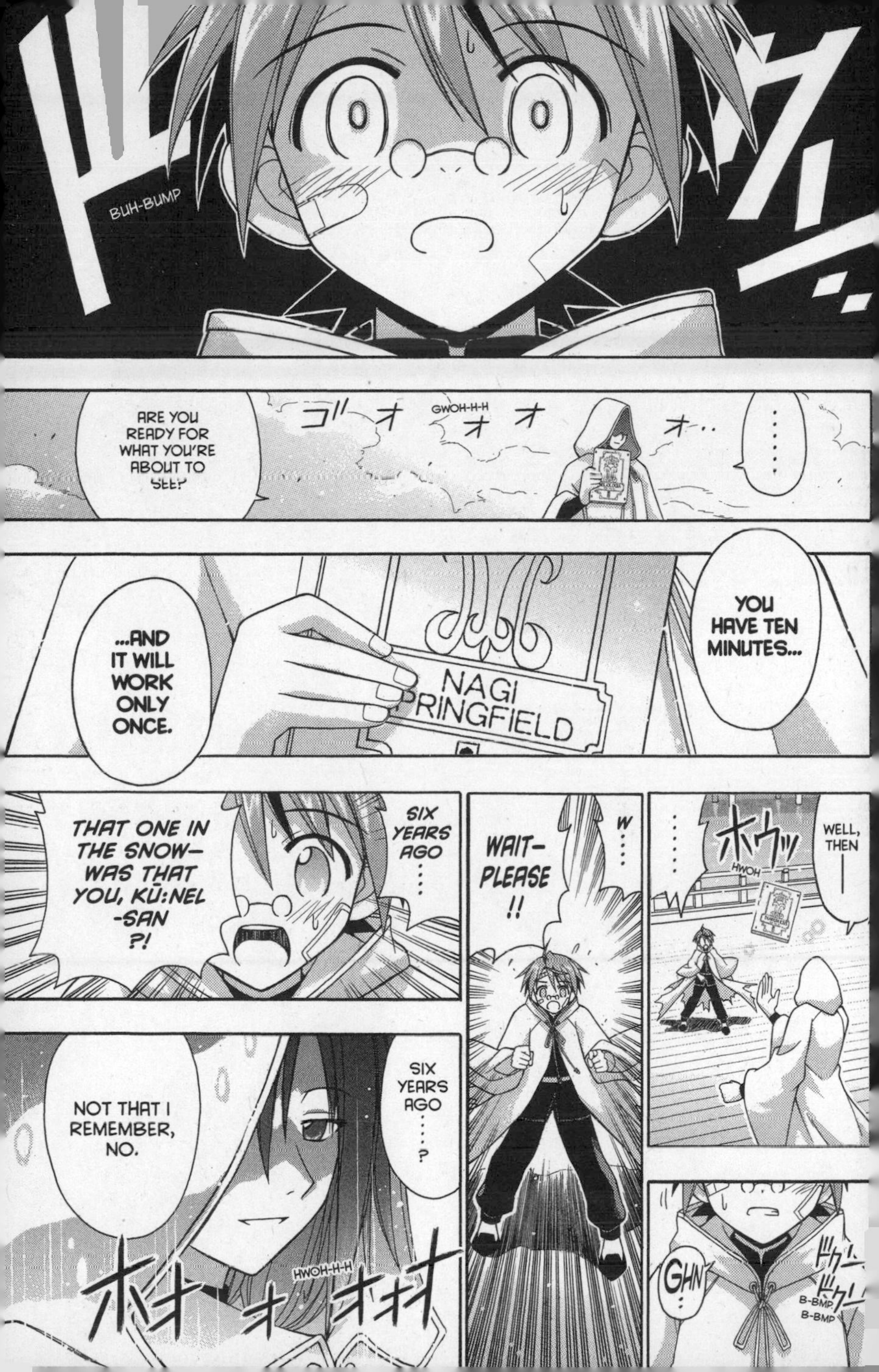
BUH-BUMP
......
ゴオオオオ..
GWOH-H-H
ARE YOU READY FOR WHAT YOU'RE ABOUT TO SEE?
YOU HAVE TEN MINUTES...
...AND IT WILL WORK ONLY ONCE.
NAGI
RINGFIELD
WELL, THEN—
ホウッ
HWOH
......
GHN
..
ドクン ドクン
B-BMP
B-BMP
W......
WAIT—PLEASE!!
SIX YEARS AGO....
THAT ONE IN THE SNOW—WAS THAT YOU, KŪ:NEL-SAN?!
SIX YEARS AGO.....?
NOT THAT I REMEMBER, NO.
ホオオオオ
HWOH-H-H

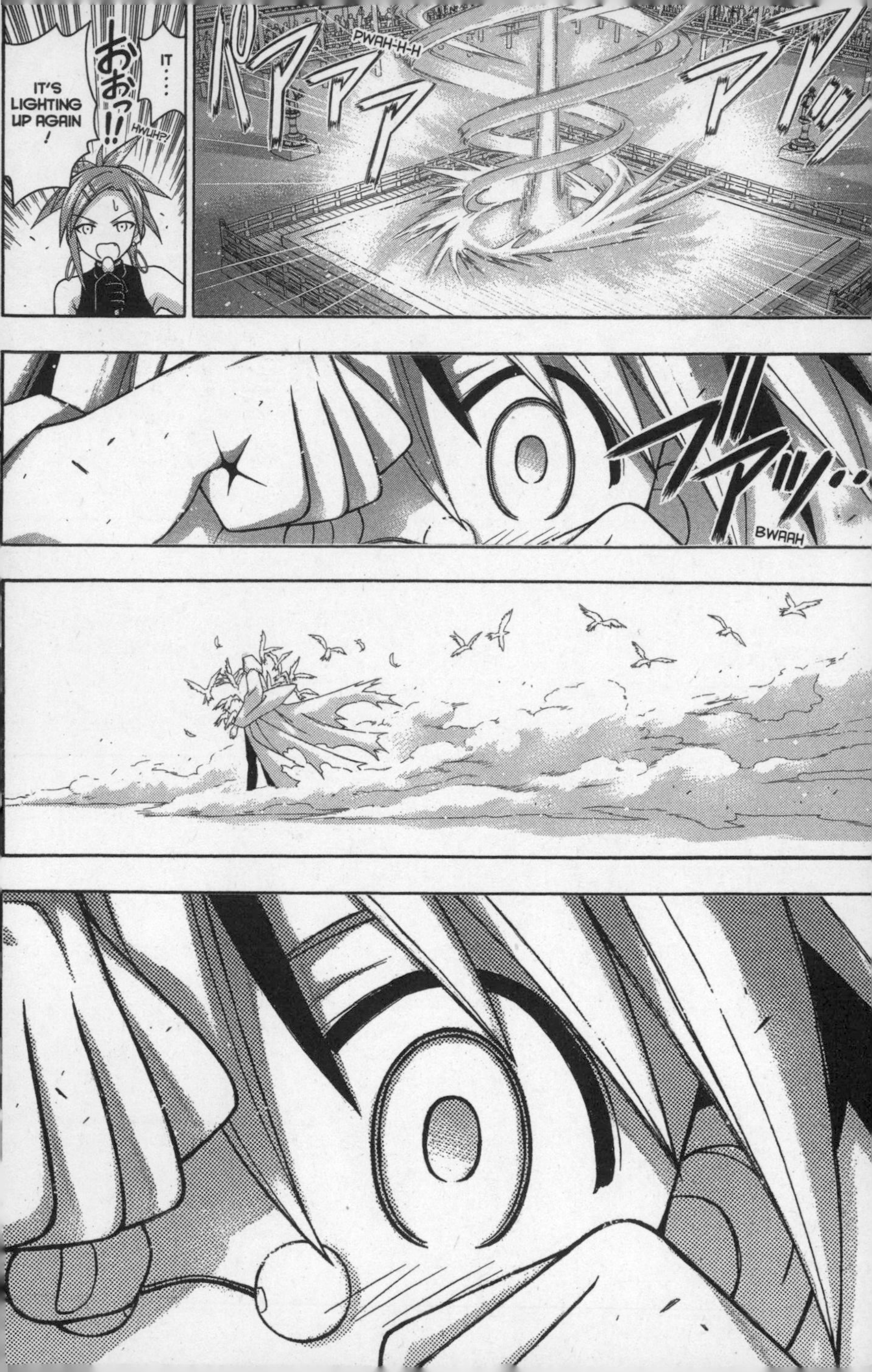
PWAH-H-H
IT.....
おおっ!!
HWUH?!
IT'S LIGHTING UP AGAIN!
BWAAH

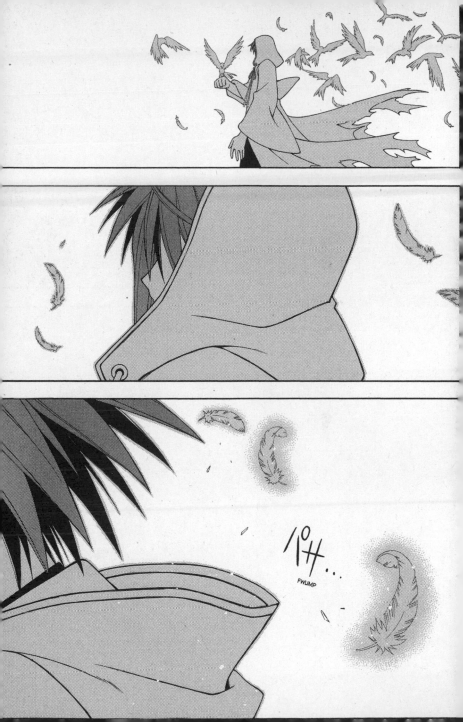

パサ...

FWUMP

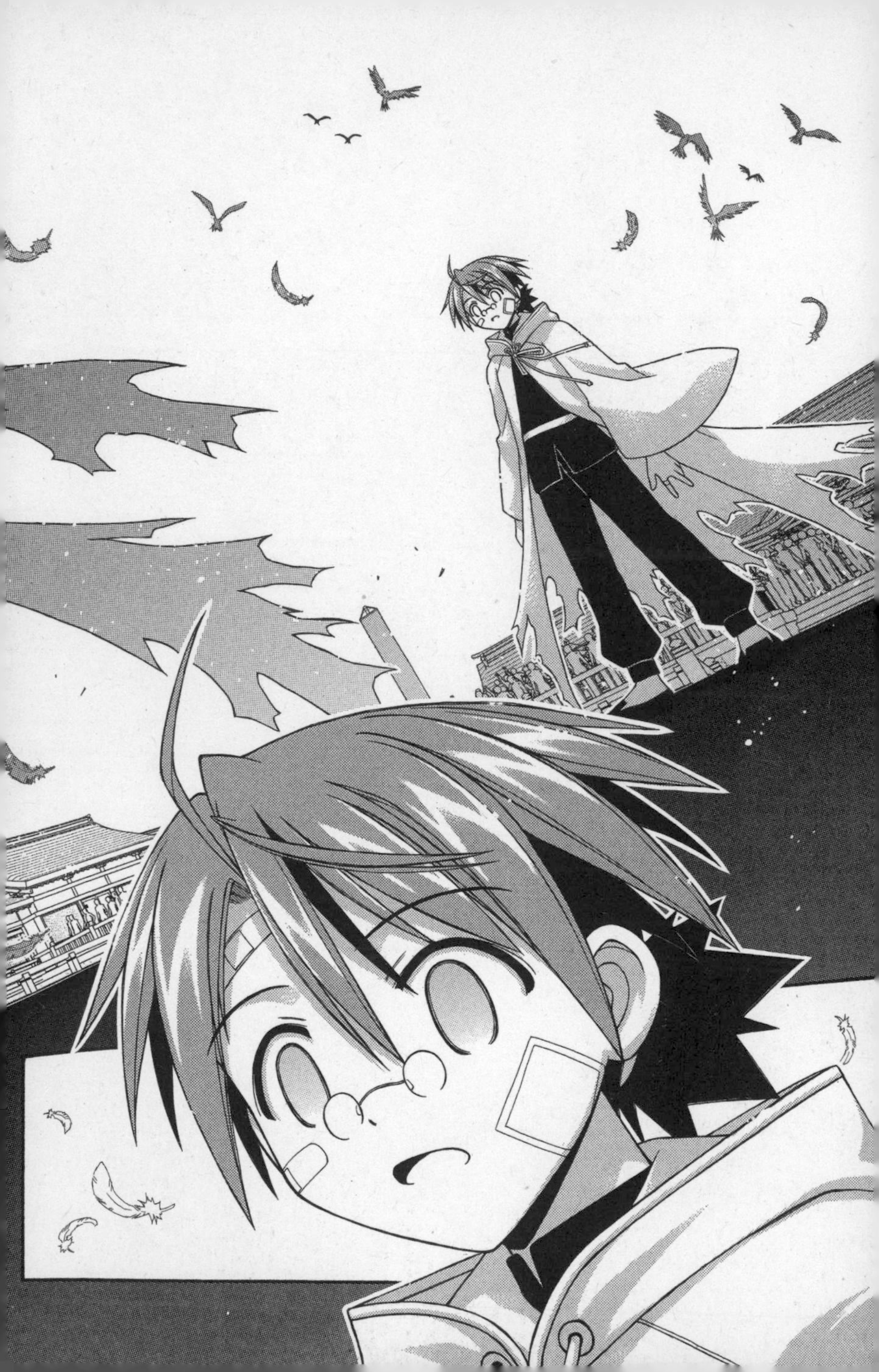

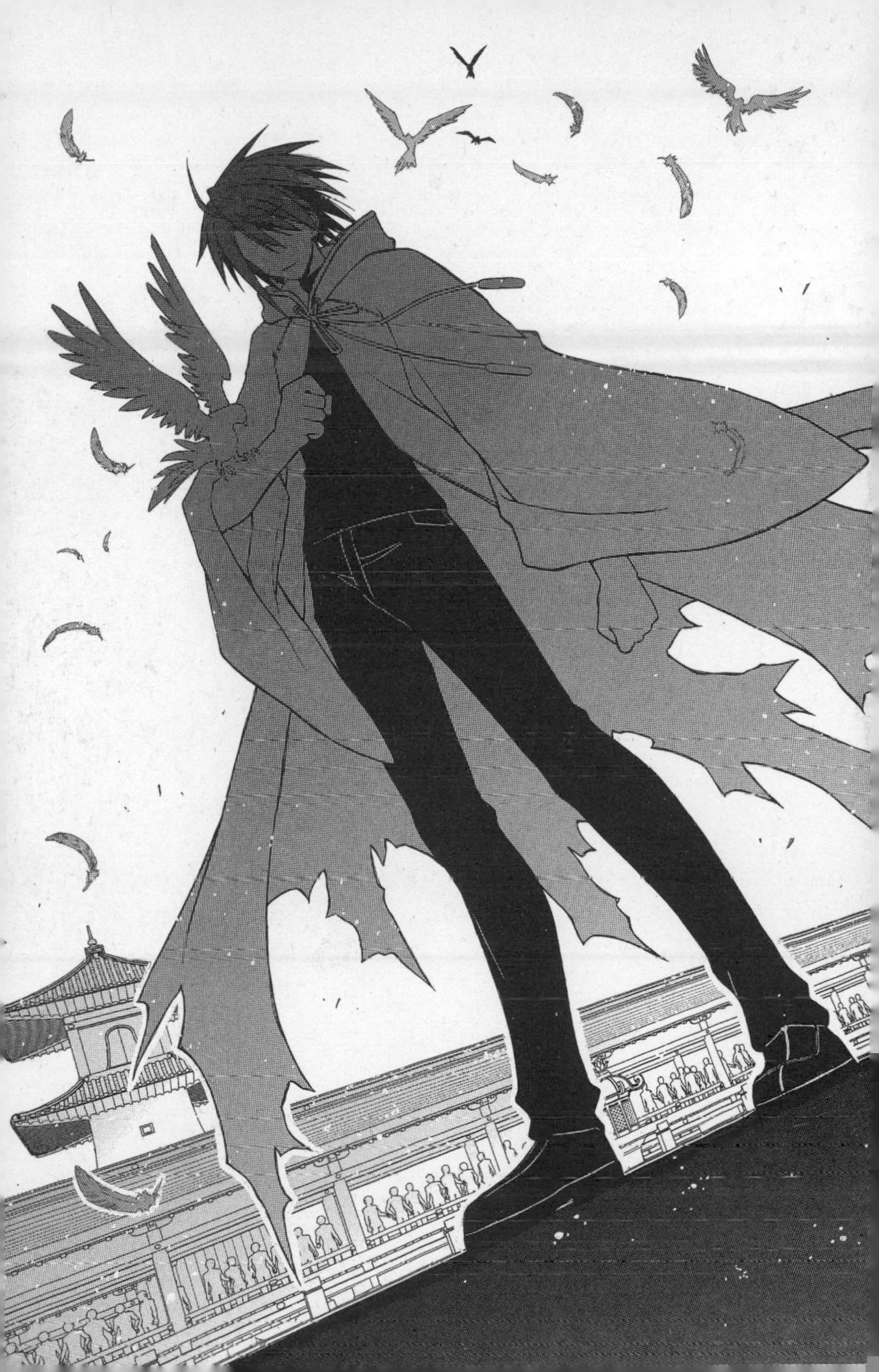

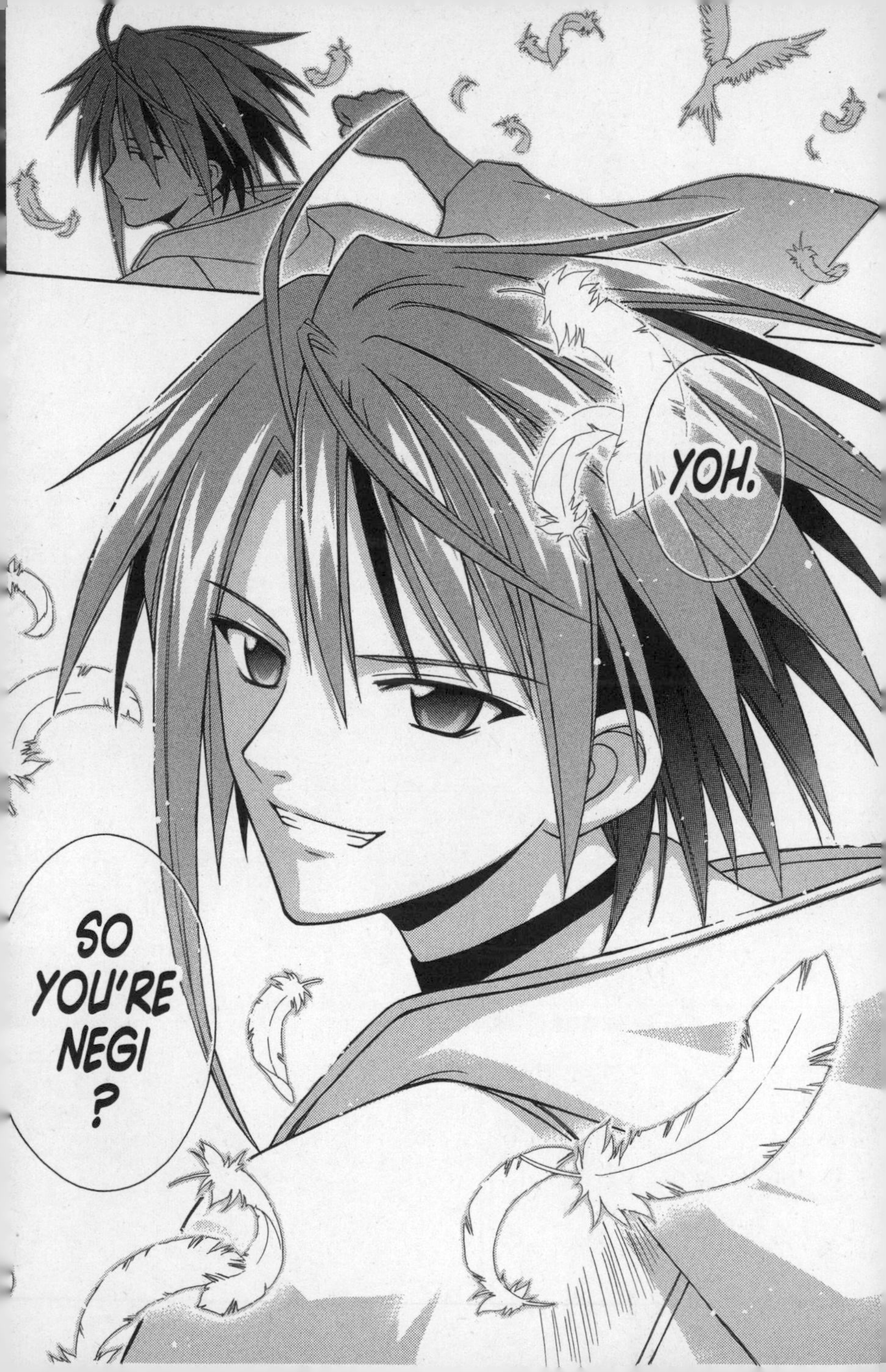
YOH.
SO YOU'RE NEGI ?

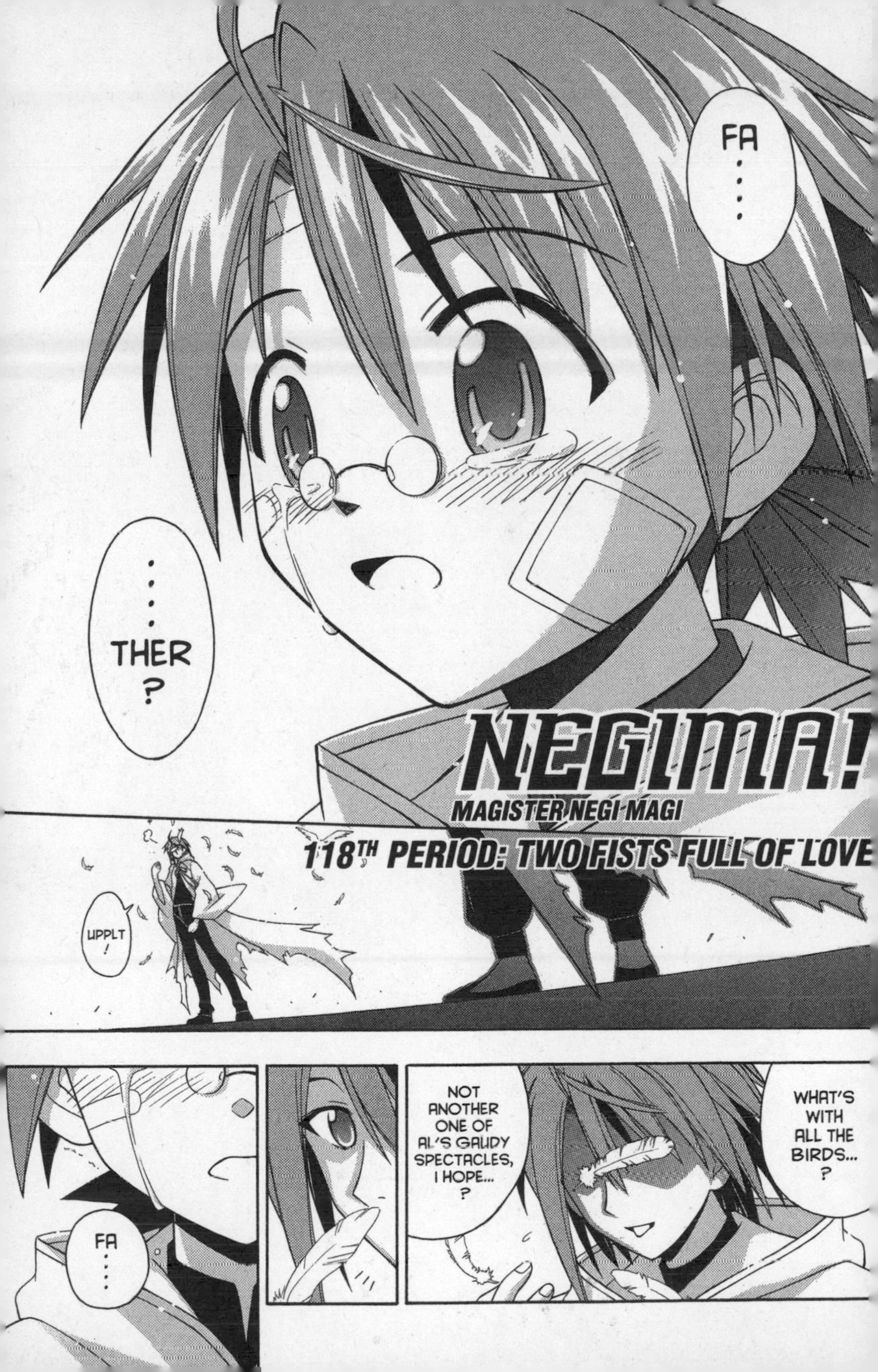
FA....
....THER?
NEGIMA!
MAGISTER NEGI MAGI
118TH PERIOD: TWO FISTS FULL OF LOVE
UPPLT!
WHAT'S WITH ALL THE BIRDS...?
NOT ANOTHER ONE OF AL'S GAUDY SPECTACLES, I HOPE...?
FA....

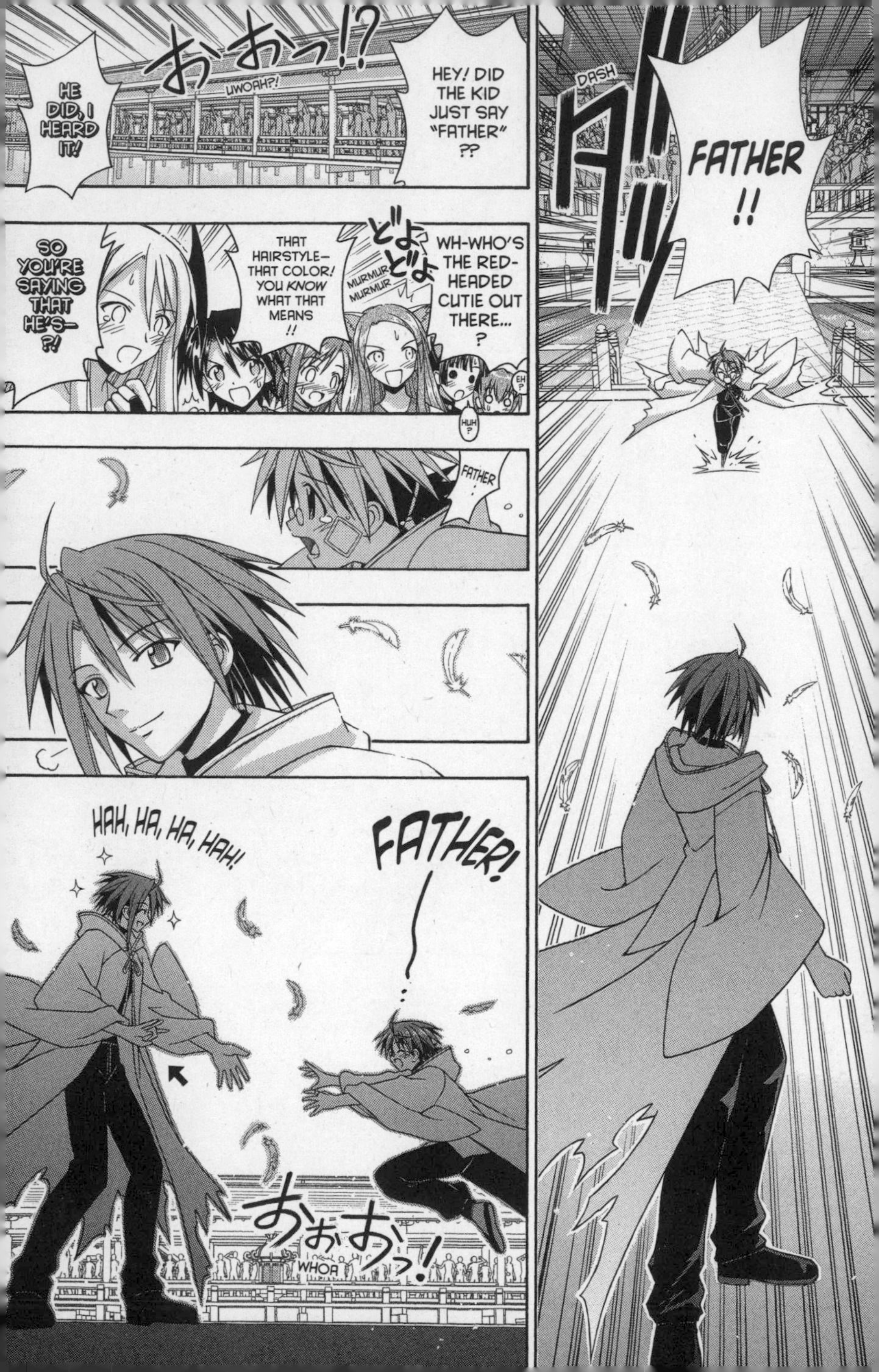
DASH
FATHER !!
おおっ!?
UWOAH?!
HEY! DID THE KID JUST SAY "FATHER" ??
HE DID, I HEARD IT!
WH-WHO'S THE RED-HEADED CUTIE OUT THERE... ?
どよどよ
MURMUR MURMUR
THAT HAIRSTYLE— THAT COLOR! YOU KNOW WHAT THAT MEANS !!
SO YOU'RE SAYING THAT HE'S— ?!
EH?
HUH?
FATHER ...
FATHER!
HAH, HA, HA, HAH!
おおおっ!
WHOA

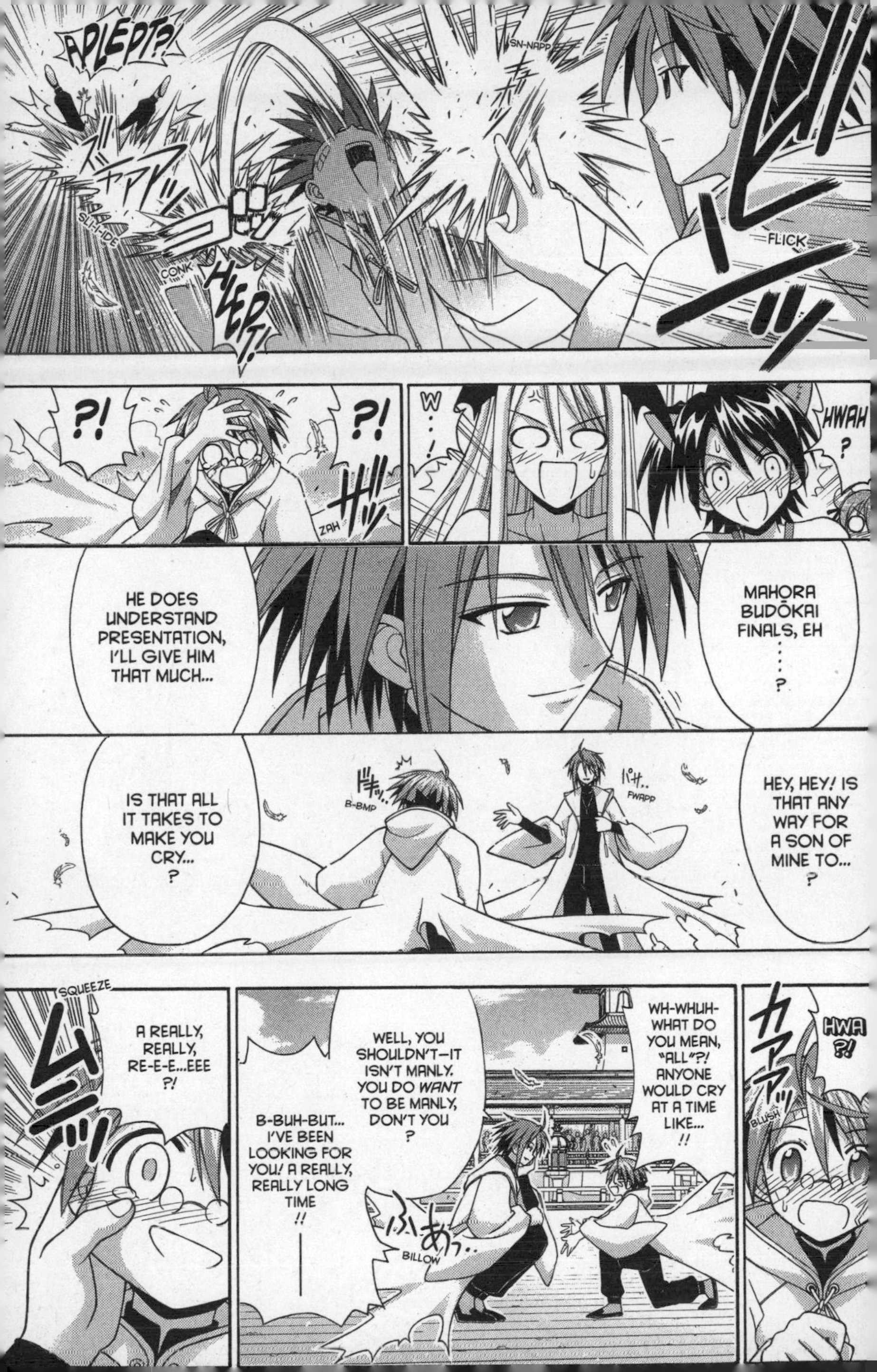
FLICK
SN-NAPP
HLEPT!
CONK
ADLEPT?!
SLIH-IDE
HWAH?
W...!
?!
?!
ZAH
MAHORA BUDŌKAI FINALS, EH.....?
HE DOES UNDERSTAND PRESENTATION, I'LL GIVE HIM THAT MUCH...
HEY, HEY! IS THAT ANY WAY FOR A SON OF MINE TO...?
FWAPP
B-BMP
IS THAT ALL IT TAKES TO MAKE YOU CRY...?
HWA?!
BLUSH
WH-WHUH-WHAT DO YOU MEAN, "ALL"?! ANYONE WOULD CRY AT A TIME LIKE...!!
WELL, YOU SHOULDN'T—IT ISN'T MANLY. YOU DO *WANT* TO BE MANLY, DON'T YOU?
B-BUH-BUT... I'VE BEEN LOOKING FOR YOU! A REALLY, REALLY LONG TIME!!
BILLOW
SQUEEZE
A REALLY, REALLY, RE-E-E...EEE?!

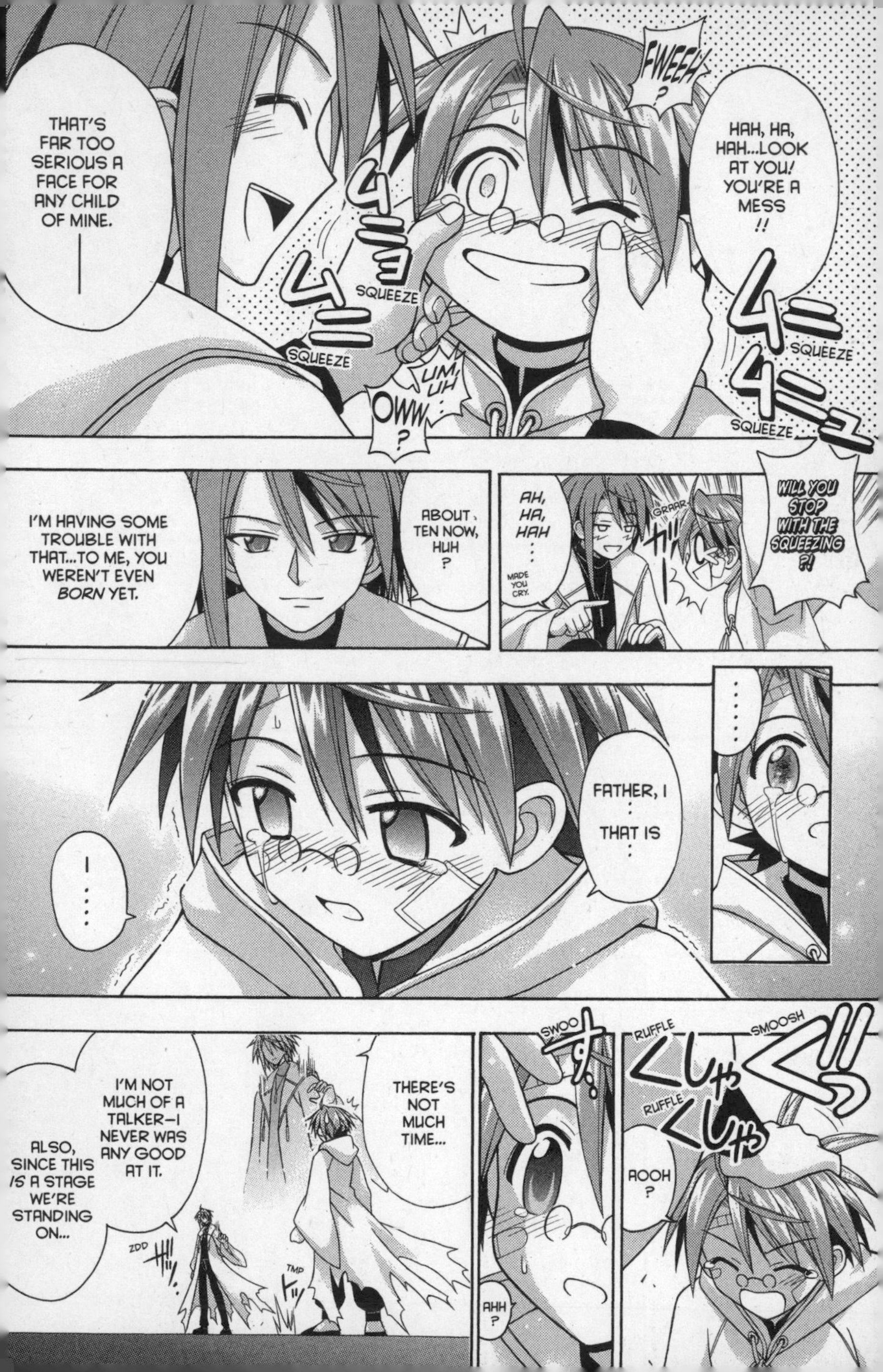
FWEEH?
HAH, HA, HAH...LOOK AT YOU! YOU'RE A MESS!!
SQUEEZE
SQUEEZE
SQUEEZE
SQUEEZE
THAT'S FAR TOO SERIOUS A FACE FOR ANY CHILD OF MINE.
UM, UH...
OWW?
WILL YOU STOP WITH THE SQUEEZING?!
GRAAR
AH, HA, HAH...
MADE YOU CRY.
ABOUT TEN NOW, HUH?
I'M HAVING SOME TROUBLE WITH THAT...TO ME, YOU WEREN'T EVEN *BORN* YET.
......
FATHER, I...THAT IS...
I......
SMOOSH
RUFFLE
RUFFLE
SWOO
AOOH?
AHH?
THERE'S NOT MUCH TIME...
I'M NOT MUCH OF A TALKER—I NEVER WAS ANY GOOD AT IT.
ALSO, SINCE THIS *IS* A STAGE WE'RE STANDING ON...
ZDD
TMP

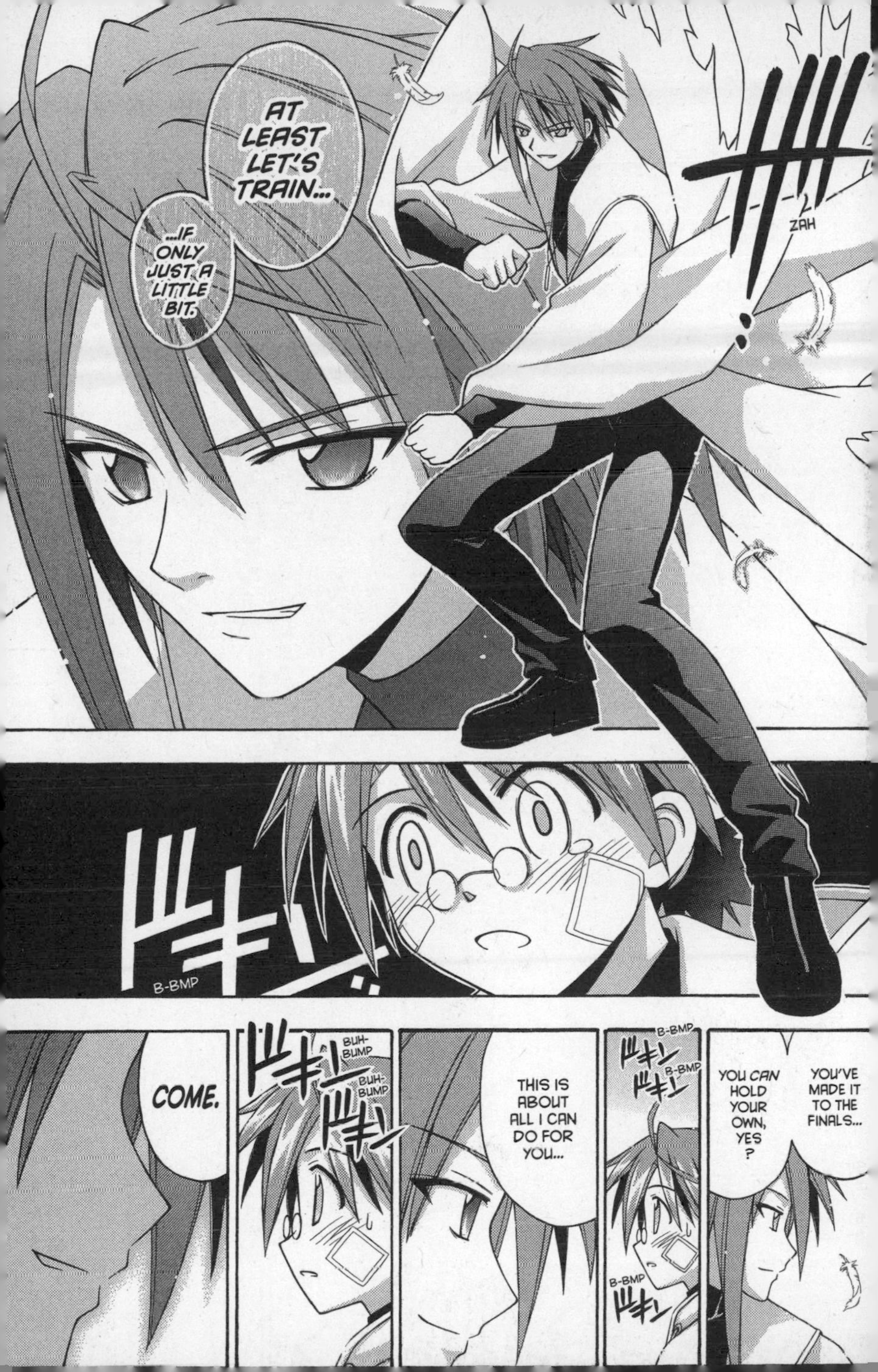
ZAH
AT LEAST LET'S TRAIN...
...IF ONLY JUST A LITTLE BIT.
B-BMP
YOU'VE MADE IT TO THE FINALS...
YOU *CAN* HOLD YOUR OWN, YES?
B-BMP
B-BMP
B-BMP
THIS IS ABOUT ALL I CAN DO FOR YOU...
BUH-BUMP
BUH-BUMP
COME.

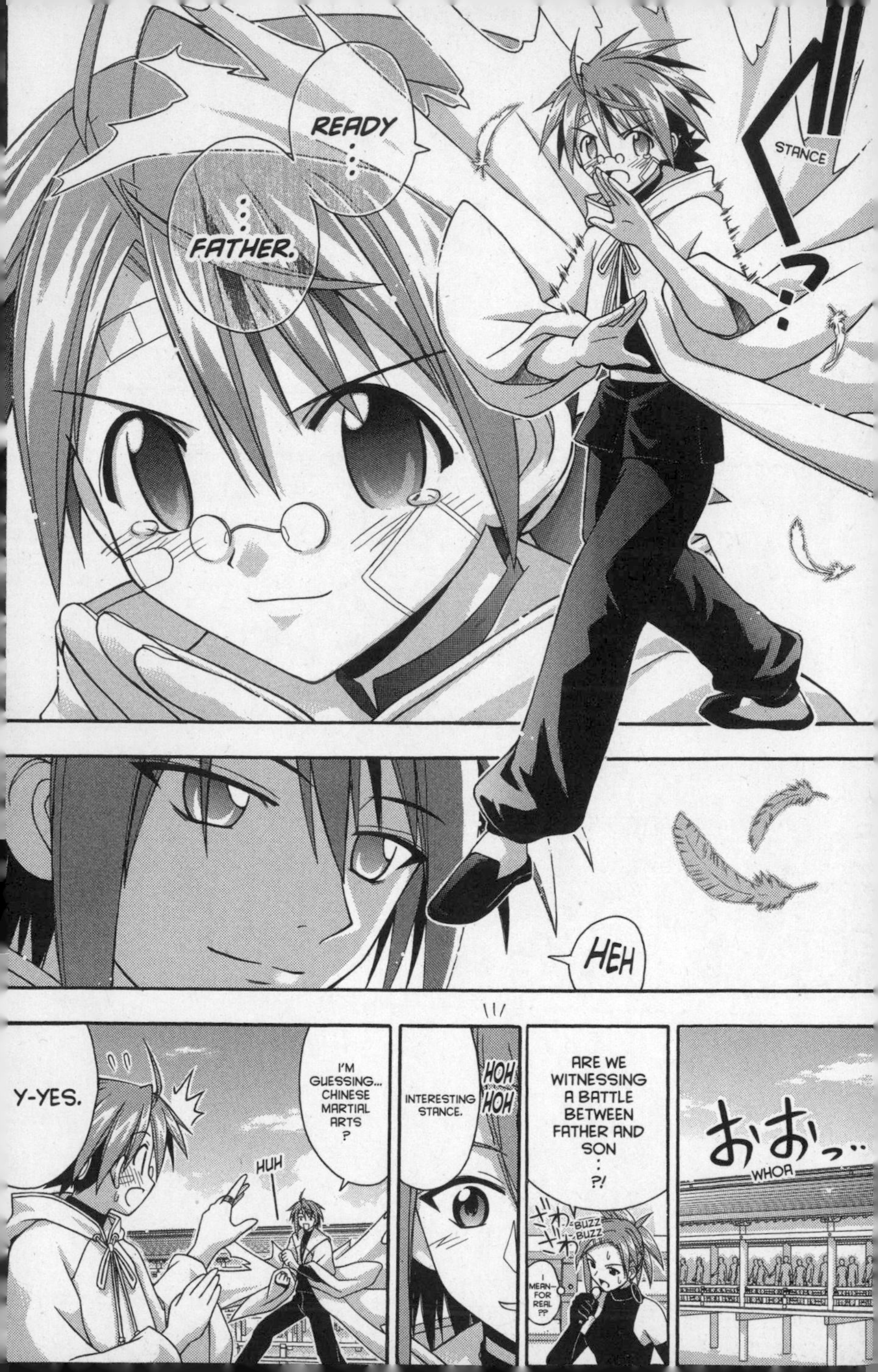
STANCE
READY...
...FATHER.
HEH
おおっ..
WHOA
ARE WE WITNESSING A BATTLE BETWEEN FATHER AND SON..?!
ざわ ざわ
BUZZ BUZZ
I MEAN—FOR REAL?!
HOH HOH
INTERESTING STANCE.
I'M GUESSING... CHINESE MARTIAL ARTS?
HUH
Y-YES.

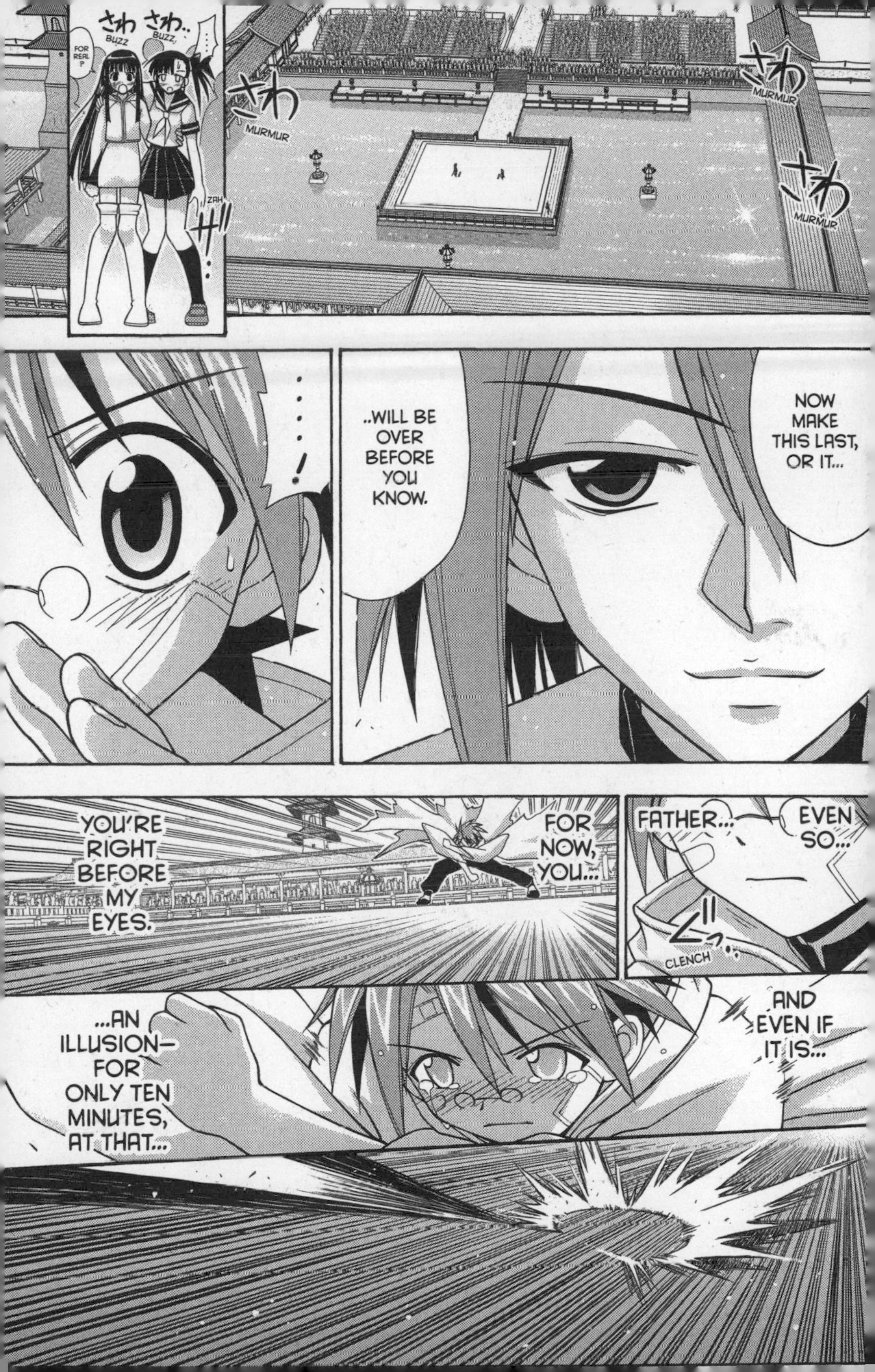
さわ
MURMUR
さわ
MURMUR
さわ
MURMUR
さわ さわ..
BUZZ BUZZ
FOR REAL ?
...
ザ
ZAH
NOW MAKE THIS LAST, OR IT...
..WILL BE OVER BEFORE YOU KNOW.
...!
FATHER...
EVEN SO...
ぐっ
CLENCH
FOR NOW, YOU...
YOU'RE RIGHT BEFORE MY EYES.
AND EVEN IF IT IS...
...AN ILLUSION— FOR ONLY TEN MINUTES, AT THAT...

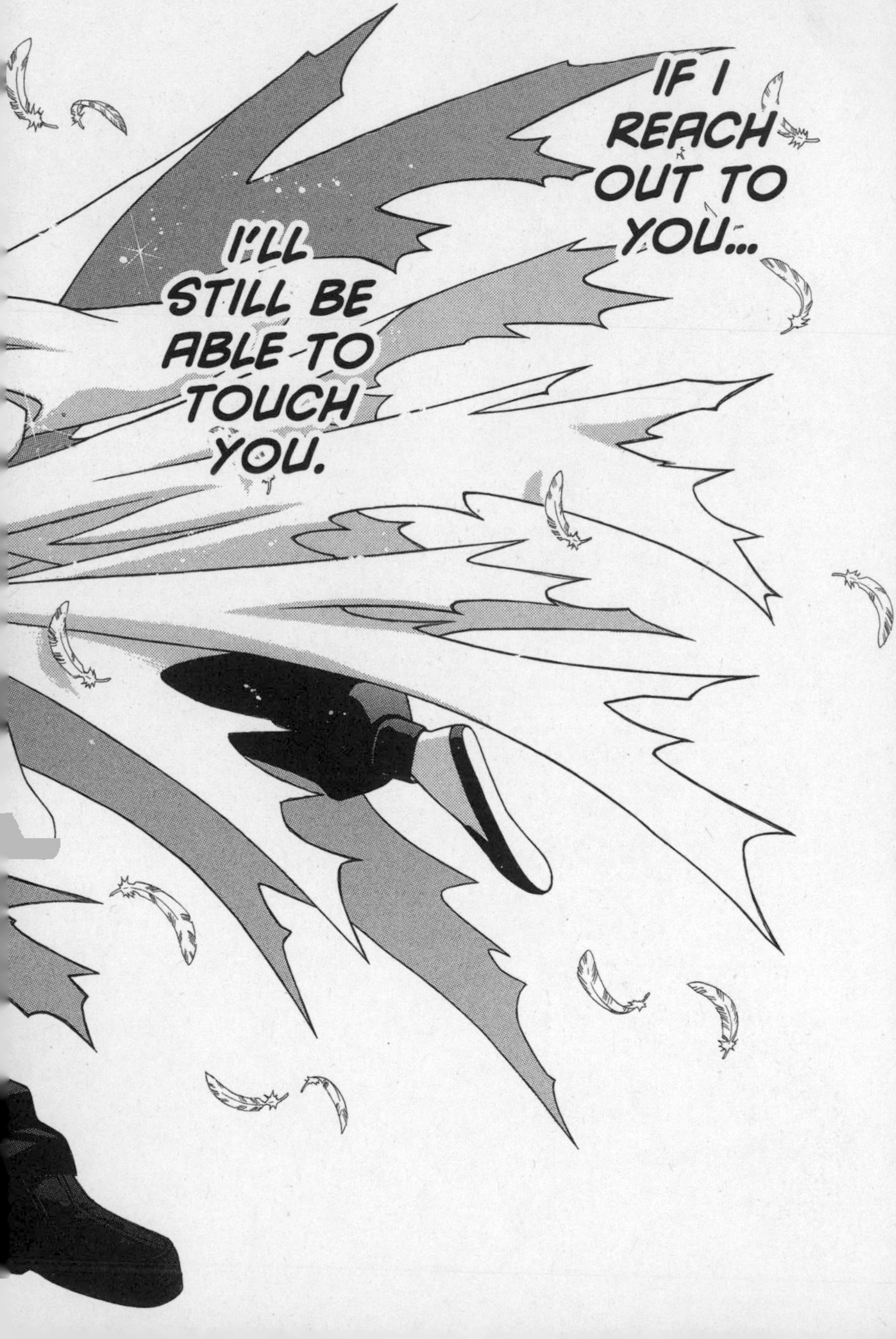
IF I REACH OUT TO YOU...
I'LL STILL BE ABLE TO TOUCH YOU.

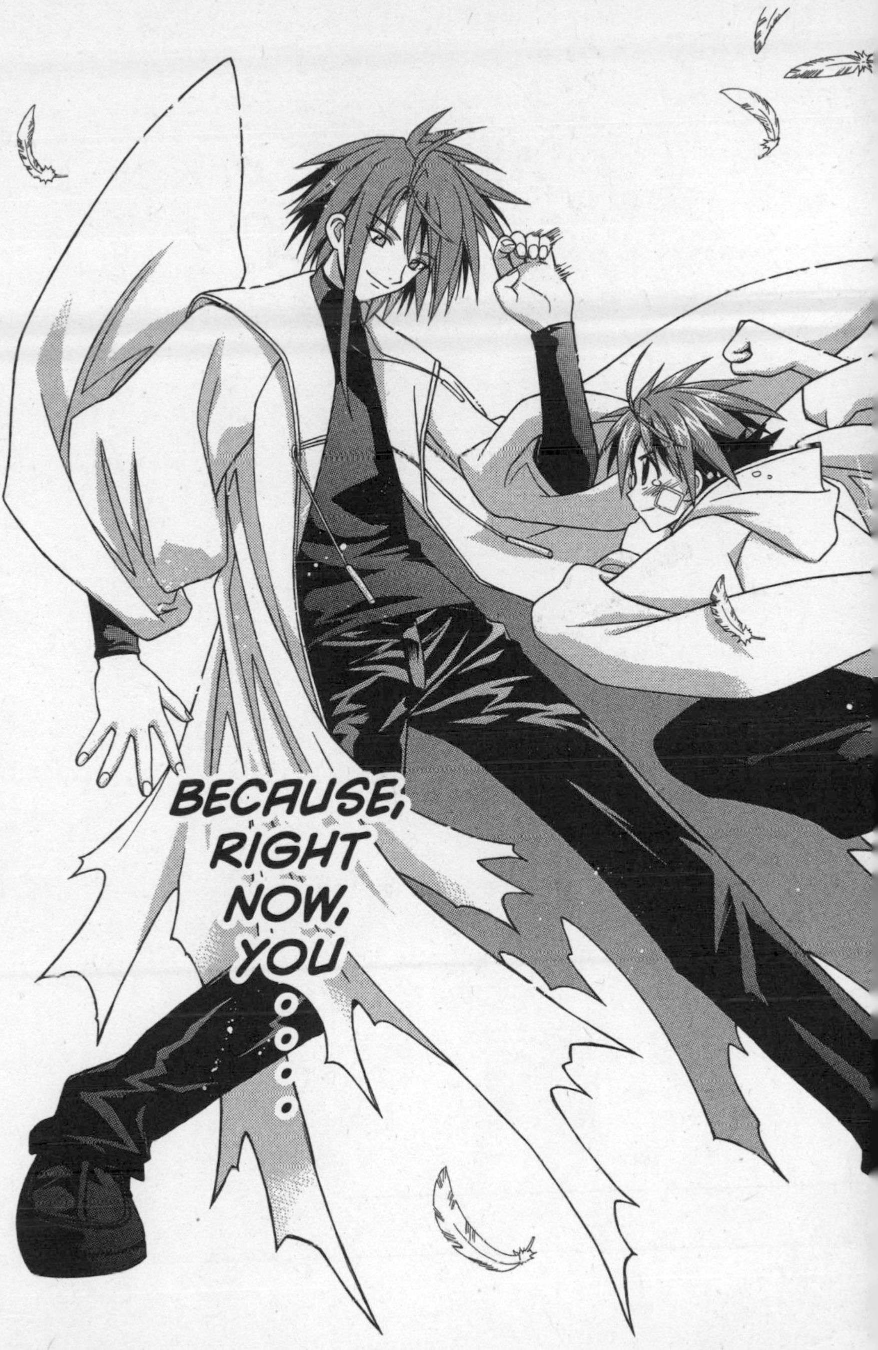
BECAUSE, RIGHT NOW, YOU . . .

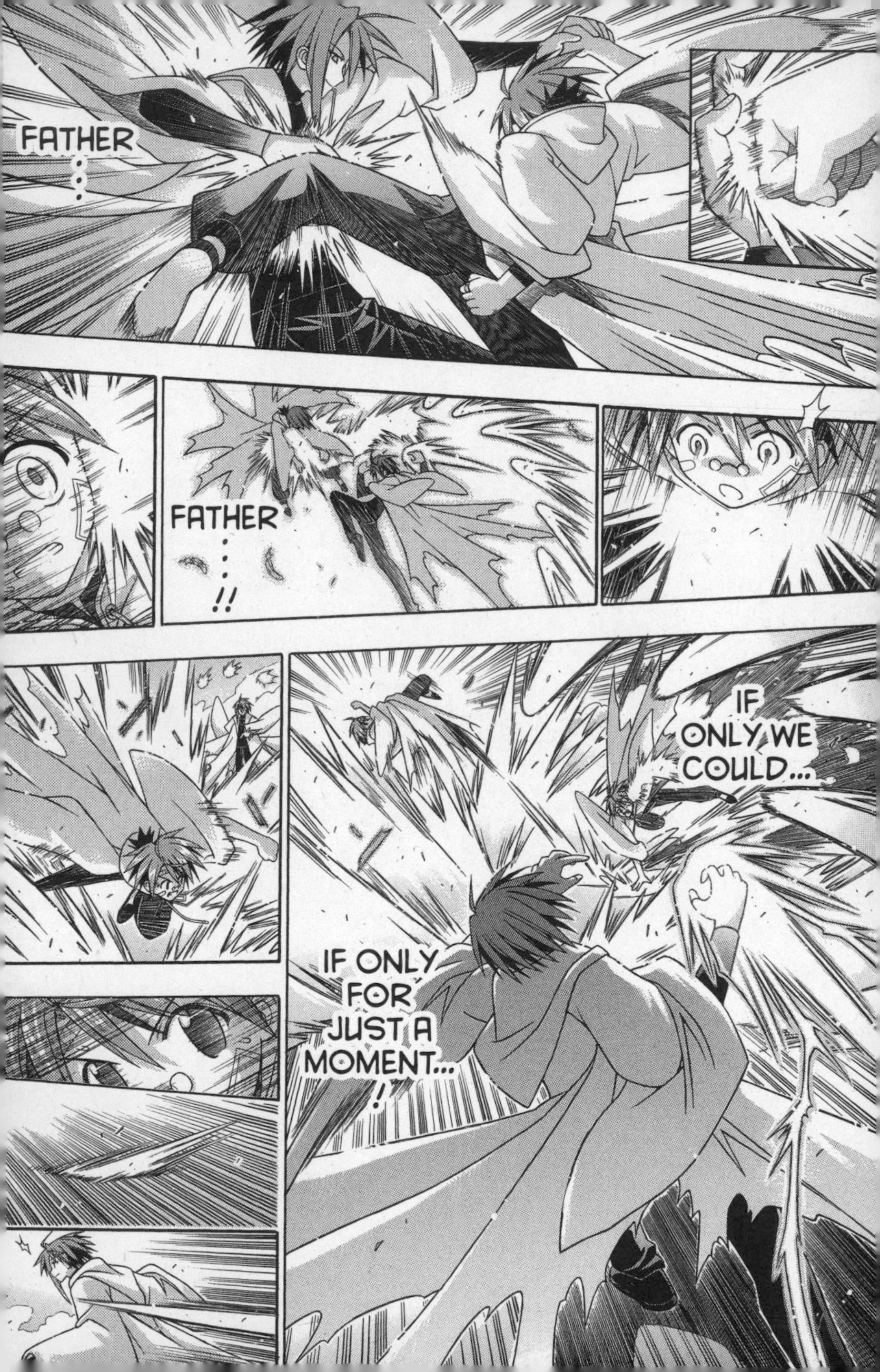
FATHER...
FATHER...!!
IF ONLY WE COULD...
IF ONLY FOR JUST A MOMENT...!

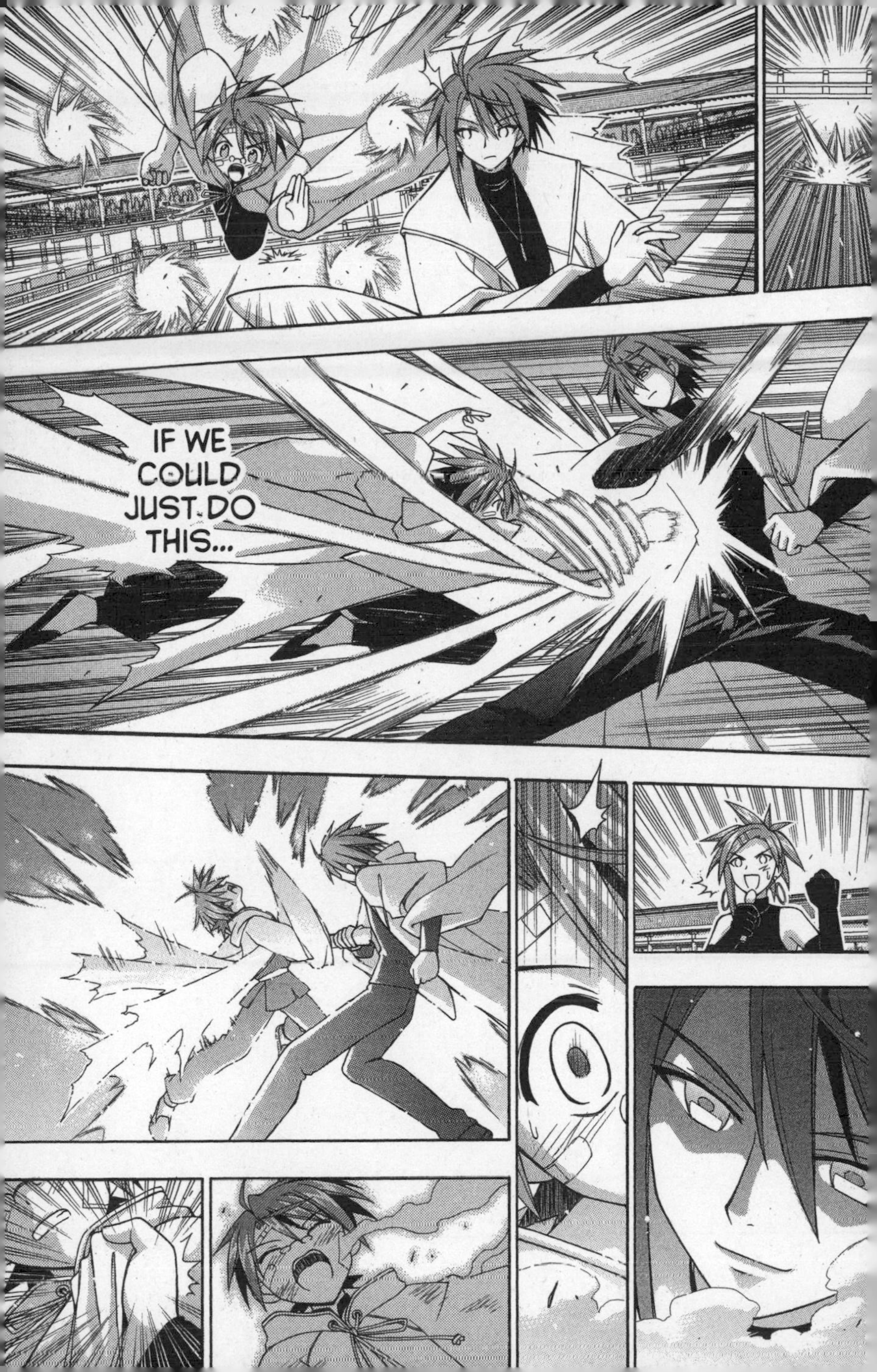
IF WE COULD JUST DO THIS...

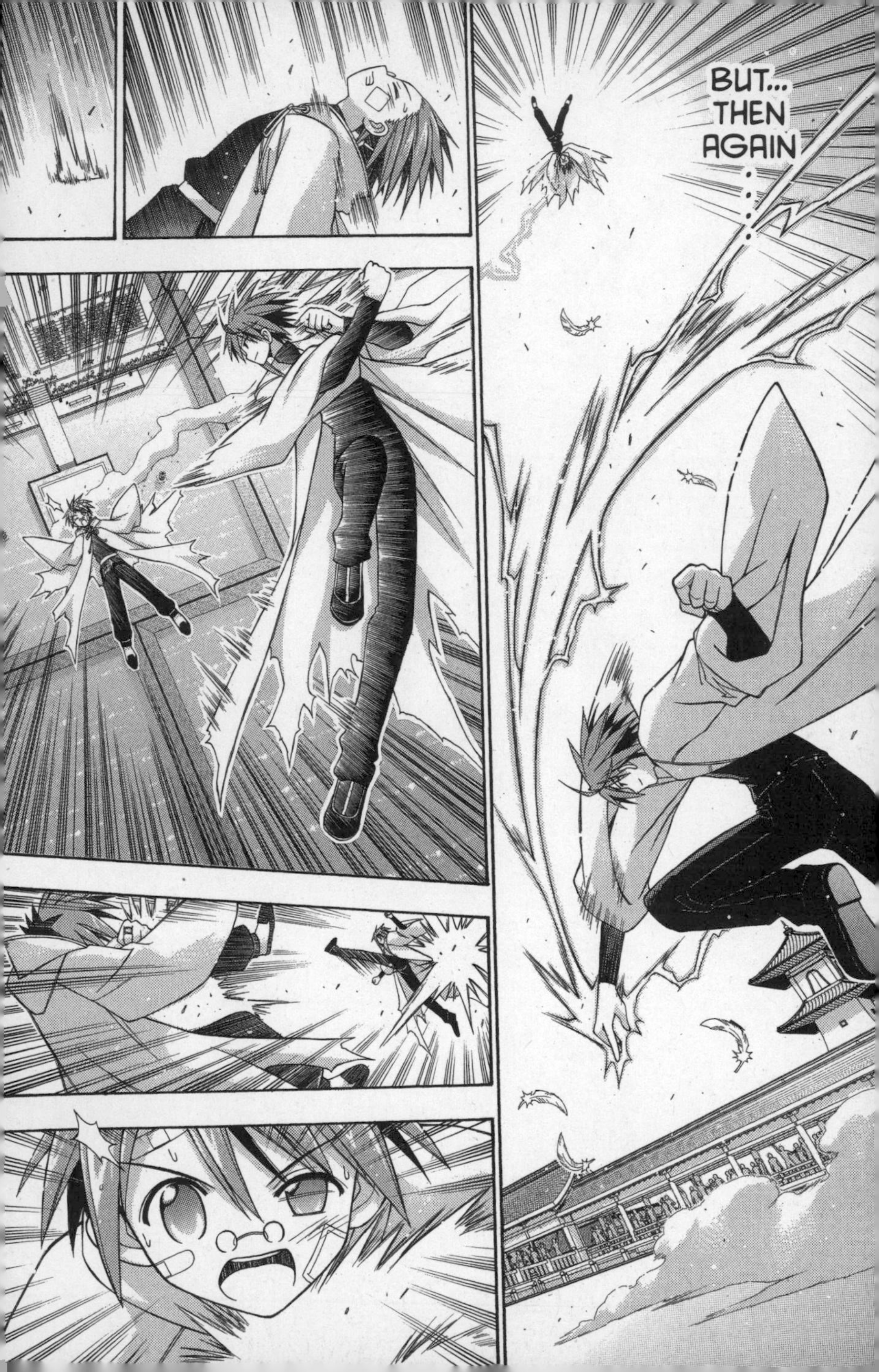
BUT... THEN AGAIN...

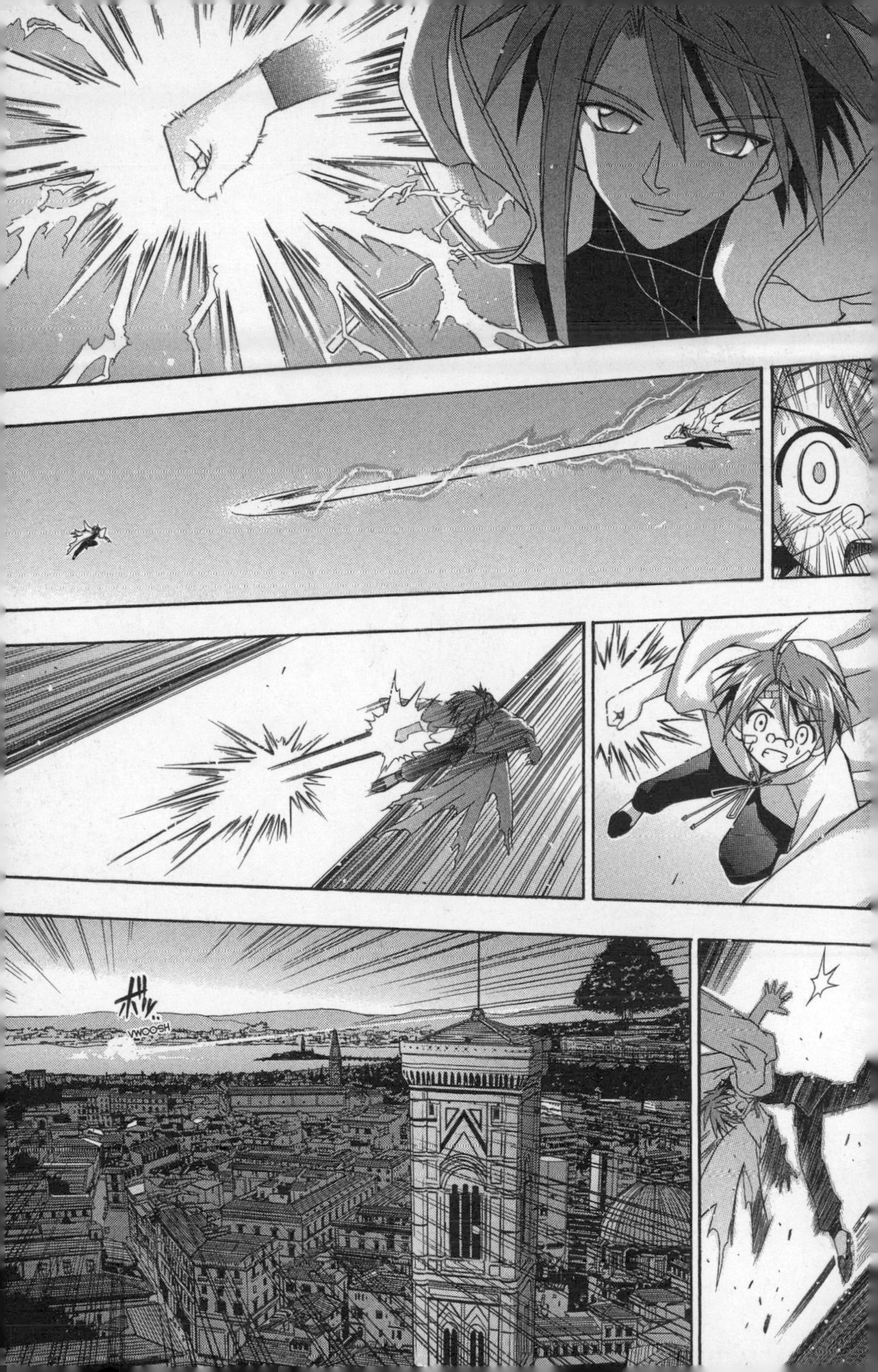
ボッ..
VWOOSH

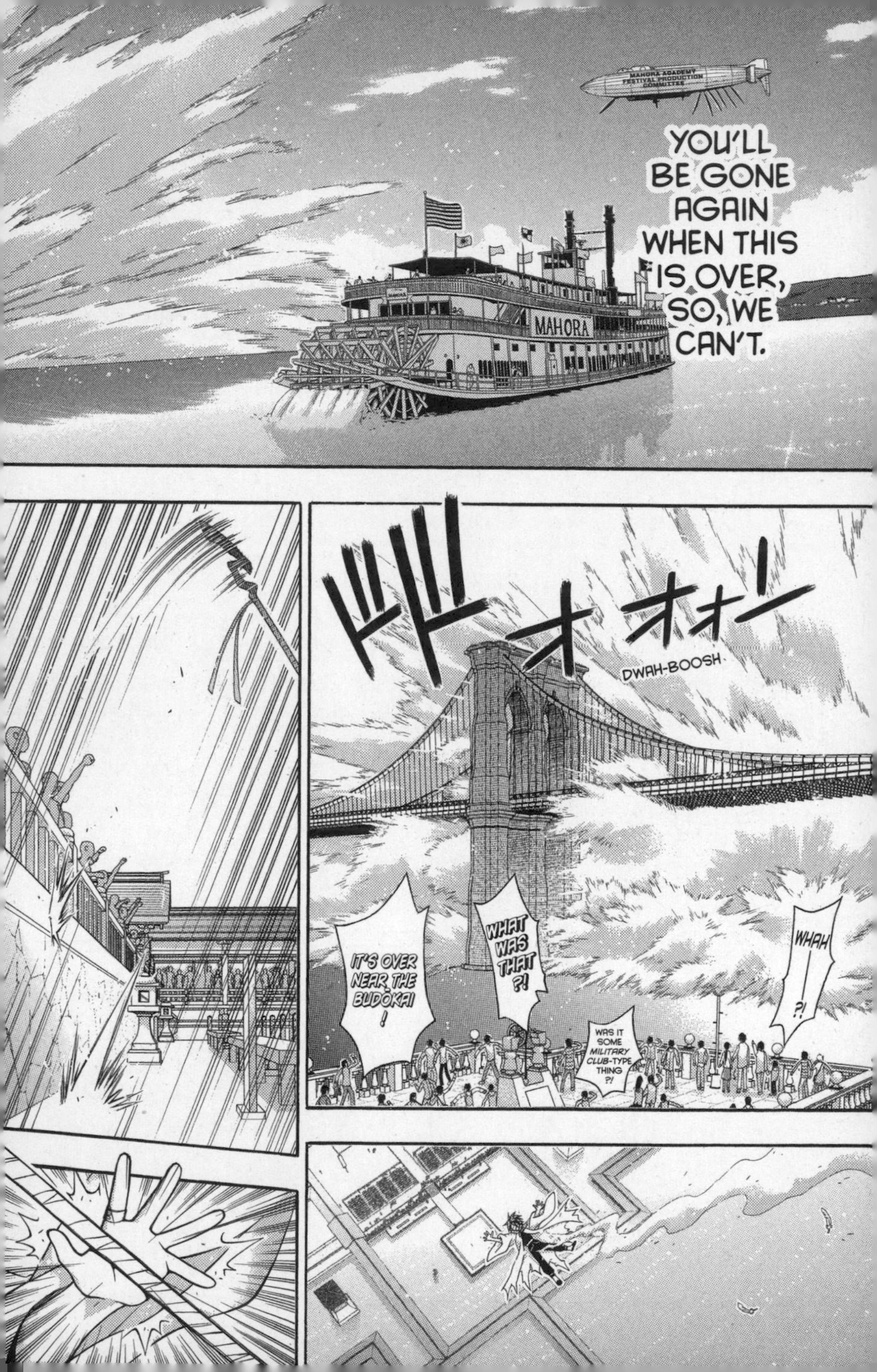
MAHORA ACADEMY FESTIVAL PRODUCTION COMMITTEE
MAHORA
YOU'LL BE GONE AGAIN WHEN THIS IS OVER, SO, WE CAN'T.
DWAH-BOOSH
WHAH—?!
WHAT WAS THAT ?!
IT'S OVER NEAR THE BUDŌKAI!
WAS IT SOME MILITARY CLUB-TYPE THING ?!

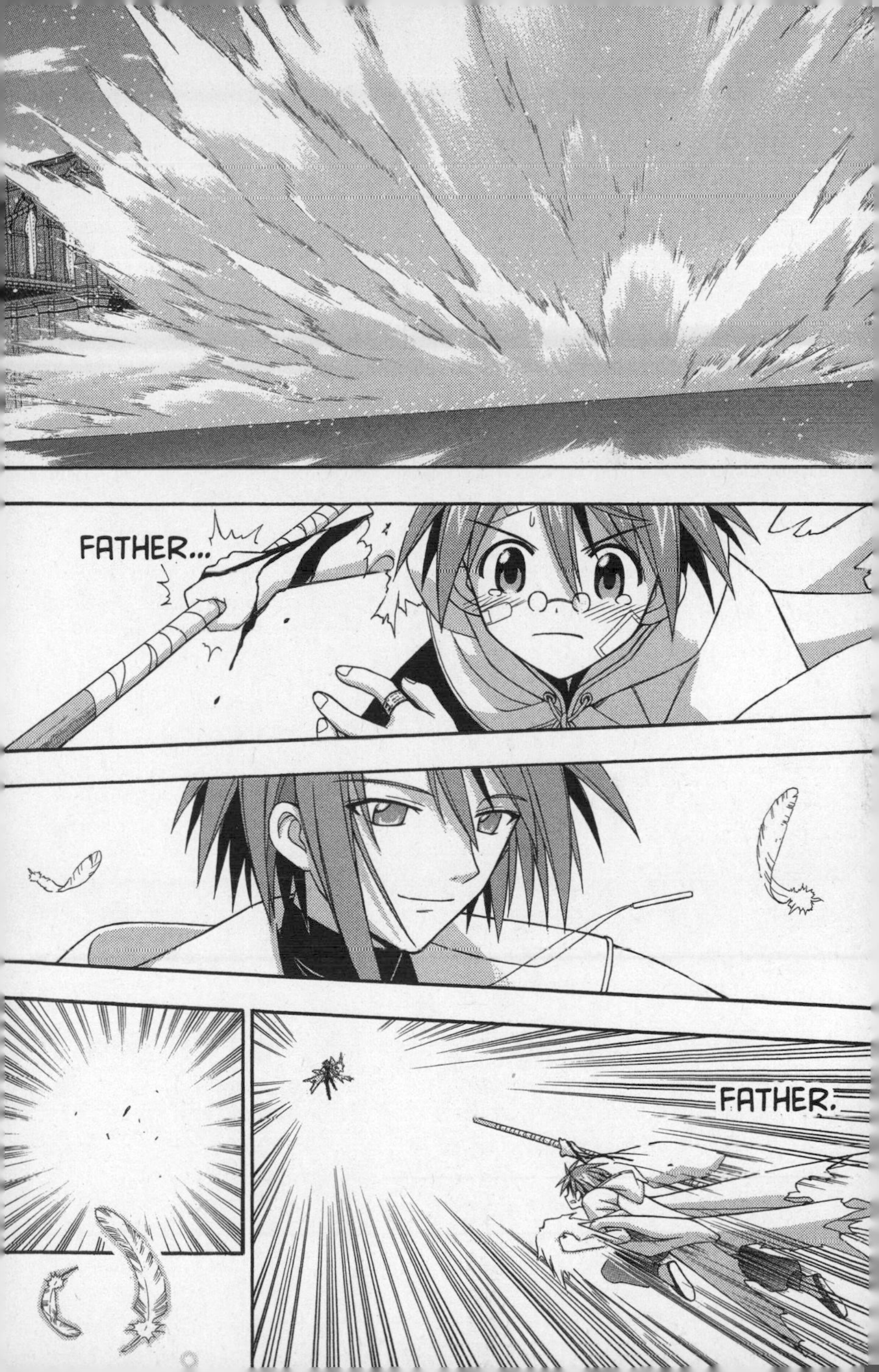
FATHER...
FATHER.

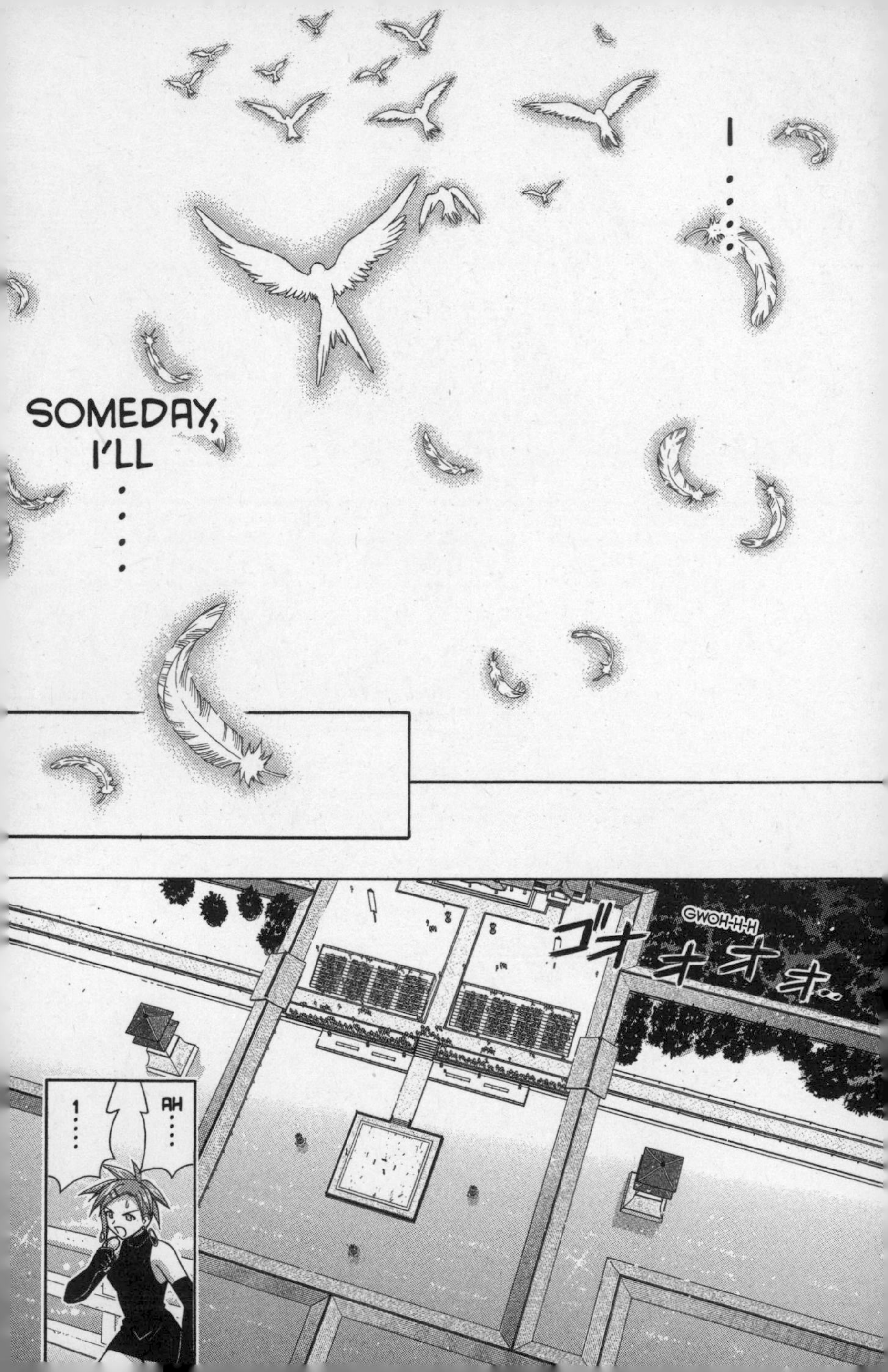
I....
SOMEDAY, I'LL....
ゴオオオオ
GWOH-H-H
AH....
I....

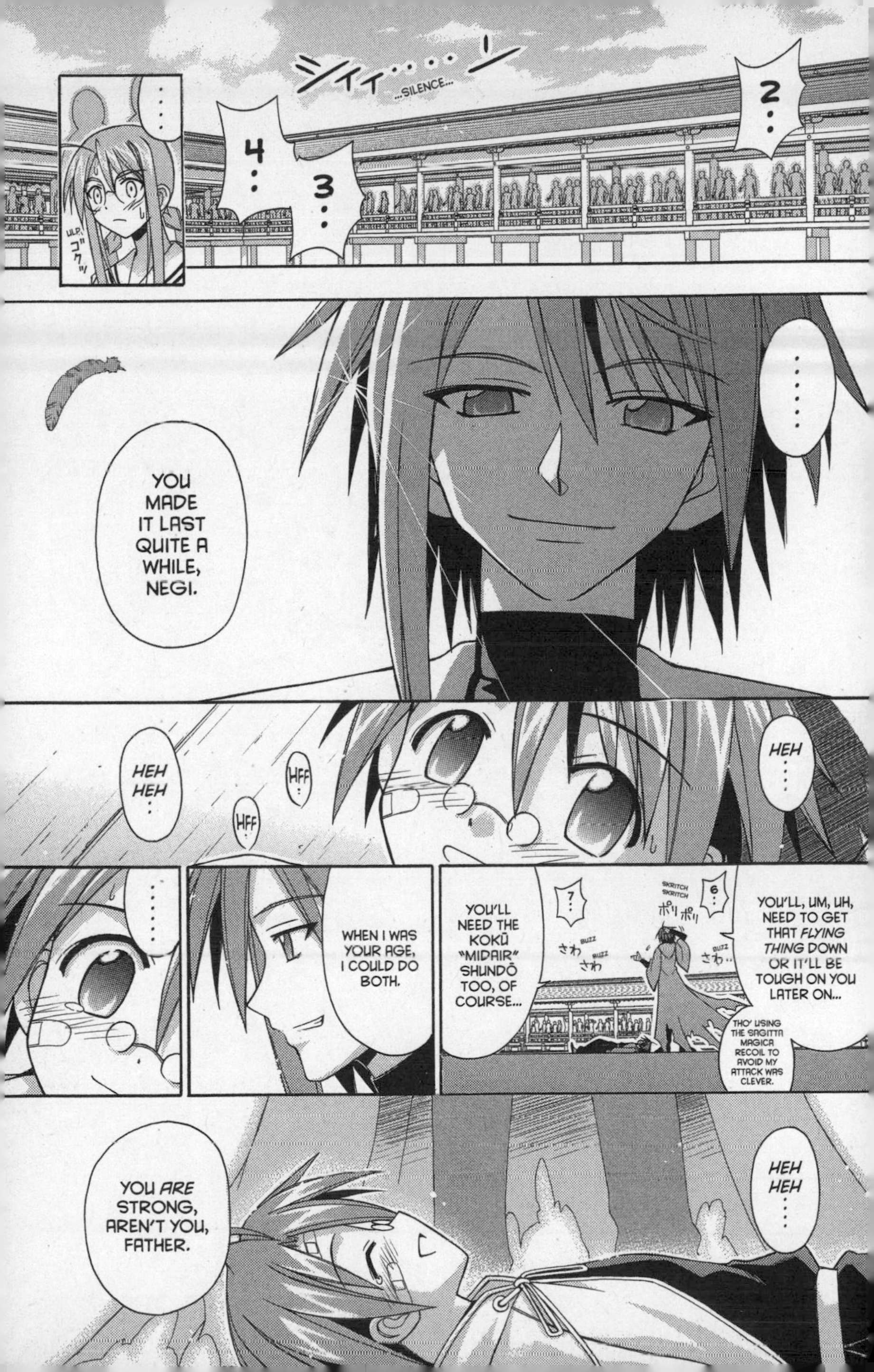
2...
シィィ...ン
...SILENCE...
3...
4...
......
ULP, ゴクッ
......
YOU MADE IT LAST QUITE A WHILE, NEGI.
HEH......
HFF...
HFF...
HEH HEH...
6...
SKRITCH SKRITCH ポリポリ
YOU'LL, UM, UH, NEED TO GET THAT *FLYING THING* DOWN OR IT'LL BE TOUGH ON YOU LATER ON...
THO' USING THE SAGITTA MAGICA RECOIL TO AVOID MY ATTACK WAS CLEVER.
BUZZ さわ...
BUZZ さわ BUZZ さわ
7...
YOU'LL NEED THE KOKŪ "MIDAIR" SHUNDŌ TOO, OF COURSE...
WHEN I WAS YOUR AGE, I COULD DO BOTH.
......
HEH HEH...
YOU *ARE* STRONG, AREN'T YOU, FATHER.

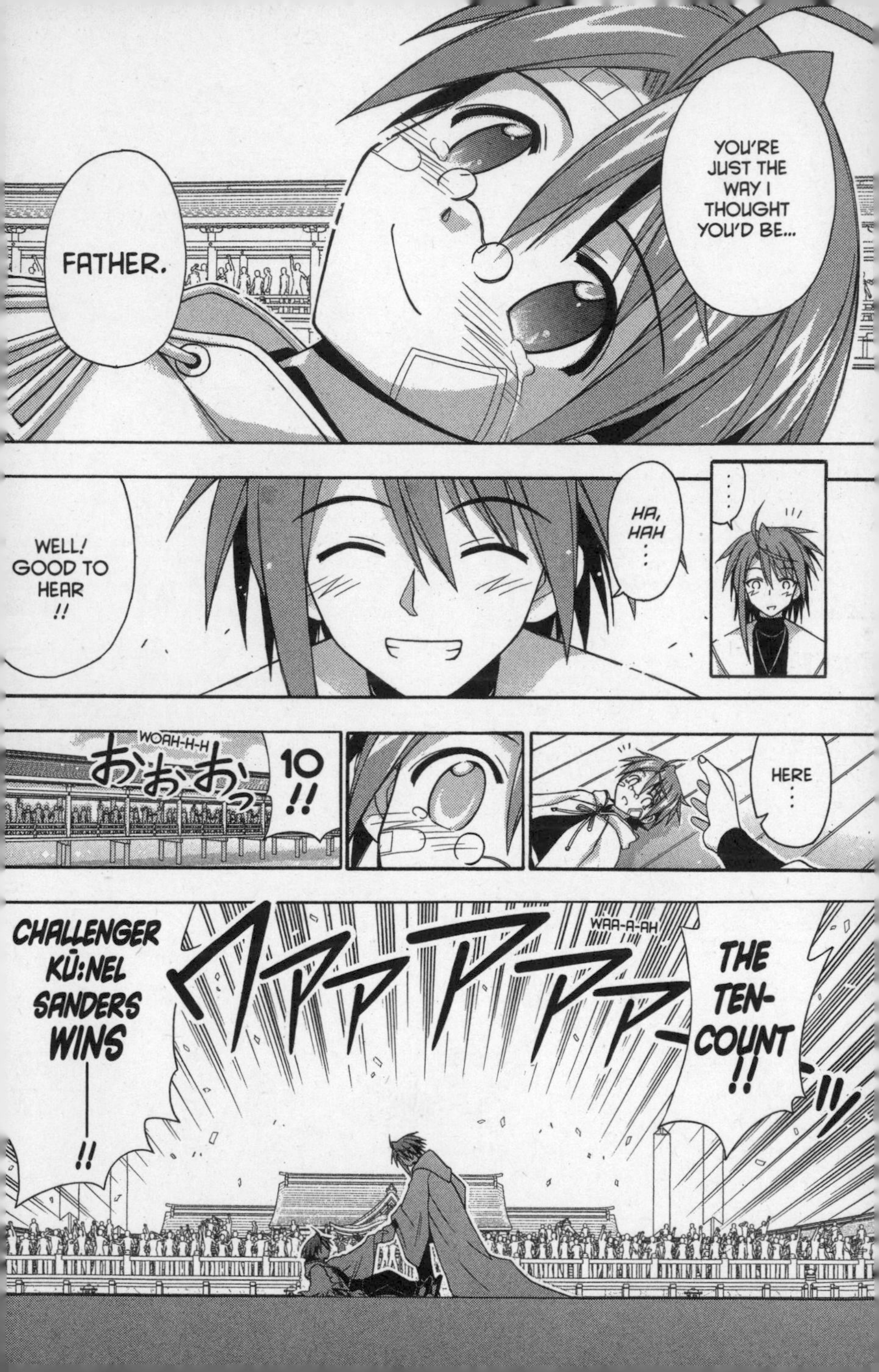

YOU'RE JUST THE WAY I THOUGHT YOU'D BE...
FATHER.
. . .
HA, HAH . . .
WELL! GOOD TO HEAR !!
HERE . . .
10 !!
WOAH-H-H
おおおっ
THE TEN-COUNT !!
WAA-A-AH
CHALLENGER KÜ:NEL SANDERS WINS — !!

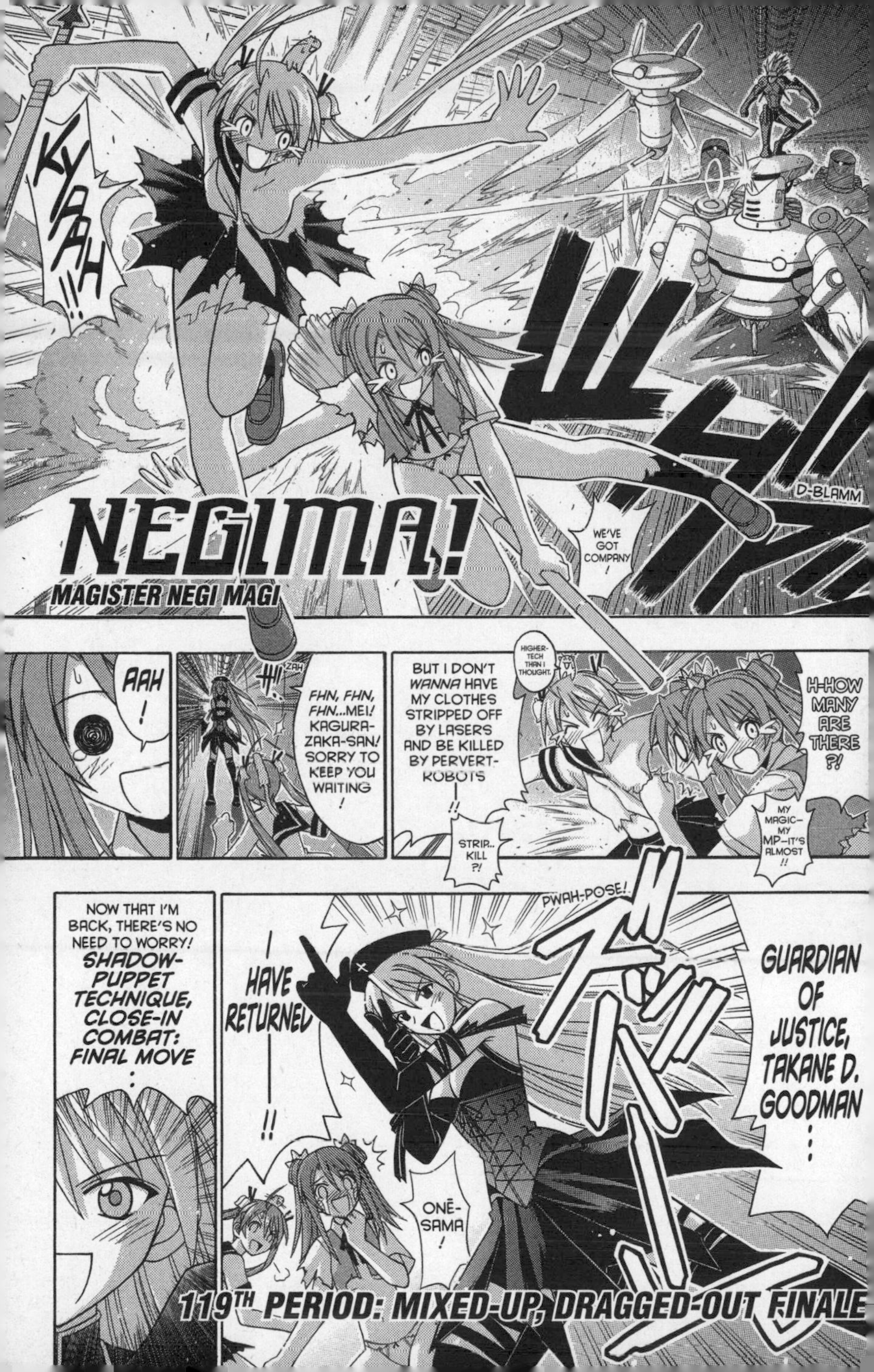
KYAAAH!!
D-BLAMM
WE'VE GOT COMPANY!
NEGIMA!
MAGISTER NEGI MAGI
H-HOW MANY ARE THERE?!
HIGHER-TECH THAN I THOUGHT.
MY MAGIC—MY MP—IT'S ALMOST!!
BUT I DON'T WANNA HAVE MY CLOTHES STRIPPED OFF BY LASERS AND BE KILLED BY PERVERT-ROBOTS!!
STRIP... KILL?!
ZAH
FHN, FHN, FHN...MEI! KAGURAZAKA-SAN! SORRY TO KEEP YOU WAITING!
AAH!
GUARDIAN OF JUSTICE, TAKANE D. GOODMAN...
PWAH-POSE!
I HAVE RETURNED—!!
ONĒ-SAMA!
119TH PERIOD: MIXED-UP, DRAGGED-OUT FINALE
NOW THAT I'M BACK, THERE'S NO NEED TO WORRY!
SHADOW-PUPPET TECHNIQUE, CLOSE-IN COMBAT: FINAL MOVE:

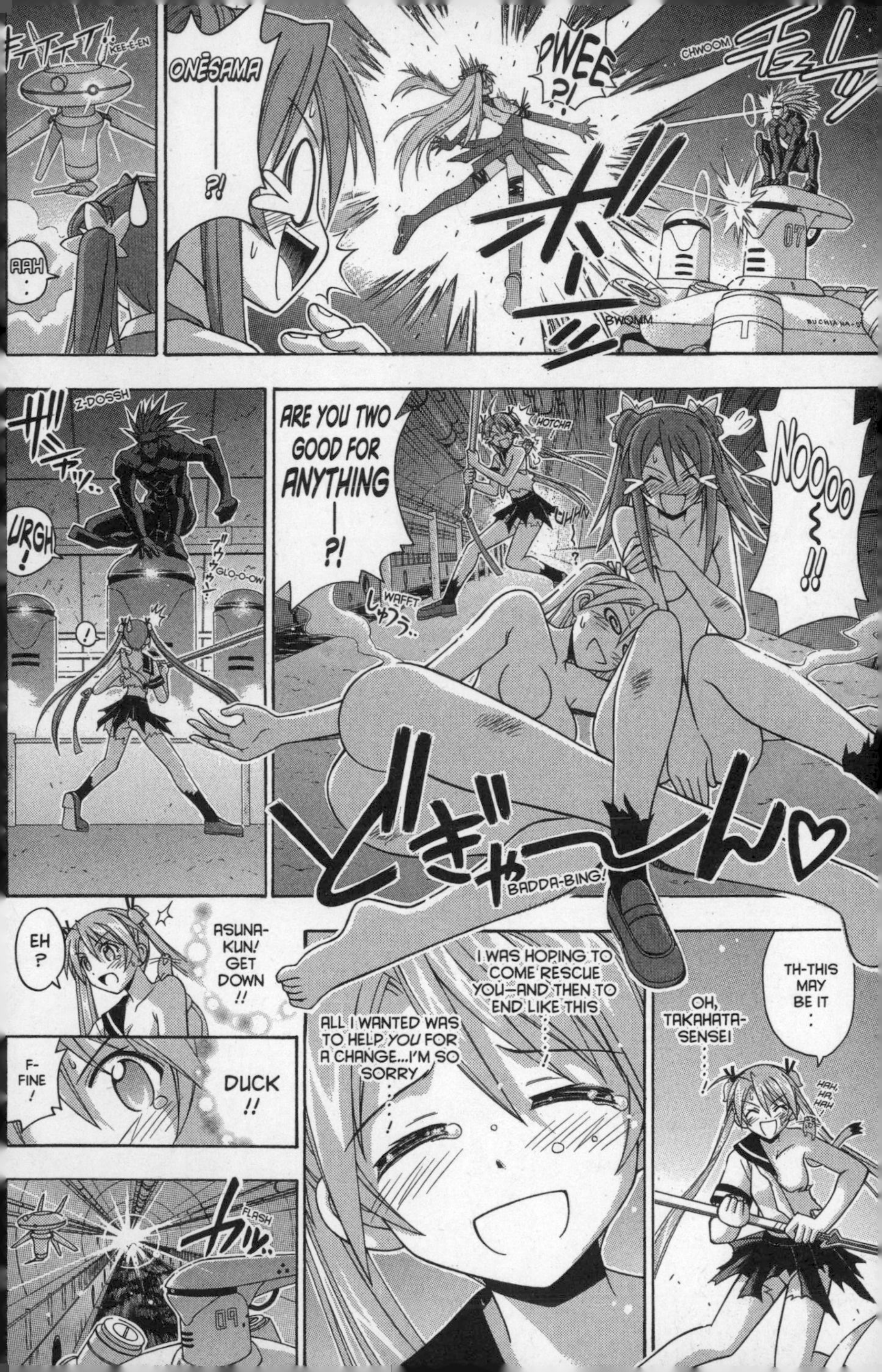

CHWOOM
PWEE ?!
BWOMM
ONĒSAMA — ?!
KEE-E-EN
AAH...
NOOOO~!!
ARE YOU TWO GOOD FOR ANYTHING — ?!
HOTCHA
UHHN
?
WAFFT
どぎゃ〜ん♡
BADDA-BING!
Z-DOSSH
URGH!
GLO-O-OW
!
TH-THIS MAY BE IT...
OH, TAKAHATA-SENSEI...!
HAH, HAH, HAH
I WAS HOPING TO COME RESCUE YOU—AND THEN TO END LIKE THIS...!
ALL I WANTED WAS TO HELP YOU FOR A CHANGE...I'M SO SORRY...!
EH?
ASUNA-KUN! GET DOWN!!
F-FINE!
DUCK!!
FLASH

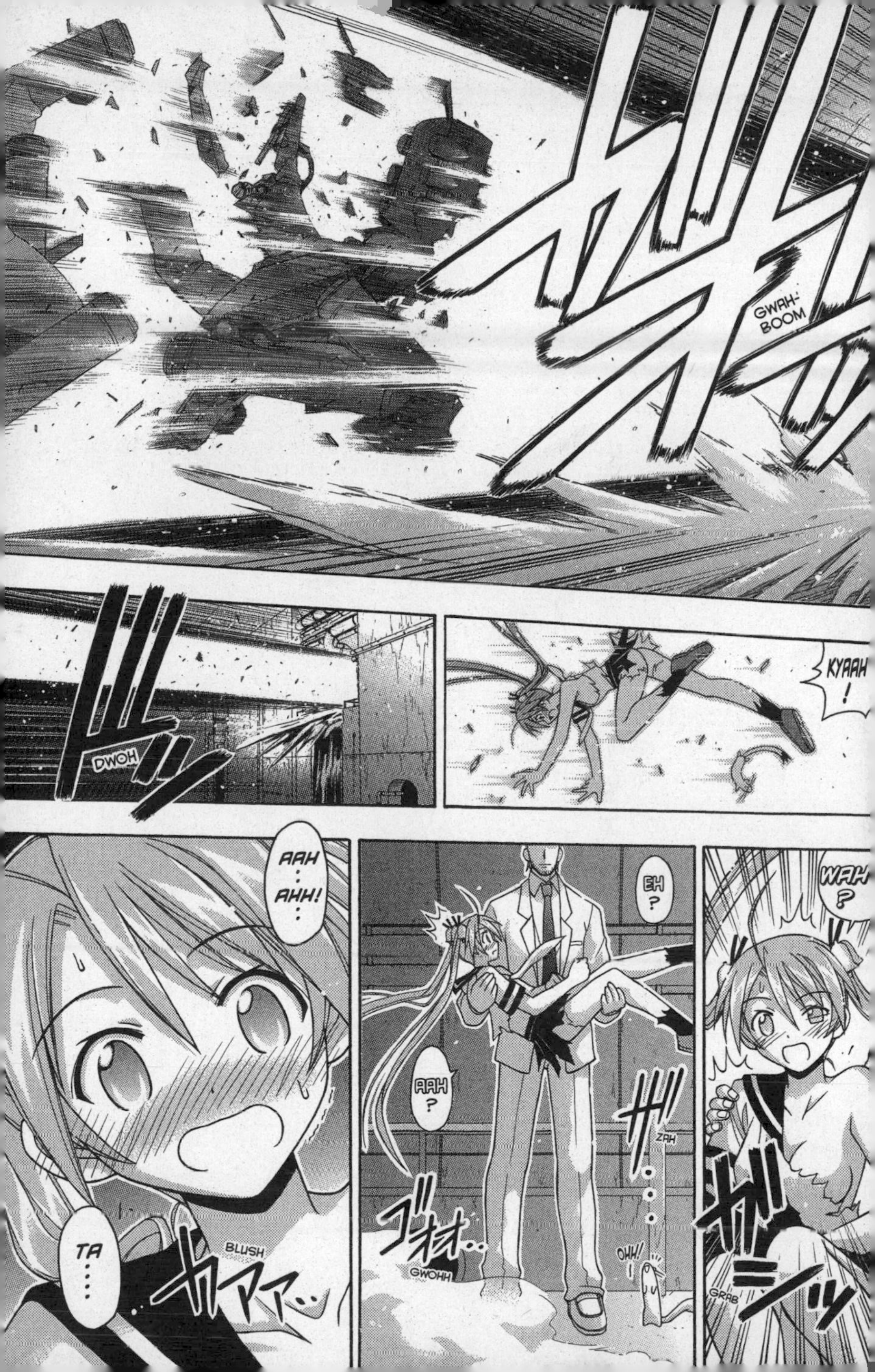
GWAH-BOOM
KYAAH!
DWOH
WAH?
GRAB
EH?
AAH?
ZAH
...
OHH!
GWOHH
AAH... AHH!...
TA.....
BLUSH

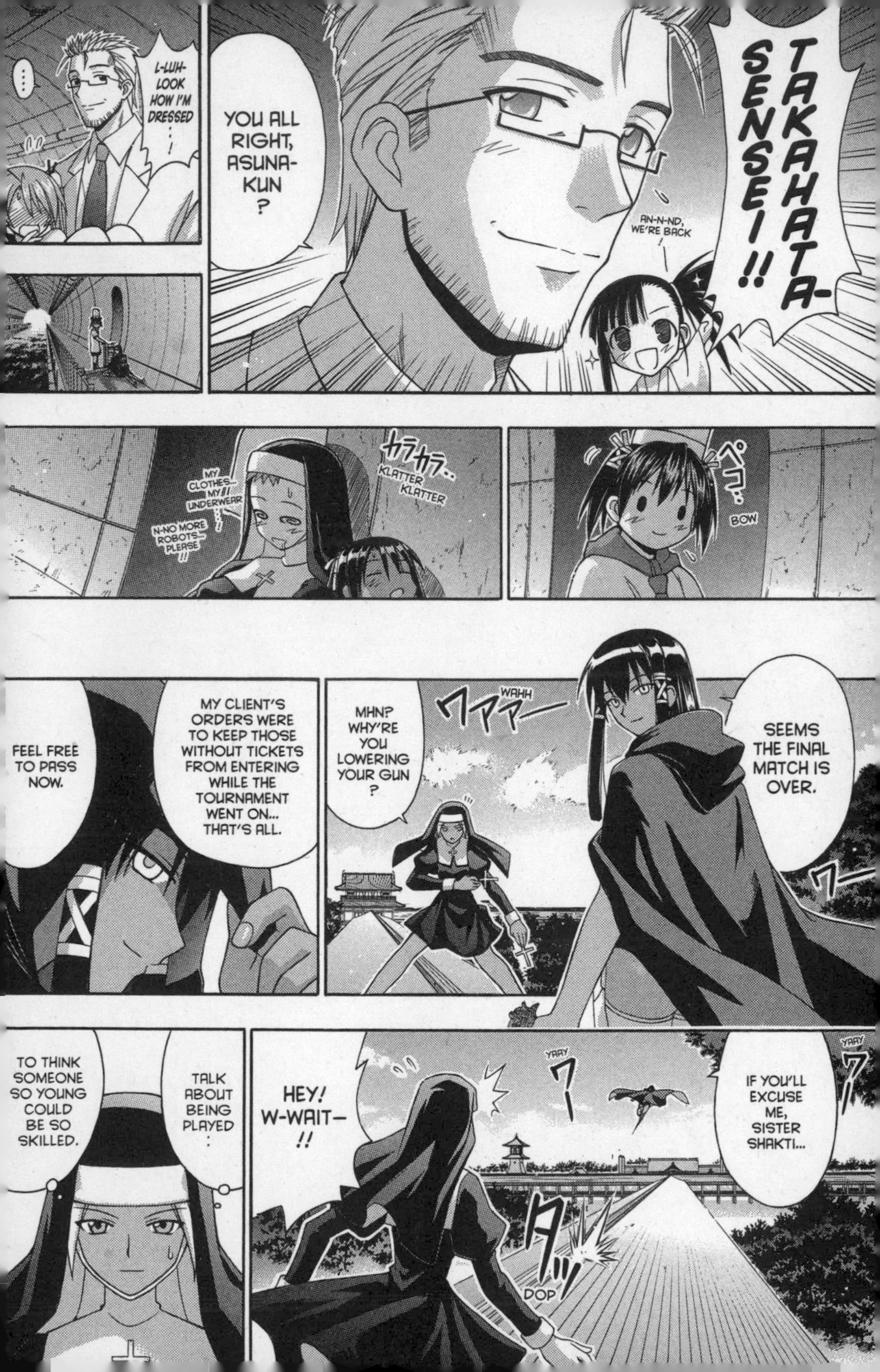
TAKAHATA-SENSEI!!
AN-N-ND, WE'RE BACK!
YOU ALL RIGHT, ASUNA-KUN?
L-LUH-LOOK HOW I'M DRESSED...!
...
ペコ
BOW
カラカラ
KLATTER KLATTER
MY CLOTHES... MY UNDERWEAR...!!
N-NO MORE ROBOTS... PLEASE!!
SEEMS THE FINAL MATCH IS OVER.
ワー
ワアアー
WAHH
MHN? WHY'RE YOU LOWERING YOUR GUN?
MY CLIENT'S ORDERS WERE TO KEEP THOSE WITHOUT TICKETS FROM ENTERING WHILE THE TOURNAMENT WENT ON... THAT'S ALL.
FEEL FREE TO PASS NOW.
ワ
YAAY
IF YOU'LL EXCUSE ME, SISTER SHAKTI...
ワ
YAAY
ダッ
DOP
HEY! W-WAIT—!!
TALK ABOUT BEING PLAYED...
TO THINK SOMEONE SO YOUNG COULD BE SO SKILLED.

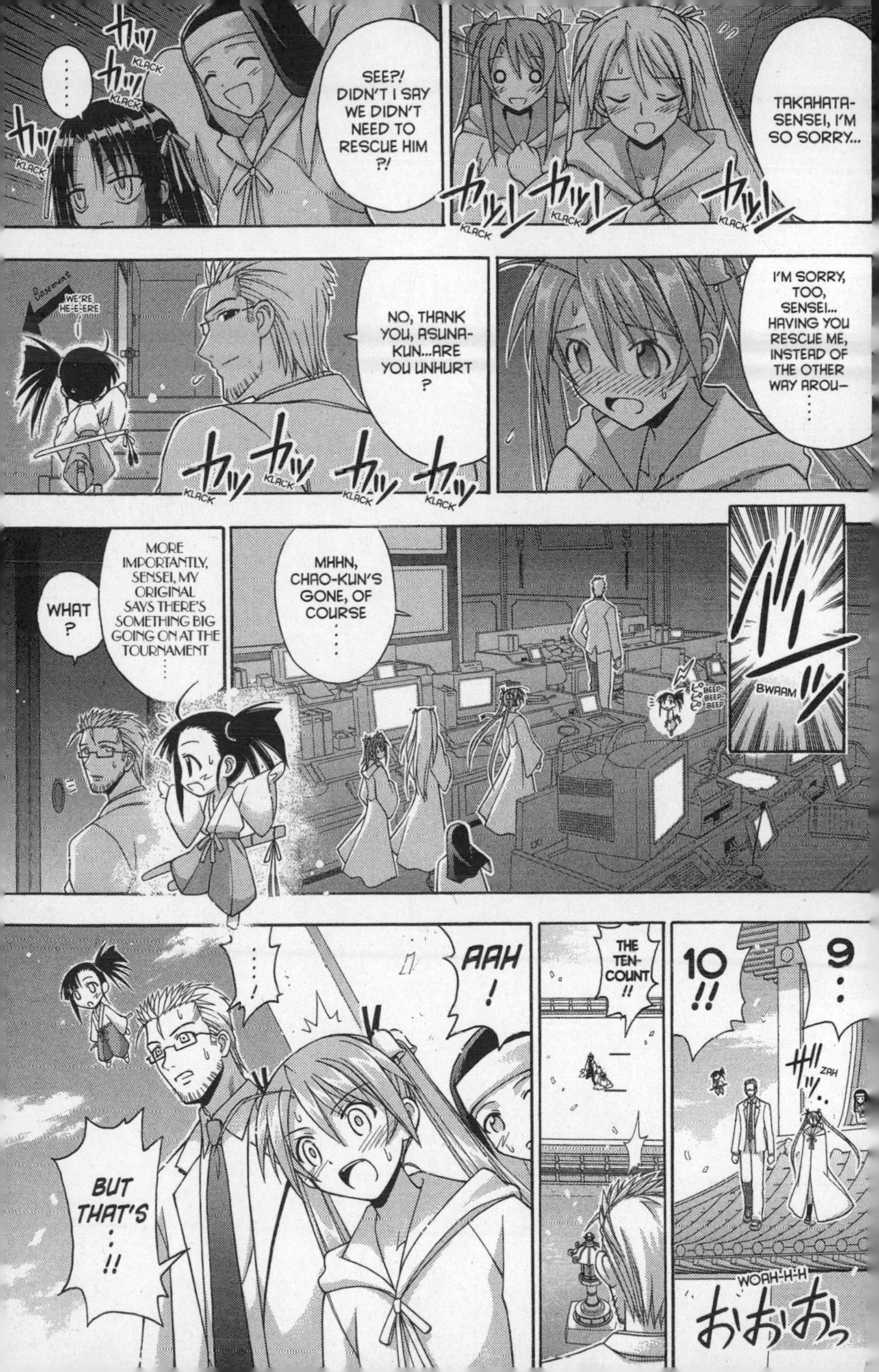
TAKAHATA-SENSEI, I'M SO SORRY...
KLACK
KLACK
KLACK
SEE?! DIDN'T I SAY WE DIDN'T NEED TO RESCUE HIM?!
......
KLACK
KLACK
KLACK
I'M SORRY, TOO, SENSEI... HAVING YOU RESCUE ME, INSTEAD OF THE OTHER WAY AROU—......
NO, THANK YOU, ASUNA-KUN...ARE YOU UNHURT?
KLACK
KLACK
KLACK
KLACK
Basement
WE'RE HE-E-ERE!
BWAAM
MHHN, CHAO-KUN'S GONE, OF COURSE....
BEEP BEEP BEEP
MORE IMPORTANTLY, SENSEI, MY ORIGINAL SAYS THERE'S SOMETHING BIG GOING ON AT THE TOURNAMENT.....
WHAT?
9...
10!!
ZAH
WOAH-H-H
おおおっ
THE TEN-COUNT!!
AAH!
....!
BUT THAT'S...!!

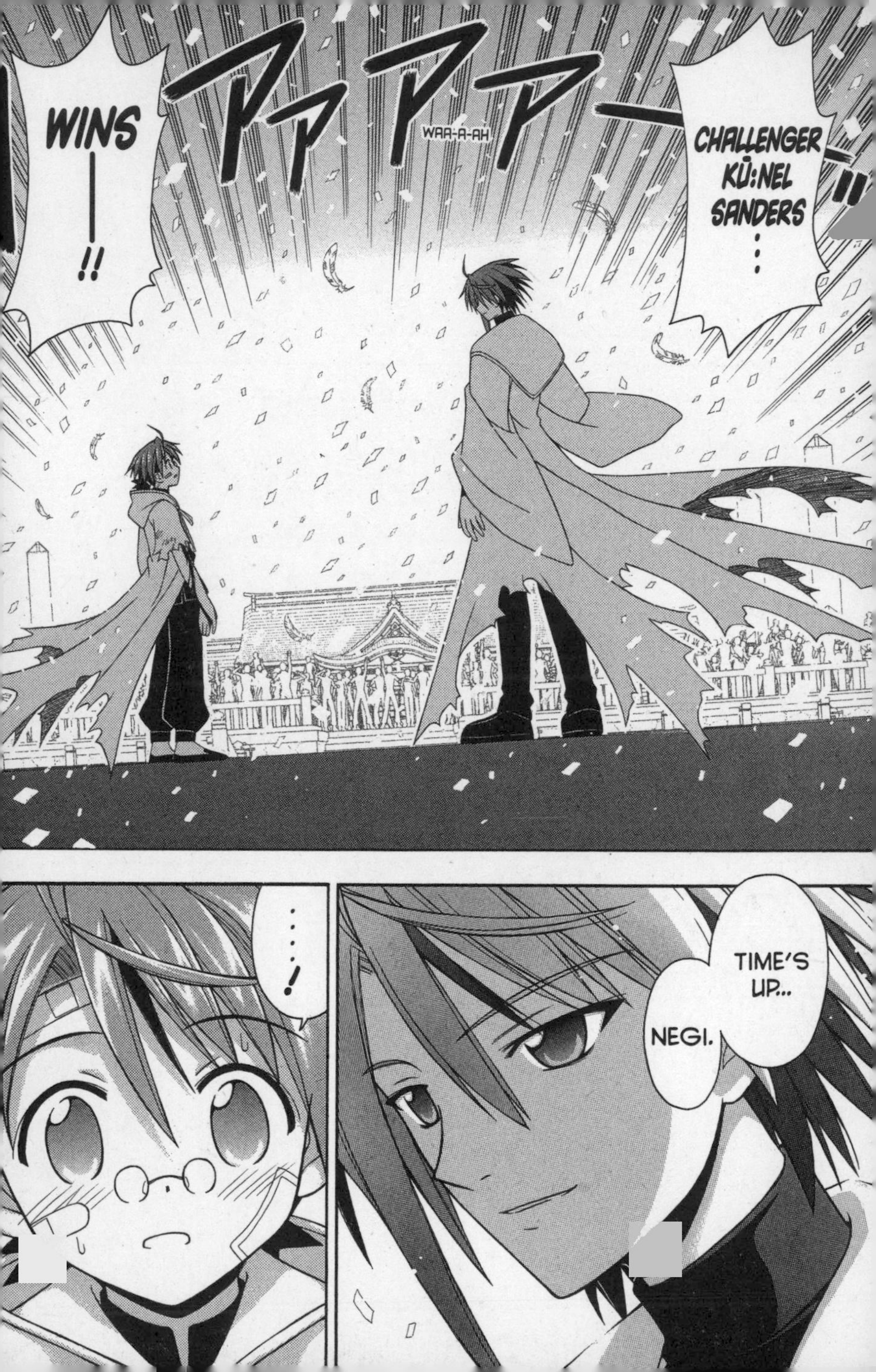
CHALLENGER KŪ:NEL SANDERS...
WAA-A-AH
WINS—!!
TIME'S UP...
NEGI.
...!

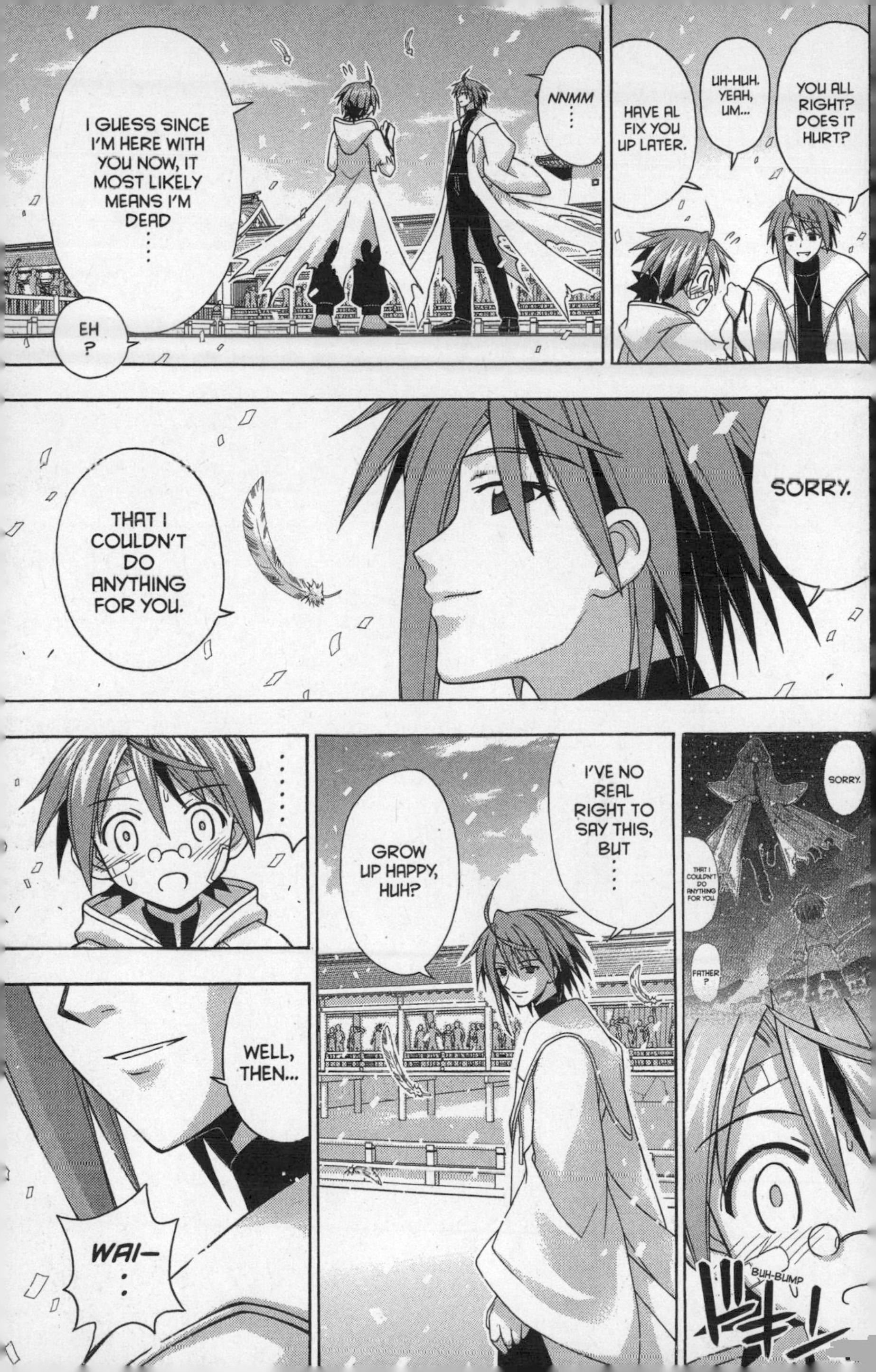
YOU ALL RIGHT? DOES IT HURT?
UH-HUH. YEAH, UM...
HAVE AL FIX YOU UP LATER.
NNMM ....
I GUESS SINCE I'M HERE WITH YOU NOW, IT MOST LIKELY MEANS I'M DEAD ....
EH ?
SORRY.
THAT I COULDN'T DO ANYTHING FOR YOU.
SORRY.
THAT I COULDN'T DO ANYTHING FOR YOU.
FATHER ?
BUH-BUMP
ドキ!
I'VE NO REAL RIGHT TO SAY THIS, BUT ....
GROW UP HAPPY, HUH?
......
WELL, THEN...
WAI- :

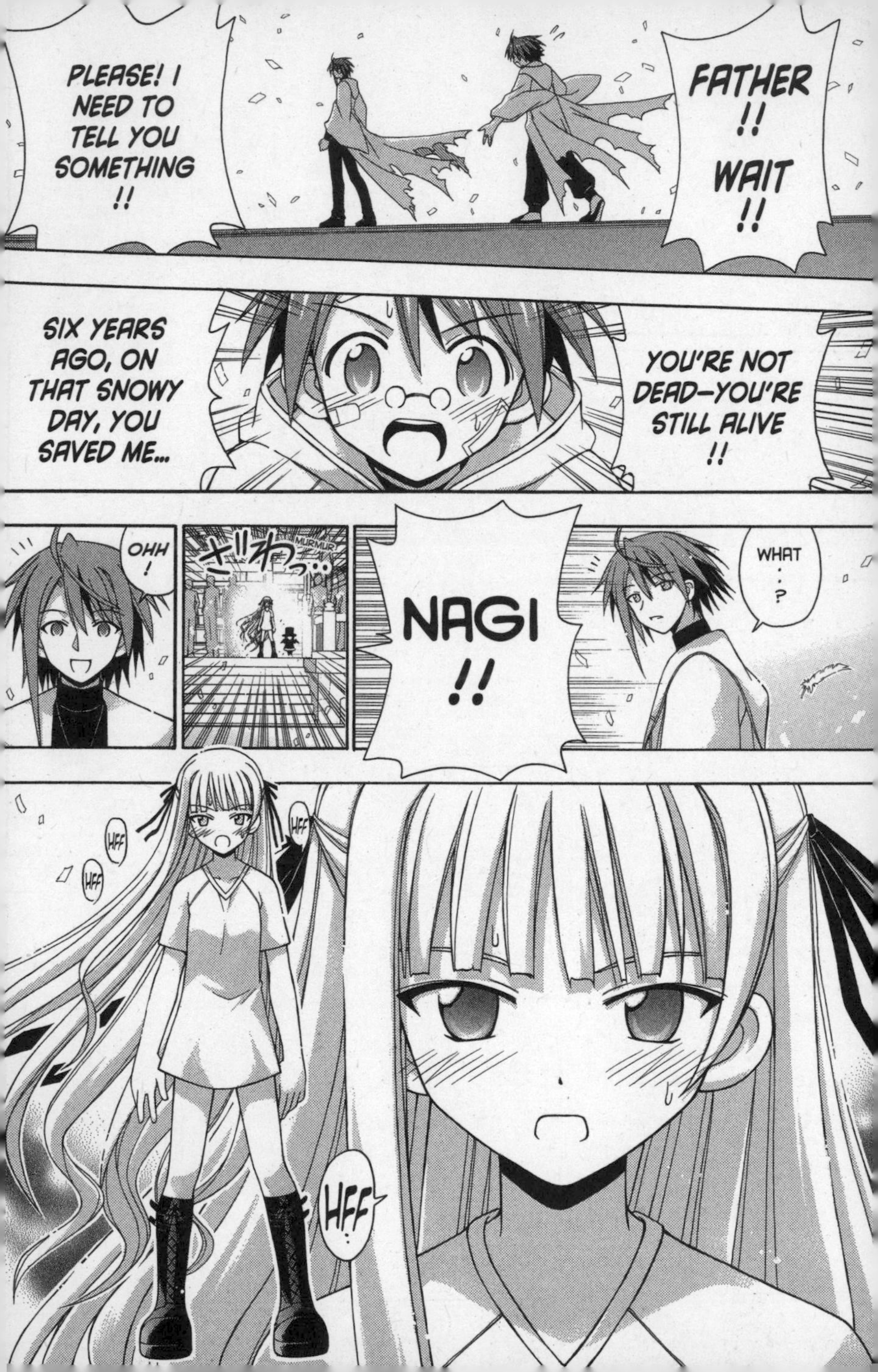
FATHER!! WAIT!!
PLEASE! I NEED TO TELL YOU SOMETHING!!
YOU'RE NOT DEAD—YOU'RE STILL ALIVE!!
SIX YEARS AGO, ON THAT SNOWY DAY, YOU SAVED ME...
WHAT...?
NAGI!!
MURMUR
OHH!
HFF
HFF
HFF
HFF

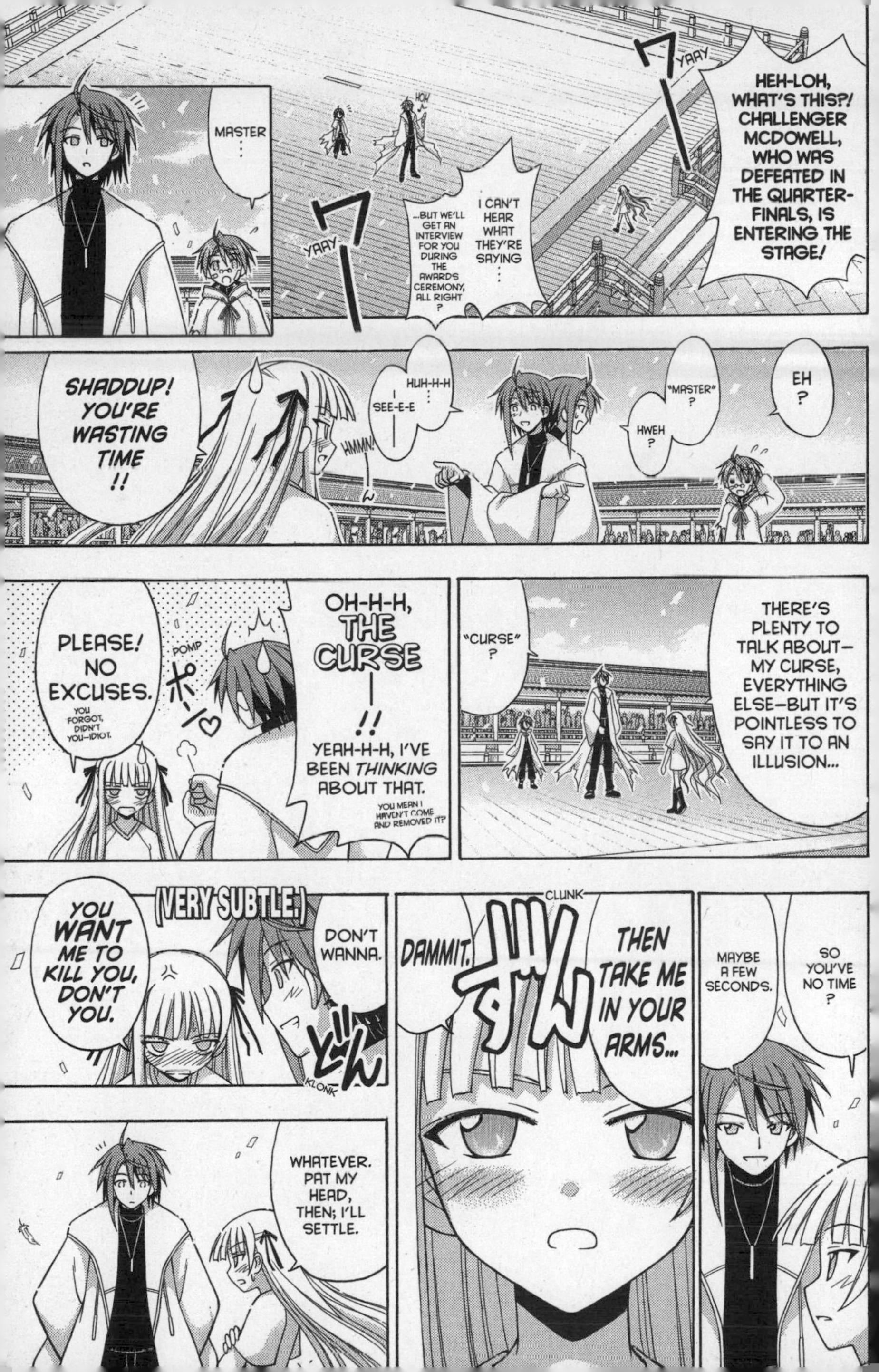

HEH-LOH, WHAT'S THIS?! CHALLENGER MCDOWELL, WHO WAS DEFEATED IN THE QUARTER-FINALS, IS ENTERING THE STAGE!
YAAY
YAAY
I CAN'T HEAR WHAT THEY'RE SAYING...
...BUT WE'LL GET AN INTERVIEW FOR YOU DURING THE AWARDS CEREMONY, ALL RIGHT?
HOH
MASTER...
EH?
"MASTER"?
HWEH?
HUH-H-H I SEE-E-E...
HMMM!
SHADDUP! YOU'RE WASTING TIME!!
THERE'S PLENTY TO TALK ABOUT—MY CURSE, EVERYTHING ELSE—BUT IT'S POINTLESS TO SAY IT TO AN ILLUSION...
"CURSE"?
OH-H-H, THE CURSE—!!
YEAH-H-H, I'VE BEEN THINKING ABOUT THAT.
YOU MEAN I HAVEN'T COME AND REMOVED IT?
POMP
PLEASE! NO EXCUSES.
YOU FORGOT, DIDN'T YOU—IDIOT.
SO YOU'VE NO TIME?
MAYBE A FEW SECONDS.
THEN TAKE ME IN YOUR ARMS...
CLUNK
DAMMIT.
DON'T WANNA.
(VERY SUBTLE.)
YOU WANT ME TO KILL YOU, DON'T YOU.
KLONK
WHATEVER. PAT MY HEAD, THEN; I'LL SETTLE.

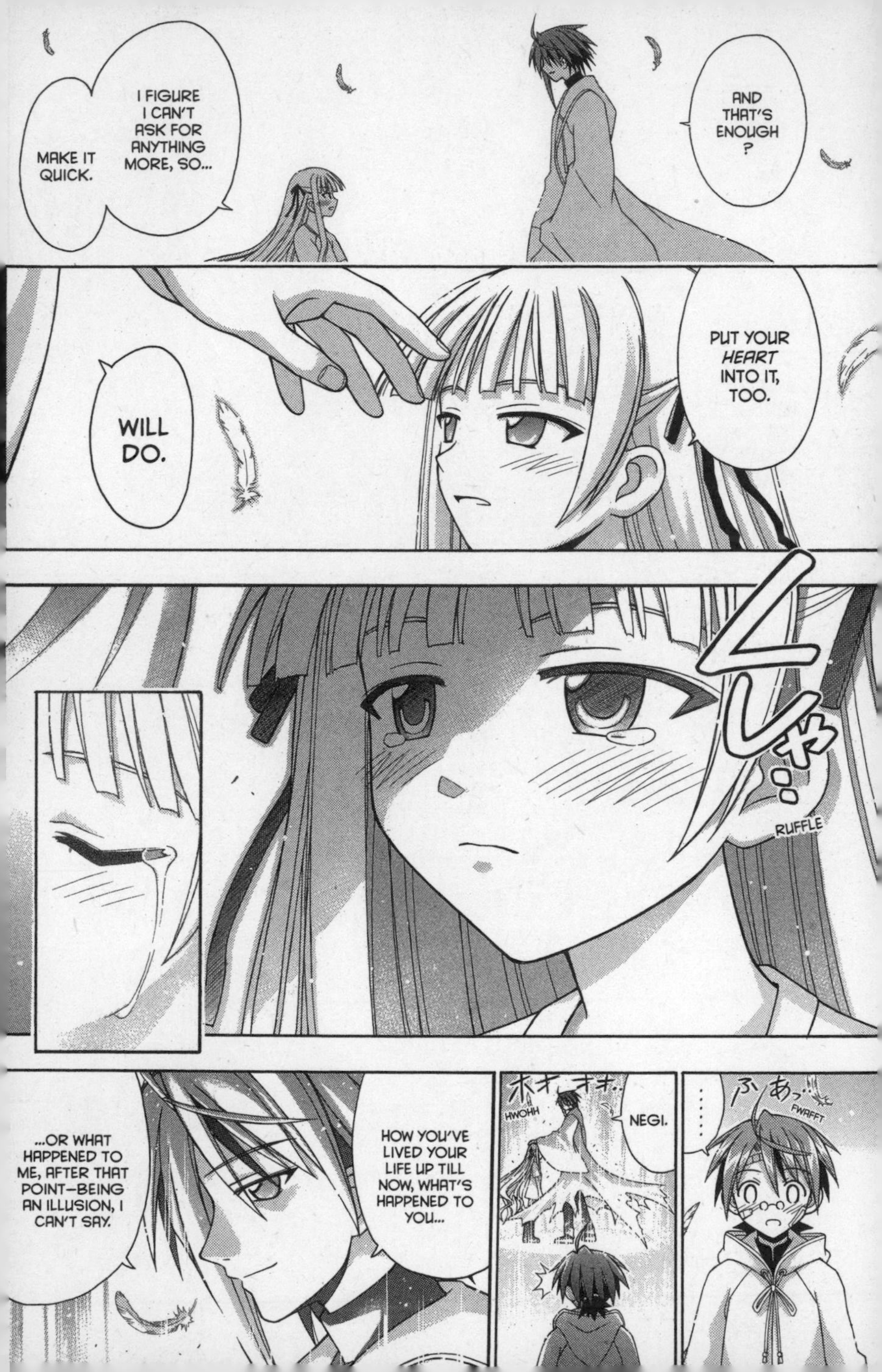
AND THAT'S ENOUGH ?
I FIGURE I CAN'T ASK FOR ANYTHING MORE, SO...
MAKE IT QUICK.
PUT YOUR *HEART* INTO IT, TOO.
WILL DO.
RUFFLE
FWAFFT
......
HWOHH
NEGI.
HOW YOU'VE LIVED YOUR LIFE UP TILL NOW, WHAT'S HAPPENED TO YOU...
...OR WHAT HAPPENED TO ME, AFTER THAT POINT—BEING AN ILLUSION, I CAN'T SAY.

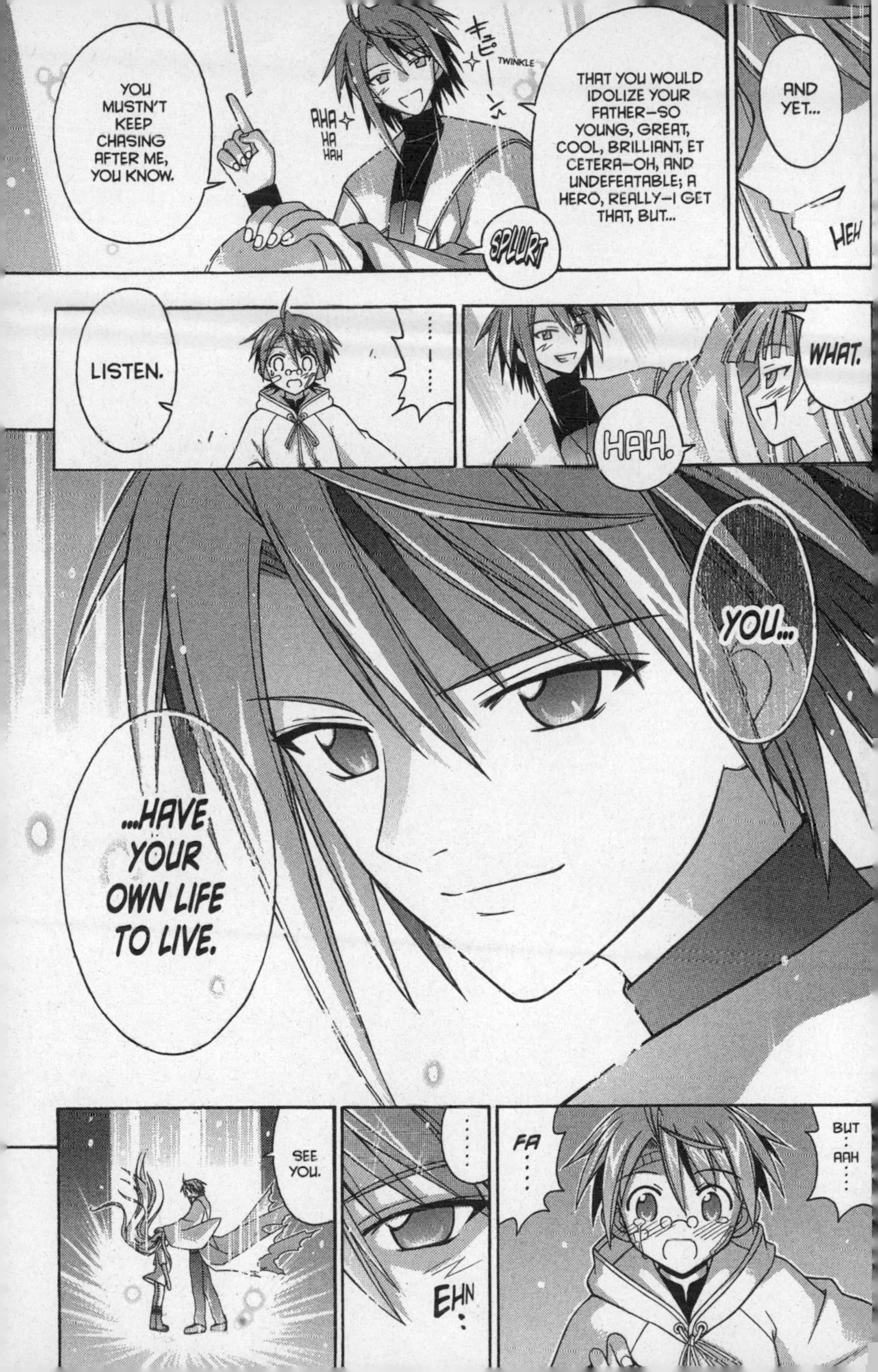

AND YET...
HEH
TWINKLE
THAT YOU WOULD IDOLIZE YOUR FATHER—SO YOUNG, GREAT, COOL, BRILLIANT, ET CETERA—OH, AND UNDEFEATABLE; A HERO, REALLY—I GET THAT, BUT...
AHA HA HAH
YOU MUSTN'T KEEP CHASING AFTER ME, YOU KNOW.
SPLURT
WHAT.
HAH.
......!
LISTEN.
YOU...
...HAVE YOUR OWN LIFE TO LIVE.
BUT... AAH......
FA......
......
EHN...
SEE YOU.

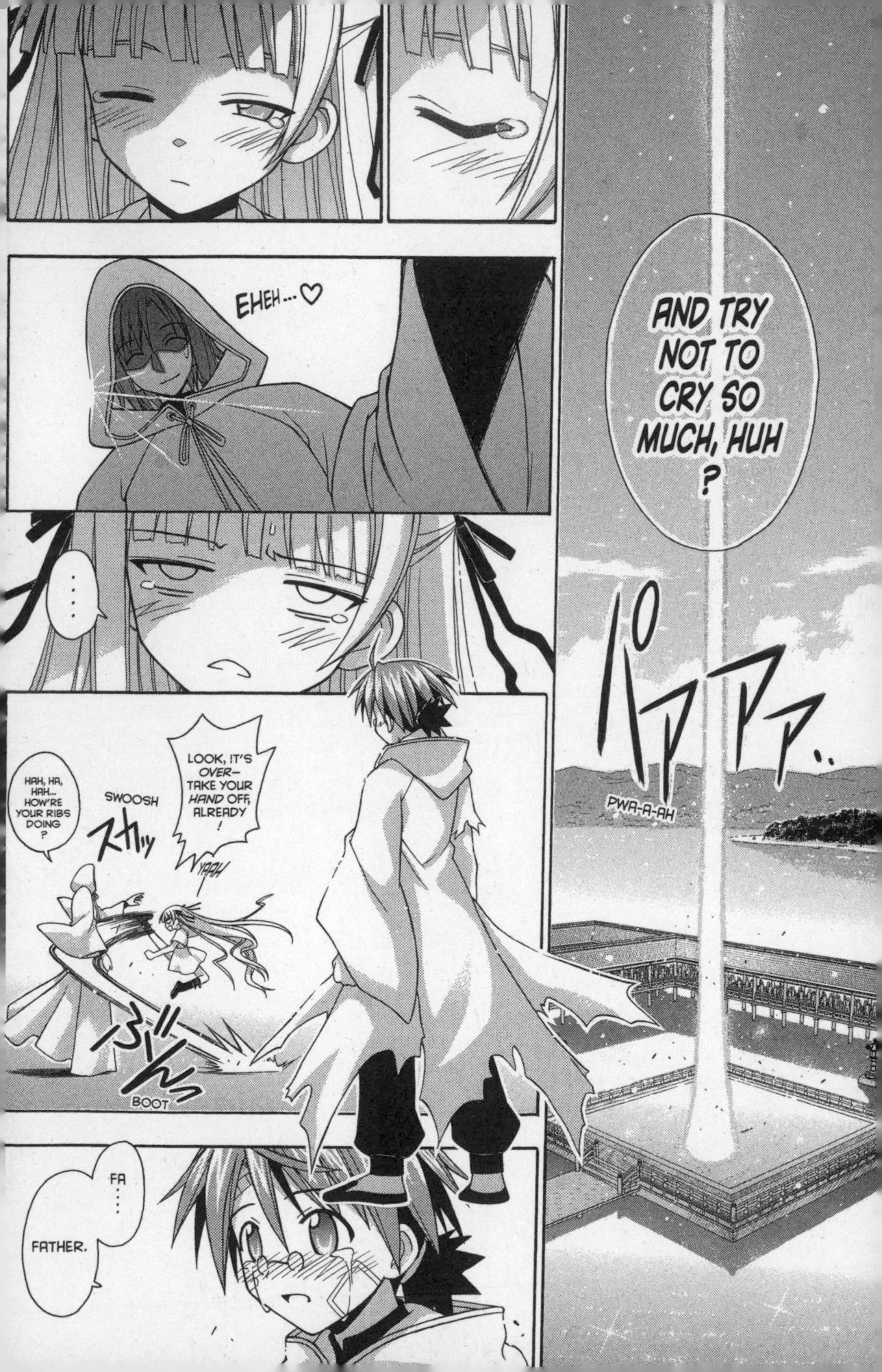
AND TRY NOT TO CRY SO MUCH, HUH?
パァァァ
PWA-A-AH
EHEH...♡
....
LOOK, IT'S OVER—TAKE YOUR HAND OFF, ALREADY!
YAAH
SWOOSH
スカッ
HAH, HA, HAH... HOW'RE YOUR RIBS DOING?
BOOT
FA.....
FATHER.

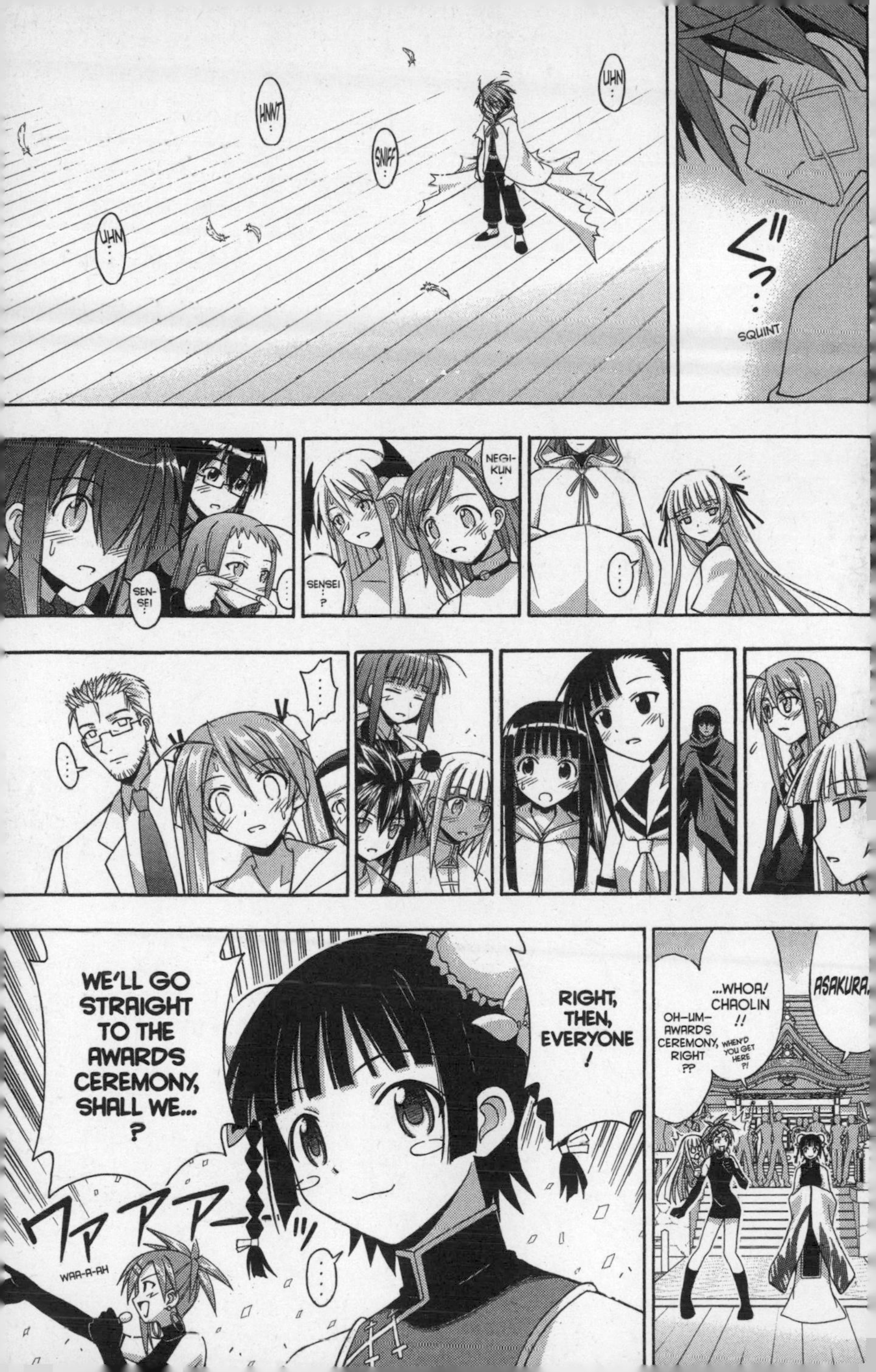
くっ
SQUINT
UHN…
SNIFF…
HNNT…
UHN…
…
NEGI-KUN…
SENSEI…?
…
SEN-SEI…
…
…
…
ASAKURA!
…WHOA! CHAOLIN!!
WHEN'D YOU GET HERE?!
OH—UM—AWARDS CEREMONY, RIGHT??
RIGHT, THEN, EVERYONE!
WE'LL GO STRAIGHT TO THE AWARDS CEREMONY, SHALL WE…?
…
ワァアアー
WAA-A-AH

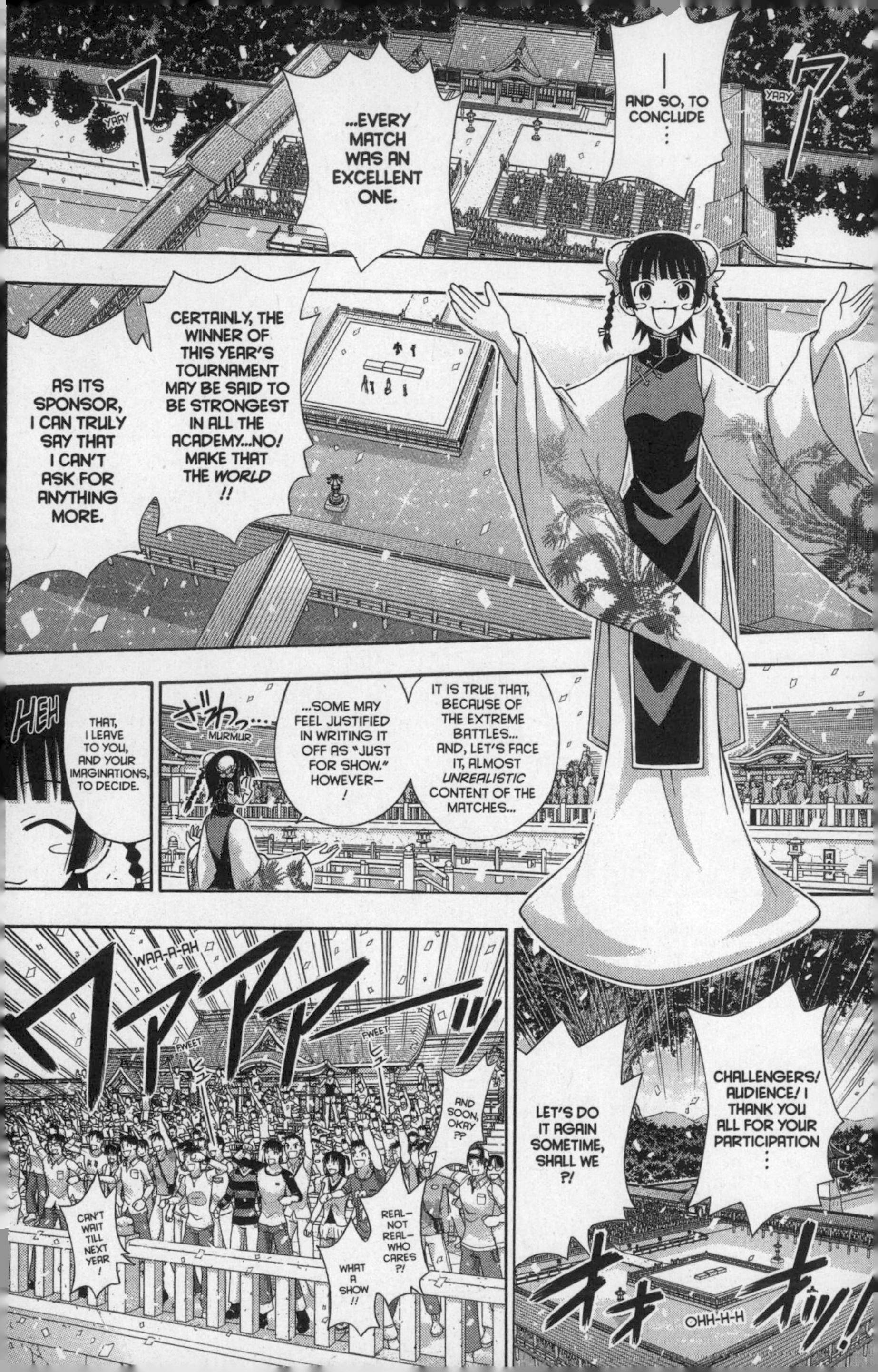
YAAY
AND SO, TO CONCLUDE . . .
...EVERY MATCH WAS AN EXCELLENT ONE.
YAAY
CERTAINLY, THE WINNER OF THIS YEAR'S TOURNAMENT MAY BE SAID TO BE STRONGEST IN ALL THE ACADEMY...NO! MAKE THAT THE *WORLD* !!
AS ITS SPONSOR, I CAN TRULY SAY THAT I CAN'T ASK FOR ANYTHING MORE.
IT IS TRUE THAT, BECAUSE OF THE EXTREME BATTLES... AND, LET'S FACE IT, ALMOST *UNREALISTIC* CONTENT OF THE MATCHES...
...SOME MAY FEEL JUSTIFIED IN WRITING IT OFF AS "JUST FOR SHOW." HOWEVER—!
ざわっ…
MURMUR
THAT, I LEAVE TO YOU, AND YOUR IMAGINATIONS, TO DECIDE.
HEH
CHALLENGERS! AUDIENCE! I THANK YOU ALL FOR YOUR PARTICIPATION . . .
LET'S DO IT AGAIN SOMETIME, SHALL WE ?!
OHH-H-H
WAA-A-AH
FWEET
FWEET
AND SOON, OKAY ??
REAL— NOT REAL— WHO CARES ?!
WHAT A SHOW !!
CAN'T WAIT TILL NEXT YEAR !

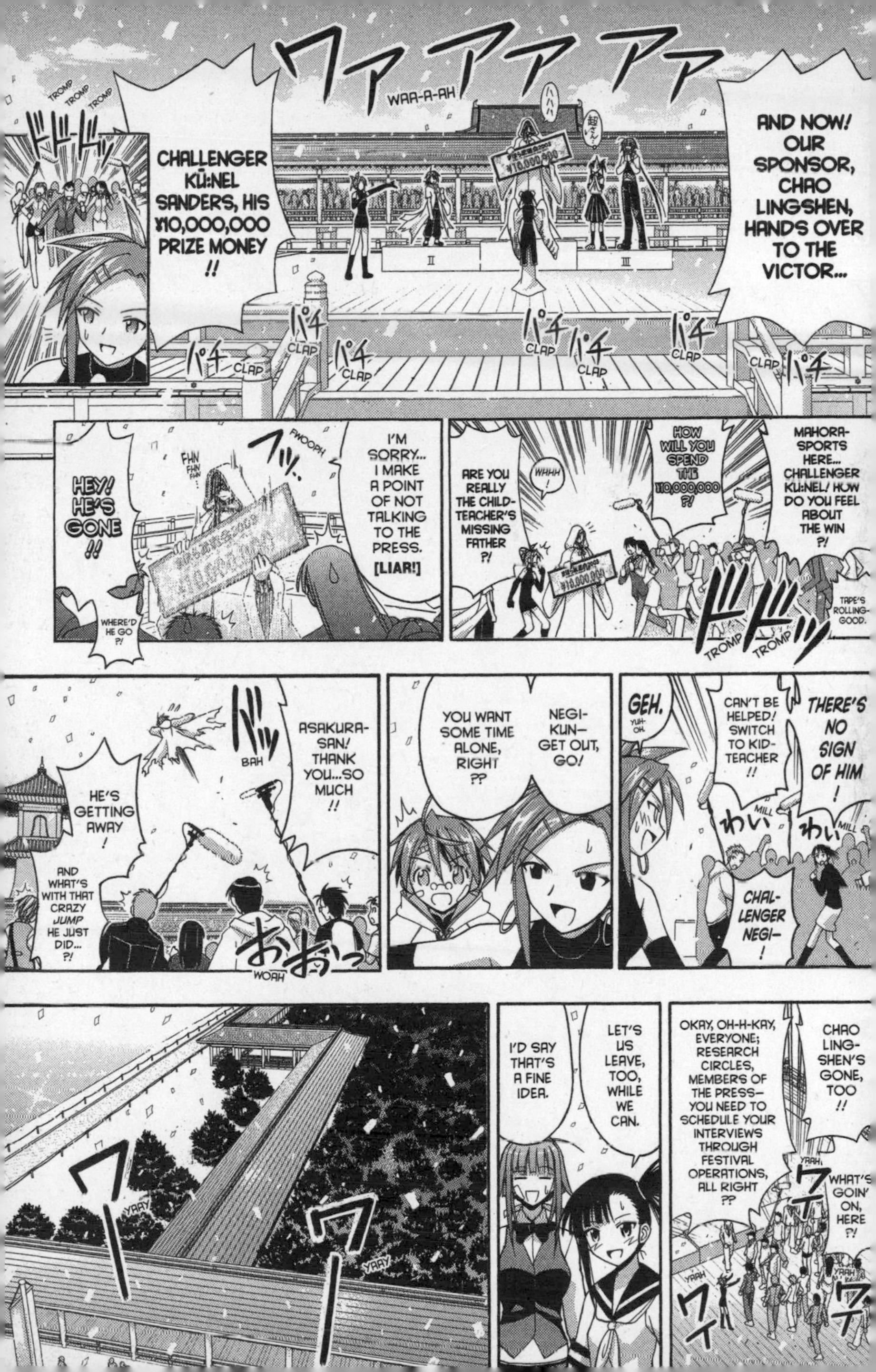

AND NOW! OUR SPONSOR, CHAO LINGSHEN, HANDS OVER TO THE VICTOR...
WAA-A-AH
CHALLENGER KŪ:NEL SANDERS, HIS ¥10,000,000 PRIZE MONEY!!
TROMP TROMP TROMP
CLAP
CLAP
CLAP
CLAP
CLAP
CLAP
MAHORA-SPORTS HERE... CHALLENGER KU:NEL! HOW DO YOU FEEL ABOUT THE WIN?!
TAPE'S ROLLING-GOOD.
HOW WILL YOU SPEND THE ¥10,000,000?!
WHHH!
ARE YOU REALLY THE CHILD-TEACHER'S MISSING FATHER?!
TROMP TROMP
I'M SORRY... I MAKE A POINT OF NOT TALKING TO THE PRESS. [LIAR!]
FWOOPH
FHN FHN FHN
HEY! HE'S GONE!!
WHERE'D HE GO?!
THERE'S NO SIGN OF HIM!
CAN'T BE HELPED! SWITCH TO KID-TEACHER!!
GEH.
YUH-OH.
MILL
MILL
CHAL-LENGER NEGI-!
NEGI-KUN— GET OUT, GO!
YOU WANT SOME TIME ALONE, RIGHT??
ASAKURA-SAN! THANK YOU...SO MUCH!!
BAH
HE'S GETTING AWAY!
AND WHAT'S WITH THAT CRAZY JUMP HE JUST DID...?!
WOAH
CHAO LING-SHEN'S GONE, TOO!!
OKAY, OH-H-KAY, EVERYONE; RESEARCH CIRCLES, MEMBERS OF THE PRESS— YOU NEED TO SCHEDULE YOUR INTERVIEWS THROUGH FESTIVAL OPERATIONS, ALL RIGHT??
YAAH
WHAT'S GOIN' ON, HERE?!
YAAH
YAAH
LET'S US LEAVE, TOO, WHILE WE CAN.
I'D SAY THAT'S A FINE IDEA.
YAAY
YAAY

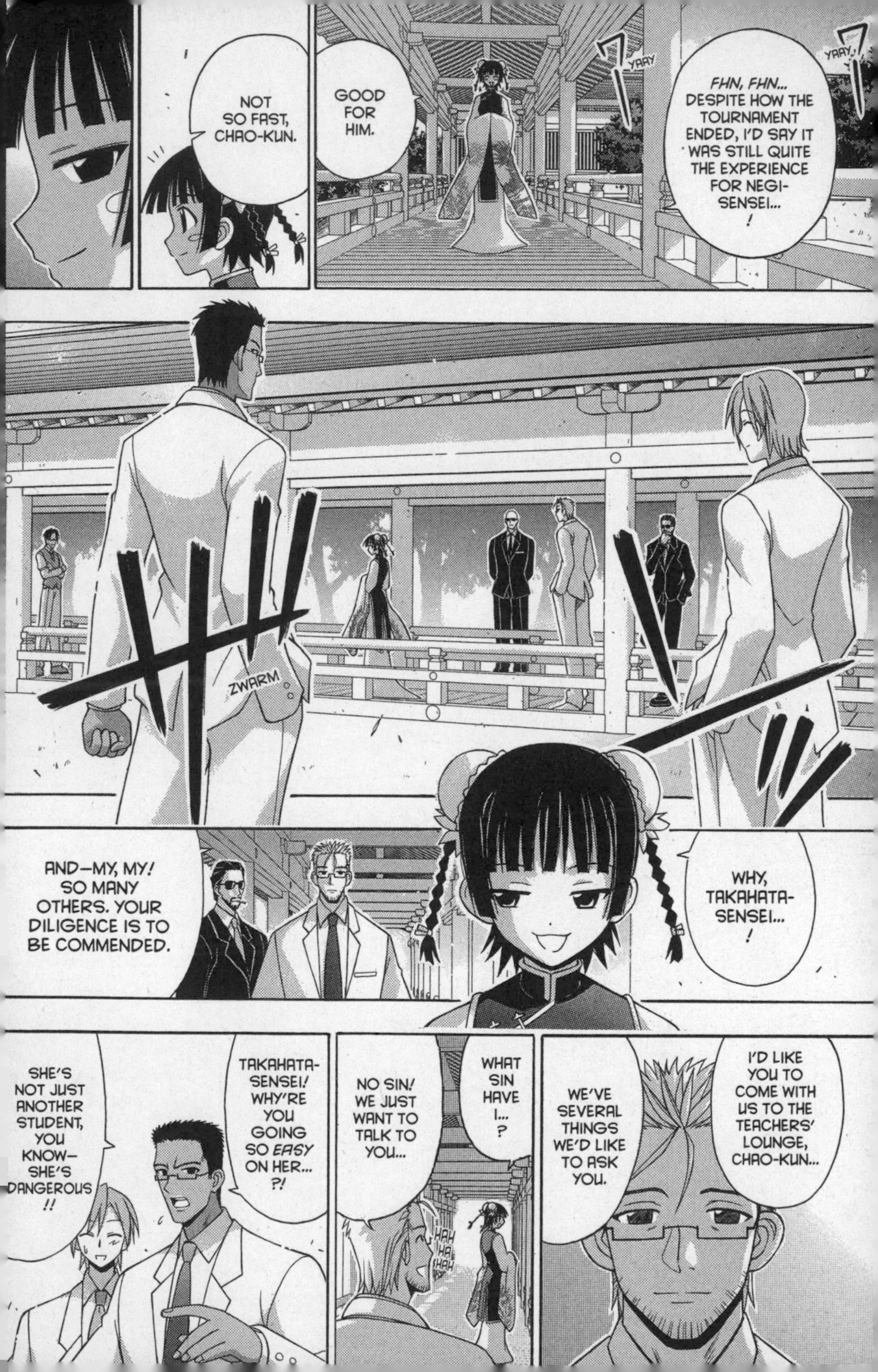
YAAY
YAAY
FHN, FHN... DESPITE HOW THE TOURNAMENT ENDED, I'D SAY IT WAS STILL QUITE THE EXPERIENCE FOR NEGI-SENSEI... !
GOOD FOR HIM.
NOT SO FAST, CHAO-KUN.
ZWARM
WHY, TAKAHATA-SENSEI... !
AND—MY, MY! SO MANY OTHERS. YOUR DILIGENCE IS TO BE COMMENDED.
I'D LIKE YOU TO COME WITH US TO THE TEACHERS' LOUNGE, CHAO-KUN...
WE'VE SEVERAL THINGS WE'D LIKE TO ASK YOU.
WHAT SIN HAVE I... ?
NO SIN! WE JUST WANT TO TALK TO YOU...
HAH HA HAH
TAKAHATA-SENSEI! WHY'RE YOU GOING SO *EASY* ON HER... ?!
SHE'S NOT JUST ANOTHER STUDENT, YOU KNOW—SHE'S DANGEROUS !!

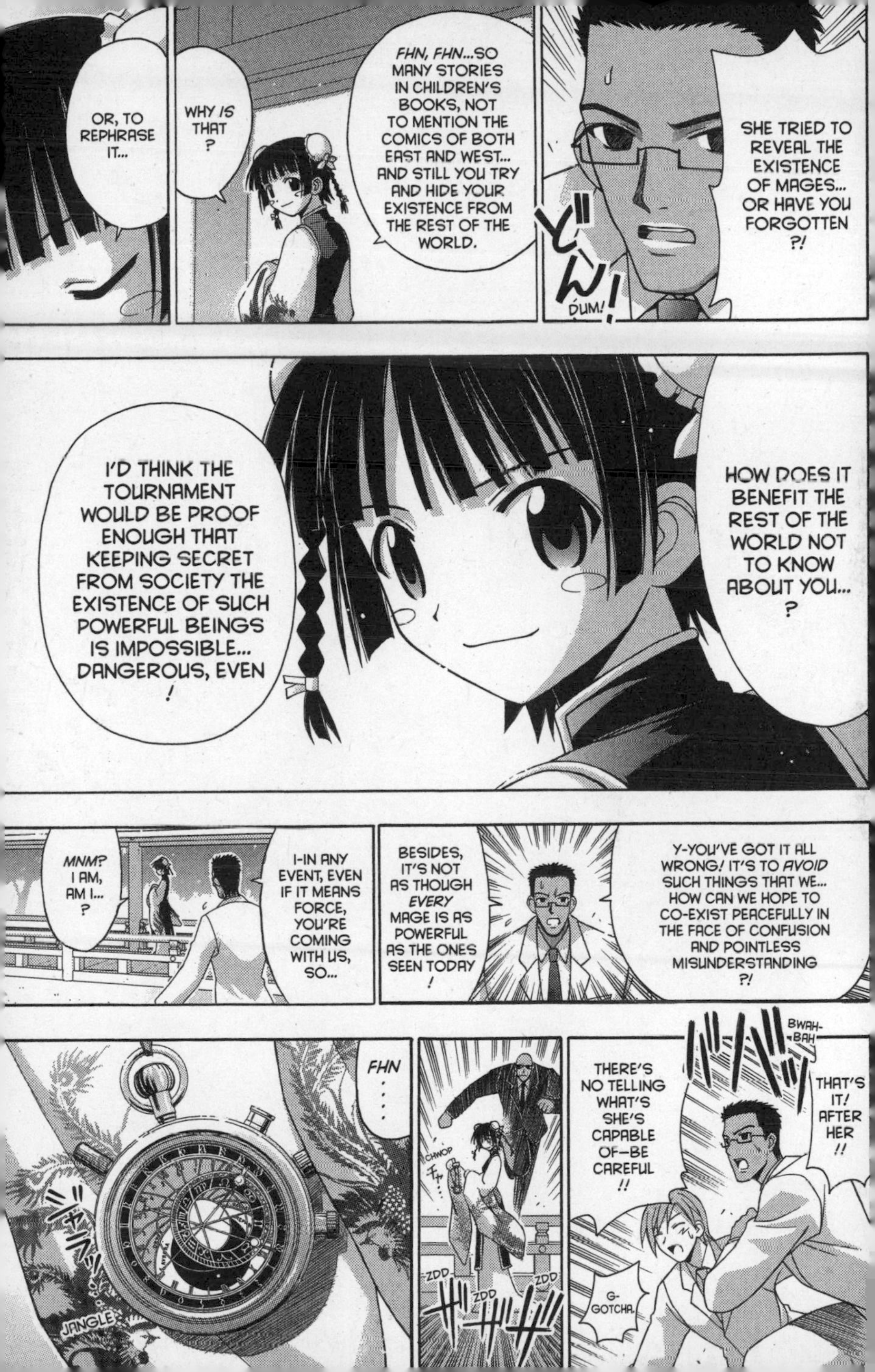
SHE TRIED TO REVEAL THE EXISTENCE OF MAGES... OR HAVE YOU FORGOTTEN ?!
DUM!
FHN, FHN...SO MANY STORIES IN CHILDREN'S BOOKS, NOT TO MENTION THE COMICS OF BOTH EAST AND WEST... AND STILL YOU TRY AND HIDE YOUR EXISTENCE FROM THE REST OF THE WORLD.
WHY IS THAT ?
OR, TO REPHRASE IT...
HOW DOES IT BENEFIT THE REST OF THE WORLD NOT TO KNOW ABOUT YOU... ?
I'D THINK THE TOURNAMENT WOULD BE PROOF ENOUGH THAT KEEPING SECRET FROM SOCIETY THE EXISTENCE OF SUCH POWERFUL BEINGS IS IMPOSSIBLE... DANGEROUS, EVEN !
Y-YOU'VE GOT IT ALL WRONG! IT'S TO AVOID SUCH THINGS THAT WE... HOW CAN WE HOPE TO CO-EXIST PEACEFULLY IN THE FACE OF CONFUSION AND POINTLESS MISUNDERSTANDING ?!
BESIDES, IT'S NOT AS THOUGH EVERY MAGE IS AS POWERFUL AS THE ONES SEEN TODAY !
I-IN ANY EVENT, EVEN IF IT MEANS FORCE, YOU'RE COMING WITH US, SO...
MNM? I AM, AM I... ?
BWAH-BAH
THAT'S IT! AFTER HER !!
THERE'S NO TELLING WHAT'S SHE'S CAPABLE OF—BE CAREFUL !!
G-GOTCHA.
CHWOP
ZDD
ZDD
ZDD
FHN ...
JANGLE

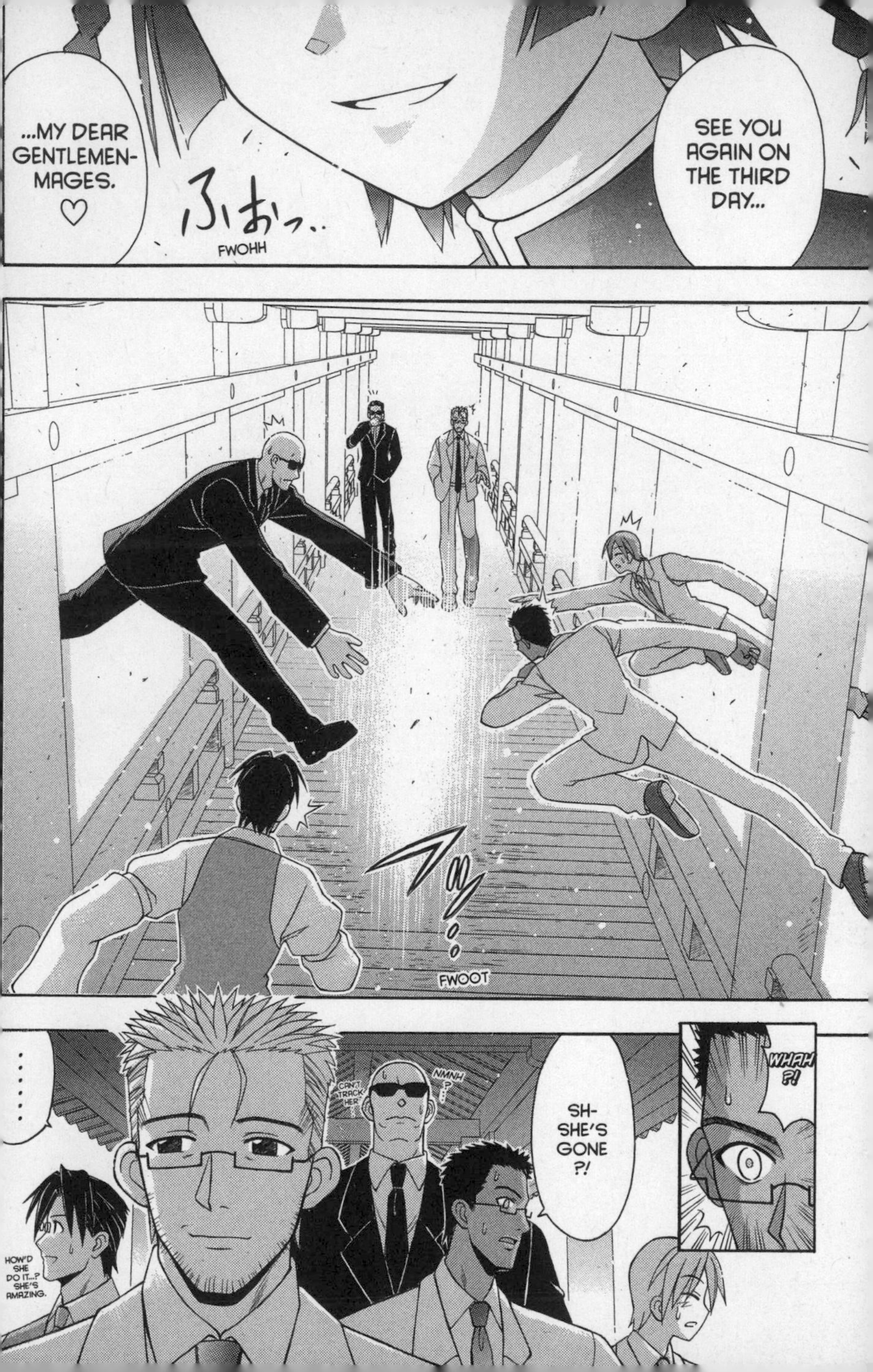
SEE YOU AGAIN ON THE THIRD DAY...
ふおっ..
FWOHH
...MY DEAR GENTLEMEN-MAGES. ♡
FWOOT
WHAH ?!
SH- SHE'S GONE ?!
NMNH ...?
CAN'T TRACK HER
......
HOW'D SHE DO IT...? SHE'S AMAZING.

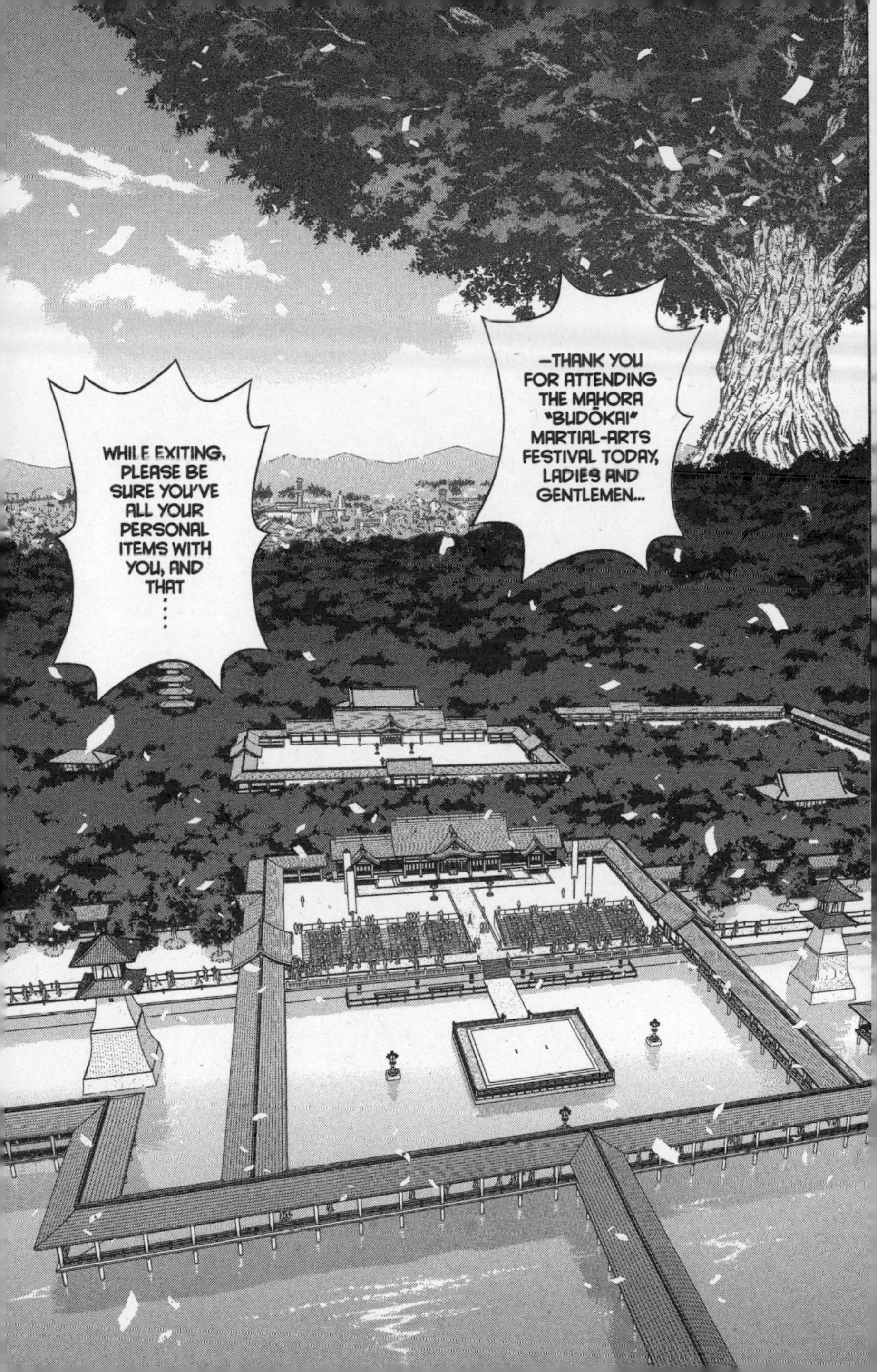
—THANK YOU FOR ATTENDING THE MAHORA "BUDŌKAI" MARTIAL-ARTS FESTIVAL TODAY, LADIES AND GENTLEMEN...
WHILE EXITING, PLEASE BE SURE YOU'VE ALL YOUR PERSONAL ITEMS WITH YOU, AND THAT
...

LEXICON MAGICUM NEGIMARIUM

—*Negima!* Volume 13—
[117th Period]

■イノチノシヘン

ハイ•ビュブロイ•ハイ•ビオグラフィカイ

(ἁι βύβλοι ἁι βιογραφικαί)

In ancient Greek, **βυβλοι** means "paper" and also "book," while **βιογραφικαί** means "to depict life," or "to illustrate life"—"biography," in this sense. [*"Paper of Life" or "Poem of Life" are possible translations for the Japanese transliteration* "Inochi no Shihen *(life + of + paper/poem)." In that* kanji *is not used, but the phonetic* katakana, *it's a safe bet that author intends for both meanings to be considered—Ed.*]

In the course of his travels, the mysterious "Kū:nel" has met many different persons, and this artifact has collected the life-information of all of them. In order for him to create a "book" of their lives, he need but ask the true name of the person, and perform a special ritual.

As British anthropologist Sir James George Frazier suggests in his book, *The Golden Bough*,

> Unable to discriminate clearly between words and things, the savage commonly fancies that the link between a name and the person or thing denominated by it is not a mere arbitrary and ideal association, but a real and substantial bond which unites the two in such a way that magic may be wrought on a man just as easily through his name as through his hair, his nails, or any other material part of his person. In fact, primitive man regards his name as a vital portion of himself and takes care of it accordingly. Thus, for example, the North American Indian regards his name, not as a mere label, but as a distinct part of his personality, just as much as are his eyes or his teeth, and believes that injury will result as surely from the malicious handling of his name as from a wound inflicted on any part of his physical organism (Chapter 22, Sec. 1).

Knowing a person's name has important significance in the creation of magic. As Frazier goes on to say, a "person's name only seems to be a part of himself when it is uttered with his own breath"—which goes to explain why one's true name must be given for the **ἁι βυβλοι ἁι βιογραφικαί** to be created. "The Tolampoos of Celebes," Frazier elaborates, "believe that if you write a man's name down, you can carry off his soul along with it."

Of all the world's cultures, Indonesia is believed to be the one with which Kū:nel's artifact is most closely affiliated, and has the power to allow him to actually become an individual—possessing all the emotions, tastes, and memories associated therein—for ten minutes' time.

It should be noted that, being an artifact of limited usefulness, the contents of the **ἁι βυβλοι ἁι βιογραφικαί** are not automatically updated, containing only the biography of the individual up to the point the book was created and no further.

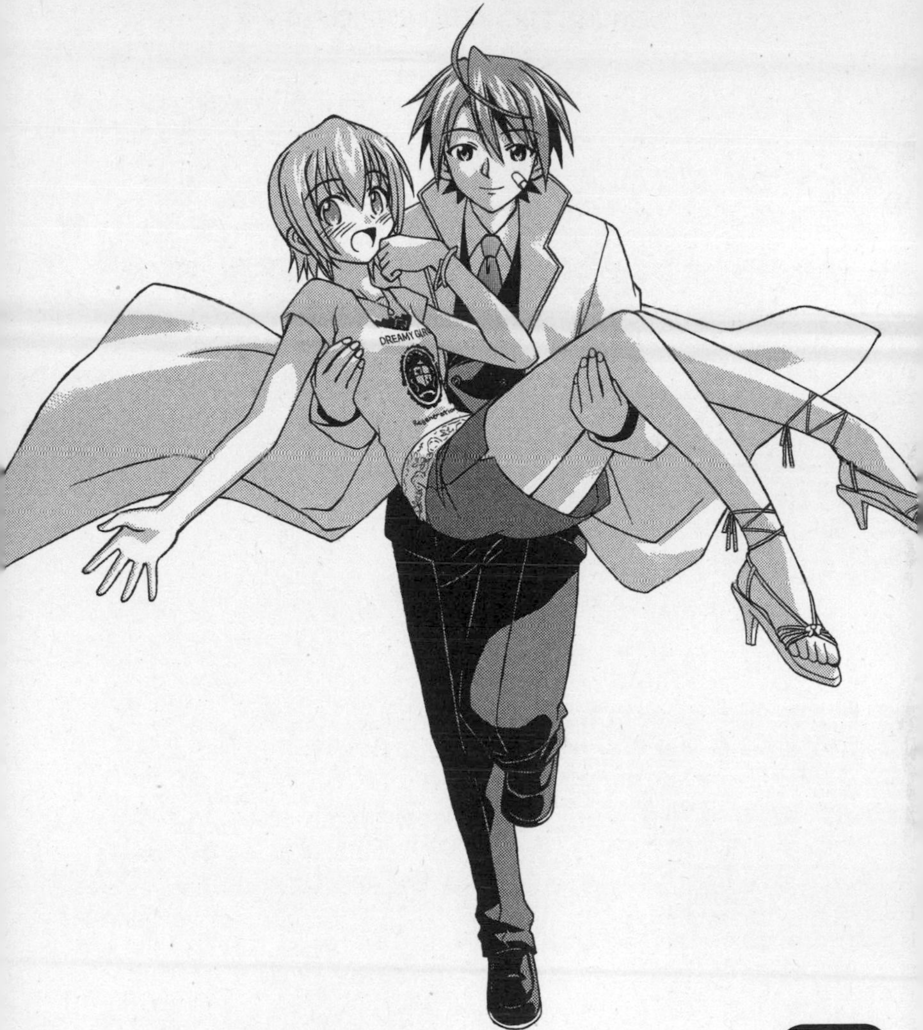

魔法先生(まほうせんせい)

ネギま!

MAGISTER NEGI MAGI

14

Ken Akamatsu

赤松(あかまつ) 健(けん)

Contents

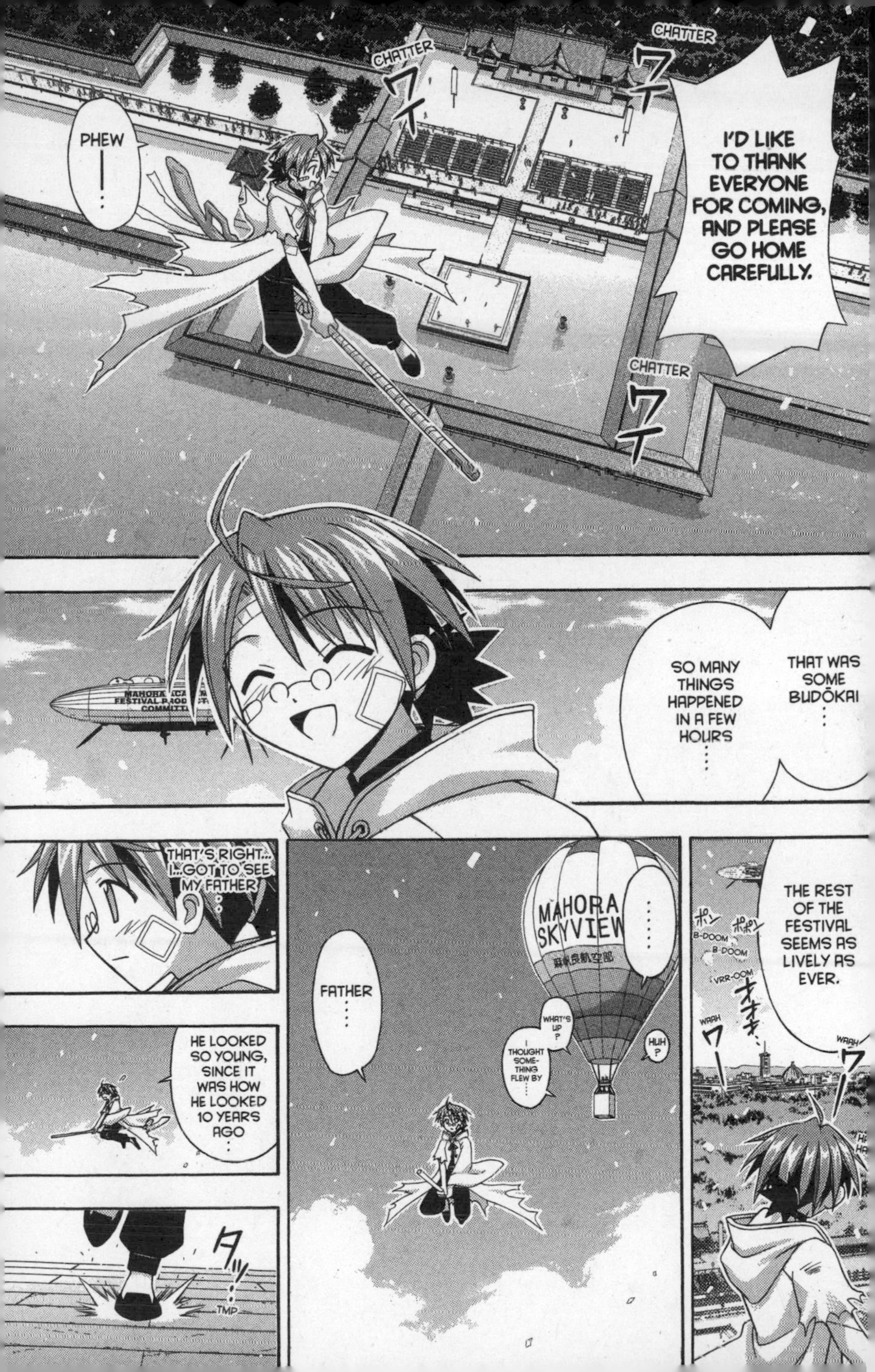
CHATTER
ワイ
I'D LIKE TO THANK EVERYONE FOR COMING, AND PLEASE GO HOME CAREFULLY.
CHATTER
ワイ
CHATTER
ワイ
PHEW—...
THAT WAS SOME BUDŌKAI...
SO MANY THINGS HAPPENED IN A FEW HOURS...
THE REST OF THE FESTIVAL SEEMS AS LIVELY AS EVER.
ポン B-DOOM
ポポン B-DOOM
VRR-OOM
オォォ
WAAH ワー
WAAH ワー
......
MAHORA SKYVIEW
FATHER...
HUH?
WHAT'S UP?
I THOUGHT SOMETHING FLEW BY...
THAT'S RIGHT... I...GOT TO SEE MY FATHER...
HE LOOKED SO YOUNG, SINCE IT WAS HOW HE LOOKED 10 YEARS AGO...
タッ
TMP

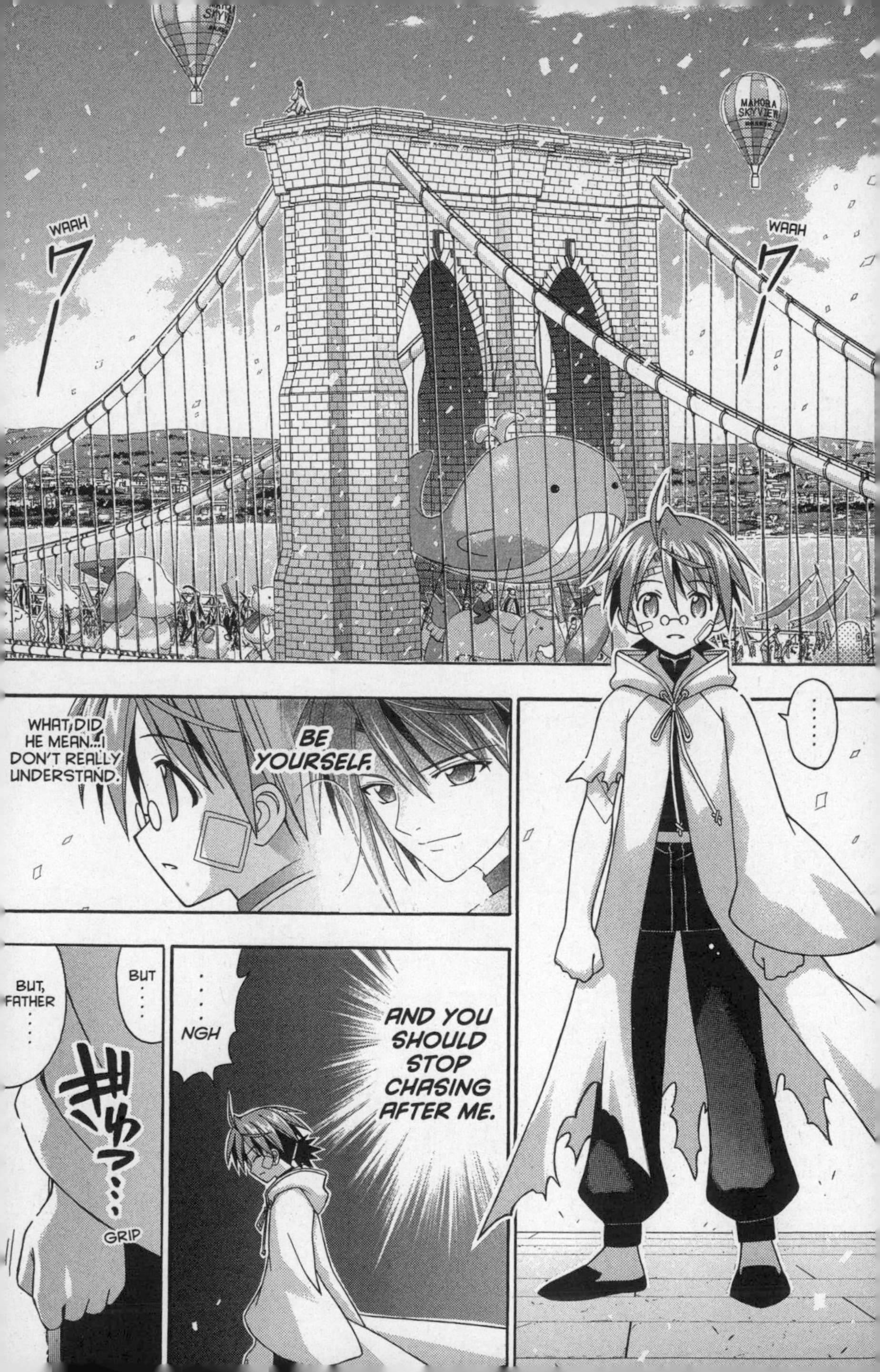
WAAH
WAAH
......
BE YOURSELF.
WHAT, DID HE MEAN...I DON'T REALLY UNDERSTAND.
AND YOU SHOULD STOP CHASING AFTER ME.
......NGH
BUT......
BUT, FATHER......
ぎゅっ...
GRIP

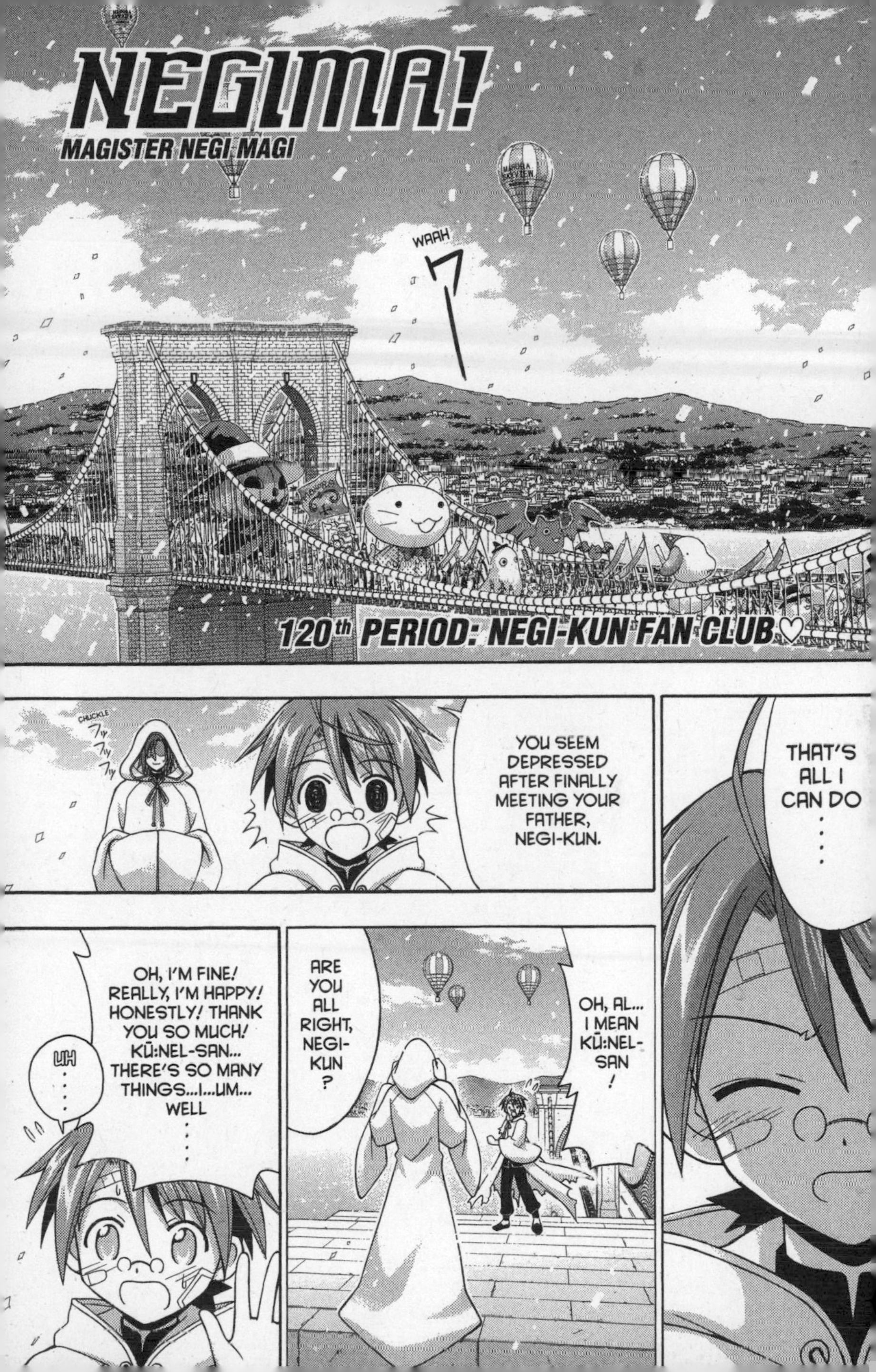
NEGIMA!
MAGISTER NEGI MAGI
MAHORA SKYVIEW
WAAH
120th PERIOD: NEGI-KUN FAN CLUB♡
THAT'S ALL I CAN DO . . . .
YOU SEEM DEPRESSED AFTER FINALLY MEETING YOUR FATHER, NEGI-KUN.
CHUCKLE
OH, AL... I MEAN KŪ:NEL-SAN !
ARE YOU ALL RIGHT, NEGI-KUN ?
OH, I'M FINE! REALLY, I'M HAPPY! HONESTLY! THANK YOU SO MUCH! KŪ:NEL-SAN... THERE'S SO MANY THINGS...I...UM... WELL . . . .
UH . . . .

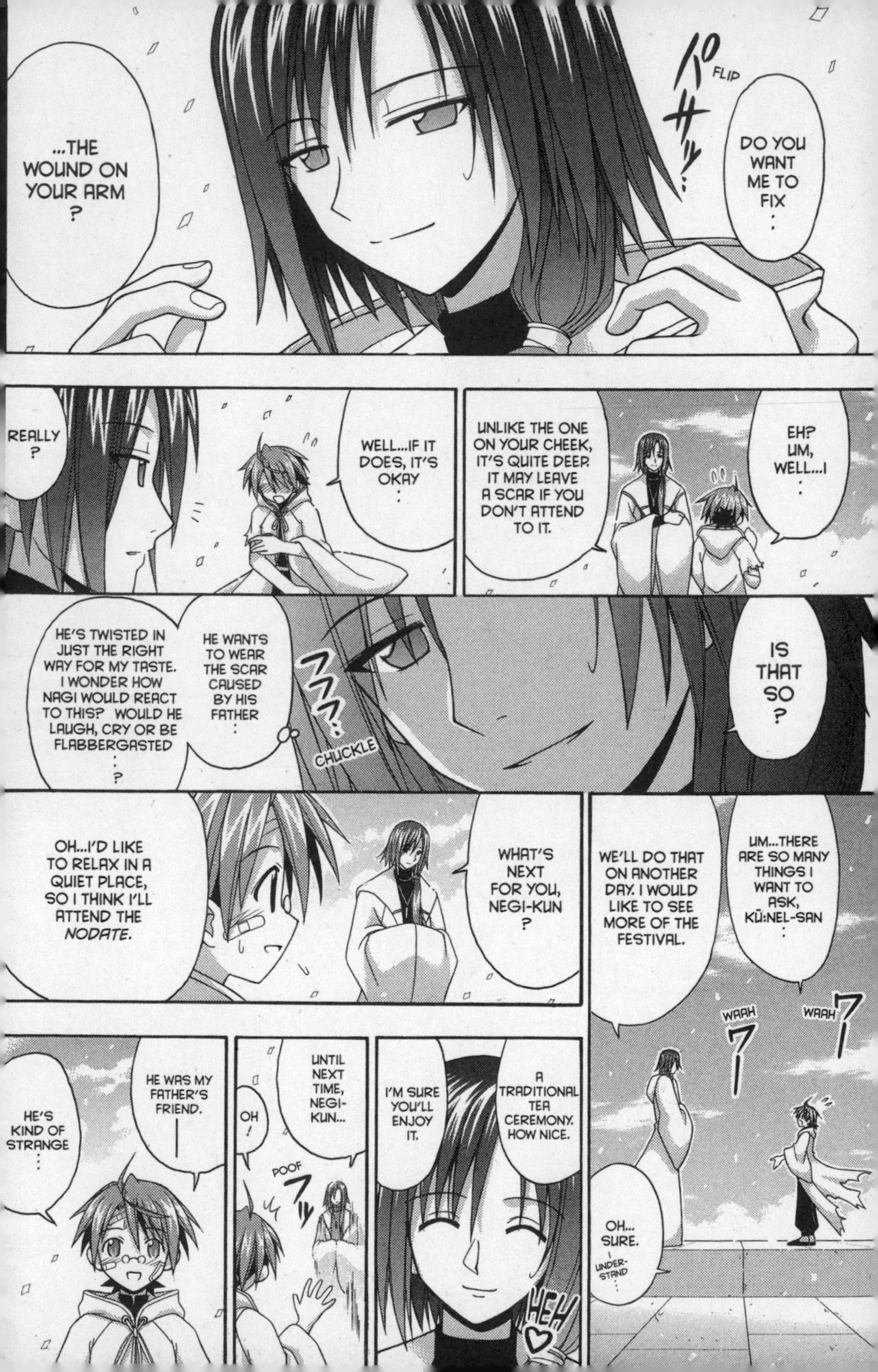

DO YOU WANT ME TO FIX :
FLIP
...THE WOUND ON YOUR ARM ?
EH? UM, WELL...I :
UNLIKE THE ONE ON YOUR CHEEK, IT'S QUITE DEEP. IT MAY LEAVE A SCAR IF YOU DON'T ATTEND TO IT.
WELL...IF IT DOES, IT'S OKAY :
REALLY ?
IS THAT SO ?
CHUCKLE
HE WANTS TO WEAR THE SCAR CAUSED BY HIS FATHER :
HE'S TWISTED IN JUST THE RIGHT WAY FOR MY TASTE. I WONDER HOW NAGI WOULD REACT TO THIS? WOULD HE LAUGH, CRY OR BE FLABBERGASTED : ?
UM...THERE ARE SO MANY THINGS I WANT TO ASK, KŪ:NEL-SAN :
WE'LL DO THAT ON ANOTHER DAY. I WOULD LIKE TO SEE MORE OF THE FESTIVAL.
WAAH
WAAH
OH... SURE.
I UNDERSTAND ...
WHAT'S NEXT FOR YOU, NEGI-KUN ?
OH...I'D LIKE TO RELAX IN A QUIET PLACE, SO I THINK I'LL ATTEND THE NODATE.
A TRADITIONAL TEA CEREMONY. HOW NICE.
I'M SURE YOU'LL ENJOY IT.
UNTIL NEXT TIME, NEGI-KUN...
OH !
POOF
HE WAS MY FATHER'S FRIEND.
HE'S KIND OF STRANGE :

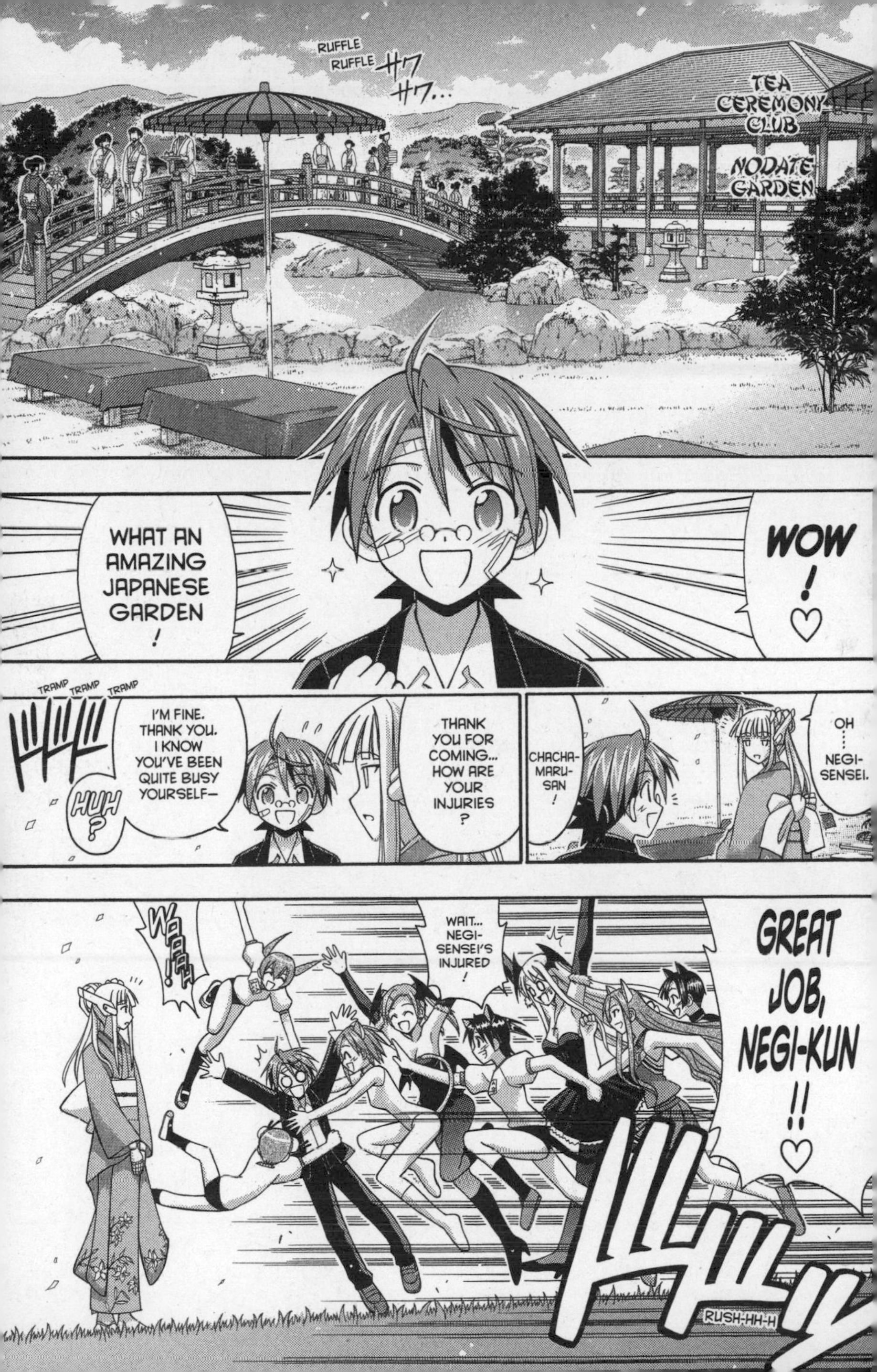
RUFFLE
RUFFLE
サワ
サワ…
TEA CEREMONY CLUB
NODATE GARDEN
WOW! ♡
WHAT AN AMAZING JAPANESE GARDEN!
OH… NEGI-SENSEI.
CHACHAMARU-SAN!
THANK YOU FOR COMING… HOW ARE YOUR INJURIES?
I'M FINE. THANK YOU. I KNOW YOU'VE BEEN QUITE BUSY YOURSELF—
HUH?
TRAMP TRAMP TRAMP
GREAT JOB, NEGI-KUN!! ♡
WAIT… NEGI-SENSEI'S INJURED!
WAAAAH!
RUSH-HH-H

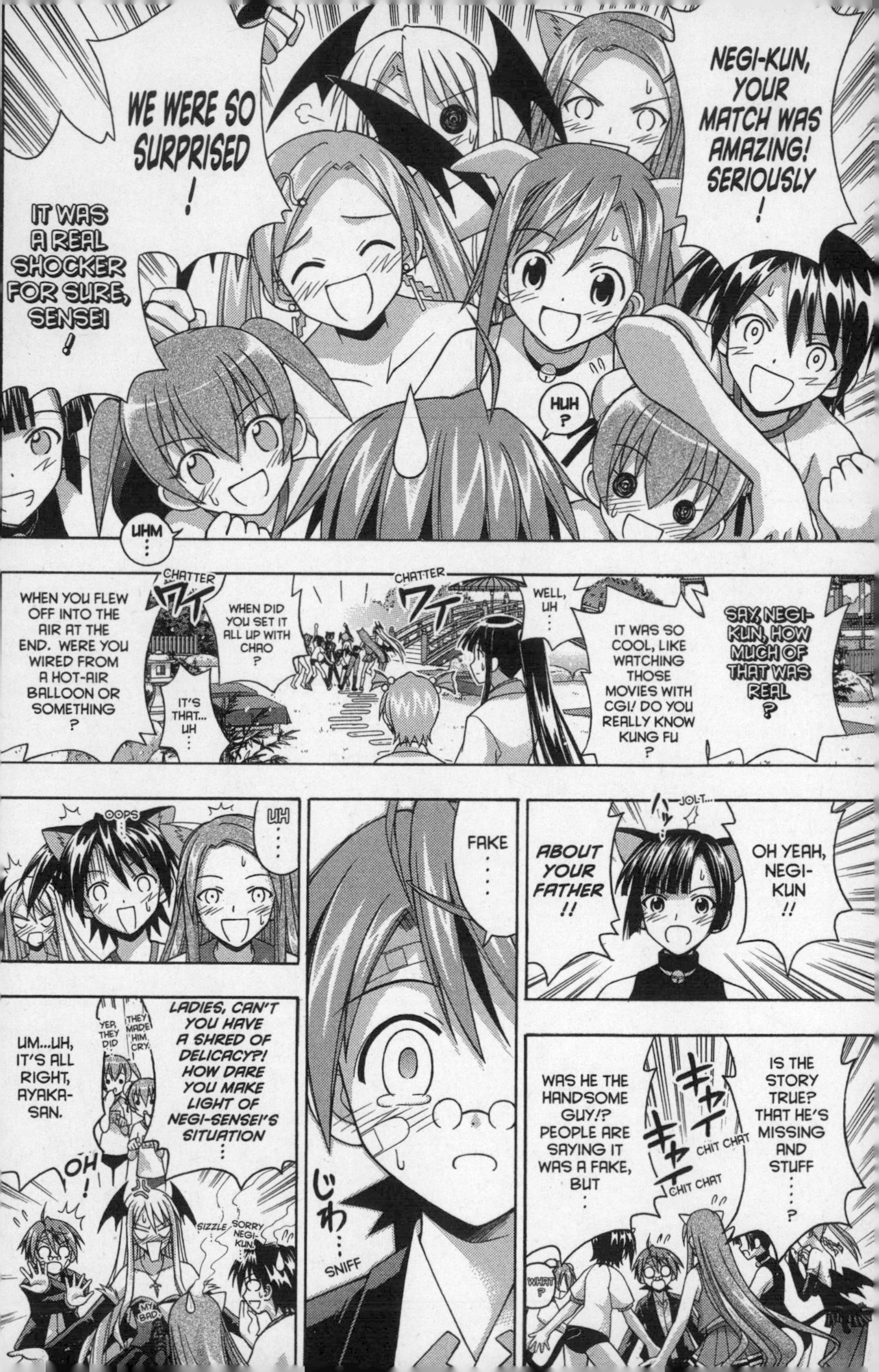
NEGI-KUN, YOUR MATCH WAS AMAZING! SERIOUSLY!
WE WERE SO SURPRISED!
IT WAS A REAL SHOCKER FOR SURE, SENSEI!
HUH?
UHM...
SAY, NEGI-KUN, HOW MUCH OF THAT WAS REAL?
IT WAS SO COOL, LIKE WATCHING THOSE MOVIES WITH CGI! DO YOU REALLY KNOW KUNG FU?
WELL, UH...
CHATTER
WHEN DID YOU SET IT ALL UP WITH CHAO?
IT'S THAT... UH...
CHATTER
WHEN YOU FLEW OFF INTO THE AIR AT THE END. WERE YOU WIRED FROM A HOT-AIR BALLOON OR SOMETHING?
JOLT...
OH YEAH, NEGI-KUN!!
ABOUT YOUR FATHER!!
IS THE STORY TRUE? THAT HE'S MISSING AND STUFF...?
WAS HE THE HANDSOME GUY!? PEOPLE ARE SAYING IT WAS A FAKE, BUT:
CHIT CHAT
CHIT CHAT
WHAT?
FAKE...
SNIFF
UH...
OOPS
LADIES, CAN'T YOU HAVE A SHRED OF DELICACY?! HOW DARE YOU MAKE LIGHT OF NEGI-SENSEI'S SITUATION...
THEY MADE HIM CRY.
YEP, THEY DID
UM...UH, IT'S ALL RIGHT, AYAKA-SAN.
OH!
SIZZLE
SORRY NEGI-KUN
MY BAD

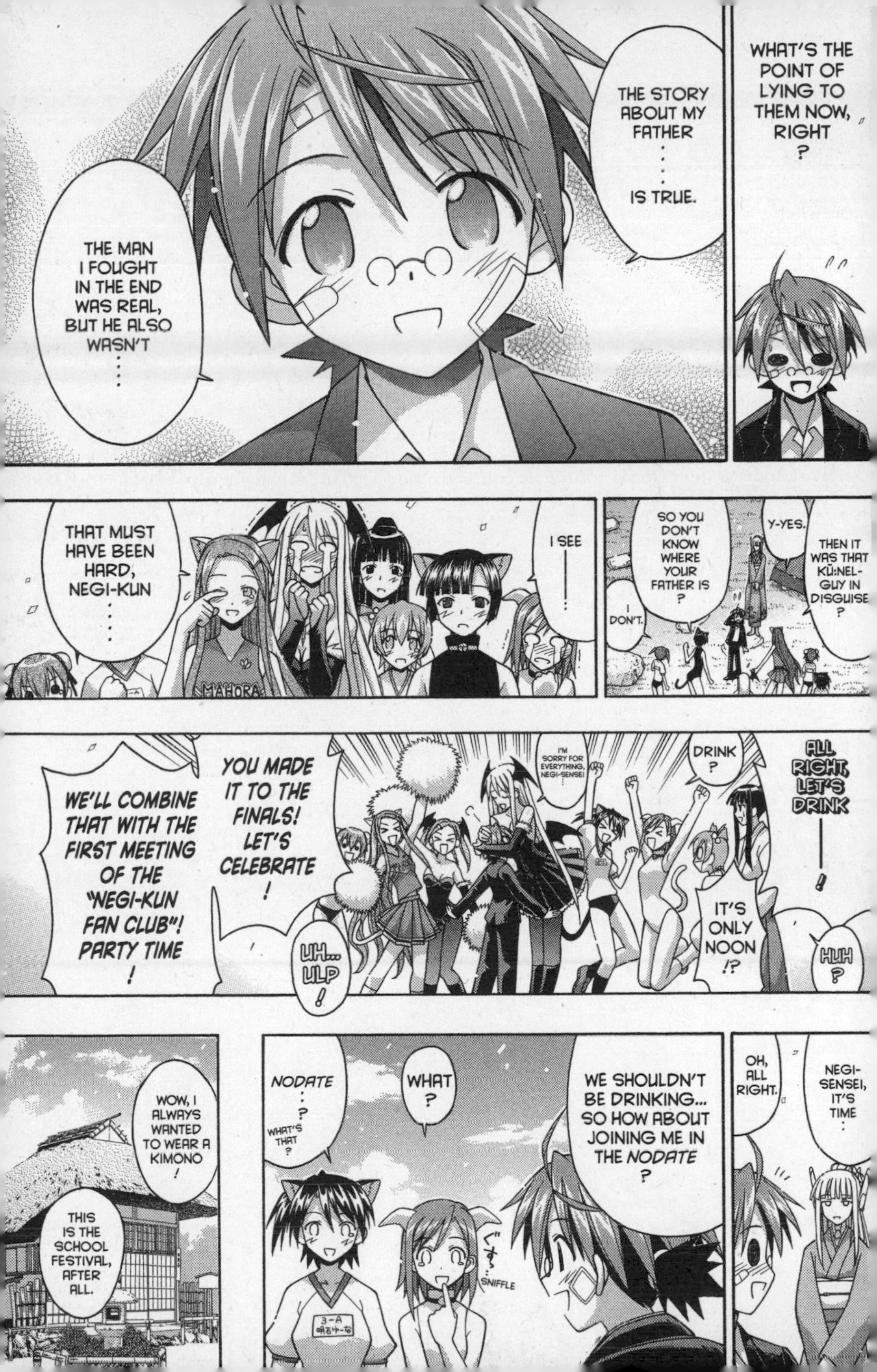
WHAT'S THE POINT OF LYING TO THEM NOW, RIGHT?
THE STORY ABOUT MY FATHER . . . IS TRUE.
THE MAN I FOUGHT IN THE END WAS REAL, BUT HE ALSO WASN'T . . .
THEN IT WAS THAT KŪ:NEL-GUY IN DISGUISE?
Y-YES.
SO YOU DON'T KNOW WHERE YOUR FATHER IS?
I DON'T.
I SEE ——!
THAT MUST HAVE BEEN HARD, NEGI-KUN . . .
ALL RIGHT, LET'S DRINK ——!
HUH?
DRINK?
IT'S ONLY NOON!?
I'M SORRY FOR EVERYTHING, NEGI-SENSEI!
YOU MADE IT TO THE FINALS! LET'S CELEBRATE!
UH... ULP!
WE'LL COMBINE THAT WITH THE FIRST MEETING OF THE "NEGI-KUN FAN CLUB"! PARTY TIME!
NEGI-SENSEI, IT'S TIME :
OH, ALL RIGHT.
WE SHOULDN'T BE DRINKING... SO HOW ABOUT JOINING ME IN THE *NODATE*?
WHAT?
NODATE . . . ?
WHAT'S THAT?
SNIFFLE
WOW, I ALWAYS WANTED TO WEAR A KIMONO!
THIS IS THE SCHOOL FESTIVAL, AFTER ALL.

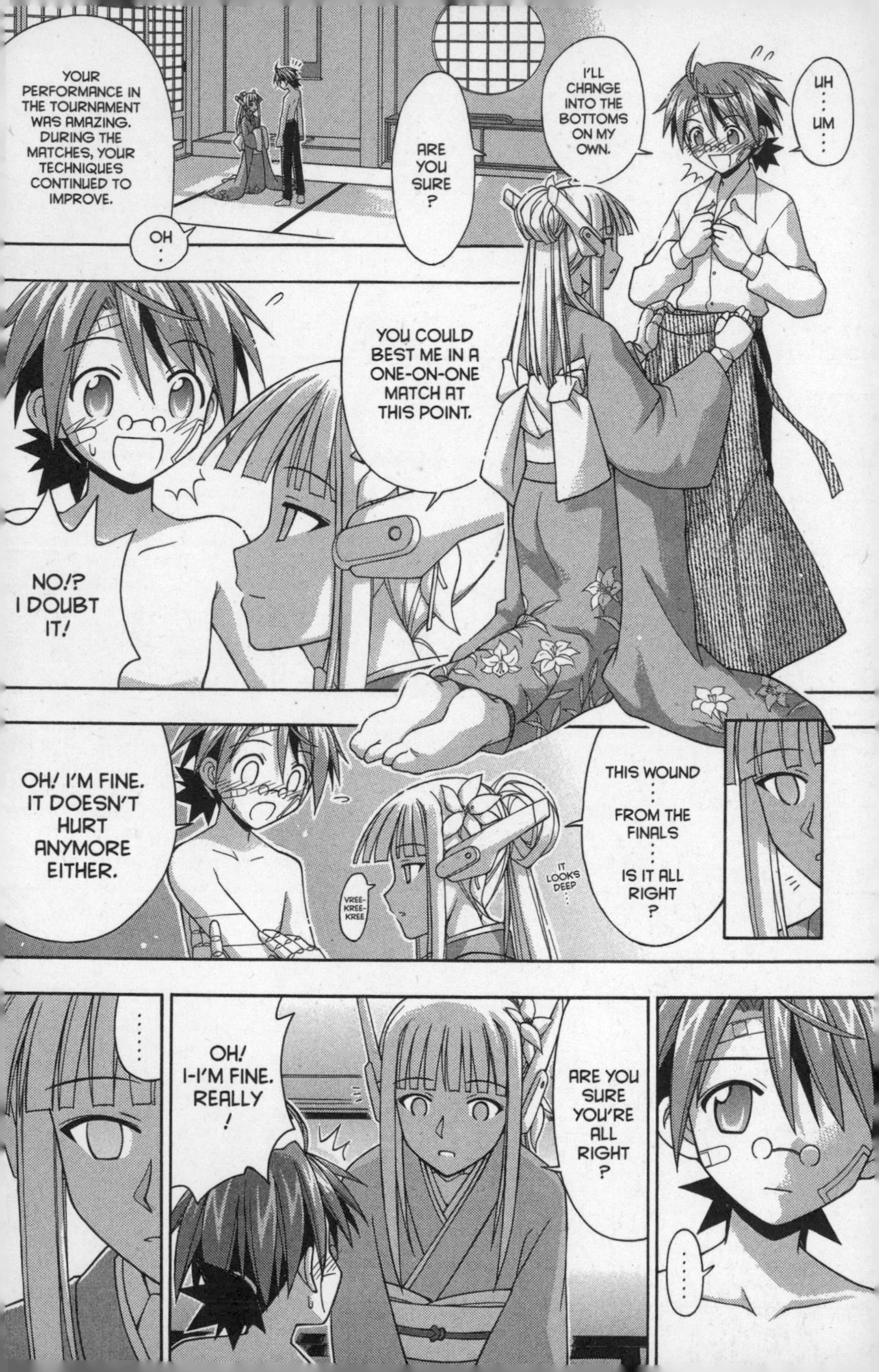
UH... UM...
I'LL CHANGE INTO THE BOTTOMS ON MY OWN.
ARE YOU SURE?
YOUR PERFORMANCE IN THE TOURNAMENT WAS AMAZING. DURING THE MATCHES, YOUR TECHNIQUES CONTINUED TO IMPROVE.
OH...
YOU COULD BEST ME IN A ONE-ON-ONE MATCH AT THIS POINT.
NO!? I DOUBT IT!
THIS WOUND... FROM THE FINALS... IS IT ALL RIGHT?
IT LOOKS DEEP...
VREE-KREE-KREE
OH! I'M FINE. IT DOESN'T HURT ANYMORE EITHER.
ARE YOU SURE YOU'RE ALL RIGHT?
......
OH! I-I'M FINE. REALLY!
......

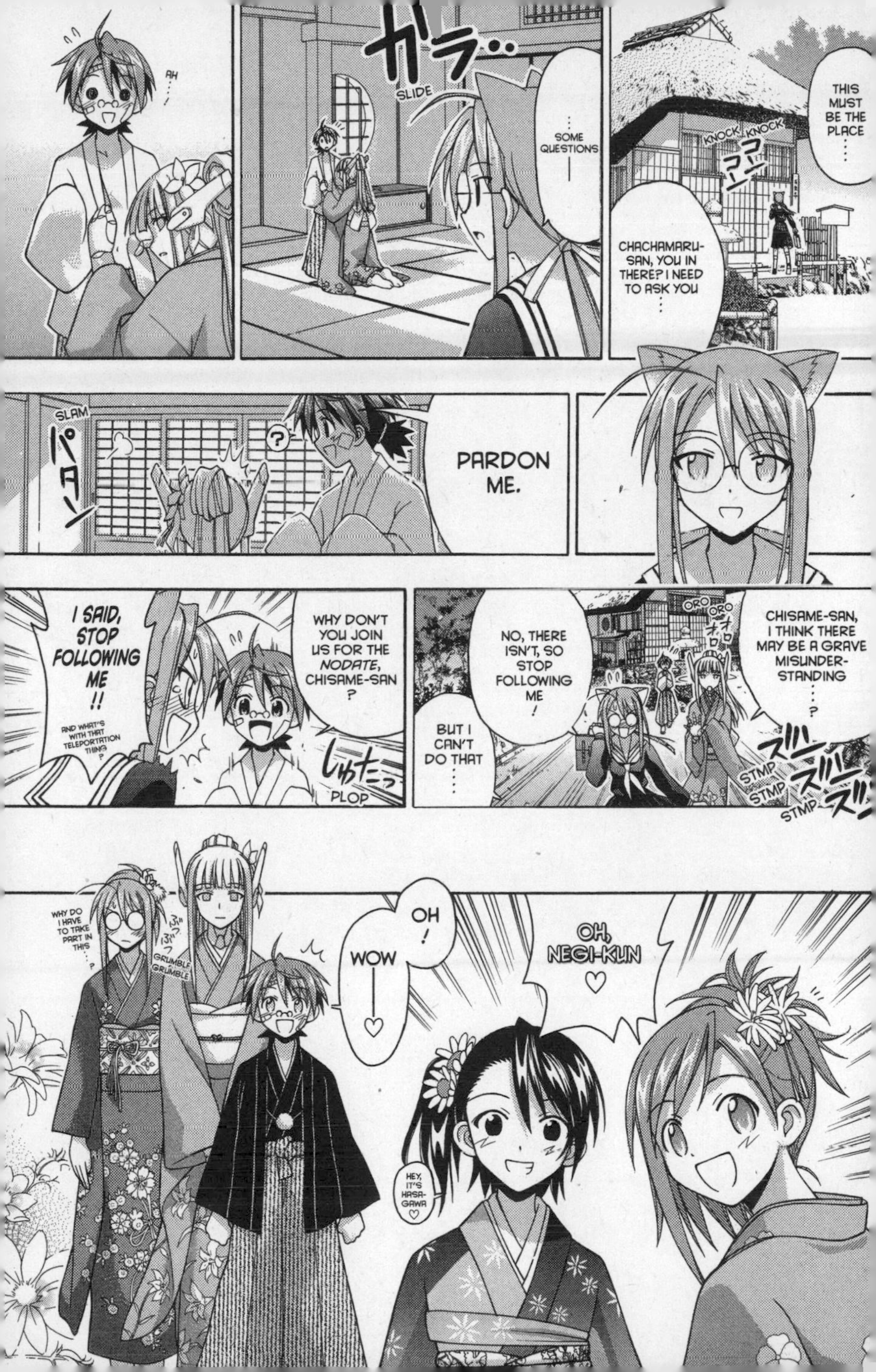
THIS MUST BE THE PLACE...
KNOCK KNOCK
CHACHAMARU-SAN, YOU IN THERE? I NEED TO ASK YOU...
SLIDE
...SOME QUESTIONS—
AH...
PARDON ME.
SLAM
?
CHISAME-SAN, I THINK THERE MAY BE A GRAVE MISUNDER-STANDING...?
ORO ORO
NO, THERE ISN'T, SO STOP FOLLOWING ME!
BUT I CAN'T DO THAT...
STMP STMP STMP
WHY DON'T YOU JOIN US FOR THE *NODATE*, CHISAME-SAN?
I SAID, STOP FOLLOWING ME!!
AND WHAT'S WITH THAT TELEPORTATION THING?
PLOP
OH, NEGI-KUN ♡
HEY, IT'S HASEGAWA ♡
OH! WOW—♡
WHY DO I HAVE TO TAKE PART IN THIS...?
GRUMBLE GRUMBLE

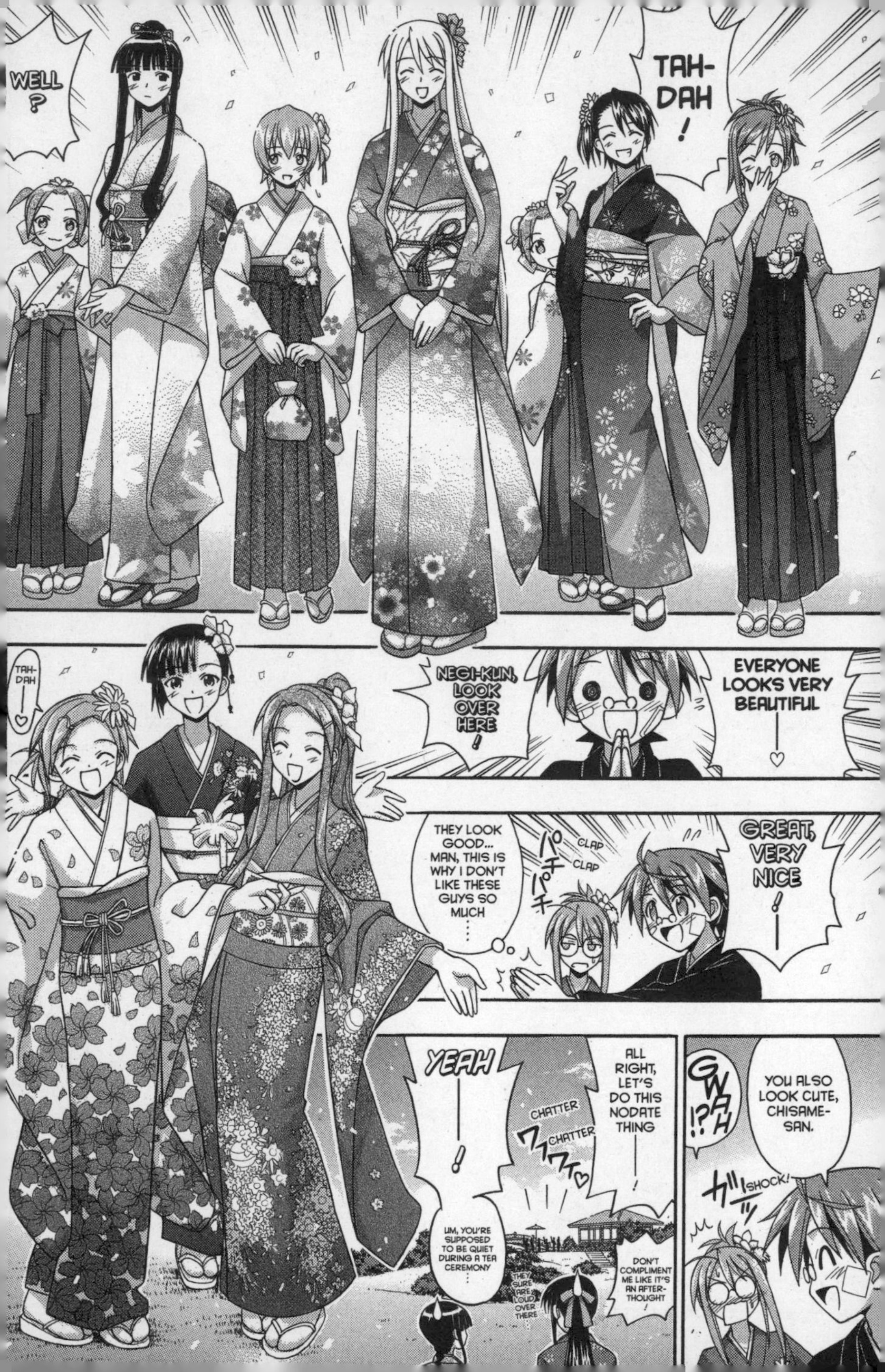

TAH-DAH!
WELL?
EVERYONE LOOKS VERY BEAUTIFUL—♡
NEGI-KUN, LOOK OVER HERE!
TAH-DAH—♡
GREAT, VERY NICE!—
CLAP CLAP
THEY LOOK GOOD... MAN, THIS IS WHY I DON'T LIKE THESE GUYS SO MUCH....
YOU ALSO LOOK CUTE, CHISAME-SAN.
GWAH!?
SHOCK!
DON'T COMPLIMENT ME LIKE IT'S AN AFTER-THOUGHT!
ALL RIGHT, LET'S DO THIS NODATE THING—!
YEAH—!
CHATTER CHATTER
THEY SURE ARE LOUD OVER THERE
UM, YOU'RE SUPPOSED TO BE QUIET DURING A TEA CEREMONY....

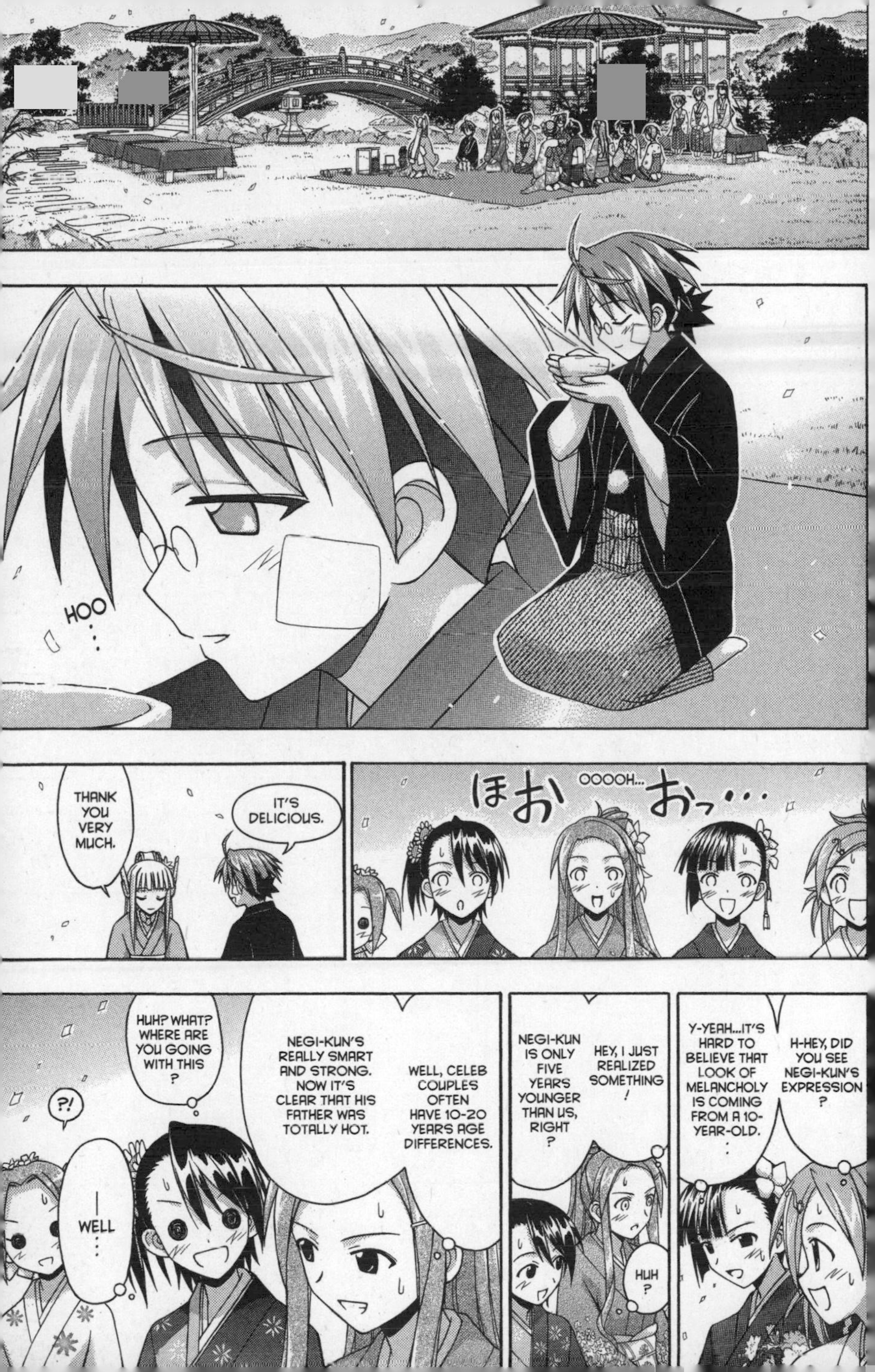
HOO...
ほお OOOOH... おっ...
IT'S DELICIOUS.
THANK YOU VERY MUCH.
H-HEY, DID YOU SEE NEGI-KUN'S EXPRESSION?
Y-YEAH...IT'S HARD TO BELIEVE THAT LOOK OF MELANCHOLY IS COMING FROM A 10-YEAR-OLD.
HEY, I JUST REALIZED SOMETHING!
NEGI-KUN IS ONLY FIVE YEARS YOUNGER THAN US, RIGHT?
HUH?
WELL, CELEB COUPLES OFTEN HAVE 10-20 YEARS AGE DIFFERENCES.
NEGI-KUN'S REALLY SMART AND STRONG. NOW IT'S CLEAR THAT HIS FATHER WAS TOTALLY HOT.
HUH? WHAT? WHERE ARE YOU GOING WITH THIS?
?!
―WELL...

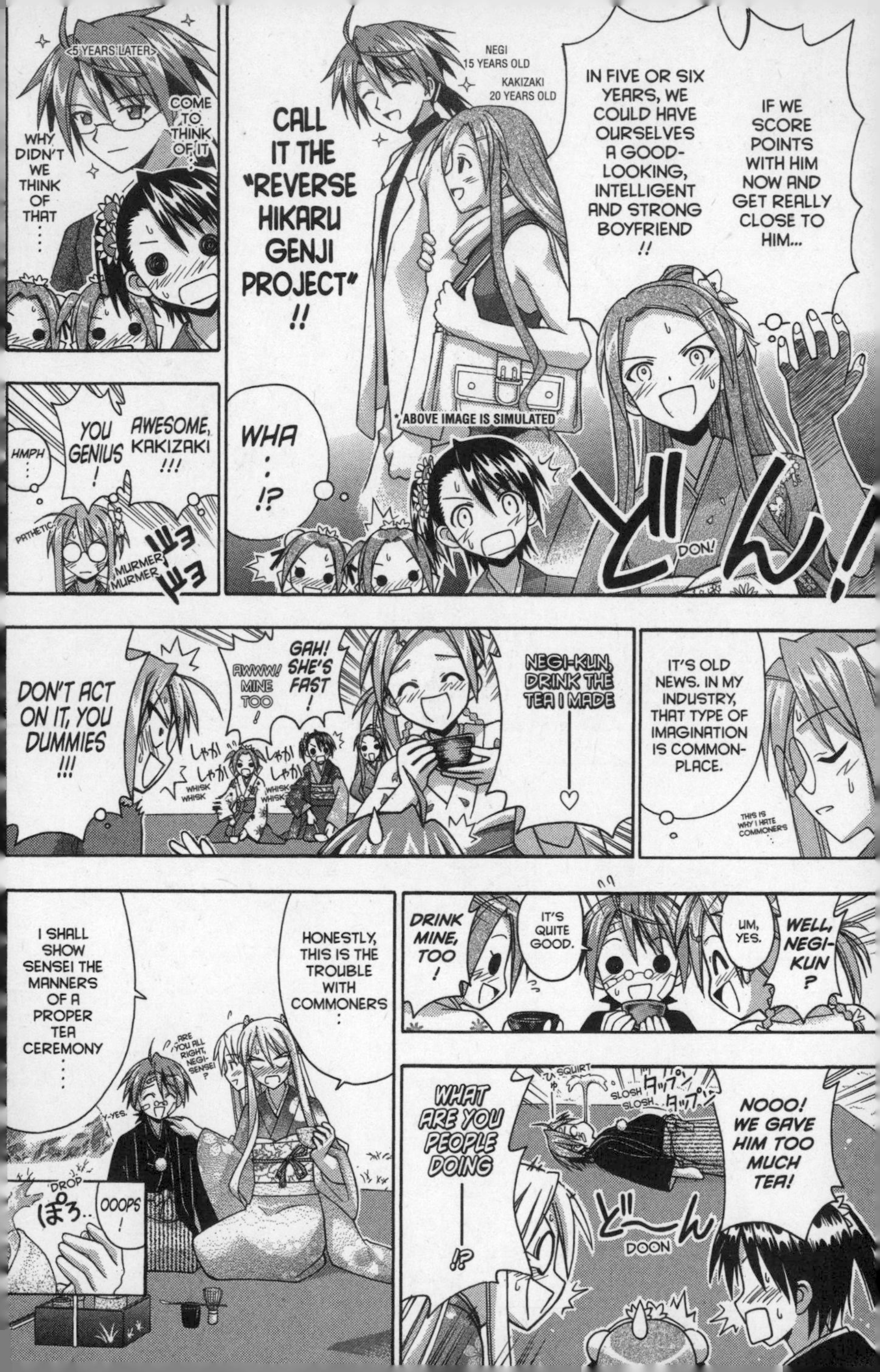
IF WE SCORE POINTS WITH HIM NOW AND GET REALLY CLOSE TO HIM...
IN FIVE OR SIX YEARS, WE COULD HAVE OURSELVES A GOOD-LOOKING, INTELLIGENT AND STRONG BOYFRIEND!!
NEGI 15 YEARS OLD
KAKIZAKI 20 YEARS OLD
CALL IT THE "REVERSE HIKARU GENJI PROJECT"!!
*ABOVE IMAGE IS SIMULATED
どん!
DON!
WHA...!?
<5 YEARS LATER>
COME TO THINK OF IT...
WHY DIDN'T WE THINK OF THAT...
AWESOME, KAKIZAKI!!!
YOU GENIUS!
HMPH...
ドヨドヨ
MURMER MURMER
PATHETIC
IT'S OLD NEWS. IN MY INDUSTRY, THAT TYPE OF IMAGINATION IS COMMONPLACE.
THIS IS WHY I HATE COMMONERS...
NEGI-KUN, DRINK THE TEA I MADE ♡
GAH! SHE'S FAST!
AWWW! MINE TOO!
しゃかしゃか
WHISK WHISK
しゃかしゃか
WHISK WHISK
DON'T ACT ON IT, YOU DUMMIES!!!
WELL, NEGI-KUN?
UM, YES.
IT'S QUITE GOOD.
DRINK MINE, TOO!
NOOO! WE GAVE HIM TOO MUCH TEA!
タップ タップ
SLOSH SLOSH
ぴゅ
SQUIRT
WHAT ARE YOU PEOPLE DOING—!?
どーん
DOON
HONESTLY, THIS IS THE TROUBLE WITH COMMONERS...
I SHALL SHOW SENSEI THE MANNERS OF A PROPER TEA CEREMONY...
ARE YOU ALL RIGHT, NEGI-SENSEI?
Y-YES.
ぽろ..
DROP
OOOPS!

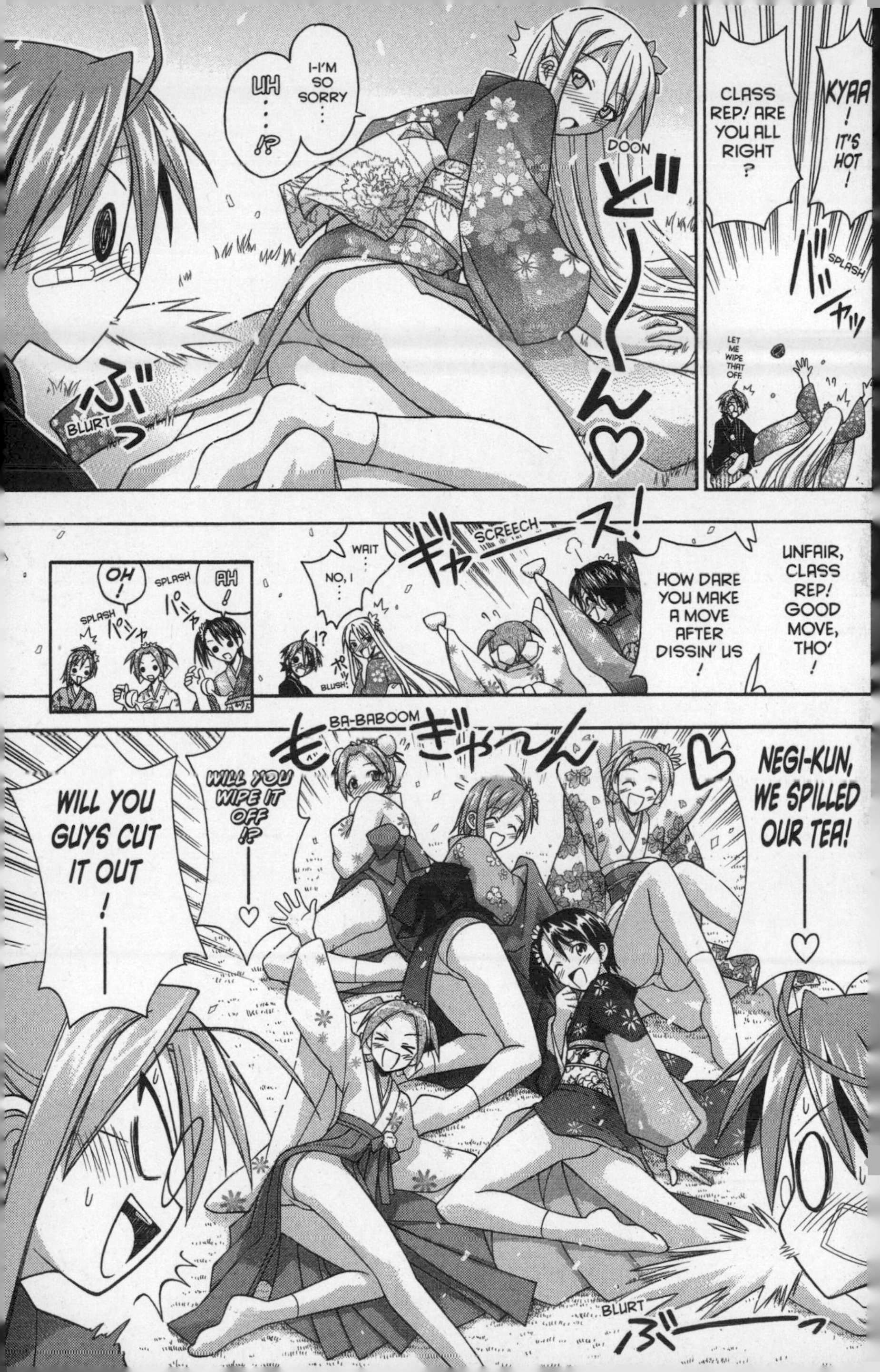
KYAA! IT'S HOT!
CLASS REP! ARE YOU ALL RIGHT?
バシャッ
SPLASH
LET ME WIPE THAT OFF.
DOON
どーーん♡
I-I'M SO SORRY...
UH...!?
ぶっ
BLURT
UNFAIR, CLASS REP! GOOD MOVE, THO'!
HOW DARE YOU MAKE A MOVE AFTER DISSIN' US!
ギャース!
SCREECH
WAIT... NO, I...
!?
ポッ
BLUSH
AH!
パシャ
SPLASH
OH!
パシャ
SPLASH
NEGI-KUN, WE SPILLED OUR TEA! ♡
もぎゃーん♡
BA-BABOOM
WILL YOU WIPE IT OFF!? ♡
WILL YOU GUYS CUT IT OUT!
ぶー
BLURT

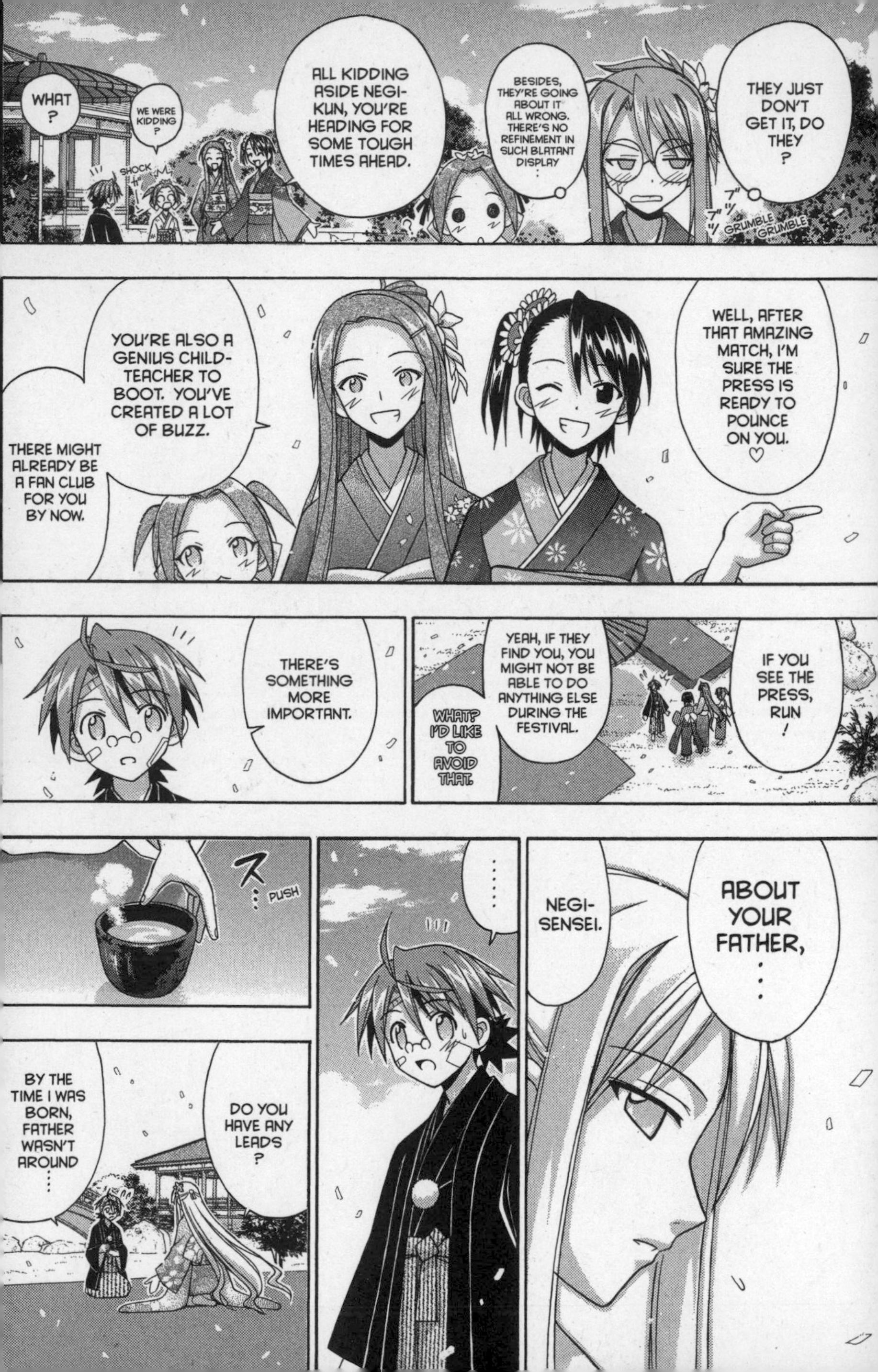
THEY JUST DON'T GET IT, DO THEY?
GRUMBLE GRUMBLE
BESIDES, THEY'RE GOING ABOUT IT ALL WRONG. THERE'S NO REFINEMENT IN SUCH BLATANT DISPLAY...
ALL KIDDING ASIDE NEGI-KUN, YOU'RE HEADING FOR SOME TOUGH TIMES AHEAD.
WE WERE KIDDING?
SHOCK
WHAT?
WELL, AFTER THAT AMAZING MATCH, I'M SURE THE PRESS IS READY TO POUNCE ON YOU. ♡
YOU'RE ALSO A GENIUS CHILD-TEACHER TO BOOT. YOU'VE CREATED A LOT OF BUZZ.
THERE MIGHT ALREADY BE A FAN CLUB FOR YOU BY NOW.
IF YOU SEE THE PRESS, RUN!
YEAH, IF THEY FIND YOU, YOU MIGHT NOT BE ABLE TO DO ANYTHING ELSE DURING THE FESTIVAL.
WHAT? I'D LIKE TO AVOID THAT.
THERE'S SOMETHING MORE IMPORTANT.
ABOUT YOUR FATHER, ...
NEGI-SENSEI.
......
PUSH
DO YOU HAVE ANY LEADS?
BY THE TIME I WAS BORN, FATHER WASN'T AROUND...

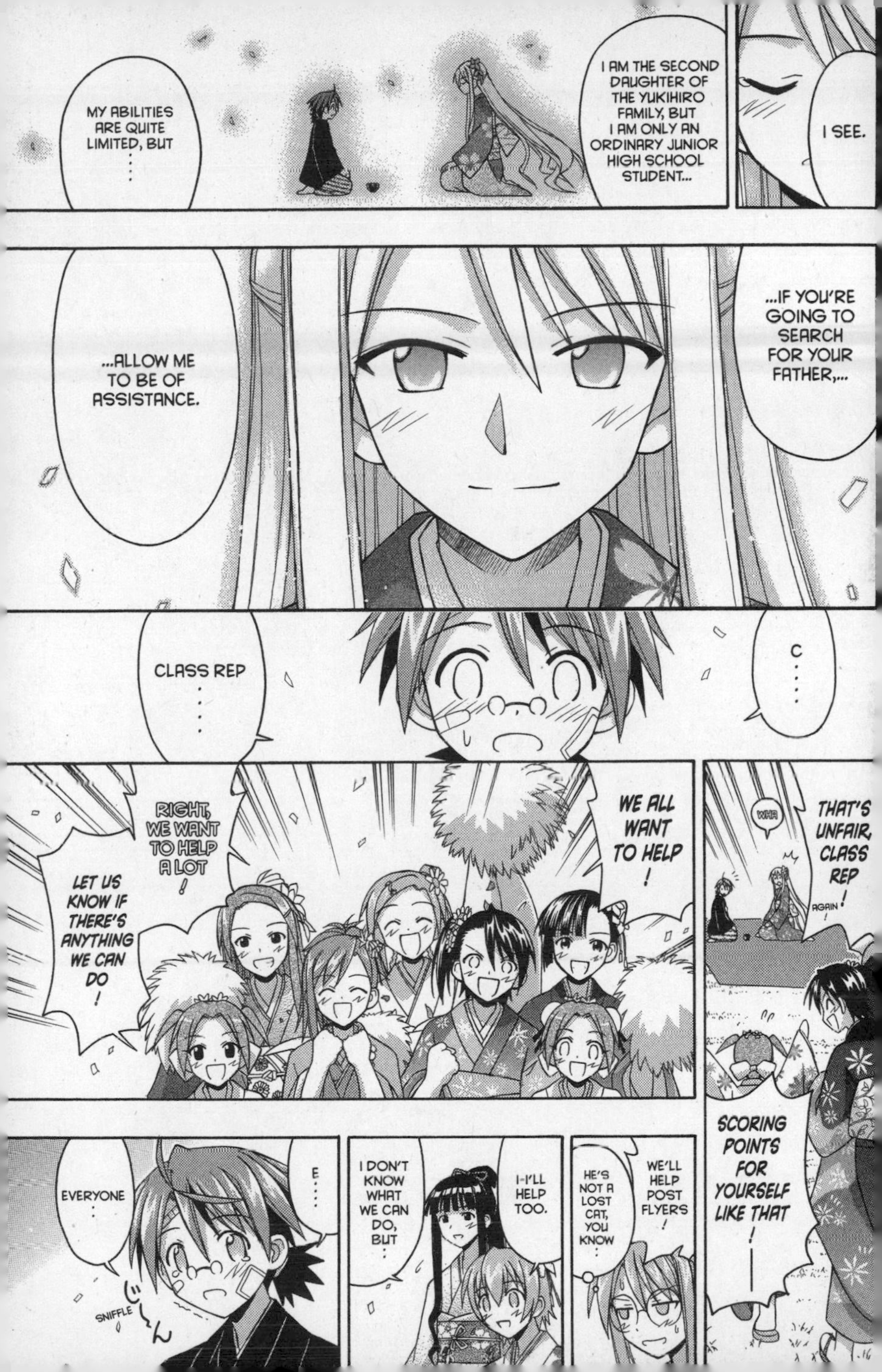
I SEE.
I AM THE SECOND DAUGHTER OF THE YUKIHIRO FAMILY, BUT I AM ONLY AN ORDINARY JUNIOR HIGH SCHOOL STUDENT...
MY ABILITIES ARE QUITE LIMITED, BUT ....
...IF YOU'RE GOING TO SEARCH FOR YOUR FATHER,...
...ALLOW ME TO BE OF ASSISTANCE.
C ....
CLASS REP ....
THAT'S UNFAIR, CLASS REP!
WHA
AGAIN!
SCORING POINTS FOR YOURSELF LIKE THAT!
WE ALL WANT TO HELP!
RIGHT, WE WANT TO HELP A LOT!
LET US KNOW IF THERE'S ANYTHING WE CAN DO!
WE'LL HELP POST FLYERS!
HE'S NOT A LOST CAT, YOU KNOW...
I-I'LL HELP TOO.
I DON'T KNOW WHAT WE CAN DO, BUT...
E....
EVERYONE...
SNIFFLE

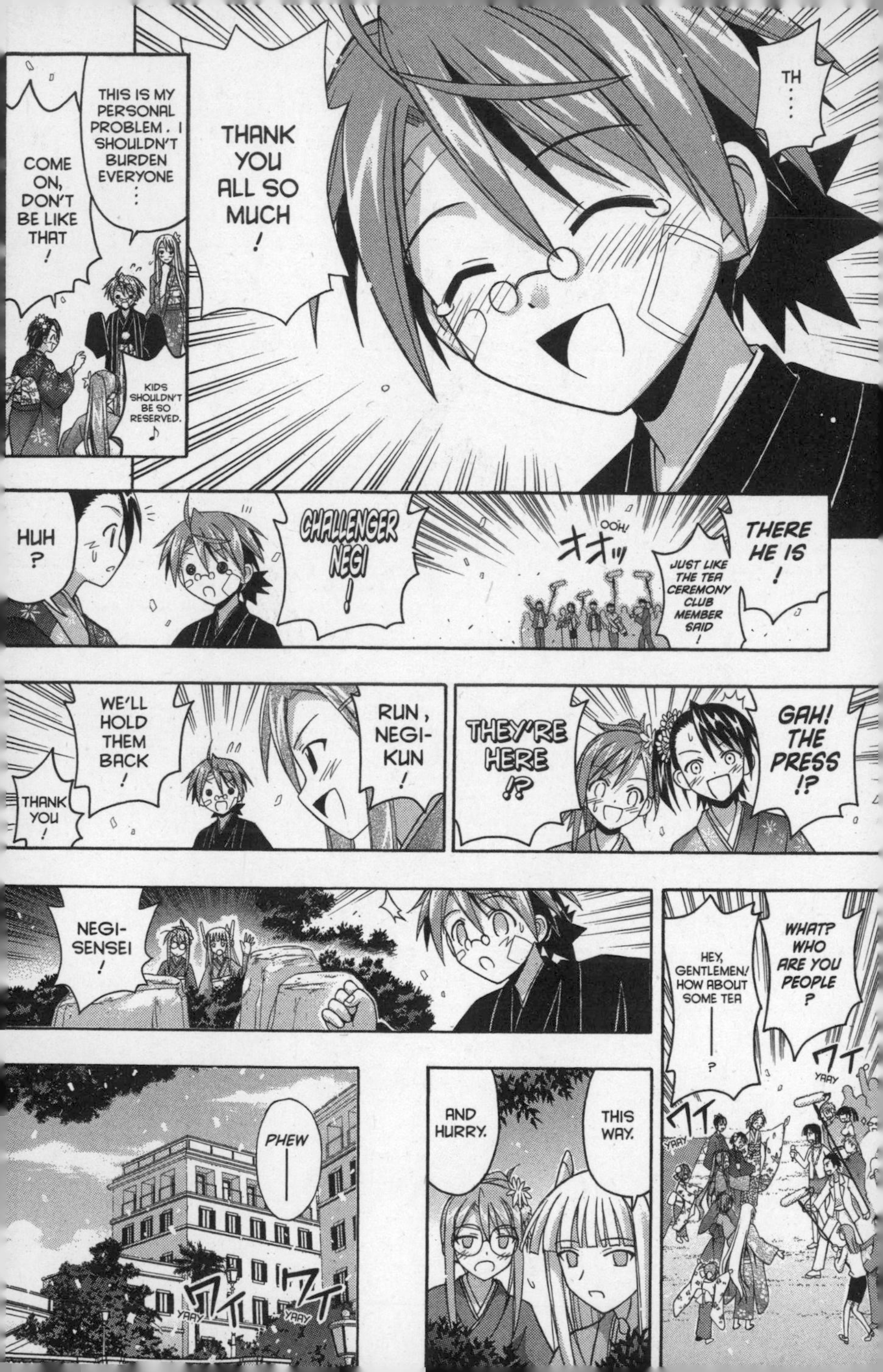
TH....
THANK YOU ALL SO MUCH!
THIS IS MY PERSONAL PROBLEM. I SHOULDN'T BURDEN EVERYONE...
COME ON, DON'T BE LIKE THAT!
KIDS SHOULDN'T BE SO RESERVED. ♪
THERE HE IS!
JUST LIKE THE TEA CEREMONY CLUB MEMBER SAID!
オオッ OOH!
CHALLENGER NEGI!
HUH?
GAH! THE PRESS!?
THEY'RE HERE!?
RUN, NEGI-KUN!
WE'LL HOLD THEM BACK!
THANK YOU!
WHAT? WHO ARE YOU PEOPLE?
HEY, GENTLEMEN! HOW ABOUT SOME TEA—?
ワイ YAAY
ワイ YAAY
NEGI-SENSEI!
THIS WAY.
AND HURRY.
PHEW—
ワイ!ワイ YAAY YAAY

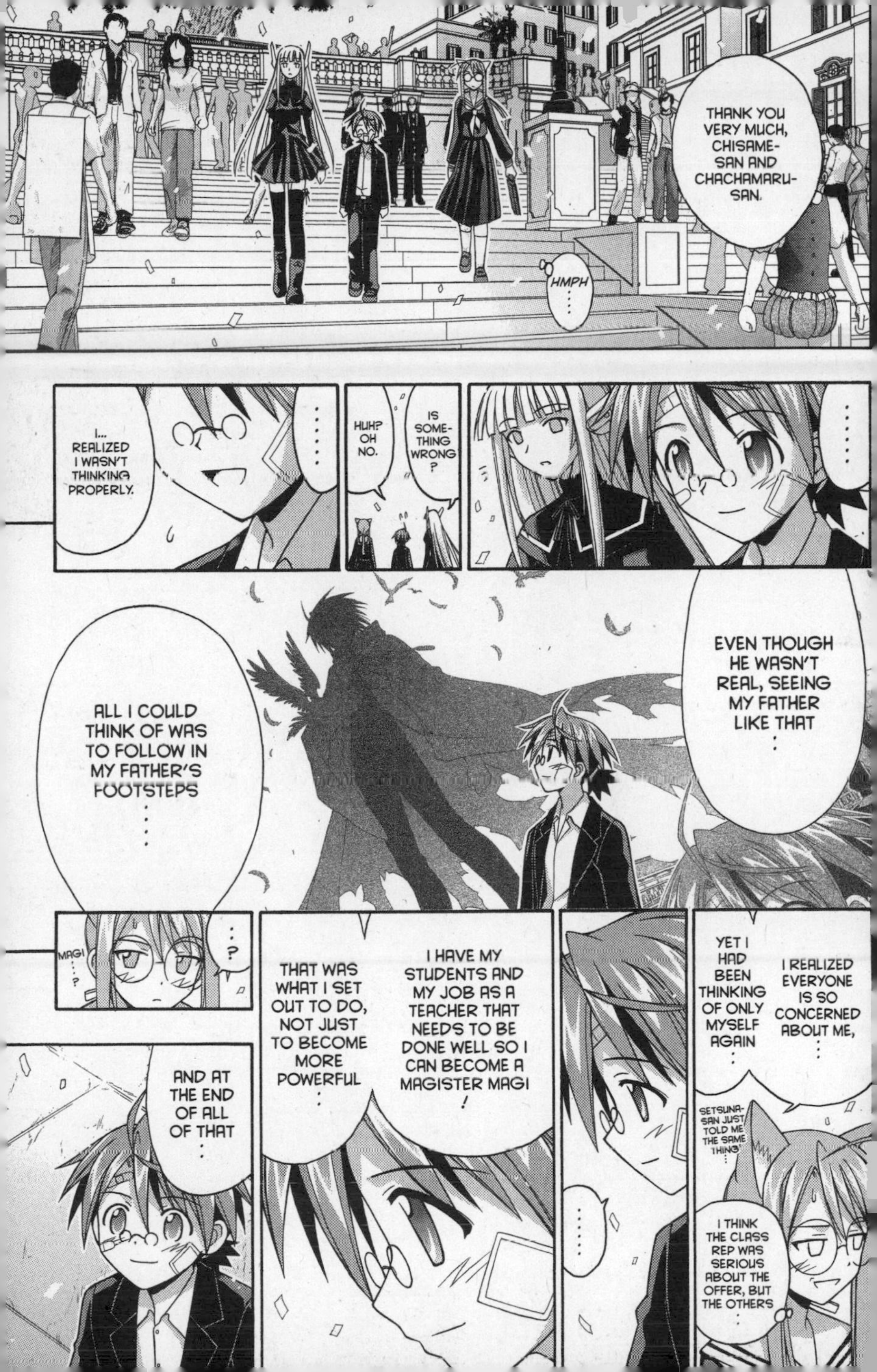
THANK YOU VERY MUCH, CHISAME-SAN AND CHACHAMARU-SAN.
HMPH ...
......
IS SOMETHING WRONG?
HUH? OH NO.
......
I... REALIZED I WASN'T THINKING PROPERLY.
EVEN THOUGH HE WASN'T REAL, SEEING MY FATHER LIKE THAT :
ALL I COULD THINK OF WAS TO FOLLOW IN MY FATHER'S FOOTSTEPS .....
I REALIZED EVERYONE IS SO CONCERNED ABOUT ME, :
YET I HAD BEEN THINKING OF ONLY MYSELF AGAIN :
SETSUNA-SAN JUST TOLD ME THE SAME THING ...
I THINK THE CLASS REP WAS SERIOUS ABOUT THE OFFER, BUT THE OTHERS :
......
I HAVE MY STUDENTS AND MY JOB AS A TEACHER THAT NEEDS TO BE DONE WELL SO I CAN BECOME A MAGISTER MAGI !
THAT WAS WHAT I SET OUT TO DO, NOT JUST TO BECOME MORE POWERFUL :
MAGI ...?
..?
AND AT THE END OF ALL OF THAT :

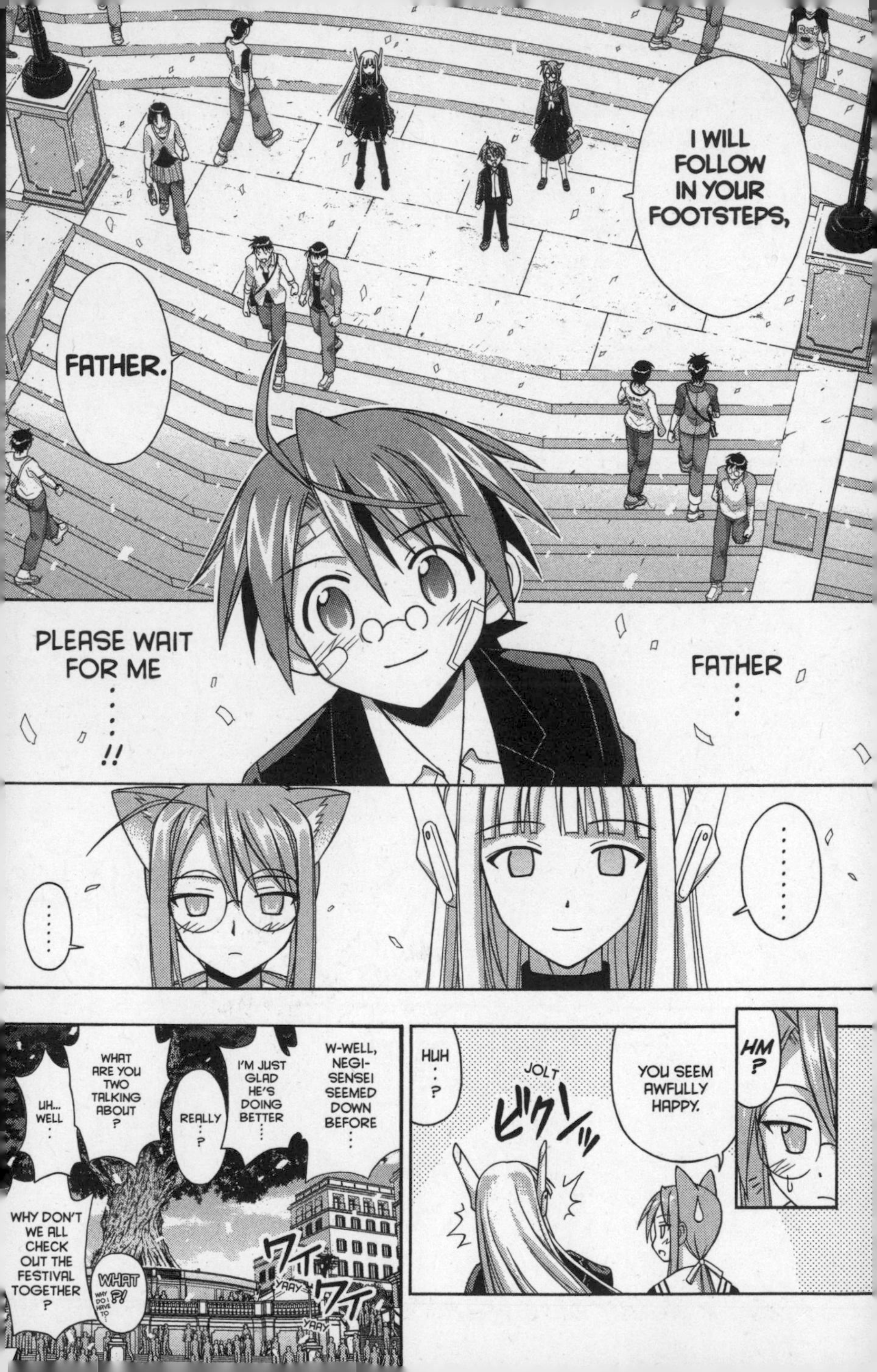
I WILL FOLLOW IN YOUR FOOTSTEPS,
FATHER.
FATHER . . .
PLEASE WAIT FOR ME . . . . . !!
. . . .
. . . . . .
HM ?
YOU SEEM AWFULLY HAPPY.
JOLT
HUH . . ?
W-WELL, NEGI-SENSEI SEEMED DOWN BEFORE . . .
I'M JUST GLAD HE'S DOING BETTER . . .
REALLY . . ?
WHAT ARE YOU TWO TALKING ABOUT ?
UH... WELL . .
WHY DON'T WE ALL CHECK OUT THE FESTIVAL TOGETHER ?
WHAT ?!
WHY DO I HAVE TO?
YAAY
YAAY

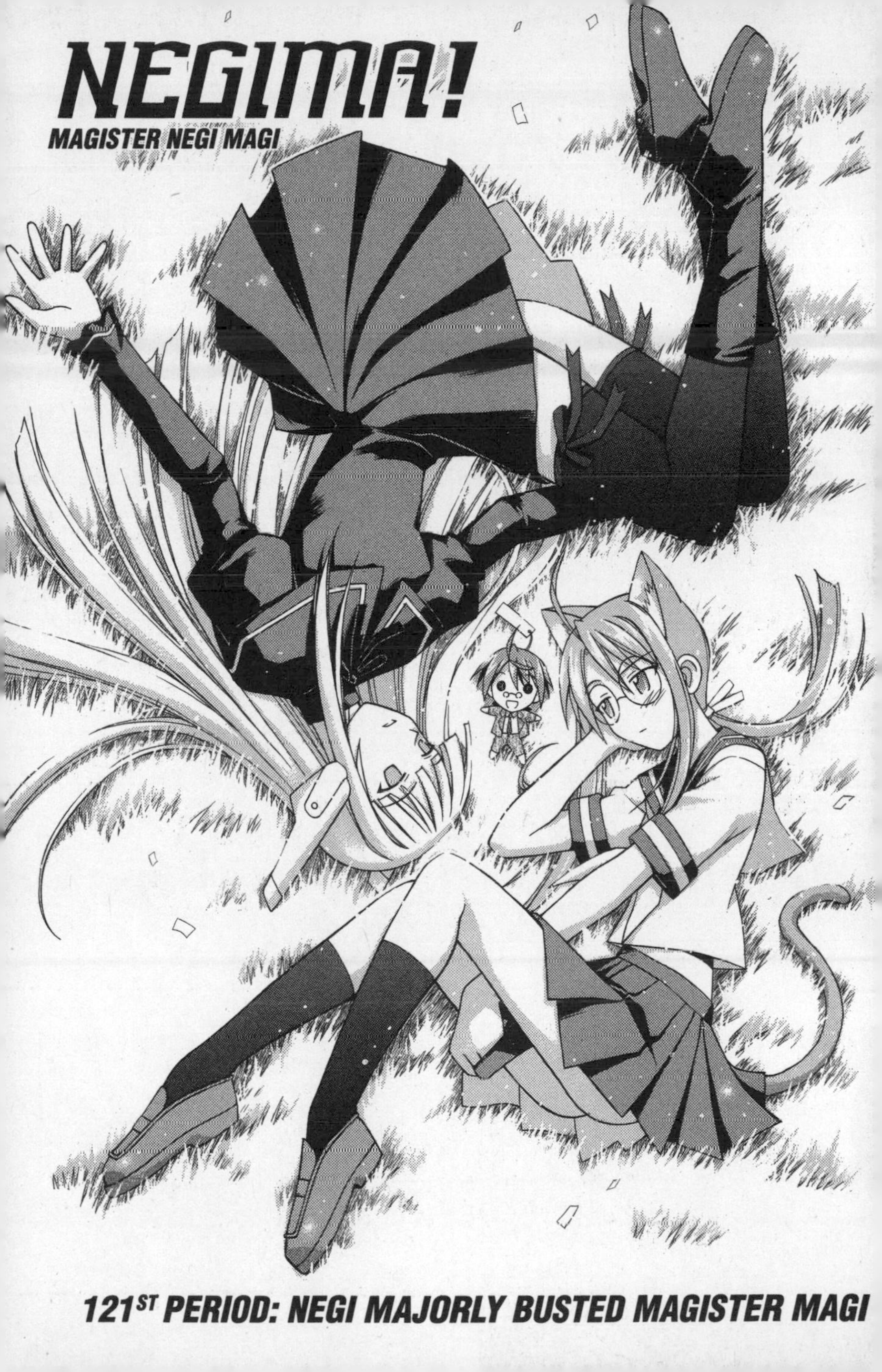
NEGIMA!
MAGISTER NEGI MAGI
121ST PERIOD: NEGI MAJORLY BUSTED MAGISTER MAGI

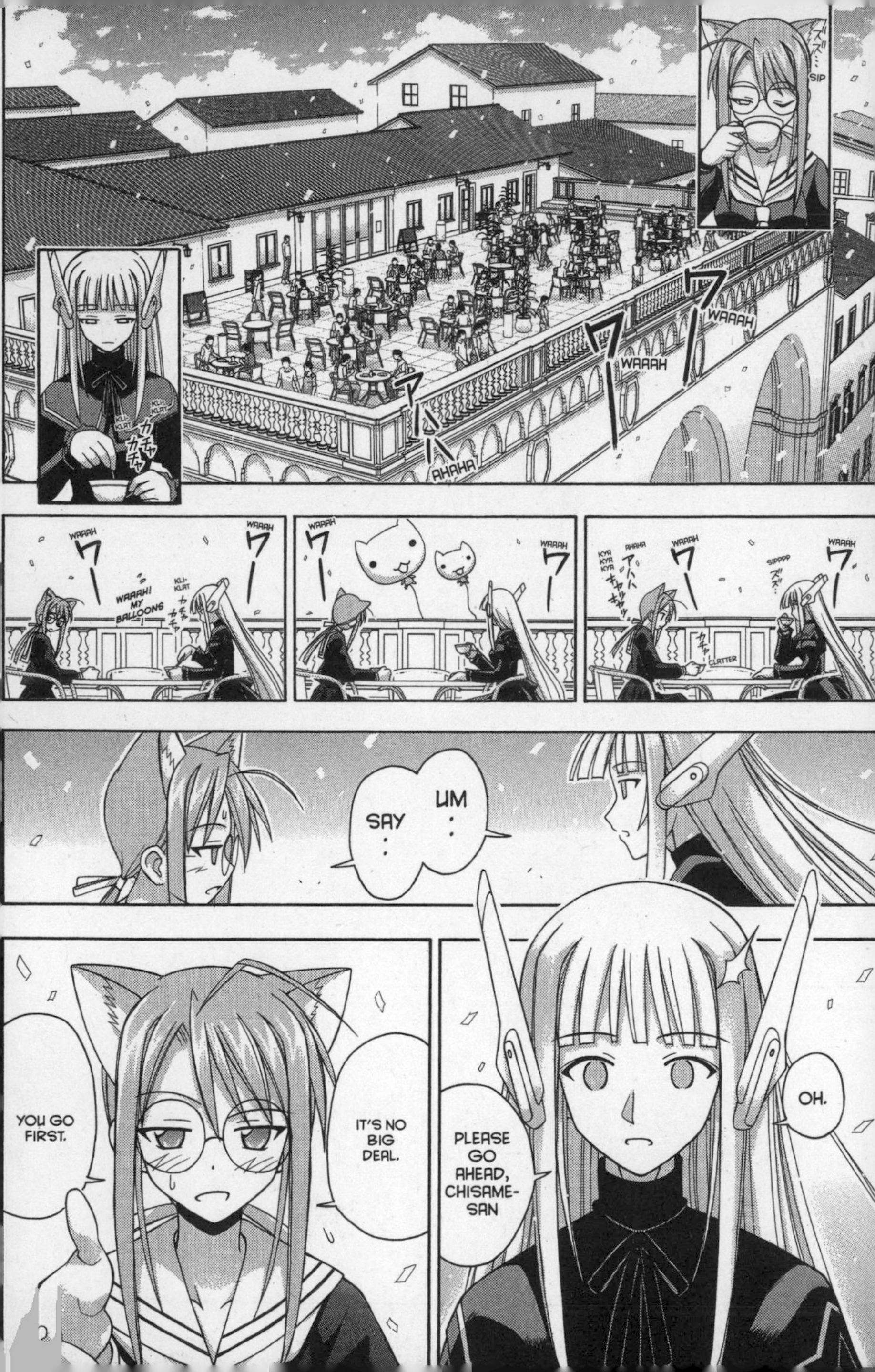
ズズ…
SIP
ワー
WAAAH
ワー
WAAAH
アハハ
AHAHA
KLI-KLAT
KLI-KLAT
カチャ カチャ
WAAAH
ワー
SIPPPP
ズズ…
WAAAH
ワー
AHAHA
アハハ
KYA KYA KYA
キャッキャッ
カチャ
CLATTER
WAAAH
ワー
WAAAH
ワー
WAAAH
ワー
KLI-KLAT
カチャ カチャ
WAAAH! MY BALLOONS!
WAAAH
ワー
UM...
SAY...
OH.
PLEASE GO AHEAD, CHISAME-SAN
IT'S NO BIG DEAL.
YOU GO FIRST.

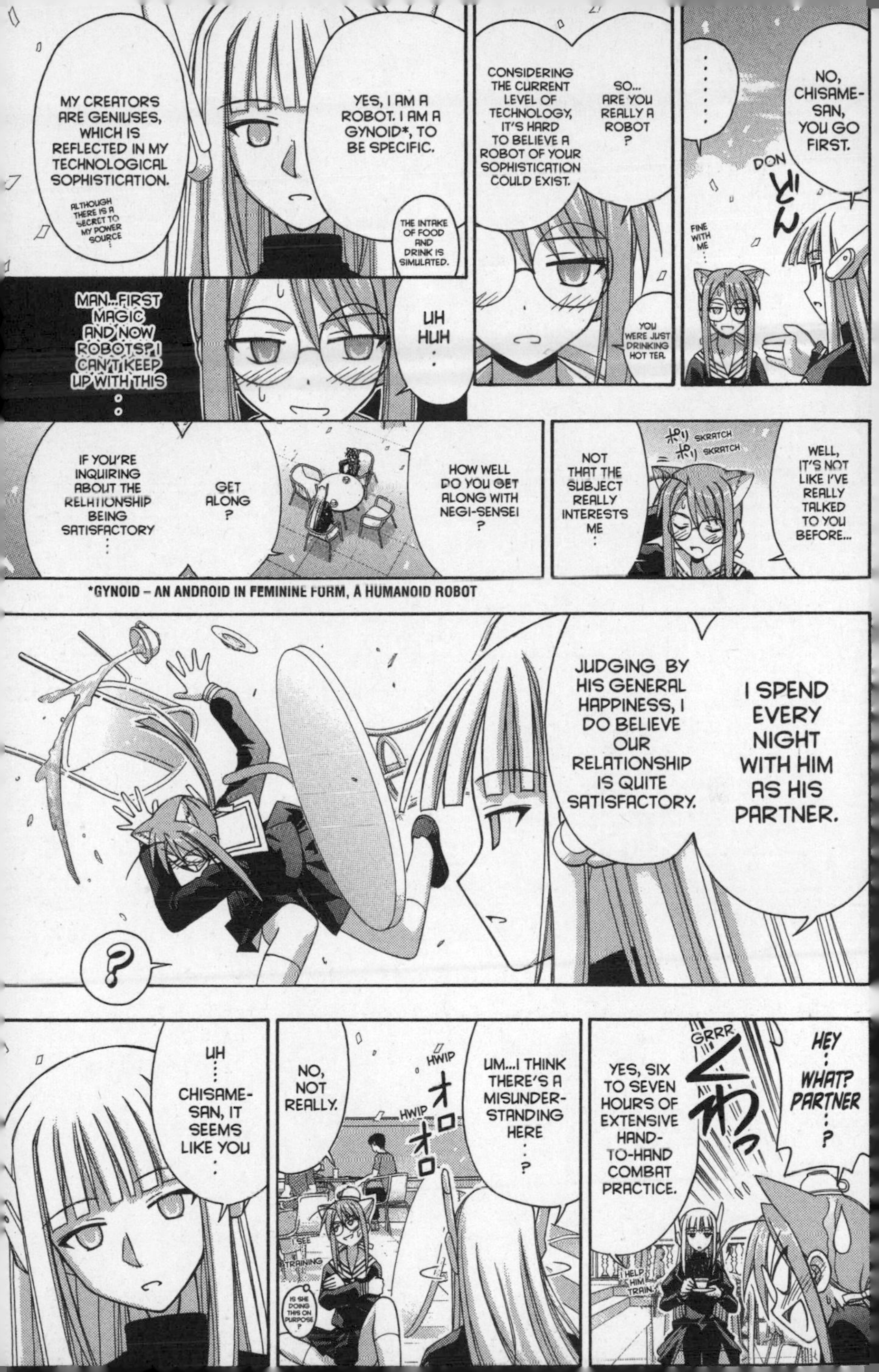
NO, CHISAME-SAN, YOU GO FIRST.
......
DON どん
FINE WITH ME...
SO... ARE YOU REALLY A ROBOT?
CONSIDERING THE CURRENT LEVEL OF TECHNOLOGY, IT'S HARD TO BELIEVE A ROBOT OF YOUR SOPHISTICATION COULD EXIST.
YOU WERE JUST DRINKING HOT TEA.
YES, I AM A ROBOT. I AM A GYNOID*, TO BE SPECIFIC.
THE INTAKE OF FOOD AND DRINK IS SIMULATED.
MY CREATORS ARE GENIUSES, WHICH IS REFLECTED IN MY TECHNOLOGICAL SOPHISTICATION.
ALTHOUGH THERE IS A SECRET TO MY POWER SOURCE...
UH HUH..
MAN...FIRST MAGIC AND NOW ROBOTS?! I CAN'T KEEP UP WITH THIS..
WELL, IT'S NOT LIKE I'VE REALLY TALKED TO YOU BEFORE...
ポリ SKRATCH
ポリ SKRATCH
NOT THAT THE SUBJECT REALLY INTERESTS ME...
HOW WELL DO YOU GET ALONG WITH NEGI-SENSEI?
GET ALONG?
IF YOU'RE INQUIRING ABOUT THE RELATIONSHIP BEING SATISFACTORY...
I SPEND EVERY NIGHT WITH HIM AS HIS PARTNER.
JUDGING BY HIS GENERAL HAPPINESS, I DO BELIEVE OUR RELATIONSHIP IS QUITE SATISFACTORY.
?
HEY... WHAT? PARTNER...?
GRRR くわっ
YES, SIX TO SEVEN HOURS OF EXTENSIVE HAND-TO-HAND COMBAT PRACTICE.
I HELP HIM TRAIN.
UM...I THINK THERE'S A MISUNDERSTANDING HERE..?
HWIP オロ
HWIP オロ
NO, NOT REALLY.
I SEE TRAINING
IS SHE DOING THIS ON PURPOSE?
UH... CHISAME-SAN, IT SEEMS LIKE YOU...

*GYNOID – AN ANDROID IN FEMININE FORM, A HUMANOID ROBOT

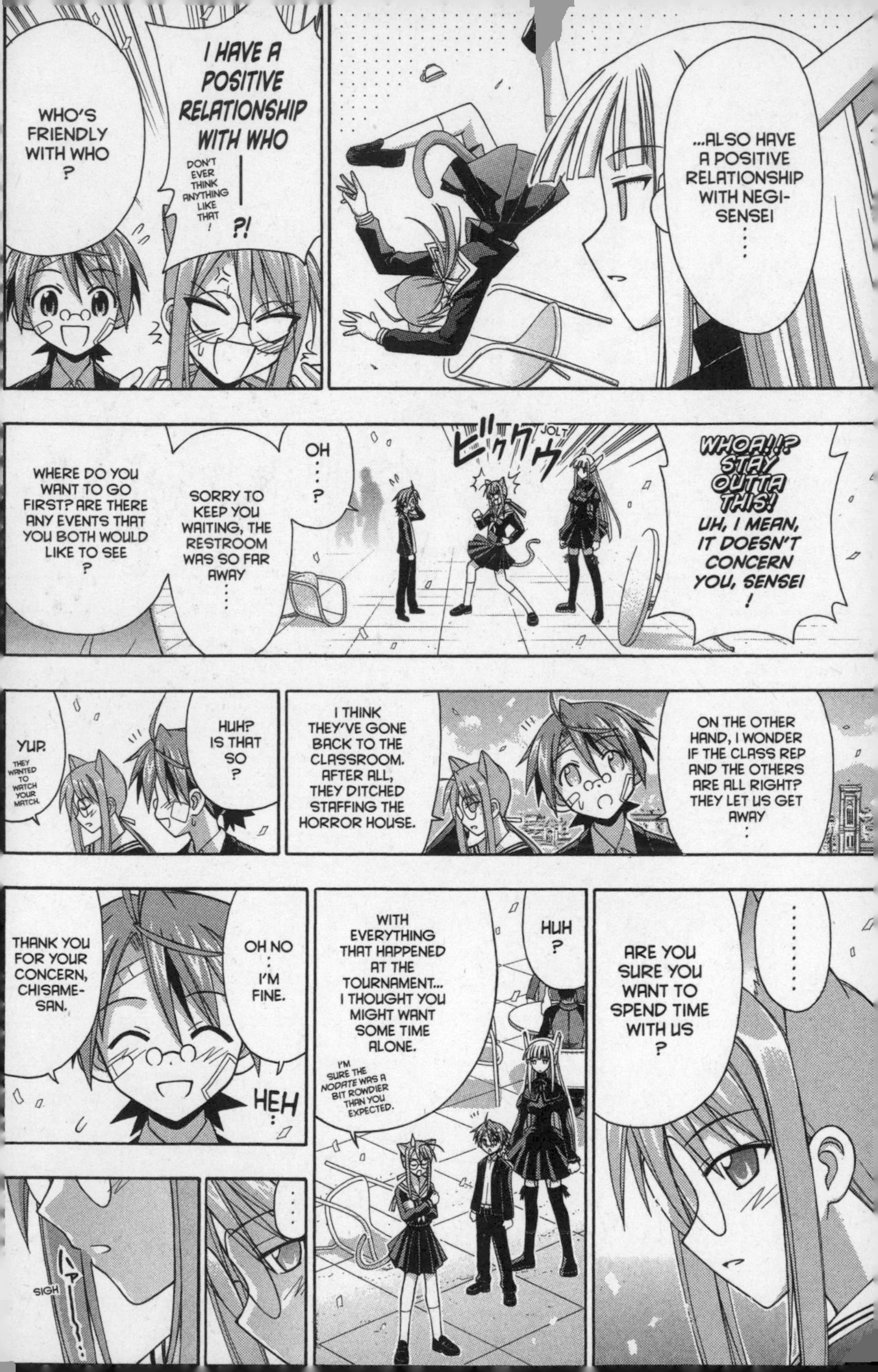
...ALSO HAVE A POSITIVE RELATIONSHIP WITH NEGI-SENSEI...
I HAVE A POSITIVE RELATIONSHIP WITH WHO—?!
DON'T EVER THINK ANYTHING LIKE THAT!
WHO'S FRIENDLY WITH WHO?
WHOA!!? STAY OUTTA THIS! UH, I MEAN, IT DOESN'T CONCERN YOU, SENSEI!
JOLT
OH...?
SORRY TO KEEP YOU WAITING, THE RESTROOM WAS SO FAR AWAY...
WHERE DO YOU WANT TO GO FIRST? ARE THERE ANY EVENTS THAT YOU BOTH WOULD LIKE TO SEE?
ON THE OTHER HAND, I WONDER IF THE CLASS REP AND THE OTHERS ARE ALL RIGHT? THEY LET US GET AWAY...
I THINK THEY'VE GONE BACK TO THE CLASSROOM. AFTER ALL, THEY DITCHED STAFFING THE HORROR HOUSE.
HUH? IS THAT SO?
YUP.
THEY WANTED TO WATCH YOUR MATCH.
......
ARE YOU SURE YOU WANT TO SPEND TIME WITH US?
HUH?
WITH EVERYTHING THAT HAPPENED AT THE TOURNAMENT... I THOUGHT YOU MIGHT WANT SOME TIME ALONE.
I'M SURE THE *NODATE* WAS A BIT ROWDIER THAN YOU EXPECTED.
OH NO... I'M FINE.
THANK YOU FOR YOUR CONCERN, CHISAME-SAN.
HEH...
...
SIGH

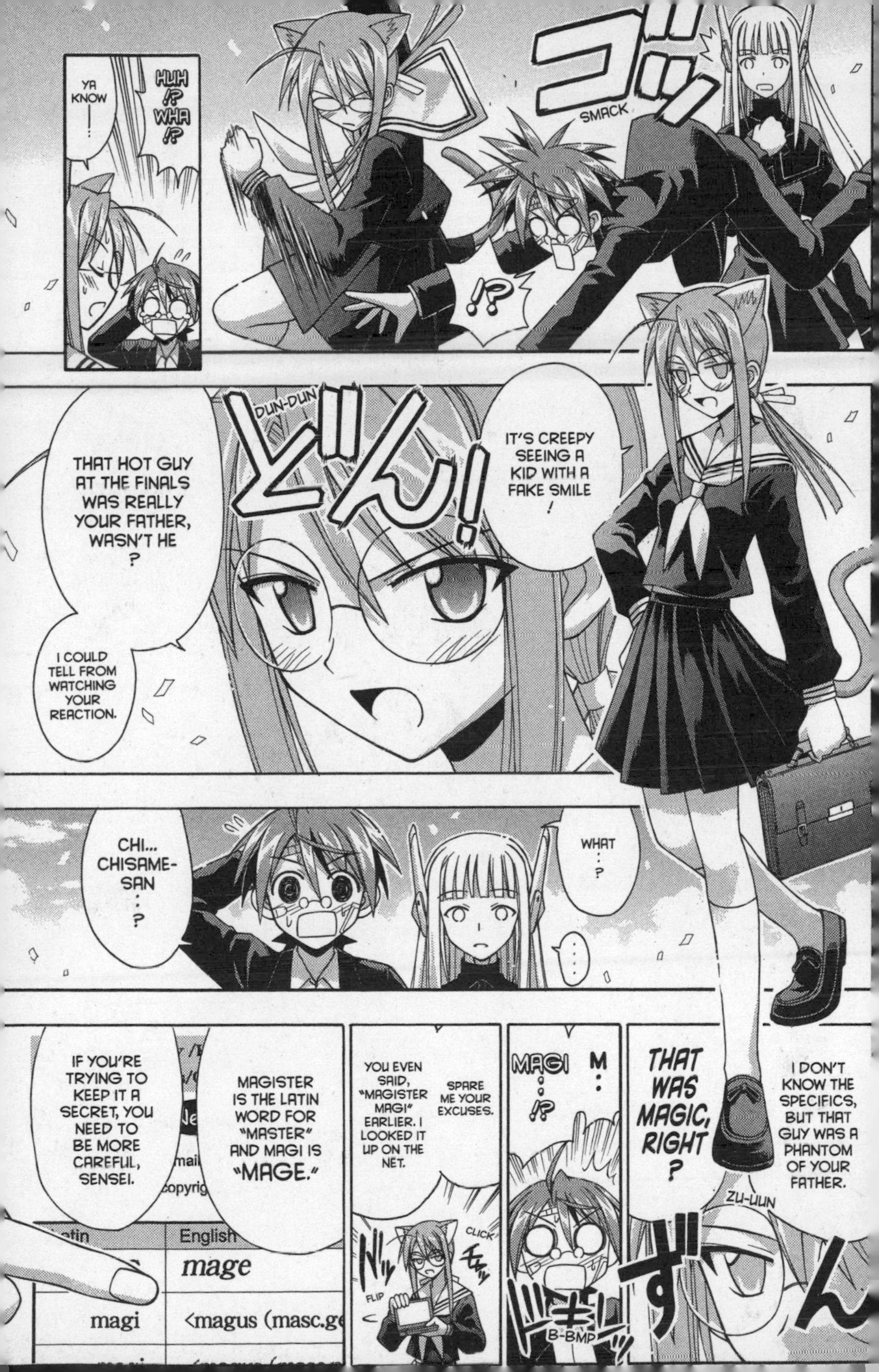
SMACK
!?
HUH!? WHA!?
YA KNOW...!
IT'S CREEPY SEEING A KID WITH A FAKE SMILE!
DUN-DUN
どん!
THAT HOT GUY AT THE FINALS WAS REALLY YOUR FATHER, WASN'T HE?
I COULD TELL FROM WATCHING YOUR REACTION.
WHAT...?
...
CHI... CHISAME-SAN...?
I DON'T KNOW THE SPECIFICS, BUT THAT GUY WAS A PHANTOM OF YOUR FATHER.
THAT WAS MAGIC, RIGHT?
ZU-UUN
M...
MAGI...!?
B-BMP
SPARE ME YOUR EXCUSES.
YOU EVEN SAID, "MAGISTER MAGI" EARLIER. I LOOKED IT UP ON THE NET.
CLICK
FLIP
MAGISTER IS THE LATIN WORD FOR "MASTER" AND MAGI IS "MAGE."
IF YOU'RE TRYING TO KEEP IT A SECRET, YOU NEED TO BE MORE CAREFUL, SENSEI.
English
mage
magi

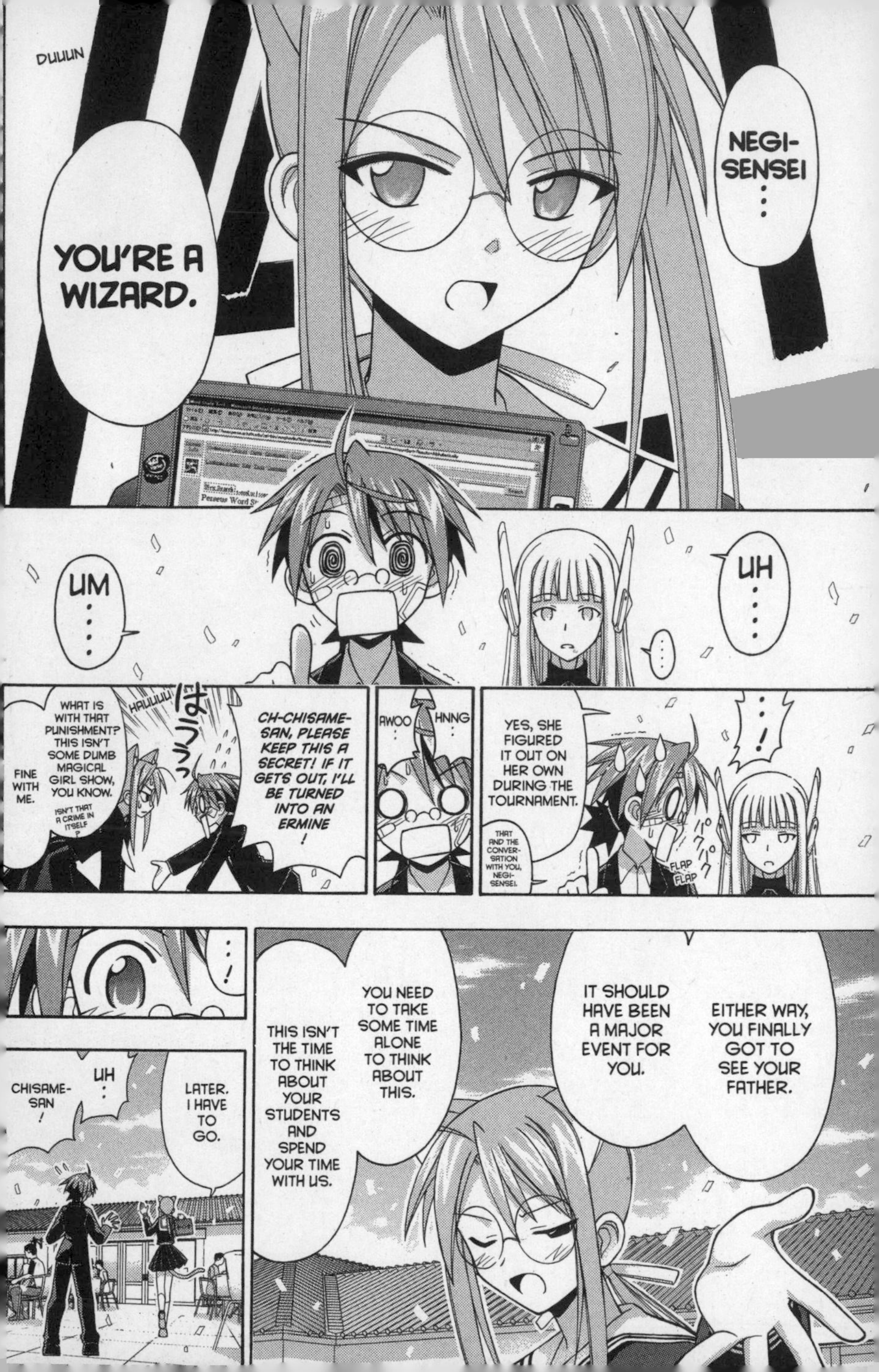
DUUUN
NEGI-SENSEI...
YOU'RE A WIZARD.
UH....
...
UM....
!!
YES, SHE FIGURED IT OUT ON HER OWN DURING THE TOURNAMENT.
THAT AND THE CONVERSATION WITH YOU, NEGI-SENSEI.
FLAP FLAP
HNNG
AWOO
CH-CHISAME-SAN, PLEASE KEEP THIS A SECRET! IF IT GETS OUT, I'LL BE TURNED INTO AN ERMINE!
HAUUUU
WHAT IS WITH THAT PUNISHMENT? THIS ISN'T SOME DUMB MAGICAL GIRL SHOW, YOU KNOW.
ISN'T THAT A CRIME IN ITSELF?
FINE WITH ME.
EITHER WAY, YOU FINALLY GOT TO SEE YOUR FATHER.
IT SHOULD HAVE BEEN A MAJOR EVENT FOR YOU.
YOU NEED TO TAKE SOME TIME ALONE TO THINK ABOUT THIS.
THIS ISN'T THE TIME TO THINK ABOUT YOUR STUDENTS AND SPEND YOUR TIME WITH US.
...!
LATER. I HAVE TO GO.
UH:
CHISAME-SAN!

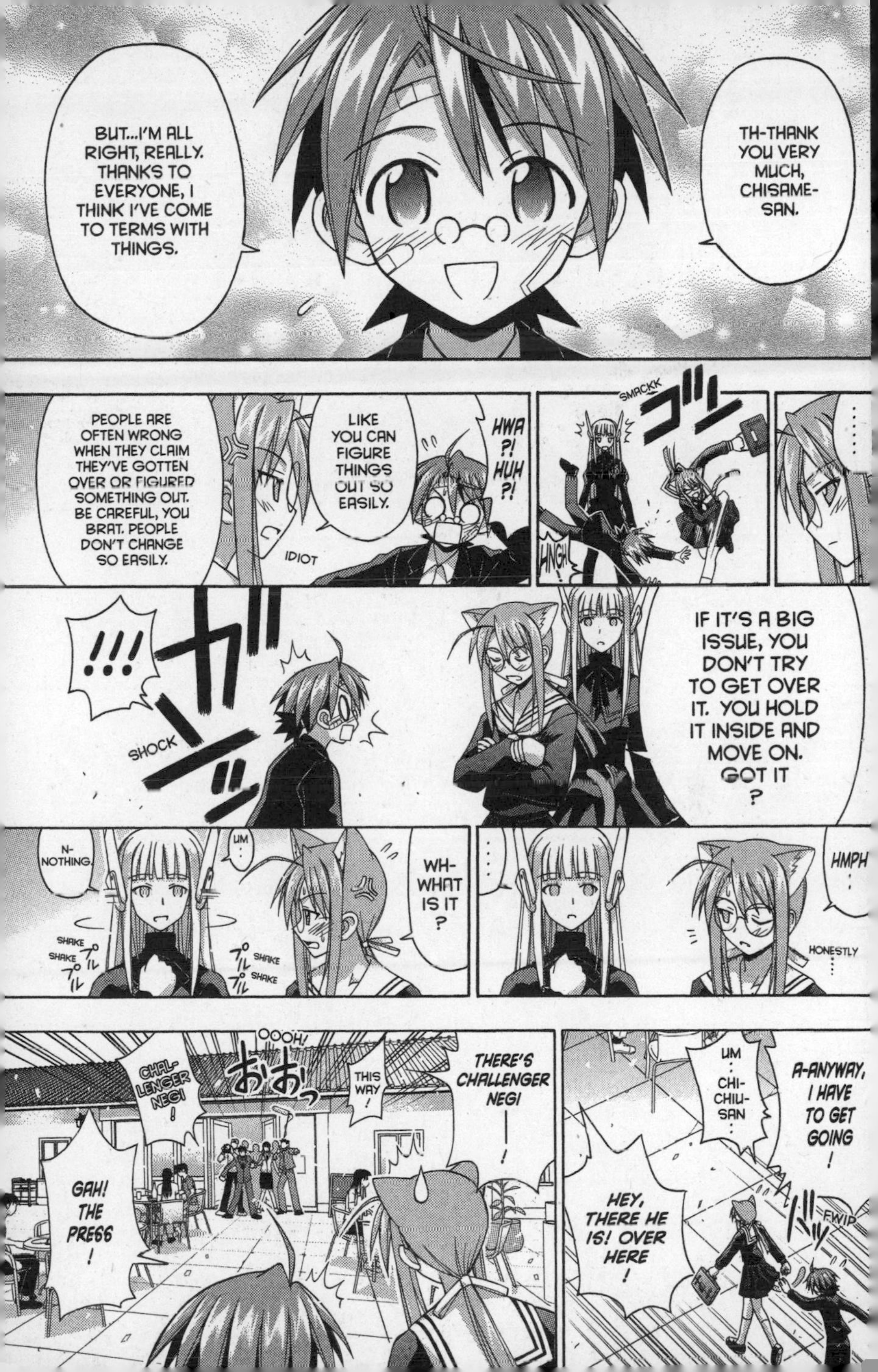
TH-THANK YOU VERY MUCH, CHISAME-SAN.
BUT...I'M ALL RIGHT, REALLY. THANKS TO EVERYONE, I THINK I'VE COME TO TERMS WITH THINGS.
....
SMACKK
HNGH!
HWA?! HUH?!
LIKE YOU CAN FIGURE THINGS OUT SO EASILY.
PEOPLE ARE OFTEN WRONG WHEN THEY CLAIM THEY'VE GOTTEN OVER OR FIGURED SOMETHING OUT. BE CAREFUL, YOU BRAT. PEOPLE DON'T CHANGE SO EASILY.
IDIOT
IF IT'S A BIG ISSUE, YOU DON'T TRY TO GET OVER IT. YOU HOLD IT INSIDE AND MOVE ON. GOT IT?
!!!
SHOCK
HMPH...
HONESTLY...
....
WH-WHAT IS IT?
UM...
N-NOTHING.
SHAKE SHAKE
SHAKE SHAKE
A-ANYWAY, I HAVE TO GET GOING!
UM... CHI-CHIU-SAN
FWIP
HEY, THERE HE IS! OVER HERE!
THERE'S CHALLENGER NEGI—!
THIS WAY!
OOOH!
CHAL-LENGER NEGI!
GAH! THE PRESS!

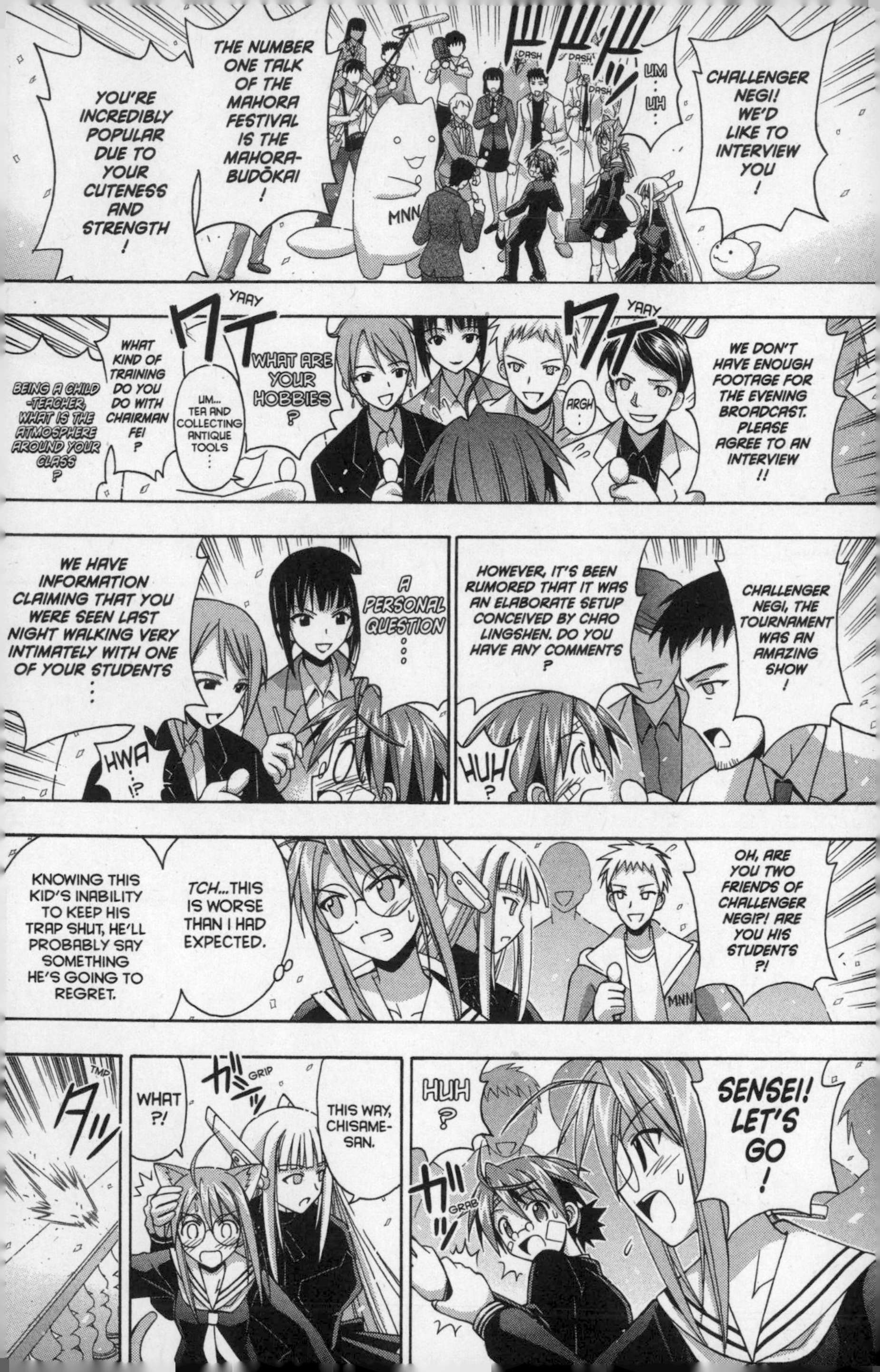
DASH
DASH
DASH
CHALLENGER NEGI! WE'D LIKE TO INTERVIEW YOU!
UM... UH...
THE NUMBER ONE TALK OF THE MAHORA FESTIVAL IS THE MAHORA-BUDŌKAI!
YOU'RE INCREDIBLY POPULAR DUE TO YOUR CUTENESS AND STRENGTH!
MNN
WE DON'T HAVE ENOUGH FOOTAGE FOR THE EVENING BROADCAST. PLEASE AGREE TO AN INTERVIEW!!
YAAY
ARGH...
YAAY
WHAT ARE YOUR HOBBIES?
UM... TEA AND COLLECTING ANTIQUE TOOLS...
WHAT KIND OF TRAINING DO YOU DO WITH CHAIRMAN FEI?
BEING A CHILD-TEACHER, WHAT IS THE ATMOSPHERE AROUND YOUR CLASS?
CHALLENGER NEGI, THE TOURNAMENT WAS AN AMAZING SHOW!
HOWEVER, IT'S BEEN RUMORED THAT IT WAS AN ELABORATE SETUP CONCEIVED BY CHAO LINGSHEN. DO YOU HAVE ANY COMMENTS?
HUH?
A PERSONAL QUESTION...
WE HAVE INFORMATION CLAIMING THAT YOU WERE SEEN LAST NIGHT WALKING VERY INTIMATELY WITH ONE OF YOUR STUDENTS...
HWA...!?
OH, ARE YOU TWO FRIENDS OF CHALLENGER NEGI?! ARE YOU HIS STUDENTS?!
MNN
TCH...THIS IS WORSE THAN I HAD EXPECTED.
KNOWING THIS KID'S INABILITY TO KEEP HIS TRAP SHUT, HE'LL PROBABLY SAY SOMETHING HE'S GOING TO REGRET.
SENSEI! LET'S GO!
HUH?
GRAB
THIS WAY, CHISAME-SAN.
GRIP
WHAT?!
TMP

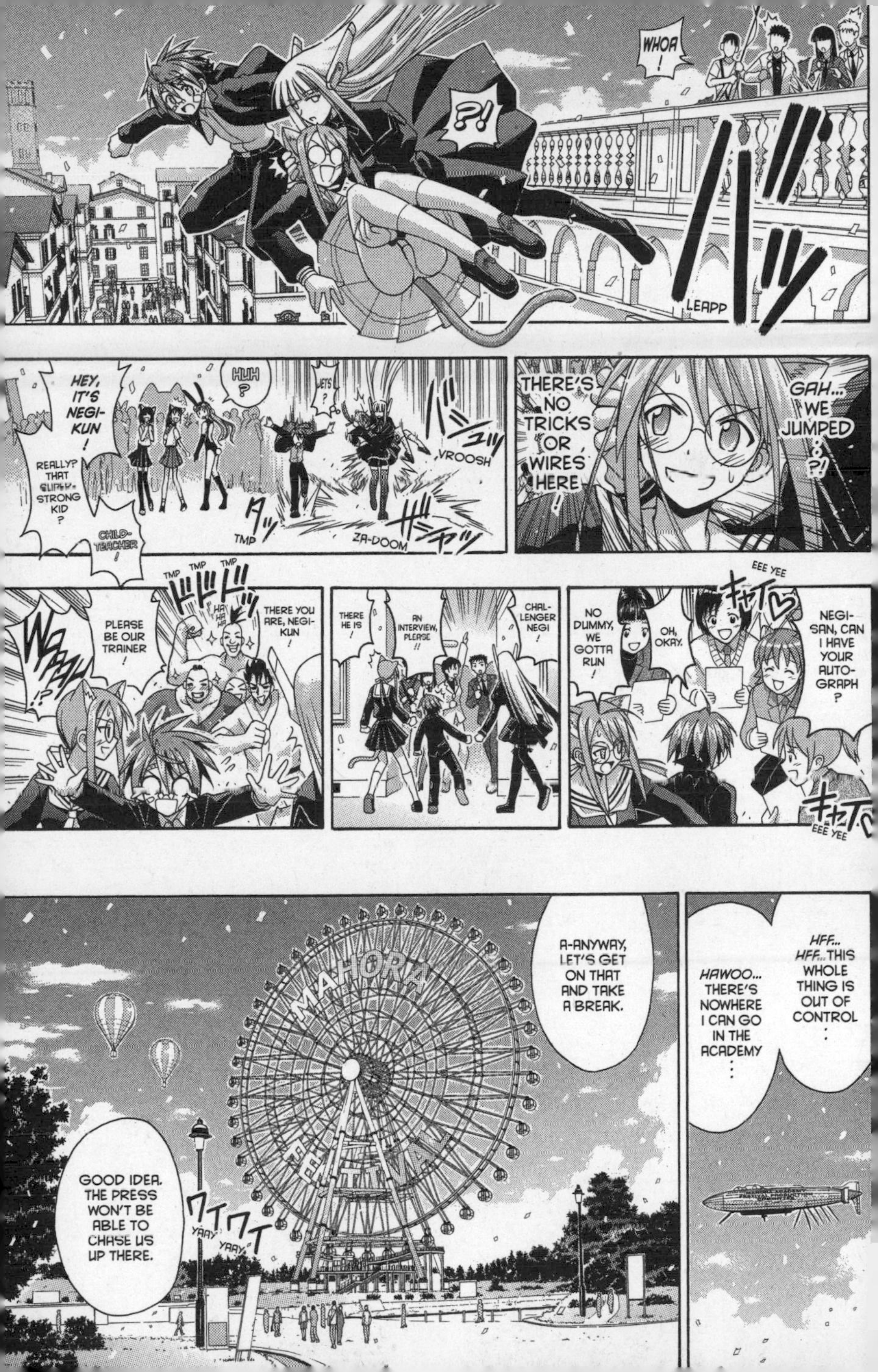
WHOA!
?!
LEAPP
GAH... WE JUMPED...?!
THERE'S NO TRICKS OR WIRES HERE!
HEY, IT'S NEGI-KUN!
HUH?
JETS?
VROOSH
REALLY? THAT SUPER-STRONG KID?
CHILD-TEACHER!
TMP
ZA-DOOM
NEGI-SAN, CAN I HAVE YOUR AUTOGRAPH?
EEE YEE
OH, OKAY.
NO DUMMY, WE GOTTA RUN!
EEE YEE
CHALLENGER NEGI!
AN INTERVIEW, PLEASE!!
THERE HE IS!
THERE YOU ARE, NEGI-KUN!
TMP TMP TMP
HA HA HA
PLEASE BE OUR TRAINER!
HFF... HFF... THIS WHOLE THING IS OUT OF CONTROL...
HAWOO... THERE'S NOWHERE I CAN GO IN THE ACADEMY...
A-ANYWAY, LET'S GET ON THAT AND TAKE A BREAK.
MAHORA
GOOD IDEA. THE PRESS WON'T BE ABLE TO CHASE US UP THERE.
YAAY YAAY

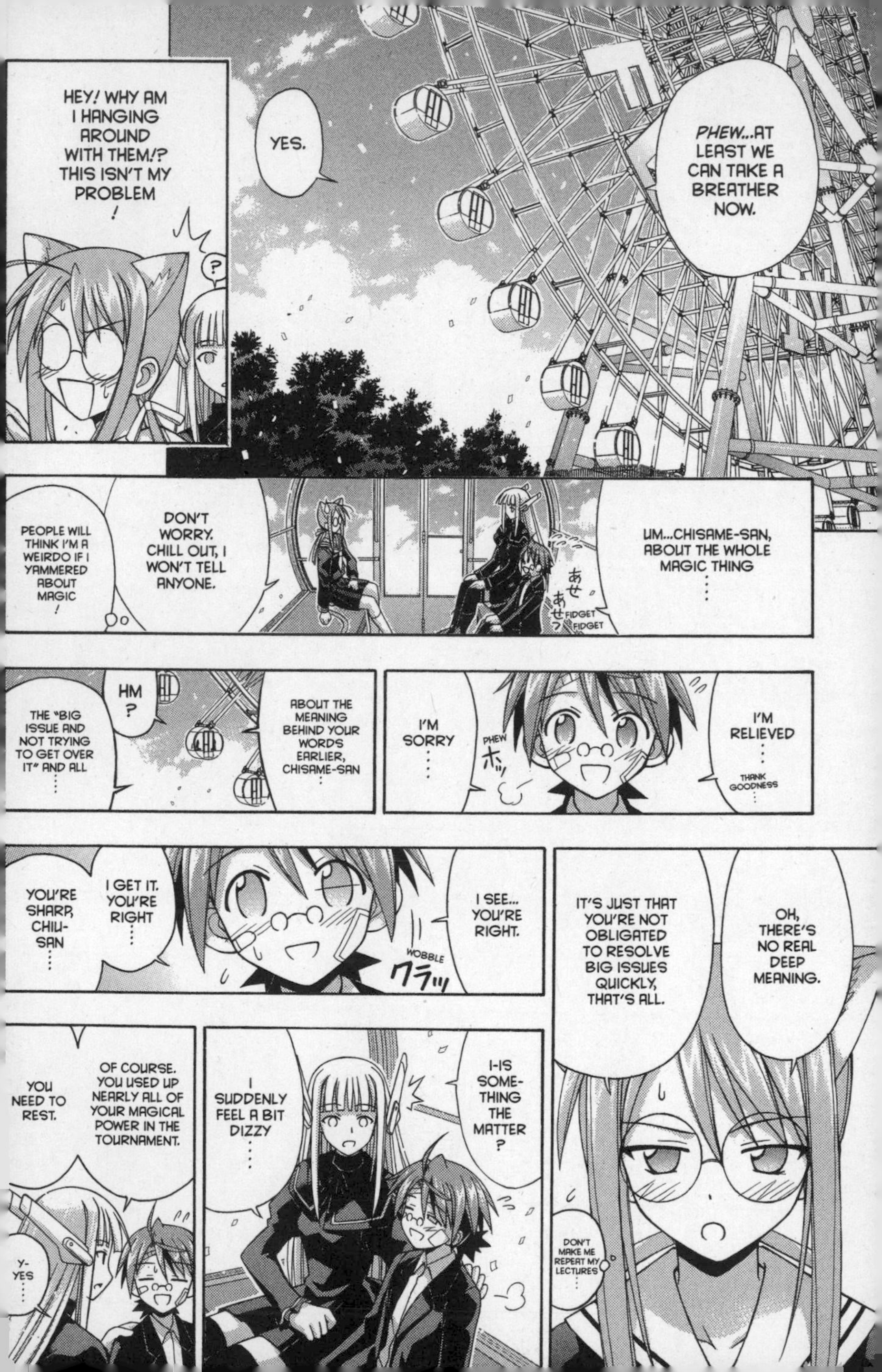
PHEW...AT LEAST WE CAN TAKE A BREATHER NOW.
YES.
HEY! WHY AM I HANGING AROUND WITH THEM!? THIS ISN'T MY PROBLEM!
?
UM...CHISAME-SAN, ABOUT THE WHOLE MAGIC THING....
あせあせ
FIDGET FIDGET
DON'T WORRY. CHILL OUT, I WON'T TELL ANYONE.
PEOPLE WILL THINK I'M A WEIRDO IF I YAMMERED ABOUT MAGIC!
I'M RELIEVED...
THANK GOODNESS...
ホッ
PHEW
I'M SORRY...
ABOUT THE MEANING BEHIND YOUR WORDS EARLIER, CHISAME-SAN...
HM?
THE "BIG ISSUE AND NOT TRYING TO GET OVER IT" AND ALL...
OH, THERE'S NO REAL DEEP MEANING.
IT'S JUST THAT YOU'RE NOT OBLIGATED TO RESOLVE BIG ISSUES QUICKLY, THAT'S ALL.
DON'T MAKE ME REPEAT MY LECTURES...
I SEE... YOU'RE RIGHT.
WOBBLE
グラッ
I GET IT. YOU'RE RIGHT...
YOU'RE SHARP, CHIU-SAN...
I-IS SOMETHING THE MATTER?
I SUDDENLY FEEL A BIT DIZZY....
OF COURSE. YOU USED UP NEARLY ALL OF YOUR MAGICAL POWER IN THE TOURNAMENT.
YOU NEED TO REST.
Y-YES....

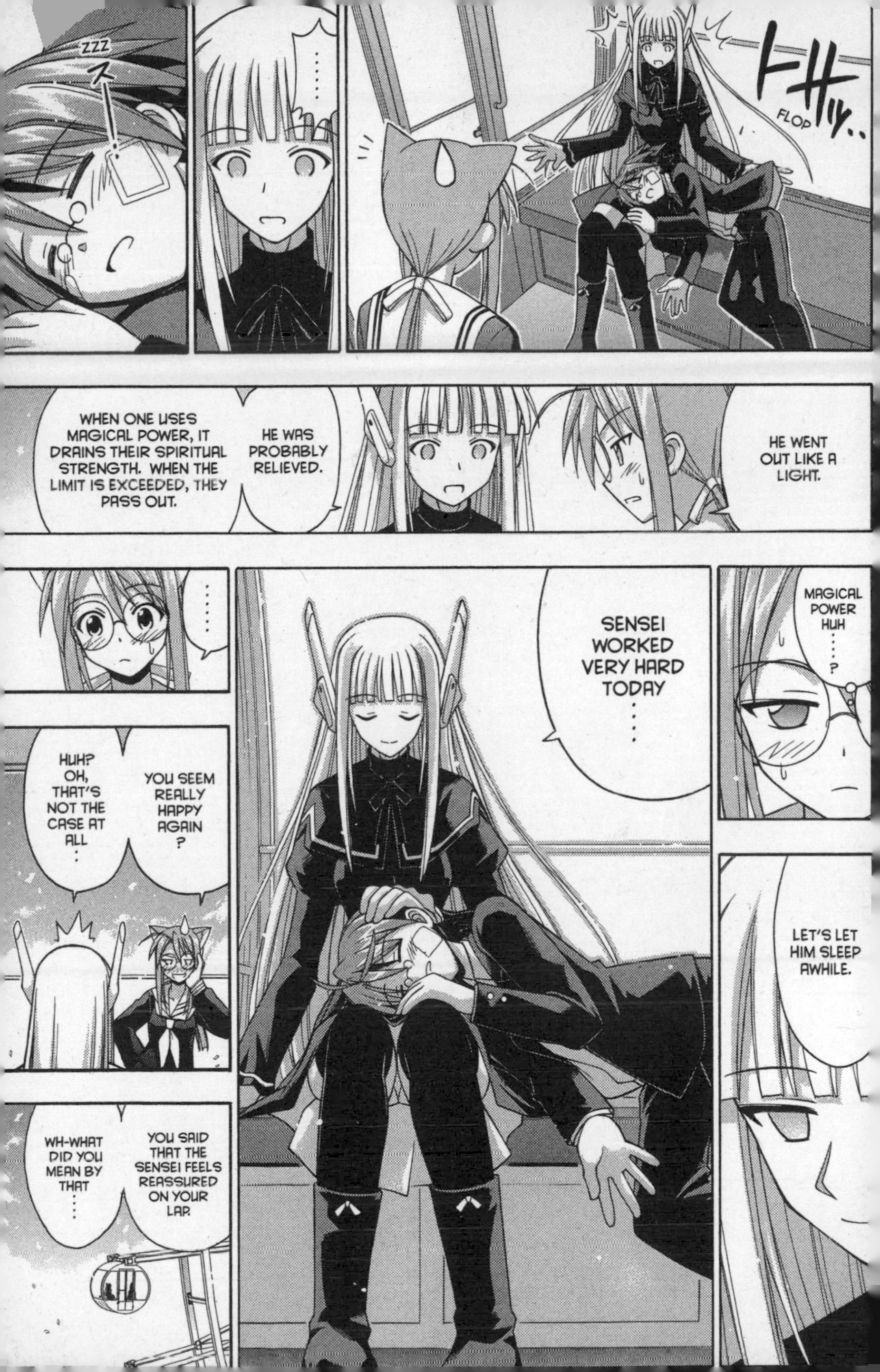
FLOP
……
ZZZ
HE WENT OUT LIKE A LIGHT.
HE WAS PROBABLY RELIEVED.
WHEN ONE USES MAGICAL POWER, IT DRAINS THEIR SPIRITUAL STRENGTH. WHEN THE LIMIT IS EXCEEDED, THEY PASS OUT.
MAGICAL POWER HUH....?
LET'S LET HIM SLEEP AWHILE.
SENSEI WORKED VERY HARD TODAY....
……
YOU SEEM REALLY HAPPY AGAIN?
HUH? OH, THAT'S NOT THE CASE AT ALL..
YOU SAID THAT THE SENSEI FEELS REASSURED ON YOUR LAP.
WH-WHAT DID YOU MEAN BY THAT....

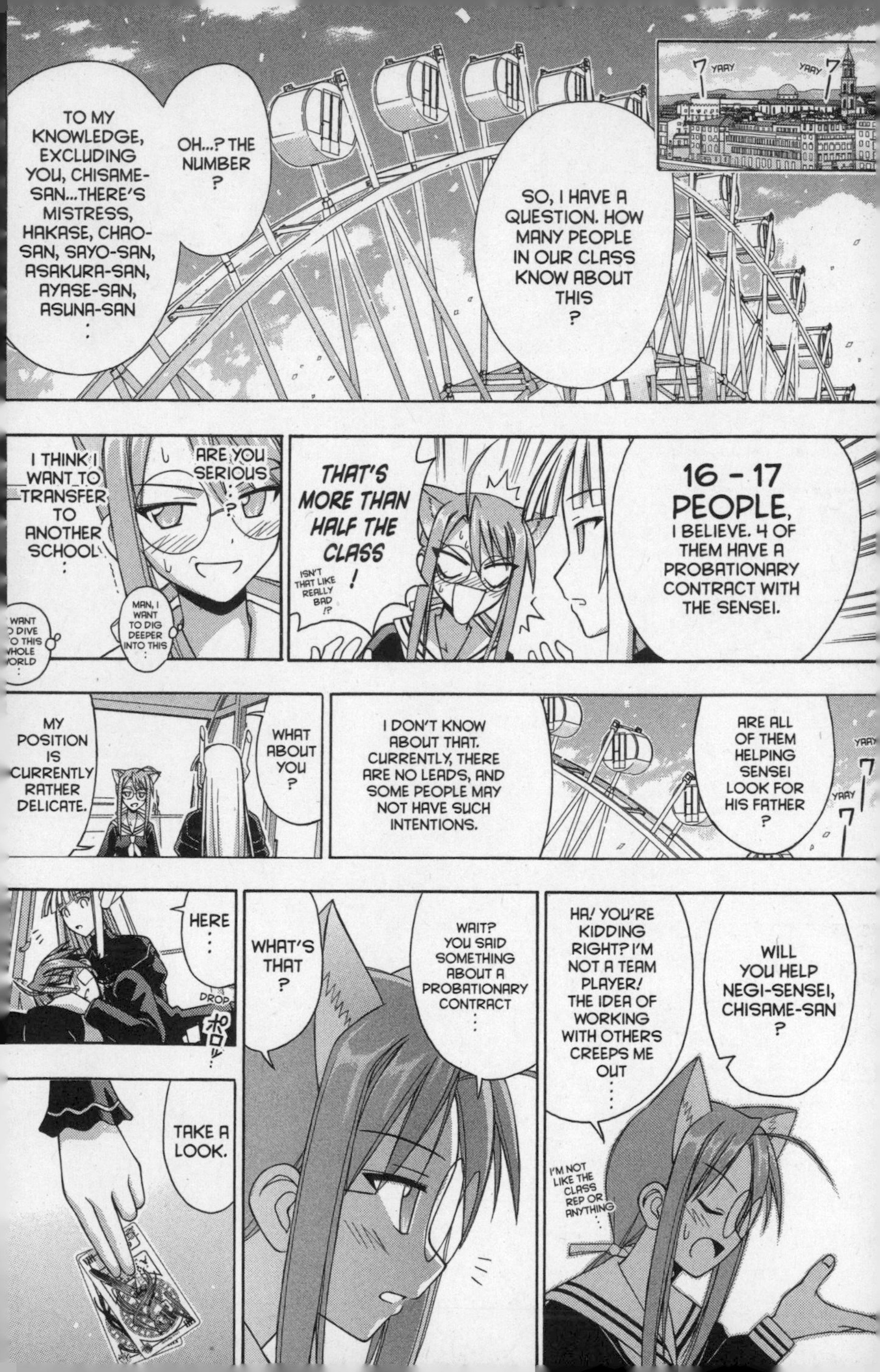
YAAY
YAAY
SO, I HAVE A QUESTION. HOW MANY PEOPLE IN OUR CLASS KNOW ABOUT THIS?
OH...? THE NUMBER?
TO MY KNOWLEDGE, EXCLUDING YOU, CHISAME-SAN...THERE'S MISTRESS, HAKASE, CHAO-SAN, SAYO-SAN, ASAKURA-SAN, AYASE-SAN, ASUNA-SAN...
16 - 17 PEOPLE, I BELIEVE. 4 OF THEM HAVE A PROBATIONARY CONTRACT WITH THE SENSEI.
THAT'S MORE THAN HALF THE CLASS!
ISN'T THAT LIKE REALLY BAD!?
ARE YOU SERIOUS...?
I THINK I WANT TO TRANSFER TO ANOTHER SCHOOL...
MAN, I WANT TO DIG DEEPER INTO THIS...
ARE ALL OF THEM HELPING SENSEI LOOK FOR HIS FATHER?
YAAY
YAAY
I DON'T KNOW ABOUT THAT. CURRENTLY, THERE ARE NO LEADS, AND SOME PEOPLE MAY NOT HAVE SUCH INTENTIONS.
WHAT ABOUT YOU?
MY POSITION IS CURRENTLY RATHER DELICATE.
WILL YOU HELP NEGI-SENSEI, CHISAME-SAN?
HA! YOU'RE KIDDING RIGHT? I'M NOT A TEAM PLAYER! THE IDEA OF WORKING WITH OTHERS CREEPS ME OUT...
I'M NOT LIKE THE CLASS REP OR ANYTHING...
WAIT? YOU SAID SOMETHING ABOUT A PROBATIONARY CONTRACT...
WHAT'S THAT?
HERE...
DROP
TAKE A LOOK.

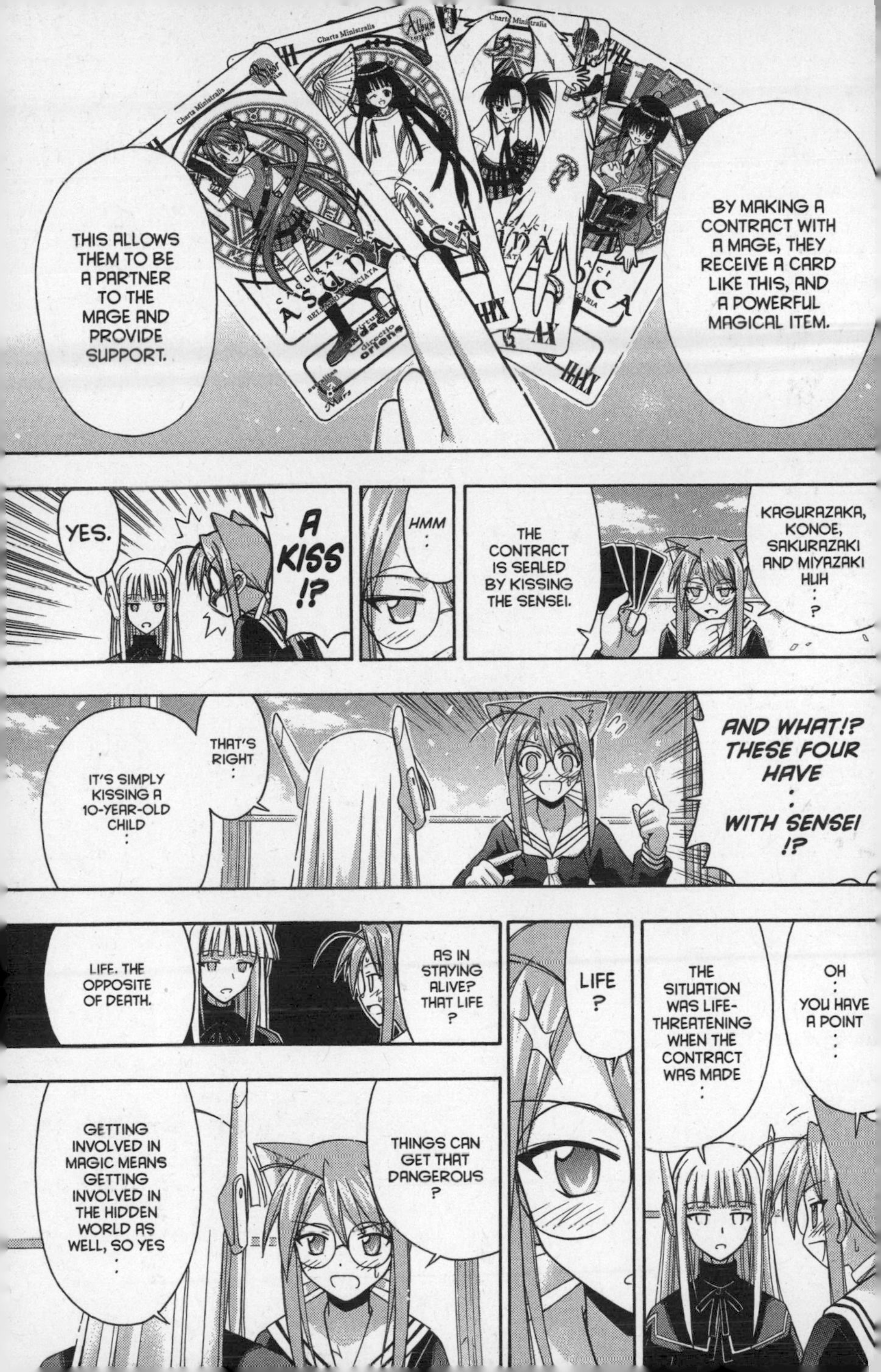
BY MAKING A CONTRACT WITH A MAGE, THEY RECEIVE A CARD LIKE THIS, AND A POWERFUL MAGICAL ITEM.
THIS ALLOWS THEM TO BE A PARTNER TO THE MAGE AND PROVIDE SUPPORT.
KAGURAZAKA, KONOE, SAKURAZAKI AND MIYAZAKI HUH . . ?
THE CONTRACT IS SEALED BY KISSING THE SENSEI.
HMM . .
A KISS !?
YES.
AND WHAT!? THESE FOUR HAVE . . WITH SENSEI !?
THAT'S RIGHT . .
IT'S SIMPLY KISSING A 10-YEAR-OLD CHILD . .
OH . . YOU HAVE A POINT . .
THE SITUATION WAS LIFE-THREATENING WHEN THE CONTRACT WAS MADE . .
LIFE ?
AS IN STAYING ALIVE? THAT LIFE ?
LIFE. THE OPPOSITE OF DEATH.
THINGS CAN GET THAT DANGEROUS ?
GETTING INVOLVED IN MAGIC MEANS GETTING INVOLVED IN THE HIDDEN WORLD AS WELL, SO YES . .

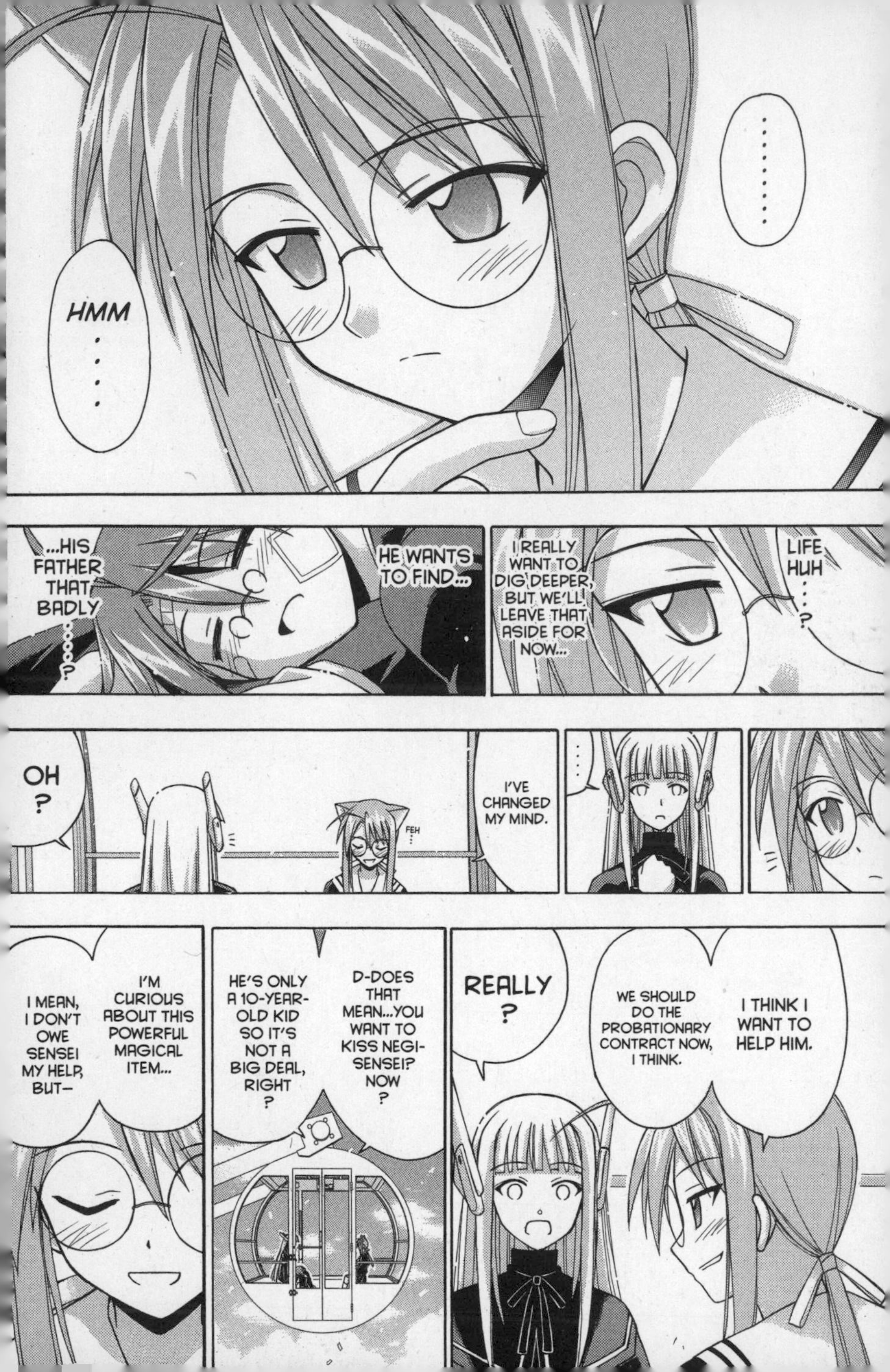
......
HMM.....
LIFE HUH...?
I REALLY WANT TO DIG DEEPER, BUT WE'LL LEAVE THAT ASIDE FOR NOW...
HE WANTS TO FIND...
...HIS FATHER THAT BADLY.....?
...
I'VE CHANGED MY MIND.
FEH...
OH?
I THINK I WANT TO HELP HIM.
WE SHOULD DO THE PROBATIONARY CONTRACT NOW, I THINK.
REALLY?
D-DOES THAT MEAN...YOU WANT TO KISS NEGI-SENSEI? NOW?
HE'S ONLY A 10-YEAR-OLD KID SO IT'S NOT A BIG DEAL, RIGHT?
I'M CURIOUS ABOUT THIS POWERFUL MAGICAL ITEM...
I MEAN, I DON'T OWE SENSEI MY HELP, BUT—

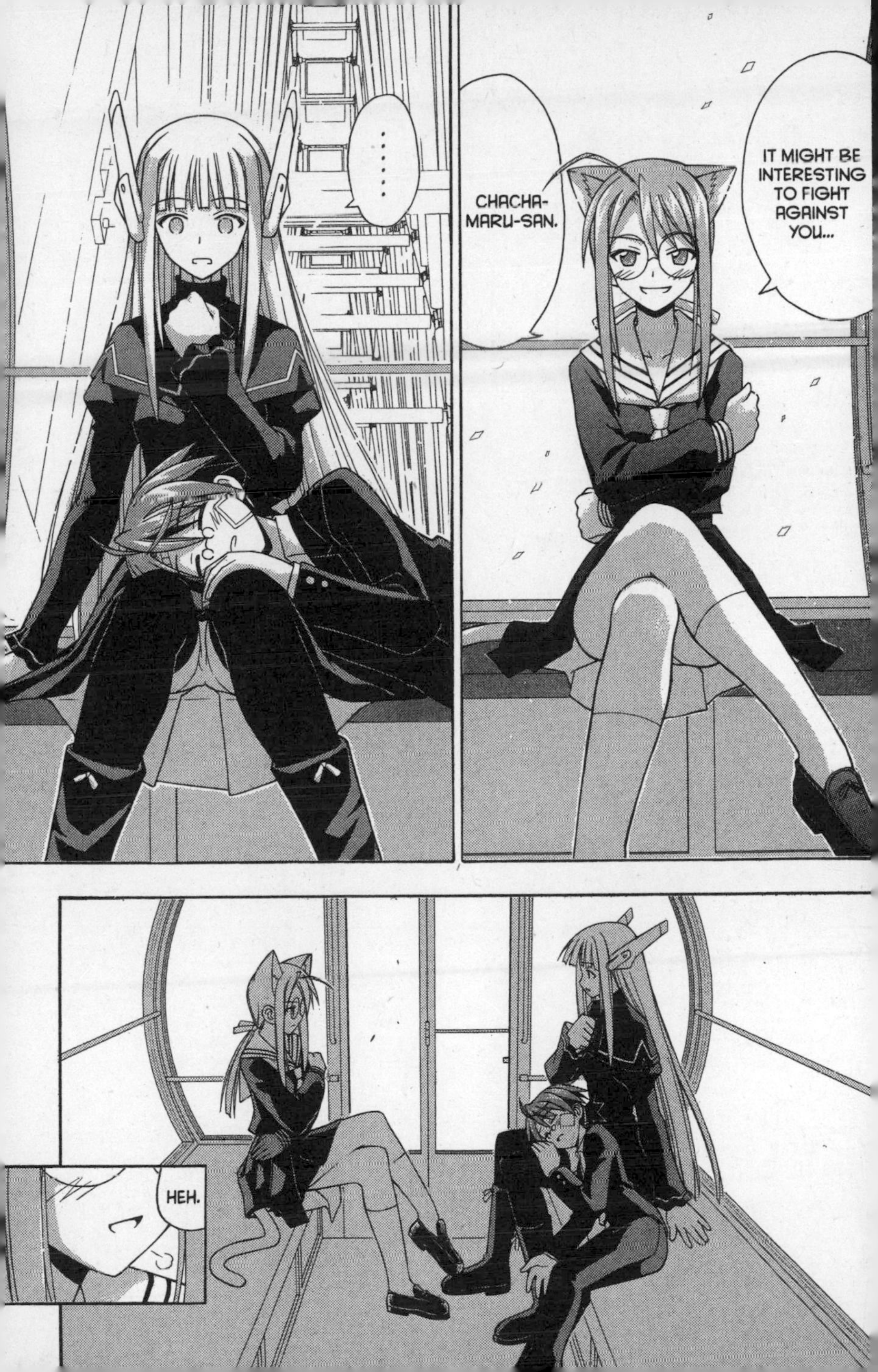
IT MIGHT BE INTERESTING TO FIGHT AGAINST YOU...
CHACHA-MARU-SAN.
......
HEH.

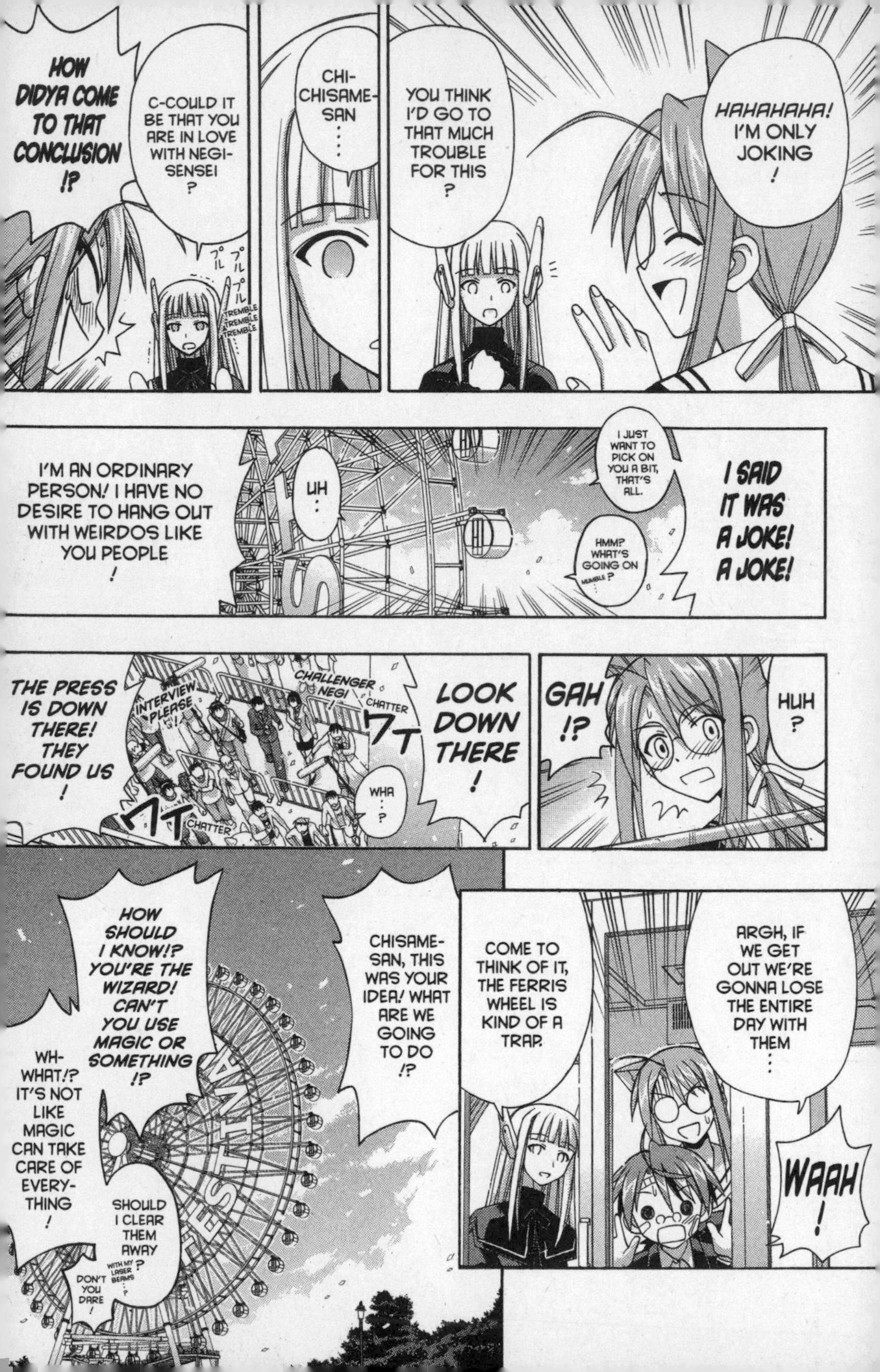
HAHAHAHA! I'M ONLY JOKING!
YOU THINK I'D GO TO THAT MUCH TROUBLE FOR THIS?
CHI-CHISAME-SAN...
C-COULD IT BE THAT YOU ARE IN LOVE WITH NEGI-SENSEI?
TREMBLE TREMBLE TREMBLE
HOW DIDYA COME TO THAT CONCLUSION!?
I SAID IT WAS A JOKE! A JOKE!
I JUST WANT TO PICK ON YOU A BIT, THAT'S ALL.
HMM? WHAT'S GOING ON MUMBLE?
UH...
I'M AN ORDINARY PERSON! I HAVE NO DESIRE TO HANG OUT WITH WEIRDOS LIKE YOU PEOPLE!
HUH?
GAH!?
LOOK DOWN THERE!
CHATTER
CHALLENGER NEGI!
INTERVIEW PLEASE!
WHA...?
THE PRESS IS DOWN THERE! THEY FOUND US!
CHATTER
ARGH, IF WE GET OUT WE'RE GONNA LOSE THE ENTIRE DAY WITH THEM...
WAAH!
COME TO THINK OF IT, THE FERRIS WHEEL IS KIND OF A TRAP.
CHISAME-SAN, THIS WAS YOUR IDEA! WHAT ARE WE GOING TO DO!?
HOW SHOULD I KNOW!? YOU'RE THE WIZARD! CAN'T YOU USE MAGIC OR SOMETHING!?
WH-WHAT!? IT'S NOT LIKE MAGIC CAN TAKE CARE OF EVERYTHING!
SHOULD I CLEAR THEM AWAY?
WITH MY LASER BEAMS...?
DON'T YOU DARE!

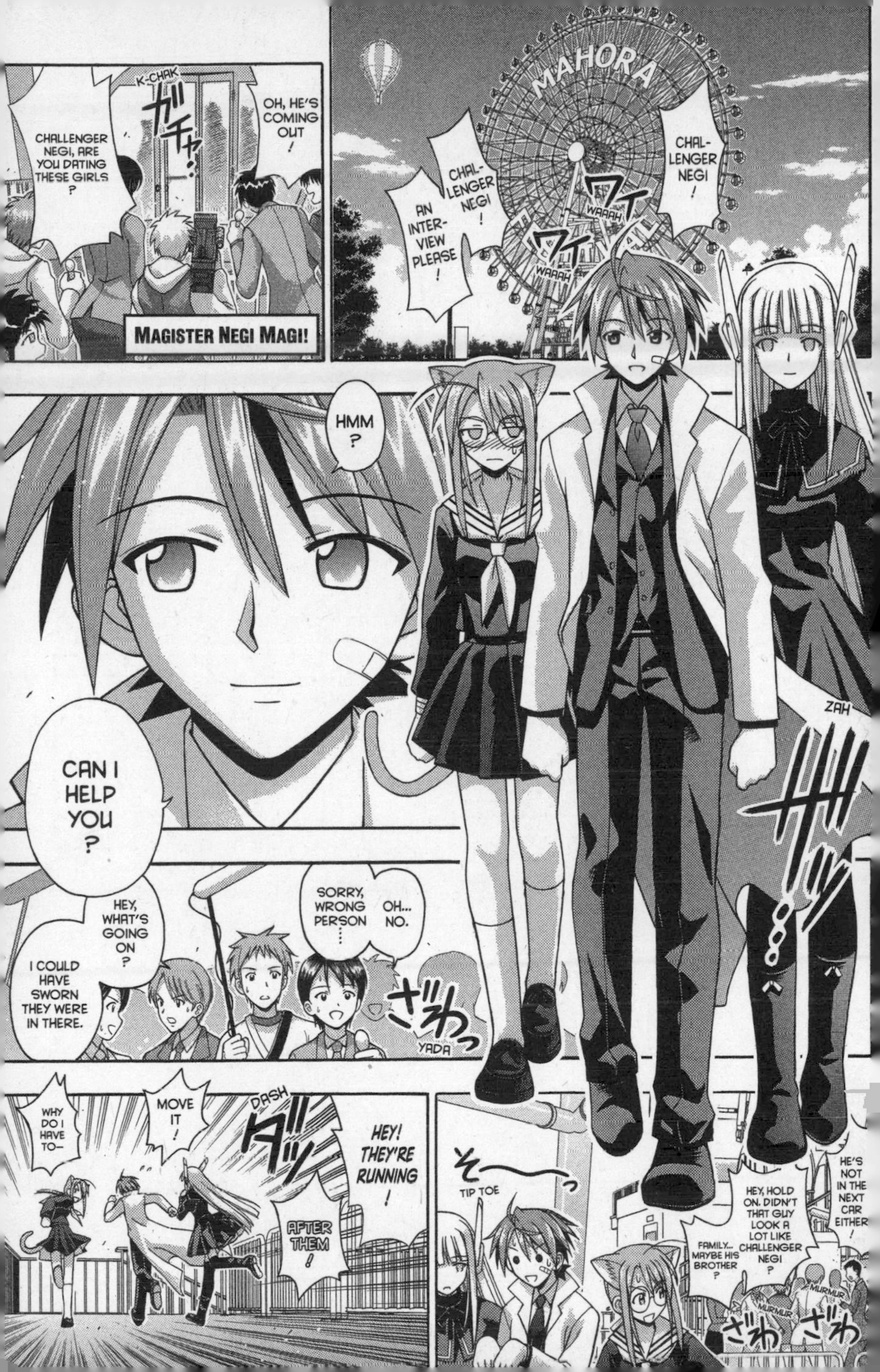
MAHORA
CHAL-LENGER NEGI!
WAAAH
WAAAH
CHAL-LENGER NEGI!
AN INTER-VIEW PLEASE!
OH, HE'S COMING OUT!
K-CHAK
CHALLENGER NEGI, ARE YOU DATING THESE GIRLS?
MAGISTER NEGI MAGI!
ZAH
HMM?
CAN I HELP YOU?
OH... NO.
SORRY, WRONG PERSON...
HEY, WHAT'S GOING ON?
I COULD HAVE SWORN THEY WERE IN THERE.
YADA
HE'S NOT IN THE NEXT CAR EITHER!
HEY, HOLD ON. DIDN'T THAT GUY LOOK A LOT LIKE CHALLENGER NEGI?
FAMILY... MAYBE HIS BROTHER?
MURMUR
MURMUR
TIP TOE
HEY! THEY'RE RUNNING!
AFTER THEM!
DASH
MOVE IT!
WHY DO I HAVE TO—

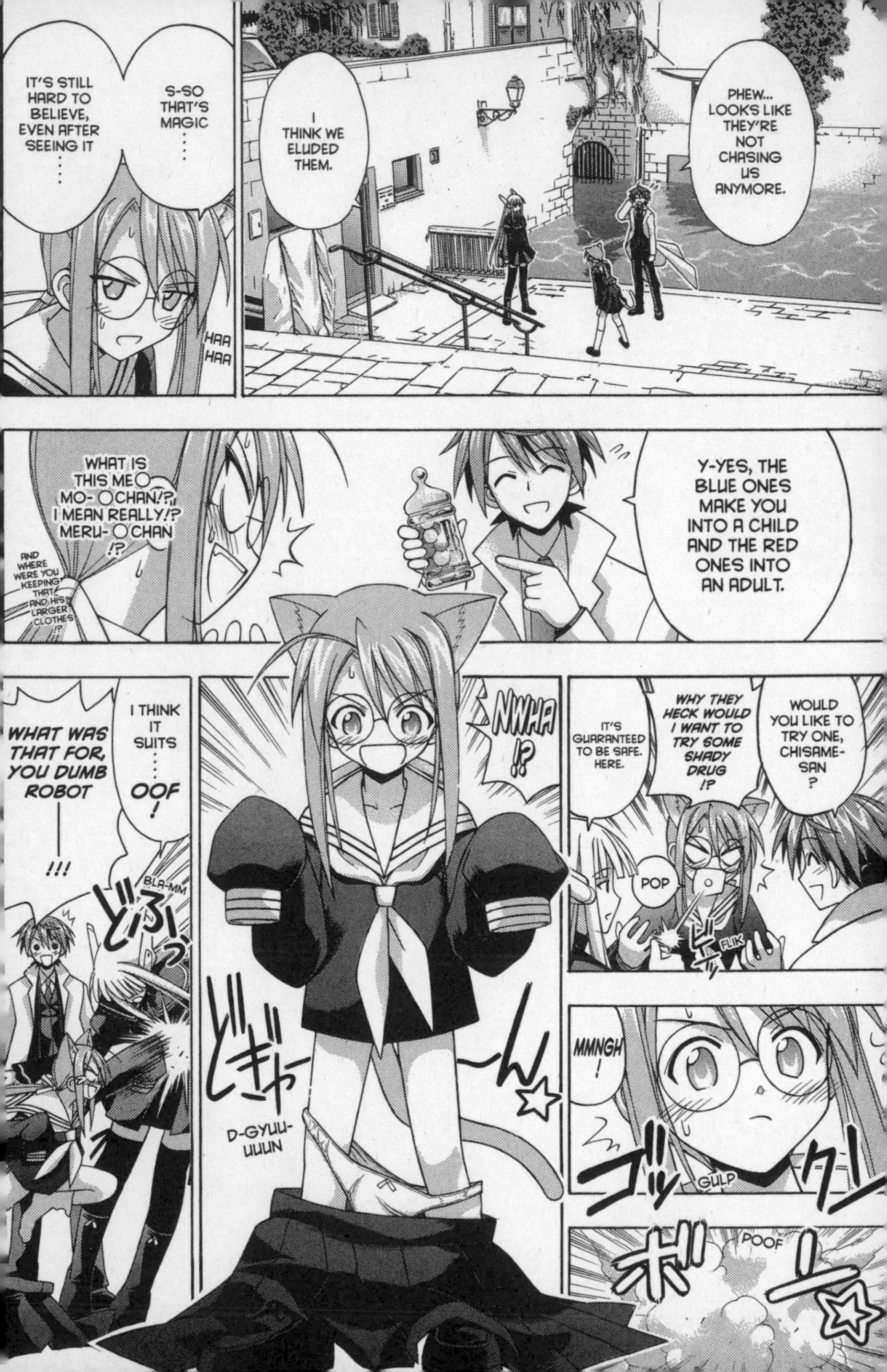
PHEW... LOOKS LIKE THEY'RE NOT CHASING US ANYMORE.
I THINK WE ELUDED THEM.
S-SO THAT'S MAGIC ....
IT'S STILL HARD TO BELIEVE, EVEN AFTER SEEING IT ....
HAA HAA
Y-YES, THE BLUE ONES MAKE YOU INTO A CHILD AND THE RED ONES INTO AN ADULT.
WHAT IS THIS ME◯ MO-◯CHAN!? I MEAN REALLY!? MERU-◯CHAN !?
AND WHERE WERE YOU KEEPING THAT AND HIS LARGER CLOTHES !?
WOULD YOU LIKE TO TRY ONE, CHISAME-SAN ?
WHY THEY HECK WOULD I WANT TO TRY SOME SHADY DRUG !?
IT'S GUARANTEED TO BE SAFE. HERE.
POP
FLIK
MMNGH !
GULP
POOF
NWHA !?
D-GYUU-UUUN
I THINK IT SUITS .... OOF !
BLA-MM
WHAT WAS THAT FOR, YOU DUMB ROBOT ——— !!!

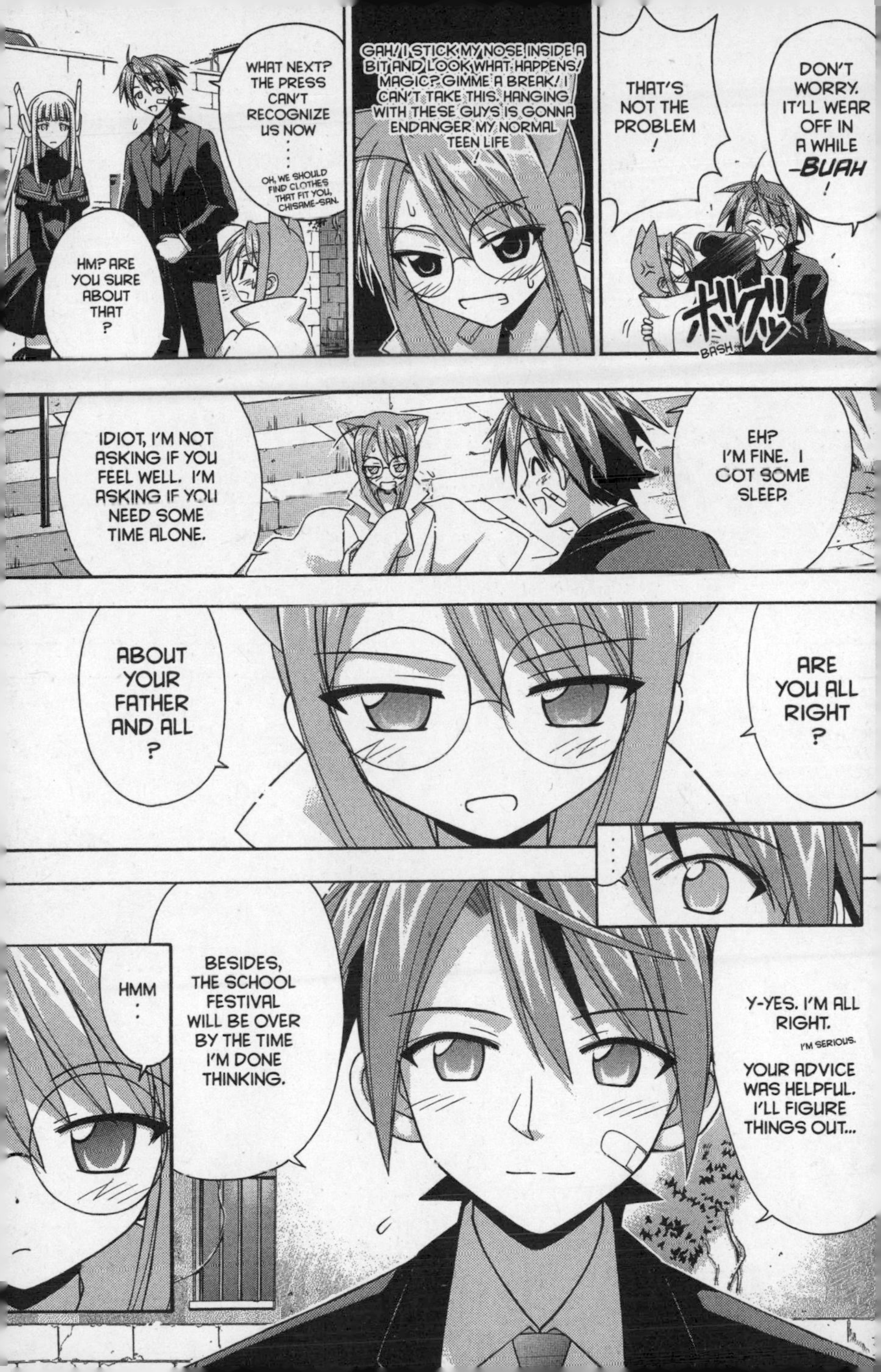
DON'T WORRY. IT'LL WEAR OFF IN A WHILE —BUAH!
THAT'S NOT THE PROBLEM!
BASH
GAH! I STICK MY NOSE INSIDE A BIT AND LOOK WHAT HAPPENS! MAGIC? GIMME A BREAK! I CAN'T TAKE THIS. HANGING WITH THESE GUYS IS GONNA ENDANGER MY NORMAL TEEN LIFE!
WHAT NEXT? THE PRESS CAN'T RECOGNIZE US NOW...
OH, WE SHOULD FIND CLOTHES THAT FIT YOU, CHISAME-SAN.
HM? ARE YOU SURE ABOUT THAT?
EH? I'M FINE. I GOT SOME SLEEP.
IDIOT, I'M NOT ASKING IF YOU FEEL WELL. I'M ASKING IF YOU NEED SOME TIME ALONE.
ARE YOU ALL RIGHT?
ABOUT YOUR FATHER AND ALL?
....
Y-YES. I'M ALL RIGHT.
I'M SERIOUS.
YOUR ADVICE WAS HELPFUL. I'LL FIGURE THINGS OUT...
BESIDES, THE SCHOOL FESTIVAL WILL BE OVER BY THE TIME I'M DONE THINKING.
HMM...

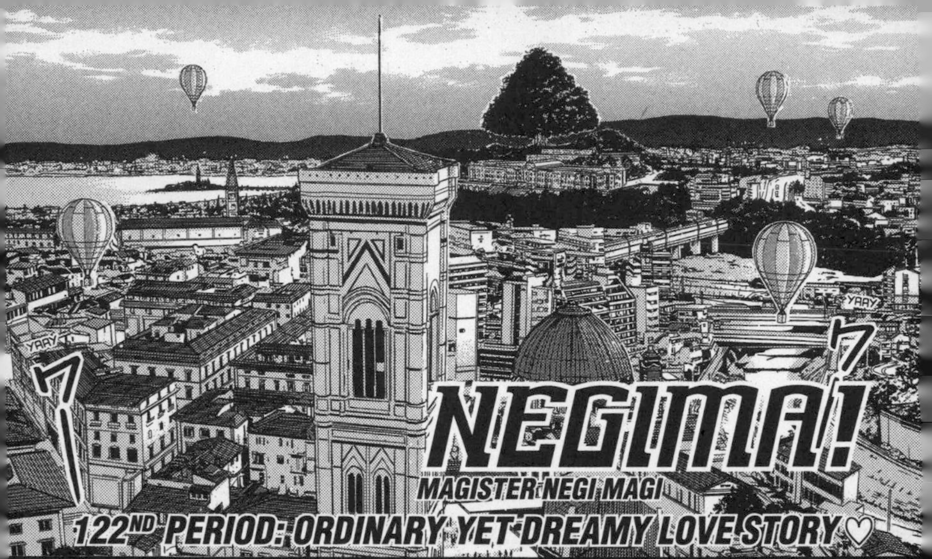
YAAY
YAAY
NEGIMA!
MAGISTER NEGI MAGI
122ND PERIOD: ORDINARY YET DREAMY LOVE STORY♡

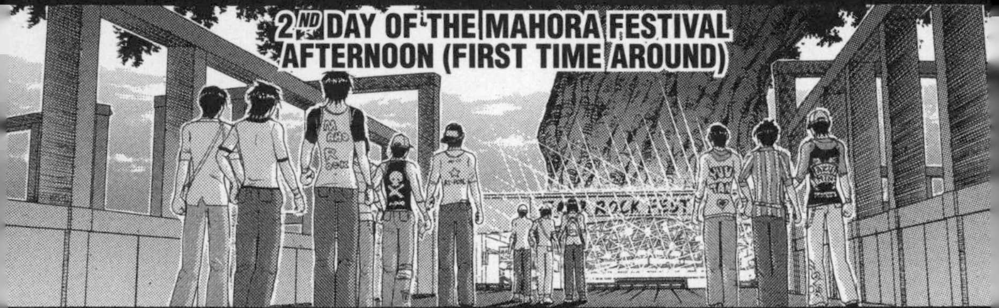
2ND DAY OF THE MAHORA FESTIVAL
AFTERNOON (FIRST TIME AROUND)

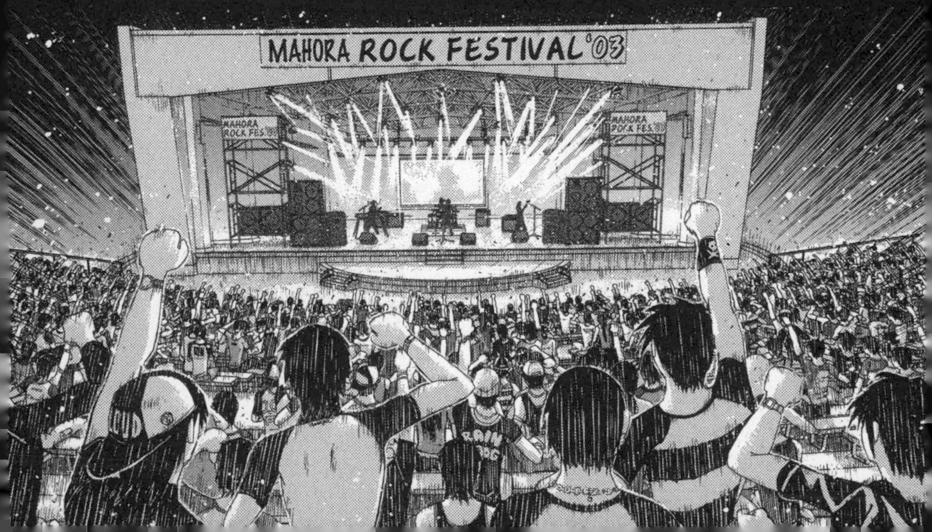
MAHORA ROCK FESTIVAL '03

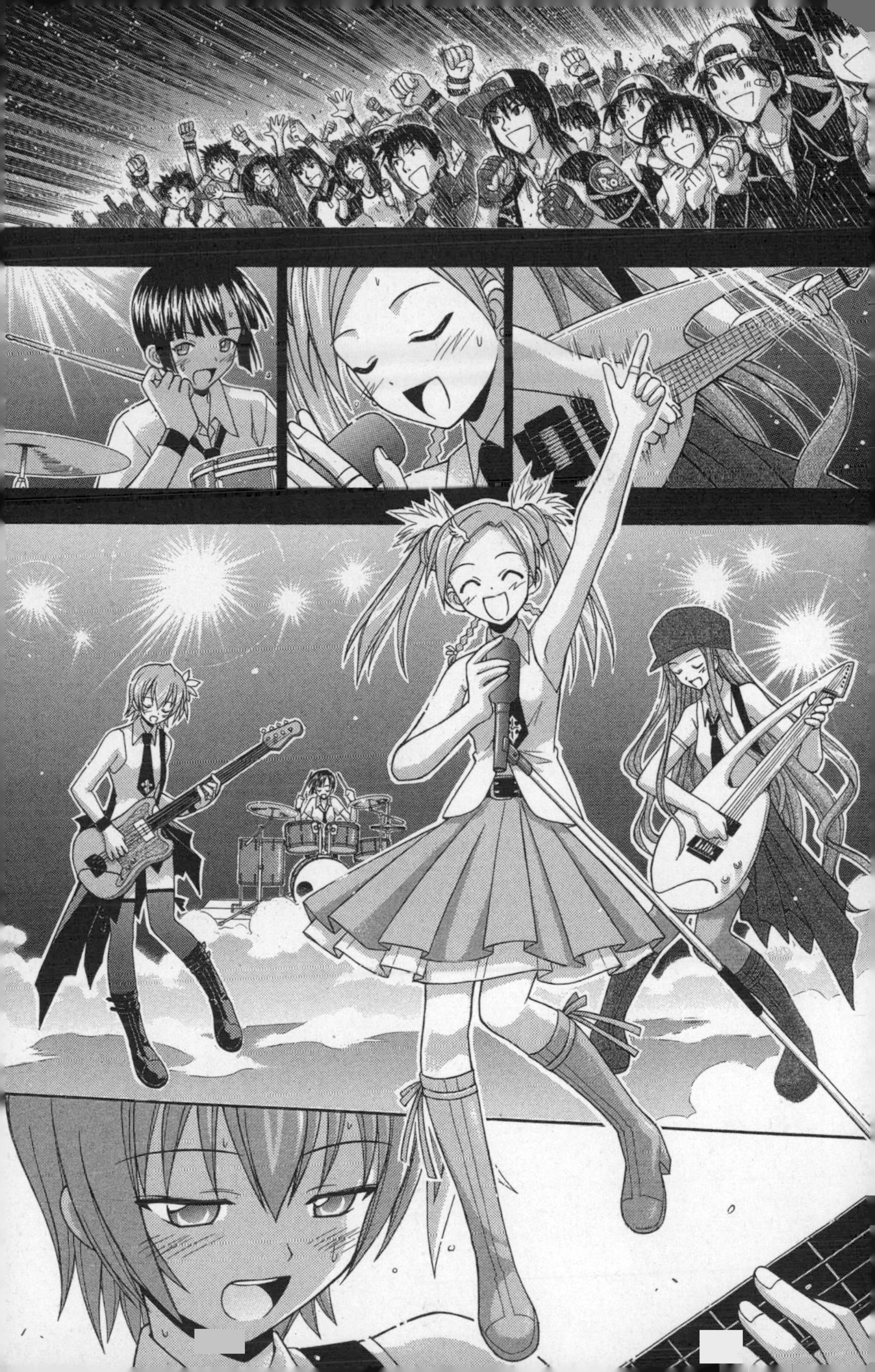

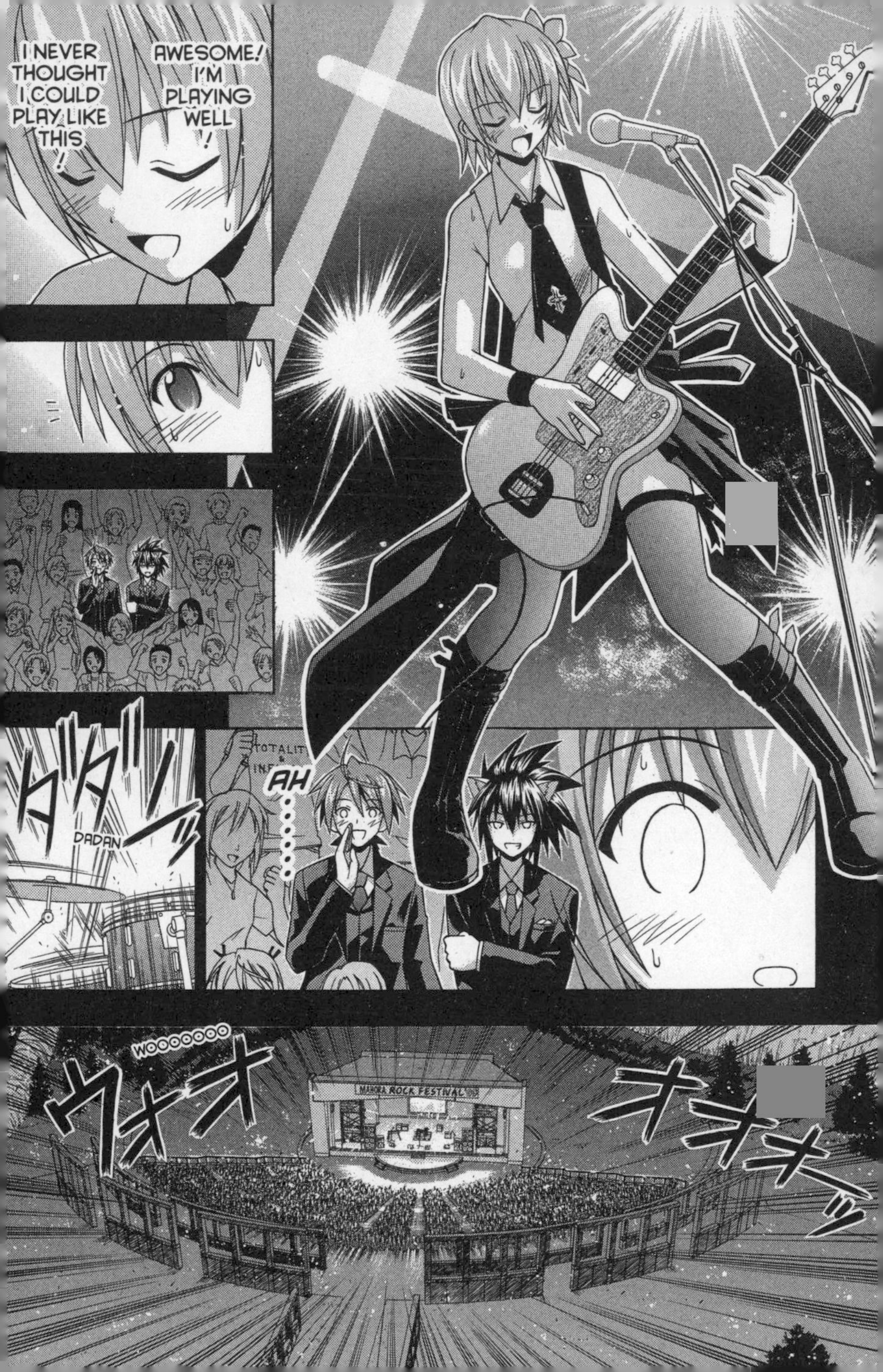
AWESOME! I'M PLAYING WELL!
I NEVER THOUGHT I COULD PLAY LIKE THIS!
AH.......
DADAN
WOOOOOOO
MAHORA ROCK FESTIVAL

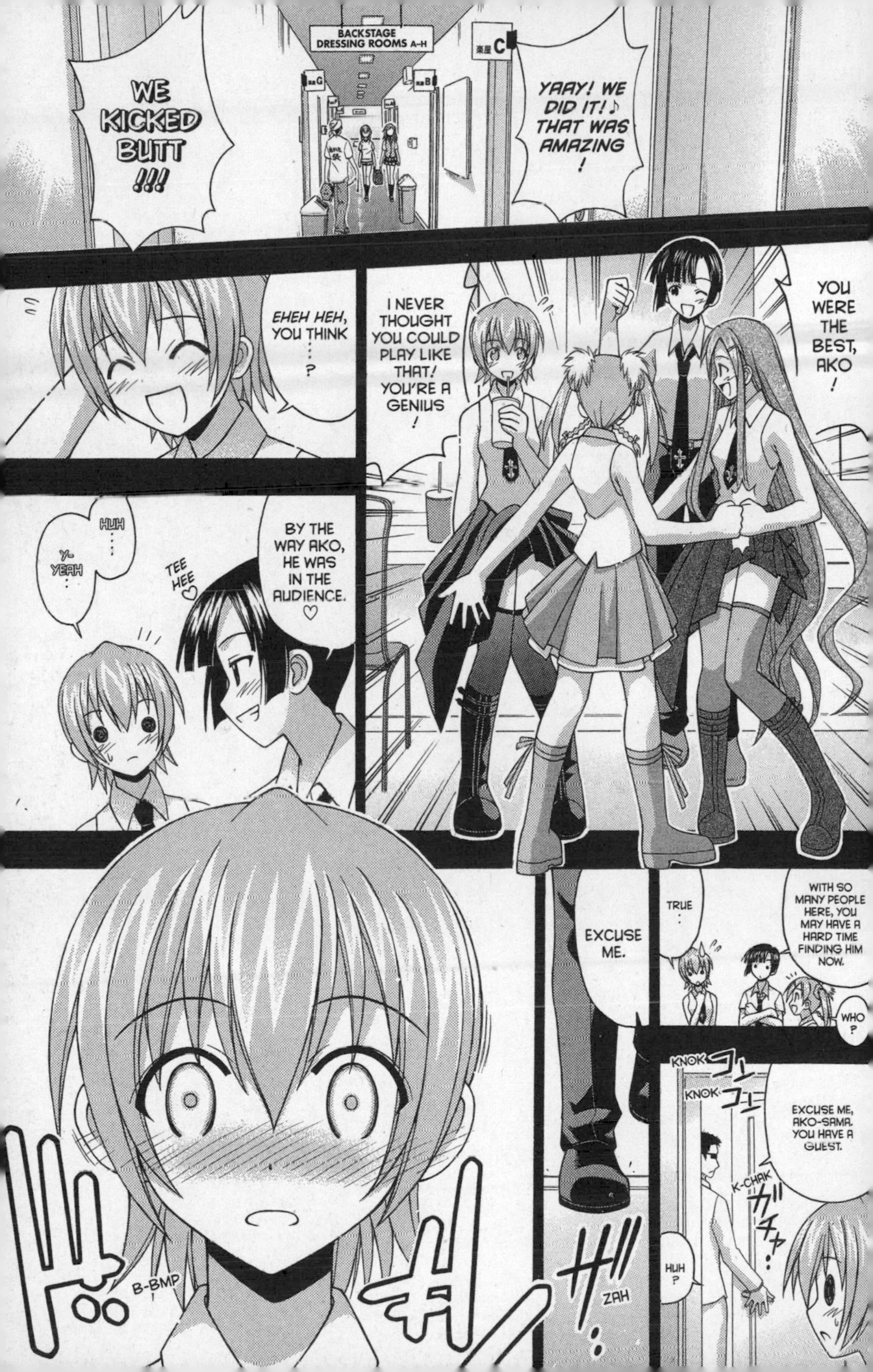

楽屋 C
YAAY! WE DID IT!♪ THAT WAS AMAZING!
BACKSTAGE DRESSING ROOMS A–H
WE KICKED BUTT!!!
YOU WERE THE BEST, AKO!
I NEVER THOUGHT YOU COULD PLAY LIKE THAT! YOU'RE A GENIUS!
EHEH HEH, YOU THINK...?
BY THE WAY AKO, HE WAS IN THE AUDIENCE.♡
TEE HEE♡
HUH... Y-YEAH...
WITH SO MANY PEOPLE HERE, YOU MAY HAVE A HARD TIME FINDING HIM NOW.
TRUE...
WHO?
KNOK KNOK
EXCUSE ME, AKO-SAMA. YOU HAVE A GUEST.
K-CHAK
HUH?
EXCUSE ME.
ZAH
B-BMP

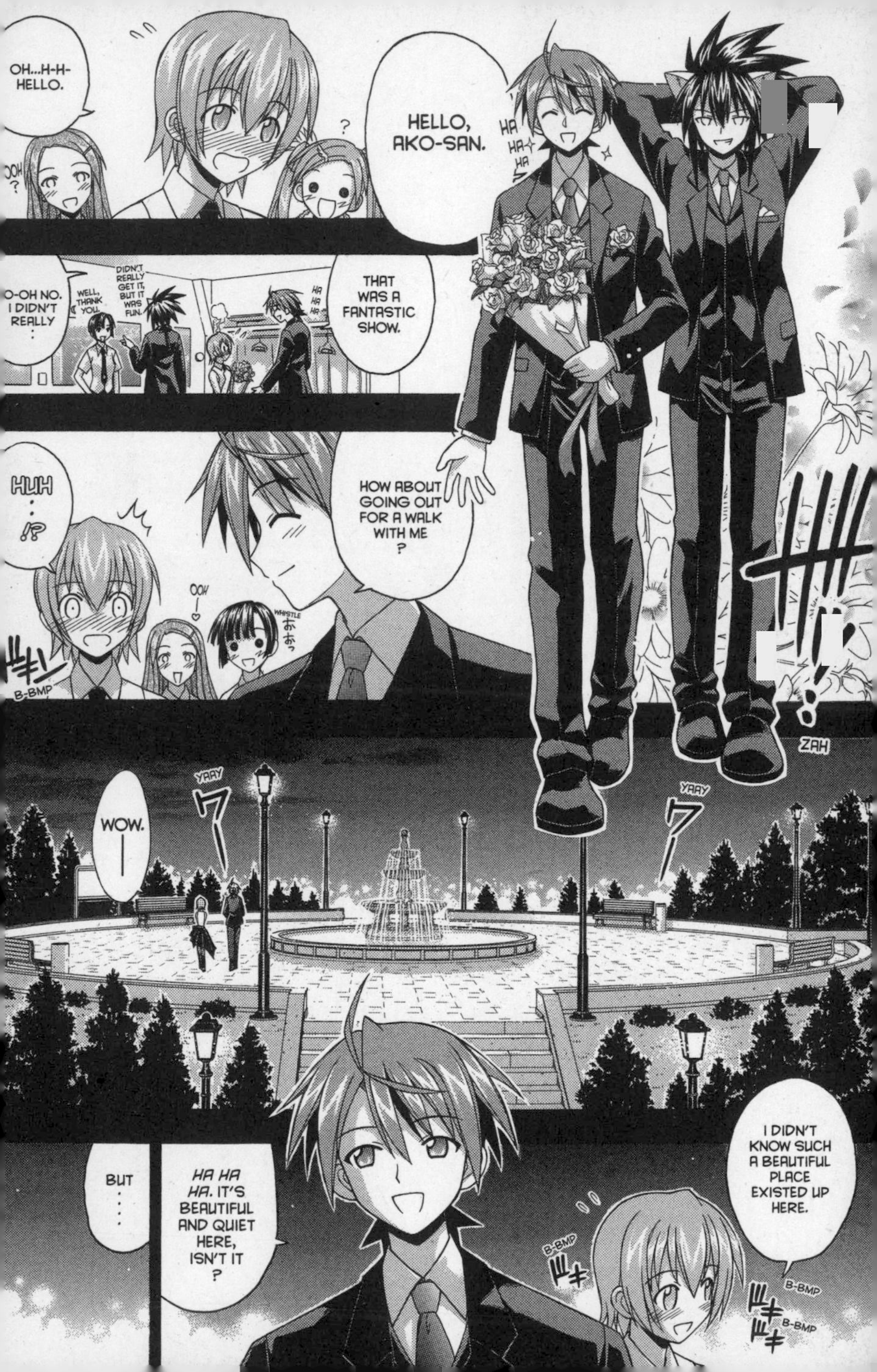
HELLO, AKO-SAN.
HA HA HA
ZAH
?
OH...H-H-HELLO.
OOH ?
THAT WAS A FANTASTIC SHOW.
HA HA
DIDN'T REALLY GET IT, BUT IT WAS FUN.
WELL, THANK YOU.
O-OH NO. I DIDN'T REALLY
HOW ABOUT GOING OUT FOR A WALK WITH ME ?
WHISTLE
OOH!
HUH . . !?
B-BMP
YAAY
WOW.
YAAY
I DIDN'T KNOW SUCH A BEAUTIFUL PLACE EXISTED UP HERE.
B-BMP
B-BMP
B-BMP
HA HA HA. IT'S BEAUTIFUL AND QUIET HERE, ISN'T IT ?
BUT . . . .

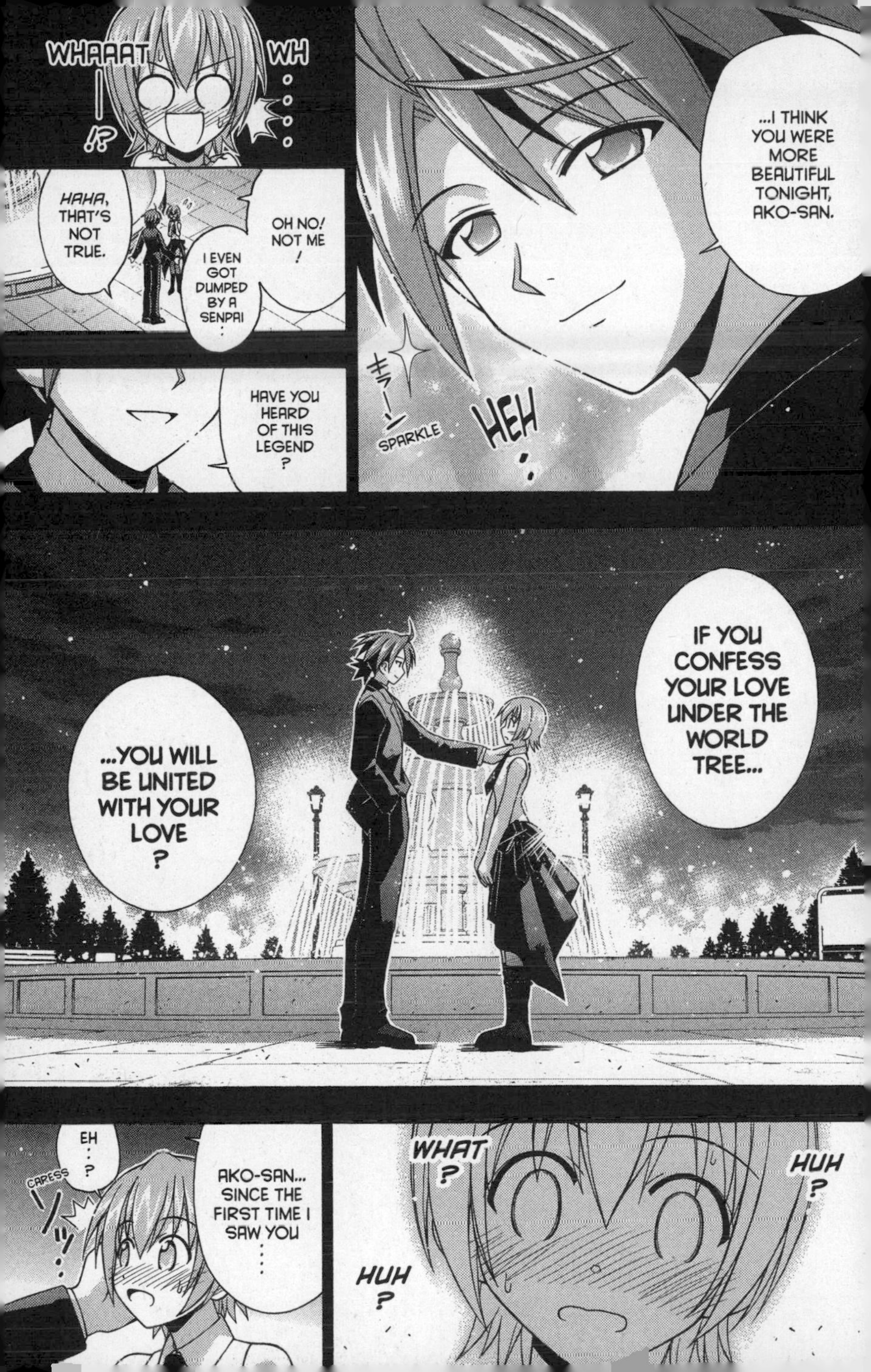
...I THINK YOU WERE MORE BEAUTIFUL TONIGHT, AKO-SAN.
SPARKLE
HEH..
WHOOOO
WHAAAT—!?
OH NO! NOT ME!
I EVEN GOT DUMPED BY A SENPAI...
HAHA, THAT'S NOT TRUE.
HAVE YOU HEARD OF THIS LEGEND?
IF YOU CONFESS YOUR LOVE UNDER THE WORLD TREE...
...YOU WILL BE UNITED WITH YOUR LOVE?
HUH?
WHAT?
HUH?
AKO-SAN... SINCE THE FIRST TIME I SAW YOU...
EH...?
CARESS

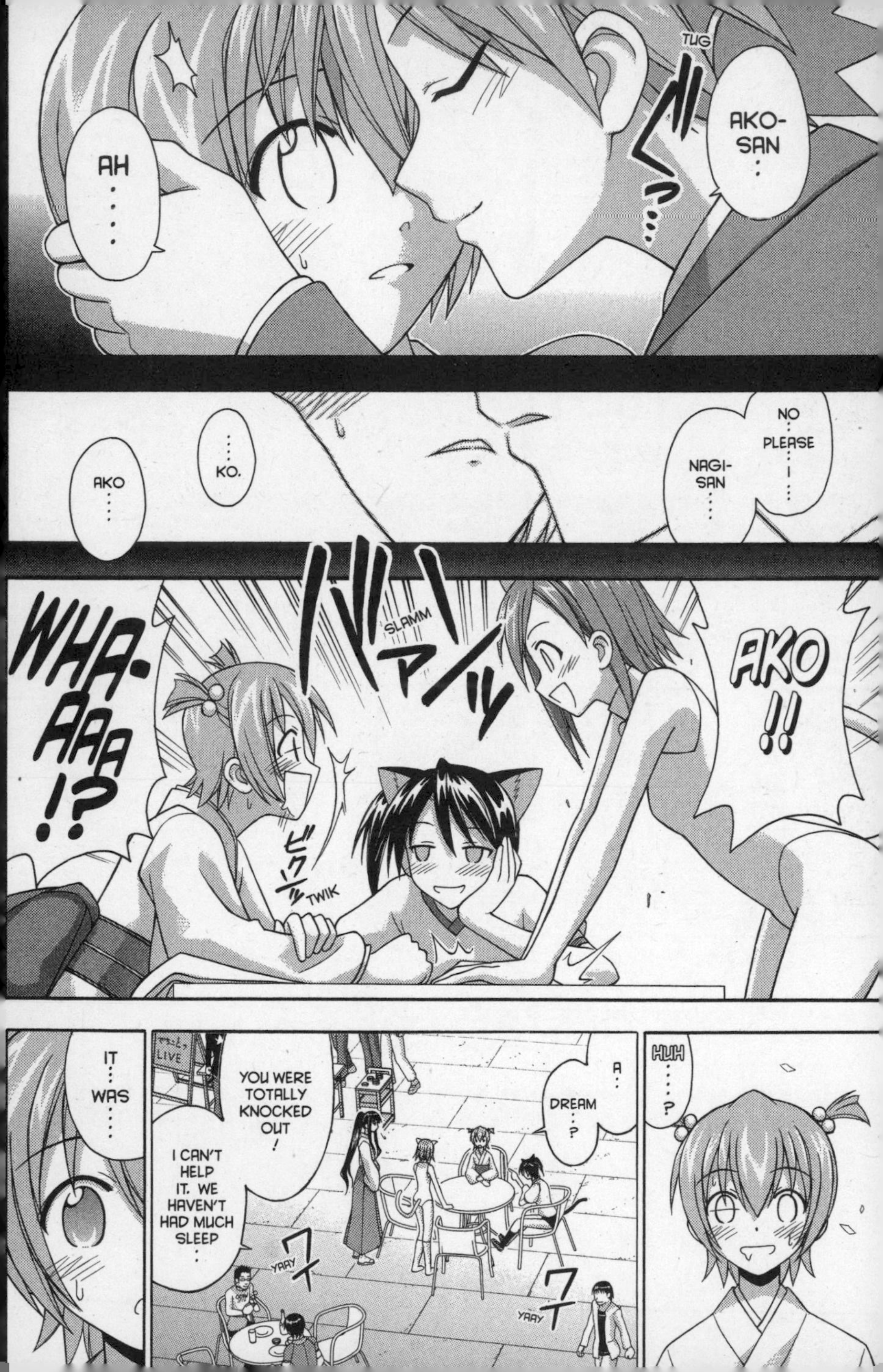
TUG
AKO-SAN...
AH.....
NO... PLEASE... I....
NAGI-SAN...
...KO.
AKO...
SLAMM
AKO!!
WHA-AAAA!?
TWIK
HUH....?
A... DREAM...?
YOU WERE TOTALLY KNOCKED OUT!
I CAN'T HELP IT. WE HAVEN'T HAD MUCH SLEEP...
LIVE
YAAY
YAAY
IT... WAS.....

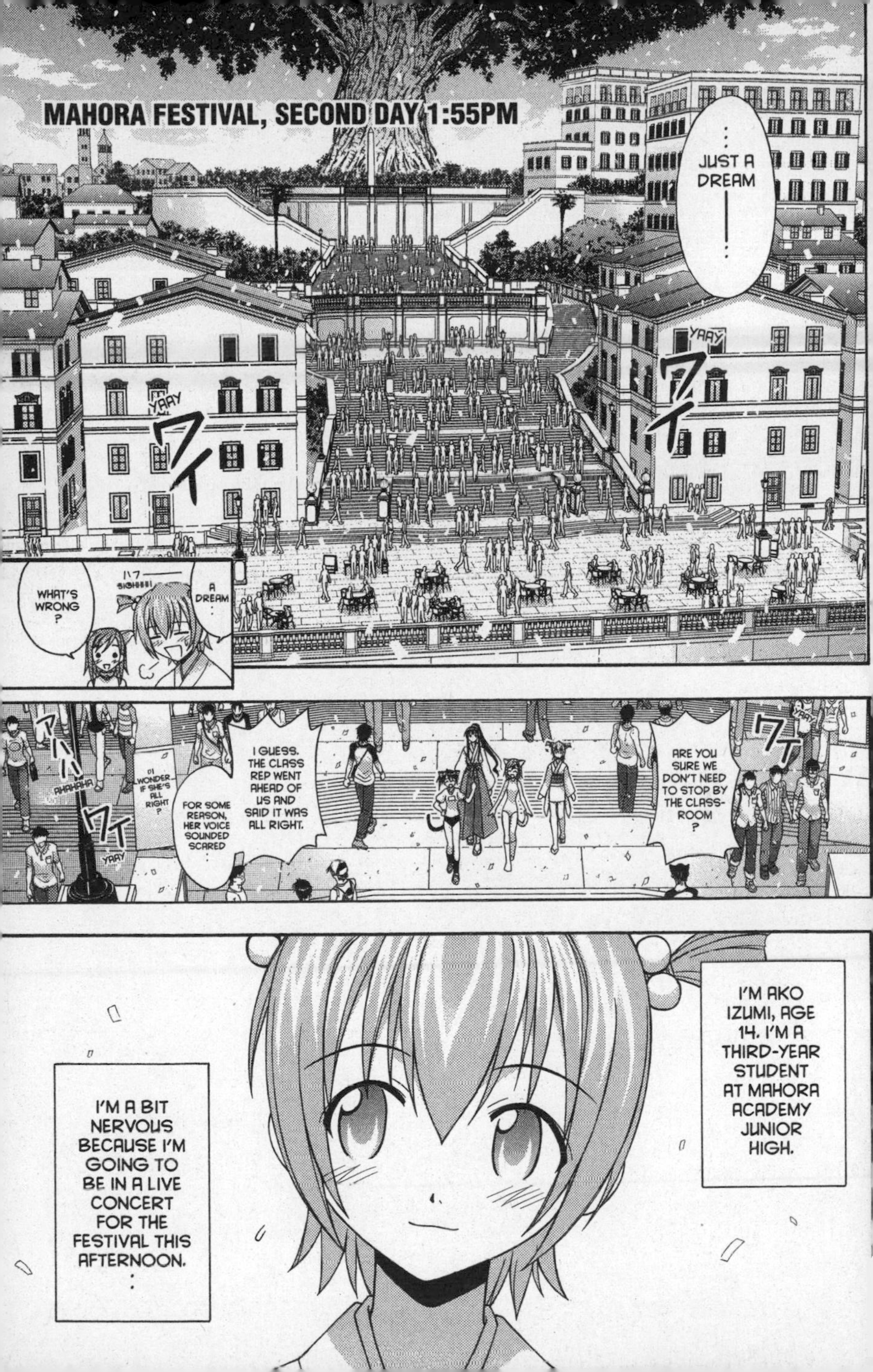
MAHORA FESTIVAL, SECOND DAY 1:55PM
...JUST A DREAM—!!
ワイ YAAY
ワイ YAAY
A DREAM...
ハフ— SIGH!!!
WHAT'S WRONG?
ワイ YAAY
ARE YOU SURE WE DON'T NEED TO STOP BY THE CLASSROOM?
I GUESS. THE CLASS REP WENT AHEAD OF US AND SAID IT WAS ALL RIGHT.
FOR SOME REASON, HER VOICE SOUNDED SCARED...
I WONDER IF SHE'S ALL RIGHT?
アハハ AHAHAHA
ワイ YAAY
I'M AKO IZUMI, AGE 14. I'M A THIRD-YEAR STUDENT AT MAHORA ACADEMY JUNIOR HIGH.
I'M A BIT NERVOUS BECAUSE I'M GOING TO BE IN A LIVE CONCERT FOR THE FESTIVAL THIS AFTERNOON...

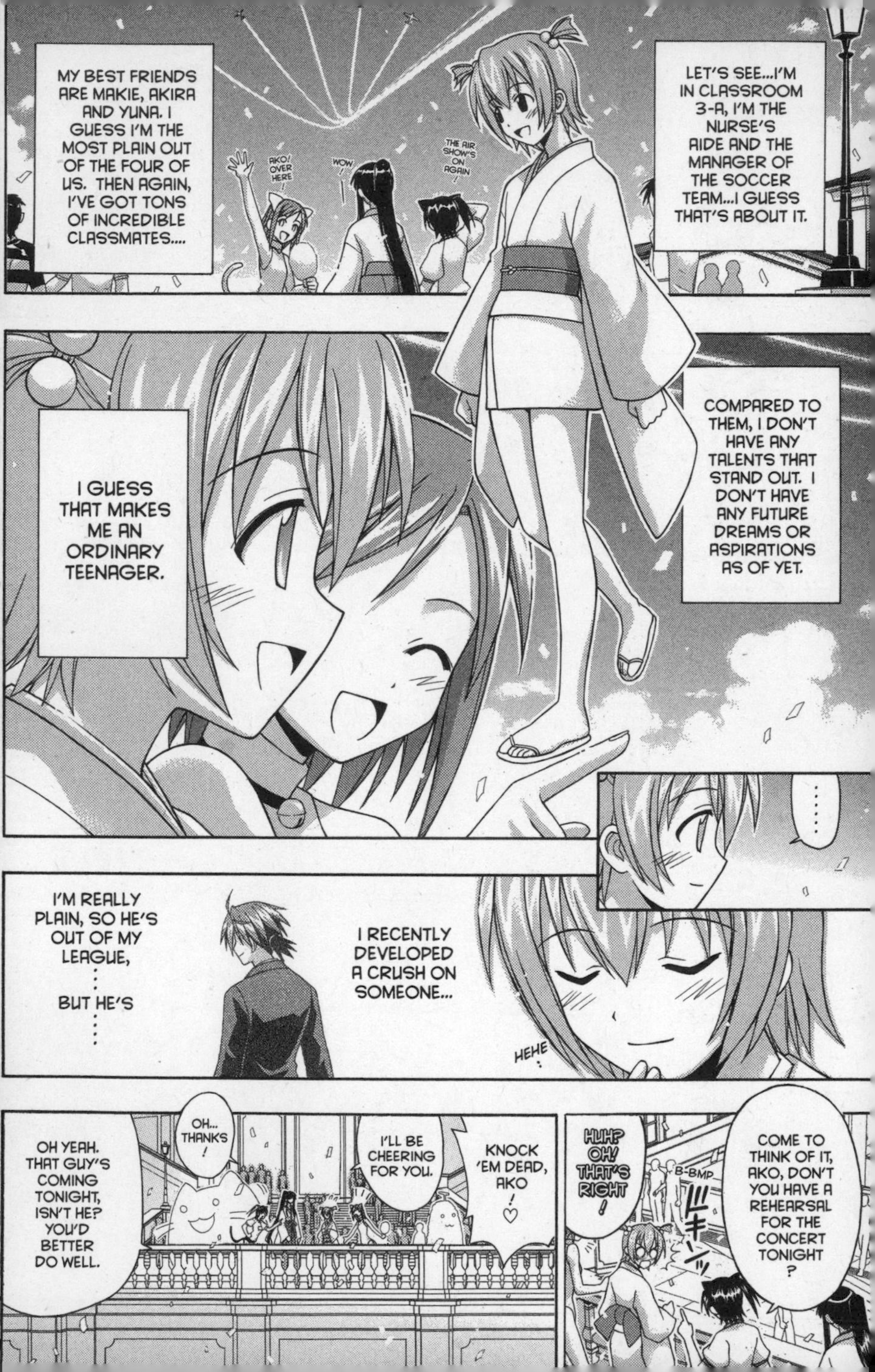
LET'S SEE...I'M IN CLASSROOM 3-A, I'M THE NURSE'S AIDE AND THE MANAGER OF THE SOCCER TEAM...I GUESS THAT'S ABOUT IT.
THE AIR SHOW'S ON AGAIN!
WOW!
AKO! OVER HERE!
MY BEST FRIENDS ARE MAKIE, AKIRA AND YUNA. I GUESS I'M THE MOST PLAIN OUT OF THE FOUR OF US. THEN AGAIN, I'VE GOT TONS OF INCREDIBLE CLASSMATES....
COMPARED TO THEM, I DON'T HAVE ANY TALENTS THAT STAND OUT. I DON'T HAVE ANY FUTURE DREAMS OR ASPIRATIONS AS OF YET.
I GUESS THAT MAKES ME AN ORDINARY TEENAGER.
......
HEHE
I RECENTLY DEVELOPED A CRUSH ON SOMEONE...
I'M REALLY PLAIN, SO HE'S OUT OF MY LEAGUE,
...
BUT HE'S ......
COME TO THINK OF IT, AKO, DON'T YOU HAVE A REHEARSAL FOR THE CONCERT TONIGHT?
B-BMP
HUH? OH! THAT'S RIGHT!
KNOCK 'EM DEAD, AKO! ♡
I'LL BE CHEERING FOR YOU.
OH... THANKS!
OH YEAH. THAT GUY'S COMING TONIGHT, ISN'T HE? YOU'D BETTER DO WELL.

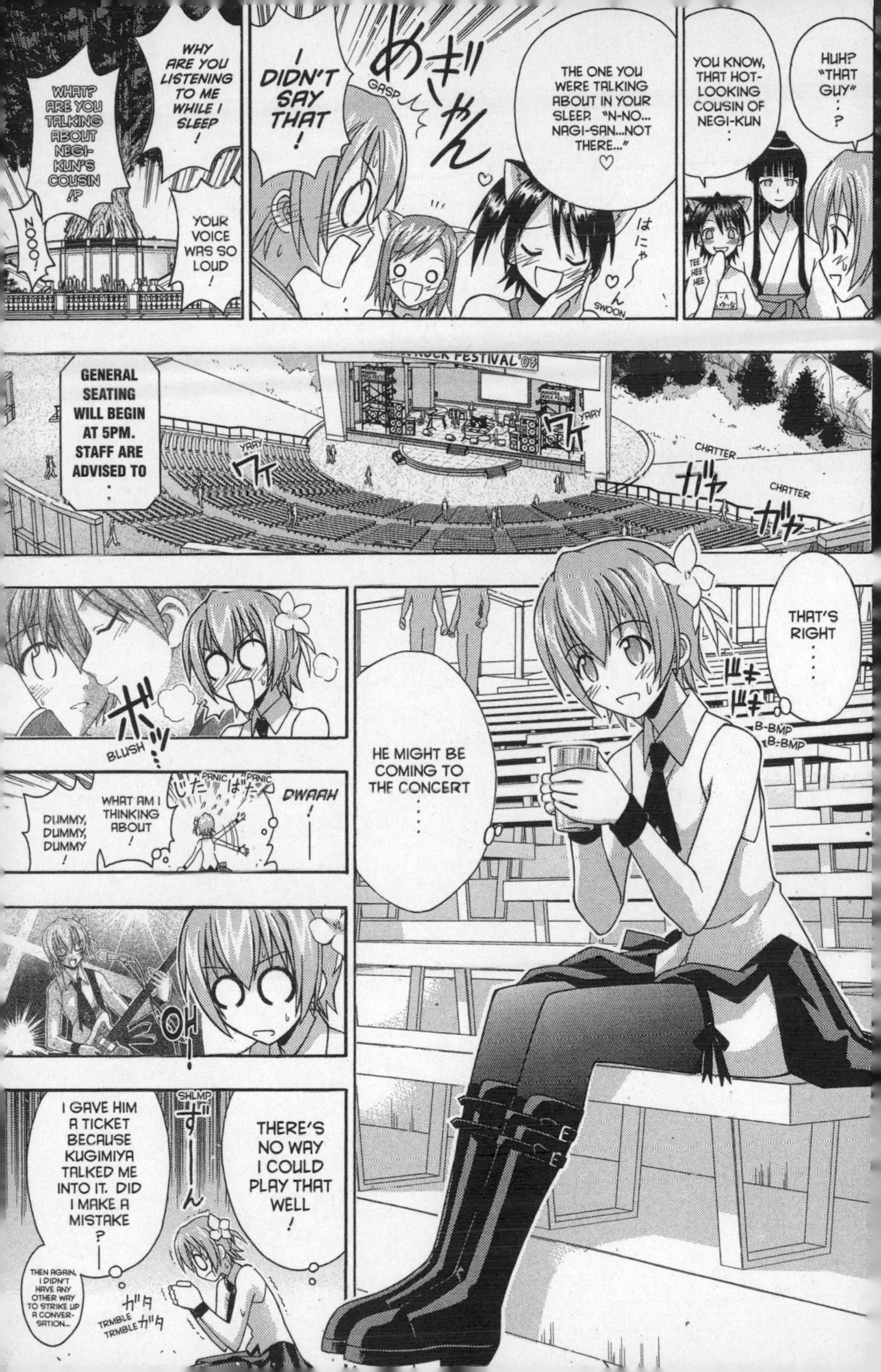
HUH? "THAT GUY" . . ?
YOU KNOW, THAT HOT-LOOKING COUSIN OF NEGI-KUN . .
TEE HEE HEE
THE ONE YOU WERE TALKING ABOUT IN YOUR SLEEP. "N-NO... NAGI-SAN...NOT THERE..." ♡
はにゃ~ん SWOON
あぎゃん GASP
I DIDN'T SAY THAT!
WHY ARE YOU LISTENING TO ME WHILE I SLEEP!
WHAT? ARE YOU TALKING ABOUT NEGI-KUN'S COUSIN!?
YOUR VOICE WAS SO LOUD!
NOOOO!
ROCK FESTIVAL '03
GENERAL SEATING WILL BEGIN AT 5PM. STAFF ARE ADVISED TO . .
ワイ YAAY
ワイ YAAY
ガヤ CHATTER
ガヤ CHATTER
THAT'S RIGHT . . .
ドキ ドキ B-BMP B-BMP
HE MIGHT BE COMING TO THE CONCERT . . .
ボッ BLUSH
DWAAH!
じたばた PANIC PANIC
WHAT AM I THINKING ABOUT!
DUMMY, DUMMY, DUMMY!
OH!
THERE'S NO WAY I COULD PLAY THAT WELL!
ずーん SHLMP
I GAVE HIM A TICKET BECAUSE KUGIMIYA TALKED ME INTO IT. DID I MAKE A MISTAKE?
THEN AGAIN, I DIDN'T HAVE ANY OTHER WAY TO STRIKE UP A CONVERSATION...
ガタ ガタ TRMBLE TRMBLE

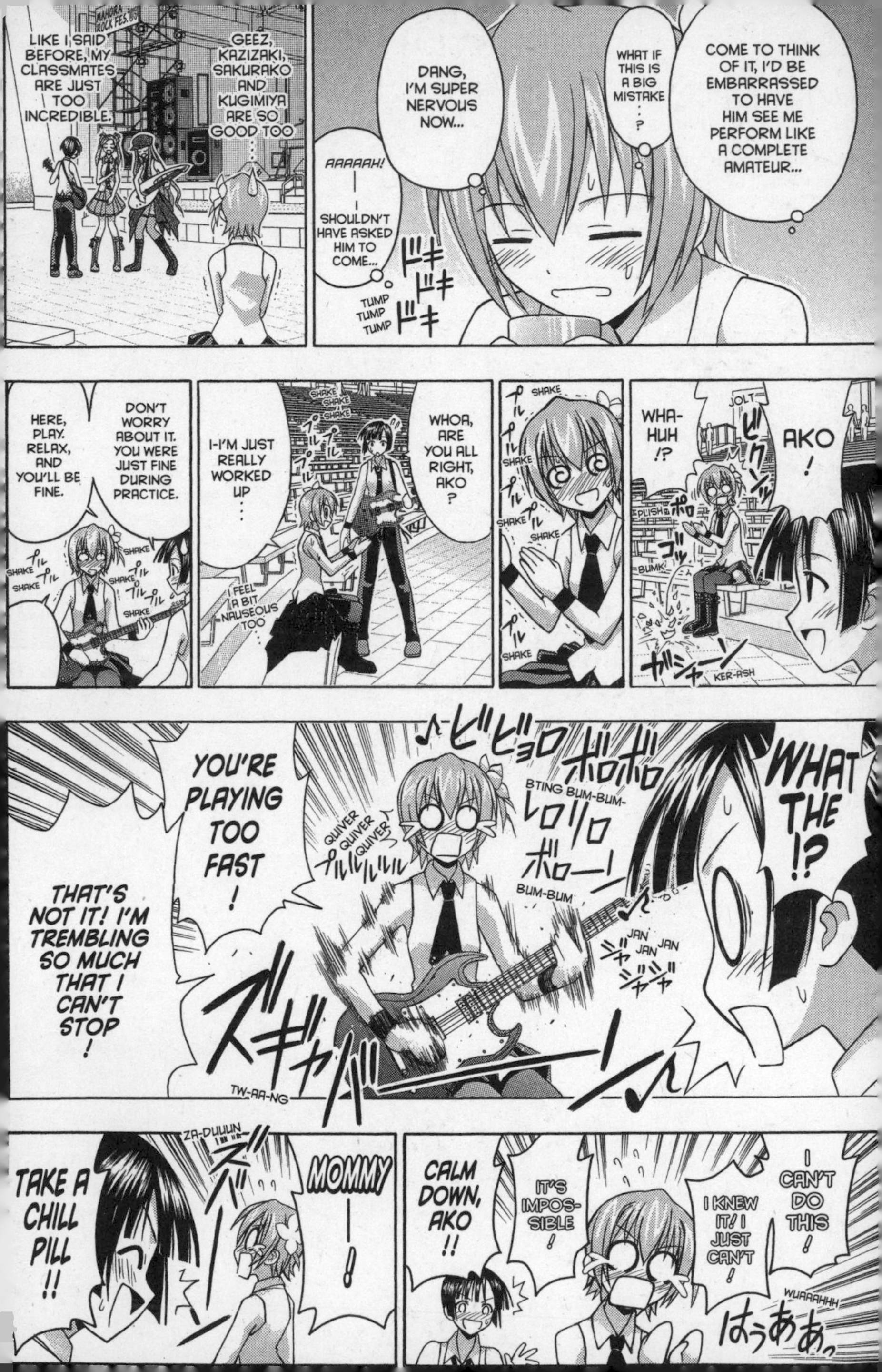

COME TO THINK OF IT, I'D BE EMBARRASSED TO HAVE HIM SEE ME PERFORM LIKE A COMPLETE AMATEUR...
WHAT IF THIS IS A BIG MISTAKE...?
DANG, I'M SUPER NERVOUS NOW...
AAAAAH!— I SHOULDN'T HAVE ASKED HIM TO COME...
TUMP TUMP TUMP
GEEZ, KAZIZAKI, SAKURAKO AND KUGIMIYA ARE SO GOOD TOO...
LIKE I SAID BEFORE, MY CLASSMATES ARE JUST TOO INCREDIBLE.
AKO!
JOLT
WHA-HUH!?
PLISH
BUMK
KER-ASH
SHAKE SHAKE SHAKE SHAKE SHAKE SHAKE
WHOA, ARE YOU ALL RIGHT, AKO?
SHAKE SHAKE SHAKE
I-I'M JUST REALLY WORKED UP...
I FEEL A BIT NAUSEOUS TOO...
DON'T WORRY ABOUT IT. YOU WERE JUST FINE DURING PRACTICE.
HERE, PLAY. RELAX, AND YOU'LL BE FINE.
SHAKE SHAKE SHAKE SHAKE SHAKE
WHAT THE!?
BTING BUM-BUM-
BUM-BUM
JAN JAN JAN
QUIVER QUIVER QUIVER
YOU'RE PLAYING TOO FAST!
THAT'S NOT IT! I'M TREMBLING SO MUCH THAT I CAN'T STOP!
TW-AA-NG
I CAN'T DO THIS!
I KNEW IT! I JUST CAN'T!
IT'S IMPOSSIBLE!
CALM DOWN, AKO!!
WUAAAHHH
MOMMY—!
ZA-DUUUN
TAKE A CHILL PILL!!

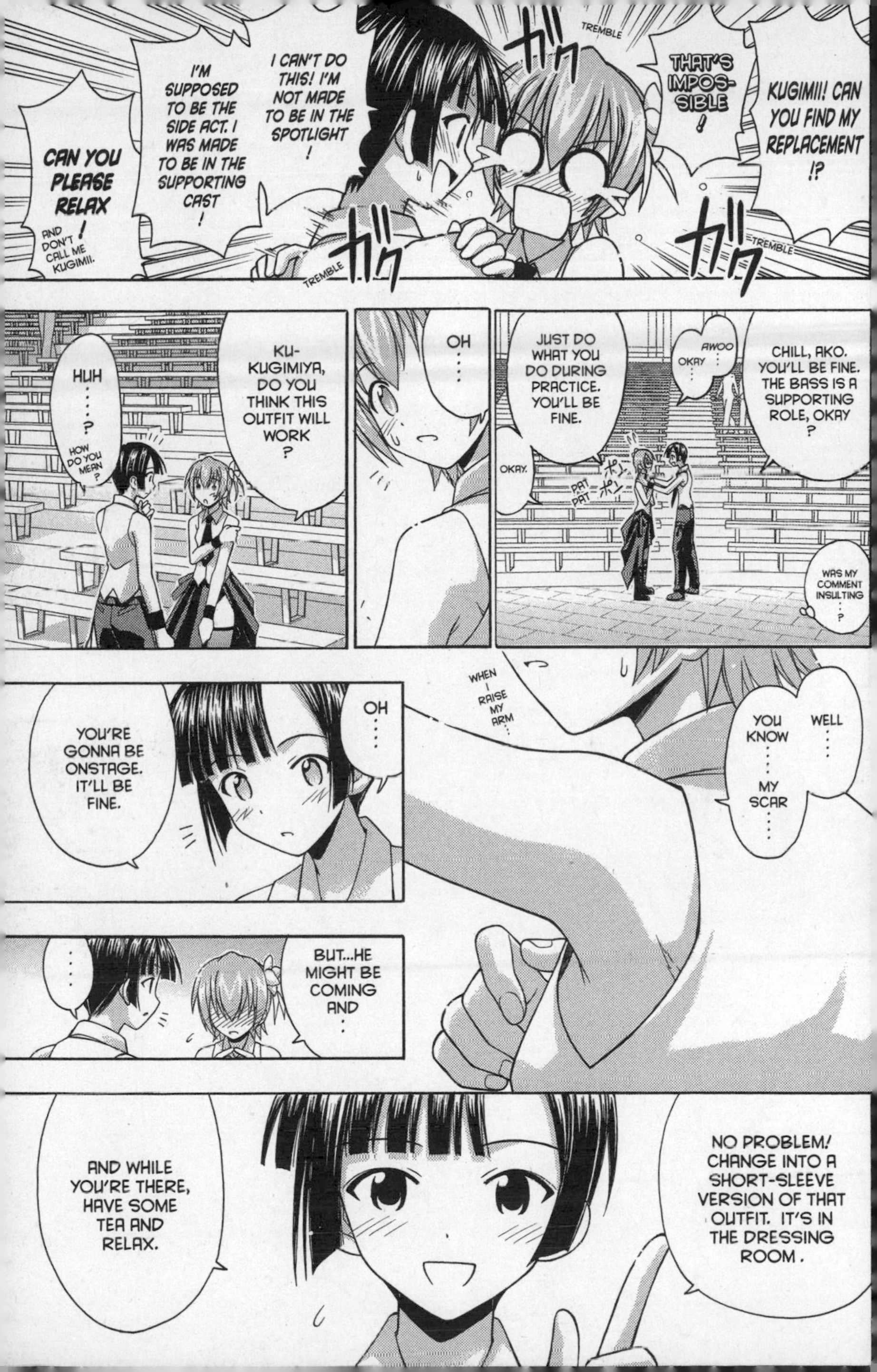
KUGIMII! CAN YOU FIND MY REPLACEMENT !?
TREMBLE
THAT'S IMPOSSIBLE !
TREMBLE
I CAN'T DO THIS! I'M NOT MADE TO BE IN THE SPOTLIGHT !
I'M SUPPOSED TO BE THE SIDE ACT. I WAS MADE TO BE IN THE SUPPORTING CAST !
TREMBLE
CAN YOU PLEASE RELAX !
AND DON'T CALL ME KUGIMII.
CHILL, AKO. YOU'LL BE FINE. THE BASS IS A SUPPORTING ROLE, OKAY ?
AWOO... OKAY...
JUST DO WHAT YOU DO DURING PRACTICE. YOU'LL BE FINE.
OKAY.
PAT PAT
WAS MY COMMENT INSULTING...?
OH...
KU-KUGIMIYA, DO YOU THINK THIS OUTFIT WILL WORK ?
HUH...?
HOW DO YOU MEAN ?
WELL...
YOU KNOW... MY SCAR...
WHEN I RAISE MY ARM...
OH...
YOU'RE GONNA BE ONSTAGE. IT'LL BE FINE.
BUT...HE MIGHT BE COMING AND...
...
NO PROBLEM! CHANGE INTO A SHORT-SLEEVE VERSION OF THAT OUTFIT. IT'S IN THE DRESSING ROOM.
AND WHILE YOU'RE THERE, HAVE SOME TEA AND RELAX.

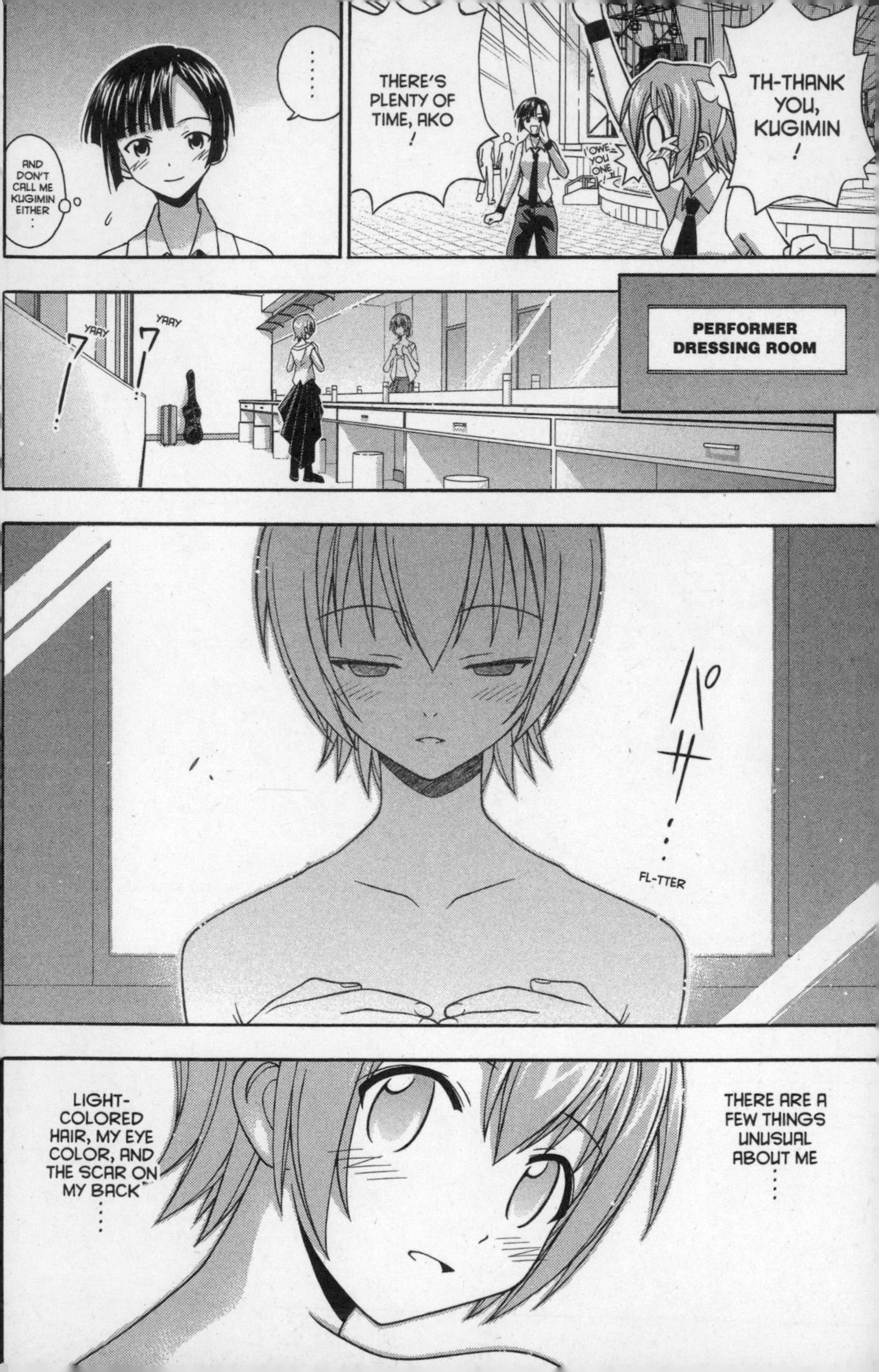
TH-THANK YOU, KUGIMIN!
I OWE YOU ONE!!
THERE'S PLENTY OF TIME, AKO!
......
AND DON'T CALL ME KUGIMIN EITHER...
PERFORMER DRESSING ROOM
YAAY
YAAY
FL-TTER
THERE ARE A FEW THINGS UNUSUAL ABOUT ME...
LIGHT-COLORED HAIR, MY EYE COLOR, AND THE SCAR ON MY BACK...

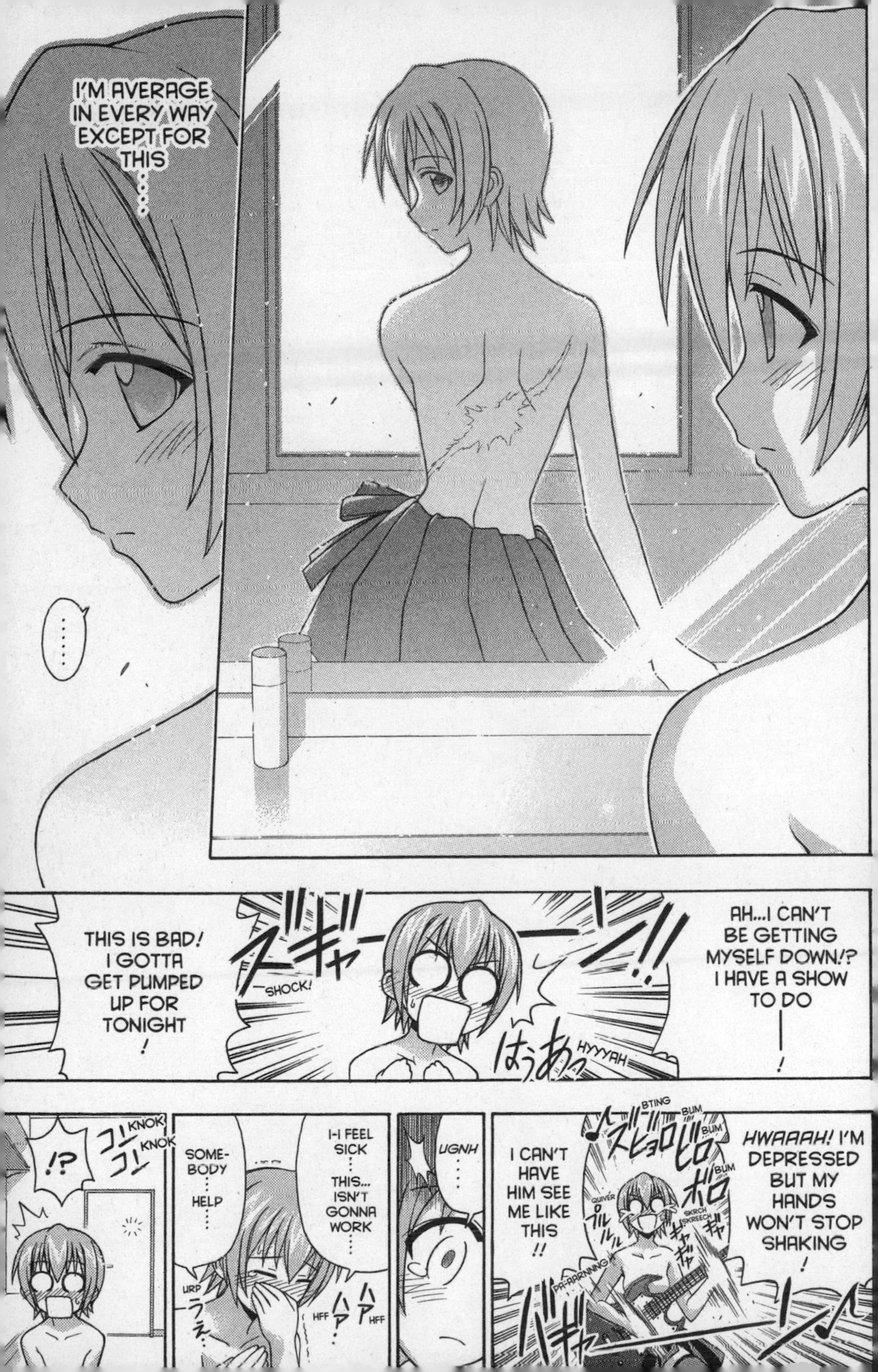
I'M AVERAGE IN EVERY WAY EXCEPT FOR THIS ...
......
AH...I CAN'T BE GETTING MYSELF DOWN!? I HAVE A SHOW TO DO—!
ズギャーン!!
SHOCK!
はうあっ
HYYYAH
THIS IS BAD! I GOTTA GET PUMPED UP FOR TONIGHT!
HWAAAH! I'M DEPRESSED BUT MY HANDS WON'T STOP SHAKING!
BTING
BUM
BUM
BUM
ズビョロビロボロ
QUIVER
プルルル
SKRCH
SKREECH
ギャギャ
PA-RARNNNG
バギャーン
I CAN'T HAVE HIM SEE ME LIKE THIS!!
UGNH ...
I-I FEEL SICK ... THIS... ISN'T GONNA WORK...
ハァ
HFF
ハァ
HFF
URP
うえ...
SOME-BODY ... HELP ...
コン!
KNOK
コン!
KNOK
!?

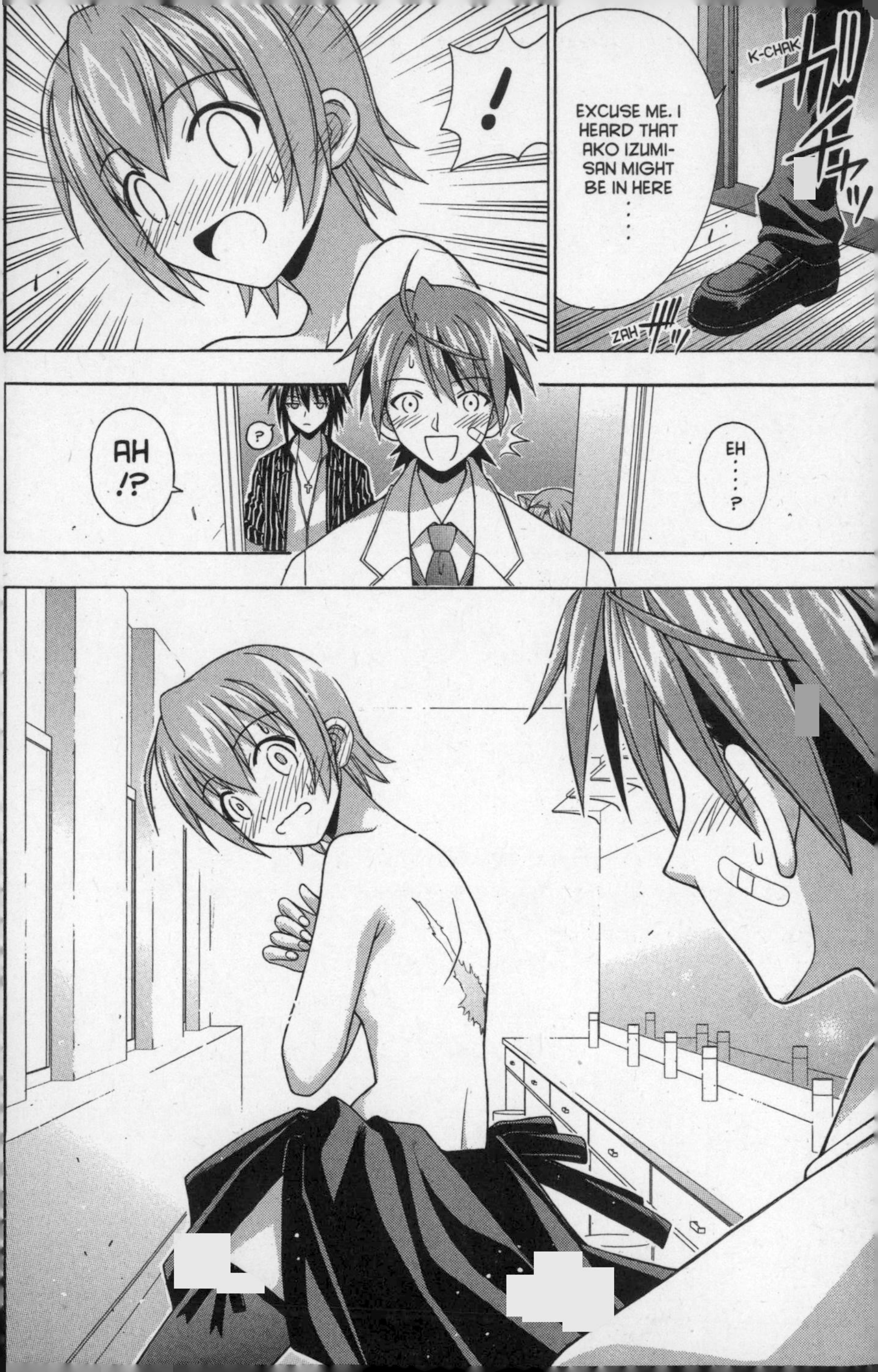
K-CHAK
EXCUSE ME. I HEARD THAT AKO IZUMI-SAN MIGHT BE IN HERE
....
ZAH
!
EH.....?
AH !?

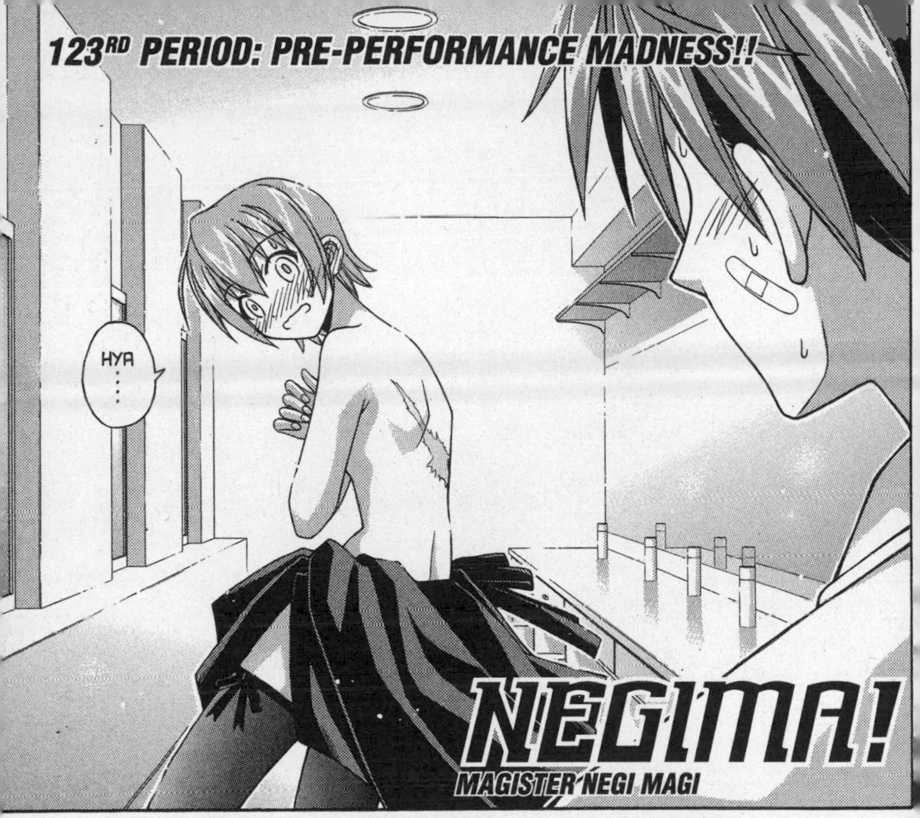
123RD PERIOD: PRE-PERFORMANCE MADNESS!!
HYA ...
NEGIMA!
MAGISTER NEGI MAGI

SEVERAL HOURS EARLIER...

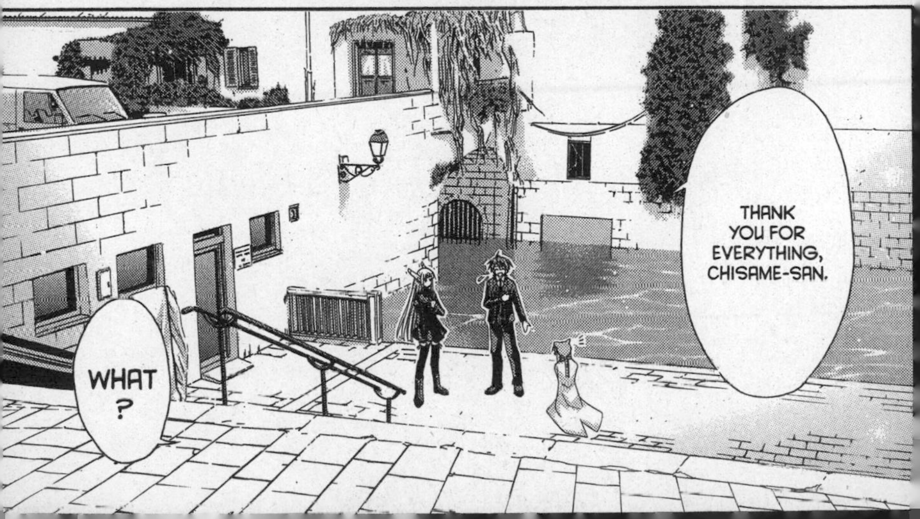
THANK YOU FOR EVERYTHING, CHISAME-SAN.
WHAT ?

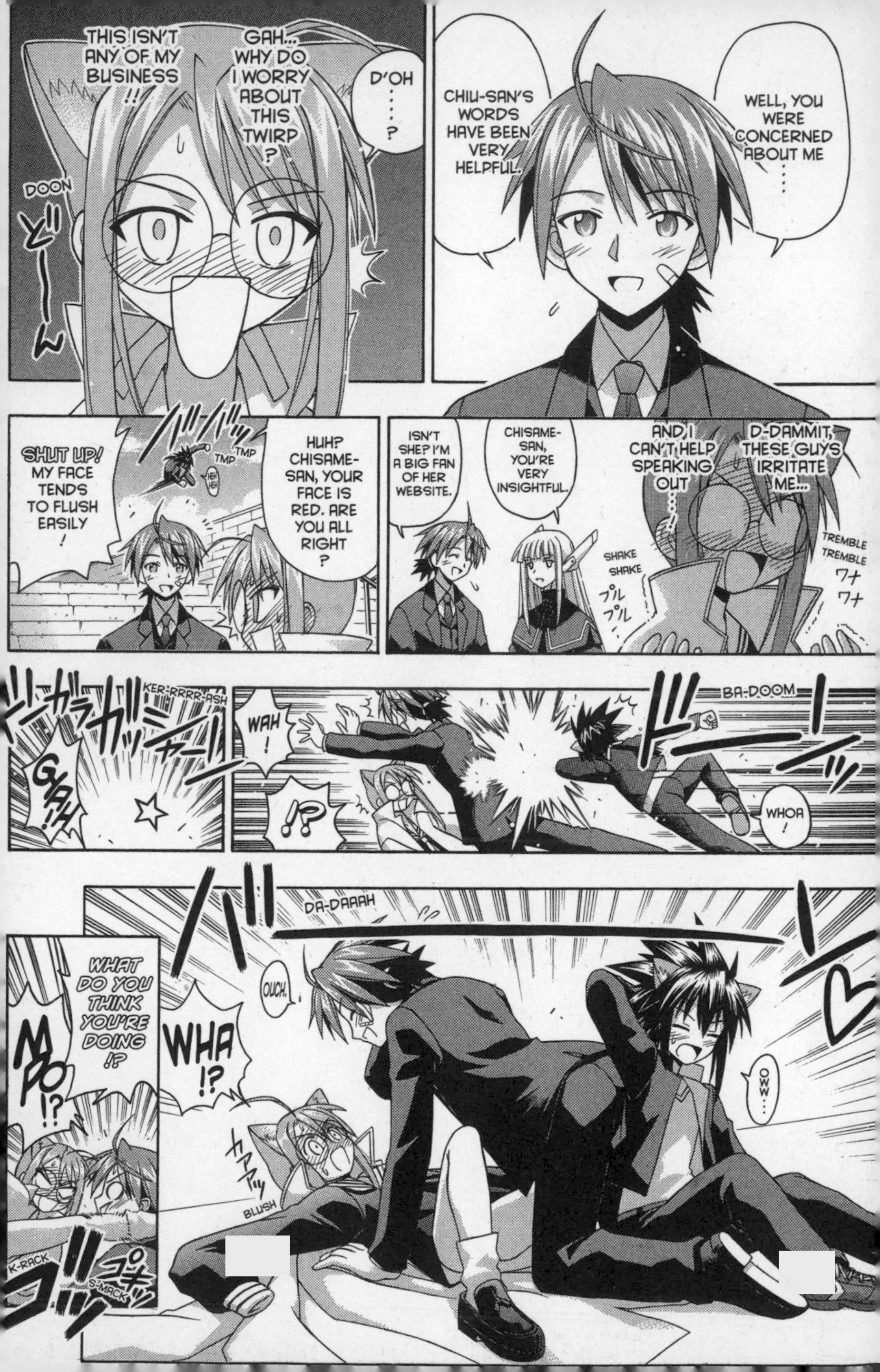
WELL, YOU WERE CONCERNED ABOUT ME ......
CHIU-SAN'S WORDS HAVE BEEN VERY HELPFUL.
D'OH .....?
GAH... WHY DO I WORRY ABOUT THIS TWIRP?
THIS ISN'T ANY OF MY BUSINESS !!
DOON
D-DAMMIT, THESE GUYS IRRITATE ME...
AND I CAN'T HELP SPEAKING OUT .....
TREMBLE TREMBLE
ワナワナ
SHAKE SHAKE
プルプル
CHISAME-SAN, YOU'RE VERY INSIGHTFUL.
ISN'T SHE? I'M A BIG FAN OF HER WEBSITE.
HUH? CHISAME-SAN, YOUR FACE IS RED. ARE YOU ALL RIGHT?
TMP TMP
SHUT UP! MY FACE TENDS TO FLUSH EASILY!
BA-DOOM
WHOA!
WAH!
!?
KER-RRRR-ASH
GYAH!?
DA-DAAAH
OWW...
OUCH.
WHA!?
BLUSH
WHAT DO YOU THINK YOU'RE DOING!?
MPO!?
S-MACK
K-RACK

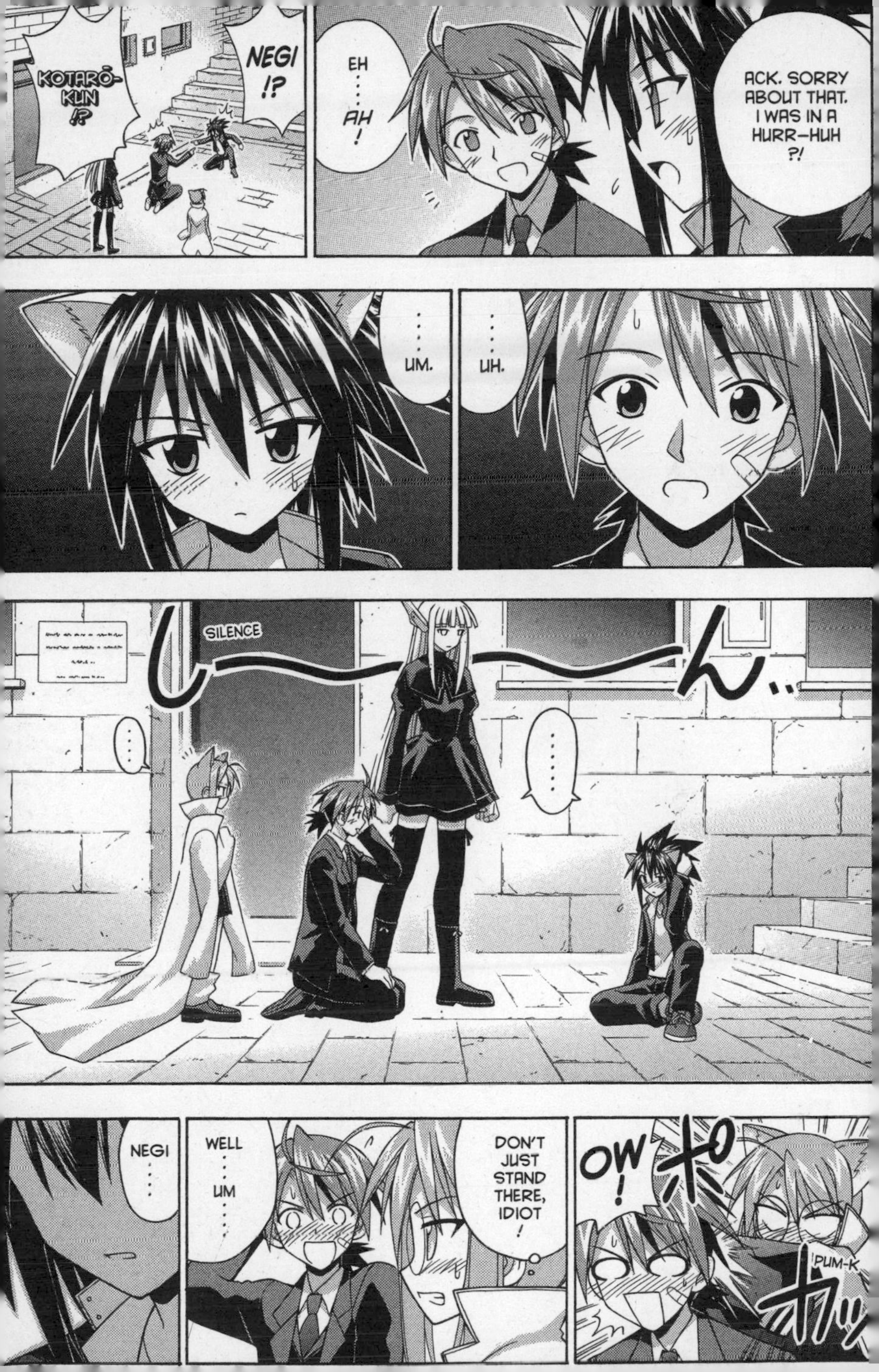
ACK. SORRY ABOUT THAT. I WAS IN A HURR—HUH ?!
EH ... AH!
NEGI !?
KOTARŌ-KUN !?
... UH.
... UM.
SILENCE
......
....
WELL ... UM ....
NEGI ...
DON'T JUST STAND THERE, IDIOT!
OW!
PUM-K

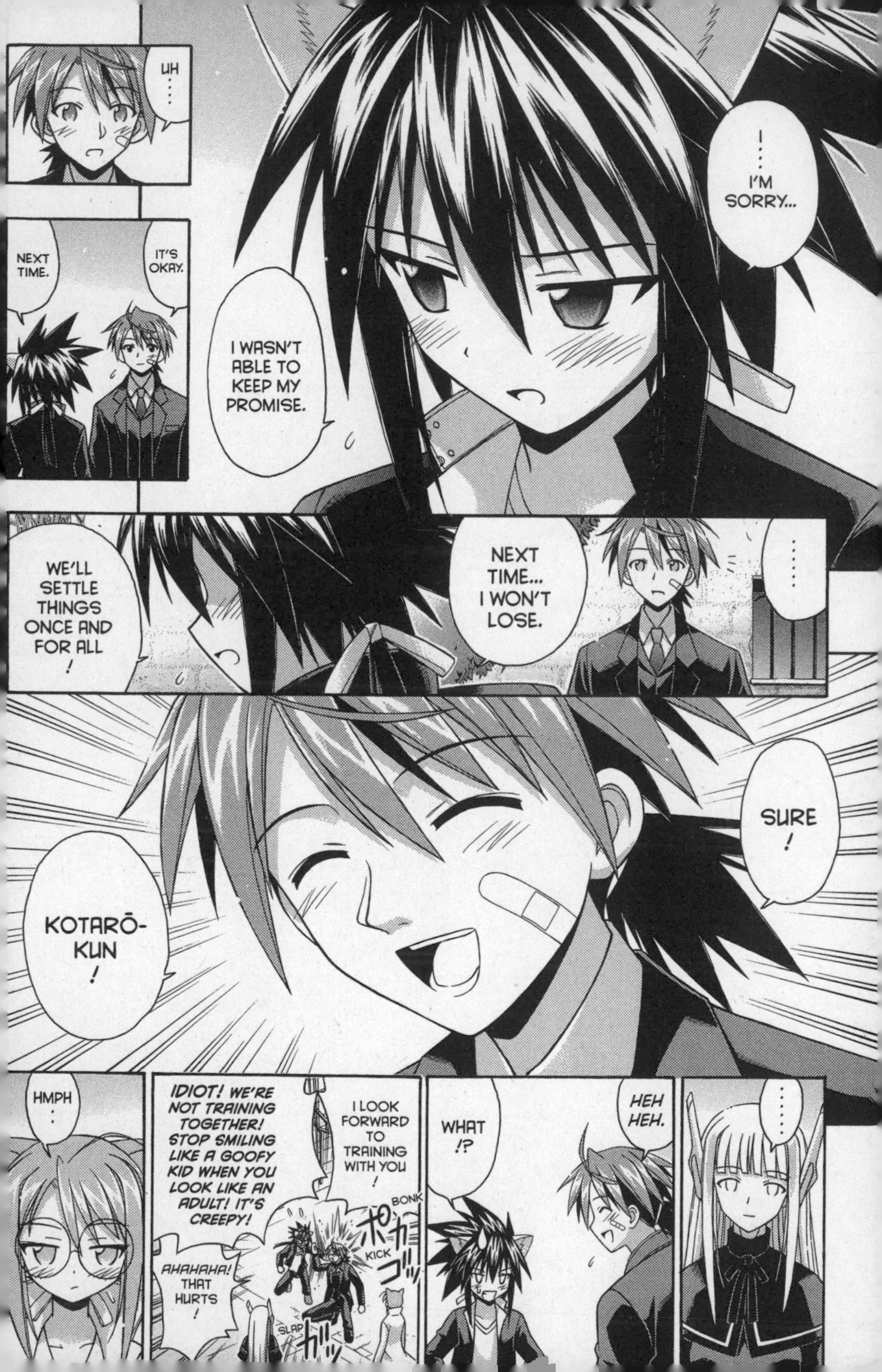
I... I'M SORRY...
I WASN'T ABLE TO KEEP MY PROMISE.
UH ....
IT'S OKAY.
NEXT TIME.
......
NEXT TIME... I WON'T LOSE.
WE'LL SETTLE THINGS ONCE AND FOR ALL!
SURE!
KOTARŌ-KUN!
......
HEH HEH.
WHAT!?
I LOOK FORWARD TO TRAINING WITH YOU!
IDIOT! WE'RE NOT TRAINING TOGETHER! STOP SMILING LIKE A GOOFY KID WHEN YOU LOOK LIKE AN ADULT! IT'S CREEPY!
BONK
KICK
AHAHAHA! THAT HURTS!
SLAP
HMPH
:

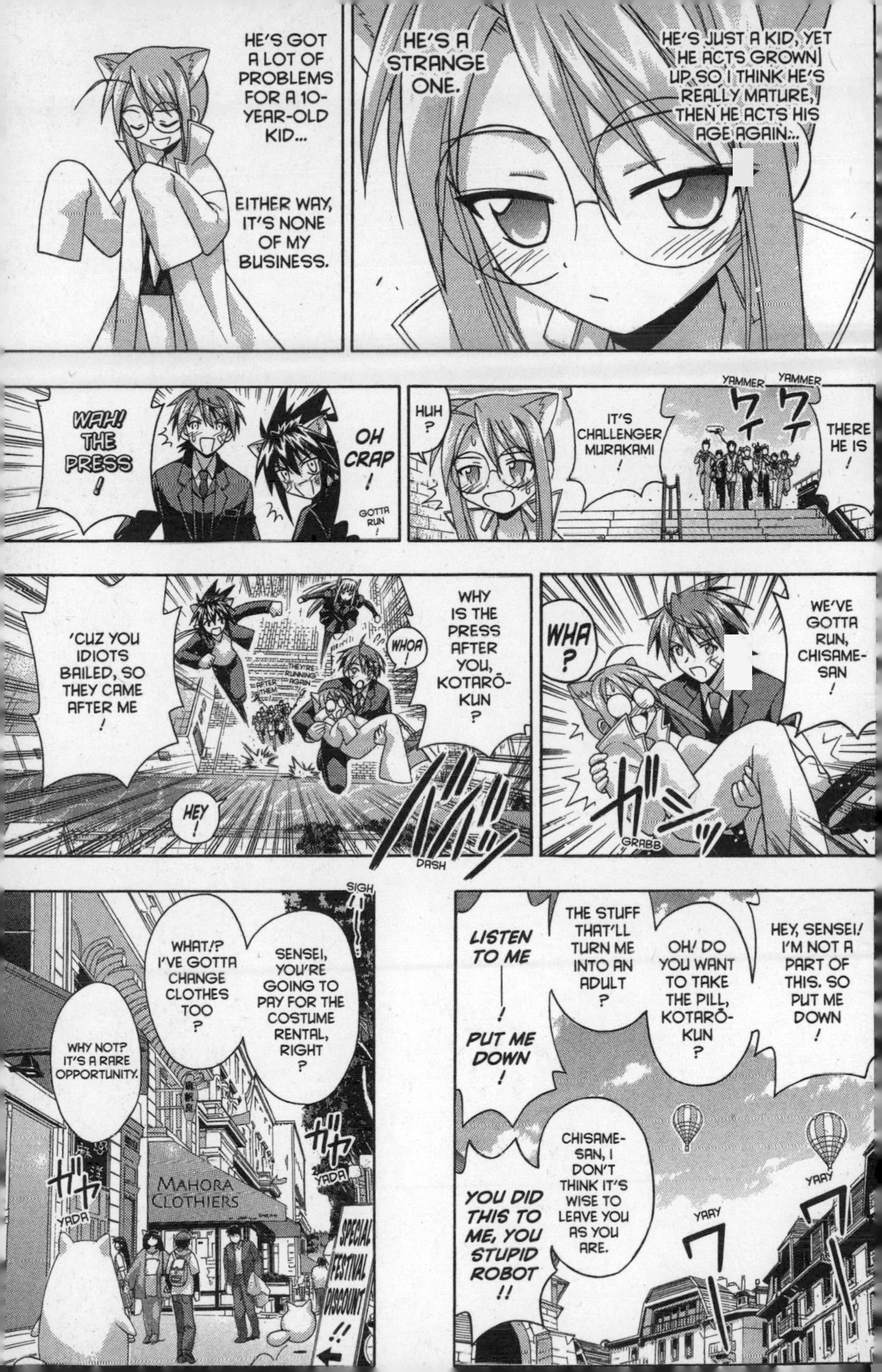

HE'S JUST A KID, YET HE ACTS GROWN UP, SO I THINK HE'S REALLY MATURE, THEN HE ACTS HIS AGE AGAIN...
HE'S A STRANGE ONE.
HE'S GOT A LOT OF PROBLEMS FOR A 10-YEAR-OLD KID...
EITHER WAY, IT'S NONE OF MY BUSINESS.
YAMMER
YAMMER
THERE HE IS!
IT'S CHALLENGER MURAKAMI!
HUH?
OH CRAP!
GOTTA RUN!
WAH! THE PRESS!
WE'VE GOTTA RUN, CHISAME-SAN!
WHA?
GRABB
WHY IS THE PRESS AFTER YOU, KOTARŌ-KUN?
WHOA!
THEY'RE RUNNING AGAIN
AFTER THEM
'CUZ YOU IDIOTS BAILED, SO THEY CAME AFTER ME!
HEY!
DASH
HEY, SENSEI! I'M NOT A PART OF THIS. SO PUT ME DOWN!
OH! DO YOU WANT TO TAKE THE PILL, KOTARŌ-KUN?
THE STUFF THAT'LL TURN ME INTO AN ADULT?
LISTEN TO ME—! PUT ME DOWN!
CHISAME-SAN, I DON'T THINK IT'S WISE TO LEAVE YOU AS YOU ARE.
YOU DID THIS TO ME, YOU STUPID ROBOT!!
YAAY
YAAY
SIGH
SENSEI, YOU'RE GOING TO PAY FOR THE COSTUME RENTAL, RIGHT?
WHAT!? I'VE GOTTA CHANGE CLOTHES TOO?
WHY NOT? IT'S A RARE OPPORTUNITY.
YADA
YADA
MAHORA CLOTHIERS
SPECIAL FESTIVAL DISCOUNT!!

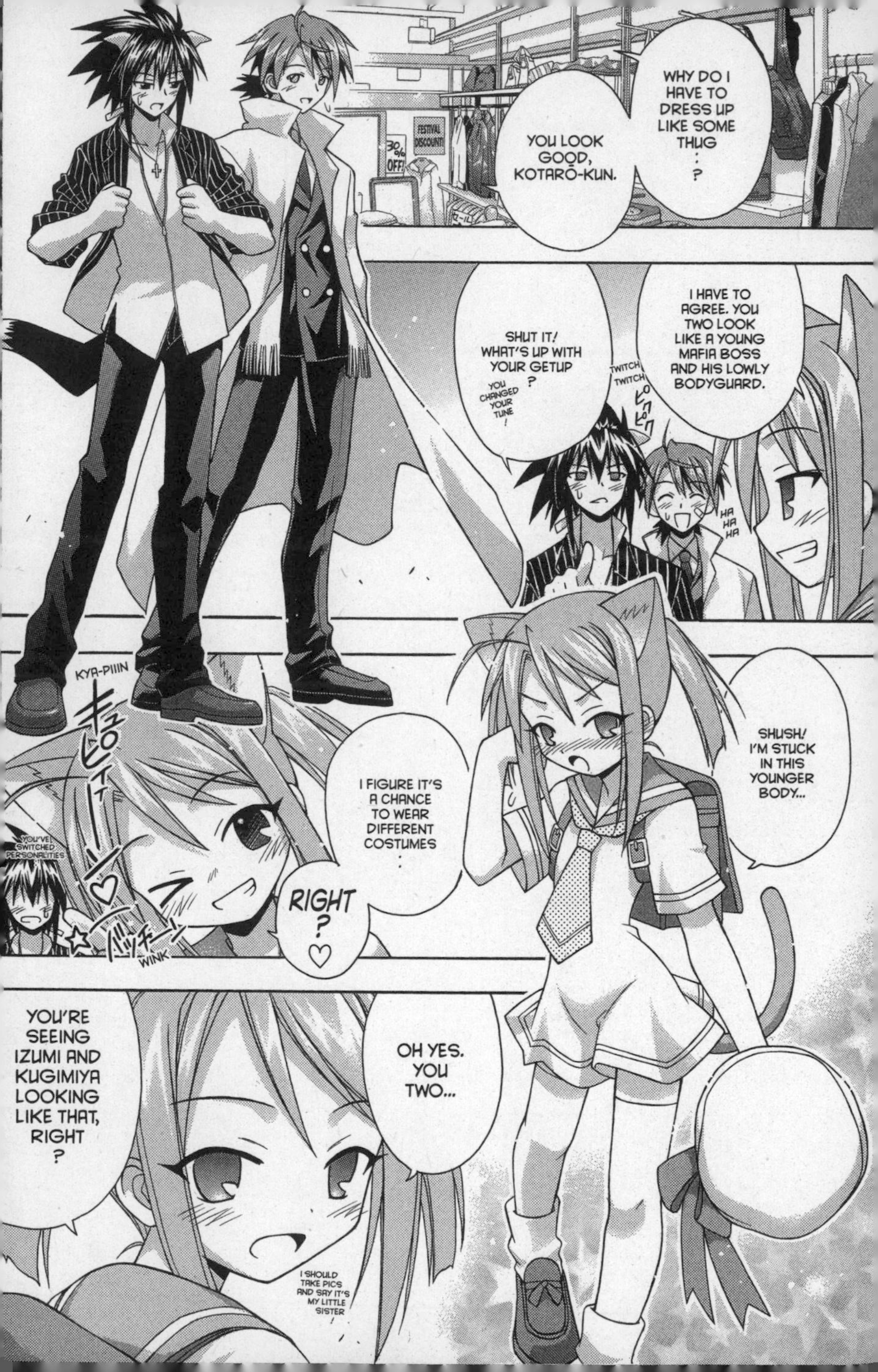
WHY DO I HAVE TO DRESS UP LIKE SOME THUG...?
YOU LOOK GOOD, KOTARŌ-KUN.
FESTIVAL DISCOUNT!
30% OFF!
I HAVE TO AGREE. YOU TWO LOOK LIKE A YOUNG MAFIA BOSS AND HIS LOWLY BODYGUARD.
HA HA HA
TWITCH TWITCH
SHUT IT! WHAT'S UP WITH YOUR GETUP?
YOU CHANGED YOUR TUNE!
SHUSH! I'M STUCK IN THIS YOUNGER BODY...
I FIGURE IT'S A CHANCE TO WEAR DIFFERENT COSTUMES...
RIGHT? ♡
WINK
KYA-PIIIN
YOU'VE SWITCHED PERSONALITIES
OH YES. YOU TWO...
YOU'RE SEEING IZUMI AND KUGIMIYA LOOKING LIKE THAT, RIGHT?
I SHOULD TAKE PICS AND SAY IT'S MY LITTLE SISTER!

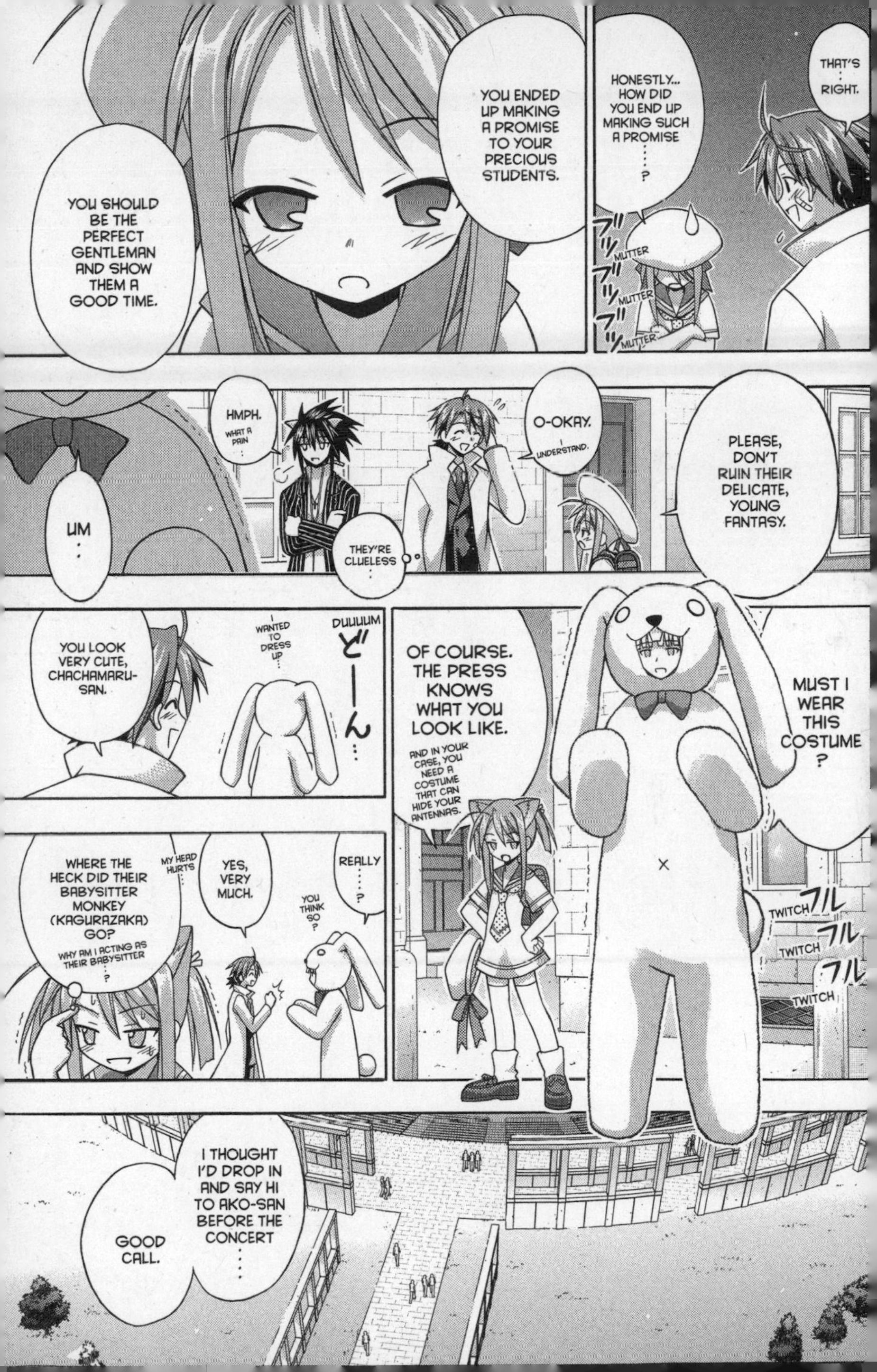
THAT'S... RIGHT.
HONESTLY... HOW DID YOU END UP MAKING SUCH A PROMISE...?
ブツ MUTTER
ブツ MUTTER
ブツ MUTTER
YOU ENDED UP MAKING A PROMISE TO YOUR PRECIOUS STUDENTS.
YOU SHOULD BE THE PERFECT GENTLEMAN AND SHOW THEM A GOOD TIME.
PLEASE, DON'T RUIN THEIR DELICATE, YOUNG FANTASY.
O-OKAY.
I UNDERSTAND.
HMPH.
WHAT A PAIN...
THEY'RE CLUELESS...
UM...
MUST I WEAR THIS COSTUME?
TWITCH フル
TWITCH フル
フル TWITCH
OF COURSE. THE PRESS KNOWS WHAT YOU LOOK LIKE.
AND IN YOUR CASE, YOU NEED A COSTUME THAT CAN HIDE YOUR ANTENNAS.
DUUUUM どーん...
I WANTED TO DRESS UP...
YOU LOOK VERY CUTE, CHACHAMARU-SAN.
REALLY...?
YOU THINK SO?
YES, VERY MUCH.
MY HEAD HURTS...
WHERE THE HECK DID THEIR BABYSITTER MONKEY (KAGURAZAKA) GO?
WHY AM I ACTING AS THEIR BABYSITTER...?
I THOUGHT I'D DROP IN AND SAY HI TO AKO-SAN BEFORE THE CONCERT...
GOOD CALL.

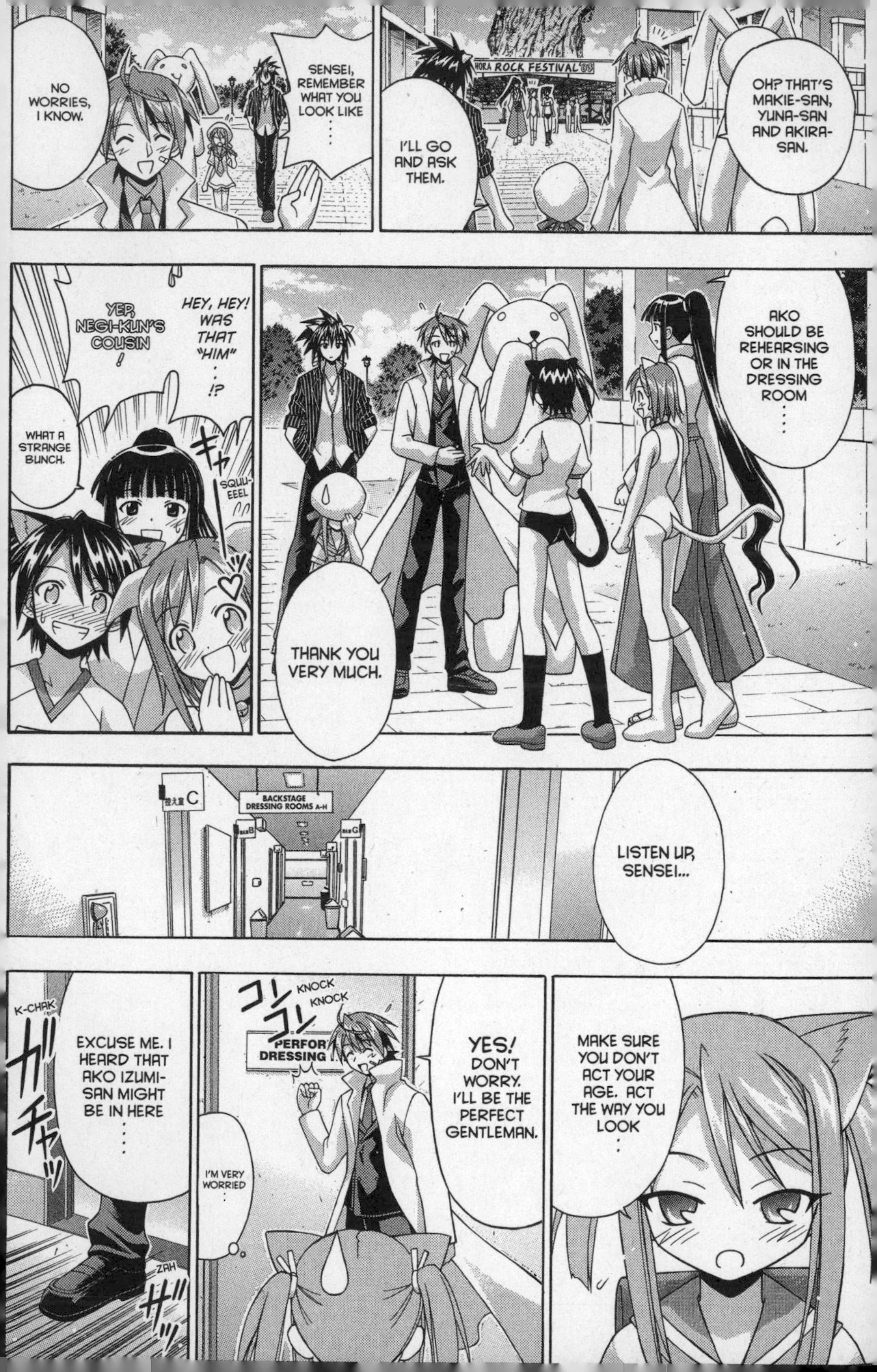
HORA ROCK FESTIVAL
OH? THAT'S MAKIE-SAN, YUNA-SAN AND AKIRA-SAN.
I'LL GO AND ASK THEM.
SENSEI, REMEMBER WHAT YOU LOOK LIKE ...
NO WORRIES, I KNOW.
AKO SHOULD BE REHEARSING OR IN THE DRESSING ROOM ...
THANK YOU VERY MUCH.
HEY, HEY! WAS THAT "HIM" ... !?
YEP, NEGI-KUN'S COUSIN!
SQUU-EEEL
WHAT A STRANGE BUNCH.
LISTEN UP, SENSEI...
BACKSTAGE DRESSING ROOMS A-H
MAKE SURE YOU DON'T ACT YOUR AGE. ACT THE WAY YOU LOOK ...
KNOCK KNOCK
PERFOR DRESSING
YES! DON'T WORRY. I'LL BE THE PERFECT GENTLEMAN.
I'M VERY WORRIED ...
K-CHAK
EXCUSE ME. I HEARD THAT AKO IZUMI-SAN MIGHT BE IN HERE ...
ZAH

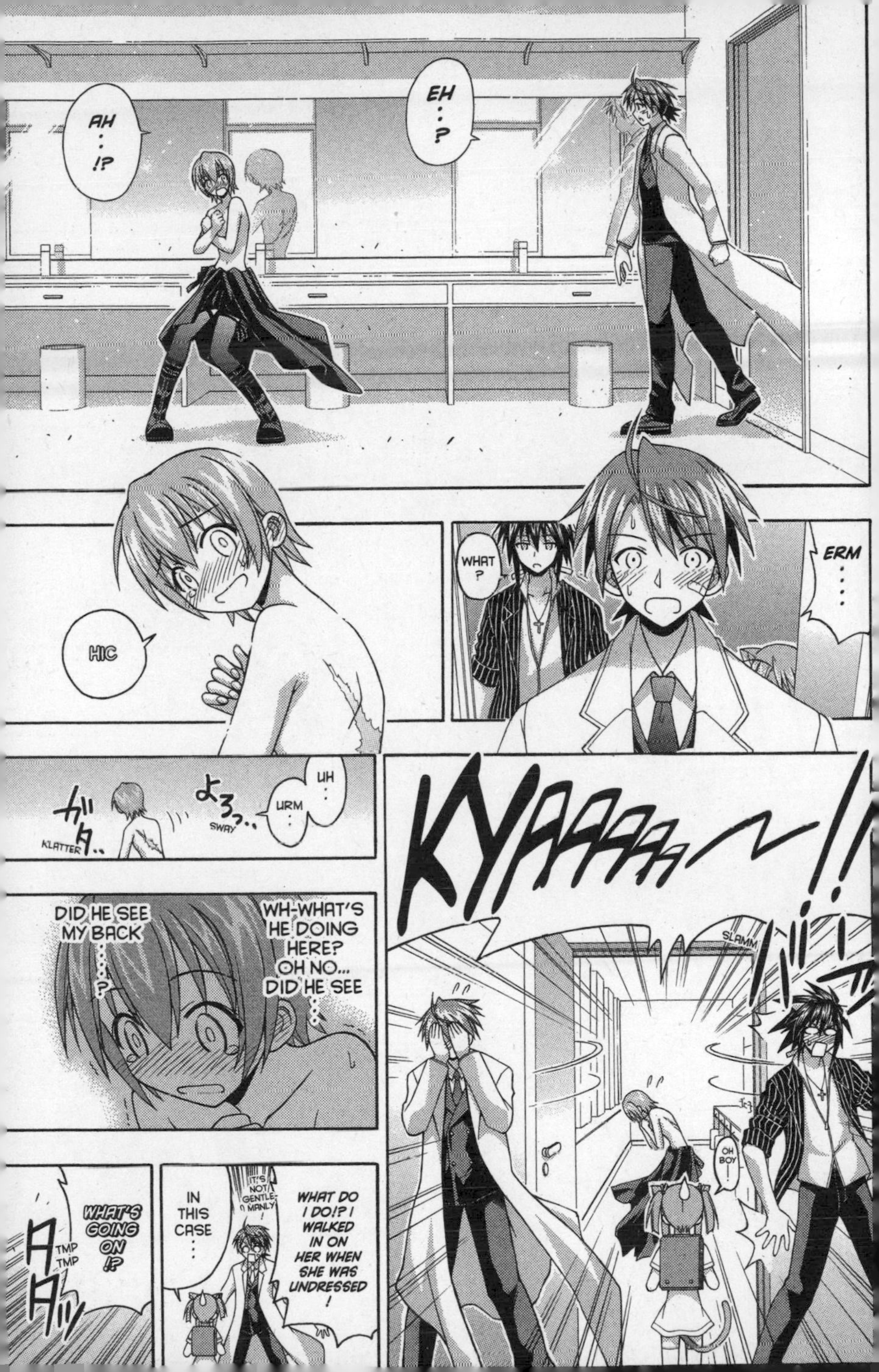

EH...?
AH...!?
ERM...
WHAT?
HIC
KYAAAAA~!!
SLAMM
OH BOY!
UH...
URM...
よろっ.. SWAY
ガタ.. KLATTER
WH-WHAT'S HE DOING HERE? OH NO... DID HE SEE...
DID HE SEE MY BACK...?
WHAT DO I DO!? I WALKED IN ON HER WHEN SHE WAS UNDRESSED!
IT'S NOT GENTLEMANLY!
IN THIS CASE...
WHAT'S GOING ON!?
TMP TMP

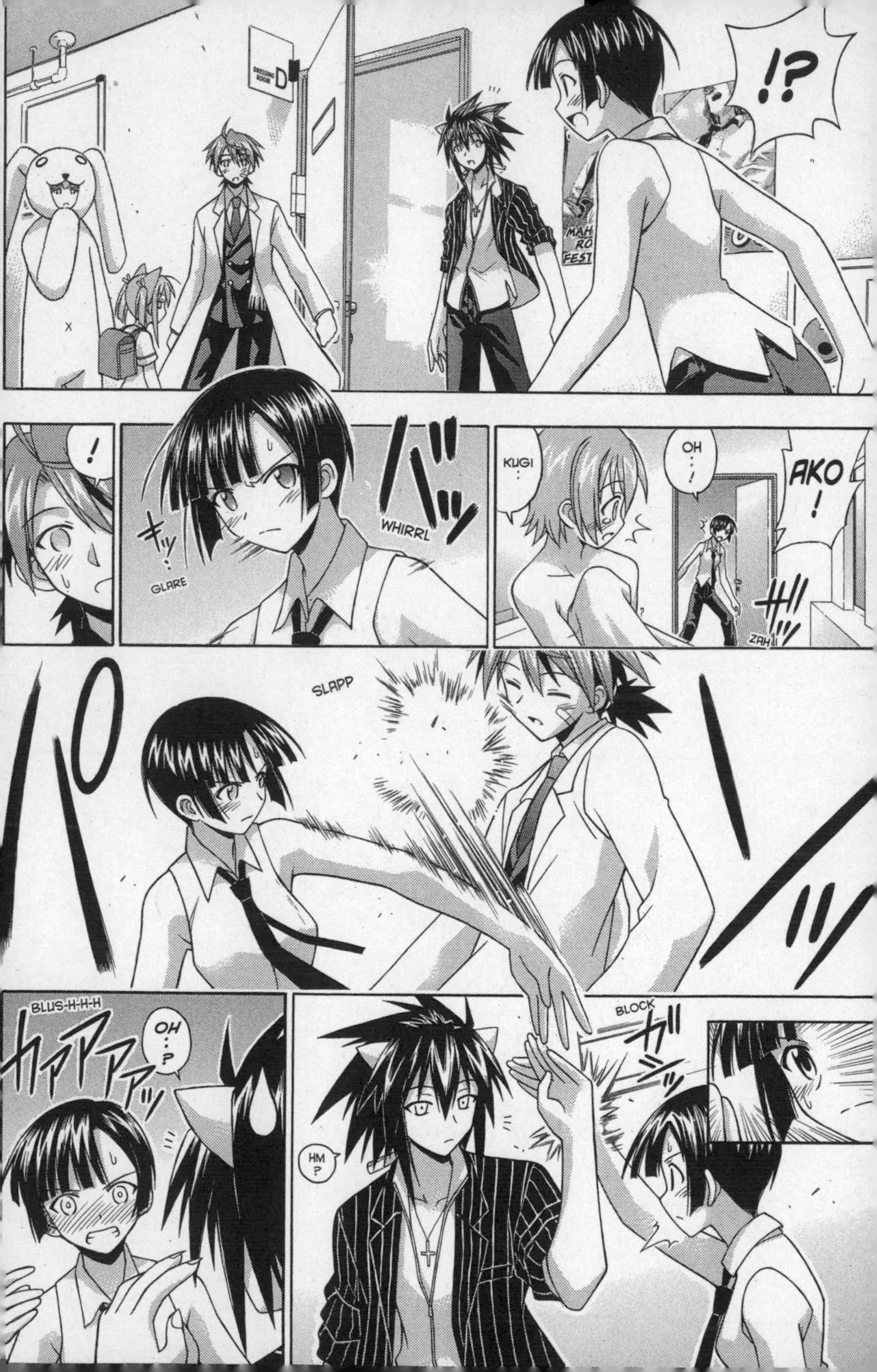

!?
DRESSING ROOM D
AKO !
OH...!
KUGI...
ZAH
WHIRRL
GLARE
!
SLAPP
BLOCK
HM?
BLUS-H-H-H
OH...?

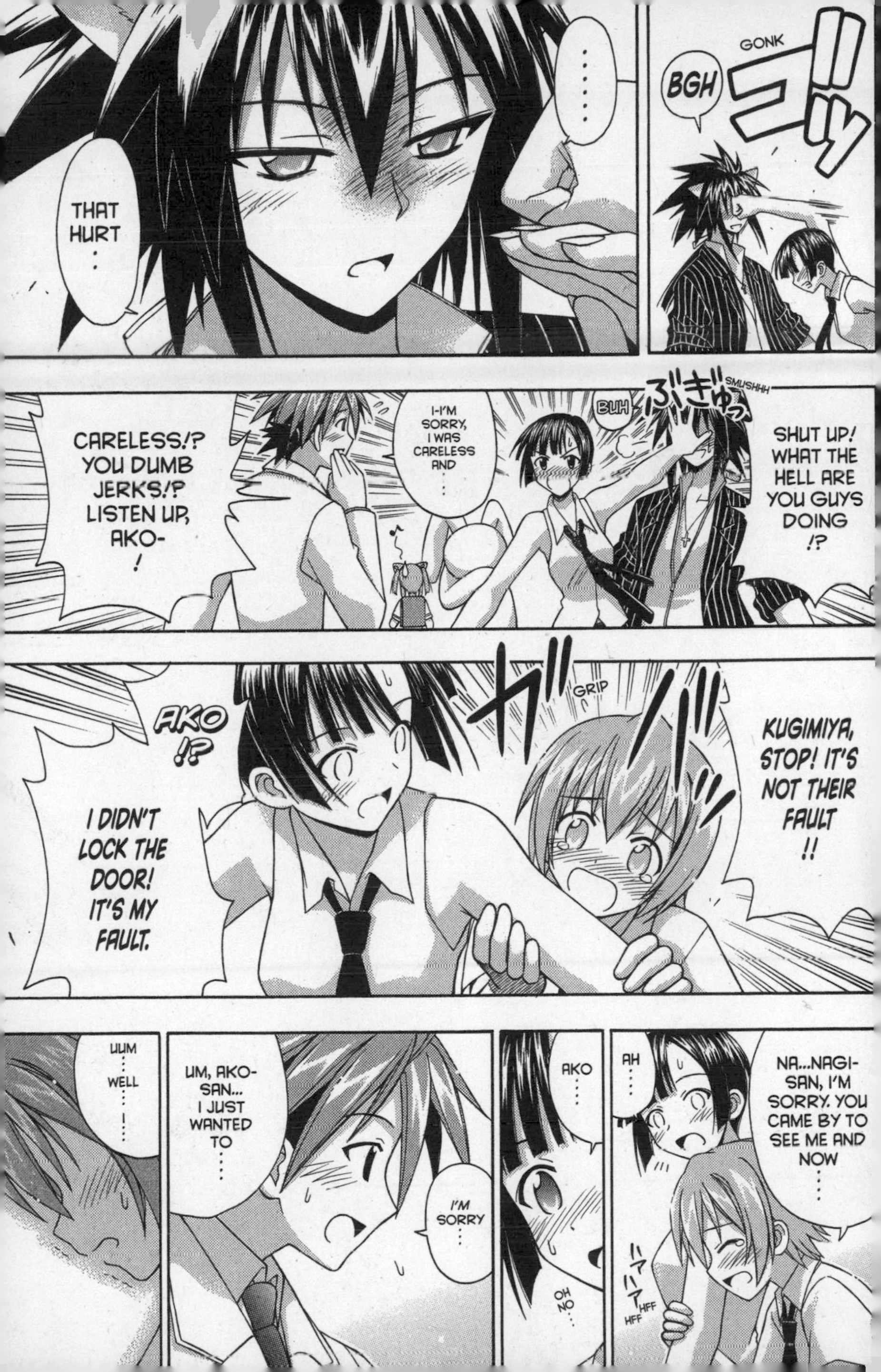
GONK
BGH
ゴッ
......
THAT HURT :
SHUT UP! WHAT THE HELL ARE YOU GUYS DOING !?
ぶぎゅっ
SMUSHHH
BUH
I-I'M SORRY, I WAS CARELESS AND ...
CARELESS!? YOU DUMB JERKS!? LISTEN UP, AKO-!
KUGIMIYA, STOP! IT'S NOT THEIR FAULT !!
GRIP
AKO !?
I DIDN'T LOCK THE DOOR! IT'S MY FAULT.
NA...NAGI-SAN, I'M SORRY. YOU CAME BY TO SEE ME AND NOW ...
ハァハァ
HFF HFF
AH ...
AKO ...
OH NO...
UM, AKO-SAN... I JUST WANTED TO ...
I'M SORRY ...
UUM ... WELL ... I ...

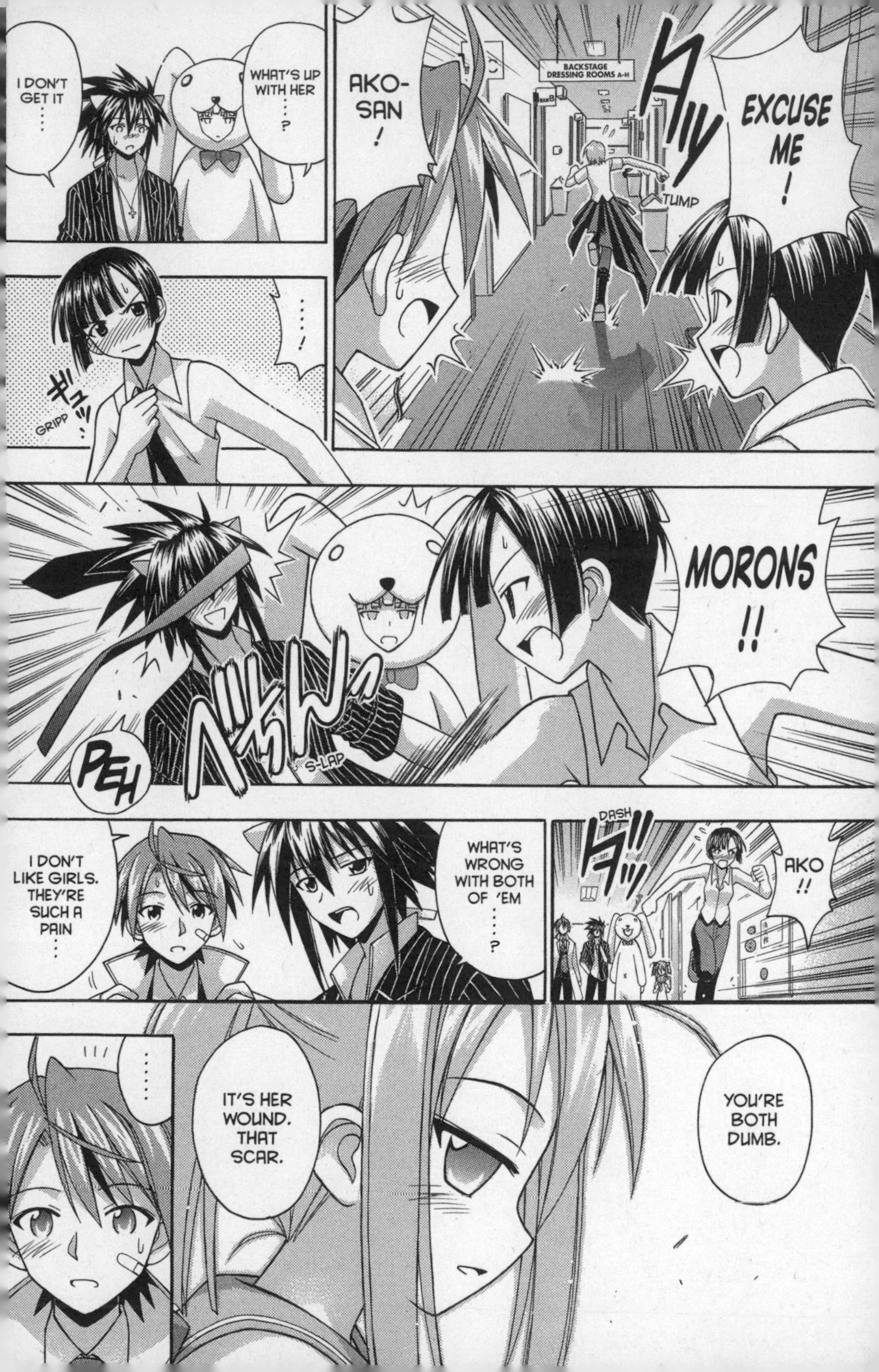
EXCUSE ME!
TUMP
AKO-SAN!
BACKSTAGE DRESSING ROOMS A-H
WHAT'S UP WITH HER ....?
I DON'T GET IT ....
....!
GRIPP
MORONS!!
S-LAP
PEH
AKO!!
DASH
WHAT'S WRONG WITH BOTH OF 'EM ....?
I DON'T LIKE GIRLS. THEY'RE SUCH A PAIN ....
YOU'RE BOTH DUMB.
IT'S HER WOUND. THAT SCAR.
......

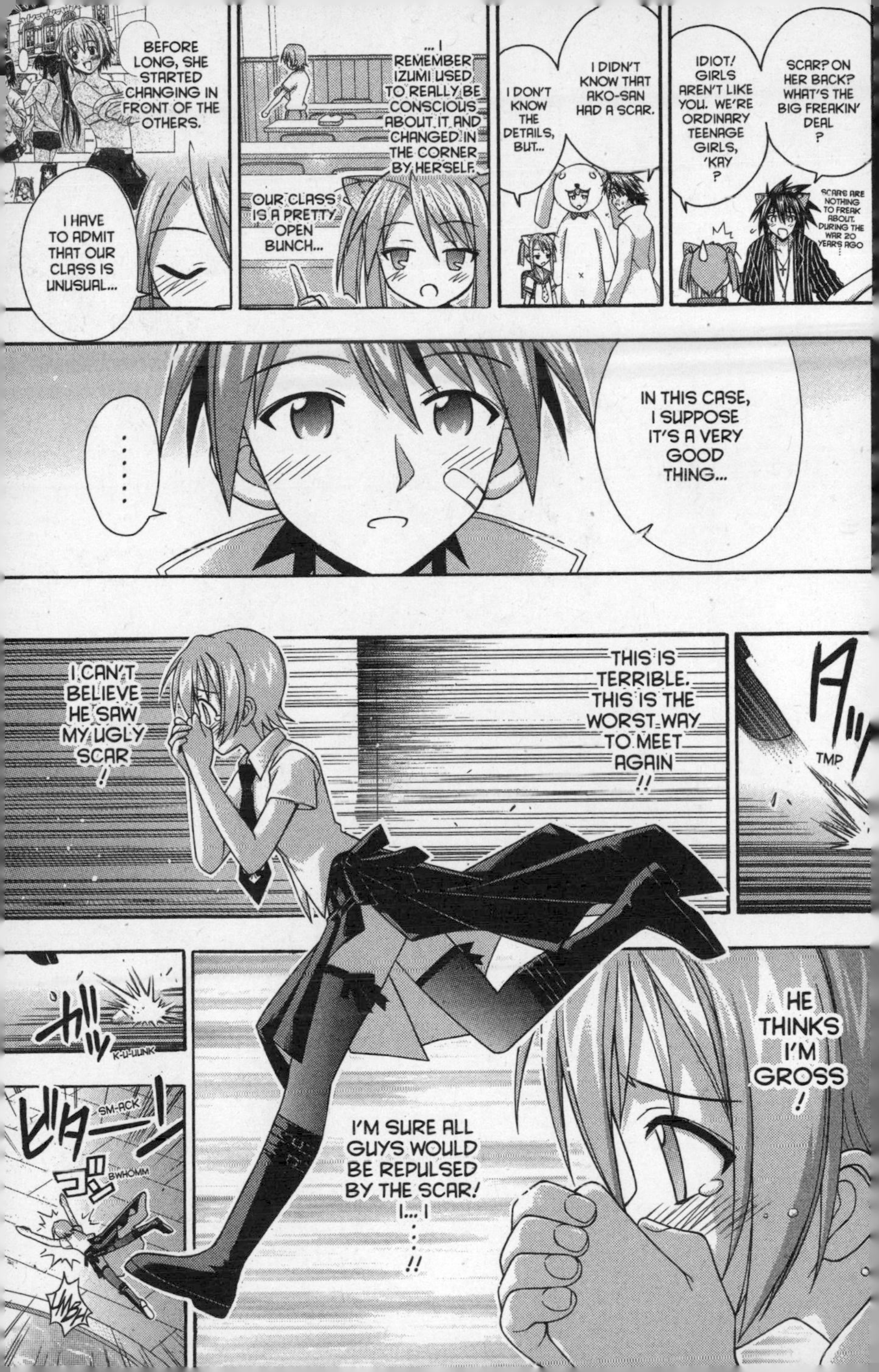
SCAR? ON HER BACK? WHAT'S THE BIG FREAKIN' DEAL?
IDIOT! GIRLS AREN'T LIKE YOU. WE'RE ORDINARY TEENAGE GIRLS, 'KAY?
SCARS ARE NOTHING TO FREAK ABOUT. DURING THE WAR 20 YEARS AGO...
I DIDN'T KNOW THAT AKO-SAN HAD A SCAR.
I DON'T KNOW THE DETAILS, BUT...
...I REMEMBER IZUMI USED TO REALLY BE CONSCIOUS ABOUT IT AND CHANGED IN THE CORNER BY HERSELF.
OUR CLASS IS A PRETTY OPEN BUNCH...
BEFORE LONG, SHE STARTED CHANGING IN FRONT OF THE OTHERS.
I HAVE TO ADMIT THAT OUR CLASS IS UNUSUAL...
IN THIS CASE, I SUPPOSE IT'S A VERY GOOD THING...
......
TMP
THIS IS TERRIBLE. THIS IS THE WORST WAY TO MEET AGAIN!!
I CAN'T BELIEVE HE SAW MY UGLY SCAR!
HE THINKS I'M GROSS!
I'M SURE ALL GUYS WOULD BE REPULSED BY THE SCAR! I... I...!!
K-U-UUNK
SM-ACK
BWHOMM

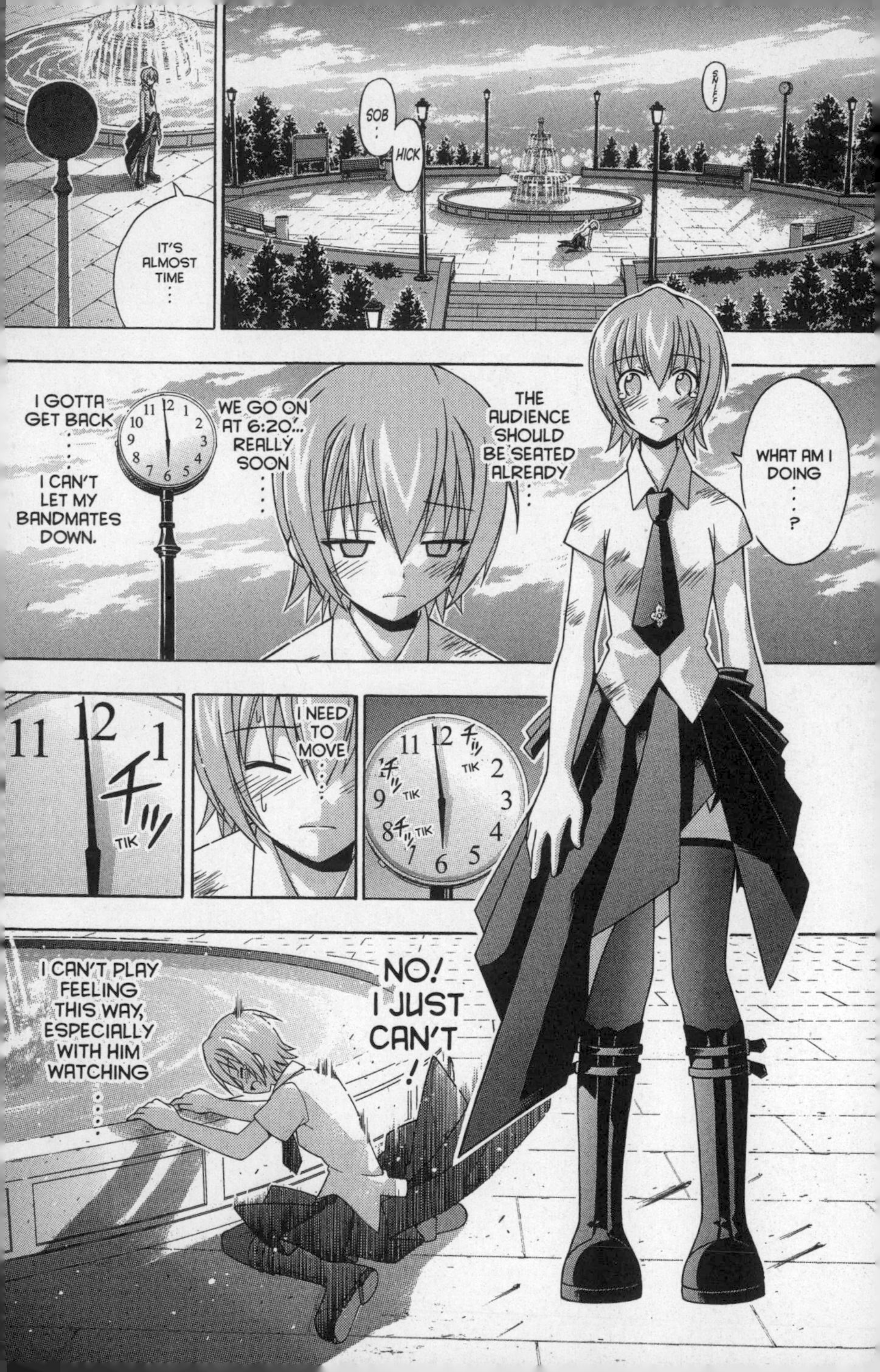
SNIFF
SOB...
HICK
IT'S ALMOST TIME...
WHAT AM I DOING...?
THE AUDIENCE SHOULD BE SEATED ALREADY...
WE GO ON AT 6:20... REALLY SOON...
I GOTTA GET BACK... I CAN'T LET MY BANDMATES DOWN.
チッ TIK
チッ TIK
チッ TIK
I NEED TO MOVE...
チッ TIK
NO! I JUST CAN'T!
I CAN'T PLAY FEELING THIS WAY, ESPECIALLY WITH HIM WATCHING...

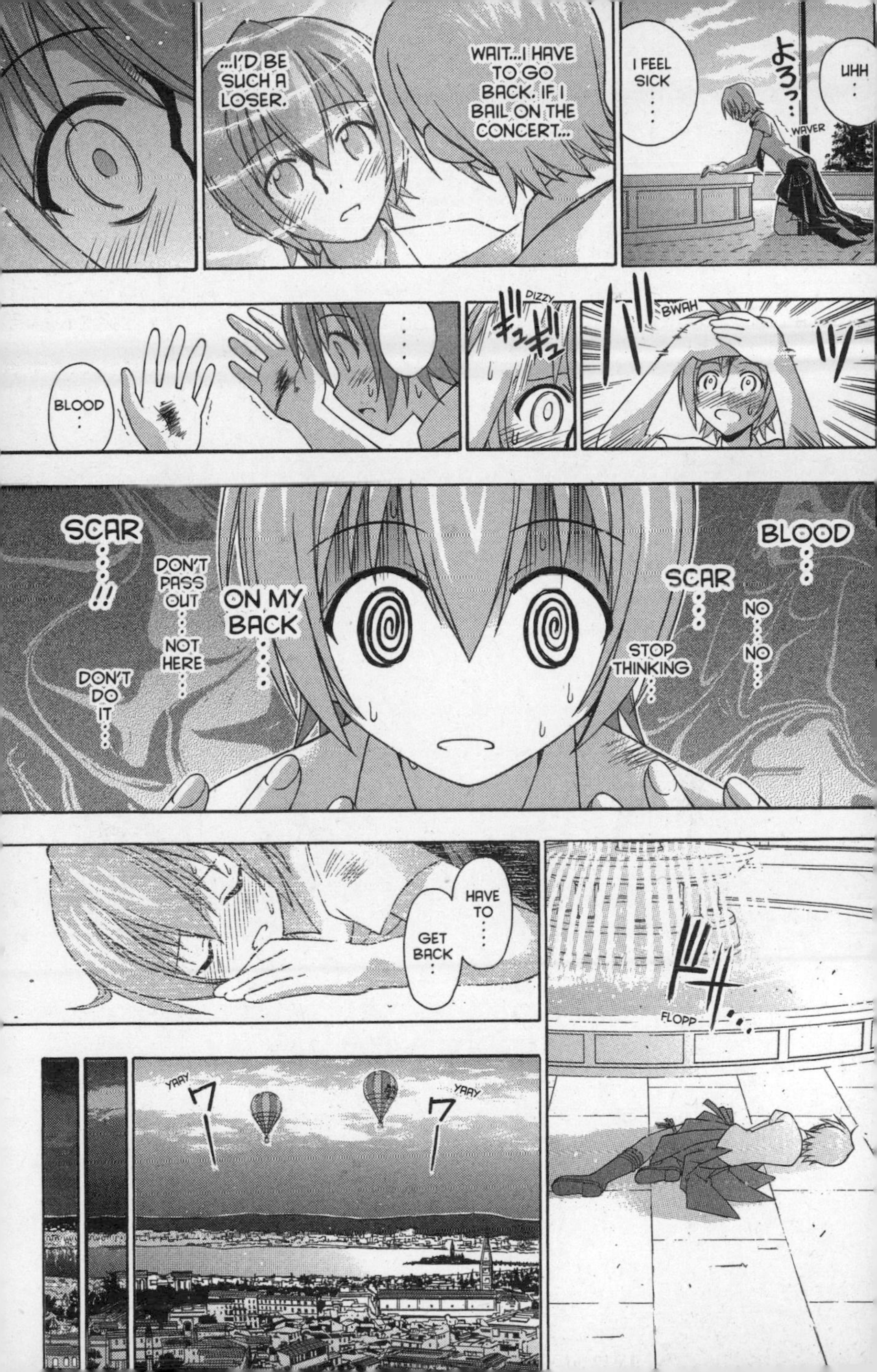
UHH...
よろっ
WAVER
I FEEL SICK...
WAIT...I HAVE TO GO BACK. IF I BAIL ON THE CONCERT...
...I'D BE SUCH A LOSER.
BWAH
DIZZY
...
BLOOD...
BLOOD...
NO...NO...
SCAR...
STOP THINKING...
ON MY BACK...
DON'T PASS OUT...
NOT HERE...
SCAR...!!
DON'T DO IT...
FLOPP
HAVE TO....
GET BACK...
YAAY
YAAY

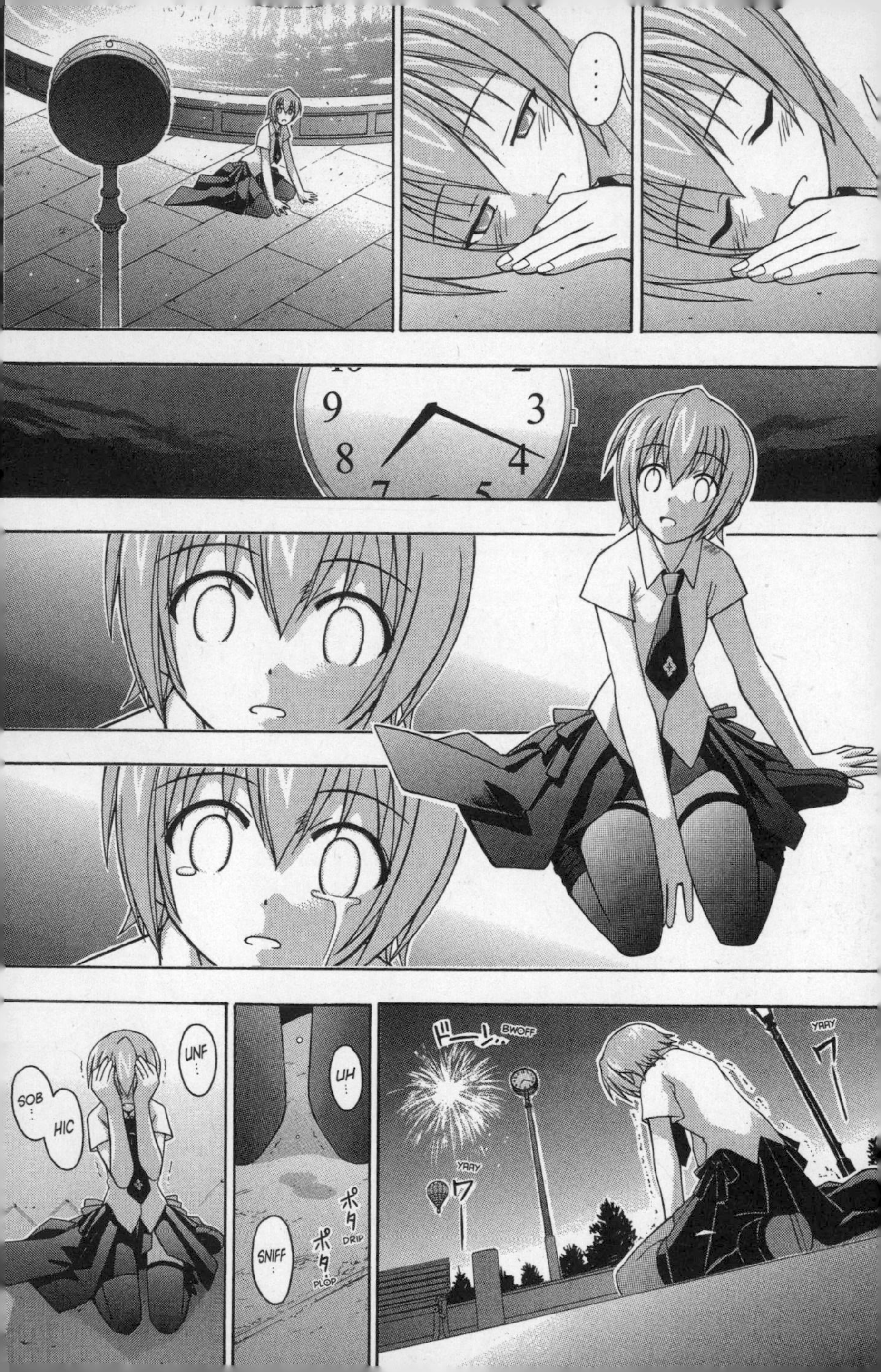

…
ワー YAAY
ドーン BWOFF
ワー YAAY
UH…
ポタ DRIP
ポタ… PLOP
SNIFF…
UNF…
SOB… HIC

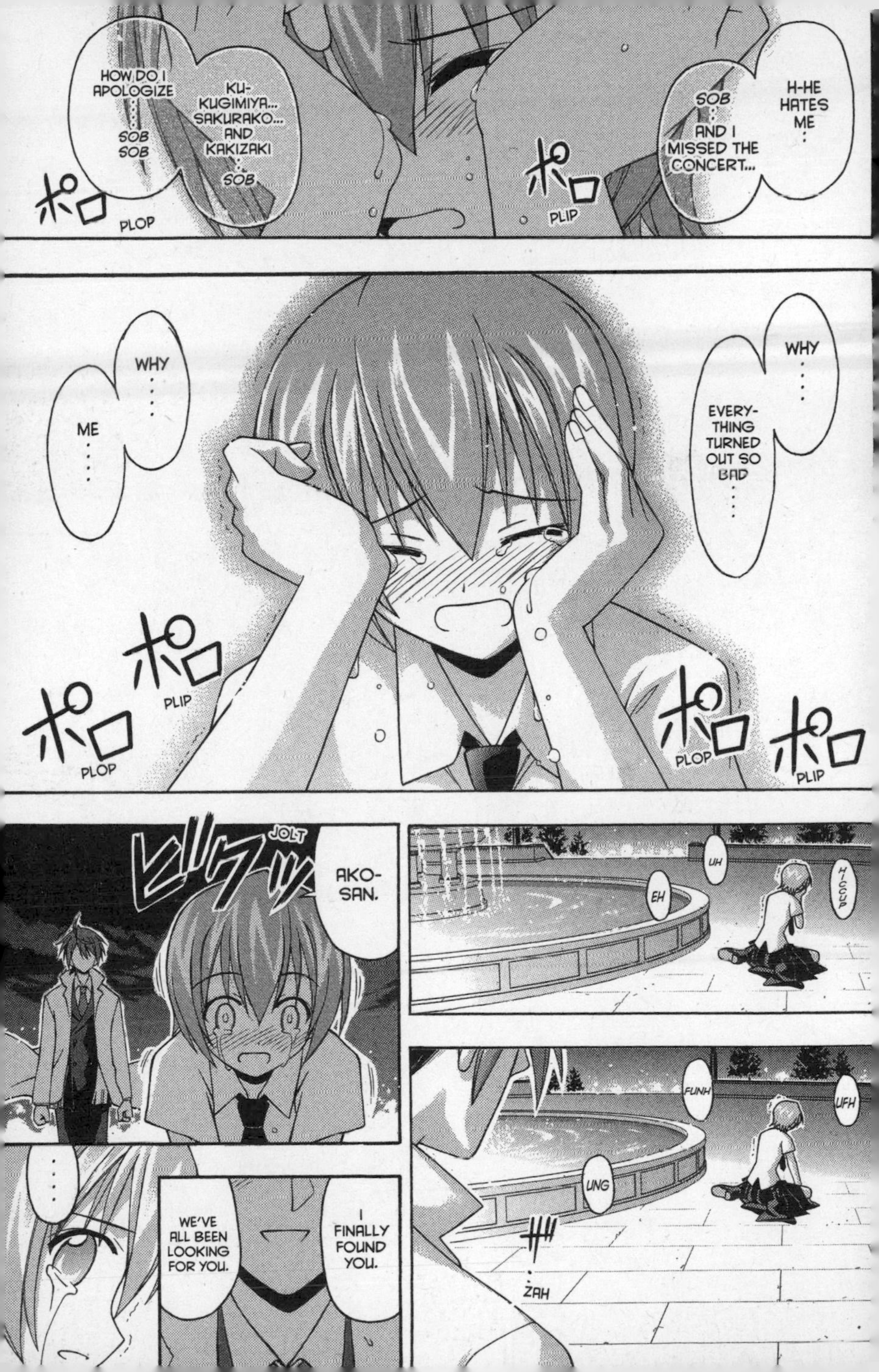
H-HE HATES ME...
SOB... AND I MISSED THE CONCERT...
PLIP
KU-KUGIMIYA... SAKURAKO... AND KAKIZAKI... SOB
HOW DO I APOLOGIZE... SOB SOB
PLOP
WHY... EVERYTHING TURNED OUT SO BAD...
PLIP
PLOP
WHY... ME...
PLIP
PLOP
HICCUP
UH
EH
UFH
FUNH
UNG
ZAH
JOLT
AKO-SAN.
I FINALLY FOUND YOU.
WE'VE ALL BEEN LOOKING FOR YOU.
...

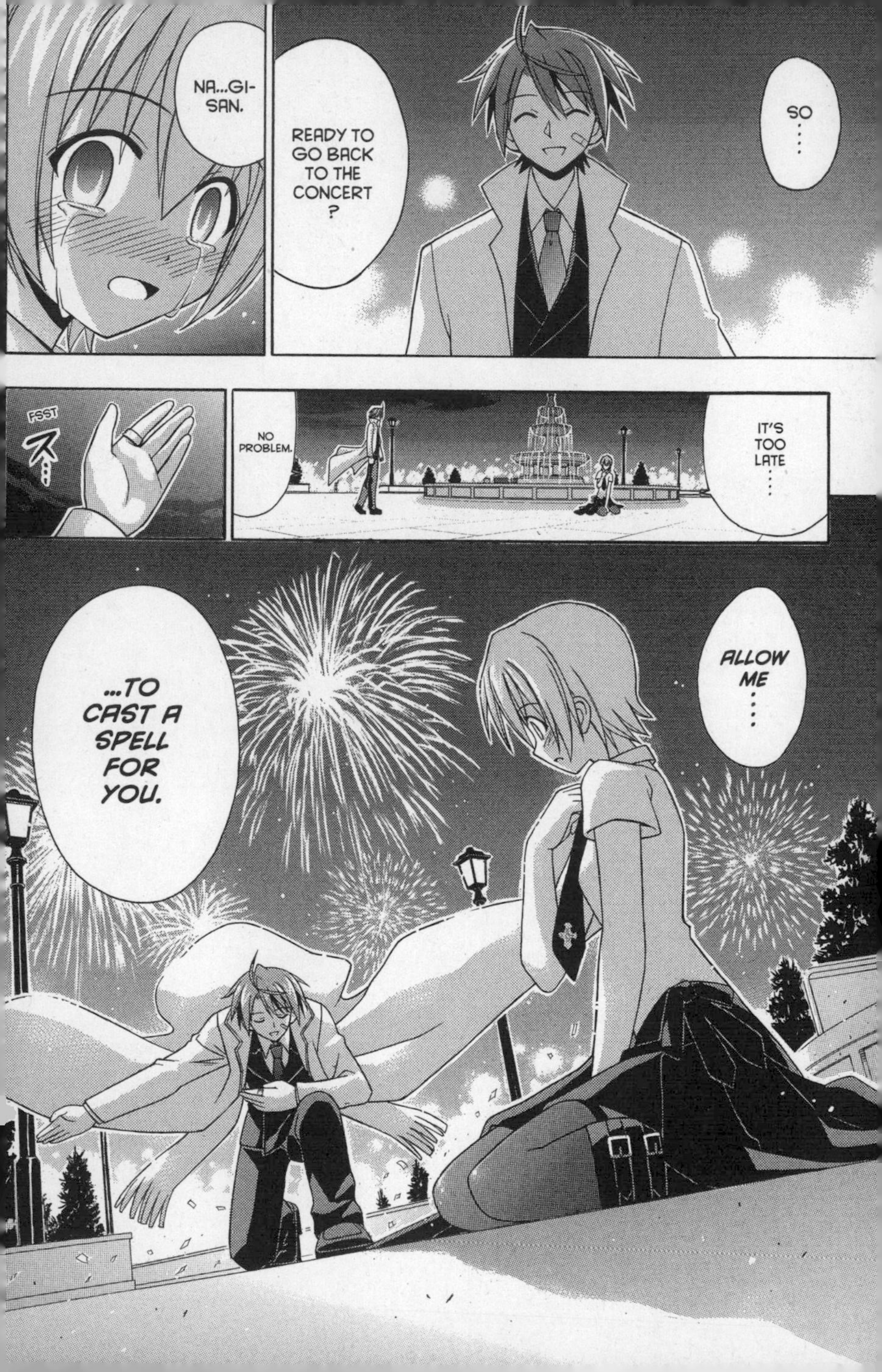
SO....
READY TO GO BACK TO THE CONCERT ?
NA...GI-SAN.
IT'S TOO LATE....
NO PROBLEM.
FSST
ス...
ALLOW ME....
...TO CAST A SPELL FOR YOU.

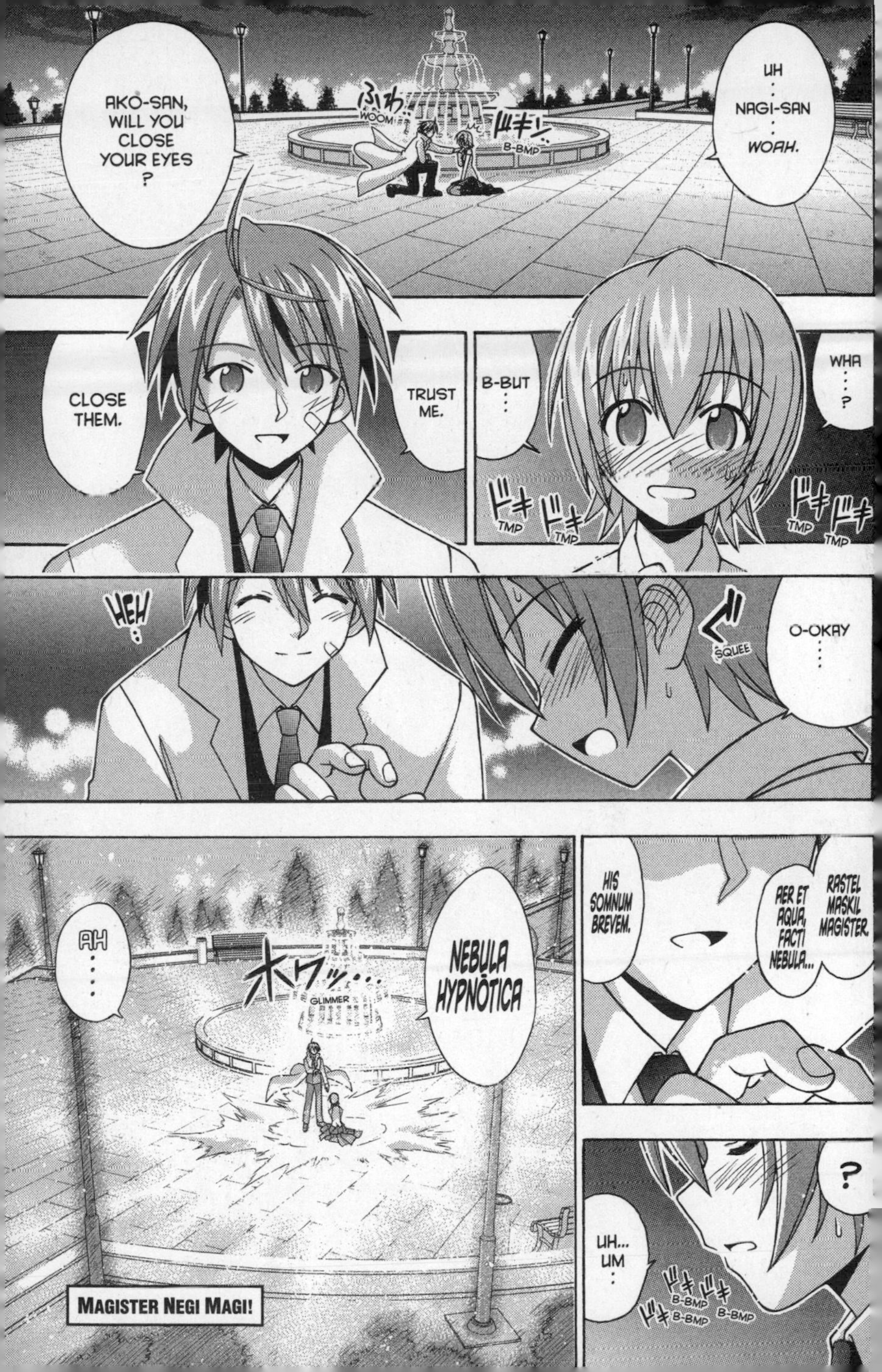
UH... NAGI-SAN... WOAH.
ドキッ B-BMP
ふわ WOOM
AKO-SAN, WILL YOU CLOSE YOUR EYES?
WHA...?
ドキドキ TMP TMP
B-BUT...
ドキドキ TMP TMP
TRUST ME.
CLOSE THEM.
O-OKAY...
ぐ SQUEE
HEH.
RASTEL MASKIL MAGISTER.
AER ET AQUA, FACTI NEBULA...
HIS SOMNUM BREVEM.
?
UH... UM...
ドキドキ B-BMP B-BMP
ドキ B-BMP
NEBULA HYPNÖTICA
ホワッ... GLIMMER
AH...
MAGISTER NEGI MAGI!

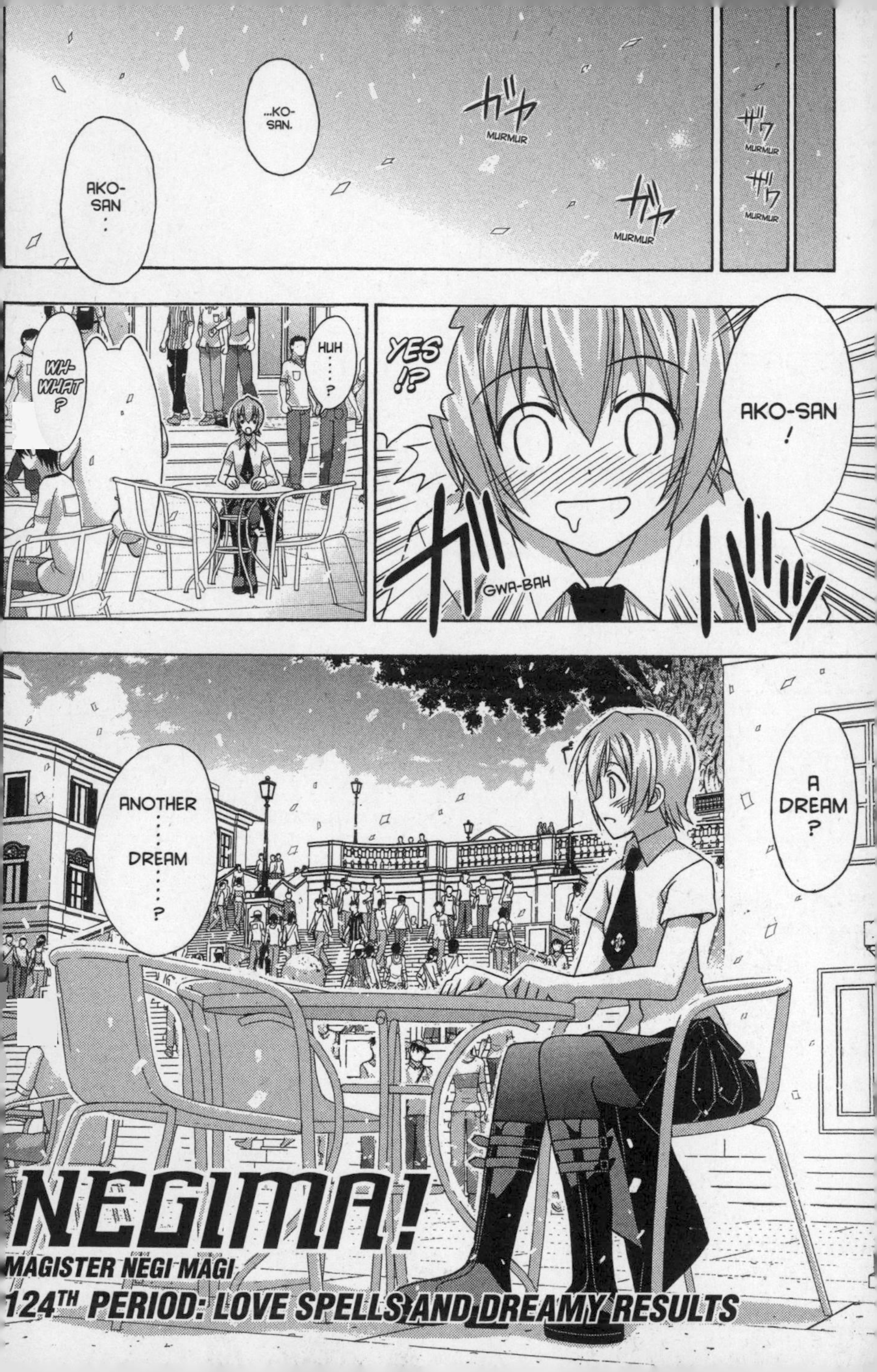
MURMUR
MURMUR
MURMUR
...KO-SAN.
MURMUR
AKO-SAN . .
AKO-SAN !
YES !?
GWA-BAH
HUH . . . ?
WH-WHAT ?
A DREAM ?
ANOTHER . . . DREAM . . . ?
NEGIMA!
MAGISTER NEGI MAGI
124TH PERIOD: LOVE SPELLS AND DREAMY RESULTS

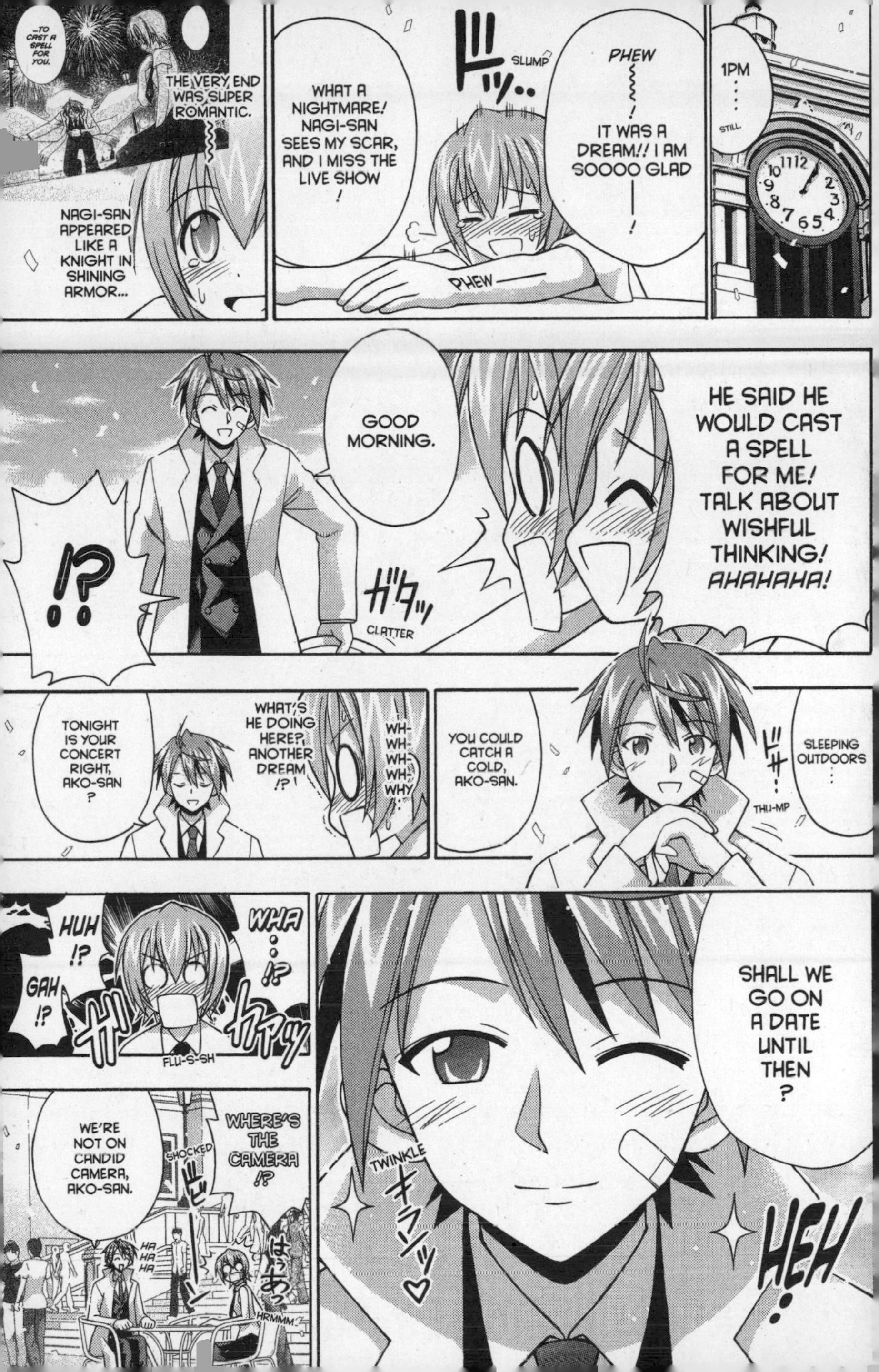
1PM
...
STILL.
PHEW ~ ! IT WAS A DREAM!! I AM SOOOO GLAD —— !
SLUMP
WHAT A NIGHTMARE! NAGI-SAN SEES MY SCAR, AND I MISS THE LIVE SHOW!
PHEW ——
THE VERY END WAS SUPER ROMANTIC.
...TO CAST A SPELL FOR YOU.
NAGI-SAN APPEARED LIKE A KNIGHT IN SHINING ARMOR...
HE SAID HE WOULD CAST A SPELL FOR ME! TALK ABOUT WISHFUL THINKING! AHAHAHA!
GOOD MORNING.
CLATTER
!?
SLEEPING OUTDOORS...
THU-MP
YOU COULD CATCH A COLD, AKO-SAN.
WH-WH-WH-WH-WHY
WHAT'S HE DOING HERE? ANOTHER DREAM!?
TONIGHT IS YOUR CONCERT RIGHT, AKO-SAN?
SHALL WE GO ON A DATE UNTIL THEN?
HEH
TWINKLE
WHA...!?
HUH!?
GAH!?
FLU-S-SH
WHERE'S THE CAMERA!?
SHOCKED
WE'RE NOT ON CANDID CAMERA, AKO-SAN.
HA HA HA
HRMMM

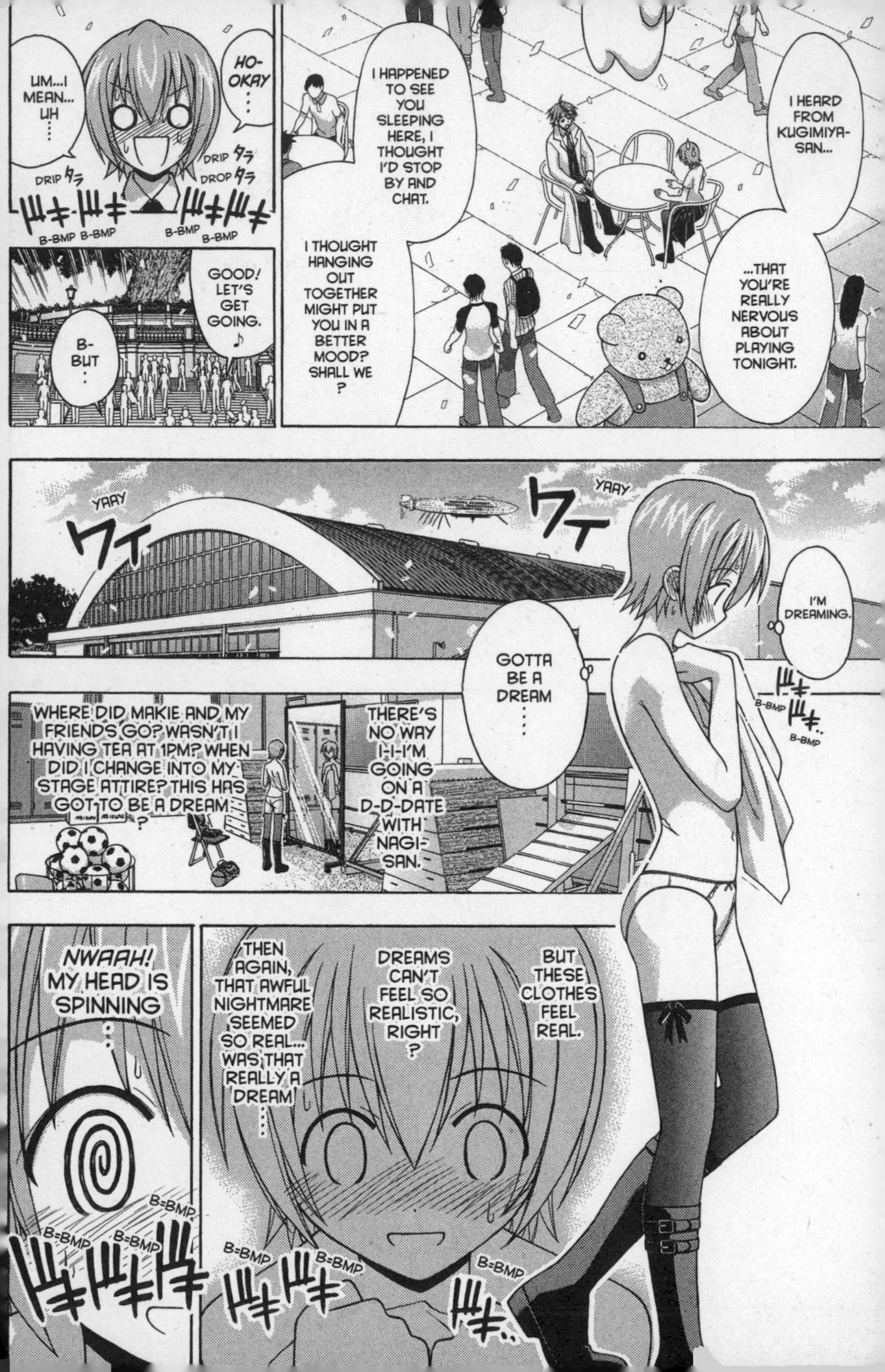
I HEARD FROM KUGIMIYA-SAN...
...THAT YOU'RE REALLY NERVOUS ABOUT PLAYING TONIGHT.
I HAPPENED TO SEE YOU SLEEPING HERE, I THOUGHT I'D STOP BY AND CHAT.
I THOUGHT HANGING OUT TOGETHER MIGHT PUT YOU IN A BETTER MOOD? SHALL WE ?
HO-OKAY ...
UM...I MEAN... UH ...
DRIP DRIP DROP
B-BMP B-BMP B-BMP B-BMP
GOOD! LET'S GET GOING. ♪
B-BUT ...
YAAY
YAAY
I'M DREAMING.
GOTTA BE A DREAM ...
B-BMP B-BMP
THERE'S NO WAY I-I-I'M GOING ON A D-D-DATE WITH NAGI-SAN.
WHERE DID MAKIE AND MY FRIENDS GO? WASN'T I HAVING TEA AT 1PM? WHEN DID I CHANGE INTO MY STAGE ATTIRE? THIS HAS GOT TO BE A DREAM ?
BUT THESE CLOTHES FEEL REAL.
DREAMS CAN'T FEEL SO REALISTIC, RIGHT ?
THEN AGAIN, THAT AWFUL NIGHTMARE SEEMED SO REAL... WAS THAT REALLY A DREAM ...
B=BMP B=BMP B=BMP
NWAAH! MY HEAD IS SPINNING ...
B=BMP B=BMP B=BMP

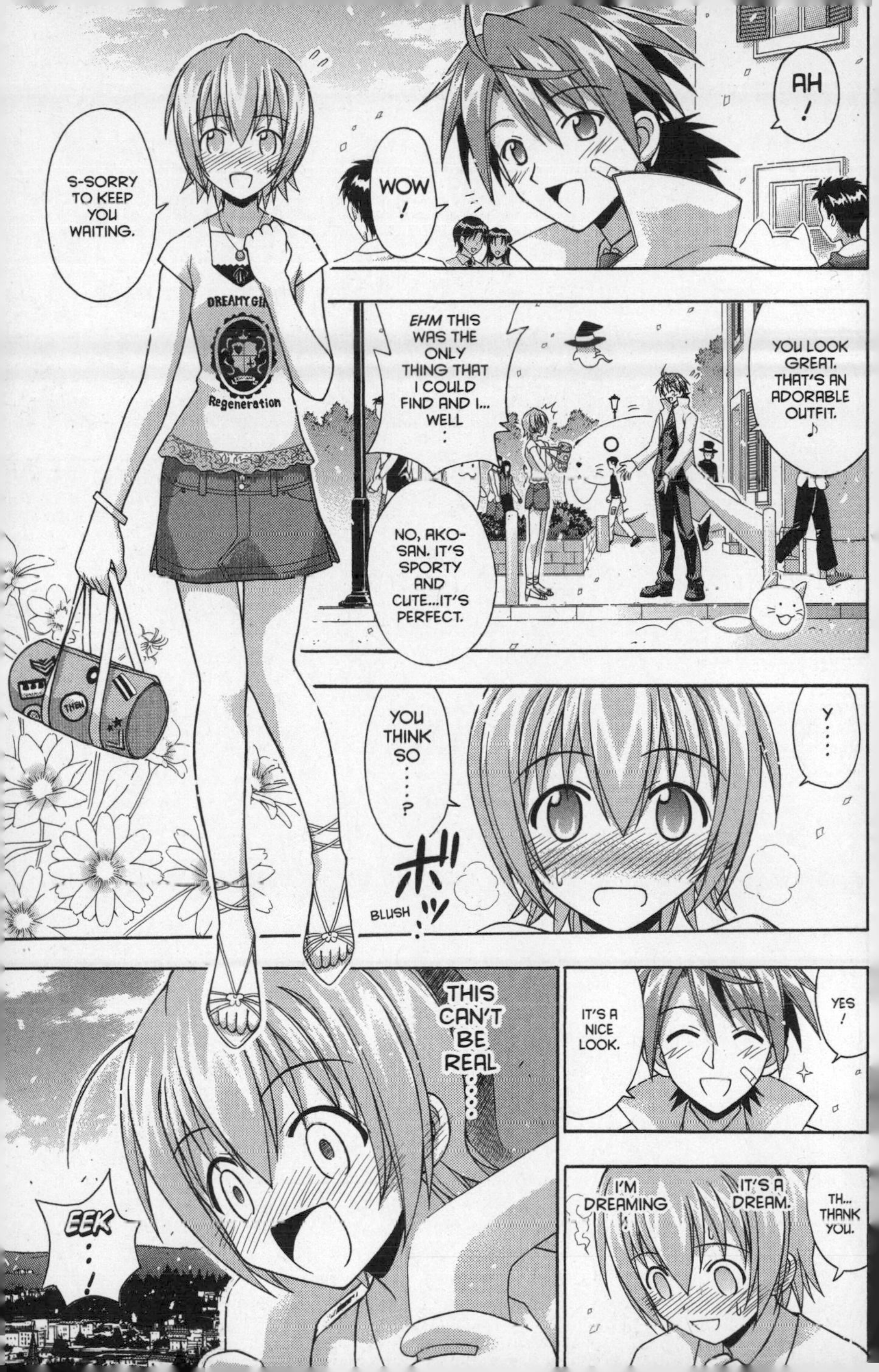
AH!
WOW!
YOU LOOK GREAT. THAT'S AN ADORABLE OUTFIT. ♪
EHM THIS WAS THE ONLY THING THAT I COULD FIND AND I... WELL :
NO, AKO-SAN. IT'S SPORTY AND CUTE...IT'S PERFECT.
Y....
YOU THINK SO.....?
BLUSH
S-SORRY TO KEEP YOU WAITING.
DREAMY GIR
Regeneration
YES!
IT'S A NICE LOOK.
TH... THANK YOU.
IT'S A DREAM.
I'M DREAMING!
THIS CAN'T BE REAL....
EEK...!

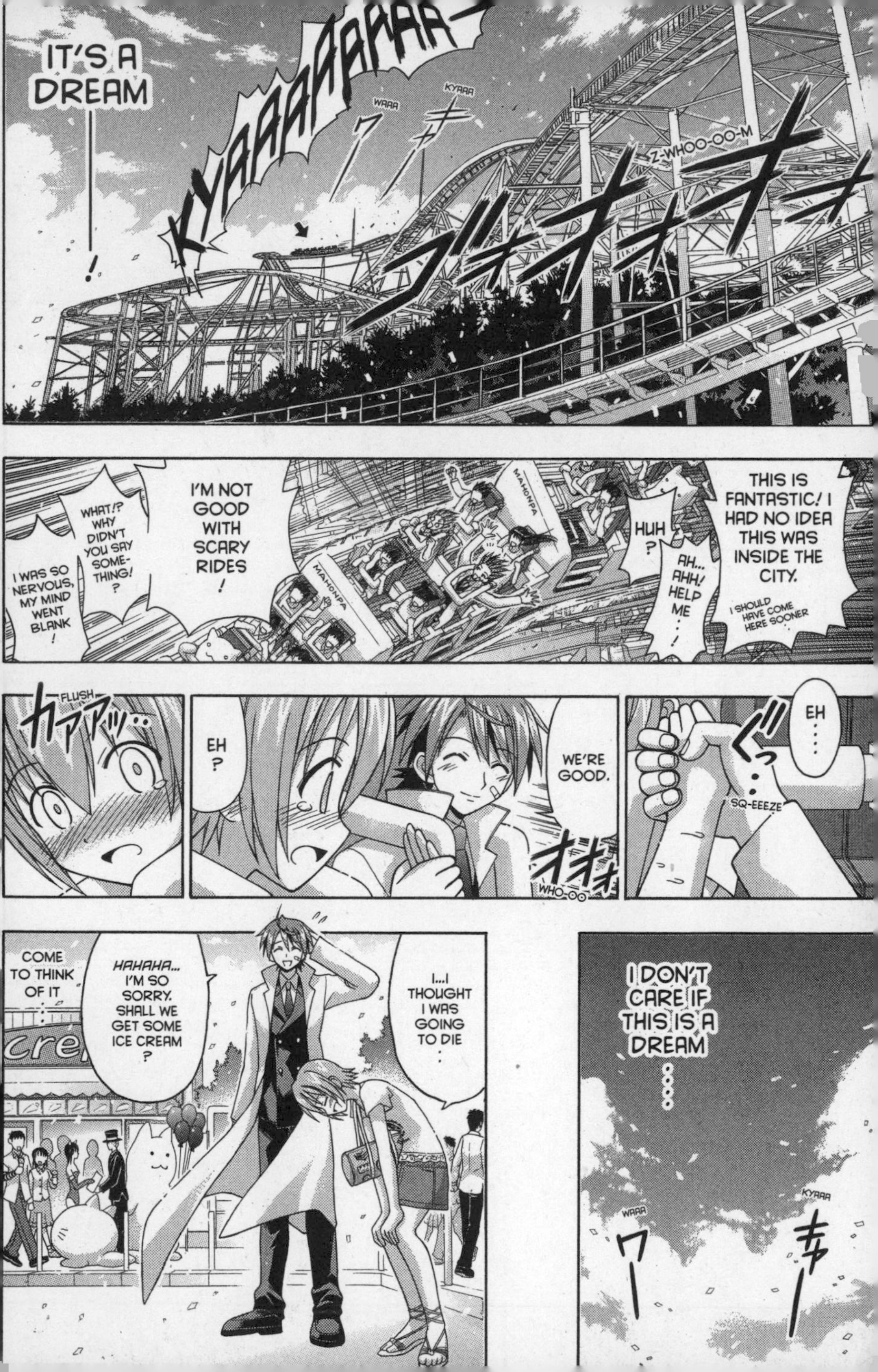
Z-WHOO-OO-M
KYAAA
WAAA
KYAAAAAAAAA—
IT'S A DREAM
!
THIS IS FANTASTIC! I HAD NO IDEA THIS WAS INSIDE THE CITY.
I SHOULD HAVE COME HERE SOONER
AH... AHH! HELP ME...!
HUH?
MAHONPA
MAHONPA
I'M NOT GOOD WITH SCARY RIDES!
WHAT!? WHY DIDN'T YOU SAY SOME-THING!?
I WAS SO NERVOUS, MY MIND WENT BLANK!
EH....
SQ-EEEZE
WE'RE GOOD.
EH?
WHO-OO
FLUSH
I DON'T CARE IF THIS IS A DREAM....
KYAAA
WAAA
I...I THOUGHT I WAS GOING TO DIE...
HAHAHA... I'M SO SORRY. SHALL WE GET SOME ICE CREAM?
COME TO THINK OF IT...

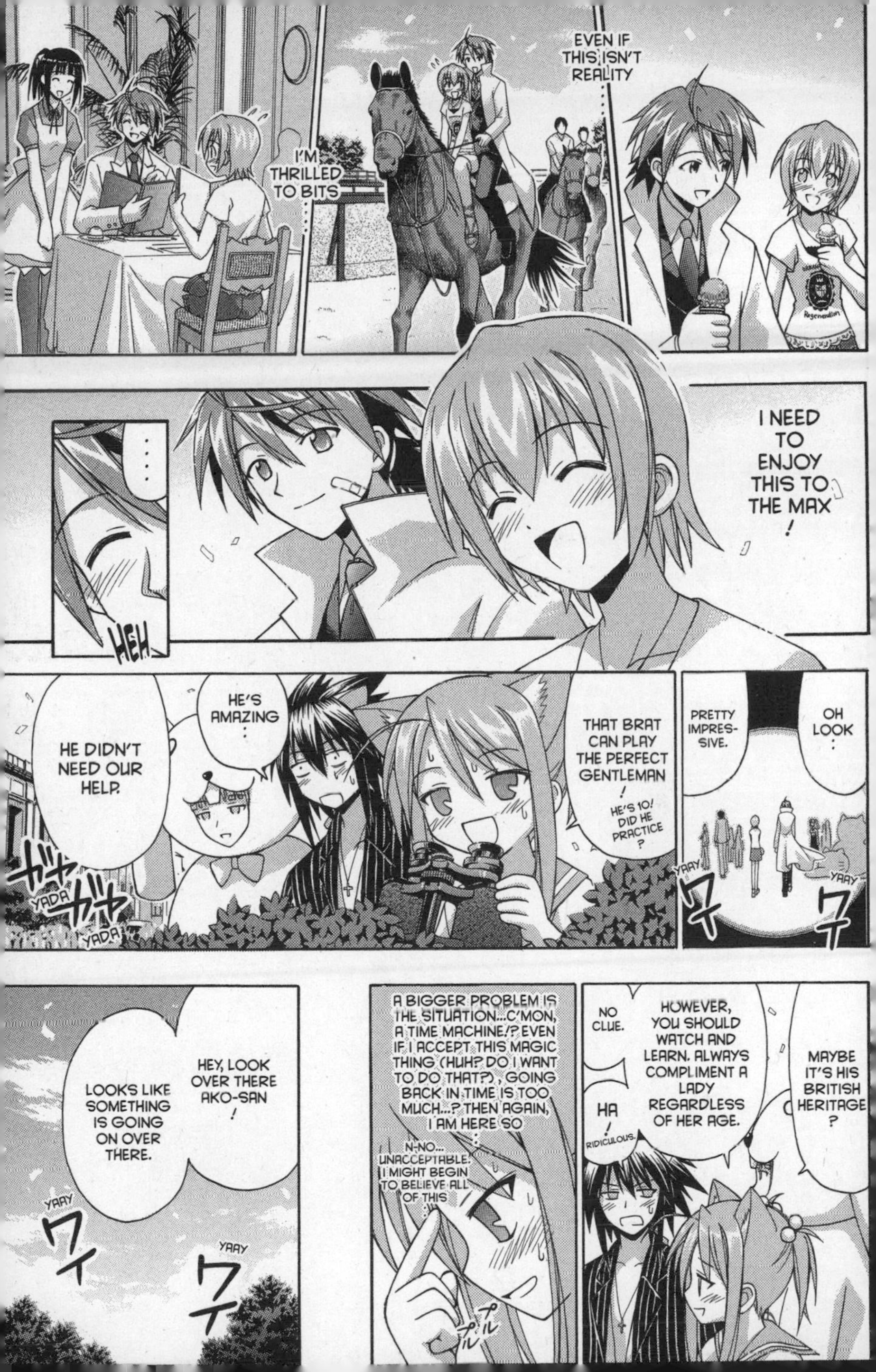
EVEN IF THIS ISN'T REALITY
I'M THRILLED TO BITS
I NEED TO ENJOY THIS TO THE MAX!
....
HEH
OH LOOK...
PRETTY IMPRES-SIVE.
YAAY ワ
YAAY ワ
THAT BRAT CAN PLAY THE PERFECT GENTLEMAN!
HE'S 10! DID HE PRACTICE?
HE'S AMAZING...
HE DIDN'T NEED OUR HELP.
YADA ガヤ
YADA ガヤ
MAYBE IT'S HIS BRITISH HERITAGE?
NO CLUE.
HOWEVER, YOU SHOULD WATCH AND LEARN. ALWAYS COMPLIMENT A LADY REGARDLESS OF HER AGE.
HA! RIDICULOUS.
A BIGGER PROBLEM IS THE SITUATION...C'MON, A TIME MACHINE!? EVEN IF I ACCEPT THIS MAGIC THING (HUH? DO I WANT TO DO THAT?), GOING BACK IN TIME IS TOO MUCH...? THEN AGAIN, I AM HERE SO...
N-NO... UNACCEPTABLE! I MIGHT BEGIN TO BELIEVE ALL OF THIS...!
プル プル
HEY, LOOK OVER THERE AKO-SAN!
LOOKS LIKE SOMETHING IS GOING ON OVER THERE.
YAAY ワイ
YAAY ワイ

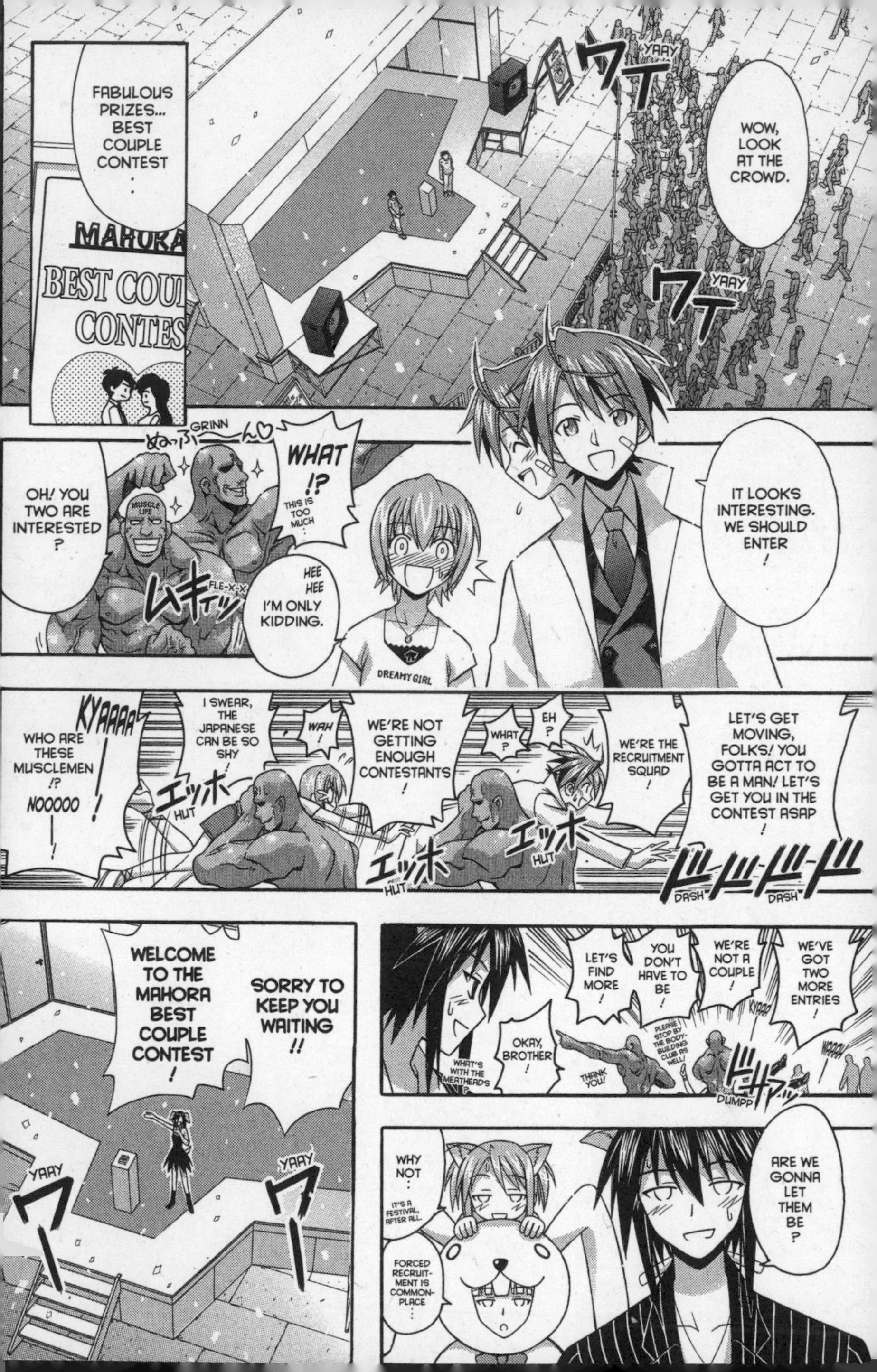

YAAY
WOW, LOOK AT THE CROWD.
YAAY
FABULOUS PRIZES... BEST COUPLE CONTEST
MAHORA
BEST COUPLE CONTEST
IT LOOKS INTERESTING. WE SHOULD ENTER!
HEE HEE I'M ONLY KIDDING.
DREAMY GIRL
WHAT!? THIS IS TOO MUCH...
GRINN
OH! YOU TWO ARE INTERESTED?
MUSCLE LIFE
FLE-X-X
LET'S GET MOVING, FOLKS! YOU GOTTA ACT TO BE A MAN! LET'S GET YOU IN THE CONTEST ASAP!
DASH DASH
WE'RE THE RECRUITMENT SQUAD!
EH?
WHAT?
HUT
WE'RE NOT GETTING ENOUGH CONTESTANTS!
WAH!
HUT
I SWEAR, THE JAPANESE CAN BE SO SHY!
KYAAAA
WHO ARE THESE MUSCLEMEN!? NOOOOO!
HUT
WE'VE GOT TWO MORE ENTRIES!
WE'RE NOT A COUPLE!
YOU DON'T HAVE TO BE!
LET'S FIND MORE!
OKAY, BROTHER!
PLEASE STOP BY THE BODY-BUILDING CLUB AS WELL!
THANK YOU!
WHAT'S WITH THE MEATHEADS?
DUMPP
ARE WE GONNA LET THEM BE?
WHY NOT... IT'S A FESTIVAL, AFTER ALL.
FORCED RECRUITMENT IS COMMONPLACE...
WELCOME TO THE MAHORA BEST COUPLE CONTEST!
SORRY TO KEEP YOU WAITING!!
YAAY
YAAY

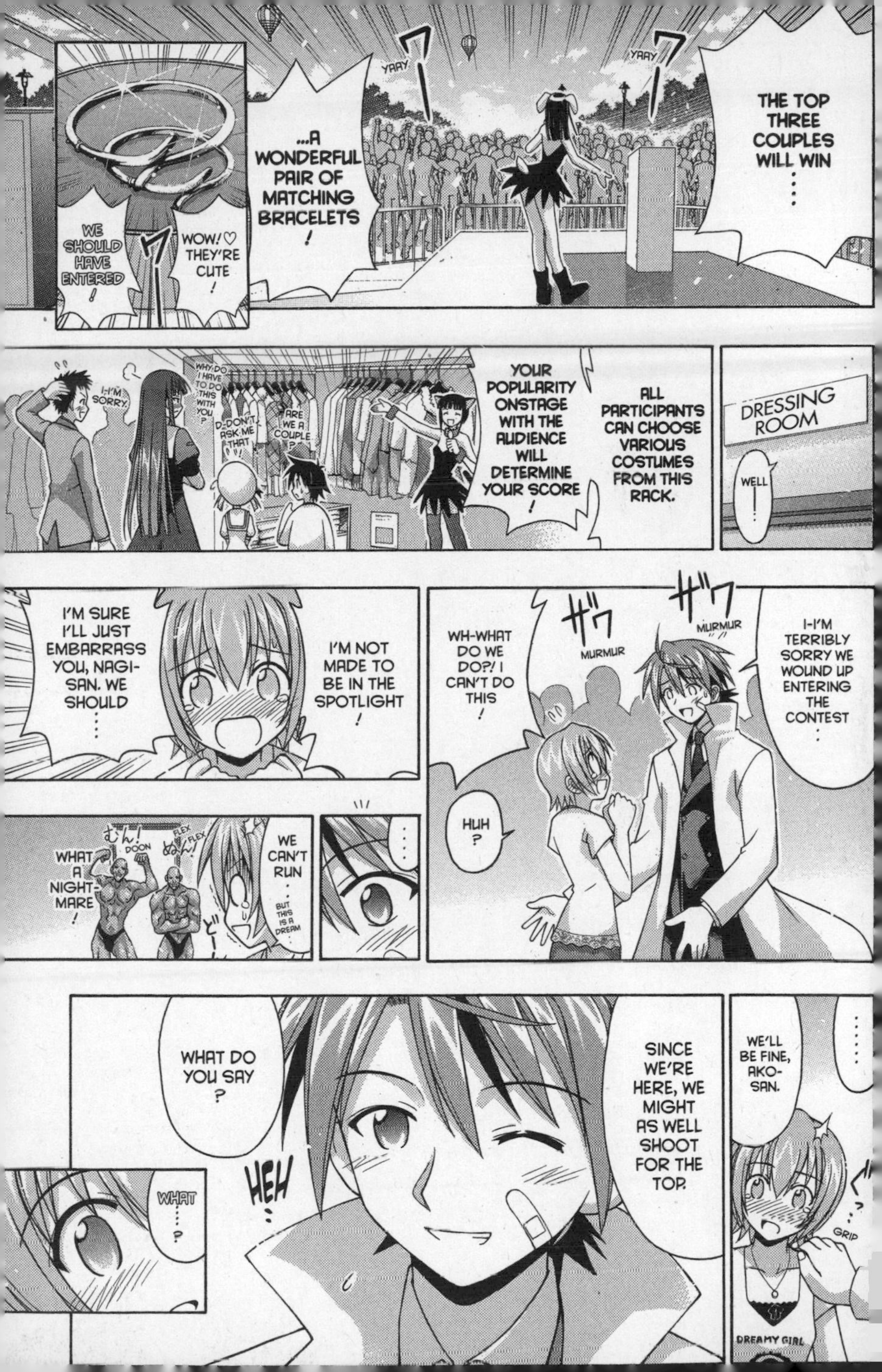

THE TOP THREE COUPLES WILL WIN....
YAAY
...A WONDERFUL PAIR OF MATCHING BRACELETS!
YAAY
WOW! ♡ THEY'RE CUTE!
WE SHOULD HAVE ENTERED!
DRESSING ROOM
WELL...!
ALL PARTICIPANTS CAN CHOOSE VARIOUS COSTUMES FROM THIS RACK.
YOUR POPULARITY ONSTAGE WITH THE AUDIENCE WILL DETERMINE YOUR SCORE!
ARE WE A COUPLE?
D-DON'T ASK ME THAT
WHY DO I HAVE TO DO THIS WITH YOU?
I-I'M SORRY.
I-I'M TERRIBLY SORRY WE WOUND UP ENTERING THE CONTEST...
MURMUR
MURMUR
WH-WHAT DO WE DO?! I CAN'T DO THIS!
HUH?
I'M NOT MADE TO BE IN THE SPOTLIGHT!
I'M SURE I'LL JUST EMBARRASS YOU, NAGI-SAN. WE SHOULD...
....
WE CAN'T RUN...
BUT THIS IS A DREAM
FLEX FLEX
DOON
WHAT A NIGHT-MARE!
......
WE'LL BE FINE, AKO-SAN.
GRIP
DREAMY GIRL
SINCE WE'RE HERE, WE MIGHT AS WELL SHOOT FOR THE TOP.
WHAT DO YOU SAY?
HEH
WHAT...?

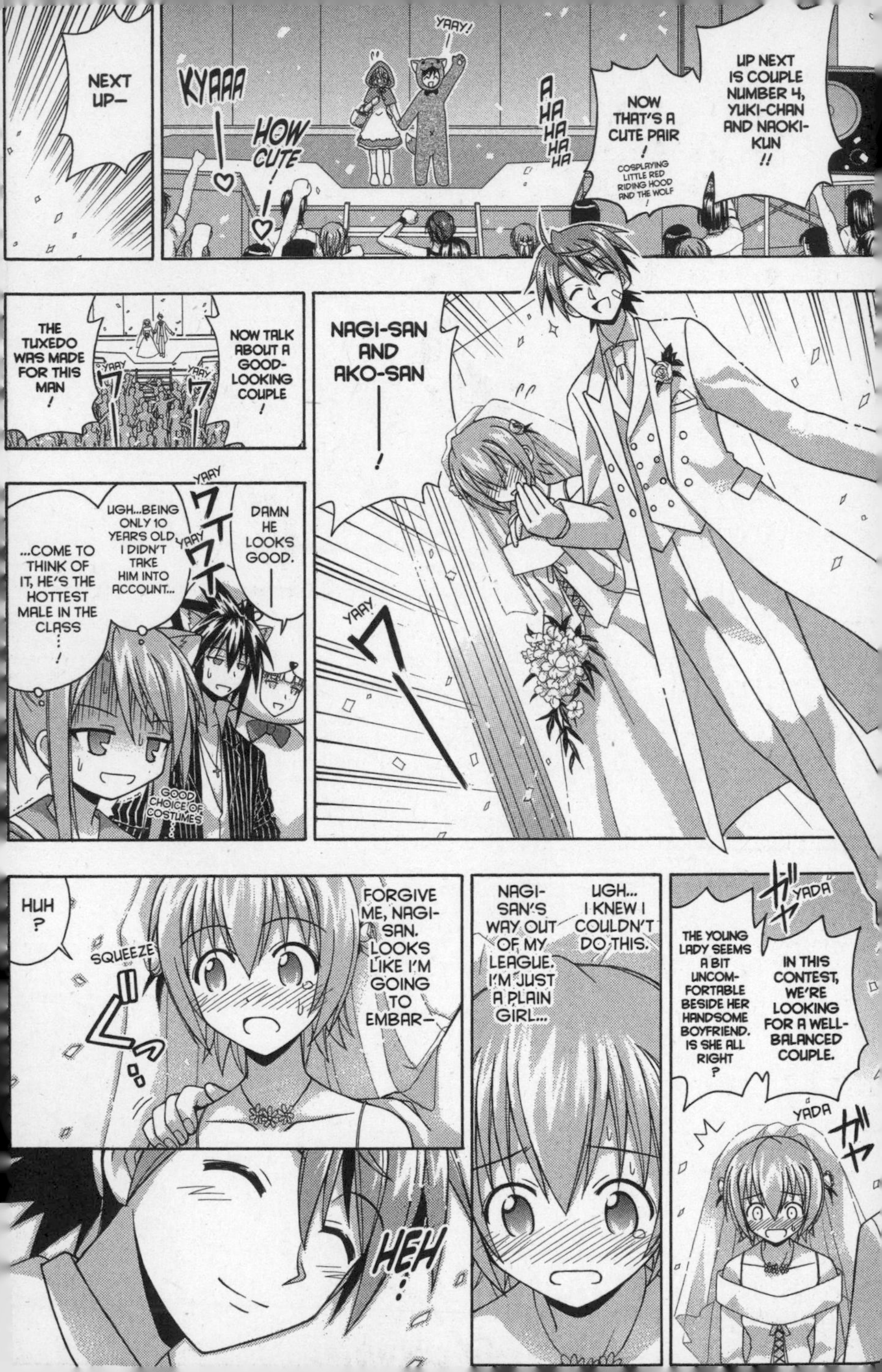
UP NEXT IS COUPLE NUMBER 4, YUKI-CHAN AND NAOKI-KUN!!
NOW THAT'S A CUTE PAIR!
COSPLAYING LITTLE RED RIDING HOOD AND THE WOLF!
AHAHAHAHA
YAAY!
HOW CUTE!♡
KYAAA—♡
NEXT UP—
NAGI-SAN AND AKO-SAN—!
YAAY
NOW TALK ABOUT A GOOD-LOOKING COUPLE!
THE TUXEDO WAS MADE FOR THIS MAN!
YAAY
YAAY
DAMN HE LOOKS GOOD.—
YAAY
YAAY
UGH...BEING ONLY 10 YEAR'S OLD I DIDN'T TAKE HIM INTO ACCOUNT...
...COME TO THINK OF IT, HE'S THE HOTTEST MALE IN THE CLASS...!
GOOD CHOICE OF COSTUMES
YADA
IN THIS CONTEST, WE'RE LOOKING FOR A WELL-BALANCED COUPLE.
THE YOUNG LADY SEEMS A BIT UNCOMFORTABLE BESIDE HER HANDSOME BOYFRIEND. IS SHE ALL RIGHT?
YADA
UGH... I KNEW I COULDN'T DO THIS.
NAGI-SAN'S WAY OUT OF MY LEAGUE. I'M JUST A PLAIN GIRL...
FORGIVE ME, NAGI-SAN. LOOKS LIKE I'M GOING TO EMBAR—
HUH?
SQUEEZE
HEH...

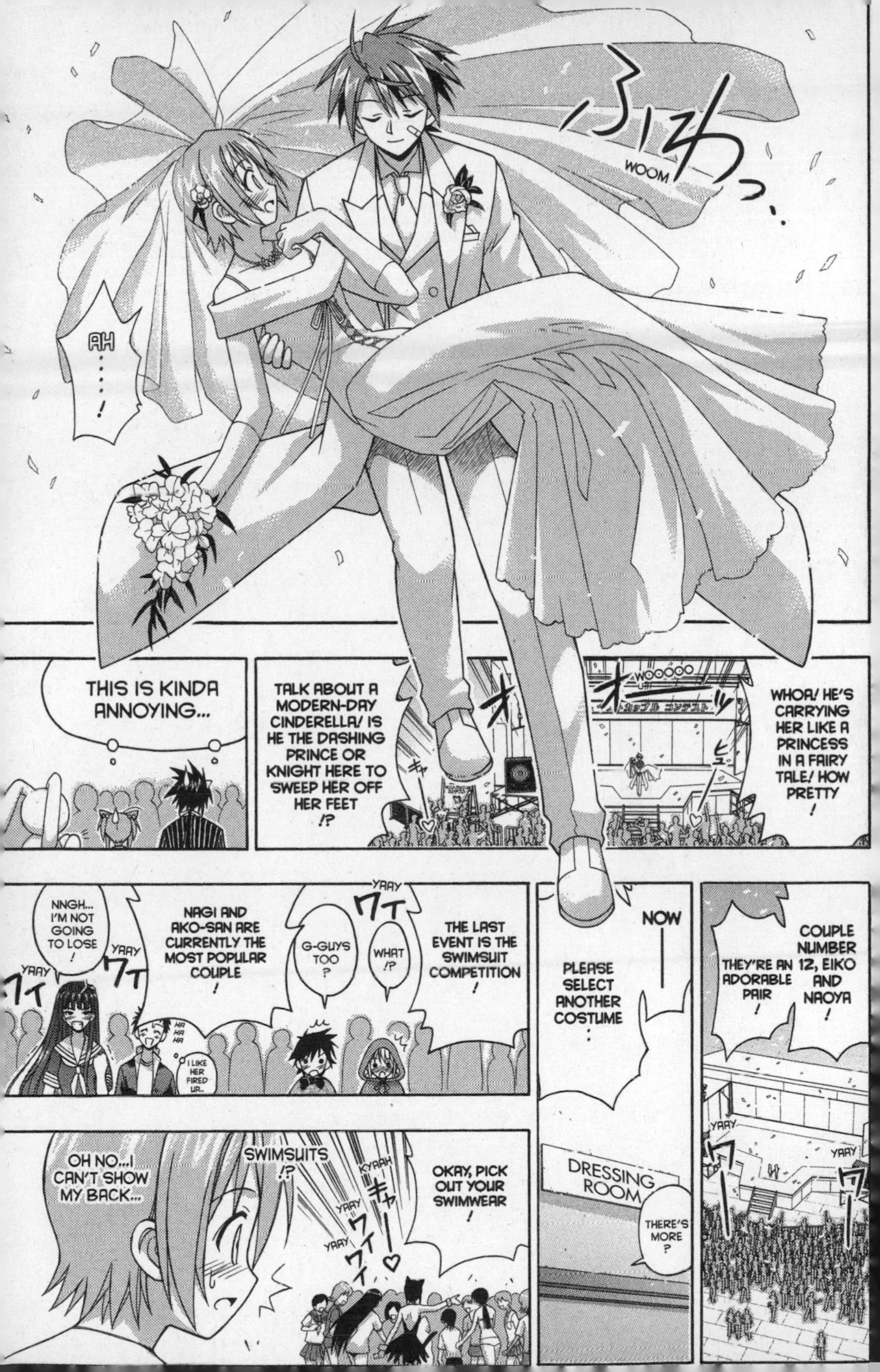
ふわっ
WOOM
AH.....!
WHOA! HE'S CARRYING HER LIKE A PRINCESS IN A FAIRY TALE! HOW PRETTY!
オーッ
WOOOOO
カップル コンテスト
ヒュ
キャ
TALK ABOUT A MODERN-DAY CINDERELLA! IS HE THE DASHING PRINCE OR KNIGHT HERE TO SWEEP HER OFF HER FEET!?
THIS IS KINDA ANNOYING...
COUPLE NUMBER 12, EIKO AND NAOYA!
THEY'RE AN ADORABLE PAIR!
YAAY
ワー
YAAY
NOW—
PLEASE SELECT ANOTHER COSTUME...
DRESSING ROOM
THERE'S MORE?
THE LAST EVENT IS THE SWIMSUIT COMPETITION!
WHAT!?
G-GUYS TOO?
YAAY
ワイ
NAGI AND AKO-SAN ARE CURRENTLY THE MOST POPULAR COUPLE!
YAAY
ワイ
NNGH... I'M NOT GOING TO LOSE!
YAAY
ワイ
HA HA HA
I LIKE HER FIRED UP..
OKAY, PICK OUT YOUR SWIMWEAR!
KYAAH
キャー♡
YAAY
YAAY
ワイワイ
SWIMSUITS!?
OH NO...I CAN'T SHOW MY BACK...

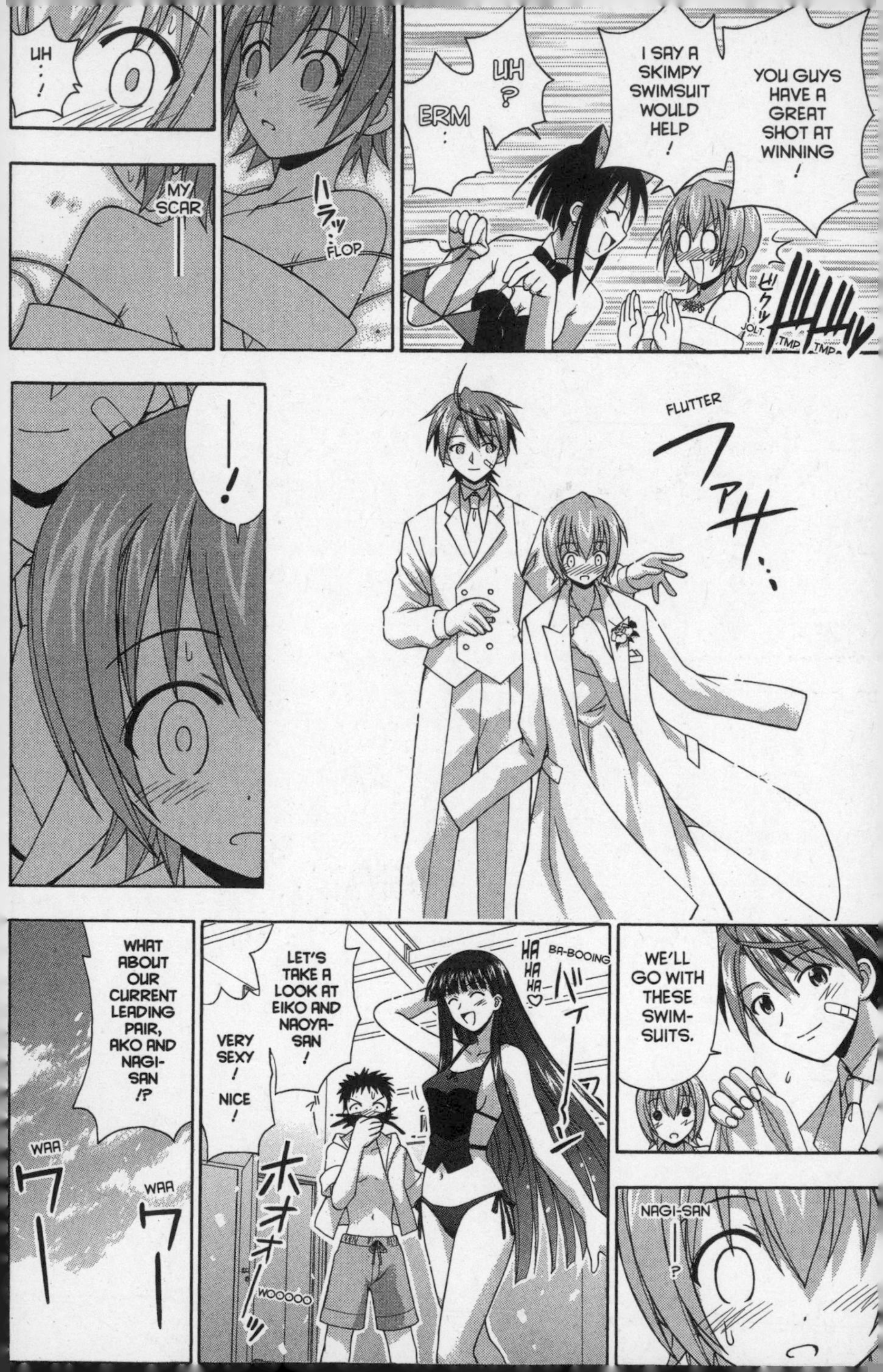
YOU GUYS HAVE A GREAT SHOT AT WINNING!
I SAY A SKIMPY SWIMSUIT WOULD HELP!
UH?
ERM...
JOLT
TMP TMP
FLOP
UH...!
MY SCAR—
FLUTTER
—!
WE'LL GO WITH THESE SWIM-SUITS.
NAGI-SAN—?
LET'S TAKE A LOOK AT EIKO AND NAOYA-SAN!
HA HA HA♡
BA-BOOING
VERY SEXY!
NICE!
WOOOOO
WHAT ABOUT OUR CURRENT LEADING PAIR, AKO AND NAGI-SAN!?
WAA
WAA

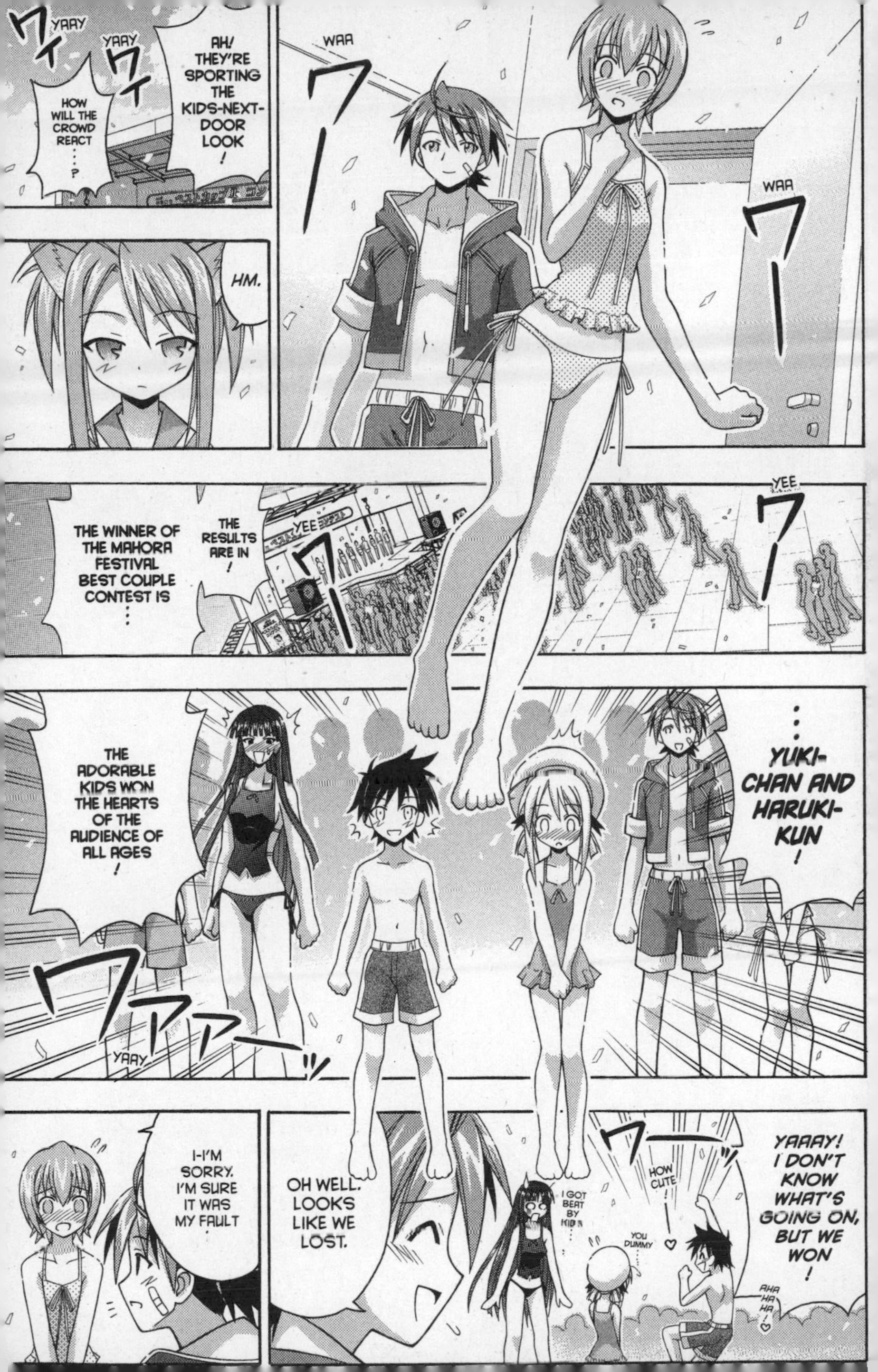
WAA
ワ
WAA
ワー
YAAY
ワイ
YAAY
ワイ
AH! THEY'RE SPORTING THE KIDS-NEXT-DOOR LOOK!
HOW WILL THE CROWD REACT...?
HM.
YEE
ワ
YEE
ワ
THE RESULTS ARE IN!
THE WINNER OF THE MAHORA FESTIVAL BEST COUPLE CONTEST IS...
...YUKI-CHAN AND HARUKI-KUN!
THE ADORABLE KIDS WON THE HEARTS OF THE AUDIENCE OF ALL AGES!
ワァアー!!
YAAY
YAAAY! I DON'T KNOW WHAT'S GOING ON, BUT WE WON!
ワー
HOW CUTE!
I GOT BEAT BY KID
YOU DUMMY...
AHAHAHA!
OH WELL. LOOKS LIKE WE LOST.
I-I'M SORRY. I'M SURE IT WAS MY FAULT.

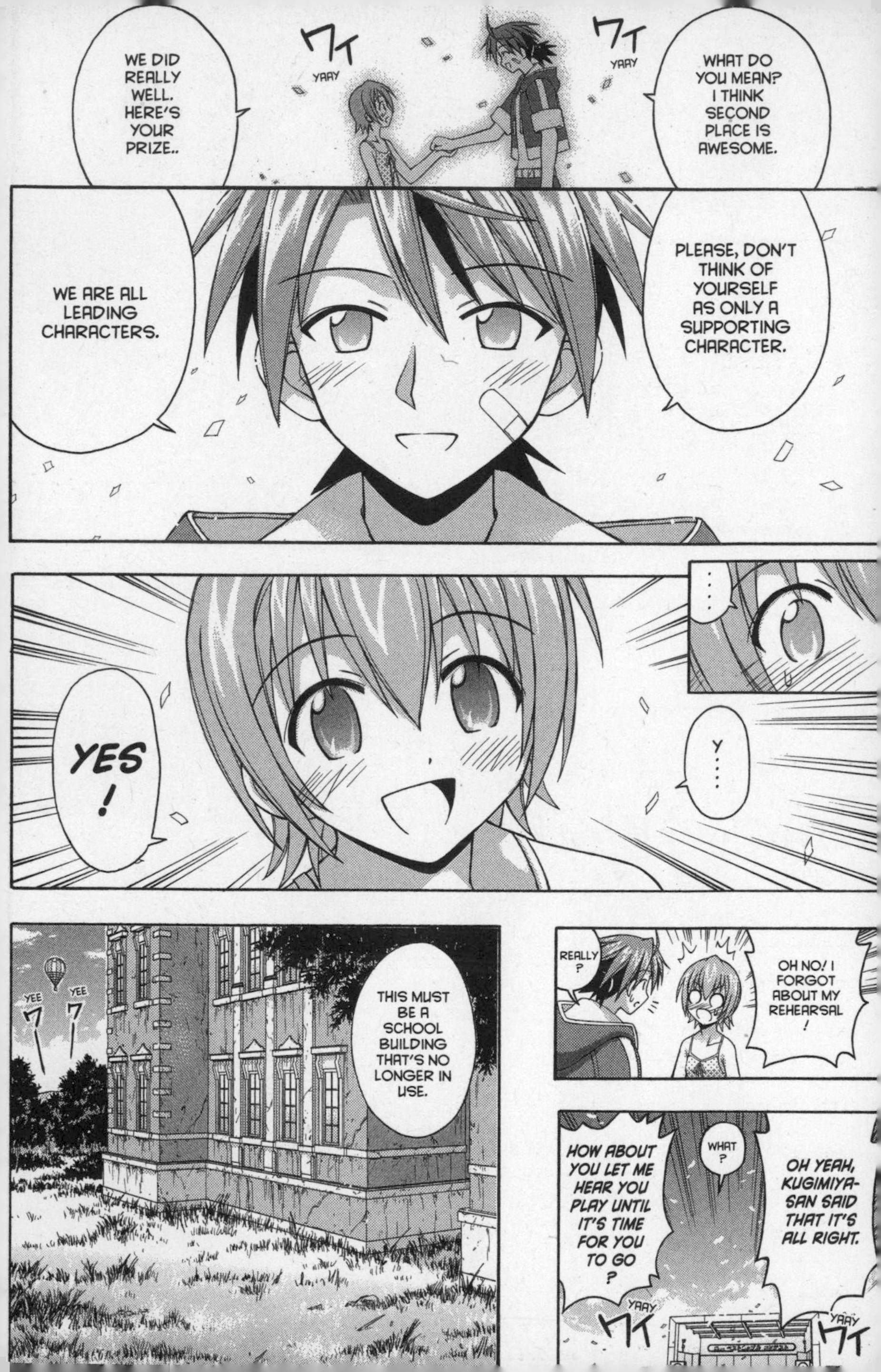
WHAT DO YOU MEAN? I THINK SECOND PLACE IS AWESOME.
ワイ YAAY
ワイ YAAY
WE DID REALLY WELL. HERE'S YOUR PRIZE..
PLEASE, DON'T THINK OF YOURSELF AS ONLY A SUPPORTING CHARACTER.
WE ARE ALL LEADING CHARACTERS.
....
Y.....
YES!
OH NO! I FORGOT ABOUT MY REHEARSAL!
REALLY?
OH YEAH, KUGIMIYA-SAN SAID THAT IT'S ALL RIGHT.
WHAT?
HOW ABOUT YOU LET ME HEAR YOU PLAY UNTIL IT'S TIME FOR YOU TO GO?
YAAY
YAAY
THIS MUST BE A SCHOOL BUILDING THAT'S NO LONGER IN USE.
YEE
YEE

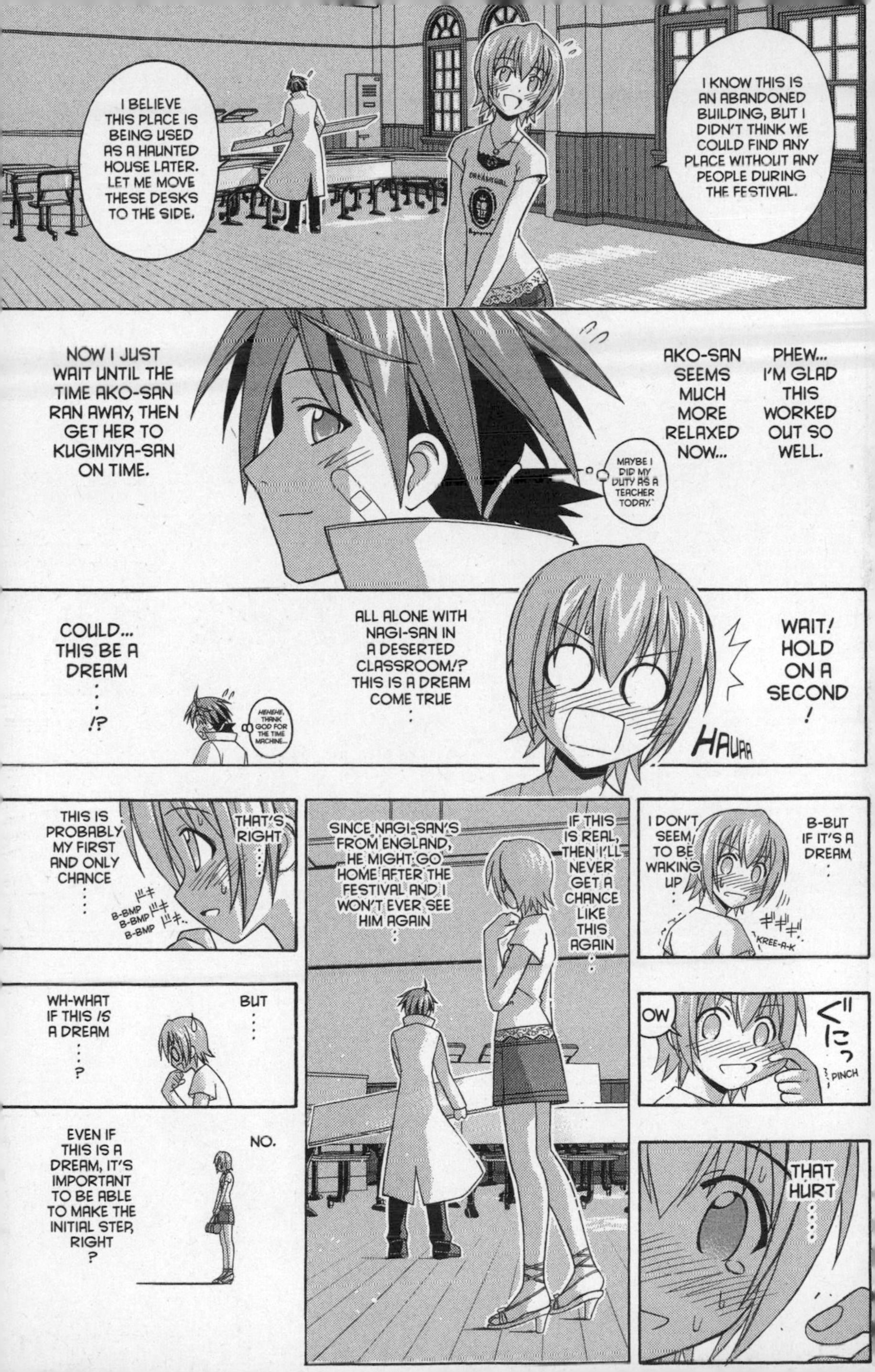
I KNOW THIS IS AN ABANDONED BUILDING, BUT I DIDN'T THINK WE COULD FIND ANY PLACE WITHOUT ANY PEOPLE DURING THE FESTIVAL.
I BELIEVE THIS PLACE IS BEING USED AS A HAUNTED HOUSE LATER. LET ME MOVE THESE DESKS TO THE SIDE.
PHEW... I'M GLAD THIS WORKED OUT SO WELL.
AKO-SAN SEEMS MUCH MORE RELAXED NOW...
MAYBE I DID MY DUTY AS A TEACHER TODAY.
NOW I JUST WAIT UNTIL THE TIME AKO-SAN RAN AWAY, THEN GET HER TO KUGIMIYA-SAN ON TIME.
WAIT! HOLD ON A SECOND!
HAURA
ALL ALONE WITH NAGI-SAN IN A DESERTED CLASSROOM!? THIS IS A DREAM COME TRUE...
HEHEHE, THANK GOD FOR THE TIME MACHINE...
COULD... THIS BE A DREAM...!?
B-BUT IF IT'S A DREAM...
I DON'T SEEM TO BE WAKING UP...
ギギギ
KREE-A-K
OW
ぐにっ
PINCH
THAT HURT....
IF THIS IS REAL, THEN I'LL NEVER GET A CHANCE LIKE THIS AGAIN...
SINCE NAGI-SAN'S FROM ENGLAND, HE MIGHT GO HOME AFTER THE FESTIVAL AND I WON'T EVER SEE HIM AGAIN...
THAT'S RIGHT...
THIS IS PROBABLY MY FIRST AND ONLY CHANCE...
ドキ B-BMP ドキ B-BMP ドキ.. B-BMP
BUT...
WH-WHAT IF THIS IS A DREAM...?
NO.
EVEN IF THIS IS A DREAM, IT'S IMPORTANT TO BE ABLE TO MAKE THE INITIAL STEP, RIGHT?

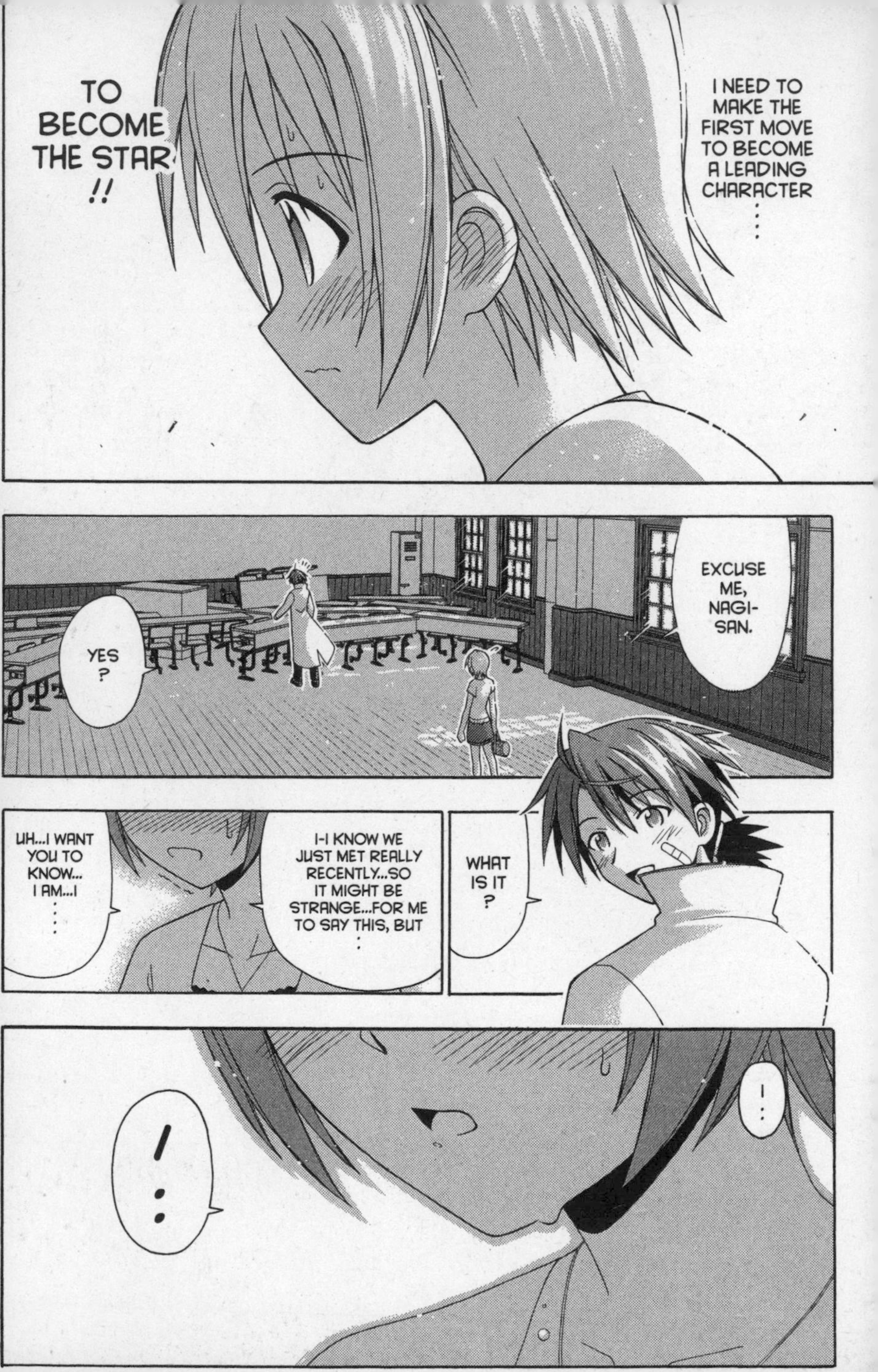
I NEED TO MAKE THE FIRST MOVE TO BECOME A LEADING CHARACTER . . .
TO BECOME THE STAR !!
EXCUSE ME, NAGI-SAN.
YES ?
WHAT IS IT ?
I-I KNOW WE JUST MET REALLY RECENTLY...SO IT MIGHT BE STRANGE...FOR ME TO SAY THIS, BUT :
UH...I WANT YOU TO KNOW... I AM...I . . .
! . .
! . .

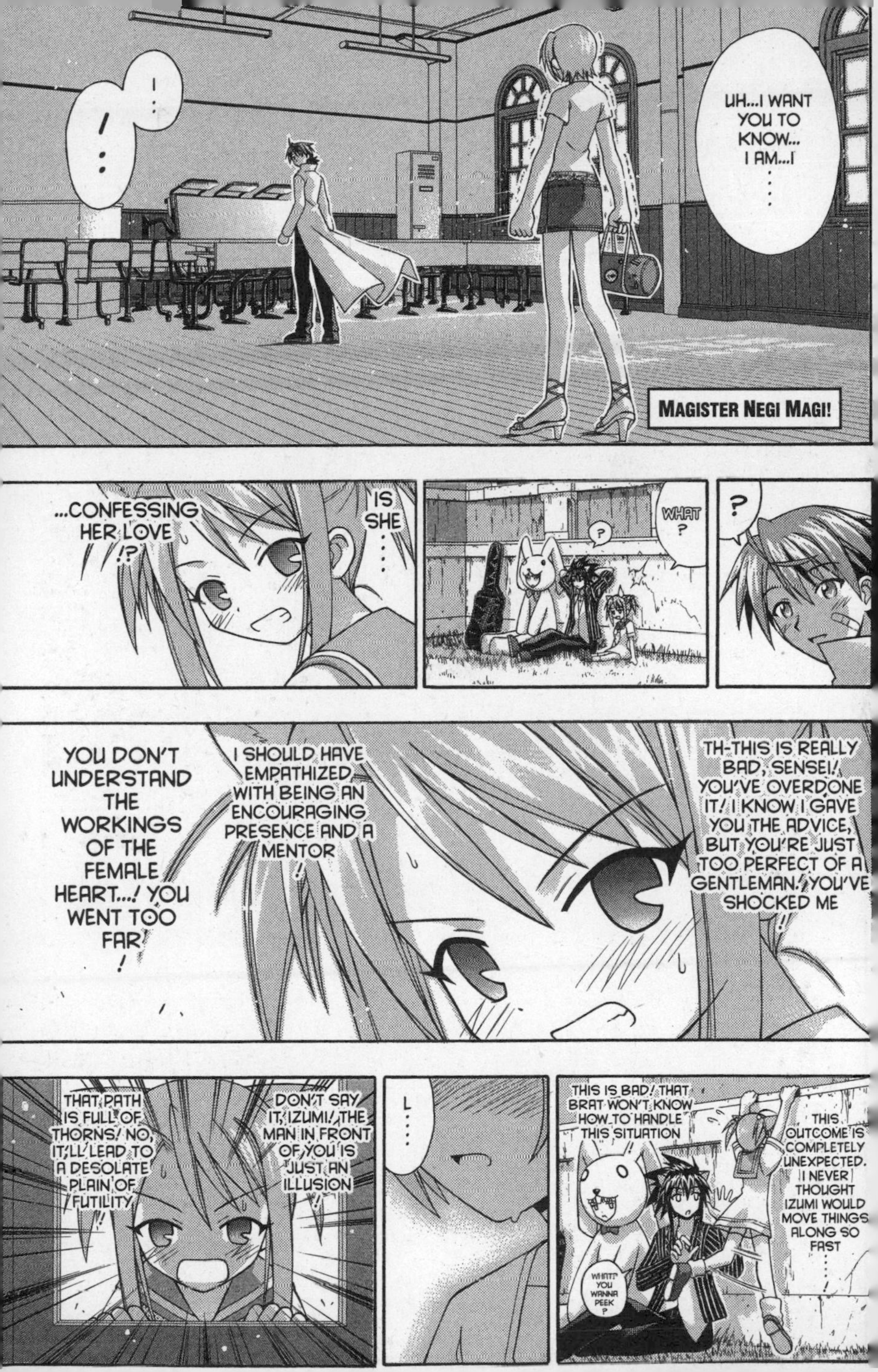
UH...I WANT YOU TO KNOW... I AM...I ....
!...!...
MAGISTER NEGI MAGI!
?
WHAT ?
?
IS SHE ....
...CONFESSING HER LOVE !?
TH-THIS IS REALLY BAD, SENSEI! YOU'VE OVERDONE IT! I KNOW I GAVE YOU THE ADVICE, BUT YOU'RE JUST TOO PERFECT OF A GENTLEMAN! YOU'VE SHOCKED ME !!
I SHOULD HAVE EMPATHIZED WITH BEING AN ENCOURAGING PRESENCE AND A MENTOR !
YOU DON'T UNDERSTAND THE WORKINGS OF THE FEMALE HEART...! YOU WENT TOO FAR !!
THIS OUTCOME IS COMPLETELY UNEXPECTED. I NEVER THOUGHT IZUMI WOULD MOVE THINGS ALONG SO FAST ....!
THIS IS BAD! THAT BRAT WON'T KNOW HOW TO HANDLE THIS SITUATION !
WHAT? YOU WANNA PEEK ?
L.....
DON'T SAY IT, IZUMI! THE MAN IN FRONT OF YOU IS JUST AN ILLUSION !
THAT PATH IS FULL OF THORNS! NO, IT'LL LEAD TO A DESOLATE PLAIN OF FUTILITY !

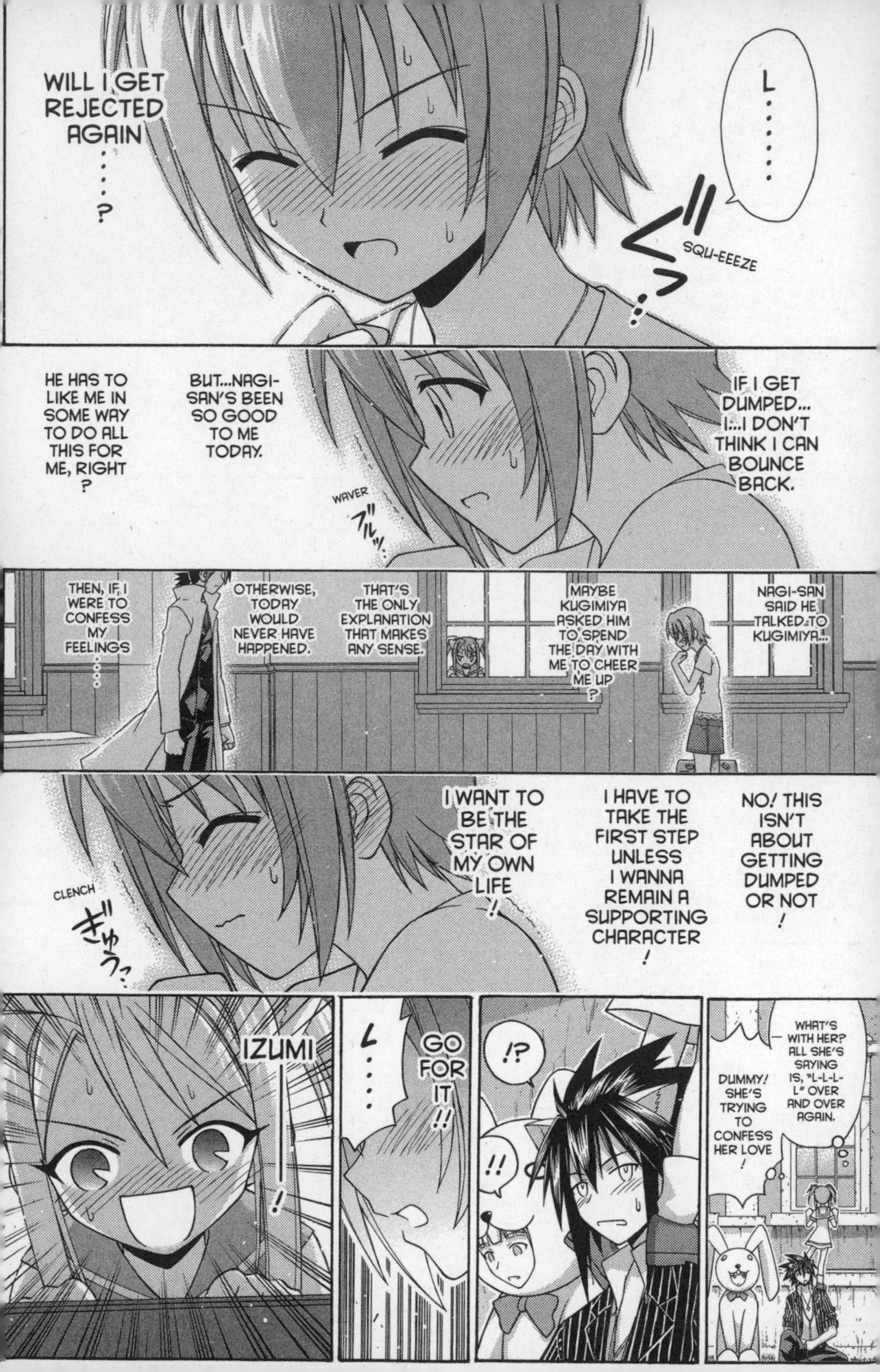

L......
SQU-EEEZE
WILL I GET REJECTED AGAIN....?
IF I GET DUMPED... I...I DON'T THINK I CAN BOUNCE BACK.
WAVER
BUT...NAGI-SAN'S BEEN SO GOOD TO ME TODAY.
HE HAS TO LIKE ME IN SOME WAY TO DO ALL THIS FOR ME, RIGHT?
NAGI-SAN SAID HE TALKED TO KUGIMIYA...
MAYBE KUGIMIYA ASKED HIM TO SPEND THE DAY WITH ME TO CHEER ME UP?
THAT'S THE ONLY EXPLANATION THAT MAKES ANY SENSE.
OTHERWISE, TODAY WOULD NEVER HAVE HAPPENED.
THEN, IF I WERE TO CONFESS MY FEELINGS....
NO! THIS ISN'T ABOUT GETTING DUMPED OR NOT!
I HAVE TO TAKE THE FIRST STEP UNLESS I WANNA REMAIN A SUPPORTING CHARACTER!
I WANT TO BE THE STAR OF MY OWN LIFE!
CLENCH
WHAT'S WITH HER? ALL SHE'S SAYING IS, "L-L-L-L" OVER AND OVER AGAIN.
DUMMY! SHE'S TRYING TO CONFESS HER LOVE!
!?
!!
GO FOR IT!!
L....
IZUMI—!

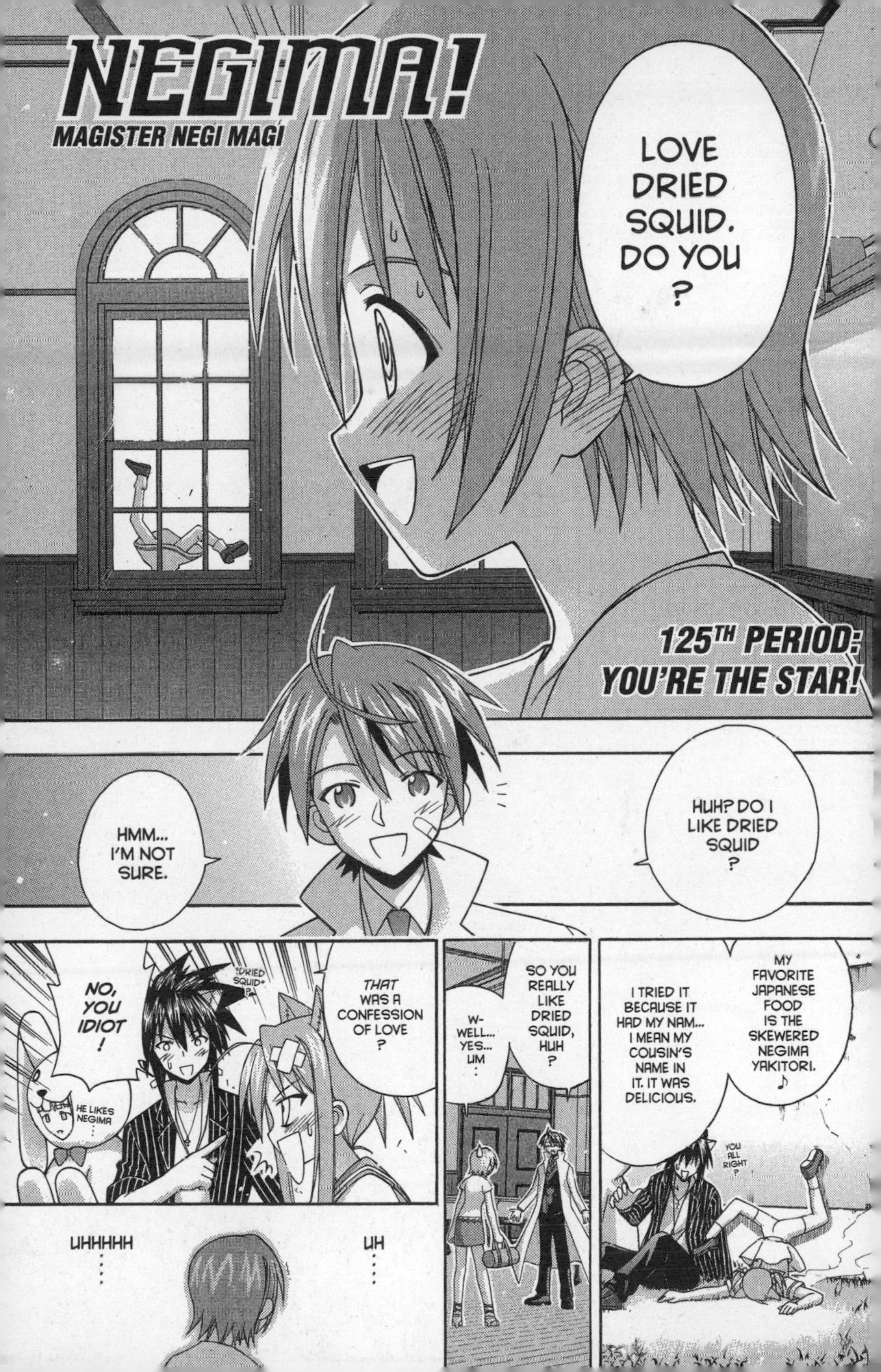
LOVE DRIED SQUID. DO YOU ?
NEGIMA!
MAGISTER NEGI MAGI
125TH PERIOD: YOU'RE THE STAR!
HUH? DO I LIKE DRIED SQUID ?
HMM... I'M NOT SURE.
MY FAVORITE JAPANESE FOOD IS THE SKEWERED NEGIMA YAKITORI. ♪
I TRIED IT BECAUSE IT HAD MY NAM... I MEAN MY COUSIN'S NAME IN IT. IT WAS DELICIOUS.
YOU ALL RIGHT ?
SO YOU REALLY LIKE DRIED SQUID, HUH ?
W-WELL... YES... UM :
THAT WAS A CONFESSION OF LOVE ?
"DRIED SQUID" ?!
NO, YOU IDIOT !
HE LIKES NEGIMA ...
UH ...
UHHHHH ...

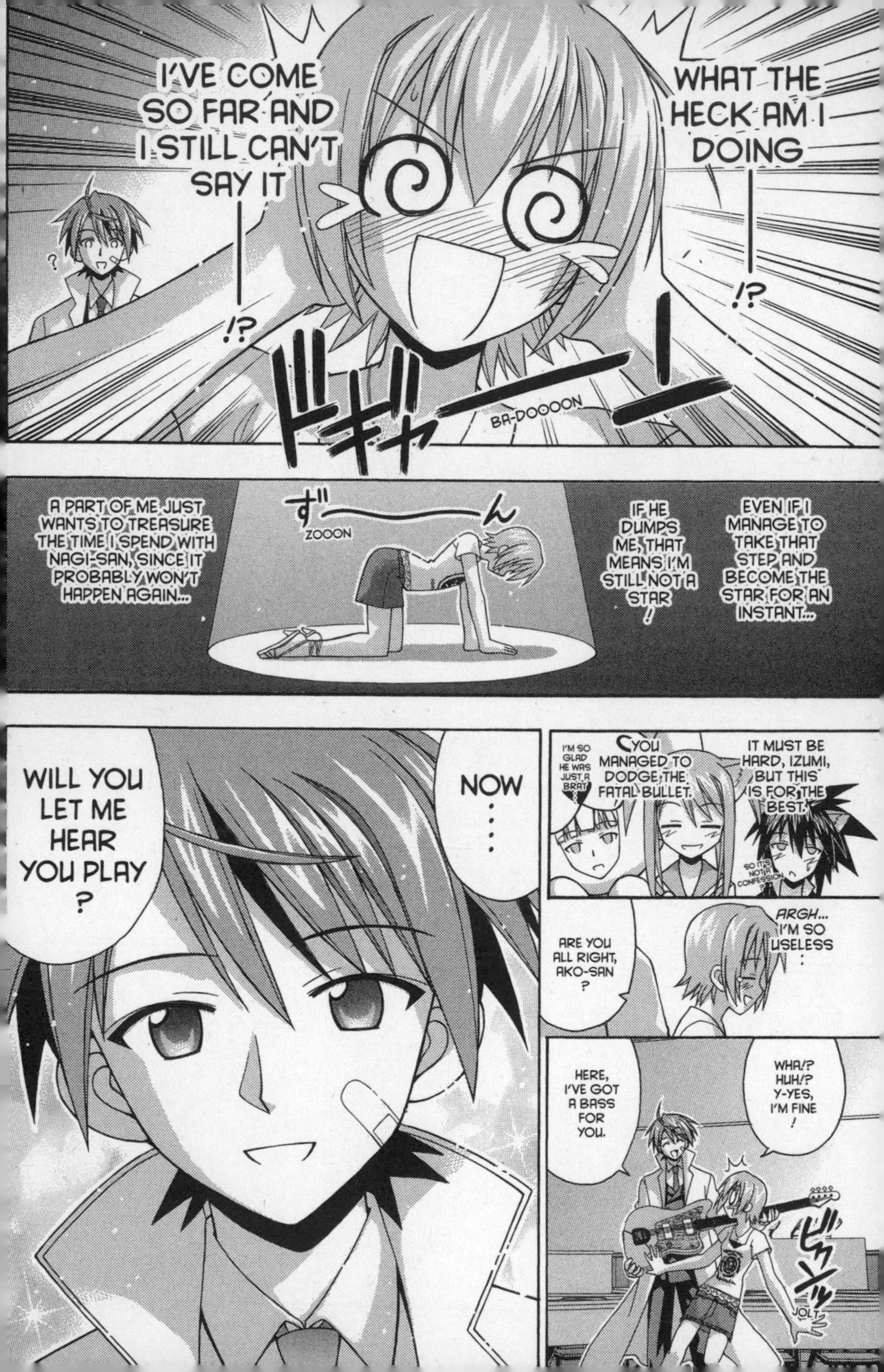
WHAT THE HECK AM I DOING !?
I'VE COME SO FAR AND I STILL CAN'T SAY IT !?
ドギャーー
BA-DOOOON
EVEN IF I MANAGE TO TAKE THAT STEP AND BECOME THE STAR FOR AN INSTANT...
IF HE DUMPS ME, THAT MEANS I'M STILL NOT A STAR !
ずーーん
ZOOON
A PART OF ME JUST WANTS TO TREASURE THE TIME I SPEND WITH NAGI-SAN, SINCE IT PROBABLY WON'T HAPPEN AGAIN...
IT MUST BE HARD, IZUMI, BUT THIS IS FOR THE BEST.
SO IT'S NOT A CONFESSION ?
YOU MANAGED TO DODGE THE FATAL BULLET.
I'M SO GLAD HE WAS JUST A BRAT
ARGH... I'M SO USELESS :
ARE YOU ALL RIGHT, AKO-SAN ?
WHA!? HUH!? Y-YES, I'M FINE !
JOLT
HERE, I'VE GOT A BASS FOR YOU.
NOW ....
WILL YOU LET ME HEAR YOU PLAY ?

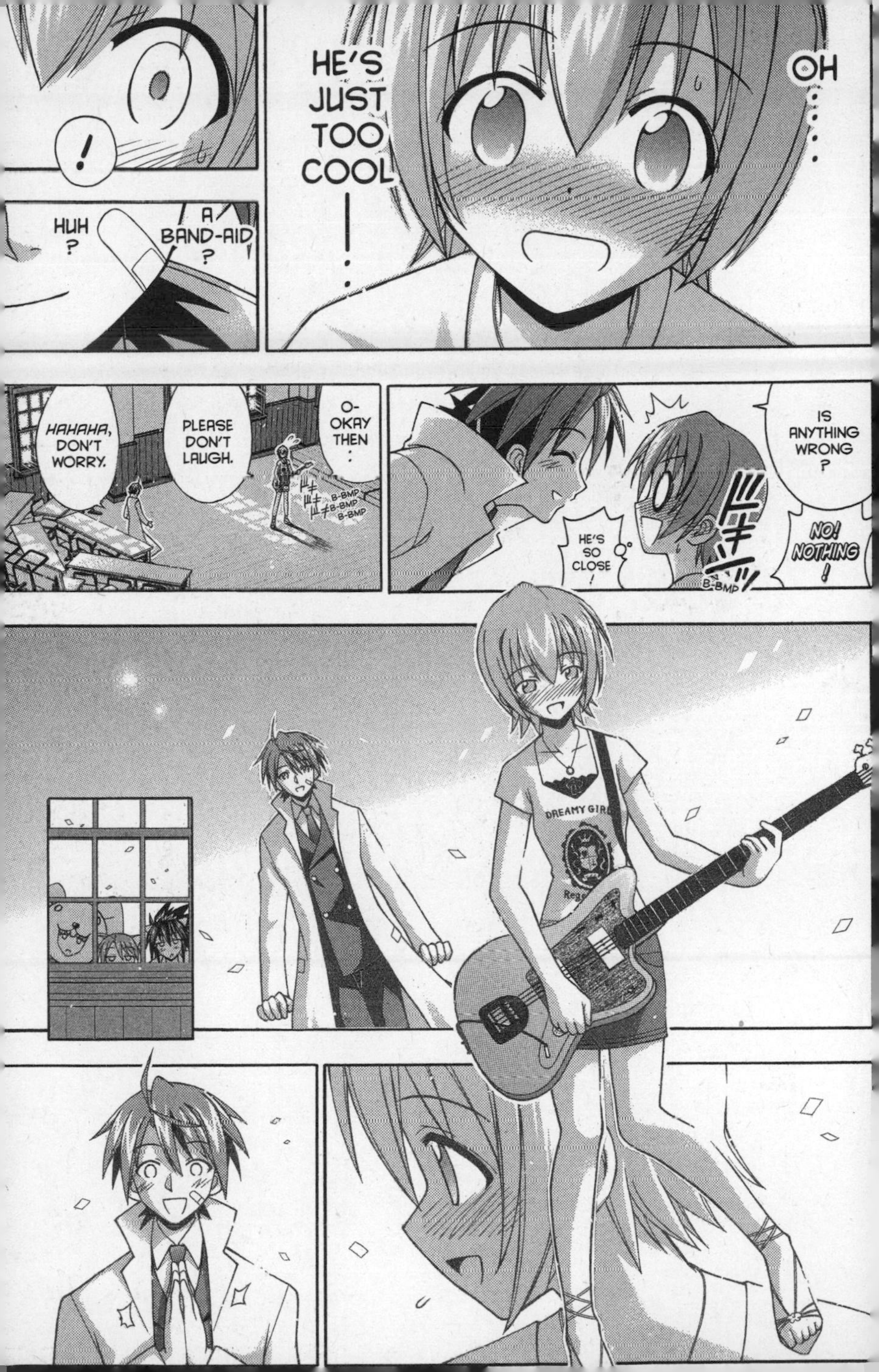
OH......
HE'S JUST TOO COOL!......
!
A BAND-AID?
HUH?
IS ANYTHING WRONG?
NO! NOTHING!
HE'S SO CLOSE!
B-BMP
O-OKAY THEN:
B-BMP B-BMP B-BMP
PLEASE DON'T LAUGH.
HAHAHA, DON'T WORRY.

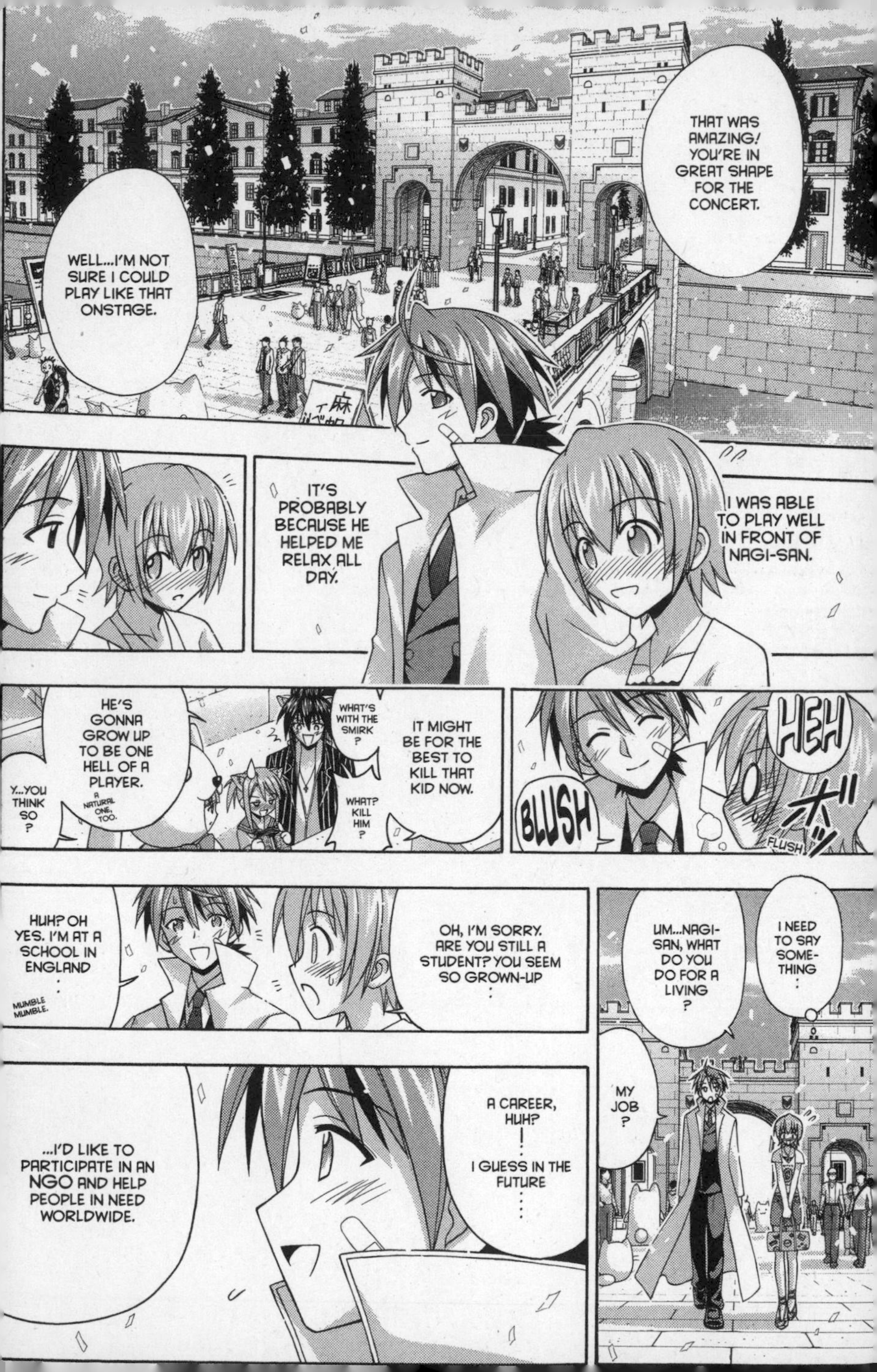
THAT WAS AMAZING! YOU'RE IN GREAT SHAPE FOR THE CONCERT.
WELL...I'M NOT SURE I COULD PLAY LIKE THAT ONSTAGE.
I WAS ABLE TO PLAY WELL IN FRONT OF NAGI-SAN.
IT'S PROBABLY BECAUSE HE HELPED ME RELAX ALL DAY.
HEH
FLUSH
BLUSH
IT MIGHT BE FOR THE BEST TO KILL THAT KID NOW.
WHAT'S WITH THE SMIRK?
WHAT? KILL HIM?
HE'S GONNA GROW UP TO BE ONE HELL OF A PLAYER.
A NATURAL ONE, TOO.
Y...YOU THINK SO?
I NEED TO SAY SOME-THING...
UM...NAGI-SAN, WHAT DO YOU DO FOR A LIVING?
MY JOB?
OH, I'M SORRY. ARE YOU STILL A STUDENT? YOU SEEM SO GROWN-UP...
HUH? OH YES. I'M AT A SCHOOL IN ENGLAND...
MUMBLE MUMBLE.
A CAREER, HUH? ! I GUESS IN THE FUTURE....
...I'D LIKE TO PARTICIPATE IN AN NGO AND HELP PEOPLE IN NEED WORLDWIDE.

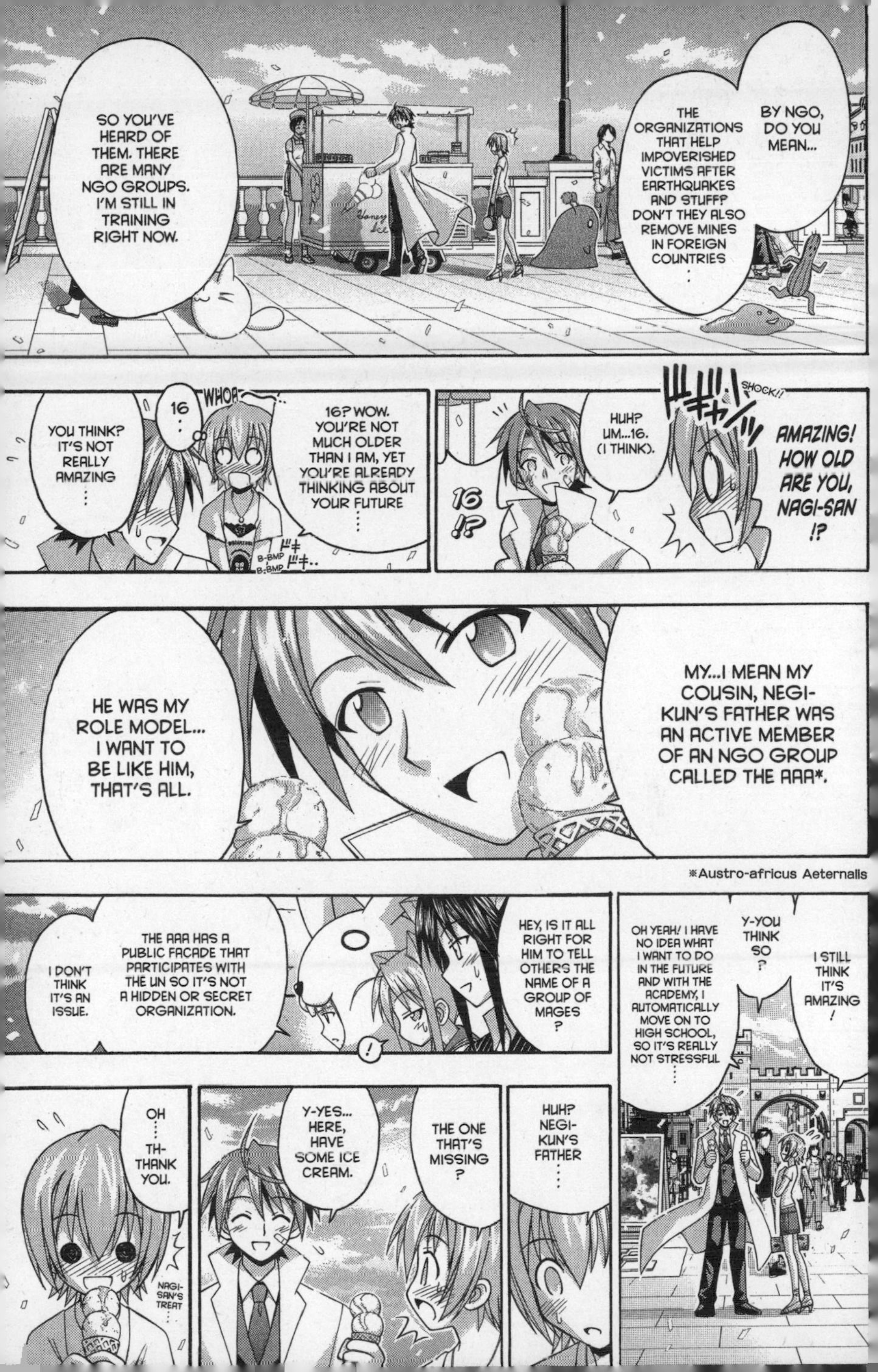
BY NGO, DO YOU MEAN...
THE ORGANIZATIONS THAT HELP IMPOVERISHED VICTIMS AFTER EARTHQUAKES AND STUFF? DON'T THEY ALSO REMOVE MINES IN FOREIGN COUNTRIES...
SO YOU'VE HEARD OF THEM. THERE ARE MANY NGO GROUPS. I'M STILL IN TRAINING RIGHT NOW.
AMAZING! HOW OLD ARE YOU, NAGI-SAN!?
SHOCK!!
HUH? UM...16. (I THINK).
16!?
16? WOW. YOU'RE NOT MUCH OLDER THAN I AM, YET YOU'RE ALREADY THINKING ABOUT YOUR FUTURE...
WHOA
16...
B-BMP B-BMP
YOU THINK? IT'S NOT REALLY AMAZING...
MY...I MEAN MY COUSIN, NEGI-KUN'S FATHER WAS AN ACTIVE MEMBER OF AN NGO GROUP CALLED THE AAA*.
HE WAS MY ROLE MODEL... I WANT TO BE LIKE HIM, THAT'S ALL.
*Austro-africus Aeternalis
I STILL THINK IT'S AMAZING!
Y-YOU THINK SO?
OH YEAH! I HAVE NO IDEA WHAT I WANT TO DO IN THE FUTURE AND WITH THE ACADEMY, I AUTOMATICALLY MOVE ON TO HIGH SCHOOL, SO IT'S REALLY NOT STRESSFUL...
HEY, IS IT ALL RIGHT FOR HIM TO TELL OTHERS THE NAME OF A GROUP OF MAGES?
!
THE AAA HAS A PUBLIC FACADE THAT PARTICIPATES WITH THE UN SO IT'S NOT A HIDDEN OR SECRET ORGANIZATION.
I DON'T THINK IT'S AN ISSUE.
HUH? NEGI-KUN'S FATHER...
THE ONE THAT'S MISSING?
Y-YES... HERE, HAVE SOME ICE CREAM.
OH... TH-THANK YOU.
NAGI-SAN'S TREAT...

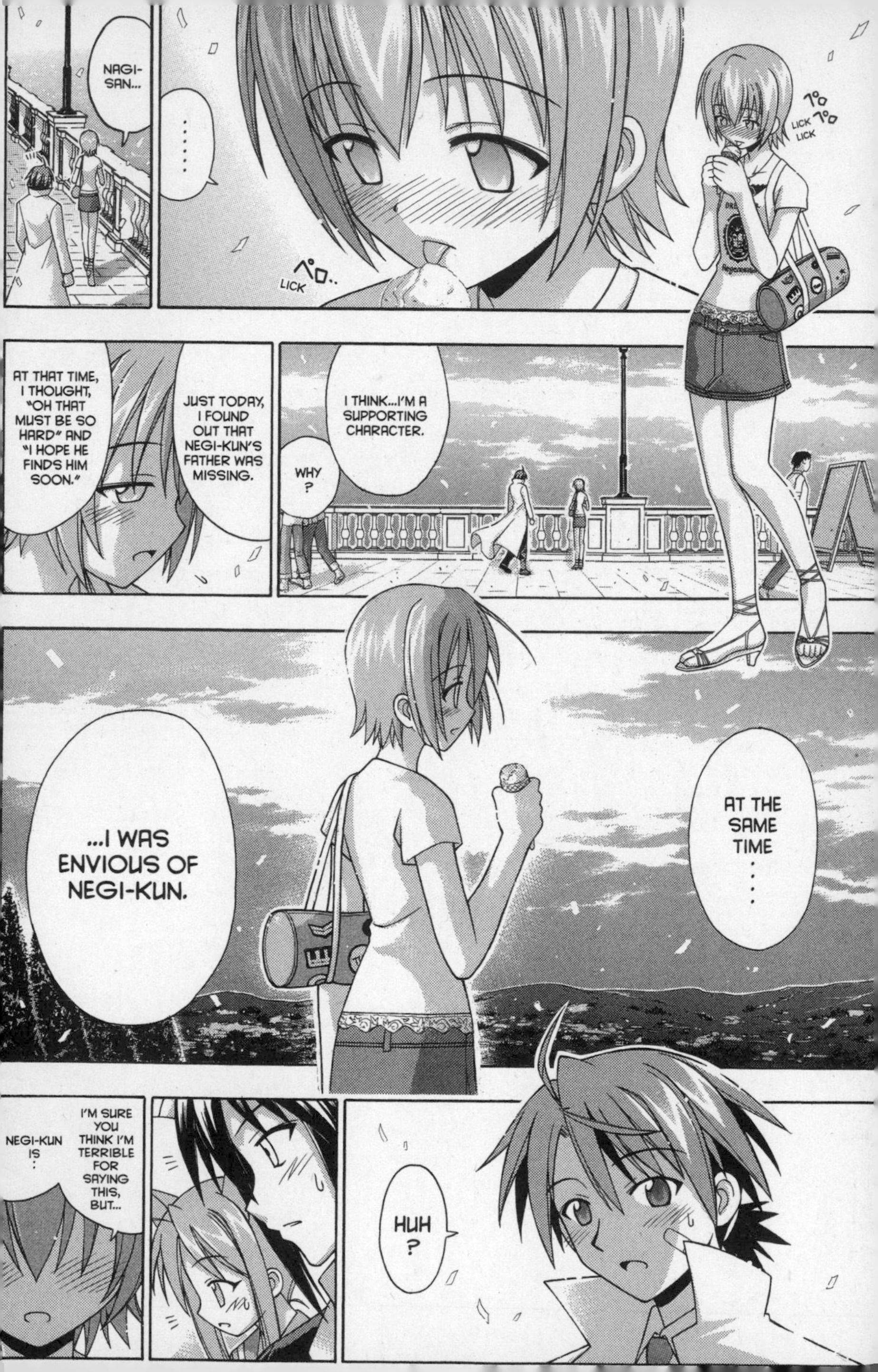

ペロ LICK ペロ LICK
......
ペロ..
LICK
NAGI-SAN...
I THINK...I'M A SUPPORTING CHARACTER.
WHY?
JUST TODAY, I FOUND OUT THAT NEGI-KUN'S FATHER WAS MISSING.
AT THAT TIME, I THOUGHT, "OH THAT MUST BE SO HARD" AND "I HOPE HE FINDS HIM SOON."
AT THE SAME TIME....
...I WAS ENVIOUS OF NEGI-KUN.
HUH?
I'M SURE YOU THINK I'M TERRIBLE FOR SAYING THIS, BUT...
NEGI-KUN IS:

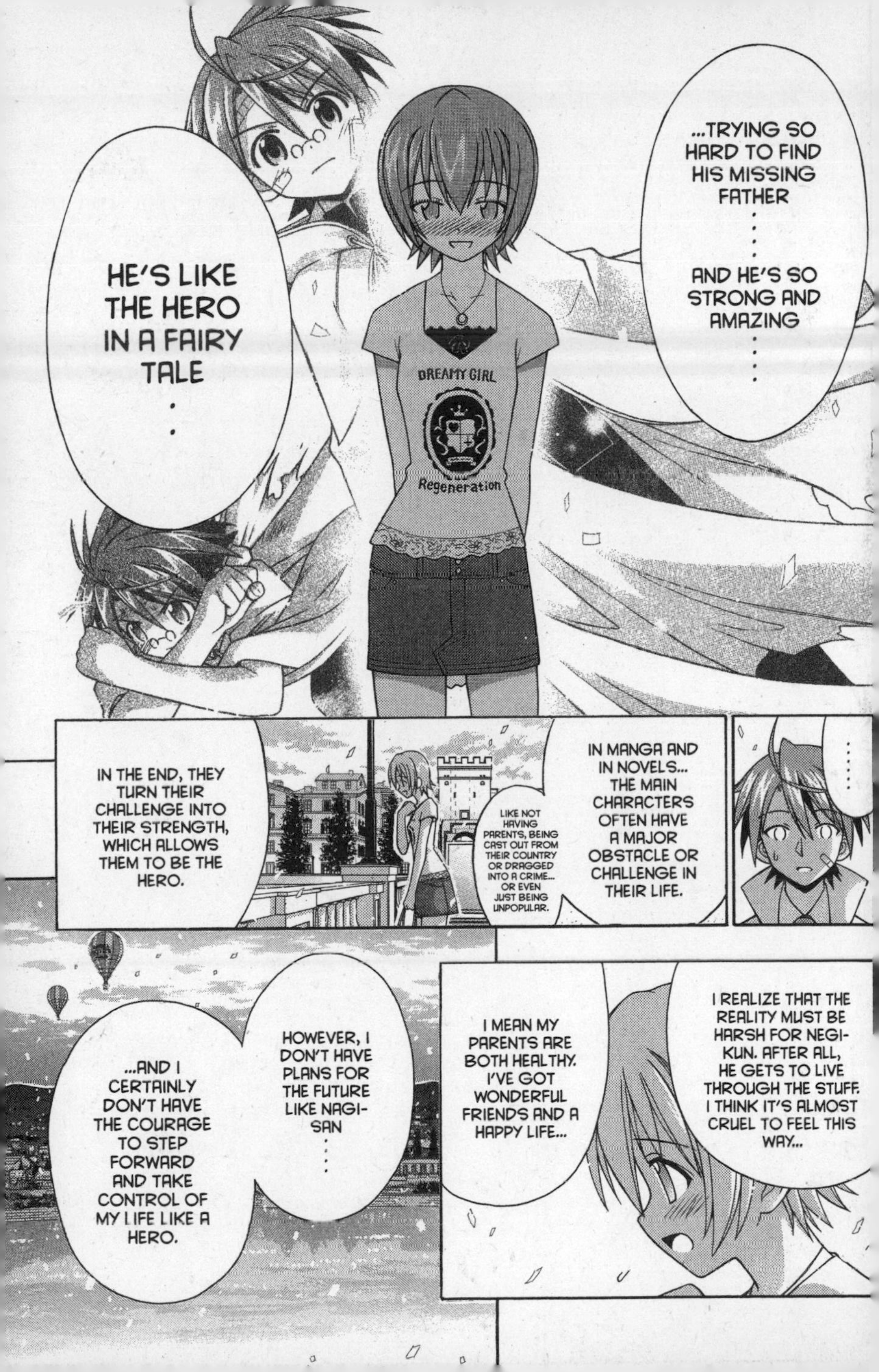
...TRYING SO HARD TO FIND HIS MISSING FATHER ...... AND HE'S SO STRONG AND AMAZING ......
HE'S LIKE THE HERO IN A FAIRY TALE ..
......
IN MANGA AND IN NOVELS... THE MAIN CHARACTERS OFTEN HAVE A MAJOR OBSTACLE OR CHALLENGE IN THEIR LIFE.
LIKE NOT HAVING PARENTS, BEING CAST OUT FROM THEIR COUNTRY OR DRAGGED INTO A CRIME... OR EVEN JUST BEING UNPOPULAR.
IN THE END, THEY TURN THEIR CHALLENGE INTO THEIR STRENGTH, WHICH ALLOWS THEM TO BE THE HERO.
I REALIZE THAT THE REALITY MUST BE HARSH FOR NEGI-KUN. AFTER ALL, HE GETS TO LIVE THROUGH THE STUFF. I THINK IT'S ALMOST CRUEL TO FEEL THIS WAY...
I MEAN MY PARENTS ARE BOTH HEALTHY. I'VE GOT WONDERFUL FRIENDS AND A HAPPY LIFE...
HOWEVER, I DON'T HAVE PLANS FOR THE FUTURE LIKE NAGI-SAN ....
...AND I CERTAINLY DON'T HAVE THE COURAGE TO STEP FORWARD AND TAKE CONTROL OF MY LIFE LIKE A HERO.

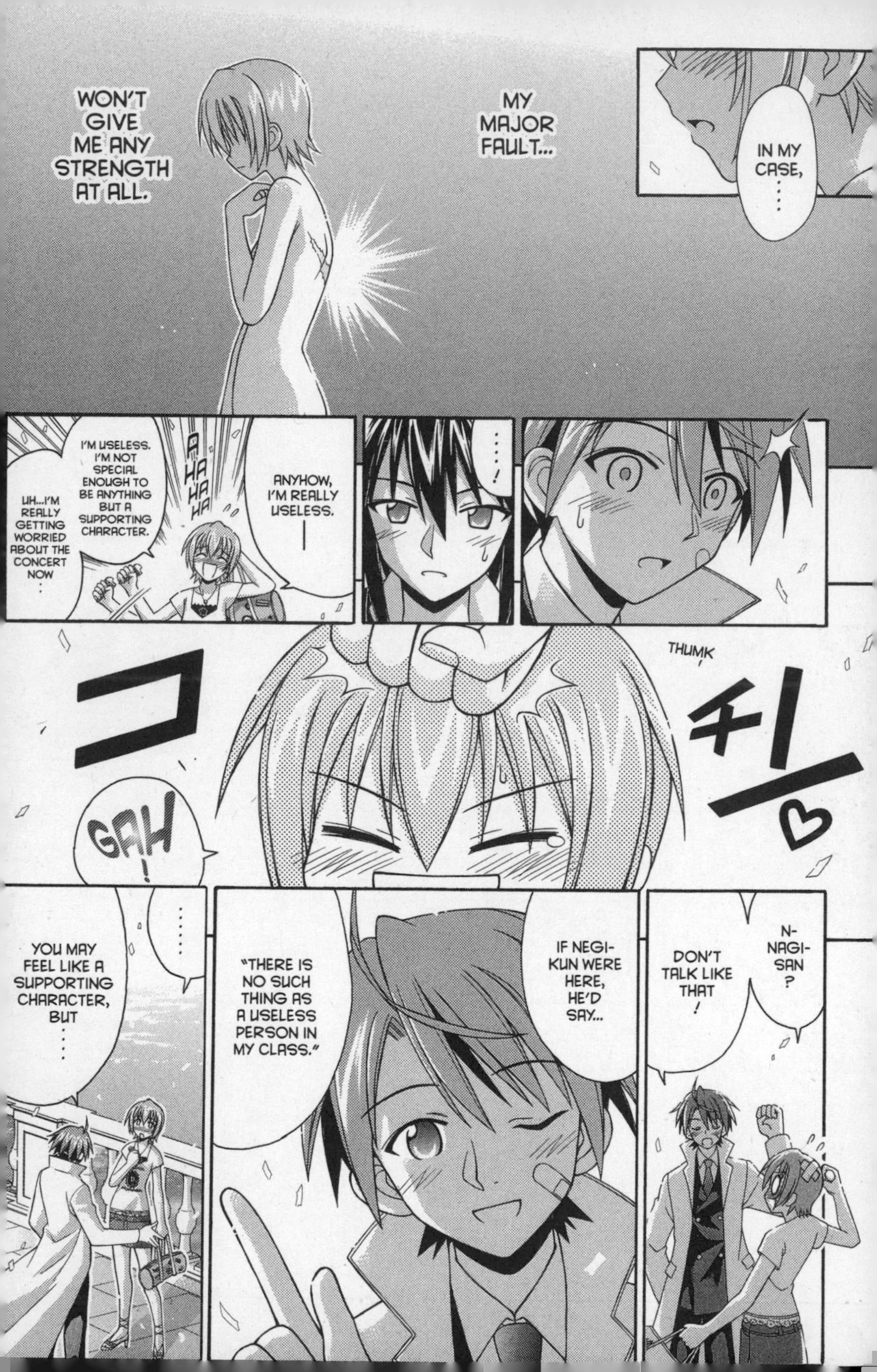
IN MY CASE, ...
MY MAJOR FAULT...
WON'T GIVE ME ANY STRENGTH AT ALL.
...!
ANYHOW, I'M REALLY USELESS.
A HA HA HA
I'M USELESS. I'M NOT SPECIAL ENOUGH TO BE ANYTHING BUT A SUPPORTING CHARACTER.
UH...I'M REALLY GETTING WORRIED ABOUT THE CONCERT NOW...
THUMK
コ
チン
GAH!
N-NAGI-SAN?
DON'T TALK LIKE THAT!
IF NEGI-KUN WERE HERE, HE'D SAY...
"THERE IS NO SUCH THING AS A USELESS PERSON IN MY CLASS."
......
YOU MAY FEEL LIKE A SUPPORTING CHARACTER, BUT ...

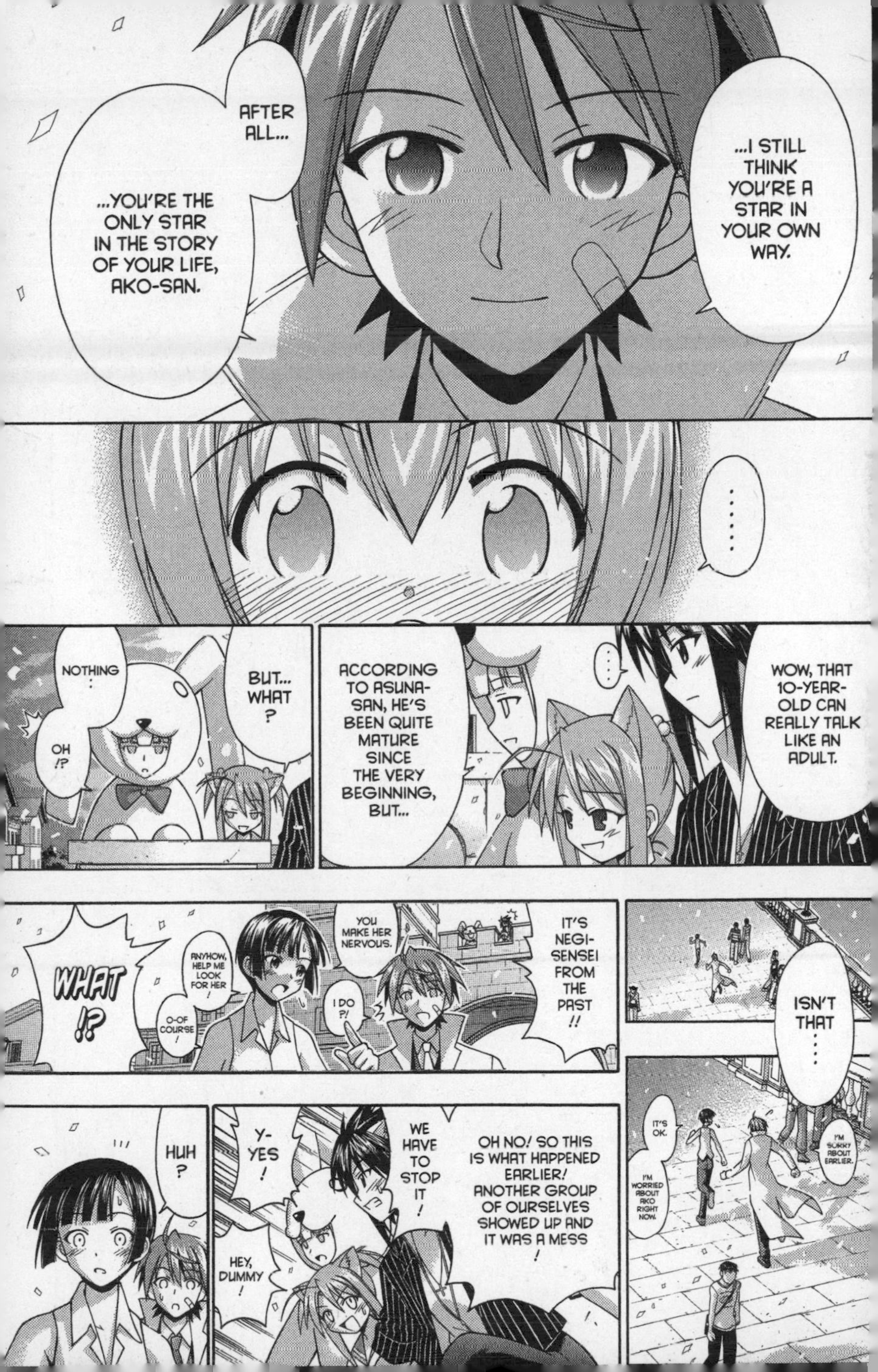
...I STILL THINK YOU'RE A STAR IN YOUR OWN WAY.
AFTER ALL...
...YOU'RE THE ONLY STAR IN THE STORY OF YOUR LIFE, AKO-SAN.
......
WOW, THAT 10-YEAR-OLD CAN REALLY TALK LIKE AN ADULT.
...
ACCORDING TO ASUNA-SAN, HE'S BEEN QUITE MATURE SINCE THE VERY BEGINNING, BUT...
BUT... WHAT?
NOTHING.
OH!?
ISN'T THAT......
IT'S NEGI-SENSEI FROM THE PAST!!
YOU MAKE HER NERVOUS.
I DO?!
ANYHOW, HELP ME LOOK FOR HER!
O-OF COURSE!
WHAT!?
I'M SORRY ABOUT EARLIER.
IT'S OK.
I'M WORRIED ABOUT AKO RIGHT NOW.
OH NO! SO THIS IS WHAT HAPPENED EARLIER! ANOTHER GROUP OF OURSELVES SHOWED UP AND IT WAS A MESS!
WE HAVE TO STOP IT!
Y-YES!
HEY, DUMMY!
HUH?

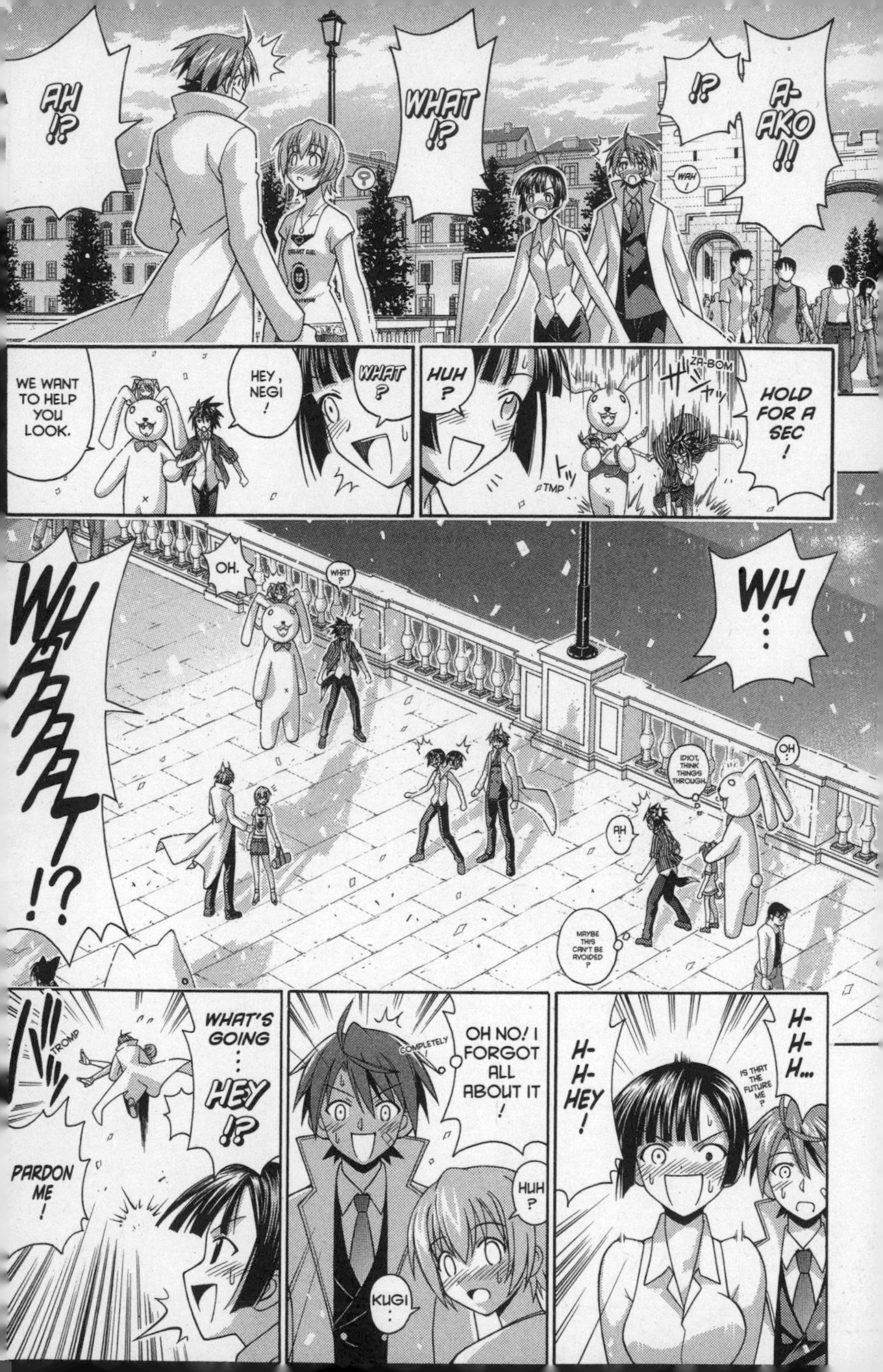
A-AKO!!
!?
WAH!
WHAT!?
?
AH!?
HOLD FOR A SEC!
ZA-BOM
HUH?
TMP
WHAT?
HEY, NEGI!
WE WANT TO HELP YOU LOOK.
WH...
OH...
IDIOT, THINK THINGS THROUGH.
WHAT?
OH.
AH...
MAYBE THIS CAN'T BE AVOIDED?
WHAAAAAT!?
H-H-H...
IS THAT THE FUTURE ME?
H-H-HEY!
COMPLETELY!
OH NO! I FORGOT ALL ABOUT IT!
HUH?
KUGI...
WHAT'S GOING... HEY!?
TROMP
PARDON ME!

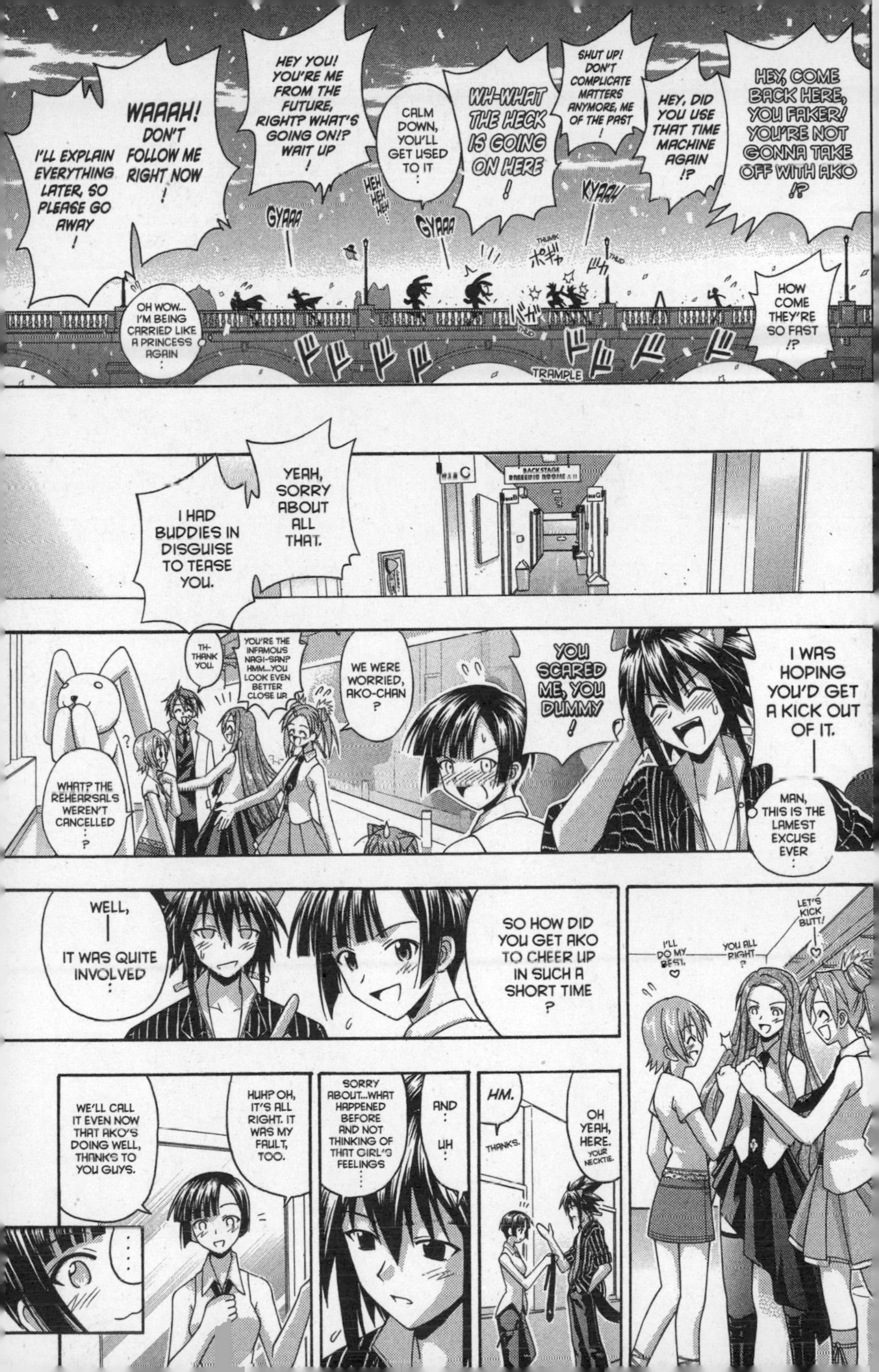
HEY, COME BACK HERE, YOU FAKER! YOU'RE NOT GONNA TAKE OFF WITH AKO!?
HEY, DID YOU USE THAT TIME MACHINE AGAIN!?
SHUT UP! DON'T COMPLICATE MATTERS ANYMORE, ME OF THE PAST!
KYAAA
WH-WHAT THE HECK IS GOING ON HERE!
CALM DOWN, YOU'LL GET USED TO IT...
HEY YOU! YOU'RE ME FROM THE FUTURE, RIGHT? WHAT'S GOING ON!? WAIT UP!
HEH HEH HEH
WAAAH! DON'T FOLLOW ME RIGHT NOW!
I'LL EXPLAIN EVERYTHING LATER, SO PLEASE GO AWAY!
GYAAA
GYAAA
THUNK
THUD
HOW COME THEY'RE SO FAST!?
THUD
TRAMPLE
OH WOW... I'M BEING CARRIED LIKE A PRINCESS AGAIN...
BACKSTAGE
YEAH, SORRY ABOUT ALL THAT.
I HAD BUDDIES IN DISGUISE TO TEASE YOU.
I WAS HOPING YOU'D GET A KICK OUT OF IT.
MAN, THIS IS THE LAMEST EXCUSE EVER...
YOU SCARED ME, YOU DUMMY!
WE WERE WORRIED, AKO-CHAN?
YOU'RE THE INFAMOUS NAGI-SAN? HMM...YOU LOOK EVEN BETTER CLOSE UP.
TH-THANK YOU.
WHAT? THE REHEARSALS WEREN'T CANCELLED...?
LET'S KICK BUTT!
YOU ALL RIGHT?
I'LL DO MY BEST.
SO HOW DID YOU GET AKO TO CHEER UP IN SUCH A SHORT TIME?
WELL, IT WAS QUITE INVOLVED...
HM.
OH YEAH, HERE. YOUR NECKTIE.
THANKS.
AND... UH
SORRY ABOUT...WHAT HAPPENED BEFORE AND NOT THINKING OF THAT GIRL'S FEELINGS...
HUH? OH, IT'S ALL RIGHT. IT WAS MY FAULT, TOO.
WE'LL CALL IT EVEN NOW THAT AKO'S DOING WELL, THANKS TO YOU GUYS.
....

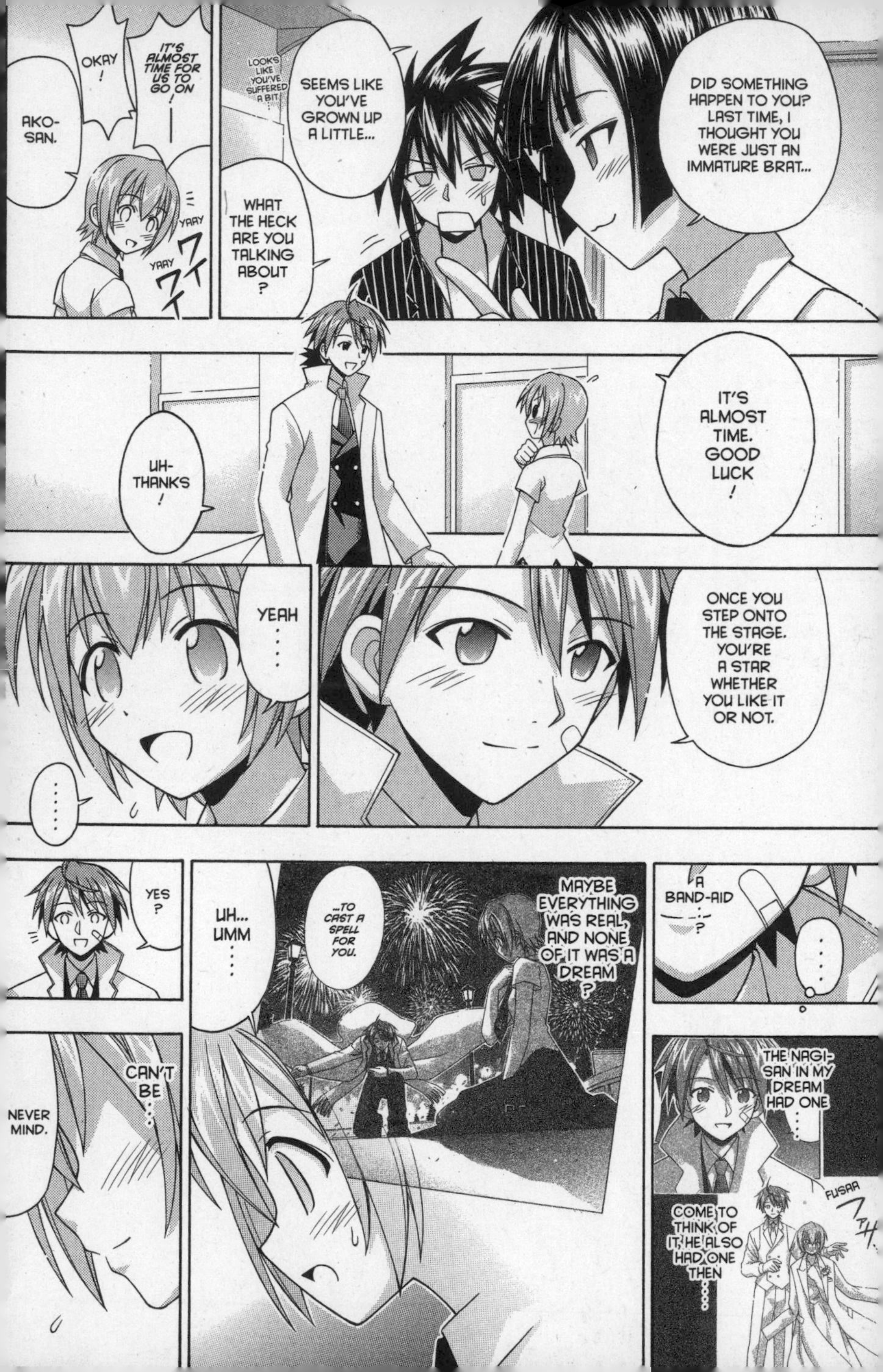
DID SOMETHING HAPPEN TO YOU? LAST TIME, I THOUGHT YOU WERE JUST AN IMMATURE BRAT...
SEEMS LIKE YOU'VE GROWN UP A LITTLE...
LOOKS LIKE YOU'VE SUFFERED A BIT
WHAT THE HECK ARE YOU TALKING ABOUT?
IT'S ALMOST TIME FOR US TO GO ON!
OKAY!
AKO-SAN.
YAAY
YAAY
IT'S ALMOST TIME. GOOD LUCK!
UH-THANKS!
ONCE YOU STEP ONTO THE STAGE. YOU'RE A STAR WHETHER YOU LIKE IT OR NOT.
YEAH....
......
A BAND-AID...?
....
MAYBE EVERYTHING WAS REAL, AND NONE OF IT WAS A DREAM?
...TO CAST A SPELL FOR YOU.
UH... UMM....
YES?
THE NAGI-SAN IN MY DREAM HAD ONE....
FUSAA
COME TO THINK OF IT, HE ALSO HAD ONE THEN......
CAN'T BE....
NEVER MIND.

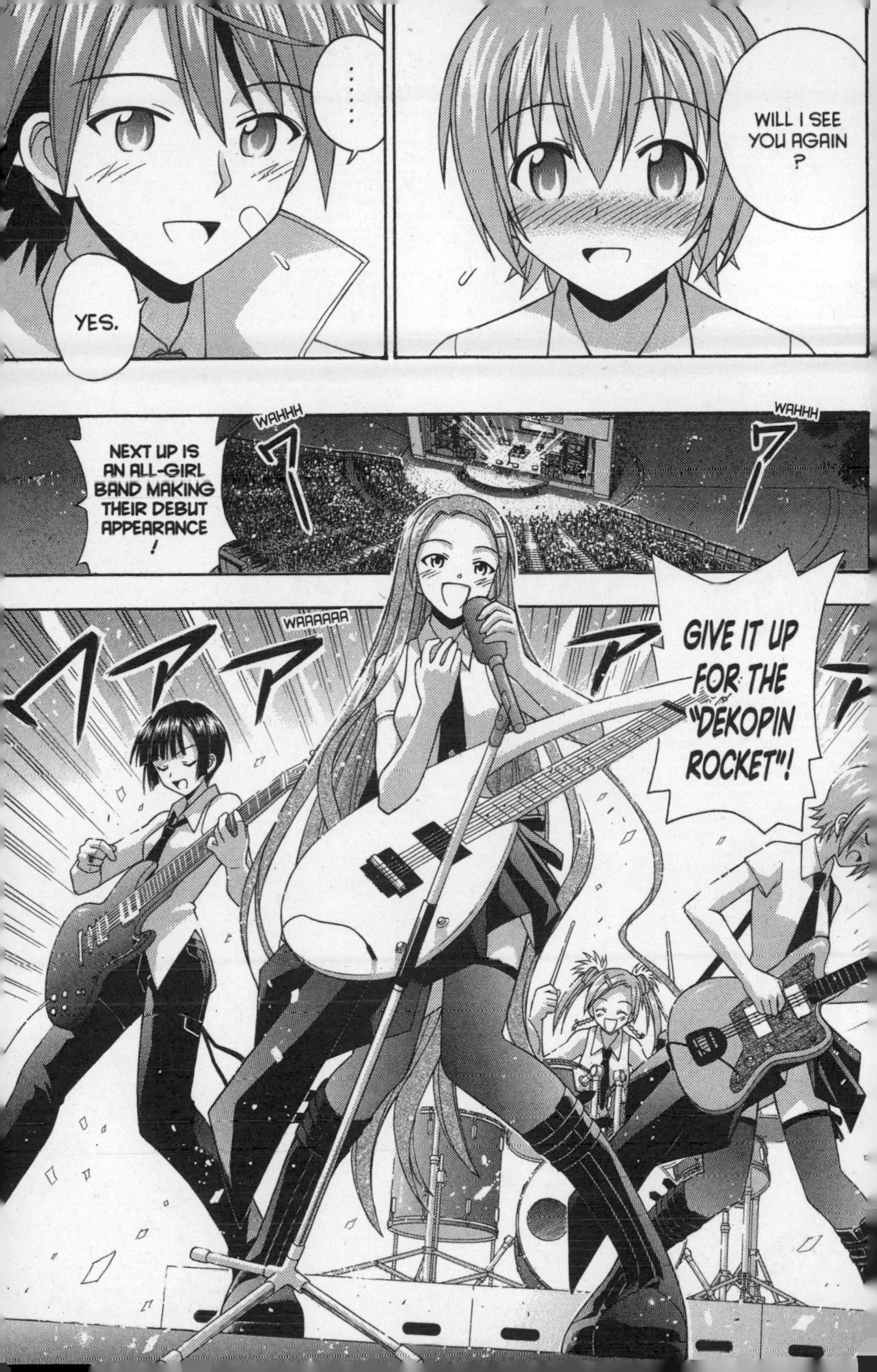
WILL I SEE YOU AGAIN ?
......
YES.
WAHHH
WAHHH
NEXT UP IS AN ALL-GIRL BAND MAKING THEIR DEBUT APPEARANCE !
GIVE IT UP FOR THE "DEKOPIN ROCKET"!
WAAAAAA

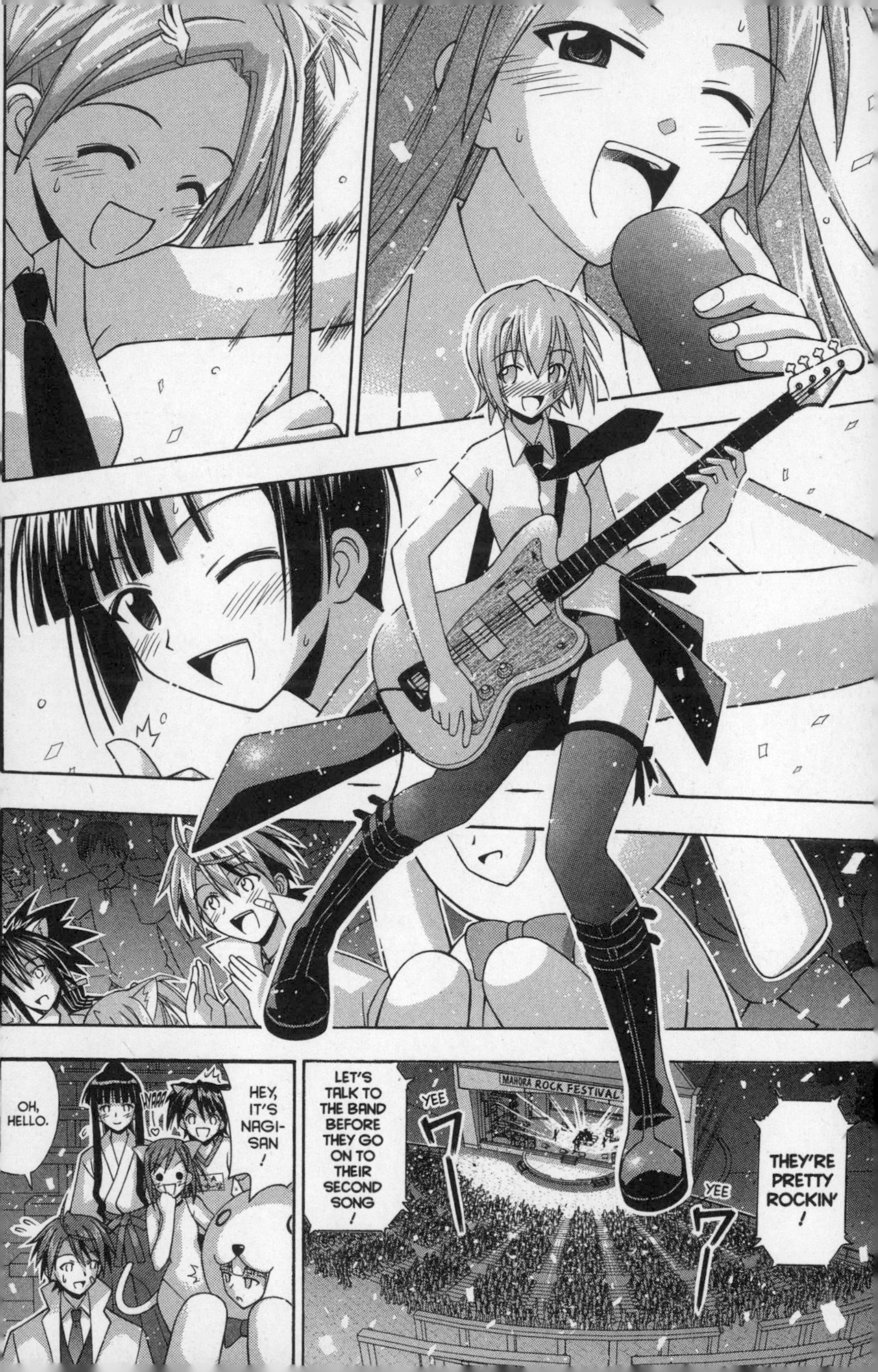
THEY'RE PRETTY ROCKIN'!
YEE
YEE
MAHORA ROCK FESTIVAL
LET'S TALK TO THE BAND BEFORE THEY GO ON TO THEIR SECOND SONG!
HEY, IT'S NAGI-SAN!
OH, HELLO.

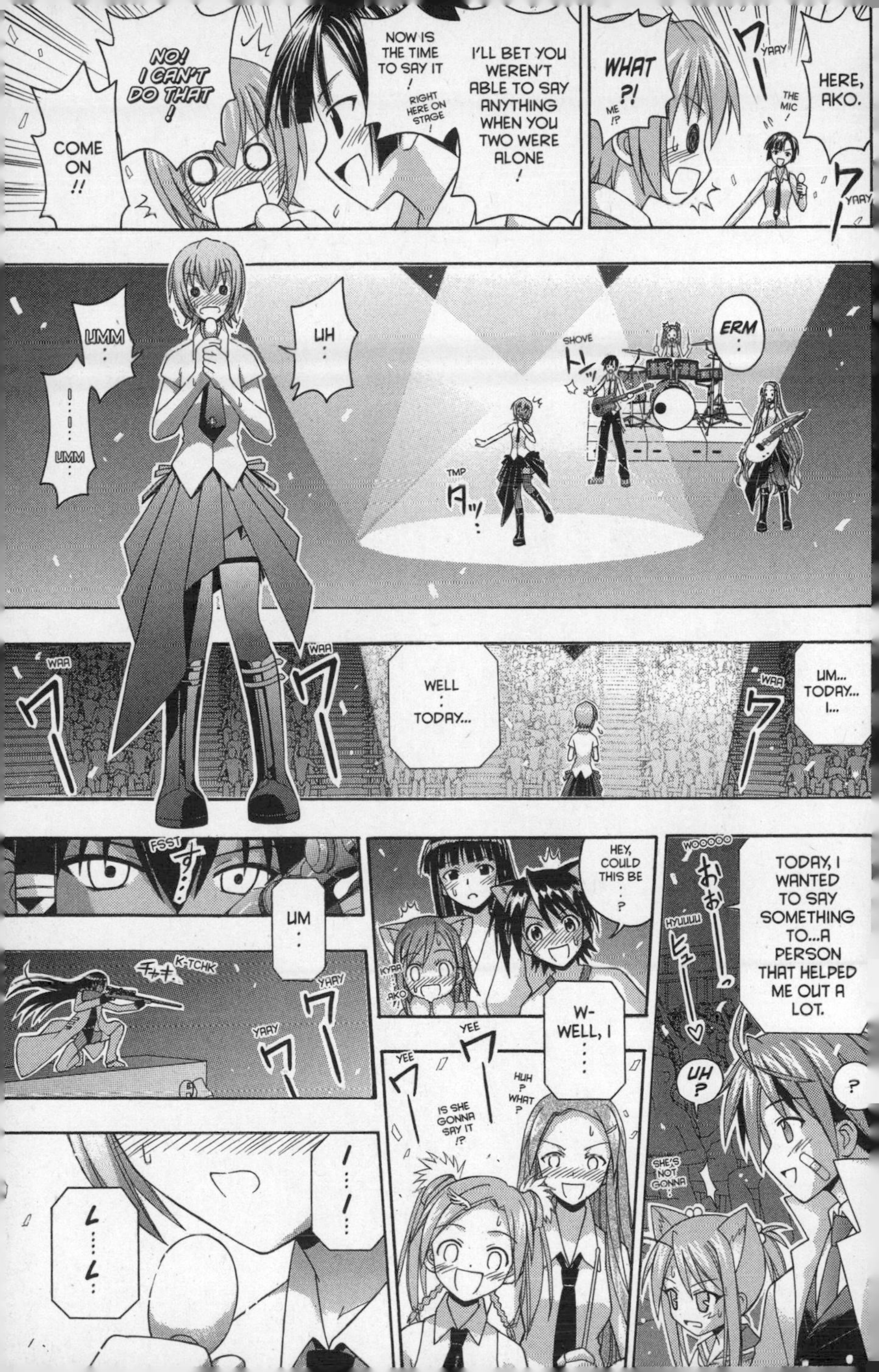
HERE, AKO.
THE MIC!
YAAY
WHAT?!
ME!?
YAAY
I'LL BET YOU WEREN'T ABLE TO SAY ANYTHING WHEN YOU TWO WERE ALONE!
NOW IS THE TIME TO SAY IT!
RIGHT HERE ON STAGE!
NO! I CAN'T DO THAT!
COME ON!!
ERM...
SHOVE
TMP
UH...
UMM...
I... I... UMM...
UM... TODAY... I...
WAA
WELL... TODAY...
WAA
WAA
WOOOOO
TODAY, I WANTED TO SAY SOMETHING TO...A PERSON THAT HELPED ME OUT A LOT.
HYUUUU
HEY, COULD THIS BE...?
KYAA
AKO
FSST
UM...
K-TCHK
YAAY
YAAY
?
UH?
SHE'S NOT GONNA...
W-WELL, I....
YEE
HUH? WHAT?
YEE
IS SHE GONNA SAY IT!?
I...I...
L...L...

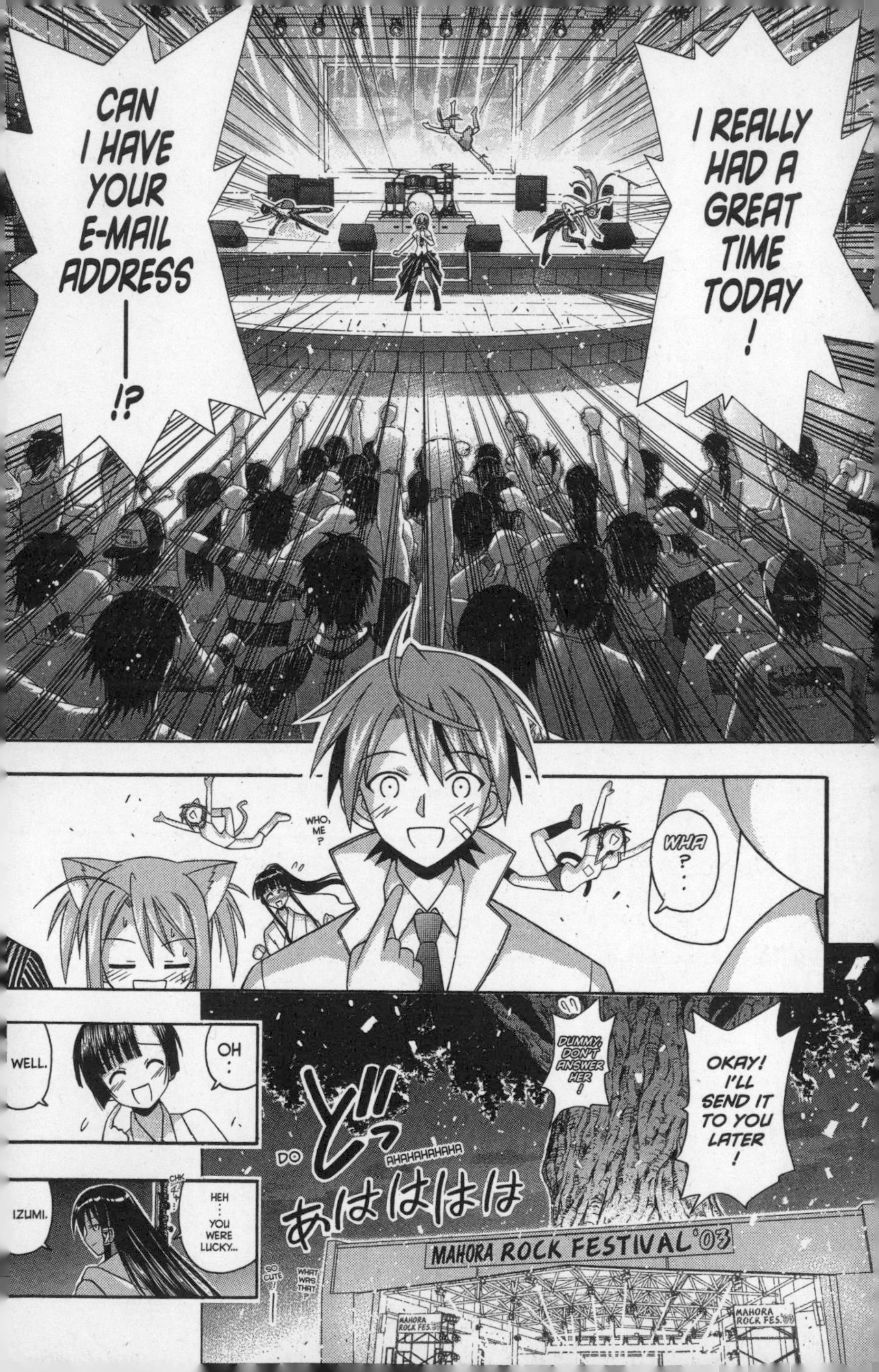
I REALLY HAD A GREAT TIME TODAY!
CAN I HAVE YOUR E-MAIL ADDRESS—!?
WHA?...
WHO, ME?
OKAY! I'LL SEND IT TO YOU LATER!
DUMMY, DON'T ANSWER HER!
DO
AHAHAHAHAHA
あはははは
MAHORA ROCK FESTIVAL '03
MAHORA ROCK FES.'03
MAHORA ROCK FES.
WHAT WAS THAT?
SO CUTE!!
OH...
WELL.
HEH... YOU WERE LUCKY...
CHK
IZUMI.

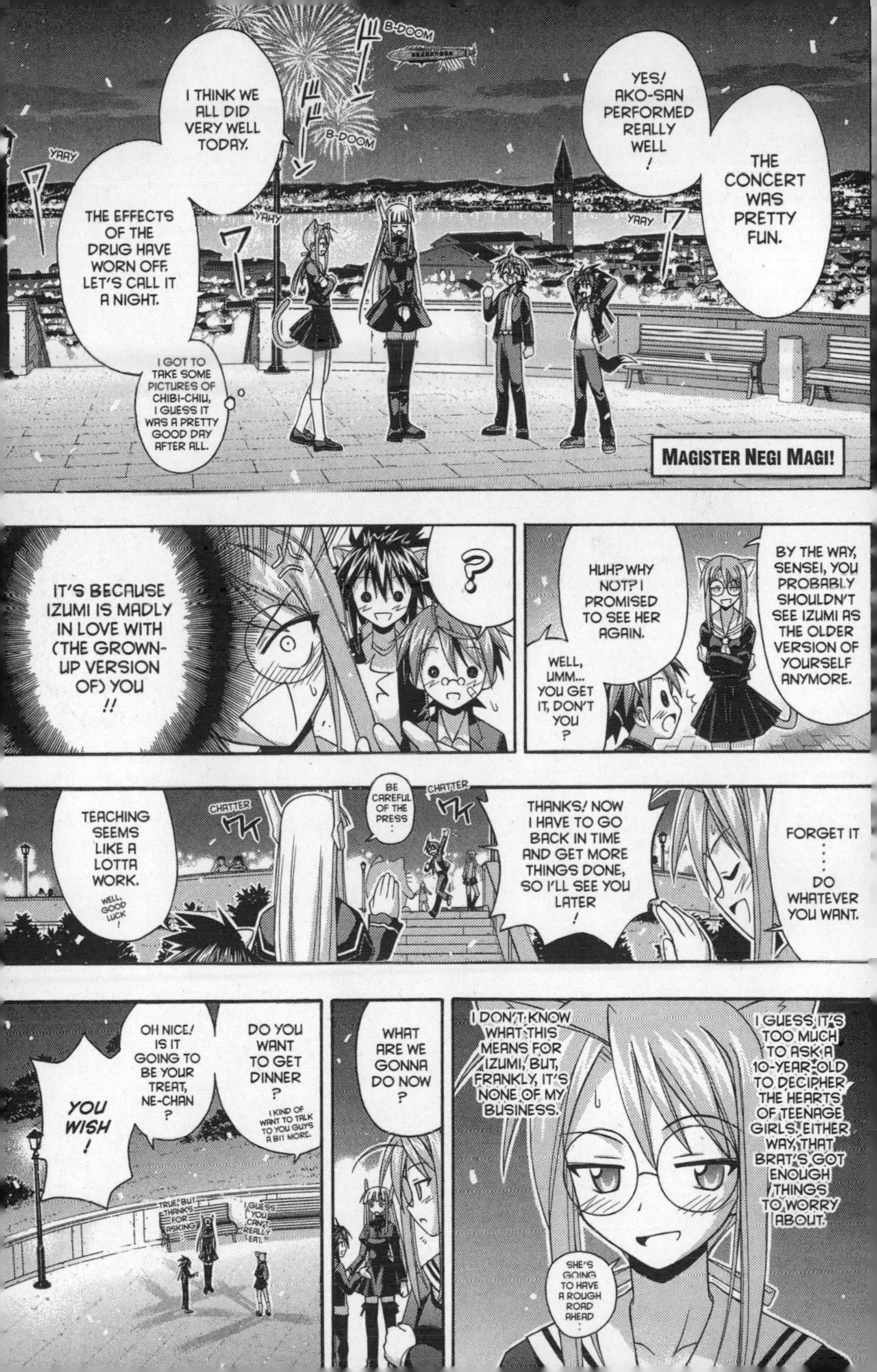
YES! AKO-SAN PERFORMED REALLY WELL!
THE CONCERT WAS PRETTY FUN.
YAAY
B-DOOM
B-DOOM
I THINK WE ALL DID VERY WELL TODAY.
YAAY
THE EFFECTS OF THE DRUG HAVE WORN OFF. LET'S CALL IT A NIGHT.
YAAY
I GOT TO TAKE SOME PICTURES OF CHIBI-CHIU, I GUESS IT WAS A PRETTY GOOD DAY AFTER ALL.
MAGISTER NEGI MAGI!
BY THE WAY, SENSEI, YOU PROBABLY SHOULDN'T SEE IZUMI AS THE OLDER VERSION OF YOURSELF ANYMORE.
HUH? WHY NOT? I PROMISED TO SEE HER AGAIN.
WELL, UMM... YOU GET IT, DON'T YOU?
?
IT'S BECAUSE IZUMI IS MADLY IN LOVE WITH (THE GROWN-UP VERSION OF) YOU!!
FORGET IT... DO WHATEVER YOU WANT.
THANKS! NOW I HAVE TO GO BACK IN TIME AND GET MORE THINGS DONE, SO I'LL SEE YOU LATER!
CHATTER
BE CAREFUL OF THE PRESS...
CHATTER
TEACHING SEEMS LIKE A LOTTA WORK.
WELL, GOOD LUCK!
I GUESS IT'S TOO MUCH TO ASK A 10-YEAR-OLD TO DECIPHER THE HEARTS OF TEENAGE GIRLS. EITHER WAY, THAT BRAT'S GOT ENOUGH THINGS TO WORRY ABOUT.
I DON'T KNOW WHAT THIS MEANS FOR IZUMI, BUT, FRANKLY, IT'S NONE OF MY BUSINESS.
SHE'S GOING TO HAVE A ROUGH ROAD AHEAD...
WHAT ARE WE GONNA DO NOW?
DO YOU WANT TO GET DINNER?
I KIND OF WANT TO TALK TO YOU GUYS A BIT MORE.
OH NICE! IS IT GOING TO BE YOUR TREAT, NE-CHAN?
YOU WISH!
I GUESS YOU CAN'T REALLY EAT.
TRUE, BUT THANKS FOR ASKING.

NEGIMA!
MAGISTER NEGI MAGI

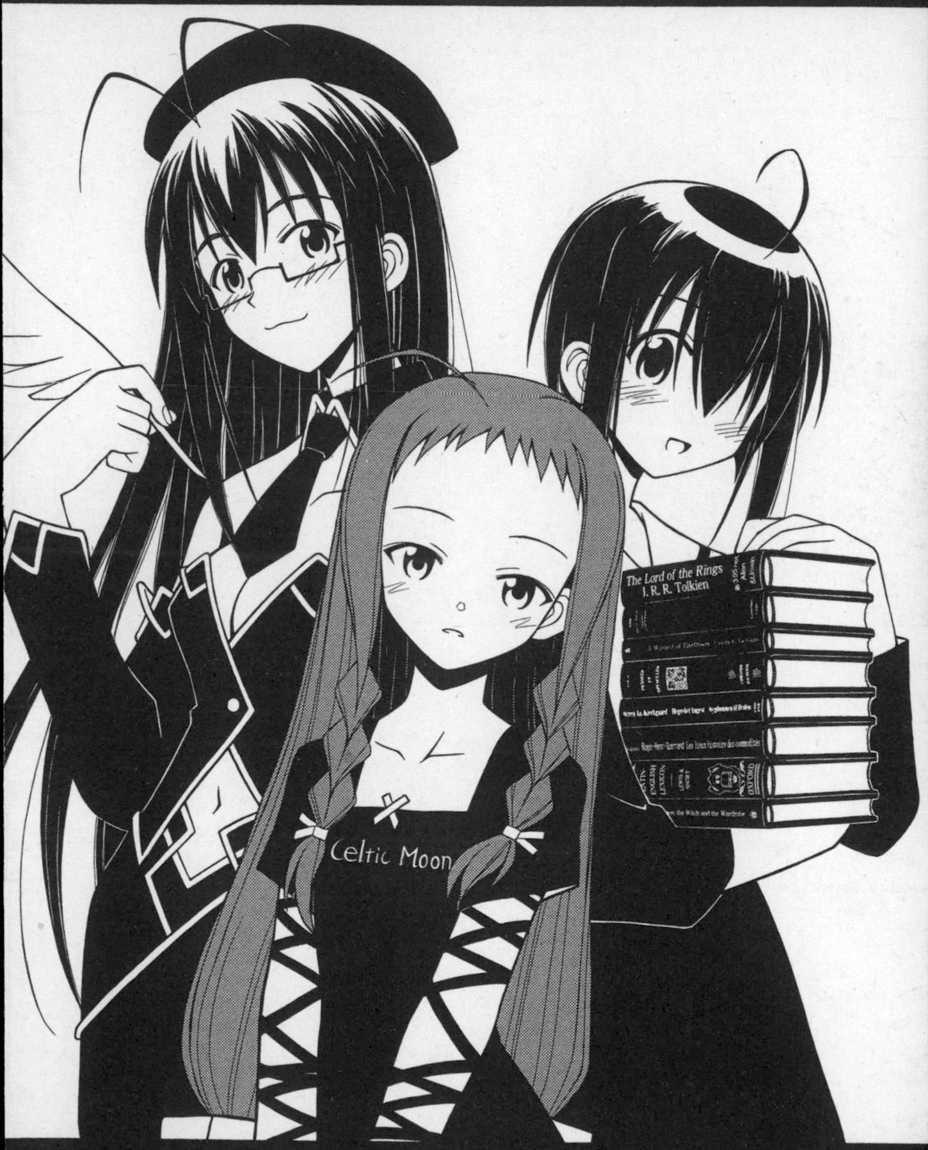
The Lord of the Rings
J. R. R. Tolkien
Celtic Moon

126TH PERIOD: FIERCE MATERIAL DESIRES♡

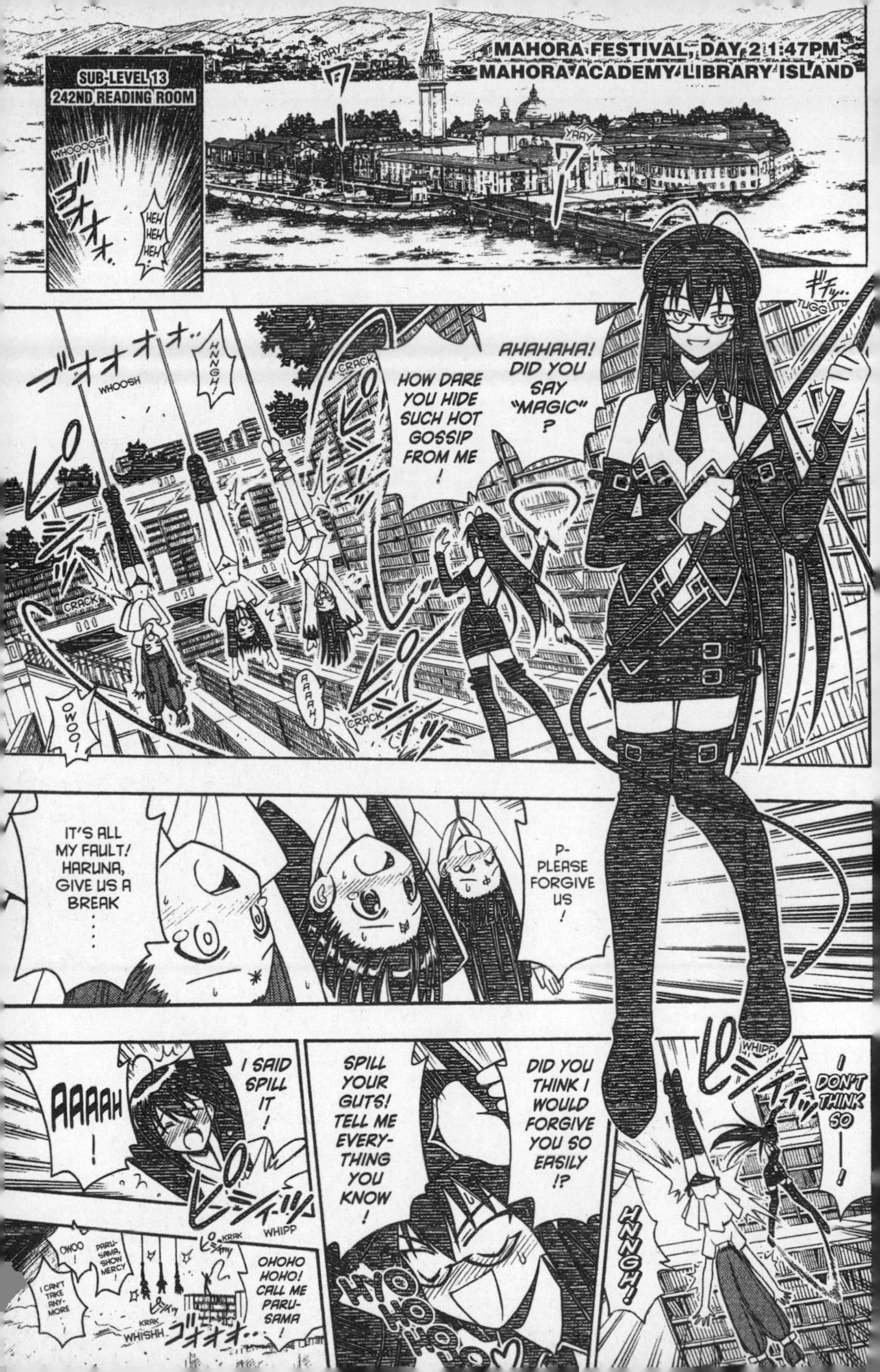
MAHORA FESTIVAL, DAY 2 1:47PM
MAHORA ACADEMY LIBRARY ISLAND
YAAY
YAAY
SUB-LEVEL 13
242ND READING ROOM
WHOOOOSH
HEH HEH HEH
TUGG
AHAHAHA! DID YOU SAY "MAGIC"?
HOW DARE YOU HIDE SUCH HOT GOSSIP FROM ME!
CRACK
HNNGH!
WHOOSH
CRACK
AAAAH!
CRACK
OWOO!
P-PLEASE FORGIVE US!
IT'S ALL MY FAULT! HARUNA, GIVE US A BREAK...
I DON'T THINK SO—!
WHIPP
HNNGH!
DID YOU THINK I WOULD FORGIVE YOU SO EASILY!?
SPILL YOUR GUTS! TELL ME EVERY-THING YOU KNOW!
I SAID SPILL IT!
AAAAH!
WHIPP
OHOHO HOHO! CALL ME PARU-SAMA!
KRAK
PARU-SAMA, SHOW MERCY!
OWOO!
I CAN'T TAKE ANY-MORE...
KRAK
WHISHH

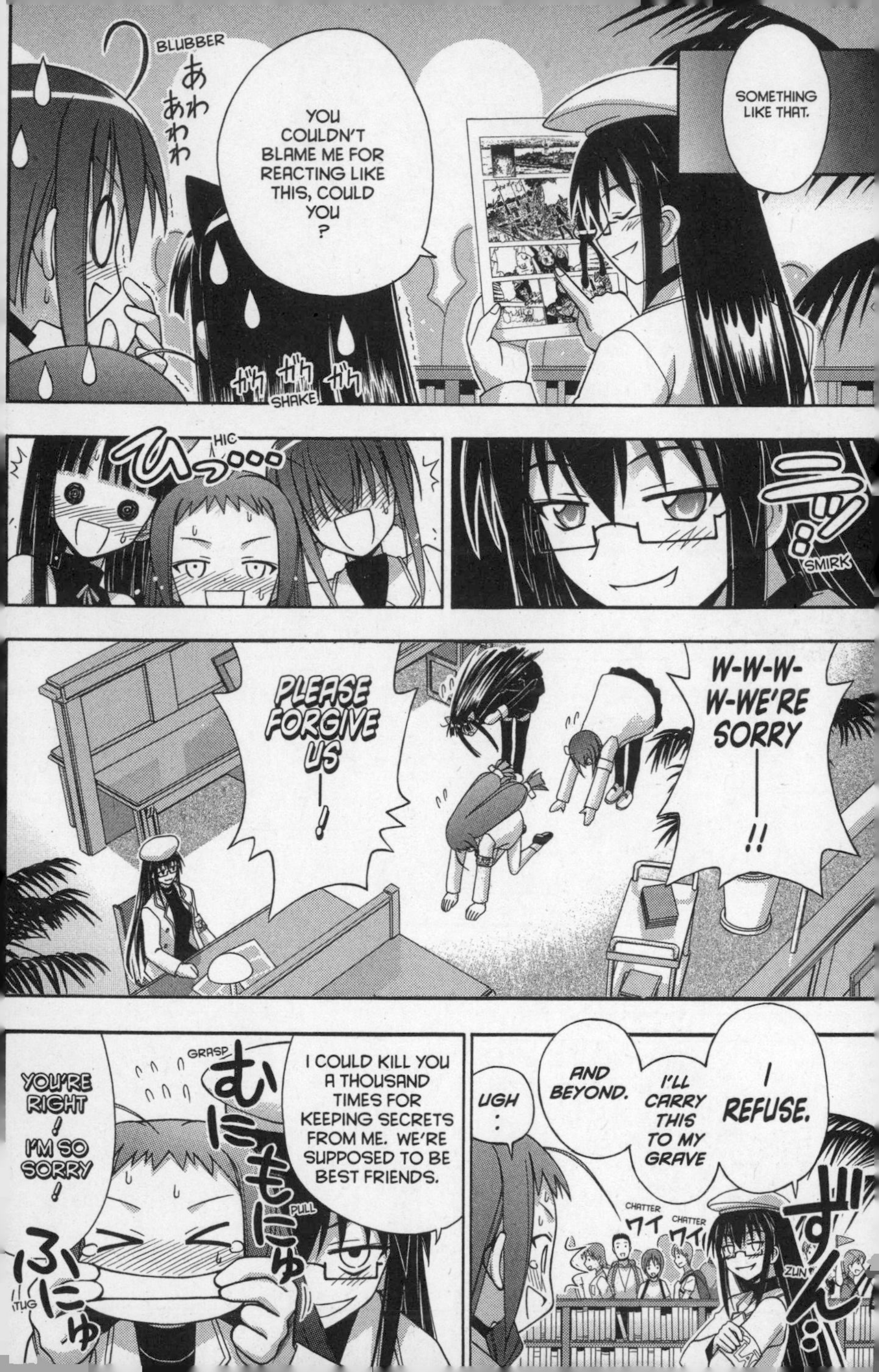
SOMETHING LIKE THAT.
YOU COULDN'T BLAME ME FOR REACTING LIKE THIS, COULD YOU ?
BLUBBER
あわあわわ
がくがくがく
SHAKE
ニッ
SMIRK
ひっ
HIC
W-W-W-W-WE'RE SORRY —!!
PLEASE FORGIVE US —!
I REFUSE.
I'LL CARRY THIS TO MY GRAVE
AND BEYOND.
UGH :
CHATTER
ワイ
CHATTER
ワイ
ずん
ZUN
I COULD KILL YOU A THOUSAND TIMES FOR KEEPING SECRETS FROM ME. WE'RE SUPPOSED TO BE BEST FRIENDS.
GRASP
むに
もにゅ
PULL
YOU'RE RIGHT! I'M SO SORRY!
ふにゅ
TUG

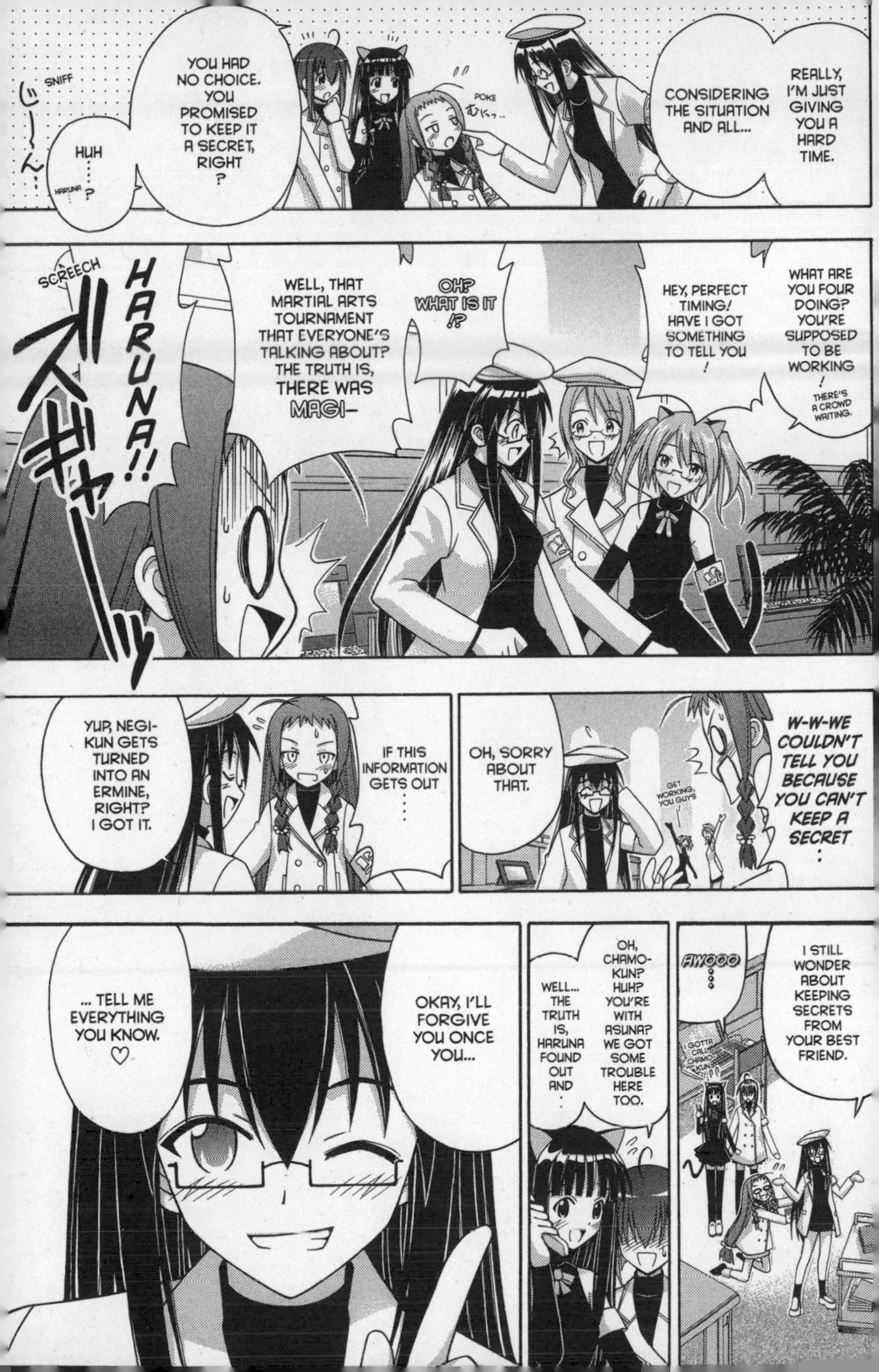
REALLY, I'M JUST GIVING YOU A HARD TIME.
CONSIDERING THE SITUATION AND ALL...
POKE
むにっ...
YOU HAD NO CHOICE. YOU PROMISED TO KEEP IT A SECRET, RIGHT?
SNIFF
じ～ん...
HUH.....?
HARUNA
WHAT ARE YOU FOUR DOING? YOU'RE SUPPOSED TO BE WORKING!
THERE'S A CROWD WAITING.
HEY, PERFECT TIMING! HAVE I GOT SOMETHING TO TELL YOU!
OH? WHAT IS IT!?
WELL, THAT MARTIAL ARTS TOURNAMENT THAT EVERYONE'S TALKING ABOUT? THE TRUTH IS, THERE WAS MAGI–
HARUNA!!
SCREECH
ズギャー
W-W-WE COULDN'T TELL YOU BECAUSE YOU CAN'T KEEP A SECRET:
OH, SORRY ABOUT THAT.
GET WORKING, YOU GUYS!
IF THIS INFORMATION GETS OUT.....
YUP, NEGI-KUN GETS TURNED INTO AN ERMINE, RIGHT? I GOT IT.
I STILL WONDER ABOUT KEEPING SECRETS FROM YOUR BEST FRIEND.
AWOOO...
I GOTTA CALL CHAMO-KUN!
OH, CHAMO-KUN? HUH? YOU'RE WITH ASUNA? WE GOT SOME TROUBLE HERE TOO.
WELL... THE TRUTH IS, HARUNA FOUND OUT AND:
OKAY, I'LL FORGIVE YOU ONCE YOU...
... TELL ME EVERYTHING YOU KNOW. ♡

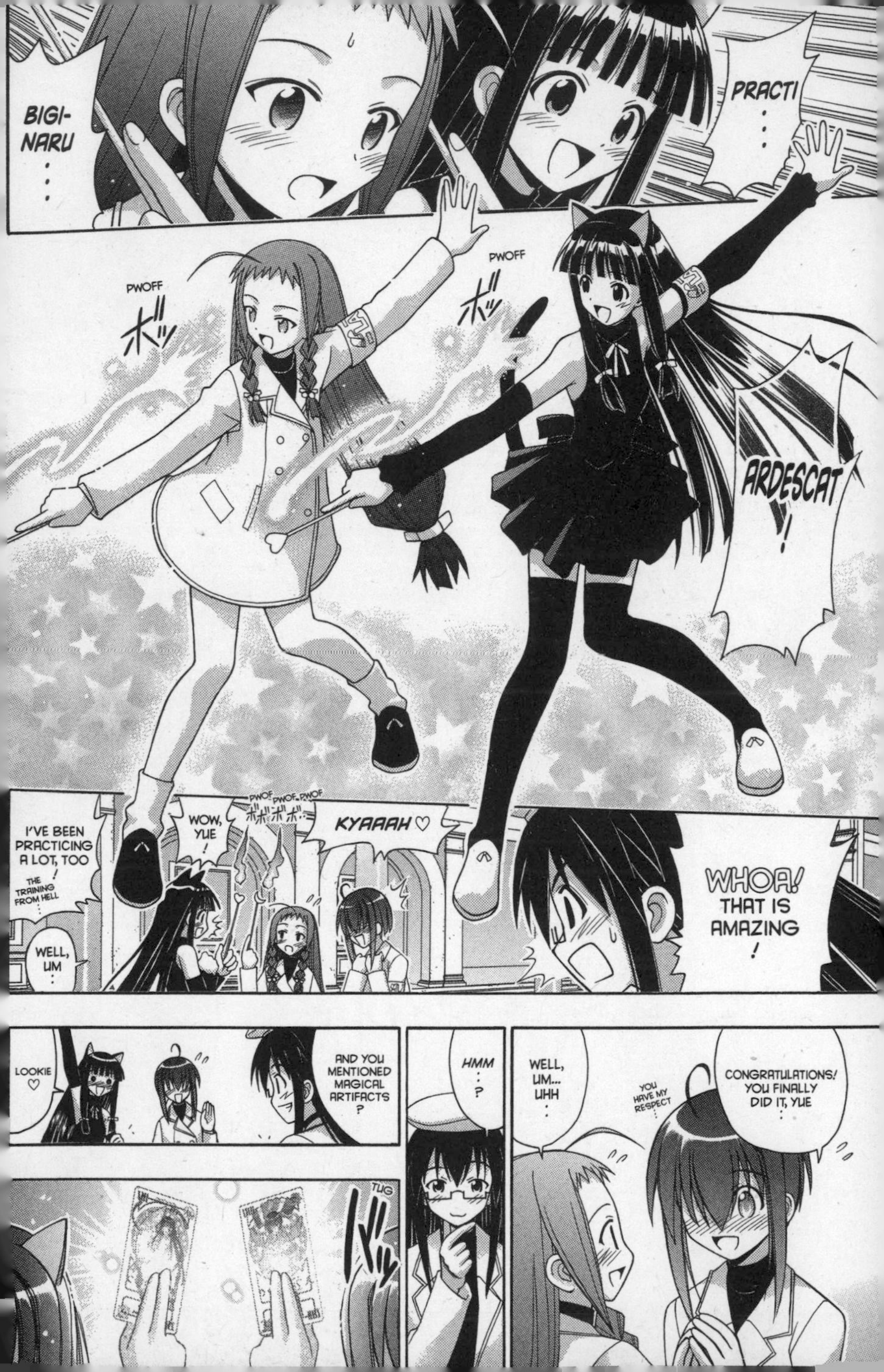
PRACTI...
BIGI-NARU...
ARDESCAT!
PWOFF
PWOFF
WHOA! THAT IS AMAZING!
KYAAAH♡
PWOF PWOF PWOF
WOW, YUE!
I'VE BEEN PRACTICING A LOT, TOO!
THE TRAINING FROM HELL...
WELL, UM...
CONGRATULATIONS! YOU FINALLY DID IT, YUE...
YOU HAVE MY RESPECT...
WELL, UM... UHH...
HMM...?
AND YOU MENTIONED MAGICAL ARTIFACTS?
LOOKIE♡
TUG

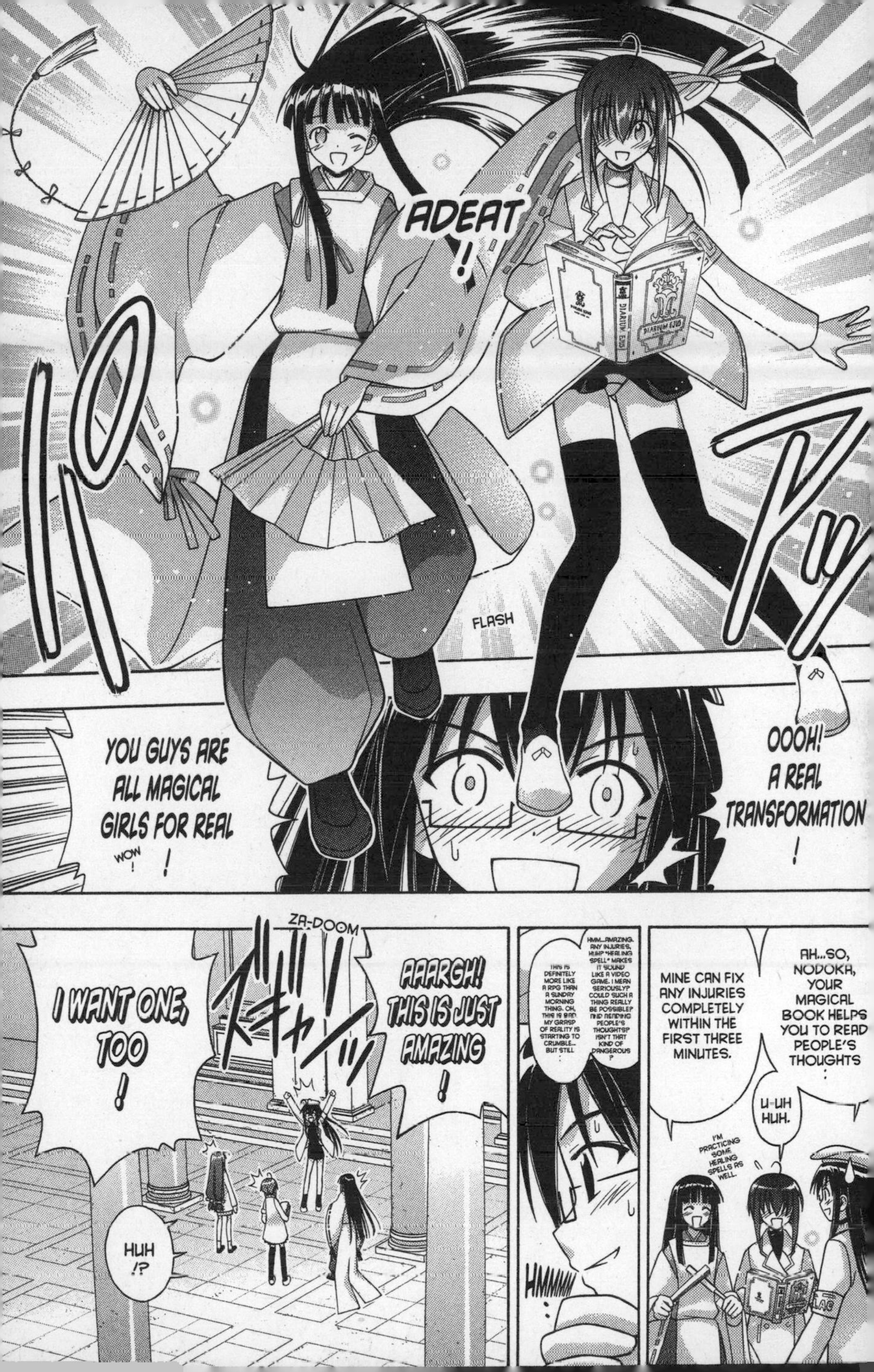
ADEAT !
FLASH
OOOH! A REAL TRANSFORMATION !
YOU GUYS ARE ALL MAGICAL GIRLS FOR REAL !
WOW !
AH...SO, NODOKA, YOUR MAGICAL BOOK HELPS YOU TO READ PEOPLE'S THOUGHTS :
MINE CAN FIX ANY INJURIES COMPLETELY WITHIN THE FIRST THREE MINUTES.
U-UH HUH.
I'M PRACTICING SOME HEALING SPELLS AS WELL.
HMM...AMAZING. ANY INJURIES, HUH? "HEALING SPELL" MAKES IT SOUND LIKE A VIDEO GAME. I MEAN SERIOUSLY? COULD SUCH A THING REALLY BE POSSIBLE? AND READING PEOPLE'S THOUGHTS? ISN'T THAT KIND OF DANGEROUS ?
THIS IS DEFINITELY MORE LIKE A RPG THAN A SUNDAY MORNING THING. OH, THIS IS BAD. MY GRASP OF REALITY IS STARTING TO CRUMBLE... BUT STILL :
HMMM :
ZA-DOOM
AAARGH! THIS IS JUST AMAZING !
I WANT ONE, TOO !
HUH !?

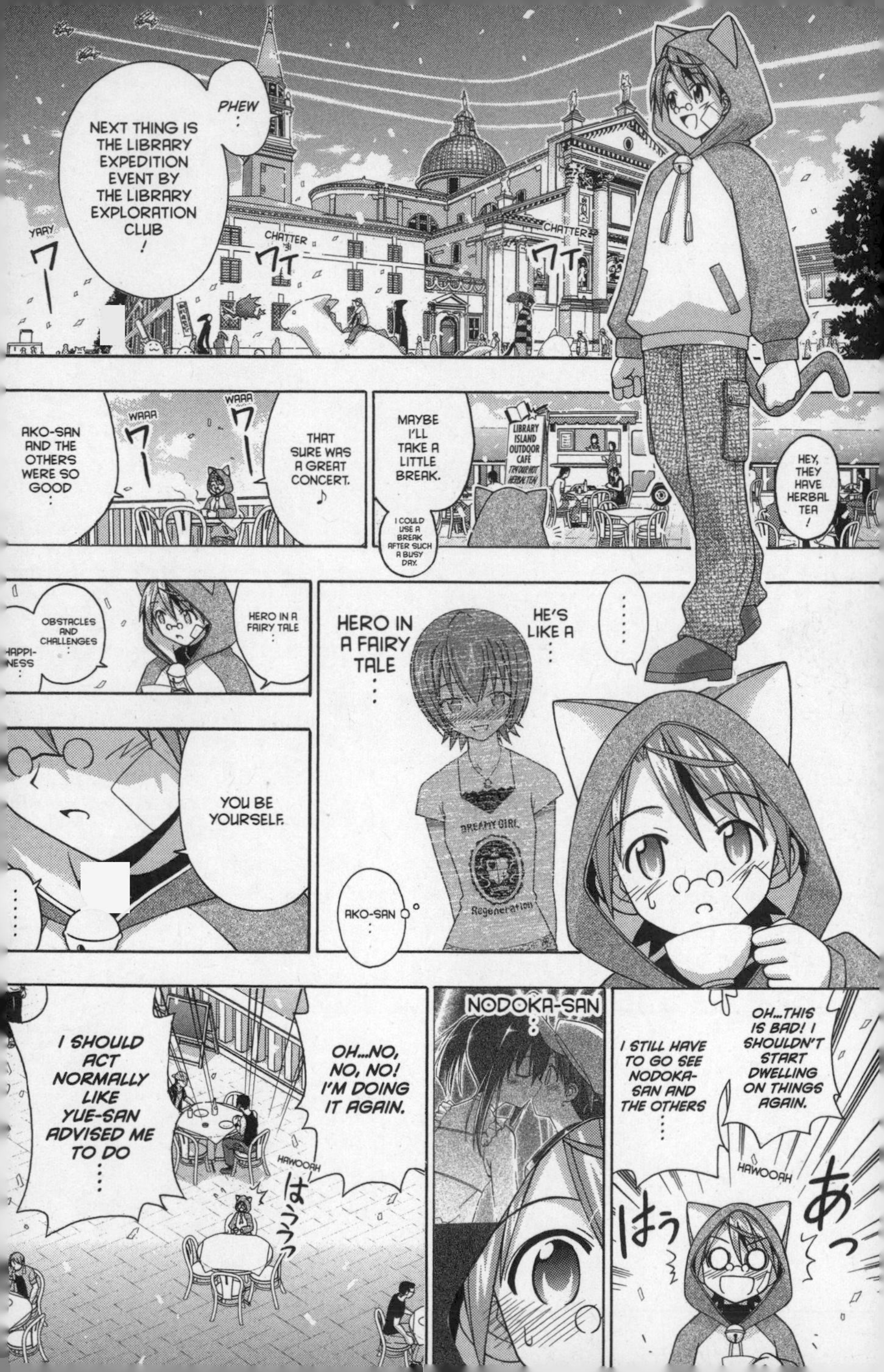
PHEW...
NEXT THING IS THE LIBRARY EXPEDITION EVENT BY THE LIBRARY EXPLORATION CLUB!
CHATTER
CHATTER
YAAY
HEY, THEY HAVE HERBAL TEA!
LIBRARY ISLAND OUTDOOR CAFÉ
MAYBE I'LL TAKE A LITTLE BREAK.
I COULD USE A BREAK AFTER SUCH A BUSY DAY.
WAAA
THAT SURE WAS A GREAT CONCERT. ♪
WAAA
AKO-SAN AND THE OTHERS WERE SO GOOD...
......
HE'S LIKE A...
HERO IN A FAIRY TALE...
AKO-SAN...
HERO IN A FAIRY TALE...
OBSTACLES AND CHALLENGES...
HAPPI-NESS...
YOU BE YOURSELF.
......
OH...THIS IS BAD! I SHOULDN'T START DWELLING ON THINGS AGAIN.
I STILL HAVE TO GO SEE NODOKA-SAN AND THE OTHERS...
HAWOOAH
NODOKA-SAN
OH...NO, NO, NO! I'M DOING IT AGAIN.
I SHOULD ACT NORMALLY LIKE YUE-SAN ADVISED ME TO DO...
HAWOOAH

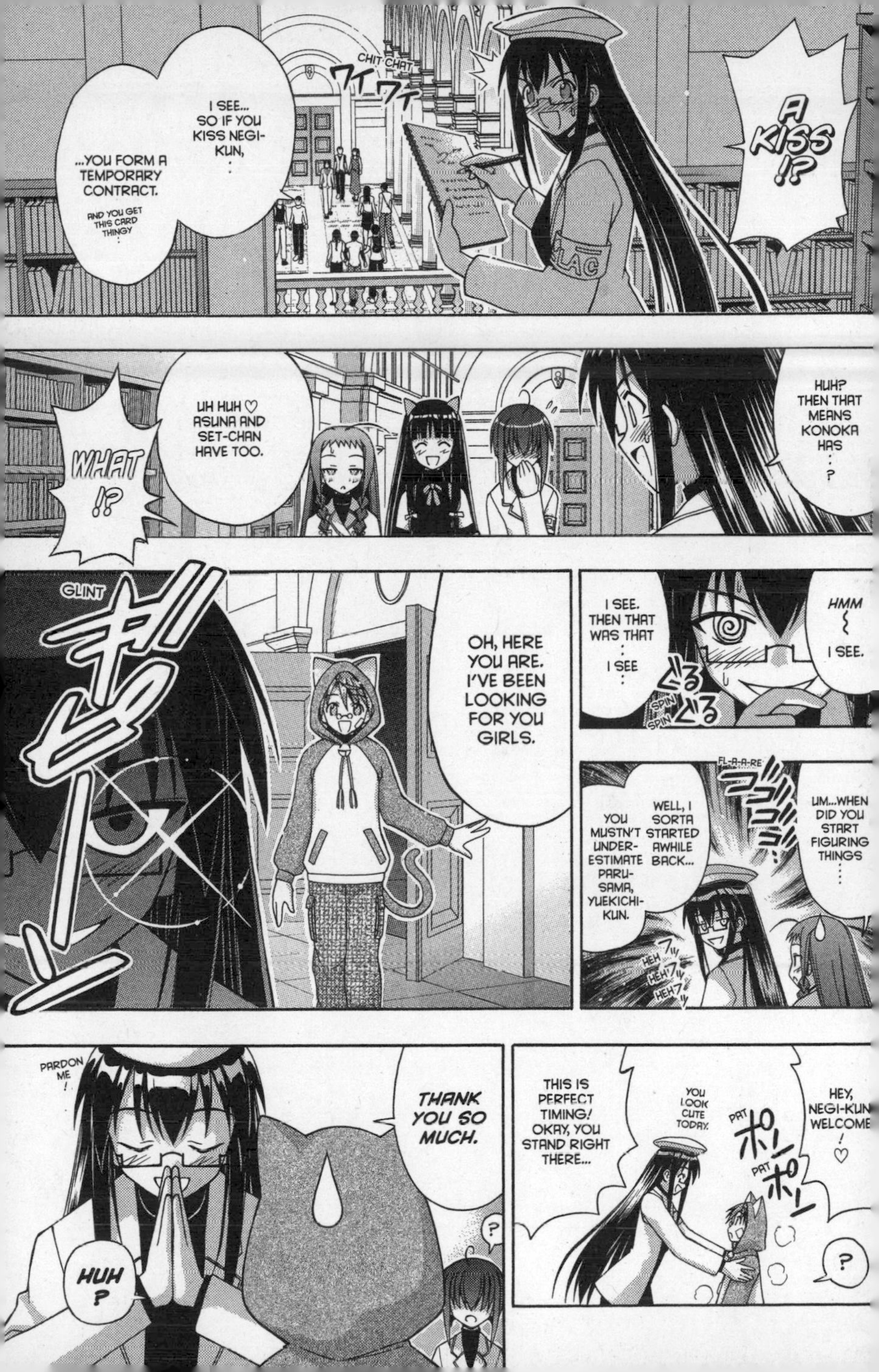
A KISS!?
CHIT CHAT
I SEE... SO IF YOU KISS NEGI-KUN, . .
...YOU FORM A TEMPORARY CONTRACT.
AND YOU GET THIS CARD THINGY . .
HUH? THEN THAT MEANS KONOKA HAS . . ?
UH HUH ♡ ASUNA AND SET-CHAN HAVE TOO.
WHAT!?
HMM~ I SEE.
I SEE. THEN THAT WAS THAT . . I SEE . .
SPIN SPIN
UM...WHEN DID YOU START FIGURING THINGS . . . .
FL-A-A-RE
WELL, I SORTA STARTED AWHILE BACK...
YOU MUSTN'T UNDER-ESTIMATE PARU-SAMA, YUEKICHI-KUN.
HEH HEH HEH
OH, HERE YOU ARE. I'VE BEEN LOOKING FOR YOU GIRLS.
GLINT
HEY, NEGI-KUN WELCOME! ♡
PAT PAT
YOU LOOK CUTE TODAY.
THIS IS PERFECT TIMING! OKAY, YOU STAND RIGHT THERE...
?
THANK YOU SO MUCH.
PARDON ME!
?
HUH?

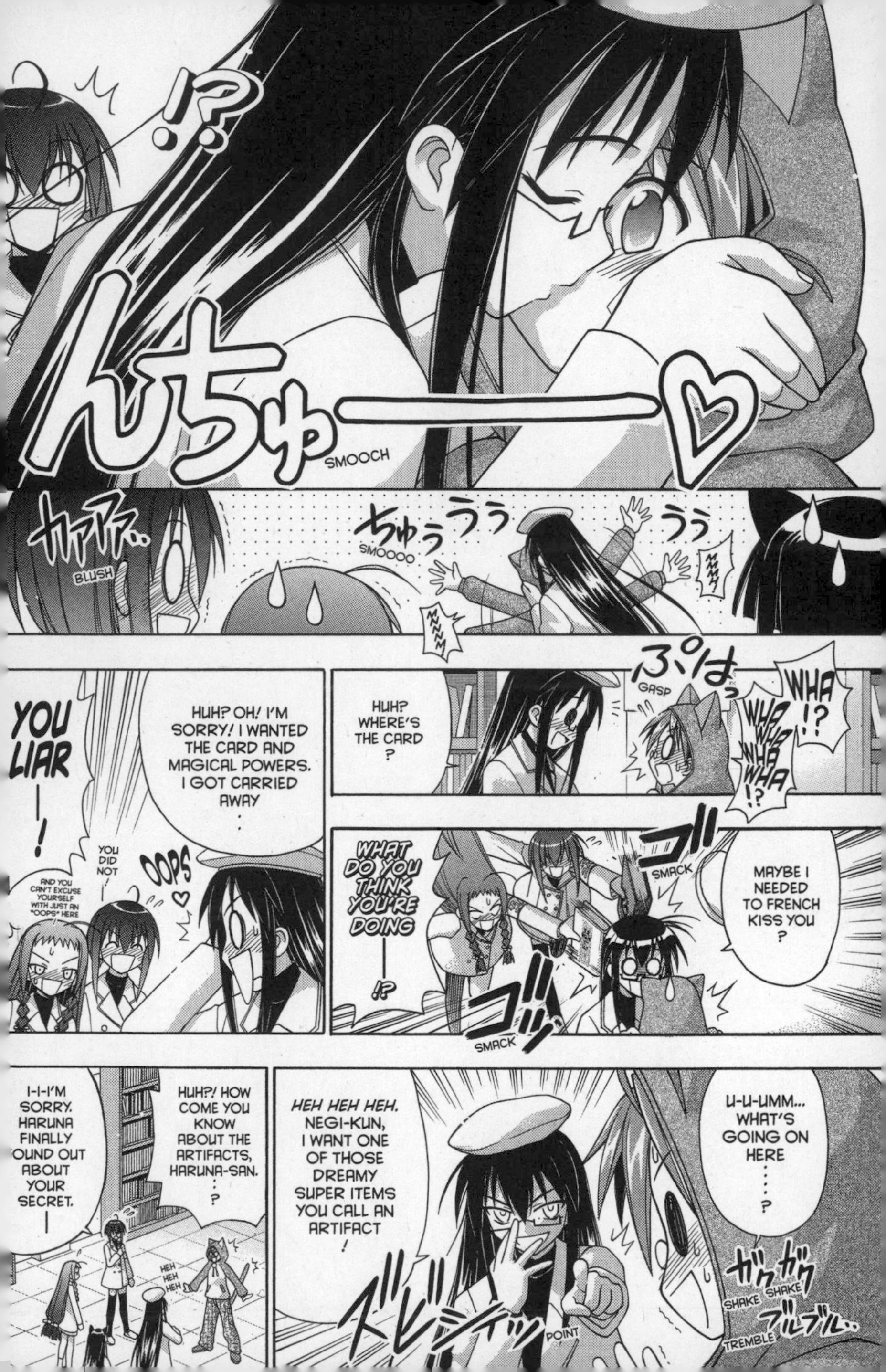
!?
んちゅーーー♡
SMOOCH
うう
MMMM!
ちゅううう
SMOOOO
MNNNM
カァァァ..
BLUSH
WHA!?
WHA WHA WHA WHA!?
ぷはっ
GASP
HUH? WHERE'S THE CARD?
MAYBE I NEEDED TO FRENCH KISS YOU?
ゴッ
SMACK
WHAT DO YOU THINK YOU'RE DOING—!?
ゴッ
SMACK
HUH? OH! I'M SORRY! I WANTED THE CARD AND MAGICAL POWERS. I GOT CARRIED AWAY...
YOU LIAR—!
YOU DID NOT!
OOPS♡
AND YOU CAN'T EXCUSE YOURSELF WITH JUST AN "OOPS" HERE
U-U-UMM... WHAT'S GOING ON HERE.....?
ガクガク
SHAKE SHAKE
ブルブル..
TREMBLE
HEH HEH HEH. NEGI-KUN, I WANT ONE OF THOSE DREAMY SUPER ITEMS YOU CALL AN ARTIFACT!
ズビシィッ
POINT
HUH?! HOW COME YOU KNOW ABOUT THE ARTIFACTS, HARUNA-SAN...?
I-I-I'M SORRY. HARUNA FINALLY OUND OUT ABOUT YOUR SECRET.—
HEH HEH HEH

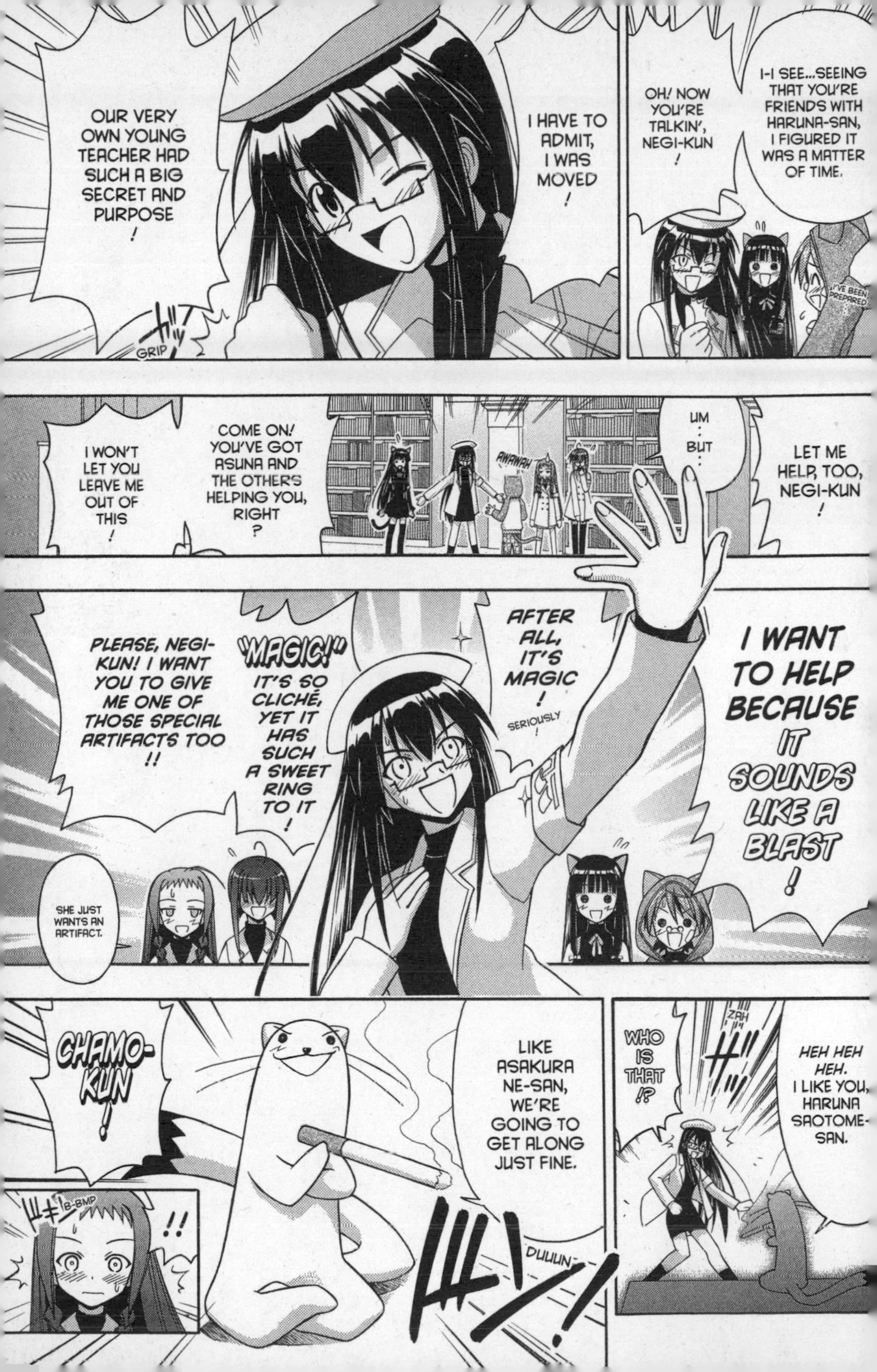
I-I SEE...SEEING THAT YOU'RE FRIENDS WITH HARUNA-SAN, I FIGURED IT WAS A MATTER OF TIME.
OH! NOW YOU'RE TALKIN', NEGI-KUN!
I'VE BEEN PREPARED
I HAVE TO ADMIT, I WAS MOVED!
OUR VERY OWN YOUNG TEACHER HAD SUCH A BIG SECRET AND PURPOSE!
GRIP
LET ME HELP, TOO, NEGI-KUN!
UM... BUT...
AWAWAH
COME ON! YOU'VE GOT ASUNA AND THE OTHERS HELPING YOU, RIGHT?
I WON'T LET YOU LEAVE ME OUT OF THIS!
I WANT TO HELP BECAUSE IT SOUNDS LIKE A BLAST!
AFTER ALL, IT'S MAGIC!
SERIOUSLY!
"MAGIC!" IT'S SO CLICHÉ, YET IT HAS SUCH A SWEET RING TO IT!
PLEASE, NEGI-KUN! I WANT YOU TO GIVE ME ONE OF THOSE SPECIAL ARTIFACTS TOO!!
SHE JUST WANTS AN ARTIFACT.
ZAH
HEH HEH HEH. I LIKE YOU, HARUNA SAOTOME-SAN.
WHO IS THAT!?
LIKE ASAKURA NE-SAN, WE'RE GOING TO GET ALONG JUST FINE.
DUUUN
CHAMO-KUN!
B-BMP
!!

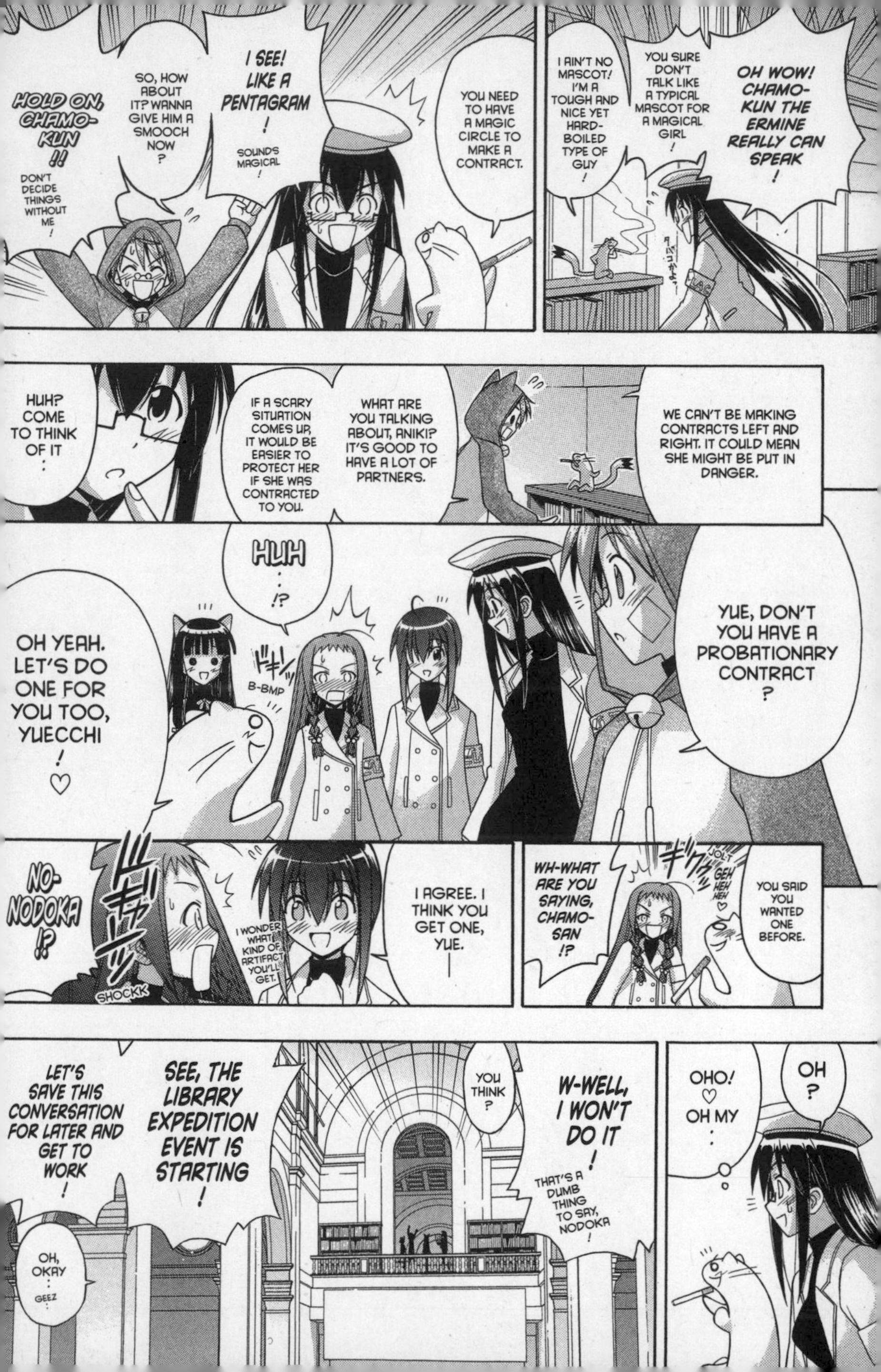

OH WOW! CHAMO-KUN THE ERMINE REALLY CAN SPEAK!
YOU SURE DON'T TALK LIKE A TYPICAL MASCOT FOR A MAGICAL GIRL!
I AIN'T NO MASCOT! I'M A TOUGH AND NICE YET HARD-BOILED TYPE OF GUY!
YOU NEED TO HAVE A MAGIC CIRCLE TO MAKE A CONTRACT.
I SEE! LIKE A PENTAGRAM!
SOUNDS MAGICAL
SO, HOW ABOUT IT? WANNA GIVE HIM A SMOOCH NOW?
HOLD ON, CHAMO-KUN!!
DON'T DECIDE THINGS WITHOUT ME!
WE CAN'T BE MAKING CONTRACTS LEFT AND RIGHT. IT COULD MEAN SHE MIGHT BE PUT IN DANGER.
WHAT ARE YOU TALKING ABOUT, ANIKI? IT'S GOOD TO HAVE A LOT OF PARTNERS.
IF A SCARY SITUATION COMES UP, IT WOULD BE EASIER TO PROTECT HER IF SHE WAS CONTRACTED TO YOU.
HUH? COME TO THINK OF IT:
YUE, DON'T YOU HAVE A PROBATIONARY CONTRACT?
HUH..!?
B-BMP
OH YEAH. LET'S DO ONE FOR YOU TOO, YUECCHI! ♡
YOU SAID YOU WANTED ONE BEFORE.
GEH HEH HEH ♡
JOLT
WH-WHAT ARE YOU SAYING, CHAMO-SAN!?
I AGREE. I THINK YOU GET ONE, YUE.
I WONDER WHAT KIND OF ARTIFACT YOU'LL GET.
NO-NODOKA!?
SHOCKK
OH?
OHO! ♡ OH MY:
W-WELL, I WON'T DO IT!
THAT'S A DUMB THING TO SAY, NODOKA!
YOU THINK?
SEE, THE LIBRARY EXPEDITION EVENT IS STARTING!
LET'S SAVE THIS CONVERSATION FOR LATER AND GET TO WORK!
OH, OKAY:
GEEZ:

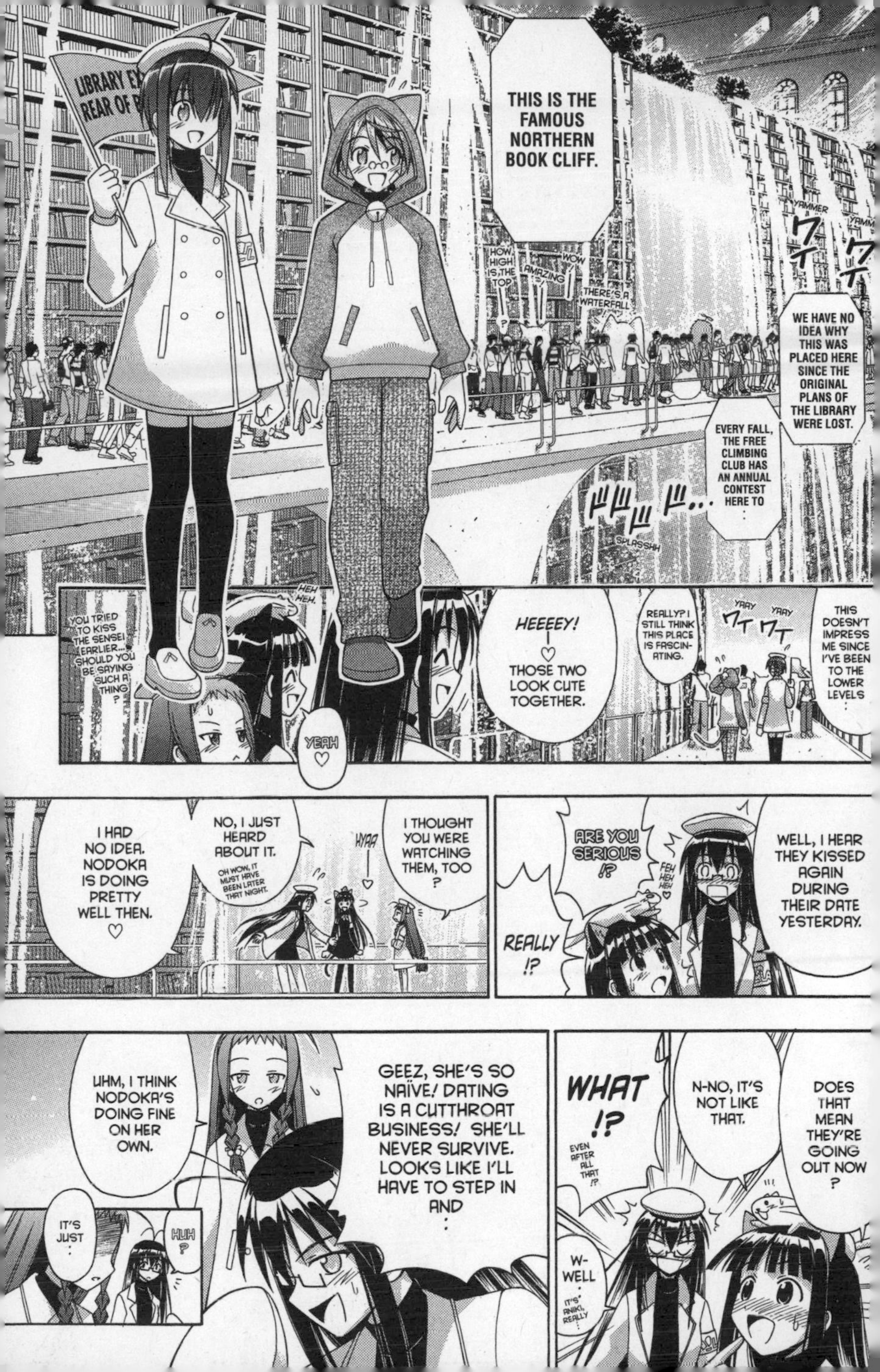
THIS IS THE FAMOUS NORTHERN BOOK CLIFF.
ワイ ワイ
YAMMER YAMM
WE HAVE NO IDEA WHY THIS WAS PLACED HERE SINCE THE ORIGINAL PLANS OF THE LIBRARY WERE LOST.
EVERY FALL, THE FREE CLIMBING CLUB HAS AN ANNUAL CONTEST HERE TO...
ドドドド…
SPLASSHH
THERE'S A WATERFALL!
WOW
AMAZING
HOW HIGH IS THE TOP?
LIBRARY EX
REAR OF B
THIS DOESN'T IMPRESS ME SINCE I'VE BEEN TO THE LOWER LEVELS...
ワイ ワイ
YAAY YAAY
REALLY? I STILL THINK THIS PLACE IS FASCINATING.
HEEEEY! ♡ THOSE TWO LOOK CUTE TOGETHER.
YEAH ♡
HEH HEH.
YOU TRIED TO KISS THE SENSEI EARLIER... SHOULD YOU BE SAYING SUCH A THING?
WELL, I HEAR THEY KISSED AGAIN DURING THEIR DATE YESTERDAY.
ARE YOU SERIOUS!?
FEH HEH HEH
REALLY!?
I THOUGHT YOU WERE WATCHING THEM, TOO?
HYAA ♡
NO, I JUST HEARD ABOUT IT.
OH WOW, IT MUST HAVE BEEN LATER THAT NIGHT.
I HAD NO IDEA. NODOKA IS DOING PRETTY WELL THEN. ♡
DOES THAT MEAN THEY'RE GOING OUT NOW?
N-NO, IT'S NOT LIKE THAT.
WHAT!?
EVEN AFTER ALL THAT!?
W-WELL...
IT'S' ANIKI, REALLY...
GEEZ, SHE'S SO NAÏVE! DATING IS A CUTTHROAT BUSINESS! SHE'LL NEVER SURVIVE. LOOKS LIKE I'LL HAVE TO STEP IN AND...
UHM, I THINK NODOKA'S DOING FINE ON HER OWN.
HUH?
IT'S JUST...

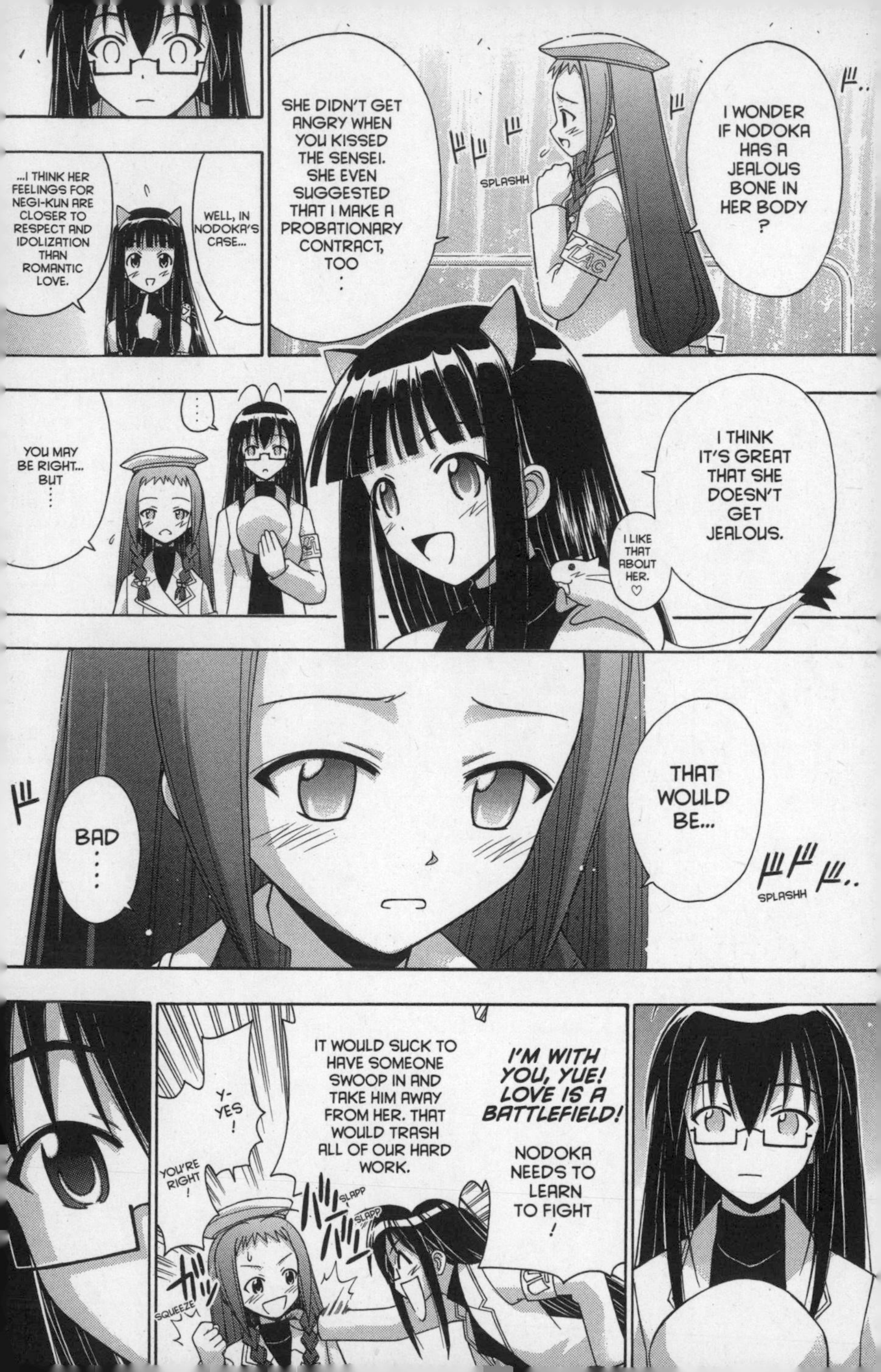
I WONDER IF NODOKA HAS A JEALOUS BONE IN HER BODY?
SPLASHH
SHE DIDN'T GET ANGRY WHEN YOU KISSED THE SENSEI. SHE EVEN SUGGESTED THAT I MAKE A PROBATIONARY CONTRACT, TOO...
WELL, IN NODOKA'S CASE...
...I THINK HER FEELINGS FOR NEGI-KUN ARE CLOSER TO RESPECT AND IDOLIZATION THAN ROMANTIC LOVE.
I THINK IT'S GREAT THAT SHE DOESN'T GET JEALOUS.
I LIKE THAT ABOUT HER. ♡
...
YOU MAY BE RIGHT... BUT ....
THAT WOULD BE...
SPLASHH
BAD ....
I'M WITH YOU, YUE! LOVE IS A BATTLEFIELD!
NODOKA NEEDS TO LEARN TO FIGHT!
IT WOULD SUCK TO HAVE SOMEONE SWOOP IN AND TAKE HIM AWAY FROM HER. THAT WOULD TRASH ALL OF OUR HARD WORK.
SLAPP
SLAPP
Y-YES!
YOU'RE RIGHT!
SQUEEZE

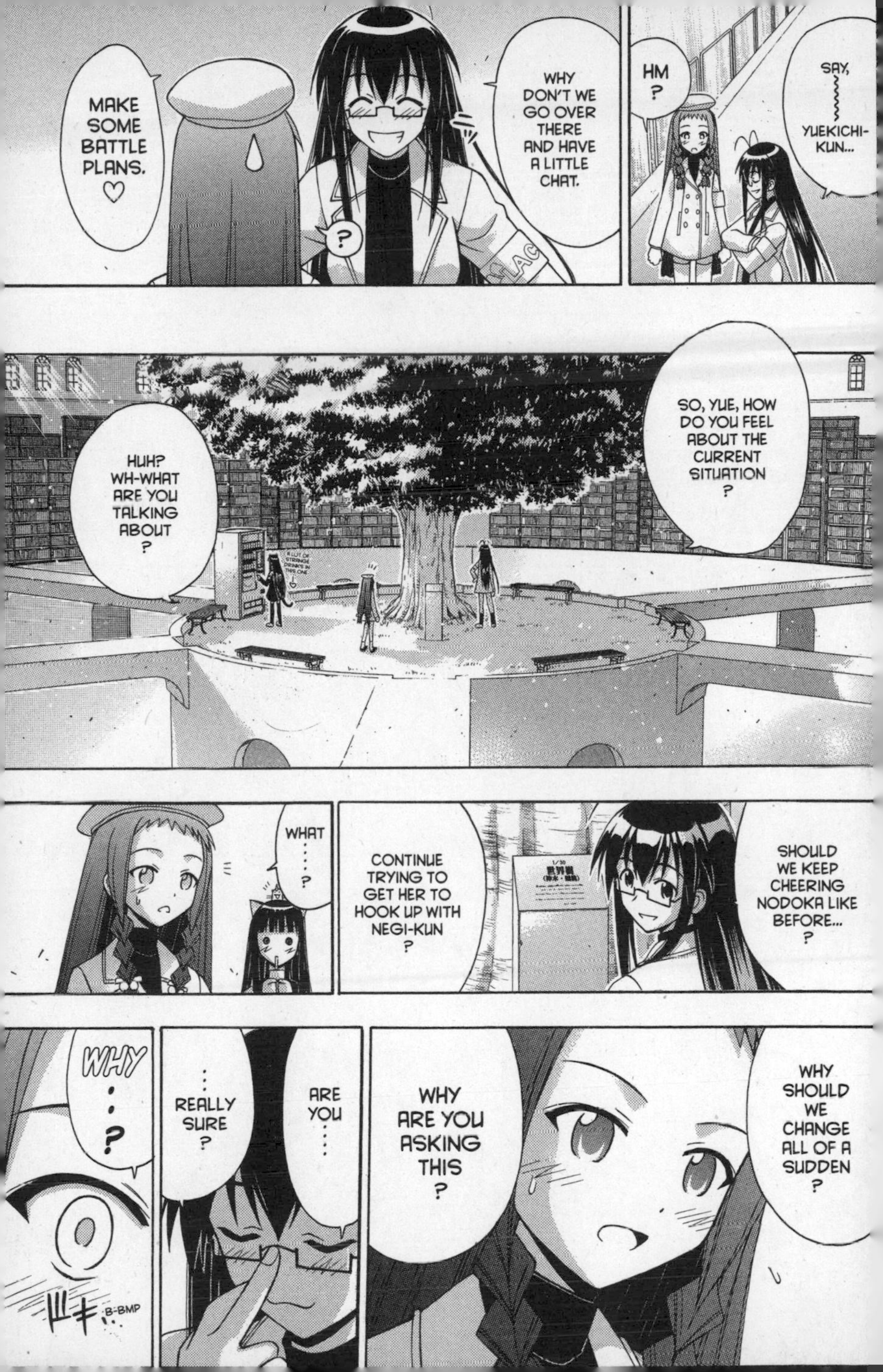
SAY, YUEKICHI-KUN...
HM?
WHY DON'T WE GO OVER THERE AND HAVE A LITTLE CHAT.
?
MAKE SOME BATTLE PLANS. ♡
SO, YUE, HOW DO YOU FEEL ABOUT THE CURRENT SITUATION?
HUH? WH-WHAT ARE YOU TALKING ABOUT?
A LOT OF STRANGE DRINKS IN THIS ONE
SHOULD WE KEEP CHEERING NODOKA LIKE BEFORE...?
CONTINUE TRYING TO GET HER TO HOOK UP WITH NEGI-KUN?
WHAT...?
WHY SHOULD WE CHANGE ALL OF A SUDDEN?
WHY ARE YOU ASKING THIS?
ARE YOU...
...REALLY SURE?
WHY..?
B-BMP

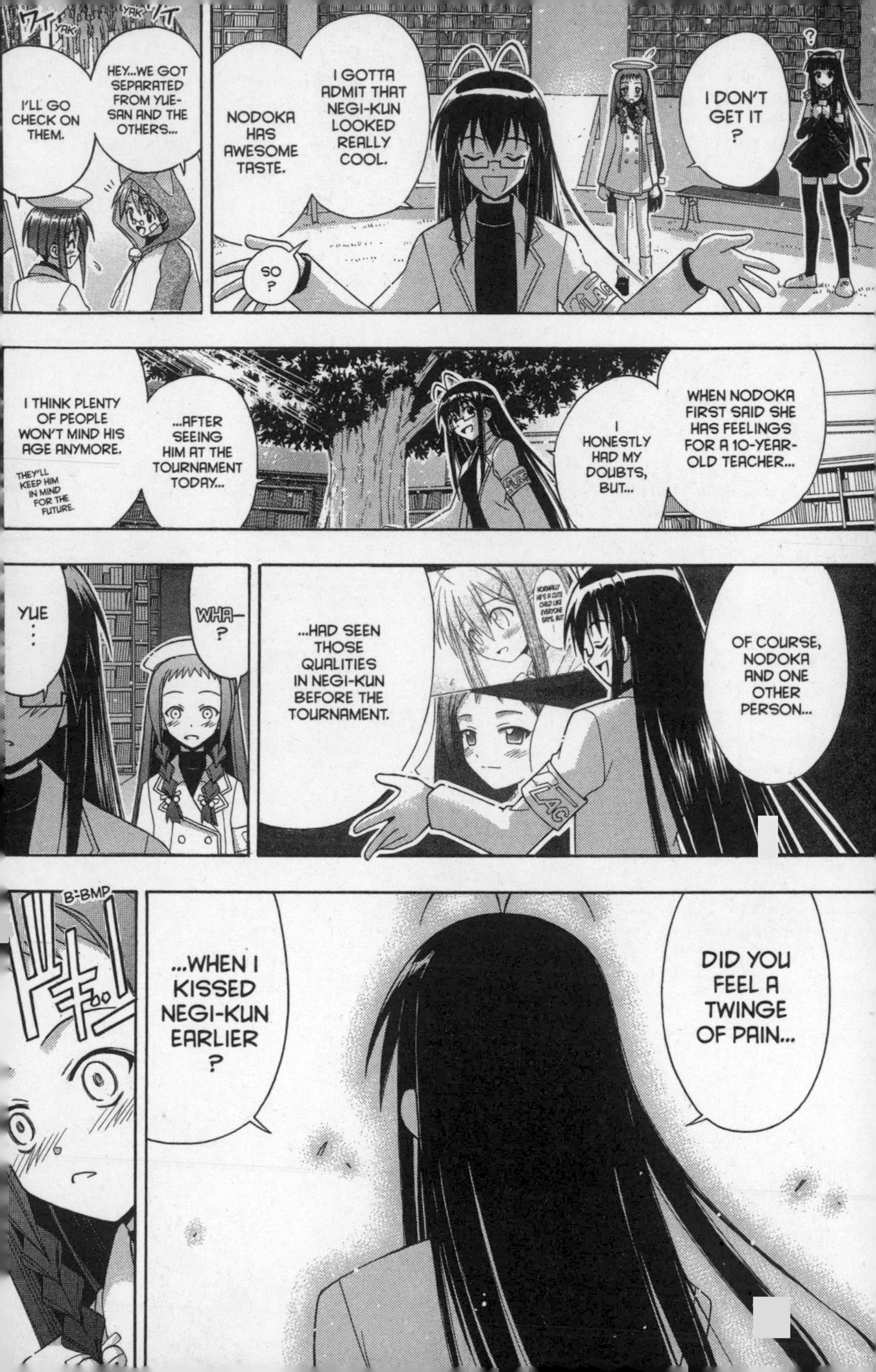
I DON'T GET IT ?
?
I GOTTA ADMIT THAT NEGI-KUN LOOKED REALLY COOL.
NODOKA HAS AWESOME TASTE.
SO ?
HEY...WE GOT SEPARATED FROM YUE-SAN AND THE OTHERS...
I'LL GO CHECK ON THEM.
WHEN NODOKA FIRST SAID SHE HAS FEELINGS FOR A 10-YEAR-OLD TEACHER...
I HONESTLY HAD MY DOUBTS, BUT...
...AFTER SEEING HIM AT THE TOURNAMENT TODAY...
I THINK PLENTY OF PEOPLE WON'T MIND HIS AGE ANYMORE.
THEY'LL KEEP HIM IN MIND FOR THE FUTURE.
OF COURSE, NODOKA AND ONE OTHER PERSON...
NORMALLY HE'S A CUTE CHILD LIKE EVERYONE SAYS, BUT !
...HAD SEEN THOSE QUALITIES IN NEGI-KUN BEFORE THE TOURNAMENT.
WHA— ?
YUE ...
DID YOU FEEL A TWINGE OF PAIN...
...WHEN I KISSED NEGI-KUN EARLIER ?
B-BMP

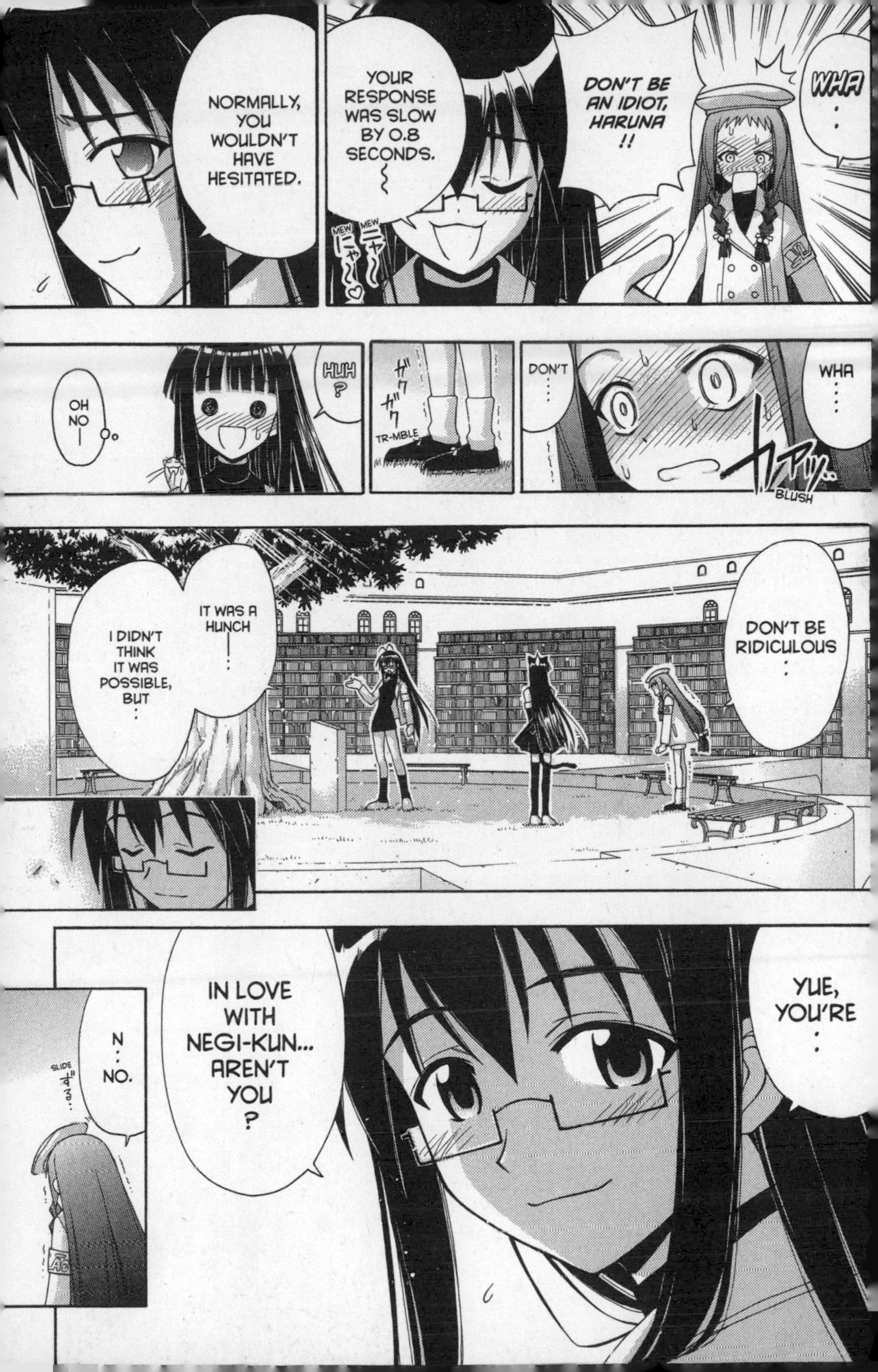

WHA :
DON'T BE AN IDIOT, HARUNA !!
YOUR RESPONSE WAS SLOW BY 0.8 SECONDS.
MEW ニャ〜
MEW にゃ〜♡
NORMALLY, YOU WOULDN'T HAVE HESITATED.
WHA ...
DON'T ...
BLUSH
TR-MBLE
HUH ?
OH NO —
DON'T BE RIDICULOUS :
IT WAS A HUNCH — ...
I DIDN'T THINK IT WAS POSSIBLE, BUT ...
YUE, YOU'RE :
IN LOVE WITH NEGI-KUN... AREN'T YOU ?
N : NO.
SLIDE

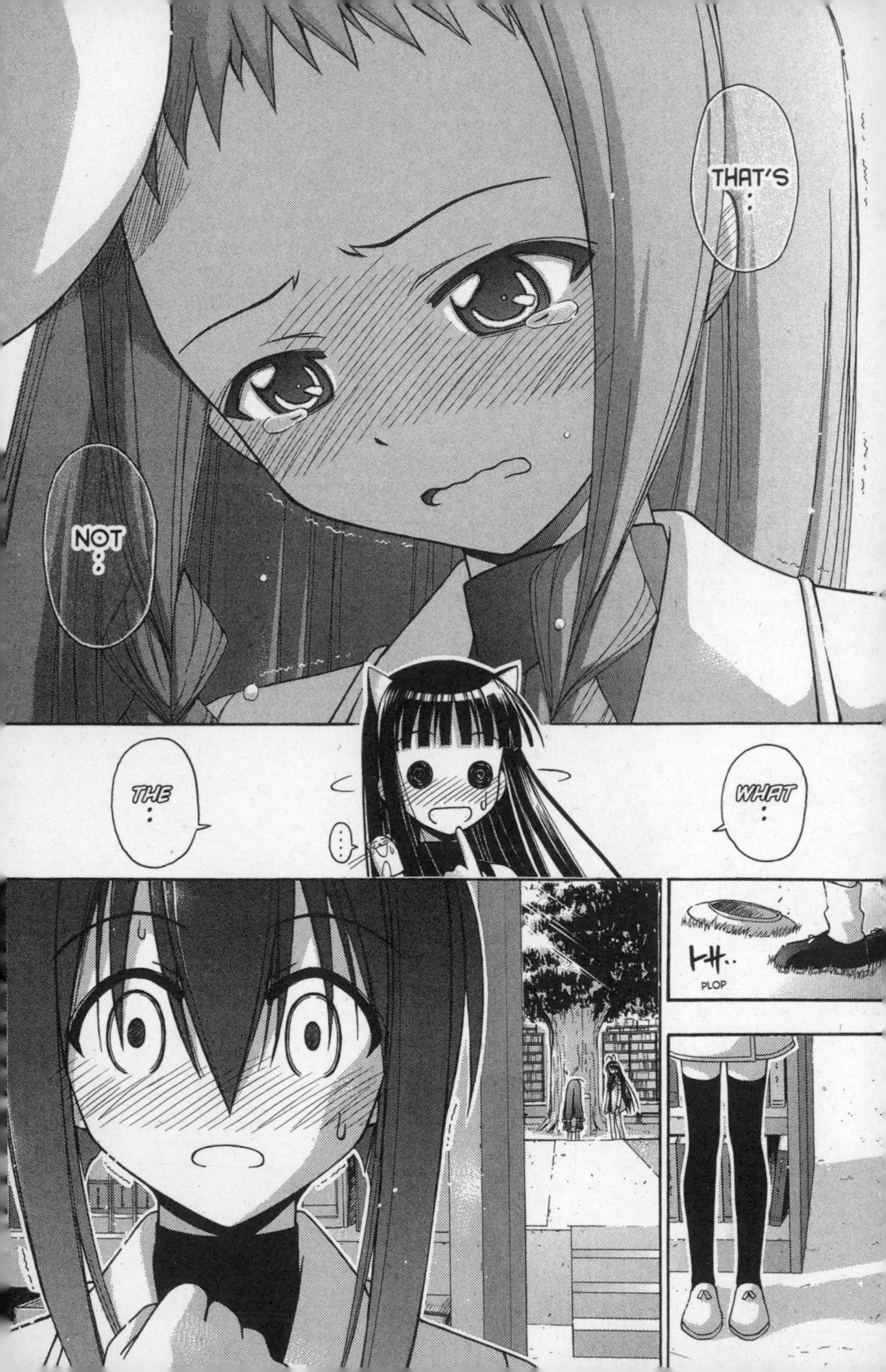
THAT'S...
NOT...
WHAT...
...
THE...
トサ..
PLOP

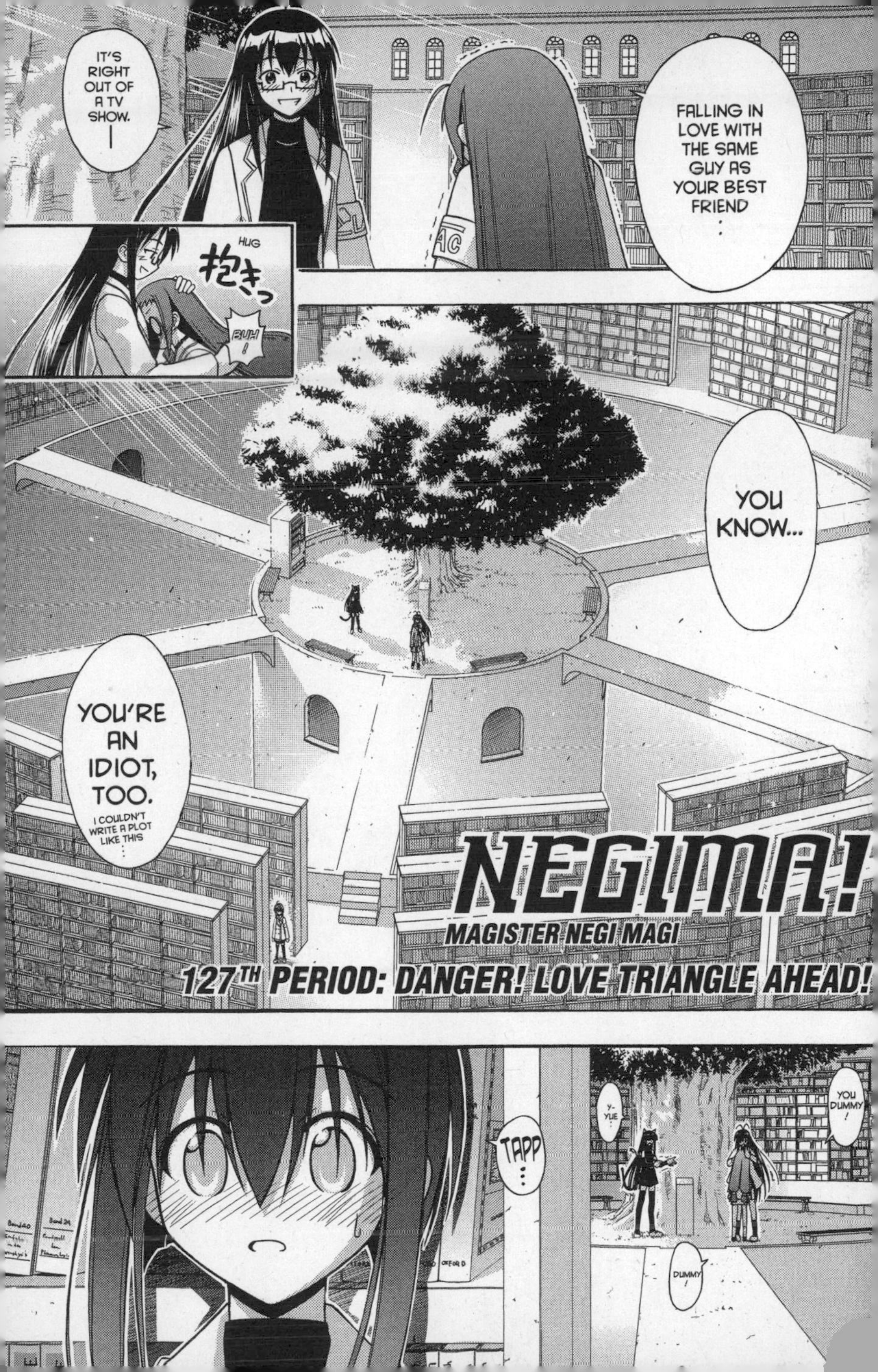
FALLING IN LOVE WITH THE SAME GUY AS YOUR BEST FRIEND...
IT'S RIGHT OUT OF A TV SHOW.
HUG
抱きっ
BUH!
YOU KNOW...
YOU'RE AN IDIOT, TOO.
I COULDN'T WRITE A PLOT LIKE THIS...
NEGIMA!
MAGISTER NEGI MAGI
127TH PERIOD: DANGER! LOVE TRIANGLE AHEAD!
YOU DUMMY!
Y-YUE...
DUMMY!
TAPP...

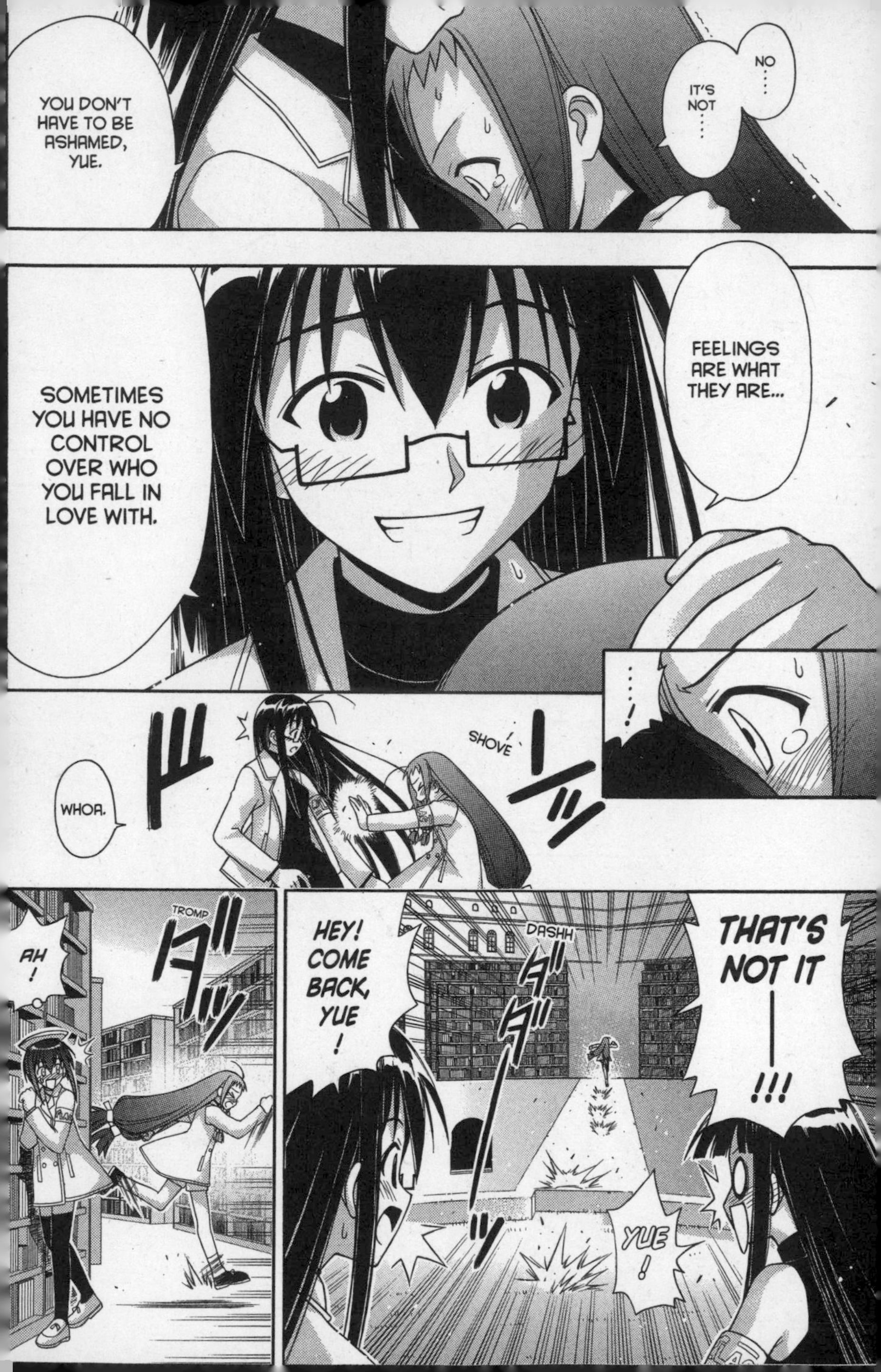
NO... IT'S NOT......
YOU DON'T HAVE TO BE ASHAMED, YUE.
FEELINGS ARE WHAT THEY ARE...
SOMETIMES YOU HAVE NO CONTROL OVER WHO YOU FALL IN LOVE WITH.
...!
SHOVE
WHOA.
THAT'S NOT IT—!!!
YUE!
DASHH
HEY! COME BACK, YUE!
TROMP
AH!

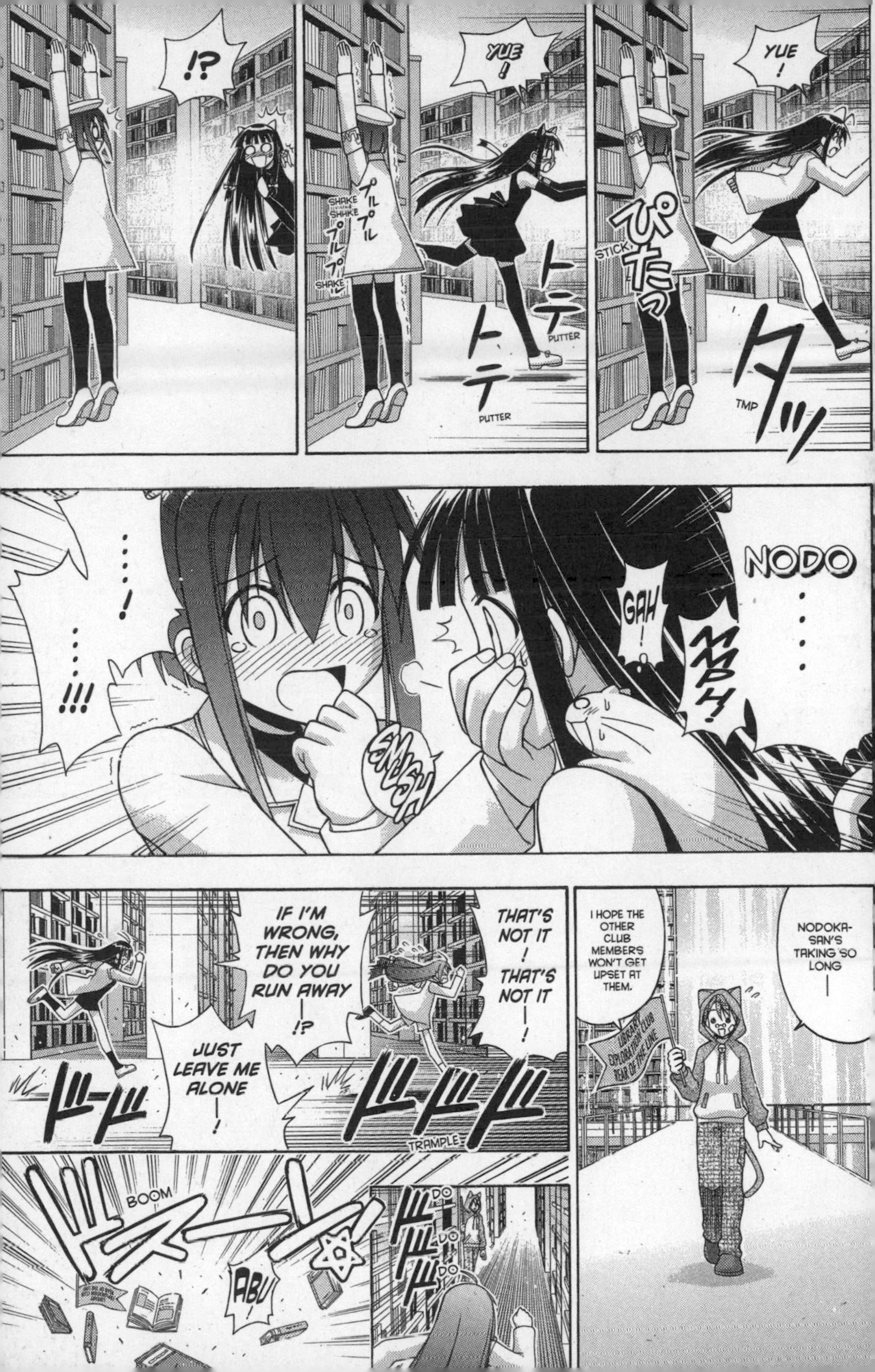
YUE !
ぴたっ
STICK
タッ
TMP
YUE !
プルプル
SHAKE SHAKE
プルプル
SHAKE
トテ
PUTTER
トテ
PUTTER
!?
NODO . . . .
GAH !
MMPH !
SMUSH
. . . . !
. . . . !!!
NODOKA-SAN'S TAKING SO LONG —
I HOPE THE OTHER CLUB MEMBERS WON'T GET UPSET AT THEM.
LIBRARY EXPLORATION CLUB REAR OF THE LINE
THAT'S NOT IT ! THAT'S NOT IT — !
IF I'M WRONG, THEN WHY DO YOU RUN AWAY — !?
ドドドド
TRAMPLE
JUST LEAVE ME ALONE — !
ドドド
DO DO DO
ドドドド
BOOM
ドスーン
ABU !

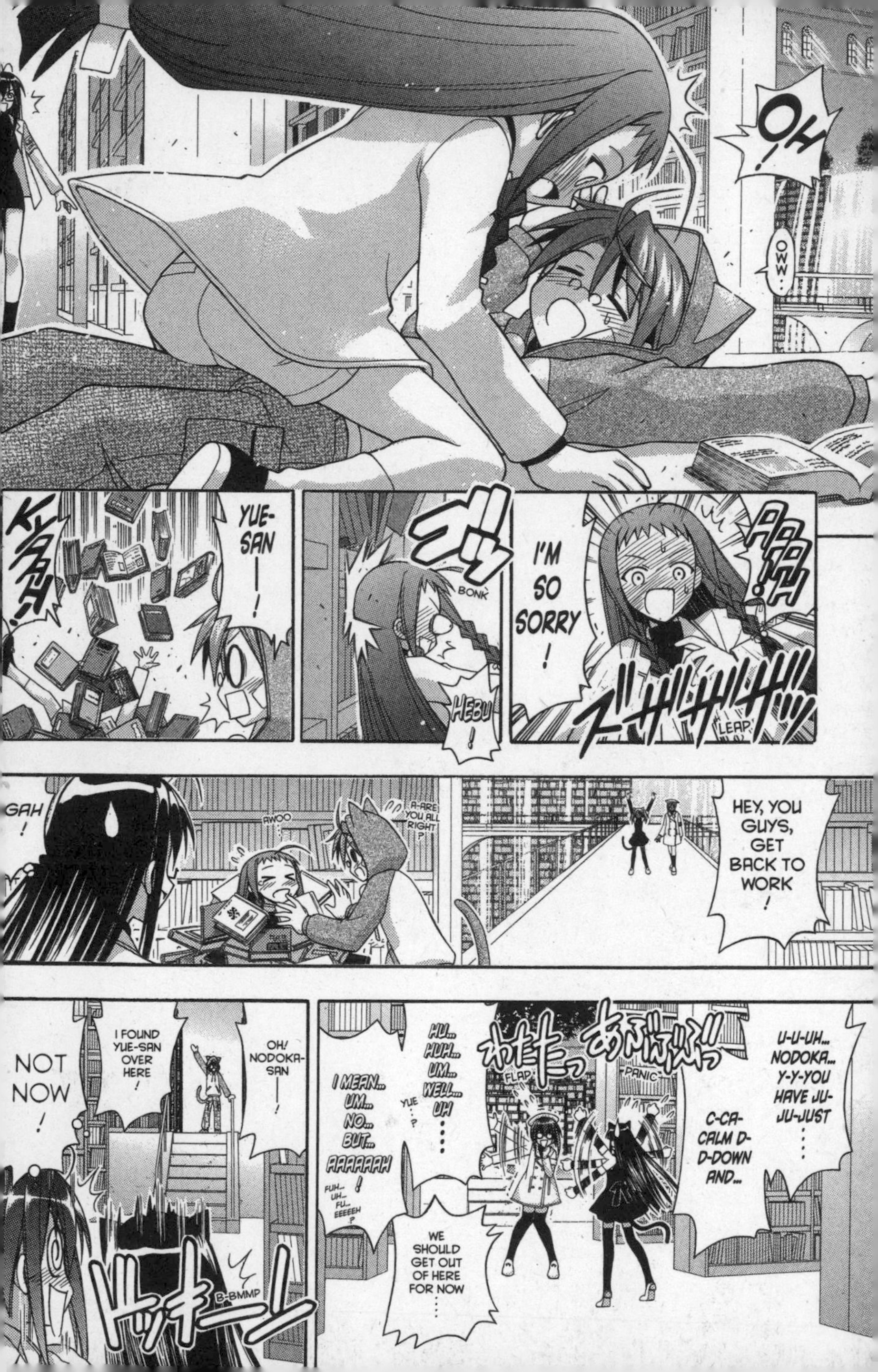
OH!
OWW...
I'M SO SORRY!
LEAP
BONK
HEBU!
YUE-SAN—!
HEY, YOU GUYS, GET BACK TO WORK!
A-ARE YOU ALL RIGHT?
AWOO
GAH!
U-U-UH... NODOKA... Y-Y-YOU HAVE JU-JU-JUST ....
C-CA-CALM D-D-DOWN AND...
PANIC
FLAP
HU... HUH... UM... WELL... UH ....
YUE...?
I MEAN... UM... NO... BUT... AAAAAAAH!
FUH... UH... FU... EEEEEH?
WE SHOULD GET OUT OF HERE FOR NOW ....
OH! NODOKA-SAN—!
I FOUND YUE-SAN OVER HERE!
NOT NOW!
B-BMMP

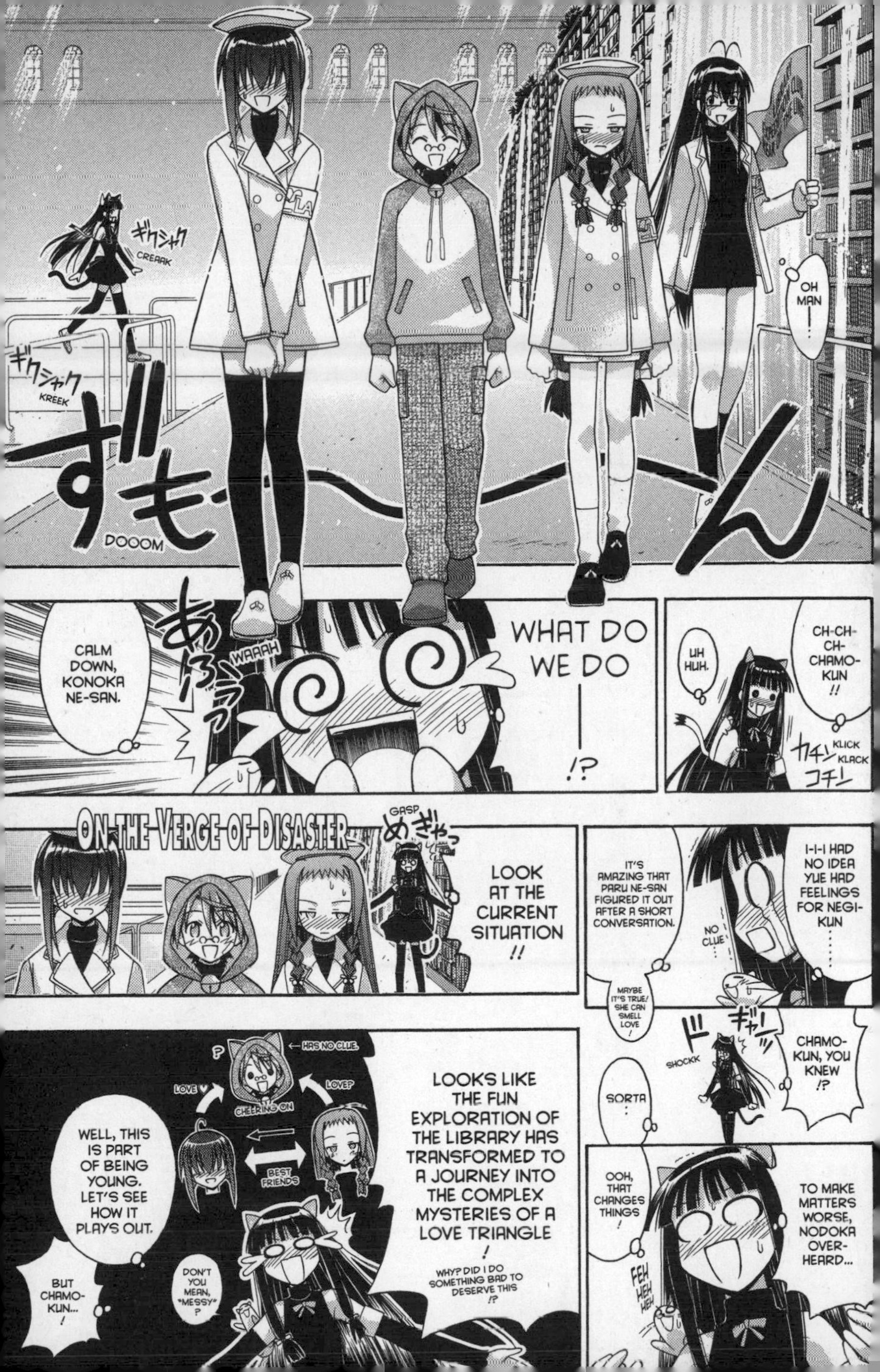
OH MAN!
ギクシャク CREAAK
ギクシャク KREEK
ずも～～ん DOOOM
CH-CH-CH-CHAMO-KUN!!
UH HUH.
カチンコチン KLICK KLACK
WHAT DO WE DO—!?
WAAAH
CALM DOWN, KONOKA NE-SAN.
I-I-I HAD NO IDEA YUE HAD FEELINGS FOR NEGI-KUN......
NO CLUE...
IT'S AMAZING THAT PARU NE-SAN FIGURED IT OUT AFTER A SHORT CONVERSATION.
MAYBE IT'S TRUE/ SHE CAN SMELL LOVE!
ON THE VERGE OF DISASTER
めぎゃっ GASP
LOOK AT THE CURRENT SITUATION!!
CHAMO-KUN, YOU KNEW!?
ド SHOCKK
SORTA...
TO MAKE MATTERS WORSE, NODOKA OVER-HEARD...
OOH, THAT CHANGES THINGS!
FEH HEH HEH
LOOKS LIKE THE FUN EXPLORATION OF THE LIBRARY HAS TRANSFORMED TO A JOURNEY INTO THE COMPLEX MYSTERIES OF A LOVE TRIANGLE!
WHY? DID I DO SOMETHING BAD TO DESERVE THIS!?
? ← HAS NO CLUE.
LOVE?
LOVE ♥
CHEERING ON
BEST FRIENDS
WELL, THIS IS PART OF BEING YOUNG. LET'S SEE HOW IT PLAYS OUT.
DON'T YOU MEAN, "MESSY"?
BUT CHAMO-KUN...!

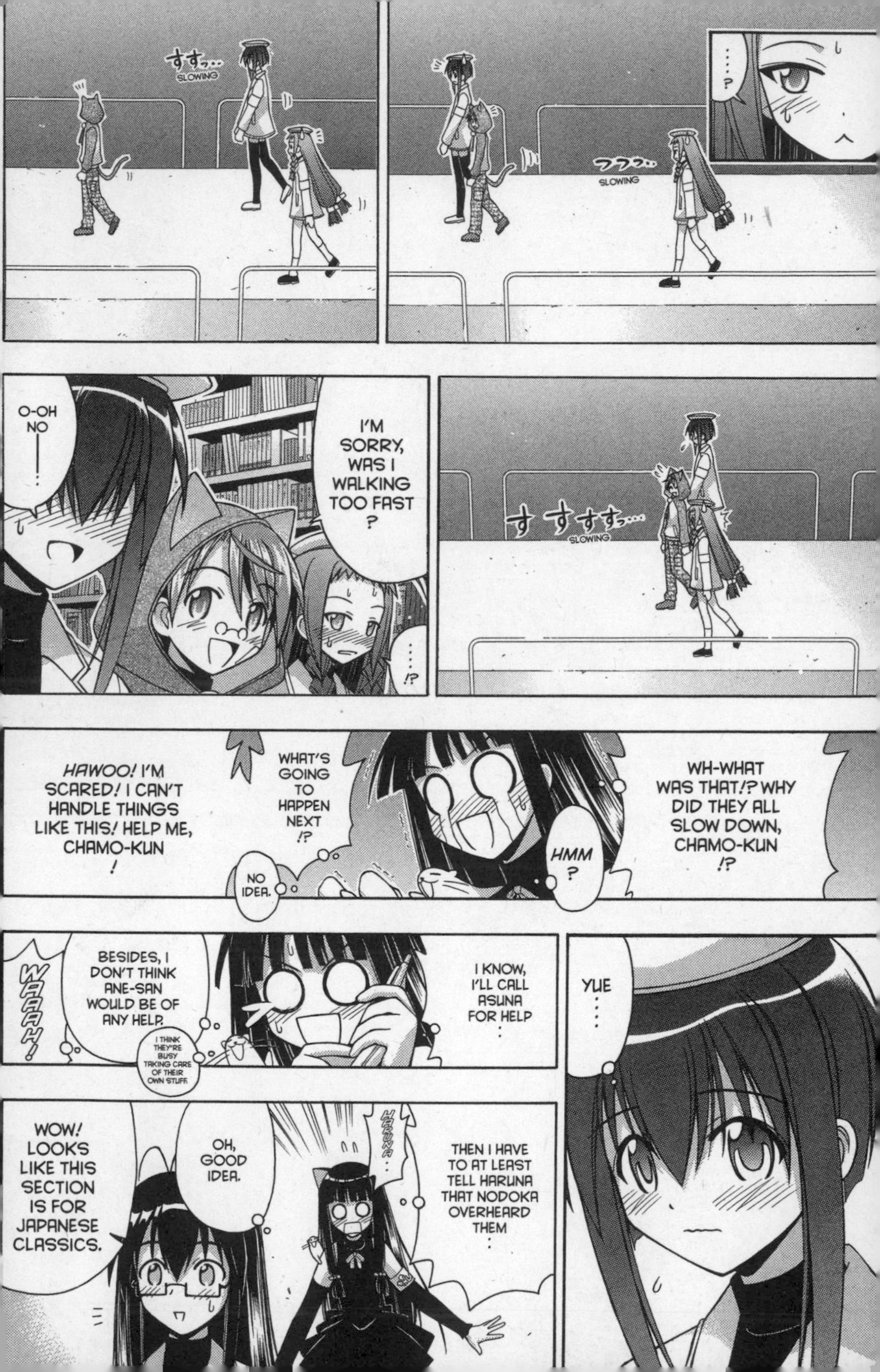
…?
フフフっ…
SLOWING
すすっ…
SLOWING
すすすすっ…
SLOWING
I'M SORRY, WAS I WALKING TOO FAST?
O-OH NO—!
…!?
WH-WHAT WAS THAT!? WHY DID THEY ALL SLOW DOWN, CHAMO-KUN!?
HMM?
WHAT'S GOING TO HAPPEN NEXT!?
NO IDEA.
HAWOO! I'M SCARED! I CAN'T HANDLE THINGS LIKE THIS! HELP ME, CHAMO-KUN!
YUE…
I KNOW, I'LL CALL ASUNA FOR HELP…
BESIDES, I DON'T THINK ANE-SAN WOULD BE OF ANY HELP.
I THINK THEY'RE BUSY TAKING CARE OF THEIR OWN STUFF.
WAAAAH!
THEN I HAVE TO AT LEAST TELL HARUNA THAT NODOKA OVERHEARD THEM…
HARUNA…
OH, GOOD IDEA.
WOW! LOOKS LIKE THIS SECTION IS FOR JAPANESE CLASSICS.

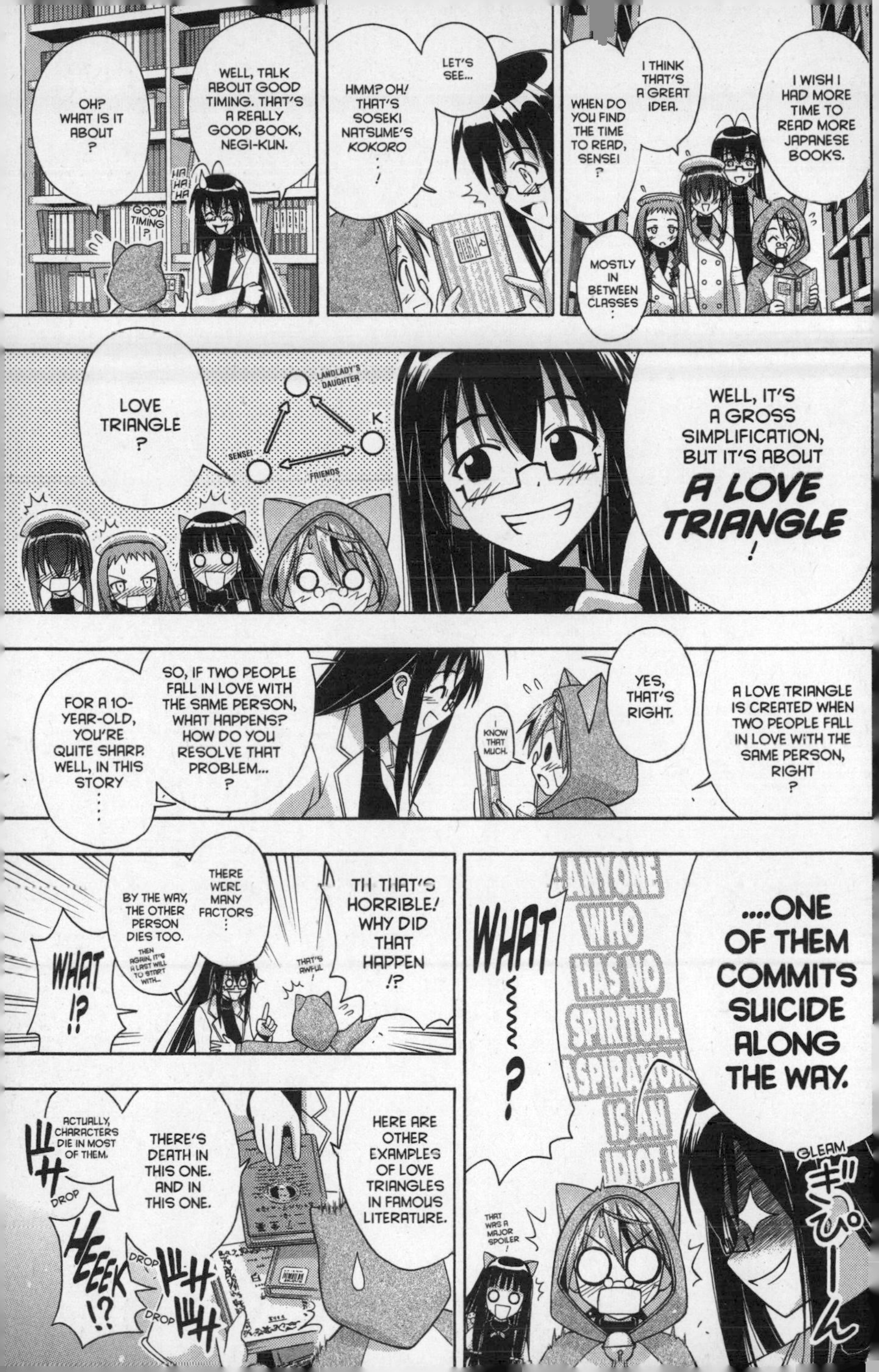
I WISH I HAD MORE TIME TO READ MORE JAPANESE BOOKS.
I THINK THAT'S A GREAT IDEA.
WHEN DO YOU FIND THE TIME TO READ, SENSEI?
MOSTLY IN BETWEEN CLASSES...
LET'S SEE...
HMM? OH! THAT'S SOSEKI NATSUME'S *KOKORO*...!
WELL, TALK ABOUT GOOD TIMING. THAT'S A REALLY GOOD BOOK, NEGI-KUN.
OH? WHAT IS IT ABOUT?
HA HA HA
GOOD TIMING?!
WELL, IT'S A GROSS SIMPLIFICATION, BUT IT'S ABOUT **A LOVE TRIANGLE**!
LANDLADY'S DAUGHTER
K
SENSEI
FRIENDS
LOVE TRIANGLE?
A LOVE TRIANGLE IS CREATED WHEN TWO PEOPLE FALL IN LOVE WITH THE SAME PERSON, RIGHT?
YES, THAT'S RIGHT.
I KNOW THAT MUCH.
SO, IF TWO PEOPLE FALL IN LOVE WITH THE SAME PERSON, WHAT HAPPENS? HOW DO YOU RESOLVE THAT PROBLEM...?
FOR A 10-YEAR-OLD, YOU'RE QUITE SHARP. WELL, IN THIS STORY...
....ONE OF THEM COMMITS SUICIDE ALONG THE WAY.
GLEAM
ANYONE WHO HAS NO SPIRITUAL ASPIRATIONS IS AN IDIOT!
WHAT~~?
THAT WAS A MAJOR SPOILER!
TH THAT'S HORRIBLE! WHY DID THAT HAPPEN!?
THERE WERE MANY FACTORS...
BY THE WAY, THE OTHER PERSON DIES TOO.
THEN AGAIN, IT'S A LAST WILL TO START WITH...
THAT'S AWFUL!
WHAT!?
HERE ARE OTHER EXAMPLES OF LOVE TRIANGLES IN FAMOUS LITERATURE.
THERE'S DEATH IN THIS ONE. AND IN THIS ONE.
ACTUALLY, CHARACTERS DIE IN MOST OF THEM.
DROP
HEEEK!?
DROP
DROP

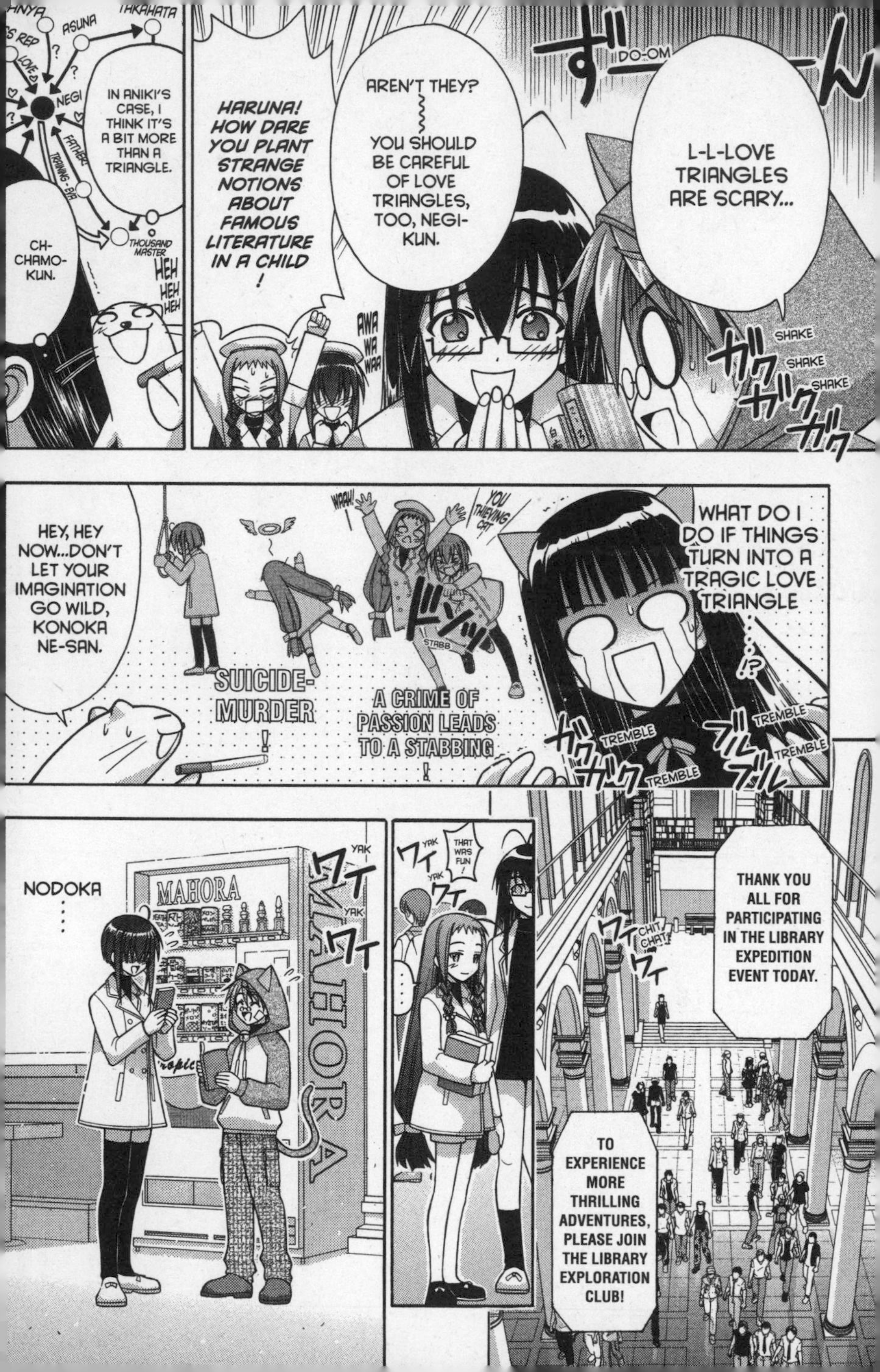
DO-OM
L-L-LOVE TRIANGLES ARE SCARY...
SHAKE
SHAKE
SHAKE
AREN'T THEY?
YOU SHOULD BE CAREFUL OF LOVE TRIANGLES, TOO, NEGI-KUN.
HARUNA! HOW DARE YOU PLANT STRANGE NOTIONS ABOUT FAMOUS LITERATURE IN A CHILD!
AWA WA WAA
TAKAHATA
ASUNA
LOVE
NEGI
FATHER
TRAINING · EVA
THOUSAND MASTER
IN ANIKI'S CASE, I THINK IT'S A BIT MORE THAN A TRIANGLE.
HEH HEH HEH
CH-CHAMO-KUN.
WHAT DO I DO IF THINGS TURN INTO A TRAGIC LOVE TRIANGLE...!?
TREMBLE
TREMBLE
TREMBLE
TREMBLE
YOU THIEVING CAT
WAAH!
STABB
A CRIME OF PASSION LEADS TO A STABBING!
SUICIDE-MURDER!
HEY, HEY NOW...DON'T LET YOUR IMAGINATION GO WILD, KONOKA NE-SAN.
THANK YOU ALL FOR PARTICIPATING IN THE LIBRARY EXPEDITION EVENT TODAY.
CHIT CHAT
TO EXPERIENCE MORE THRILLING ADVENTURES, PLEASE JOIN THE LIBRARY EXPLORATION CLUB!
YAK
YAK
THAT WAS FUN!
...
YAK
YAK
MAHORA
NODOKA...

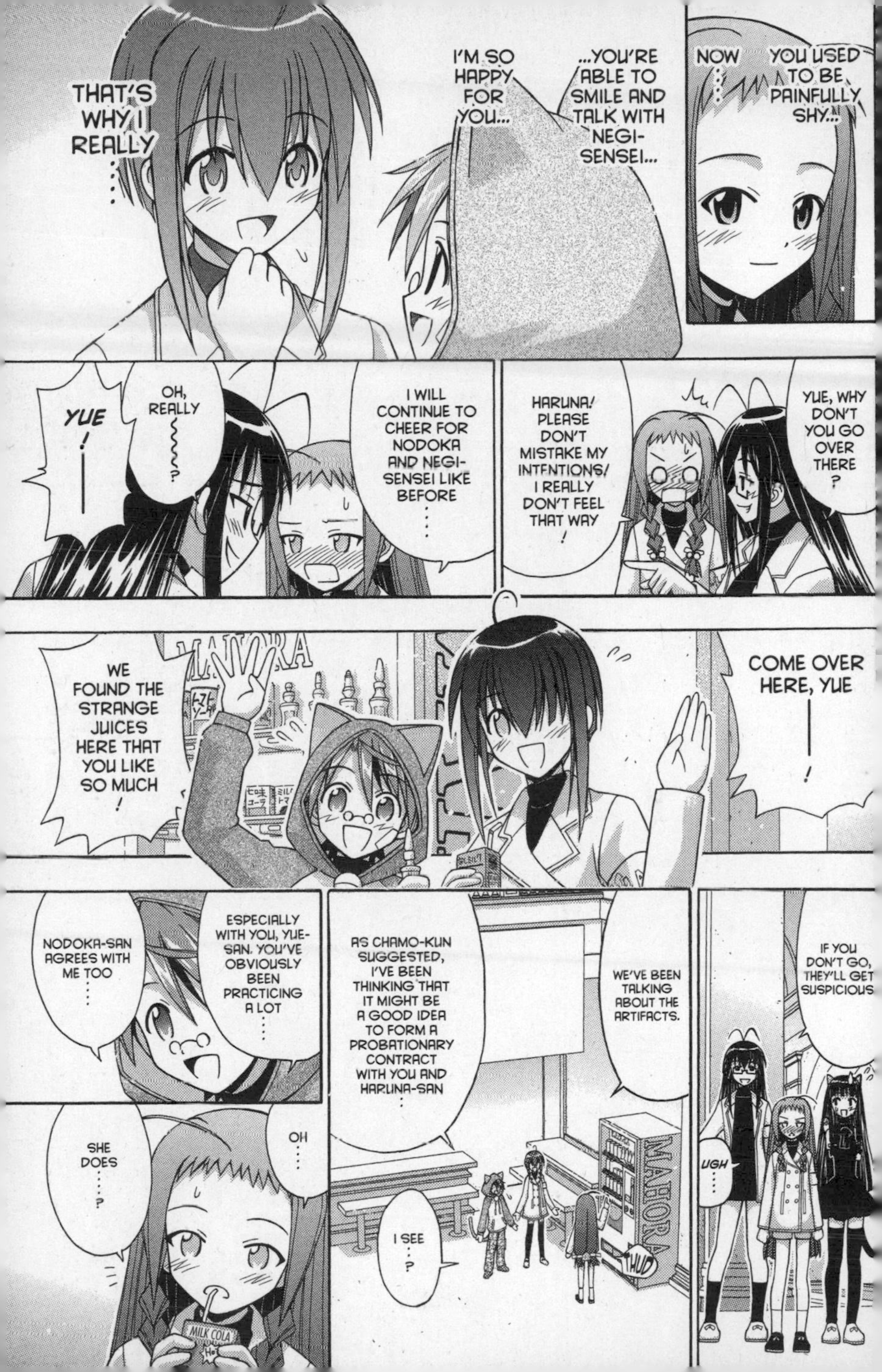
YOU USED TO BE PAINFULLY SHY...
NOW...
...YOU'RE ABLE TO SMILE AND TALK WITH NEGI-SENSEI...
I'M SO HAPPY FOR YOU...
THAT'S WHY I REALLY...
YUE, WHY DON'T YOU GO OVER THERE?
HARUNA! PLEASE DON'T MISTAKE MY INTENTIONS! I REALLY DON'T FEEL THAT WAY!
I WILL CONTINUE TO CHEER FOR NODOKA AND NEGI-SENSEI LIKE BEFORE...
OH, REALLY~?
YUE!—
COME OVER HERE, YUE—!
WE FOUND THE STRANGE JUICES HERE THAT YOU LIKE SO MUCH!
IF YOU DON'T GO, THEY'LL GET SUSPICIOUS
UGH...
WE'VE BEEN TALKING ABOUT THE ARTIFACTS.
AS CHAMO-KUN SUGGESTED, I'VE BEEN THINKING THAT IT MIGHT BE A GOOD IDEA TO FORM A PROBATIONARY CONTRACT WITH YOU AND HARUNA-SAN:
MAHORA
THUD
I SEE...?
ESPECIALLY WITH YOU, YUE-SAN. YOU'VE OBVIOUSLY BEEN PRACTICING A LOT...
NODOKA-SAN AGREES WITH ME TOO...
OH...
SHE DOES...?
MILK COLA

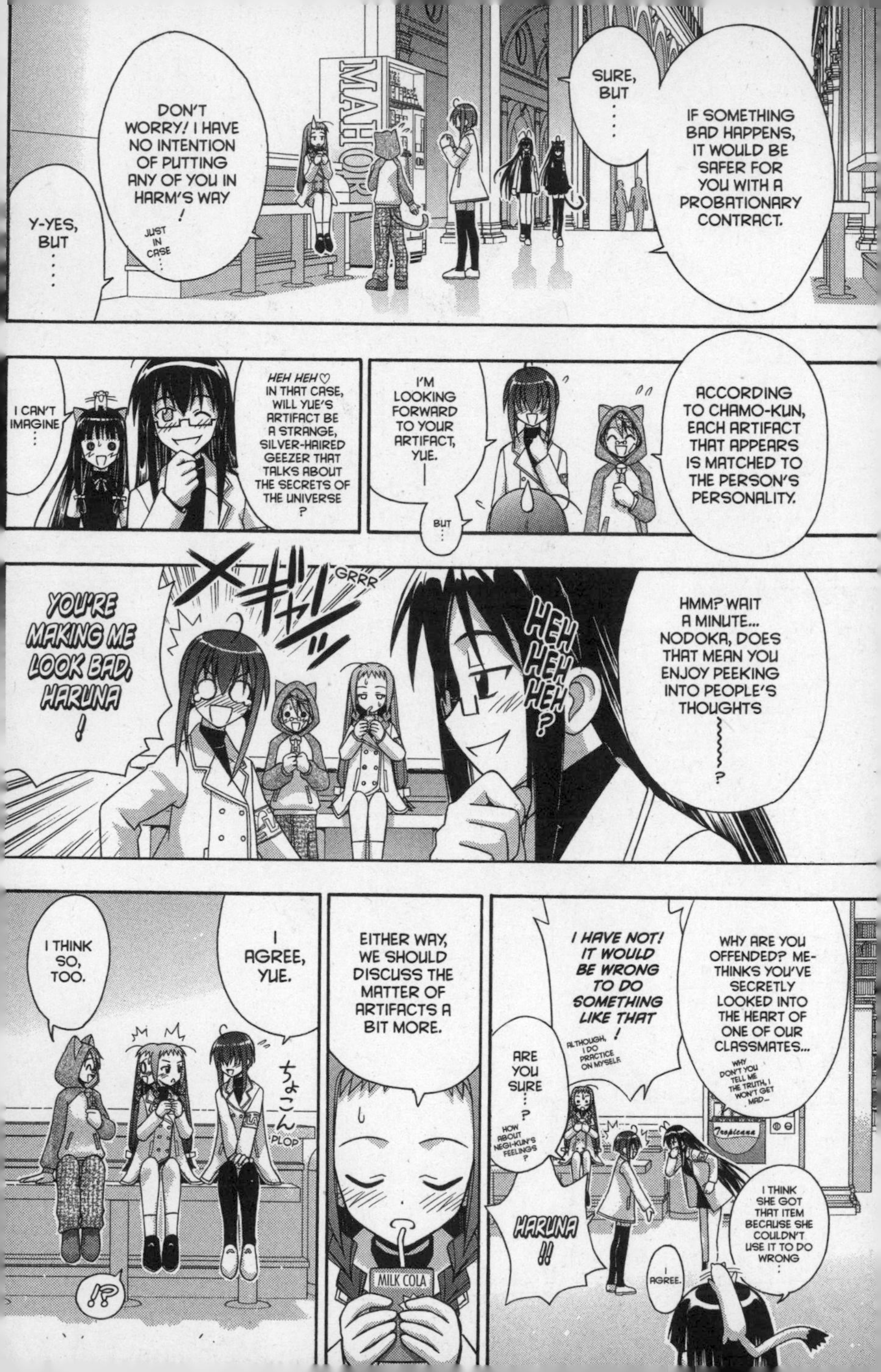

SURE, BUT....
IF SOMETHING BAD HAPPENS, IT WOULD BE SAFER FOR YOU WITH A PROBATIONARY CONTRACT.
MAHORA
DON'T WORRY! I HAVE NO INTENTION OF PUTTING ANY OF YOU IN HARM'S WAY!
JUST IN CASE...
Y-YES, BUT....
ACCORDING TO CHAMO-KUN, EACH ARTIFACT THAT APPEARS IS MATCHED TO THE PERSON'S PERSONALITY.
I'M LOOKING FORWARD TO YOUR ARTIFACT, YUE—
BUT...
HEH HEH♡ IN THAT CASE, WILL YUE'S ARTIFACT BE A STRANGE, SILVER-HAIRED GEEZER THAT TALKS ABOUT THE SECRETS OF THE UNIVERSE?
I CAN'T IMAGINE...
HMM? WAIT A MINUTE... NODOKA, DOES THAT MEAN YOU ENJOY PEEKING INTO PEOPLE'S THOUGHTS~~~?
HEH HEH HEH?
GRRR
ギャンッ
YOU'RE MAKING ME LOOK BAD, HARUNA!
WHY ARE YOU OFFENDED? METHINKS YOU'VE SECRETLY LOOKED INTO THE HEART OF ONE OF OUR CLASSMATES...
WHY DON'T YOU TELL ME THE TRUTH, I WON'T GET MAD...
I HAVE NOT! IT WOULD BE WRONG TO DO SOMETHING LIKE THAT!
ALTHOUGH, I DO PRACTICE ON MYSELF.
ARE YOU SURE...?
HOW ABOUT NEGI-KUN'S FEELINGS?
Tropicana
I THINK SHE GOT THAT ITEM BECAUSE SHE COULDN'T USE IT TO DO WRONG:
I AGREE.
HARUNA!!
EITHER WAY, WE SHOULD DISCUSS THE MATTER OF ARTIFACTS A BIT MORE.
MILK COLA
I AGREE, YUE.
I THINK SO, TOO.
ちょこん
PLOP
!?

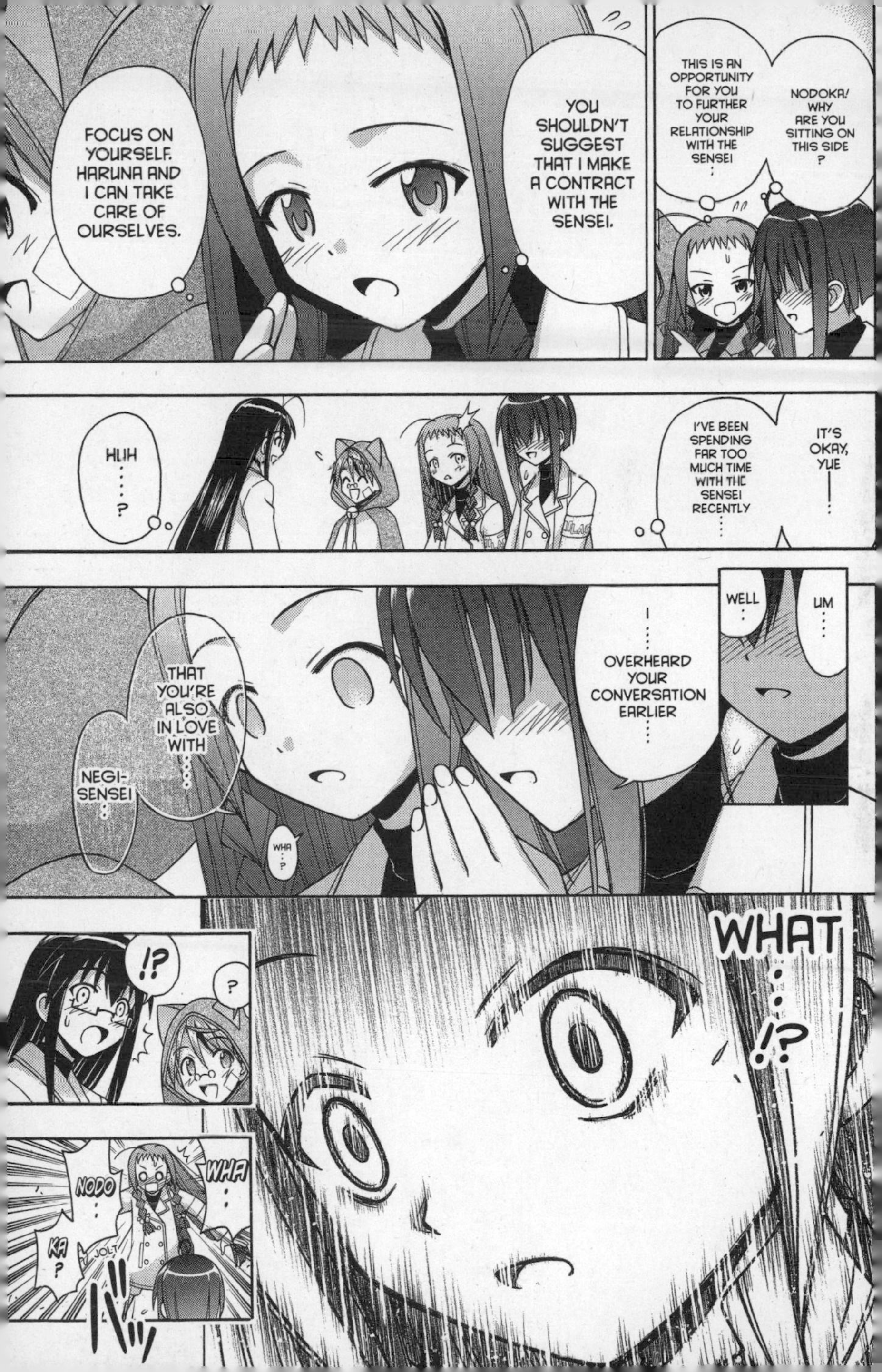
NODOKA! WHY ARE YOU SITTING ON THIS SIDE?
THIS IS AN OPPORTUNITY FOR YOU TO FURTHER YOUR RELATIONSHIP WITH THE SENSEI...
YOU SHOULDN'T SUGGEST THAT I MAKE A CONTRACT WITH THE SENSEI.
FOCUS ON YOURSELF. HARUNA AND I CAN TAKE CARE OF OURSELVES.
IT'S OKAY, YUE—...
I'VE BEEN SPENDING FAR TOO MUCH TIME WITH THE SENSEI RECENTLY...
HUH....?
UM...
WELL..
I.... OVERHEARD YOUR CONVERSATION EARLIER.....
THAT YOU'RE ALSO IN LOVE WITH....
NEGI-SENSEI..
WHA..?
WHAT...!?
!?
?
WHA..
NODO.. KA?
JOLT

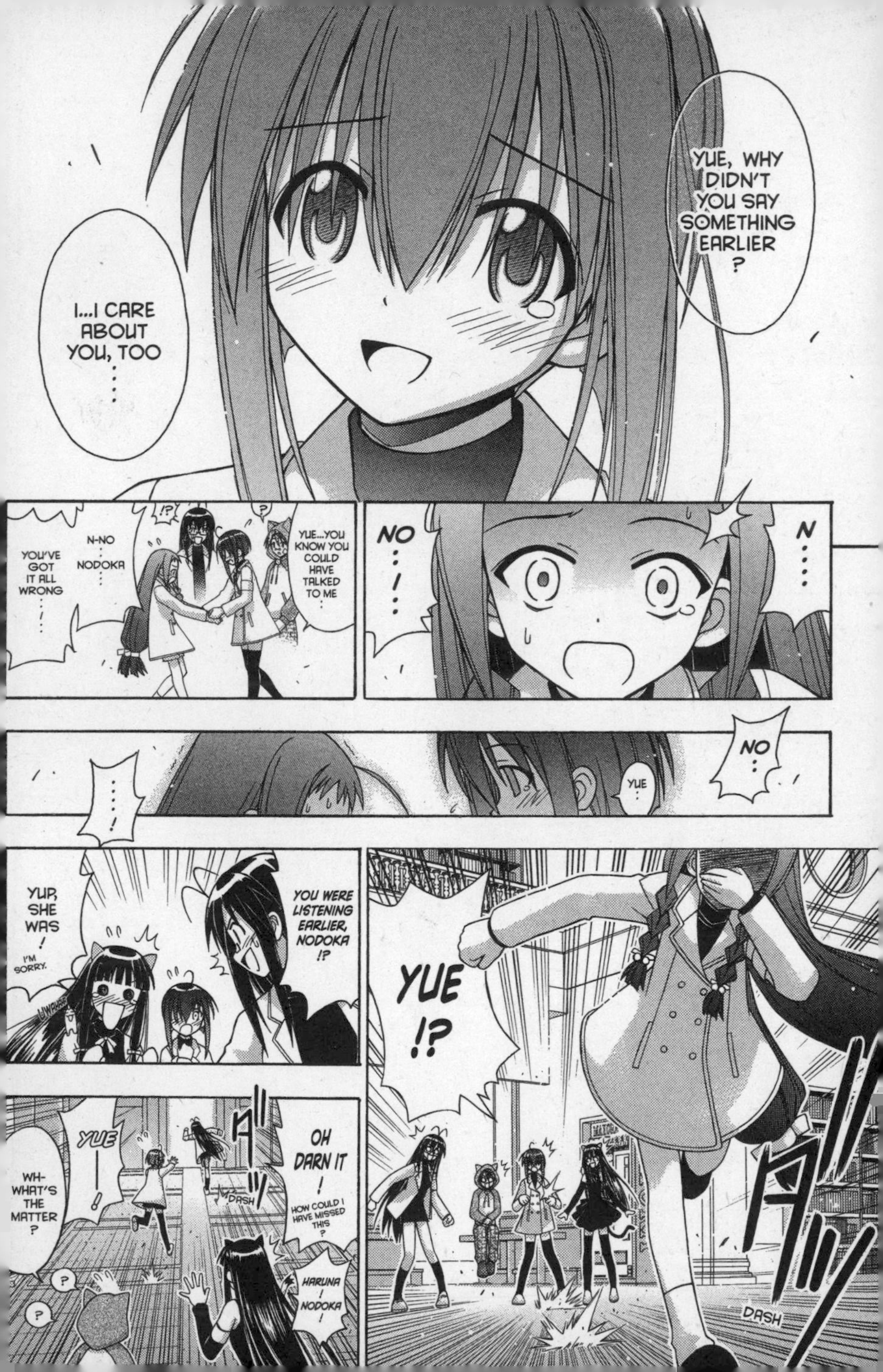
YUE, WHY DIDN'T YOU SAY SOMETHING EARLIER ?
I...I CARE ABOUT YOU, TOO ....
N....
NO ..!...
YUE...YOU KNOW YOU COULD HAVE TALKED TO ME ..
?
!?
N-NO .. NODOKA ..
YOU'VE GOT IT ALL WRONG ...!...
NO ..
YUE ..
....!
YUE !?
YOU WERE LISTENING EARLIER, NODOKA !?
YUP, SHE WAS !
I'M SORRY.
DASH
OH DARN IT !
HOW COULD I HAVE MISSED THIS ?
HARUNA ! NODOKA !
DASH
YUE ——!
WH-WHAT'S THE MATTER ?
?
?

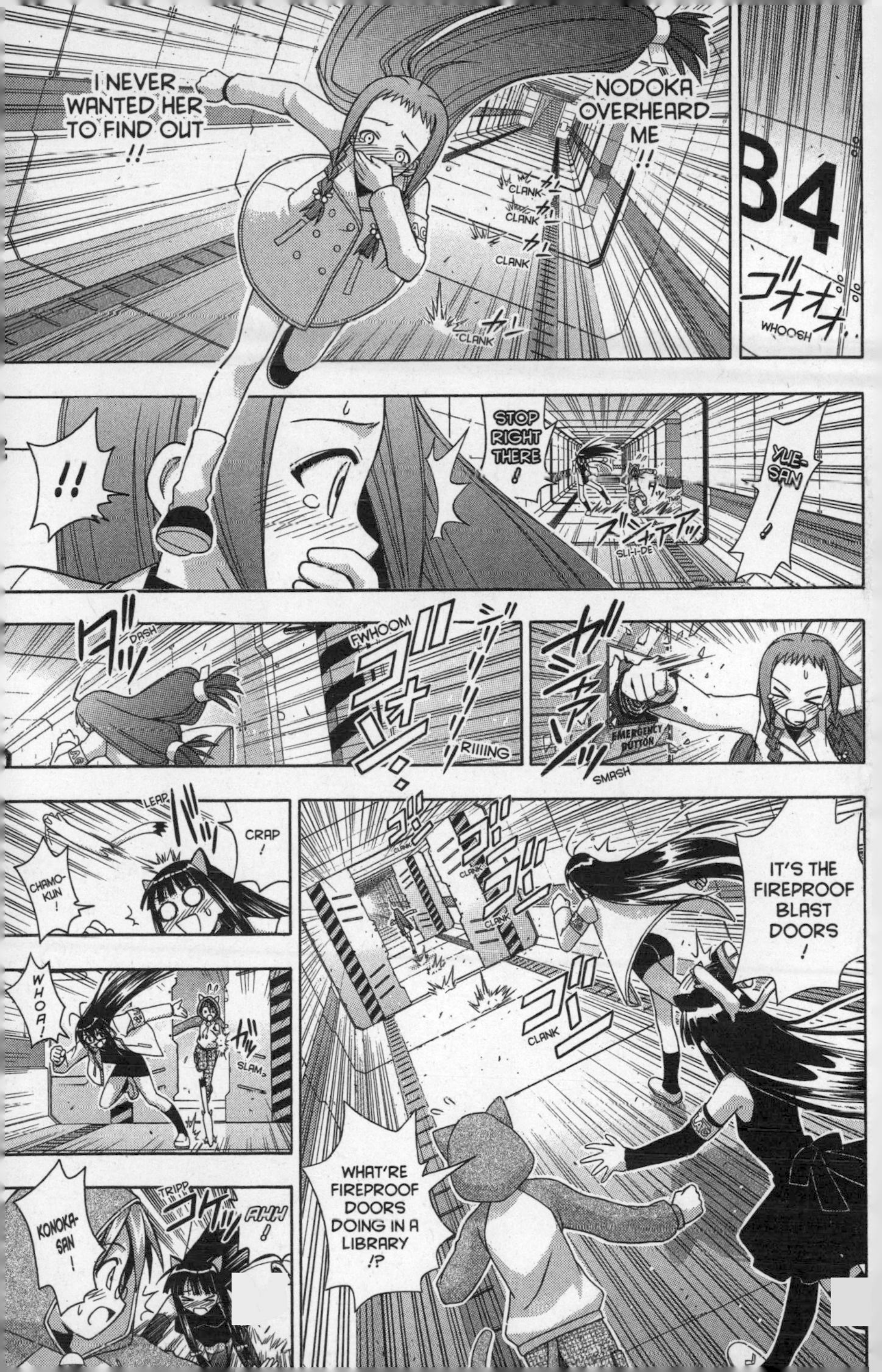
34
WHOOSH
NODOKA OVERHEARD ME!!
I NEVER WANTED HER TO FIND OUT!!
CLANK
CLANK
CLANK
CLANK
YUE-SAN!
STOP RIGHT THERE!
TMP
SLI-I-DE
!!
EMERGENCY BUTTON
SMASH
FWHOOM
RIIING
DASH
IT'S THE FIREPROOF BLAST DOORS!
CLANK
CLANK
CLANK
CLANK
WHAT'RE FIREPROOF DOORS DOING IN A LIBRARY!?
CRAP!
LEAP
CHAMO-KUN!
WHOA!
SLAM
AHH!
TRIPP
KONOKA-SAN!

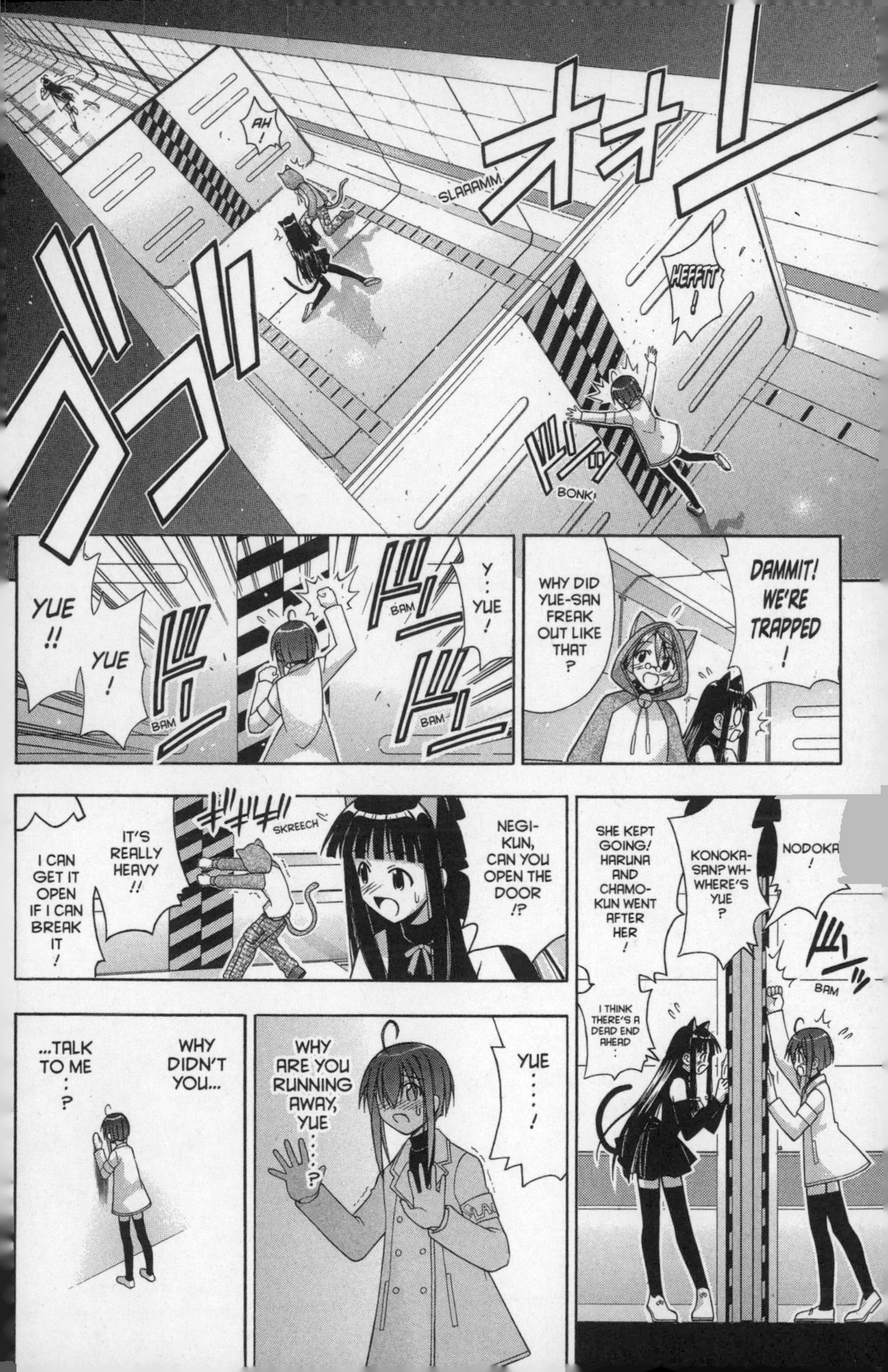
HEFFTT!
SLAAAMM
AH!
BONK
DAMMIT! WE'RE TRAPPED!
WHY DID YUE-SAN FREAK OUT LIKE THAT?
Y... YUE!
BAM
BAM
YUE!!
YUE!
BAM
NODOKA!
KONOKA-SAN? WH-WHERE'S YUE?
SHE KEPT GOING! HARUNA AND CHAMO-KUN WENT AFTER HER!
BAM
I THINK THERE'S A DEAD END AHEAD...
NEGI-KUN, CAN YOU OPEN THE DOOR!?
SKREECH
IT'S REALLY HEAVY!!
I CAN GET IT OPEN IF I CAN BREAK IT!
YUE...!
WHY ARE YOU RUNNING AWAY, YUE...?
WHY DIDN'T YOU...
...TALK TO ME...?

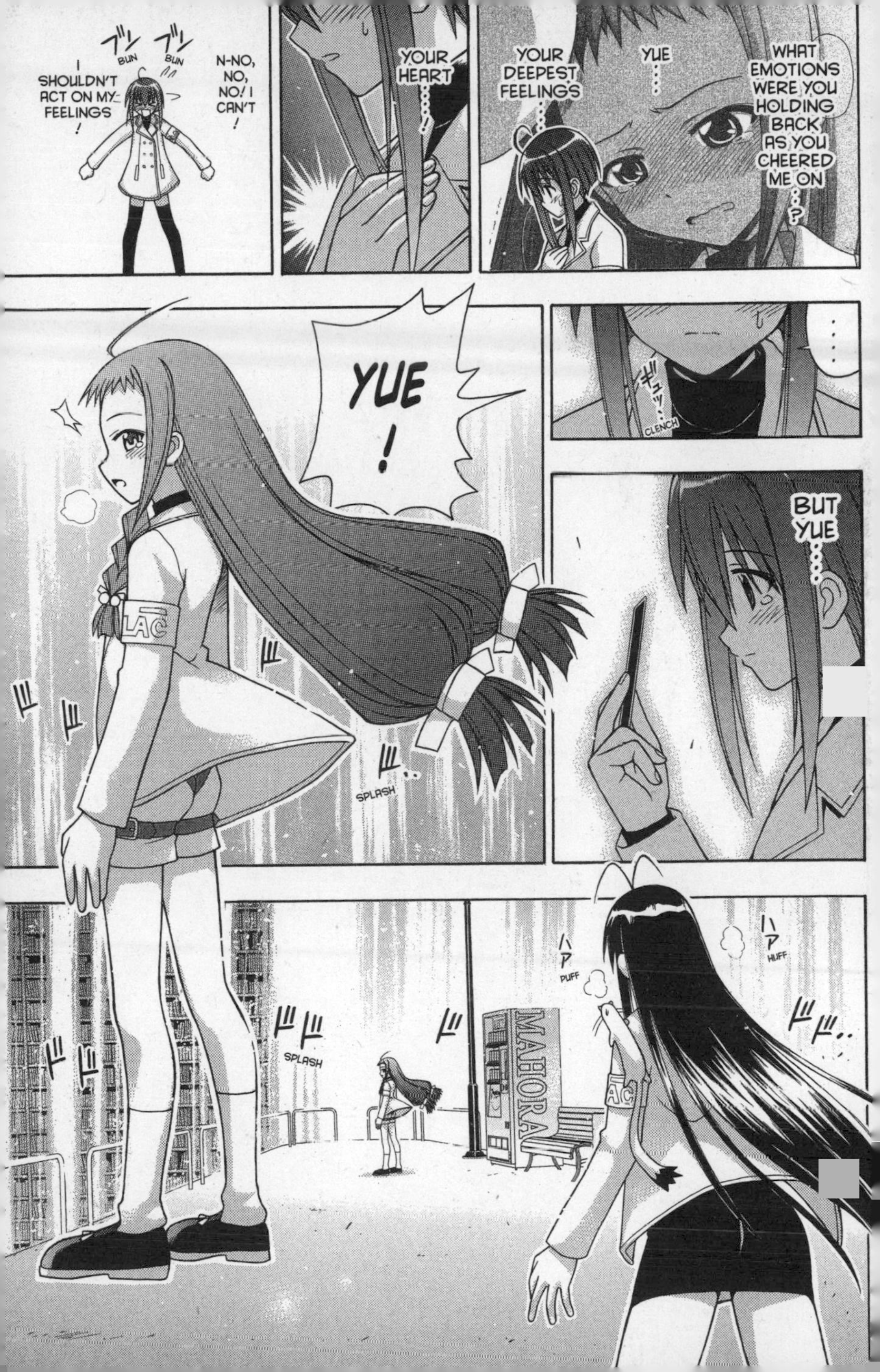

WHAT EMOTIONS WERE YOU HOLDING BACK AS YOU CHEERED ME ON ...?
YUE ...
YOUR DEEPEST FEELINGS
YOUR HEART ...!
N-NO, NO, NO! I CAN'T!
ブン BUN
ブン BUN
I SHOULDN'T ACT ON MY FEELINGS!
...
ギュッ CLENCH
BUT YUE ...
YUE!
SPLASH
ハァ HUFF
ハァ PUFF
SPLASH
MAHORA

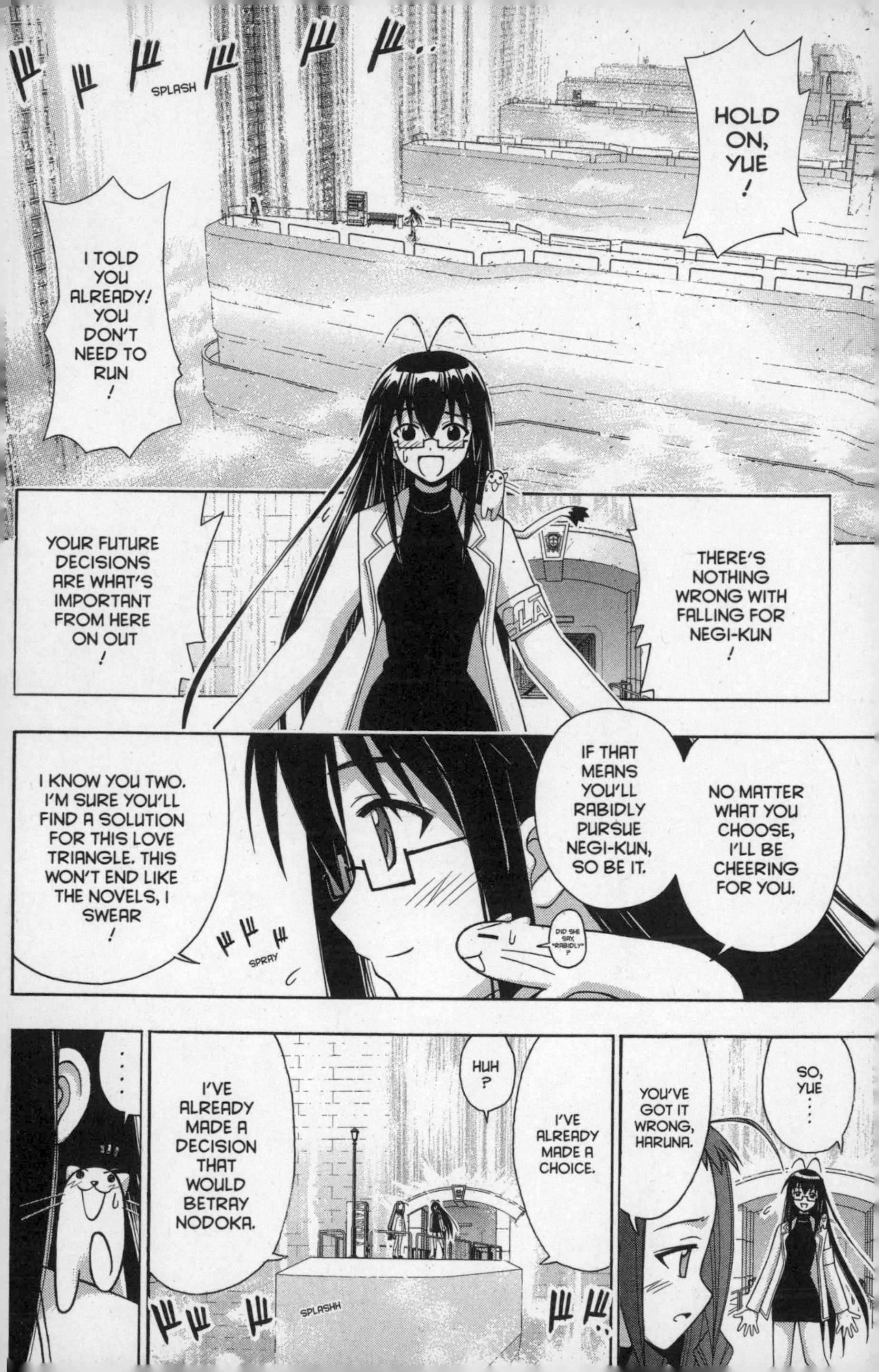
HOLD ON, YUE!
SPLASH
I TOLD YOU ALREADY! YOU DON'T NEED TO RUN!
THERE'S NOTHING WRONG WITH FALLING FOR NEGI-KUN!
YOUR FUTURE DECISIONS ARE WHAT'S IMPORTANT FROM HERE ON OUT!
NO MATTER WHAT YOU CHOOSE, I'LL BE CHEERING FOR YOU.
IF THAT MEANS YOU'LL RABIDLY PURSUE NEGI-KUN, SO BE IT.
DID SHE SAY, "RABIDLY"?
I KNOW YOU TWO. I'M SURE YOU'LL FIND A SOLUTION FOR THIS LOVE TRIANGLE. THIS WON'T END LIKE THE NOVELS, I SWEAR!
SPRAY
SO, YUE....
YOU'VE GOT IT WRONG, HARUNA.
HUH?
I'VE ALREADY MADE A CHOICE.
I'VE ALREADY MADE A DECISION THAT WOULD BETRAY NODOKA.
SPLASHH
....

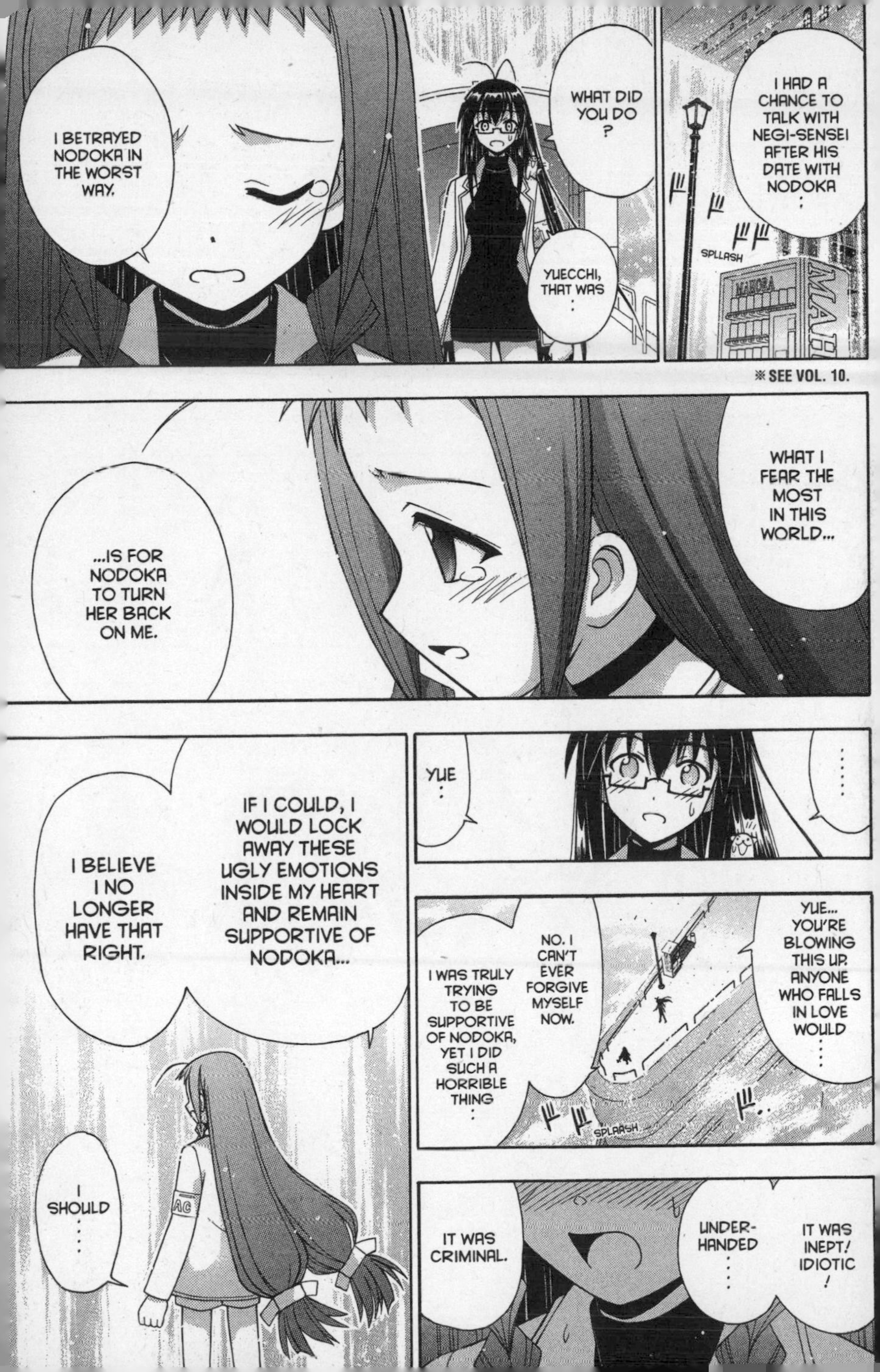
I HAD A CHANCE TO TALK WITH NEGI-SENSEI AFTER HIS DATE WITH NODOKA...
SPLLASH
WHAT DID YOU DO?
YUECCHI, THAT WAS...
I BETRAYED NODOKA IN THE WORST WAY.
※ SEE VOL. 10.
WHAT I FEAR THE MOST IN THIS WORLD...
...IS FOR NODOKA TO TURN HER BACK ON ME.
......
YUE...
YUE... YOU'RE BLOWING THIS UP. ANYONE WHO FALLS IN LOVE WOULD...
NO. I CAN'T EVER FORGIVE MYSELF NOW.
I WAS TRULY TRYING TO BE SUPPORTIVE OF NODOKA, YET I DID SUCH A HORRIBLE THING...
SPLAASH
IT WAS INEPT! IDIOTIC!
UNDER-HANDED...
IT WAS CRIMINAL.
IF I COULD, I WOULD LOCK AWAY THESE UGLY EMOTIONS INSIDE MY HEART AND REMAIN SUPPORTIVE OF NODOKA...
I BELIEVE I NO LONGER HAVE THAT RIGHT.
I SHOULD......

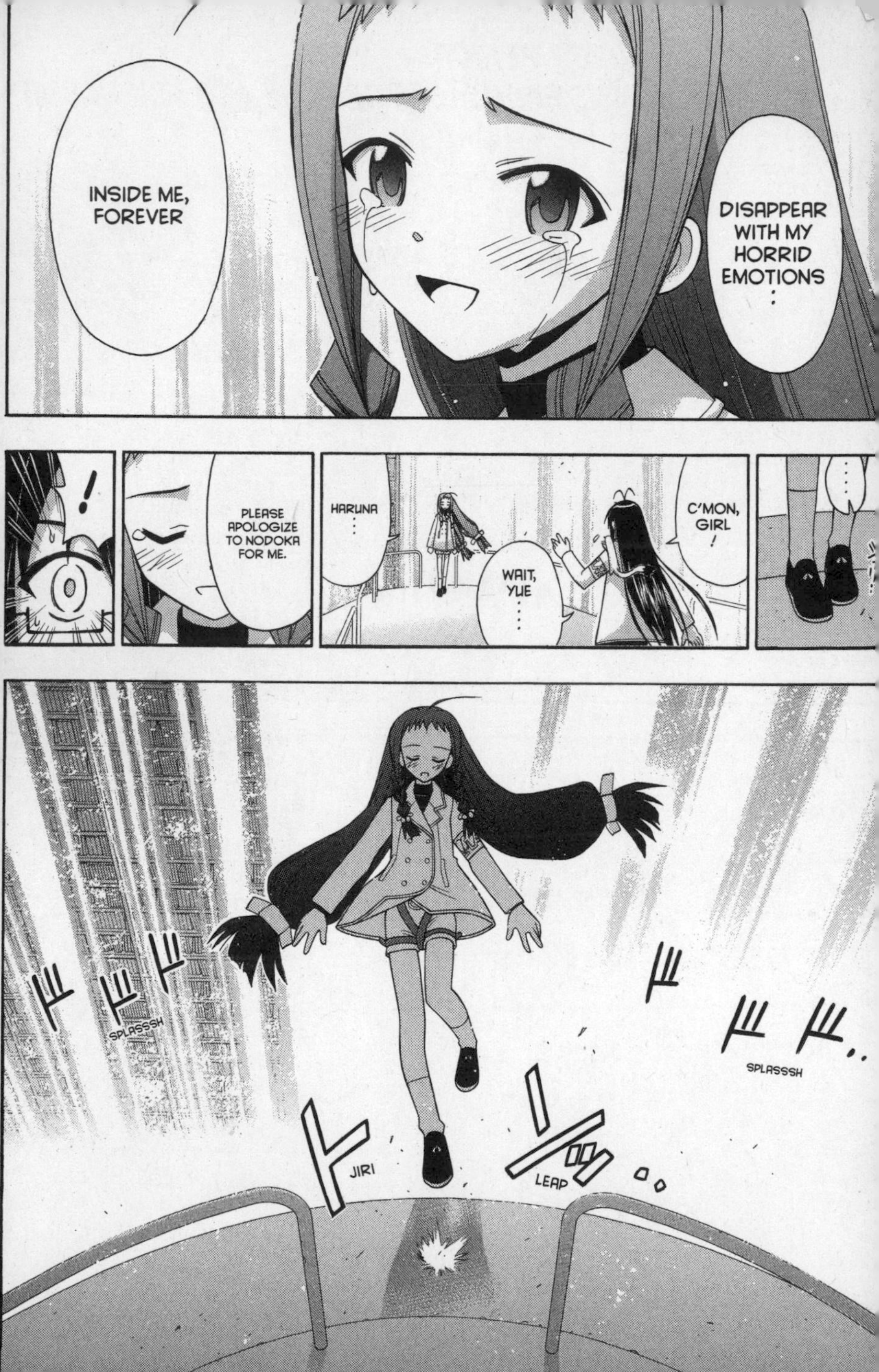
DISAPPEAR WITH MY HORRID EMOTIONS
:
INSIDE ME, FOREVER
...
C'MON, GIRL
!
HARUNA
...
WAIT, YUE
...
PLEASE APOLOGIZE TO NODOKA FOR ME.
!
ドドド..
SPLASSSH
LEAP
JIRI
ドドド
SPLASSSH

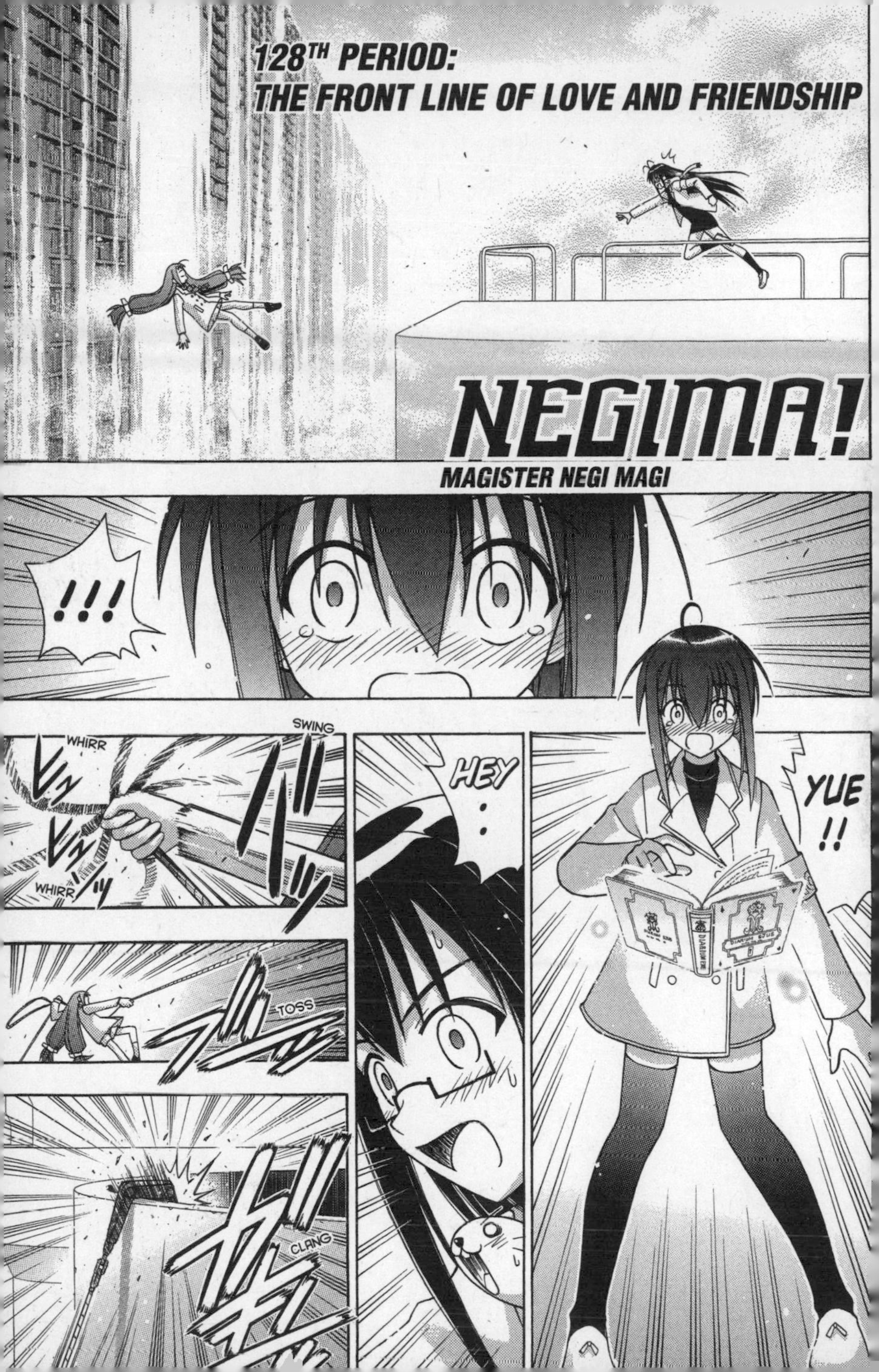
128TH PERIOD:
THE FRONT LINE OF LOVE AND FRIENDSHIP
NEGIMA!
MAGISTER NEGI MAGI
!!!
YUE !!
HEY :
SWING
WHIRR
WHIRR
TOSS
CLANG

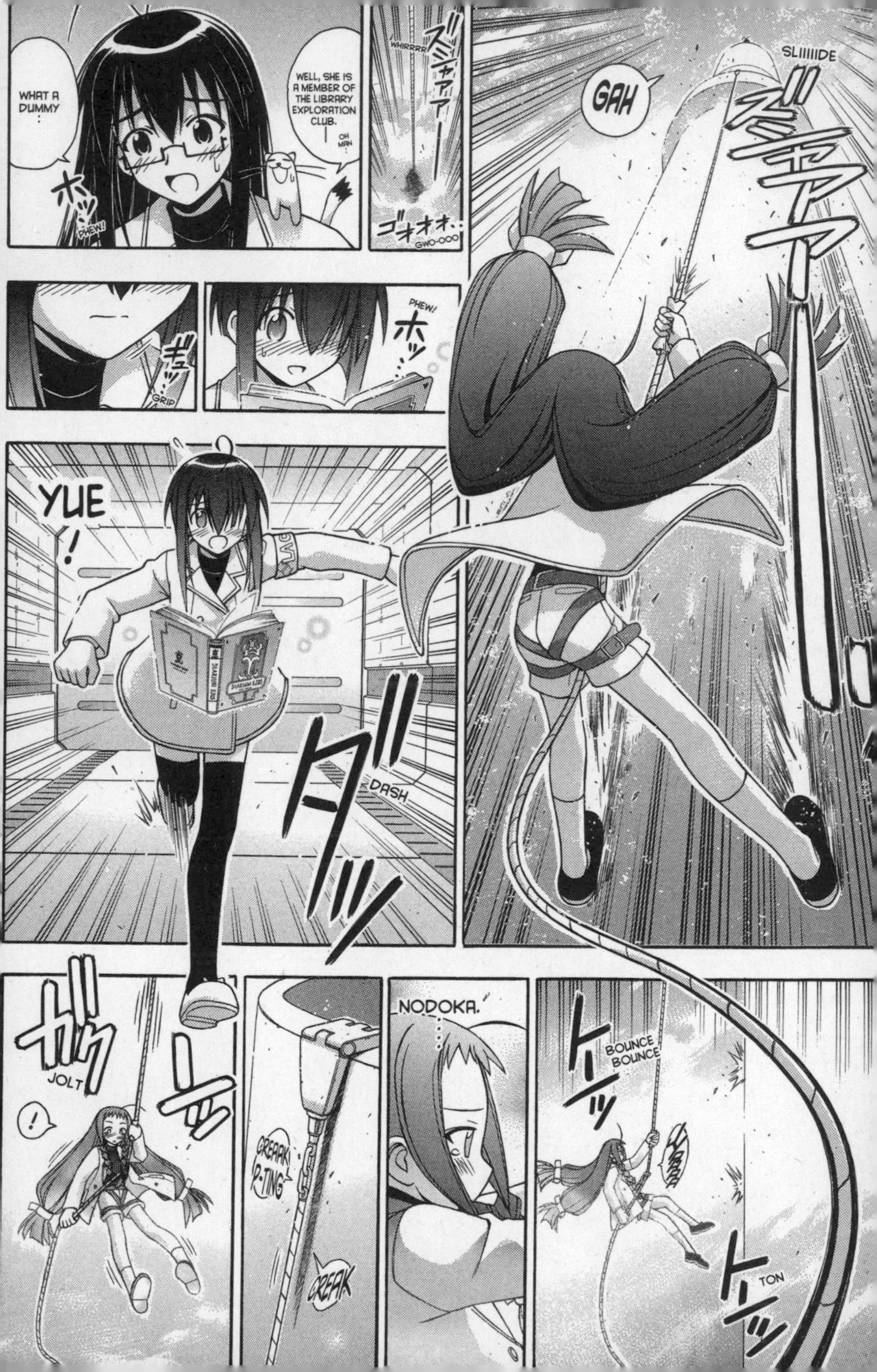
SLIIIIDE
GAH
WELL, SHE IS A MEMBER OF THE LIBRARY EXPLORATION CLUB.
WHIRRRR
OH MAN
GWO-OOO
WHAT A DUMMY
PHEW!
PHEW!
GRIP
YUE!
DASH
BOUNCE BOUNCE
TON
NODOKA.
CREAK! D-TING
CREAK
JOLT
!

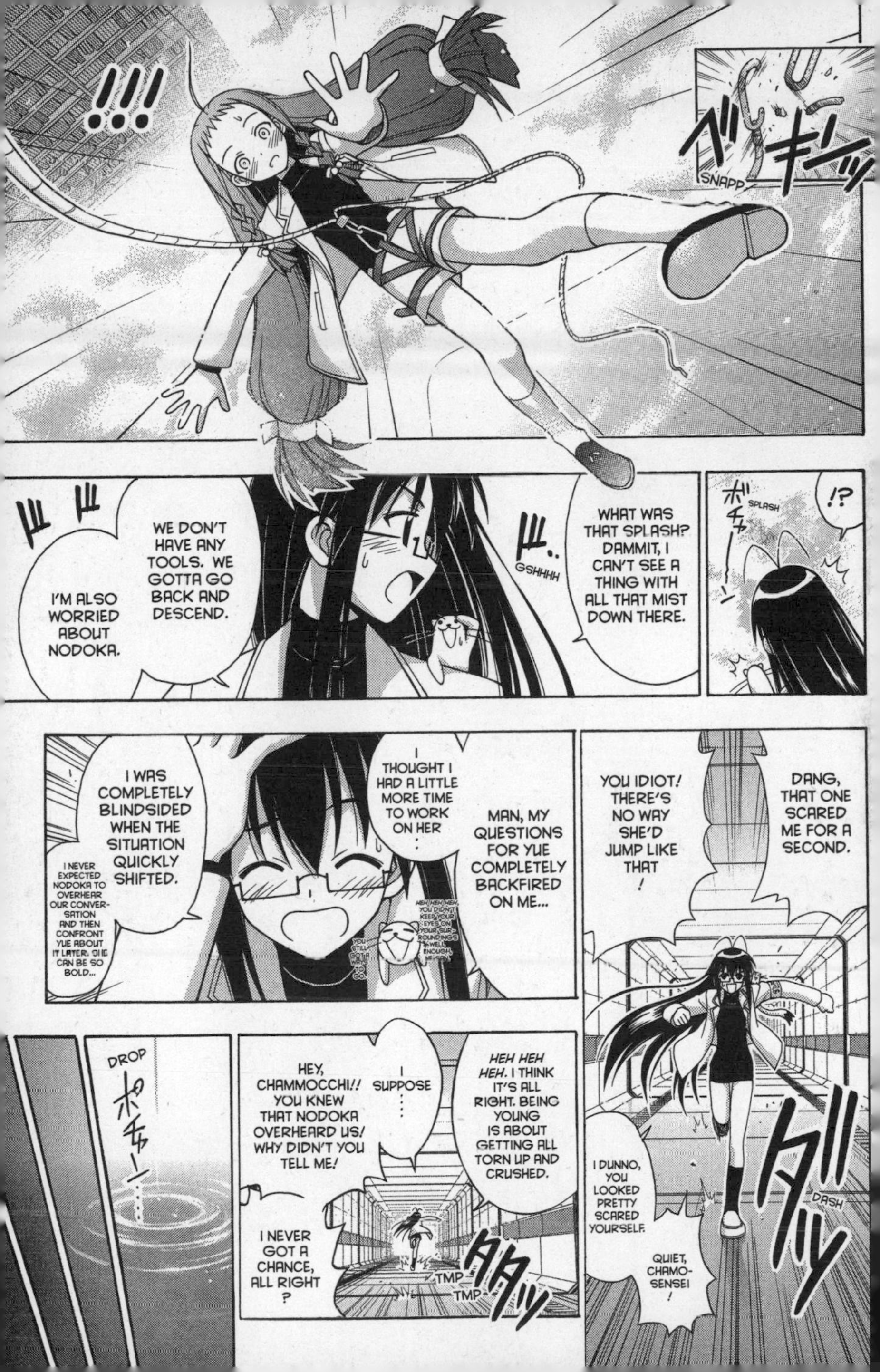
!!!
SNAPP
!?
SPLASH
WHAT WAS THAT SPLASH? DAMMIT, I CAN'T SEE A THING WITH ALL THAT MIST DOWN THERE.
GSHHHH
WE DON'T HAVE ANY TOOLS. WE GOTTA GO BACK AND DESCEND.
I'M ALSO WORRIED ABOUT NODOKA.
DANG, THAT ONE SCARED ME FOR A SECOND.
YOU IDIOT! THERE'S NO WAY SHE'D JUMP LIKE THAT!
DASH
I DUNNO, YOU LOOKED PRETTY SCARED YOURSELF.
QUIET, CHAMO-SENSEI!
I THOUGHT I HAD A LITTLE MORE TIME TO WORK ON HER...
MAN, MY QUESTIONS FOR YUE COMPLETELY BACKFIRED ON ME...
I WAS COMPLETELY BLINDSIDED WHEN THE SITUATION QUICKLY SHIFTED.
I NEVER EXPECTED NODOKA TO OVERHEAR OUR CONVERSATION AND THEN CONFRONT YUE ABOUT IT LATER. SHE CAN BE SO BOLD...
HEH HEH HEH, YOU DIDN'T KEEP YOUR EYES ON YOUR SURROUNDINGS WELL ENOUGH,
YOU STILL GOT A WAYS TO GO.
HEH HEH HEH. I THINK IT'S ALL RIGHT. BEING YOUNG IS ABOUT GETTING ALL TORN UP AND CRUSHED.
I SUPPOSE...
HEY, CHAMMOCCHI!! YOU KNEW THAT NODOKA OVERHEARD US! WHY DIDN'T YOU TELL ME!
I NEVER GOT A CHANCE, ALL RIGHT?
TMP
TMP
DROP

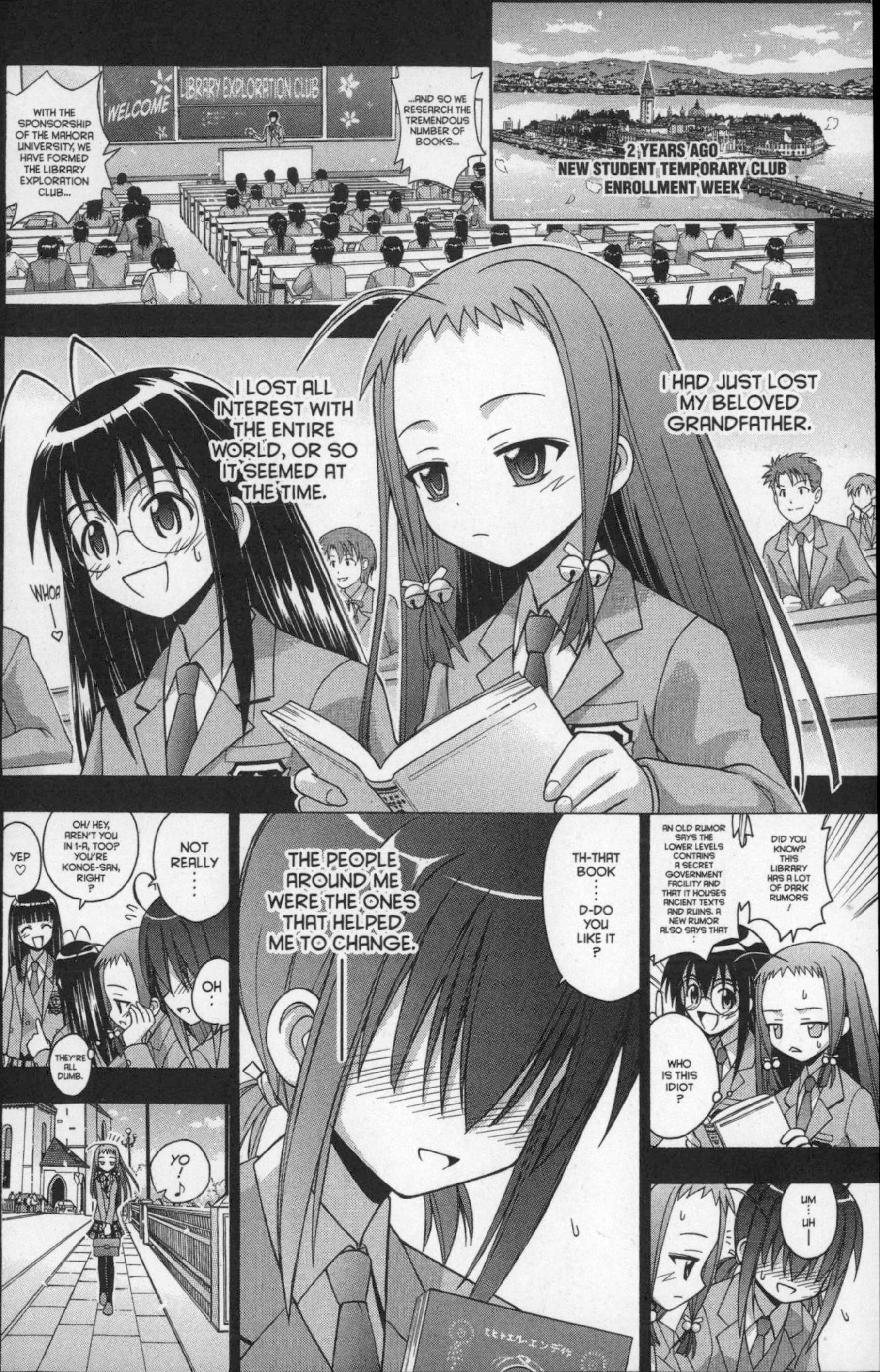
2 YEARS AGO
NEW STUDENT TEMPORARY CLUB ENROLLMENT WEEK
LIBRARY EXPLORATION CLUB
WELCOME
...AND SO WE RESEARCH THE TREMENDOUS NUMBER OF BOOKS...
WITH THE SPONSORSHIP OF THE MAHORA UNIVERSITY, WE HAVE FORMED THE LIBRARY EXPLORATION CLUB...
I HAD JUST LOST MY BELOVED GRANDFATHER.
I LOST ALL INTEREST WITH THE ENTIRE WORLD, OR SO IT SEEMED AT THE TIME.
WHOA ! ♡
DID YOU KNOW? THIS LIBRARY HAS A LOT OF DARK RUMORS!
AN OLD RUMOR SAYS THE LOWER LEVELS CONTAINS A SECRET GOVERNMENT FACILITY AND THAT IT HOUSES ANCIENT TEXTS AND RUINS. A NEW RUMOR ALSO SAYS THAT ...
WHO IS THIS IDIOT ?
UM... UH !
TH-THAT BOOK... D-DO YOU LIKE IT ?
THE PEOPLE AROUND ME WERE THE ONES THAT HELPED ME TO CHANGE.
NOT REALLY...
OH! HEY, AREN'T YOU IN 1-A, TOO? YOU'RE KONOE-SAN, RIGHT ?
YEP ♡
OH...
THEY'RE ALL DUMB.
YO-! ♪

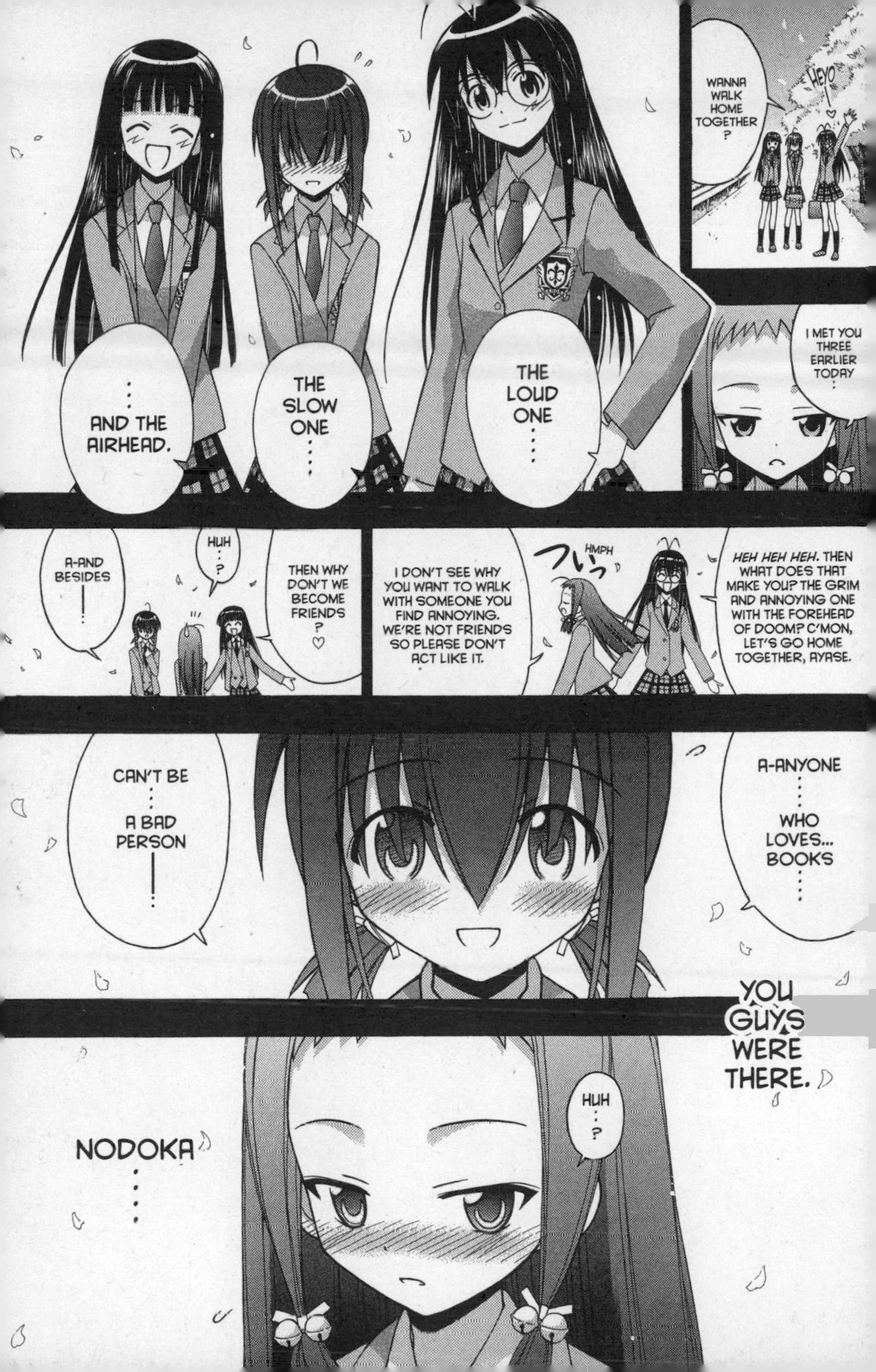
WANNA WALK HOME TOGETHER ?
HEYO
I MET YOU THREE EARLIER TODAY ...
THE LOUD ONE ....
THE SLOW ONE ....
... AND THE AIRHEAD.
HEH HEH HEH. THEN WHAT DOES THAT MAKE YOU? THE GRIM AND ANNOYING ONE WITH THE FOREHEAD OF DOOM? C'MON, LET'S GO HOME TOGETHER, AYASE.
HMPH
I DON'T SEE WHY YOU WANT TO WALK WITH SOMEONE YOU FIND ANNOYING. WE'RE NOT FRIENDS SO PLEASE DON'T ACT LIKE IT.
THEN WHY DON'T WE BECOME FRIENDS ? ♡
HUH ...?
A-AND BESIDES ―!
A-ANYONE ... WHO LOVES... BOOKS ...
CAN'T BE ... A BAD PERSON ―!
YOU GUYS WERE THERE.
HUH ...?
NODOKA ....

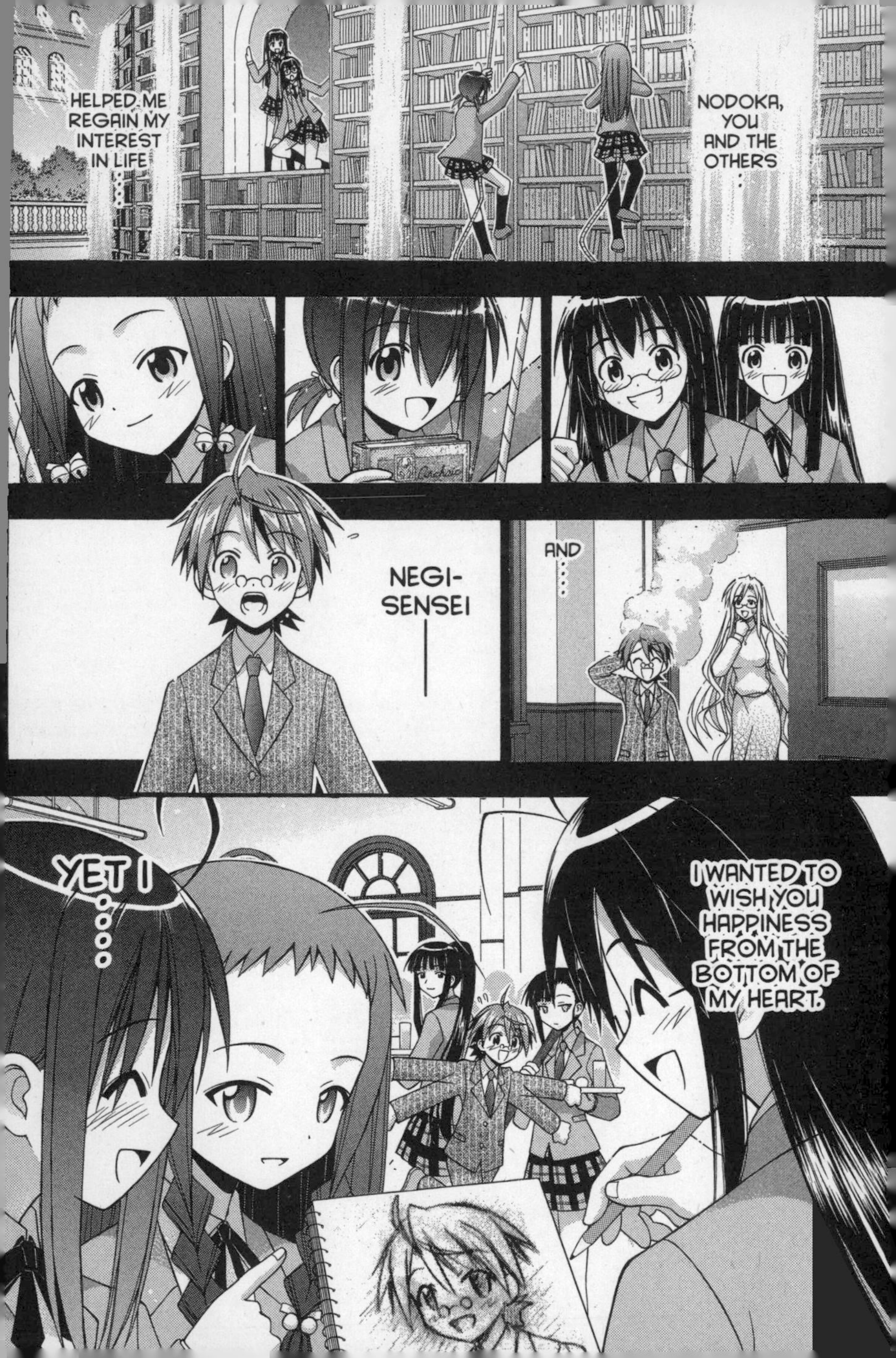
NODOKA, YOU AND THE OTHERS :
HELPED ME REGAIN MY INTEREST IN LIFE ...
AND ....
NEGI-SENSEI —
I WANTED TO WISH YOU HAPPINESS FROM THE BOTTOM OF MY HEART.
YET I ....

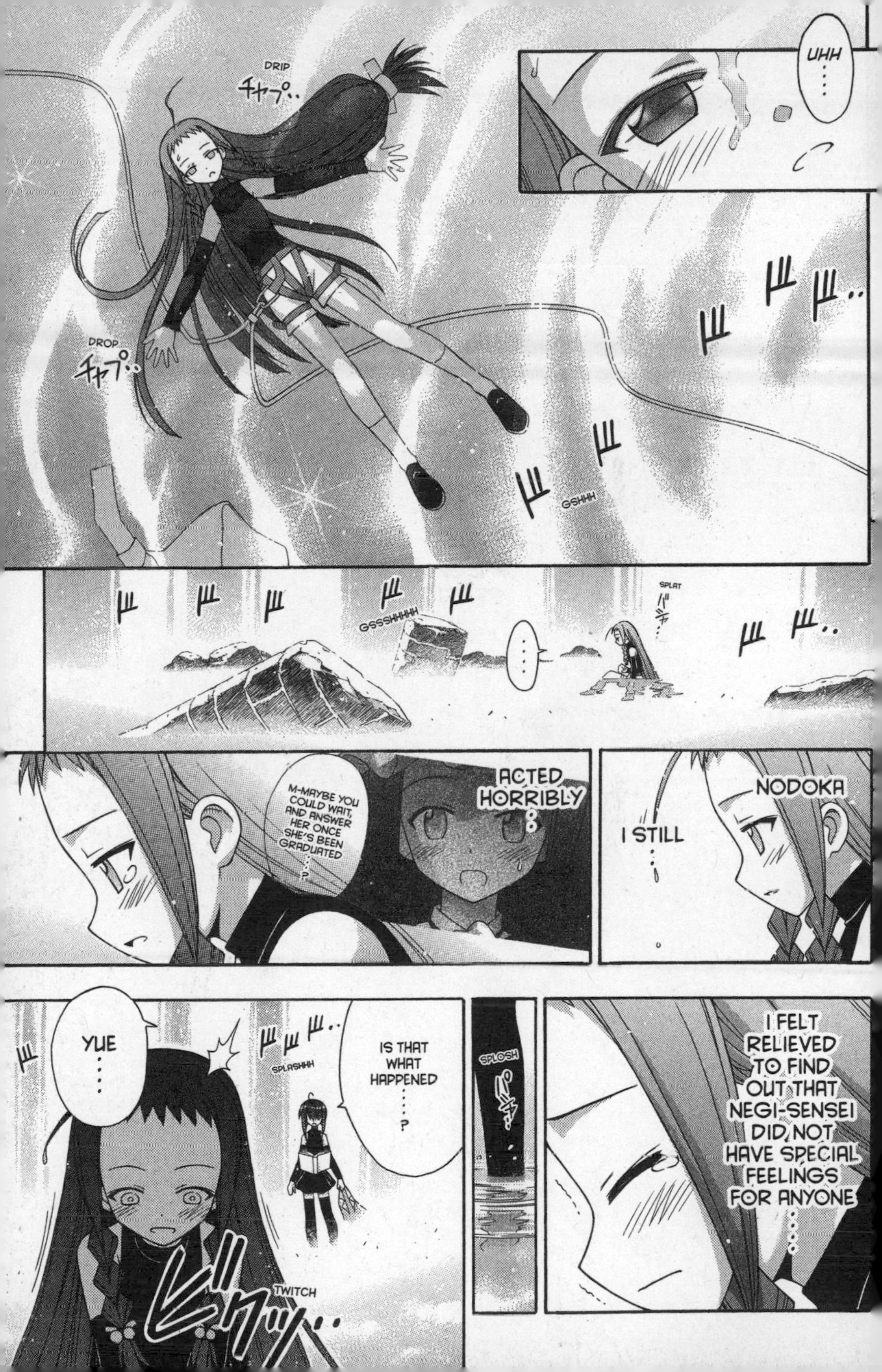
UHH.....
ザ ザ ザ..
DRIP
チャプ..
DROP
チャプ..
ザ ザ
GSHHH
ザ ザ..
SPLAT
バシャ...
......
GSSSHHHH
ザ ザ ザ ザ ザ
NODOKA
I STILL...
ACTED HORRIBLY..
M-MAYBE YOU COULD WAIT, AND ANSWER HER ONCE SHE'S BEEN GRADUATED...?
I FELT RELIEVED TO FIND OUT THAT NEGI-SENSEI DID NOT HAVE SPECIAL FEELINGS FOR ANYONE....
SPLOSH
IS THAT WHAT HAPPENED....?
ザザザ..
SPLASHHH
YUE....
ザ
TWITCH
ビクッ..

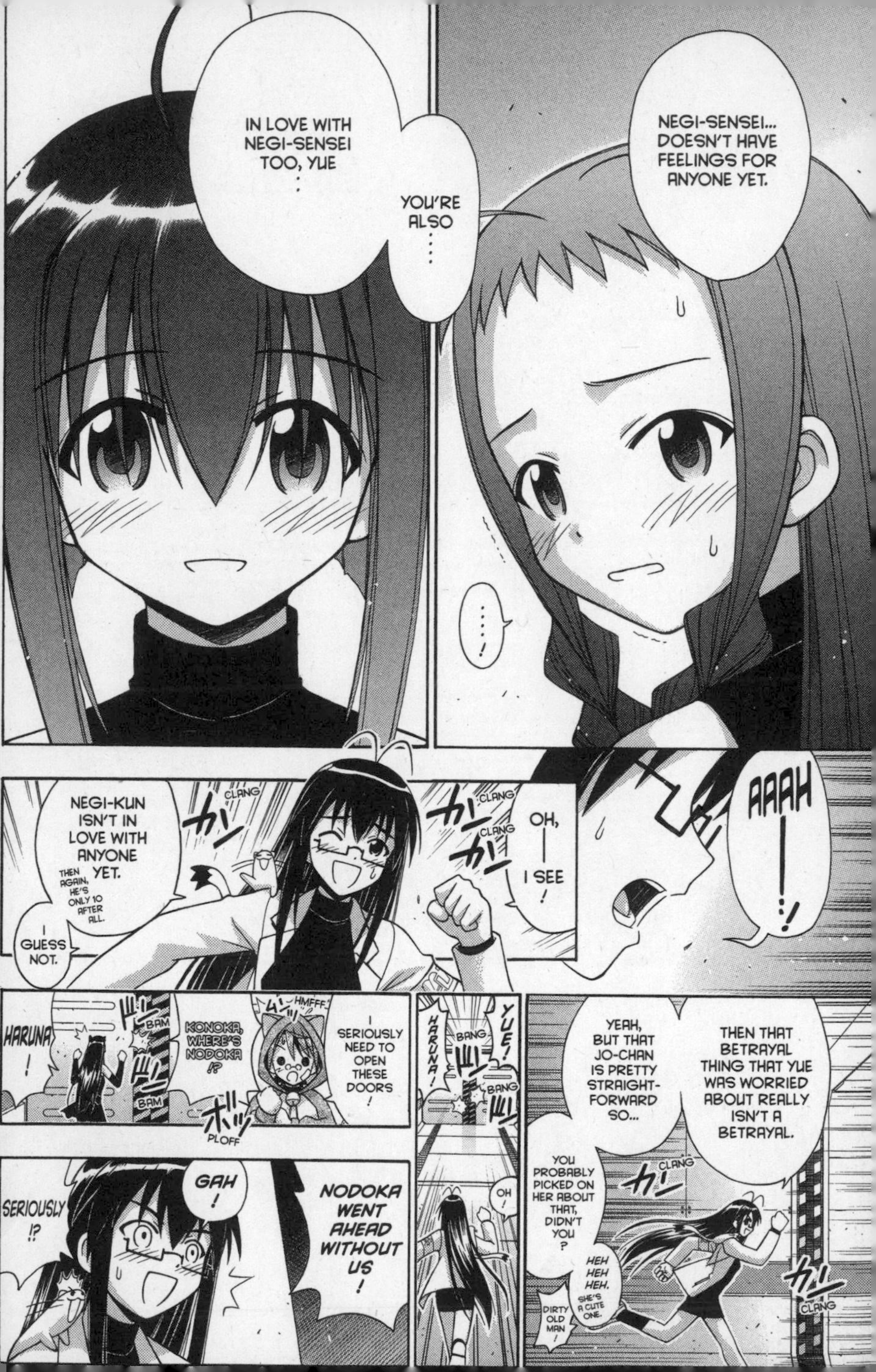
NEGI-SENSEI... DOESN'T HAVE FEELINGS FOR ANYONE YET.
....!
YOU'RE ALSO ....
IN LOVE WITH NEGI-SENSEI TOO, YUE ...
AAAH!!
OH, I SEE!
CLANG
CLANG
CLANG
NEGI-KUN ISN'T IN LOVE WITH ANYONE YET.
THEN AGAIN, HE'S ONLY 10 AFTER ALL.
I GUESS NOT.
THEN THAT BETRAYAL THING THAT YUE WAS WORRIED ABOUT REALLY ISN'T A BETRAYAL.
YEAH, BUT THAT JO-CHAN IS PRETTY STRAIGHT-FORWARD SO...
CLANG
YOU PROBABLY PICKED ON HER ABOUT THAT, DIDN'T YOU?
HEH HEH HEH.
SHE'S A CUTE ONE.
DIRTY OLD MAN!
CLANG
YUE!
HARUNA!
BANG
BANG
OH!
I SERIOUSLY NEED TO OPEN THESE DOORS!
HMFFF
KONOKA, WHERE'S NODOKA!?
BAM
BAM
HARUNA!
PLOFF
NODOKA WENT AHEAD WITHOUT US!
GAH!
SERIOUSLY!?

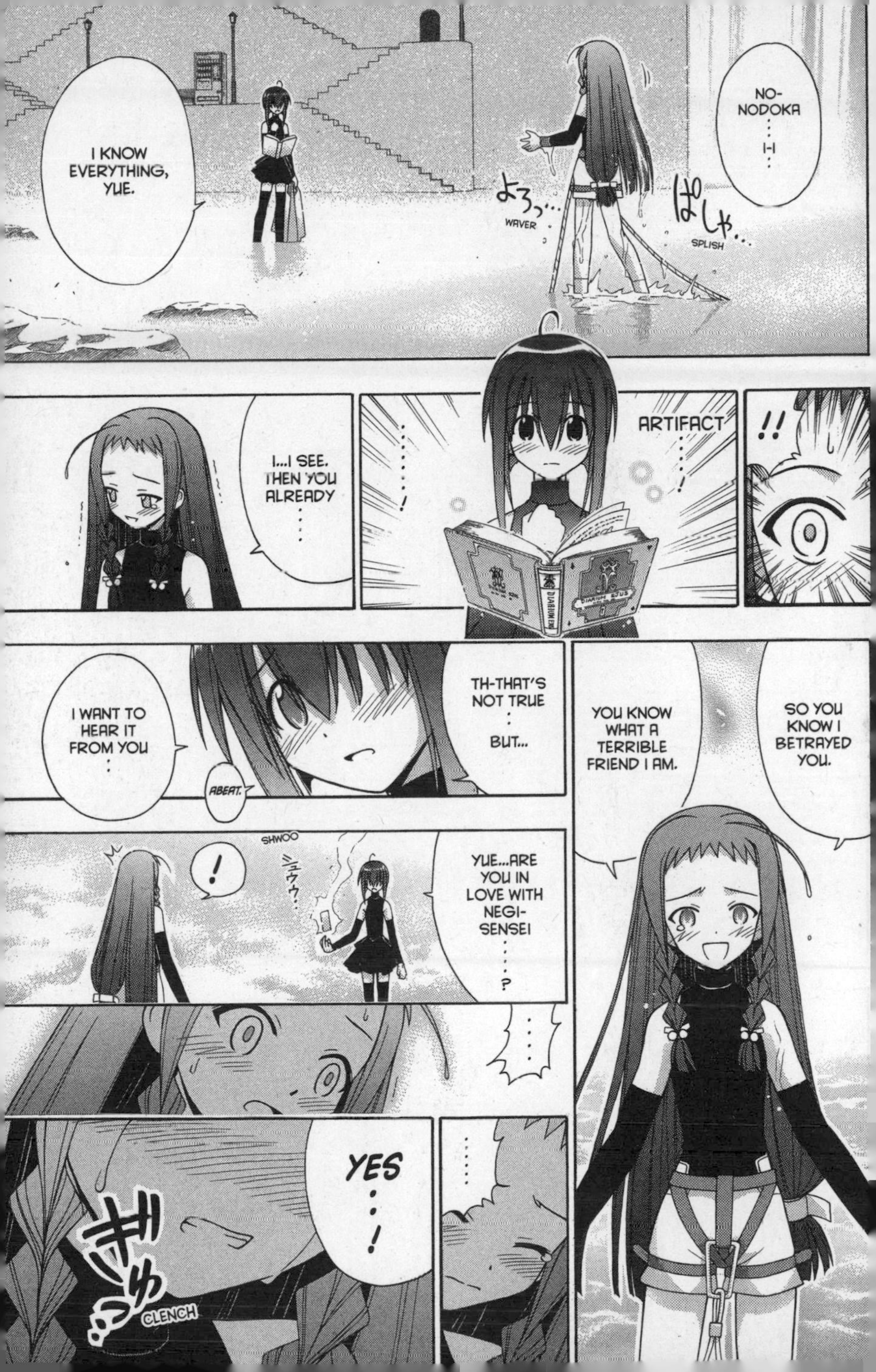
NO-NODOKA... I-I...
ぱしゃ…
SPLISH
よろっ…
WAVER
I KNOW EVERYTHING, YUE.
!!
ARTIFACT...!
...!
I...I SEE. THEN YOU ALREADY...
SO YOU KNOW I BETRAYED YOU.
YOU KNOW WHAT A TERRIBLE FRIEND I AM.
TH-THAT'S NOT TRUE... BUT...
I WANT TO HEAR IT FROM YOU...
ABEAT.
YUE...ARE YOU IN LOVE WITH NEGI-SENSEI...?
シュウゥ…
SHWOO
!
....!
....
YES...!
ぎゅっ
CLENCH

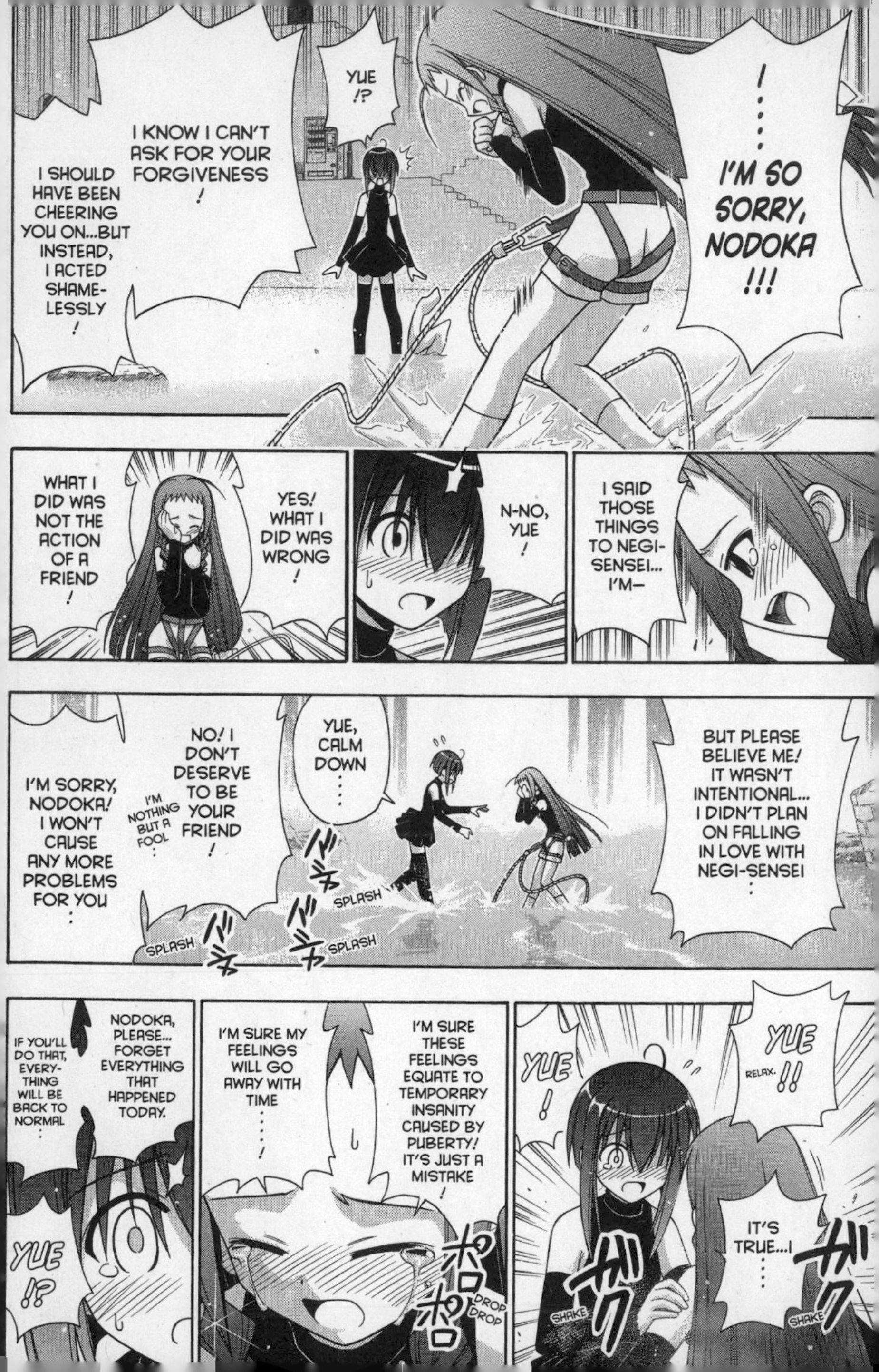
I......! I'M SO SORRY, NODOKA!!!
YUE!?
I KNOW I CAN'T ASK FOR YOUR FORGIVENESS!
I SHOULD HAVE BEEN CHEERING YOU ON...BUT INSTEAD, I ACTED SHAMELESSLY!
I SAID THOSE THINGS TO NEGI-SENSEI... I'M—
N-NO, YUE!
YES! WHAT I DID WAS WRONG!
WHAT I DID WAS NOT THE ACTION OF A FRIEND!
BUT PLEASE BELIEVE ME! IT WASN'T INTENTIONAL... I DIDN'T PLAN ON FALLING IN LOVE WITH NEGI-SENSEI...
YUE, CALM DOWN....
NO! I DON'T DESERVE TO BE YOUR FRIEND!
I'M NOTHING BUT A FOOL...
I'M SORRY, NODOKA! I WON'T CAUSE ANY MORE PROBLEMS FOR YOU...
SPLASH
SPLASH
SPLASH
YUE!!
RELAX.
YUE!
IT'S TRUE...I...
SHAKE
SHAKE
I'M SURE THESE FEELINGS EQUATE TO TEMPORARY INSANITY CAUSED BY PUBERTY! IT'S JUST A MISTAKE!
I'M SURE MY FEELINGS WILL GO AWAY WITH TIME...!
DROP DROP
NODOKA, PLEASE... FORGET EVERYTHING THAT HAPPENED TODAY.
IF YOU'LL DO THAT, EVERYTHING WILL BE BACK TO NORMAL...
YUE!?

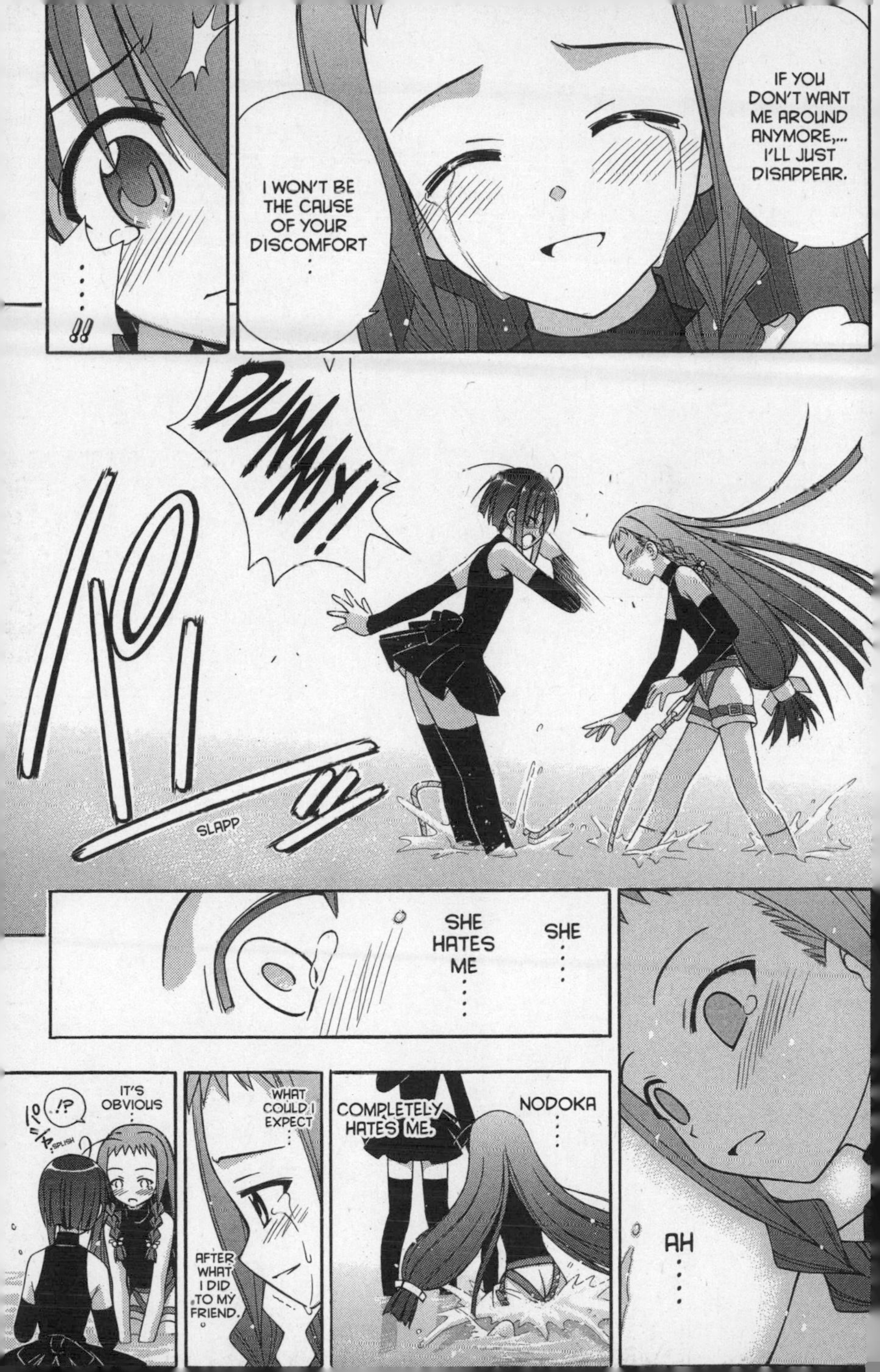
IF YOU DON'T WANT ME AROUND ANYMORE,... I'LL JUST DISAPPEAR.
I WON'T BE THE CAUSE OF YOUR DISCOMFORT ...
....!!
DUMMY!
SLAPP
AH ....
SHE ....
SHE HATES ME ....
NODOKA ....
COMPLETELY HATES ME.
WHAT COULD I EXPECT ...
AFTER WHAT I DID TO MY FRIEND.
IT'S OBVIOUS ...
!?
SPLISH

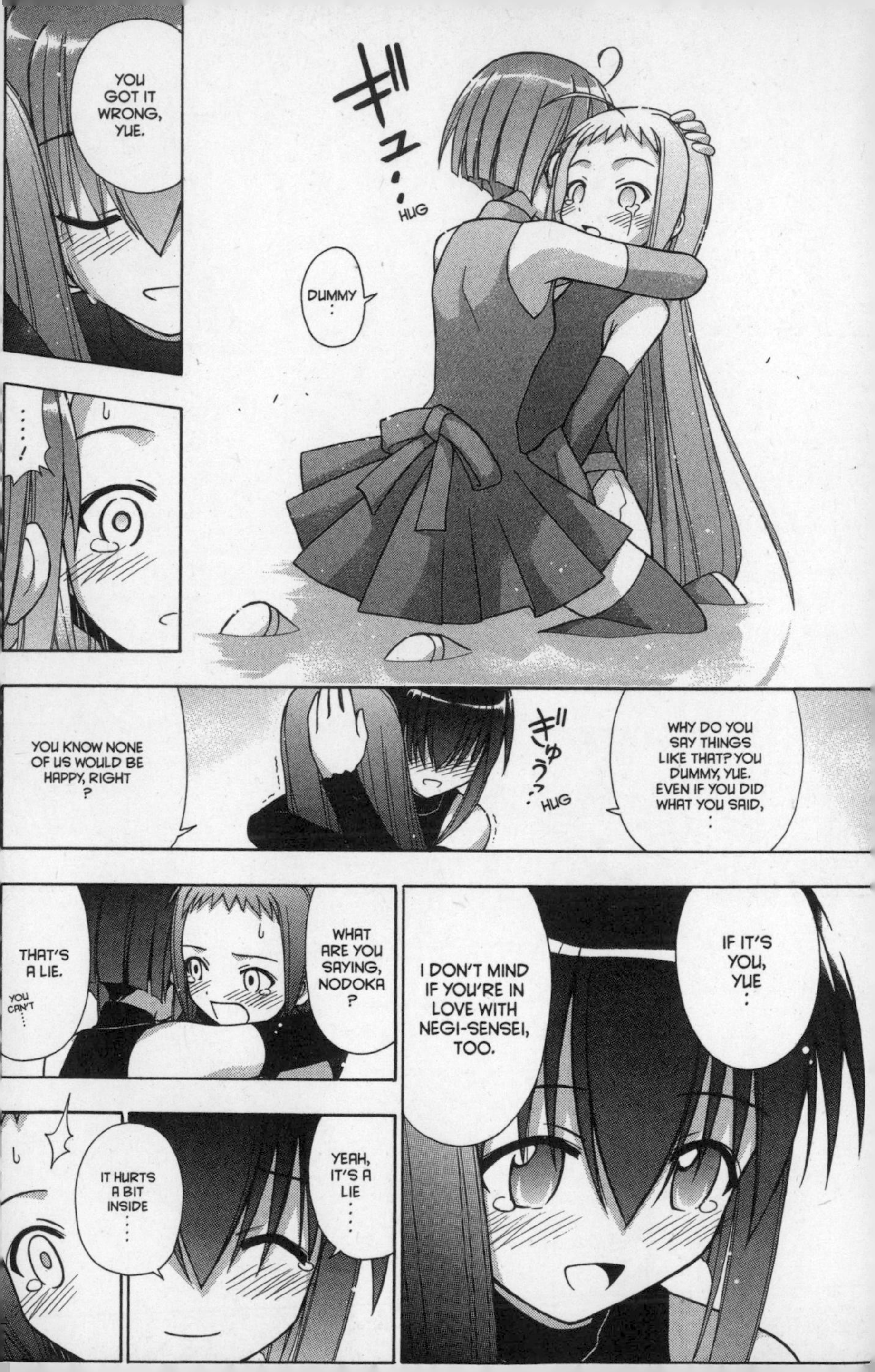
ギュ‥
HUG
DUMMY…
YOU GOT IT WRONG, YUE.
…!
WHY DO YOU SAY THINGS LIKE THAT? YOU DUMMY, YUE. EVEN IF YOU DID WHAT YOU SAID, …
ぎゅう…
HUG
YOU KNOW NONE OF US WOULD BE HAPPY, RIGHT?
IF IT'S YOU, YUE…
I DON'T MIND IF YOU'RE IN LOVE WITH NEGI-SENSEI, TOO.
WHAT ARE YOU SAYING, NODOKA?
THAT'S A LIE.
YOU CAN'T…
YEAH, IT'S A LIE…
IT HURTS A BIT INSIDE…

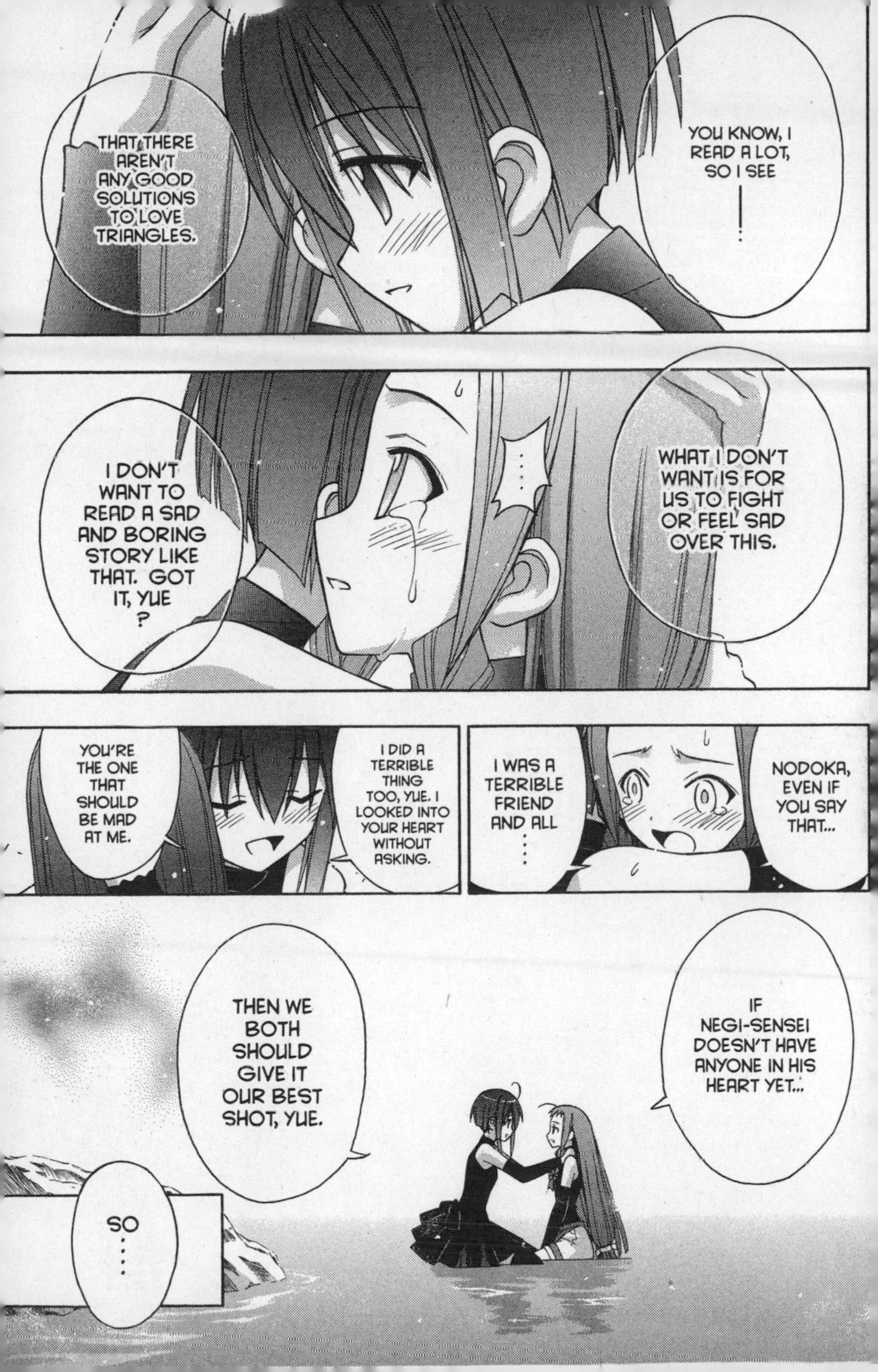
YOU KNOW, I READ A LOT, SO I SEE—!
THAT THERE AREN'T ANY GOOD SOLUTIONS TO LOVE TRIANGLES.
WHAT I DON'T WANT IS FOR US TO FIGHT OR FEEL SAD OVER THIS.
...
I DON'T WANT TO READ A SAD AND BORING STORY LIKE THAT. GOT IT, YUE?
NODOKA, EVEN IF YOU SAY THAT...
I WAS A TERRIBLE FRIEND AND ALL...
I DID A TERRIBLE THING TOO, YUE. I LOOKED INTO YOUR HEART WITHOUT ASKING.
YOU'RE THE ONE THAT SHOULD BE MAD AT ME.
IF NEGI-SENSEI DOESN'T HAVE ANYONE IN HIS HEART YET...
THEN WE BOTH SHOULD GIVE IT OUR BEST SHOT, YUE.
SO...

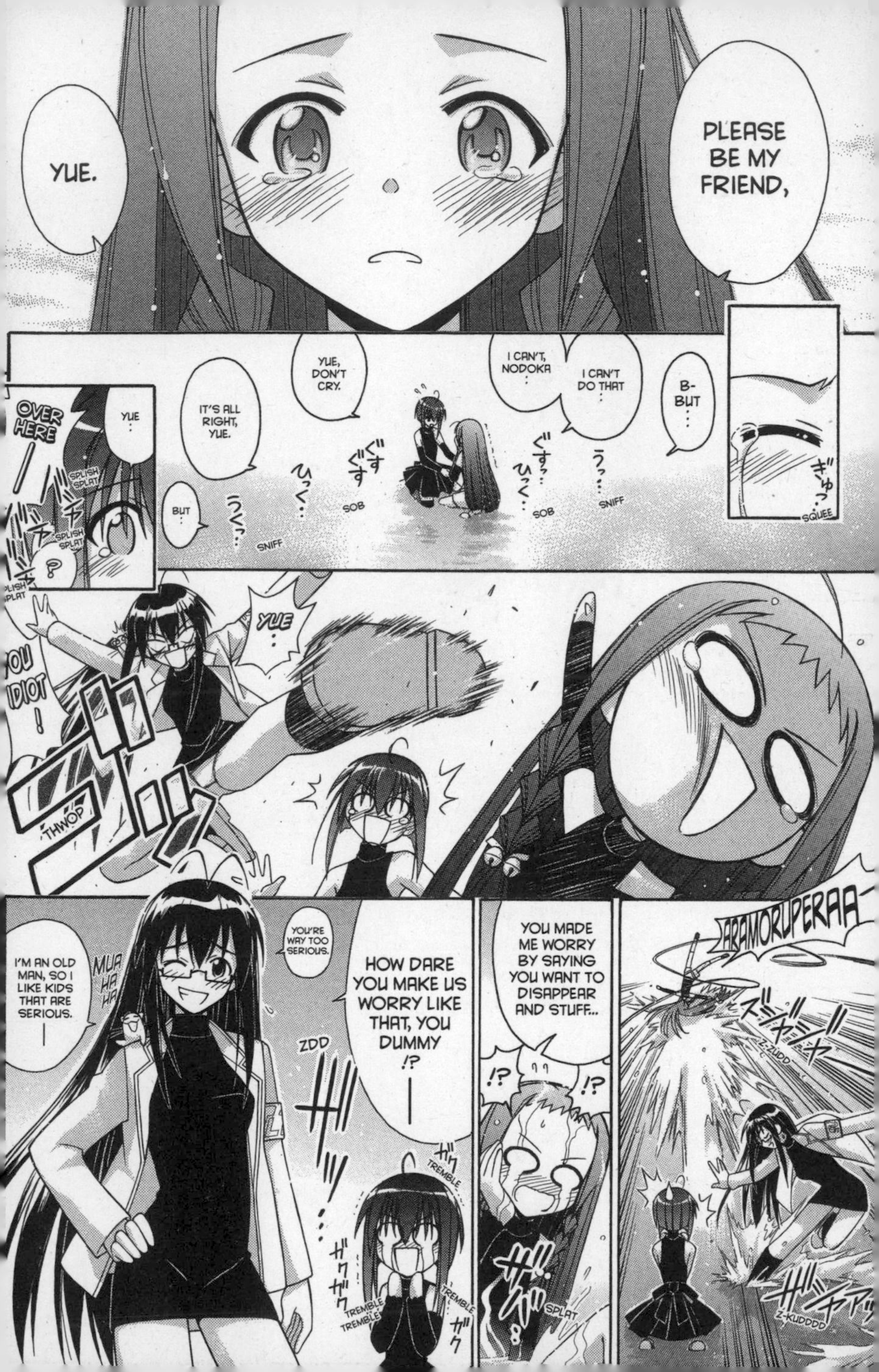
PLEASE BE MY FRIEND,
YUE.
SQUEE
B-BUT...
うっ…
SNIFF
I CAN'T DO THAT...
I CAN'T, NODOKA...
SOB
YUE, DON'T CRY.
ぐす ぐす
SOB
IT'S ALL RIGHT, YUE.
BUT...
SNIFF
YUE...
OVER HERE
SPLISH SPLAT
SPLISH SPLAT
?
SPLISH SPLAT
YUE...
YOU IDIOT!
THWOP
ARAMORUPERAA
Z-ZUDD
Z-KUDDDD
YOU MADE ME WORRY BY SAYING YOU WANT TO DISAPPEAR AND STUFF...
!?
!?
SPLAT
HOW DARE YOU MAKE US WORRY LIKE THAT, YOU DUMMY!?
YOU'RE WAY TOO SERIOUS.
ZDD
TREMBLE
TREMBLE
TREMBLE TREMBLE
I'M AN OLD MAN, SO I LIKE KIDS THAT ARE SERIOUS.
MUA HA HA

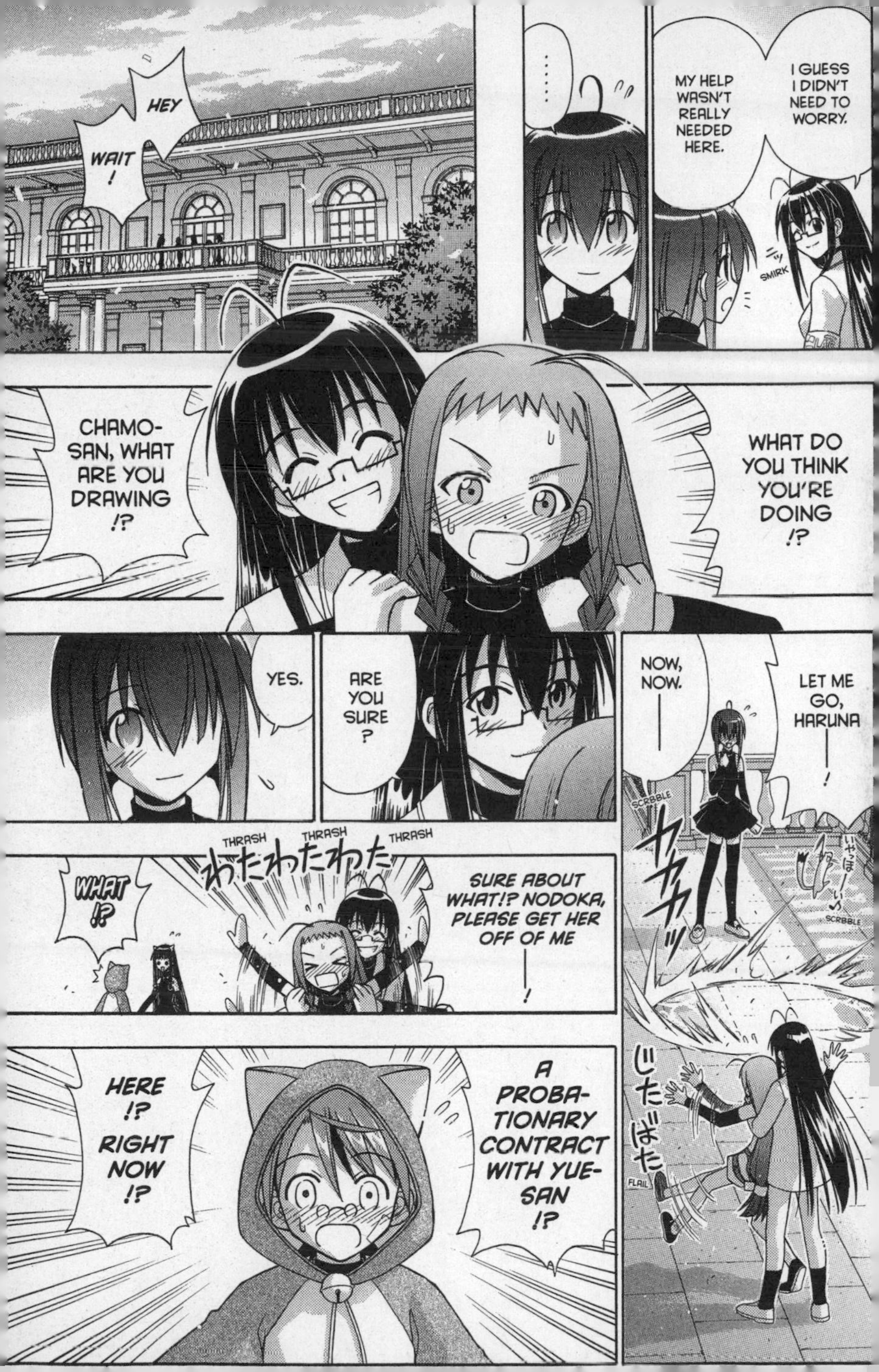
I GUESS I DIDN'T NEED TO WORRY.
MY HELP WASN'T REALLY NEEDED HERE.
SMIRK
......
HEY
WAIT!
WHAT DO YOU THINK YOU'RE DOING!?
CHAMO-SAN, WHAT ARE YOU DRAWING!?
LET ME GO, HARUNA—!
NOW, NOW.—
SCRBBLE
SCRBBLE
FLAIL
ARE YOU SURE?
YES.
THRASH THRASH THRASH
わたわたわた
SURE ABOUT WHAT!? NODOKA, PLEASE GET HER OFF OF ME—!
WHAT!?
A PROBATIONARY CONTRACT WITH YUE-SAN!?
HERE!? RIGHT NOW!?

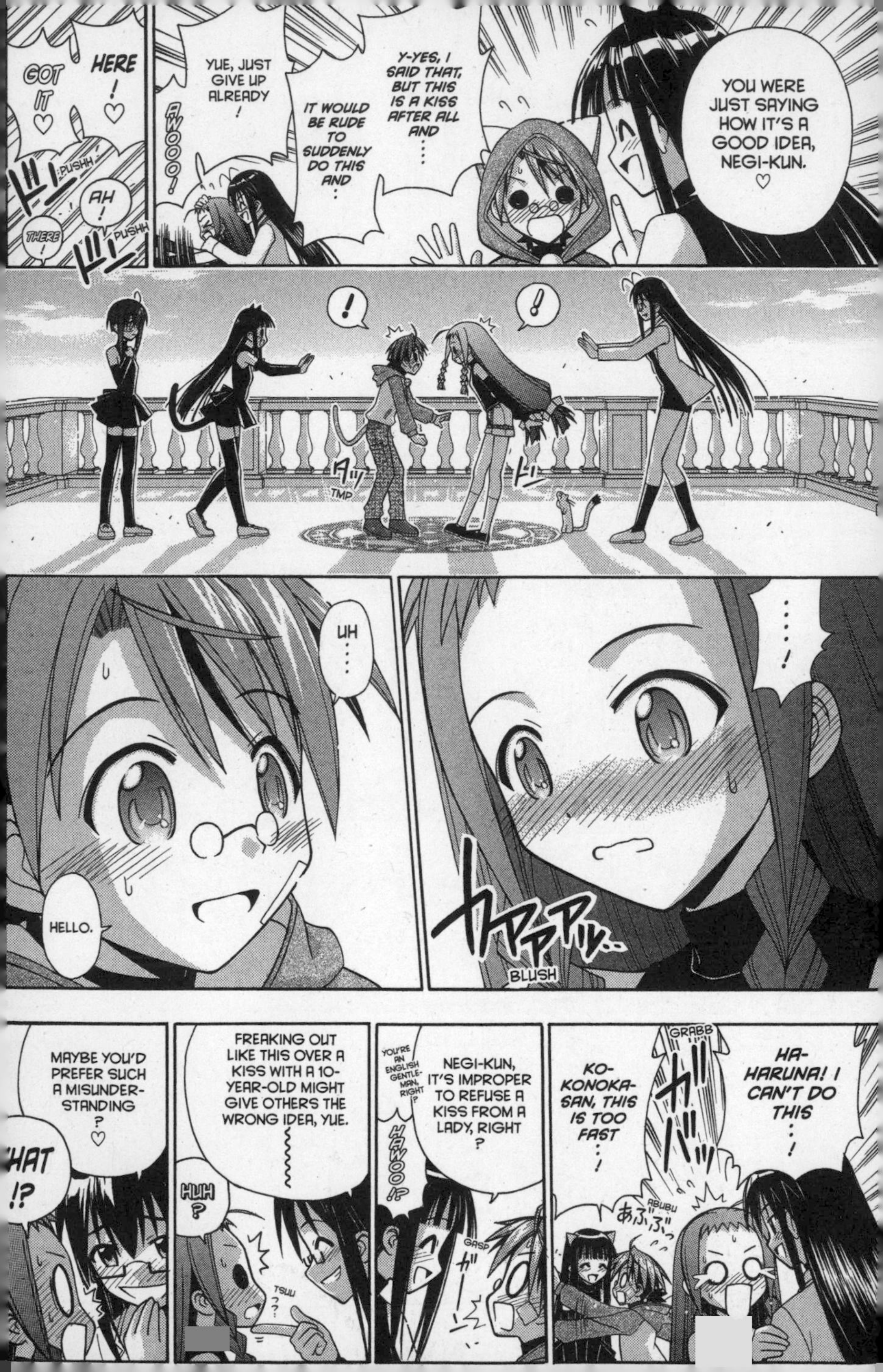
YOU WERE JUST SAYING HOW IT'S A GOOD IDEA, NEGI-KUN. ♡
Y-YES, I SAID THAT, BUT THIS IS A KISS AFTER ALL AND ....
IT WOULD BE RUDE TO SUDDENLY DO THIS AND ...
YUE, JUST GIVE UP ALREADY!
AWOOO!
HERE! ♡
GOT IT ♡
PUSHH
AH!
THERE!
PUSHH
!
!
TMP
....!
BLUSH
UH ....
HELLO.
HA-HARUNA! I CAN'T DO THIS ...!
GRABB
KO-KONOKA-SAN, THIS IS TOO FAST ...!
ABUBU
あぶぶ
NEGI-KUN, IT'S IMPROPER TO REFUSE A KISS FROM A LADY, RIGHT?
YOU'RE AN ENGLISH GENTLEMAN, RIGHT?
HAWOO!?
GASP
FREAKING OUT LIKE THIS OVER A KISS WITH A 10-YEAR-OLD MIGHT GIVE OTHERS THE WRONG IDEA, YUE.
HUH?
TSUU ??
MAYBE YOU'D PREFER SUCH A MISUNDERSTANDING? ♡
HAT !?

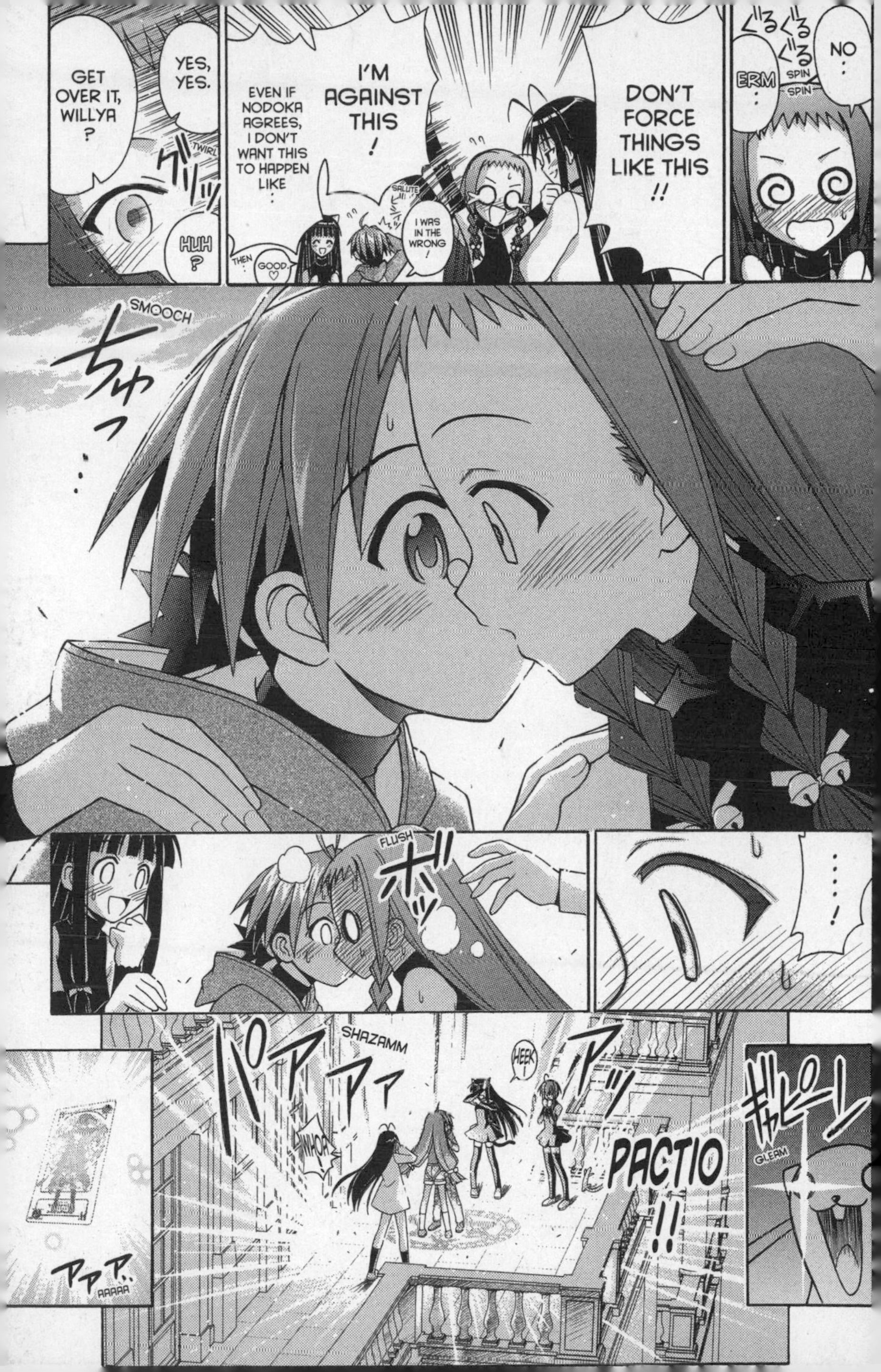
NO...
ERM...
SPIN SPIN
DON'T FORCE THINGS LIKE THIS!!
I'M AGAINST THIS!
EVEN IF NODOKA AGREES, I DON'T WANT THIS TO HAPPEN LIKE...
SALUTE
I WAS IN THE WRONG!
THEN... GOOD. ♡
YES, YES.
GET OVER IT, WILLYA?
TWIRL
HUH?
SMOOCH
ちゅっ
...
....!
FLUSH
GLEAM
PACTIO!!
SHAZAMM
HEEK!
AAAAA

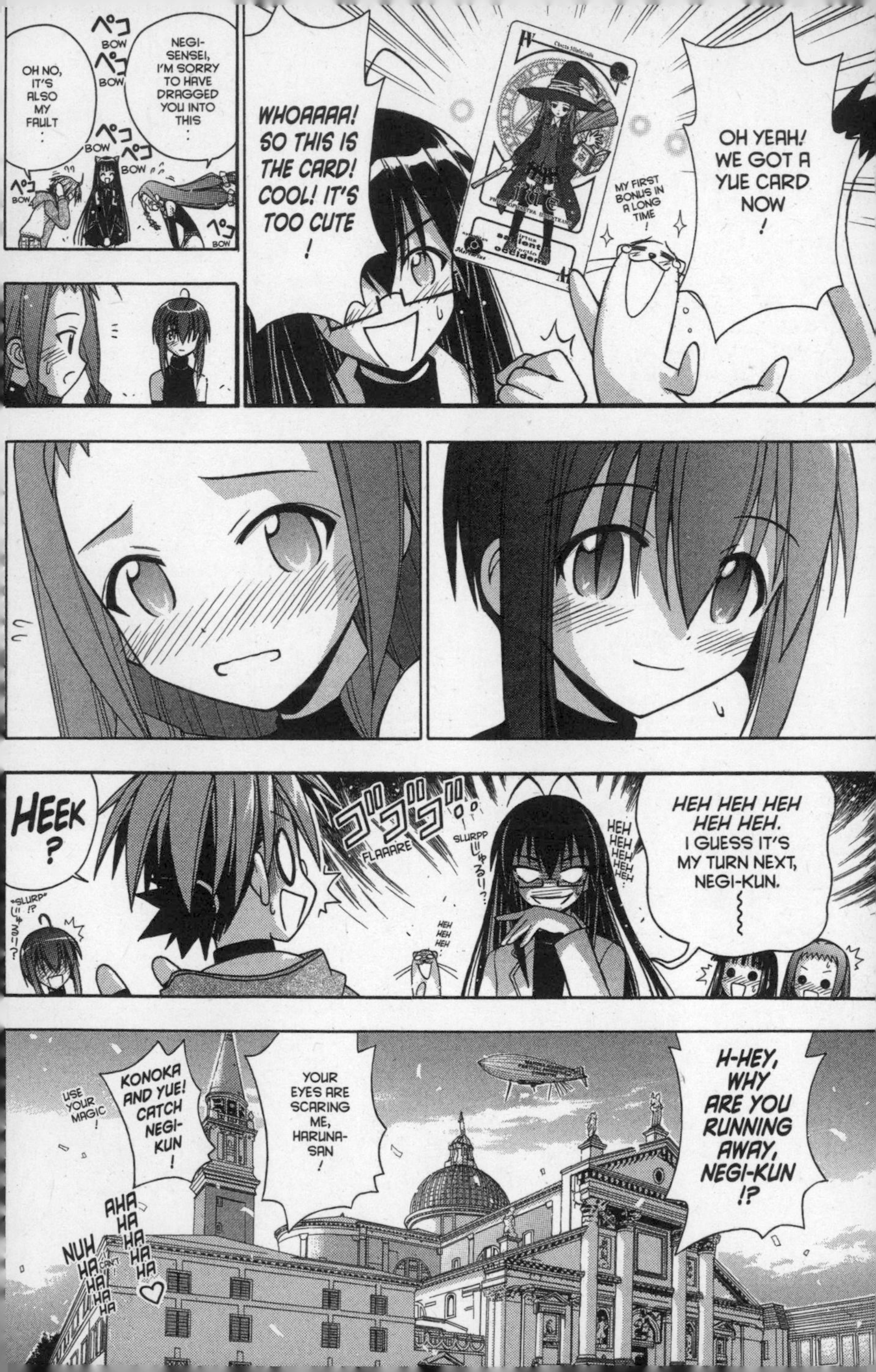
OH YEAH! WE GOT A YUE CARD NOW!
MY FIRST BONUS IN A LONG TIME!
WHOAAAA! SO THIS IS THE CARD! COOL! IT'S TOO CUTE!
NEGI-SENSEI, I'M SORRY TO HAVE DRAGGED YOU INTO THIS...
ペコ BOW
ペコ BOW
ペコ BOW
ペコ BOW
OH NO, IT'S ALSO MY FAULT...
ペコ BOW
ペコ BOW
HEH HEH HEH HEH HEH. I GUESS IT'S MY TURN NEXT, NEGI-KUN.
HEH HEH HEH HEH HEH
SLURP じゅるり!?
ゴゴゴ FLAAARE
HEH HEH HEH
HEEK?
"SLURP" じゅるり!?
H-HEY, WHY ARE YOU RUNNING AWAY, NEGI-KUN!?
YOUR EYES ARE SCARING ME, HARUNA-SAN!
KONOKA AND YUE! CATCH NEGI-KUN!
USE YOUR MAGIC!
AHA HA HA HA HA
NUH HA HA HA HA

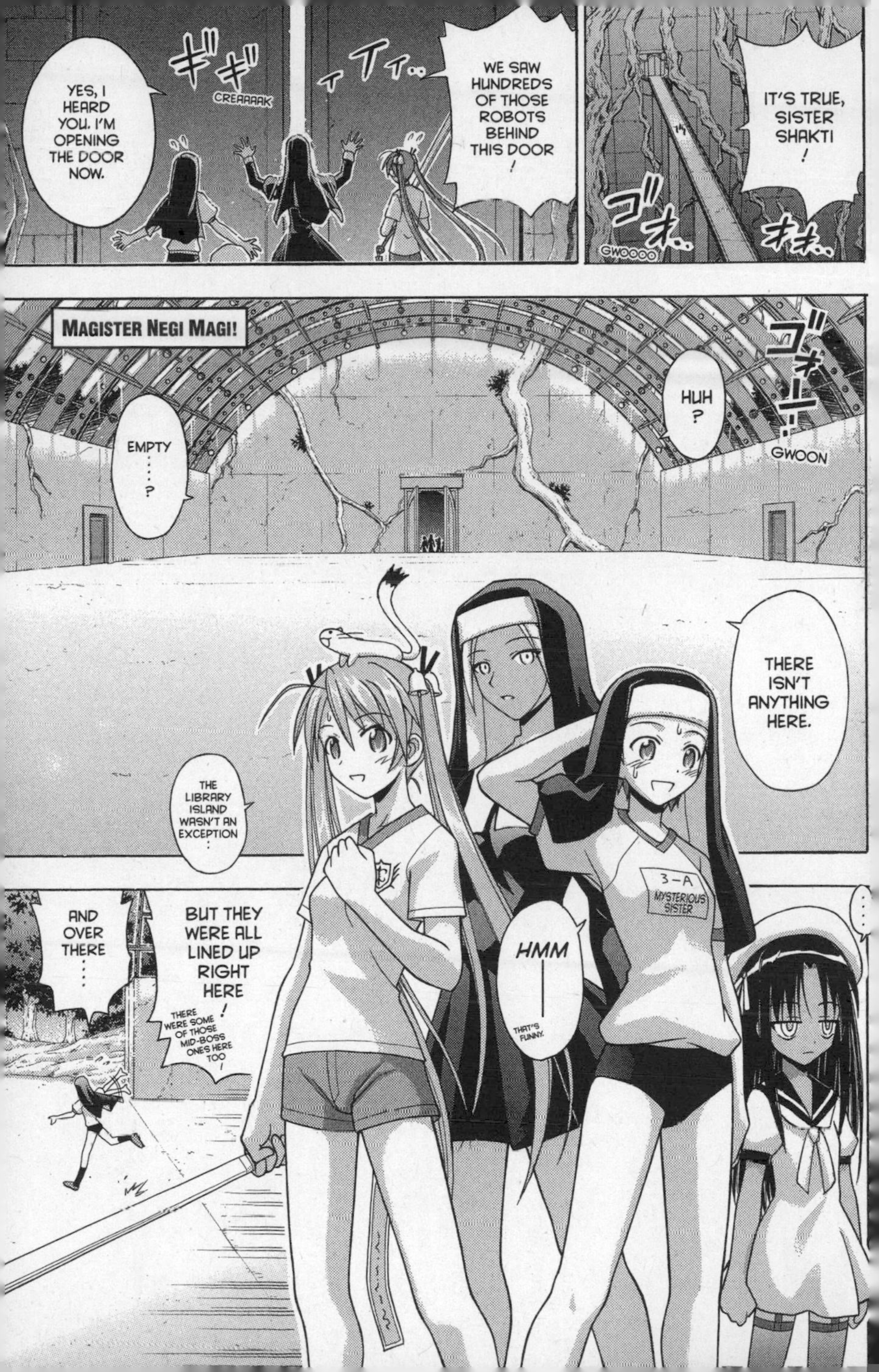
IT'S TRUE, SISTER SHAKTI!
GWOOOO
WE SAW HUNDREDS OF THOSE ROBOTS BEHIND THIS DOOR!
CREAAAAK
YES, I HEARD YOU. I'M OPENING THE DOOR NOW.
MAGISTER NEGI MAGI!
GWOON
HUH?
EMPTY....?
...
THERE ISN'T ANYTHING HERE.
3-A MYSTERIOUS SISTER
HMM—
THAT'S FUNNY.
THE LIBRARY ISLAND WASN'T AN EXCEPTION...
BUT THEY WERE ALL LINED UP RIGHT HERE!
THERE WERE SOME OF THOSE MID-BOSS ONES HERE TOO!
AND OVER THERE....

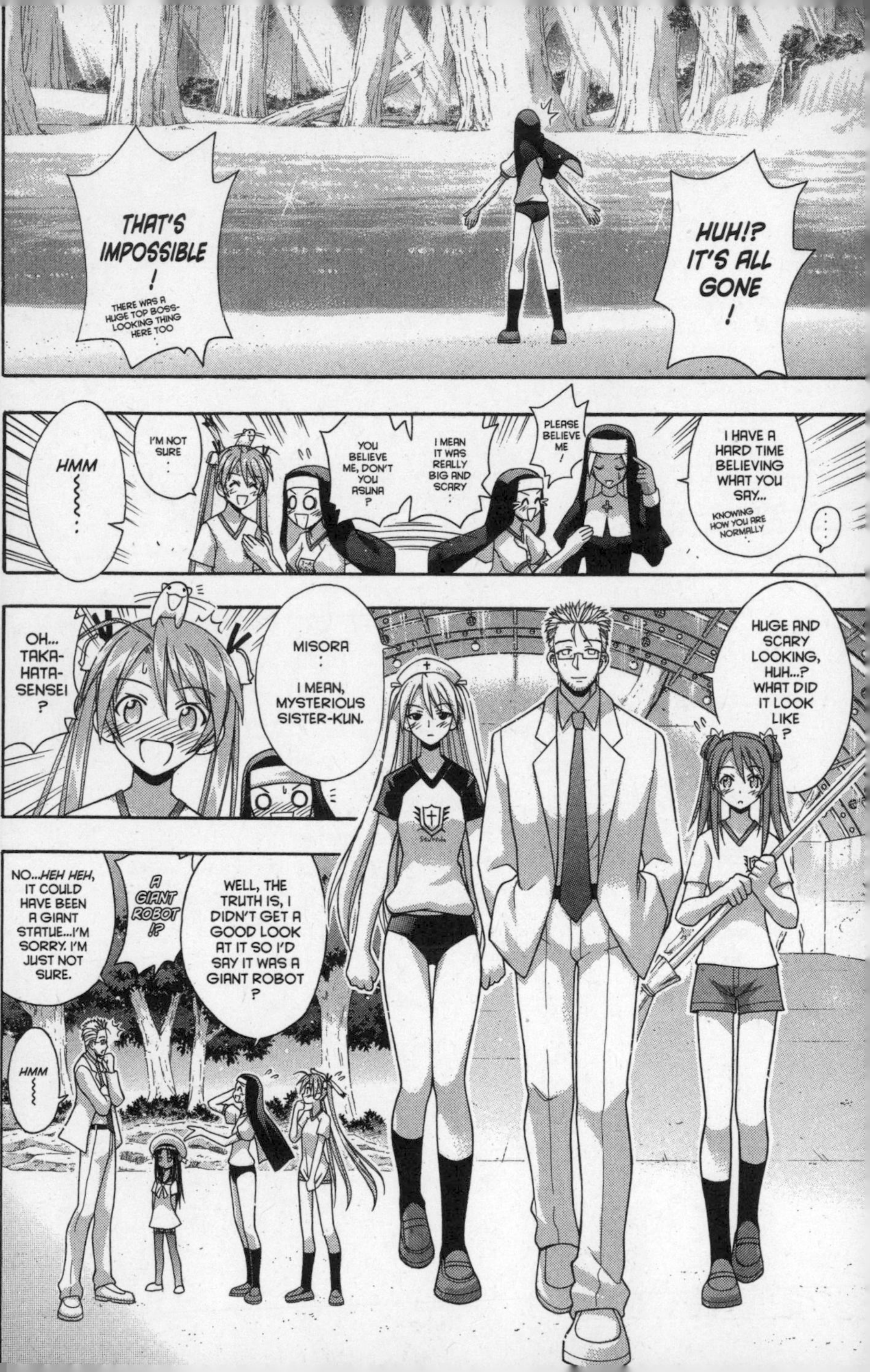
HUH!? IT'S ALL GONE!
THAT'S IMPOSSIBLE!
THERE WAS A HUGE TOP BOSS-LOOKING THING HERE TOO...
I HAVE A HARD TIME BELIEVING WHAT YOU SAY...
KNOWING HOW YOU ARE NORMALLY
...
PLEASE BELIEVE ME!
I MEAN IT WAS REALLY BIG AND SCARY...
YOU BELIEVE ME, DON'T YOU ASUNA?
I'M NOT SURE...
HMM
HUGE AND SCARY LOOKING, HUH...? WHAT DID IT LOOK LIKE?
MISORA... I MEAN, MYSTERIOUS SISTER-KUN.
OH... TAKA-HATA-SENSEI?
WELL, THE TRUTH IS, I DIDN'T GET A GOOD LOOK AT IT SO I'D SAY IT WAS A GIANT ROBOT?
A GIANT ROBOT!?
NO...HEH HEH, IT COULD HAVE BEEN A GIANT STATUE...I'M SORRY. I'M JUST NOT SURE.
HMM

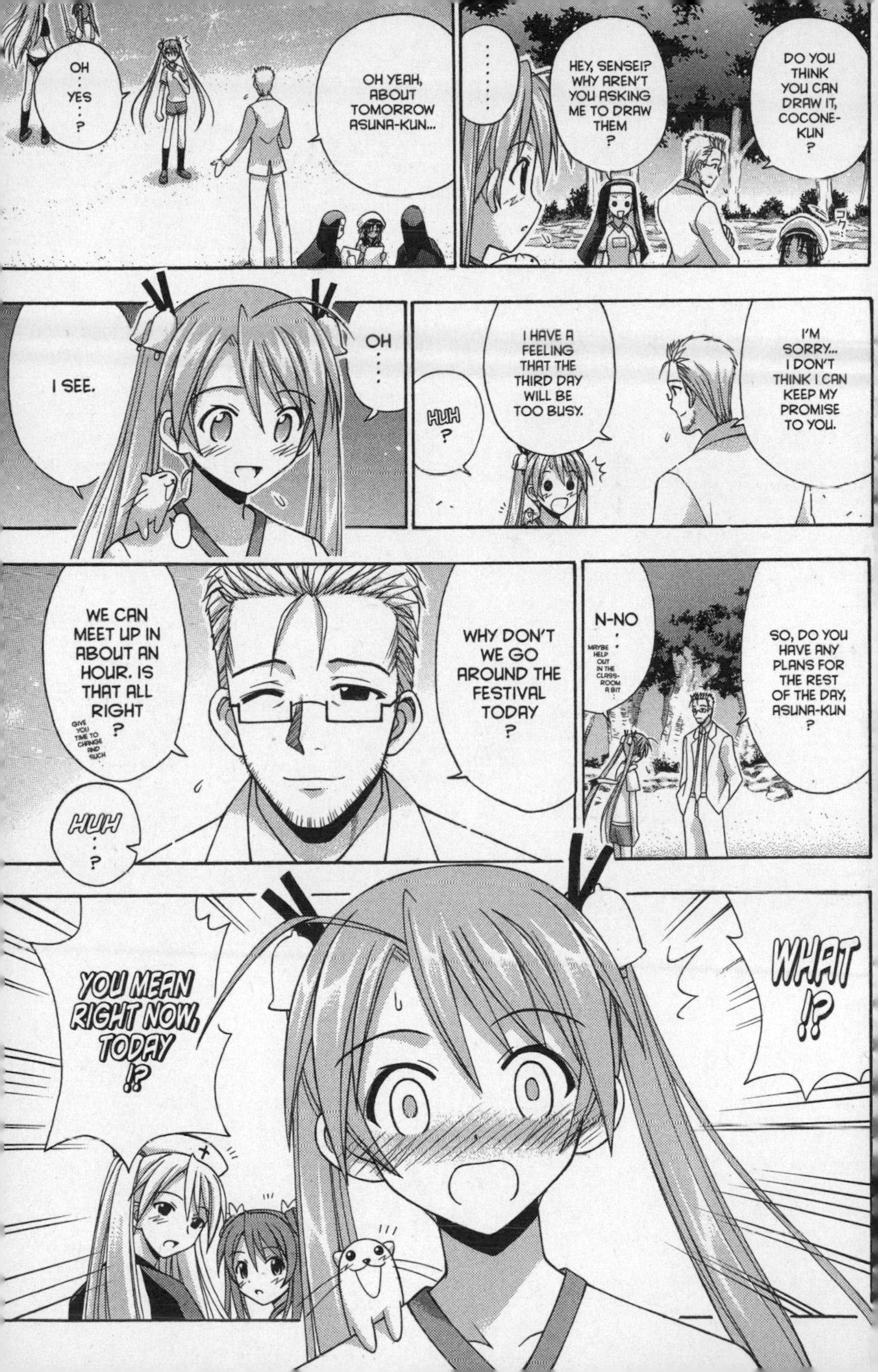
DO YOU THINK YOU CAN DRAW IT, COCONE-KUN ?
HEY, SENSEI? WHY AREN'T YOU ASKING ME TO DRAW THEM ?
......
OH YEAH, ABOUT TOMORROW ASUNA-KUN...
OH... YES...?
I'M SORRY... I DON'T THINK I CAN KEEP MY PROMISE TO YOU.
I HAVE A FEELING THAT THE THIRD DAY WILL BE TOO BUSY.
HUH ?
OH...
I SEE.
SO, DO YOU HAVE ANY PLANS FOR THE REST OF THE DAY, ASUNA-KUN ?
N-NO...
MAYBE HELP OUT IN THE CLASSROOM A BIT
WHY DON'T WE GO AROUND THE FESTIVAL TODAY ?
WE CAN MEET UP IN ABOUT AN HOUR. IS THAT ALL RIGHT ?
GIVE YOU TIME TO CHANGE AND SUCH
HUH...?
WHAT !?
YOU MEAN RIGHT NOW, TODAY !?

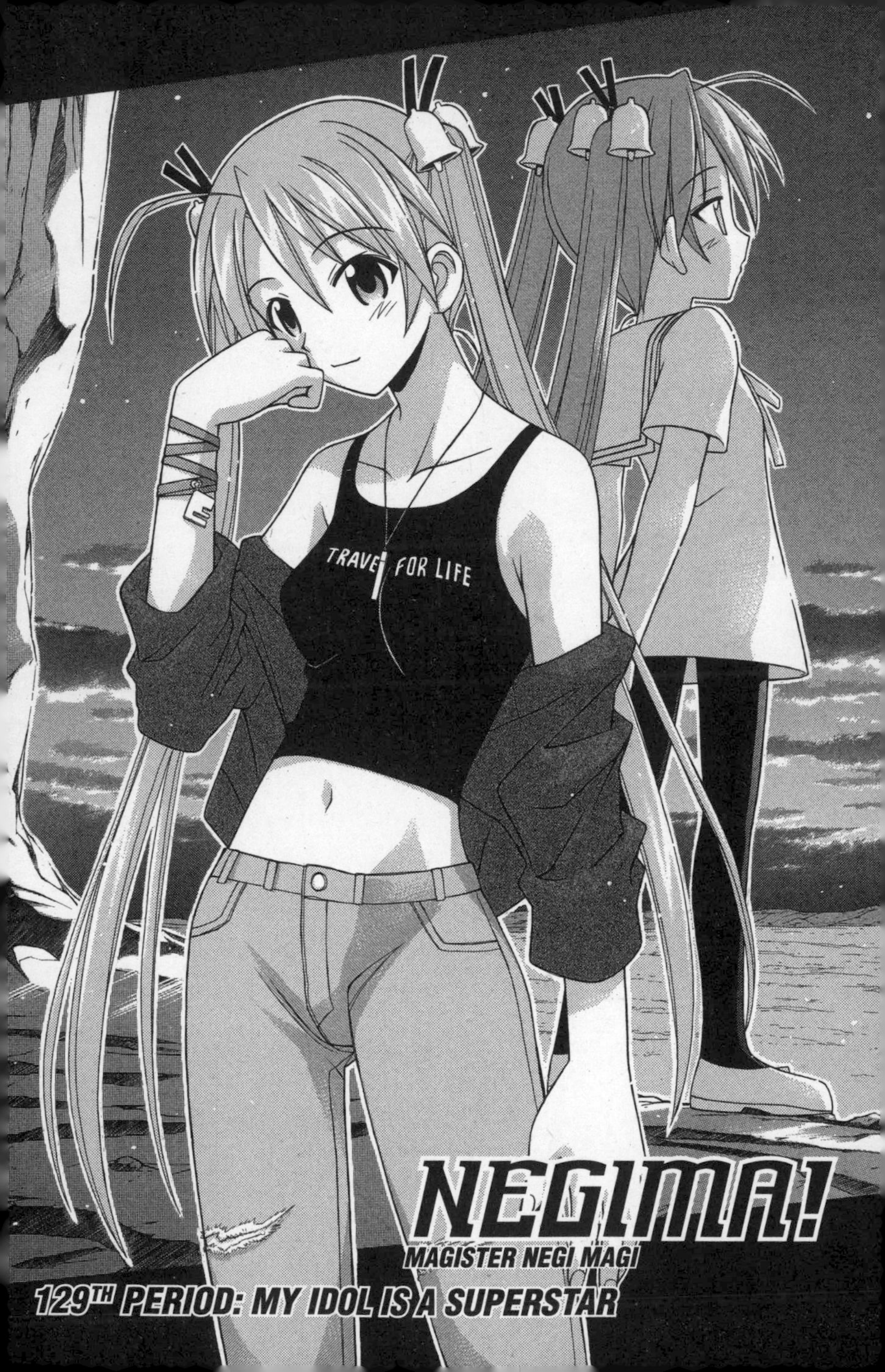
TRAVEL FOR LIFE
NEGIMA!
MAGISTER NEGI MAGI
129TH PERIOD: MY IDOL IS A SUPERSTAR

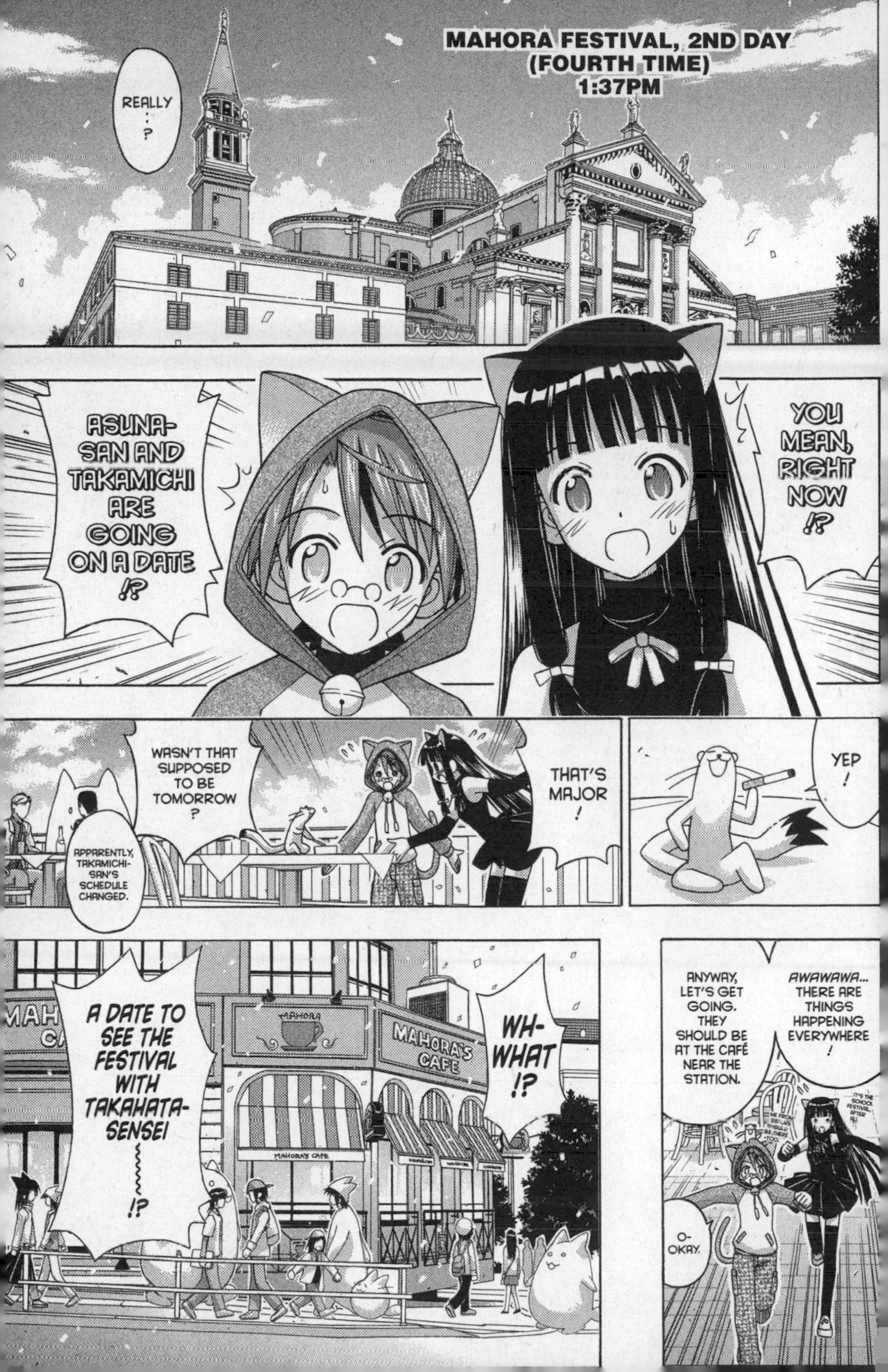
MAHORA FESTIVAL, 2ND DAY (FOURTH TIME) 1:37PM
REALLY..?
YOU MEAN, RIGHT NOW!?
ASUNA-SAN AND TAKAMICHI ARE GOING ON A DATE!?
YEP!
THAT'S MAJOR!
WASN'T THAT SUPPOSED TO BE TOMORROW?
APPARENTLY, TAKAMICHI-SAN'S SCHEDULE CHANGED.
AWAWAWA... THERE ARE THINGS HAPPENING EVERYWHERE!
ANYWAY, LET'S GET GOING. THEY SHOULD BE AT THE CAFÉ NEAR THE STATION.
IT'S THE SCHOOL FESTIVAL, AFTER ALL.
O-OKAY.
WH-WHAT!?
A DATE TO SEE THE FESTIVAL WITH TAKAHATA-SENSEI~~~!?
MAHORA
MAHORA'S CAFE

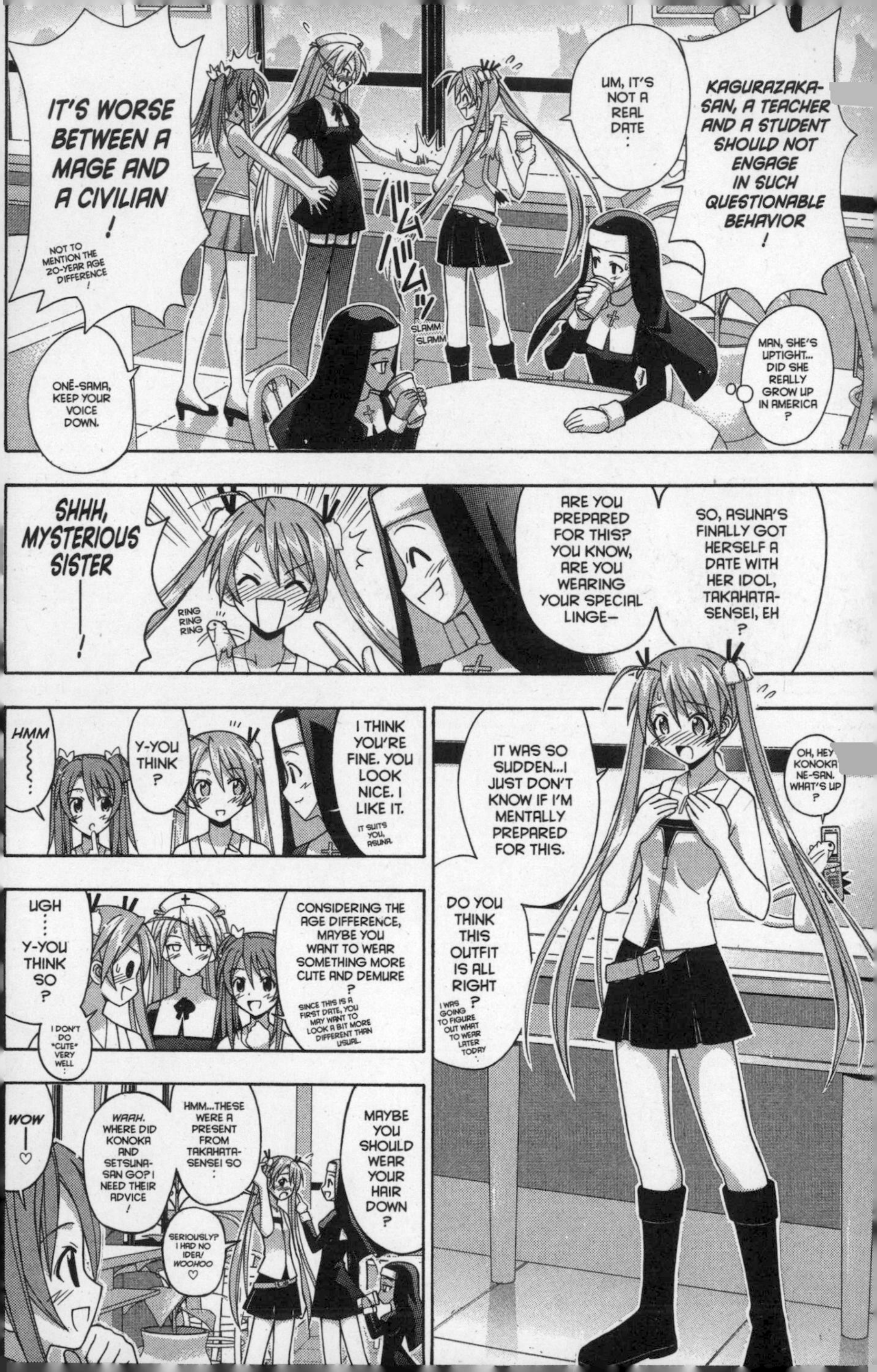
KAGURAZAKA-SAN, A TEACHER AND A STUDENT SHOULD NOT ENGAGE IN SUCH QUESTIONABLE BEHAVIOR!
UM, IT'S NOT A REAL DATE...
SLAMM SLAMM
IT'S WORSE BETWEEN A MAGE AND A CIVILIAN!
NOT TO MENTION THE 20-YEAR AGE DIFFERENCE!
MAN, SHE'S UPTIGHT... DID SHE REALLY GROW UP IN AMERICA?
ONĒ-SAMA, KEEP YOUR VOICE DOWN.
SO, ASUNA'S FINALLY GOT HERSELF A DATE WITH HER IDOL, TAKAHATA-SENSEI, EH?
ARE YOU PREPARED FOR THIS? YOU KNOW, ARE YOU WEARING YOUR SPECIAL LINGE—
SHHH, MYSTERIOUS SISTER—!
RING RING RING
OH, HEY KONOKA NE-SAN. WHAT'S UP?
IT WAS SO SUDDEN...I JUST DON'T KNOW IF I'M MENTALLY PREPARED FOR THIS.
DO YOU THINK THIS OUTFIT IS ALL RIGHT?
I WAS GOING TO FIGURE OUT WHAT TO WEAR LATER TODAY...
I THINK YOU'RE FINE. YOU LOOK NICE. I LIKE IT.
IT SUITS YOU, ASUNA.
Y-YOU THINK?
HMM~~...
CONSIDERING THE AGE DIFFERENCE, MAYBE YOU WANT TO WEAR SOMETHING MORE CUTE AND DEMURE?
SINCE THIS IS A FIRST DATE, YOU MAY WANT TO LOOK A BIT MORE DIFFERENT THAN USUAL.
UGH... Y-YOU THINK SO?
I DON'T DO "CUTE" VERY WELL...
MAYBE YOU SHOULD WEAR YOUR HAIR DOWN?
HMM...THESE WERE A PRESENT FROM TAKAHATA-SENSEI SO...
WAAH. WHERE DID KONOKA AND SETSUNA-SAN GO? I NEED THEIR ADVICE!
SERIOUSLY? I HAD NO IDEA! WOOHOO ♡
WOW—♡

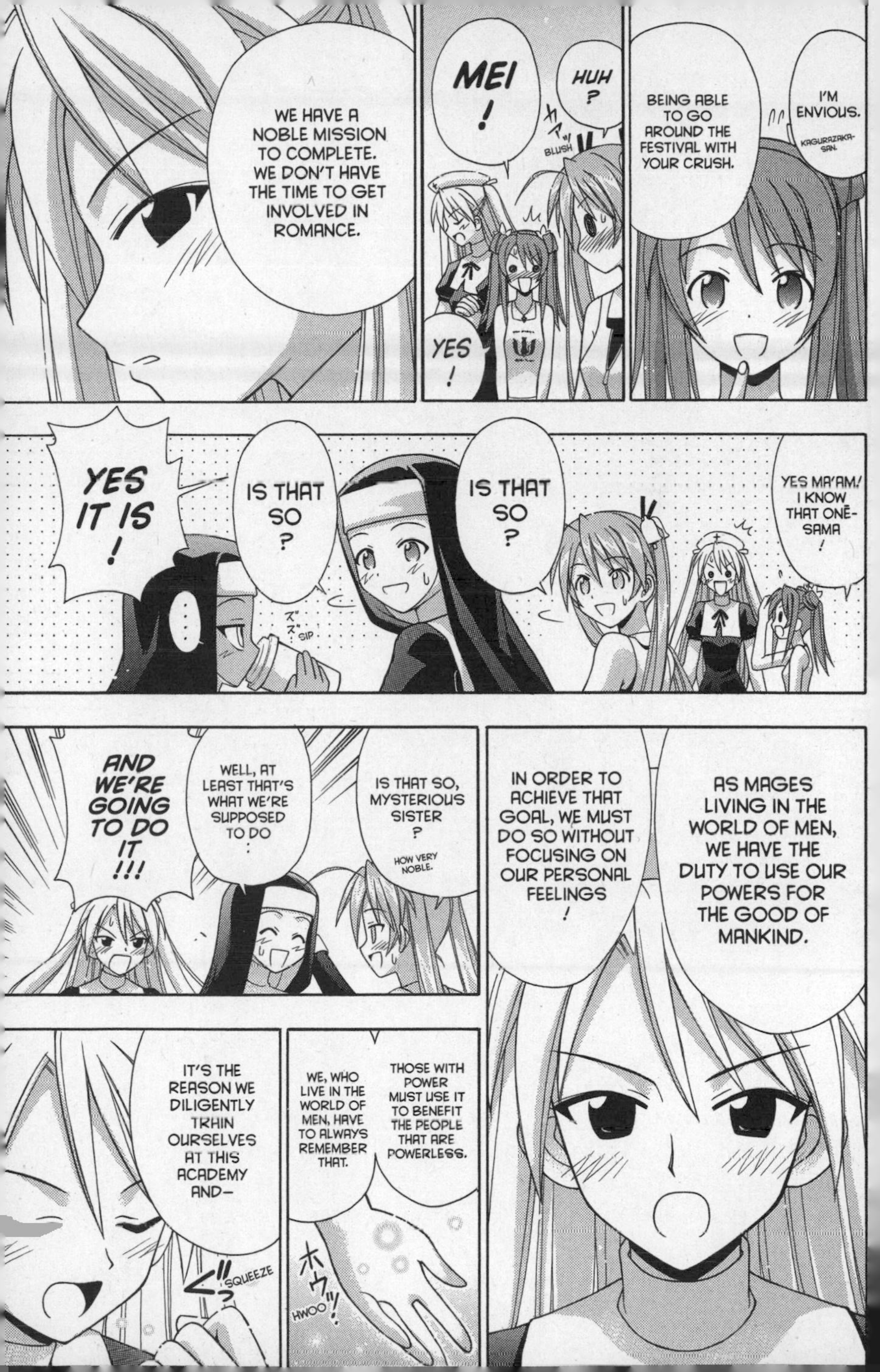
I'M ENVIOUS.
KAGURAZAKA-SAN.
BEING ABLE TO GO AROUND THE FESTIVAL WITH YOUR CRUSH.
HUH?
BLUSH
MEI!
YES!
WE HAVE A NOBLE MISSION TO COMPLETE. WE DON'T HAVE THE TIME TO GET INVOLVED IN ROMANCE.
YES MA'AM! I KNOW THAT ONĒ-SAMA!
IS THAT SO?
IS THAT SO?
SIP
YES IT IS!
AS MAGES LIVING IN THE WORLD OF MEN, WE HAVE THE DUTY TO USE OUR POWERS FOR THE GOOD OF MANKIND.
IN ORDER TO ACHIEVE THAT GOAL, WE MUST DO SO WITHOUT FOCUSING ON OUR PERSONAL FEELINGS!
IS THAT SO, MYSTERIOUS SISTER?
HOW VERY NOBLE.
WELL, AT LEAST THAT'S WHAT WE'RE SUPPOSED TO DO:
AND WE'RE GOING TO DO IT!!!
THOSE WITH POWER MUST USE IT TO BENEFIT THE PEOPLE THAT ARE POWERLESS.
WE, WHO LIVE IN THE WORLD OF MEN, HAVE TO ALWAYS REMEMBER THAT.
HWOO
IT'S THE REASON WE DILIGENTLY TRAIN OURSELVES AT THIS ACADEMY AND—
SQUEEZE

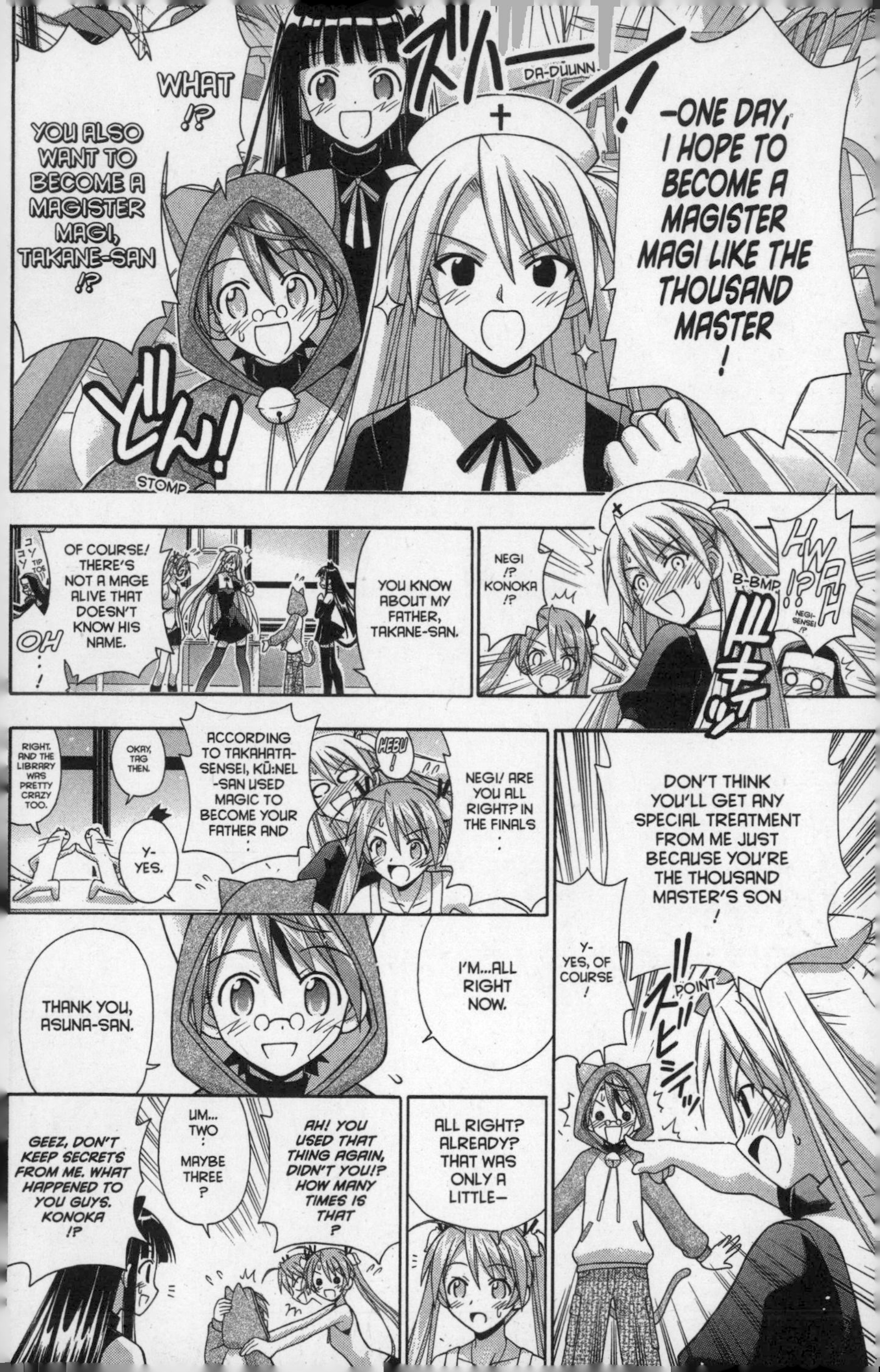
DA-DUUNN
-ONE DAY, I HOPE TO BECOME A MAGISTER MAGI LIKE THE THOUSAND MASTER!
WHAT!?
YOU ALSO WANT TO BECOME A MAGISTER MAGI, TAKANE-SAN!?
STOMP
HWAH!?
B-BMP
NEGI-SENSEI!?
NEGI!? KONOKA!?
YOU KNOW ABOUT MY FATHER, TAKANE-SAN.
OF COURSE! THERE'S NOT A MAGE ALIVE THAT DOESN'T KNOW HIS NAME.
TIP TOE
OH...!
DON'T THINK YOU'LL GET ANY SPECIAL TREATMENT FROM ME JUST BECAUSE YOU'RE THE THOUSAND MASTER'S SON!
Y-YES, OF COURSE!
POINT
NEGI! ARE YOU ALL RIGHT? IN THE FINALS:
HEBU!
ACCORDING TO TAKAHATA-SENSEI, KŪ:NEL-SAN USED MAGIC TO BECOME YOUR FATHER AND:
Y-YES.
OKAY, TAG THEN.
RIGHT. AND THE LIBRARY WAS PRETTY CRAZY TOO.
I'M...ALL RIGHT NOW.
THANK YOU, ASUNA-SAN.
ALL RIGHT? ALREADY? THAT WAS ONLY A LITTLE—
AH! YOU USED THAT THING AGAIN, DIDN'T YOU!? HOW MANY TIMES IS THAT?
UM... TWO: MAYBE THREE?
GEEZ, DON'T KEEP SECRETS FROM ME. WHAT HAPPENED TO YOU GUYS. KONOKA!?

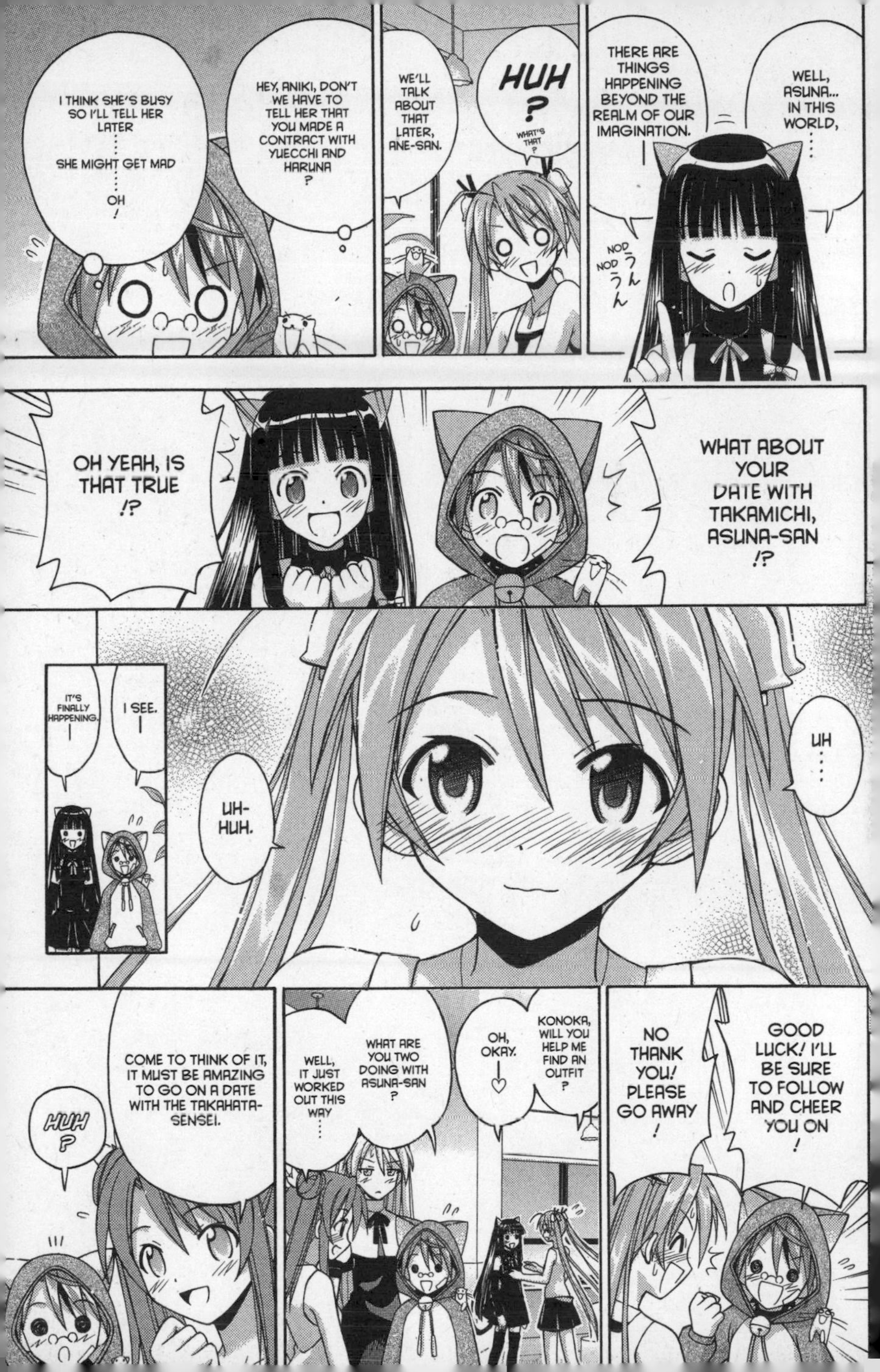
WELL, ASUNA... IN THIS WORLD, ...
THERE ARE THINGS HAPPENING BEYOND THE REALM OF OUR IMAGINATION. —
NOD うん NOD うん
HUH?
WHAT'S THAT?
WE'LL TALK ABOUT THAT LATER, ANE-SAN.
HEY, ANIKI, DON'T WE HAVE TO TELL HER THAT YOU MADE A CONTRACT WITH YUECCHI AND HARUNA?
I THINK SHE'S BUSY SO I'LL TELL HER LATER ... SHE MIGHT GET MAD ... OH!
WHAT ABOUT YOUR DATE WITH TAKAMICHI, ASUNA-SAN!?
OH YEAH, IS THAT TRUE!?
UH...
I SEE. —
IT'S FINALLY HAPPENING. —
UH-HUH.
GOOD LUCK! I'LL BE SURE TO FOLLOW AND CHEER YOU ON!
NO THANK YOU! PLEASE GO AWAY!
KONOKA, WILL YOU HELP ME FIND AN OUTFIT?
OH, OKAY. —♡
WHAT ARE YOU TWO DOING WITH ASUNA-SAN?
WELL, IT JUST WORKED OUT THIS WAY...
COME TO THINK OF IT, IT MUST BE AMAZING TO GO ON A DATE WITH THE TAKAHATA-SENSEI.
HUH?

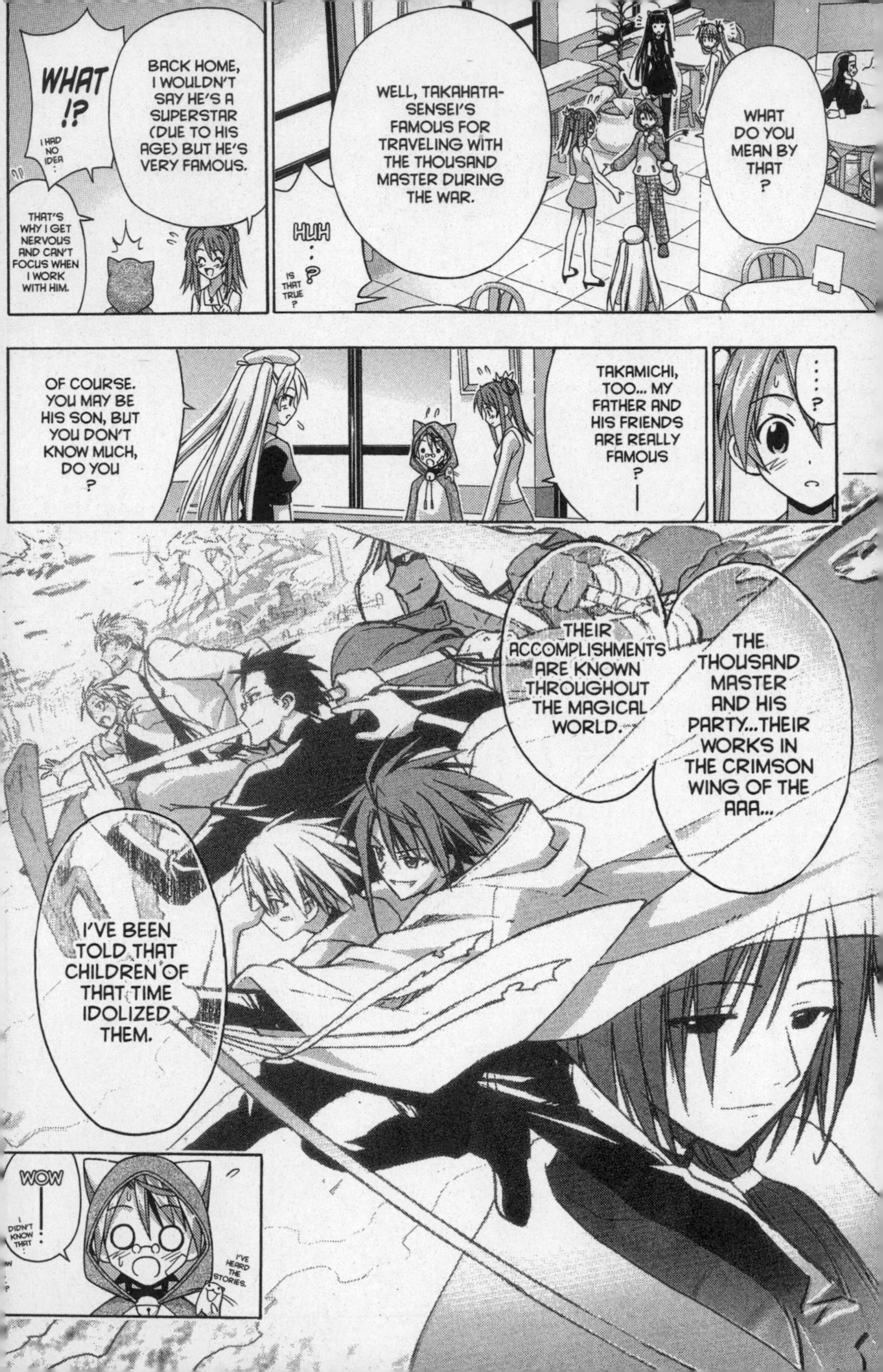
WHAT DO YOU MEAN BY THAT?
WELL, TAKAHATA-SENSEI'S FAMOUS FOR TRAVELING WITH THE THOUSAND MASTER DURING THE WAR.
HUH...?
IS THAT TRUE?
BACK HOME, I WOULDN'T SAY HE'S A SUPERSTAR (DUE TO HIS AGE) BUT HE'S VERY FAMOUS.
WHAT!?
I HAD NO IDEA...
THAT'S WHY I GET NERVOUS AND CAN'T FOCUS WHEN I WORK WITH HIM.
...?
TAKAMICHI, TOO... MY FATHER AND HIS FRIENDS ARE REALLY FAMOUS?
OF COURSE. YOU MAY BE HIS SON, BUT YOU DON'T KNOW MUCH, DO YOU?
THE THOUSAND MASTER AND HIS PARTY...THEIR WORKS IN THE CRIMSON WING OF THE AAA...
THEIR ACCOMPLISHMENTS ARE KNOWN THROUGHOUT THE MAGICAL WORLD.
I'VE BEEN TOLD THAT CHILDREN OF THAT TIME IDOLIZED THEM.
WOW!
I DIDN'T KNOW THAT...
I'VE HEARD THE STORIES.

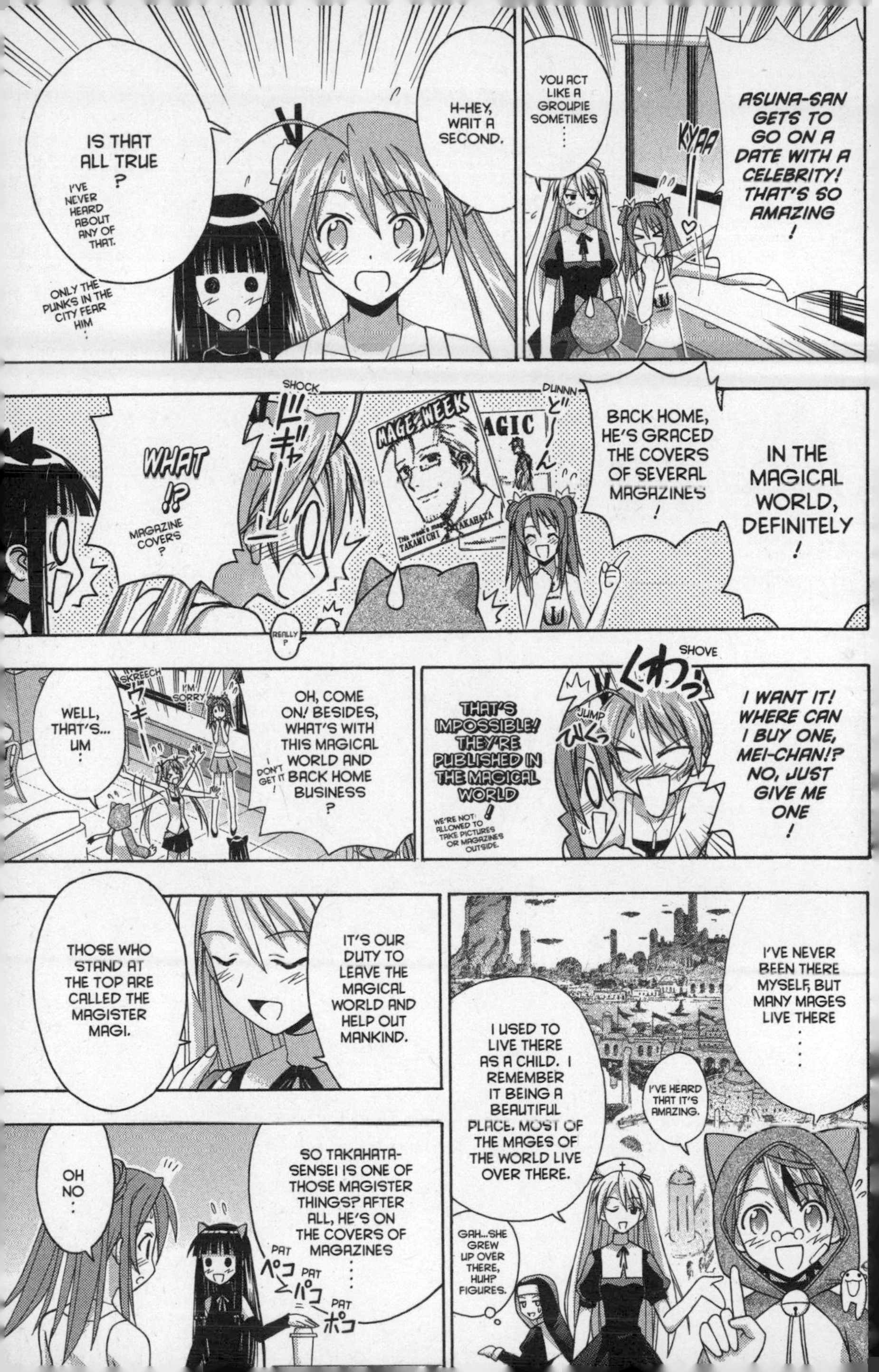
ASUNA-SAN GETS TO GO ON A DATE WITH A CELEBRITY! THAT'S SO AMAZING!
KYAA
YOU ACT LIKE A GROUPIE SOMETIMES...
H-HEY, WAIT A SECOND.
IS THAT ALL TRUE?
I'VE NEVER HEARD ABOUT ANY OF THAT.
ONLY THE PUNKS IN THE CITY FEAR HIM...
IN THE MAGICAL WORLD, DEFINITELY!
BACK HOME, HE'S GRACED THE COVERS OF SEVERAL MAGAZINES!
DUNNN
MAGE WEEK
AGIC
TAKAMICHI TAKAHATA
SHOCK
WHAT!?
MAGAZINE COVERS?
REALLY?
I WANT IT! WHERE CAN I BUY ONE, MEI-CHAN!? NO, JUST GIVE ME ONE!
SHOVE
くわっ
JUMP
THAT'S IMPOSSIBLE! THEY'RE PUBLISHED IN THE MAGICAL WORLD!
WE'RE NOT ALLOWED TO TAKE PICTURES OR MAGAZINES OUTSIDE.
OH, COME ON! BESIDES, WHAT'S WITH THIS MAGICAL WORLD AND BACK HOME BUSINESS?
I DON'T GET IT!
I'M SORRY
SKREECH
WELL, THAT'S... UM...
I'VE NEVER BEEN THERE MYSELF, BUT MANY MAGES LIVE THERE...
I USED TO LIVE THERE AS A CHILD. I REMEMBER IT BEING A BEAUTIFUL PLACE. MOST OF THE MAGES OF THE WORLD LIVE OVER THERE.
I'VE HEARD THAT IT'S AMAZING.
GAH...SHE GREW UP OVER THERE, HUH? FIGURES.
IT'S OUR DUTY TO LEAVE THE MAGICAL WORLD AND HELP OUT MANKIND.
THOSE WHO STAND AT THE TOP ARE CALLED THE MAGISTER MAGI.
SO TAKAHATA-SENSEI IS ONE OF THOSE MAGISTER THINGS? AFTER ALL, HE'S ON THE COVERS OF MAGAZINES...
PAT ペコ
PAT パコ
PAT ポコ
OH NO...

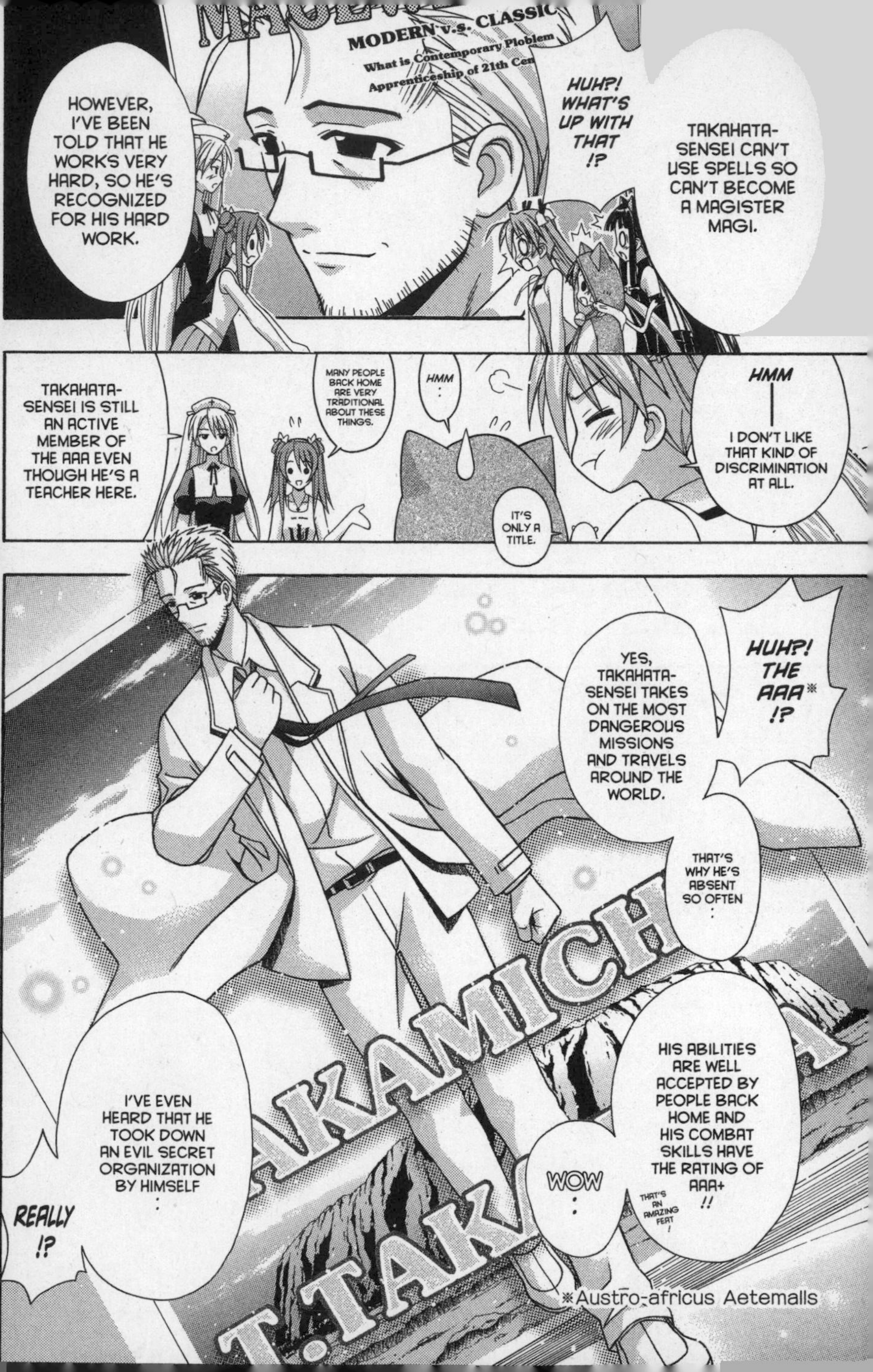
MODERN v.s. CLASSIC
What is Contemporary Ploblem
Apprenticeship of 21th Cen
TAKAHATA-SENSEI CAN'T USE SPELLS SO CAN'T BECOME A MAGISTER MAGI.
HUH?! WHAT'S UP WITH THAT !?
HOWEVER, I'VE BEEN TOLD THAT HE WORKS VERY HARD, SO HE'S RECOGNIZED FOR HIS HARD WORK.
HMM I DON'T LIKE THAT KIND OF DISCRIMINATION AT ALL.
IT'S ONLY A TITLE.
HMM :
MANY PEOPLE BACK HOME ARE VERY TRADITIONAL ABOUT THESE THINGS.
TAKAHATA-SENSEI IS STILL AN ACTIVE MEMBER OF THE AAA EVEN THOUGH HE'S A TEACHER HERE.
HUH?! THE AAA※ !?
YES, TAKAHATA-SENSEI TAKES ON THE MOST DANGEROUS MISSIONS AND TRAVELS AROUND THE WORLD.
THAT'S WHY HE'S ABSENT SO OFTEN :
HIS ABILITIES ARE WELL ACCEPTED BY PEOPLE BACK HOME AND HIS COMBAT SKILLS HAVE THE RATING OF AAA+ !!
THAT'S AN AMAZING FEAT!
WOW :
I'VE EVEN HEARD THAT HE TOOK DOWN AN EVIL SECRET ORGANIZATION BY HIMSELF :
REALLY !?
※Austro-africus Aetemalls

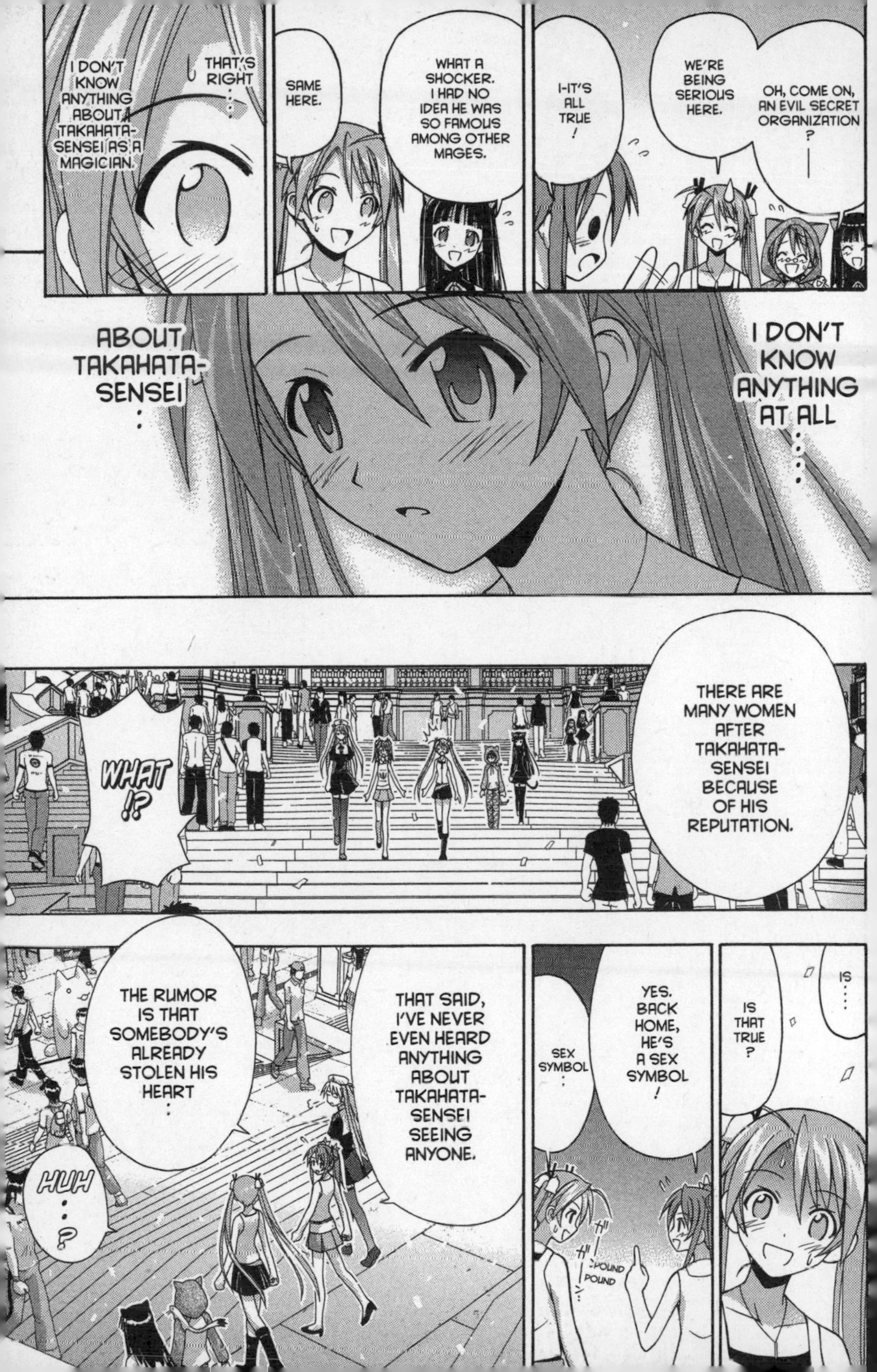
OH, COME ON, AN EVIL SECRET ORGANIZATION?
WE'RE BEING SERIOUS HERE.
I-IT'S ALL TRUE!
WHAT A SHOCKER. I HAD NO IDEA HE WAS SO FAMOUS AMONG OTHER MAGES.
SAME HERE.
THAT'S RIGHT...
I DON'T KNOW ANYTHING ABOUT TAKAHATA-SENSEI AS A MAGICIAN.
I DON'T KNOW ANYTHING AT ALL...
ABOUT TAKAHATA-SENSEI:
THERE ARE MANY WOMEN AFTER TAKAHATA-SENSEI BECAUSE OF HIS REPUTATION.
WHAT!?
IS...
IS THAT TRUE?
YES. BACK HOME, HE'S A SEX SYMBOL!
SEX SYMBOL:
POUND POUND
THAT SAID, I'VE NEVER EVEN HEARD ANYTHING ABOUT TAKAHATA-SENSEI SEEING ANYONE.
THE RUMOR IS THAT SOMEBODY'S ALREADY STOLEN HIS HEART:
HUH...?

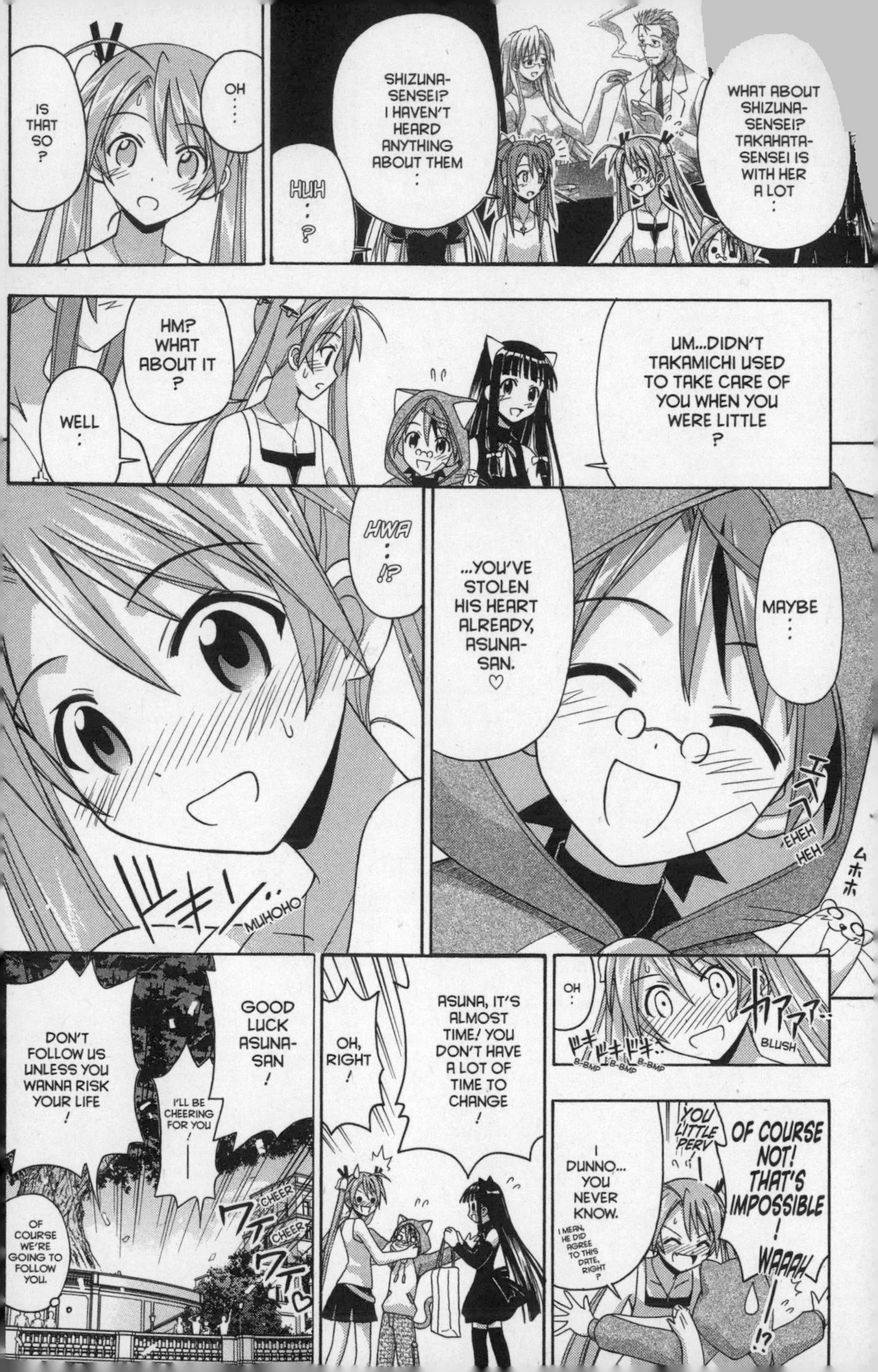
WHAT ABOUT SHIZUNA-SENSEI? TAKAHATA-SENSEI IS WITH HER A LOT...
SHIZUNA-SENSEI? I HAVEN'T HEARD ANYTHING ABOUT THEM...
HUH...?
OH...
IS THAT SO?
UM...DIDN'T TAKAMICHI USED TO TAKE CARE OF YOU WHEN YOU WERE LITTLE?
HM? WHAT ABOUT IT?
WELL...
MAYBE...
...YOU'VE STOLEN HIS HEART ALREADY, ASUNA-SAN. ♡
EHEH HEH
HWA...!?
MUHOHO
OH...
BLUSH
B-BMP B-BMP B-BMP
OF COURSE NOT! THAT'S IMPOSSIBLE! WAAAH!!?
YOU LITTLE PERV!
I DUNNO... YOU NEVER KNOW.
I MEAN, HE DID AGREE TO THIS DATE, RIGHT?
ASUNA, IT'S ALMOST TIME! YOU DON'T HAVE A LOT OF TIME TO CHANGE!
OH, RIGHT!
GOOD LUCK ASUNA-SAN!
I'LL BE CHEERING FOR YOU!
DON'T FOLLOW US UNLESS YOU WANNA RISK YOUR LIFE!
CHEER
CHEER
OF COURSE WE'RE GOING TO FOLLOW YOU.

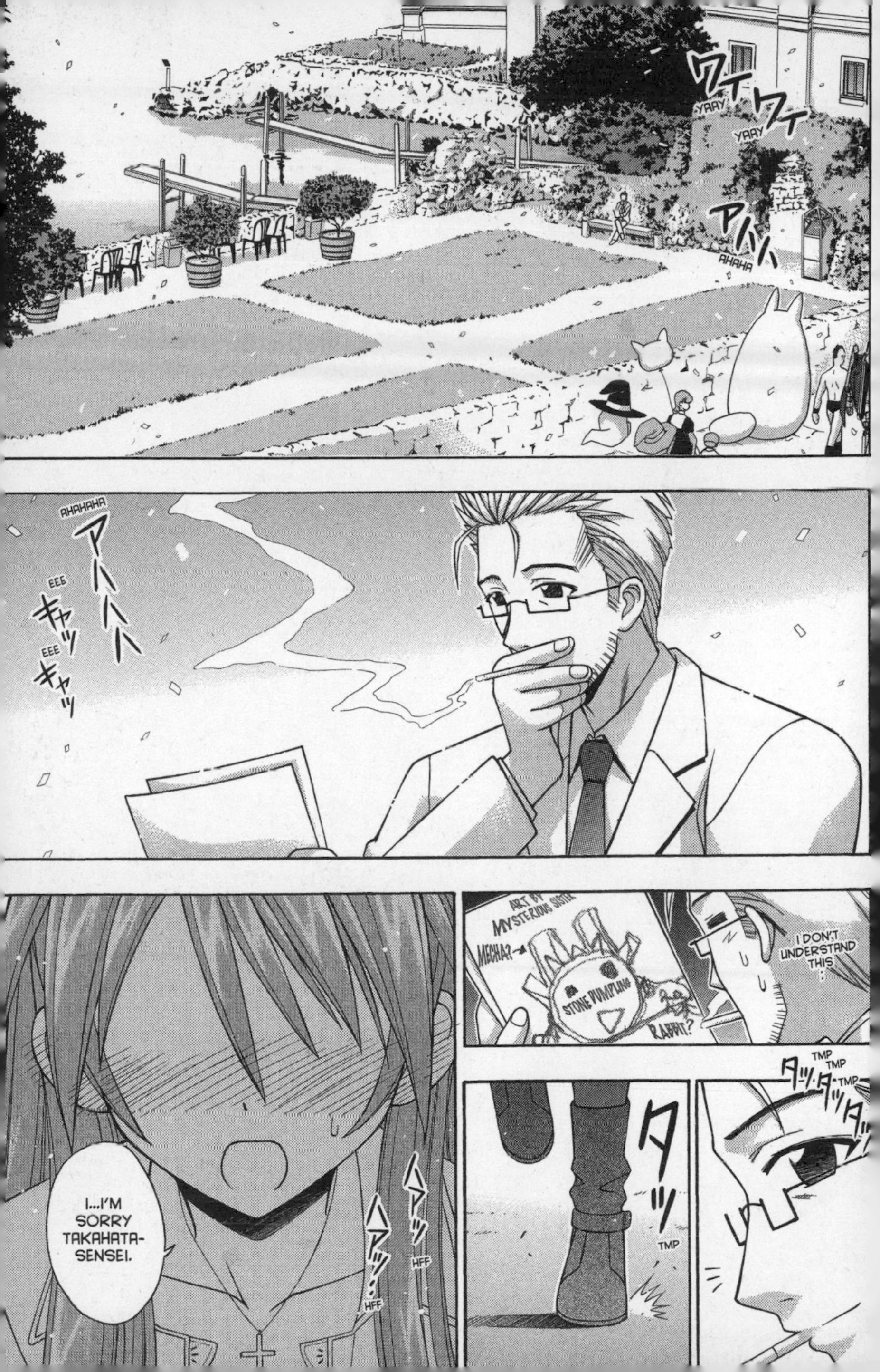
ワイワイ
YAAY
YAAY
アハハ
AHAHA
アハハハ
AHAHAHA
キャッ
EEE
キャッ
EEE
ART BY
MYSTERIOUS SISTE
MECHA?
STONE DUMPLING
RABBIT?
I DON'T UNDERSTAND THIS...
タッタッタッ
TMP
TMP
TMP
タッ
TMP
ハァッ
HFF
ハァッ
HFF
I...I'M SORRY TAKAHATA-SENSEI.

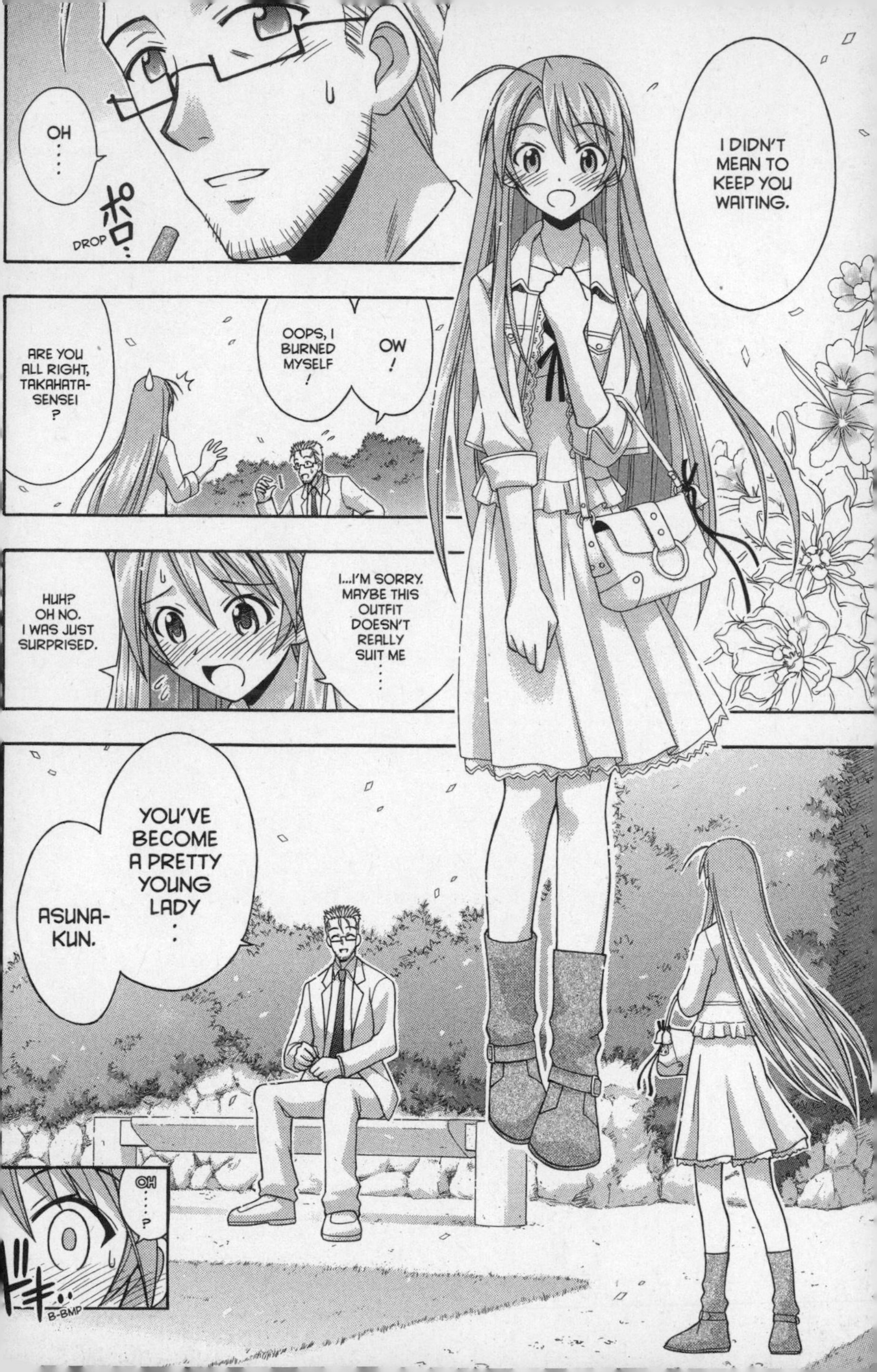
I DIDN'T MEAN TO KEEP YOU WAITING.
OH.....
ポロ
DROP
OOPS, I BURNED MYSELF!
OW!
ARE YOU ALL RIGHT, TAKAHATA-SENSEI?
I...I'M SORRY. MAYBE THIS OUTFIT DOESN'T REALLY SUIT ME.....
HUH? OH NO. I WAS JUST SURPRISED.
YOU'VE BECOME A PRETTY YOUNG LADY.. ASUNA-KUN.
OH....?
B-BMP

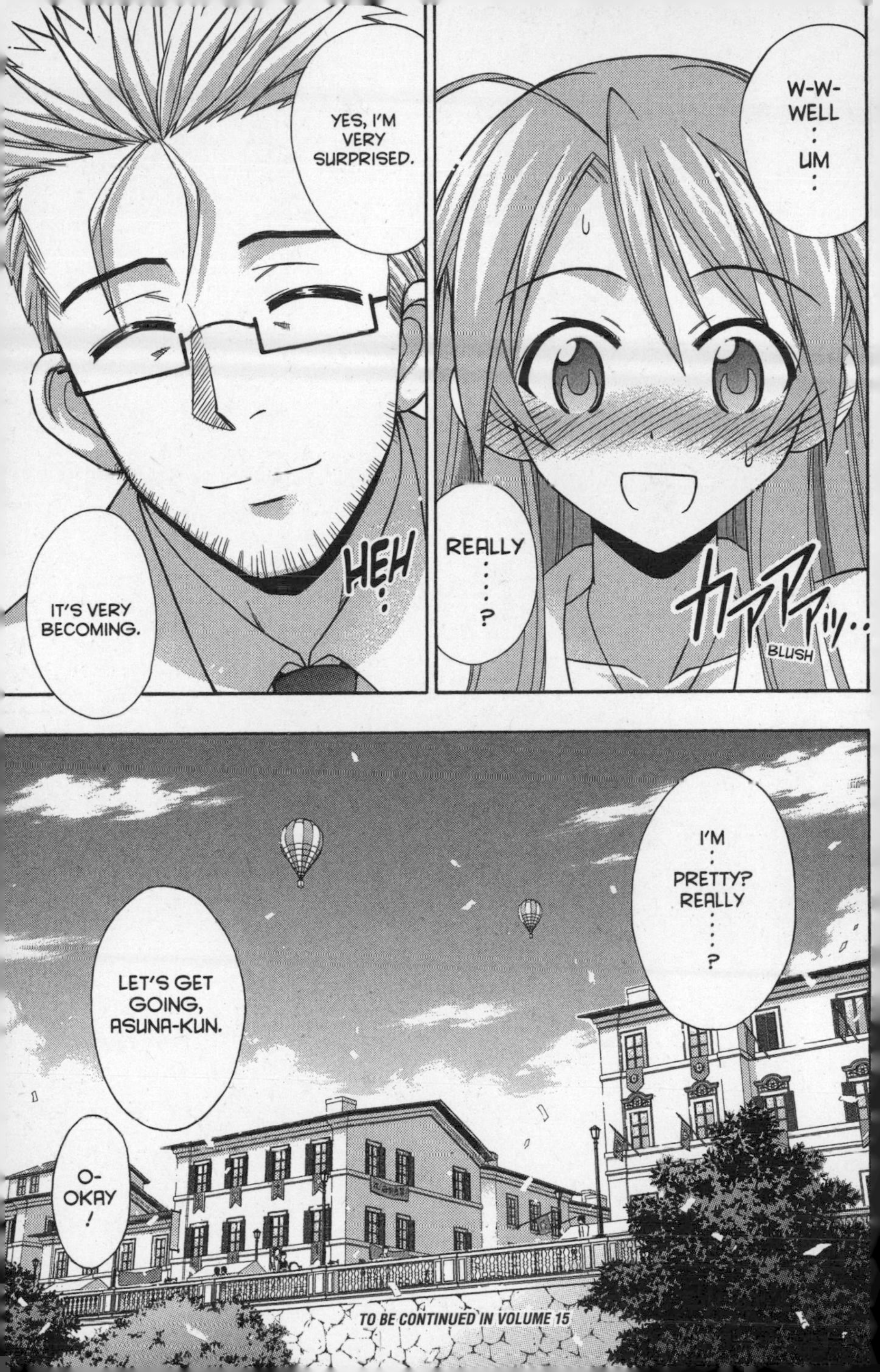
W-W-WELL . . . UM . . .
REALLY . . . . ?
BLUSH
YES, I'M VERY SURPRISED.
HEH
IT'S VERY BECOMING.
I'M . . . PRETTY? REALLY . . . . ?
LET'S GET GOING, ASUNA-KUN.
O-OKAY!

TO BE CONTINUED IN VOLUME 15

まほうせんせい
魔法先生ネギま!
MAGISTER NEGI MAGI

15

あかまつ けん
赤松 健
Ken Akamatsu

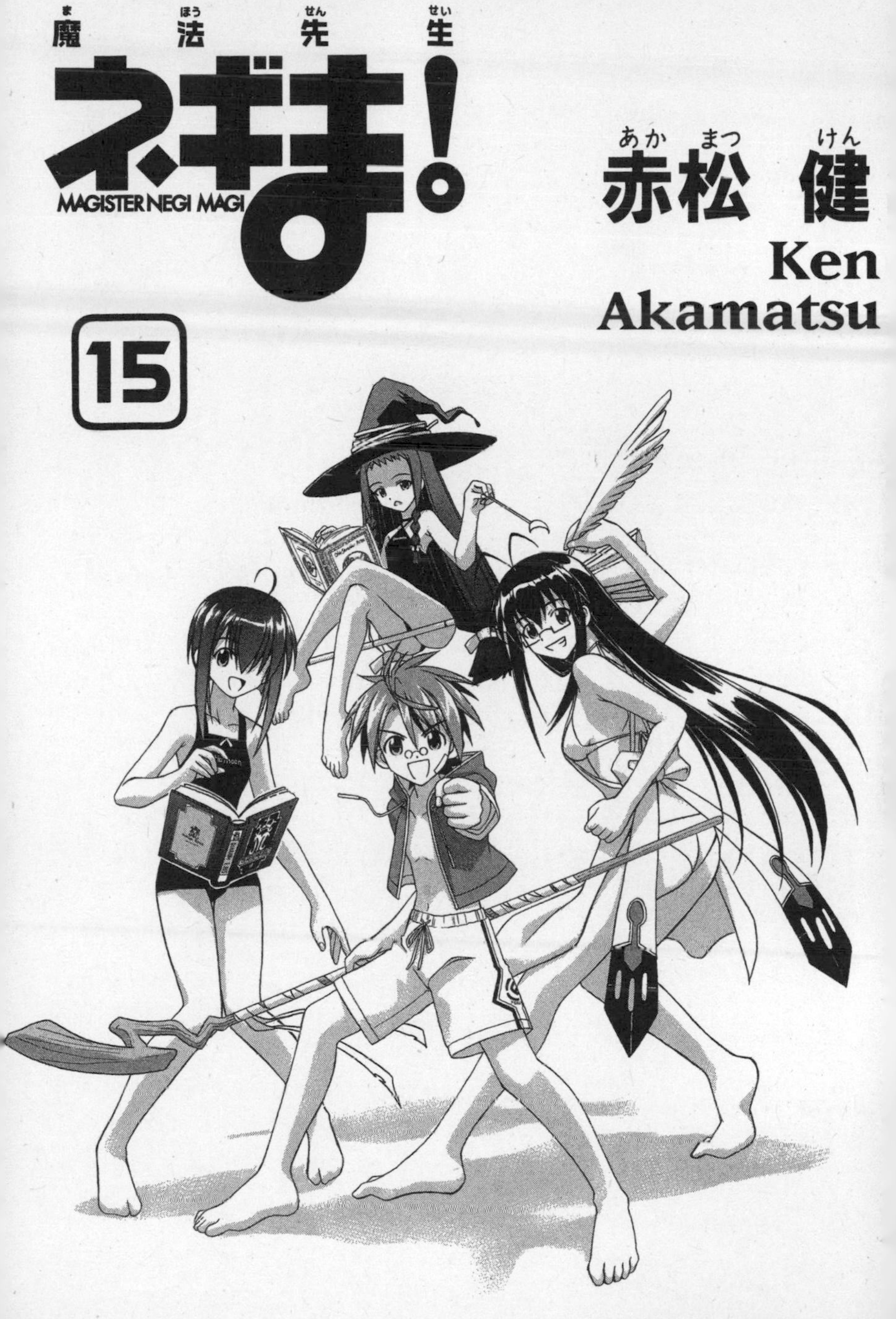

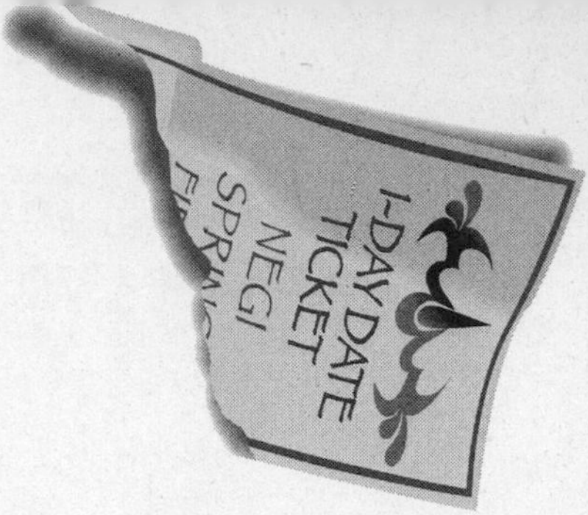
1-DAY DATE
TICKET
NEGI

Contents

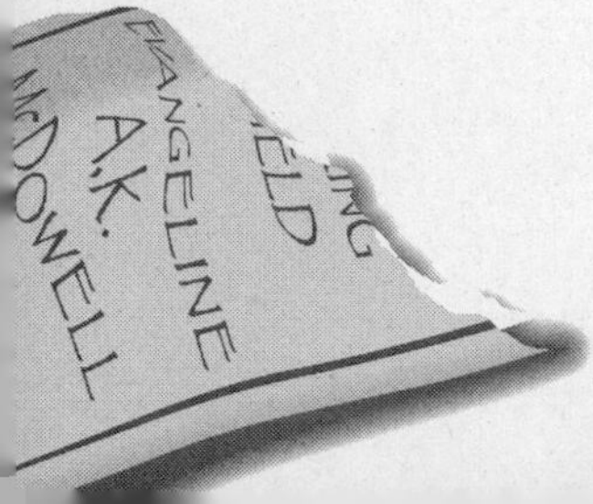
EVANGELINE
A.K.
McDOWELL

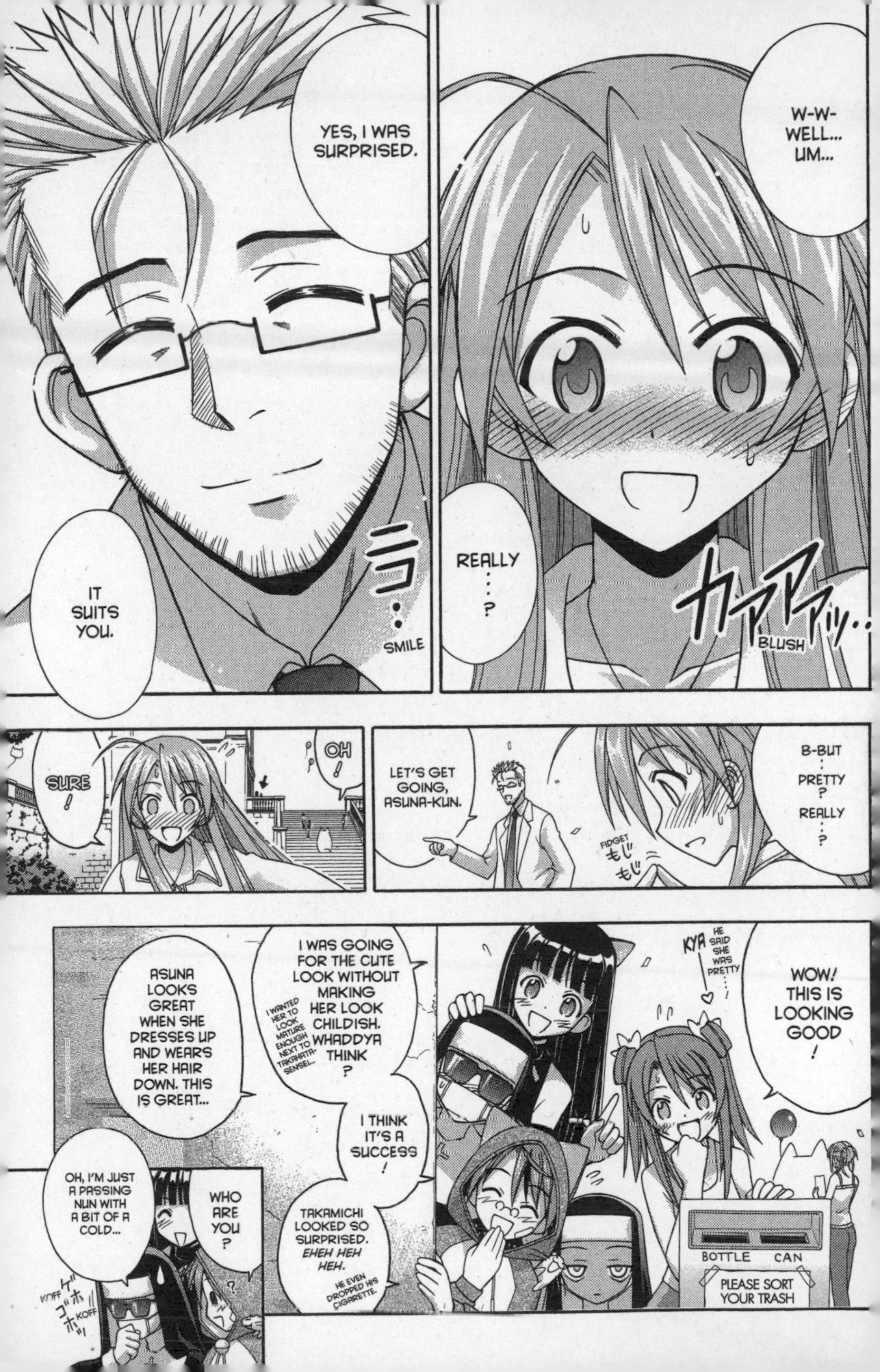
W-W-WELL... UM...
REALLY...?
カァァァッ.. BLUSH
YES, I WAS SURPRISED.
IT SUITS YOU.
ニコ.. SMILE
B-BUT... PRETTY? REALLY...?
LET'S GET GOING, ASUNA-KUN.
FIDGET もじもじ
OH!
SURE!
WOW! THIS IS LOOKING GOOD!
KYA
HE SAID SHE WAS PRETTY...!
BOTTLE CAN
PLEASE SORT YOUR TRASH
I WAS GOING FOR THE CUTE LOOK WITHOUT MAKING HER LOOK CHILDISH. WHADDYA THINK?
I WANTED HER TO LOOK MATURE ENOUGH NEXT TO TAKAHATA-SENSEI...
ASUNA LOOKS GREAT WHEN SHE DRESSES UP AND WEARS HER HAIR DOWN. THIS IS GREAT...
I THINK IT'S A SUCCESS!
TAKAMICHI LOOKED SO SURPRISED. EHEH HEH HEH.
HE EVEN DROPPED HIS CIGARETTE.
WHO ARE YOU?
OH, I'M JUST A PASSING NUN WITH A BIT OF A COLD...
ゲホ KOFF ゴホ KOFF

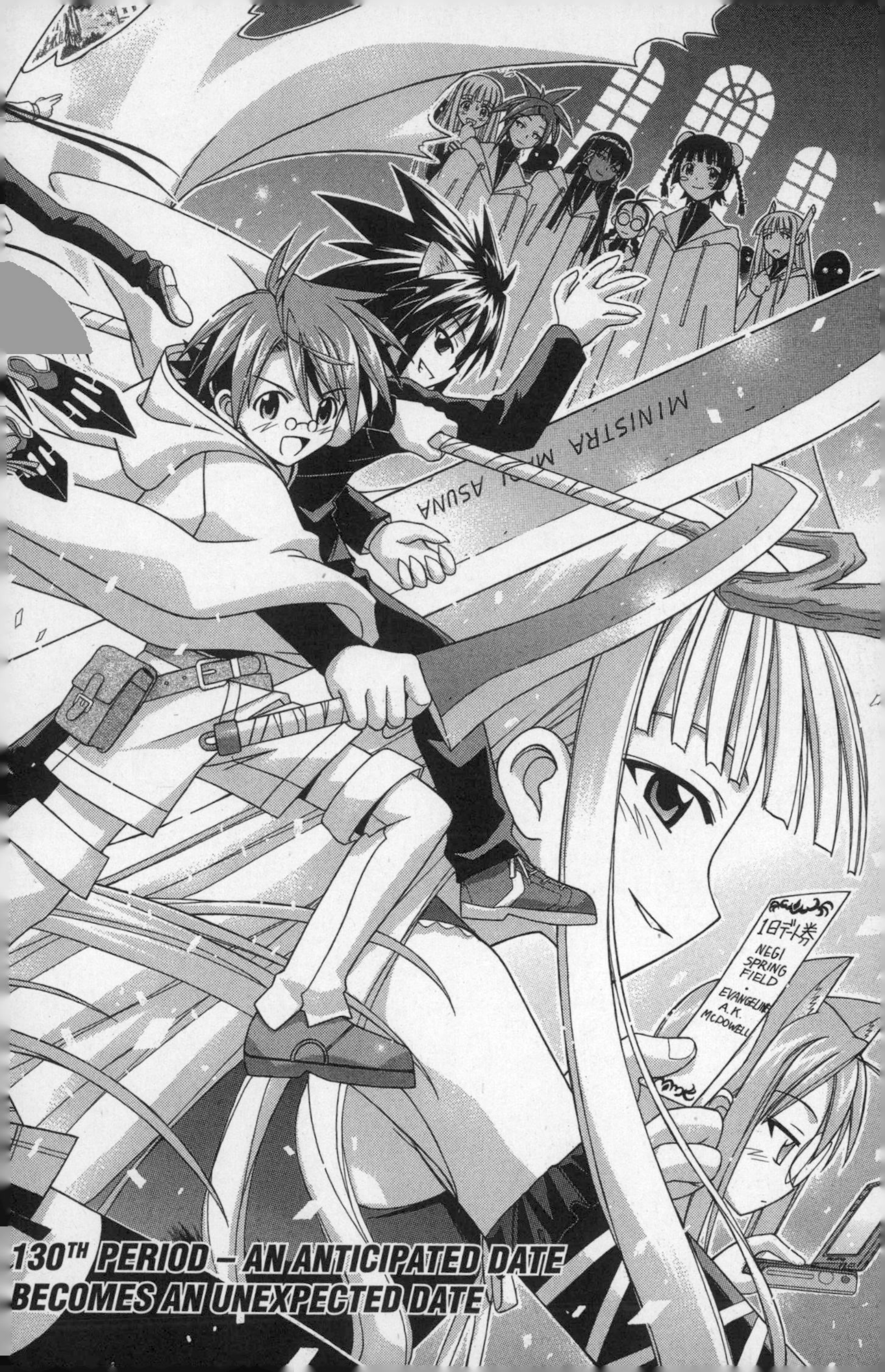
MINISTRA MI
I ASUNA
1日デート券
NEGI
SPRING
FIELD
·
EVANGELINE
A.K.
McDOWELL

130TH PERIOD – AN ANTICIPATED DATE BECOMES AN UNEXPECTED DATE

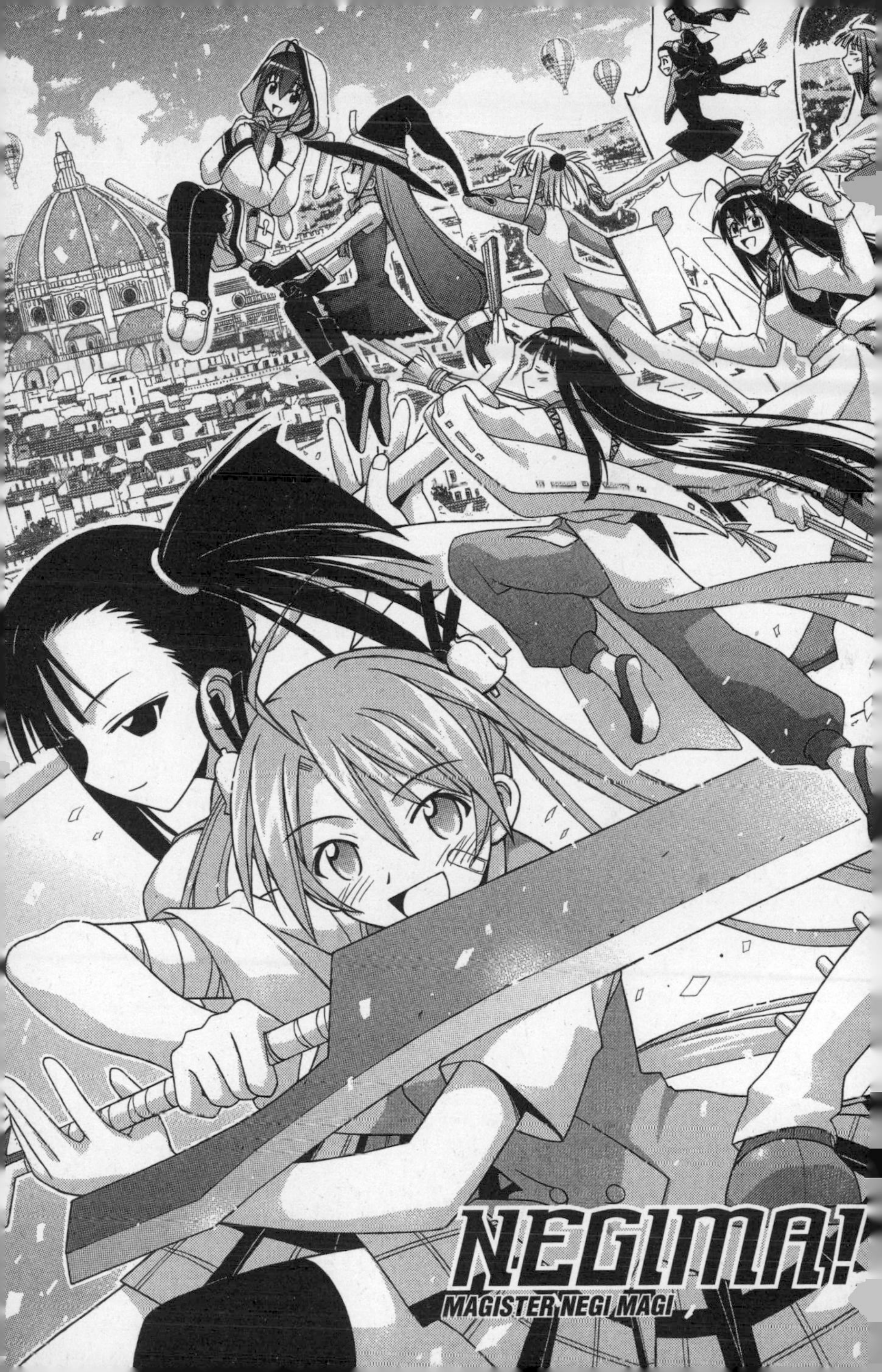
NEGIMA!
MAGISTER NEGI MAGI

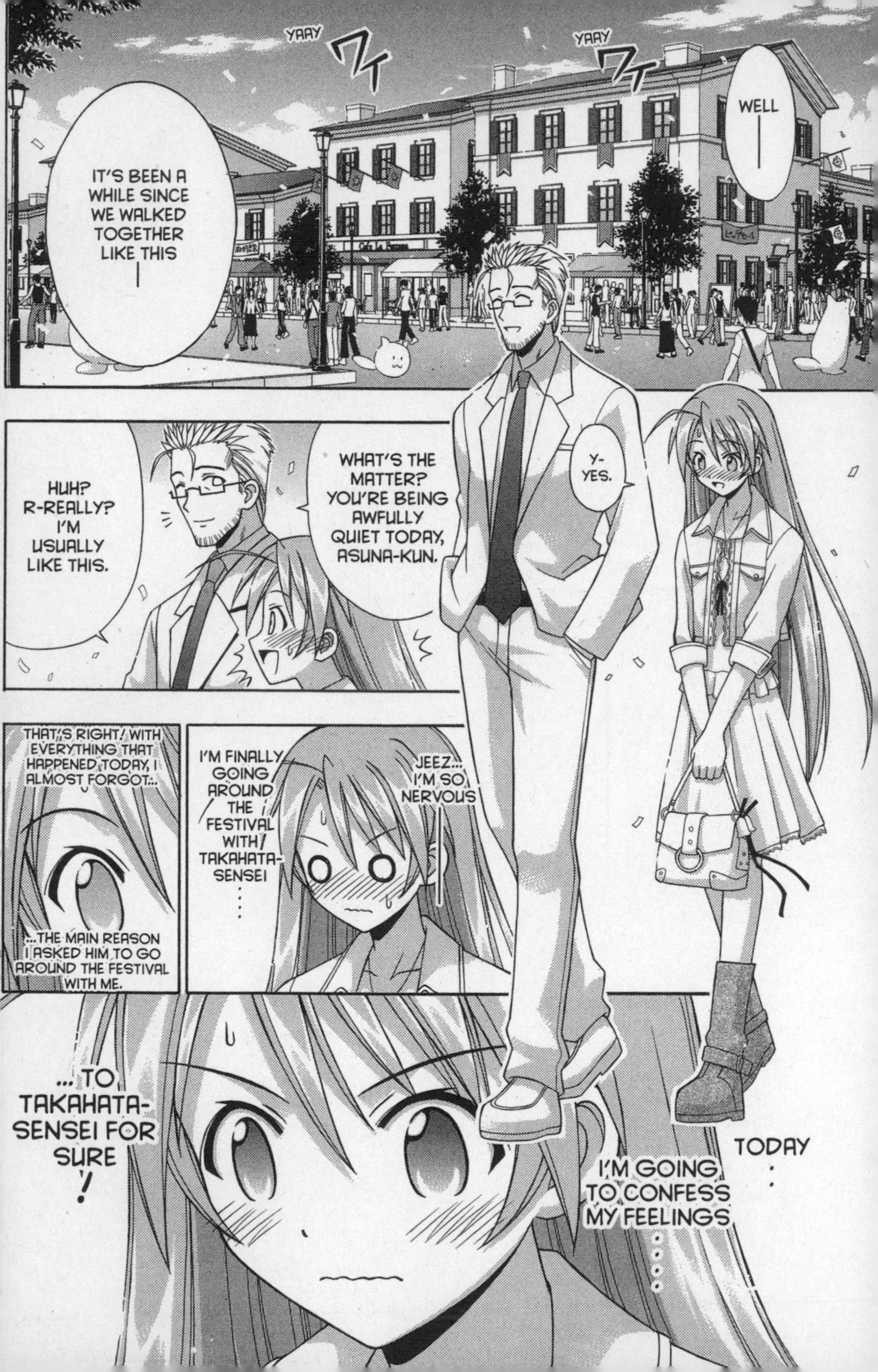
YAAY
YAAY
WELL —
IT'S BEEN A WHILE SINCE WE WALKED TOGETHER LIKE THIS —
Y-YES.
WHAT'S THE MATTER? YOU'RE BEING AWFULLY QUIET TODAY, ASUNA-KUN.
HUH? R-REALLY? I'M USUALLY LIKE THIS.
JEEZ... I'M SO NERVOUS
I'M FINALLY GOING AROUND THE FESTIVAL WITH TAKAHATA-SENSEI ...
THAT'S RIGHT! WITH EVERYTHING THAT HAPPENED TODAY, I ALMOST FORGOT...
...THE MAIN REASON I ASKED HIM TO GO AROUND THE FESTIVAL WITH ME.
TODAY :
I'M GOING TO CONFESS MY FEELINGS .....
... TO TAKAHATA-SENSEI FOR SURE !

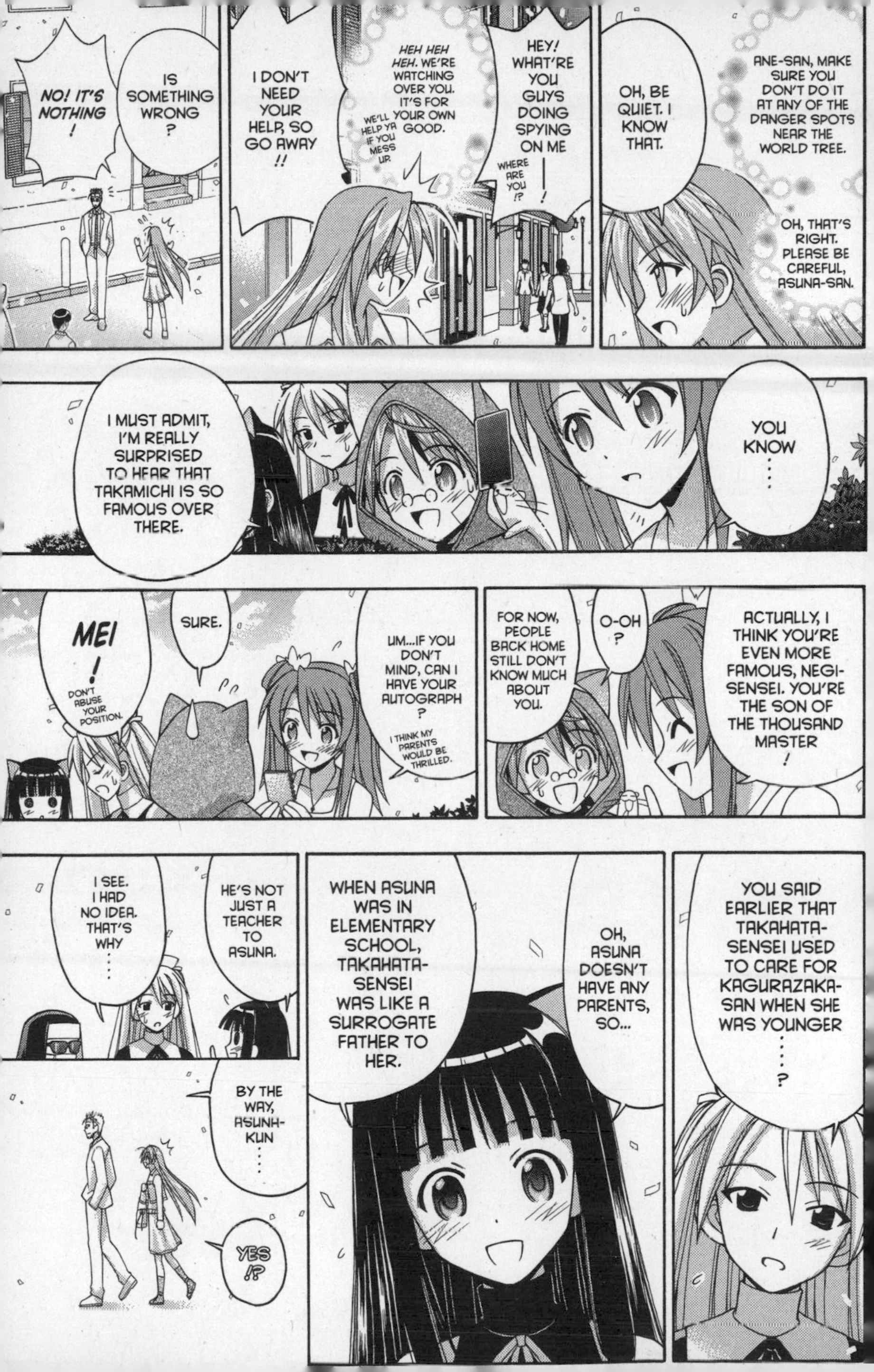
ANE-SAN, MAKE SURE YOU DON'T DO IT AT ANY OF THE DANGER SPOTS NEAR THE WORLD TREE.
OH, THAT'S RIGHT. PLEASE BE CAREFUL, ASUNA-SAN.
OH, BE QUIET. I KNOW THAT.
HEY! WHAT'RE YOU GUYS DOING SPYING ON ME!
WHERE ARE YOU!?
HEH HEH HEH. WE'RE WATCHING OVER YOU. IT'S FOR YOUR OWN GOOD.
WE'LL HELP YA IF YOU MESS UP.
I DON'T NEED YOUR HELP, SO GO AWAY!!
IS SOMETHING WRONG?
NO! IT'S NOTHING!
YOU KNOW...
I MUST ADMIT, I'M REALLY SURPRISED TO HEAR THAT TAKAMICHI IS SO FAMOUS OVER THERE.
ACTUALLY, I THINK YOU'RE EVEN MORE FAMOUS, NEGI-SENSEI. YOU'RE THE SON OF THE THOUSAND MASTER!
O-OH?
FOR NOW, PEOPLE BACK HOME STILL DON'T KNOW MUCH ABOUT YOU.
UM...IF YOU DON'T MIND, CAN I HAVE YOUR AUTOGRAPH?
I THINK MY PARENTS WOULD BE THRILLED.
SURE.
MEI!
DON'T ABUSE YOUR POSITION.
YOU SAID EARLIER THAT TAKAHATA-SENSEI USED TO CARE FOR KAGURAZAKA-SAN WHEN SHE WAS YOUNGER...?
OH, ASUNA DOESN'T HAVE ANY PARENTS, SO...
WHEN ASUNA WAS IN ELEMENTARY SCHOOL, TAKAHATA-SENSEI WAS LIKE A SURROGATE FATHER TO HER.
HE'S NOT JUST A TEACHER TO ASUNA.
I SEE. I HAD NO IDEA. THAT'S WHY...
BY THE WAY, ASUNA-KUN...
YES!?

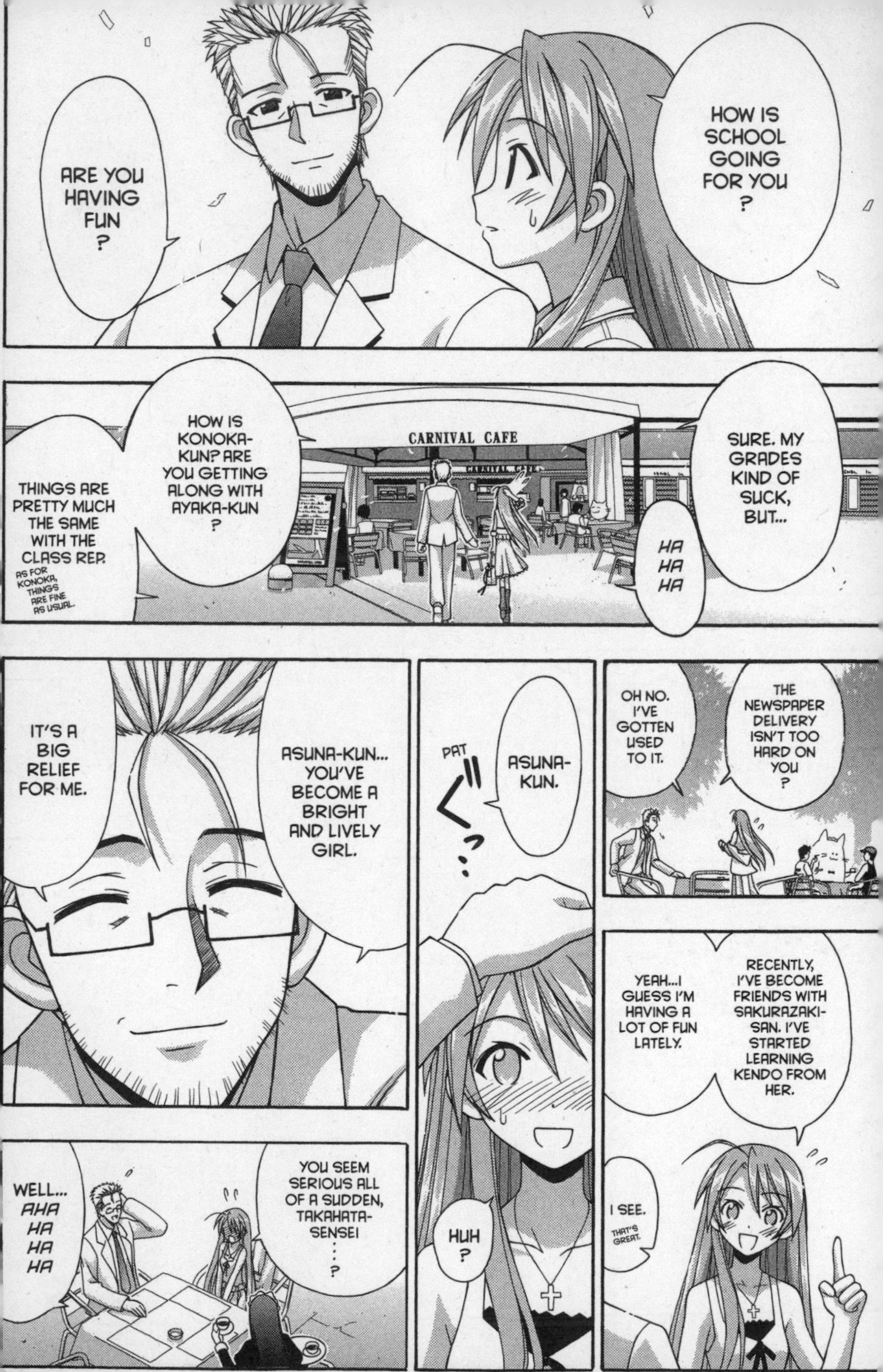
HOW IS SCHOOL GOING FOR YOU?
ARE YOU HAVING FUN?
SURE. MY GRADES KIND OF SUCK, BUT...
HA HA HA
HOW IS KONOKA-KUN? ARE YOU GETTING ALONG WITH AYAKA-KUN?
CARNIVAL CAFE
THINGS ARE PRETTY MUCH THE SAME WITH THE CLASS REP.
AS FOR KONOKA, THINGS ARE FINE AS USUAL.
THE NEWSPAPER DELIVERY ISN'T TOO HARD ON YOU?
OH NO. I'VE GOTTEN USED TO IT.
RECENTLY, I'VE BECOME FRIENDS WITH SAKURAZAKI-SAN. I'VE STARTED LEARNING KENDO FROM HER.
YEAH...I GUESS I'M HAVING A LOT OF FUN LATELY.
I SEE.
THAT'S GREAT.
ASUNA-KUN.
PAT
HUH?
ASUNA-KUN... YOU'VE BECOME A BRIGHT AND LIVELY GIRL.
IT'S A BIG RELIEF FOR ME.
YOU SEEM SERIOUS ALL OF A SUDDEN, TAKAHATA-SENSEI...?
WELL... AHA HA HA HA

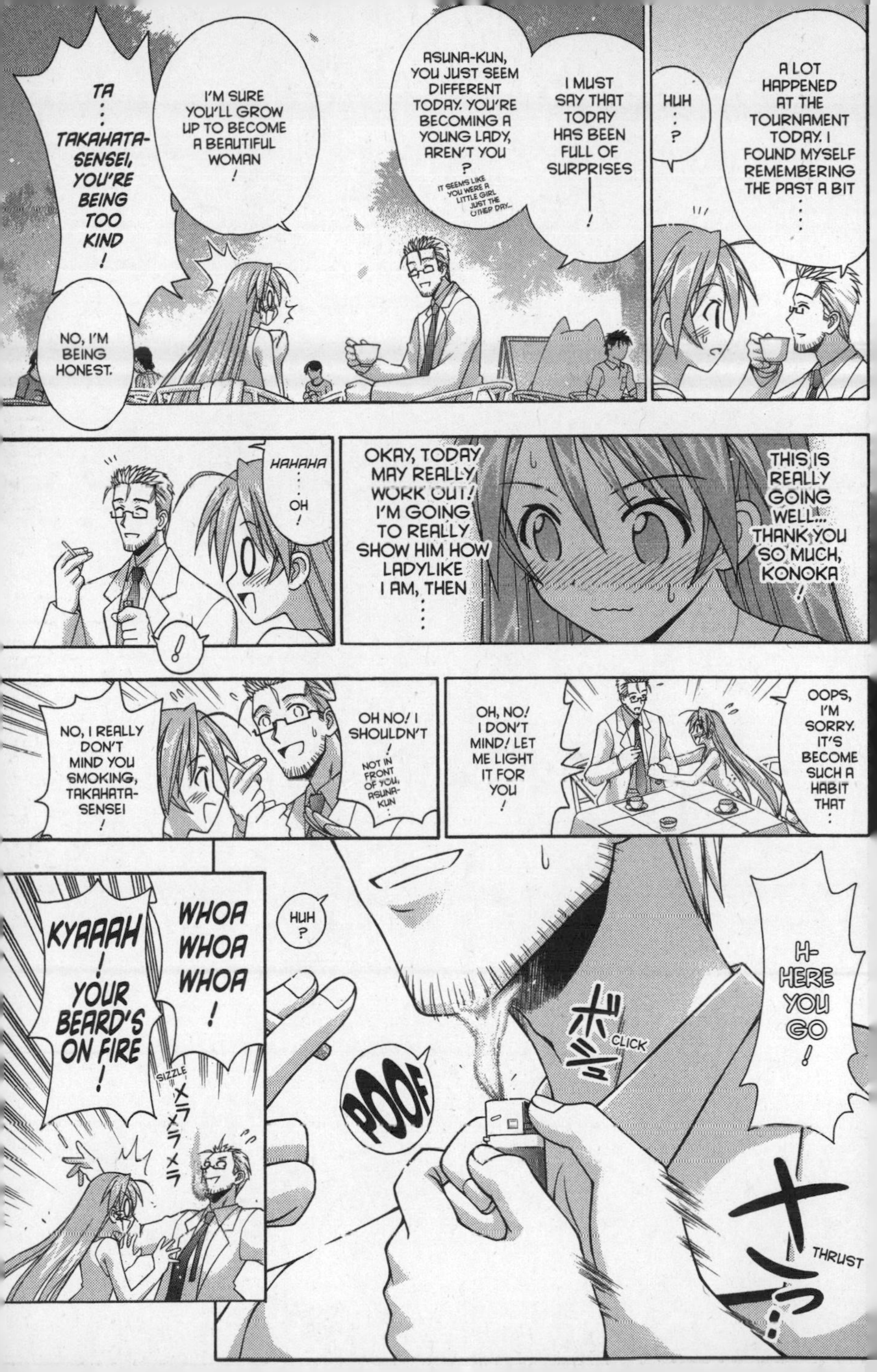
A LOT HAPPENED AT THE TOURNAMENT TODAY. I FOUND MYSELF REMEMBERING THE PAST A BIT...
HUH...?
I MUST SAY THAT TODAY HAS BEEN FULL OF SURPRISES—!
ASUNA-KUN, YOU JUST SEEM DIFFERENT TODAY. YOU'RE BECOMING A YOUNG LADY, AREN'T YOU?
IT SEEMS LIKE YOU WERE A LITTLE GIRL JUST THE OTHER DAY...
I'M SURE YOU'LL GROW UP TO BECOME A BEAUTIFUL WOMAN!
TA... TAKAHATA-SENSEI, YOU'RE BEING TOO KIND!
NO, I'M BEING HONEST.
THIS IS REALLY GOING WELL... THANK YOU SO MUCH, KONOKA!
OKAY, TODAY MAY REALLY WORK OUT! I'M GOING TO REALLY SHOW HIM HOW LADYLIKE I AM, THEN...
HAHAHA... OH!
!
OOPS, I'M SORRY. IT'S BECOME SUCH A HABIT THAT...
OH, NO! I DON'T MIND! LET ME LIGHT IT FOR YOU!
OH NO! I SHOULDN'T!
NOT IN FRONT OF YOU, ASUNA-KUN...
NO, I REALLY DON'T MIND YOU SMOKING, TAKAHATA-SENSEI!
H-HERE YOU GO!
THRUST
CLICK
POOF
HUH?
WHOA WHOA WHOA!
KYAAAH! YOUR BEARD'S ON FIRE!
SIZZLE

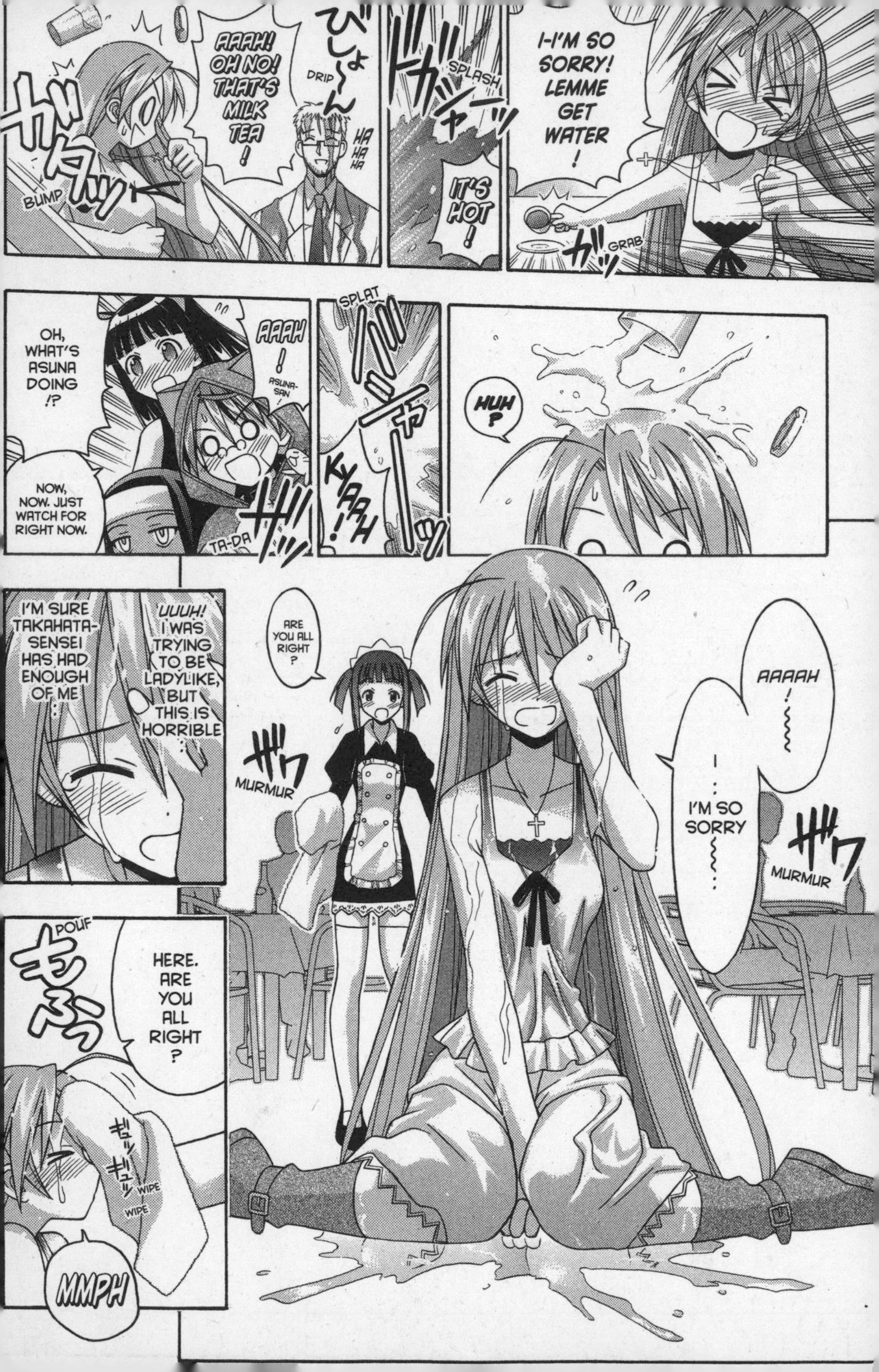
I-I'M SO SORRY! LEMME GET WATER!
GRAB
SPLASH
IT'S HOT!
びしょ～ん
DRIP
AAAH! OH NO! THAT'S MILK TEA!
HA HA HA HA
BUMP
HUH?
SPLAT
AAAH!
ASUNA-SAN!
KYAAAH!
OH, WHAT'S ASUNA DOING!?
NOW, NOW. JUST WATCH FOR RIGHT NOW.
TA-DA
ARE YOU ALL RIGHT?
AAAAH!
I... I'M SO SORRY...
MURMUR
MURMUR
UUUH! I WAS TRYING TO BE LADYLIKE, BUT THIS IS HORRIBLE...
I'M SURE TAKAHATA-SENSEI HAS HAD ENOUGH OF ME...
HERE. ARE YOU ALL RIGHT?
もふっ
POUF
ギュッギュッ
WIPE
WIPE
MMPH

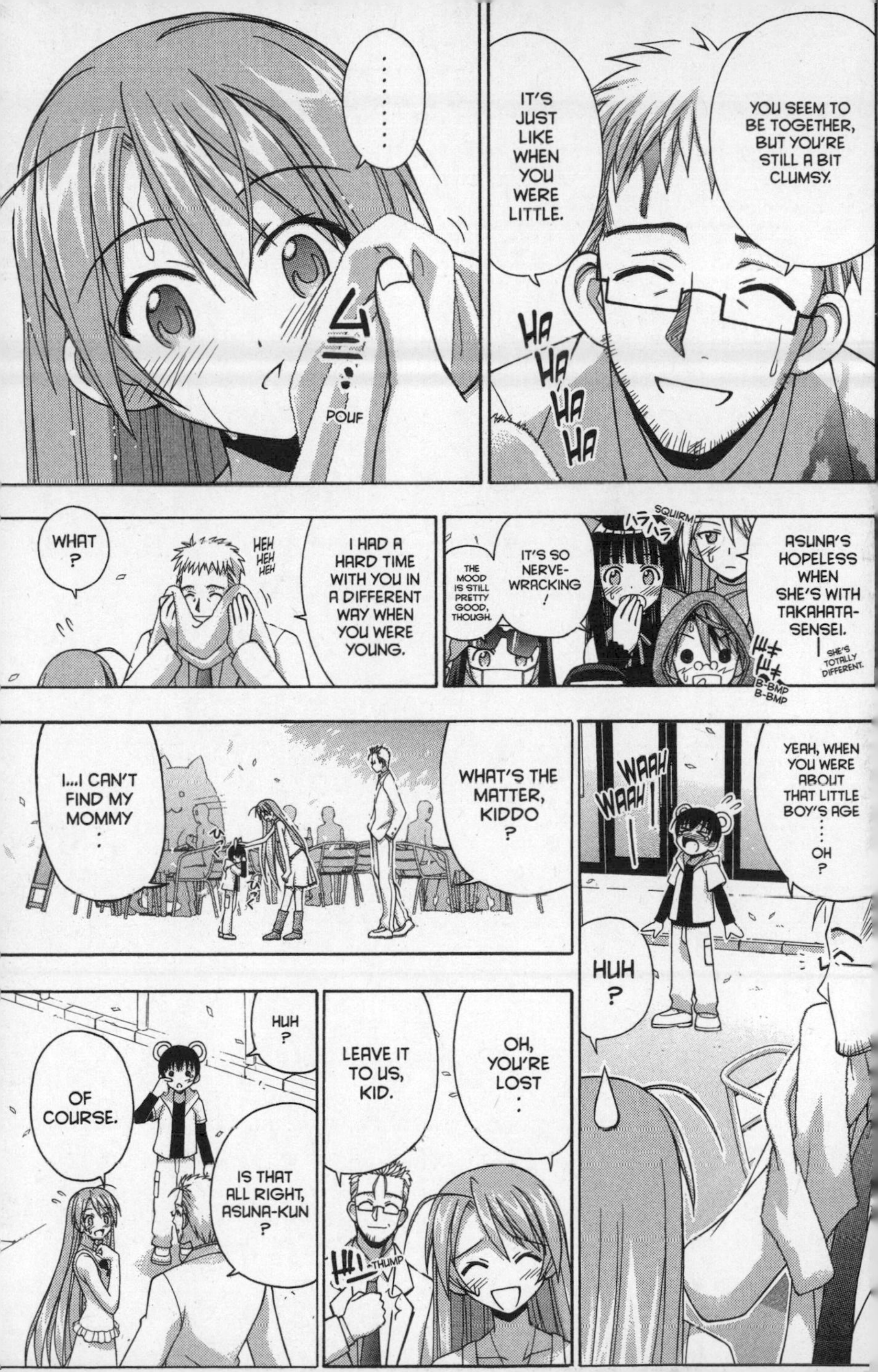
YOU SEEM TO BE TOGETHER, BUT YOU'RE STILL A BIT CLUMSY.
IT'S JUST LIKE WHEN YOU WERE LITTLE.
HA HA HA HA HA
......
POUF
ASUNA'S HOPELESS WHEN SHE'S WITH TAKAHATA-SENSEI.
SHE'S TOTALLY DIFFERENT.
B-BMP B-BMP
SQUIRM
IT'S SO NERVE-WRACKING!
THE MOOD IS STILL PRETTY GOOD, THOUGH.
I HAD A HARD TIME WITH YOU IN A DIFFERENT WAY WHEN YOU WERE YOUNG.
HEH HEH HEH
WHAT?
YEAH, WHEN YOU WERE ABOUT THAT LITTLE BOY'S AGE......
OH?
WAAH WAAH!
HUH?
WHAT'S THE MATTER, KIDDO?
I...I CAN'T FIND MY MOMMY...
OH, YOU'RE LOST...
LEAVE IT TO US, KID.
THUMP
HUH?
IS THAT ALL RIGHT, ASUNA-KUN?
OF COURSE.

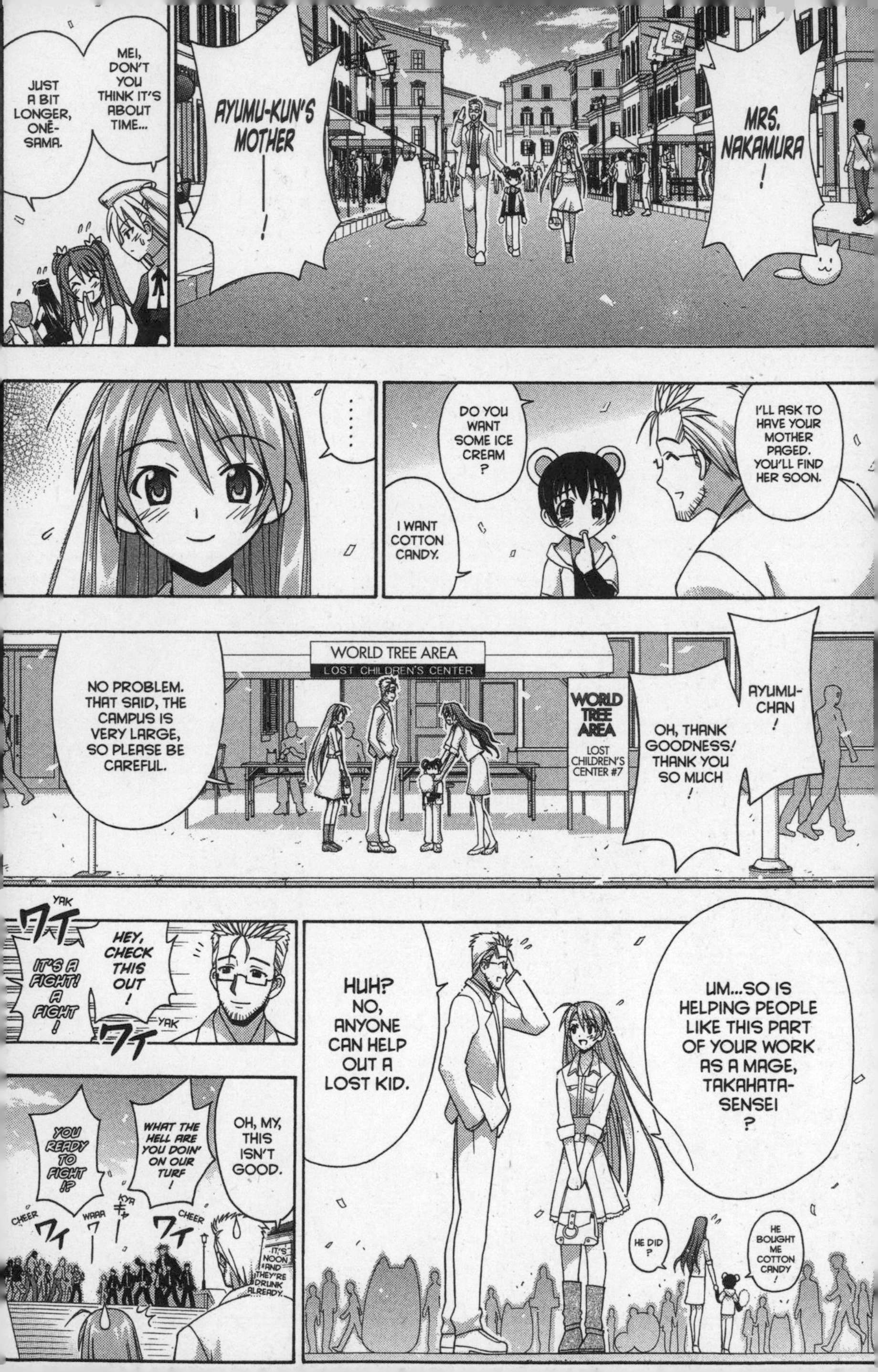
MRS. NAKAMURA!
AYUMU-KUN'S MOTHER!
MEI, DON'T YOU THINK IT'S ABOUT TIME...
JUST A BIT LONGER, ONĒ-SAMA.
I'LL ASK TO HAVE YOUR MOTHER PAGED. YOU'LL FIND HER SOON.
DO YOU WANT SOME ICE CREAM?
I WANT COTTON CANDY.
......
AYUMU-CHAN!
OH, THANK GOODNESS! THANK YOU SO MUCH!
WORLD TREE AREA
LOST CHILDREN'S CENTER #7
WORLD TREE AREA
LOST CHILDREN'S CENTER
NO PROBLEM. THAT SAID, THE CAMPUS IS VERY LARGE, SO PLEASE BE CAREFUL.
UM...SO IS HELPING PEOPLE LIKE THIS PART OF YOUR WORK AS A MAGE, TAKAHATA-SENSEI?
HE BOUGHT ME COTTON CANDY!
HE DID?
HUH? NO, ANYONE CAN HELP OUT A LOST KID.
YAK ワイ
HEY, CHECK THIS OUT!
IT'S A FIGHT! A FIGHT!
YAK ワイ
OH, MY, THIS ISN'T GOOD.
WHAT THE HELL ARE YOU DOIN' ON OUR TURF!
YOU READY TO FIGHT!?
CHEER ワイ
KYA キャ
WAAA ワー
CHEER ワイ
IT'S NOON AND THEY'RE DRUNK ALREADY.

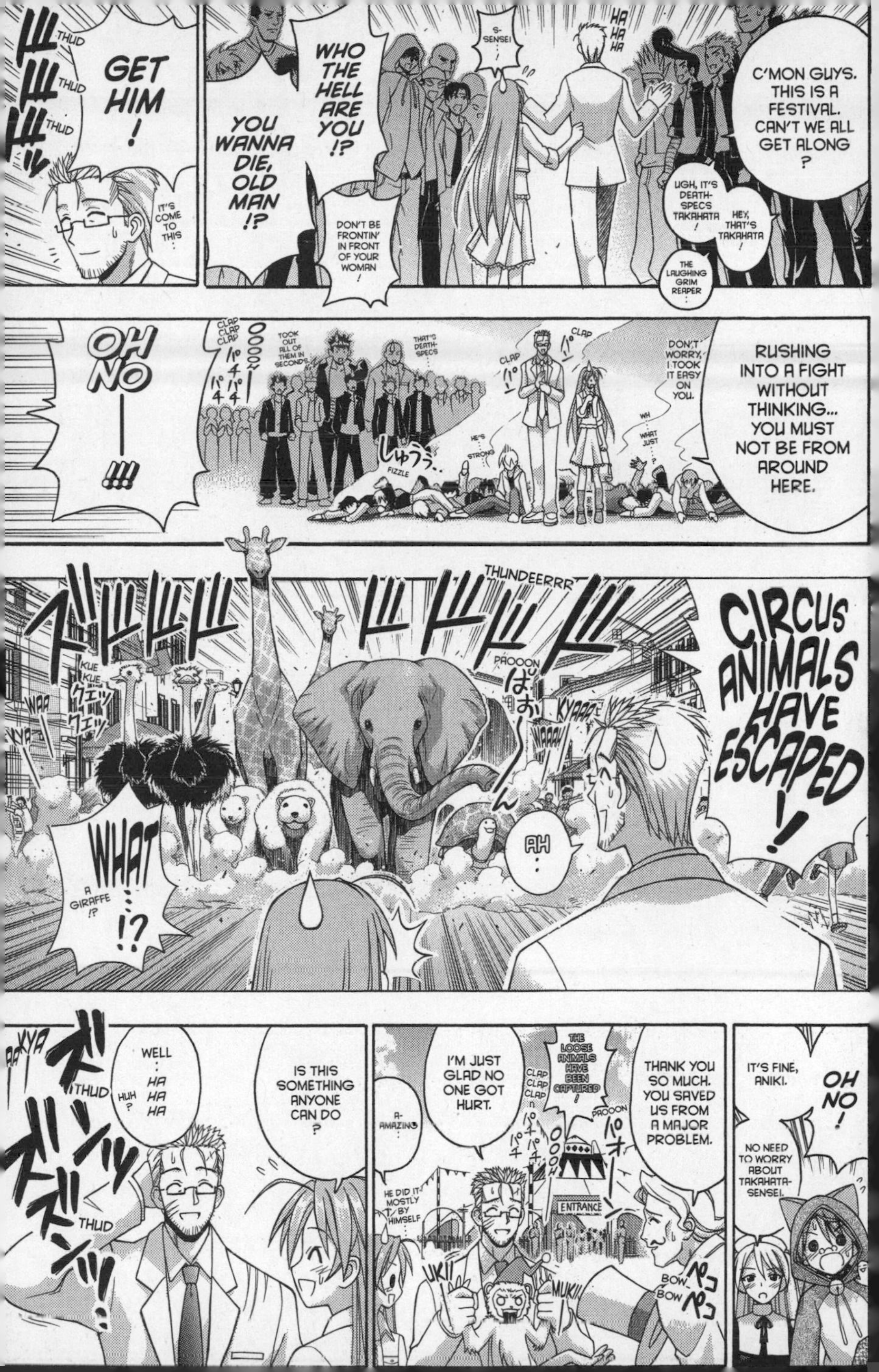

C'MON GUYS. THIS IS A FESTIVAL. CAN'T WE ALL GET ALONG?
HA HA HA
UGH, IT'S DEATH-SPECS TAKAHATA!
HEY, THAT'S TAKAHATA!
THE LAUGHING GRIM REAPER...
S-SENSEI...!
WHO THE HELL ARE YOU!?
YOU WANNA DIE, OLD MAN!?
DON'T BE FRONTIN' IN FRONT OF YOUR WOMAN!
GET HIM!
THUD
THUD
THUD
IT'S COME TO THIS...
RUSHING INTO A FIGHT WITHOUT THINKING... YOU MUST NOT BE FROM AROUND HERE.
DON'T WORRY, I TOOK IT EASY ON YOU.
CLAP
CLAP
WH WHAT JUST...?
HE'S STRONG
FIZZLE
THAT'S DEATH-SPECS...
TOOK OUT ALL OF THEM IN SECONDS
OOOOH!
CLAP CLAP CLAP
OH NO—!!!
CIRCUS ANIMALS HAVE ESCAPED!
THUNDEERRR
PROOON
KYAAA
WAAAH
AH...
KUE KUE
WAA
KYA
WHAT!?
A GIRAFFE!?
OH NO!
IT'S FINE, ANIKI.
NO NEED TO WORRY ABOUT TAKAHATA-SENSEI.
THANK YOU SO MUCH. YOU SAVED US FROM A MAJOR PROBLEM.
PROOON
BOW BOW
THE LOOSE ANIMALS HAVE BEEN CAPTURED!
OOOH
CLAP CLAP CLAP
I'M JUST GLAD NO ONE GOT HURT.
A-AMAZING
HE DID IT MOSTLY BY HIMSELF
ENTRANCE
UKI!
MUKI!
IS THIS SOMETHING ANYONE CAN DO?
WELL... HA HA HA
HUH?
THUD
THUD
KYA
AA

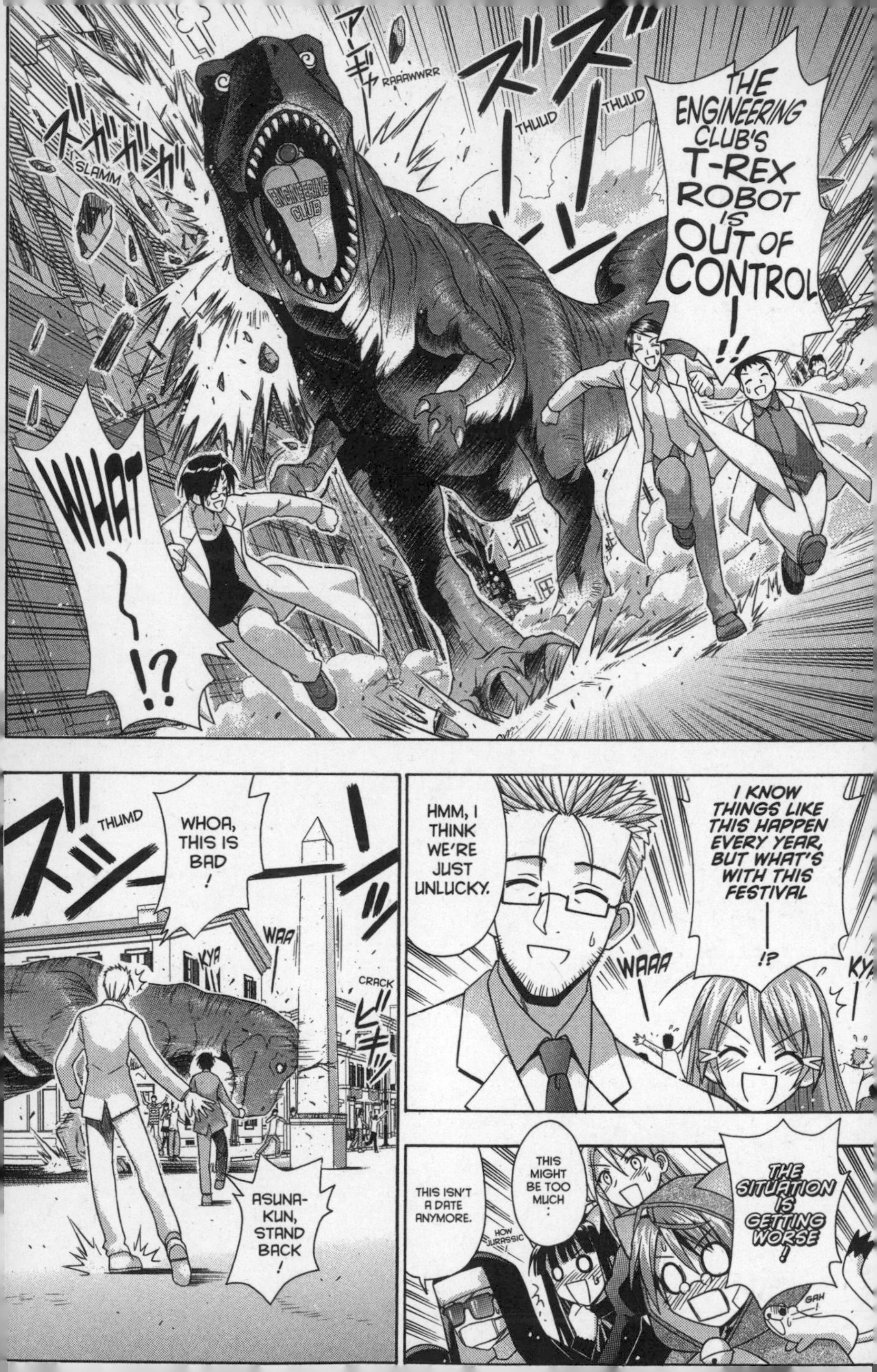
THUUD
THUUD
THE ENGINEERING CLUB'S T-REX ROBOT IS OUT OF CONTROL—!!
RAAAWWRR
ENGINEERING CLUB
SLAMM
WHAT~~!?
I KNOW THINGS LIKE THIS HAPPEN EVERY YEAR, BUT WHAT'S WITH THIS FESTIVAL—!?
KYA
HMM, I THINK WE'RE JUST UNLUCKY.
WAAA!
THE SITUATION IS GETTING WORSE!
THIS MIGHT BE TOO MUCH...
THIS ISN'T A DATE ANYMORE.
HOW JURASSIC!
GAH!
WAA!
CRACK
WHOA, THIS IS BAD!
THUMD
KYA
ASUNA-KUN, STAND BACK!

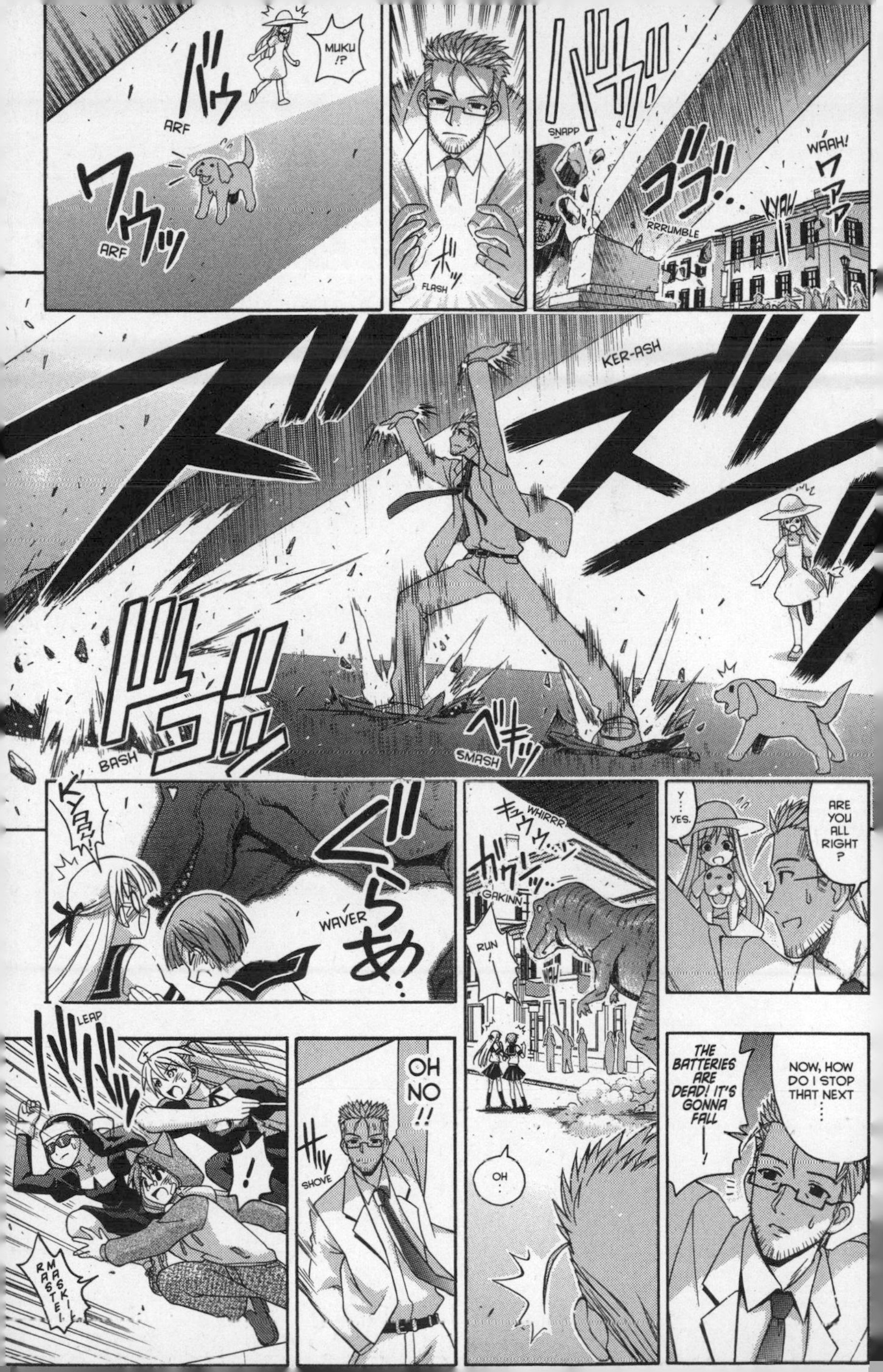
SNAPP
RRRUMBLE
WAAH!
KYAH
FLASH
MUKU !?
ARF
ARF
KER-ASH
SMASH
BASH
ARE YOU ALL RIGHT?
Y... YES.
WHIRRR
GAKINN
RUN!
WAH
KYAAH!
WAVER
NOW, HOW DO I STOP THAT NEXT...
THE BATTERIES ARE DEAD! IT'S GONNA FALL!
OH...
OH NO!!
SHOVE
LEAP
!
MASKI! RASTE!

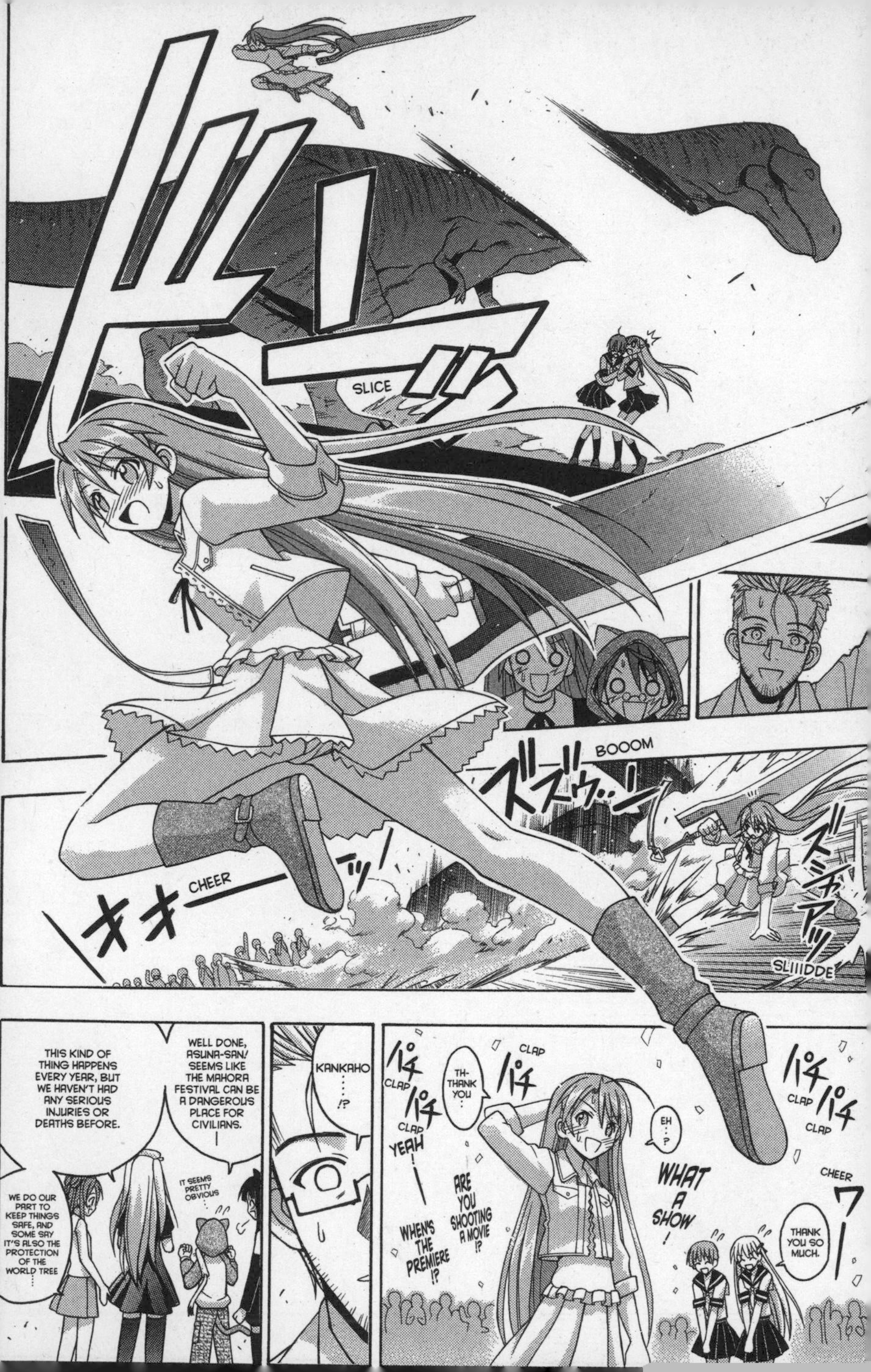
SLICE
SLIIIDDE
BOOOM
CHEER
CLAP
CLAP
CHEER
THANK YOU SO MUCH.
WHAT A SHOW!
EH...?
TH-THANK YOU...
CLAP
CLAP
CLAP
YEAH!
ARE YOU SHOOTING A MOVIE!?
WHEN'S THE PREMIERE!?
KANKAHO......!?
WELL DONE, ASUNA-SAN! SEEMS LIKE THE MAHORA FESTIVAL CAN BE A DANGEROUS PLACE FOR CIVILIANS.
THIS KIND OF THING HAPPENS EVERY YEAR, BUT WE HAVEN'T HAD ANY SERIOUS INJURIES OR DEATHS BEFORE.
IT SEEMS PRETTY OBVIOUS...
WE DO OUR PART TO KEEP THINGS SAFE, AND SOME SAY IT'S ALSO THE PROTECTION OF THE WORLD TREE...

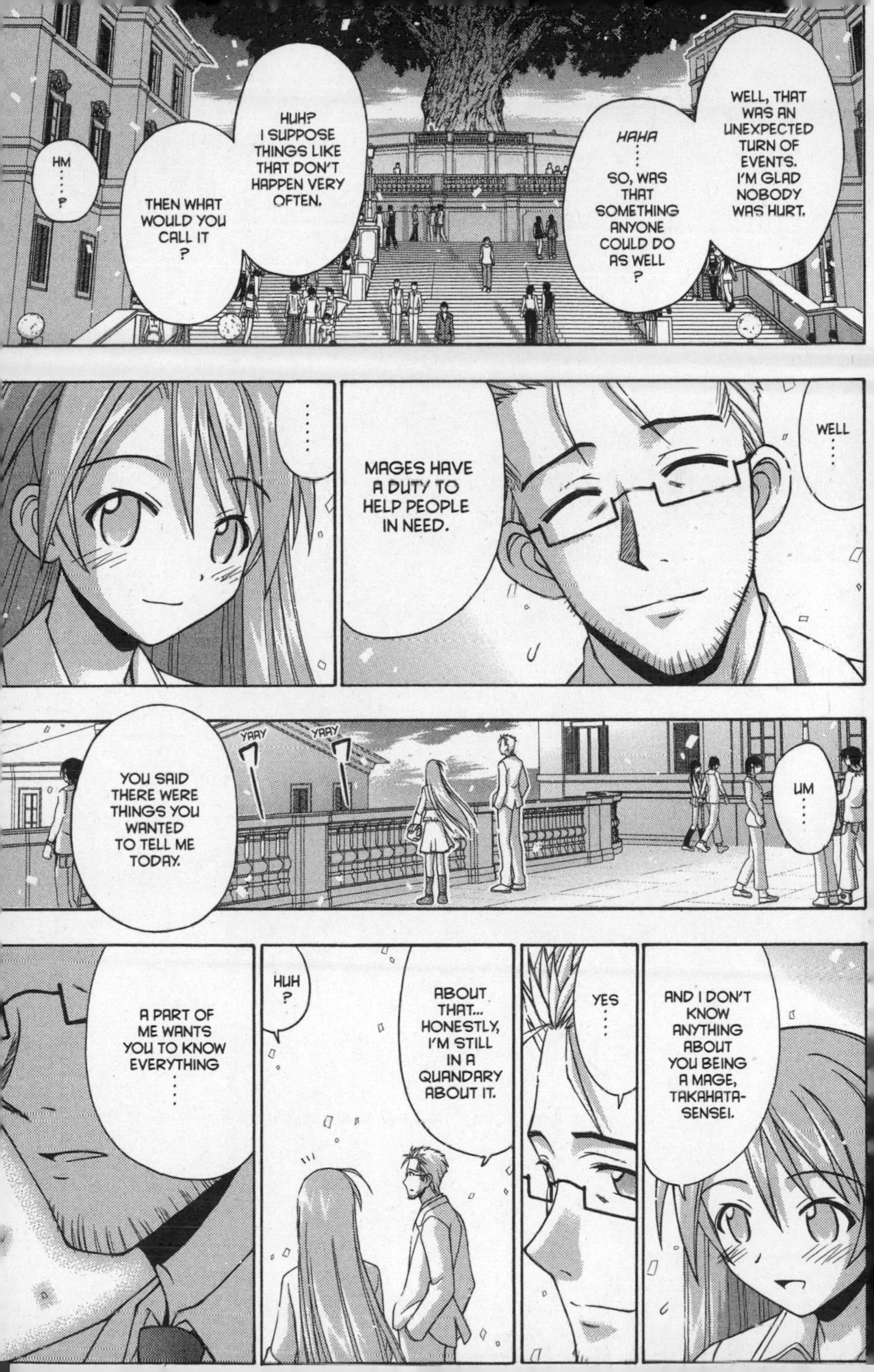

WELL, THAT WAS AN UNEXPECTED TURN OF EVENTS. I'M GLAD NOBODY WAS HURT.
HAHA... SO, WAS THAT SOMETHING ANYONE COULD DO AS WELL?
HUH? I SUPPOSE THINGS LIKE THAT DON'T HAPPEN VERY OFTEN.
THEN WHAT WOULD YOU CALL IT?
HM...?
WELL...
MAGES HAVE A DUTY TO HELP PEOPLE IN NEED.
......
UM...
YAAY
YAAY
YOU SAID THERE WERE THINGS YOU WANTED TO TELL ME TODAY.
AND I DON'T KNOW ANYTHING ABOUT YOU BEING A MAGE, TAKAHATA-SENSEI.
YES...
ABOUT THAT... HONESTLY, I'M STILL IN A QUANDARY ABOUT IT.
HUH?
A PART OF ME WANTS YOU TO KNOW EVERYTHING...

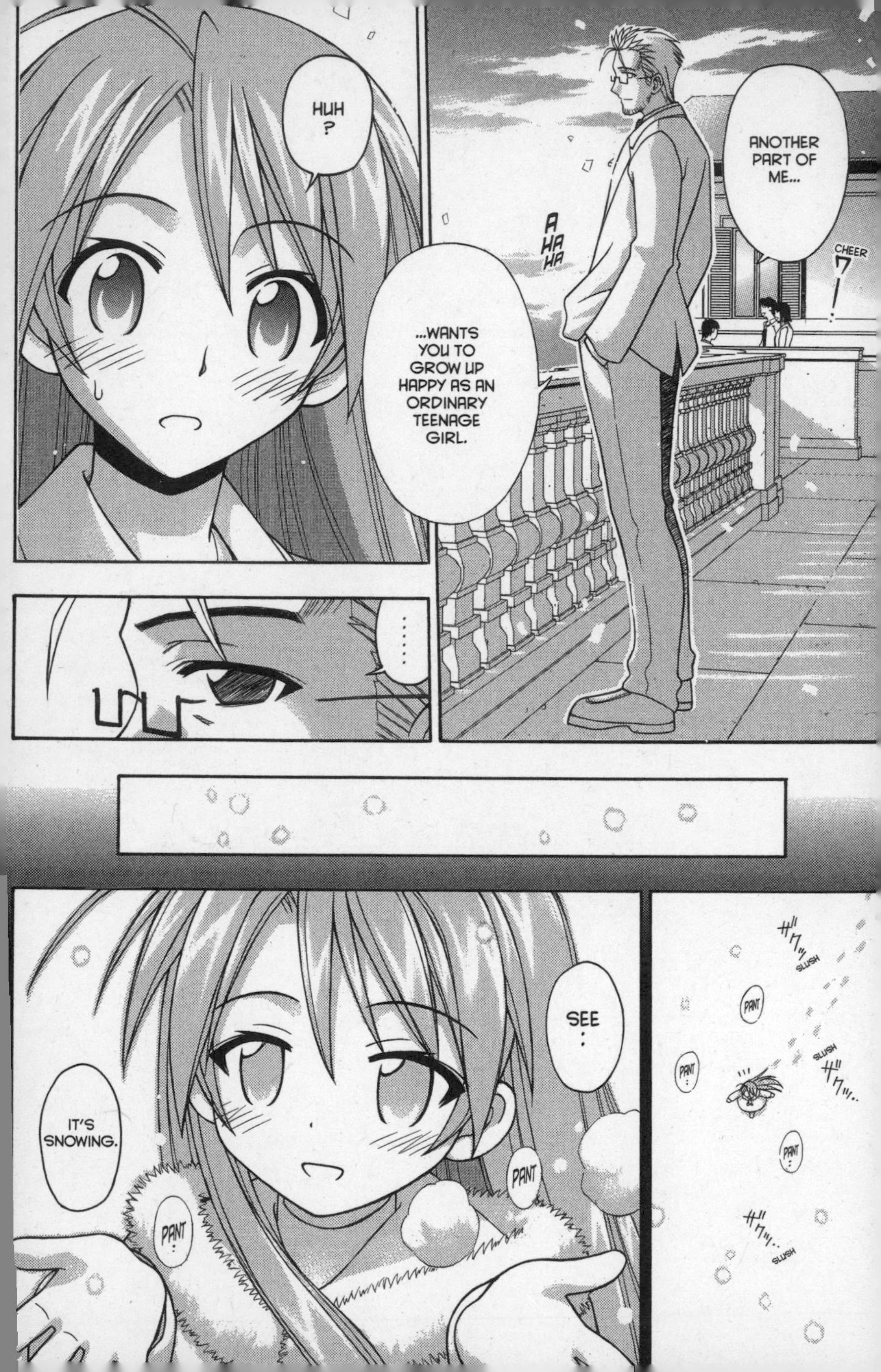
ANOTHER PART OF ME...
A HA HA
CHEER
...WANTS YOU TO GROW UP HAPPY AS AN ORDINARY TEENAGE GIRL.
HUH ?
......
SLUSH
PANT
SLUSH
PANT
PANT
SLUSH
SEE...
IT'S SNOWING.
PANT
PANT

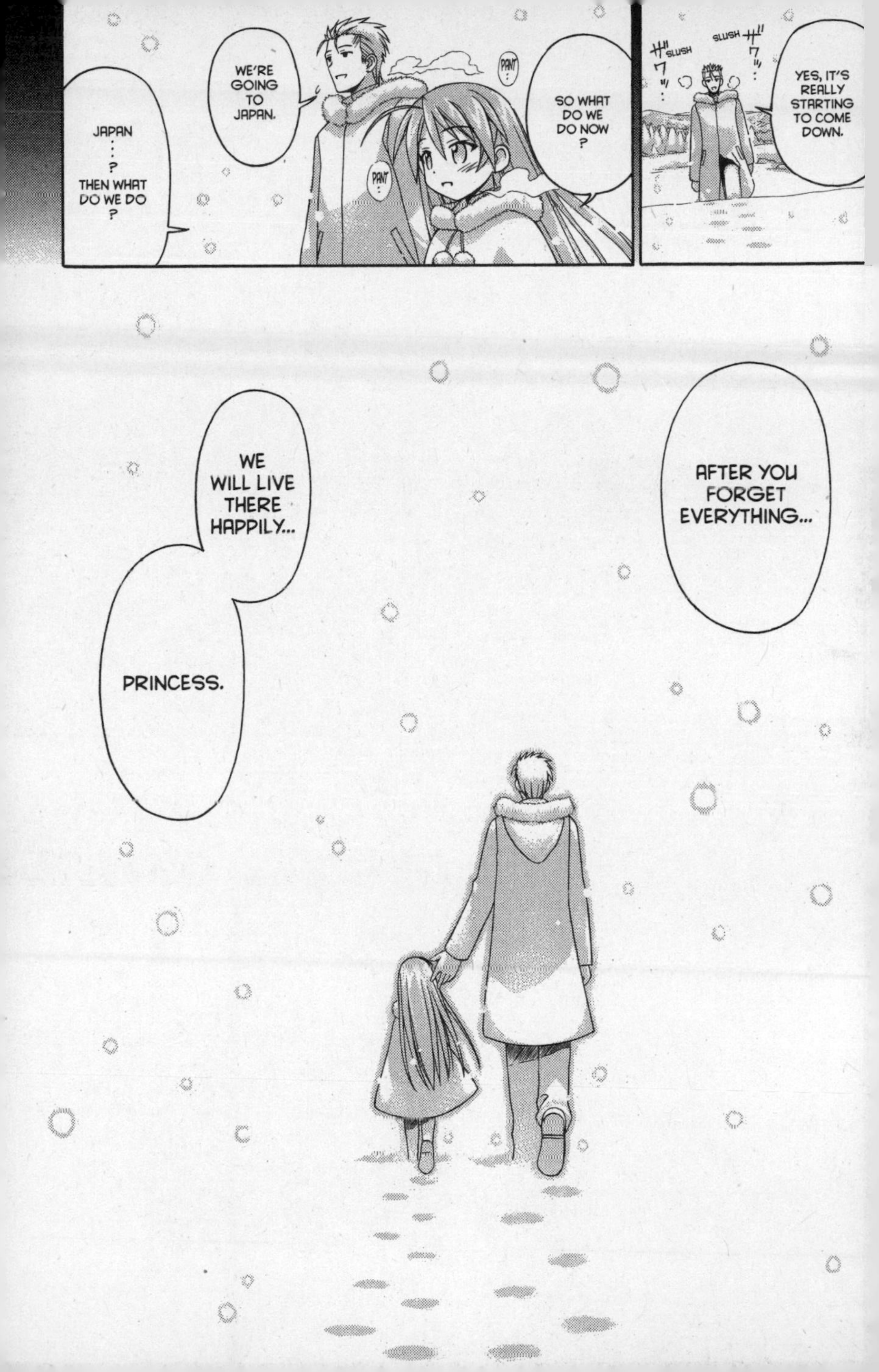
SLUSH
SLUSH
YES, IT'S REALLY STARTING TO COME DOWN.
SO WHAT DO WE DO NOW ?
PANT
WE'RE GOING TO JAPAN.
PANT
JAPAN . . . ? THEN WHAT DO WE DO ?
AFTER YOU FORGET EVERYTHING...
WE WILL LIVE THERE HAPPILY...
PRINCESS.

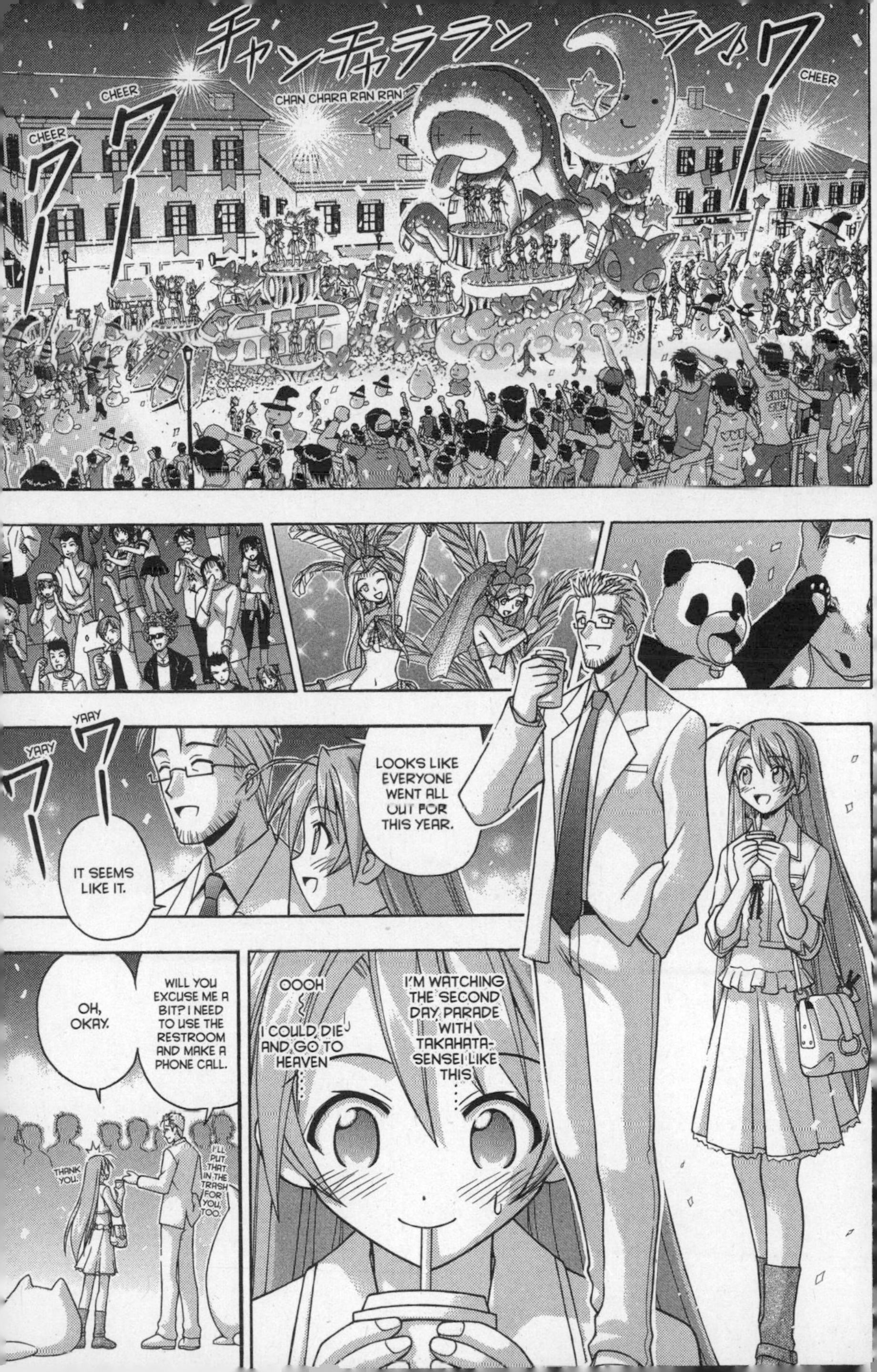
CHEER
ラン♪ワ
CHAN CHARA RAN RAN
チャンチャララン
CHEER
CHEER
LOOKS LIKE EVERYONE WENT ALL OUT FOR THIS YEAR.
YAAY
YAAY
IT SEEMS LIKE IT.
I'M WATCHING THE SECOND DAY PARADE WITH TAKAHATA-SENSEI LIKE THIS...
OOOH~ I COULD DIE AND GO TO HEAVEN...
WILL YOU EXCUSE ME A BIT? I NEED TO USE THE RESTROOM AND MAKE A PHONE CALL.
OH, OKAY.
I'LL PUT THAT IN THE TRASH FOR YOU, TOO.
THANK YOU.

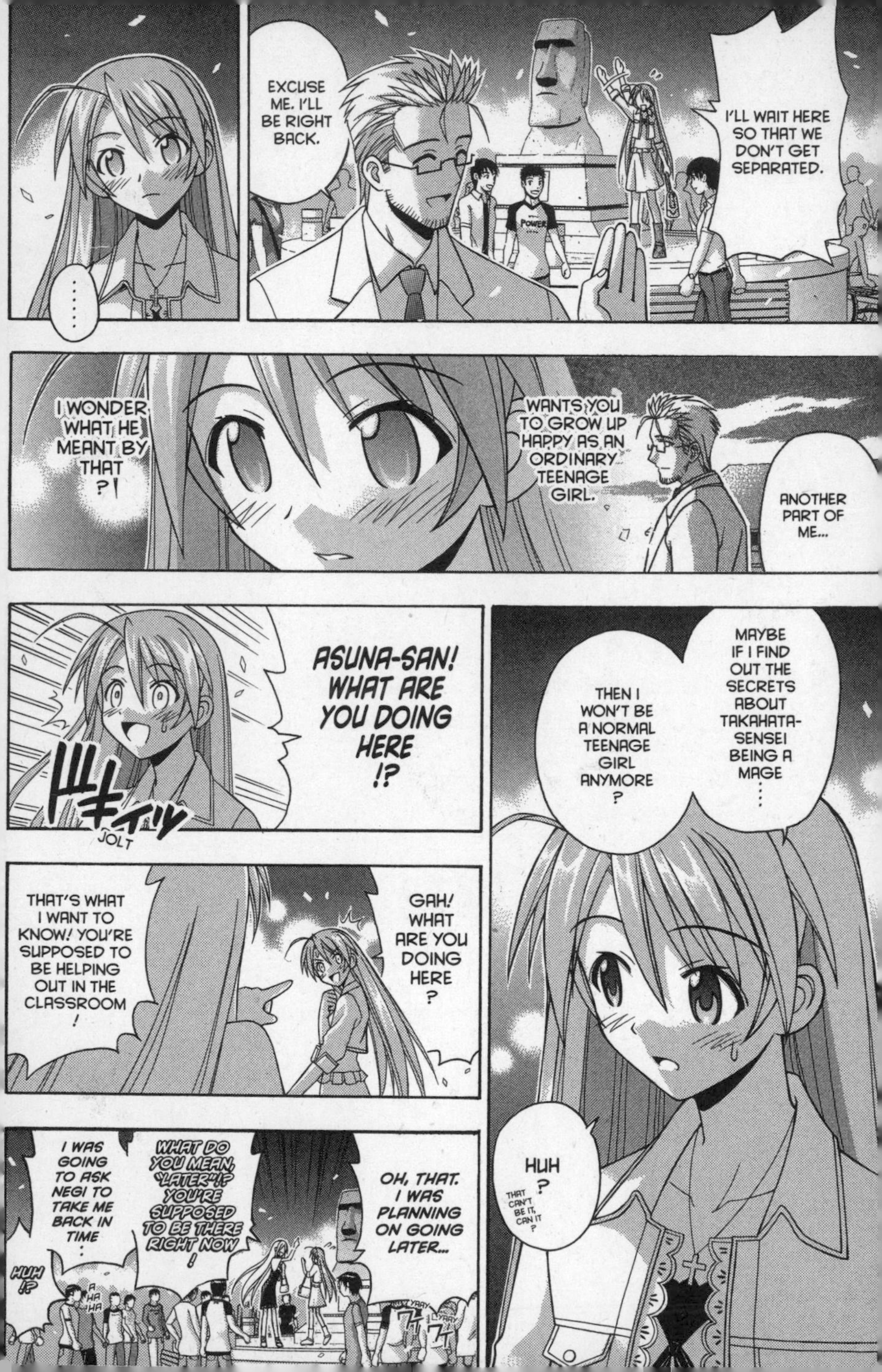

I'LL WAIT HERE SO THAT WE DON'T GET SEPARATED.
POWER
EXCUSE ME. I'LL BE RIGHT BACK.
......
ANOTHER PART OF ME...
WANTS YOU TO GROW UP HAPPY AS AN ORDINARY TEENAGE GIRL.
I WONDER WHAT HE MEANT BY THAT?!
MAYBE IF I FIND OUT THE SECRETS ABOUT TAKAHATA-SENSEI BEING A MAGE...
THEN I WON'T BE A NORMAL TEENAGE GIRL ANYMORE?
HUH?
THAT CAN'T BE IT, CAN IT?
ASUNA-SAN! WHAT ARE YOU DOING HERE!?
JOLT
GAH! WHAT ARE YOU DOING HERE?
THAT'S WHAT I WANT TO KNOW! YOU'RE SUPPOSED TO BE HELPING OUT IN THE CLASSROOM!
OH, THAT. I WAS PLANNING ON GOING LATER...
WHAT DO YOU MEAN, "LATER"!? YOU'RE SUPPOSED TO BE THERE RIGHT NOW!
I WAS GOING TO ASK NEGI TO TAKE ME BACK IN TIME...
HUH!?
A HA HA

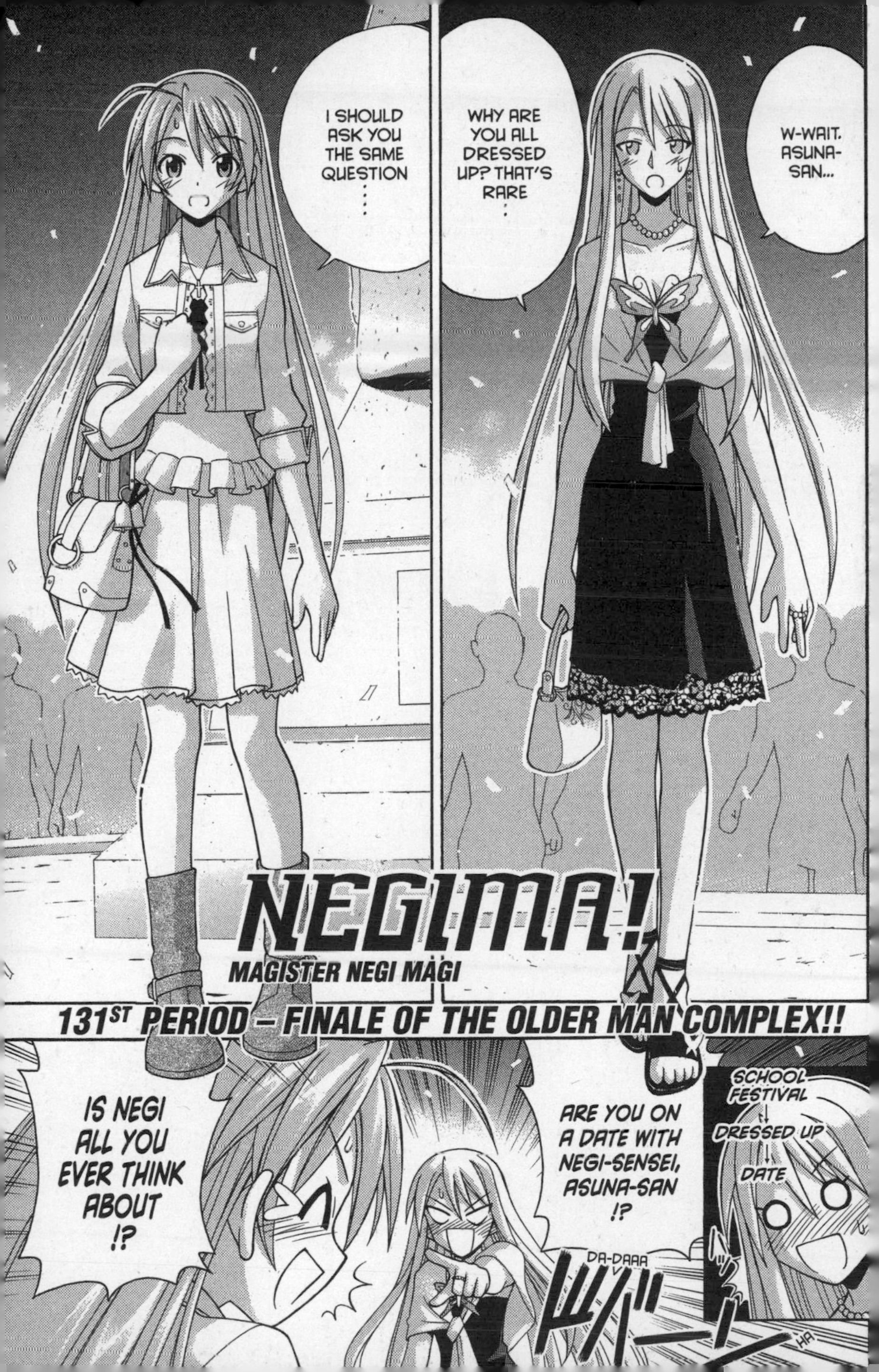
W-WAIT. ASUNA-SAN...
WHY ARE YOU ALL DRESSED UP? THAT'S RARE...
I SHOULD ASK YOU THE SAME QUESTION...
NEGIMA!
MAGISTER NEGI MAGI
131ST PERIOD – FINALE OF THE OLDER MAN COMPLEX!!
SCHOOL FESTIVAL ↓ DRESSED UP ↓ DATE
HA
ARE YOU ON A DATE WITH NEGI-SENSEI, ASUNA-SAN!?
DA-DAAA
IS NEGI ALL YOU EVER THINK ABOUT!?

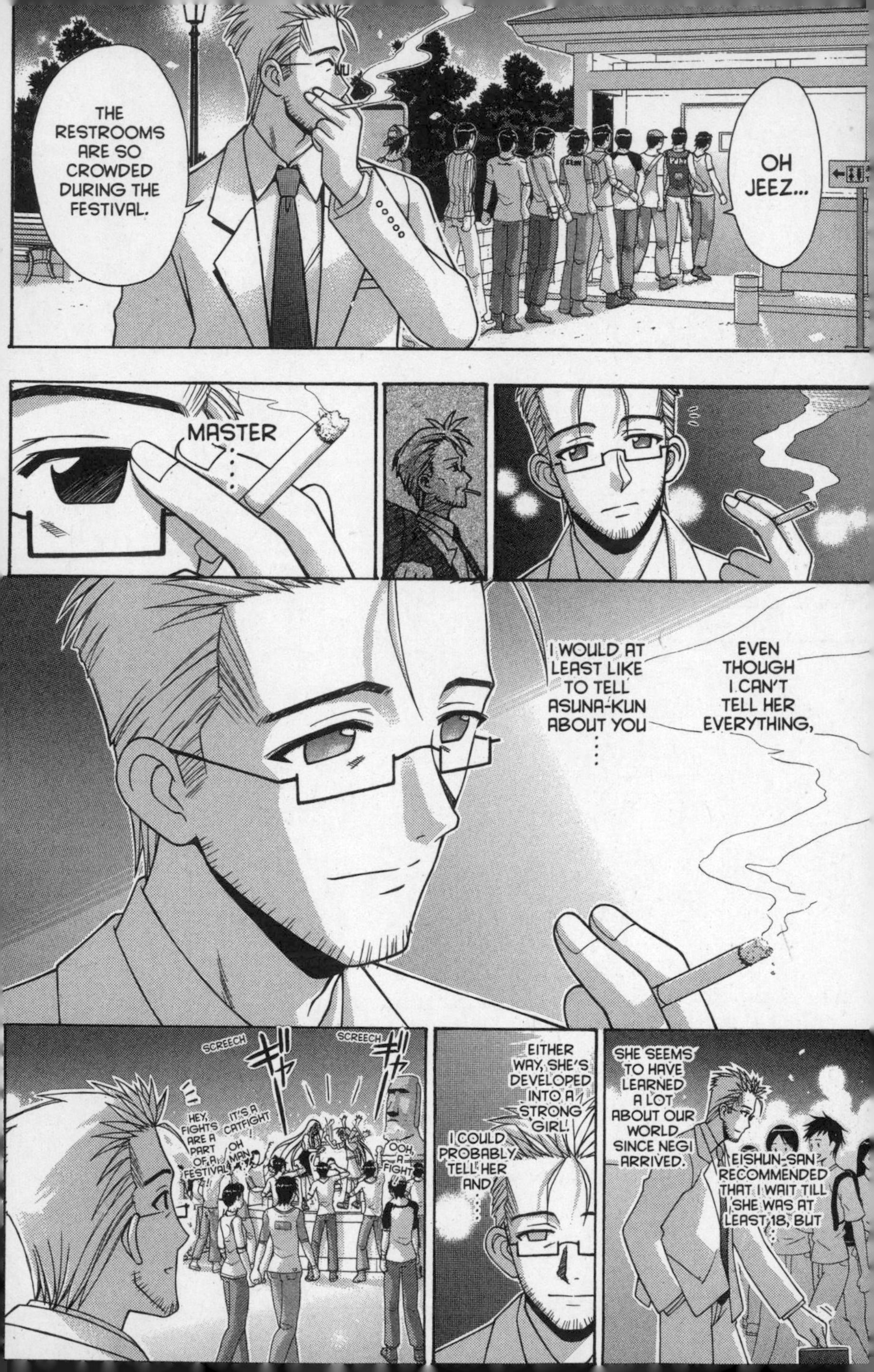
OH JEEZ...
NU
THE RESTROOMS ARE SO CROWDED DURING THE FESTIVAL.
MASTER ...
EVEN THOUGH I CAN'T TELL HER EVERYTHING,
I WOULD AT LEAST LIKE TO TELL ASUNA-KUN ABOUT YOU ...
SHE SEEMS TO HAVE LEARNED A LOT ABOUT OUR WORLD SINCE NEGI ARRIVED.
EISHUN-SAN RECOMMENDED THAT I WAIT TILL SHE WAS AT LEAST 18, BUT ...
EITHER WAY, SHE'S DEVELOPED INTO A STRONG GIRL.
I COULD PROBABLY TELL HER AND ...
SCREECH
SCREECH
OOH, A FIGHT
IT'S A CATFIGHT
OH MAN
HEY, FIGHTS ARE A PART OF A FESTIVAL!!

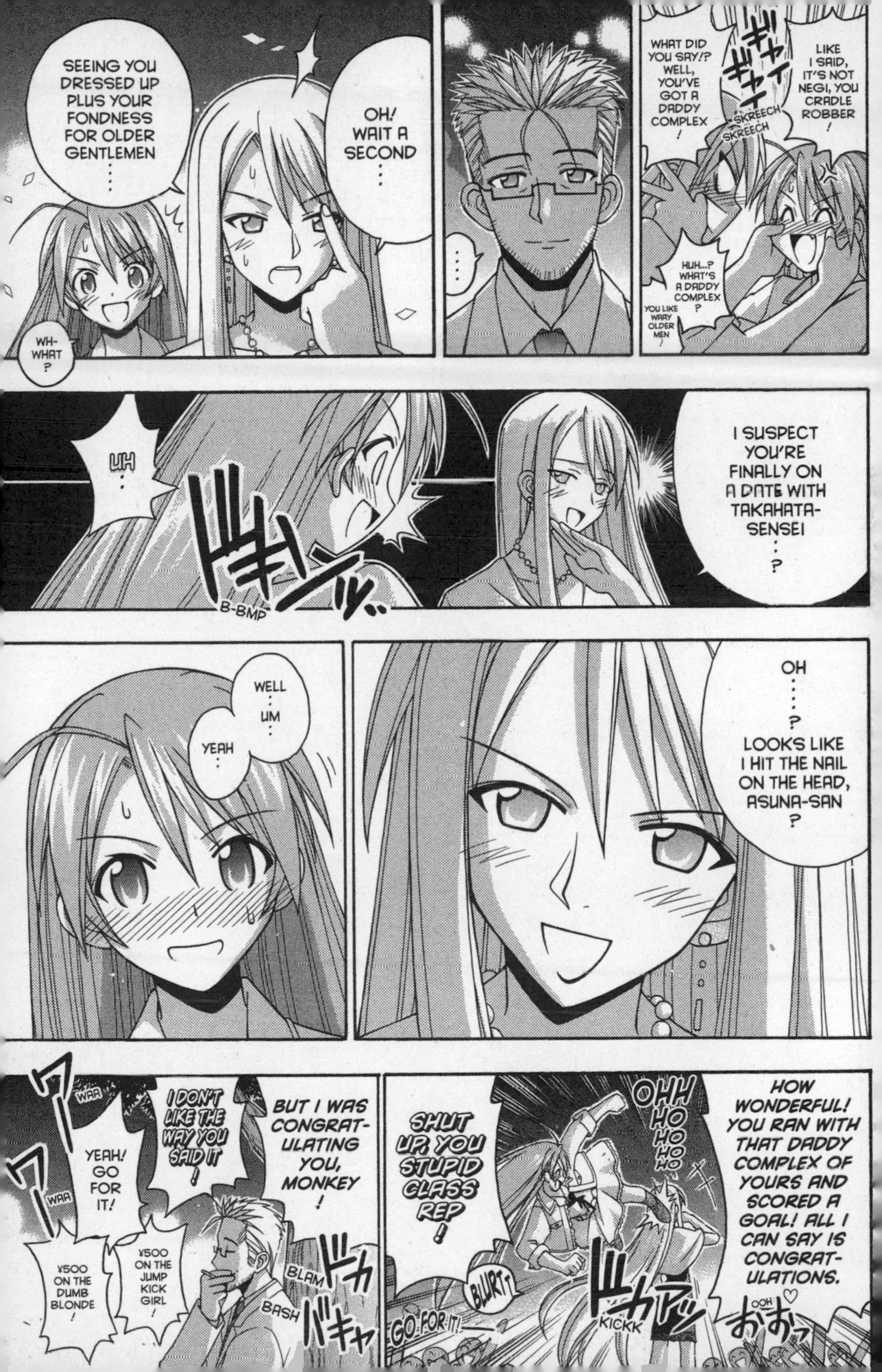
LIKE I SAID, IT'S NOT NEGI, YOU CRADLE ROBBER!
WHAT DID YOU SAY!? WELL, YOU'VE GOT A DADDY COMPLEX!
SKREECH SKREECH
HUH...? WHAT'S A DADDY COMPLEX?
YOU LIKE WAAY OLDER MEN!
....
OH! WAIT A SECOND...
SEEING YOU DRESSED UP PLUS YOUR FONDNESS FOR OLDER GENTLEMEN...
WH-WHAT?
I SUSPECT YOU'RE FINALLY ON A DATE WITH TAKAHATA-SENSEI...?
UH...
B-BMP
OH.....? LOOKS LIKE I HIT THE NAIL ON THE HEAD, ASUNA-SAN?
WELL... UM...
YEAH...
HOW WONDERFUL! YOU RAN WITH THAT DADDY COMPLEX OF YOURS AND SCORED A GOAL! ALL I CAN SAY IS CONGRATULATIONS.
OOH
OHH HO HO HO HO HO
SHUT UP, YOU STUPID CLASS REP!
KICKK
BLURT
GO FOR IT!
BUT I WAS CONGRATULATING YOU, MONKEY!
I DON'T LIKE THE WAY YOU SAID IT!
WAA
WAA
YEAH! GO FOR IT!
BLAM
BASH
¥500 ON THE JUMP KICK GIRL!
¥500 ON THE DUMB BLONDE!

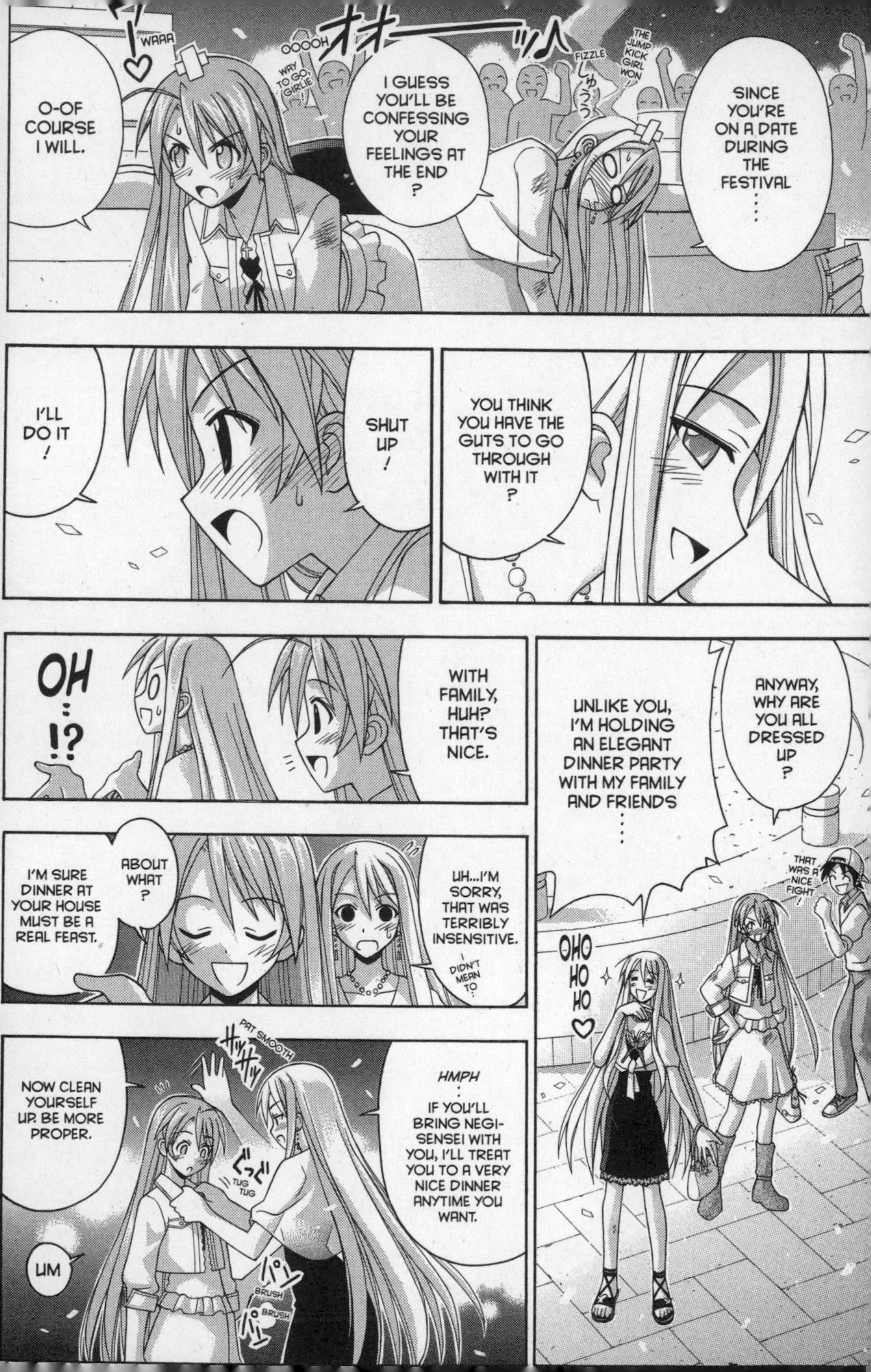
SINCE YOU'RE ON A DATE DURING THE FESTIVAL ....
THE JUMP KICK GIRL WON
FIZZLE
OOOOH
I GUESS YOU'LL BE CONFESSING YOUR FEELINGS AT THE END ?
WAY TO GO, GIRLIE!
WAAA
O-OF COURSE I WILL.
YOU THINK YOU HAVE THE GUTS TO GO THROUGH WITH IT ?
SHUT UP !
I'LL DO IT !
ANYWAY, WHY ARE YOU ALL DRESSED UP ?
UNLIKE YOU, I'M HOLDING AN ELEGANT DINNER PARTY WITH MY FAMILY AND FRIENDS ....
THAT WAS A NICE FIGHT !
OHO HO HO ♡
WITH FAMILY, HUH? THAT'S NICE.
OH ...!?
UH...I'M SORRY, THAT WAS TERRIBLY INSENSITIVE.
I DIDN'T MEAN TO...
ABOUT WHAT ?
I'M SURE DINNER AT YOUR HOUSE MUST BE A REAL FEAST.
HMPH : IF YOU'LL BRING NEGI-SENSEI WITH YOU, I'LL TREAT YOU TO A VERY NICE DINNER ANYTIME YOU WANT.
PAT SMOOTH
NOW CLEAN YOURSELF UP. BE MORE PROPER.
TUG TUG
BRUSH
BRUSH
UM

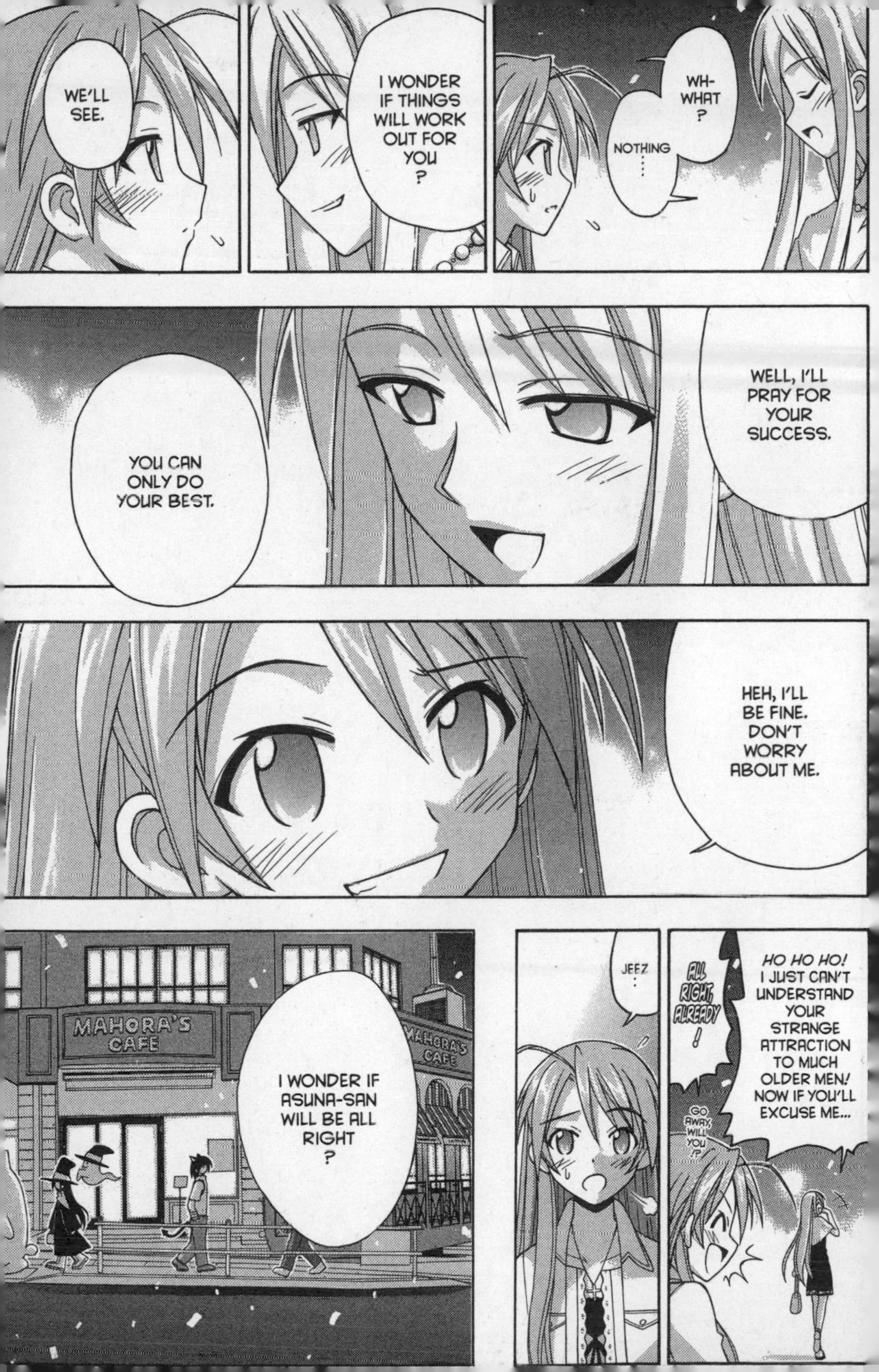
WH-WHAT?
NOTHING...
I WONDER IF THINGS WILL WORK OUT FOR YOU?
WE'LL SEE.
WELL, I'LL PRAY FOR YOUR SUCCESS.
YOU CAN ONLY DO YOUR BEST.
HEH, I'LL BE FINE. DON'T WORRY ABOUT ME.
HO HO HO! I JUST CAN'T UNDERSTAND YOUR STRANGE ATTRACTION TO MUCH OLDER MEN! NOW IF YOU'LL EXCUSE ME...
ALL RIGHT, ALREADY!
GO AWAY, WILL YOU!?
JEEZ...
MAHORA'S CAFE
MAHORA'S CAFE
I WONDER IF ASUNA-SAN WILL BE ALL RIGHT?

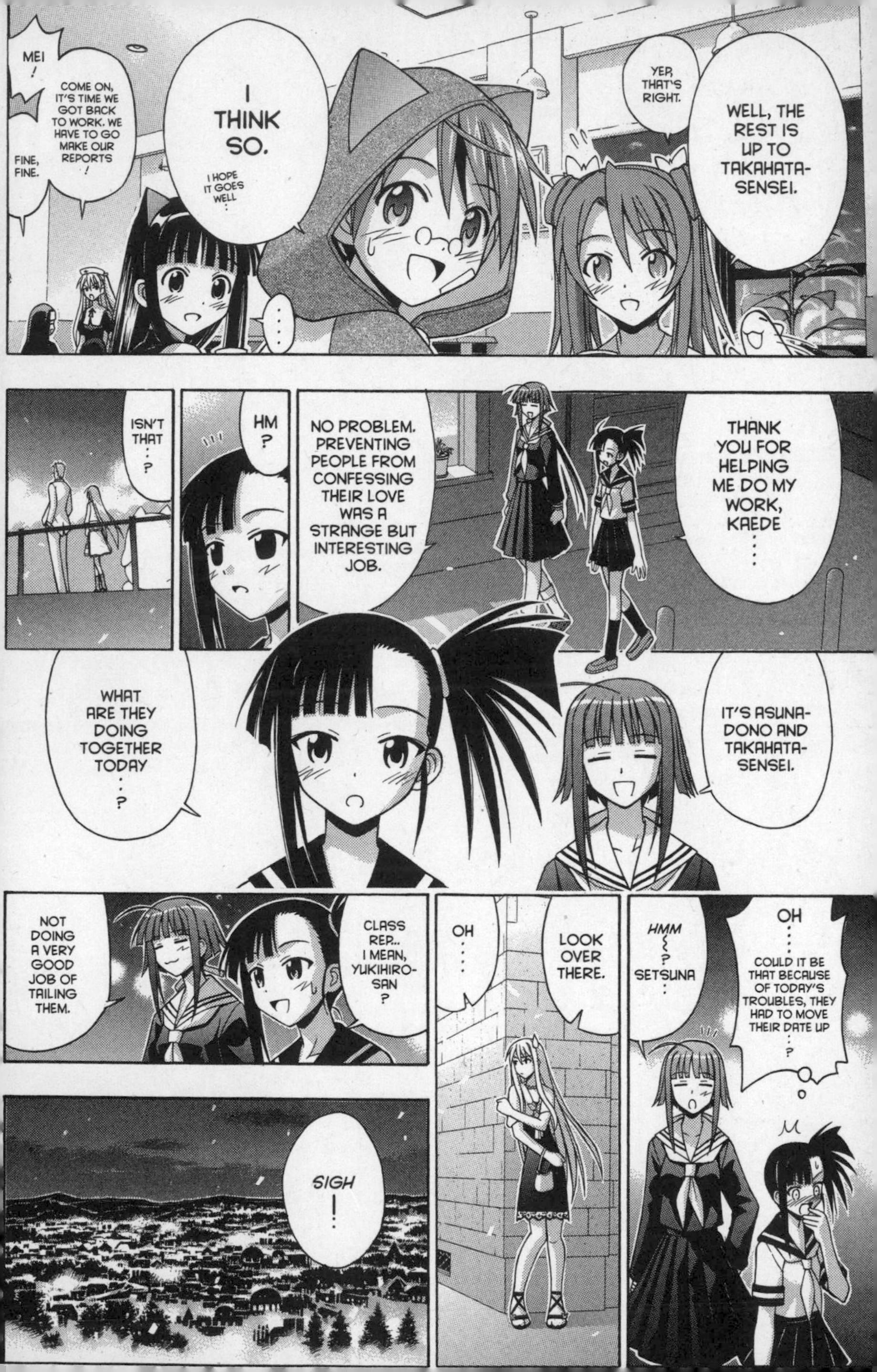
WELL, THE REST IS UP TO TAKAHATA-SENSEI.
YEP, THAT'S RIGHT.
I THINK SO.
I HOPE IT GOES WELL...
....
MEI!
COME ON, IT'S TIME WE GOT BACK TO WORK. WE HAVE TO GO MAKE OUR REPORTS!
FINE, FINE.
THANK YOU FOR HELPING ME DO MY WORK, KAEDE....
NO PROBLEM. PREVENTING PEOPLE FROM CONFESSING THEIR LOVE WAS A STRANGE BUT INTERESTING JOB.
HM?
ISN'T THAT...?
IT'S ASUNA-DONO AND TAKAHATA-SENSEI.
WHAT ARE THEY DOING TOGETHER TODAY...?
OH....
COULD IT BE THAT BECAUSE OF TODAY'S TROUBLES, THEY HAD TO MOVE THEIR DATE UP...?
HMM~? SETSUNA...
LOOK OVER THERE.
OH....
CLASS REP... I MEAN, YUKIHIRO-SAN?
NOT DOING A VERY GOOD JOB OF TAILING THEM.
SIGH!

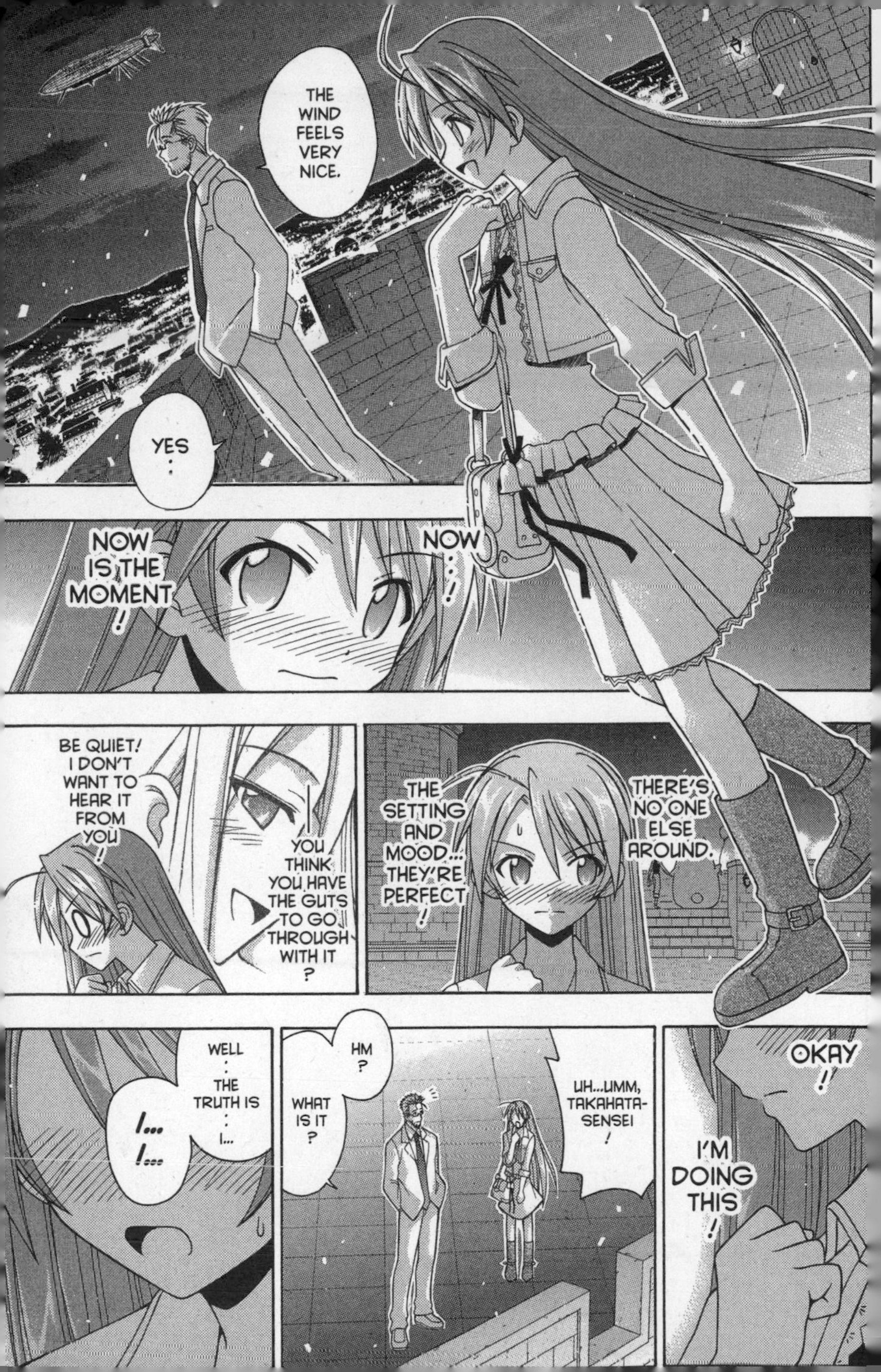
THE WIND FEELS VERY NICE.
YES :
NOW : !
NOW IS THE MOMENT !
THERE'S NO ONE ELSE AROUND.
THE SETTING AND MOOD... THEY'RE PERFECT !
YOU THINK YOU HAVE THE GUTS TO GO THROUGH WITH IT ?
BE QUIET! I DON'T WANT TO HEAR IT FROM YOU !
OKAY !
I'M DOING THIS !
UH...UMM, TAKAHATA-SENSEI !
HM ?
WHAT IS IT ?
WELL : THE TRUTH IS : I...
I... I...

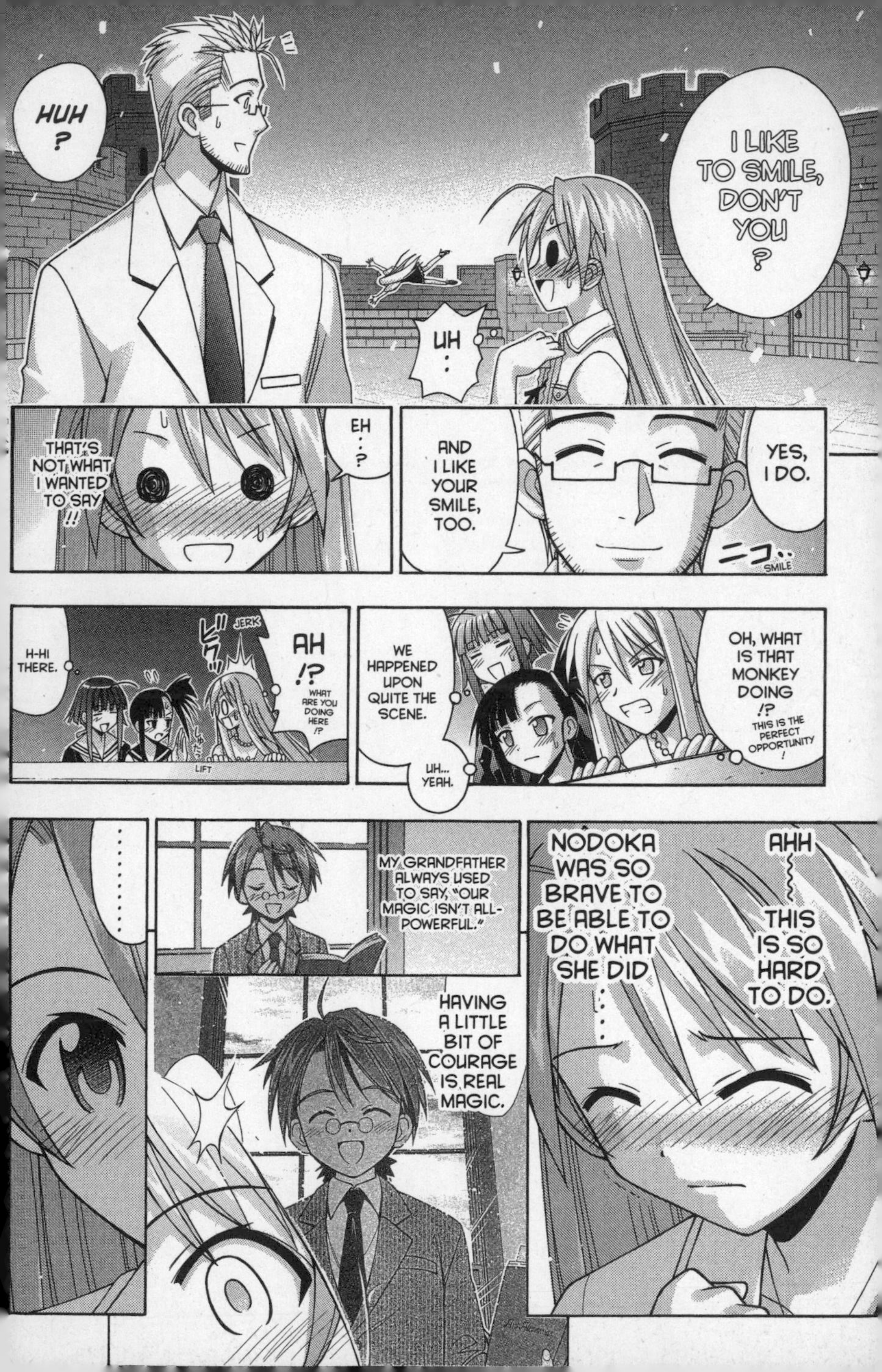
I LIKE TO SMILE, DON'T YOU?
HUH?
UH...
YES, I DO.
ニコ.. SMILE
AND I LIKE YOUR SMILE, TOO.
EH...?
THAT'S NOT WHAT I WANTED TO SAY!!
OH, WHAT IS THAT MONKEY DOING!?
THIS IS THE PERFECT OPPORTUNITY!
WE HAPPENED UPON QUITE THE SCENE.
UH... YEAH.
AH!?
WHAT ARE YOU DOING HERE!?
JERK
H-HI THERE.
LIFT
AHH~ THIS IS SO HARD TO DO.
NODOKA WAS SO BRAVE TO BE ABLE TO DO WHAT SHE DID...
MY GRANDFATHER ALWAYS USED TO SAY, "OUR MAGIC ISN'T ALL-POWERFUL."
HAVING A LITTLE BIT OF COURAGE IS REAL MAGIC.
......

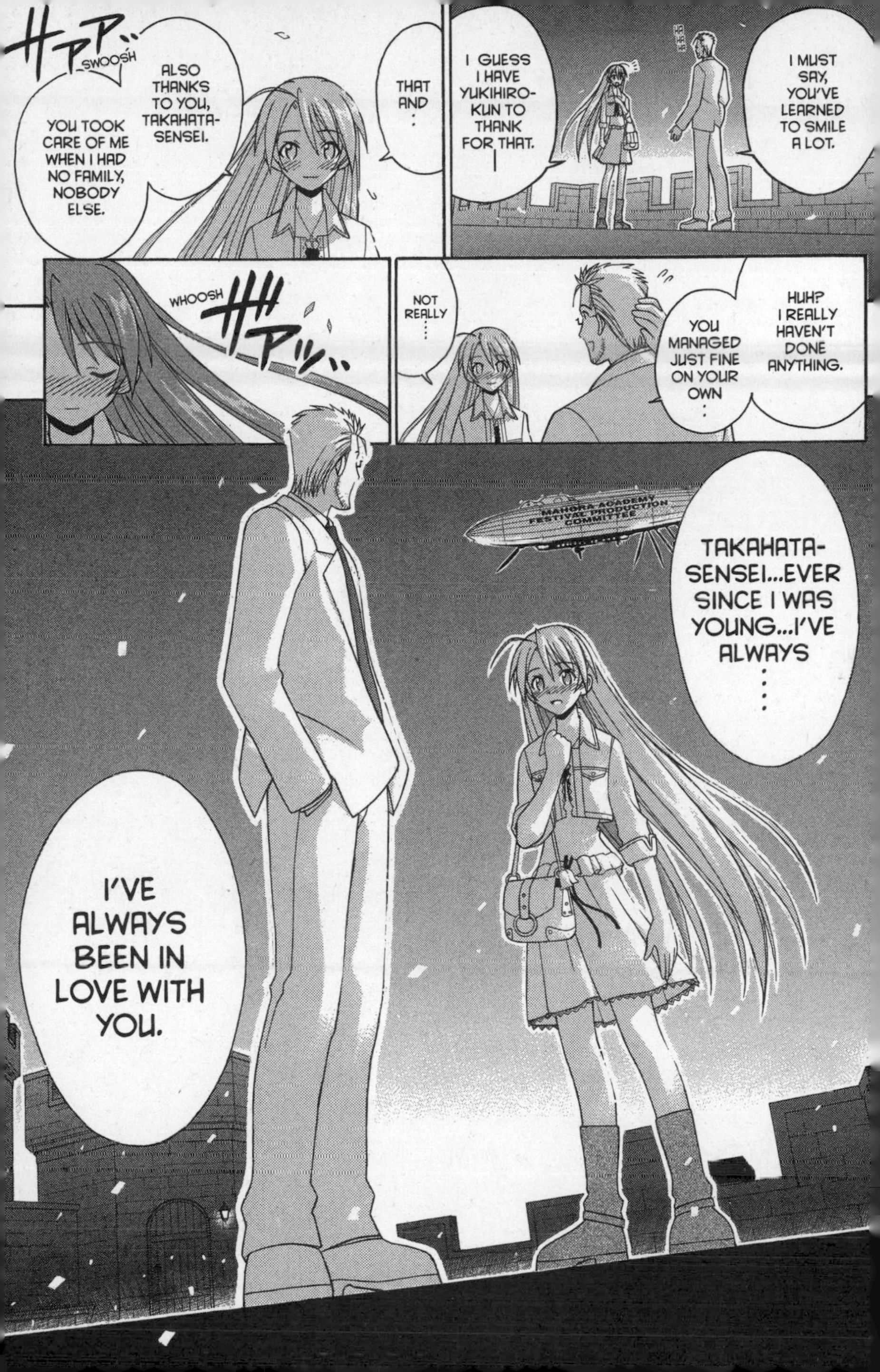
I MUST SAY, YOU'VE LEARNED TO SMILE A LOT.
I GUESS I HAVE YUKIHIRO-KUN TO THANK FOR THAT.
THAT AND...
SWOOSH
ALSO THANKS TO YOU, TAKAHATA-SENSEI.
YOU TOOK CARE OF ME WHEN I HAD NO FAMILY, NOBODY ELSE.
HUH? I REALLY HAVEN'T DONE ANYTHING.
YOU MANAGED JUST FINE ON YOUR OWN...
NOT REALLY...
WHOOSH
MAHORA ACADEMY FESTIVAL PRODUCTION COMMITTEE
TAKAHATA-SENSEI...EVER SINCE I WAS YOUNG...I'VE ALWAYS...
I'VE ALWAYS BEEN IN LOVE WITH YOU.

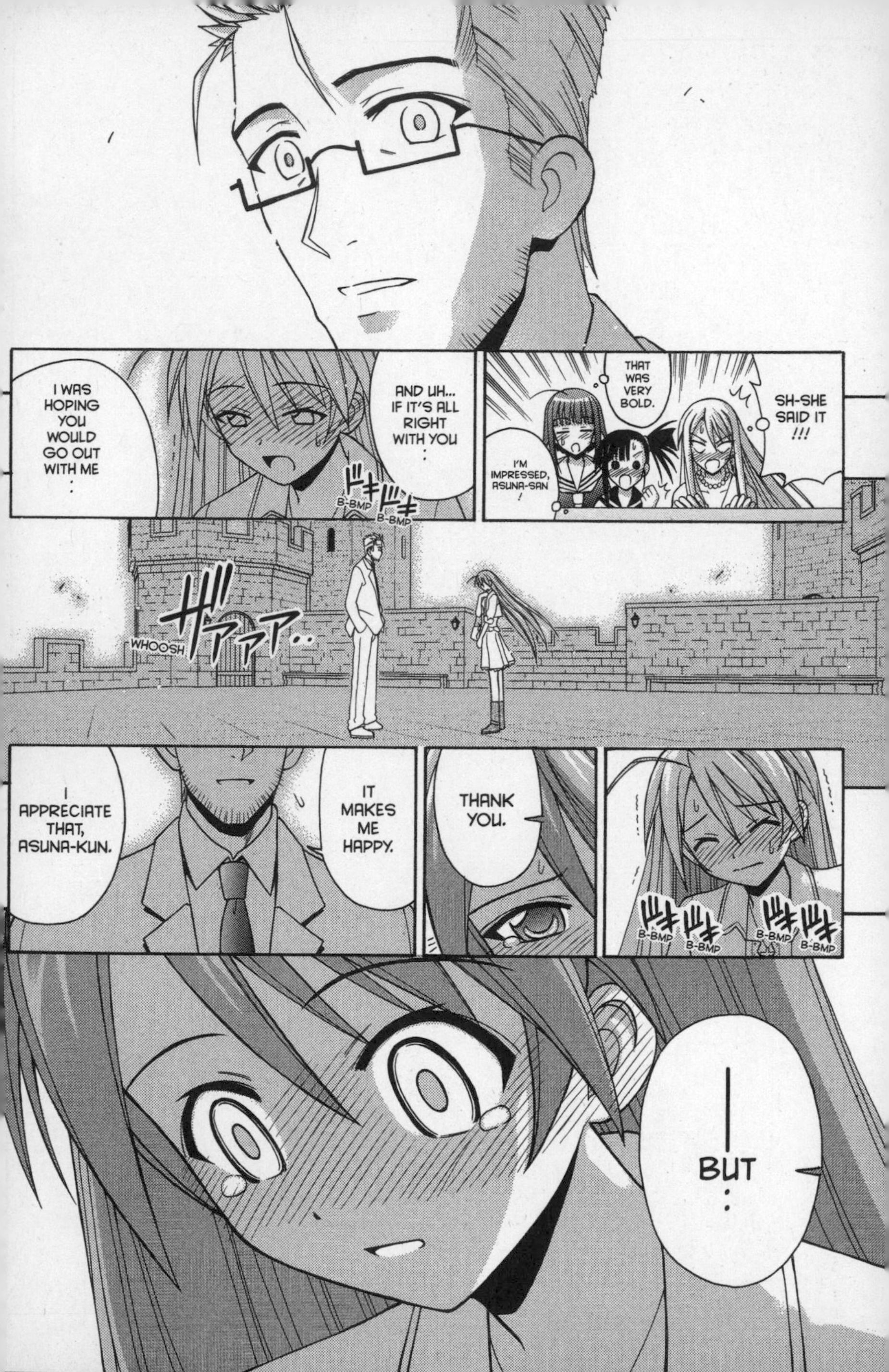
SH-SHE SAID IT !!!
THAT WAS VERY BOLD.
I'M IMPRESSED, ASUNA-SAN !
AND UH... IF IT'S ALL RIGHT WITH YOU :
I WAS HOPING YOU WOULD GO OUT WITH ME :
B-BMP B-BMP
WHOOSH
B-BMP B-BMP B-BMP B-BMP
THANK YOU.
IT MAKES ME HAPPY.
I APPRECIATE THAT, ASUNA-KUN.
BUT :

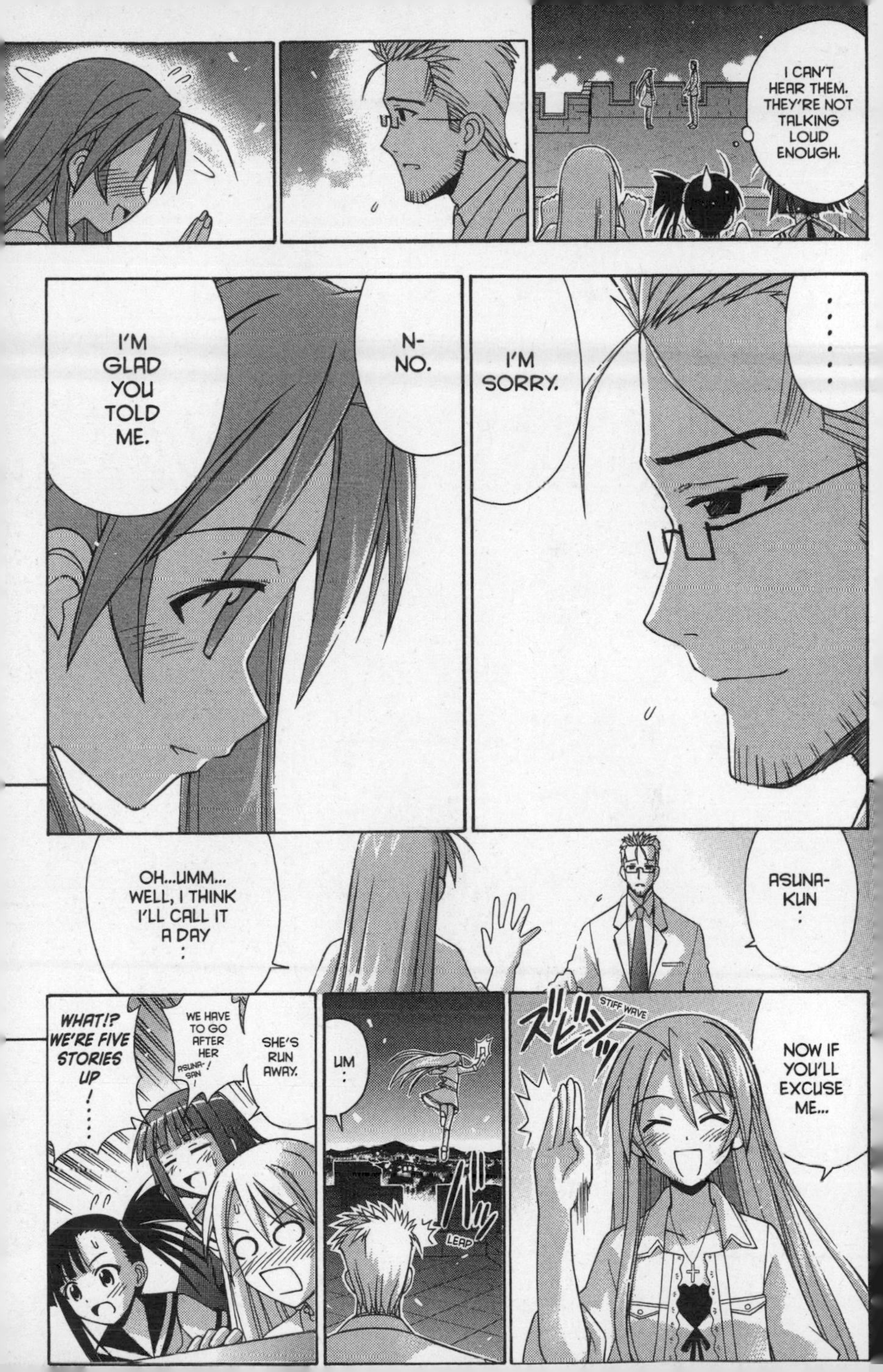
I CAN'T HEAR THEM. THEY'RE NOT TALKING LOUD ENOUGH.
......
I'M SORRY.
N-NO.
I'M GLAD YOU TOLD ME.
ASUNA-KUN...
OH...UMM... WELL, I THINK I'LL CALL IT A DAY...
STIFF WAVE
NOW IF YOU'LL EXCUSE ME...
UM...
LEAP
SHE'S RUN AWAY.
WE HAVE TO GO AFTER HER
ASUNA-SAN!
WHAT!? WE'RE FIVE STORIES UP!.....

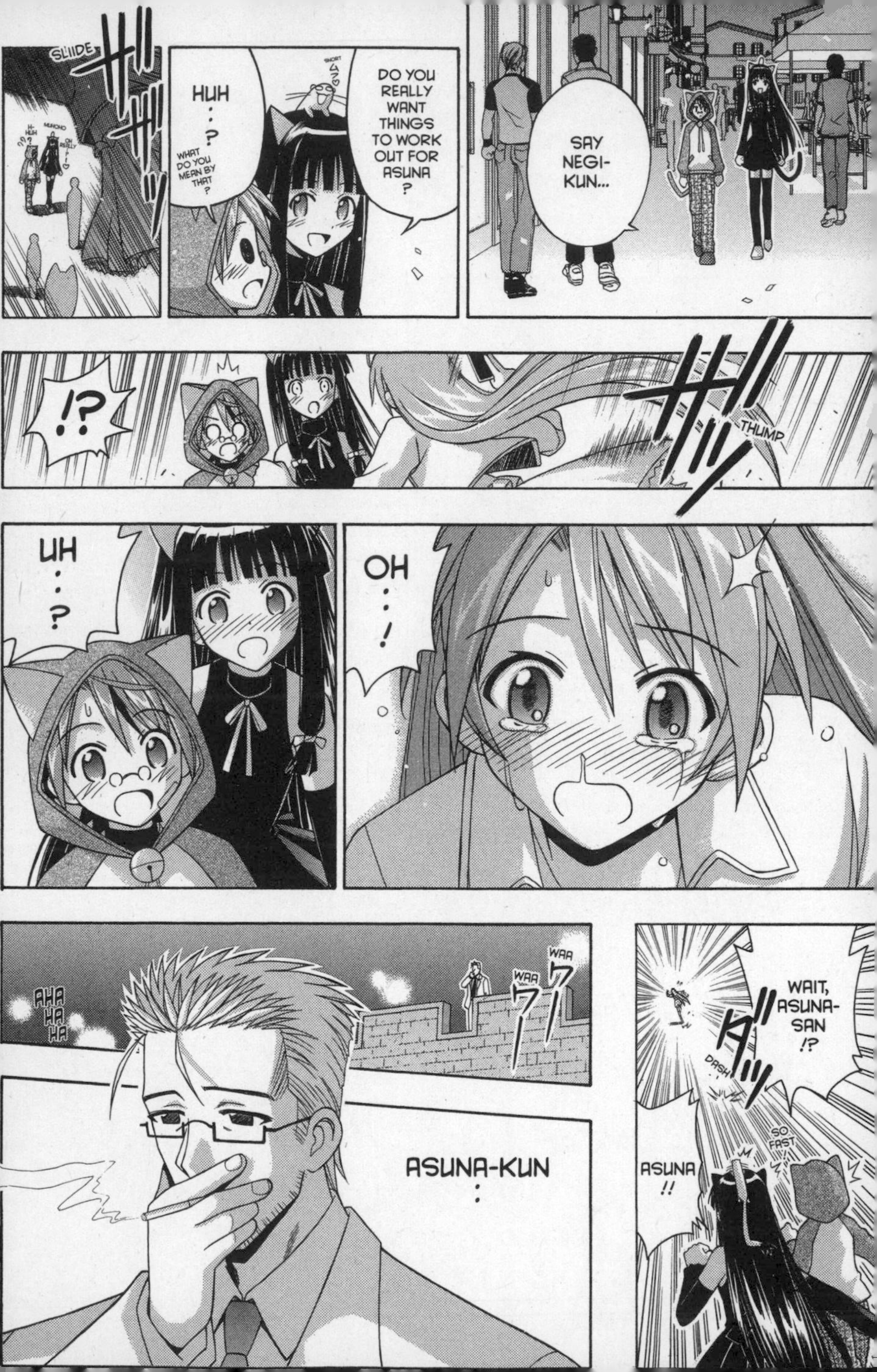
SAY NEGI-KUN...
DO YOU REALLY WANT THINGS TO WORK OUT FOR ASUNA?
SNORT
HUH...?
WHAT DO YOU MEAN BY THAT?
SLIIDE
H-HUH?
MUHOHO
OH REALLY?
THUMP
!?
OH...!
UH...?
WAIT, ASUNA-SAN!?
DASH
SO FAST
ASUNA!!
WAA
WAA
AHA HA HA
ASUNA-KUN...

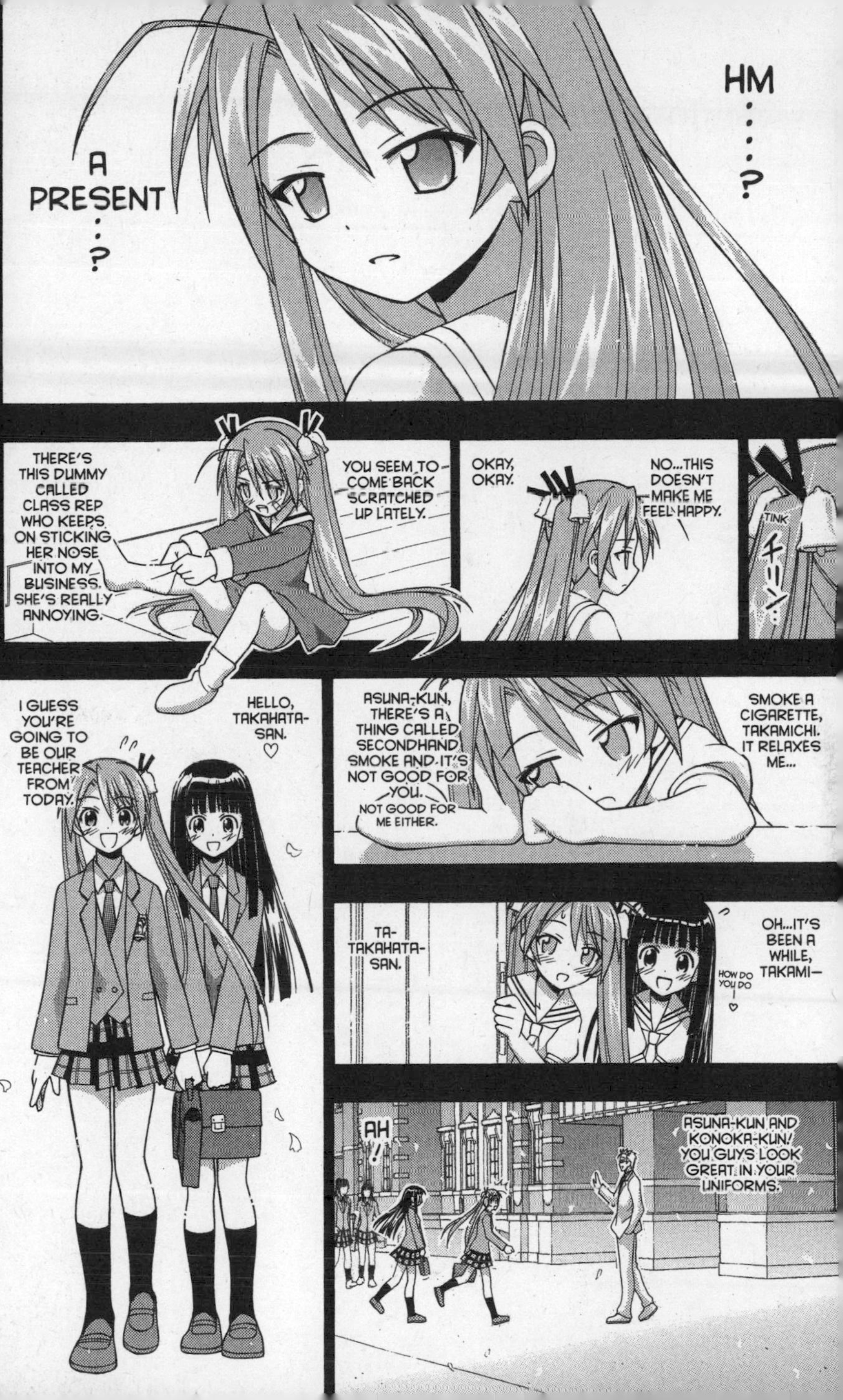
HM...?
A PRESENT...?
TINK
チリーン...
NO...THIS DOESN'T MAKE ME FEEL HAPPY.
OKAY, OKAY.
YOU SEEM TO COME BACK SCRATCHED UP LATELY.
THERE'S THIS DUMMY CALLED CLASS REP WHO KEEPS ON STICKING HER NOSE INTO MY BUSINESS. SHE'S REALLY ANNOYING.
SMOKE A CIGARETTE, TAKAMICHI. IT RELAXES ME...
ASUNA-KUN, THERE'S A THING CALLED SECONDHAND SMOKE AND IT'S NOT GOOD FOR YOU.
NOT GOOD FOR ME EITHER.
OH...IT'S BEEN A WHILE, TAKAMI—
HOW DO YOU DO ♡
TA-TAKAHATA-SAN.
ASUNA-KUN AND KONOKA-KUN! YOU GUYS LOOK GREAT IN YOUR UNIFORMS.
AH!
HELLO, TAKAHATA-SAN. ♡
I GUESS YOU'RE GOING TO BE OUR TEACHER FROM TODAY.

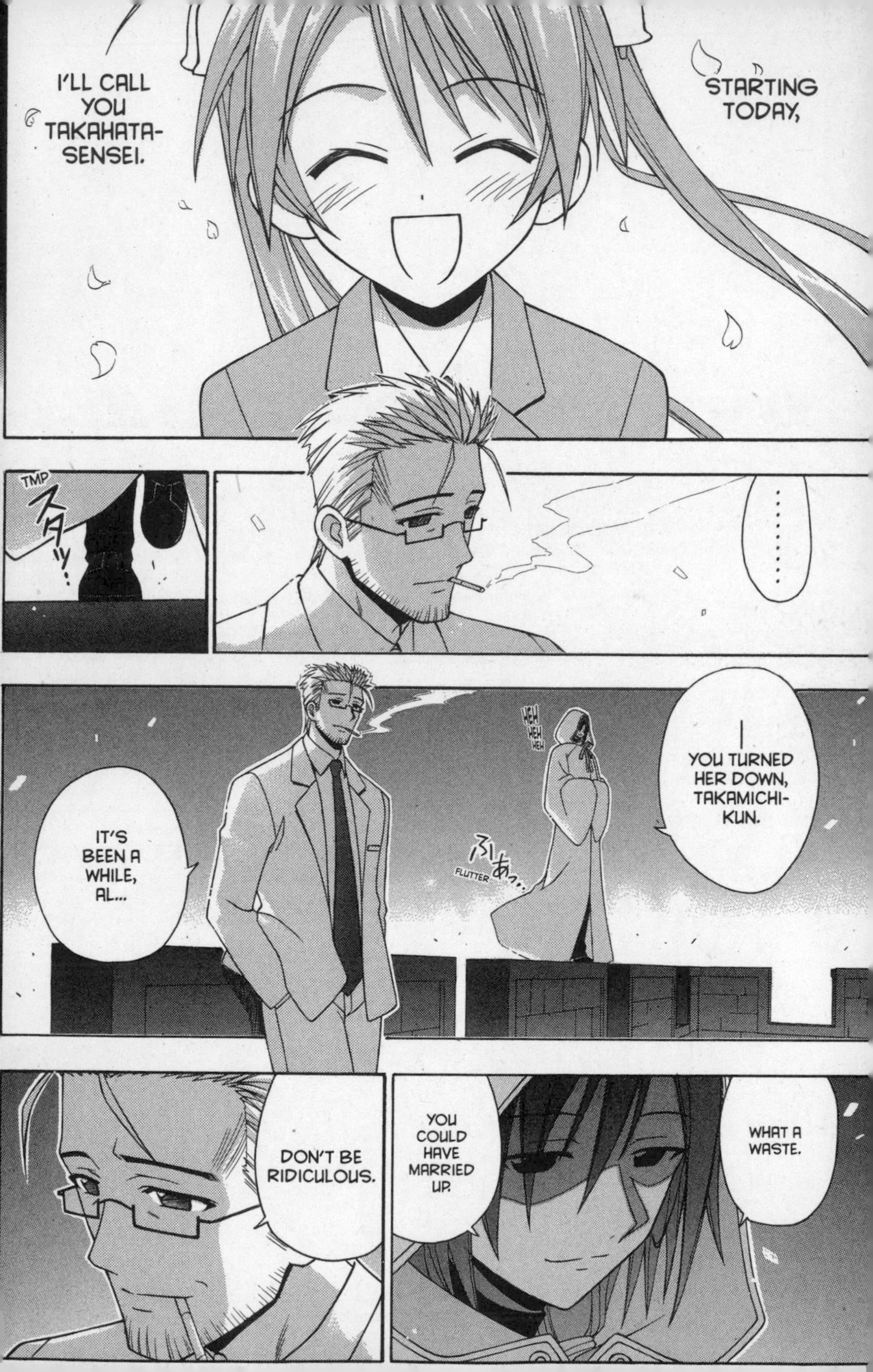
STARTING TODAY,
I'LL CALL YOU TAKAHATA-SENSEI.
......
TMP
スタッ
YOU TURNED HER DOWN, TAKAMICHI-KUN.
HEH HEH HEH
ふぁっ
FLUTTER
IT'S BEEN A WHILE, AL...
WHAT A WASTE.
YOU COULD HAVE MARRIED UP.
DON'T BE RIDICULOUS.

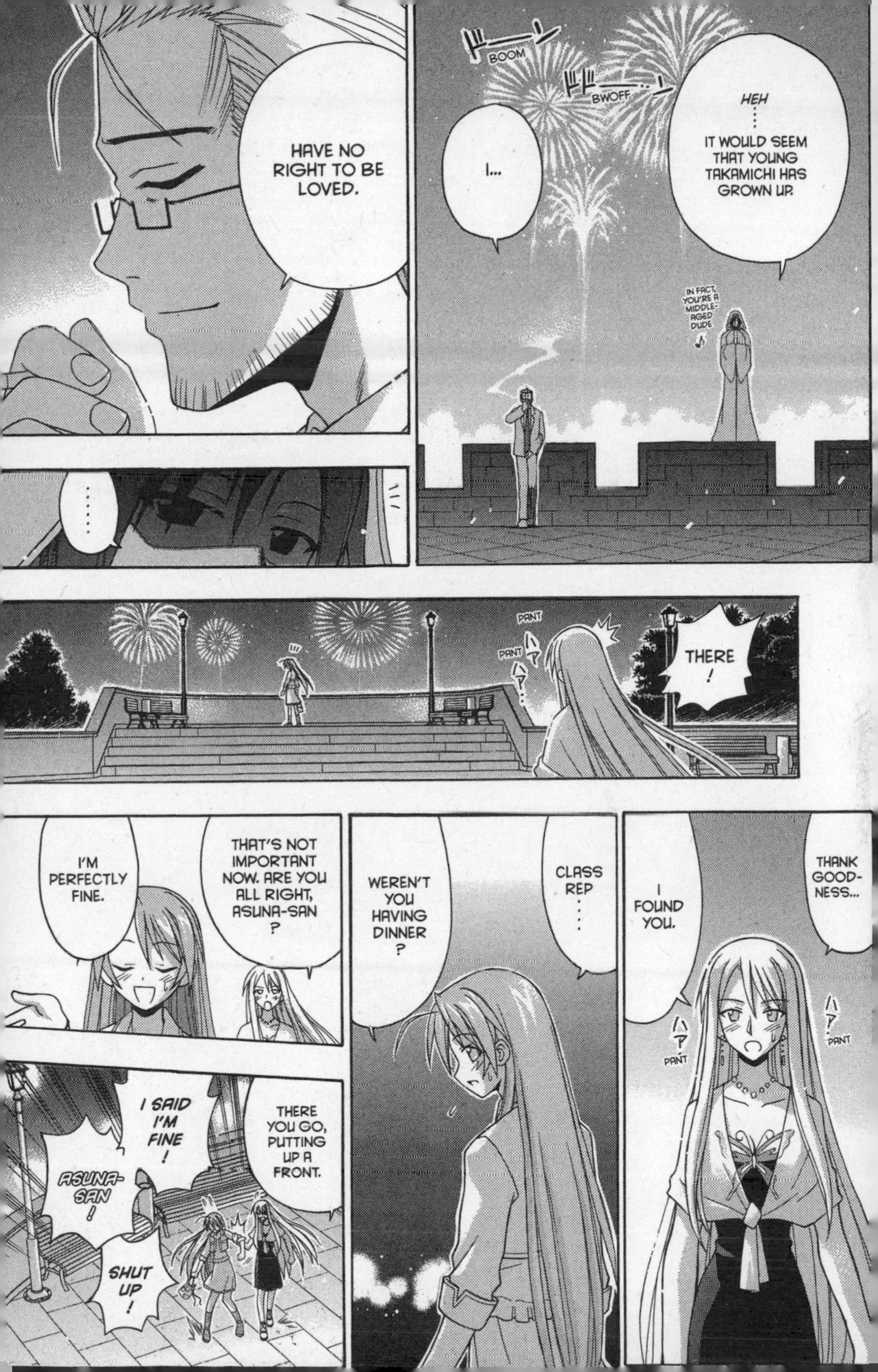
BOOM
BWOFF
HEH... IT WOULD SEEM THAT YOUNG TAKAMICHI HAS GROWN UP.
I...
IN FACT, YOU'RE A MIDDLE-AGED DUDE ♪
HAVE NO RIGHT TO BE LOVED.
......
PANT
PANT
THERE!
THANK GOODNESS...
I FOUND YOU.
PANT
PANT
CLASS REP....
WEREN'T YOU HAVING DINNER?
THAT'S NOT IMPORTANT NOW. ARE YOU ALL RIGHT, ASUNA-SAN?
I'M PERFECTLY FINE.
THERE YOU GO, PUTTING UP A FRONT.
I SAID I'M FINE!
ASUNA-SAN!
SHUT UP!

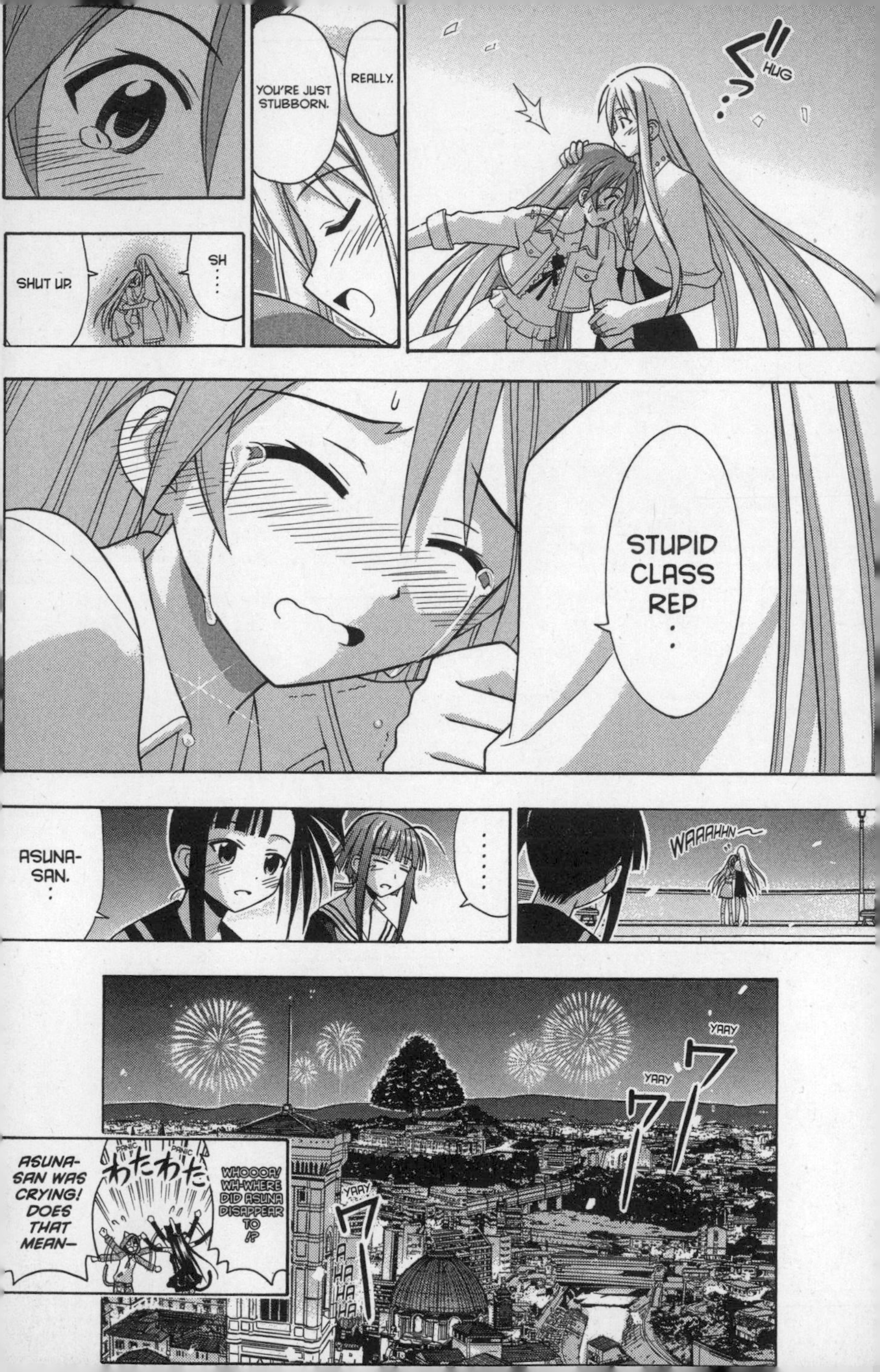
HUG
REALLY.
YOU'RE JUST STUBBORN.
SH ....
SHUT UP.
STUPID CLASS REP ..
WAAAHHN~
......
ASUNA-SAN. ..
YAAY
YAAY
YAAY
A HA HA HA
WHOOOA! WH-WHERE DID ASUNA DISAPPEAR TO !?
PANIC PANIC
わたわた
ASUNA-SAN WAS CRYING! DOES THAT MEAN—

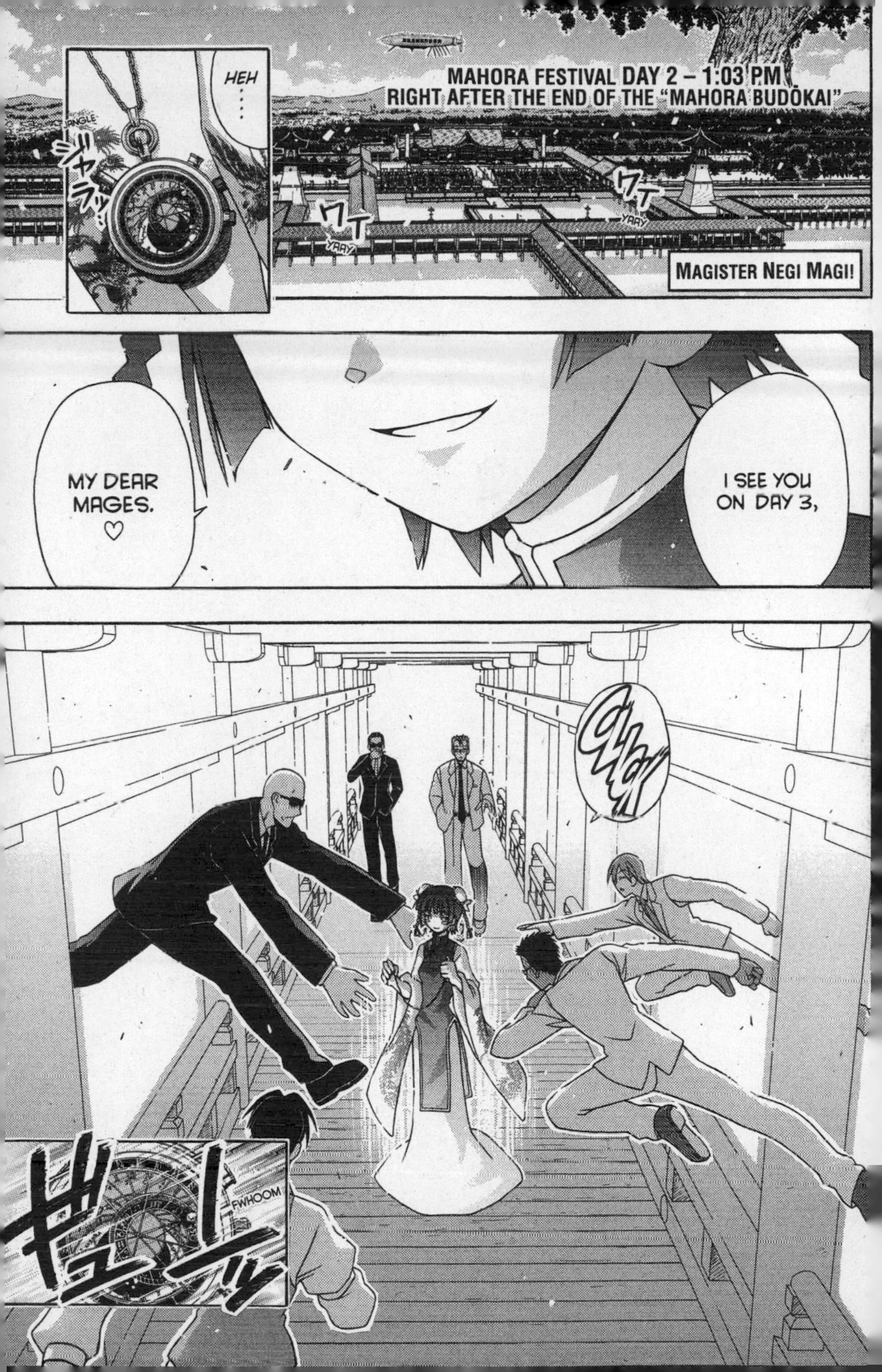
MAHORA FESTIVAL DAY 2 – 1:03 PM
RIGHT AFTER THE END OF THE "MAHORA BUDŌKAI"
YAAY
YAAY
MAGISTER NEGI MAGI!
HEH
....
JANGLE
I SEE YOU ON DAY 3,
MY DEAR MAGES. ♡
FWHOOM

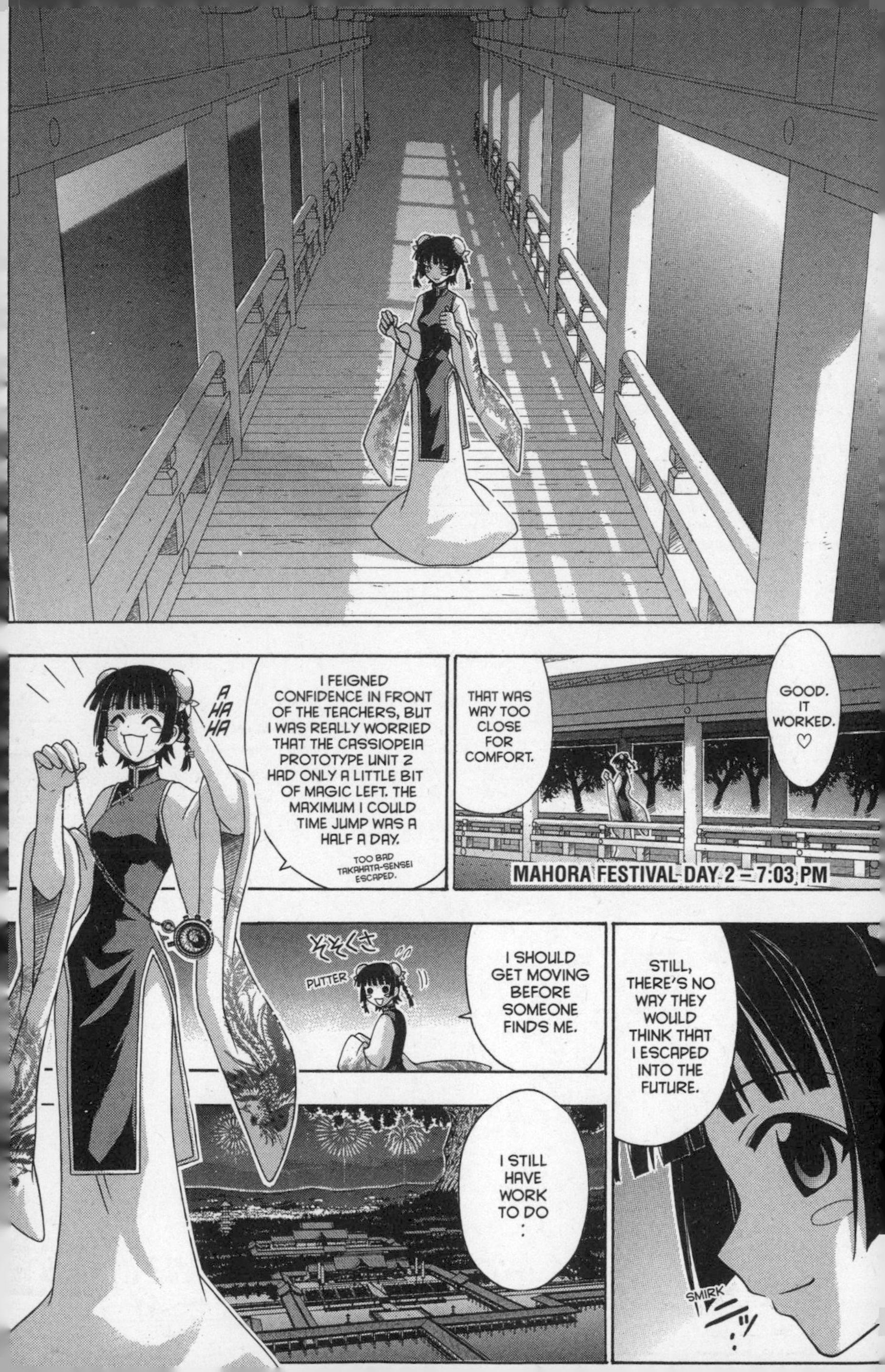

GOOD. IT WORKED. ♡
MAHORA FESTIVAL DAY 2 – 7:03 PM
THAT WAS WAY TOO CLOSE FOR COMFORT.
A HA HA
I FEIGNED CONFIDENCE IN FRONT OF THE TEACHERS, BUT I WAS REALLY WORRIED THAT THE CASSIOPEIA PROTOTYPE UNIT 2 HAD ONLY A LITTLE BIT OF MAGIC LEFT. THE MAXIMUM I COULD TIME JUMP WAS A HALF A DAY.
TOO BAD TAKAHATA-SENSEI ESCAPED.
STILL, THERE'S NO WAY THEY WOULD THINK THAT I ESCAPED INTO THE FUTURE.
SMIRK
そそくさ
PUTTER
I SHOULD GET MOVING BEFORE SOMEONE FINDS ME.
I STILL HAVE WORK TO DO

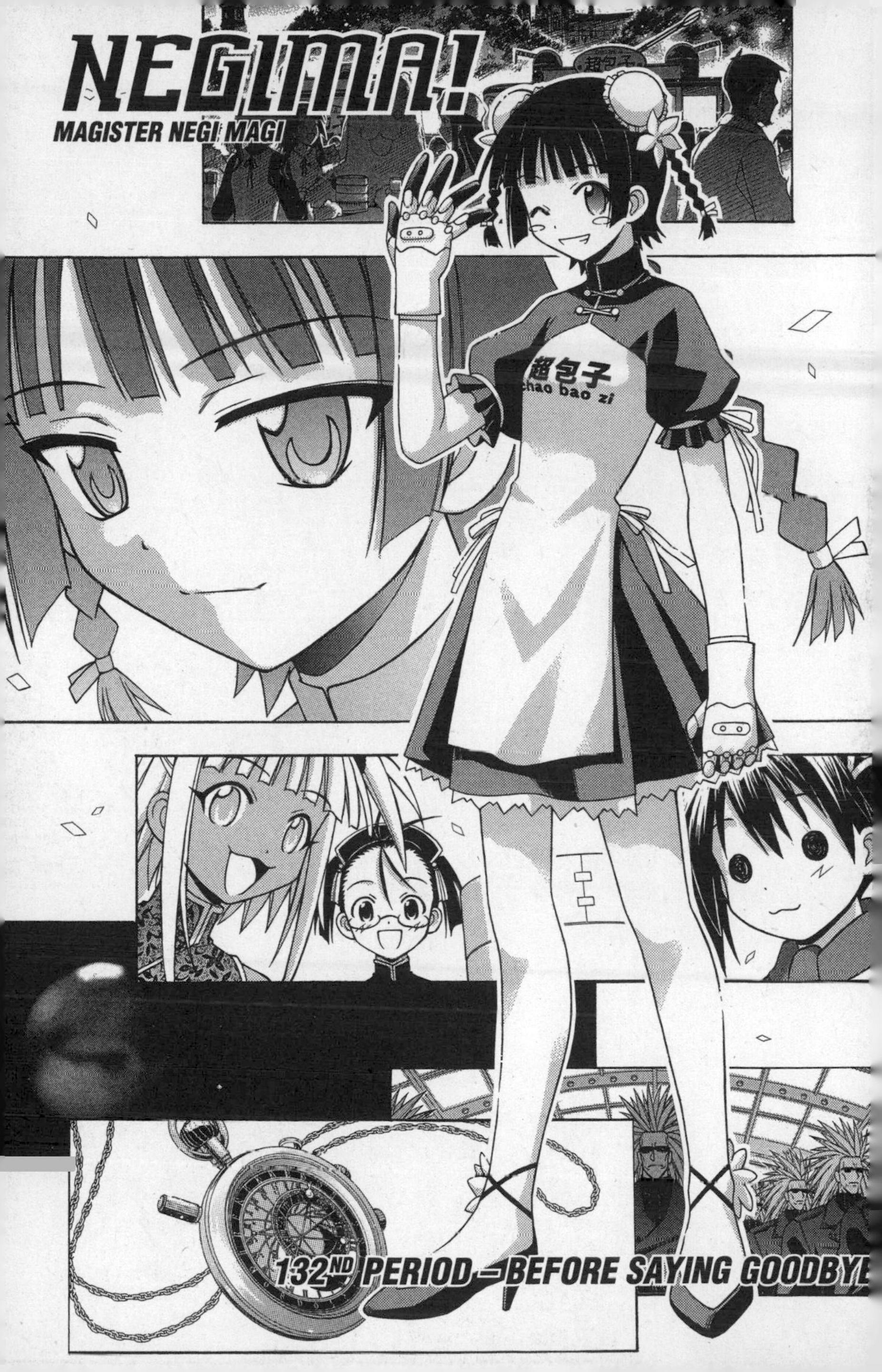
NEGIMA!
MAGISTER NEGI MAGI
超包子
超包子
chao bao zi
132ND PERIOD – BEFORE SAYING GOODBYE

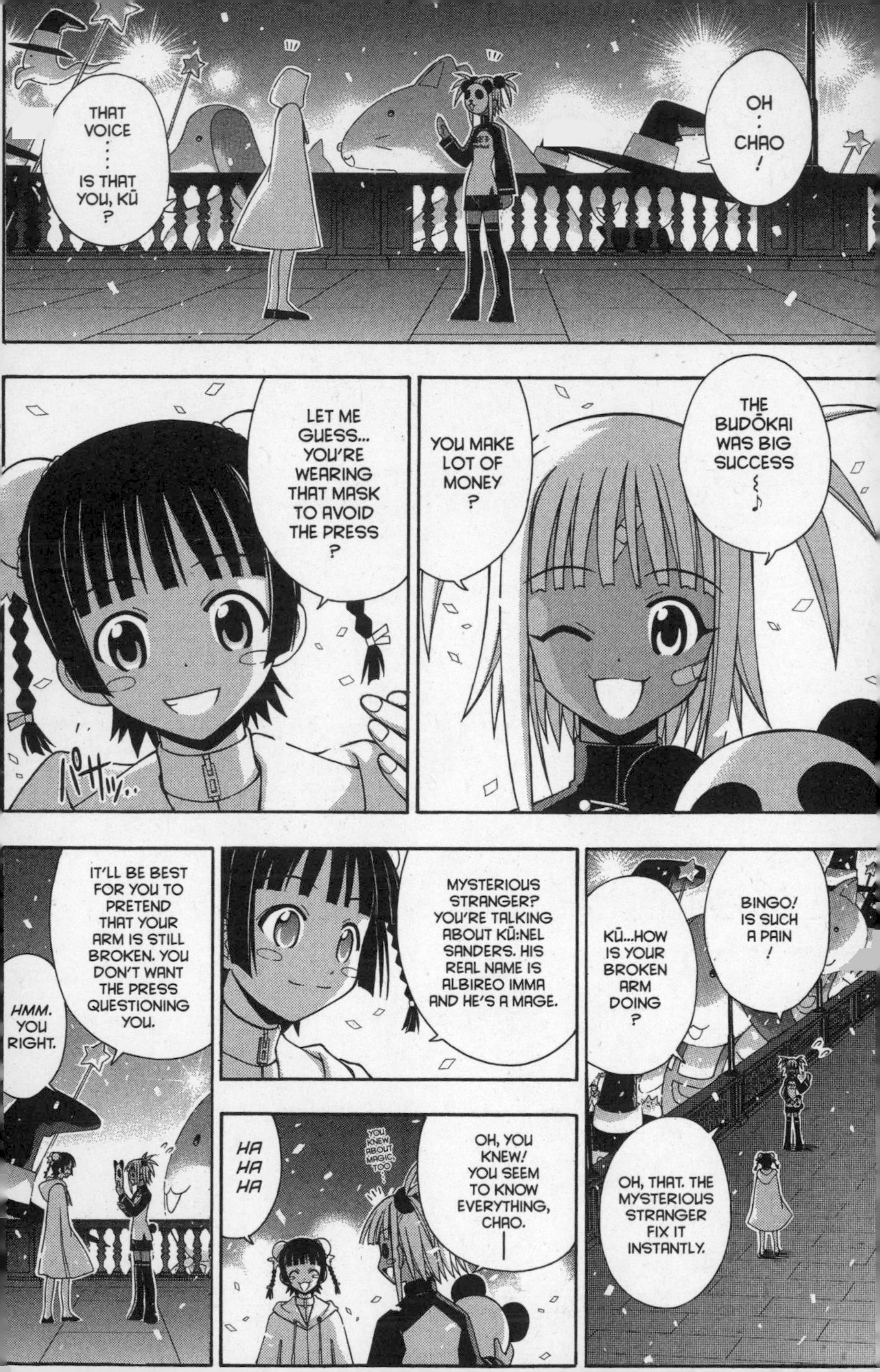
OH... CHAO!
THAT VOICE...... IS THAT YOU, KŪ?
THE BUDŌKAI WAS BIG SUCCESS~♪
YOU MAKE LOT OF MONEY?
LET ME GUESS... YOU'RE WEARING THAT MASK TO AVOID THE PRESS?
パサッ..
BINGO! IS SUCH A PAIN!
KŪ...HOW IS YOUR BROKEN ARM DOING?
OH, THAT. THE MYSTERIOUS STRANGER FIX IT INSTANTLY.
MYSTERIOUS STRANGER? YOU'RE TALKING ABOUT KŪ:NEL SANDERS. HIS REAL NAME IS ALBIREO IMMA AND HE'S A MAGE.
OH, YOU KNEW! YOU SEEM TO KNOW EVERYTHING, CHAO.
YOU KNEW ABOUT MAGIC, TOO?
HA HA HA
IT'LL BE BEST FOR YOU TO PRETEND THAT YOUR ARM IS STILL BROKEN. YOU DON'T WANT THE PRESS QUESTIONING YOU.
HMM. YOU RIGHT.

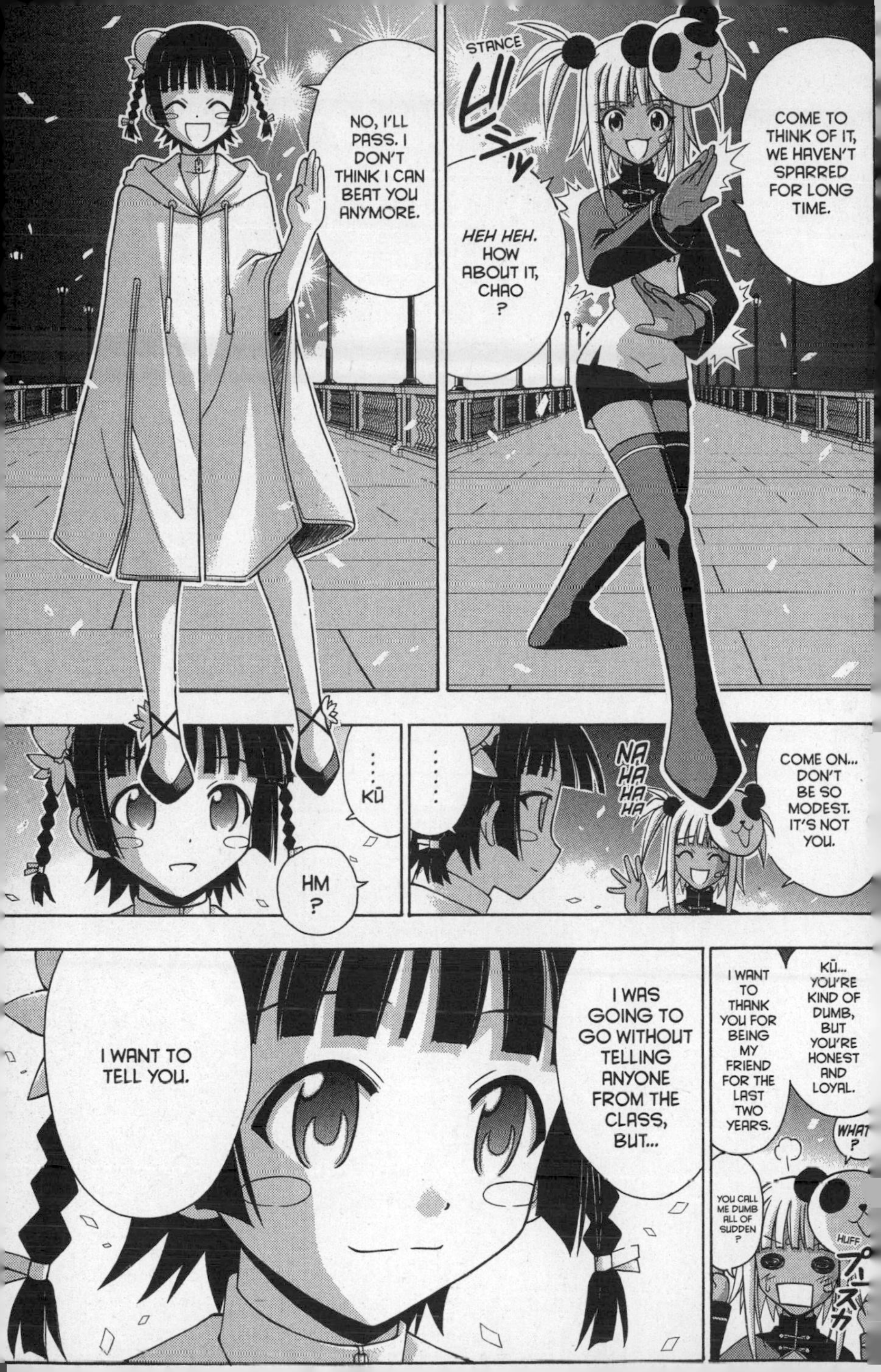
COME TO THINK OF IT, WE HAVEN'T SPARRED FOR LONG TIME.
HEH HEH. HOW ABOUT IT, CHAO?
STANCE
NO, I'LL PASS. I DON'T THINK I CAN BEAT YOU ANYMORE.
COME ON... DON'T BE SO MODEST. IT'S NOT YOU.
NAHAHAHAHA
......
...... KŪ
HM?
KŪ... YOU'RE KIND OF DUMB, BUT YOU'RE HONEST AND LOYAL.
I WANT TO THANK YOU FOR BEING MY FRIEND FOR THE LAST TWO YEARS.
WHAT?
YOU CALL ME DUMB ALL OF SUDDEN?
HUFF
プースカ
I WAS GOING TO GO WITHOUT TELLING ANYONE FROM THE CLASS, BUT...
I WANT TO TELL YOU.

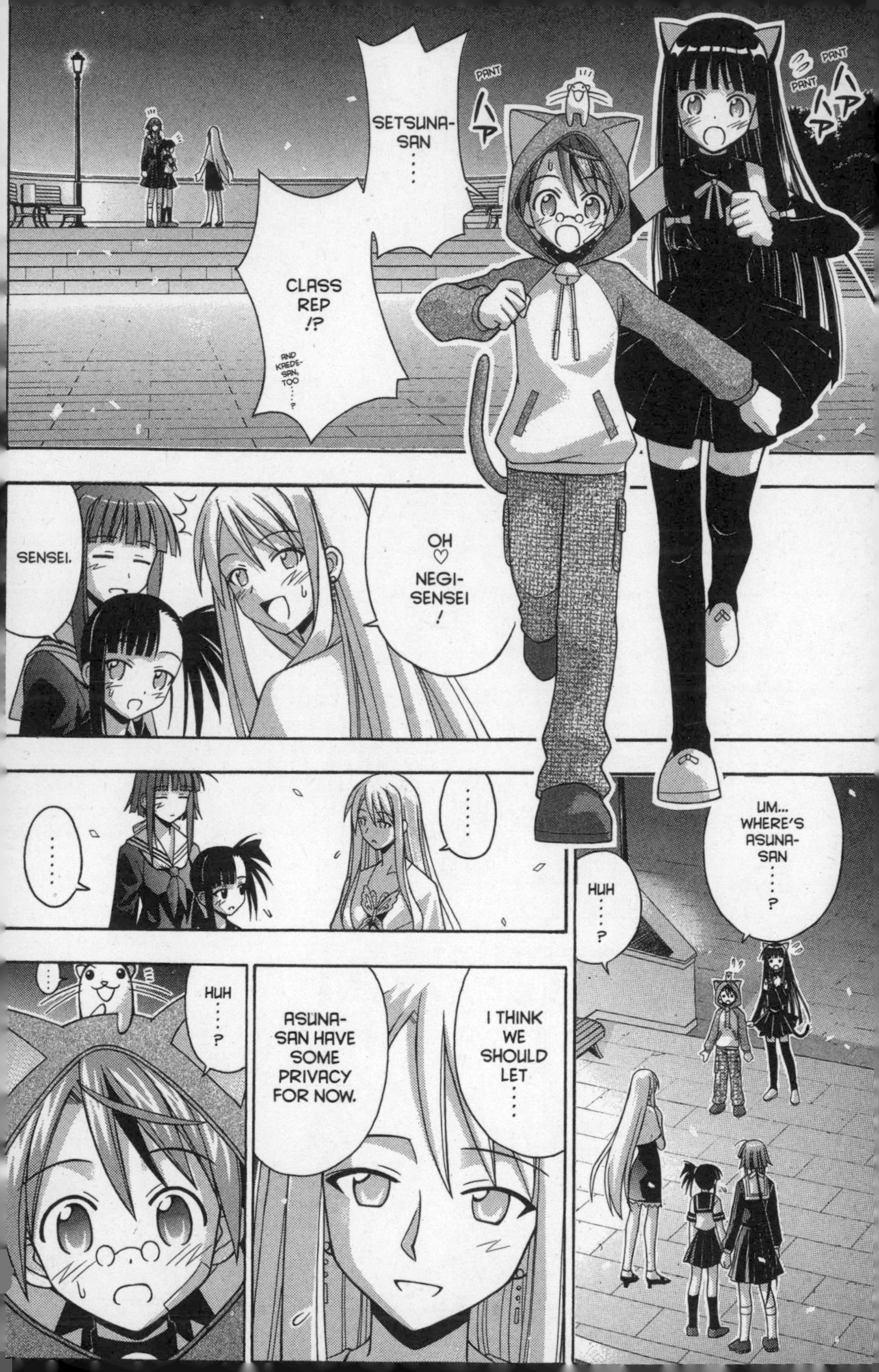
PANT ハァ
PANT ハァ
PANT ハァ
SETSUNA-SAN....
CLASS REP !?
AND KAEDE-SAN, TOO....?
OH ♡ NEGI-SENSEI!
SENSEI.
UM... WHERE'S ASUNA-SAN....?
HUH....?
......
......
I THINK WE SHOULD LET....
ASUNA-SAN HAVE SOME PRIVACY FOR NOW.
HUH....?
...

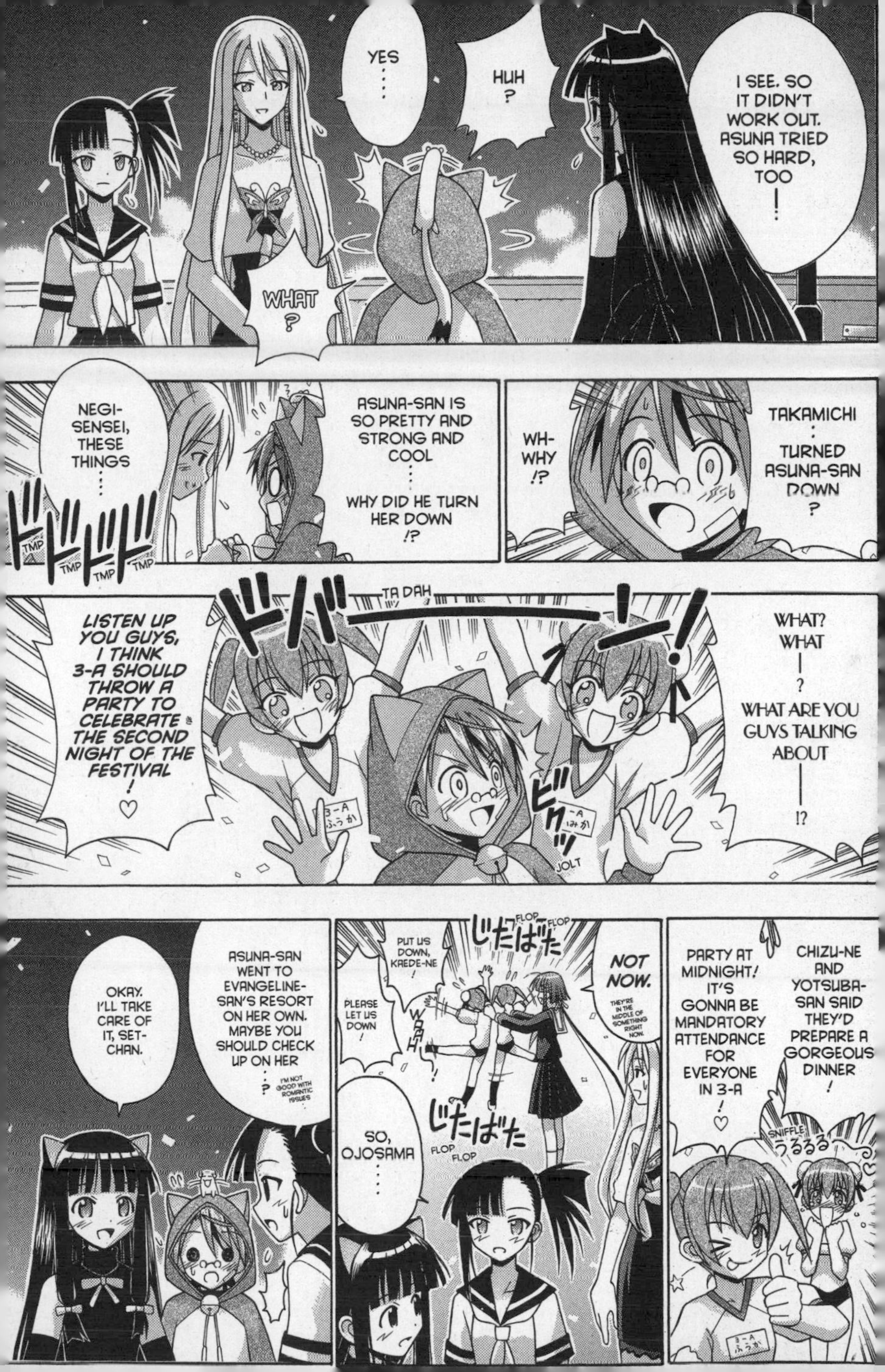
I SEE. SO IT DIDN'T WORK OUT. ASUNA TRIED SO HARD, TOO!
HUH?
YES...
WHAT?
TAKAMICHI: TURNED ASUNA-SAN DOWN?
WH-WHY!?
ASUNA-SAN IS SO PRETTY AND STRONG AND COOL... WHY DID HE TURN HER DOWN!?
NEGI-SENSEI, THESE THINGS...
ドドドド
TMP TMP TMP TMP
WHAT? WHAT—? WHAT ARE YOU GUYS TALKING ABOUT—!?
ドバーン!
TA DAH
LISTEN UP YOU GUYS, I THINK 3-A SHOULD THROW A PARTY TO CELEBRATE THE SECOND NIGHT OF THE FESTIVAL! ♡
3-A ふうか
-A みか
ビクッ
JOLT
CHIZU-NE AND YOTSUBA-SAN SAID THEY'D PREPARE A GORGEOUS DINNER!
PARTY AT MIDNIGHT! IT'S GONNA BE MANDATORY ATTENDANCE FOR EVERYONE IN 3-A! ♡
SNIFFLE
うるるる
3-A ふうか
NOT NOW.
THEY'RE IN THE MIDDLE OF SOMETHING RIGHT NOW.
じたばた
FLOP FLOP
PUT US DOWN, KAEDE-NE!
PLEASE LET US DOWN!
じたばた
FLOP FLOP
SO, OJOSAMA...
ASUNA-SAN WENT TO EVANGELINE-SAN'S RESORT ON HER OWN. MAYBE YOU SHOULD CHECK UP ON HER...?
I'M NOT GOOD WITH ROMANTIC ISSUES
OKAY. I'LL TAKE CARE OF IT, SET-CHAN.

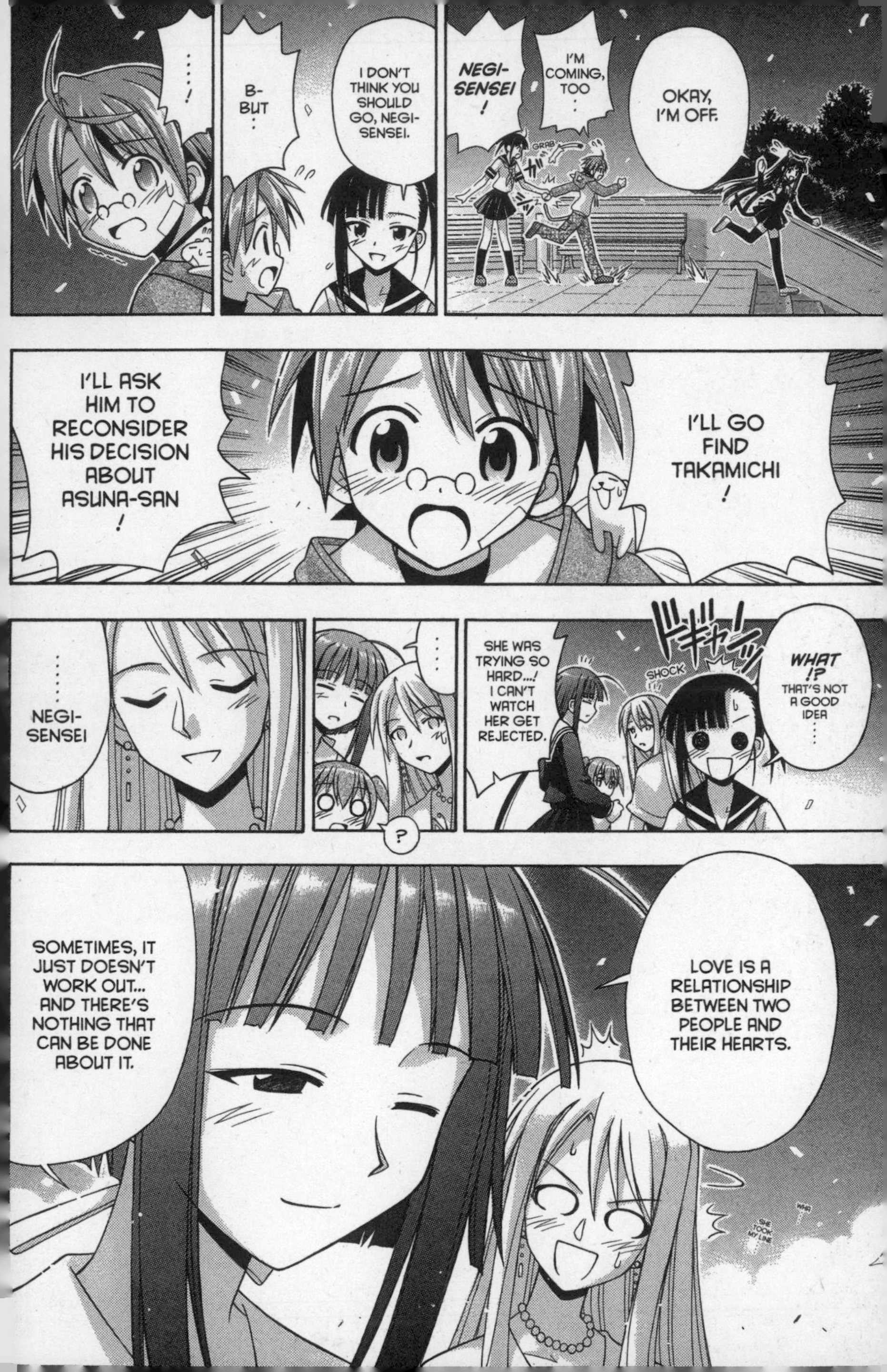
OKAY, I'M OFF.
I'M COMING, TOO...
NEGI-SENSEI!
GRAB
I DON'T THINK YOU SHOULD GO, NEGI-SENSEI.
B-BUT...
......!
I'LL GO FIND TAKAMICHI!
I'LL ASK HIM TO RECONSIDER HIS DECISION ABOUT ASUNA-SAN!
WHAT!? THAT'S NOT A GOOD IDEA...
SHOCK
SHE WAS TRYING SO HARD...! I CAN'T WATCH HER GET REJECTED.
....
?
......NEGI-SENSEI
LOVE IS A RELATIONSHIP BETWEEN TWO PEOPLE AND THEIR HEARTS.
WHA
SHE TOOK MY LINE
SOMETIMES, IT JUST DOESN'T WORK OUT... AND THERE'S NOTHING THAT CAN BE DONE ABOUT IT.

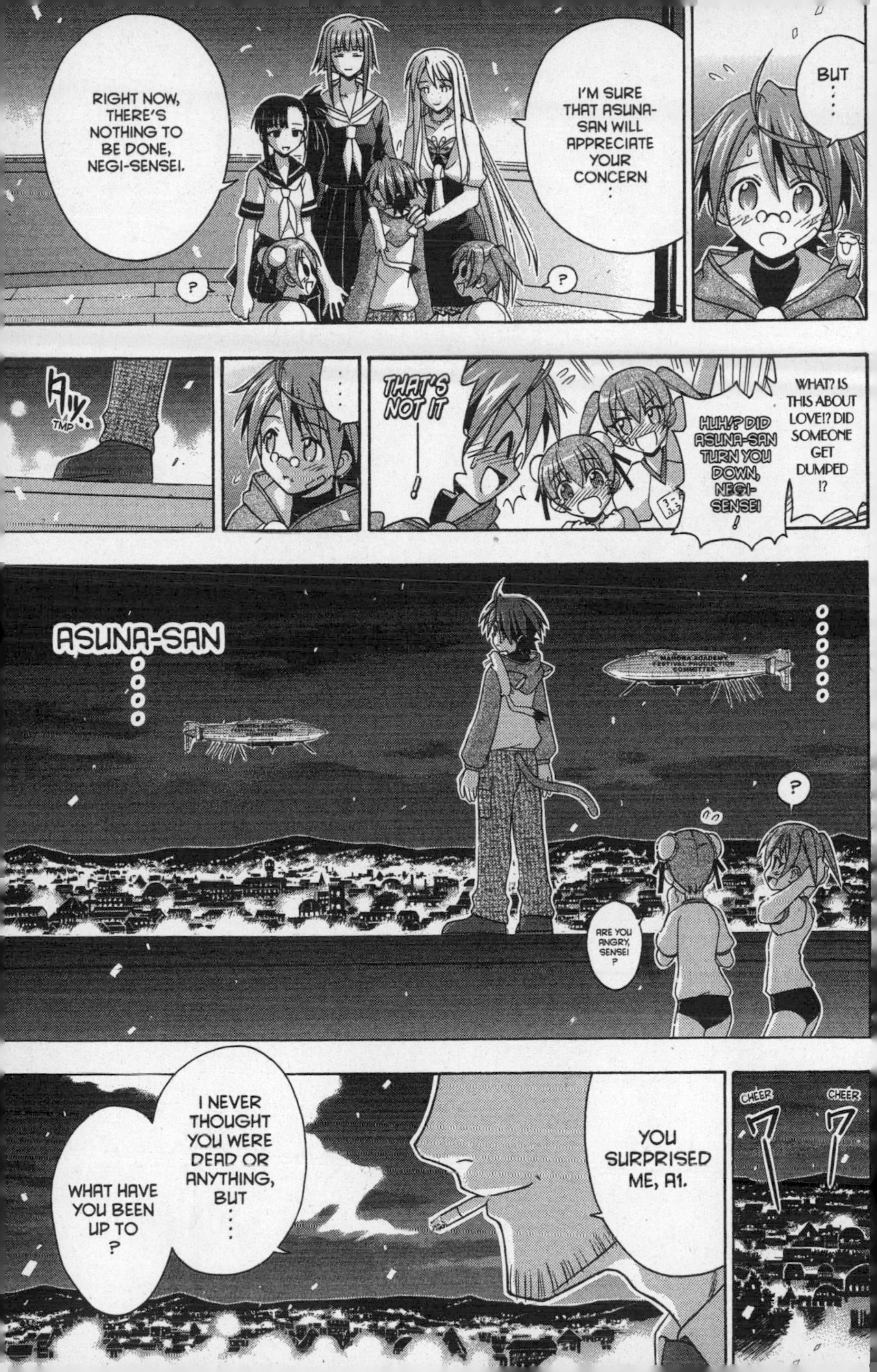
BUT ....
I'M SURE THAT ASUNA-SAN WILL APPRECIATE YOUR CONCERN :
RIGHT NOW, THERE'S NOTHING TO BE DONE, NEGI-SENSEI.
?
?
WHAT? IS THIS ABOUT LOVE!? DID SOMEONE GET DUMPED !?
HUH!? DID ASUNA-SAN TURN YOU DOWN, NEGI-SENSEI !
THAT'S NOT IT —— !
....
TMP
ASUNA-SAN OOOO
OOOOOO
MAHORA ACADEMY FESTIVAL PRODUCTION COMMITTEE
?
ARE YOU ANGRY, SENSEI ?
CHEER
CHEER
YOU SURPRISED ME, A1.
I NEVER THOUGHT YOU WERE DEAD OR ANYTHING, BUT ....
WHAT HAVE YOU BEEN UP TO ?

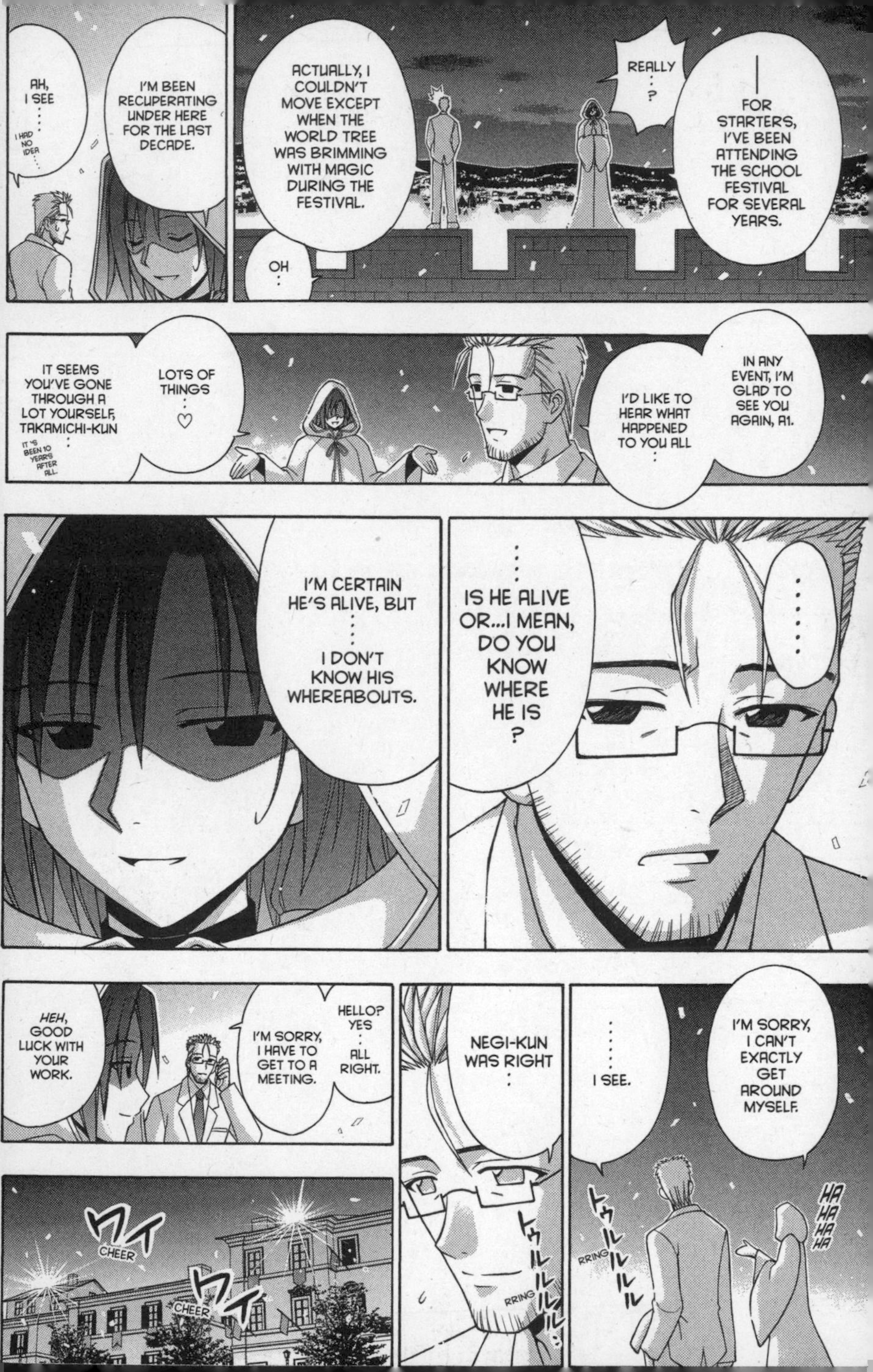
FOR STARTERS, I'VE BEEN ATTENDING THE SCHOOL FESTIVAL FOR SEVERAL YEARS.
REALLY...?
ACTUALLY, I COULDN'T MOVE EXCEPT WHEN THE WORLD TREE WAS BRIMMING WITH MAGIC DURING THE FESTIVAL.
OH...
I'M BEEN RECUPERATING UNDER HERE FOR THE LAST DECADE.
AH, I SEE...
I HAD NO IDEA...
IN ANY EVENT, I'M GLAD TO SEE YOU AGAIN, A1.
I'D LIKE TO HEAR WHAT HAPPENED TO YOU ALL...
LOTS OF THINGS...♡
IT SEEMS YOU'VE GONE THROUGH A LOT YOURSELF, TAKAMICHI-KUN...
IT'S BEEN 10 YEARS AFTER ALL.
......
...IS HE ALIVE OR...I MEAN, DO YOU KNOW WHERE HE IS?
I'M CERTAIN HE'S ALIVE, BUT... I DON'T KNOW HIS WHEREABOUTS.
I'M SORRY, I CAN'T EXACTLY GET AROUND MYSELF.
...I SEE.
HAHAHAHA
RRING
NEGI-KUN WAS RIGHT...
RRING
HELLO? YES... ALL RIGHT.
I'M SORRY, I HAVE TO GET TO A MEETING.
HEH, GOOD LUCK WITH YOUR WORK.
CHEER
CHEER

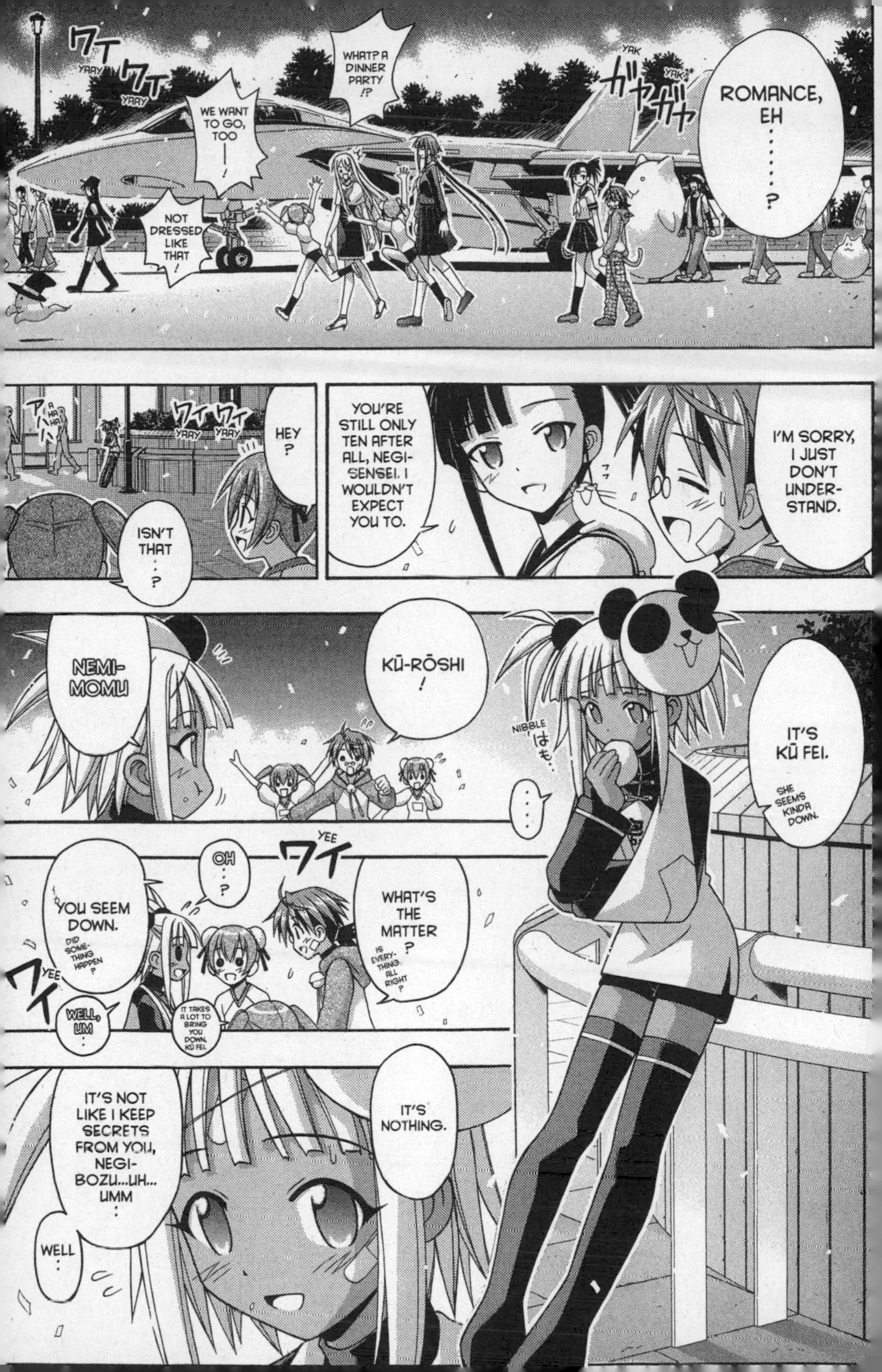
ROMANCE, EH......?
YAK ガヤ YAK ガヤ
WHAT? A DINNER PARTY!?
WE WANT TO GO, TOO—!
NOT DRESSED LIKE THAT!
ワイ YAAY ワイ YAAY
I'M SORRY, I JUST DON'T UNDER-STAND.
YOU'RE STILL ONLY TEN AFTER ALL, NEGI-SENSEI. I WOULDN'T EXPECT YOU TO.
HEY?
ISN'T THAT...?
ワイワイ YAAY YAAY
A HA HA
IT'S KŪ FEI.
SHE SEEMS KINDA DOWN.
NIBBLE はむ...
...
KŪ-RŌSHI!
NEMI-MOMU
WHAT'S THE MATTER?
IS EVERYTHING ALL RIGHT?
ワイ YEE
OH...?
YOU SEEM DOWN.
DID SOMETHING HAPPEN?
ワイ YEE
IT TAKES A LOT TO BRING YOU DOWN, KŪ FEI.
WELL, UM...
IT'S NOTHING.
IT'S NOT LIKE I KEEP SECRETS FROM YOU, NEGI-BOZU...UH... UMM...
WELL...

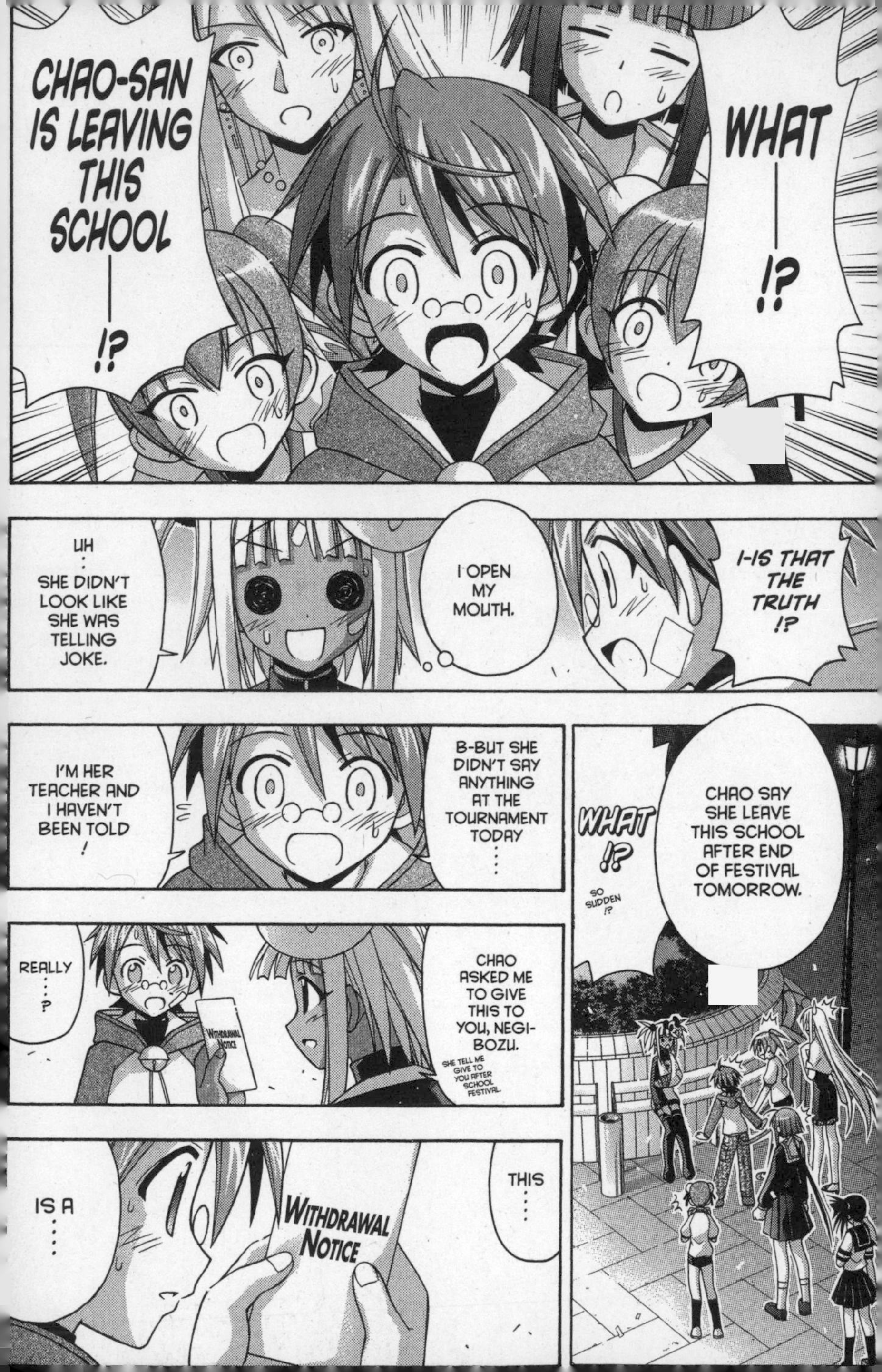
WHAT —— !?
CHAO-SAN IS LEAVING THIS SCHOOL —— !?
I-IS THAT THE TRUTH !?
I OPEN MY MOUTH.
UH... SHE DIDN'T LOOK LIKE SHE WAS TELLING JOKE.
CHAO SAY SHE LEAVE THIS SCHOOL AFTER END OF FESTIVAL TOMORROW.
WHAT !?
SO SUDDEN !?
B-BUT SHE DIDN'T SAY ANYTHING AT THE TOURNAMENT TODAY....
I'M HER TEACHER AND I HAVEN'T BEEN TOLD !
CHAO ASKED ME TO GIVE THIS TO YOU, NEGI-BOZU.
SHE TELL ME GIVE TO YOU AFTER SCHOOL FESTIVAL.
REALLY...?
WITHDRAWAL NOTICE
THIS...
WITHDRAWAL NOTICE
IS A...

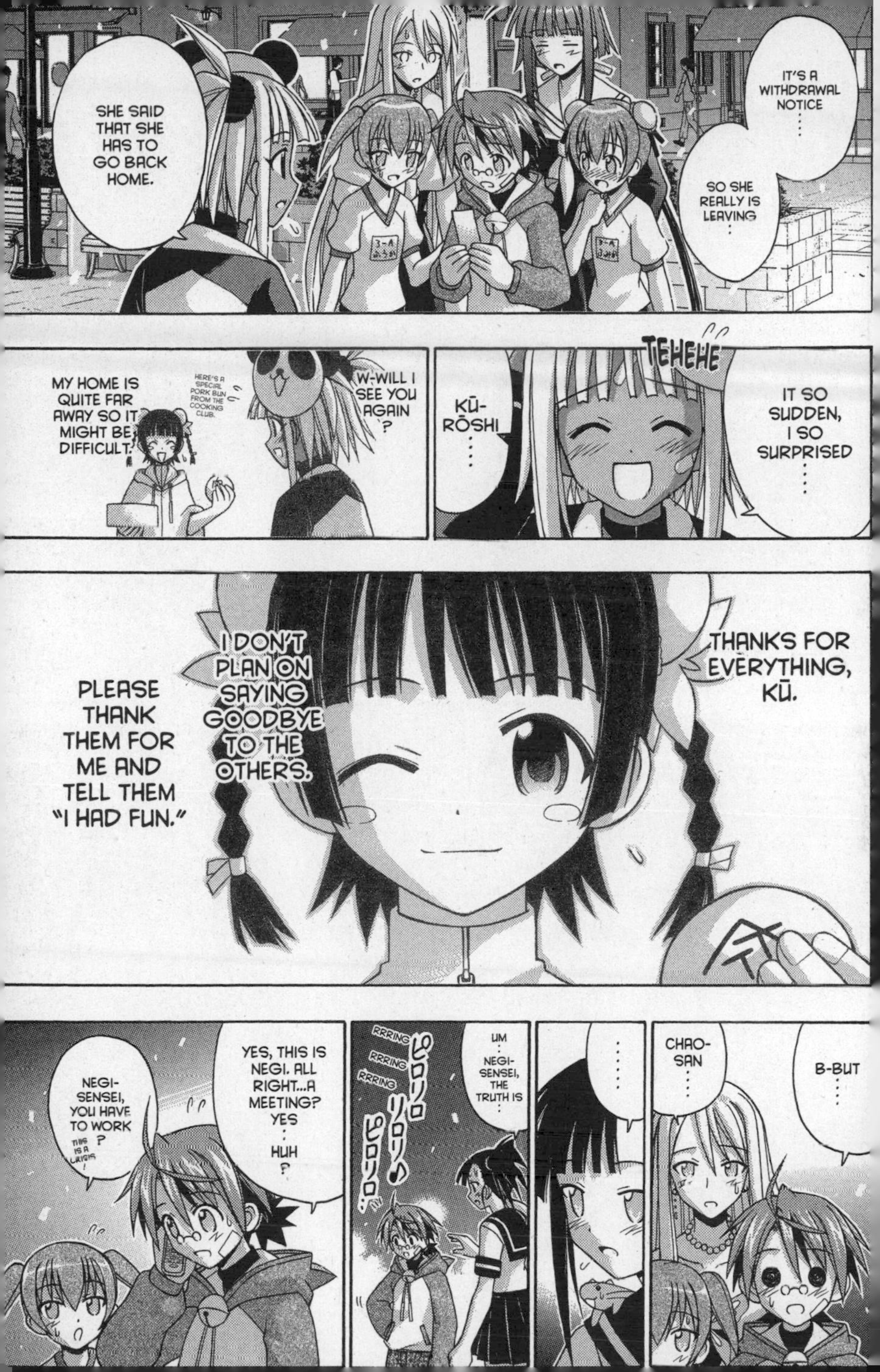
IT'S A WITHDRAWAL NOTICE…
SO SHE REALLY IS LEAVING…
SHE SAID THAT SHE HAS TO GO BACK HOME.
TEHEHE
IT SO SUDDEN, I SO SURPRISED…
KŪ-RŌSHI…
W-WILL I SEE YOU AGAIN?
HERE'S A SPECIAL PORK BUN FROM THE COOKING CLUB.
MY HOME IS QUITE FAR AWAY SO IT MIGHT BE DIFFICULT.
THANKS FOR EVERYTHING, KŪ.
I DON'T PLAN ON SAYING GOODBYE TO THE OTHERS.
PLEASE THANK THEM FOR ME AND TELL THEM "I HAD FUN."
B-BUT…
CHAO-SAN…
……
UM… NEGI-SENSEI, THE TRUTH IS…
RRRING
RRRING
RRRING
ピロリロ リロリ♪ ピロリロ…
YES, THIS IS NEGI. ALL RIGHT...A MEETING? YES… HUH?
NEGI-SENSEI, YOU HAVE TO WORK?
THIS IS A CRISIS!

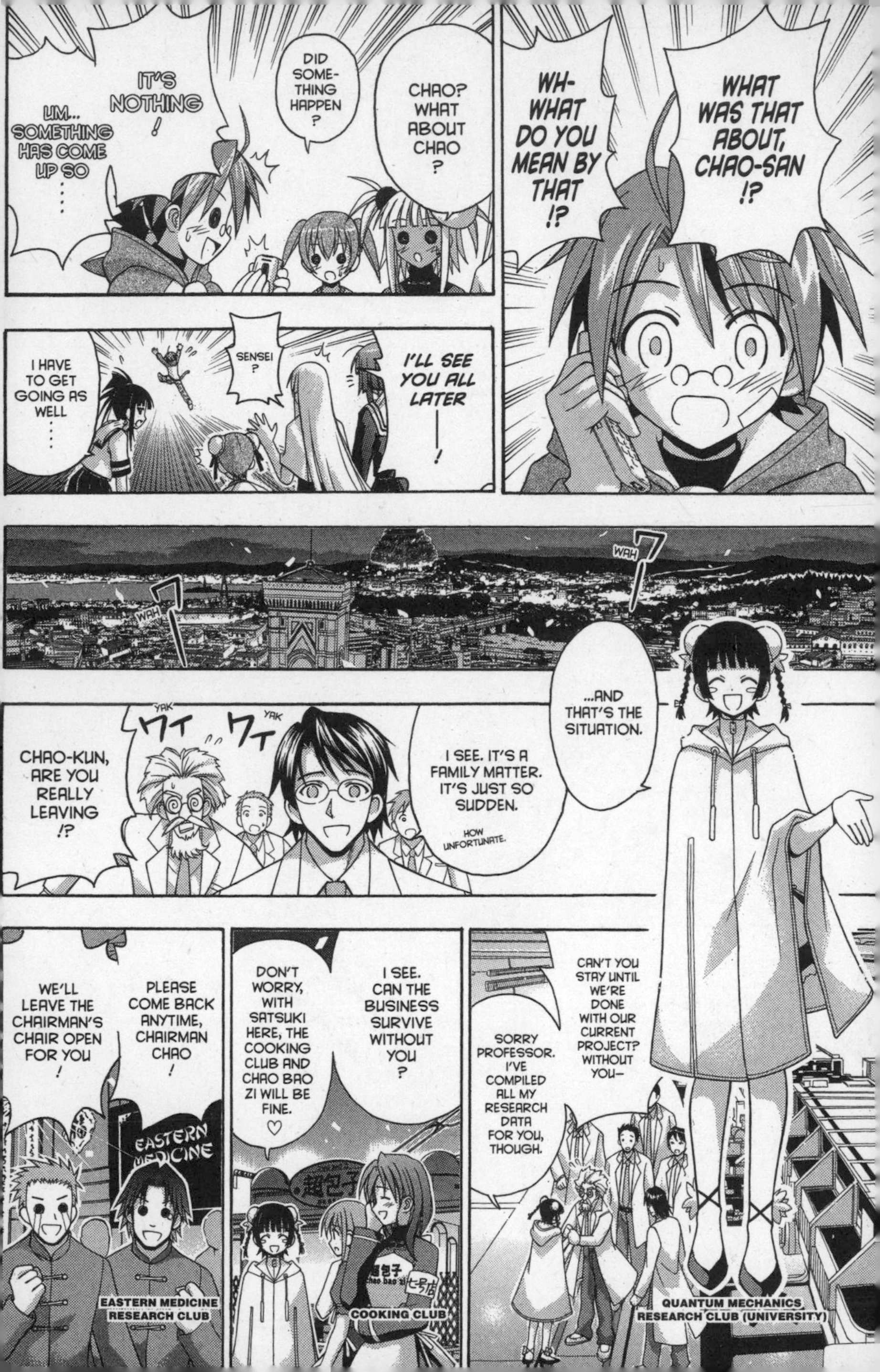
WHAT WAS THAT ABOUT, CHAO-SAN!?
WH-WHAT DO YOU MEAN BY THAT!?
CHAO? WHAT ABOUT CHAO?
DID SOMETHING HAPPEN?
IT'S NOTHING!
UM... SOMETHING HAS COME UP SO......
I'LL SEE YOU ALL LATER—!
SENSEI?
I HAVE TO GET GOING AS WELL......
WAH
WAH
...AND THAT'S THE SITUATION.
I SEE. IT'S A FAMILY MATTER. IT'S JUST SO SUDDEN.
HOW UNFORTUNATE.
YAK
YAK
CHAO-KUN, ARE YOU REALLY LEAVING!?
CAN'T YOU STAY UNTIL WE'RE DONE WITH OUR CURRENT PROJECT? WITHOUT YOU—
SORRY PROFESSOR. I'VE COMPILED ALL MY RESEARCH DATA FOR YOU, THOUGH.
QUANTUM MECHANICS RESEARCH CLUB (UNIVERSITY)
I SEE. CAN THE BUSINESS SURVIVE WITHOUT YOU?
DON'T WORRY, WITH SATSUKI HERE, THE COOKING CLUB AND CHAO BAO ZI WILL BE FINE. ♡
COOKING CLUB
PLEASE COME BACK ANYTIME, CHAIRMAN CHAO!
WE'LL LEAVE THE CHAIRMAN'S CHAIR OPEN FOR YOU!
EASTERN MEDICINE
EASTERN MEDICINE RESEARCH CLUB

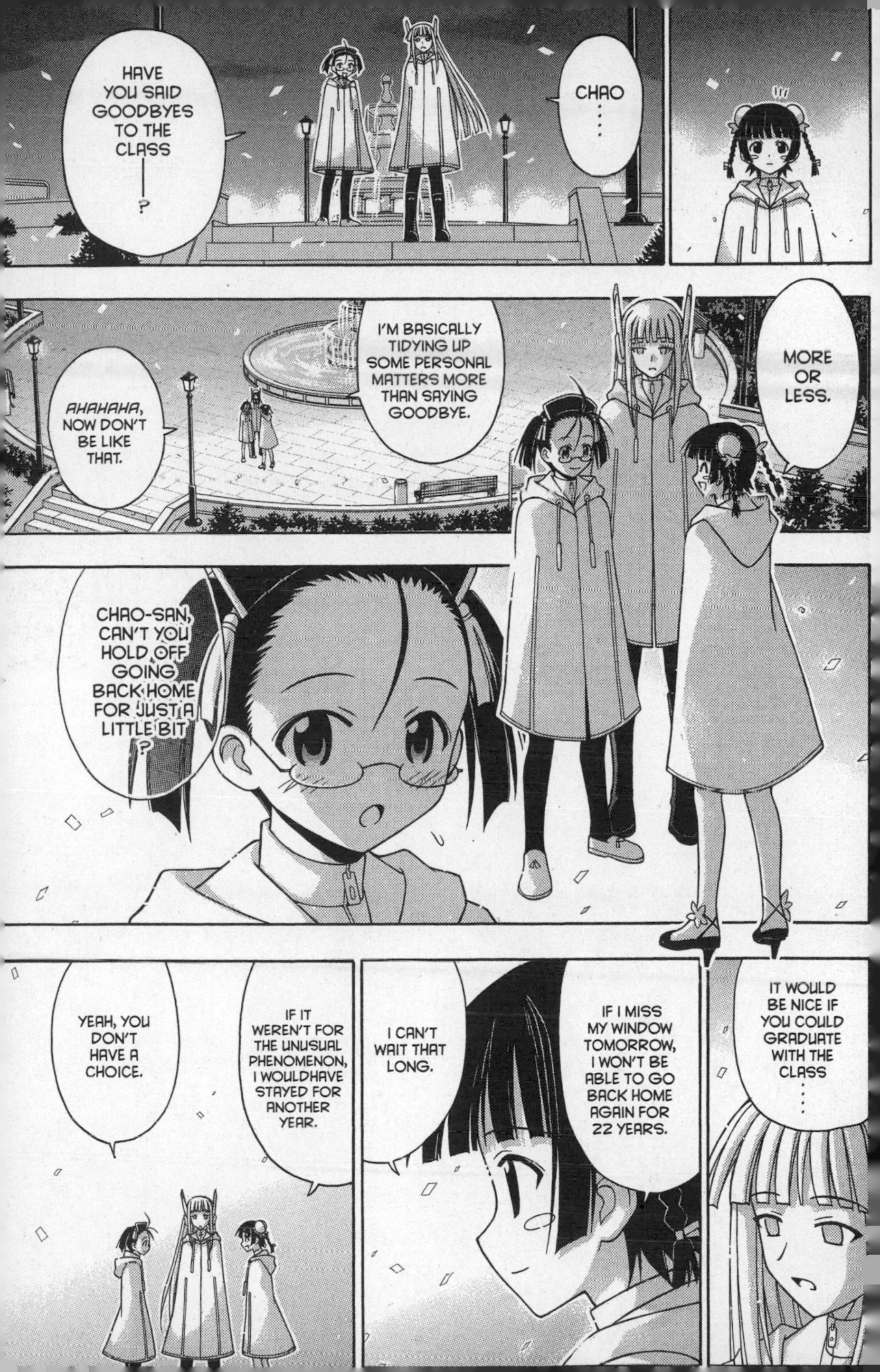
CHAO ....
HAVE YOU SAID GOODBYES TO THE CLASS—?
MORE OR LESS.
I'M BASICALLY TIDYING UP SOME PERSONAL MATTERS MORE THAN SAYING GOODBYE.
AHAHAHA, NOW DON'T BE LIKE THAT.
CHAO-SAN, CAN'T YOU HOLD OFF GOING BACK HOME FOR JUST A LITTLE BIT?
IT WOULD BE NICE IF YOU COULD GRADUATE WITH THE CLASS...
IF I MISS MY WINDOW TOMORROW, I WON'T BE ABLE TO GO BACK HOME AGAIN FOR 22 YEARS.
I CAN'T WAIT THAT LONG.
IF IT WEREN'T FOR THE UNUSUAL PHENOMENON, I WOULDHAVE STAYED FOR ANOTHER YEAR.
YEAH, YOU DON'T HAVE A CHOICE.

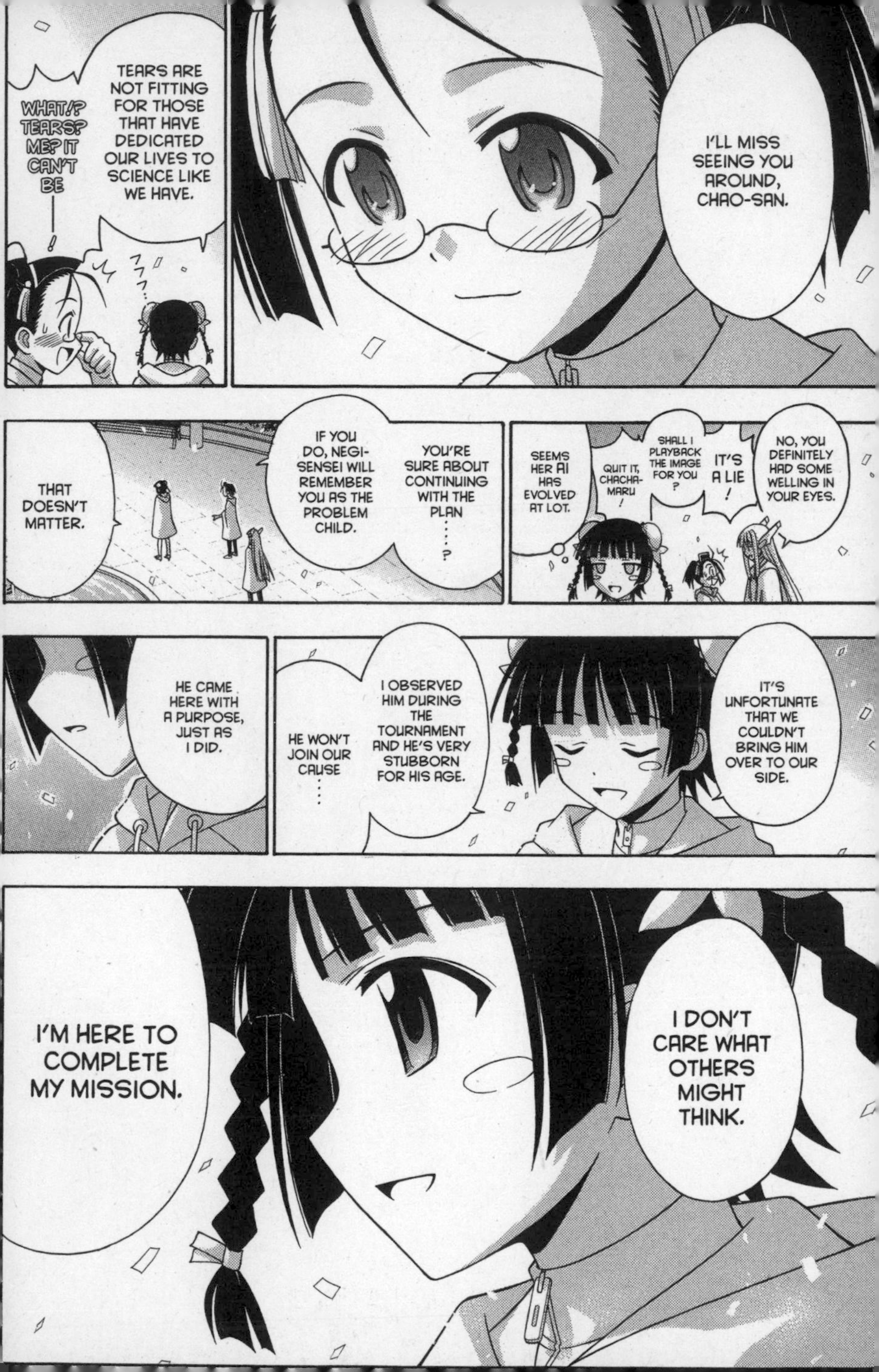
I'LL MISS SEEING YOU AROUND, CHAO-SAN.
TEARS ARE NOT FITTING FOR THOSE THAT HAVE DEDICATED OUR LIVES TO SCIENCE LIKE WE HAVE.
WHAT!? TEARS? ME? IT CAN'T BE —!
NO, YOU DEFINITELY HAD SOME WELLING IN YOUR EYES.
IT'S A LIE!
SHALL I PLAYBACK THE IMAGE FOR YOU?
QUIT IT, CHACHAMARU!
SEEMS HER AI HAS EVOLVED AT LOT.
YOU'RE SURE ABOUT CONTINUING WITH THE PLAN.....?
IF YOU DO, NEGI-SENSEI WILL REMEMBER YOU AS THE PROBLEM CHILD.
THAT DOESN'T MATTER.
IT'S UNFORTUNATE THAT WE COULDN'T BRING HIM OVER TO OUR SIDE.
I OBSERVED HIM DURING THE TOURNAMENT AND HE'S VERY STUBBORN FOR HIS AGE.
HE WON'T JOIN OUR CAUSE.....
HE CAME HERE WITH A PURPOSE, JUST AS I DID.
I DON'T CARE WHAT OTHERS MIGHT THINK.
I'M HERE TO COMPLETE MY MISSION.

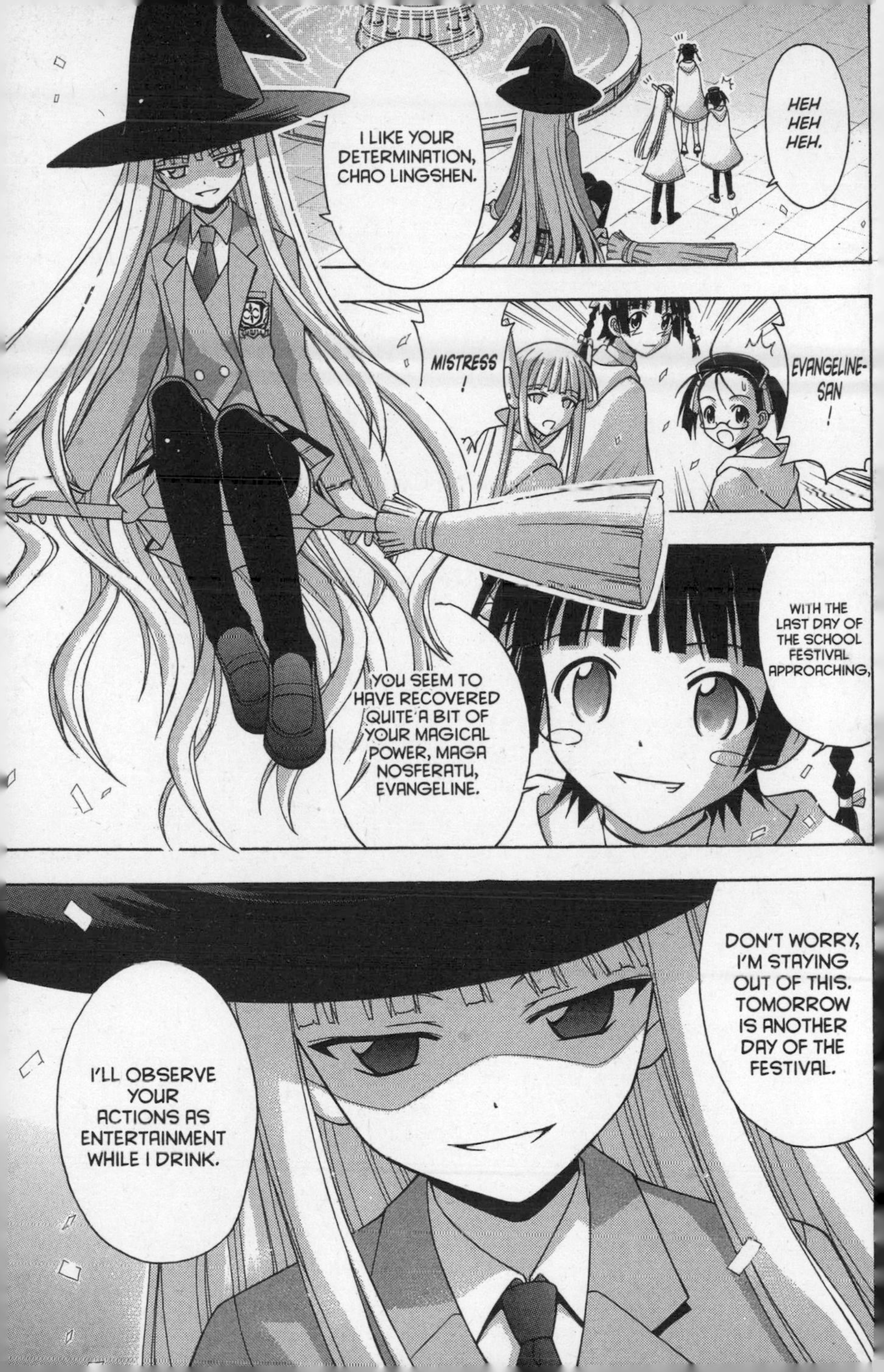
HEH HEH HEH.
EVANGELINE-SAN!
MISTRESS!
WITH THE LAST DAY OF THE SCHOOL FESTIVAL APPROACHING,
YOU SEEM TO HAVE RECOVERED QUITE A BIT OF YOUR MAGICAL POWER, MAGA NOSFERATU, EVANGELINE.
I LIKE YOUR DETERMINATION, CHAO LINGSHEN.
DON'T WORRY, I'M STAYING OUT OF THIS. TOMORROW IS ANOTHER DAY OF THE FESTIVAL.
I'LL OBSERVE YOUR ACTIONS AS ENTERTAINMENT WHILE I DRINK.

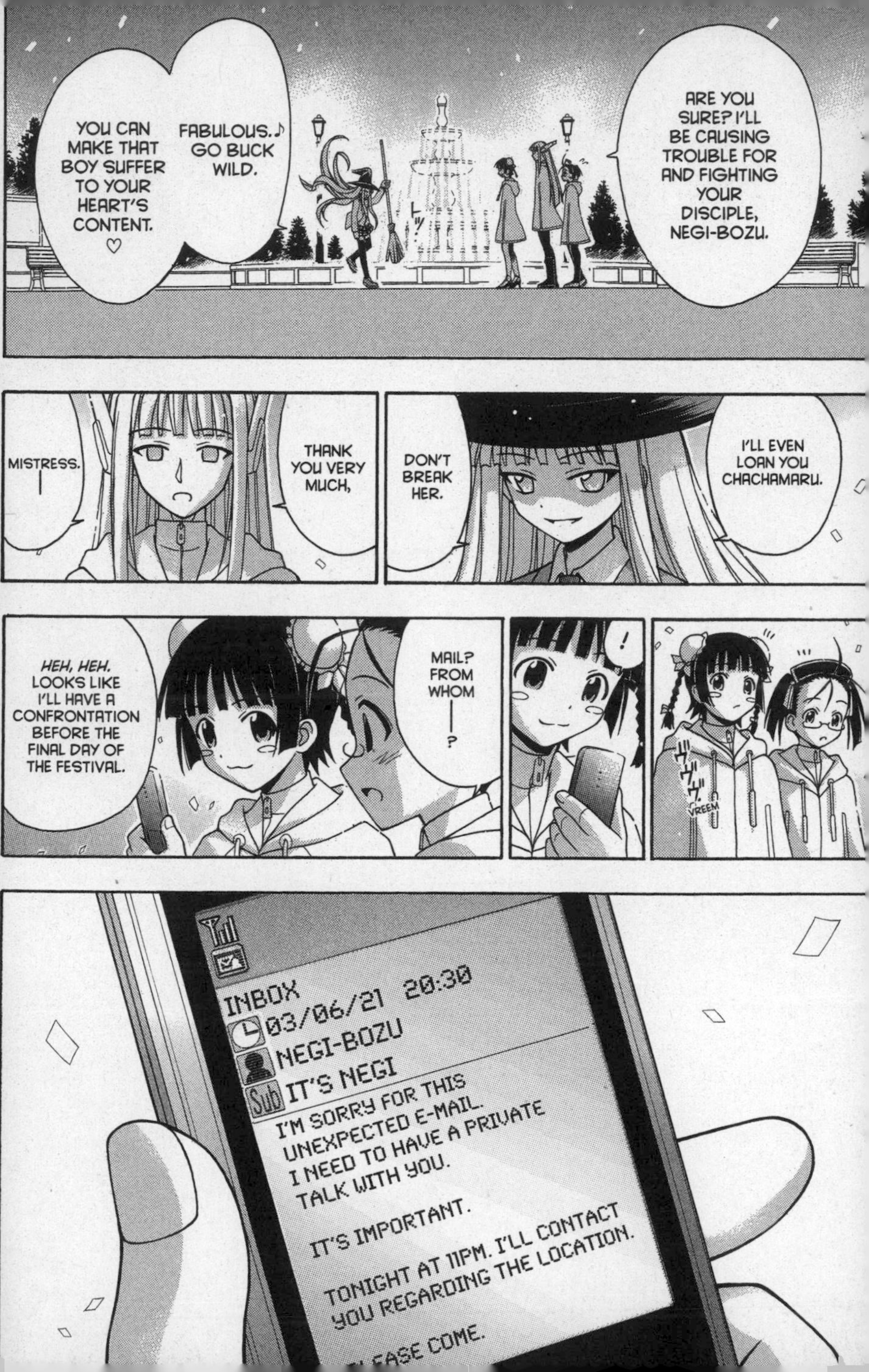
ARE YOU SURE? I'LL BE CAUSING TROUBLE FOR AND FIGHTING YOUR DISCIPLE, NEGI-BOZU.
FABULOUS.♪ GO BUCK WILD.
YOU CAN MAKE THAT BOY SUFFER TO YOUR HEART'S CONTENT. ♡
I'LL EVEN LOAN YOU CHACHAMARU.
DON'T BREAK HER.
THANK YOU VERY MUCH,
MISTRESS.
VREEM
!
MAIL? FROM WHOM—?
HEH, HEH. LOOKS LIKE I'LL HAVE A CONFRONTATION BEFORE THE FINAL DAY OF THE FESTIVAL.
INBOX
03/06/21 20:30
NEGI-BOZU
Sub IT'S NEGI
I'M SORRY FOR THIS UNEXPECTED E-MAIL. I NEED TO HAVE A PRIVATE TALK WITH YOU.
IT'S IMPORTANT.
TONIGHT AT 11PM. I'LL CONTACT YOU REGARDING THE LOCATION.
LEASE COME.

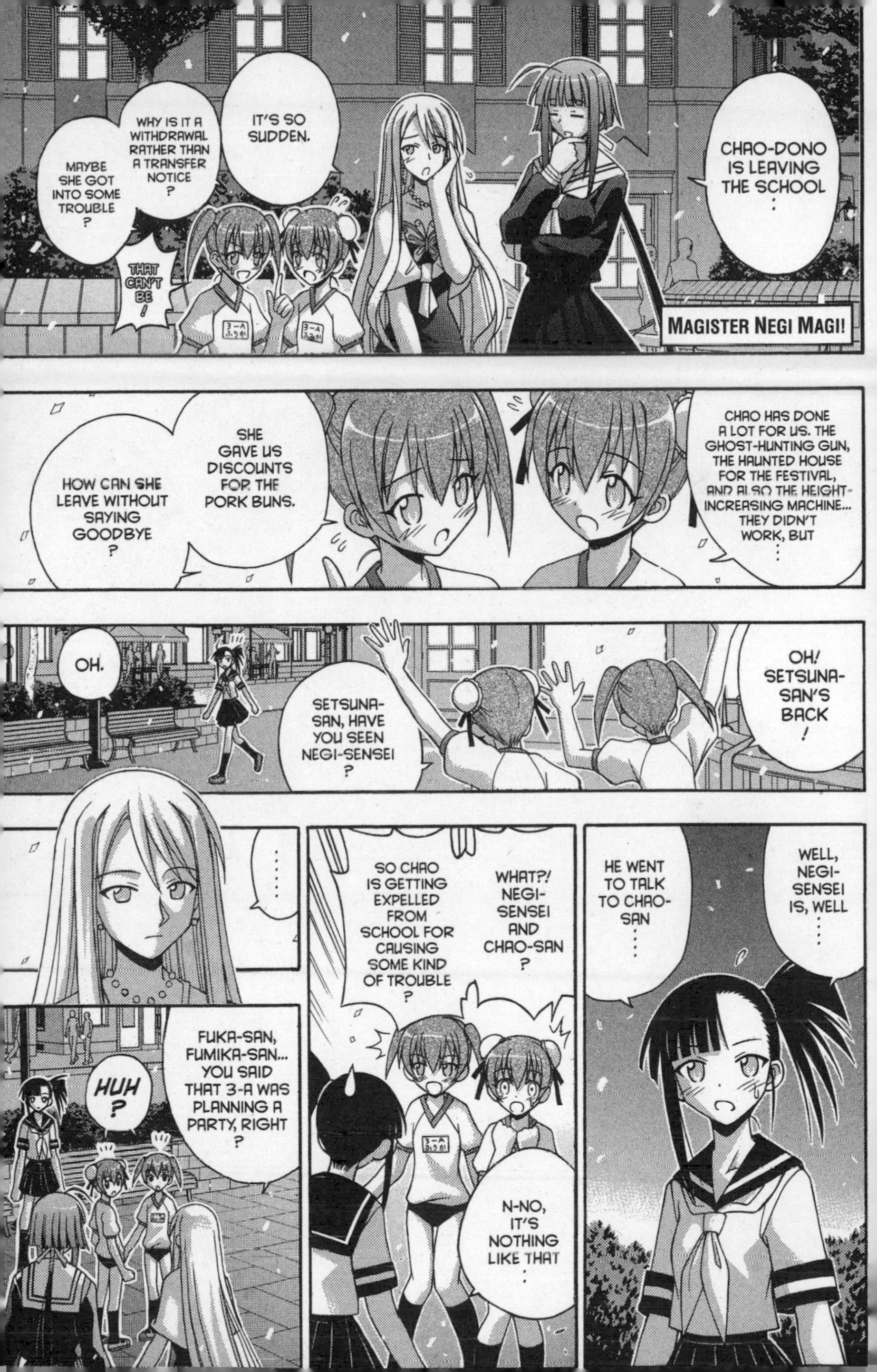
CHAO-DONO IS LEAVING THE SCHOOL...
IT'S SO SUDDEN.
WHY IS IT A WITHDRAWAL RATHER THAN A TRANSFER NOTICE?
MAYBE SHE GOT INTO SOME TROUBLE?
THAT CAN'T BE!
MAGISTER NEGI MAGI!
CHAO HAS DONE A LOT FOR US. THE GHOST-HUNTING GUN, THE HAUNTED HOUSE FOR THE FESTIVAL, AND ALSO THE HEIGHT-INCREASING MACHINE... THEY DIDN'T WORK, BUT...
SHE GAVE US DISCOUNTS FOR THE PORK BUNS.
HOW CAN SHE LEAVE WITHOUT SAYING GOODBYE?
OH! SETSUNA-SAN'S BACK!
SETSUNA-SAN, HAVE YOU SEEN NEGI-SENSEI?
OH.
WELL, NEGI-SENSEI IS, WELL...
HE WENT TO TALK TO CHAO-SAN...
WHAT?! NEGI-SENSEI AND CHAO-SAN?
SO CHAO IS GETTING EXPELLED FROM SCHOOL FOR CAUSING SOME KIND OF TROUBLE?
N-NO, IT'S NOTHING LIKE THAT...
.....
FUKA-SAN, FUMIKA-SAN... YOU SAID THAT 3-A WAS PLANNING A PARTY, RIGHT?
HUH?

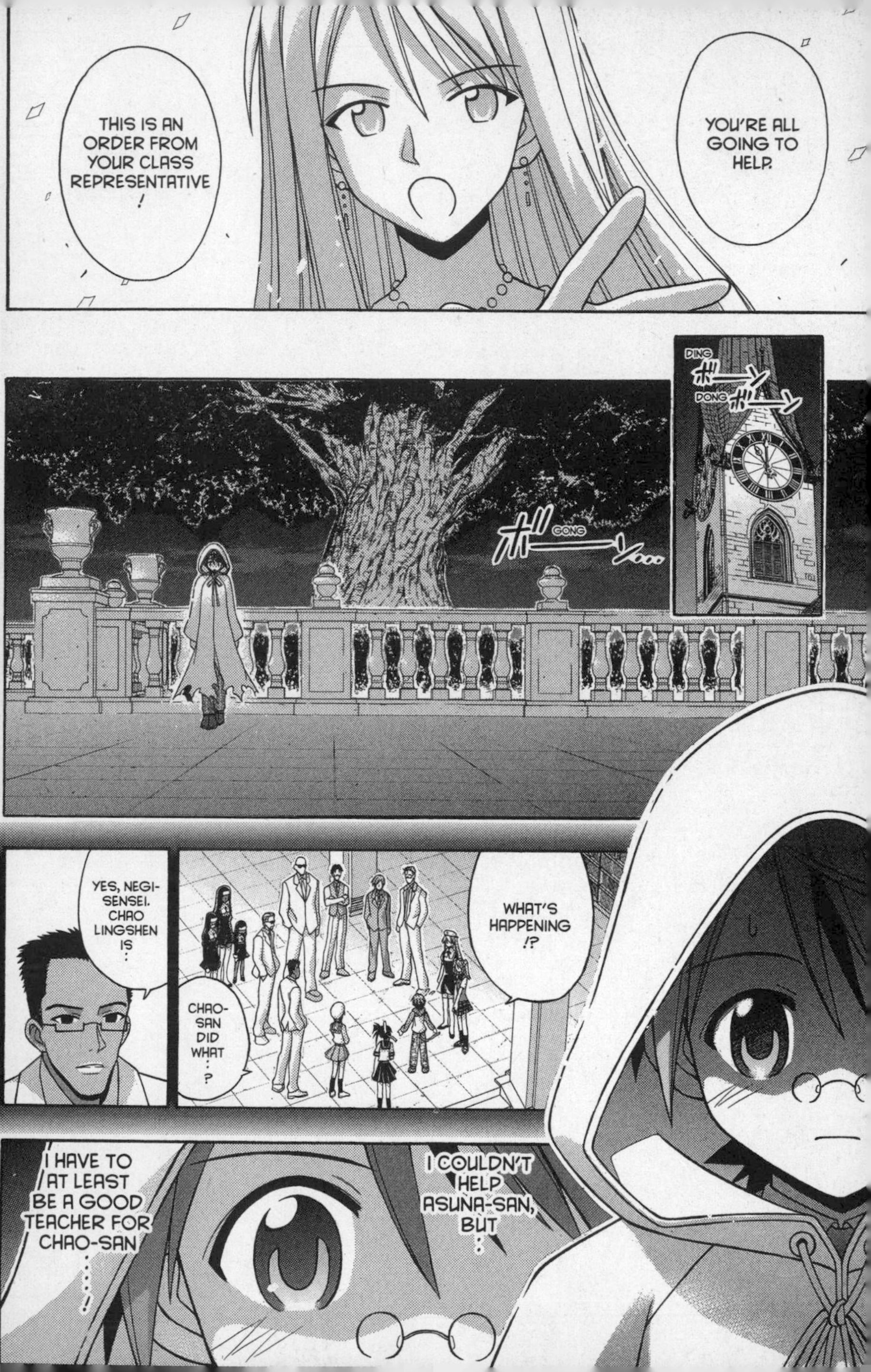
YOU'RE ALL GOING TO HELP.
THIS IS AN ORDER FROM YOUR CLASS REPRESENTATIVE!
DING
ボーン
DONG
ボーン
GONG
ボーン…
WHAT'S HAPPENING!?
CHAO-SAN DID WHAT...?
YES, NEGI-SENSEI. CHAO LINGSHEN IS...
I COULDN'T HELP ASUNA-SAN, BUT...
I HAVE TO AT LEAST BE A GOOD TEACHER FOR CHAO-SAN...!

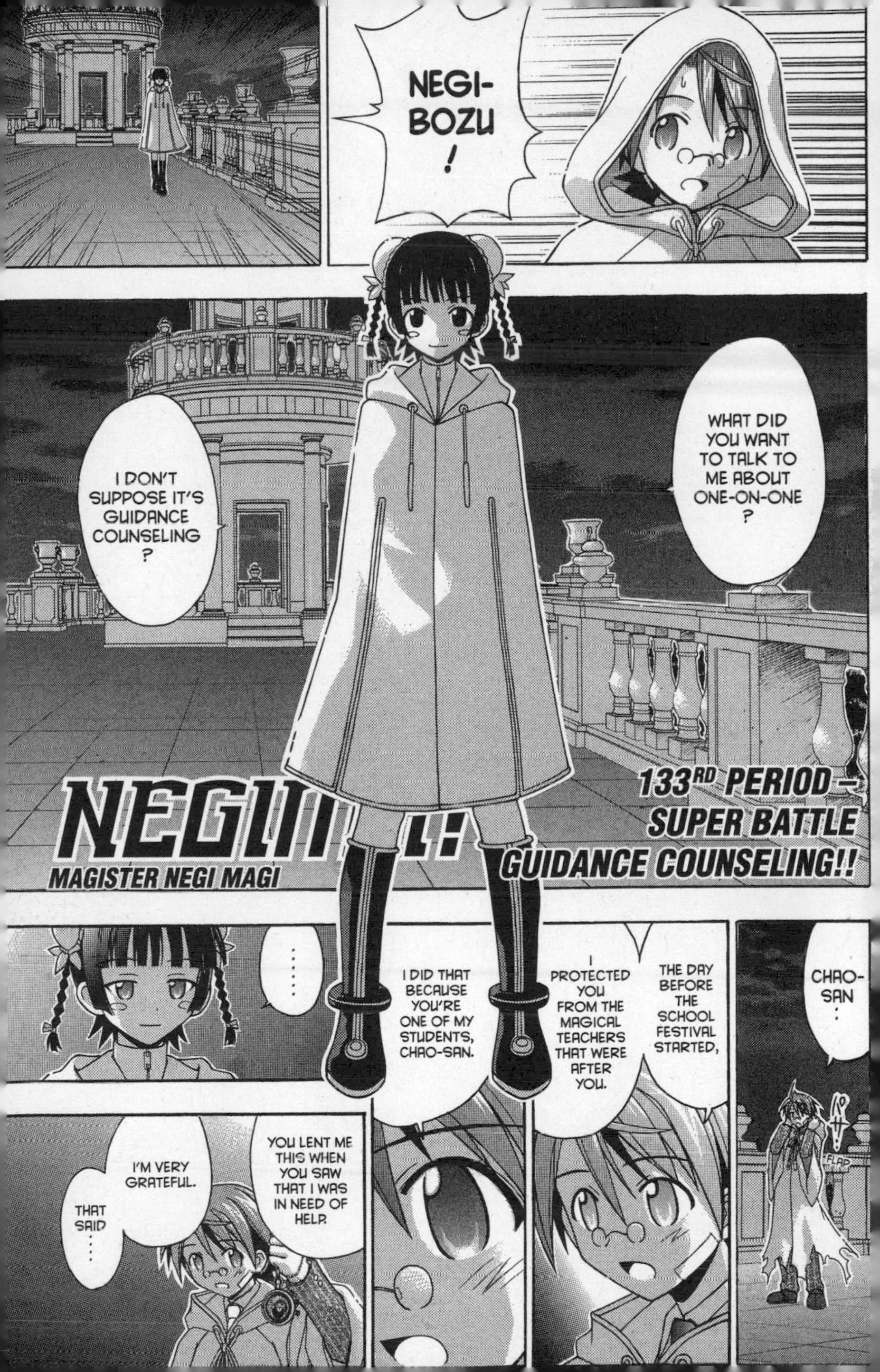
NEGI-BOZU!
WHAT DID YOU WANT TO TALK TO ME ABOUT ONE-ON-ONE?
I DON'T SUPPOSE IT'S GUIDANCE COUNSELING?
133RD PERIOD – SUPER BATTLE GUIDANCE COUNSELING!!
MAGISTER NEGI MAGI
CHAO-SAN...
FLAP
THE DAY BEFORE THE SCHOOL FESTIVAL STARTED,
I PROTECTED YOU FROM THE MAGICAL TEACHERS THAT WERE AFTER YOU.
I DID THAT BECAUSE YOU'RE ONE OF MY STUDENTS, CHAO-SAN.
......
YOU LENT ME THIS WHEN YOU SAW THAT I WAS IN NEED OF HELP.
I'M VERY GRATEFUL.
THAT SAID...

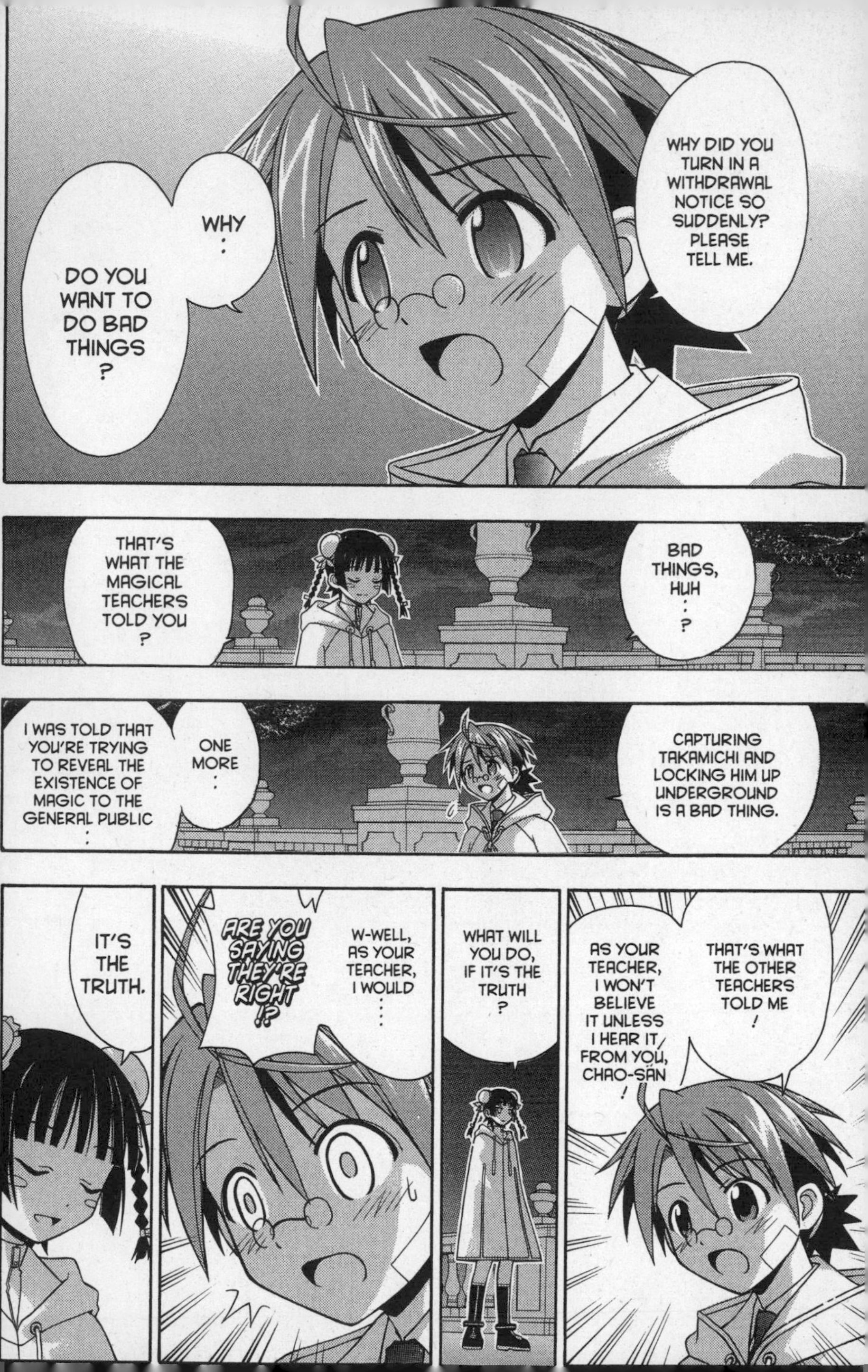
WHY DID YOU TURN IN A WITHDRAWAL NOTICE SO SUDDENLY? PLEASE TELL ME.
WHY... DO YOU WANT TO DO BAD THINGS?
BAD THINGS, HUH...?
THAT'S WHAT THE MAGICAL TEACHERS TOLD YOU?
CAPTURING TAKAMICHI AND LOCKING HIM UP UNDERGROUND IS A BAD THING.
ONE MORE...
I WAS TOLD THAT YOU'RE TRYING TO REVEAL THE EXISTENCE OF MAGIC TO THE GENERAL PUBLIC...
THAT'S WHAT THE OTHER TEACHERS TOLD ME!
AS YOUR TEACHER, I WON'T BELIEVE IT UNLESS I HEAR IT FROM YOU, CHAO-SAN!
WHAT WILL YOU DO, IF IT'S THE TRUTH?
W-WELL, AS YOUR TEACHER, I WOULD....
ARE YOU SAYING THEY'RE RIGHT!?
IT'S THE TRUTH.

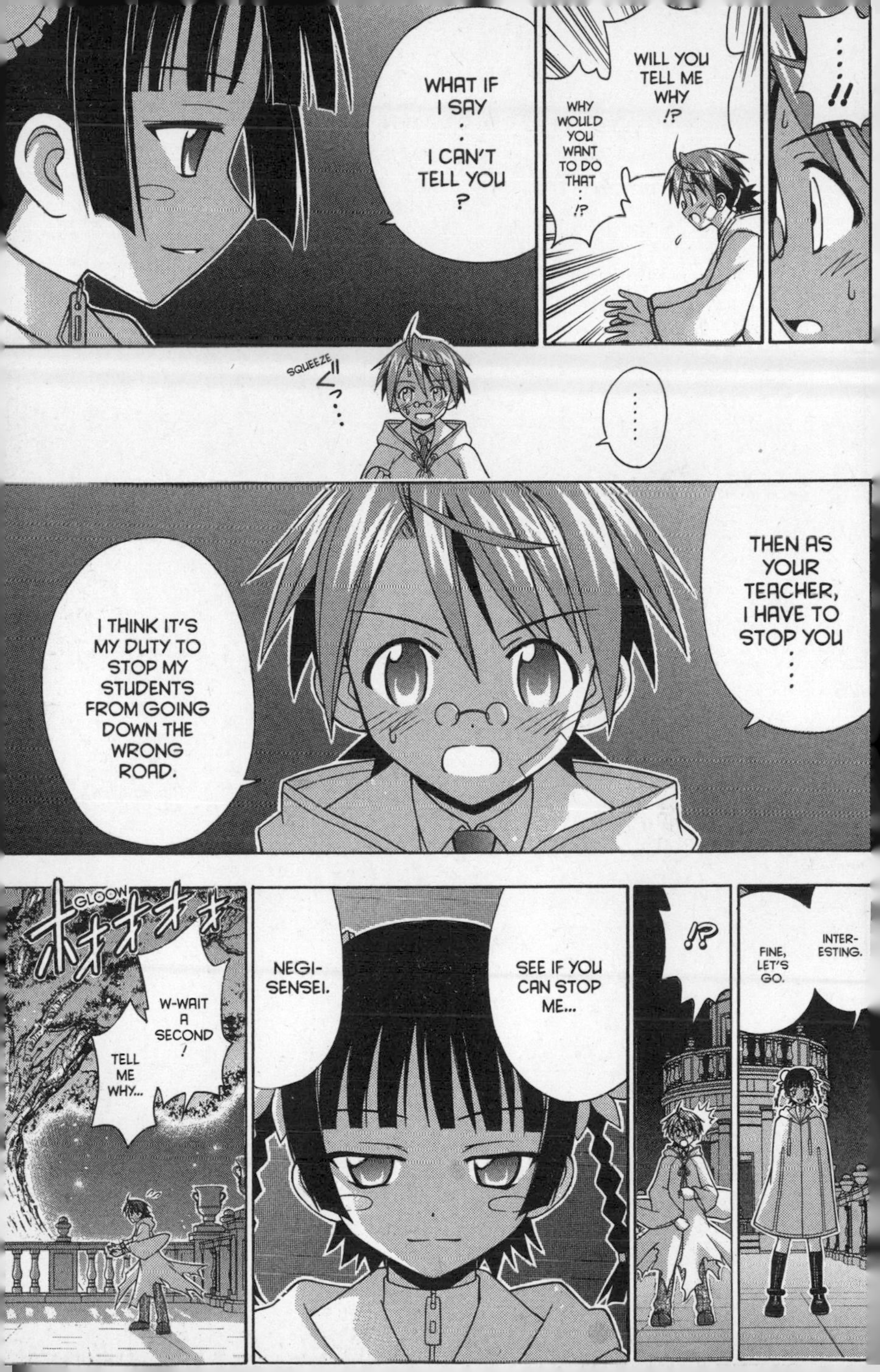
......!!
WILL YOU TELL ME WHY !?
WHY WOULD YOU WANT TO DO THAT ...!?
WHAT IF I SAY... I CAN'T TELL YOU?
......
SQUEEZE
...
THEN AS YOUR TEACHER, I HAVE TO STOP YOU...
I THINK IT'S MY DUTY TO STOP MY STUDENTS FROM GOING DOWN THE WRONG ROAD.
INTER-ESTING.
FINE, LET'S GO.
!?
SEE IF YOU CAN STOP ME...
NEGI-SENSEI.
ホオオオオ
GLOOW
W-WAIT A SECOND!
TELL ME WHY...

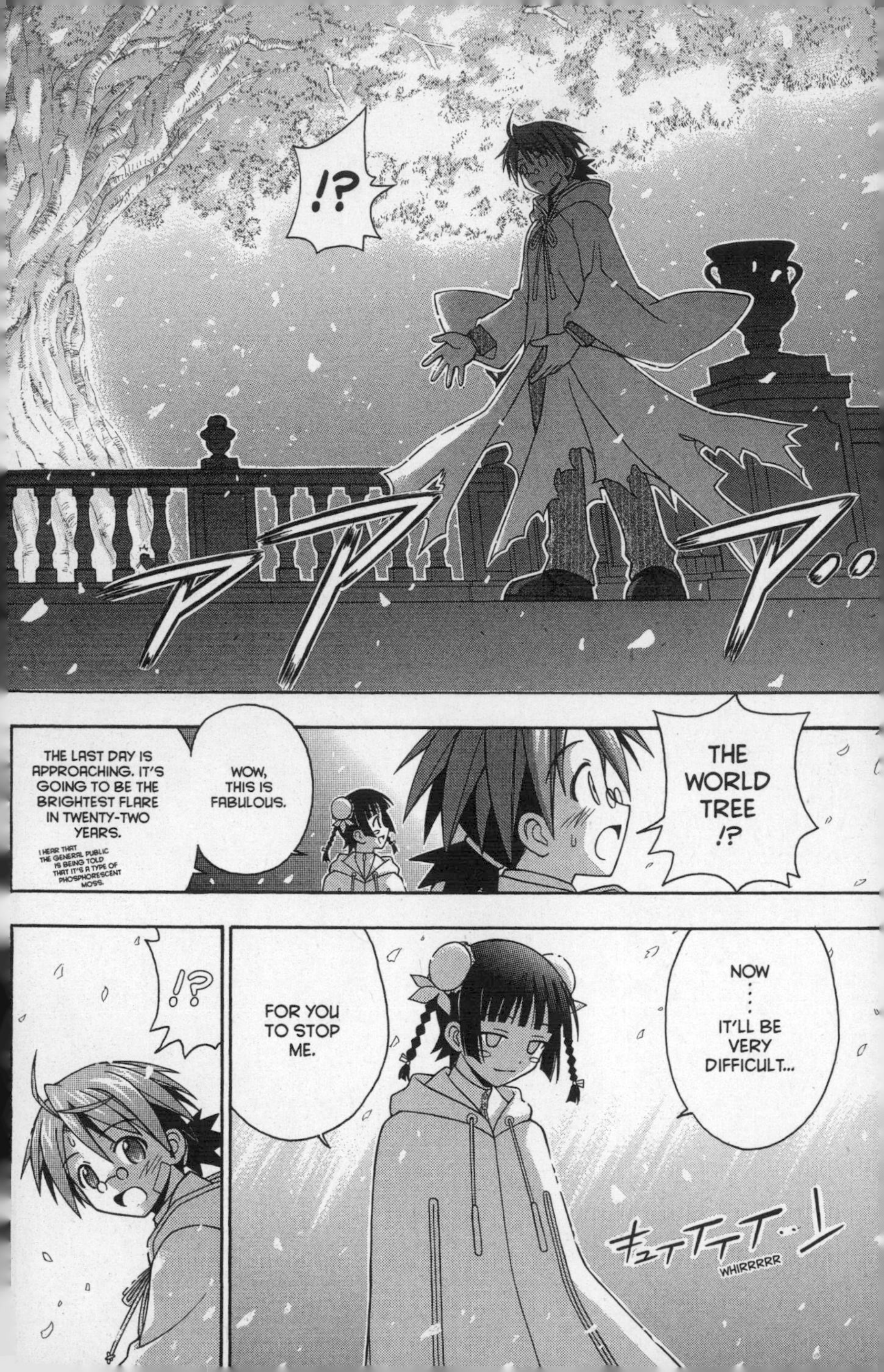
!?
THE WORLD TREE !?
WOW, THIS IS FABULOUS.
THE LAST DAY IS APPROACHING. IT'S GOING TO BE THE BRIGHTEST FLARE IN TWENTY-TWO YEARS.
I HEAR THAT THE GENERAL PUBLIC IS BEING TOLD THAT IT'S A TYPE OF PHOSPHORESCENT MOSS.
NOW . . . IT'LL BE VERY DIFFICULT...
FOR YOU TO STOP ME.
WHIRRRRR
!?

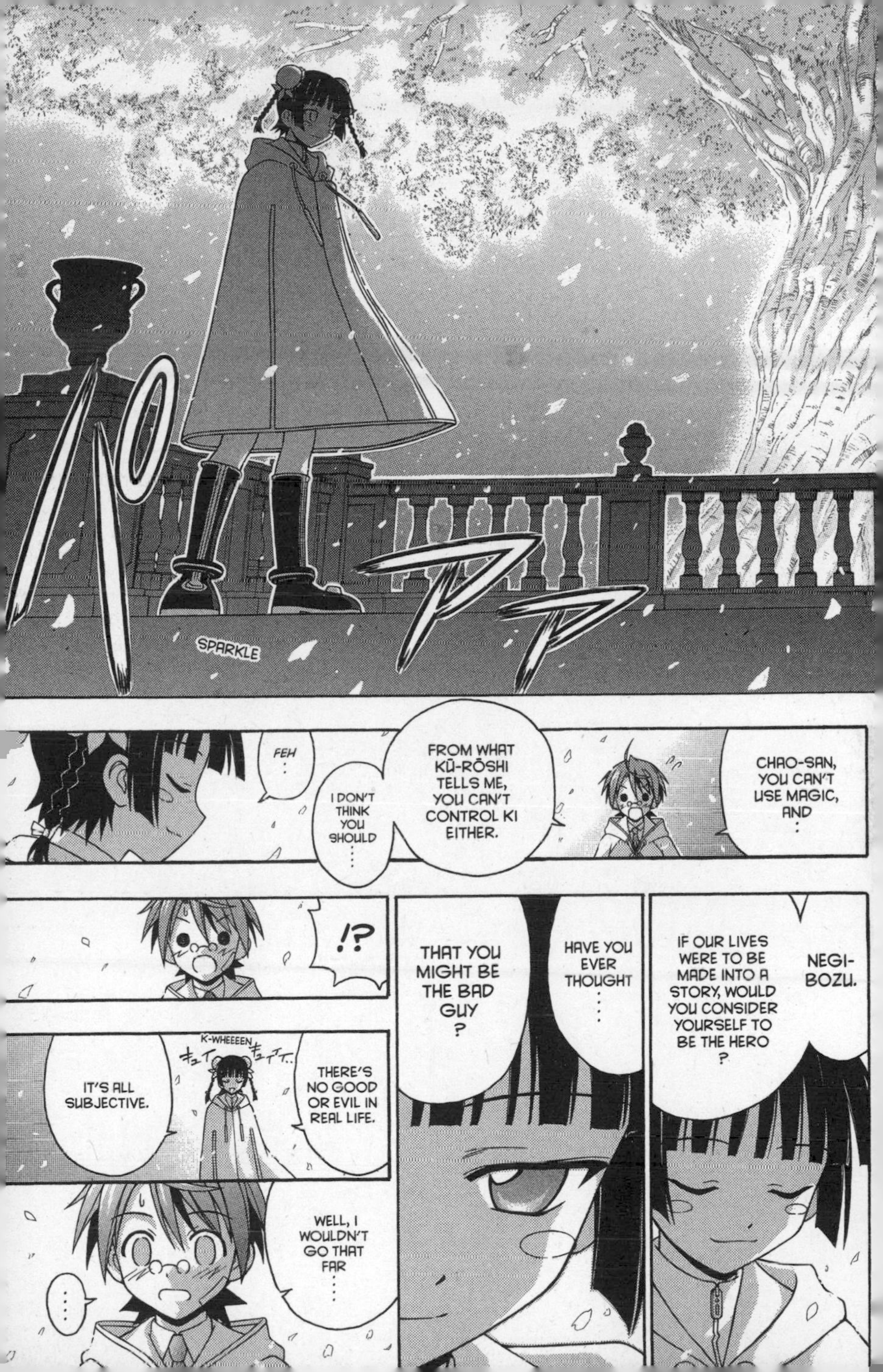
SPARKLE
CHAO-SAN, YOU CAN'T USE MAGIC, AND ...
FROM WHAT KŪ-RŌSHI TELLS ME, YOU CAN'T CONTROL KI EITHER.
I DON'T THINK YOU SHOULD ....
FEH ...
NEGI-BOZU.
IF OUR LIVES WERE TO BE MADE INTO A STORY, WOULD YOU CONSIDER YOURSELF TO BE THE HERO ?
HAVE YOU EVER THOUGHT ....
THAT YOU MIGHT BE THE BAD GUY ?
!?
THERE'S NO GOOD OR EVIL IN REAL LIFE.
K-WHEEEEN
IT'S ALL SUBJECTIVE.
WELL, I WOULDN'T GO THAT FAR ....
....

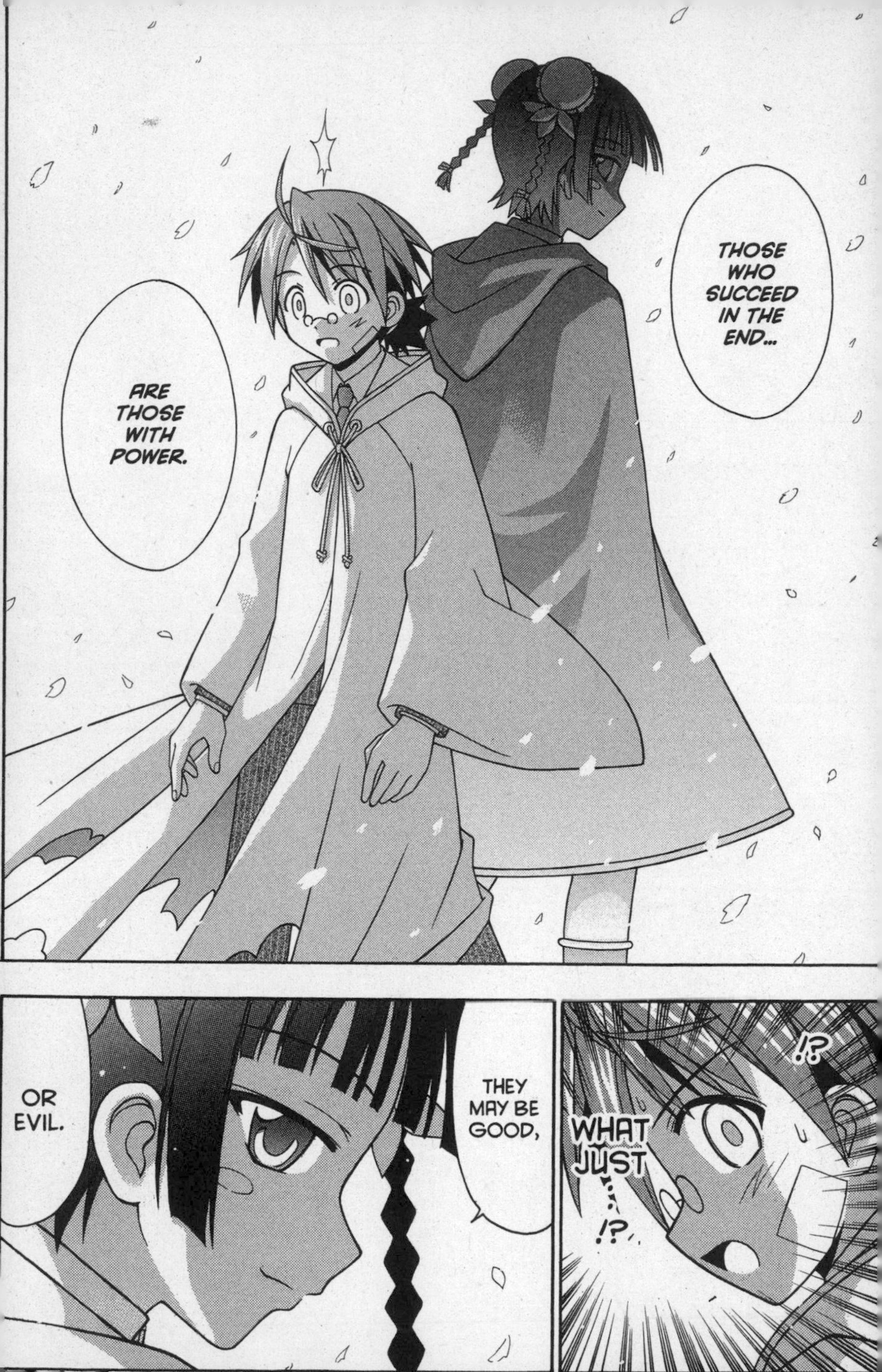
THOSE WHO SUCCEED IN THE END...
ARE THOSE WITH POWER.
!?
WHAT JUST ...!?
THEY MAY BE GOOD,
OR EVIL.

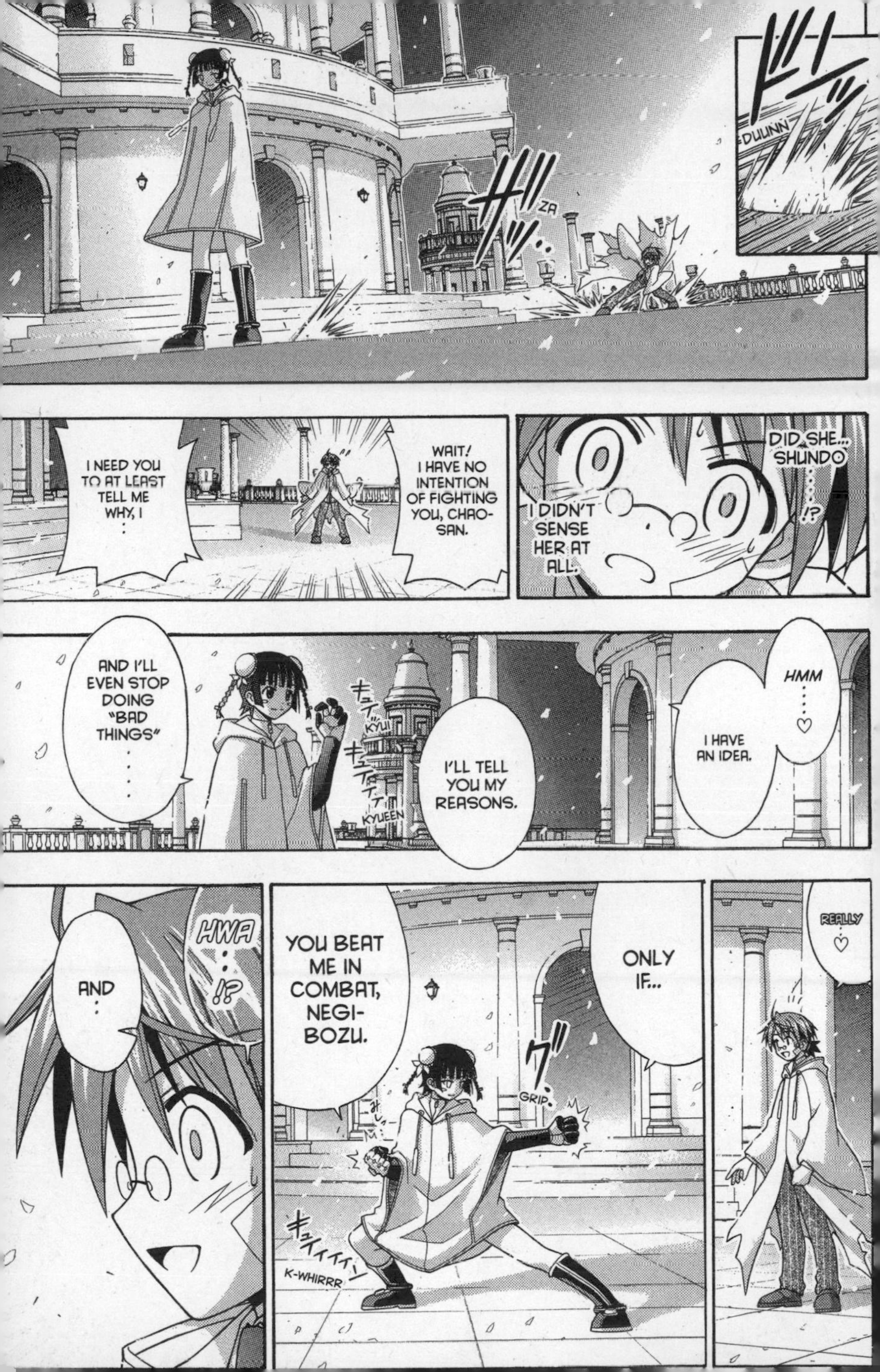
DUUNN
ZA
DID SHE... SHUNDO ...!?
I DIDN'T SENSE HER AT ALL.
WAIT! I HAVE NO INTENTION OF FIGHTING YOU, CHAO-SAN.
I NEED YOU TO AT LEAST TELL ME WHY, I ...
HMM ...♡
I HAVE AN IDEA.
I'LL TELL YOU MY REASONS.
KYUI
KYUEEN
AND I'LL EVEN STOP DOING "BAD THINGS" ...
REALLY ♡
ONLY IF...
YOU BEAT ME IN COMBAT, NEGI-BOZU.
GRIP
K-WHIRRR
HWA ...!?
AND ...

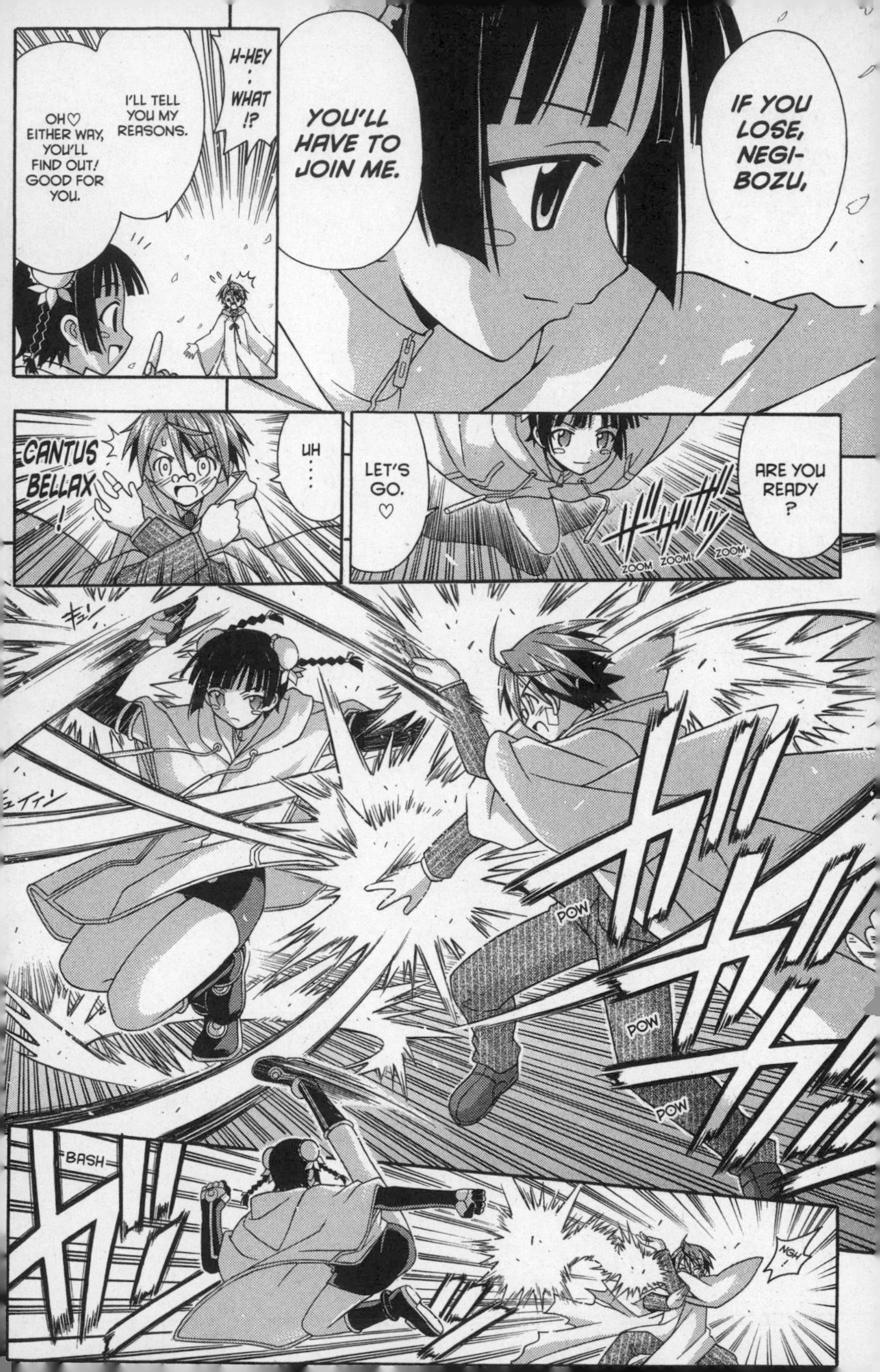
IF YOU LOSE, NEGI-BOZU,
YOU'LL HAVE TO JOIN ME.
H-HEY : WHAT !?
I'LL TELL YOU MY REASONS.
OH♡ EITHER WAY, YOU'LL FIND OUT! GOOD FOR YOU.
ARE YOU READY ?
ZOOM ZOOM ZOOM
LET'S GO. ♡
UH ....
CANTUS BELLAX !
POW
POW
POW
BASH
NGH !

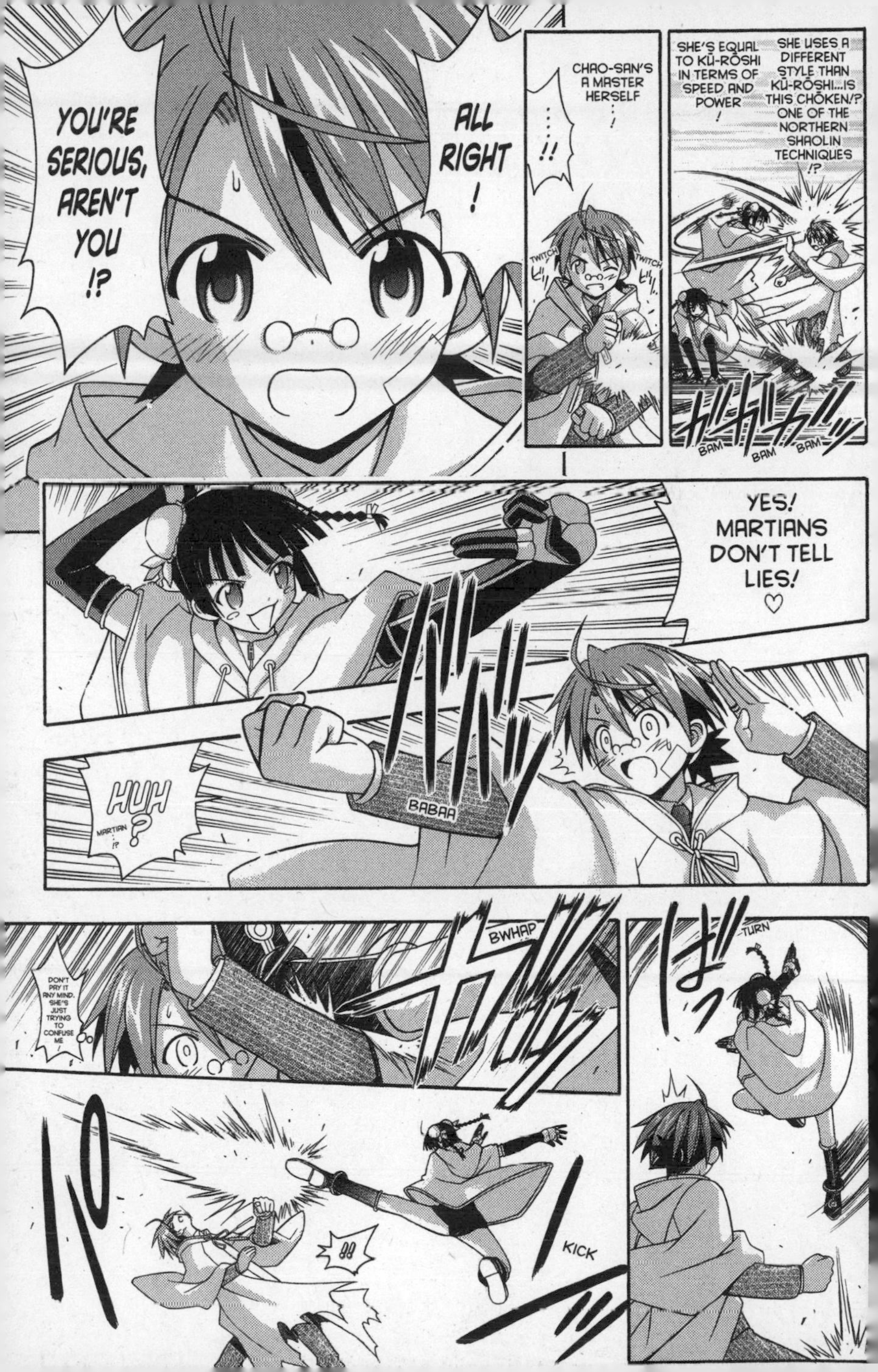
SHE USES A DIFFERENT STYLE THAN KŪ-RŌSHI...IS THIS CHŌKEN!? ONE OF THE NORTHERN SHAOLIN TECHNIQUES!?
SHE'S EQUAL TO KŪ-RŌSHI IN TERMS OF SPEED AND POWER!
BAM BAM BAM
CHAO-SAN'S A MASTER HERSELF...!
...!!
TWITCH TWITCH
ALL RIGHT!
YOU'RE SERIOUS, AREN'T YOU!?
YES! MARTIANS DON'T TELL LIES! ♡
BABAA
HUH?
MARTIAN...!?
TURN
BWHAP
DON'T PAY IT ANY MIND. SHE'S JUST TRYING TO CONFUSE ME!
KICK
!!

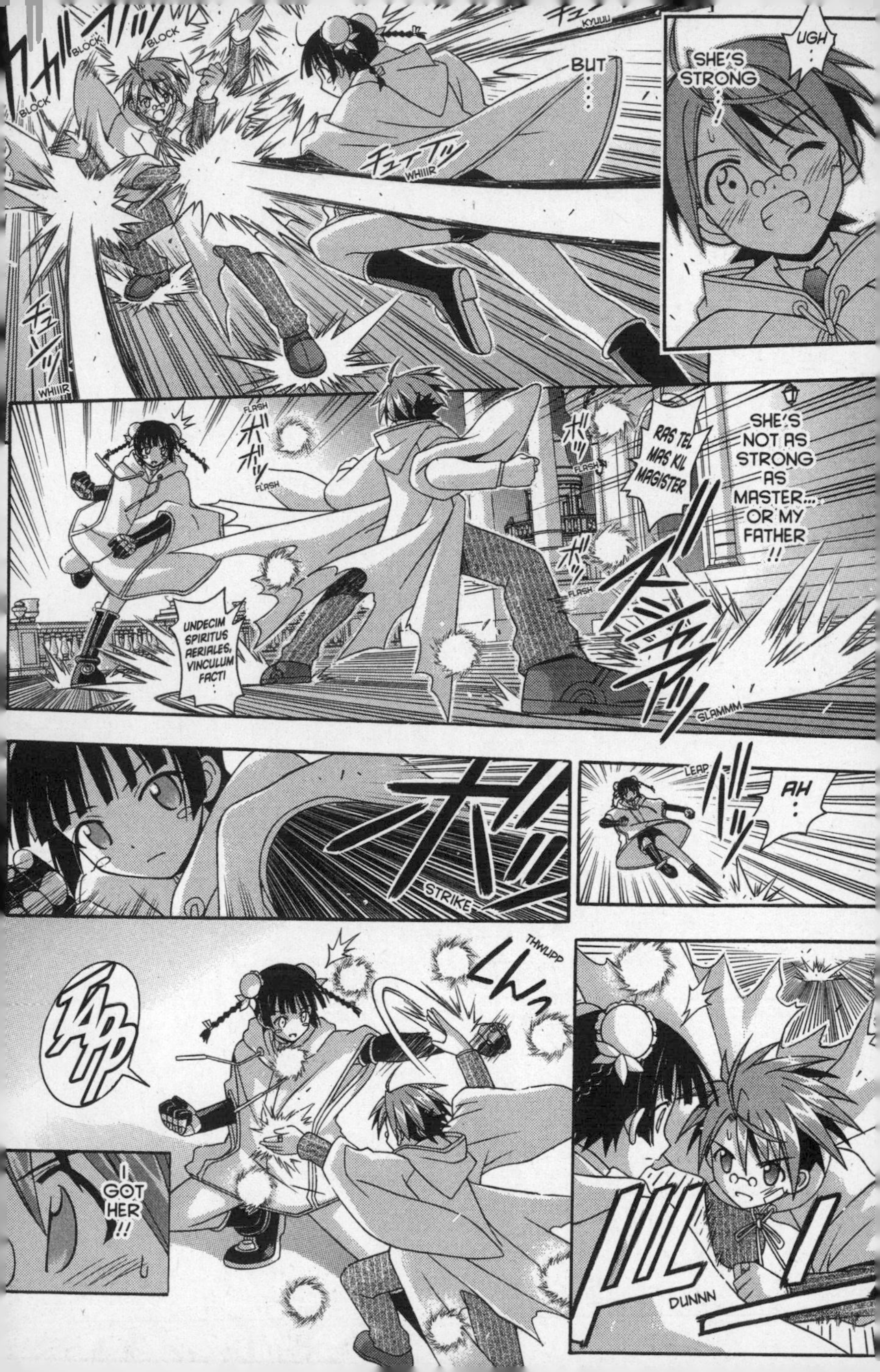
UGH ...
SHE'S STRONG ...!
KYUUU
BUT ......
BLOCK
BLOCK
BLOCK
WHIIIR
WHIIIR
SHE'S NOT AS STRONG AS MASTER... OR MY FATHER !!
RAS TEL MAS KIL MAGISTER
FLASH
FLASH
FLASH
FLASH
UNDECIM SPIRITUS AERIALES, VINCULUM FACTI
SLAMMM
AH ...
LEAP
STRIKE
DUNNN
THWUPP
TAP
I GOT HER !!

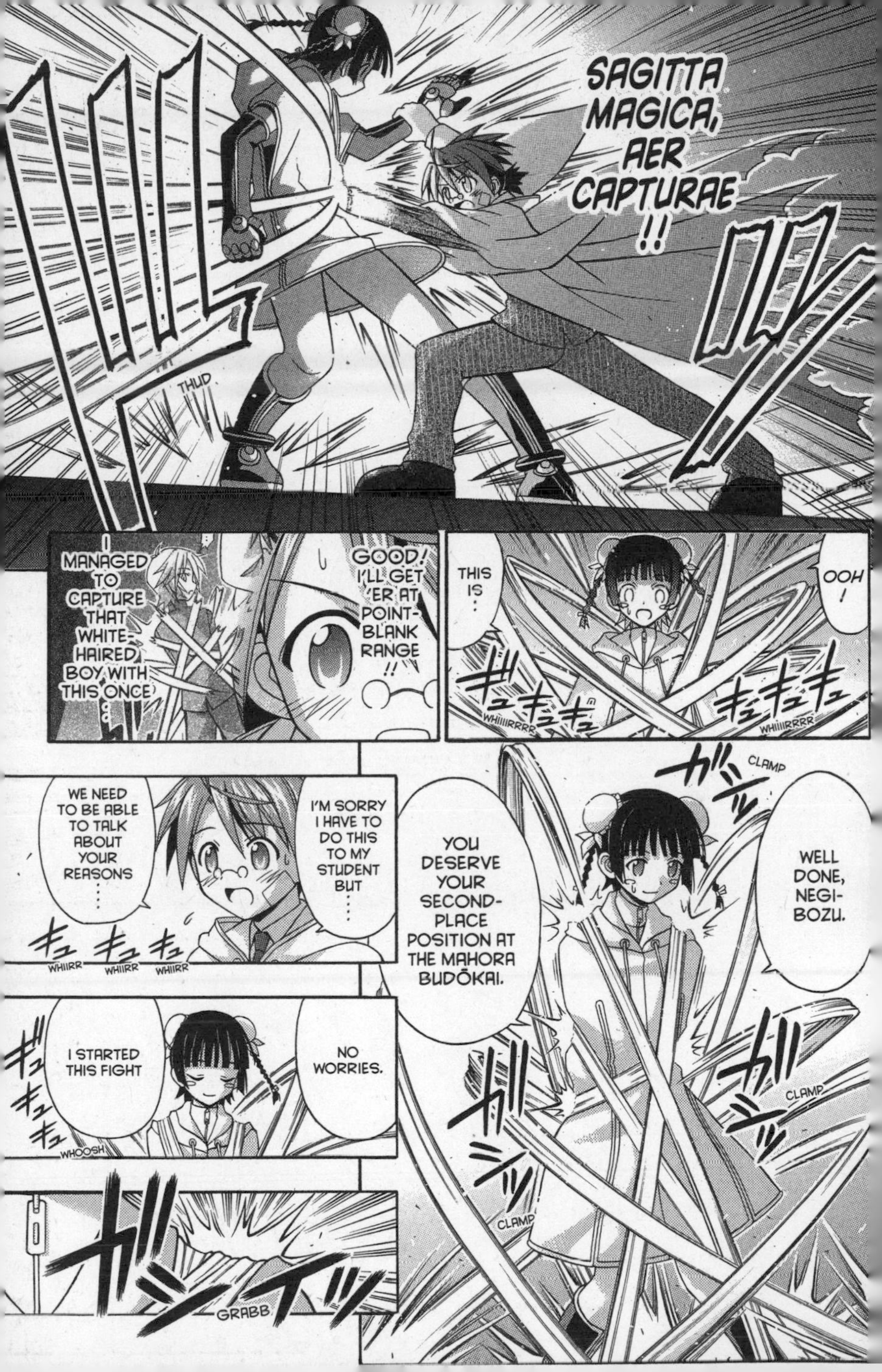
SAGITTA MAGICA, AER CAPTURAE!!
THUD
OOH!
THIS IS...
WHIIIIRRRR
WHIIIRRRR
GOOD! I'LL GET 'ER AT POINT-BLANK RANGE!!
I MANAGED TO CAPTURE THAT WHITE-HAIRED BOY WITH THIS ONCE...
CLAMP
WELL DONE, NEGI-BOZU.
YOU DESERVE YOUR SECOND-PLACE POSITION AT THE MAHORA BUDŌKAI.
CLAMP
CLAMP
I'M SORRY I HAVE TO DO THIS TO MY STUDENT BUT...
WE NEED TO BE ABLE TO TALK ABOUT YOUR REASONS...
WHIIRR
WHIIRR
WHIIRR
NO WORRIES.
I STARTED THIS FIGHT
WHOOSH
GRABB

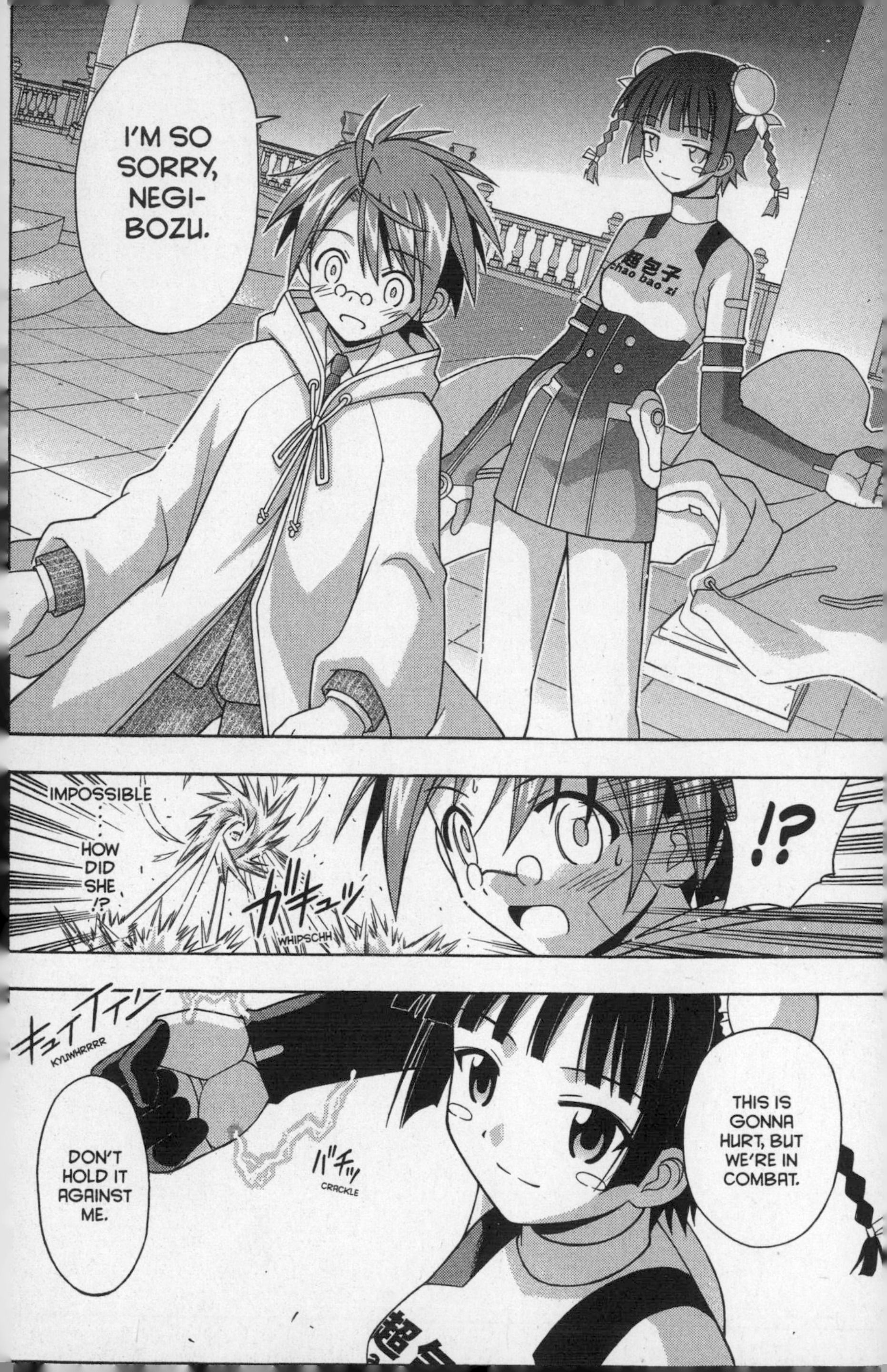

I'M SO SORRY, NEGI-BOZU.
chao bao zi
!?
ガギュッ
WHIPSCHH
IMPOSSIBLE... HOW DID SHE !?
THIS IS GONNA HURT, BUT WE'RE IN COMBAT.
バチッ
CRACKLE
DON'T HOLD IT AGAINST ME.
キュイイイン
KYUWHRRRR

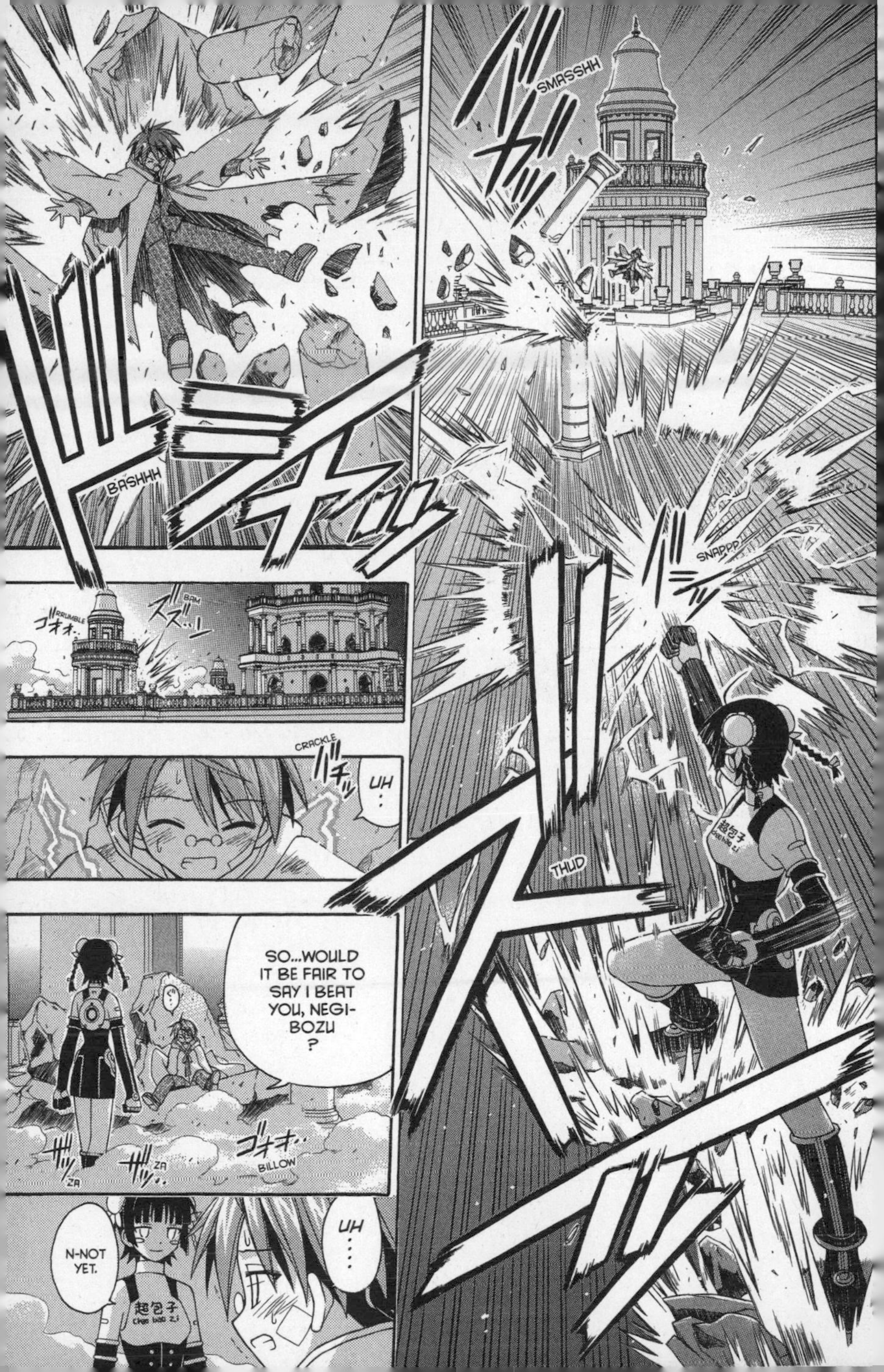
SMASSHH
SNAPPP
超包子
THUD
BASHHH
RRUMBLE
ゴオオ…
BAM
CRACKLE
UH …
SO...WOULD IT BE FAIR TO SAY I BEAT YOU, NEGI-BOZU ?
ゴオオ…
BILLOW
ZA
ZA
UH . . . .
N-NOT YET.
超包子

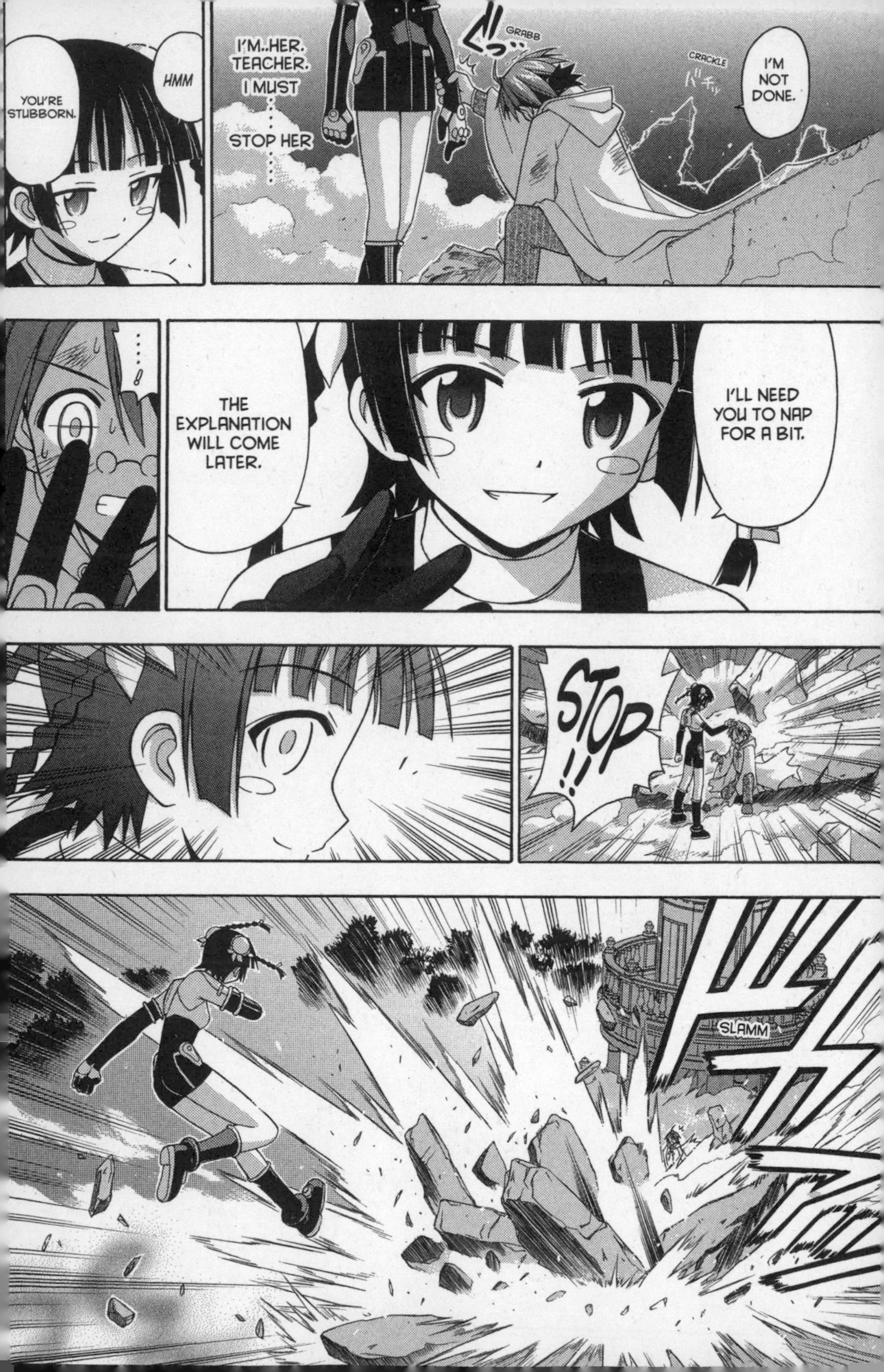
I'M NOT DONE.
CRACKLE
GRABB
I'M..HER. TEACHER. I MUST ... STOP HER ...
HMM
YOU'RE STUBBORN.
I'LL NEED YOU TO NAP FOR A BIT.
THE EXPLANATION WILL COME LATER.
...!
STOP!!
SLAMM

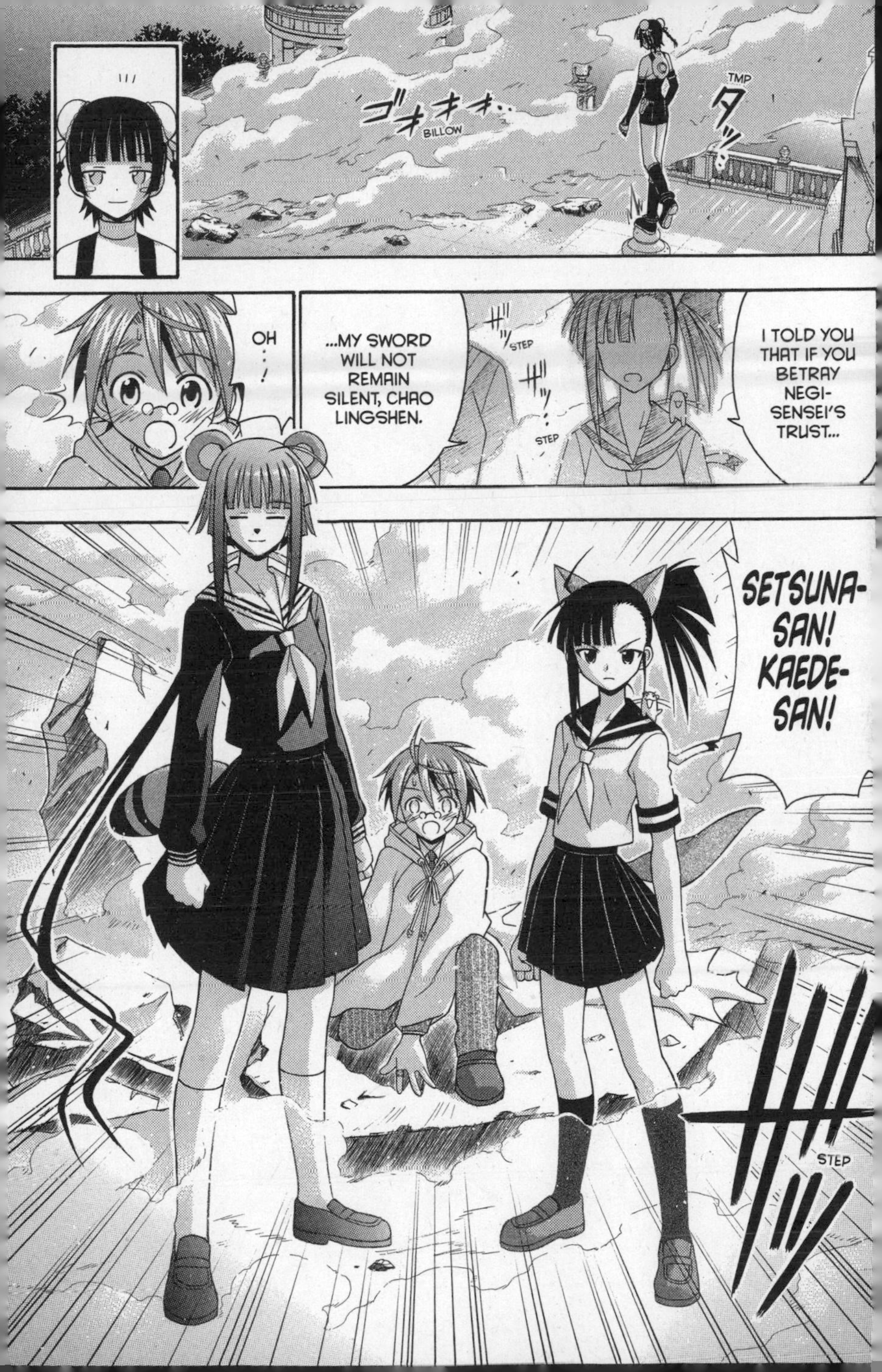
TMP
BILLOW
I TOLD YOU THAT IF YOU BETRAY NEGI-SENSEI'S TRUST...
STEP
STEP
...MY SWORD WILL NOT REMAIN SILENT, CHAO LINGSHEN.
OH...!
SETSUNA-SAN! KAEDE-SAN!
STEP

STUDENT NUMBER 19
CHAO LINGSHEN

BORN: DECEMBER 1, 1988
BLOOD TYPE: O
LIKES: WORLD DOMINATION
DISLIKES: WAR, CYCLES OF HATRED,
    UNILATERAL WORLD DOMINATION
    BY A SINGLE NATION
AFFILIATIONS: COOKING CLUB, CHINESE
    MARTIAL ARTS RESEARCH CLUB,
    ROBOT ENGINEERING RESEARCH
    CLUB, EASTERN MEDICINE
    RESEARCH CLUB, BIOENGINEERING
    RESEARCH CLUB, QUANTUM
    MECHANICS RESEARCH CLUB
    (UNIVERSITY)

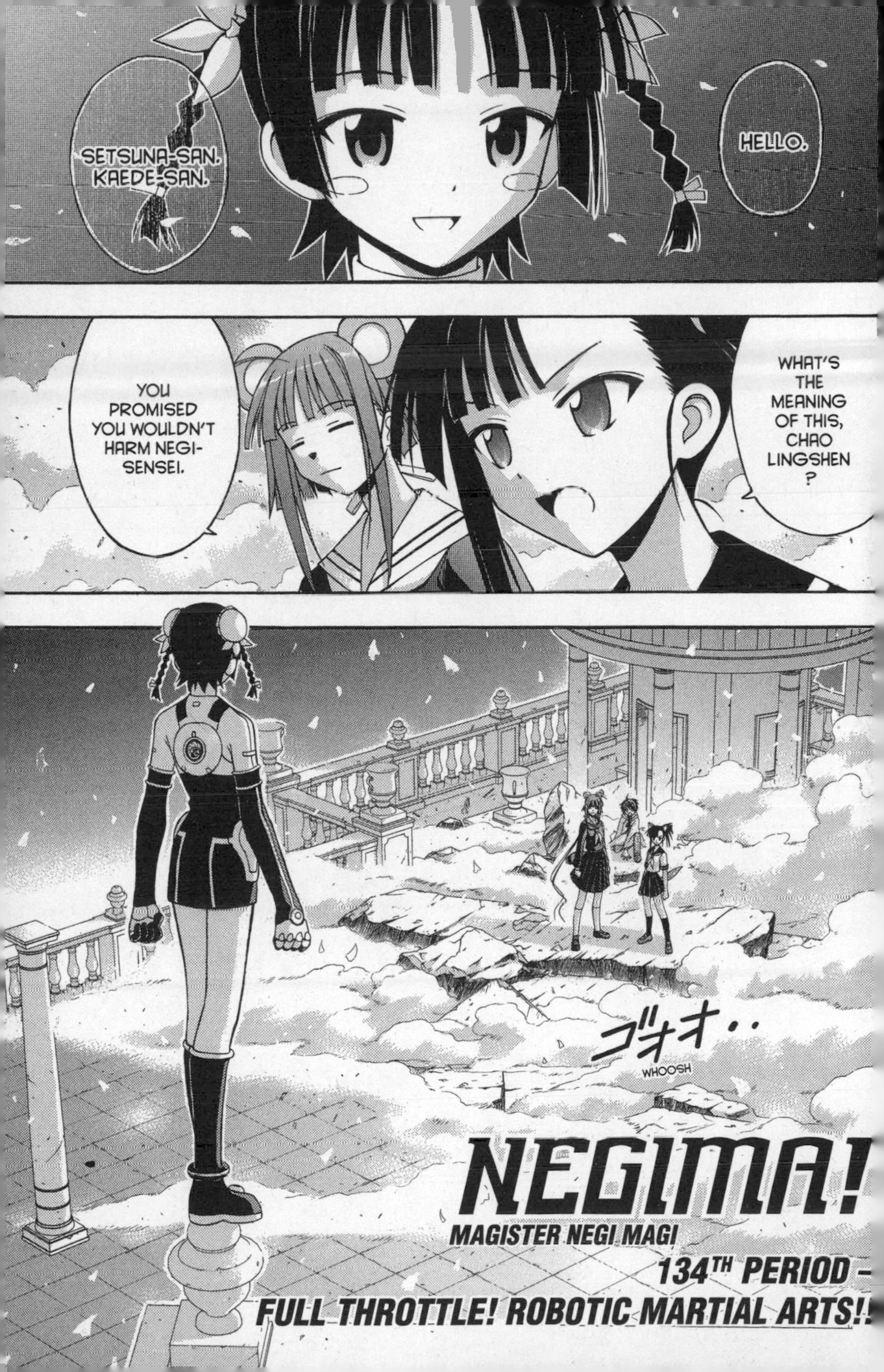
HELLO.
SETSUNA-SAN. KAEDE-SAN.
WHAT'S THE MEANING OF THIS, CHAO LINGSHEN?
YOU PROMISED YOU WOULDN'T HARM NEGI-SENSEI.
ゴオオ・・
WHOOSH
NEGIMA!
MAGISTER NEGI MAGI
134TH PERIOD –
FULL THROTTLE! ROBOTIC MARTIAL ARTS!!

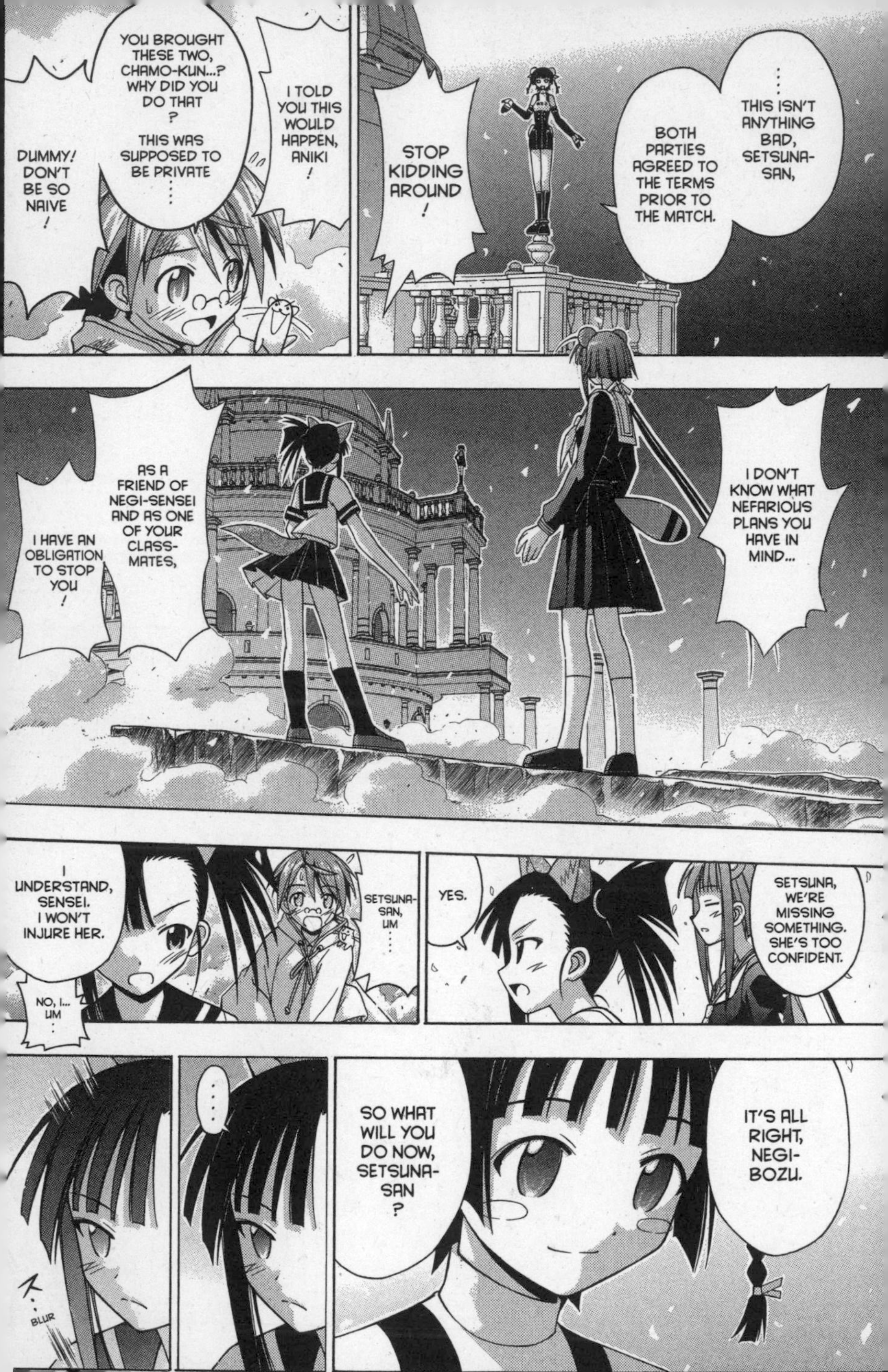
... THIS ISN'T ANYTHING BAD, SETSUNA-SAN,
BOTH PARTIES AGREED TO THE TERMS PRIOR TO THE MATCH.
STOP KIDDING AROUND!
I TOLD YOU THIS WOULD HAPPEN, ANIKI!
YOU BROUGHT THESE TWO, CHAMO-KUN...? WHY DID YOU DO THAT? THIS WAS SUPPOSED TO BE PRIVATE...
DUMMY! DON'T BE SO NAIVE!
I DON'T KNOW WHAT NEFARIOUS PLANS YOU HAVE IN MIND...
AS A FRIEND OF NEGI-SENSEI AND AS ONE OF YOUR CLASSMATES,
I HAVE AN OBLIGATION TO STOP YOU!
SETSUNA, WE'RE MISSING SOMETHING. SHE'S TOO CONFIDENT.
YES.
SETSUNA-SAN, UM...
I UNDERSTAND, SENSEI. I WON'T INJURE HER.
NO, I... UM...
IT'S ALL RIGHT, NEGI-BOZU.
SO WHAT WILL YOU DO NOW, SETSUNA-SAN?
...
BLUR

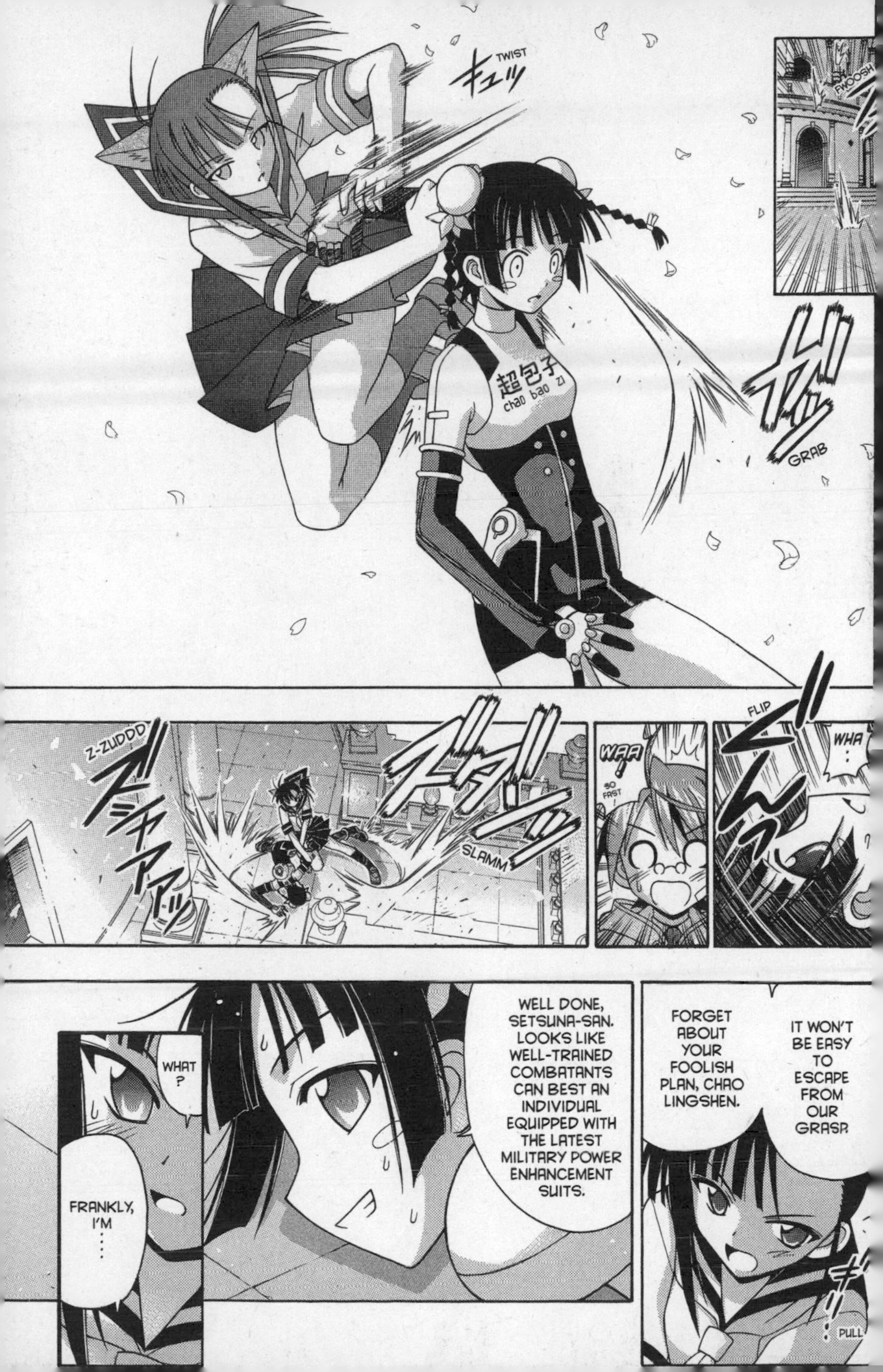

FWOOSH
TWIST
GRAB
FLIP
WHA...
WAA!
SO FAST!
SLAMM
Z-ZUDDD
IT WON'T BE EASY TO ESCAPE FROM OUR GRASP.
FORGET ABOUT YOUR FOOLISH PLAN, CHAO LINGSHEN.
PULL
WELL DONE, SETSUNA-SAN. LOOKS LIKE WELL-TRAINED COMBATANTS CAN BEST AN INDIVIDUAL EQUIPPED WITH THE LATEST MILITARY POWER ENHANCEMENT SUITS.
WHAT?
FRANKLY, I'M.....

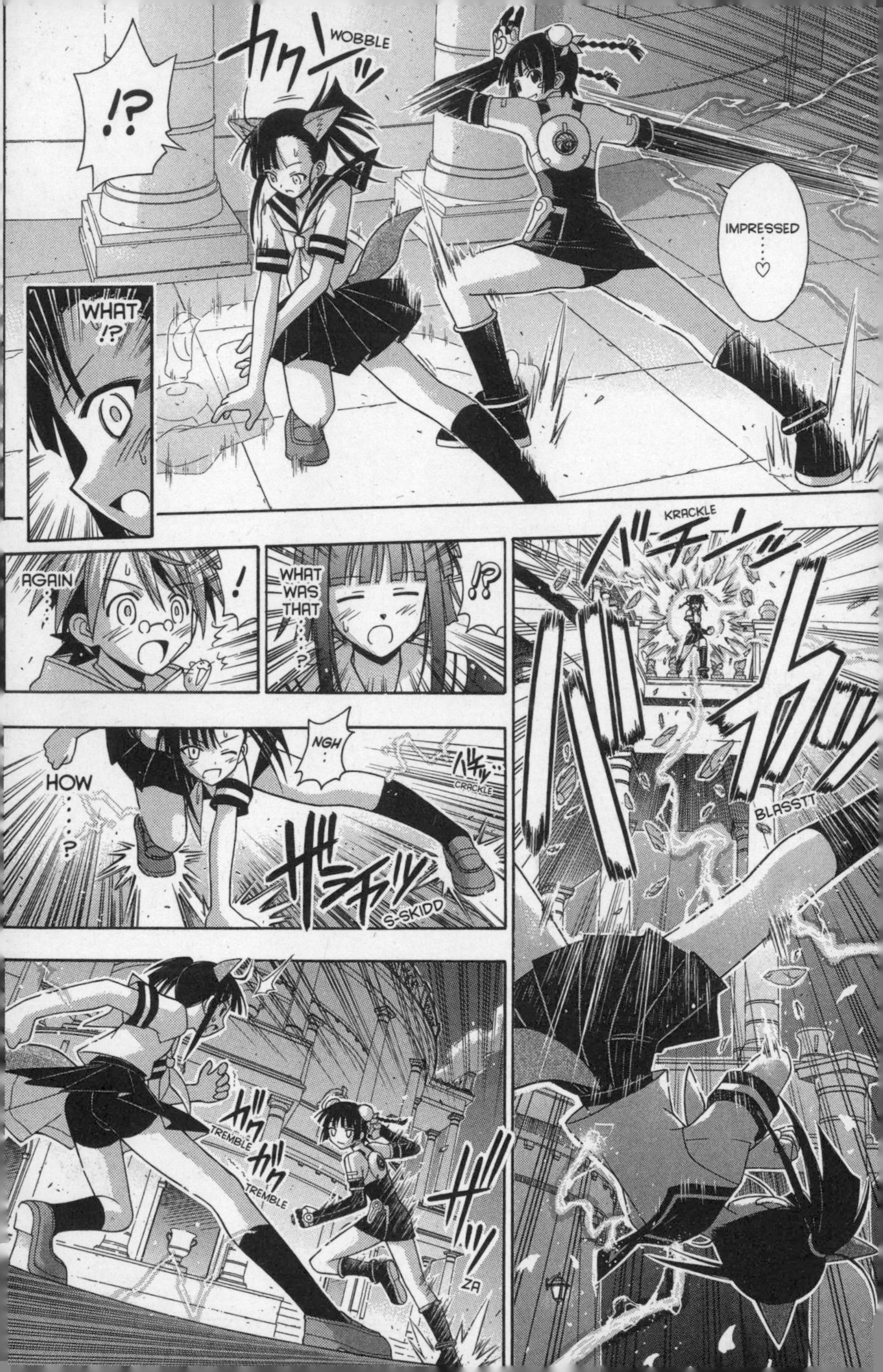
WOBBLE
IMPRESSED.....♡
!?
WHAT !?
KRACKLE
BLASSTT
!?
WHAT WAS THAT.....?
!
AGAIN.....
NGH.
CRACKLE
HOW.....?
S-SKIDD
ZA
TREMBLE
TREMBLE

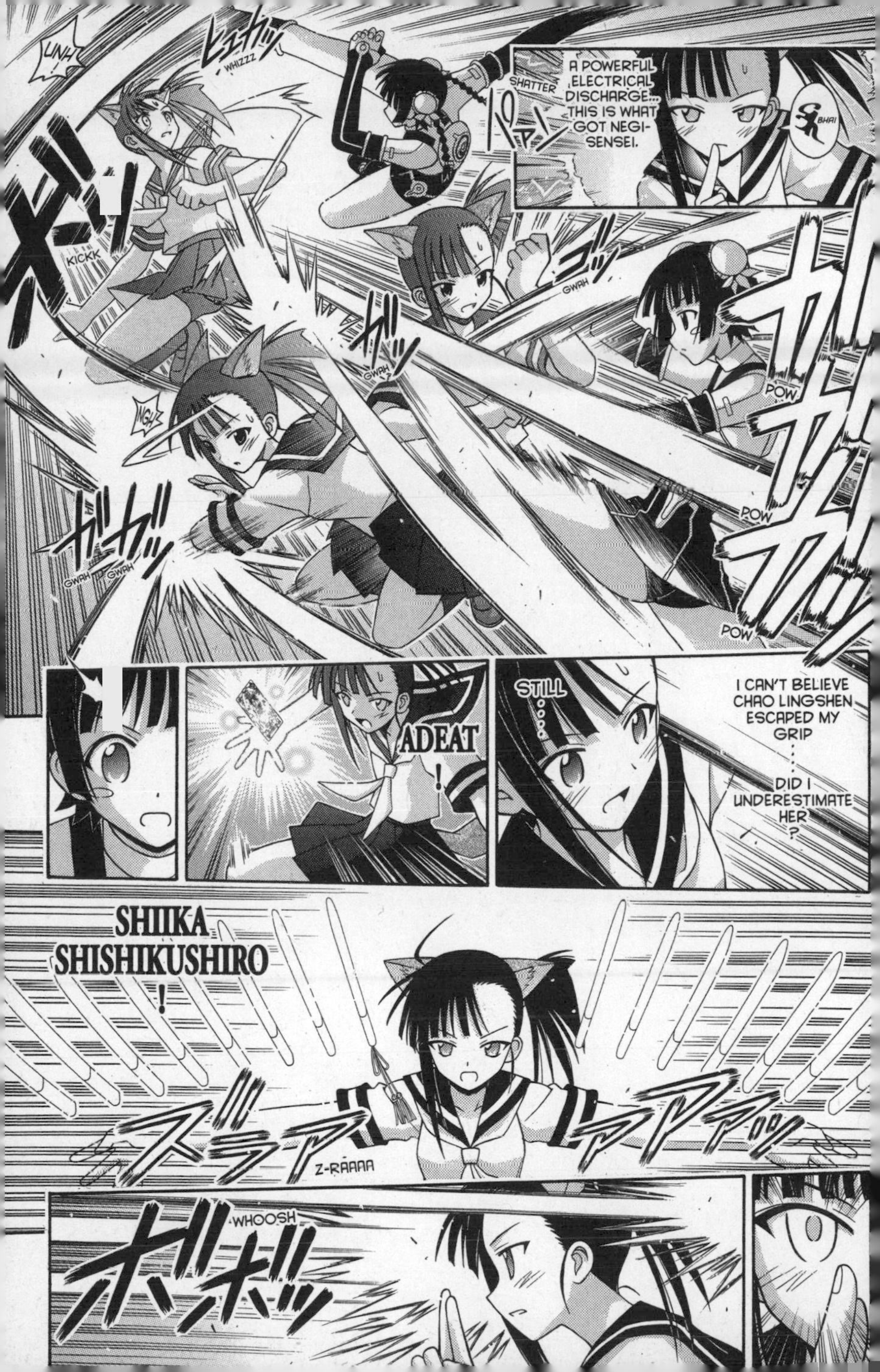
BHAI
A POWERFUL ELECTRICAL DISCHARGE... THIS IS WHAT GOT NEGI-SENSEI.
SHATTER
POW
POW
POW
GWAH
GWAH
WHIZZZ
UNH!
KICKK
NGH!
GWAH GWAH
I CAN'T BELIEVE CHAO LINGSHEN ESCAPED MY GRIP......
DID I UNDERESTIMATE HER?
STILL.....
ADEAT!
SHIIKA SHISHIKUSHIRO!
Z-RAAAA
WHOOSH

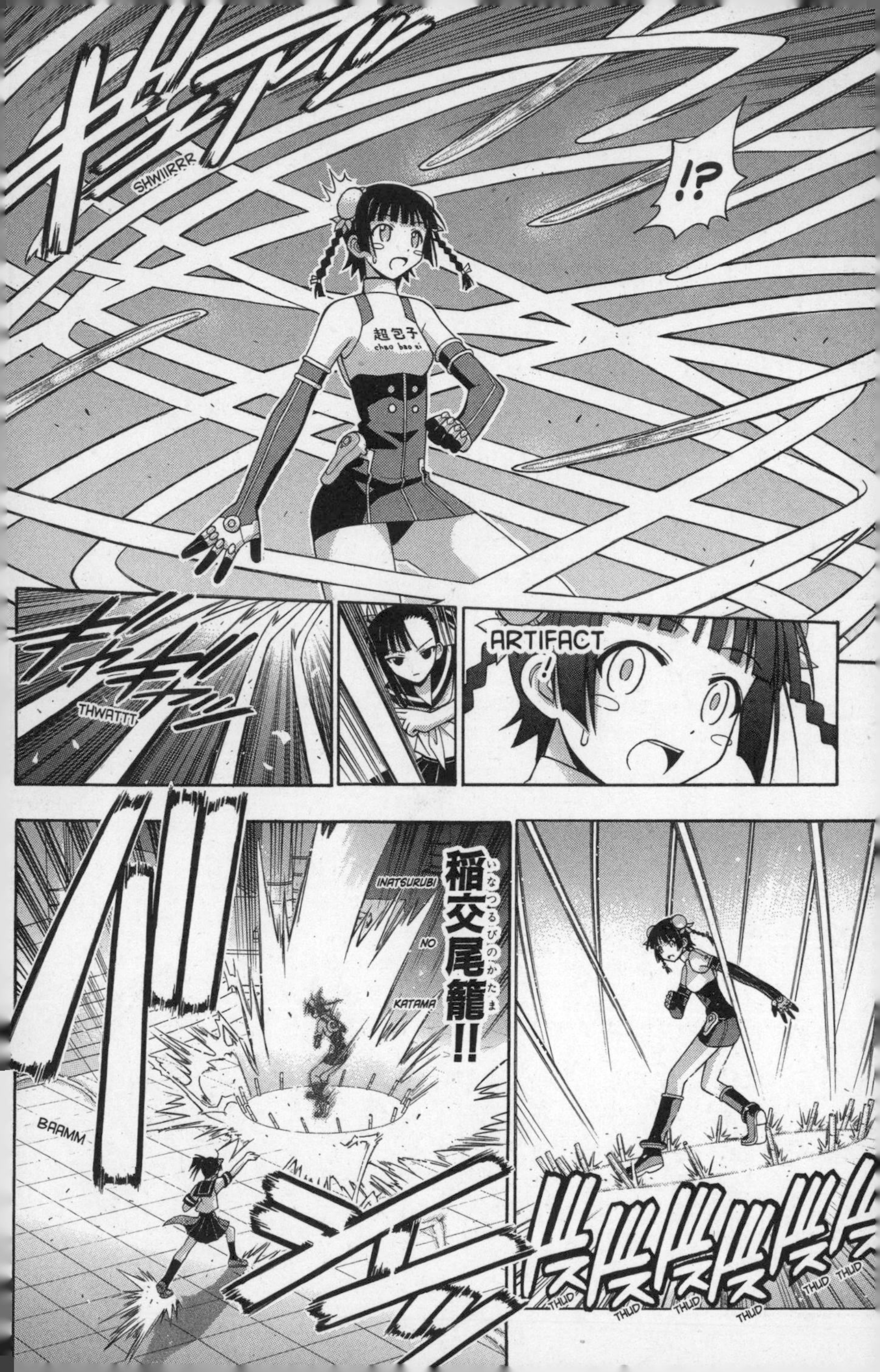
!?
SHWIIRRR
ARTIFACT!
THWATTT
THUD THUD THUD THUD THUD THUD
稲交尾籠!!
INATSURUBI NO KATAMA
BRAMM

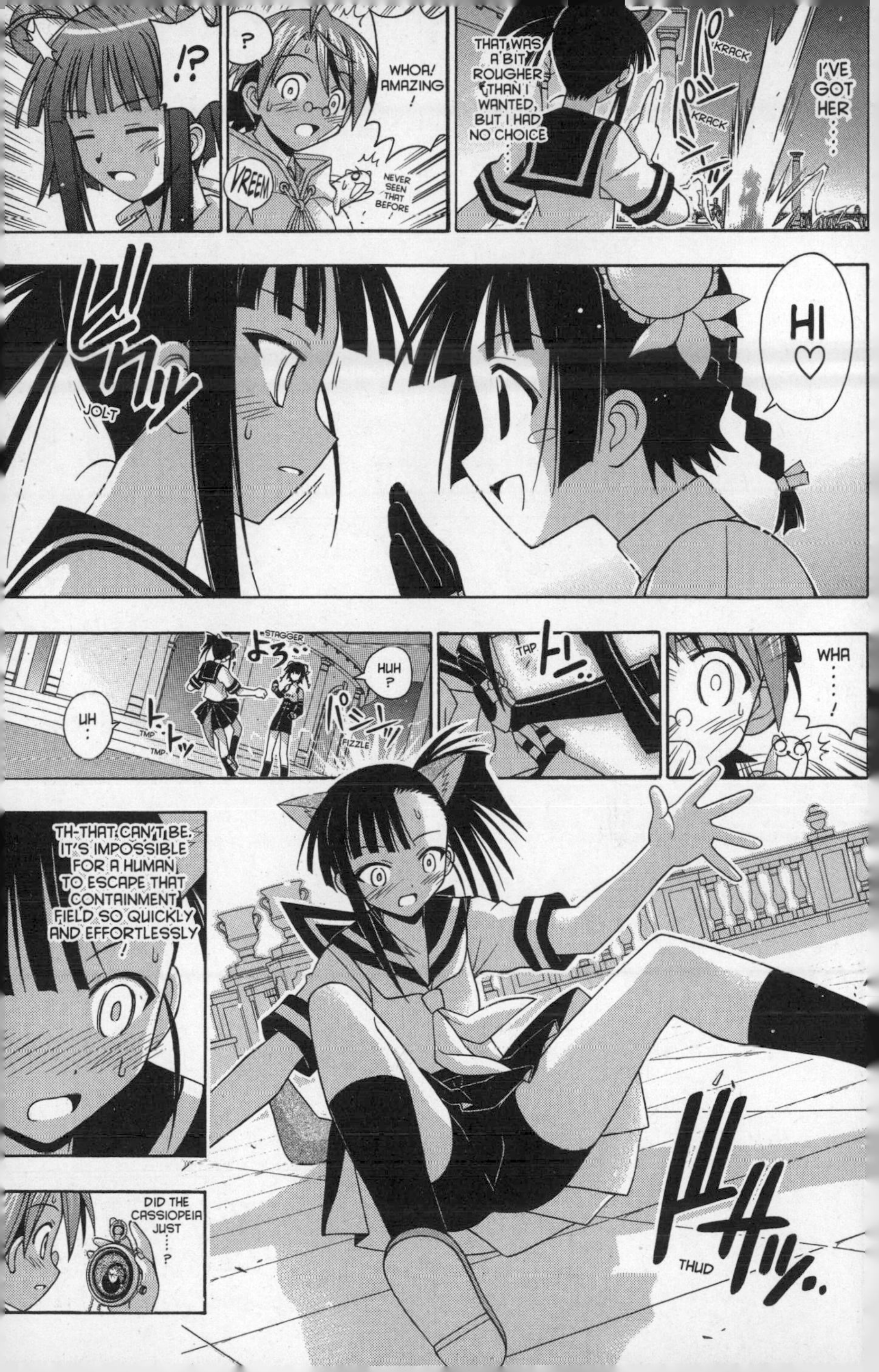
I'VE GOT HER...
KRACK
KRACK
THAT WAS A BIT ROUGHER THAN I WANTED, BUT I HAD NO CHOICE...
?
WHOA! AMAZING!
VREEM
NEVER SEEN THAT BEFORE!
!?
HI ♡
JOLT
WHA.....!
TAP
STAGGER
HUH?
FIZZLE
UH...
TMP
TMP
THUD
TH-THAT CAN'T BE, IT'S IMPOSSIBLE FOR A HUMAN TO ESCAPE THAT CONTAINMENT FIELD SO QUICKLY AND EFFORTLESSLY!
DID THE CASSIOPEIA JUST.....?

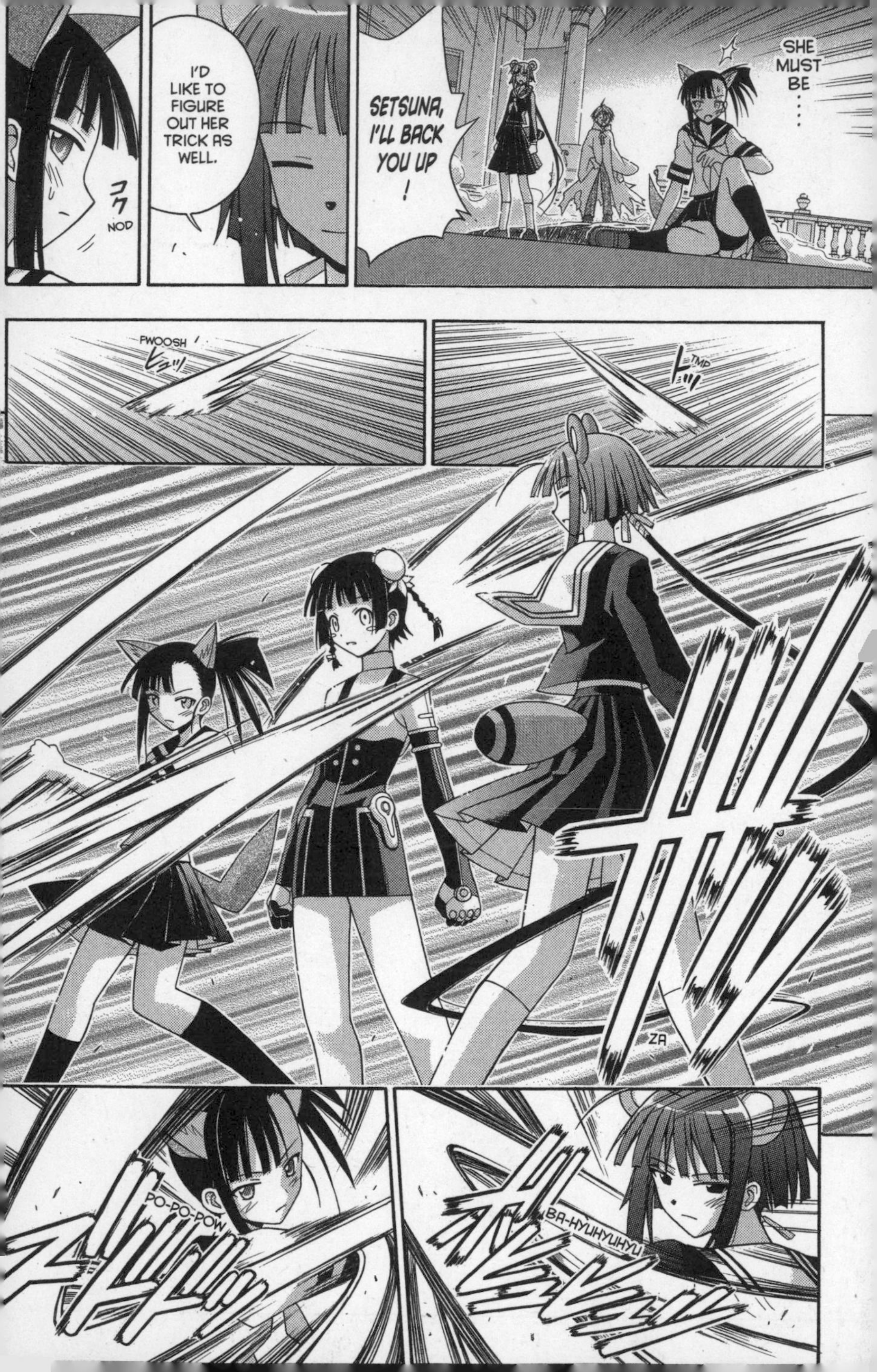
SHE MUST BE . . . .
SETSUNA, I'LL BACK YOU UP!
I'D LIKE TO FIGURE OUT HER TRICK AS WELL.
コク
NOD
TMP
FWOOSH
ヒュッ
ZA
BA-HYUHYUHYU
PO-PO-POW

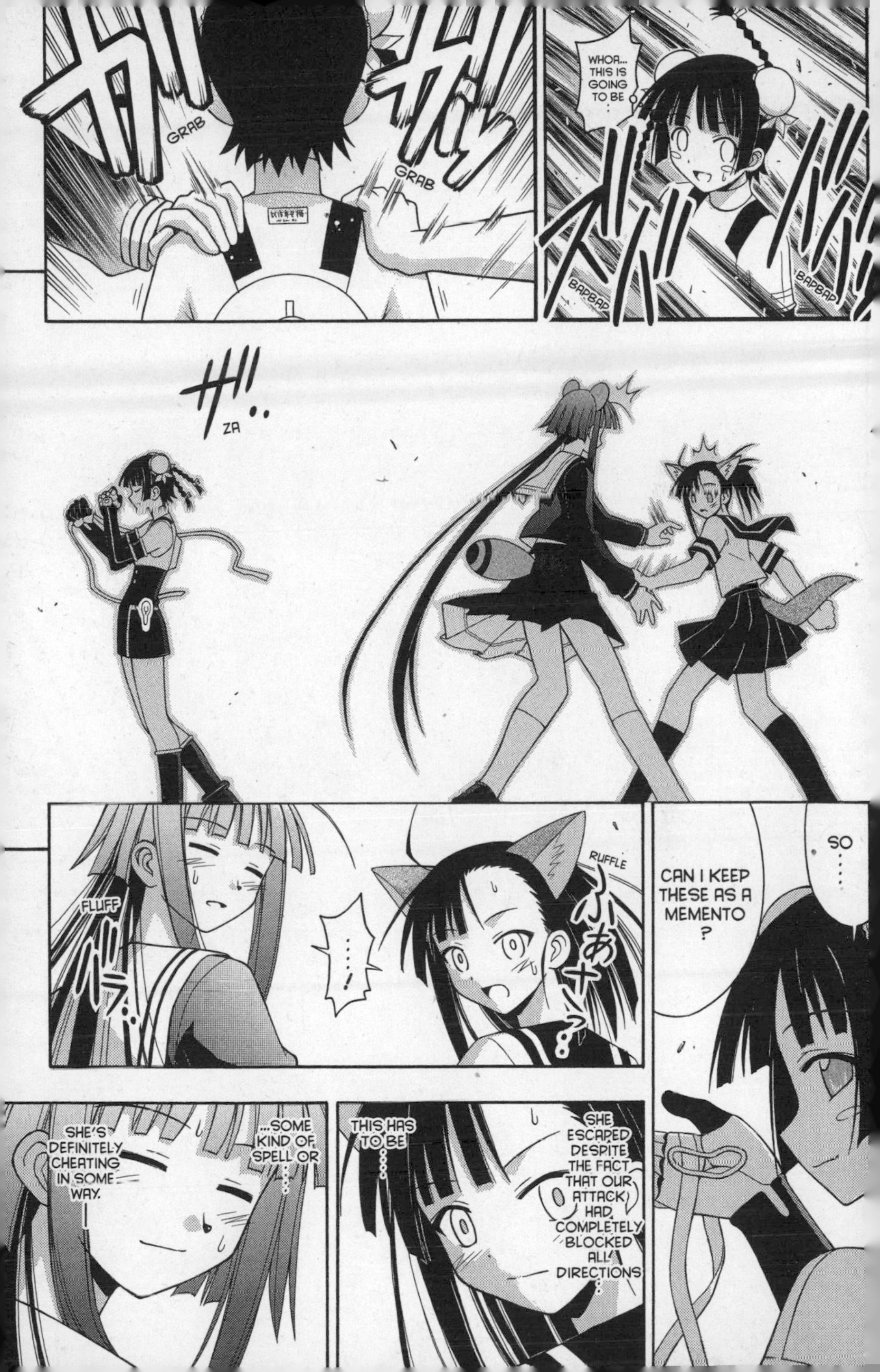
WHOA... THIS IS GOING TO BE ...
BAPBAP
BAPBAP
GRAB
GRAB
ZA
SO ....
CAN I KEEP THESE AS A MEMENTO ?
RUFFLE
...!
FLUFF
SHE ESCAPED DESPITE THE FACT THAT OUR ATTACK HAD COMPLETELY BLOCKED ALL DIRECTIONS...
THIS HAS TO BE ...
...SOME KIND OF SPELL OR ...
SHE'S DEFINITELY CHEATING IN SOME WAY. ─

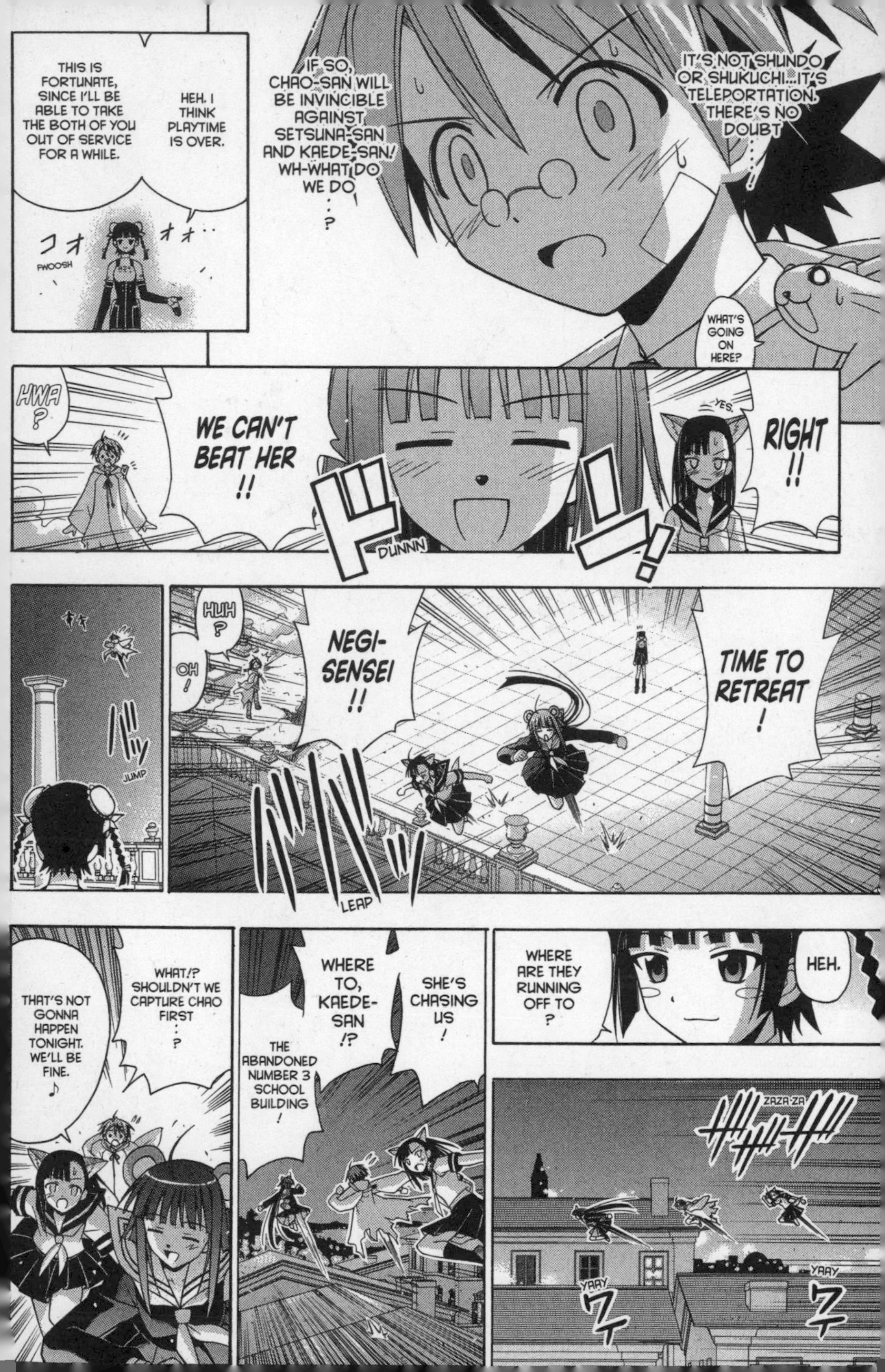
IT'S NOT SHUNDO OR SHUKUCHI...IT'S TELEPORTATION. THERE'S NO DOUBT
IF SO, CHAO-SAN WILL BE INVINCIBLE AGAINST SETSUNA-SAN AND KAEDE-SAN! WH-WHAT DO WE DO...?
WHAT'S GOING ON HERE?
HEH. I THINK PLAYTIME IS OVER.
THIS IS FORTUNATE, SINCE I'LL BE ABLE TO TAKE THE BOTH OF YOU OUT OF SERVICE FOR A WHILE.
コオオオ‥
FWOOSH
—YES.
RIGHT!!
WE CAN'T BEAT HER!!
DUNNN
HWA?
TIME TO RETREAT!
NEGI-SENSEI!!
HUH?
OH!
LEAP
JUMP
HEH.
WHERE ARE THEY RUNNING OFF TO?
ZAZA-ZA
YAAY
YAAY
SHE'S CHASING US!
WHERE TO, KAEDE-SAN!?
THE ABANDONED NUMBER 3 SCHOOL BUILDING!
WHAT!? SHOULDN'T WE CAPTURE CHAO FIRST...?
THAT'S NOT GONNA HAPPEN TONIGHT. WE'LL BE FINE. ♪

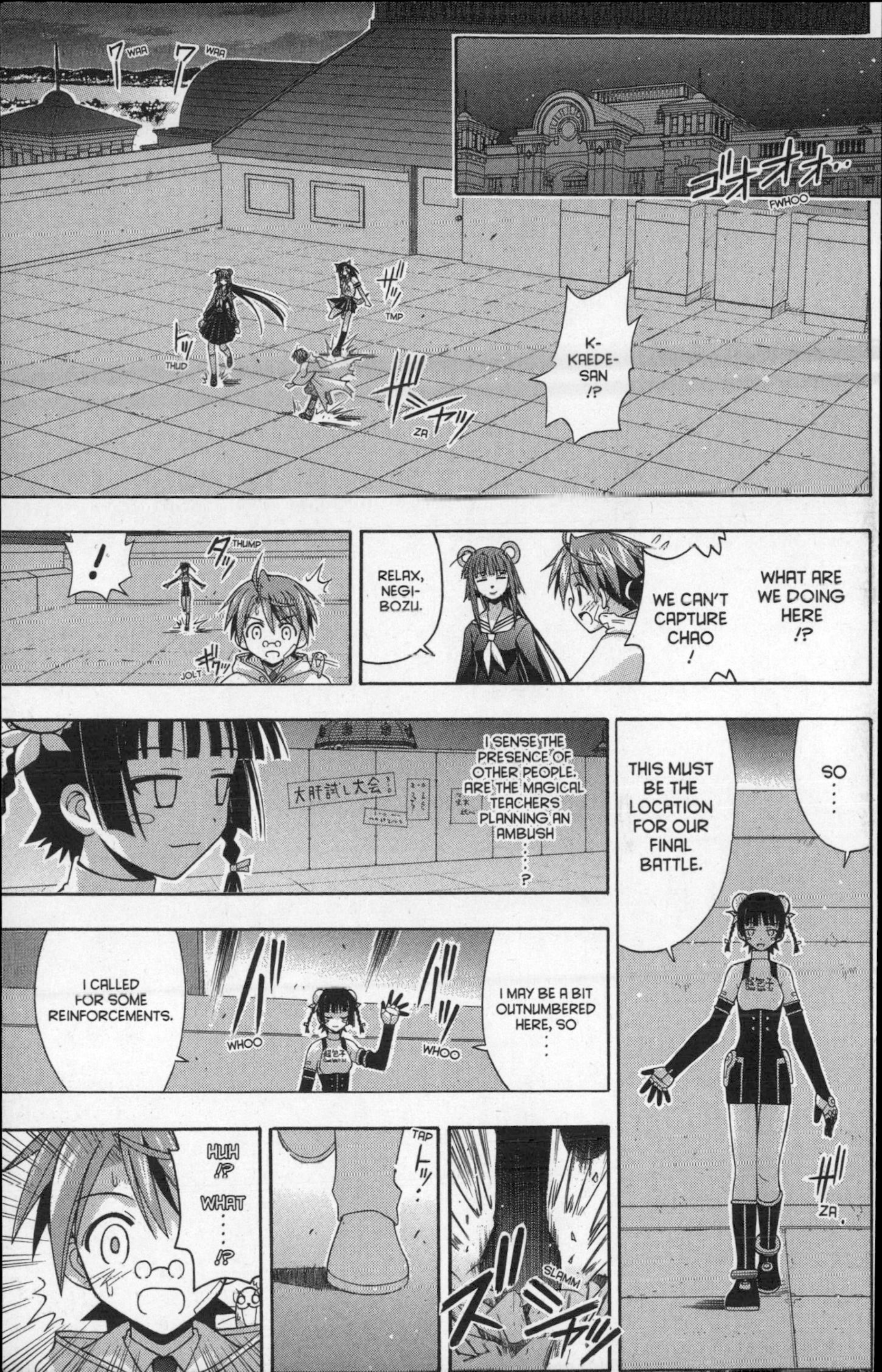

FWHOO
WAA
WAA
K-KAEDE-SAN!?
TMP
THUD
ZA
WHAT ARE WE DOING HERE!?
WE CAN'T CAPTURE CHAO!
RELAX, NEGI-BOZU.
!
THUMP
JOLT
SO....
THIS MUST BE THE LOCATION FOR OUR FINAL BATTLE.
ZA
I SENSE THE PRESENCE OF OTHER PEOPLE. ARE THE MAGICAL TEACHERS PLANNING AN AMBUSH...?
I MAY BE A BIT OUTNUMBERED HERE, SO...
WHOO
WHOO
I CALLED FOR SOME REINFORCEMENTS.
SLAMM
TAP
HUH!? WHAT....!?

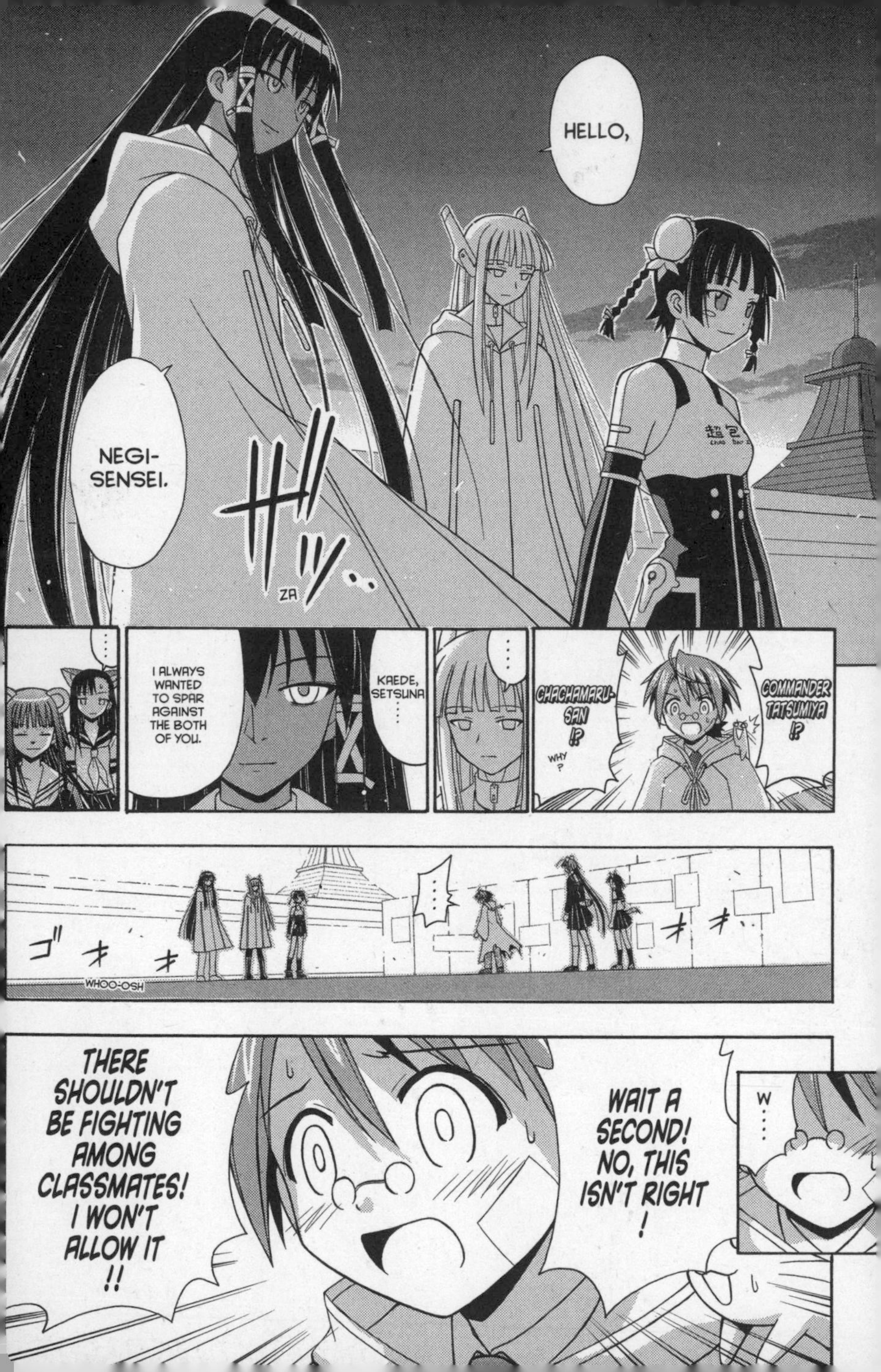
HELLO,
NEGI-SENSEI.
ZA
COMMANDER TATSUMIYA !?
CHACHAMARU-SAN !?
WHY ?
...
KAEDE, SETSUNA ...
I ALWAYS WANTED TO SPAR AGAINST THE BOTH OF YOU.
...
...
WHOO-OSH
W....
WAIT A SECOND! NO, THIS ISN'T RIGHT !
THERE SHOULDN'T BE FIGHTING AMONG CLASSMATES! I WON'T ALLOW IT !!

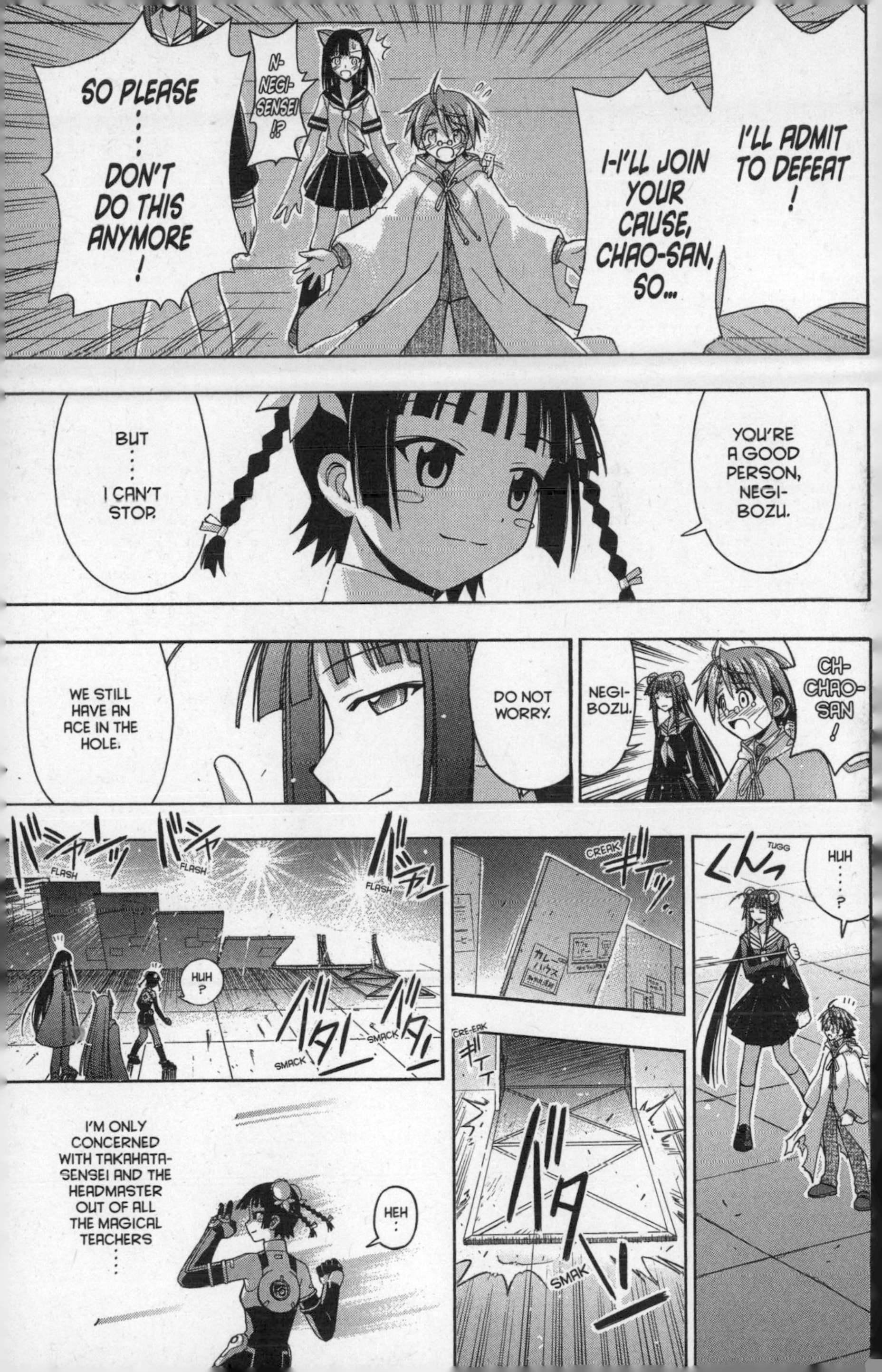

I'LL ADMIT TO DEFEAT!
I-I'LL JOIN YOUR CAUSE, CHAO-SAN, SO...
N-NEGI-SENSEI!?
SO PLEASE... DON'T DO THIS ANYMORE!
YOU'RE A GOOD PERSON, NEGI-BOZU.
BUT... I CAN'T STOP.
CH-CHAO-SAN!
NEGI-BOZU.
DO NOT WORRY.
WE STILL HAVE AN ACE IN THE HOLE.
TUGG
HUH...?
CREAK
CRE-EAK
SMAK
FLASH
FLASH
FLASH
HUH?
SMACK
SMACK
I'M ONLY CONCERNED WITH TAKAHATA-SENSEI AND THE HEADMASTER OUT OF ALL THE MAGICAL TEACHERS...
HEH...

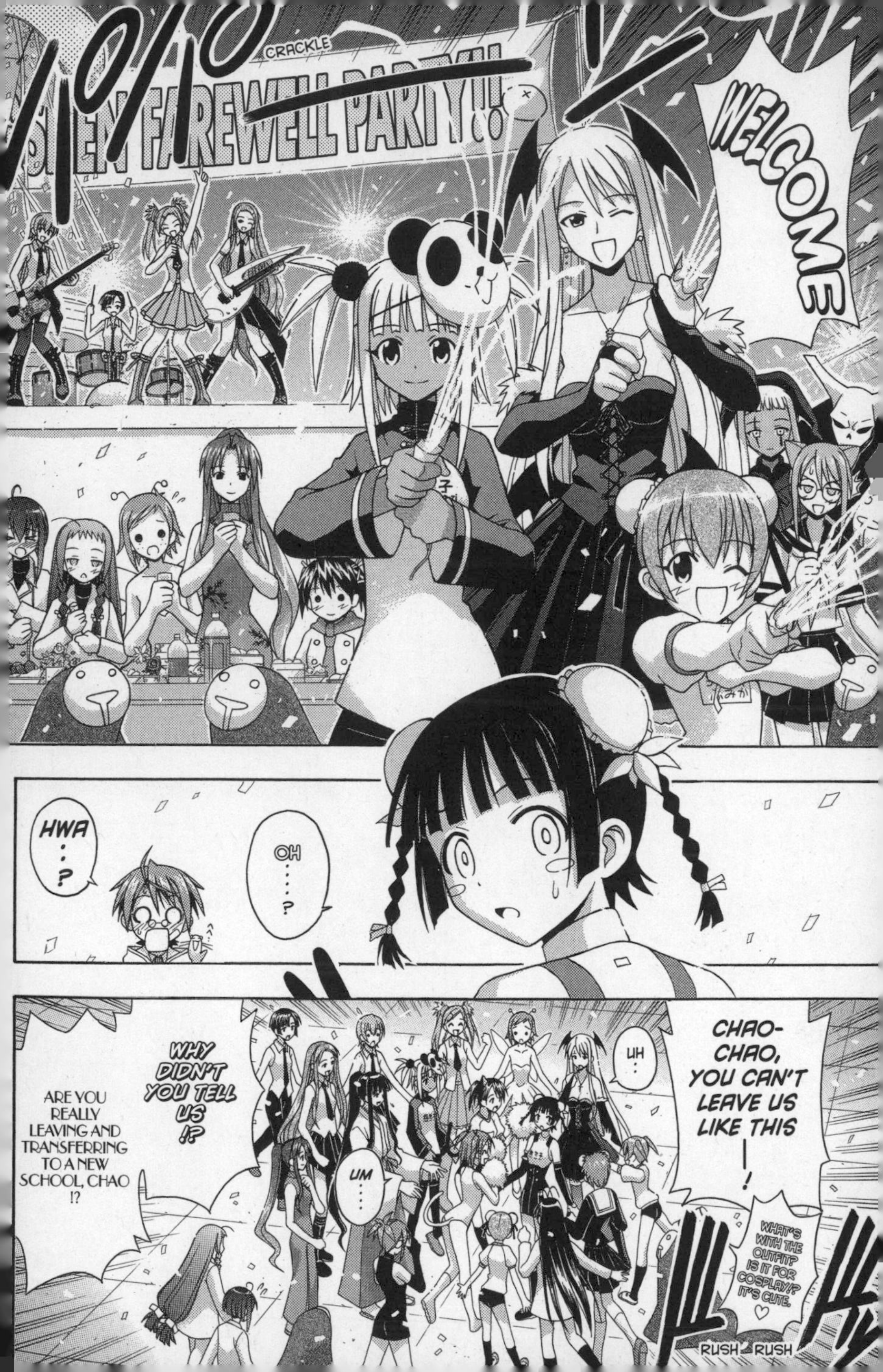
WELCOME
SIEN FAREWELL PARTY!!
CRACKLE
OH.....?
HWA...?
CHAO-CHAO, YOU CAN'T LEAVE US LIKE THIS!
UH...
WHAT'S WITH THE OUTFIT!? IS IT FOR COSPLAY!? IT'S CUTE. ♡
WHY DIDN'T YOU TELL US!?
UM.....
ARE YOU REALLY LEAVING AND TRANSFERRING TO A NEW SCHOOL, CHAO!?
RUSH RUSH

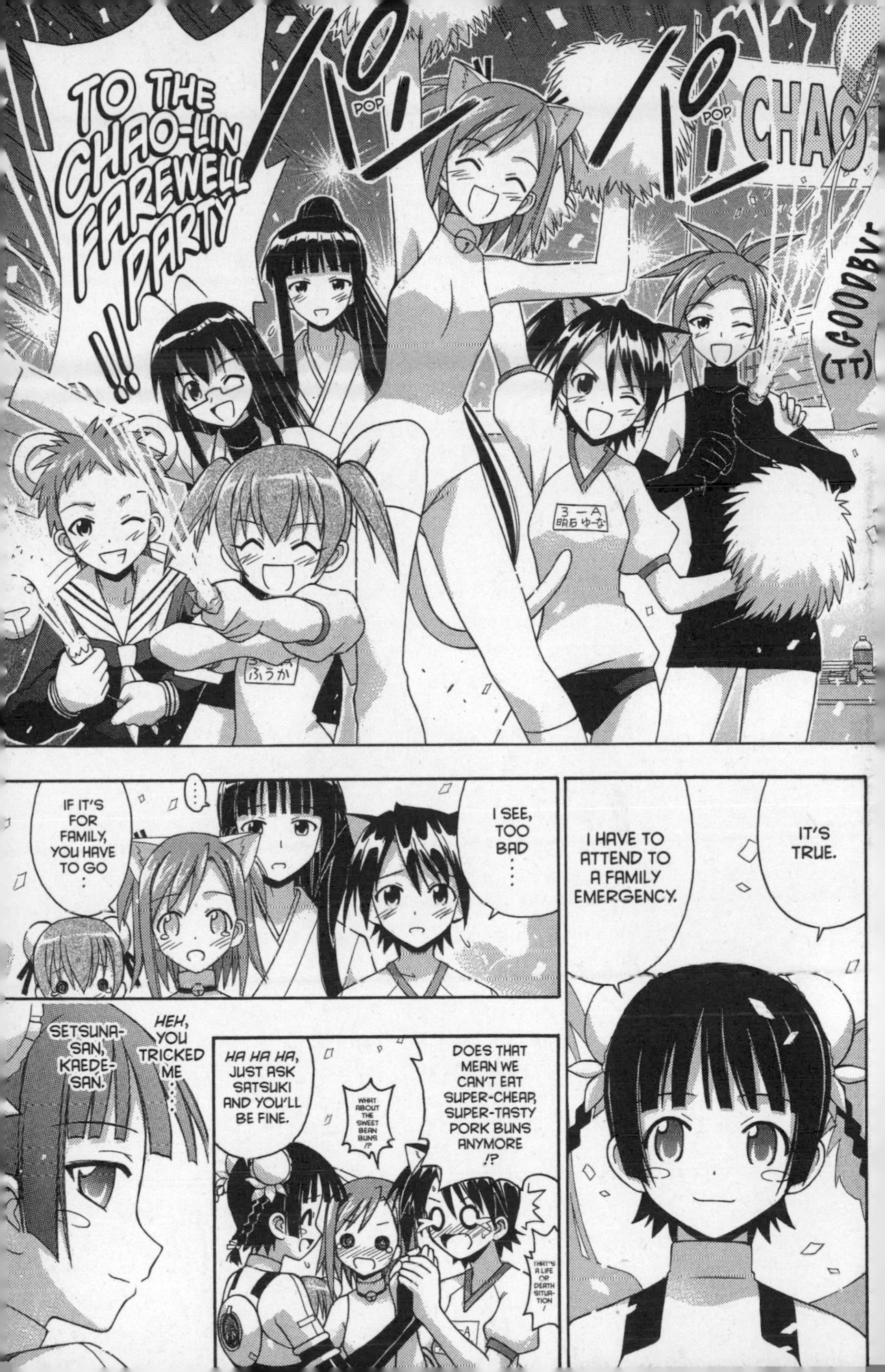
CHAO
GOODBYE (TT)
POP
POP
TO THE CHAO-LIN FAREWELL PARTY !!
3-A 明石ゆーな
ふうか
IT'S TRUE.
I HAVE TO ATTEND TO A FAMILY EMERGENCY.
I SEE, TOO BAD ...
...
IF IT'S FOR FAMILY, YOU HAVE TO GO ...
DOES THAT MEAN WE CAN'T EAT SUPER-CHEAP, SUPER-TASTY PORK BUNS ANYMORE !?
WHAT ABOUT THE SWEET BEAN BUNS !?
THAT'S A LIFE OF DEATH SITUATION!
HA HA HA, JUST ASK SATSUKI AND YOU'LL BE FINE.
HEH, YOU TRICKED ME ...
SETSUNA-SAN, KAEDE-SAN.

LEXICON MAGICUM NEGIMARUM

Negima! 134th Period

■「𑖭」

BHAI

   In Genjyou's (Xuanzang, AD 602–664) translation of *Yakushi Rurikounyorai Hongan Kudokukyou* (Sutra of the Medicine Buddha), there is a passage that reads "East of the world—past countless Buddha-lands—more numerous than the grains of sand in ten Ganges Rivers, there exists a world called Pure Lapiz Lazuli. The Buddha of that world is called the Medicine Buddha...When the World-Honored Medicine Buddha was treading the Bodhisattva path, he solemnly made Twelve Great Vows to grant sentient beings whatever they desired...'Seventh Great Vow. I vow that in a future life, when I have attained Supreme Enlightenment, sentient beings afflicted with various illnesses—with no one to help them—nowhere to turn, no physicians, no medicine, no family, no home, who are destitute and miserable, will, as soon as my name passes through their ears, be relieved of all their illnesses. With mind and body peaceful and content, they will enjoy home, family, and property in abundance and eventually realize Unsurpassed Supreme Enlightenment.'" The text says Yakushi Nyorai (Bhaisajyaguru) is the Buddha who made the Great Vow saying that anyone who hears his name will be cured of all illnesses. 𑖭 is a *shuji,* or seed syllable, of Yakushi Nyorai and takes the place of the Buddha's name. Hence, by uttering this seed syllable, the speaker is able to make a connection to the Yakushi Nyorai.

   In the story, Setsuna uttered the seed syllable 𑖭 to rid herself of the effects of Chao's electrical attack. As you can, her knees are shaking and she's unable to stand in one panel, but in the next panel, her agility is back.

■稲交尾籠

INATSURUBI NO KATAMA

   This is one of Setsuna's anti-demon spells. By throwing a *shuriken* or *vajra* around the target, a spiritual zone is formed, trapping it inside. *Katama* refers to "an extremely tightly woven basket," and *inatsurubi* means "lightning." Hence, this is a high-level technique in which the target is surrounded, then stunned, with lightning strikes.

   In the story, this technique was performed using the *tanto,* Setsuna's artifact. The artifact's ability to split into multiple blades midair and remain under control is ideal for casting this spell. Now whether or not the magical properties of the artifact conflicts with Setsuna's ki-based abilities remains unknown.

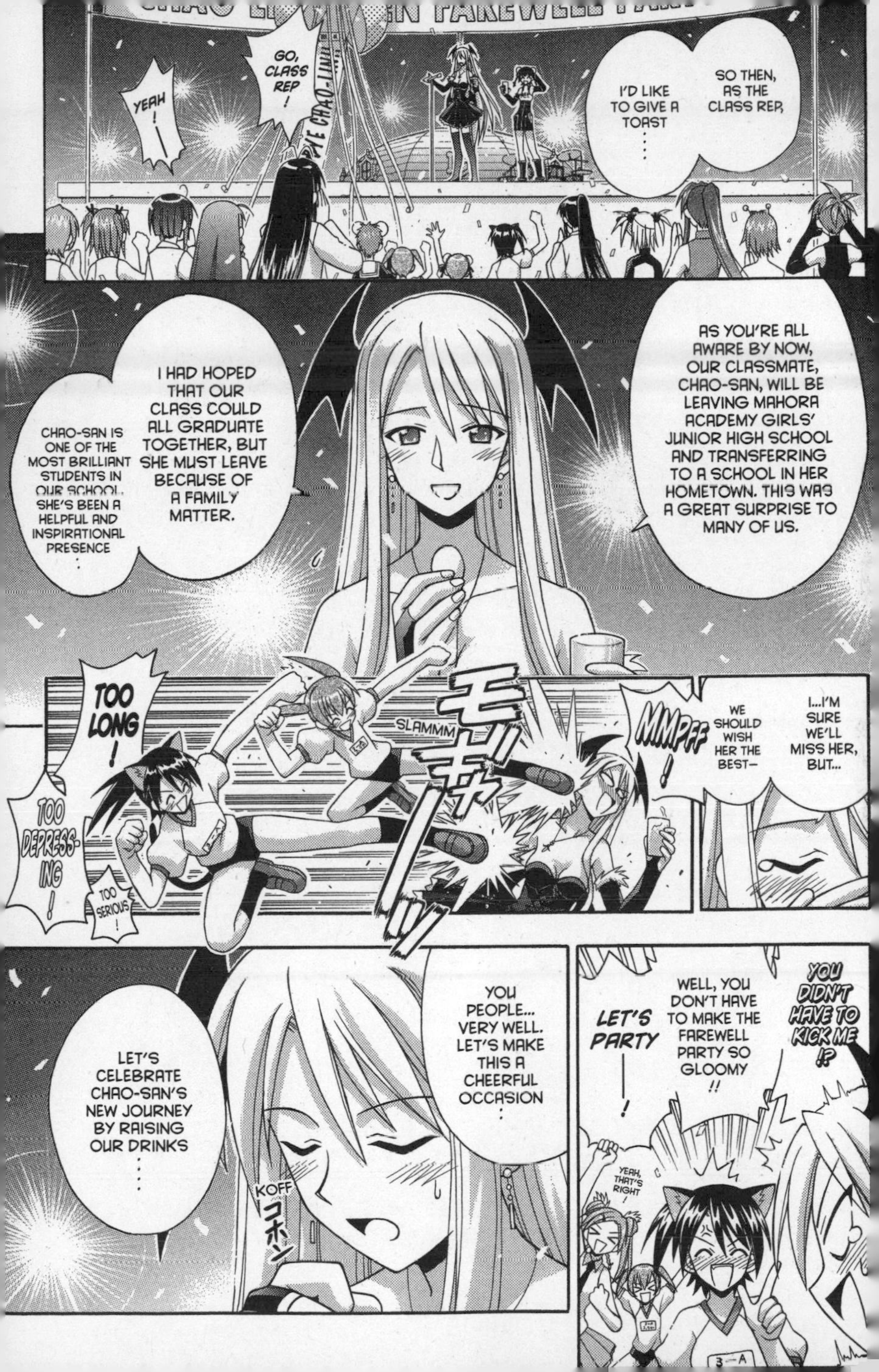
SO THEN, AS THE CLASS REP,
I'D LIKE TO GIVE A TOAST...
GO, CLASS REP!
YEAH!
AS YOU'RE ALL AWARE BY NOW, OUR CLASSMATE, CHAO-SAN, WILL BE LEAVING MAHORA ACADEMY GIRLS' JUNIOR HIGH SCHOOL AND TRANSFERRING TO A SCHOOL IN HER HOMETOWN. THIS WAS A GREAT SURPRISE TO MANY OF US.
I HAD HOPED THAT OUR CLASS COULD ALL GRADUATE TOGETHER, BUT SHE MUST LEAVE BECAUSE OF A FAMILY MATTER.
CHAO-SAN IS ONE OF THE MOST BRILLIANT STUDENTS IN OUR SCHOOL. SHE'S BEEN A HELPFUL AND INSPIRATIONAL PRESENCE...
I...I'M SURE WE'LL MISS HER, BUT...
WE SHOULD WISH HER THE BEST—
MMPFF!
SLAMMM
TOO LONG!
TOO DEPRESSING!
TOO SERIOUS!
YOU DIDN'T HAVE TO KICK ME!?
WELL, YOU DON'T HAVE TO MAKE THE FAREWELL PARTY SO GLOOMY!!
LET'S PARTY—!
YEAH, THAT'S RIGHT!
3-A
YOU PEOPLE... VERY WELL. LET'S MAKE THIS A CHEERFUL OCCASION...
KOFF
LET'S CELEBRATE CHAO-SAN'S NEW JOURNEY BY RAISING OUR DRINKS...

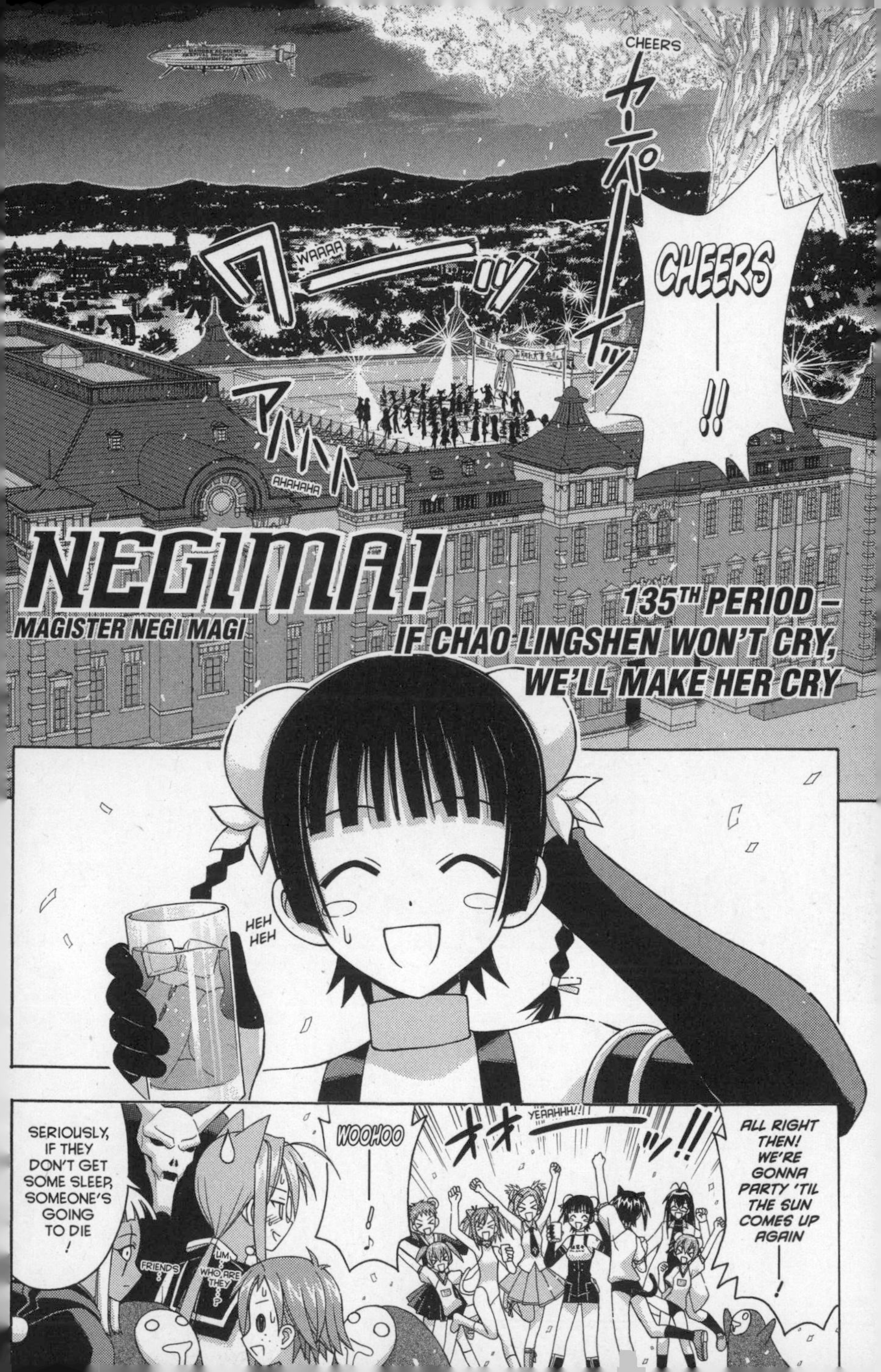
CHEERS
CHEERS——!!
WAAAA
AHAHAHA
NEGIMA!
MAGISTER NEGI MAGI
135TH PERIOD – IF CHAO LINGSHEN WON'T CRY, WE'LL MAKE HER CRY
HEH HEH
ALL RIGHT THEN! WE'RE GONNA PARTY 'TIL THE SUN COMES UP AGAIN—!
YEAAHHH!!
WOOHOO—!♪
UM... WHO ARE THEY...?
FRIENDS...
SERIOUSLY, IF THEY DON'T GET SOME SLEEP, SOMEONE'S GOING TO DIE!

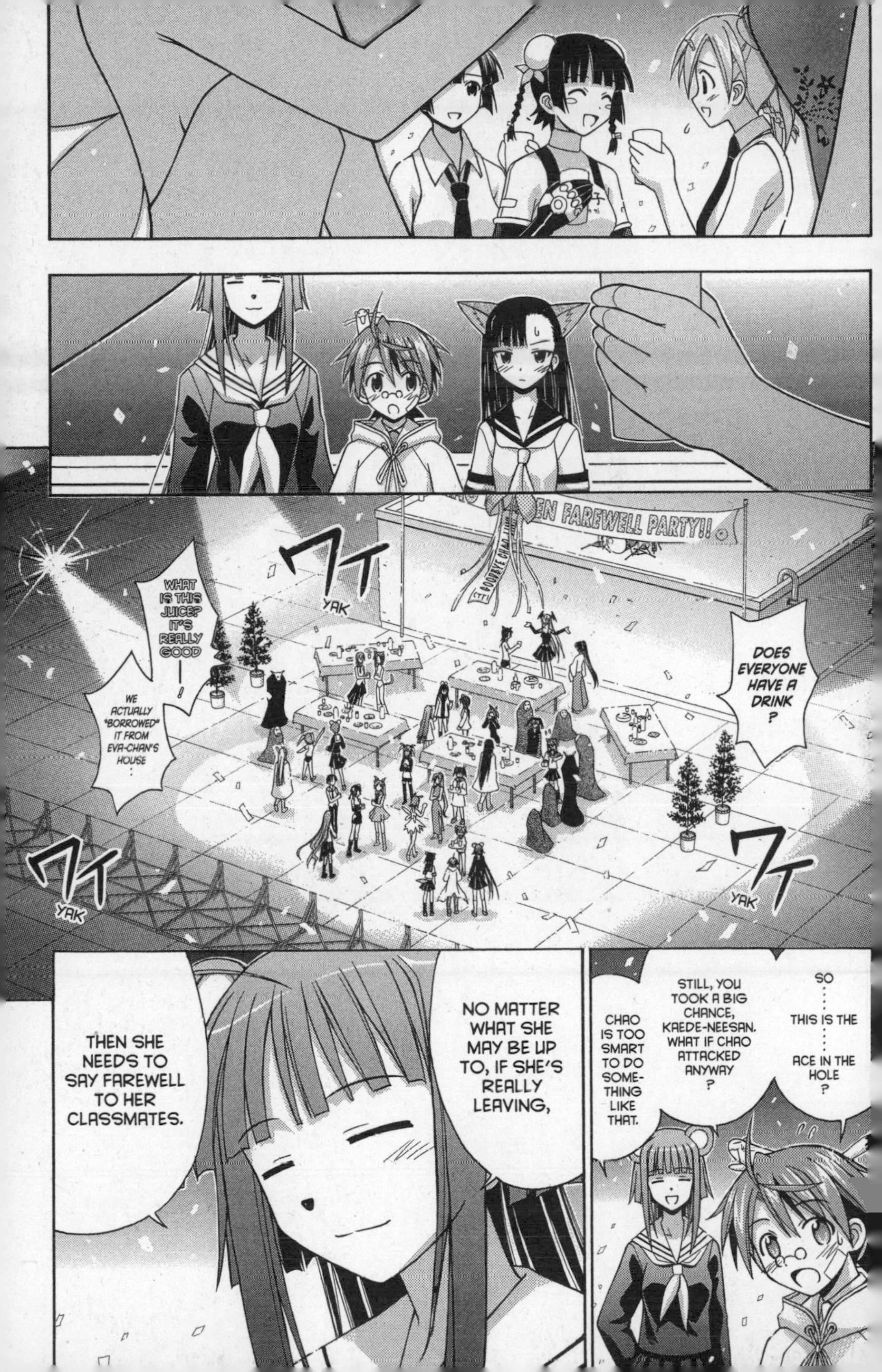
FAREWELL PARTY!!
ワイ
YAK
DOES EVERYONE HAVE A DRINK?
WHAT IS THIS JUICE? IT'S REALLY GOOD!
WE ACTUALLY "BORROWED" IT FROM EVA-CHAN'S HOUSE...
ワイ
YAK
ワイ
YAK
SO... THIS IS THE... ACE IN THE HOLE?
STILL, YOU TOOK A BIG CHANCE, KAEDE-NEESAN. WHAT IF CHAO ATTACKED ANYWAY?
CHAO IS TOO SMART TO DO SOMETHING LIKE THAT.
NO MATTER WHAT SHE MAY BE UP TO, IF SHE'S REALLY LEAVING,
THEN SHE NEEDS TO SAY FAREWELL TO HER CLASSMATES.

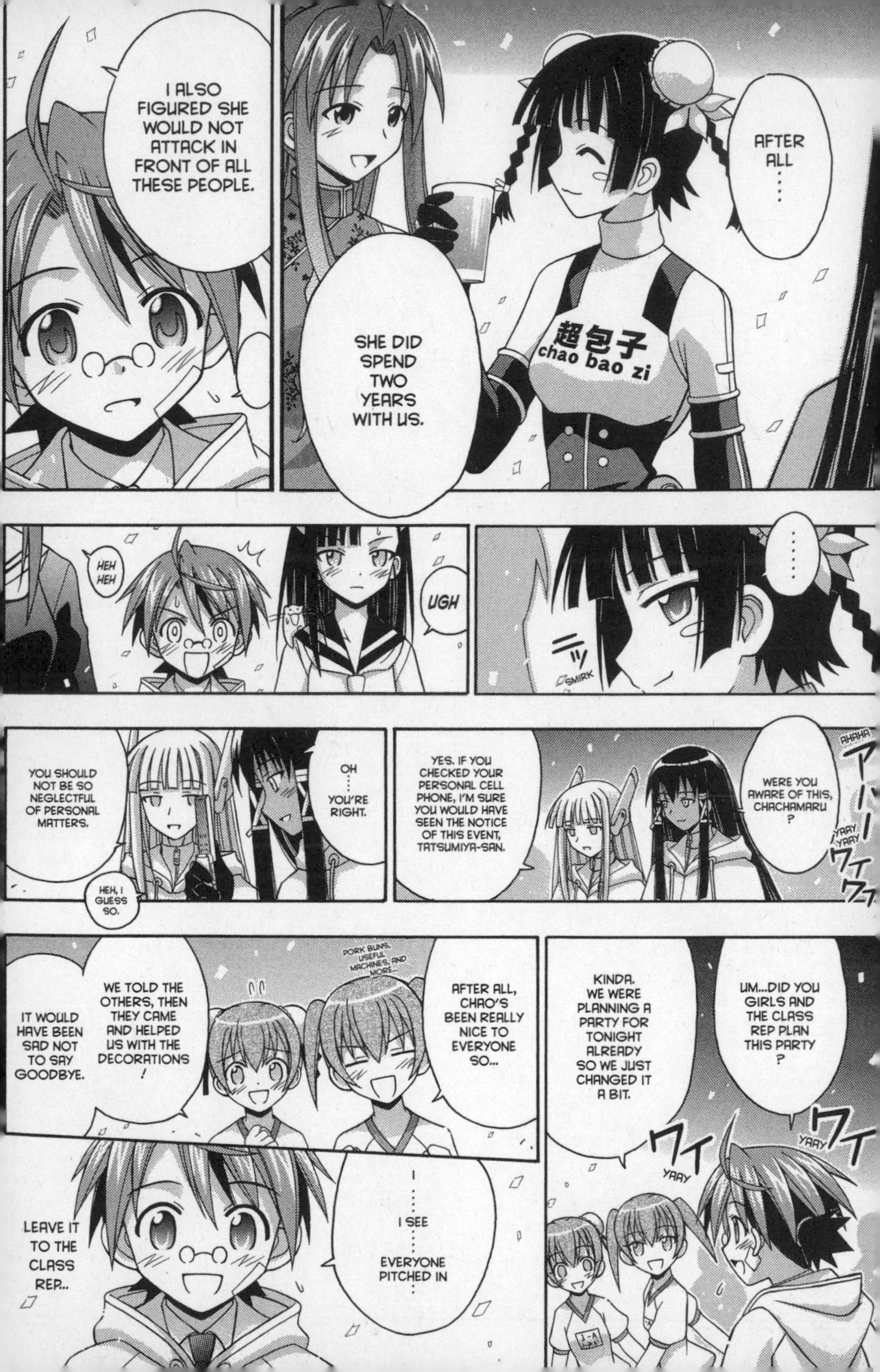
AFTER ALL......
超包子 chao bao zi
SHE DID SPEND TWO YEARS WITH US.
I ALSO FIGURED SHE WOULD NOT ATTACK IN FRONT OF ALL THESE PEOPLE.
......
ニッ SMIRK
UGH
HEH HEH
アーハー AHAHA
WERE YOU AWARE OF THIS, CHACHAMARU?
ワイワイ YAAY YAAY
YES. IF YOU CHECKED YOUR PERSONAL CELL PHONE, I'M SURE YOU WOULD HAVE SEEN THE NOTICE OF THIS EVENT, TATSUMIYA-SAN.
OH...... YOU'RE RIGHT.
YOU SHOULD NOT BE SO NEGLECTFUL OF PERSONAL MATTERS.
HEH, I GUESS SO.
UM...DID YOU GIRLS AND THE CLASS REP PLAN THIS PARTY?
KINDA. WE WERE PLANNING A PARTY FOR TONIGHT ALREADY SO WE JUST CHANGED IT A BIT.
ワイ YAAY
ワイ YAAY
AFTER ALL, CHAO'S BEEN REALLY NICE TO EVERYONE SO...
PORK BUNS, USEFUL MACHINES, AND MORE...
WE TOLD THE OTHERS, THEN THEY CAME AND HELPED US WITH THE DECORATIONS!
IT WOULD HAVE BEEN SAD NOT TO SAY GOODBYE.
I...... I SEE...... EVERYONE PITCHED IN......
LEAVE IT TO THE CLASS REP...

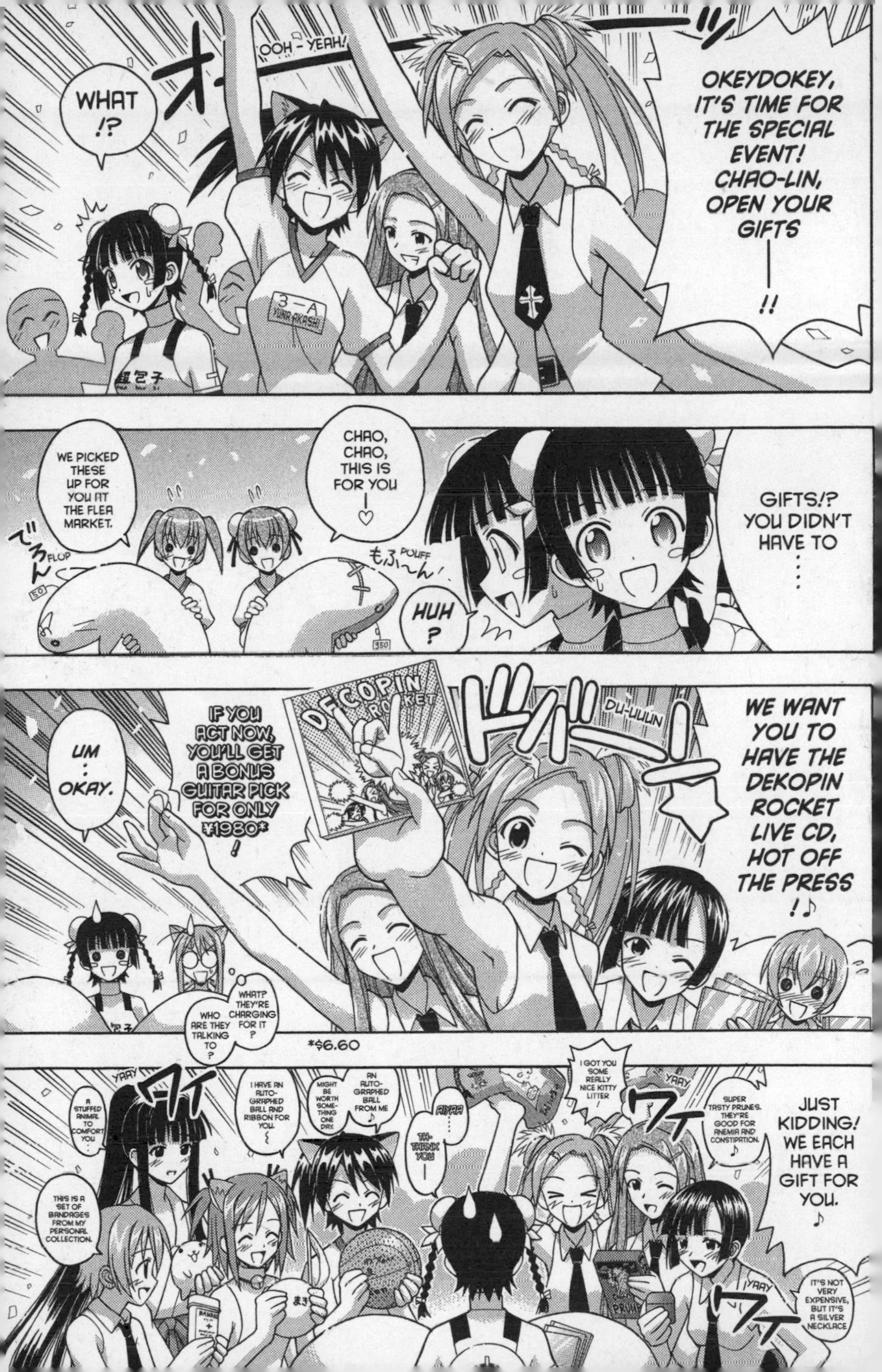
OKEYDOKEY, IT'S TIME FOR THE SPECIAL EVENT! CHAO-LIN, OPEN YOUR GIFTS —!!
OOH - YEAH!
WHAT !?
GIFTS!? YOU DIDN'T HAVE TO ...
CHAO, CHAO, THIS IS FOR YOU —♡
もふ〜ん POUFF
HUH ?
WE PICKED THESE UP FOR YOU AT THE FLEA MARKET.
でろん FLOP
WE WANT YOU TO HAVE THE DEKOPIN ROCKET LIVE CD, HOT OFF THE PRESS !♪
DU-UUUN
DECOPIN ROCKET
IF YOU ACT NOW, YOU'LL GET A BONUS GUITAR PICK FOR ONLY ¥1980* !
UM : OKAY.
WHAT? THEY'RE CHARGING FOR IT ?
WHO ARE THEY TALKING TO ?
*$6.60
JUST KIDDING! WE EACH HAVE A GIFT FOR YOU. ♪
IT'S NOT VERY EXPENSIVE, BUT IT'S A SILVER NECKLACE
YAAY
SUPER TASTY PRUNES. THEY'RE GOOD FOR ANEMIA AND CONSTIPATION. ♪
YAAY
I GOT YOU SOME REALLY NICE KITTY LITTER !
AIYAA ...
TH-THANK YOU —
AN AUTO-GRAPHED BALL FROM ME ♪
MIGHT BE WORTH SOME-THING ONE DAY.
I HAVE AN AUTO-GRAPHED BALL AND RIBBON FOR YOU. ~
YAAY
A STUFFED ANIMAL TO COMFORT YOU ..
THIS IS A SET OF BANDAGES FROM MY PERSONAL COLLECTION.

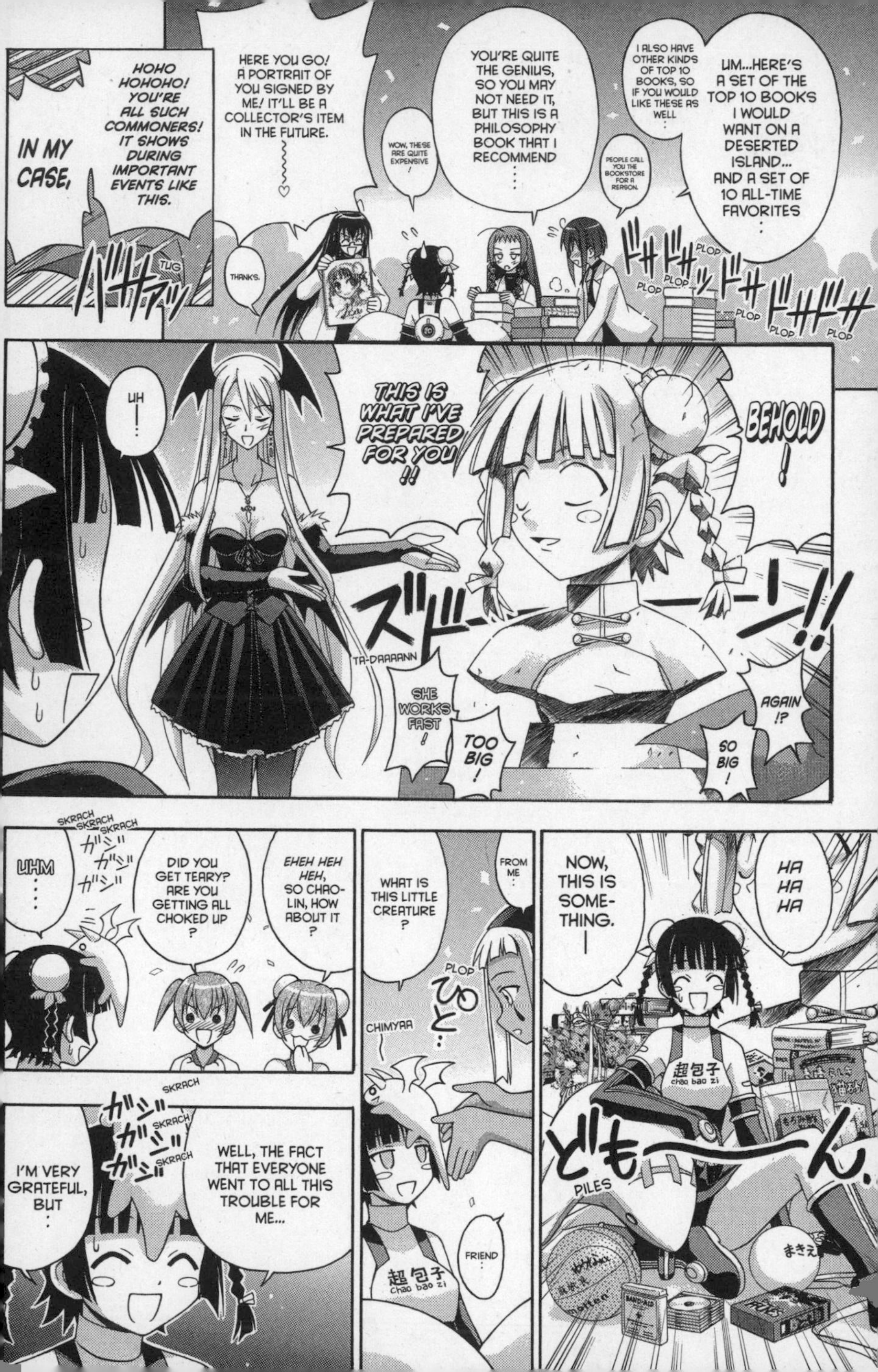
UM...HERE'S A SET OF THE TOP 10 BOOKS I WOULD WANT ON A DESERTED ISLAND... AND A SET OF 10 ALL-TIME FAVORITES...
I ALSO HAVE OTHER KINDS OF TOP 10 BOOKS, SO IF YOU WOULD LIKE THESE AS WELL...
PEOPLE CALL YOU THE BOOKSTORE FOR A REASON.
PLOP PLOP PLOP PLOP PLOP PLOP
YOU'RE QUITE THE GENIUS, SO YOU MAY NOT NEED IT, BUT THIS IS A PHILOSOPHY BOOK THAT I RECOMMEND...
HERE YOU GO! A PORTRAIT OF YOU SIGNED BY ME! IT'LL BE A COLLECTOR'S ITEM IN THE FUTURE.
WOW, THESE ARE QUITE EXPENSIVE!
THANKS.
HOHO HOHOHO! YOU'RE ALL SUCH COMMONERS! IT SHOWS DURING IMPORTANT EVENTS LIKE THIS.
IN MY CASE,
TUG
BEHOLD!
THIS IS WHAT I'VE PREPARED FOR YOU!!
UH...!
TA-DAAAANN
AGAIN!?
SO BIG!
TOO BIG!
SHE WORKS FAST!
HA HA HA
NOW, THIS IS SOME-THING.
超包子 chao bao zi
PILES
まきえ
FROM ME...
WHAT IS THIS LITTLE CREATURE?
PLOP
CHIMYAA
FRIEND...
超包子 chao bao zi
EHEH HEH HEH, SO CHAO-LIN, HOW ABOUT IT?
DID YOU GET TEARY? ARE YOU GETTING ALL CHOKED UP?
UHM...
SKRACH SKRACH SKRACH
WELL, THE FACT THAT EVERYONE WENT TO ALL THIS TROUBLE FOR ME...
I'M VERY GRATEFUL, BUT...
SKRACH SKRACH SKRACH

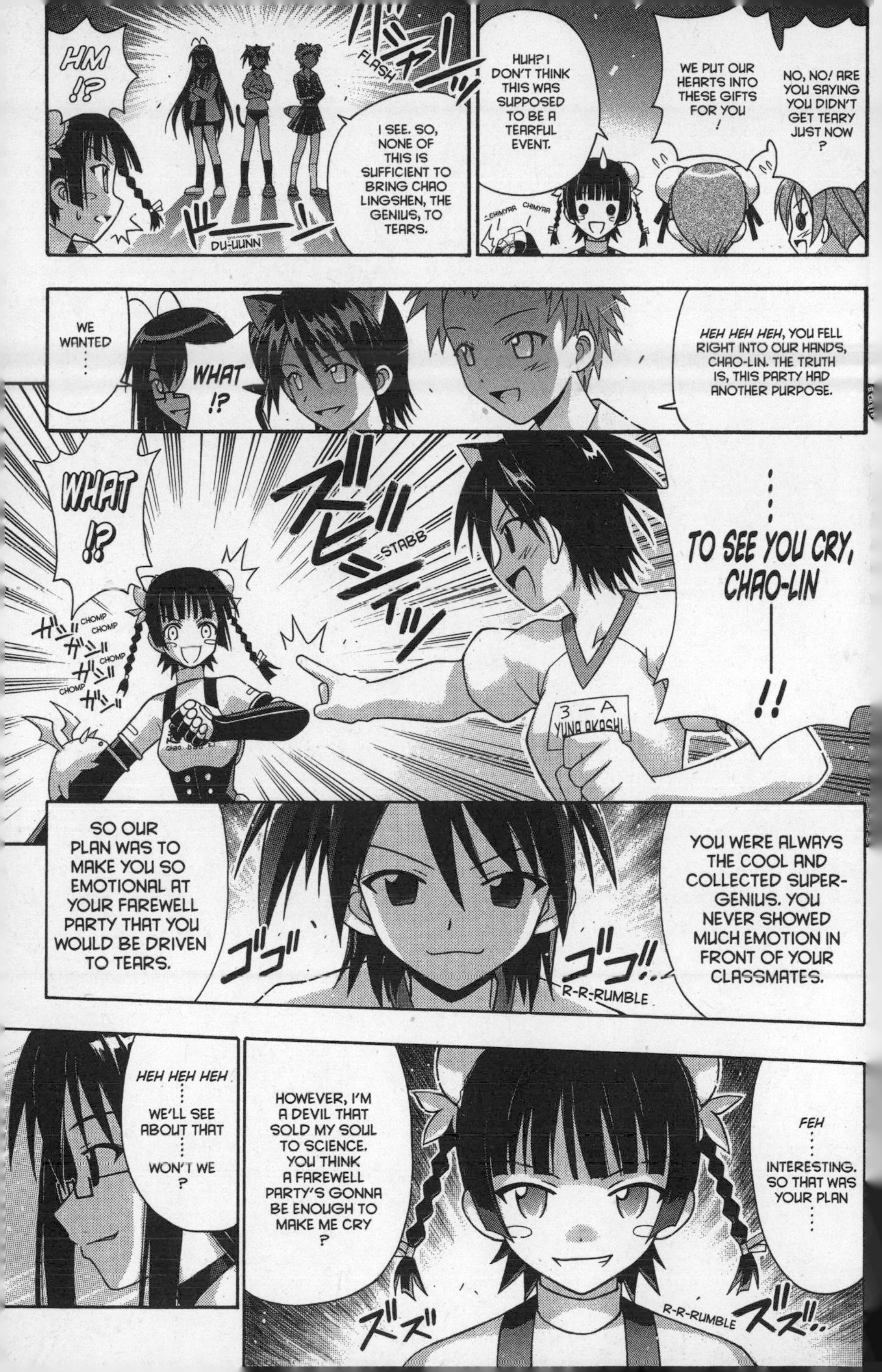
NO, NO! ARE YOU SAYING YOU DIDN'T GET TEARY JUST NOW?
WE PUT OUR HEARTS INTO THESE GIFTS FOR YOU!
HUH? I DON'T THINK THIS WAS SUPPOSED TO BE A TEARFUL EVENT.
CHIMYAA CHIMYAA
FLASH
I SEE. SO, NONE OF THIS IS SUFFICIENT TO BRING CHAO LINGSHEN, THE GENIUS, TO TEARS.
HM!?
DU-UUNN
HEH HEH HEH, YOU FELL RIGHT INTO OUR HANDS, CHAO-LIN. THE TRUTH IS, THIS PARTY HAD ANOTHER PURPOSE.
WHAT!?
WE WANTED...
...TO SEE YOU CRY, CHAO-LIN—!!
STABB
3—A YUNA AKASHI
WHAT!?
CHOMP CHOMP CHOMP CHOMP
YOU WERE ALWAYS THE COOL AND COLLECTED SUPER-GENIUS. YOU NEVER SHOWED MUCH EMOTION IN FRONT OF YOUR CLASSMATES.
R-R-RUMBLE
SO OUR PLAN WAS TO MAKE YOU SO EMOTIONAL AT YOUR FAREWELL PARTY THAT YOU WOULD BE DRIVEN TO TEARS.
FEH... INTERESTING. SO THAT WAS YOUR PLAN...
HOWEVER, I'M A DEVIL THAT SOLD MY SOUL TO SCIENCE. YOU THINK A FAREWELL PARTY'S GONNA BE ENOUGH TO MAKE ME CRY?
R-R-RUMBLE
HEH HEH HEH... WE'LL SEE ABOUT THAT... WON'T WE?

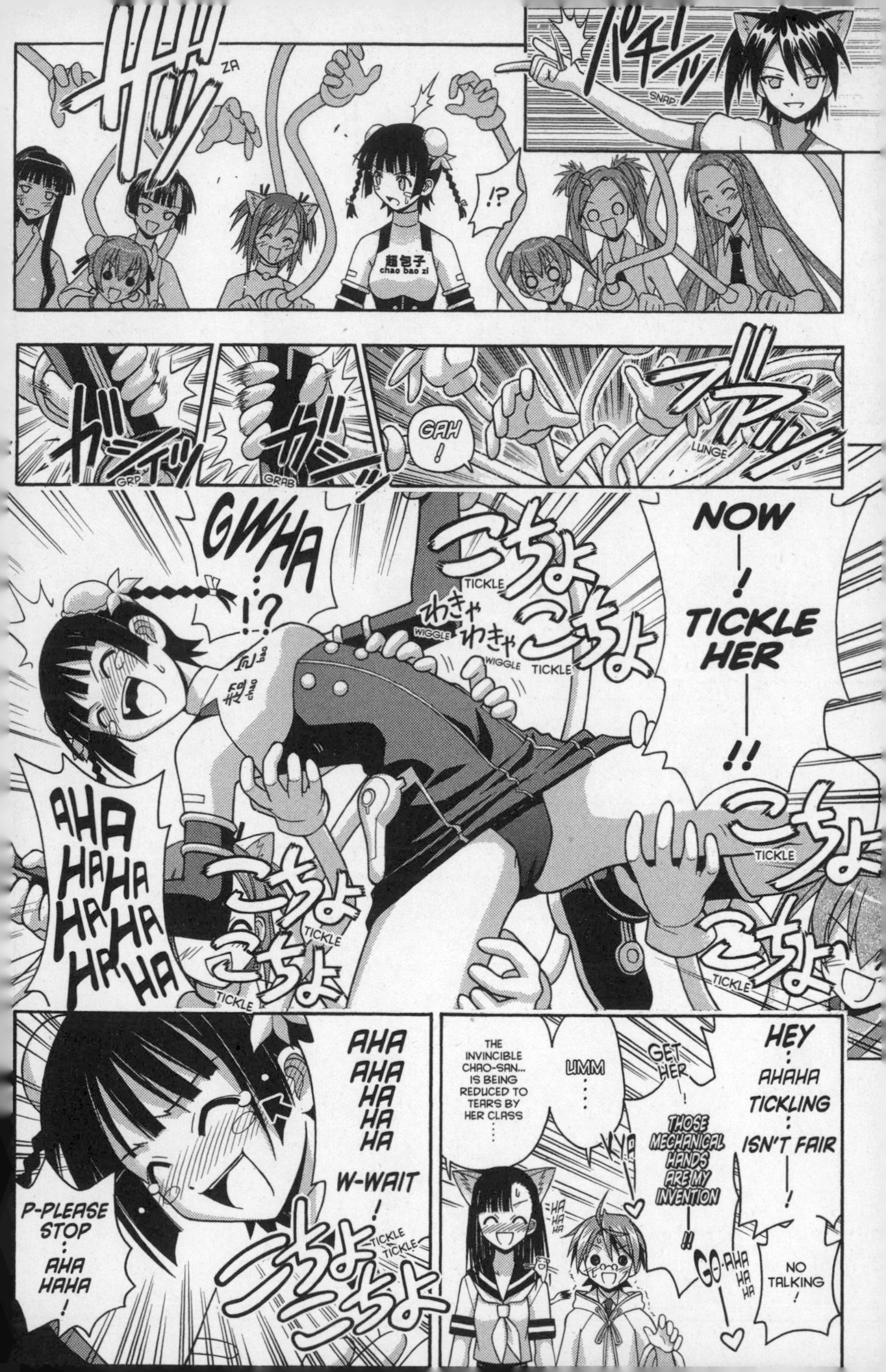

パチーンッ
SNAP
ザザッ
ZA
!?
超包子
chao bao zi
ブァッ
LUNGE
GAH!
ガシッ
GRAB
ガシッ
GRP
NOW—! TICKLE HER—!!
こちょこちょ
TICKLE TICKLE
GWHA...!?
こちょこちょ
TICKLE TICKLE
わきゃわきゃ
WIGGLE WIGGLE
超包
chao bao
AHA HA HA HA HA HA HA HA HA
こちょこちょ
TICKLE TICKLE
HEY... AHAHA TICKLING... ISN'T FAIR—!
NO TALKING!
THOSE MECHANICAL HANDS ARE MY INVENTION—!!
GET HER!
GO—♡
AHA HA HA
UMM...
THE INVINCIBLE CHAO-SAN... IS BEING REDUCED TO TEARS BY HER CLASS...
KYA♡
HA HA HA
AHA AHA HA HA HA
W-WAIT!
P-PLEASE STOP... AHA HAHA!
こちょこちょ
TICKLE TICKLE

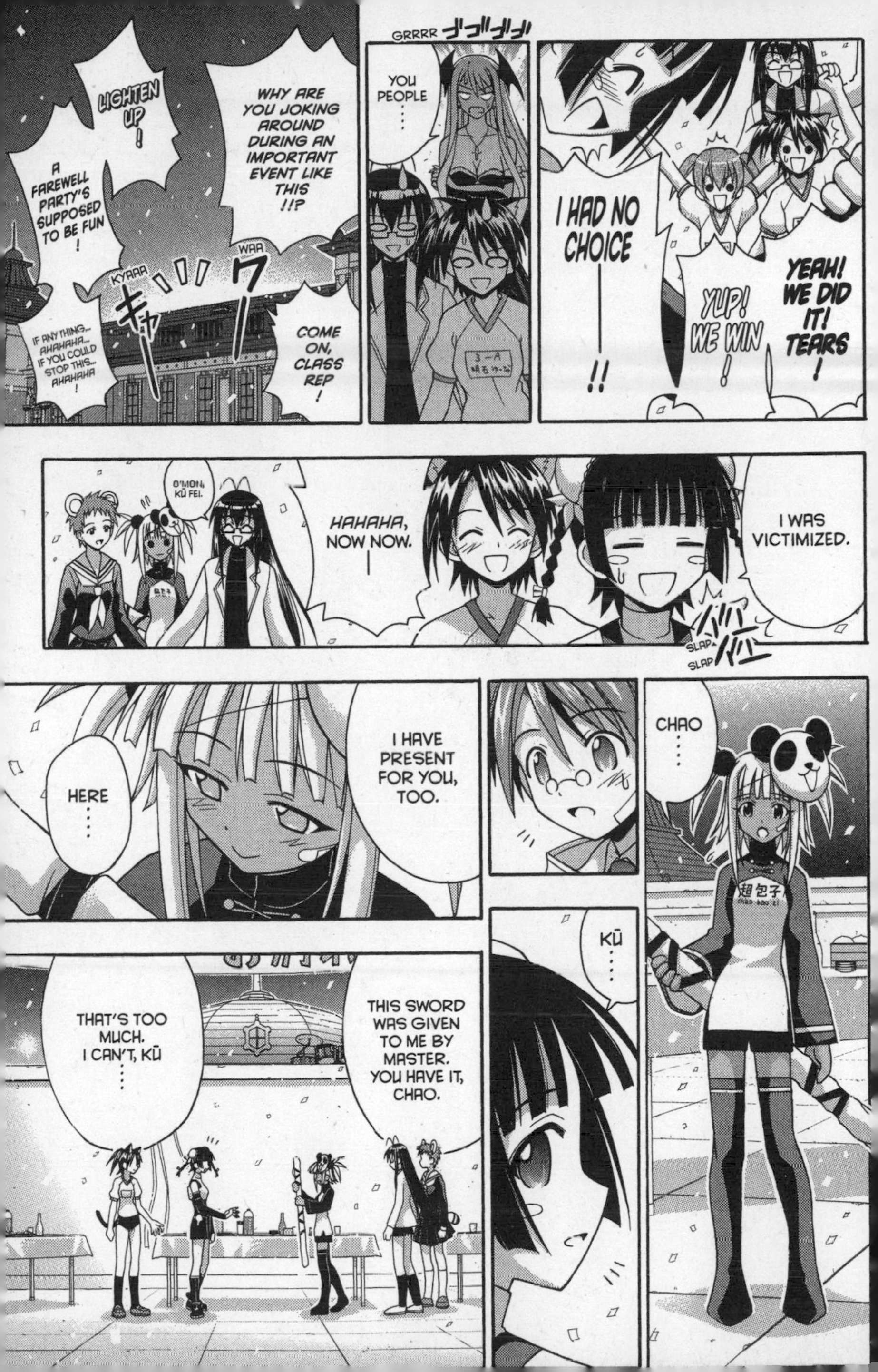
I HAD NO CHOICE―!!
YUP! WE WIN!
YEAH! WE DID IT! TEARS!
GRRRR
YOU PEOPLE....
WHY ARE YOU JOKING AROUND DURING AN IMPORTANT EVENT LIKE THIS!!?
LIGHTEN UP!
A FAREWELL PARTY'S SUPPOSED TO BE FUN!
WAA
KYAAA
COME ON, CLASS REP!
IF ANYTHING... AHAHAHA... IF YOU COULD STOP THIS... AHAHAHA!
I WAS VICTIMIZED.
SLAP
SLAP
HAHAHA, NOW NOW.
C'MON, KŪ FEI.
CHAO....
I HAVE PRESENT FOR YOU, TOO.
HERE....
KŪ....
THIS SWORD WAS GIVEN TO ME BY MASTER. YOU HAVE IT, CHAO.
THAT'S TOO MUCH. I CAN'T, KŪ....

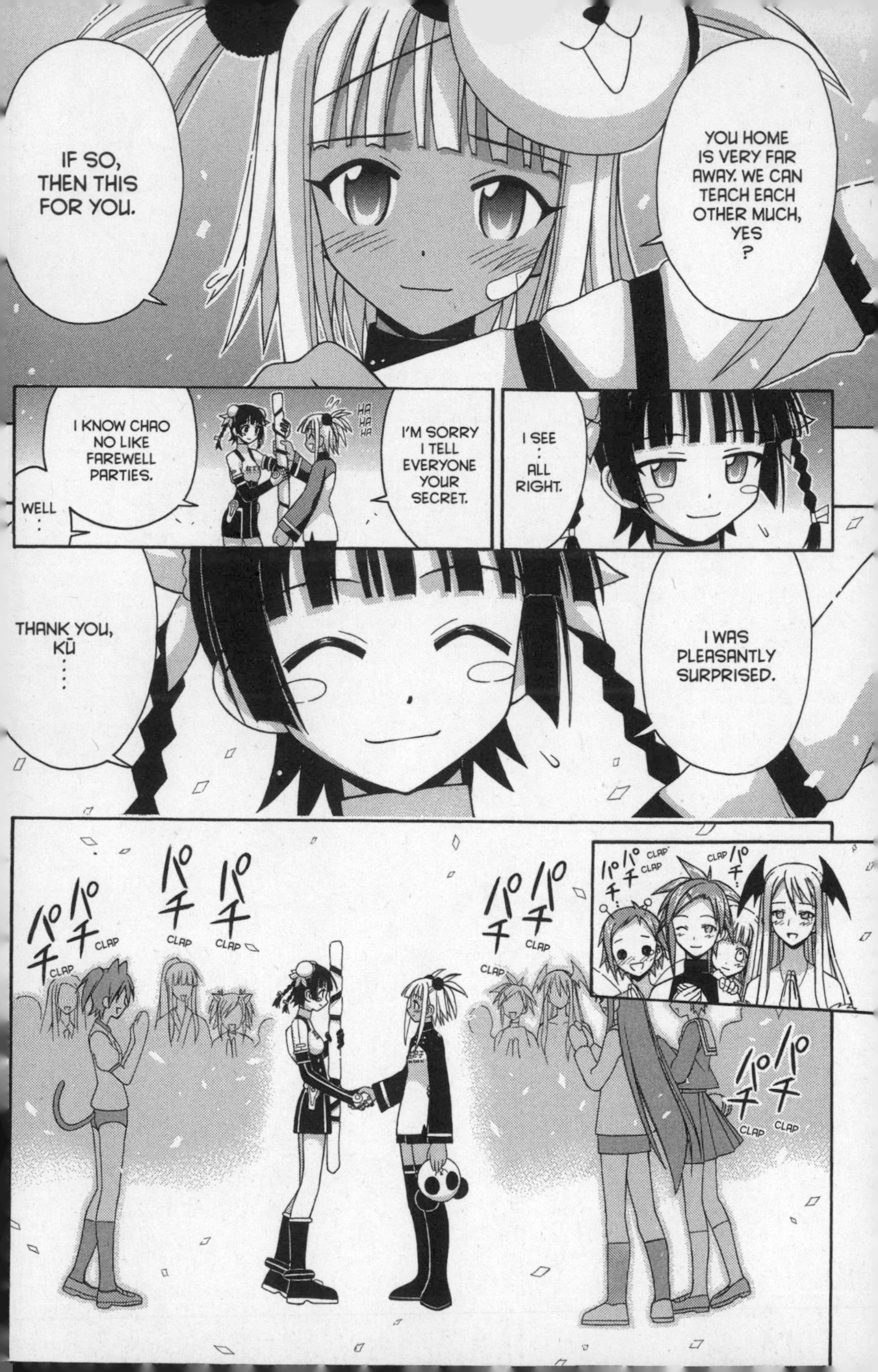

YOU HOME IS VERY FAR AWAY. WE CAN TEACH EACH OTHER MUCH, YES ?
IF SO, THEN THIS FOR YOU.
I SEE : ALL RIGHT.
I'M SORRY I TELL EVERYONE YOUR SECRET.
HA HA HA
I KNOW CHAO NO LIKE FAREWELL PARTIES.
WELL :
I WAS PLEASANTLY SURPRISED.
THANK YOU, KŪ ....
パチ CLAP
パチ CLAP
パチ CLAP
パチ CLAP
パチパチ CLAP CLAP
パチパチ CLAP
パチ CLAP
パチ CLAP
パチパチ CLAP

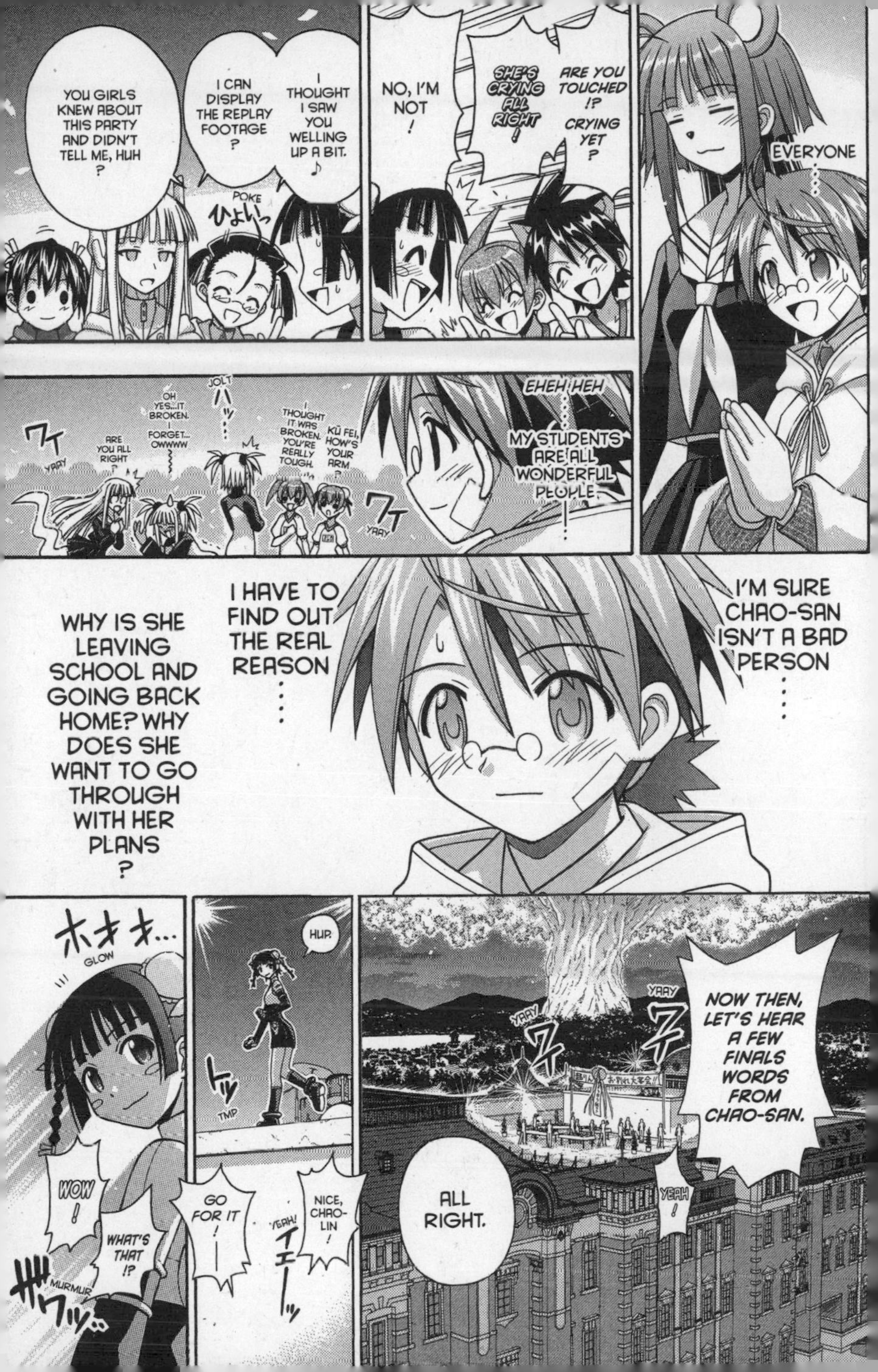
EVERYONE...
ARE YOU TOUCHED!? CRYING YET?
SHE'S CRYING ALL RIGHT!
NO, I'M NOT!
I THOUGHT I SAW YOU WELLING UP A BIT. ♪
ひょいっ
POKE
I CAN DISPLAY THE REPLAY FOOTAGE?
YOU GIRLS KNEW ABOUT THIS PARTY AND DIDN'T TELL ME, HUH?
EHEH HEH...
MY STUDENTS ARE ALL WONDERFUL PEOPLE...!
YAAY
KŪ FEI, HOW'S YOUR ARM?
I THOUGHT IT WAS BROKEN. YOU'RE REALLY TOUGH.
JOLT
OH YES... IT BROKEN. I FORGET... OWWWW
ARE YOU ALL RIGHT?
YAAY
I'M SURE CHAO-SAN ISN'T A BAD PERSON...
I HAVE TO FIND OUT THE REAL REASON...
WHY IS SHE LEAVING SCHOOL AND GOING BACK HOME? WHY DOES SHE WANT TO GO THROUGH WITH HER PLANS?
NOW THEN, LET'S HEAR A FEW FINALS WORDS FROM CHAO-SAN.
YAAY
YAAY
YEAH!
ALL RIGHT.
HUP.
TMP
NICE, CHAO-LIN!
YEAH!
GO FOR IT!
GLOW
WOW!
WHAT'S THAT!?
MURMUR

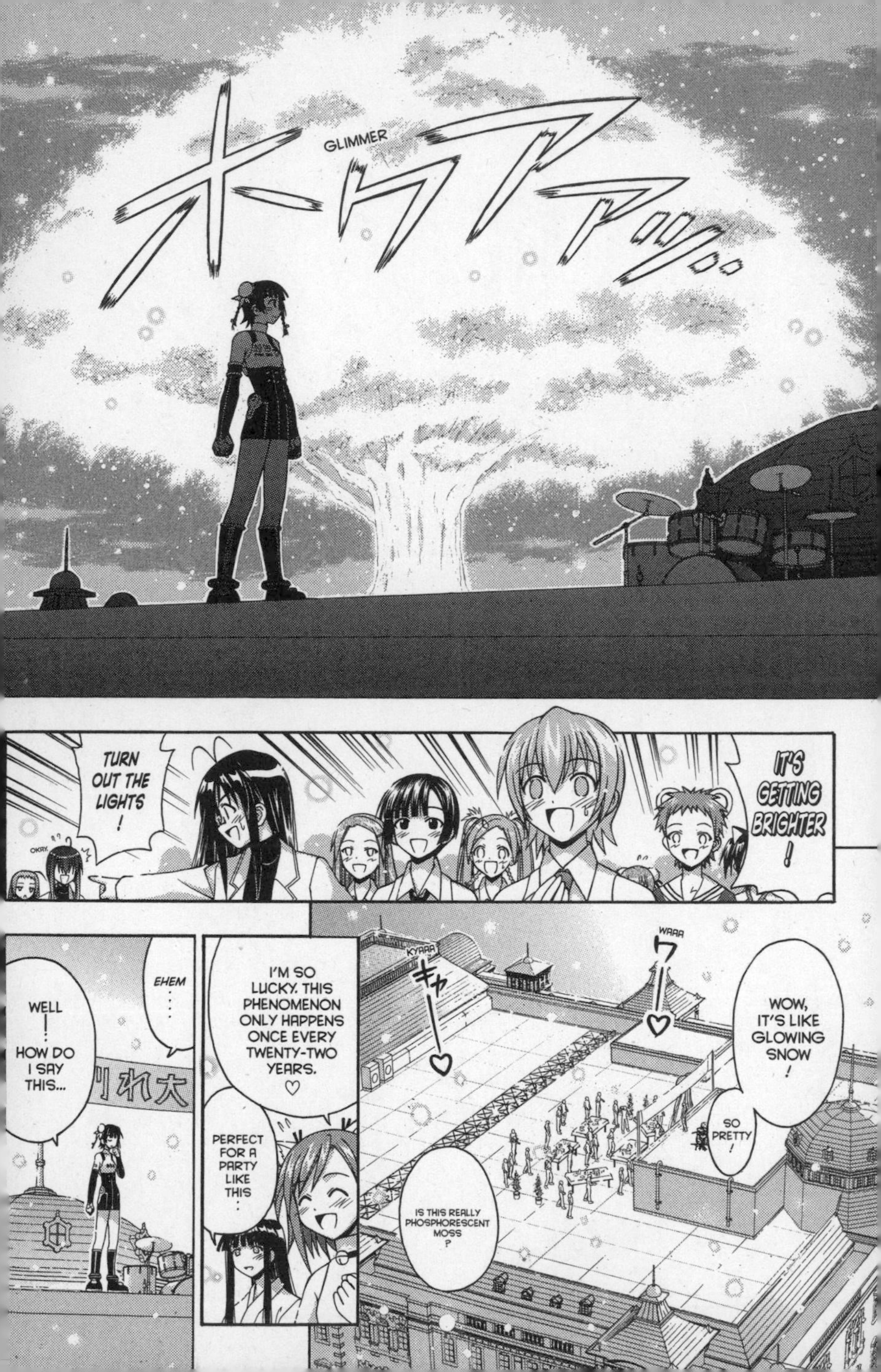
GLIMMER
IT'S GETTING BRIGHTER!
TURN OUT THE LIGHTS!
OKAY.
WAAA
KYAAA
WOW, IT'S LIKE GLOWING SNOW!
SO PRETTY!
IS THIS REALLY PHOSPHORESCENT MOSS?
I'M SO LUCKY. THIS PHENOMENON ONLY HAPPENS ONCE EVERY TWENTY-TWO YEARS. ♡
PERFECT FOR A PARTY LIKE THIS...
EHEM...
WELL! HOW DO I SAY THIS...

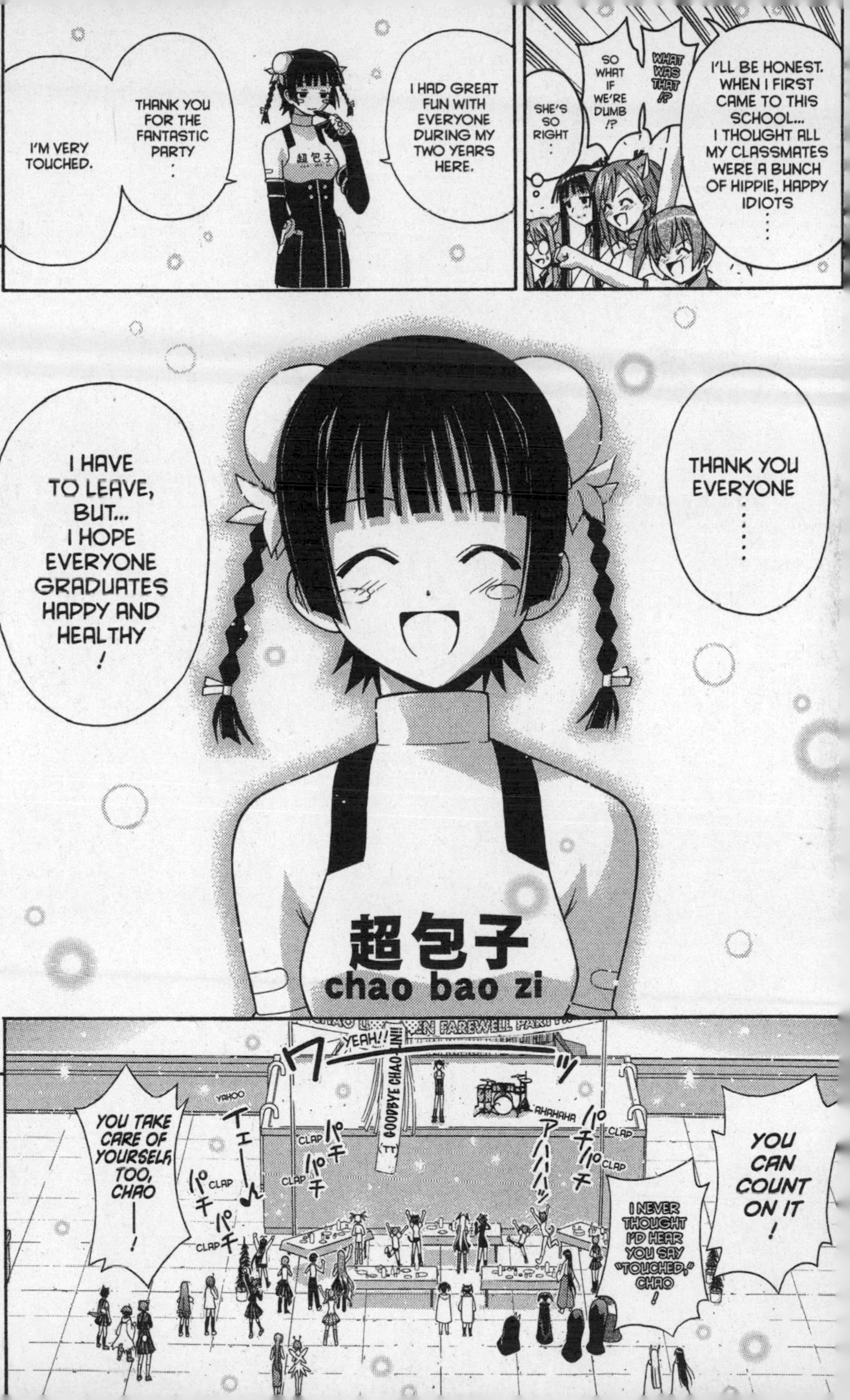
I'LL BE HONEST. WHEN I FIRST CAME TO THIS SCHOOL... I THOUGHT ALL MY CLASSMATES WERE A BUNCH OF HIPPIE, HAPPY IDIOTS ......
WHAT WAS THAT !?
SO WHAT IF WE'RE DUMB !?
SHE'S SO RIGHT ...
I HAD GREAT FUN WITH EVERYONE DURING MY TWO YEARS HERE.
THANK YOU FOR THE FANTASTIC PARTY ...
I'M VERY TOUCHED.
超包子
THANK YOU EVERYONE ......
I HAVE TO LEAVE, BUT... I HOPE EVERYONE GRADUATES HAPPY AND HEALTHY !
超包子
chao bao zi
ワーッ
YEAH!!
GOODBYE CHAO-LIN!!
(TT)
YOU CAN COUNT ON IT !
I NEVER THOUGHT I'D HEAR YOU SAY "TOUCHED," CHAO !
パチパチ CLAP CLAP
アハハハッ AHAHAHA
パチパチ CLAP CLAP
イェーイ YAHOO
パチパチ CLAP CLAP
YOU TAKE CARE OF YOURSELF, TOO, CHAO—!

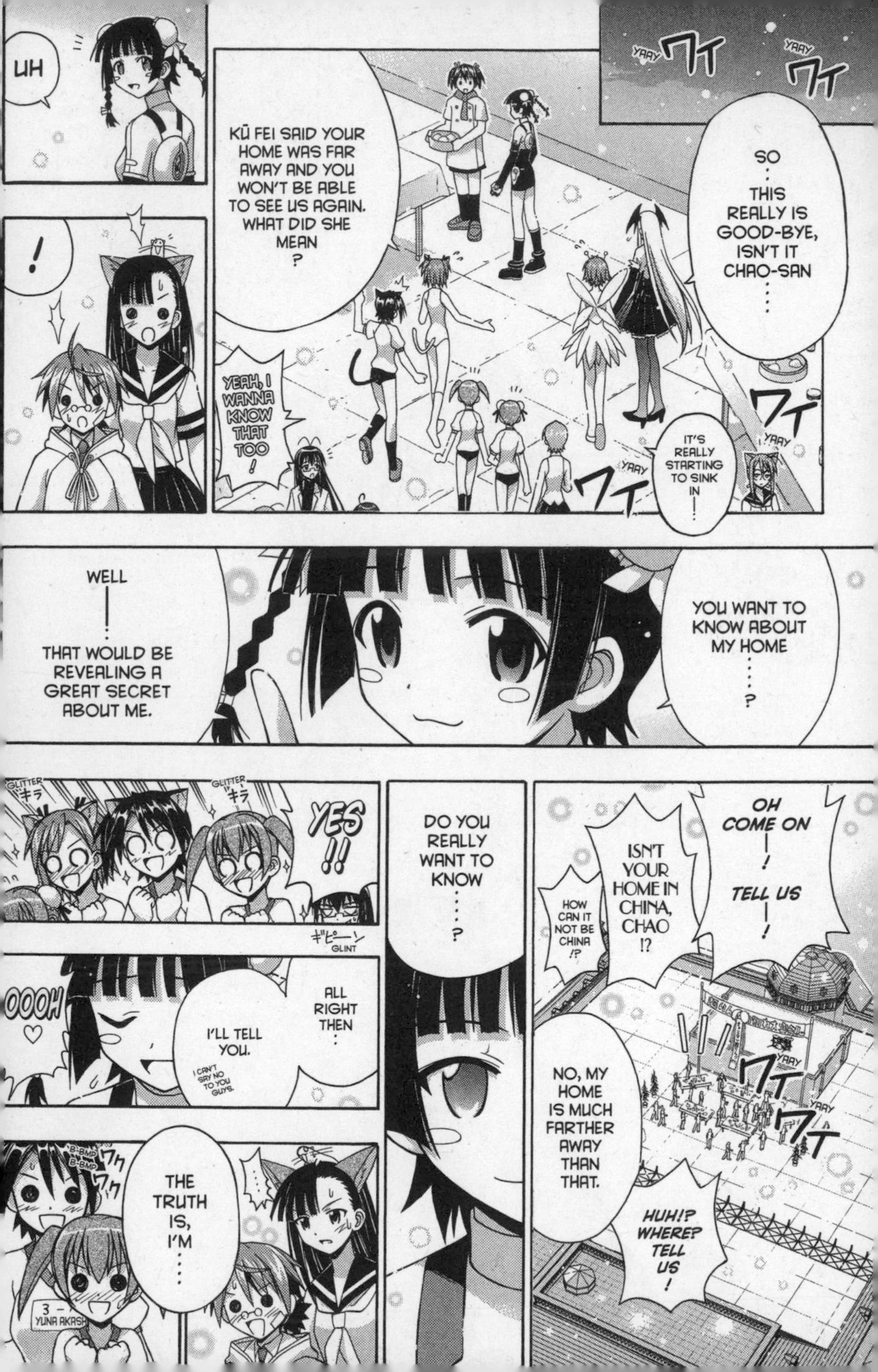
YAAY ワイ
YAAY ワイ
SO... THIS REALLY IS GOOD-BYE, ISN'T IT CHAO-SAN....
ワイ YAAY
IT'S REALLY STARTING TO SINK IN...!
YAAY ワイ
KŪ FEI SAID YOUR HOME WAS FAR AWAY AND YOU WON'T BE ABLE TO SEE US AGAIN. WHAT DID SHE MEAN?
YEAH, I WANNA KNOW THAT TOO!
UH
!
YOU WANT TO KNOW ABOUT MY HOME....?
WELL— THAT WOULD BE REVEALING A GREAT SECRET ABOUT ME.
OH COME ON—! TELL US—!
ISN'T YOUR HOME IN CHINA, CHAO!?
HOW CAN IT NOT BE CHINA!?
YAAY ワイ
YAAY ワイ
NO, MY HOME IS MUCH FARTHER AWAY THAN THAT.
HUH!? WHERE? TELL US!
DO YOU REALLY WANT TO KNOW....?
GLITTER キラ
GLITTER キラ
YES!!
ギピーン GLINT
ALL RIGHT THEN...
I'LL TELL YOU.
I CAN'T SAY NO TO YOU GUYS.
OOOH ♡
B-BMP B-BMP ワク ワク
THE TRUTH IS, I'M....

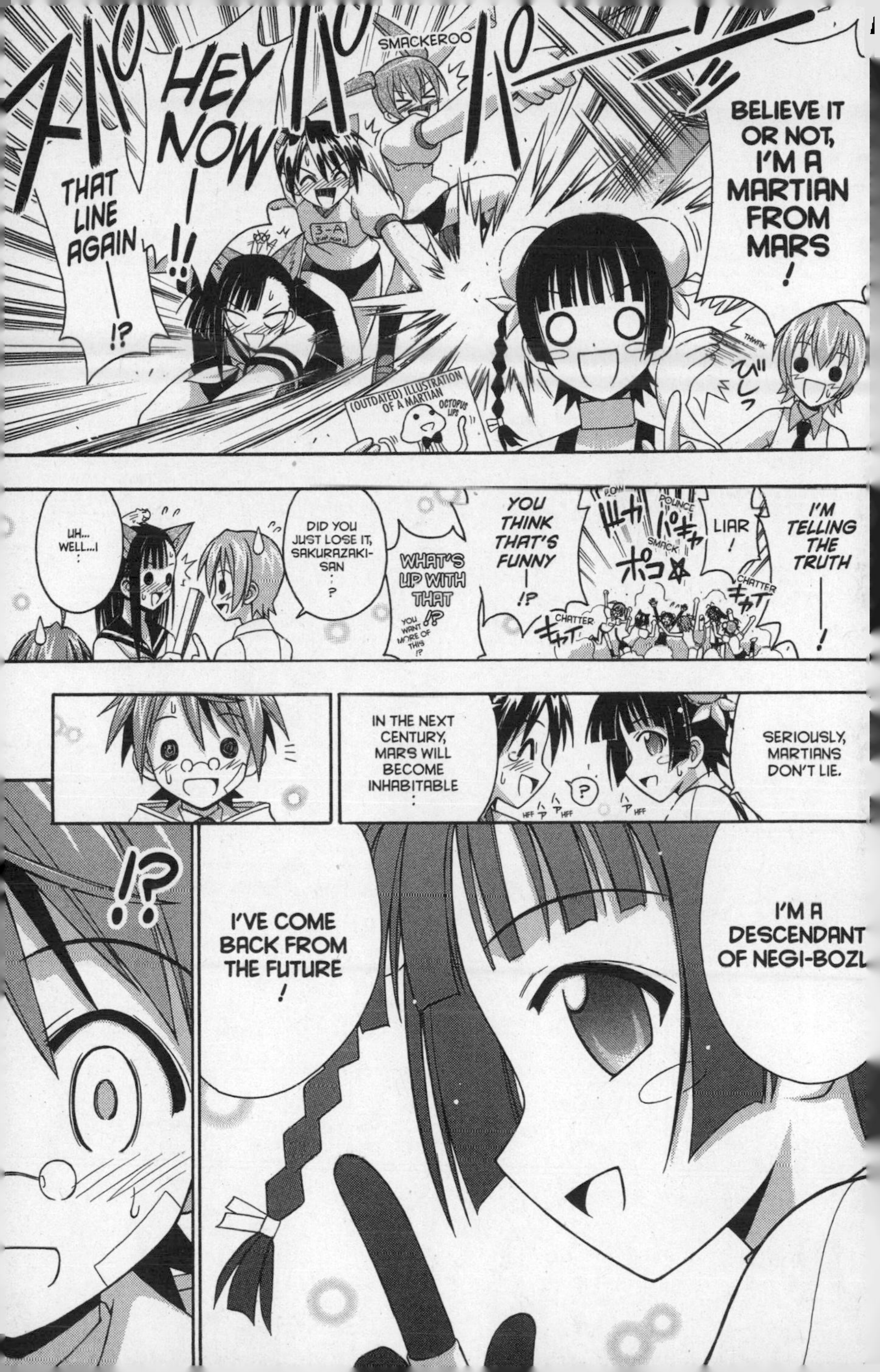
BELIEVE IT OR NOT, I'M A MARTIAN FROM MARS!
THWAK
SMACKEROO
HEY NOW!!
THAT LINE AGAIN!?
(OUTDATED) ILLUSTRATION OF A MARTIAN
OCTOPUS LIPS
I'M TELLING THE TRUTH!
LIAR!
CHATTER
POUNCE
SMACK
POW
CHATTER
YOU THINK THAT'S FUNNY!?
WHAT'S UP WITH THAT!?
YOU WANT MORE OF THIS!?
DID YOU JUST LOSE IT, SAKURAZAKI-SAN...?
UH... WELL...I...
SERIOUSLY, MARTIANS DON'T LIE.
HFF
HFF
HFF
IN THE NEXT CENTURY, MARS WILL BECOME INHABITABLE...
I'M A DESCENDANT OF NEGI-BOZU
I'VE COME BACK FROM THE FUTURE!
!?

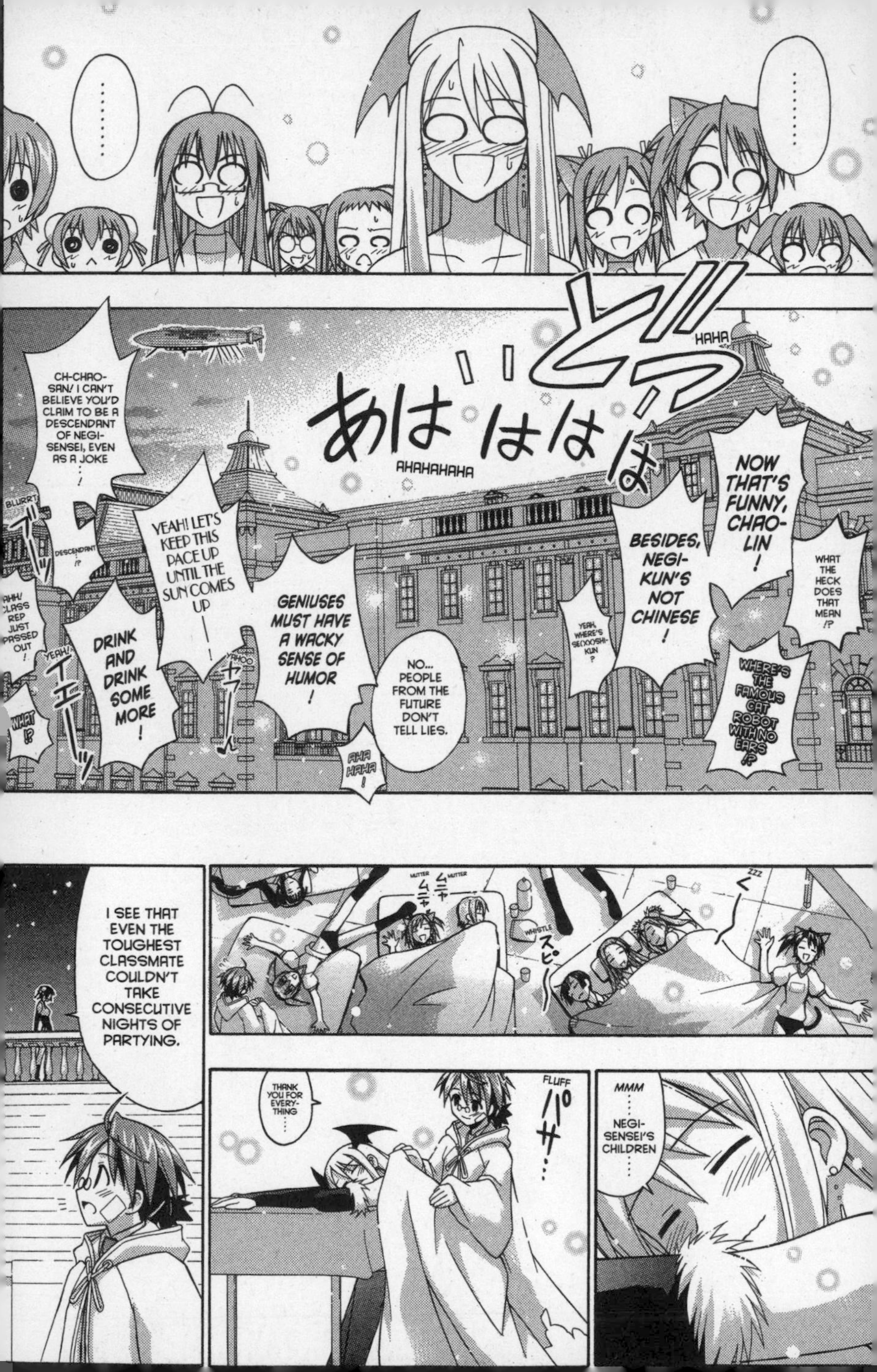
……
……
WHAT THE HECK DOES THAT MEAN!?
NOW THAT'S FUNNY, CHAO-LIN!
WHERE'S THE FAMOUS CAT ROBOT WITH NO EARS!?
HAHA
どっ
あはははは AHAHAHAHA
BESIDES, NEGI-KUN'S NOT CHINESE!
YEAH, WHERE'S SE(XX)SHI-KUN?
NO... PEOPLE FROM THE FUTURE DON'T TELL LIES.
AHA HAHA!
GENIUSES MUST HAVE A WACKY SENSE OF HUMOR!
YEAH! LET'S KEEP THIS PACE UP UNTIL THE SUN COMES UP!
YAHOO
DRINK AND DRINK SOME MORE!
YEAH!
CH-CHAO-SAN! I CAN'T BELIEVE YOU'D CLAIM TO BE A DESCENDANT OF NEGI-SENSEI, EVEN AS A JOKE…!
DESCENDANT…!?
BLURRT
AHH! CLASS REP JUST PASSED OUT!
WHAT!?
ZZZ
WHISTLE
MUTTER MUTTER
MMM… NEGI-SENSEI'S CHILDREN…
FLUFF
THANK YOU FOR EVERYTHING…
I SEE THAT EVEN THE TOUGHEST CLASSMATE COULDN'T TAKE CONSECUTIVE NIGHTS OF PARTYING.

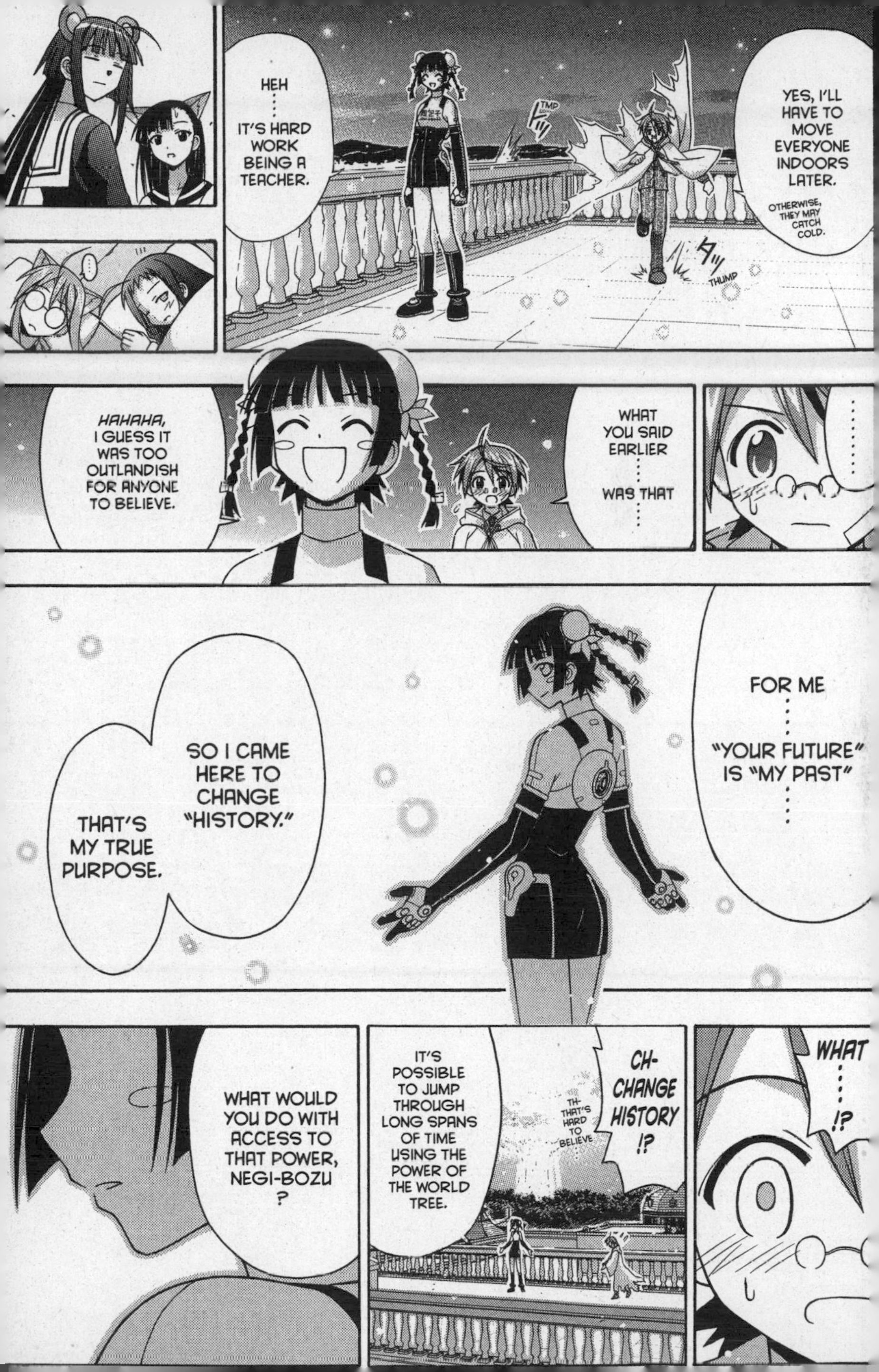
YES, I'LL HAVE TO MOVE EVERYONE INDOORS LATER.
OTHERWISE, THEY MAY CATCH COLD.
THUMP
TMP
HEH ... IT'S HARD WORK BEING A TEACHER.
...
......
WHAT YOU SAID EARLIER ...... WAS THAT ......
HAHAHA, I GUESS IT WAS TOO OUTLANDISH FOR ANYONE TO BELIEVE.
FOR ME ...... "YOUR FUTURE" IS "MY PAST" ......
SO I CAME HERE TO CHANGE "HISTORY."
THAT'S MY TRUE PURPOSE.
WHAT ...... !?
CH- CHANGE HISTORY !?
TH- THAT'S HARD TO BELIEVE ...
IT'S POSSIBLE TO JUMP THROUGH LONG SPANS OF TIME USING THE POWER OF THE WORLD TREE.
WHAT WOULD YOU DO WITH ACCESS TO THAT POWER, NEGI-BOZU ?

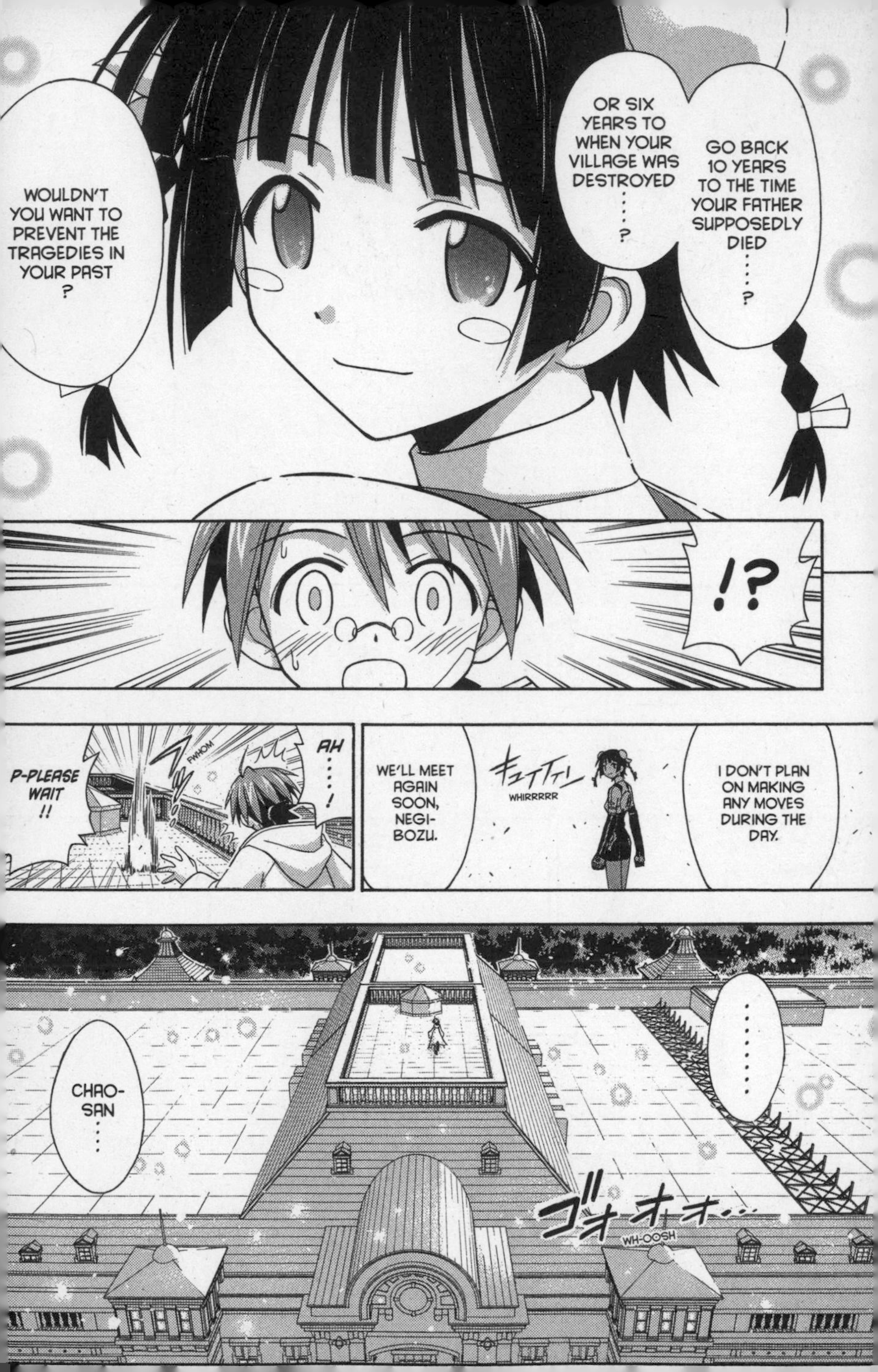

GO BACK 10 YEARS TO THE TIME YOUR FATHER SUPPOSEDLY DIED ....?
OR SIX YEARS TO WHEN YOUR VILLAGE WAS DESTROYED ....?
WOULDN'T YOU WANT TO PREVENT THE TRAGEDIES IN YOUR PAST ?
!?
I DON'T PLAN ON MAKING ANY MOVES DURING THE DAY.
WHIRRRRR
WE'LL MEET AGAIN SOON, NEGI-BOZU.
AH ....!
FWHOM
P-PLEASE WAIT !!
......
WH-OOSH
CHAO-SAN ....

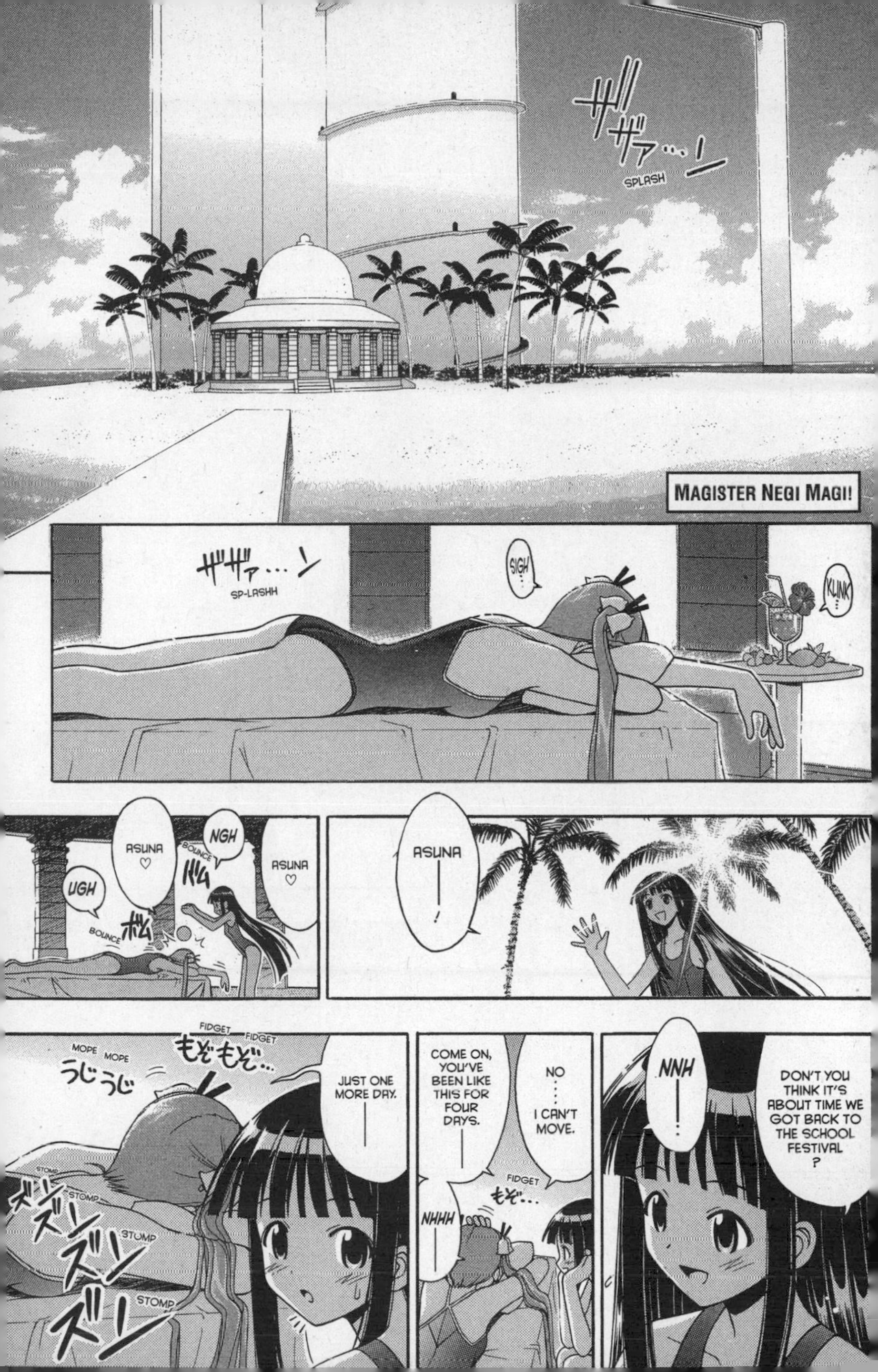
ザザァ…ン
SPLASH
MAGISTER NEGI MAGI!
KLINK…
SIGH…
ザザァ…ン
SP-LASHH
ASUNA—!
ASUNA ♡
NGH
BOUNCE ボム
ASUNA ♡
UGH
BOUNCE ボム
DON'T YOU THINK IT'S ABOUT TIME WE GOT BACK TO THE SCHOOL FESTIVAL?
NNH—!
NO… I CAN'T MOVE.
COME ON, YOU'VE BEEN LIKE THIS FOR FOUR DAYS.—
FIDGET もぞ…
NHHH—
JUST ONE MORE DAY.—
FIDGET FIDGET もぞもぞ…
MOPE MOPE うじうじ
STOMP STOMP STOMP STOMP ズーンズーンズーン

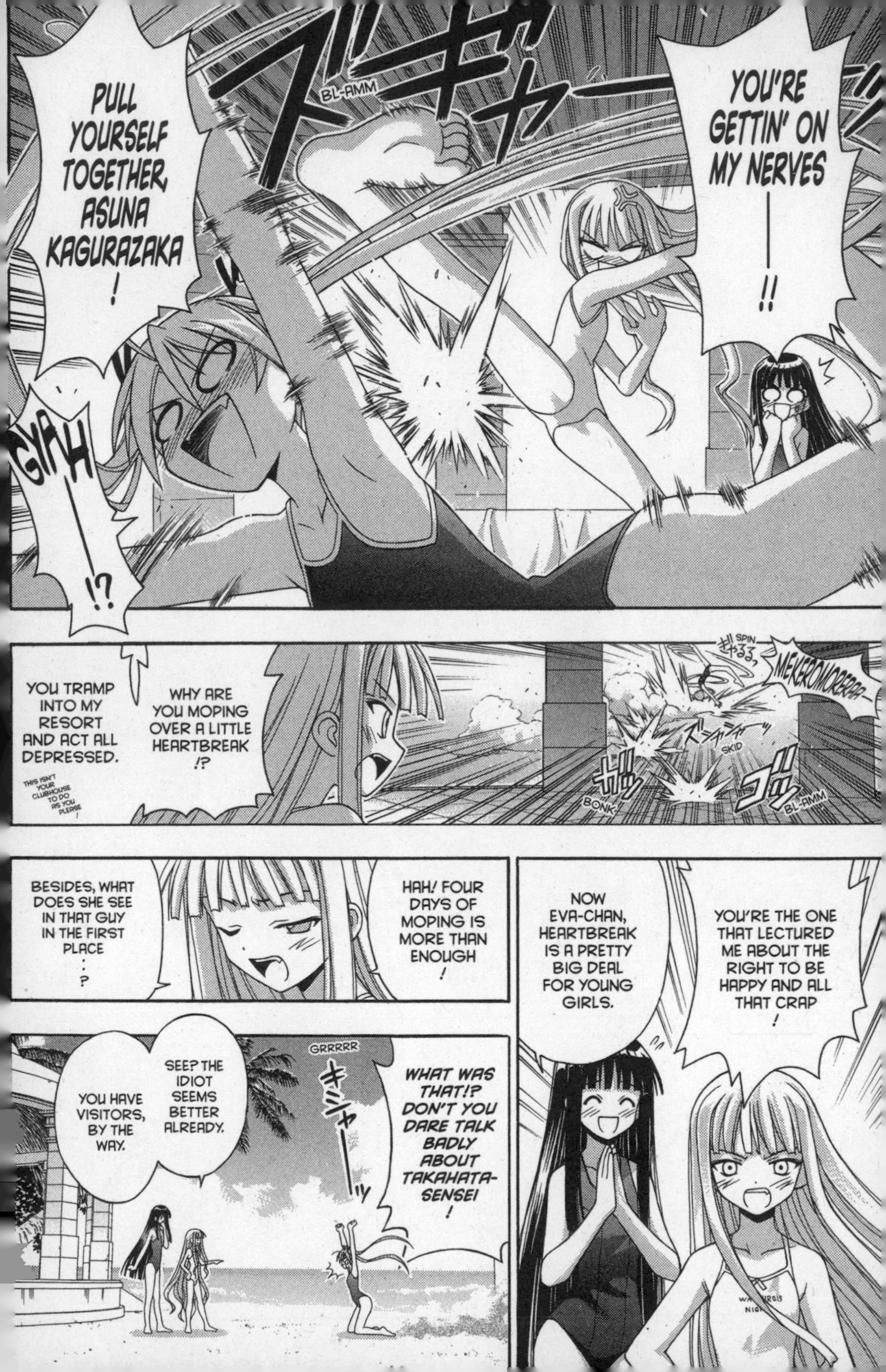

YOU'RE GETTIN' ON MY NERVES——!!
BL-AMM
PULL YOURSELF TOGETHER, ASUNA KAGURAZAKA!
GYAH——!?
SPIN
MEKEROMOREBRA—
SKID
BONK
BL-AMM
WHY ARE YOU MOPING OVER A LITTLE HEARTBREAK!?
YOU TRAMP INTO MY RESORT AND ACT ALL DEPRESSED.
THIS ISN'T YOUR CLUBHOUSE TO DO AS YOU PLEASE!
YOU'RE THE ONE THAT LECTURED ME ABOUT THE RIGHT TO BE HAPPY AND ALL THAT CRAP!
NOW EVA-CHAN, HEARTBREAK IS A PRETTY BIG DEAL FOR YOUNG GIRLS.
HAH! FOUR DAYS OF MOPING IS MORE THAN ENOUGH!
BESIDES, WHAT DOES SHE SEE IN THAT GUY IN THE FIRST PLACE...?
WHAT WAS THAT!? DON'T YOU DARE TALK BADLY ABOUT TAKAHATA-SENSEI!
GRRRRR
SEE? THE IDIOT SEEMS BETTER ALREADY.
YOU HAVE VISITORS, BY THE WAY.

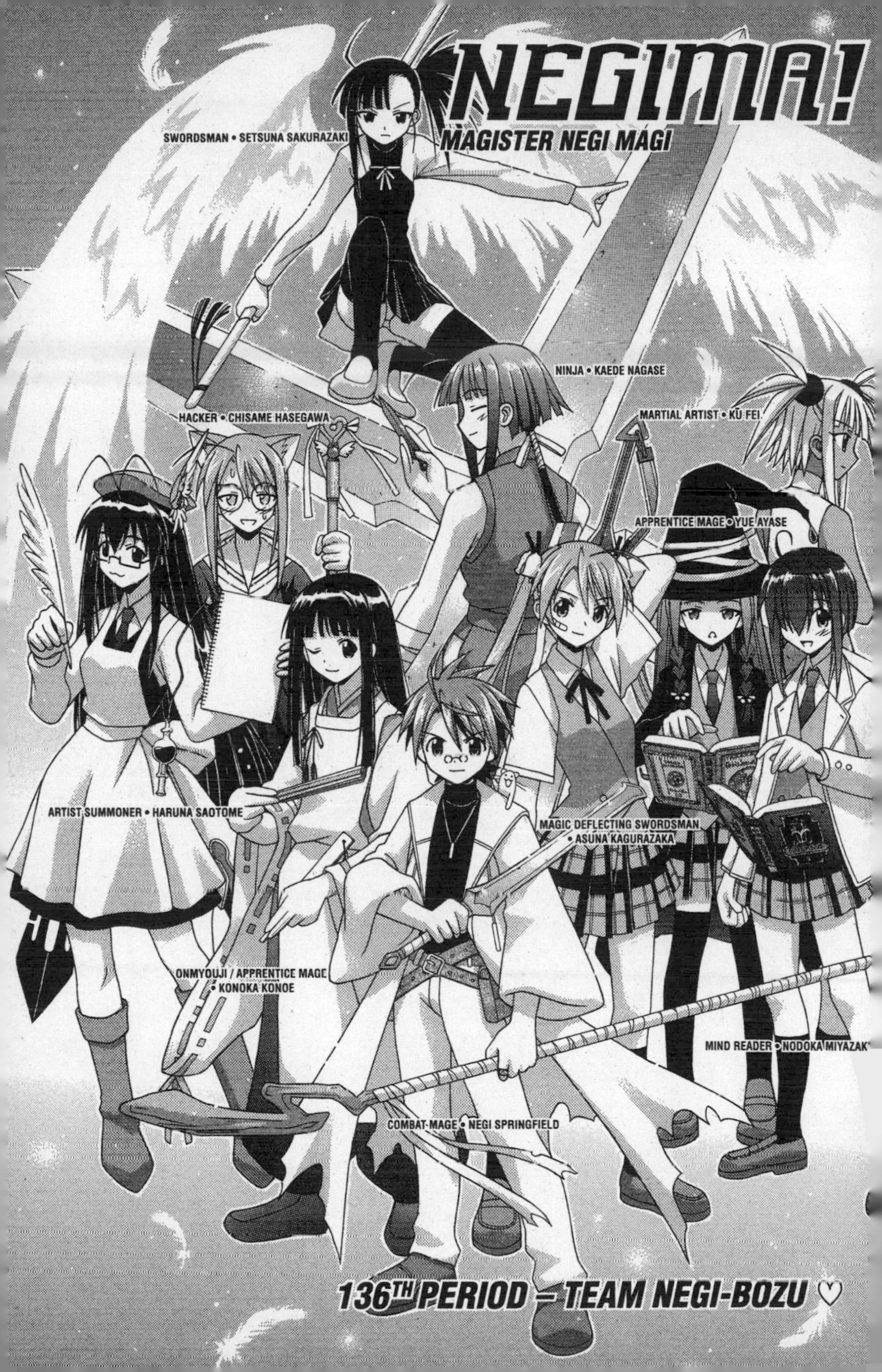
NEGIMA!
MAGISTER NEGI MAGI
SWORDSMAN • SETSUNA SAKURAZAKI
NINJA • KAEDE NAGASE
HACKER • CHISAME HASEGAWA
MARTIAL ARTIST • KU FEI
APPRENTICE MAGE • YUE AYASE
ARTIST SUMMONER • HARUNA SAOTOME
MAGIC DEFLECTING SWORDSMAN
• ASUNA KAGURAZAKA
ONMYOUJI / APPRENTICE MAGE
• KONOKA KONOE
MIND READER • NODOKA MIYAZAKI
COMBAT MAGE • NEGI SPRINGFIELD
136TH PERIOD – TEAM NEGI-BOZU ♡

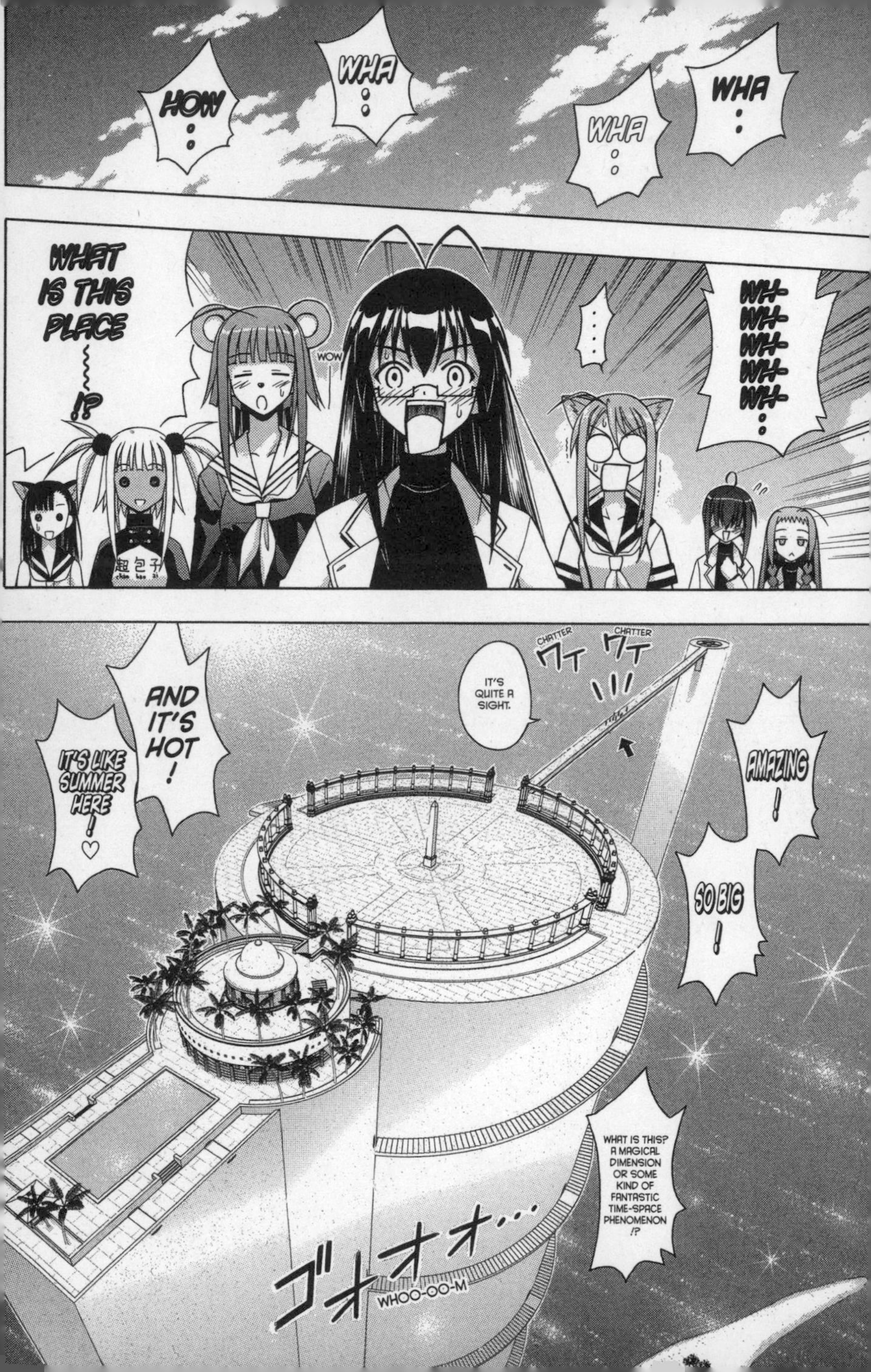
WHA . .
WHA . .
WHA . .
HOW . .
WH- WH- WH- WH- WH- . .
. . . .
WOW
WHAT IS THIS PLACE ~~~!?
超包子
CHATTER ワイ CHATTER ワイ
AMAZING!
IT'S QUITE A SIGHT.
SO BIG!
AND IT'S HOT!
IT'S LIKE SUMMER HERE! ♡
WHAT IS THIS? A MAGICAL DIMENSION OR SOME KIND OF FANTASTIC TIME-SPACE PHENOMENON !?
ゴオオオ… WHOO-OO-M

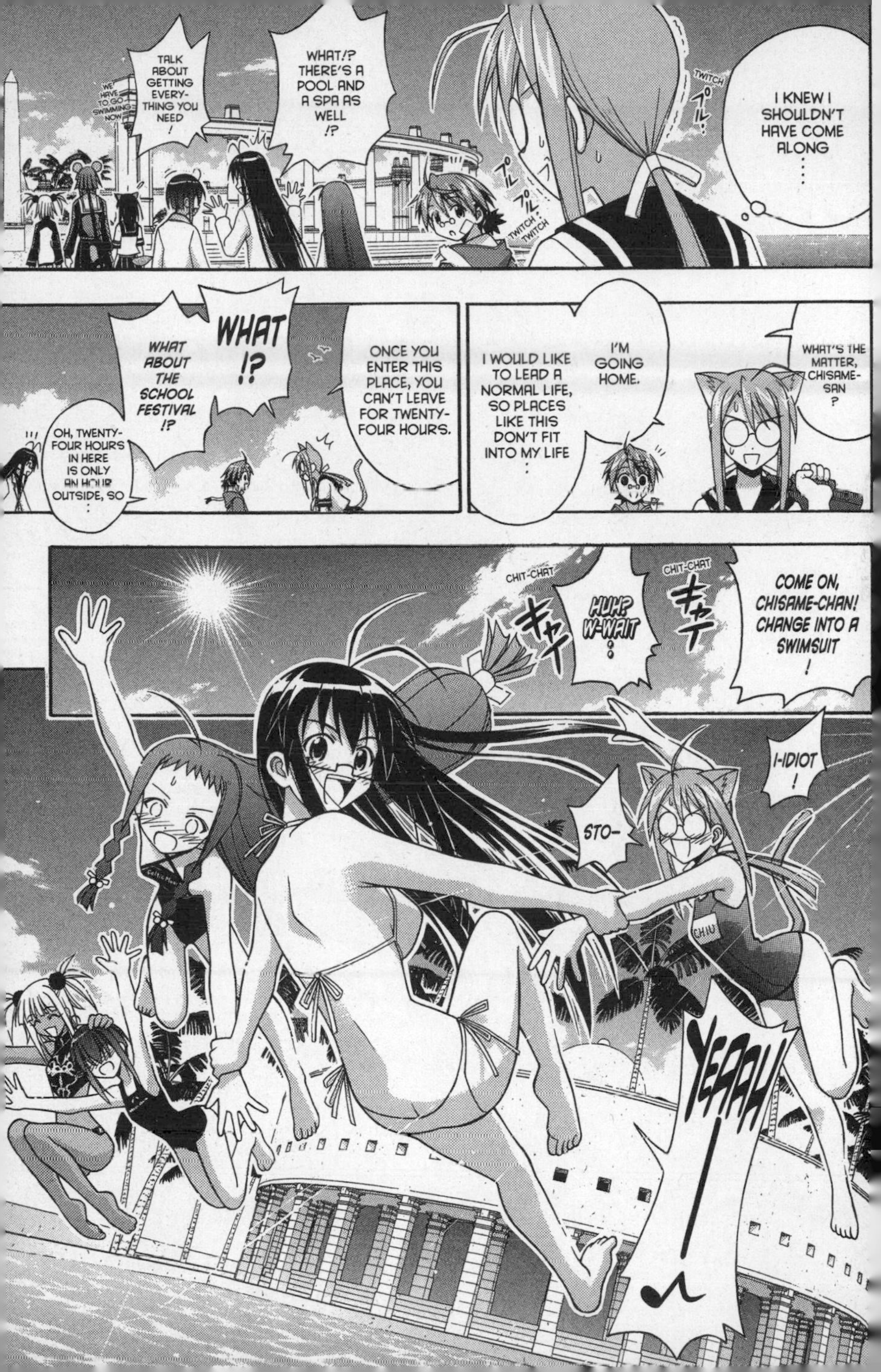

TWITCH
I KNEW I SHOULDN'T HAVE COME ALONG ...
WHAT!? THERE'S A POOL AND A SPA AS WELL !?
TALK ABOUT GETTING EVERY-THING YOU NEED !
WE HAVE TO GO SWIMMING NOW!
TWITCH TWITCH
WHAT'S THE MATTER, CHISAME-SAN ?
I'M GOING HOME.
I WOULD LIKE TO LEAD A NORMAL LIFE, SO PLACES LIKE THIS DON'T FIT INTO MY LIFE ...
ONCE YOU ENTER THIS PLACE, YOU CAN'T LEAVE FOR TWENTY-FOUR HOURS.
WHAT !?
WHAT ABOUT THE SCHOOL FESTIVAL !?
OH, TWENTY-FOUR HOURS IN HERE IS ONLY AN HOUR OUTSIDE, SO ...
COME ON, CHISAME-CHAN! CHANGE INTO A SWIMSUIT !
CHIT-CHAT
HUH? W-WAIT ...
CHIT-CHAT
I-IDIOT !
STO-
YEAAH !

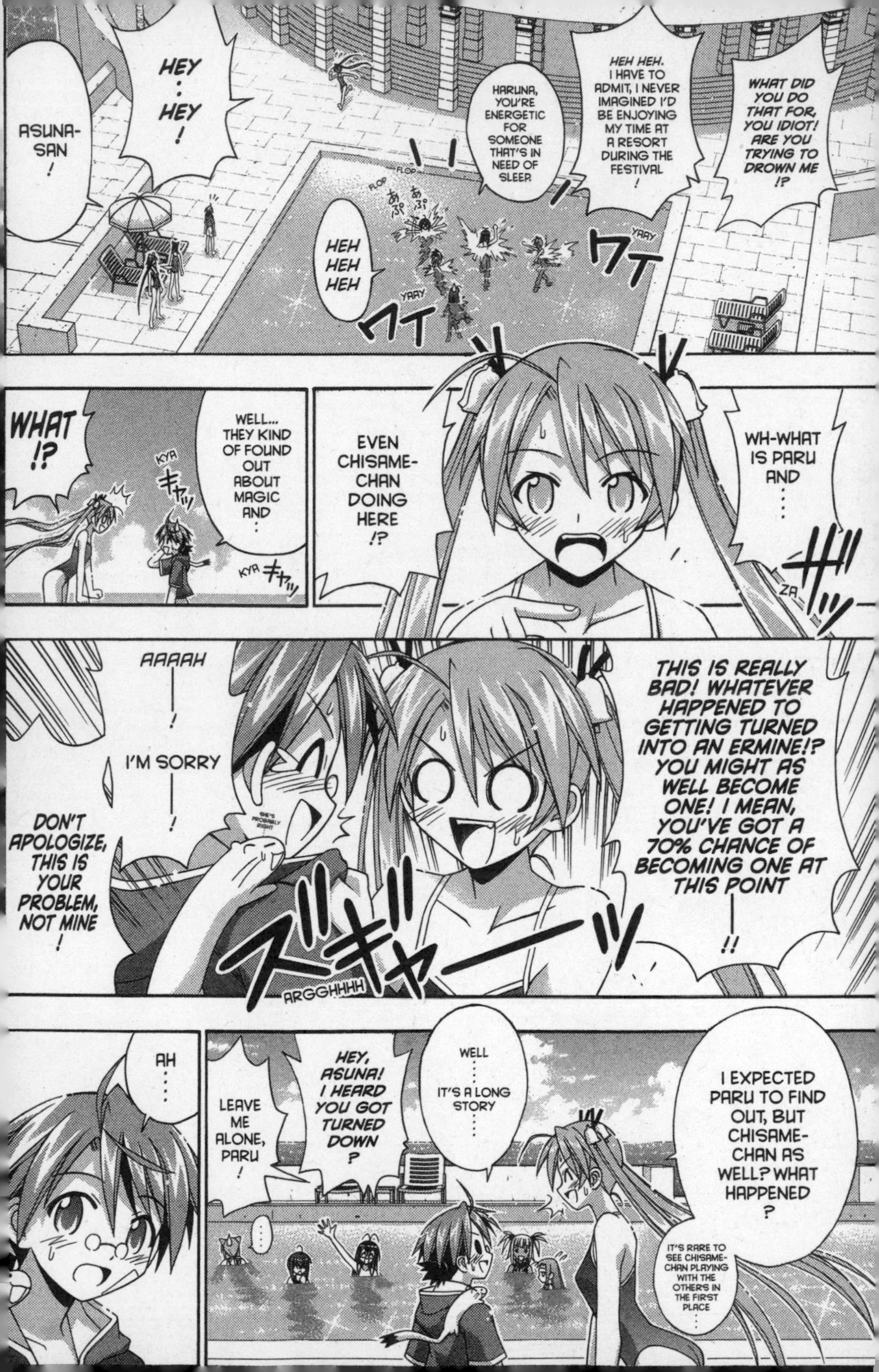
WHAT DID YOU DO THAT FOR, YOU IDIOT! ARE YOU TRYING TO DROWN ME!?
HEH HEH. I HAVE TO ADMIT, I NEVER IMAGINED I'D BE ENJOYING MY TIME AT A RESORT DURING THE FESTIVAL!
YAAY
HARUNA, YOU'RE ENERGETIC FOR SOMEONE THAT'S IN NEED OF SLEEP.
FLOP
FLOP
HEY...HEY!
HEH HEH HEH
YAAY
ASUNA-SAN!
WH-WHAT IS PARU AND....
ZA
EVEN CHISAME-CHAN DOING HERE!?
WELL... THEY KIND OF FOUND OUT ABOUT MAGIC AND...
WHAT!?
KYA
KYA
THIS IS REALLY BAD! WHATEVER HAPPENED TO GETTING TURNED INTO AN ERMINE!? YOU MIGHT AS WELL BECOME ONE! I MEAN, YOU'VE GOT A 70% CHANCE OF BECOMING ONE AT THIS POINT!!
AAAAH!
I'M SORRY!
SHE'S PROBABLY RIGHT
DON'T APOLOGIZE, THIS IS YOUR PROBLEM, NOT MINE!
ARGGHHHH
I EXPECTED PARU TO FIND OUT, BUT CHISAME-CHAN AS WELL? WHAT HAPPENED?
IT'S RARE TO SEE CHISAME-CHAN PLAYING WITH THE OTHERS IN THE FIRST PLACE...
WELL... IT'S A LONG STORY...
HEY, ASUNA! I HEARD YOU GOT TURNED DOWN?
LEAVE ME ALONE, PARU!
...
AH....

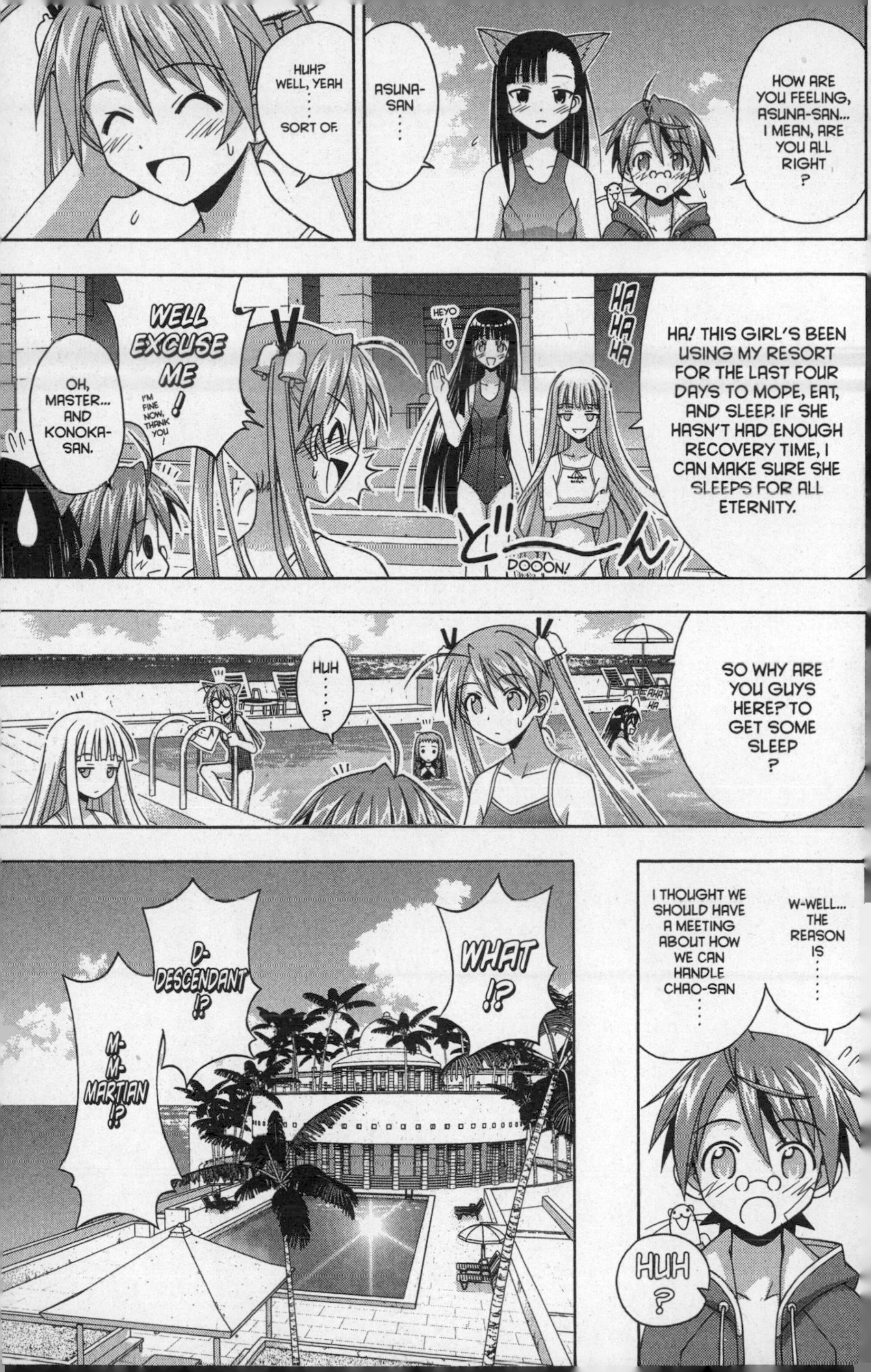
HOW ARE YOU FEELING, ASUNA-SAN... I MEAN, ARE YOU ALL RIGHT ?
ASUNA-SAN ....
HUH? WELL, YEAH ... SORT OF.
HA HA HA HA
HA! THIS GIRL'S BEEN USING MY RESORT FOR THE LAST FOUR DAYS TO MOPE, EAT, AND SLEEP. IF SHE HASN'T HAD ENOUGH RECOVERY TIME, I CAN MAKE SURE SHE SLEEPS FOR ALL ETERNITY.
HEYO ! ♥
どーーん
DOOON!
WELL EXCUSE ME !
I'M FINE NOW, THANK YOU !
OH, MASTER... AND KONOKA-SAN.
SO WHY ARE YOU GUYS HERE? TO GET SOME SLEEP ?
AHA HA
HUH .....?
W-WELL... THE REASON IS ......
I THOUGHT WE SHOULD HAVE A MEETING ABOUT HOW WE CAN HANDLE CHAO-SAN ....
HUH ?
WHAT !?
D-DESCENDANT !?
M-M-MARTIAN !?

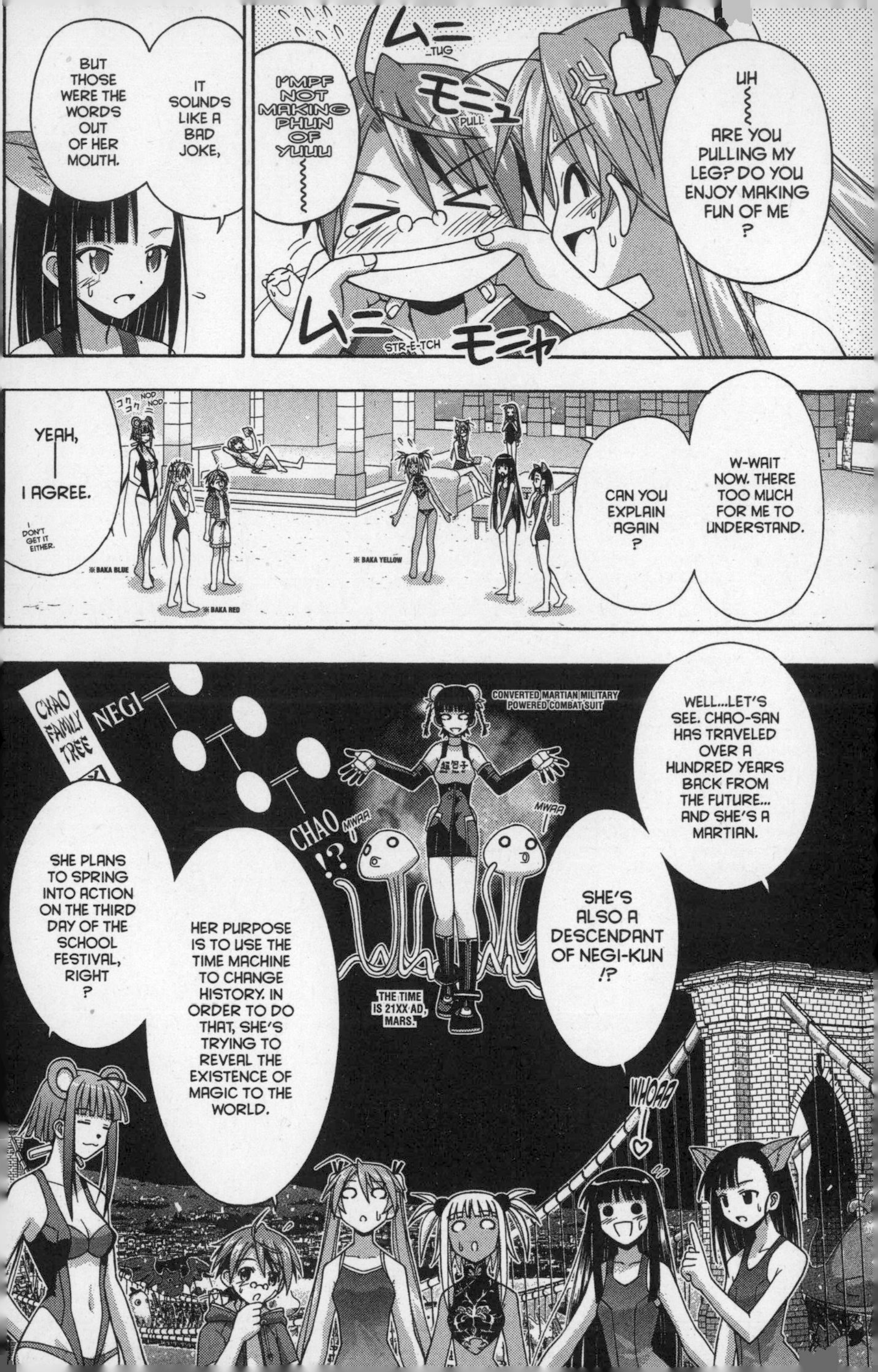

UH ~ ARE YOU PULLING MY LEG? DO YOU ENJOY MAKING FUN OF ME ?
ムニ
TUG
モニュ
PULL
I'MPF NOT MAKING PHUN OF YUUU ~
ムニ
STR-E-TCH
モニャ
IT SOUNDS LIKE A BAD JOKE,
BUT THOSE WERE THE WORDS OUT OF HER MOUTH.
W-WAIT NOW. THERE TOO MUCH FOR ME TO UNDERSTAND.
CAN YOU EXPLAIN AGAIN ?
※BAKA YELLOW
NOD NOD
YEAH, I AGREE.
I DON'T GET IT EITHER.
※BAKA BLUE
※BAKA RED
WELL...LET'S SEE. CHAO-SAN HAS TRAVELED OVER A HUNDRED YEARS BACK FROM THE FUTURE... AND SHE'S A MARTIAN.
CONVERTED MARTIAN MILITARY POWERED COMBAT SUIT
MWAA
MWAA
THE TIME IS 21XX AD, MARS.
SHE'S ALSO A DESCENDANT OF NEGI-KUN !?
CHAO FAMILY TREE
NEGI
CHAO !?
HER PURPOSE IS TO USE THE TIME MACHINE TO CHANGE HISTORY. IN ORDER TO DO THAT, SHE'S TRYING TO REVEAL THE EXISTENCE OF MAGIC TO THE WORLD.
SHE PLANS TO SPRING INTO ACTION ON THE THIRD DAY OF THE SCHOOL FESTIVAL, RIGHT ?
WHOAA

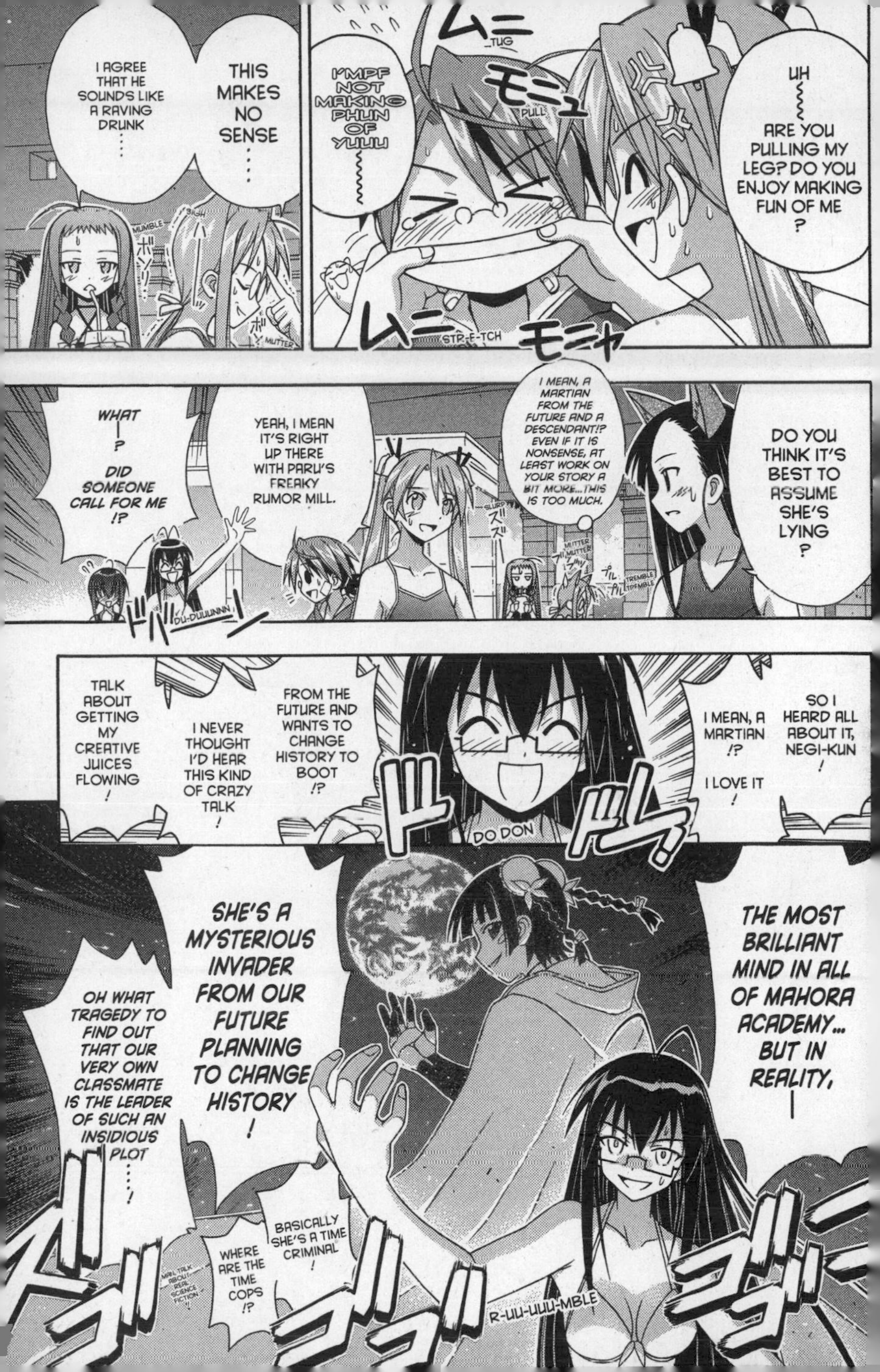
TUG
PULL
UH ~ ARE YOU PULLING MY LEG? DO YOU ENJOY MAKING FUN OF ME?
I'MPF NOT MAKING PHUN OF YUUU ~
STR-E-TCH
THIS MAKES NO SENSE ...
I AGREE THAT HE SOUNDS LIKE A RAVING DRUNK ...
SIGH
MUMBLE
MUTTER
DO YOU THINK IT'S BEST TO ASSUME SHE'S LYING?
I MEAN, A MARTIAN FROM THE FUTURE AND A DESCENDANT!? EVEN IF IT IS NONSENSE, AT LEAST WORK ON YOUR STORY A BIT MORE...THIS IS TOO MUCH.
TREMBLE TREMBLE
MUTTER MUTTER
SLURP
YEAH, I MEAN IT'S RIGHT UP THERE WITH PARU'S FREAKY RUMOR MILL.
WHAT!? DID SOMEONE CALL FOR ME!?
DU-DUUUNNN
SO I HEARD ALL ABOUT IT, NEGI-KUN!
I MEAN, A MARTIAN!?
I LOVE IT!
FROM THE FUTURE AND WANTS TO CHANGE HISTORY TO BOOT!?
I NEVER THOUGHT I'D HEAR THIS KIND OF CRAZY TALK!
TALK ABOUT GETTING MY CREATIVE JUICES FLOWING!
DO DON
THE MOST BRILLIANT MIND IN ALL OF MAHORA ACADEMY... BUT IN REALITY, I
SHE'S A MYSTERIOUS INVADER FROM OUR FUTURE PLANNING TO CHANGE HISTORY!
OH WHAT TRAGEDY TO FIND OUT THAT OUR VERY OWN CLASSMATE IS THE LEADER OF SUCH AN INSIDIOUS PLOT ...!
BASICALLY SHE'S A TIME CRIMINAL!
WHERE ARE THE TIME COPS!?
MAN, TALK ABOUT REAL SCIENCE FICTION!
R-UU-UUU-MBLE

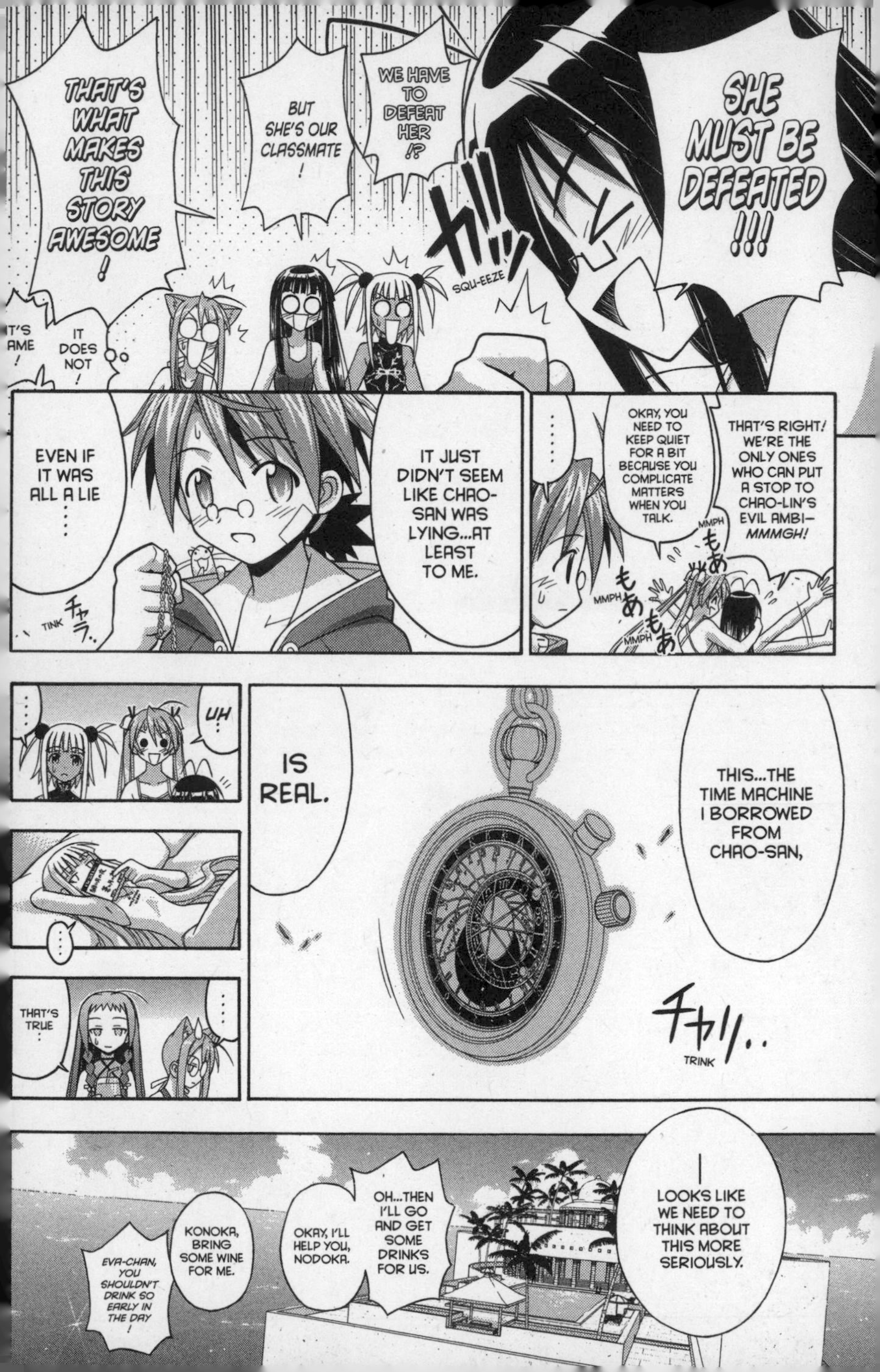

SHE MUST BE DEFEATED!!!
カッ!!
SQU-EEZE
WE HAVE TO DEFEAT HER!?
BUT SHE'S OUR CLASSMATE!
THAT'S WHAT MAKES THIS STORY AWESOME!
IT DOES NOT!
THAT'S RIGHT! WE'RE THE ONLY ONES WHO CAN PUT A STOP TO CHAO-LIN'S EVIL AMBI— MMMGH!
OKAY, YOU NEED TO KEEP QUIET FOR A BIT BECAUSE YOU COMPLICATE MATTERS WHEN YOU TALK.
......
もあ MMPH
もあ MMPH
もあ MMPH
IT JUST DIDN'T SEEM LIKE CHAO-SAN WAS LYING...AT LEAST TO ME.
EVEN IF IT WAS ALL A LIE....
チャラ.. TINK
THIS...THE TIME MACHINE I BORROWED FROM CHAO-SAN,
IS REAL.
チャリ.. TRINK
UH...
......
...
.....
THAT'S TRUE...
LOOKS LIKE WE NEED TO THINK ABOUT THIS MORE SERIOUSLY.
OH...THEN I'LL GO AND GET SOME DRINKS FOR US.
OKAY, I'LL HELP YOU, NODOKA.
KONOKA, BRING SOME WINE FOR ME.
EVA-CHAN, YOU SHOULDN'T DRINK SO EARLY IN THE DAY!

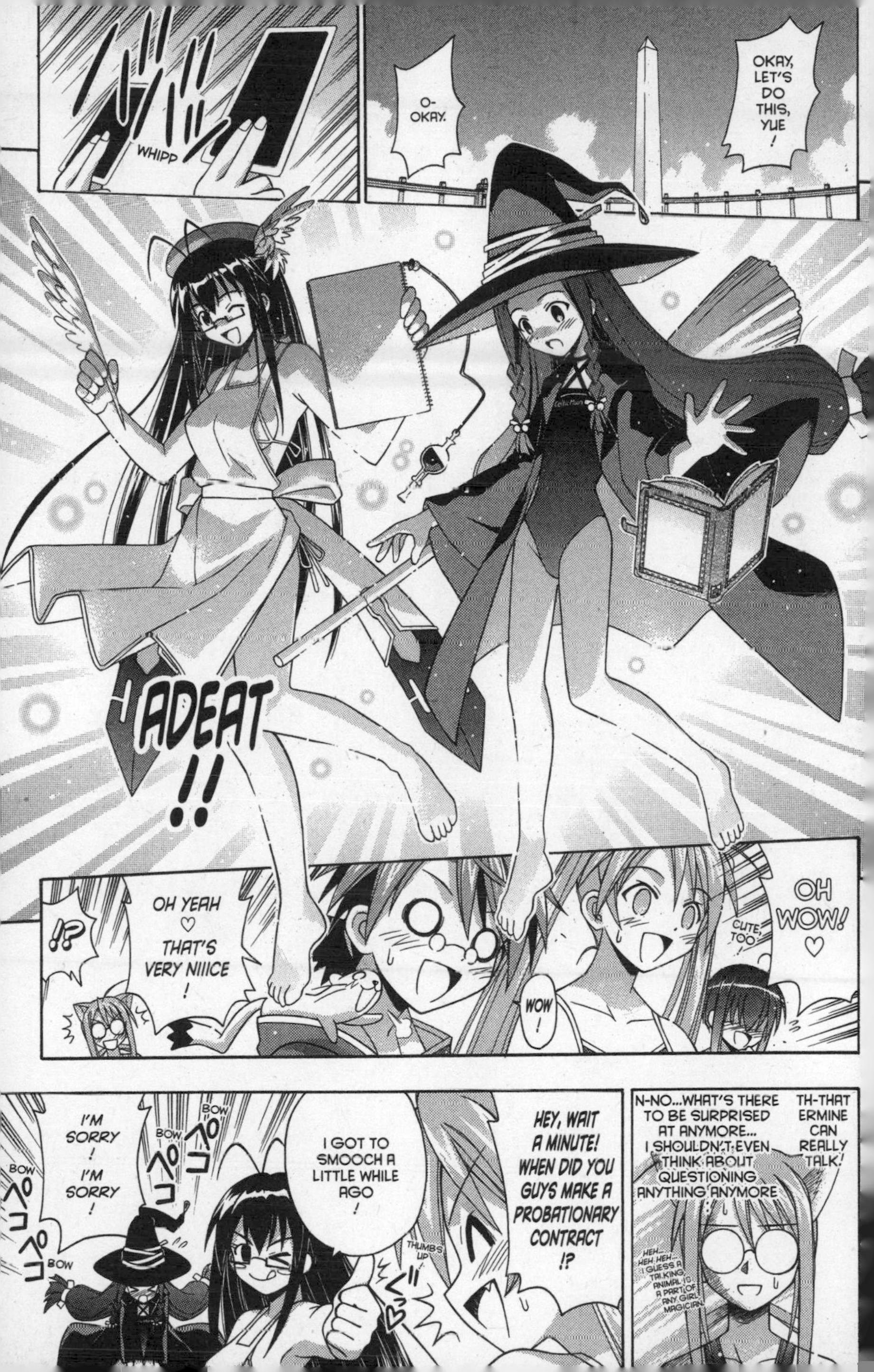

OKAY, LET'S DO THIS, YUE!
O- OKAY.
WHIPP
ADEAT!!
OH WOW! ♡
CUTE, TOO!
WOW!
OH YEAH ♡ THAT'S VERY NIIICE!
!?
TH-THAT ERMINE CAN REALLY TALK!
N-NO...WHAT'S THERE TO BE SURPRISED AT ANYMORE... I SHOULDN'T EVEN THINK ABOUT QUESTIONING ANYTHING ANYMORE
HEH... HEH HEH... I GUESS A TALKING ANIMAL IS A PART OF ANY GIRL MAGICIAN
HEY, WAIT A MINUTE! WHEN DID YOU GUYS MAKE A PROBATIONARY CONTRACT!?
I GOT TO SMOOCH A LITTLE WHILE AGO!
THUMBS UP
BOW
BOW
I'M SORRY! I'M SORRY!
BOW
BOW

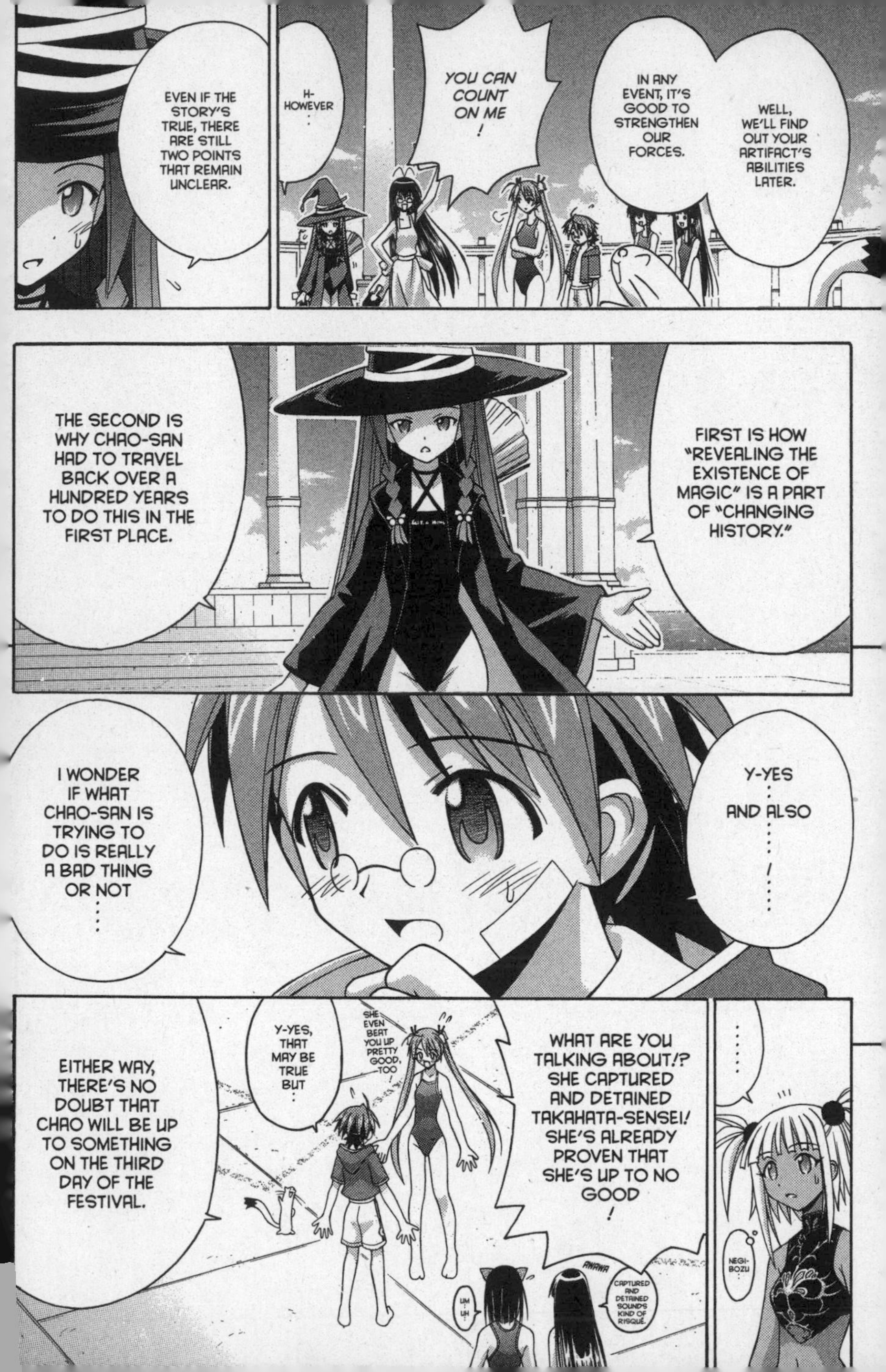
WELL, WE'LL FIND OUT YOUR ARTIFACT'S ABILITIES LATER.
IN ANY EVENT, IT'S GOOD TO STRENGTHEN OUR FORCES.
YOU CAN COUNT ON ME!
H-HOWEVER...
EVEN IF THE STORY'S TRUE, THERE ARE STILL TWO POINTS THAT REMAIN UNCLEAR.
FIRST IS HOW "REVEALING THE EXISTENCE OF MAGIC" IS A PART OF "CHANGING HISTORY."
THE SECOND IS WHY CHAO-SAN HAD TO TRAVEL BACK OVER A HUNDRED YEARS TO DO THIS IN THE FIRST PLACE.
Y-YES... AND ALSO......!.....
I WONDER IF WHAT CHAO-SAN IS TRYING TO DO IS REALLY A BAD THING OR NOT...
......
NEGI-BOZU
WHAT ARE YOU TALKING ABOUT!? SHE CAPTURED AND DETAINED TAKAHATA-SENSEI! SHE'S ALREADY PROVEN THAT SHE'S UP TO NO GOOD!
SHE EVEN BEAT YOU UP PRETTY GOOD, TOO!
Y-YES, THAT MAY BE TRUE BUT..
AWAWA
CAPTURED AND DETAINED SOUNDS KIND OF RISQUÉ.
UM... UH
EITHER WAY, THERE'S NO DOUBT THAT CHAO WILL BE UP TO SOMETHING ON THE THIRD DAY OF THE FESTIVAL.

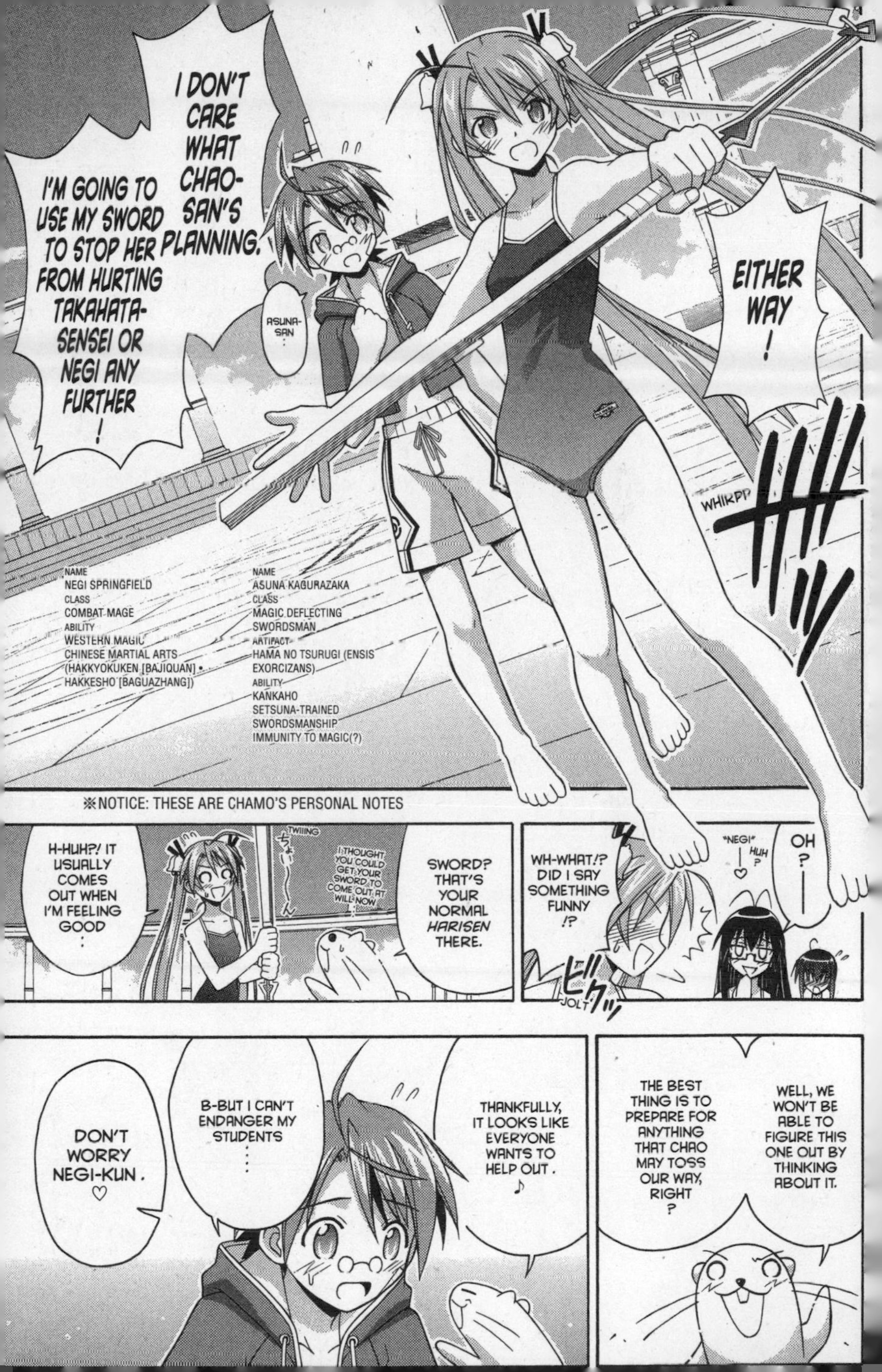
I DON'T CARE WHAT CHAO-SAN'S PLANNING.
I'M GOING TO USE MY SWORD TO STOP HER FROM HURTING TAKAHATA-SENSEI OR NEGI ANY FURTHER!
EITHER WAY!
ASUNA-SAN...
WHIKPP
NAME
NEGI SPRINGFIELD
CLASS
COMBAT MAGE
ABILITY
WESTERN MAGIC
CHINESE MARTIAL ARTS
(HAKKYOKUKEN [BAJIQUAN] •
HAKKESHO [BAGUAZHANG])
NAME
ASUNA KAGURAZAKA
CLASS
MAGIC DEFLECTING
SWORDSMAN
ARTIFACT
HAMA NO TSURUGI (ENSIS
EXORCIZANS)
ABILITY
KANKAHO
SETSUNA-TRAINED
SWORDSMANSHIP
IMMUNITY TO MAGIC(?)
※NOTICE: THESE ARE CHAMO'S PERSONAL NOTES
OH?
"NEGI" HUH? ♡
WH-WHAT!? DID I SAY SOMETHING FUNNY!?
JOLT
SWORD? THAT'S YOUR NORMAL *HARISEN* THERE.
I THOUGHT YOU COULD GET YOUR SWORD TO COME OUT AT WILL NOW...
TWIIING
H-HUH?! IT USUALLY COMES OUT WHEN I'M FEELING GOOD...
WELL, WE WON'T BE ABLE TO FIGURE THIS ONE OUT BY THINKING ABOUT IT.
THE BEST THING IS TO PREPARE FOR ANYTHING THAT CHAO MAY TOSS OUR WAY, RIGHT?
THANKFULLY, IT LOOKS LIKE EVERYONE WANTS TO HELP OUT. ♪
B-BUT I CAN'T ENDANGER MY STUDENTS...
DON'T WORRY NEGI-KUN. ♡

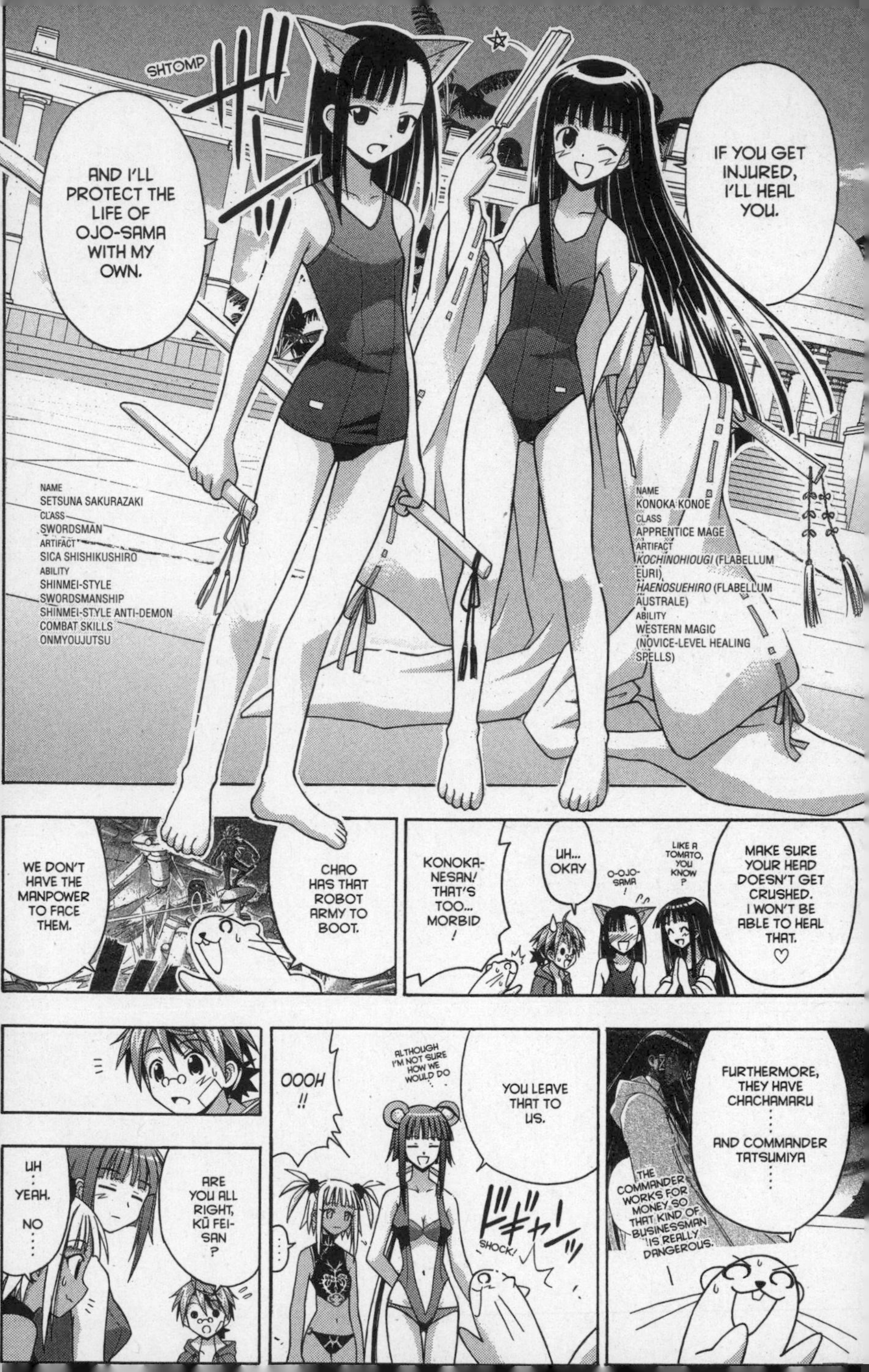
IF YOU GET INJURED, I'LL HEAL YOU.
SHTOMP
AND I'LL PROTECT THE LIFE OF OJO-SAMA WITH MY OWN.
NAME
KONOKA KONOE
CLASS
APPRENTICE MAGE
ARTIFACT
KOCHINOHIOUGI (FLABELLUM EURI)
HAENOSUEHIRO (FLABELLUM AUSTRALE)
ABILITY
WESTERN MAGIC (NOVICE-LEVEL HEALING SPELLS)
NAME
SETSUNA SAKURAZAKI
CLASS
SWORDSMAN
ARTIFACT
SICA SHISHIKUSHIRO
ABILITY
SHINMEI-STYLE SWORDSMANSHIP
SHINMEI-STYLE ANTI-DEMON COMBAT SKILLS
ONMYOUJUTSU
MAKE SURE YOUR HEAD DOESN'T GET CRUSHED. I WON'T BE ABLE TO HEAL THAT. ♡
LIKE A TOMATO, YOU KNOW?
O-OJO-SAMA!
UH... OKAY
KONOKA-NESAN! THAT'S TOO... MORBID!
CHAO HAS THAT ROBOT ARMY TO BOOT.
WE DON'T HAVE THE MANPOWER TO FACE THEM.
FURTHERMORE, THEY HAVE CHACHAMARU ... AND COMMANDER TATSUMIYA ...
THE COMMANDER WORKS FOR MONEY, SO THAT KIND OF BUSINESSMAN IS REALLY DANGEROUS.
YOU LEAVE THAT TO US.
ALTHOUGH I'M NOT SURE HOW WE WOULD DO...
OOOH!!
ドギャーッ
SHOCK!
...
ARE YOU ALL RIGHT, KŪ FEI-SAN?
UH... YEAH.
NO......

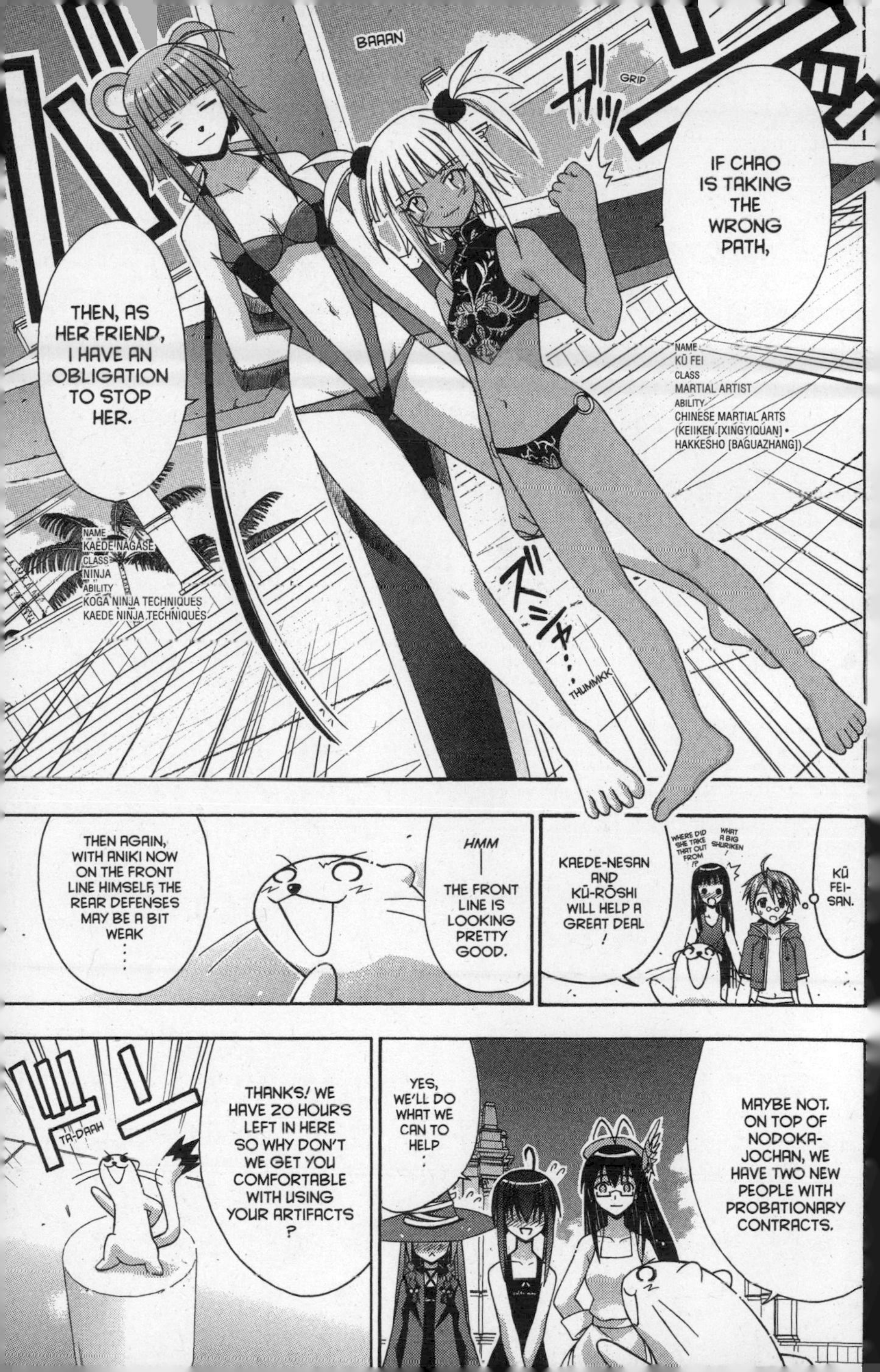
BAAAN
GRIP
IF CHAO IS TAKING THE WRONG PATH,
THEN, AS HER FRIEND, I HAVE AN OBLIGATION TO STOP HER.
NAME KŪ FEI CLASS MARTIAL ARTIST ABILITY CHINESE MARTIAL ARTS (KEIIKEN [XINGYIQUAN] • HAKKESHO [BAGUAZHANG])
NAME KAEDE NAGASE CLASS NINJA ABILITY KOGA NINJA TECHNIQUES KAEDE NINJA TECHNIQUES
THUMMKK
KŪ FEI-SAN.
WHERE DID SHE TAKE THAT OUT FROM !?
WHAT A BIG SHURIKEN !
KAEDE-NESAN AND KŪ-RŌSHI WILL HELP A GREAT DEAL !
HMM
THE FRONT LINE IS LOOKING PRETTY GOOD.
THEN AGAIN, WITH ANIKI NOW ON THE FRONT LINE HIMSELF, THE REAR DEFENSES MAY BE A BIT WEAK...
MAYBE NOT. ON TOP OF NODOKA-JOCHAN, WE HAVE TWO NEW PEOPLE WITH PROBATIONARY CONTRACTS.
YES, WE'LL DO WHAT WE CAN TO HELP...
THANKS! WE HAVE 20 HOURS LEFT IN HERE SO WHY DON'T WE GET YOU COMFORTABLE WITH USING YOUR ARTIFACTS ?
TA-DAAH

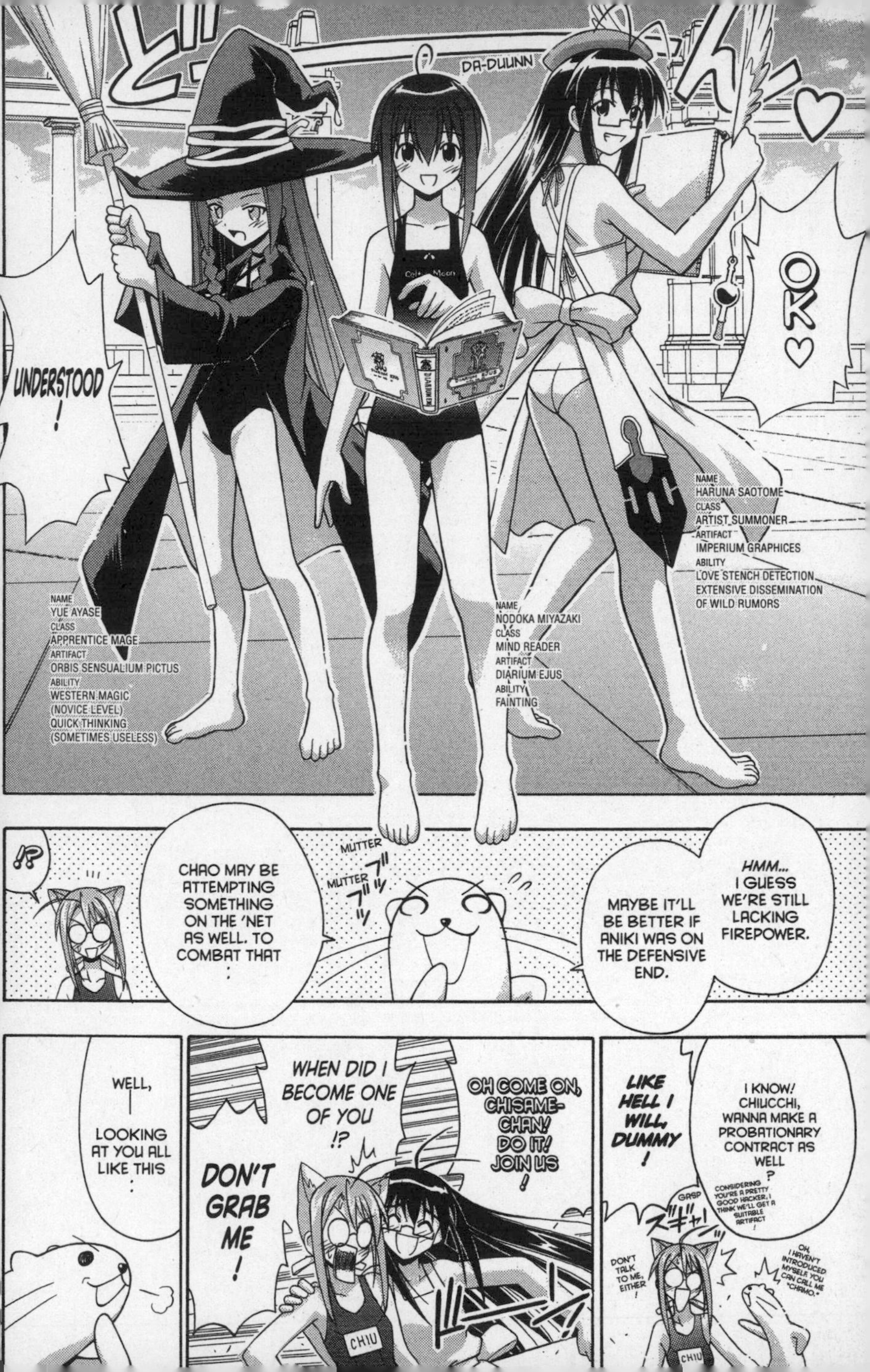
OK ♥
DA-DUUNN
NAME HARUNA SAOTOME CLASS ARTIST SUMMONER ARTIFACT IMPERIUM GRAPHICES ABILITY LOVE STENCH DETECTION EXTENSIVE DISSEMINATION OF WILD RUMORS
NAME NODOKA MIYAZAKI CLASS MIND READER ARTIFACT DIARIUM EJUS ABILITY FAINTING
UNDERSTOOD !
NAME YUE AYASE CLASS APPRENTICE MAGE ARTIFACT ORBIS SENSUALIUM PICTUS ABILITY WESTERN MAGIC (NOVICE LEVEL) QUICK THINKING (SOMETIMES USELESS)
HMM... I GUESS WE'RE STILL LACKING FIREPOWER.
MAYBE IT'LL BE BETTER IF ANIKI WAS ON THE DEFENSIVE END.
MUTTER MUTTER
CHAO MAY BE ATTEMPTING SOMETHING ON THE 'NET AS WELL. TO COMBAT THAT :
!?
I KNOW! CHIUCCHI, WANNA MAKE A PROBATIONARY CONTRACT AS WELL ?
CONSIDERING YOU'RE A PRETTY GOOD HACKER, I THINK WE'LL GET A SUITABLE ARTIFACT
LIKE HELL I WILL, DUMMY !
GASP
OH, I HAVEN'T INTRODUCED MYSELF. YOU CAN CALL ME "CHAMO."
DON'T TALK TO ME, EITHER !
CHIU
OH COME ON, CHISAME-CHAN! DO IT! JOIN US !
WHEN DID I BECOME ONE OF YOU !?
DON'T GRAB ME !
CHIU
WELL, LOOKING AT YOU ALL LIKE THIS :

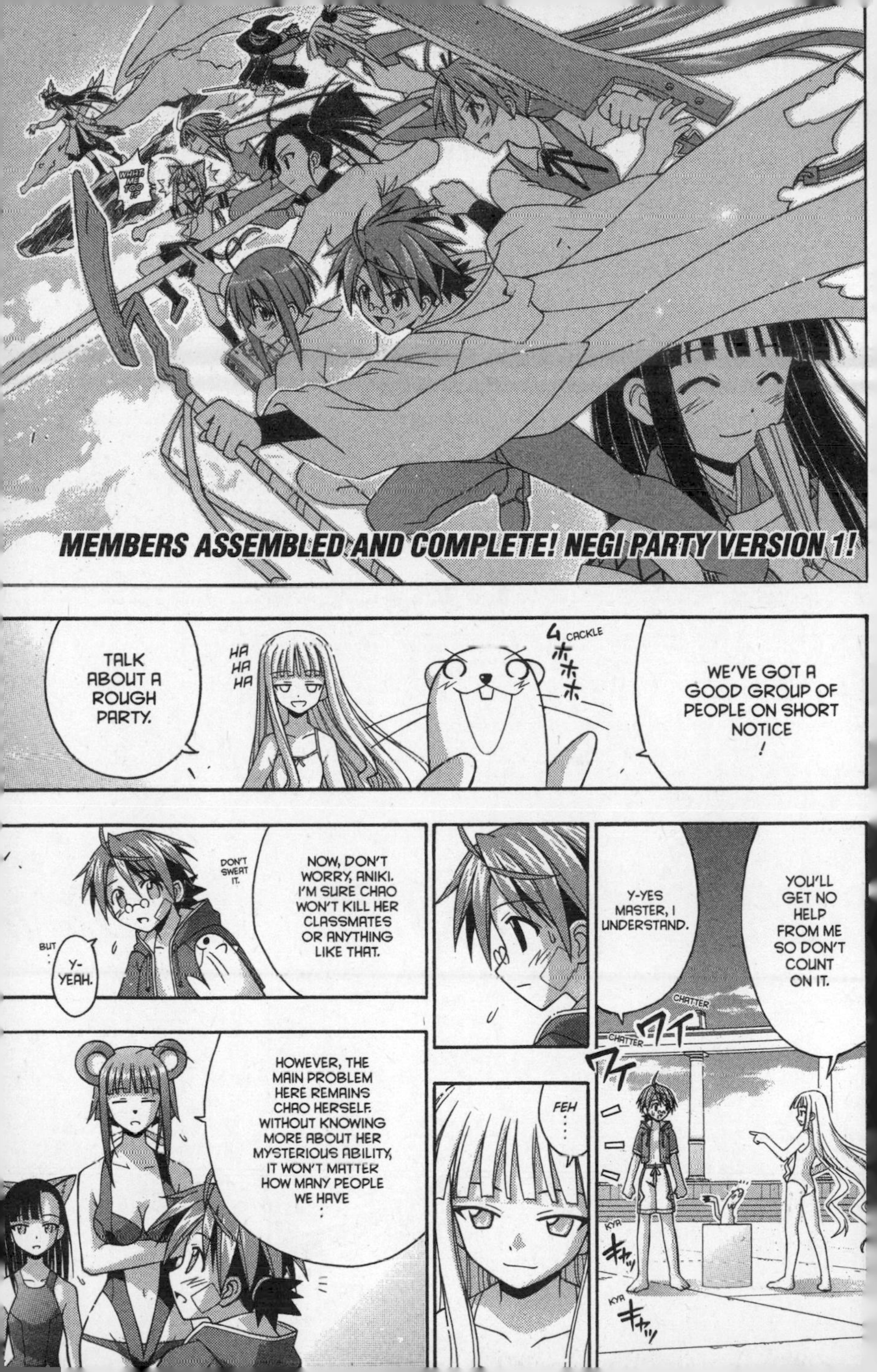
WHAT, ME TOO!?
MEMBERS ASSEMBLED AND COMPLETE! NEGI PARTY VERSION 1!
WE'VE GOT A GOOD GROUP OF PEOPLE ON SHORT NOTICE!
CACKLE
HA HA HA
TALK ABOUT A ROUGH PARTY.
YOU'LL GET NO HELP FROM ME SO DON'T COUNT ON IT.
Y-YES MASTER, I UNDERSTAND.
CHATTER
CHATTER
KYA
KYA
FEH...
NOW, DON'T WORRY, ANIKI. I'M SURE CHAO WON'T KILL HER CLASSMATES OR ANYTHING LIKE THAT.
DON'T SWEAT IT.
Y-YEAH.
BUT...
HOWEVER, THE MAIN PROBLEM HERE REMAINS CHAO HERSELF. WITHOUT KNOWING MORE ABOUT HER MYSTERIOUS ABILITY, IT WON'T MATTER HOW MANY PEOPLE WE HAVE...

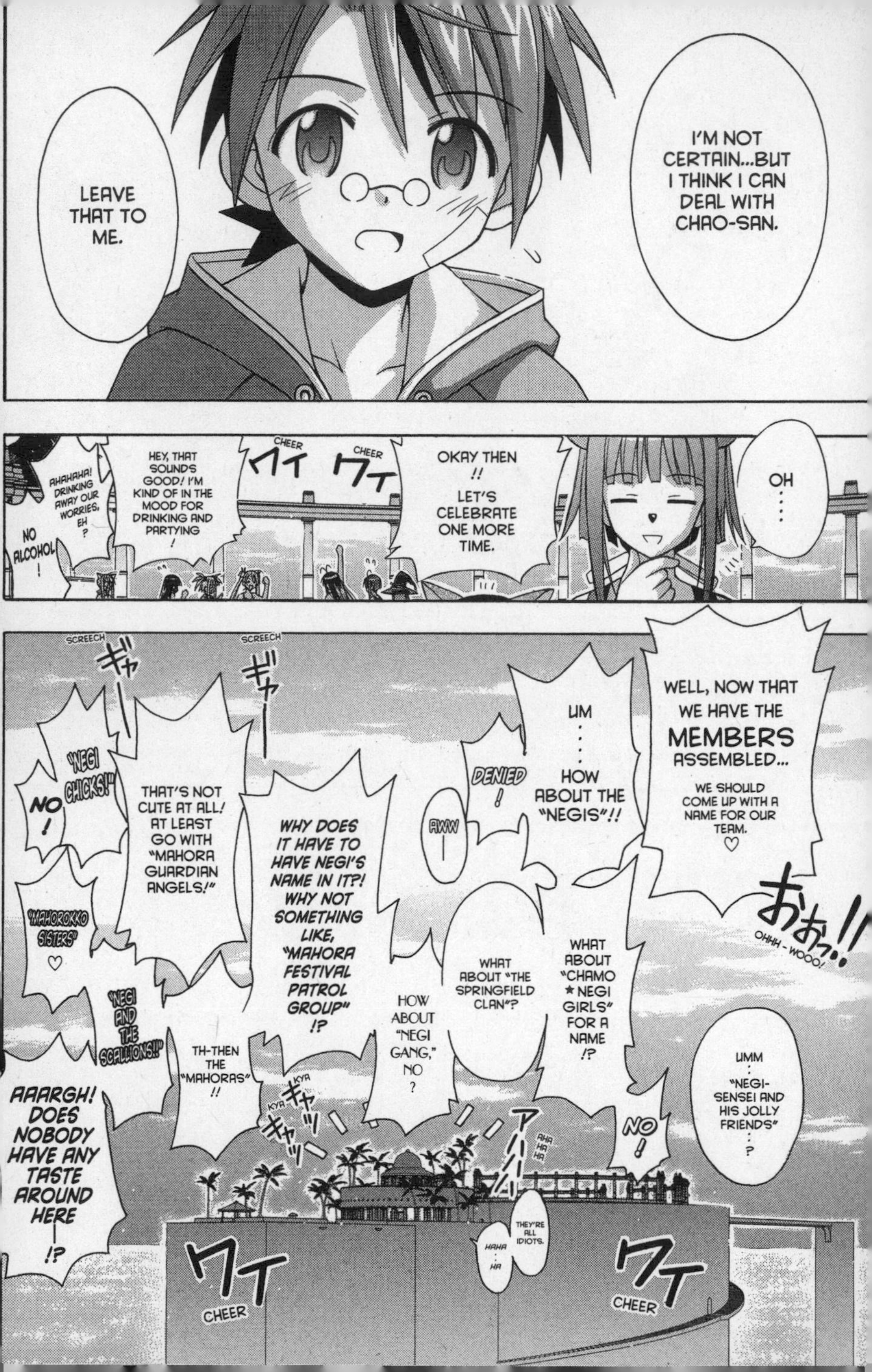
I'M NOT CERTAIN...BUT I THINK I CAN DEAL WITH CHAO-SAN.
LEAVE THAT TO ME.
OH ....
OKAY THEN !! LET'S CELEBRATE ONE MORE TIME.
CHEER
CHEER
HEY, THAT SOUND'S GOOD! I'M KIND OF IN THE MOOD FOR DRINKING AND PARTYING !
AHAHAHA! DRINKING AWAY OUR WORRIES, EH ?
NO ALCOHOL !
WELL, NOW THAT WE HAVE THE MEMBERS ASSEMBLED... WE SHOULD COME UP WITH A NAME FOR OUR TEAM. ♡
OHHH - WOOO!
UM ... HOW ABOUT THE "NEGIS"!!
DENIED !
AWW —
WHAT ABOUT "CHAMO ★ NEGI GIRLS" FOR A NAME !?
WHAT ABOUT "THE SPRINGFIELD CLAN"?
WHY DOES IT HAVE TO HAVE NEGI'S NAME IN IT?! WHY NOT SOMETHING LIKE, "MAHORA FESTIVAL PATROL GROUP" !?
SCREECH
THAT'S NOT CUTE AT ALL! AT LEAST GO WITH "MAHORA GUARDIAN ANGELS!"
SCREECH
"NEGI CHICKS!"
NO !
"MAHOROKKO SISTERS" ♡
UMM : "NEGI-SENSEI AND HIS JOLLY FRIENDS" ...?
NO !
HOW ABOUT "NEGI GANG," NO ?
TH-THEN THE "MAHORAS" !!
"NEGI AND THE SCALLIONS!!"
KYA KYA
AHA HA HA
THEY'RE ALL IDIOTS.
HAHA . HA
AAARGH! DOES NOBODY HAVE ANY TASTE AROUND HERE — !?
CHEER
CHEER

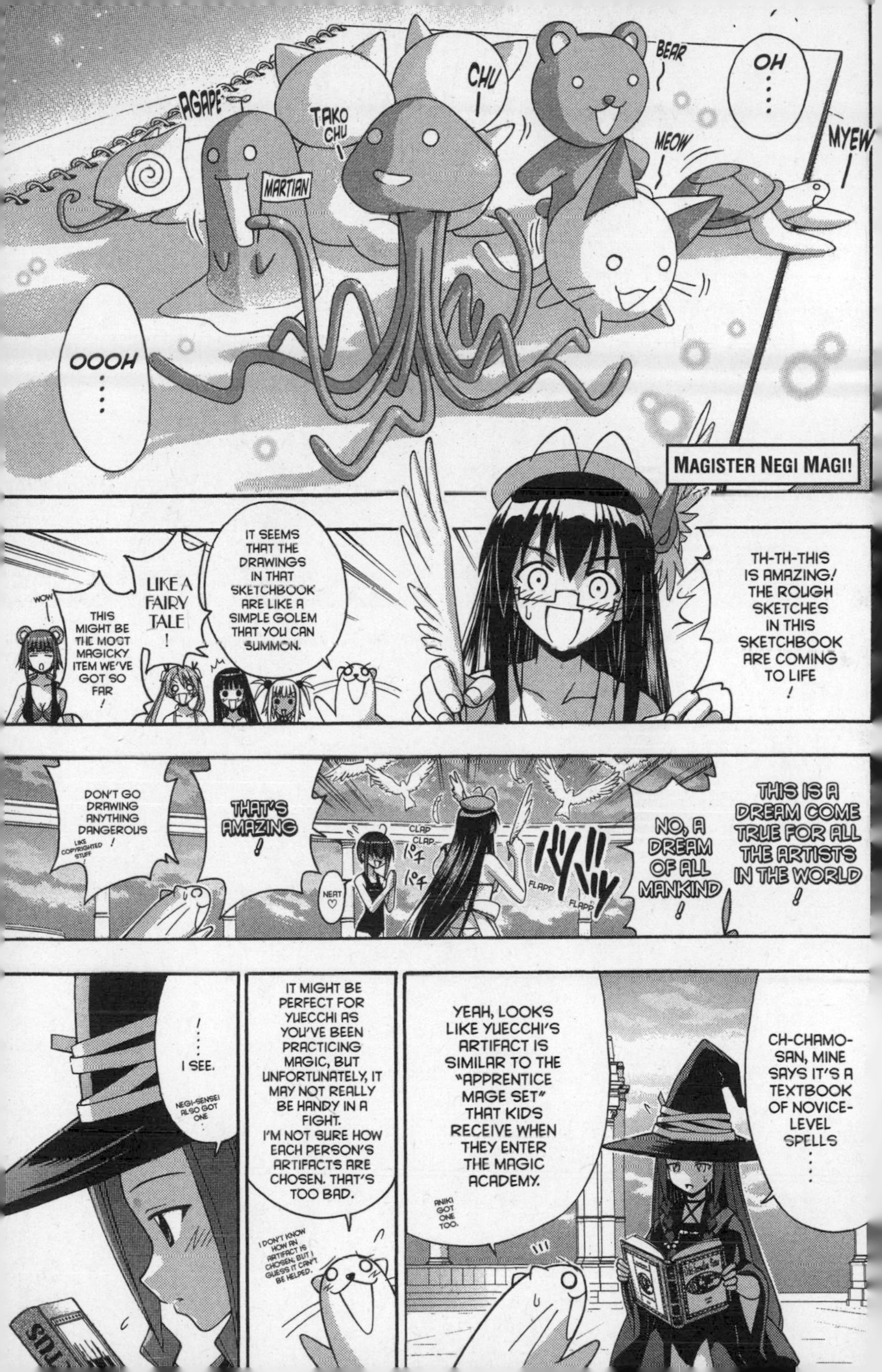
MAGISTER NEGI MAGI!
OH...
MYEW!
BEAR~
MEOW~
CHU!
TAKO CHU!
AGAPE
MARTIAN
OOOH...
TH-TH-THIS IS AMAZING! THE ROUGH SKETCHES IN THIS SKETCHBOOK ARE COMING TO LIFE!
IT SEEMS THAT THE DRAWINGS IN THAT SKETCHBOOK ARE LIKE A SIMPLE GOLEM THAT YOU CAN SUMMON.
LIKE A FAIRY TALE!
WOW!
THIS MIGHT BE THE MOST MAGICKY ITEM WE'VE GOT SO FAR!
THIS IS A DREAM COME TRUE FOR ALL THE ARTISTS IN THE WORLD!
NO, A DREAM OF ALL MANKIND!
FLAPP
FLAPP
CLAP CLAP
NEAT♡
THAT'S AMAZING!
DON'T GO DRAWING ANYTHING DANGEROUS!
LIKE COPYRIGHTED STUFF!
CH-CHAMO-SAN, MINE SAYS IT'S A TEXTBOOK OF NOVICE-LEVEL SPELLS...
YEAH, LOOKS LIKE YUECCHI'S ARTIFACT IS SIMILAR TO THE "APPRENTICE MAGE SET" THAT KIDS RECEIVE WHEN THEY ENTER THE MAGIC ACADEMY.
ANIKI GOT ONE TOO.
IT MIGHT BE PERFECT FOR YUECCHI AS YOU'VE BEEN PRACTICING MAGIC, BUT UNFORTUNATELY, IT MAY NOT REALLY BE HANDY IN A FIGHT. I'M NOT SURE HOW EACH PERSON'S ARTIFACTS ARE CHOSEN. THAT'S TOO BAD.
I DON'T KNOW HOW AN ARTIFACT IS CHOSEN; BUT I GUESS IT CAN'T BE HELPED.
...!
I SEE.
NEGI-SENSEI ALSO GOT ONE

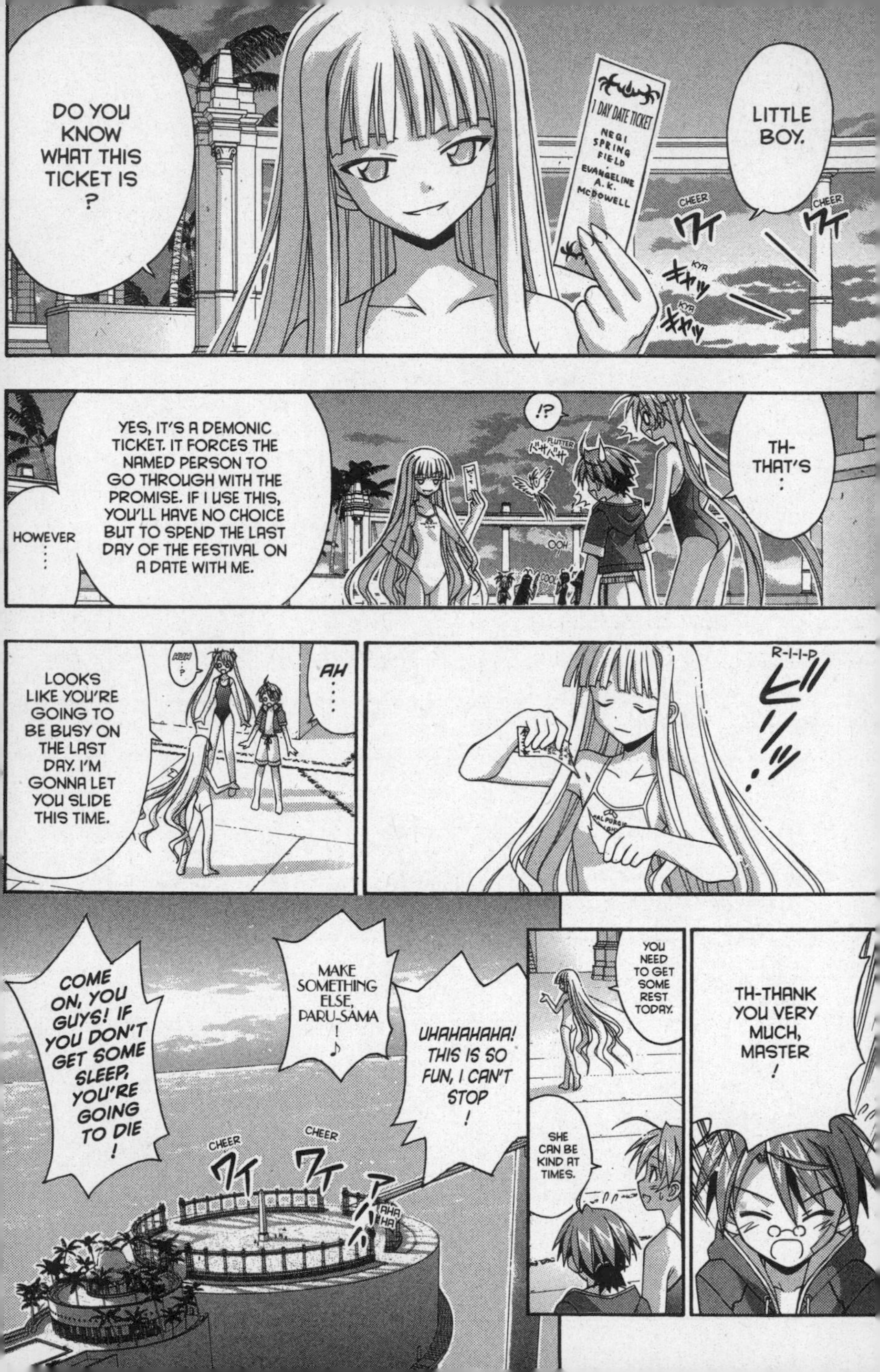
LITTLE BOY.
DO YOU KNOW WHAT THIS TICKET IS?
1 DAY DATE TICKET
NEGI SPRING FIELD
EVANGELINE A.K. McDOWELL
CHEER
CHEER
KYA
KYA
TH- THAT'S...
!?
FLUTTER
OOH
COOL
YES, IT'S A DEMONIC TICKET. IT FORCES THE NAMED PERSON TO GO THROUGH WITH THE PROMISE. IF I USE THIS, YOU'LL HAVE NO CHOICE BUT TO SPEND THE LAST DAY OF THE FESTIVAL ON A DATE WITH ME.
HOWEVER...
R-I-I-P
AH...
HUH...?
LOOKS LIKE YOU'RE GOING TO BE BUSY ON THE LAST DAY. I'M GONNA LET YOU SLIDE THIS TIME.
TH-THANK YOU VERY MUCH, MASTER!
YOU NEED TO GET SOME REST TODAY.
SHE CAN BE KIND AT TIMES.
UHAHAHAHA! THIS IS SO FUN, I CAN'T STOP!
MAKE SOMETHING ELSE, PARU-SAMA!♪
COME ON, YOU GUYS! IF YOU DON'T GET SOME SLEEP, YOU'RE GOING TO DIE!
CHEER
CHEER
AHA HA

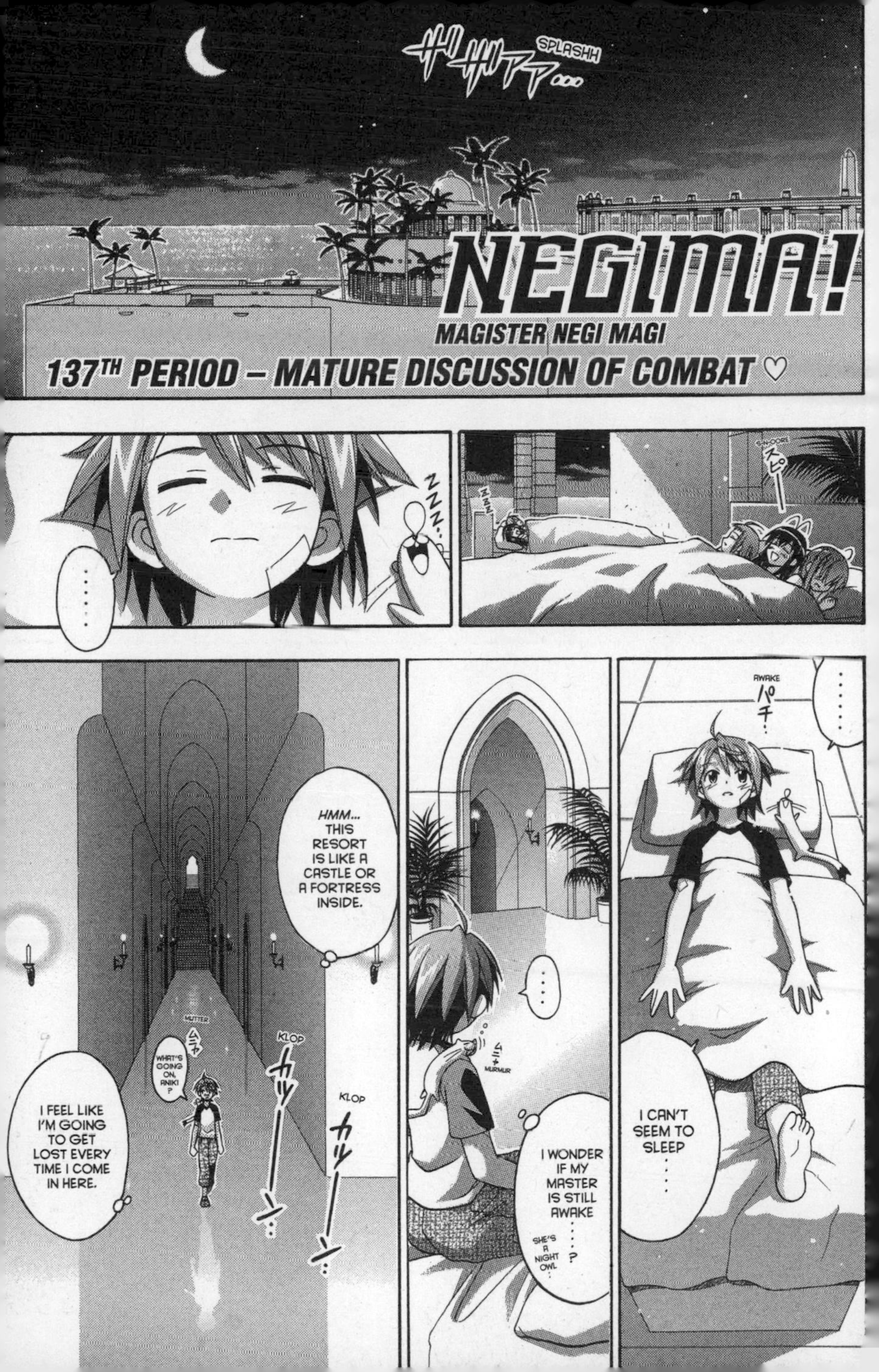
SPLASHH
NEGIMA!
MAGISTER NEGI MAGI
137TH PERIOD – MATURE DISCUSSION OF COMBAT ♡
S-N-OORE
MMM
ZZZ...
......
AWAKE
......
I CAN'T SEEM TO SLEEP......
......
MURMUR
I WONDER IF MY MASTER IS STILL AWAKE......?
SHE'S A NIGHT OWL...
HMM... THIS RESORT IS LIKE A CASTLE OR A FORTRESS INSIDE.
MUTTER
WHAT'S GOING ON, ANIKI?
KLOP
KLOP
I FEEL LIKE I'M GOING TO GET LOST EVERY TIME I COME IN HERE.

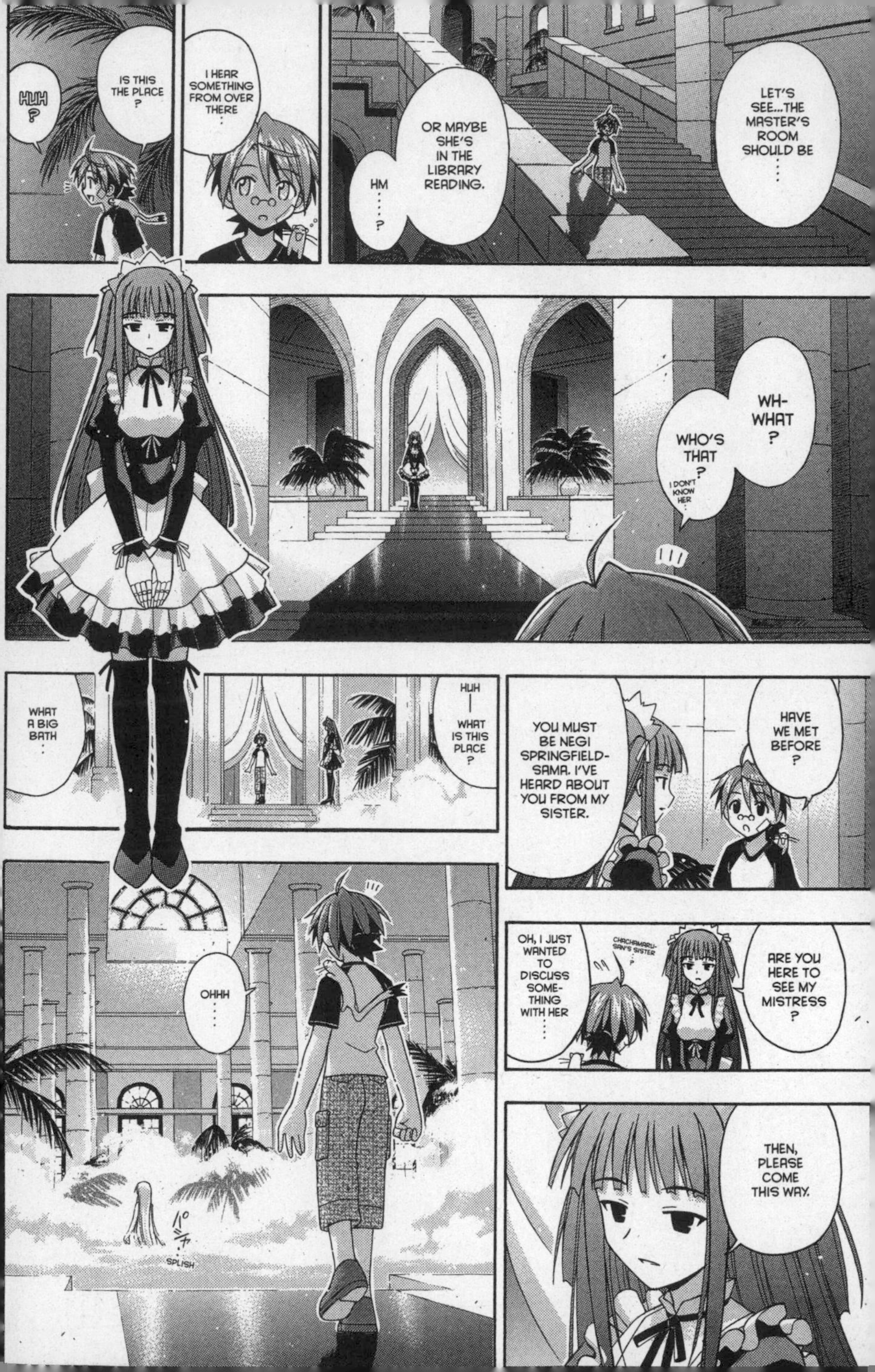
LET'S SEE...THE MASTER'S ROOM SHOULD BE ....
OR MAYBE SHE'S IN THE LIBRARY READING.
HM ....?
I HEAR SOMETHING FROM OVER THERE ...
IS THIS THE PLACE ?
HUH ?
WH- WHAT ?
WHO'S THAT ?
I DON'T KNOW HER ...
HAVE WE MET BEFORE ?
YOU MUST BE NEGI SPRINGFIELD-SAMA. I'VE HEARD ABOUT YOU FROM MY SISTER.
HUH — WHAT IS THIS PLACE ?
WHAT A BIG BATH ...
ARE YOU HERE TO SEE MY MISTRESS ?
CHACHAMARU-SAN'S SISTER ...?
OH, I JUST WANTED TO DISCUSS SOME-THING WITH HER ....
THEN, PLEASE COME THIS WAY.
OHHH ....
SPLISH

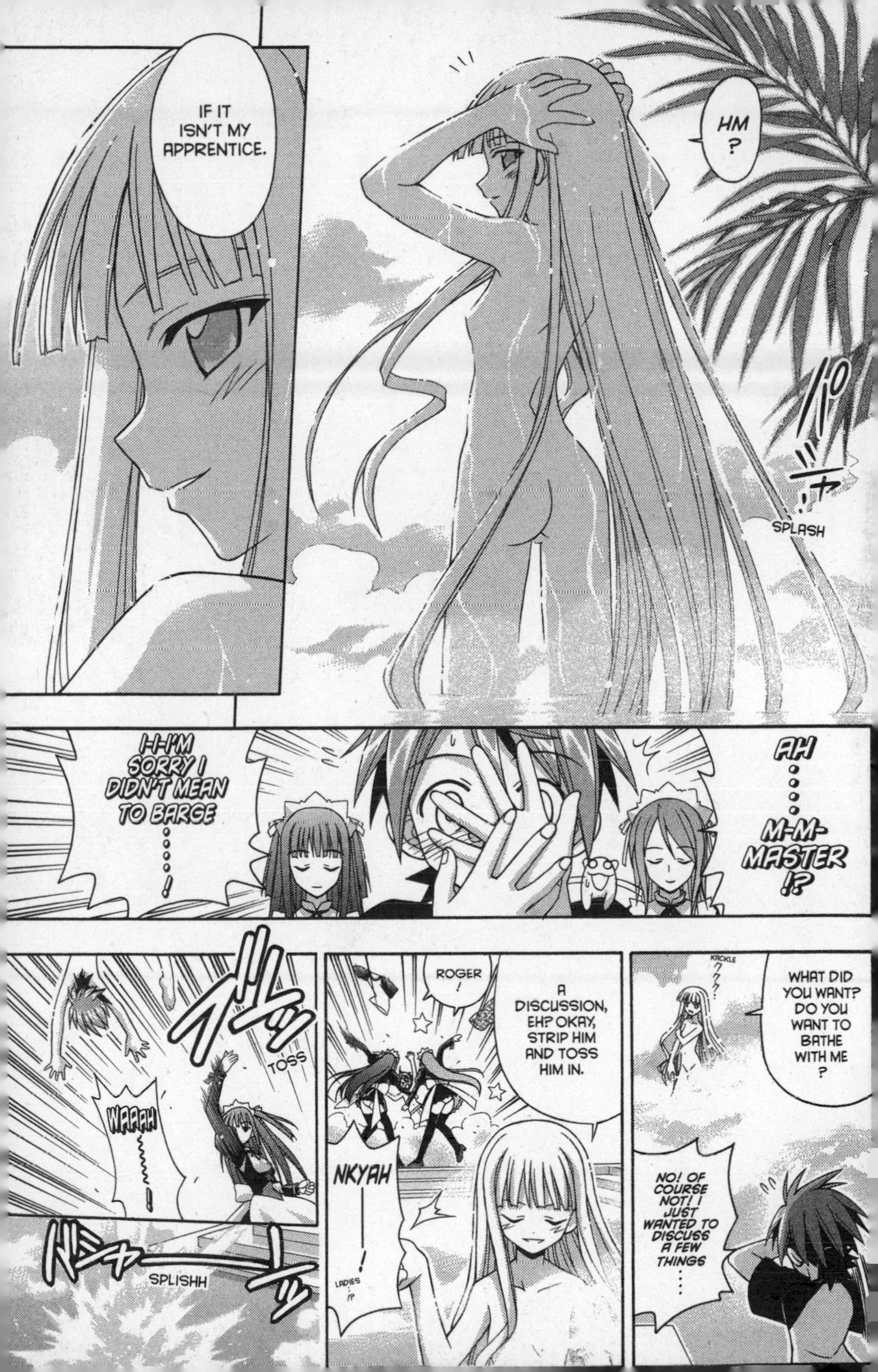
HM ?
SPLASH
IF IT ISN'T MY APPRENTICE.
AH..... M-M-MASTER !?
I-I-I'M SORRY I DIDN'T MEAN TO BARGE.....!
KRACKLE
WHAT DID YOU WANT? DO YOU WANT TO BATHE WITH ME ?
NO! OF COURSE NOT! I JUST WANTED TO DISCUSS A FEW THINGS....
A DISCUSSION, EH? OKAY, STRIP HIM AND TOSS HIM IN.
ROGER !
NKYAH !
LADIES !?
TOSS
WAAAH !
SPLISHH

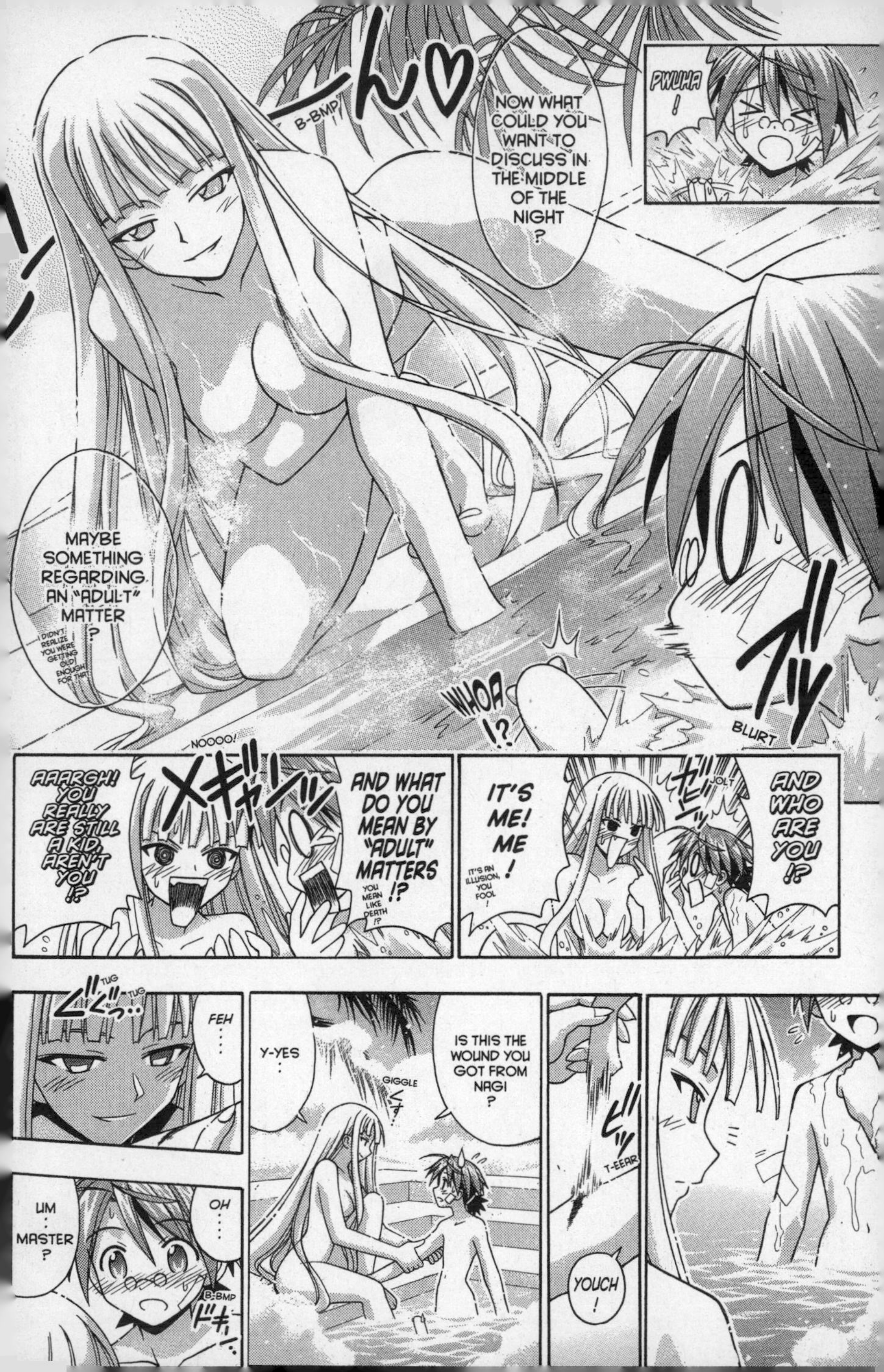
PWUHA
!
NOW WHAT COULD YOU WANT TO DISCUSS IN THE MIDDLE OF THE NIGHT
?
B-BMP
MAYBE SOMETHING REGARDING AN "ADULT" MATTER
?
I DIDN'T REALIZE YOU WERE GETTING OLD ENOUGH FOR THAT
BLURT
WHOA
!?
AND WHO ARE YOU
!?
JOLT
IT'S ME! ME
!
IT'S AN ILLUSION, YOU FOOL
!
AND WHAT DO YOU MEAN BY "ADULT" MATTERS
!?
YOU MEAN LIKE DEATH
!?
AAARGH! YOU REALLY ARE STILL A KID, AREN'T YOU
!?
NOOOO!
T-EEAR
YOUCH
!
IS THIS THE WOUND YOU GOT FROM NAGI
?
GIGGLE
Y-YES
...
FEH
...
TUG
TUG
OH
...
UM
:
MASTER
?
B-BMP

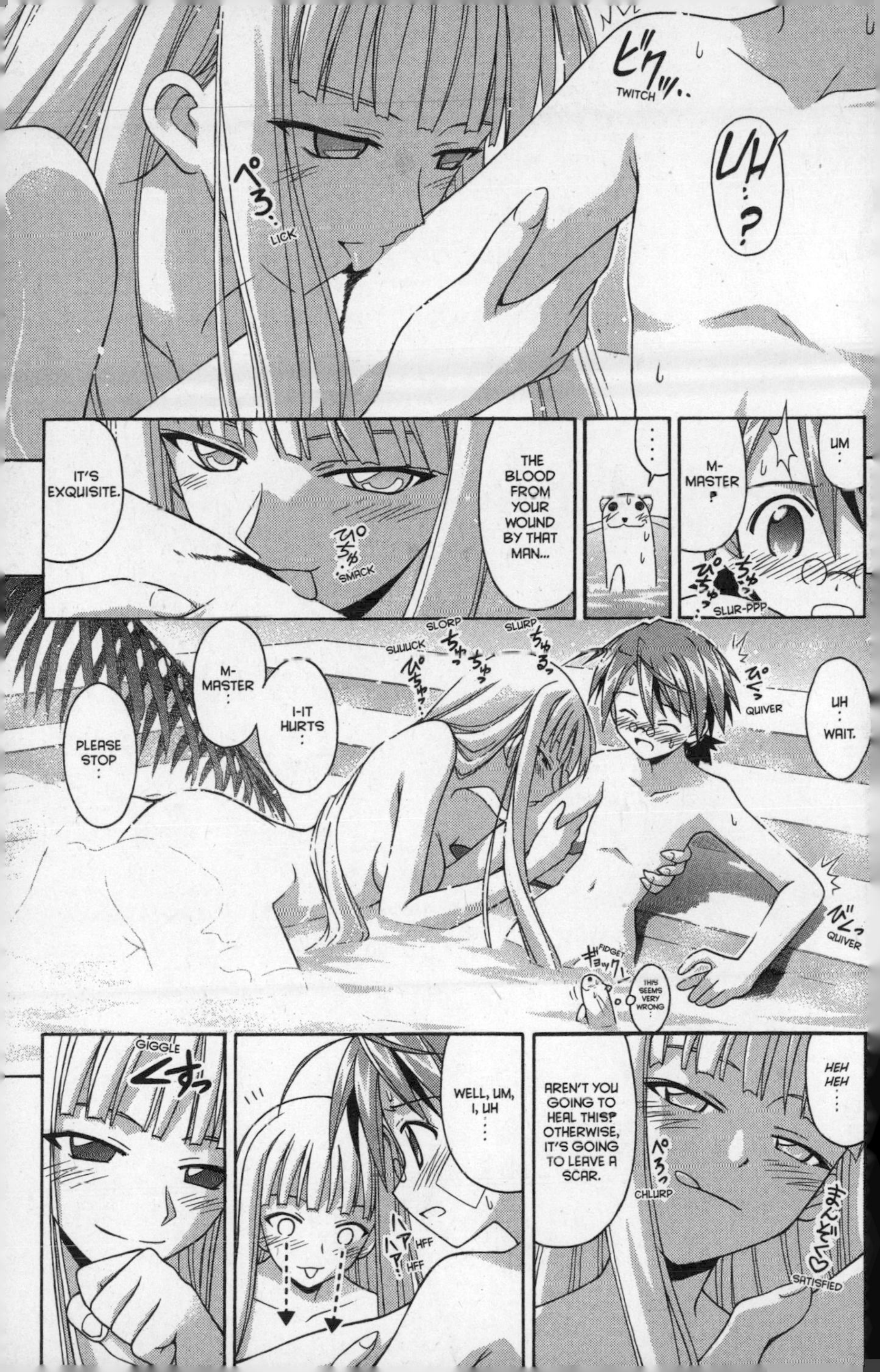

TWITCH
UH..?
LICK
UM...
M-MASTER?
SLUR-PPP
...
THE BLOOD FROM YOUR WOUND BY THAT MAN...
IT'S EXQUISITE.
SMACK
UH... WAIT.
QUIVER
SLURP
SLORP
SUUUCK
M-MASTER...
I-IT HURTS...
PLEASE STOP...
QUIVER
FIDGET
THIS SEEMS VERY WRONG
HEH HEH...
AREN'T YOU GOING TO HEAL THIS? OTHERWISE, IT'S GOING TO LEAVE A SCAR.
CHLURP
SATISFIED
WELL, UM, I, UH...
HFF
HFF
GIGGLE

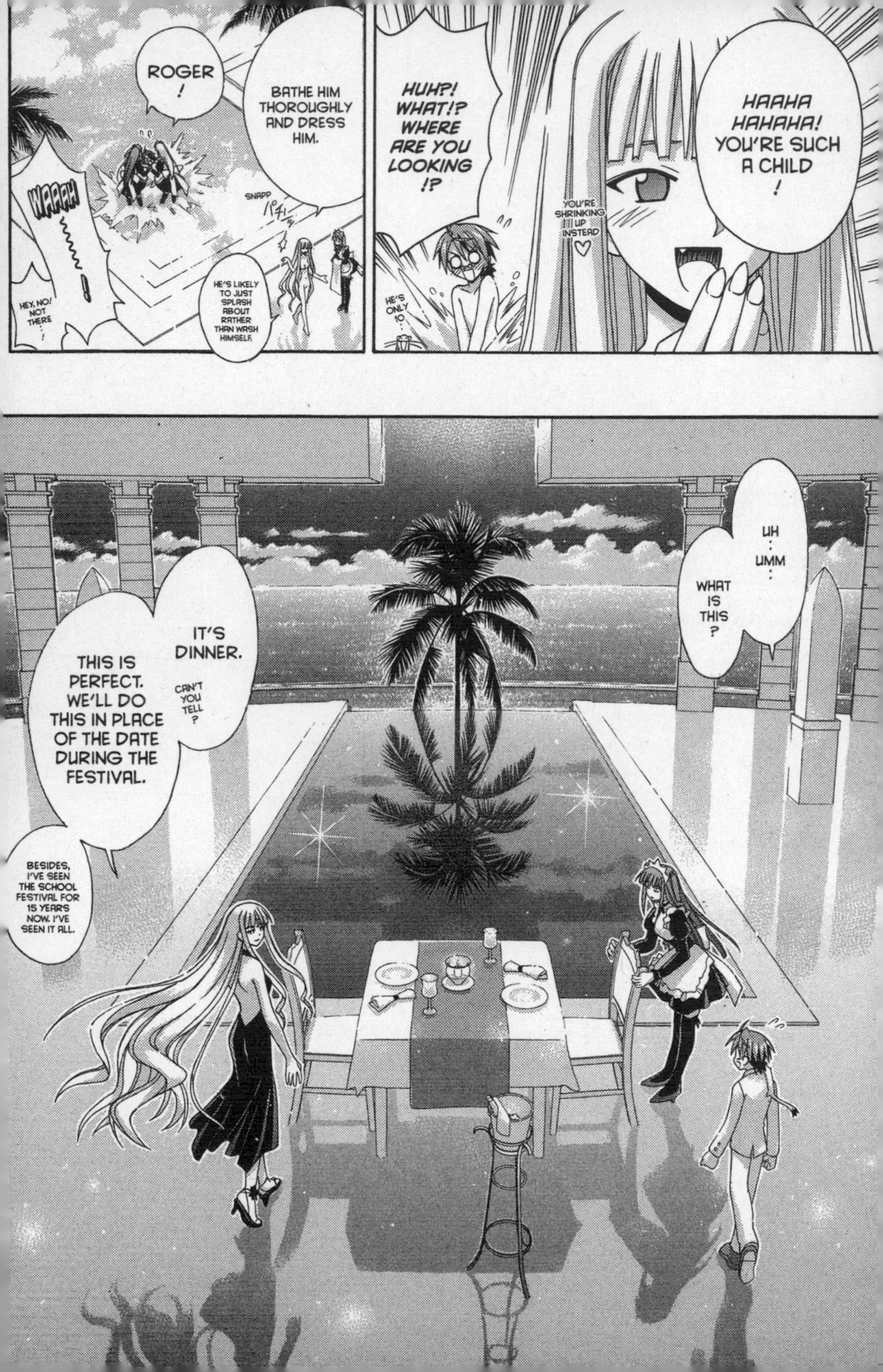
HAAHA HAHAHA! YOU'RE SUCH A CHILD!
YOU'RE SHRINKING UP INSTEAD ♡
HUH?! WHAT!? WHERE ARE YOU LOOKING!?
HE'S ONLY 10...
BATHE HIM THOROUGHLY AND DRESS HIM.
ROGER!
SNAPP
HE'S LIKELY TO JUST SPLASH ABOUT RATHER THAN WASH HIMSELF.
WAAAH
HEY, NO! NOT THERE...!
UH... UMM... WHAT IS THIS?
IT'S DINNER.
CAN'T YOU TELL?
THIS IS PERFECT. WE'LL DO THIS IN PLACE OF THE DATE DURING THE FESTIVAL.
BESIDES, I'VE SEEN THE SCHOOL FESTIVAL FOR 15 YEARS NOW. I'VE SEEN IT ALL.

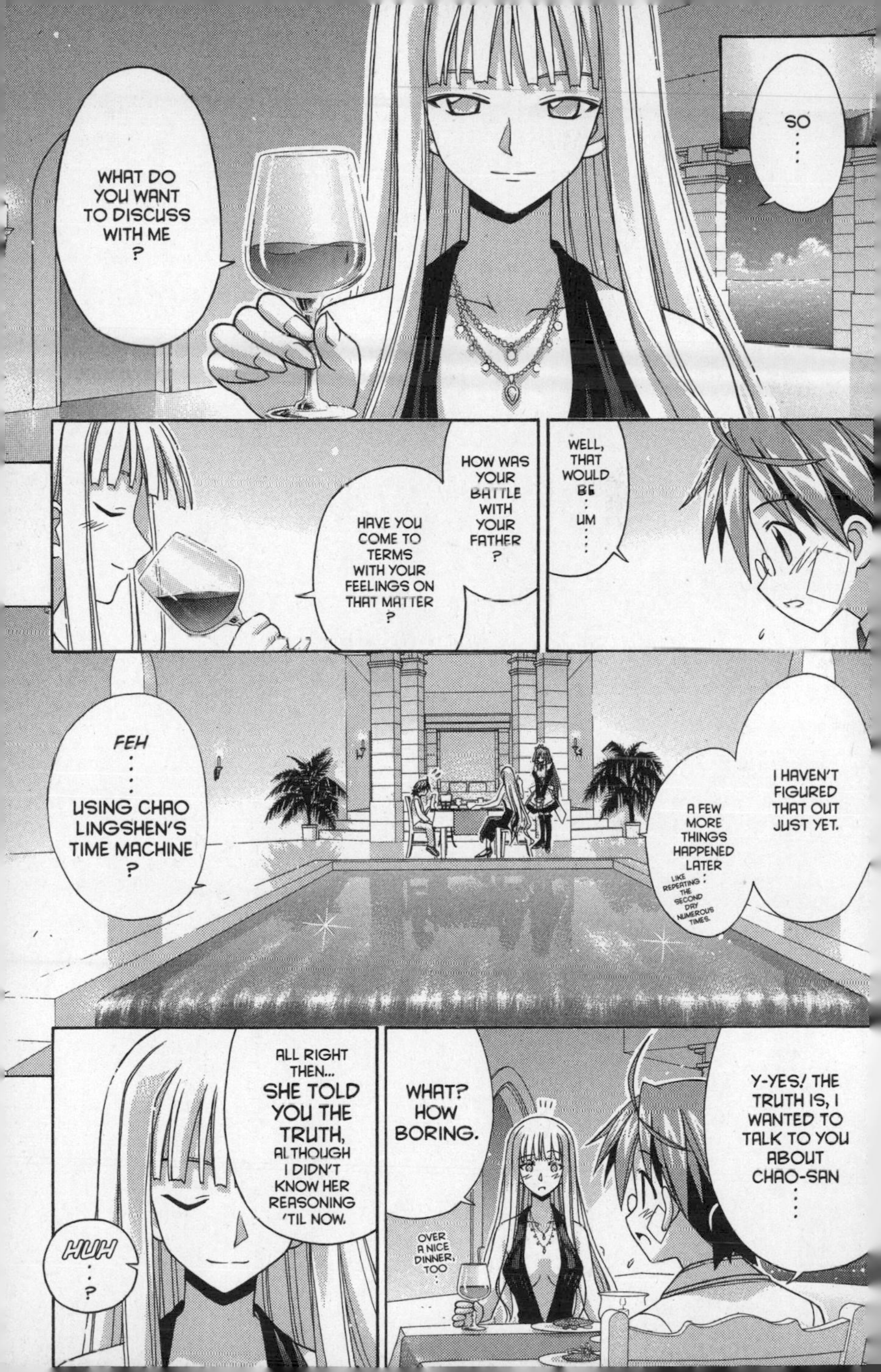
SO....
WHAT DO YOU WANT TO DISCUSS WITH ME?
WELL, THAT WOULD BE... UM...
HOW WAS YOUR BATTLE WITH YOUR FATHER?
HAVE YOU COME TO TERMS WITH YOUR FEELINGS ON THAT MATTER?
I HAVEN'T FIGURED THAT OUT JUST YET.
A FEW MORE THINGS HAPPENED LATER:
LIKE REPEATING THE SECOND DAY NUMEROUS TIMES.
FEH.... USING CHAO LINGSHEN'S TIME MACHINE?
Y-YES! THE TRUTH IS, I WANTED TO TALK TO YOU ABOUT CHAO-SAN....
WHAT? HOW BORING.
OVER A NICE DINNER, TOO...
ALL RIGHT THEN... SHE TOLD YOU THE TRUTH, ALTHOUGH I DIDN'T KNOW HER REASONING 'TIL NOW.
HUH..?

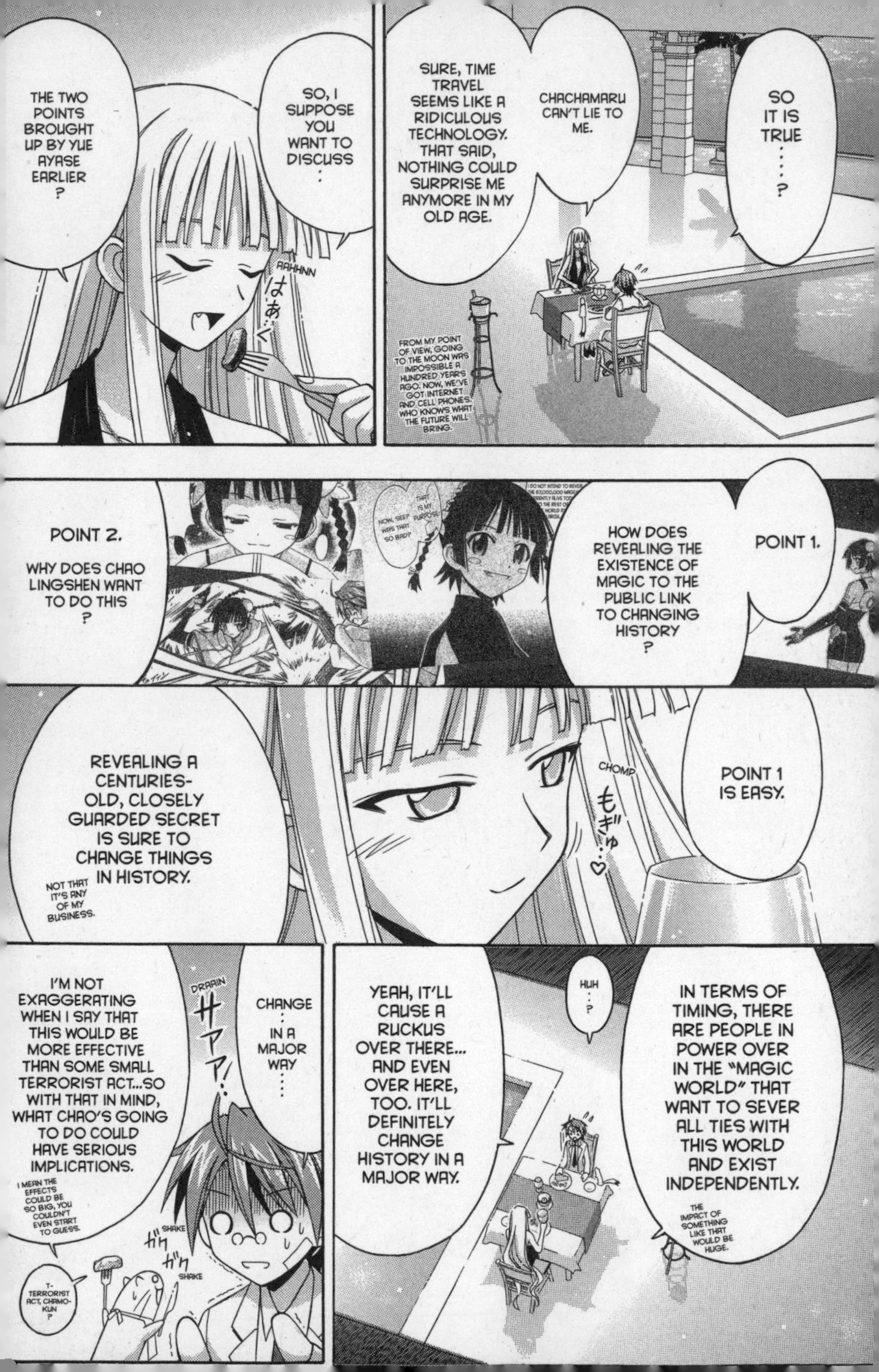
SO IT IS TRUE....?
CHACHAMARU CAN'T LIE TO ME.
SURE, TIME TRAVEL SEEMS LIKE A RIDICULOUS TECHNOLOGY. THAT SAID, NOTHING COULD SURPRISE ME ANYMORE IN MY OLD AGE.
FROM MY POINT OF VIEW, GOING TO THE MOON WAS IMPOSSIBLE A HUNDRED YEARS AGO. NOW, WE'VE GOT INTERNET AND CELL PHONES. WHO KNOWS WHAT THE FUTURE WILL BRING.
SO, I SUPPOSE YOU WANT TO DISCUSS...
AAHHNN
はあ~く
THE TWO POINTS BROUGHT UP BY YUE AYASE EARLIER?
POINT 1.
HOW DOES REVEALING THE EXISTENCE OF MAGIC TO THE PUBLIC LINK TO CHANGING HISTORY?
THAT IS MY PURPOSE
NOW, SEE? WAS THAT SO BAD?
POINT 2.
WHY DOES CHAO LINGSHEN WANT TO DO THIS?
POINT 1 IS EASY.
CHOMP
もぎゅ…♡
REVEALING A CENTURIES-OLD, CLOSELY GUARDED SECRET IS SURE TO CHANGE THINGS IN HISTORY.
NOT THAT IT'S ANY OF MY BUSINESS.
IN TERMS OF TIMING, THERE ARE PEOPLE IN POWER OVER IN THE "MAGIC WORLD" THAT WANT TO SEVER ALL TIES WITH THIS WORLD AND EXIST INDEPENDENTLY.
THE IMPACT OF SOMETHING LIKE THAT WOULD BE HUGE.
HUH...?
YEAH, IT'LL CAUSE A RUCKUS OVER THERE... AND EVEN OVER HERE, TOO. IT'LL DEFINITELY CHANGE HISTORY IN A MAJOR WAY.
CHANGE... IN A MAJOR WAY....
DRAAIN
サァア!..
I'M NOT EXAGGERATING WHEN I SAY THAT THIS WOULD BE MORE EFFECTIVE THAN SOME SMALL TERRORIST ACT...SO WITH THAT IN MIND, WHAT CHAO'S GOING TO DO COULD HAVE SERIOUS IMPLICATIONS.
I MEAN THE EFFECTS COULD BE SO BIG, YOU COULDN'T EVEN START TO GUESS.
SHAKE
ガク
ガク
SHAKE
T-TERRORIST ACT, CHAMO-KUN?

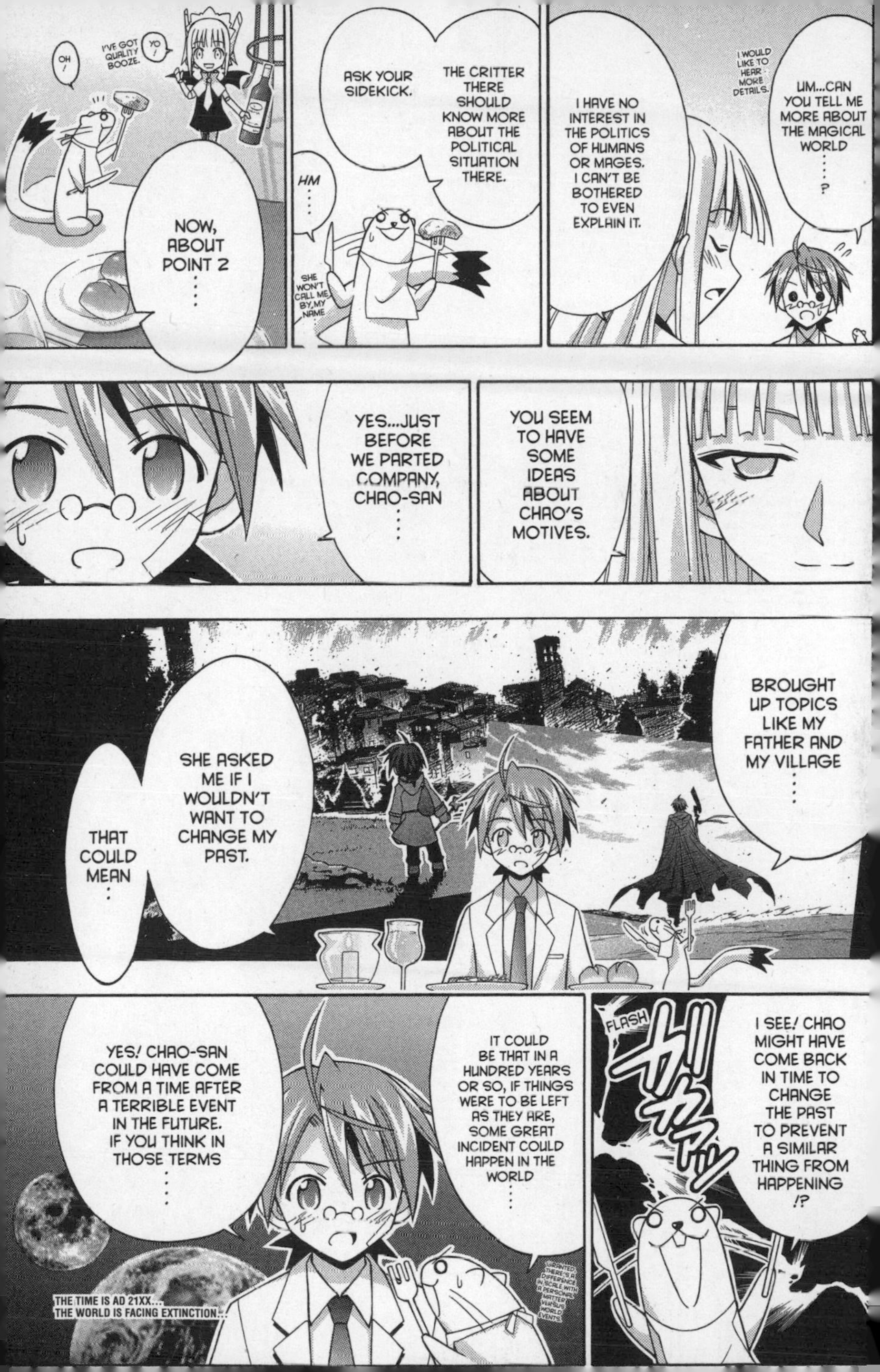
I WOULD LIKE TO HEAR MORE DETAILS.
UM...CAN YOU TELL ME MORE ABOUT THE MAGICAL WORLD ...?
I HAVE NO INTEREST IN THE POLITICS OF HUMANS OR MAGES. I CAN'T BE BOTHERED TO EVEN EXPLAIN IT.
THE CRITTER THERE SHOULD KNOW MORE ABOUT THE POLITICAL SITUATION THERE.
ASK YOUR SIDEKICK.
HM ...
SHE WON'T CALL ME BY MY NAME ...
YO!
I'VE GOT QUALITY BOOZE.
OH!
NOW, ABOUT POINT 2 ...
YOU SEEM TO HAVE SOME IDEAS ABOUT CHAO'S MOTIVES.
YES...JUST BEFORE WE PARTED COMPANY, CHAO-SAN ...
BROUGHT UP TOPICS LIKE MY FATHER AND MY VILLAGE ...
SHE ASKED ME IF I WOULDN'T WANT TO CHANGE MY PAST.
THAT COULD MEAN ...
FLASH
I SEE! CHAO MIGHT HAVE COME BACK IN TIME TO CHANGE THE PAST TO PREVENT A SIMILAR THING FROM HAPPENING !?
IT COULD BE THAT IN A HUNDRED YEARS OR SO, IF THINGS WERE TO BE LEFT AS THEY ARE, SOME GREAT INCIDENT COULD HAPPEN IN THE WORLD ...
GRANTED, THERE'S A DIFFERENCE IN SCALE WITH A PERSONAL MATTER VERSUS WORLD EVENTS.
YES! CHAO-SAN COULD HAVE COME FROM A TIME AFTER A TERRIBLE EVENT IN THE FUTURE. IF YOU THINK IN THOSE TERMS ...
THE TIME IS AD 21XX... THE WORLD IS FACING EXTINCTION...

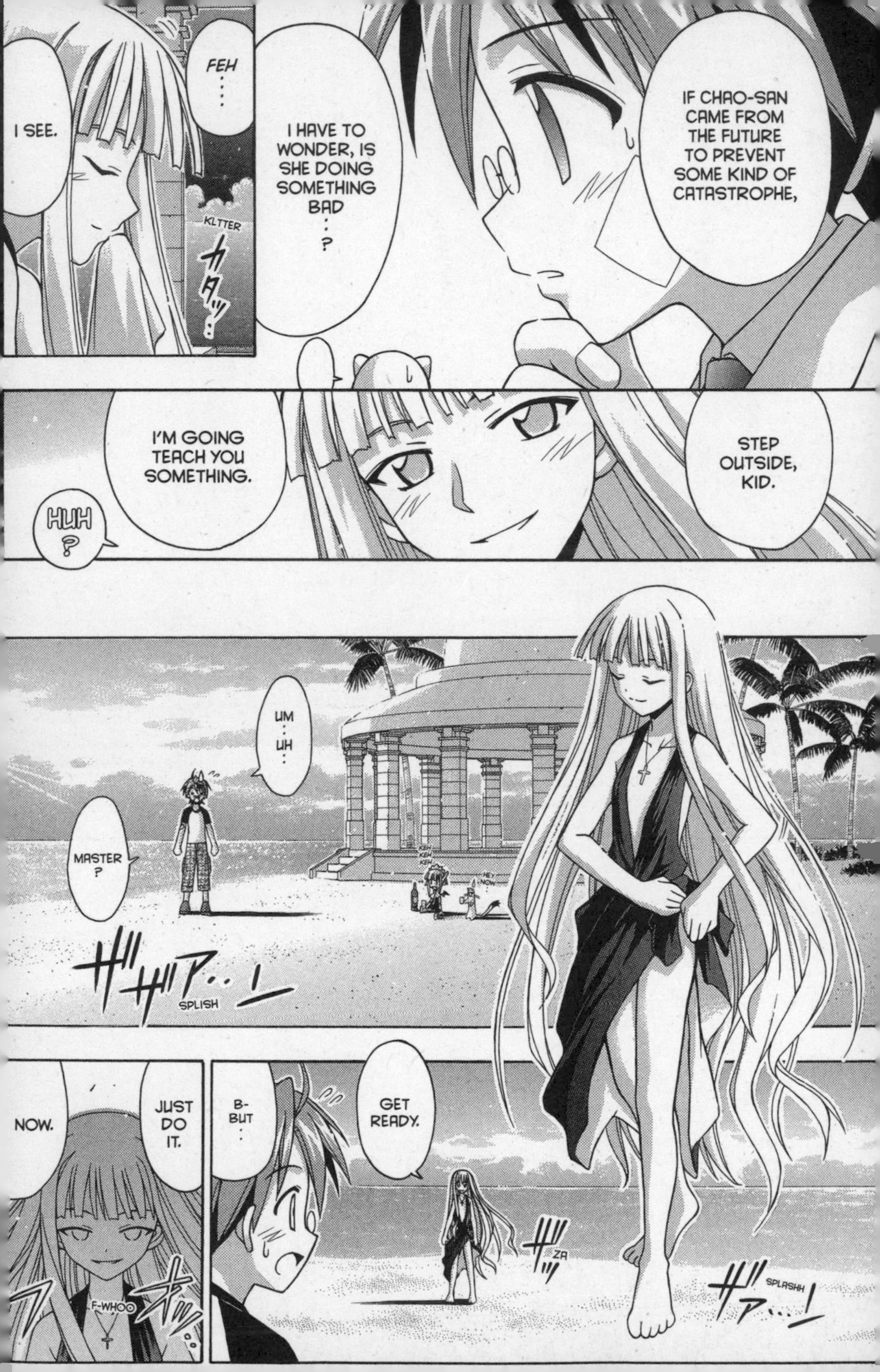
IF CHAO-SAN CAME FROM THE FUTURE TO PREVENT SOME KIND OF CATASTROPHE,
I HAVE TO WONDER, IS SHE DOING SOMETHING BAD...?
FEH....
KLTTER
I SEE.
STEP OUTSIDE, KID.
I'M GOING TEACH YOU SOMETHING.
HUH?
SPLASHH
UM... UH...
KEH KEH KEH
HEY NOW...
MASTER?
SPLISH
GET READY.
B-BUT...
JUST DO IT.
NOW.
ZA
F-WHOO

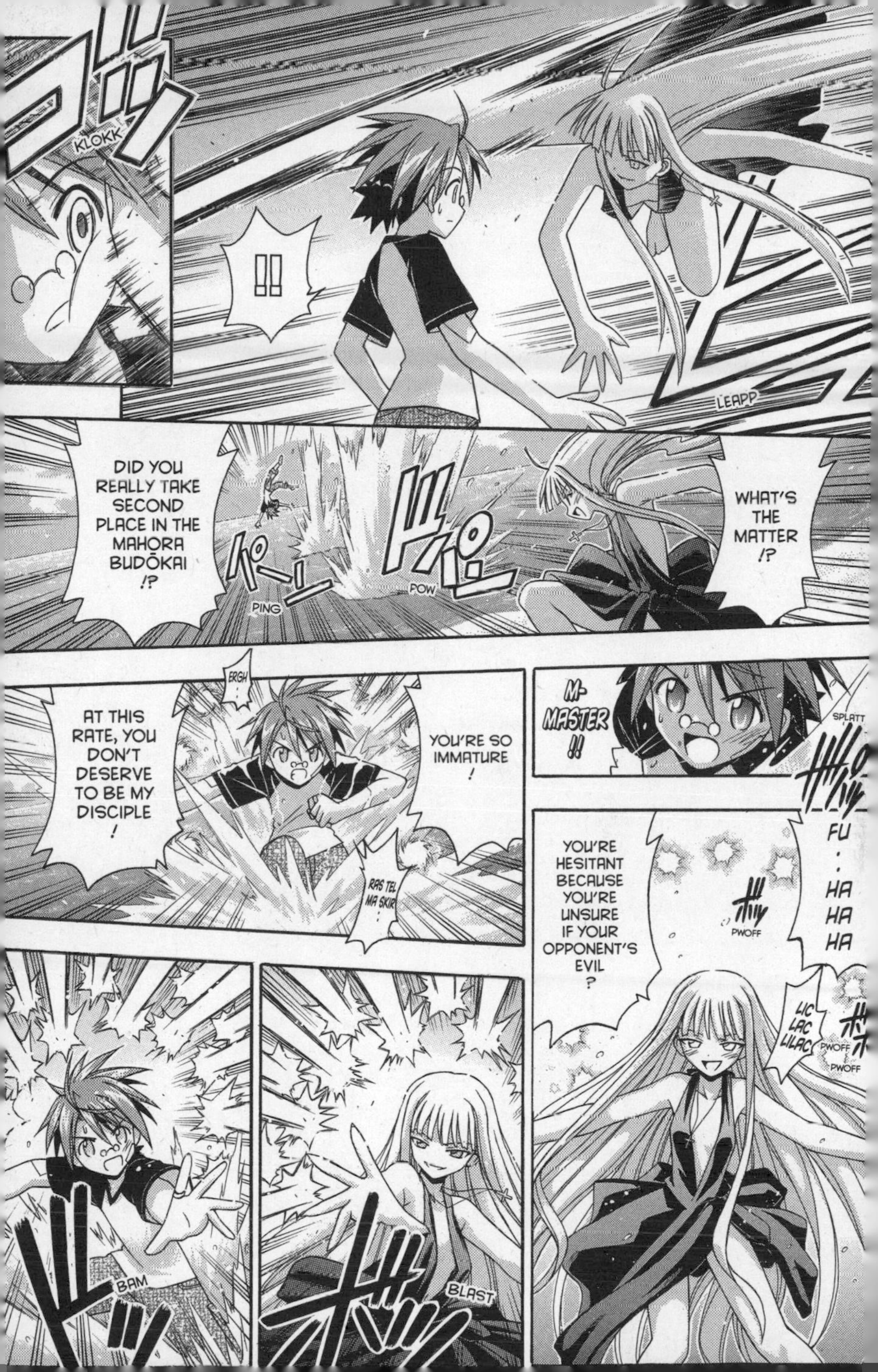
LEAPP
!!
KLOKK
WHAT'S THE MATTER!?
POW
PING
DID YOU REALLY TAKE SECOND PLACE IN THE MAHORA BUDŌKAI!?
M-MASTER!!
SPLATT
FU... HA HA HA
YOU'RE HESITANT BECAUSE YOU'RE UNSURE IF YOUR OPPONENT'S EVIL?
PWOFF
LIC LAC LILAC
PWOFF
PWOFF
YOU'RE SO IMMATURE!
ERGH...
AT THIS RATE, YOU DON'T DESERVE TO BE MY DISCIPLE!
RAS TEL MA SKIR...
BLAST
BAM

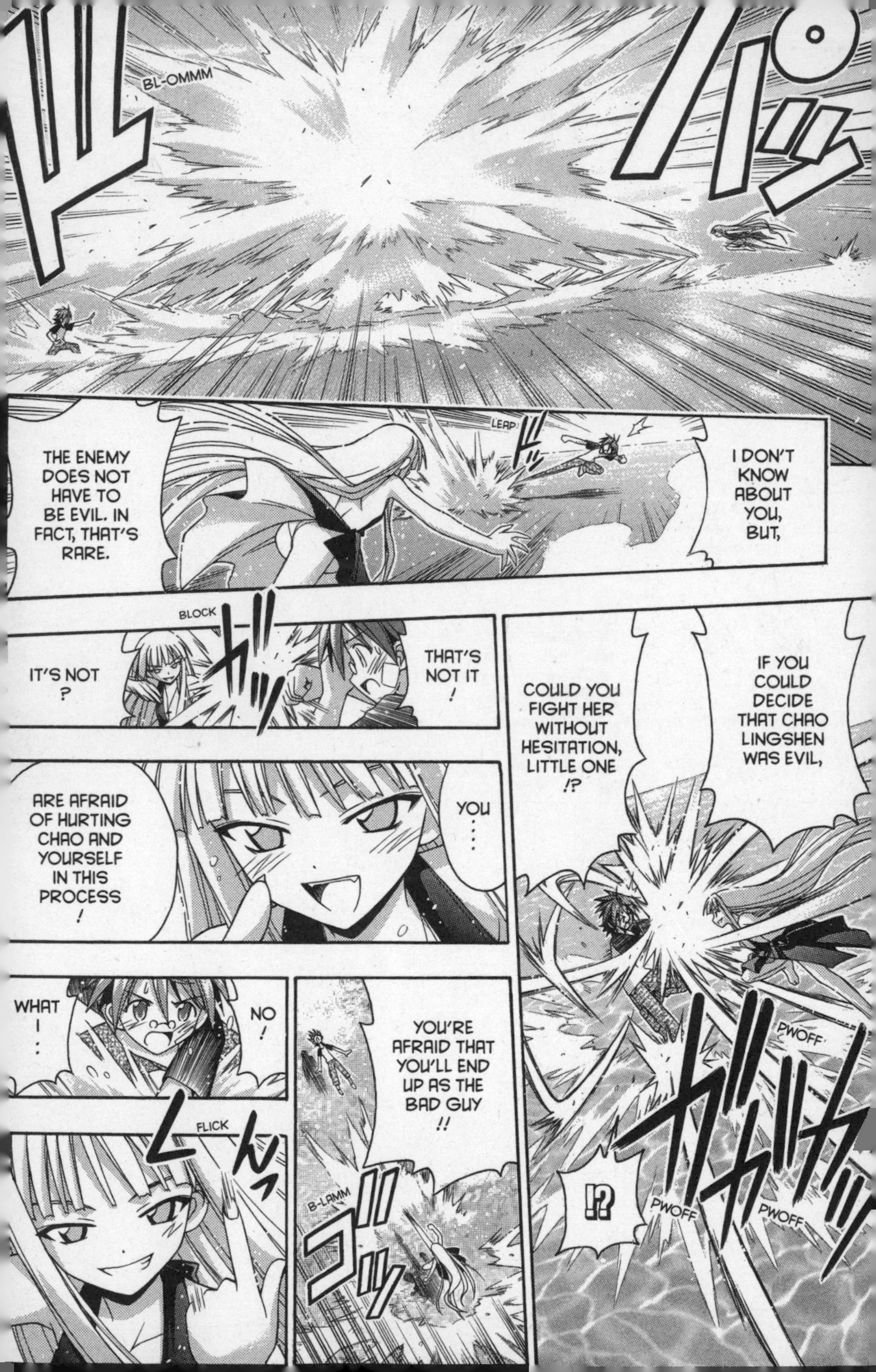
BL-OMMM
I DON'T KNOW ABOUT YOU, BUT,
LEAP
THE ENEMY DOES NOT HAVE TO BE EVIL. IN FACT, THAT'S RARE.
IF YOU COULD DECIDE THAT CHAO LINGSHEN WAS EVIL,
COULD YOU FIGHT HER WITHOUT HESITATION, LITTLE ONE !?
PWOFF
!?
PWOFF
PWOFF
THAT'S NOT IT !
BLOCK
IT'S NOT ?
YOU .....
ARE AFRAID OF HURTING CHAO AND YOURSELF IN THIS PROCESS !
YOU'RE AFRAID THAT YOU'LL END UP AS THE BAD GUY !!
B-LAMM
NO !
WHAT ! . .
FLICK

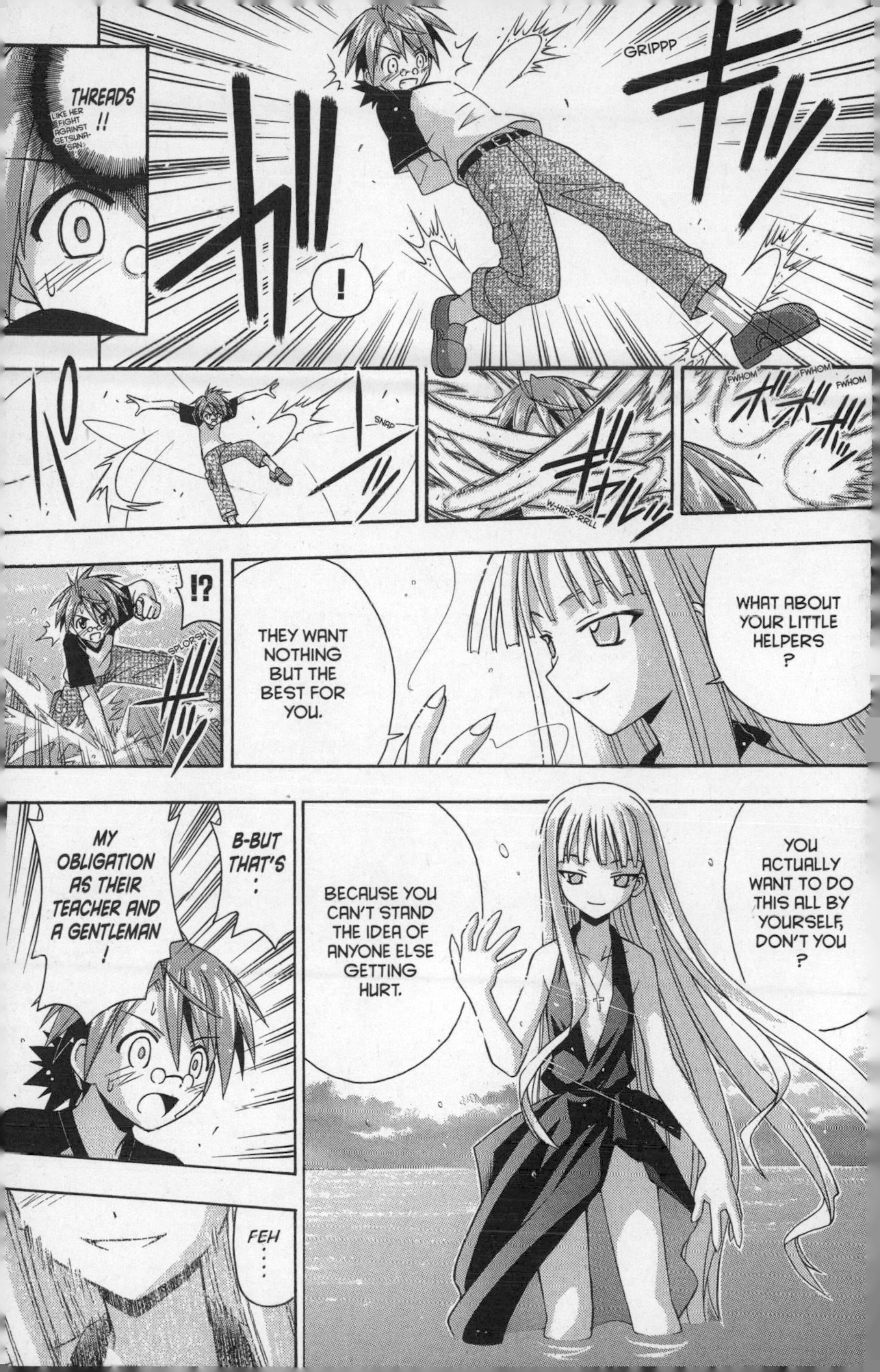
GRIPPP
!
THREADS!!
LIKE HER FIGHT AGAINST SETSUNA-SAN
FWHOM FWHOM FWHOM
W-HIRR-RRLL
SNAP
WHAT ABOUT YOUR LITTLE HELPERS?
THEY WANT NOTHING BUT THE BEST FOR YOU.
!?
SPLORSH
YOU ACTUALLY WANT TO DO THIS ALL BY YOURSELF, DON'T YOU?
BECAUSE YOU CAN'T STAND THE IDEA OF ANYONE ELSE GETTING HURT.
B-BUT THAT'S:
MY OBLIGATION AS THEIR TEACHER AND A GENTLEMAN!
FEH....

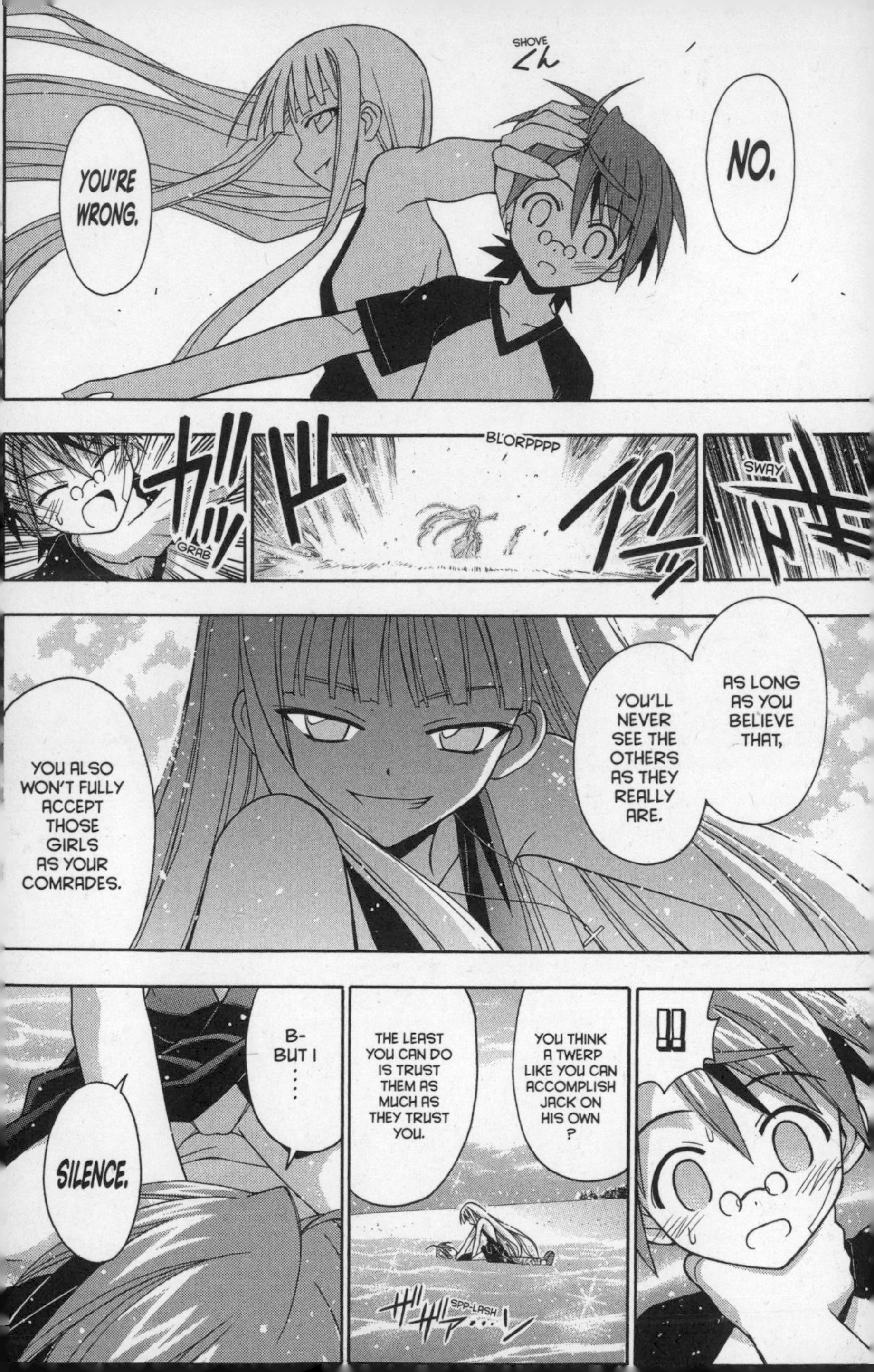
NO.
SHOVE
YOU'RE WRONG.
SWAY
BLORPPPP
GRAB
AS LONG AS YOU BELIEVE THAT,
YOU'LL NEVER SEE THE OTHERS AS THEY REALLY ARE.
YOU ALSO WON'T FULLY ACCEPT THOSE GIRLS AS YOUR COMRADES.
!!
YOU THINK A TWERP LIKE YOU CAN ACCOMPLISH JACK ON HIS OWN?
THE LEAST YOU CAN DO IS TRUST THEM AS MUCH AS THEY TRUST YOU.
SPP-LASH
B-BUT I....
SILENCE.

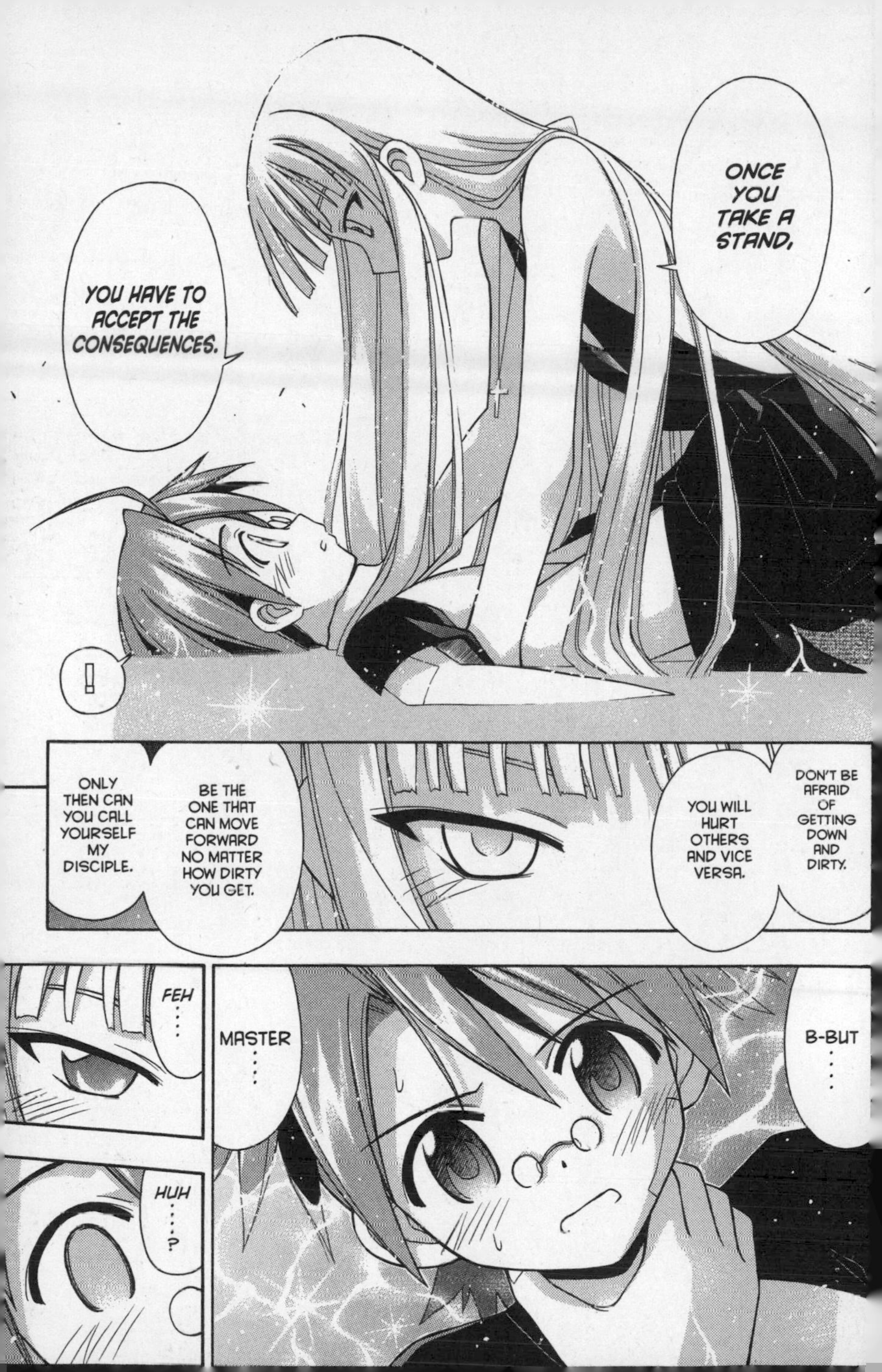
ONCE YOU TAKE A STAND,
YOU HAVE TO ACCEPT THE CONSEQUENCES.
!
DON'T BE AFRAID OF GETTING DOWN AND DIRTY.
YOU WILL HURT OTHERS AND VICE VERSA.
BE THE ONE THAT CAN MOVE FORWARD NO MATTER HOW DIRTY YOU GET.
ONLY THEN CAN YOU CALL YOURSELF MY DISCIPLE.
B-BUT....
MASTER....
FEH....
HUH....?

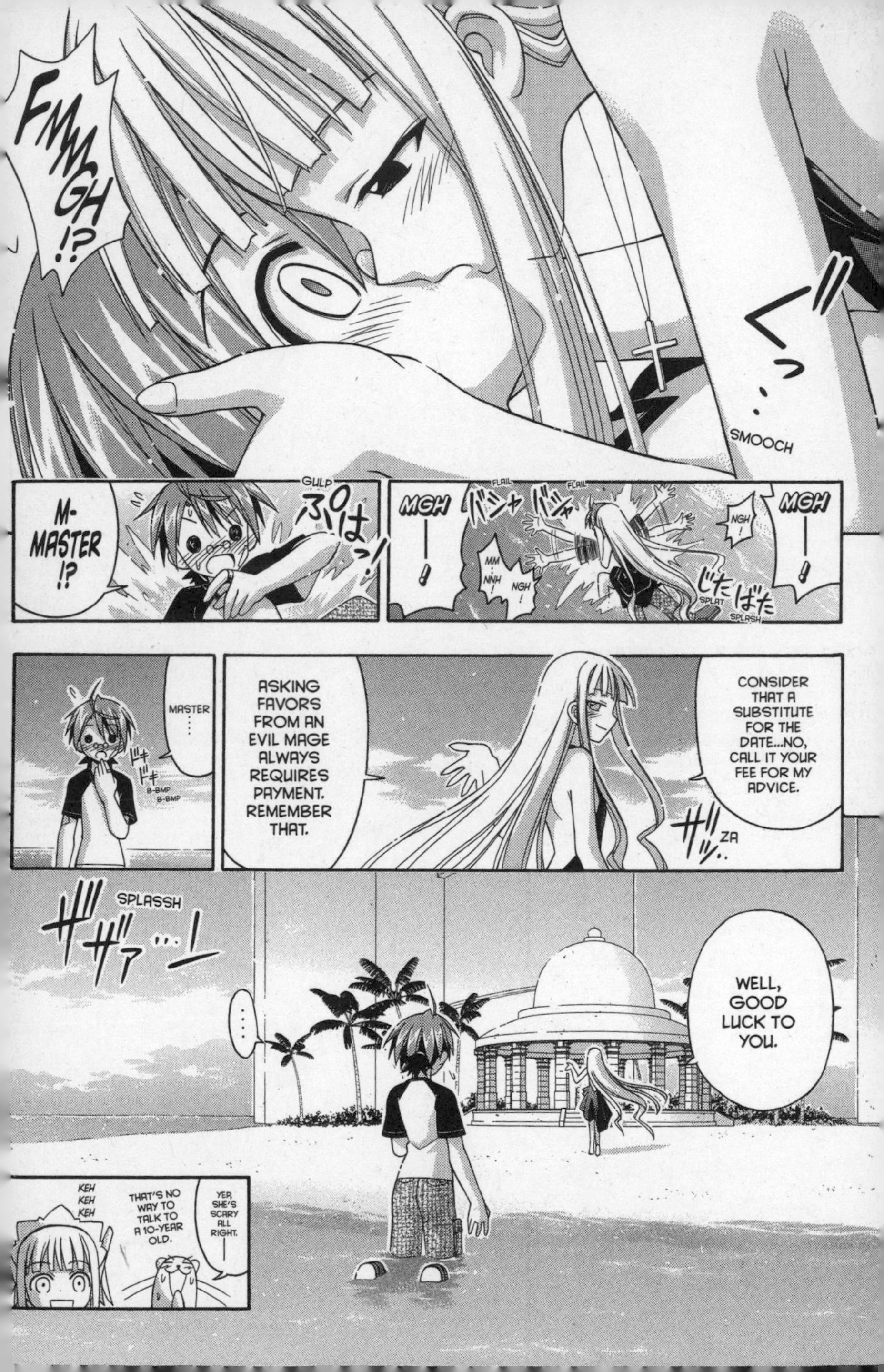
くっ…
SMOOCH
FMMGH!?
MGH—!
NGH!
バシャ
FLAIL
バシャ
FLAIL
MGH—!
MM…NNH!
NGH!
じたばた
SPLAT
SPLASH
ぷはっ!
GULP
M-MASTER!?
CONSIDER THAT A SUBSTITUTE FOR THE DATE...NO, CALL IT YOUR FEE FOR MY ADVICE.
ザッ..
ZA
ASKING FAVORS FROM AN EVIL MAGE ALWAYS REQUIRES PAYMENT. REMEMBER THAT.
MASTER…
ドキドキ
B-BMP
B-BMP
WELL, GOOD LUCK TO YOU.
……
ザザァ…!
SPLASSH
YEP, SHE'S SCARY ALL RIGHT.—
THAT'S NO WAY TO TALK TO A 10-YEAR OLD.
KEH KEH KEH

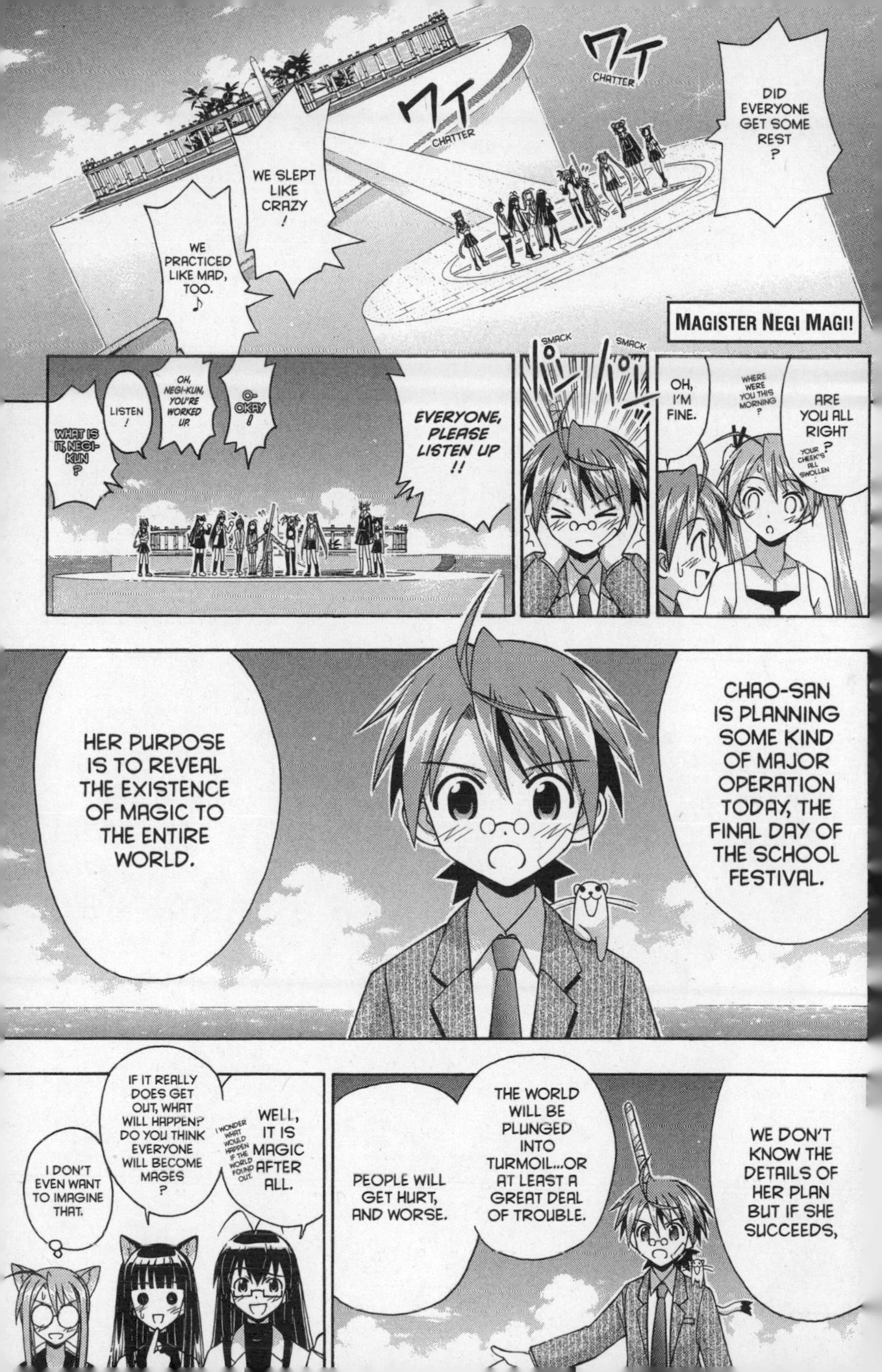
DID EVERYONE GET SOME REST?
CHATTER
CHATTER
WE SLEPT LIKE CRAZY!
WE PRACTICED LIKE MAD, TOO. ♪
MAGISTER NEGI MAGI!
ARE YOU ALL RIGHT?
WHERE WERE YOU THIS MORNING?
YOUR CHEEK'S ALL SWOLLEN
OH, I'M FINE.
SMACK
SMACK
EVERYONE, PLEASE LISTEN UP!!
O-OKAY!
OH, NEGI-KUN, YOU'RE WORKED UP.
LISTEN!
WHAT IS IT, NEGI-KUN?
CHAO-SAN IS PLANNING SOME KIND OF MAJOR OPERATION TODAY, THE FINAL DAY OF THE SCHOOL FESTIVAL.
HER PURPOSE IS TO REVEAL THE EXISTENCE OF MAGIC TO THE ENTIRE WORLD.
WE DON'T KNOW THE DETAILS OF HER PLAN BUT IF SHE SUCCEEDS,
THE WORLD WILL BE PLUNGED INTO TURMOIL...OR AT LEAST A GREAT DEAL OF TROUBLE.
PEOPLE WILL GET HURT, AND WORSE.
WELL, IT IS MAGIC AFTER ALL.
I WONDER WHAT WOULD HAPPEN IF THE WORLD FOUND OUT.
IF IT REALLY DOES GET OUT, WHAT WILL HAPPEN? DO YOU THINK EVERYONE WILL BECOME MAGES?
I DON'T EVEN WANT TO IMAGINE THAT.

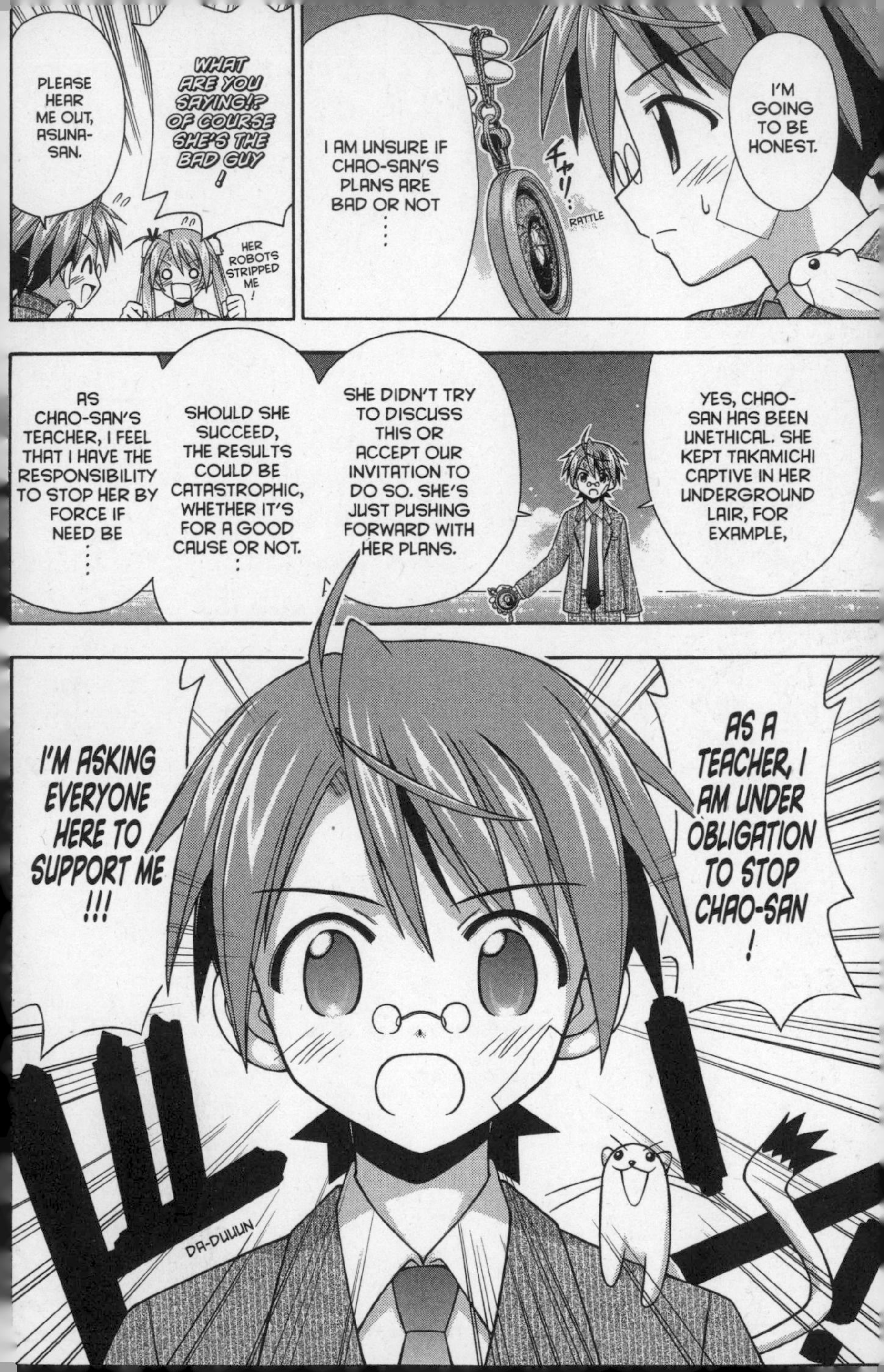
I'M GOING TO BE HONEST.
チャリ…
RATTLE
I AM UNSURE IF CHAO-SAN'S PLANS ARE BAD OR NOT ...
WHAT ARE YOU SAYING!? OF COURSE SHE'S THE BAD GUY!
PLEASE HEAR ME OUT, ASUNA-SAN.
HER ROBOTS STRIPPED ME!
YES, CHAO-SAN HAS BEEN UNETHICAL. SHE KEPT TAKAMICHI CAPTIVE IN HER UNDERGROUND LAIR, FOR EXAMPLE,
SHE DIDN'T TRY TO DISCUSS THIS OR ACCEPT OUR INVITATION TO DO SO. SHE'S JUST PUSHING FORWARD WITH HER PLANS.
SHOULD SHE SUCCEED, THE RESULTS COULD BE CATASTROPHIC, WHETHER IT'S FOR A GOOD CAUSE OR NOT. ...
AS CHAO-SAN'S TEACHER, I FEEL THAT I HAVE THE RESPONSIBILITY TO STOP HER BY FORCE IF NEED BE ...
AS A TEACHER, I AM UNDER OBLIGATION TO STOP CHAO-SAN!
I'M ASKING EVERYONE HERE TO SUPPORT ME!!!
DA-DUUUN

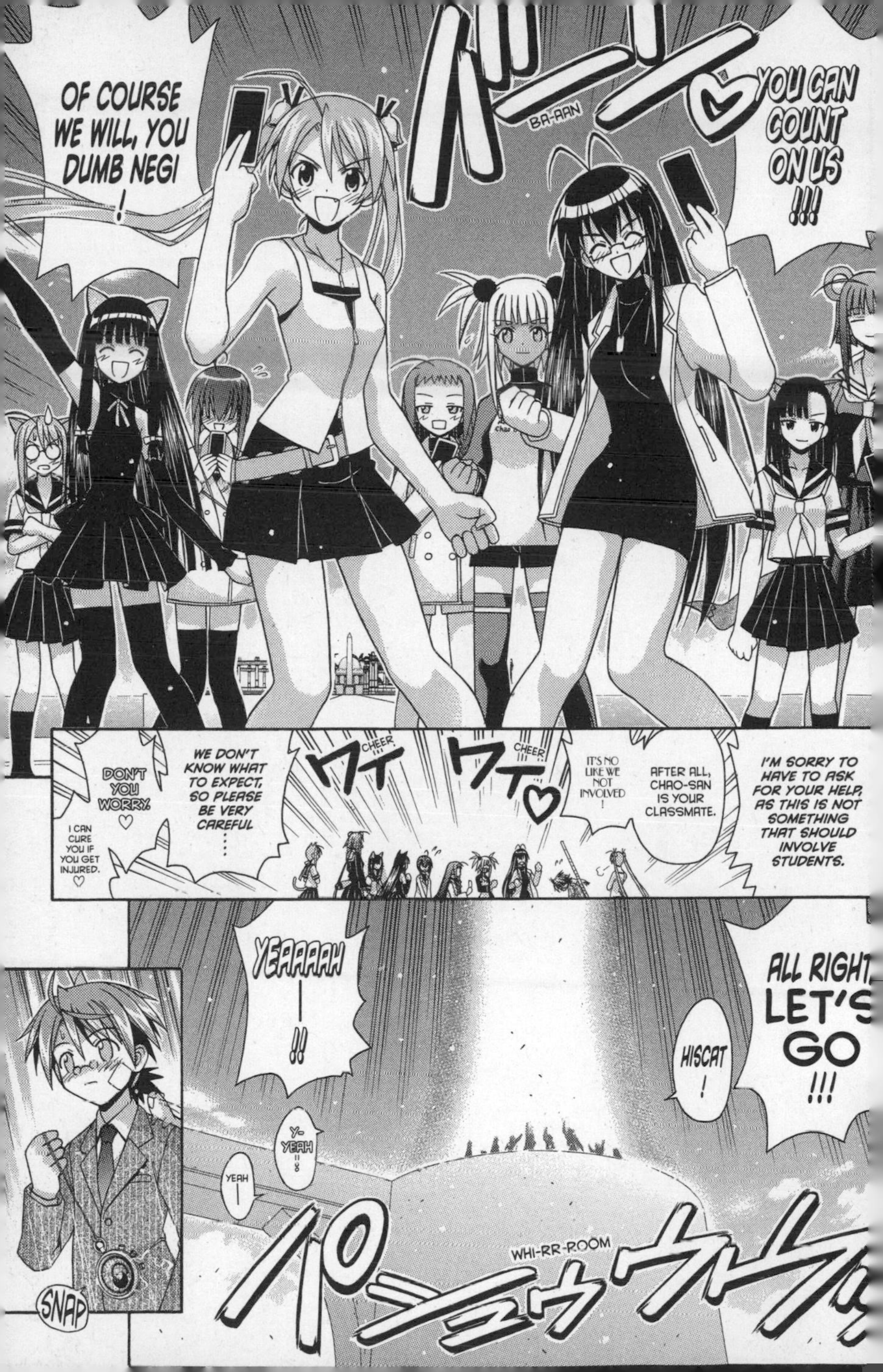
YOU CAN COUNT ON US !!!
BA-AAN
OF COURSE WE WILL, YOU DUMB NEGI !
I'M SORRY TO HAVE TO ASK FOR YOUR HELP, AS THIS IS NOT SOMETHING THAT SHOULD INVOLVE STUDENTS.
AFTER ALL, CHAO-SAN IS YOUR CLASSMATE.
IT'S NO LIKE WE NOT INVOLVED !
CHEER
CHEER
WE DON'T KNOW WHAT TO EXPECT, SO PLEASE BE VERY CAREFUL ...
DON'T YOU WORRY. ♡
I CAN CURE YOU IF YOU GET INJURED. ♡
ALL RIGHT, LET'S GO !!!
HISCAT !
YEAAAAH — !!
Y-YEAH !!
YEAH —
WHI-RR-ROOM
SNAP

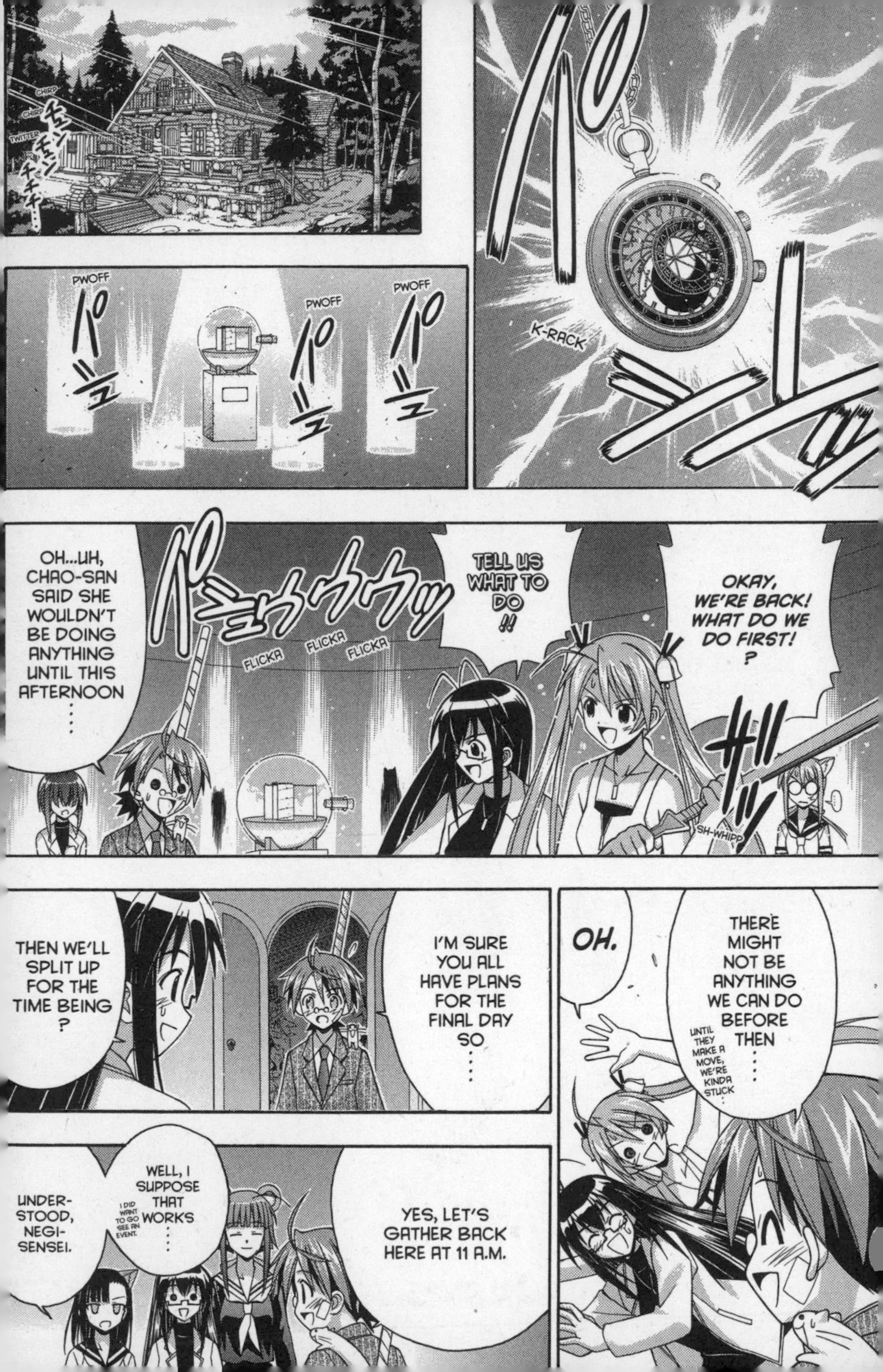
K-RACK
CHIRP
CHIRP
TWITTER
PWOFF
PWOFF
PWOFF
OKAY, WE'RE BACK! WHAT DO WE DO FIRST!?
SH-WHIPP
TELL US WHAT TO DO!!
FLICKA
FLICKA
FLICKA
OH...UH, CHAO-SAN SAID SHE WOULDN'T BE DOING ANYTHING UNTIL THIS AFTERNOON....
OH.
THERE MIGHT NOT BE ANYTHING WE CAN DO BEFORE THEN...
UNTIL THEY MAKE A MOVE, WE'RE KINDA STUCK.
I'M SURE YOU ALL HAVE PLANS FOR THE FINAL DAY SO...
THEN WE'LL SPLIT UP FOR THE TIME BEING?
YES, LET'S GATHER BACK HERE AT 11 A.M.
WELL, I SUPPOSE THAT WORKS...
I DID WANT TO GO SEE AN EVENT.
UNDER-STOOD, NEGI-SENSEI.

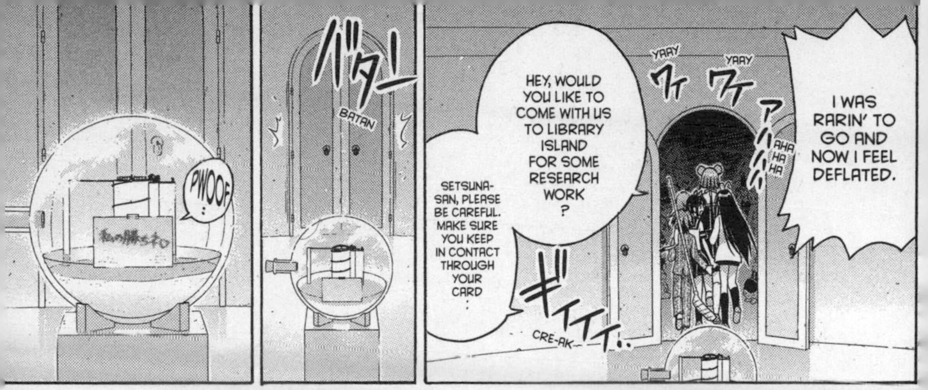
I WAS RARIN' TO GO AND NOW I FEEL DEFLATED.
YAAY
YAAY
AHA HA HA
HEY, WOULD YOU LIKE TO COME WITH US TO LIBRARY ISLAND FOR SOME RESEARCH WORK ?
SETSUNA-SAN, PLEASE BE CAREFUL. MAKE SURE YOU KEEP IN CONTACT THROUGH YOUR CARD
CRE-AK
BATAN
PWOOF

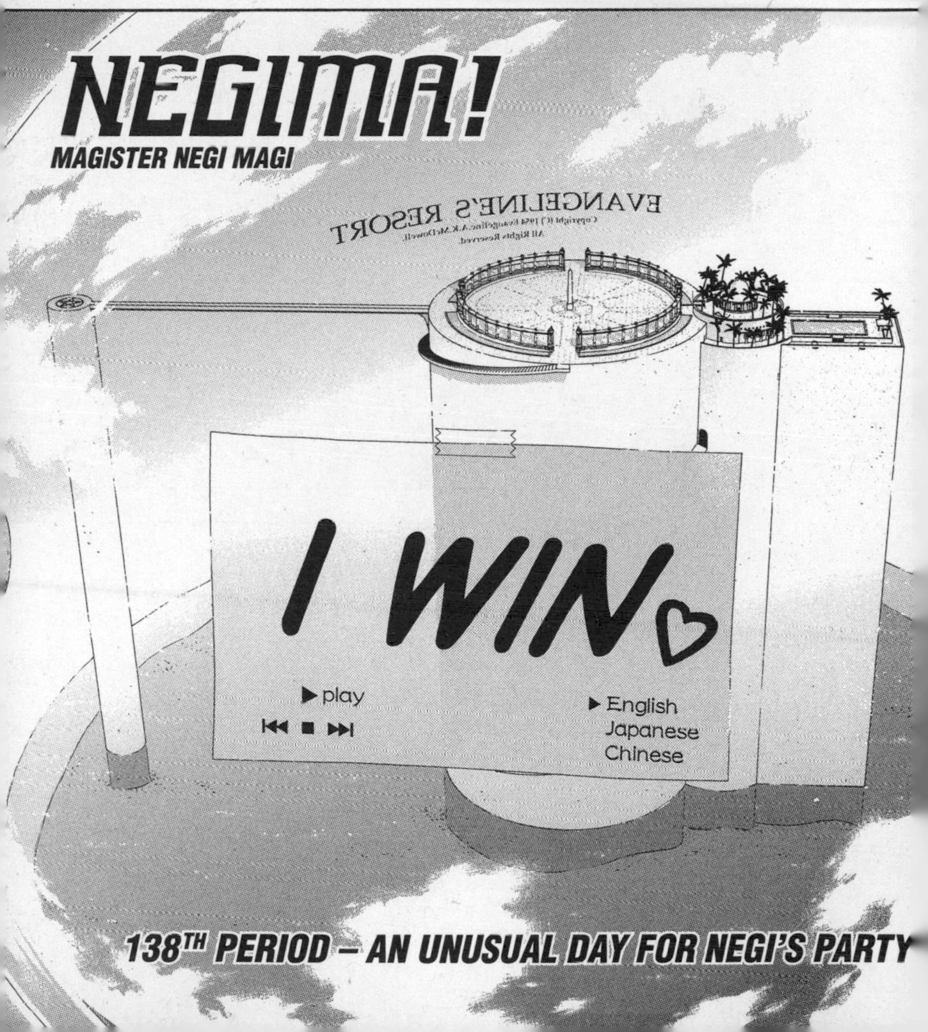
NEGIMA!
MAGISTER NEGI MAGI
EVANGELINE'S RESORT
I WIN♡
▶play
▶English
Japanese
Chinese
138TH PERIOD – AN UNUSUAL DAY FOR NEGI'S PARTY

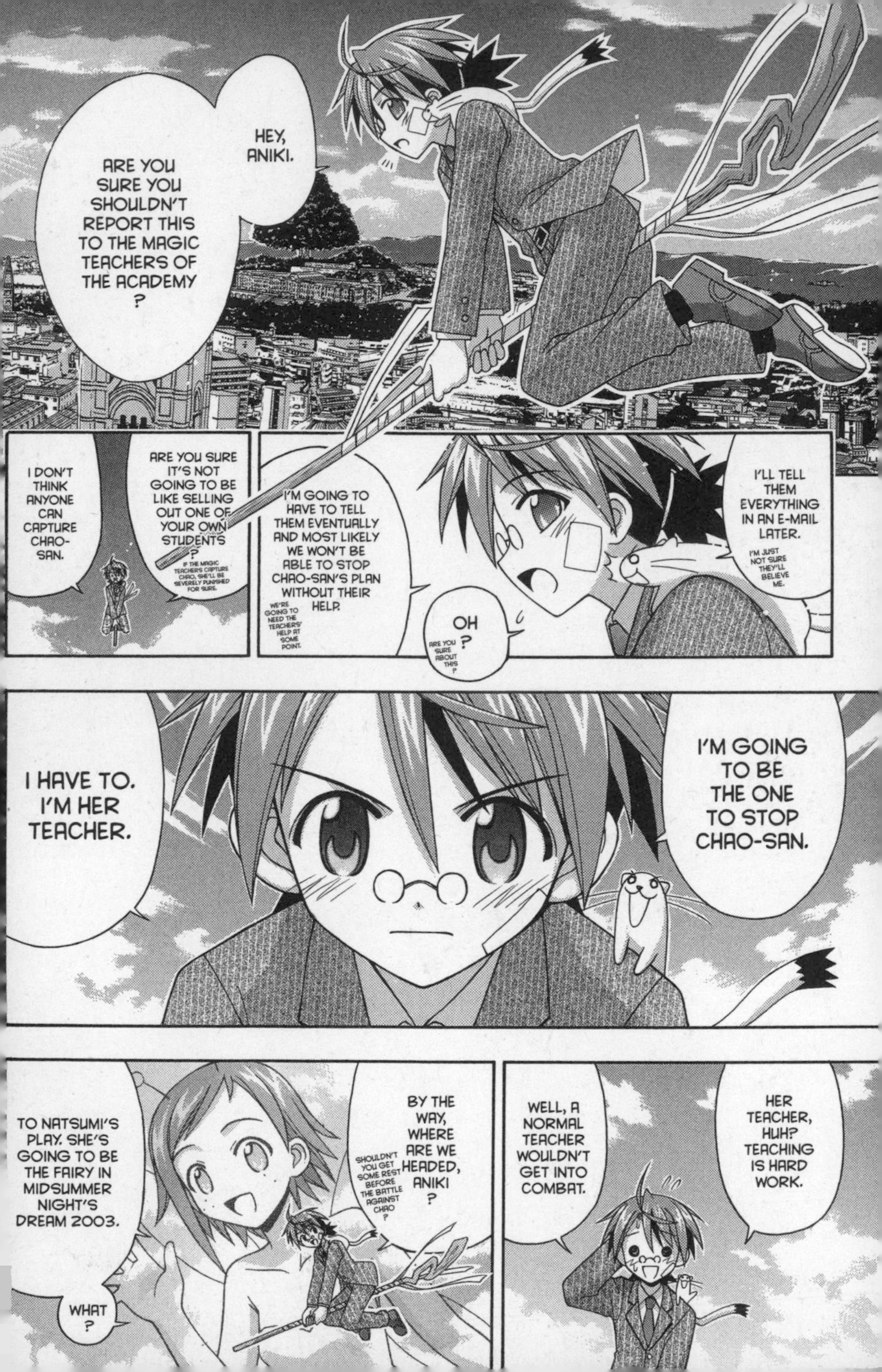
HEY, ANIKI.
ARE YOU SURE YOU SHOULDN'T REPORT THIS TO THE MAGIC TEACHERS OF THE ACADEMY ?
I'LL TELL THEM EVERYTHING IN AN E-MAIL LATER.
I'M JUST NOT SURE THEY'LL BELIEVE ME.
OH ?
ARE YOU SURE ABOUT THIS ?
I'M GOING TO HAVE TO TELL THEM EVENTUALLY AND MOST LIKELY WE WON'T BE ABLE TO STOP CHAO-SAN'S PLAN WITHOUT THEIR HELP.
WE'RE GOING TO NEED THE TEACHERS' HELP AT SOME POINT.
ARE YOU SURE IT'S NOT GOING TO BE LIKE SELLING OUT ONE OF YOUR OWN STUDENTS ?
IF THE MAGIC TEACHERS CAPTURE CHAO, SHE'LL BE SEVERELY PUNISHED FOR SURE.
I DON'T THINK ANYONE CAN CAPTURE CHAO-SAN.
I'M GOING TO BE THE ONE TO STOP CHAO-SAN.
I HAVE TO. I'M HER TEACHER.
HER TEACHER, HUH? TEACHING IS HARD WORK.
WELL, A NORMAL TEACHER WOULDN'T GET INTO COMBAT.
BY THE WAY, WHERE ARE WE HEADED, ANIKI ?
SHOULDN'T YOU GET SOME REST BEFORE THE BATTLE AGAINST CHAO ?
TO NATSUMI'S PLAY. SHE'S GOING TO BE THE FAIRY IN MIDSUMMER NIGHT'S DREAM 2003.
WHAT ?

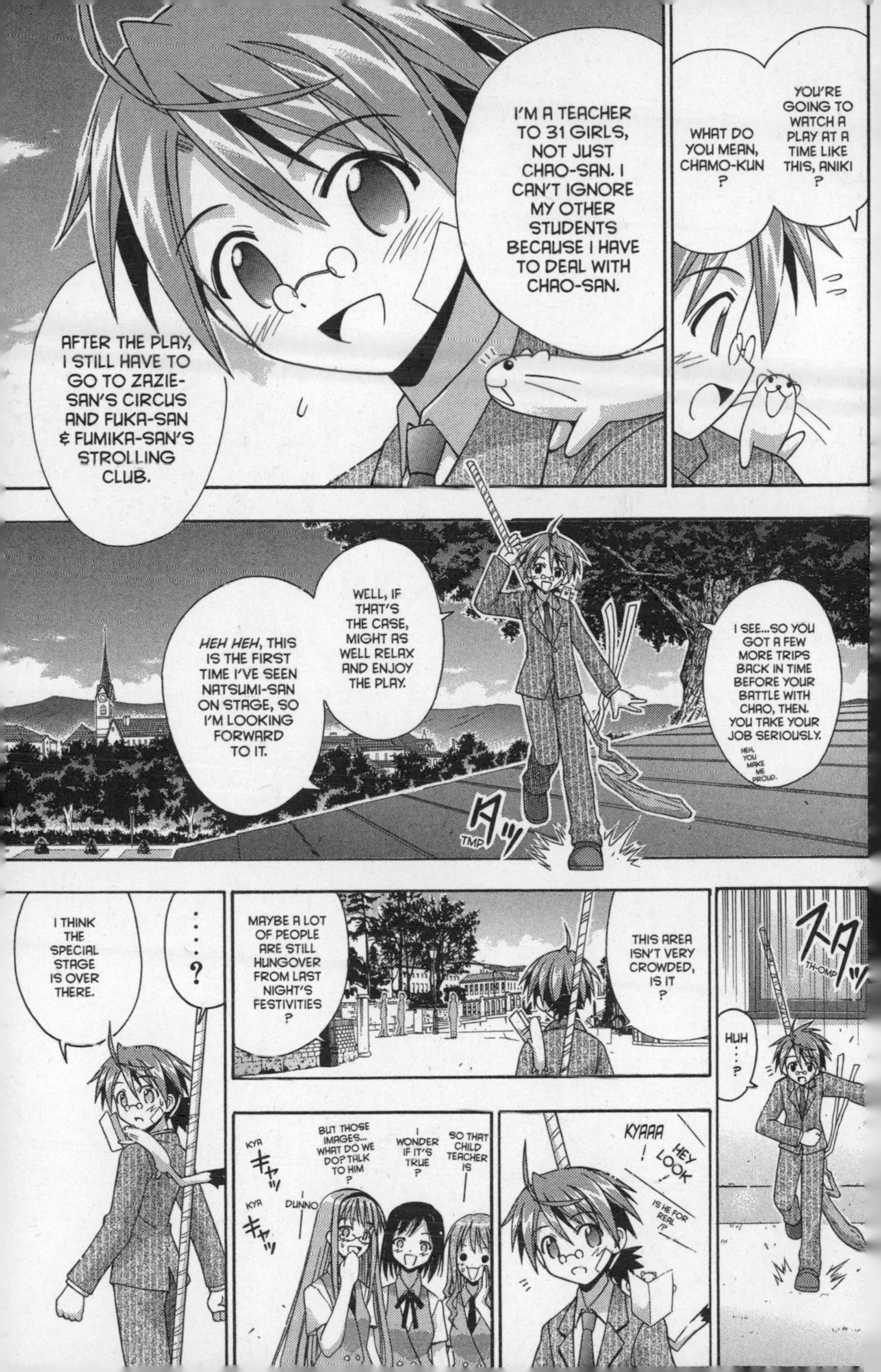

YOU'RE GOING TO WATCH A PLAY AT A TIME LIKE THIS, ANIKI?
WHAT DO YOU MEAN, CHAMO-KUN?
I'M A TEACHER TO 31 GIRLS, NOT JUST CHAO-SAN. I CAN'T IGNORE MY OTHER STUDENTS BECAUSE I HAVE TO DEAL WITH CHAO-SAN.
AFTER THE PLAY, I STILL HAVE TO GO TO ZAZIE-SAN'S CIRCUS AND FUKA-SAN & FUMIKA-SAN'S STROLLING CLUB.
I SEE...SO YOU GOT A FEW MORE TRIPS BACK IN TIME BEFORE YOUR BATTLE WITH CHAO, THEN. YOU TAKE YOUR JOB SERIOUSLY.
HEH, YOU MAKE ME PROUD.
WELL, IF THAT'S THE CASE, MIGHT AS WELL RELAX AND ENJOY THE PLAY.
HEH HEH, THIS IS THE FIRST TIME I'VE SEEN NATSUMI-SAN ON STAGE, SO I'M LOOKING FORWARD TO IT.
TMP
TH-OMP
HUH...?
THIS AREA ISN'T VERY CROWDED, IS IT?
MAYBE A LOT OF PEOPLE ARE STILL HUNGOVER FROM LAST NIGHT'S FESTIVITIES?
KYAAA!
HEY LOOK!
IS HE FOR REAL!?
SO THAT CHILD TEACHER IS—
I WONDER IF IT'S TRUE
BUT THOSE IMAGES... WHAT DO WE DO? TALK TO HIM?
I DUNNO—
KYA
KYA
....
?
I THINK THE SPECIAL STAGE IS OVER THERE.

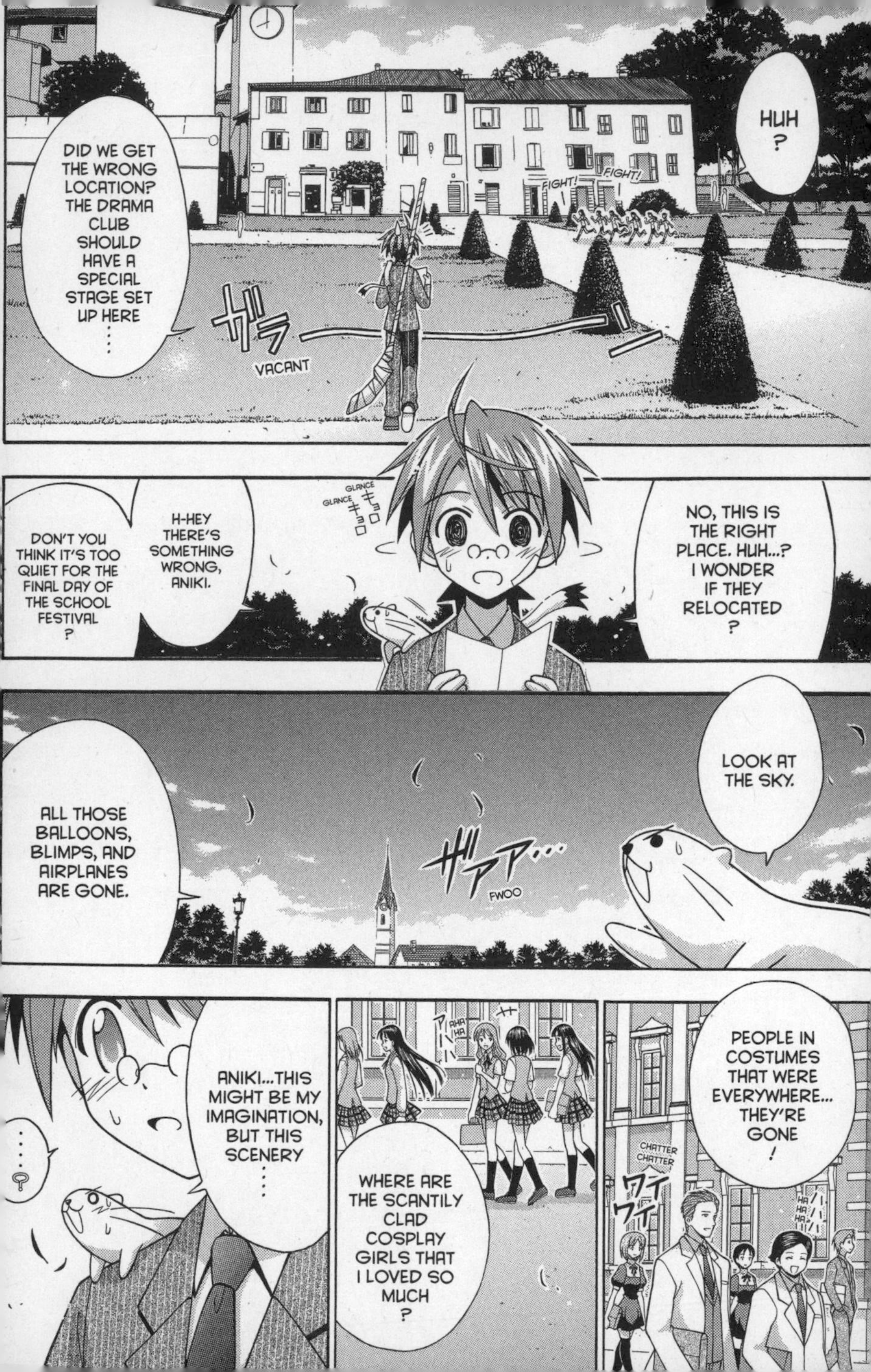
HUH?
FIGHT! FIGHT!
DID WE GET THE WRONG LOCATION? THE DRAMA CLUB SHOULD HAVE A SPECIAL STAGE SET UP HERE.....
VACANT
NO, THIS IS THE RIGHT PLACE. HUH...? I WONDER IF THEY RELOCATED?
GLANCE GLANCE
H-HEY THERE'S SOMETHING WRONG, ANIKI.
DON'T YOU THINK IT'S TOO QUIET FOR THE FINAL DAY OF THE SCHOOL FESTIVAL?
LOOK AT THE SKY.
FWOO
ALL THOSE BALLOONS, BLIMPS, AND AIRPLANES ARE GONE.
PEOPLE IN COSTUMES THAT WERE EVERYWHERE... THEY'RE GONE!
CHATTER CHATTER
HA HA HA
AHA HA
WHERE ARE THE SCANTILY CLAD COSPLAY GIRLS THAT I LOVED SO MUCH?
ANIKI...THIS MIGHT BE MY IMAGINATION, BUT THIS SCENERY...
.....?

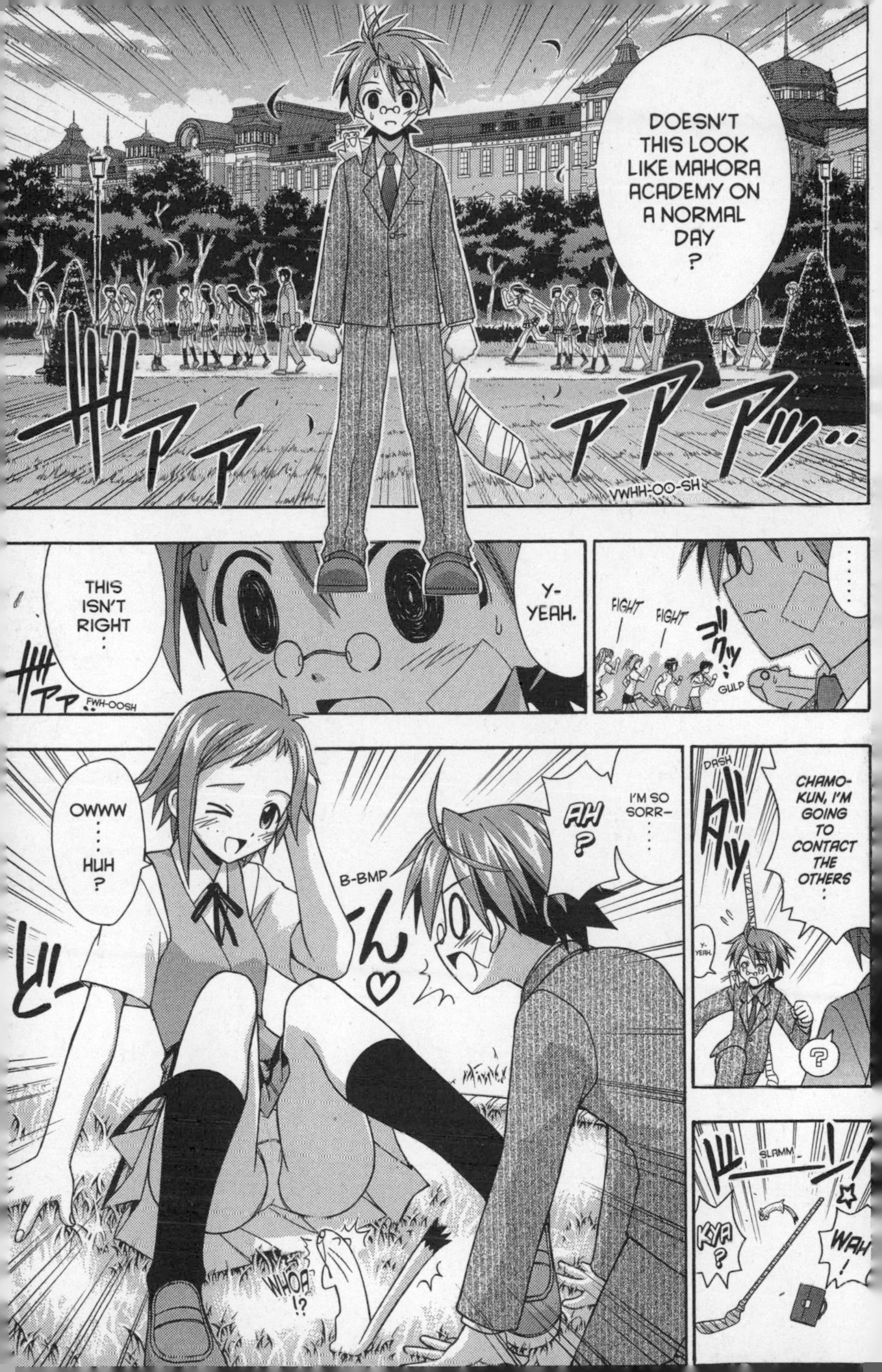
DOESN'T THIS LOOK LIKE MAHORA ACADEMY ON A NORMAL DAY ?
VWHH-OO-SH
......
FIGHT
FIGHT
GULP
Y-YEAH.
THIS ISN'T RIGHT ...
FWH-OOSH
CHAMO-KUN, I'M GOING TO CONTACT THE OTHERS ...
DASH
Y-YEAH.
?
SLAMM
KYA ?
WAH !
I'M SO SORR- ...
AH ?
B-BMP
OWWW ... HUH ?
WHOA !?

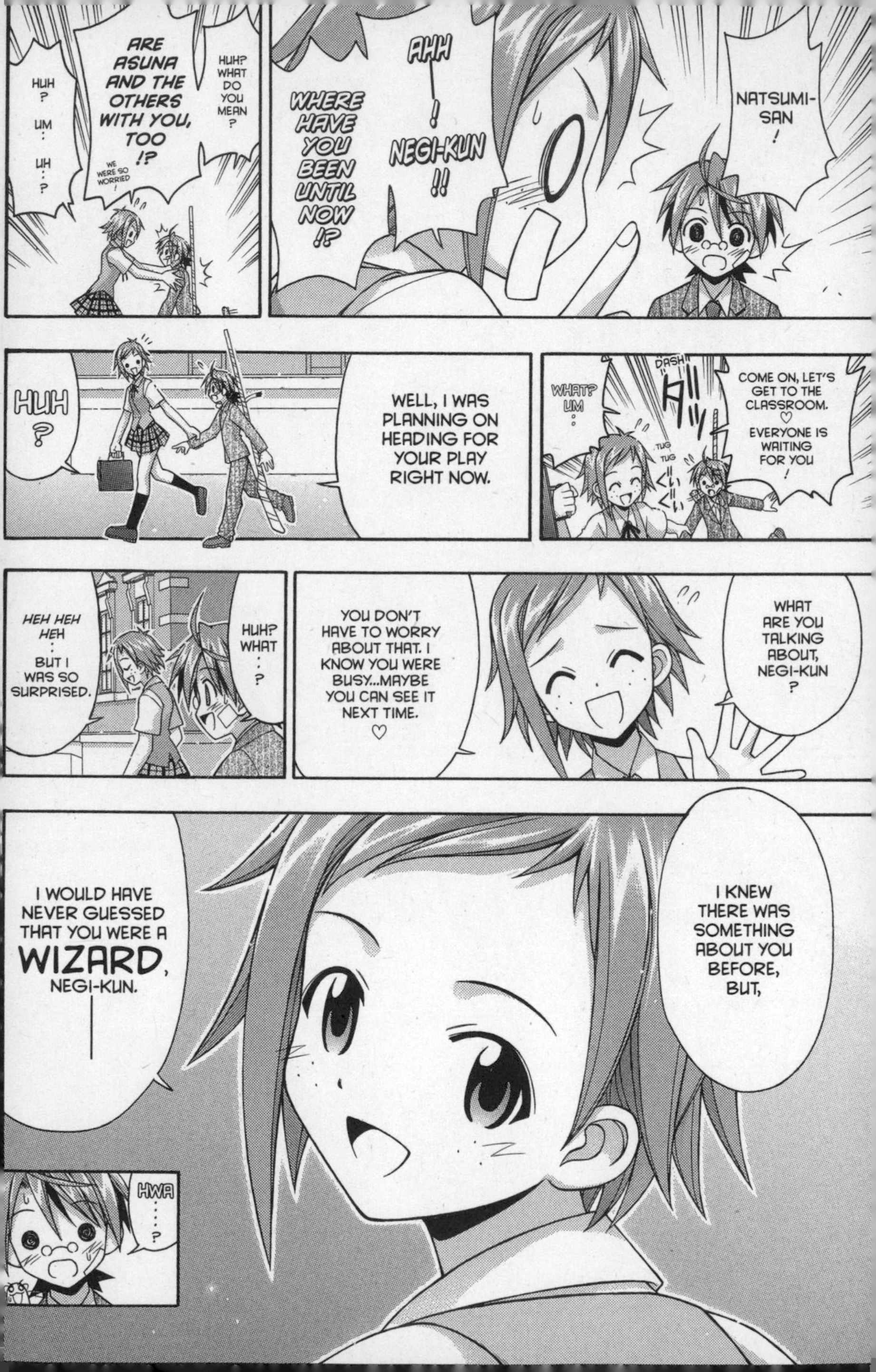
NATSUMI-SAN!
AHH...! NEGI-KUN!!
WHERE HAVE YOU BEEN UNTIL NOW!?
ARE ASUNA AND THE OTHERS WITH YOU, TOO!?
WE WERE SO WORRIED!
HUH? WHAT DO YOU MEAN?
HUH? UM... UH...?
COME ON, LET'S GET TO THE CLASSROOM. ♡
EVERYONE IS WAITING FOR YOU!
DASH
WHAT? UM...
TUG TUG
WELL, I WAS PLANNING ON HEADING FOR YOUR PLAY RIGHT NOW.
HUH?
WHAT ARE YOU TALKING ABOUT, NEGI-KUN?
YOU DON'T HAVE TO WORRY ABOUT THAT. I KNOW YOU WERE BUSY...MAYBE YOU CAN SEE IT NEXT TIME. ♡
HUH? WHAT...?
HEH HEH HEH... BUT I WAS SO SURPRISED.
I KNEW THERE WAS SOMETHING ABOUT YOU BEFORE, BUT,
I WOULD HAVE NEVER GUESSED THAT YOU WERE A WIZARD, NEGI-KUN.
HWA....?

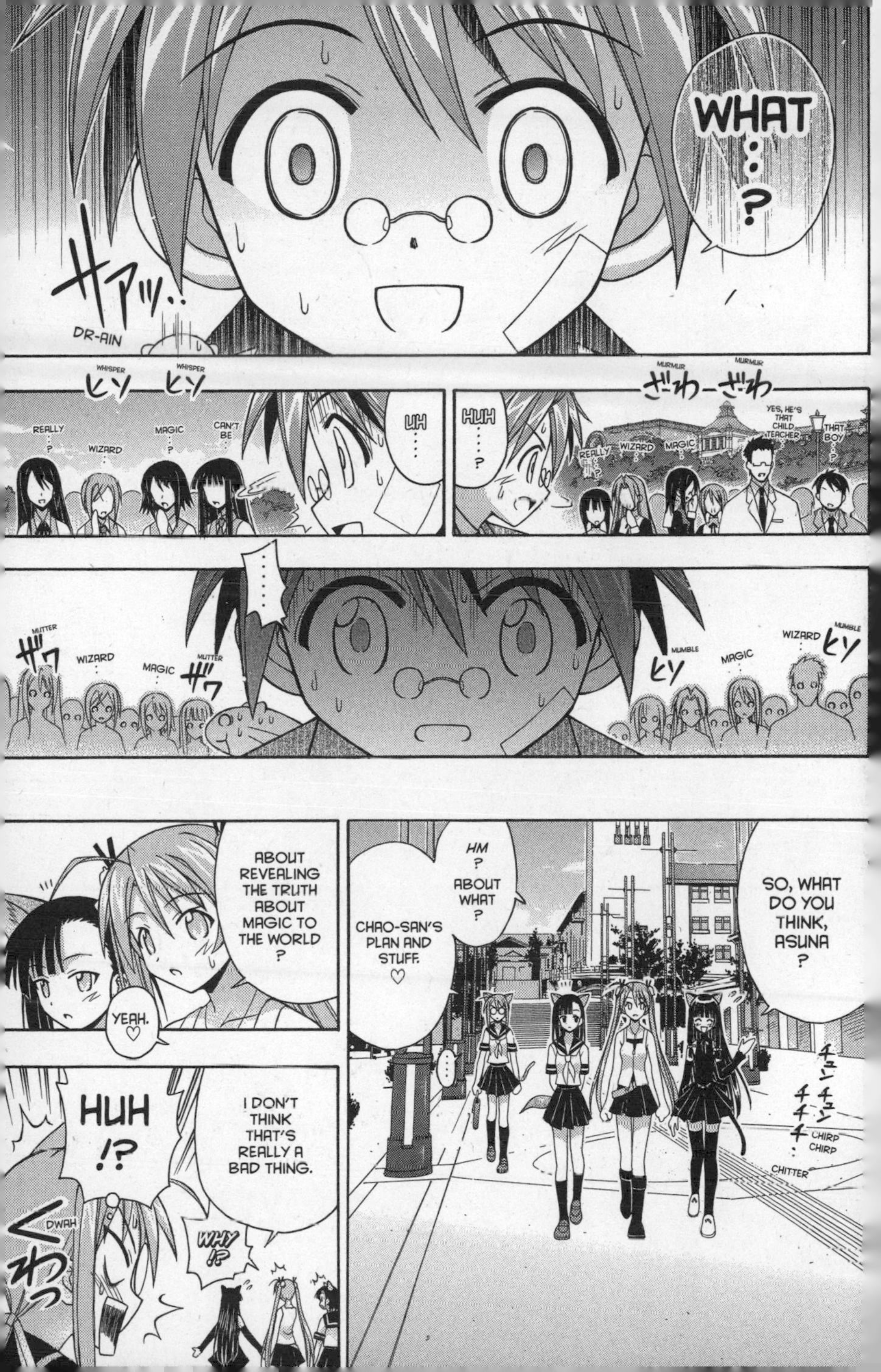
WHAT ...?
ザアッ..
DR-AIN
ざわーざわ
MURMUR MURMUR
HUH ....?
YES, HE'S THAT CHILD TEACHER
THAT BOY ...?
MAGIC
WIZARD
REALLY ...?
ヒソ ヒソ
WHISPER WHISPER
UH ....
CAN'T BE
MAGIC ...?
WIZARD ...
REALLY ...?
......
ヒソ
MUMBLE
WIZARD ...
MAGIC ...
ヒソ
MUMBLE
ザワ
MUTTER
MAGIC ...
WIZARD ...
ザワ
MUTTER
SO, WHAT DO YOU THINK, ASUNA?
チュン チュン チチチ...
CHIRP CHIRP
CHITTER
HM? ABOUT WHAT?
CHAO-SAN'S PLAN AND STUFF. ♡
...
ABOUT REVEALING THE TRUTH ABOUT MAGIC TO THE WORLD?
YEAH. ♡
I DON'T THINK THAT'S REALLY A BAD THING.
HUH !?
WHY !?
くわっ
DWAH

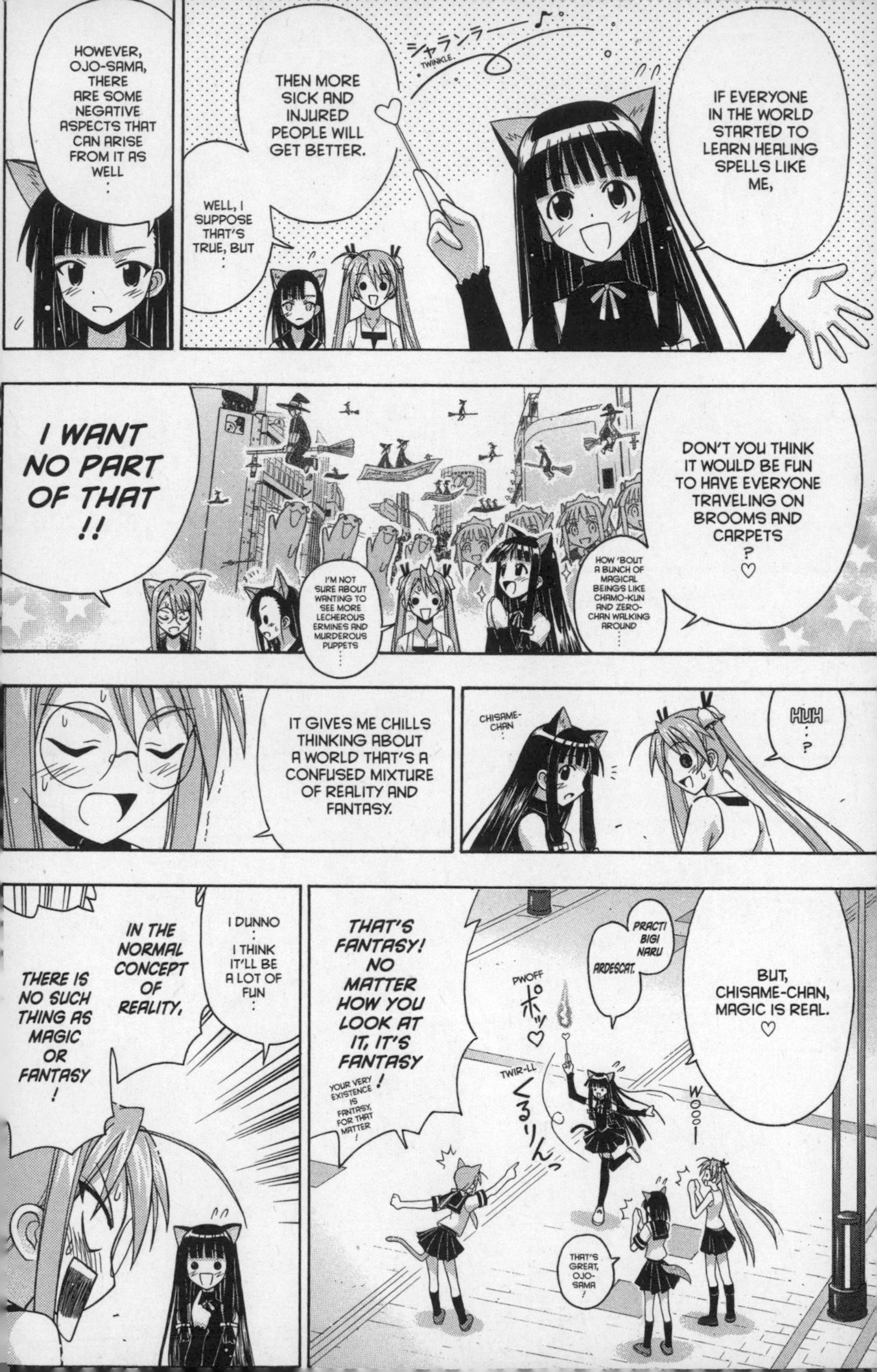
IF EVERYONE IN THE WORLD STARTED TO LEARN HEALING SPELLS LIKE ME,
シャランラー♪ TWINKLE
THEN MORE SICK AND INJURED PEOPLE WILL GET BETTER.
WELL, I SUPPOSE THAT'S TRUE, BUT...
HOWEVER, OJO-SAMA, THERE ARE SOME NEGATIVE ASPECTS THAT CAN ARISE FROM IT AS WELL...
DON'T YOU THINK IT WOULD BE FUN TO HAVE EVERYONE TRAVELING ON BROOMS AND CARPETS?♡
HOW 'BOUT A BUNCH OF MAGICAL BEINGS LIKE CHAMO-KUN AND ZERO-CHAN WALKING AROUND...
I'M NOT SURE ABOUT WANTING TO SEE MORE LECHEROUS ERMINES AND MURDEROUS PUPPETS...
I WANT NO PART OF THAT!!
HUH..?
CHISAME-CHAN...
IT GIVES ME CHILLS THINKING ABOUT A WORLD THAT'S A CONFUSED MIXTURE OF REALITY AND FANTASY.
BUT, CHISAME-CHAN, MAGIC IS REAL.♡
PRACTI BIGI NARU ARDESCAT.
PWOFF ポッ♡
TWIR-LL くるりんっ
WOOO!
THAT'S GREAT, OJO-SAMA!
THAT'S FANTASY! NO MATTER HOW YOU LOOK AT IT, IT'S FANTASY!
YOUR VERY EXISTENCE IS FANTASY, FOR THAT MATTER!
I DUNNO... I THINK IT'LL BE A LOT OF FUN...
IN THE NORMAL CONCEPT OF REALITY,
THERE IS NO SUCH THING AS MAGIC OR FANTASY!

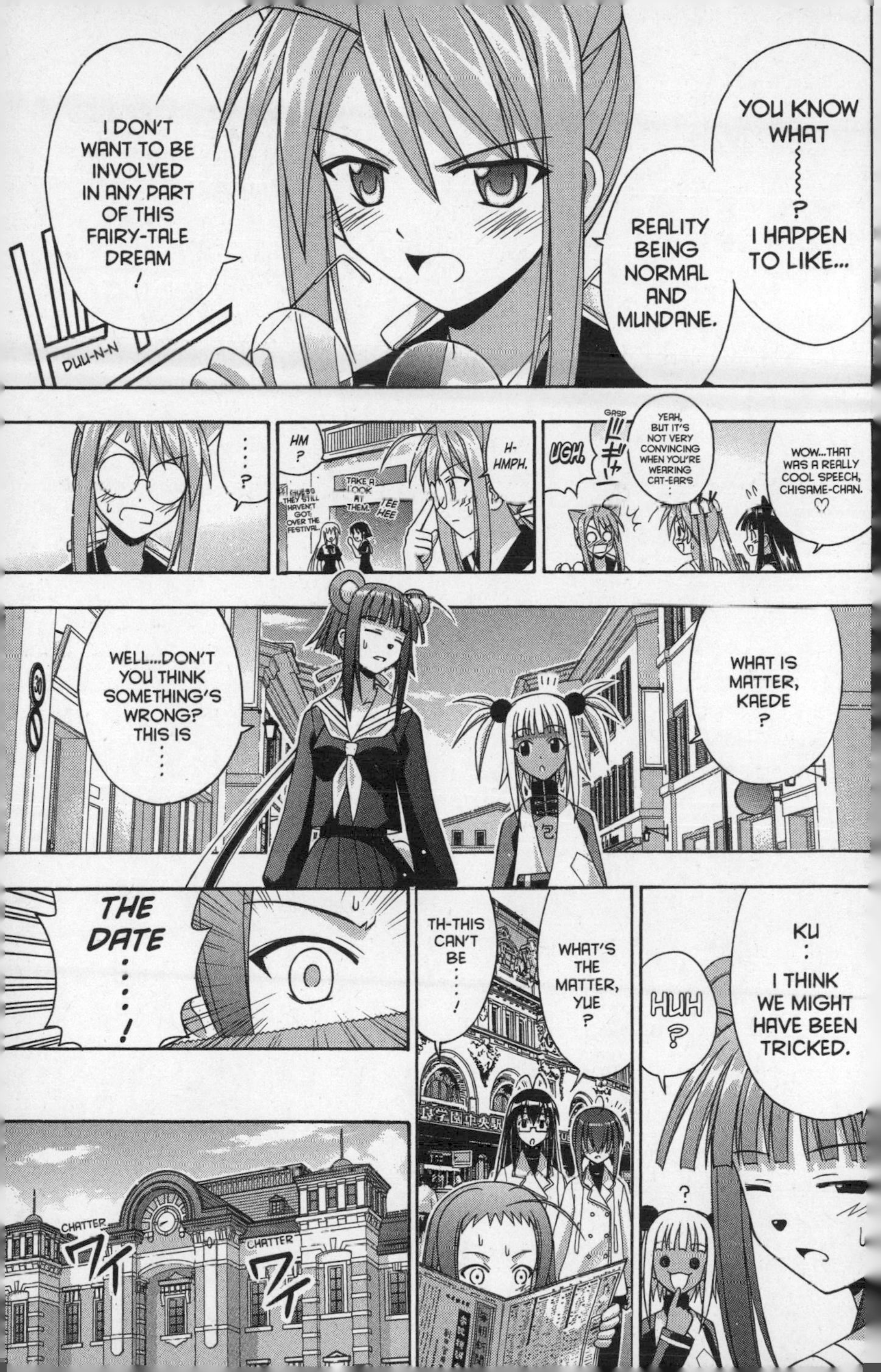

YOU KNOW WHAT ~~~~~?
I HAPPEN TO LIKE...
REALITY BEING NORMAL AND MUNDANE.
I DON'T WANT TO BE INVOLVED IN ANY PART OF THIS FAIRY-TALE DREAM!
DUU-N-N
WOW...THAT WAS A REALLY COOL SPEECH, CHISAME-CHAN. ♡
YEAH, BUT IT'S NOT VERY CONVINCING WHEN YOU'RE WEARING CAT-EARS...
GASP
UGH.
H-HMPH.
HM?
TAKE A LOOK AT THEM.
TEE HEE
GUESS THEY STILL HAVEN'T GOT OVER THE FESTIVAL.
....?
WHAT IS MATTER, KAEDE?
WELL...DON'T YOU THINK SOMETHING'S WRONG? THIS IS....
KU: I THINK WE MIGHT HAVE BEEN TRICKED.
HUH?
?
WHAT'S THE MATTER, YUE?
TH-THIS CAN'T BE....!
THE DATE....!
CHATTER
CHATTER

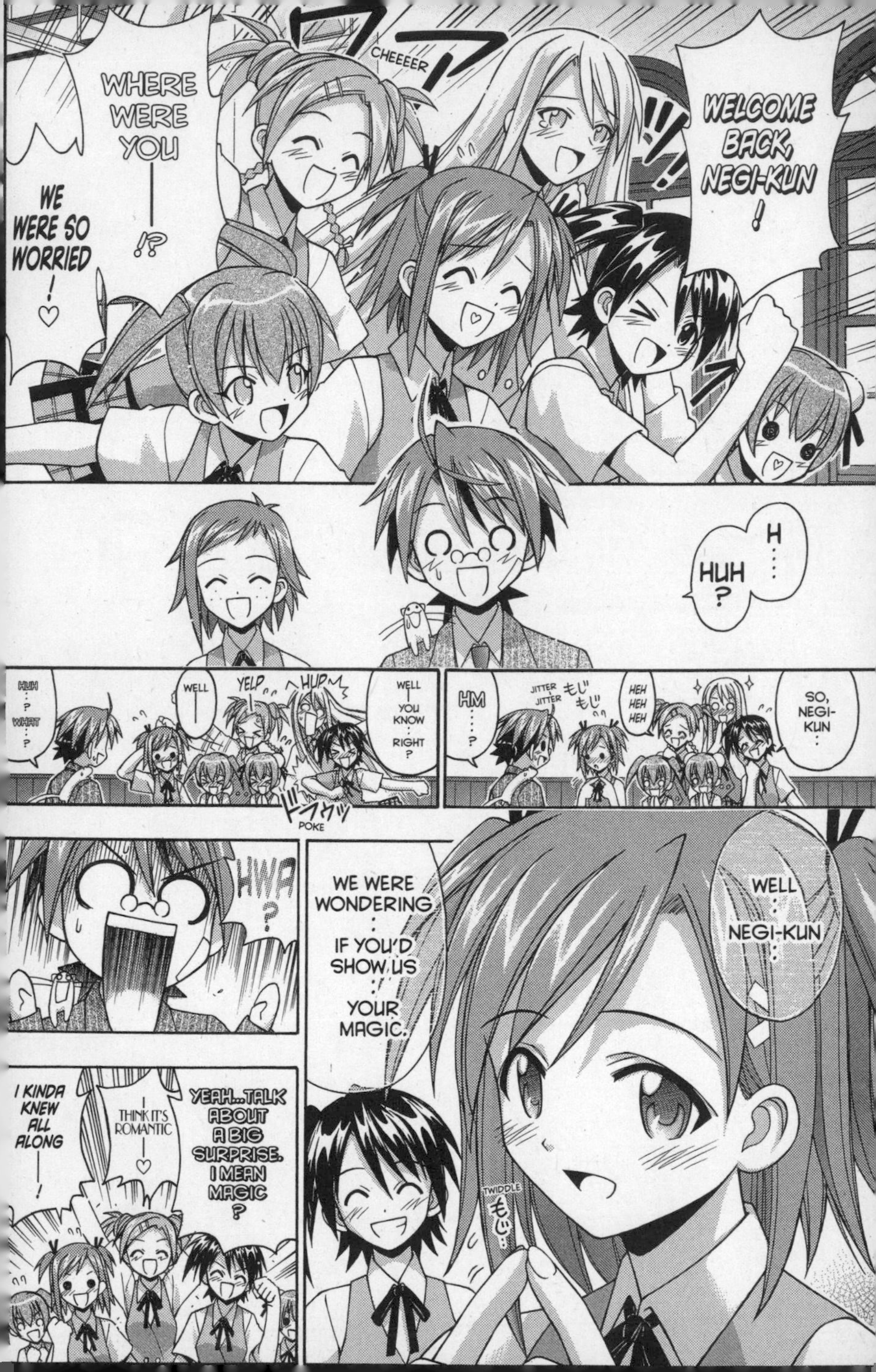
WELCOME BACK, NEGI-KUN!
ワァ CHEEEER
WHERE WERE YOU—!?
WE WERE SO WORRIED! ♡
H... HUH?
SO, NEGI-KUN...
HEH HEH HEH
もじもじ JITTER JITTER
HM...?
WELL—YOU KNOW... RIGHT?
HUP
YELP!
WELL—
HUH...? WHAT...?
ドスッ POKE
WELL... NEGI-KUN...
WE WERE WONDERING... IF YOU'D SHOW US... YOUR MAGIC.
もじ... TWIDDLE
HWA?
YEAH...TALK ABOUT A BIG SURPRISE. I MEAN MAGIC?
I THINK IT'S ROMANTIC—♡
I KINDA KNEW ALL ALONG—!

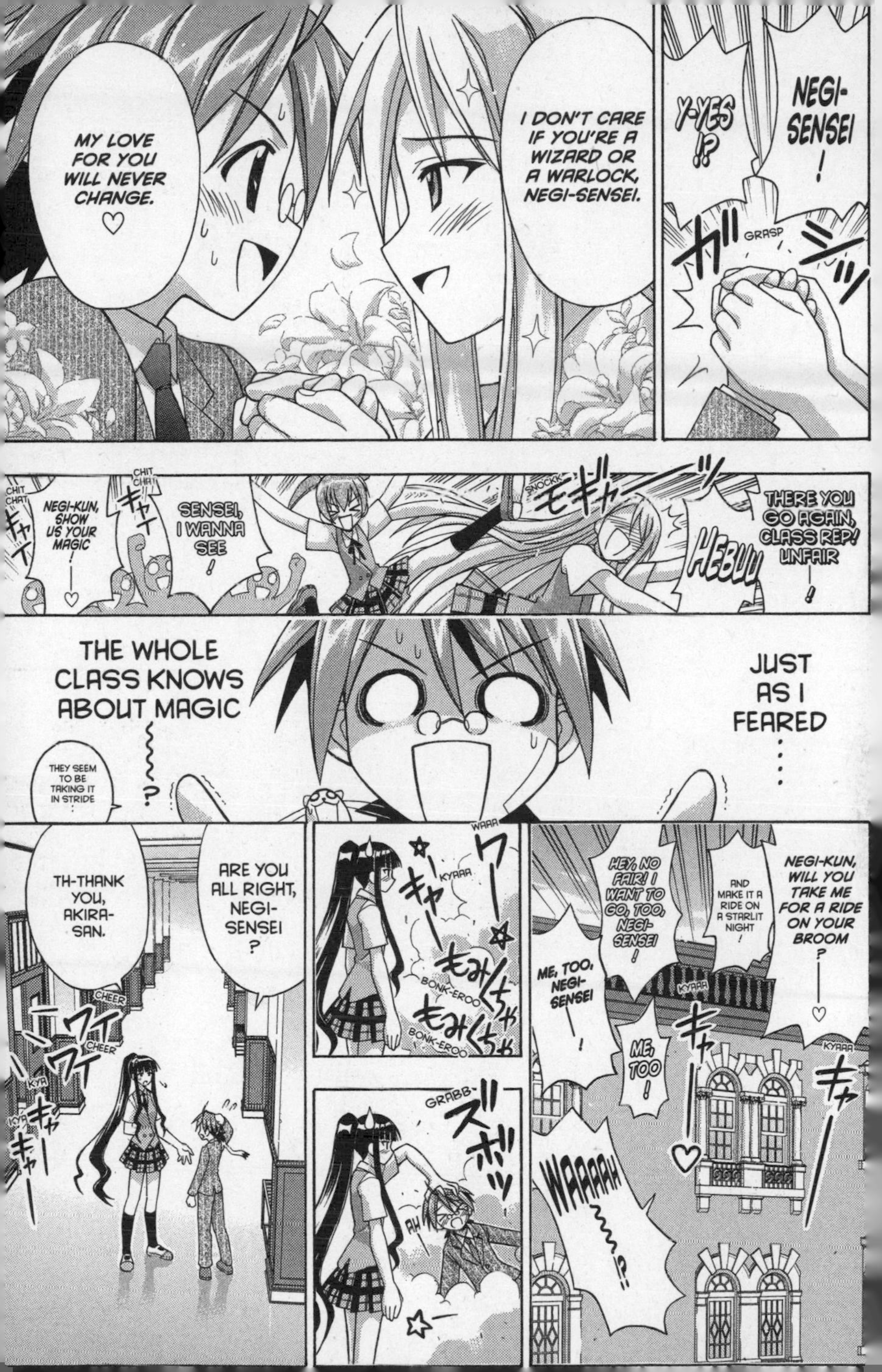
NEGI-SENSEI!
Y-YES!?
GRASP
I DON'T CARE IF YOU'RE A WIZARD OR A WARLOCK, NEGI-SENSEI.
MY LOVE FOR YOU WILL NEVER CHANGE. ♡
THERE YOU GO AGAIN, CLASS REP! UNFAIR!
HEBUU
SNOCKK
SENSEI, I WANNA SEE!
CHIT CHAT
NEGI-KUN, SHOW US YOUR MAGIC! ♡
CHIT CHAT
JUST AS I FEARED...
THE WHOLE CLASS KNOWS ABOUT MAGIC~?
THEY SEEM TO BE TAKING IT IN STRIDE
NEGI-KUN, WILL YOU TAKE ME FOR A RIDE ON YOUR BROOM? ♡
AND MAKE IT A RIDE ON A STARLIT NIGHT!
HEY, NO FAIR! I WANT TO GO, TOO, NEGI-SENSEI!
KYAAA
ME, TOO, NEGI-SENSEI!
ME, TOO!
KYAAA
WAAAAH~?
WAAA
KYAAA
BONK-EROO
BONK-EROO
GRABB
AH
ARE YOU ALL RIGHT, NEGI-SENSEI?
TH-THANK YOU, AKIRA-SAN.
CHEER
CHEER
KYA
KYA

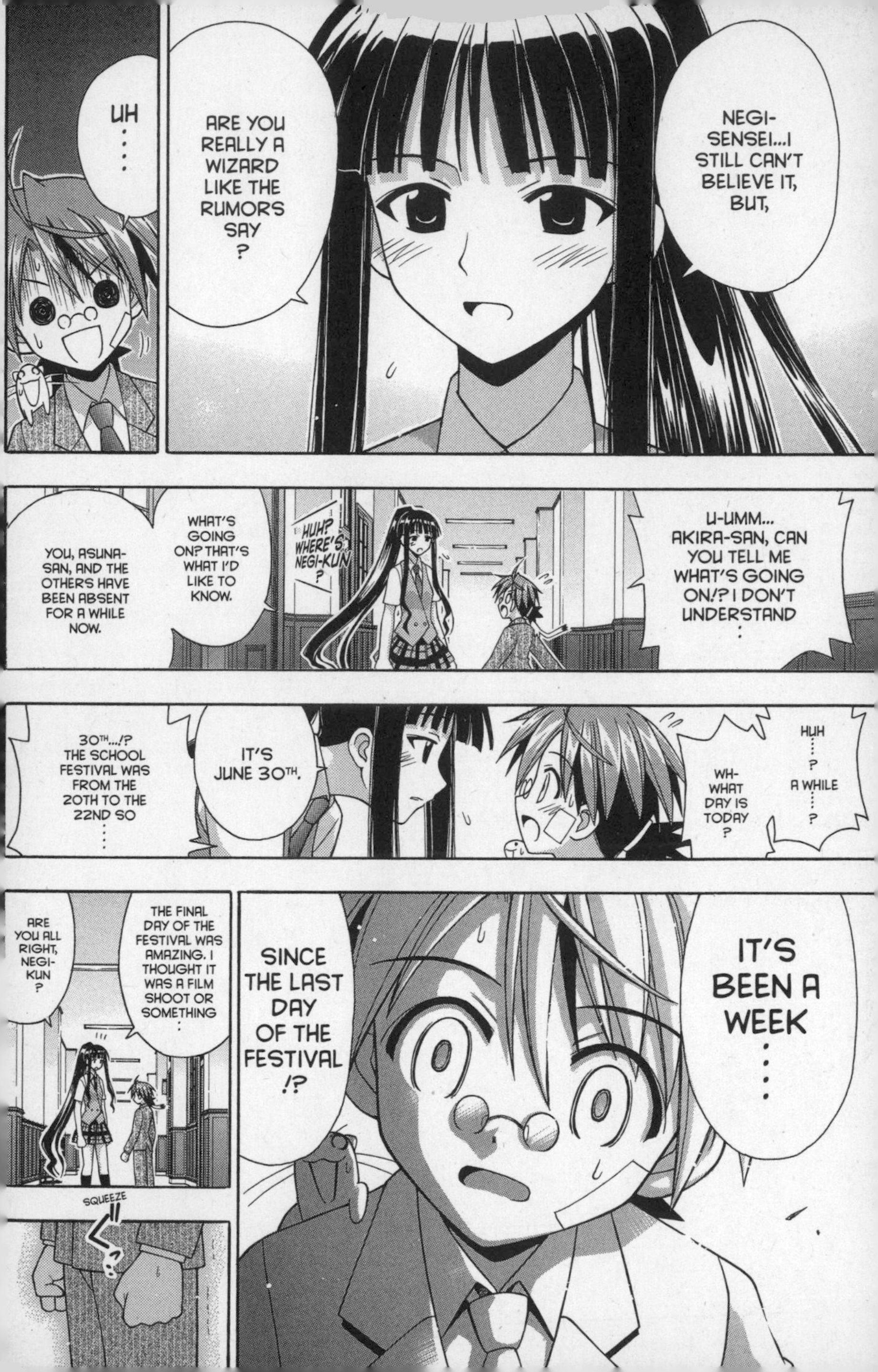
NEGI-SENSEI...I STILL CAN'T BELIEVE IT, BUT,
ARE YOU REALLY A WIZARD LIKE THE RUMORS SAY?
UH...
U-UMM... AKIRA-SAN, CAN YOU TELL ME WHAT'S GOING ON!? I DON'T UNDERSTAND...
HUH? WHERE'S NEGI-KUN?
WHAT'S GOING ON? THAT'S WHAT I'D LIKE TO KNOW.
YOU, ASUNA-SAN, AND THE OTHERS HAVE BEEN ABSENT FOR A WHILE NOW.
HUH...? A WHILE...?
WH-WHAT DAY IS TODAY?
IT'S JUNE 30TH.
30TH...!? THE SCHOOL FESTIVAL WAS FROM THE 20TH TO THE 22ND SO...
IT'S BEEN A WEEK...
SINCE THE LAST DAY OF THE FESTIVAL!?
THE FINAL DAY OF THE FESTIVAL WAS AMAZING. I THOUGHT IT WAS A FILM SHOOT OR SOMETHING...
ARE YOU ALL RIGHT, NEGI-KUN?
SQUEEZE

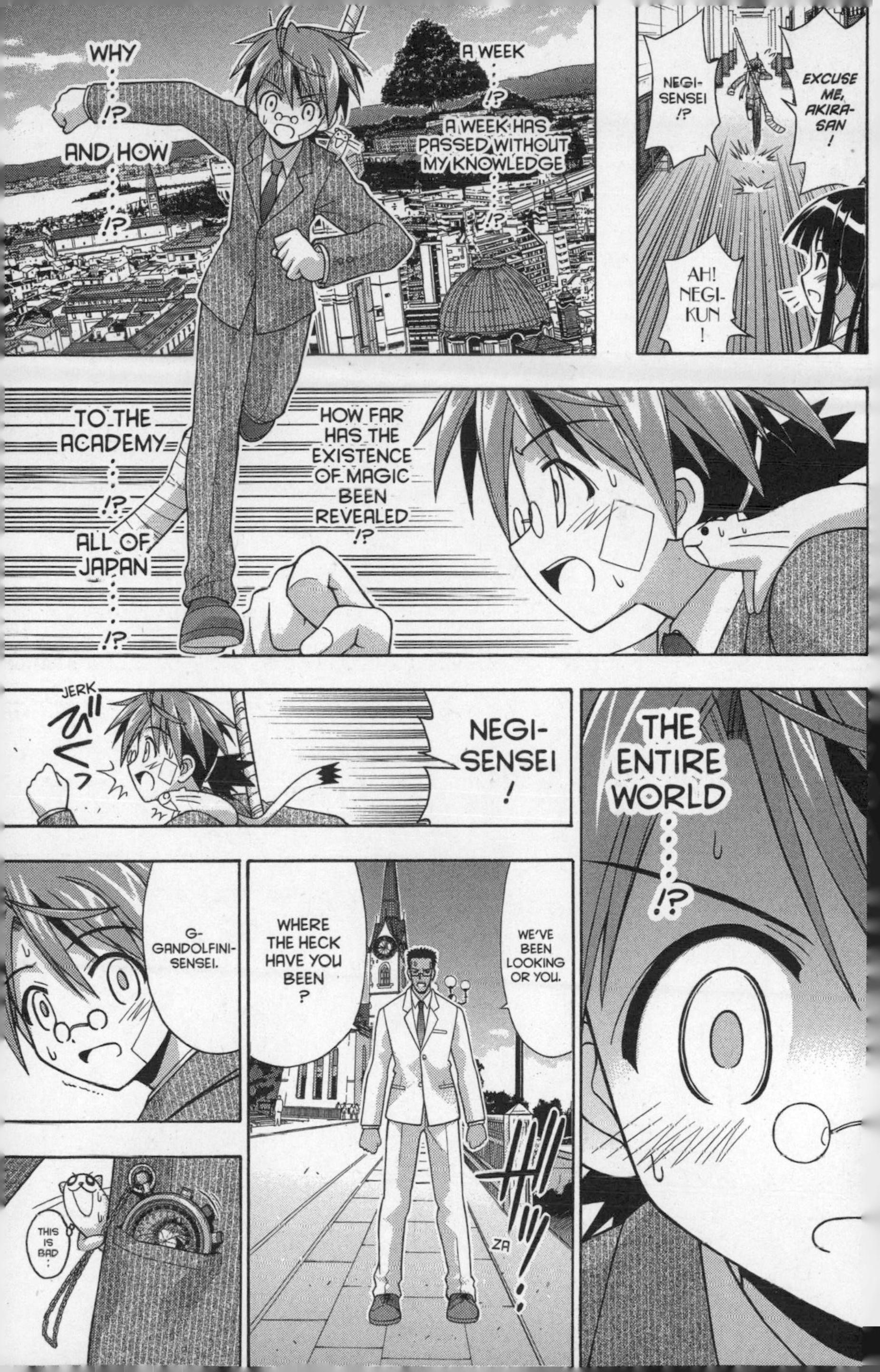
EXCUSE ME, AKIRA-SAN!
NEGI-SENSEI!?
AH! NEGI-KUN!
A WEEK...!?
A WEEK HAS PASSED WITHOUT MY KNOWLEDGE...!?
WHY...!?
AND HOW...!?
HOW FAR HAS THE EXISTENCE OF MAGIC BEEN REVEALED!?
TO THE ACADEMY...!?
ALL OF JAPAN......!?
THE ENTIRE WORLD......!?
NEGI-SENSEI!
JERK
WE'VE BEEN LOOKING OR YOU.
WHERE THE HECK HAVE YOU BEEN?
G-GANDOLFINI-SENSEI.
ZA
THIS IS BAD...

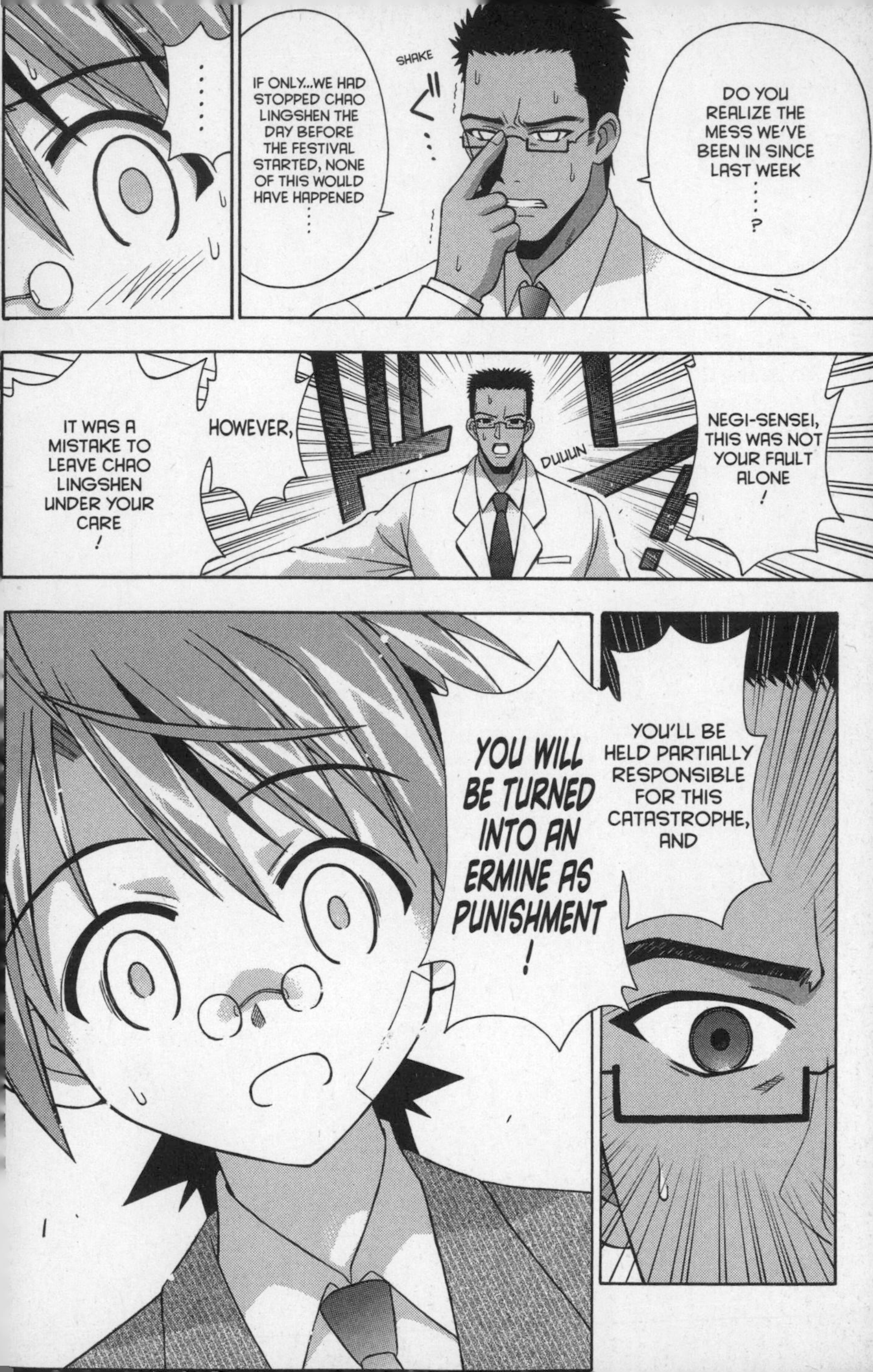
DO YOU REALIZE THE MESS WE'VE BEEN IN SINCE LAST WEEK...?
SHAKE
IF ONLY...WE HAD STOPPED CHAO LINGSHEN THE DAY BEFORE THE FESTIVAL STARTED, NONE OF THIS WOULD HAVE HAPPENED...
......
NEGI-SENSEI, THIS WAS NOT YOUR FAULT ALONE!
DUUUN
HOWEVER,
IT WAS A MISTAKE TO LEAVE CHAO LINGSHEN UNDER YOUR CARE!
YOU'LL BE HELD PARTIALLY RESPONSIBLE FOR THIS CATASTROPHE, AND
YOU WILL BE TURNED INTO AN ERMINE AS PUNISHMENT!

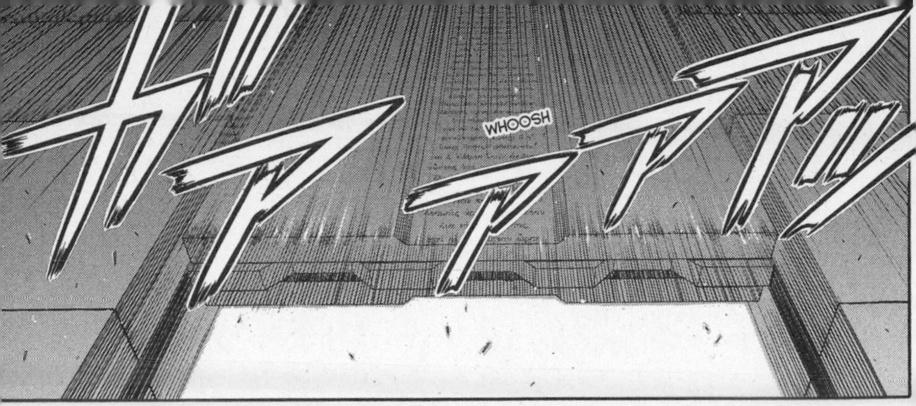
ガアアアアッ
WHOOSH

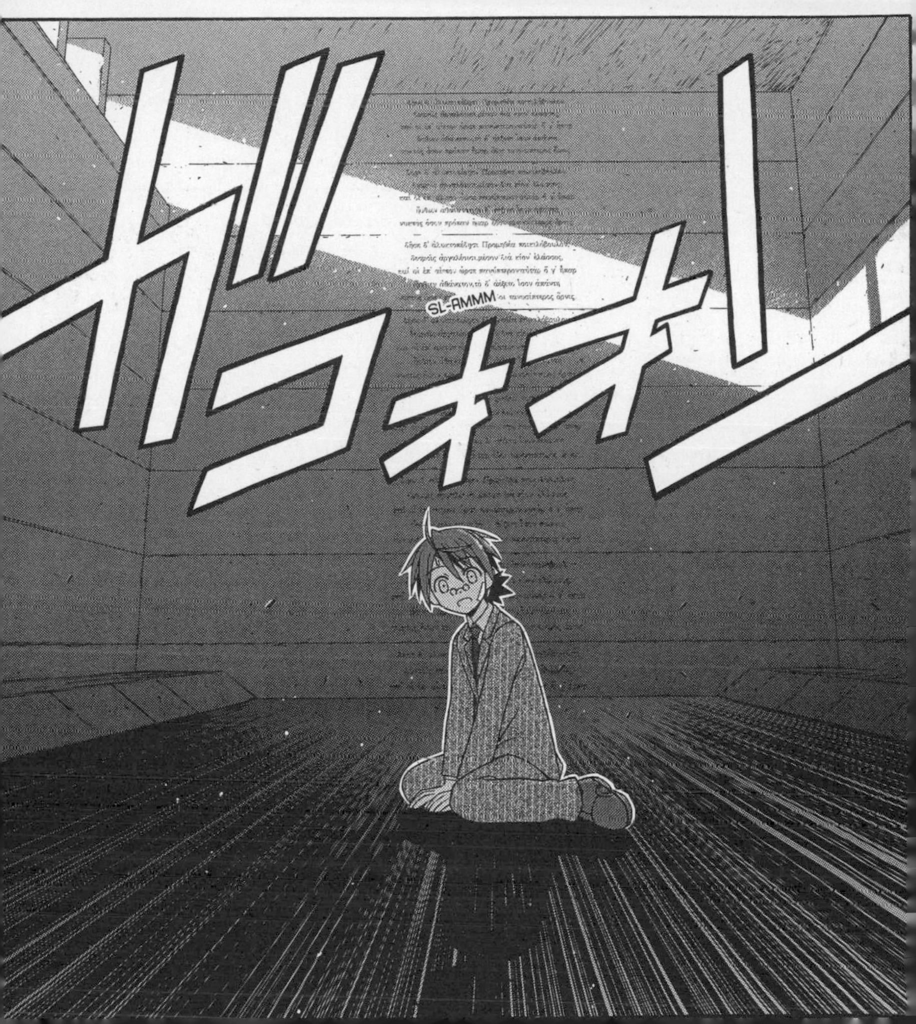
ガコォオン
SL-AMMM

LEXICON MAGICUM NEGIMARUM

■マギステース
（μαγιστής）
MAGISTER

The English words "mage," "magician," "magic," etc. are derived from the the Latin word *magus*, which means "wizard." The root of the Latin word comes from an ancient Greek word μάγος and the ancient Persian word *magu**. An excerpt from Herodotus's *The Histories*, volume ɪ, chapter ɪoɪ, reads: "The Median tribes are these: the Busae, the Paretaceni, the Struchates, the Arizanti, the Budii, the Magi [μάγοι]. Their tribes are this many." The μάγος, magus, mage, etc. were originally one of the tribes of the Mede Empire. They were in charge of dream divination, astrology, ritual sacrifices, and other priestly duties. (In chapter ɪo7 of the same book, there is a record of a μάγος performing a dream divination, and in chapter ɪ32 are records of ritual sacrifice. In volume 7, chapter 37, there is a record of the observations and interpretations of a solar eclipse.)

Magic and magic users exist in various cultures around the world. For example, in Latin: *incantator* (a person who can cast a spell, "enchanter" in English), *pharmacus* (maker of medicines, "pharmacist" in English), *praecantator* (one who can see the future), *sortilegus* (one who divinates with raffle tickets, "sorcerer" in English), *theurgus* (one who see the movements of God), and *venefiscus* ("apothecary" in English) were all related to "magic" in a Latin dictionary. "Magicians" were the priests, artists, doctors, scientists, and teachers of various cultures.

In the world of *Negima!*, the mages are called μαγιστής. The usage is similar to the Median and Persian cultures' word for magic. The ending ‑ιστής means "people who do/use." For example, the word "artist" is *artista* in Latin and τεχγιστής in Greek.

* Ancient Persian characters cannot be depicted so they have been Latinized.

■魔法界

MAGIANITAS

This word means "the Society of the Mages." The Society of the Mages has its own systems of law, economy, transportation, communication, and education. Even so, looking over the long history of human civilization, nearly all pre-modern societies can be seen to have been based in magic and mysticism. However, the arrival of the major world religions, such as Islam and Christianity, pushed aside much of the mysticism found in ancient societies and played a role, beginning in Europe in the Middle Ages, in creating modern culture.

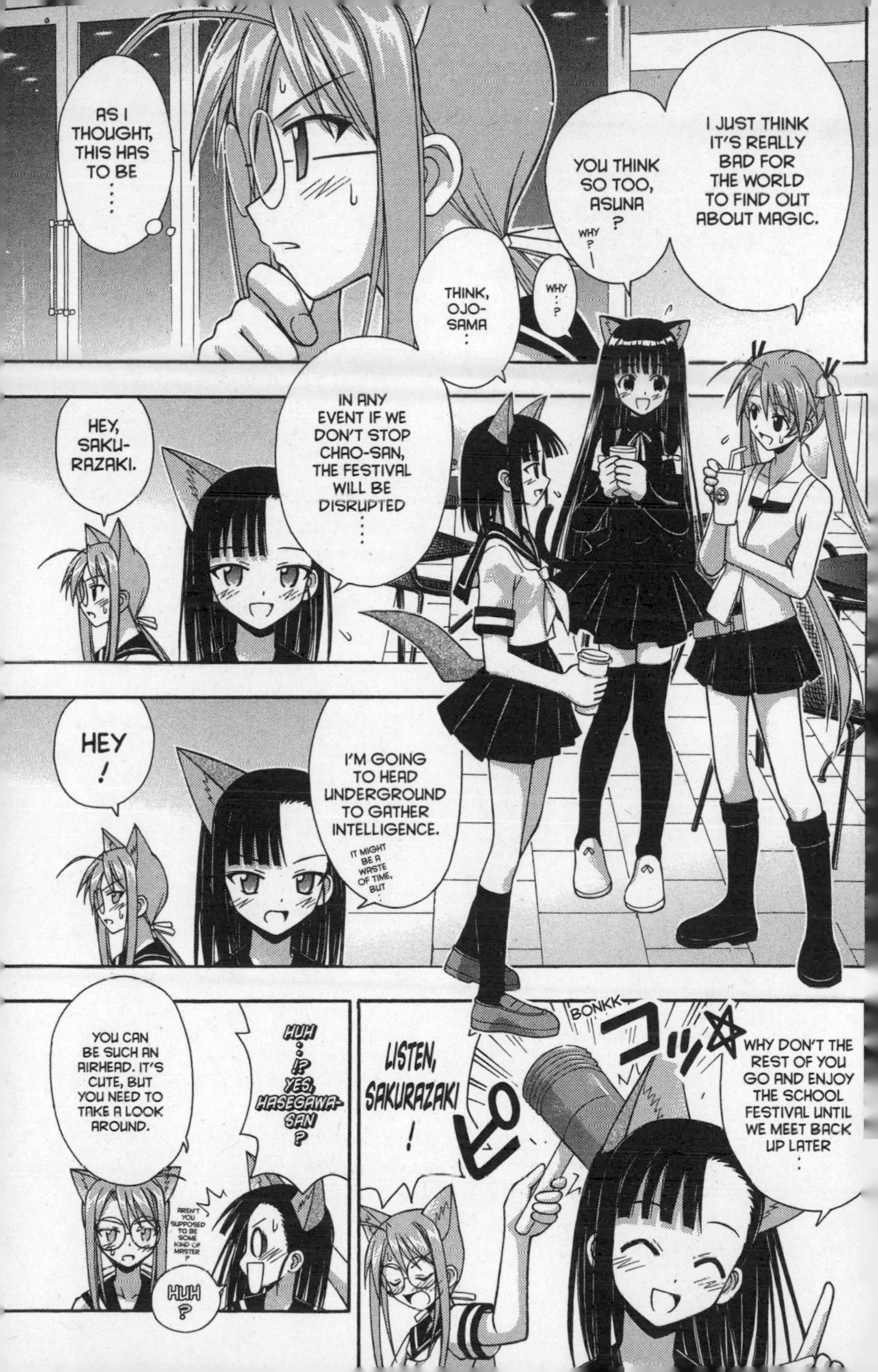

I JUST THINK IT'S REALLY BAD FOR THE WORLD TO FIND OUT ABOUT MAGIC.
YOU THINK SO TOO, ASUNA?
WHY?
WHY..?
THINK, OJO-SAMA...
AS I THOUGHT, THIS HAS TO BE...
IN ANY EVENT IF WE DON'T STOP CHAO-SAN, THE FESTIVAL WILL BE DISRUPTED...
HEY, SAKURAZAKI.
I'M GOING TO HEAD UNDERGROUND TO GATHER INTELLIGENCE.
IT MIGHT BE A WASTE OF TIME, BUT...
HEY!
WHY DON'T THE REST OF YOU GO AND ENJOY THE SCHOOL FESTIVAL UNTIL WE MEET BACK UP LATER...
BONKK
ゴッ
LISTEN, SAKURAZAKI!
HUH..!? YES, HASEGAWA-SAN?
YOU CAN BE SUCH AN AIRHEAD. IT'S CUTE, BUT YOU NEED TO TAKE A LOOK AROUND.
AREN'T YOU SUPPOSED TO BE SOME KIND OF MASTER?
HUH?

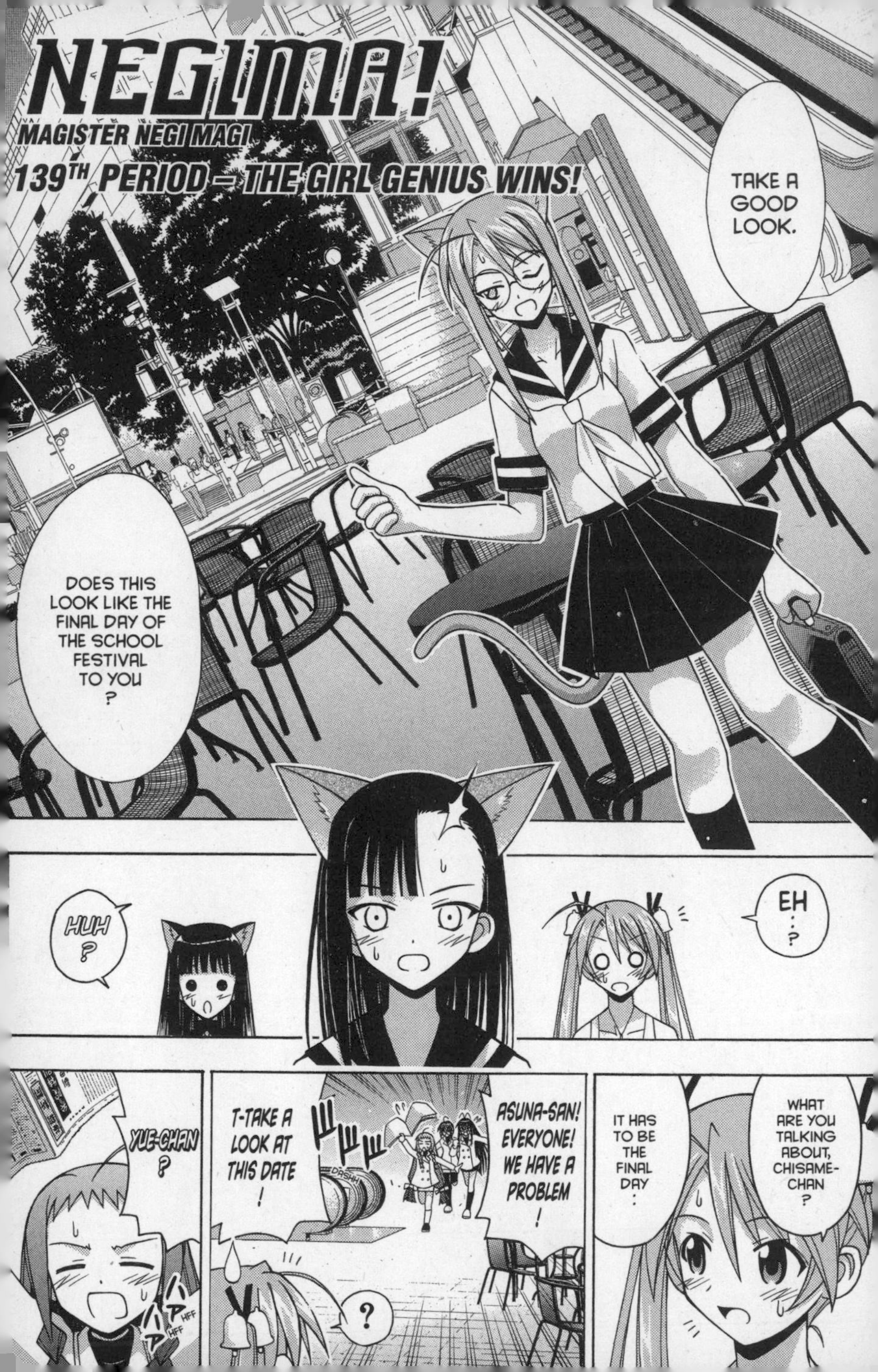
NEGIMA!
MAGISTER NEGI MAGI
139TH PERIOD – THE GIRL GENIUS WINS!
TAKE A GOOD LOOK.
DOES THIS LOOK LIKE THE FINAL DAY OF THE SCHOOL FESTIVAL TO YOU?
EH..?
HUH?
WHAT ARE YOU TALKING ABOUT, CHISAME-CHAN?
IT HAS TO BE THE FINAL DAY:
ASUNA-SAN! EVERYONE! WE HAVE A PROBLEM!
T-TAKE A LOOK AT THIS DATE!
DASHH
?
YUE-CHAN?
HFF
HFF

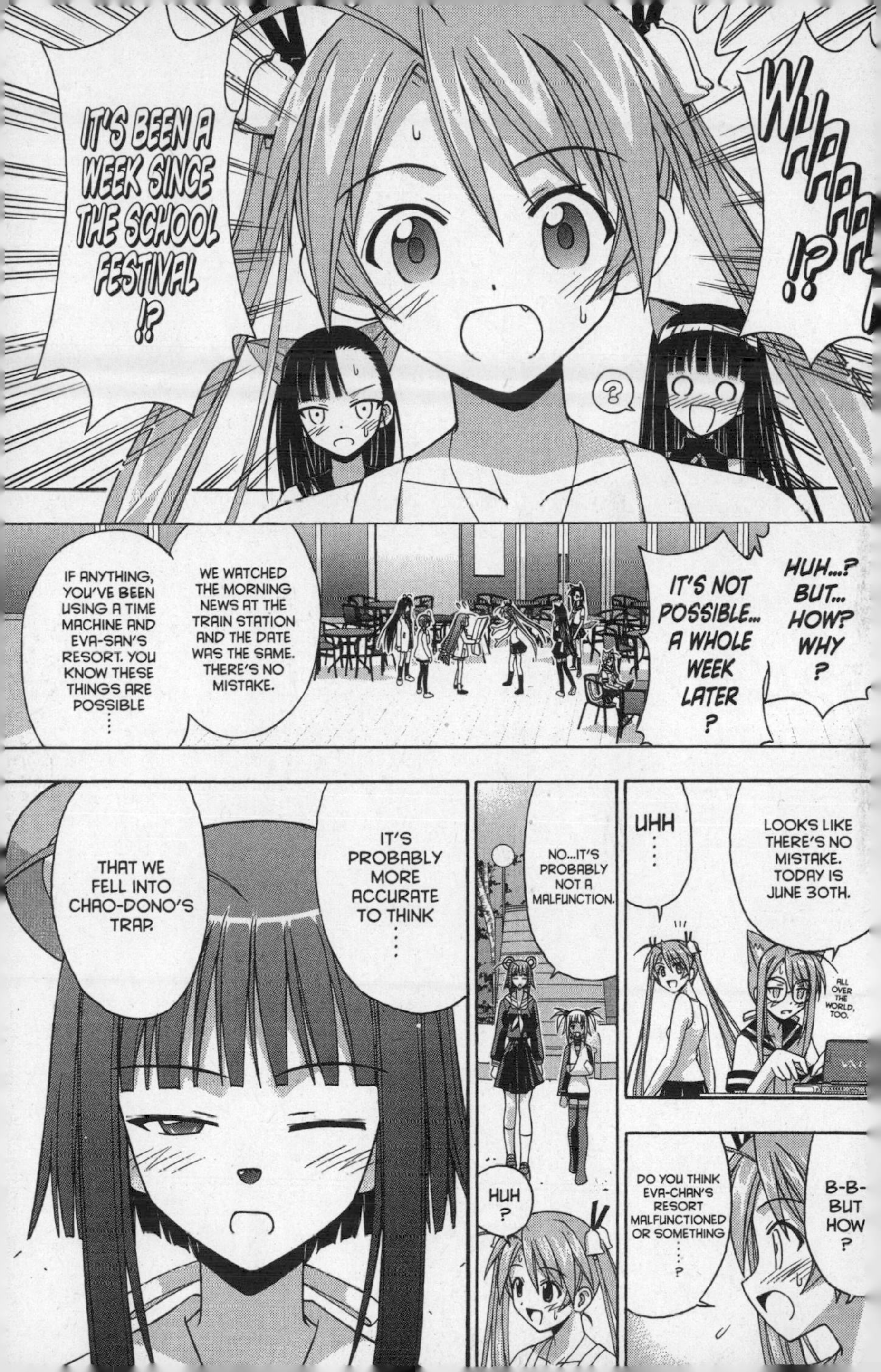
WHAAAA !?
IT'S BEEN A WEEK SINCE THE SCHOOL FESTIVAL !?
?
HUH...? BUT... HOW? WHY ?
IT'S NOT POSSIBLE... A WHOLE WEEK LATER ?
WE WATCHED THE MORNING NEWS AT THE TRAIN STATION AND THE DATE WAS THE SAME. THERE'S NO MISTAKE.
IF ANYTHING, YOU'VE BEEN USING A TIME MACHINE AND EVA-SAN'S RESORT. YOU KNOW THESE THINGS ARE POSSIBLE ...
LOOKS LIKE THERE'S NO MISTAKE. TODAY IS JUNE 30TH.
ALL OVER THE WORLD, TOO.
UHH ...
B-B-BUT HOW ?
DO YOU THINK EVA-CHAN'S RESORT MALFUNCTIONED OR SOMETHING ...?
NO...IT'S PROBABLY NOT A MALFUNCTION.
HUH ?
IT'S PROBABLY MORE ACCURATE TO THINK ...
THAT WE FELL INTO CHAO-DONO'S TRAP.

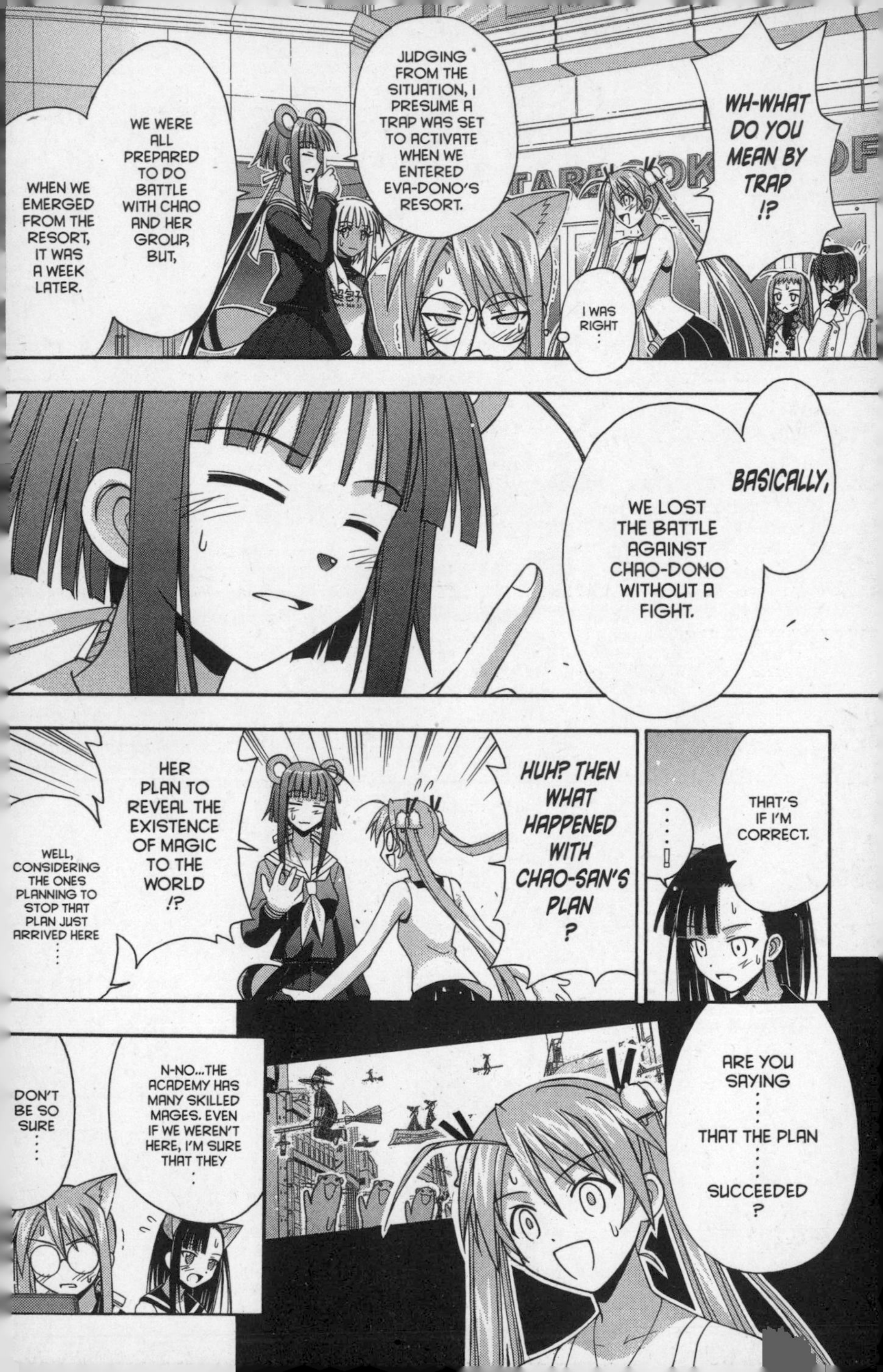
WH-WHAT DO YOU MEAN BY TRAP !?
I WAS RIGHT . . .
JUDGING FROM THE SITUATION, I PRESUME A TRAP WAS SET TO ACTIVATE WHEN WE ENTERED EVA-DONO'S RESORT.
WE WERE ALL PREPARED TO DO BATTLE WITH CHAO AND HER GROUP, BUT,
WHEN WE EMERGED FROM THE RESORT, IT WAS A WEEK LATER.
BASICALLY,
WE LOST THE BATTLE AGAINST CHAO-DONO WITHOUT A FIGHT.
THAT'S IF I'M CORRECT.
. . . . !
HUH? THEN WHAT HAPPENED WITH CHAO-SAN'S PLAN ?
HER PLAN TO REVEAL THE EXISTENCE OF MAGIC TO THE WORLD !?
WELL, CONSIDERING THE ONES PLANNING TO STOP THAT PLAN JUST ARRIVED HERE . . . .
ARE YOU SAYING . . . . THAT THE PLAN . . . . SUCCEEDED ?
N-NO...THE ACADEMY HAS MANY SKILLED MAGES. EVEN IF WE WEREN'T HERE, I'M SURE THAT THEY . .
DON'T BE SO SURE . . . .

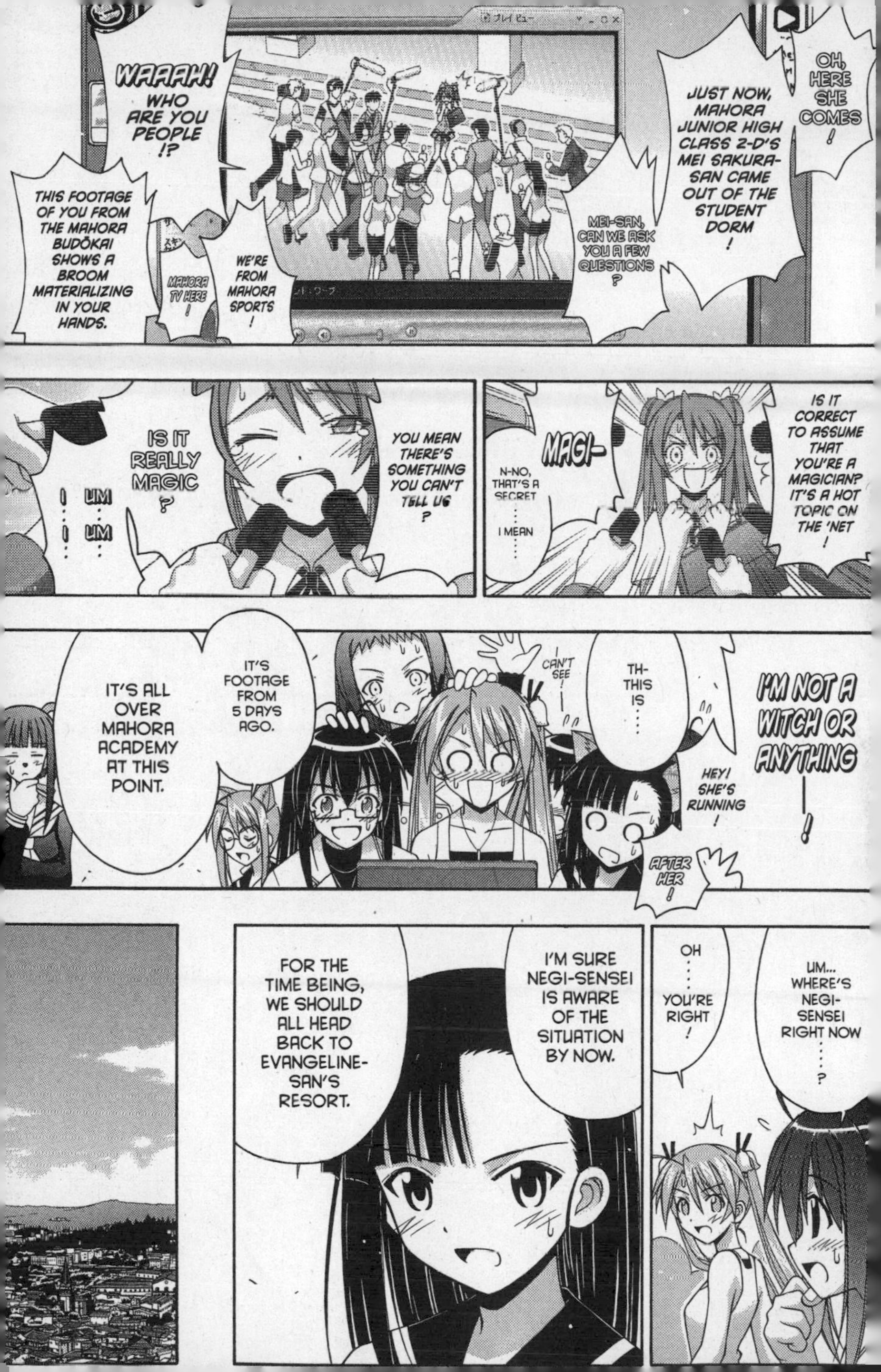
OH, HERE SHE COMES!
JUST NOW, MAHORA JUNIOR HIGH CLASS 2-D'S MEI SAKURA-SAN CAME OUT OF THE STUDENT DORM!
MEI-SAN, CAN WE ASK YOU A FEW QUESTIONS?
WAAAAH! WHO ARE YOU PEOPLE!?
WE'RE FROM MAHORA SPORTS!
MAHORA TV HERE!
THIS FOOTAGE OF YOU FROM THE MAHORA BUDŌKAI SHOWS A BROOM MATERIALIZING IN YOUR HANDS.
IS IT CORRECT TO ASSUME THAT YOU'RE A MAGICIAN? IT'S A HOT TOPIC ON THE 'NET!
MAGI-
N-NO, THAT'S A SECRET... I MEAN...
YOU MEAN THERE'S SOMETHING YOU CAN'T TELL US?
IS IT REALLY MAGIC?
I... UM... I... UM...
I'M NOT A WITCH OR ANYTHING—!
TH-THIS IS...
I CAN'T SEE!
HEY! SHE'S RUNNING!
AFTER HER!
IT'S FOOTAGE FROM 5 DAYS AGO.
IT'S ALL OVER MAHORA ACADEMY AT THIS POINT.
UM... WHERE'S NEGI-SENSEI RIGHT NOW...?
OH... YOU'RE RIGHT!
I'M SURE NEGI-SENSEI IS AWARE OF THE SITUATION BY NOW.
FOR THE TIME BEING, WE SHOULD ALL HEAD BACK TO EVANGELINE-SAN'S RESORT.

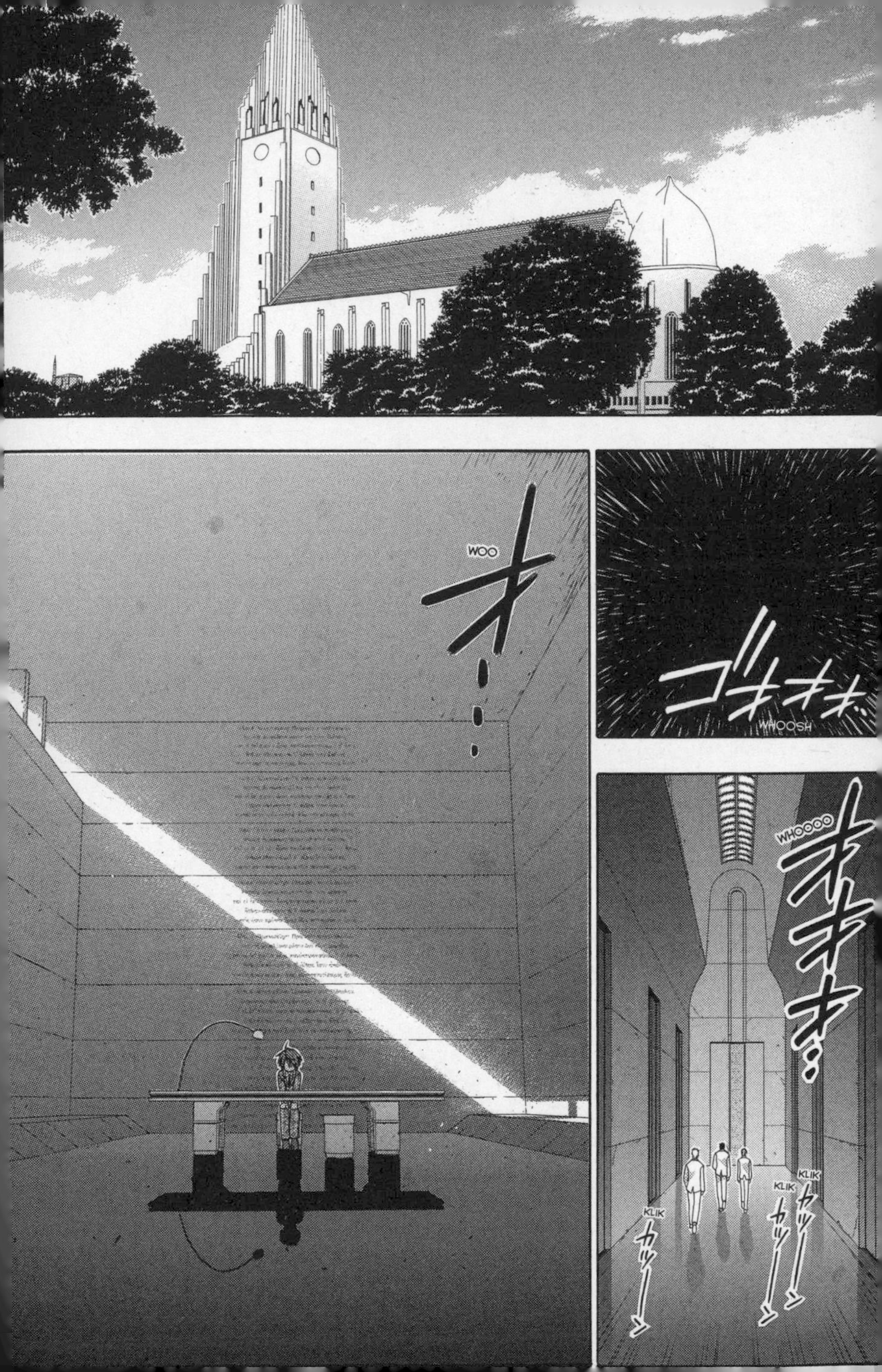
WHOOSH
WHOOOO
KLIK
KLIK
KLIK
WOO

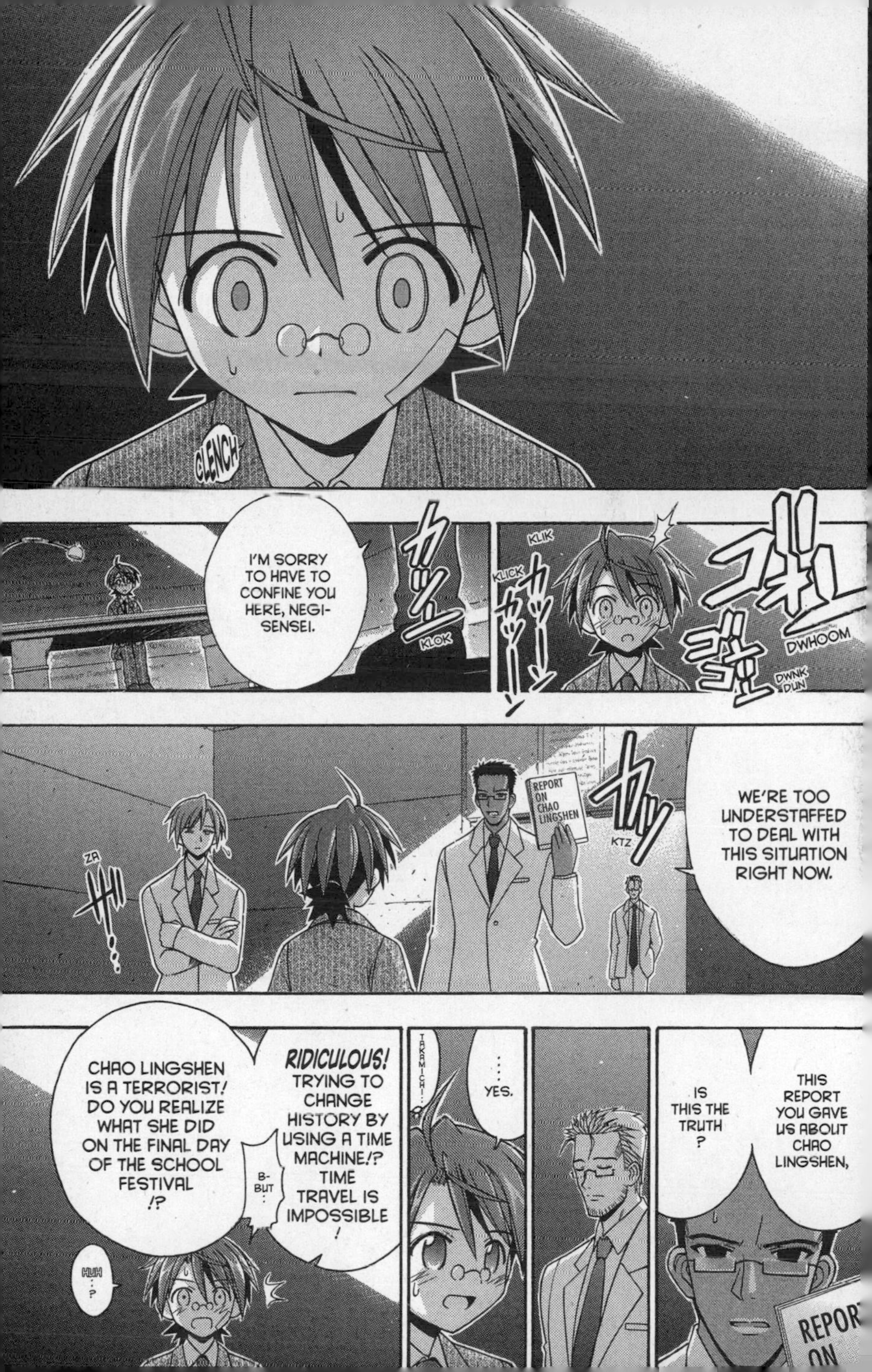
CLENCH
DWHOOM
DWNK DUN
KLIK
KLICK
KLOK
I'M SORRY TO HAVE TO CONFINE YOU HERE, NEGI-SENSEI.
WE'RE TOO UNDERSTAFFED TO DEAL WITH THIS SITUATION RIGHT NOW.
KTZ
REPORT ON CHAO LINGSHEN
ZA
THIS REPORT YOU GAVE US ABOUT CHAO LINGSHEN,
IS THIS THE TRUTH?
REPORT ON
...YES.
TAKAMICHI...
RIDICULOUS! TRYING TO CHANGE HISTORY BY USING A TIME MACHINE!? TIME TRAVEL IS IMPOSSIBLE!
B-BUT...
CHAO LINGSHEN IS A TERRORIST! DO YOU REALIZE WHAT SHE DID ON THE FINAL DAY OF THE SCHOOL FESTIVAL!?
HUH...?

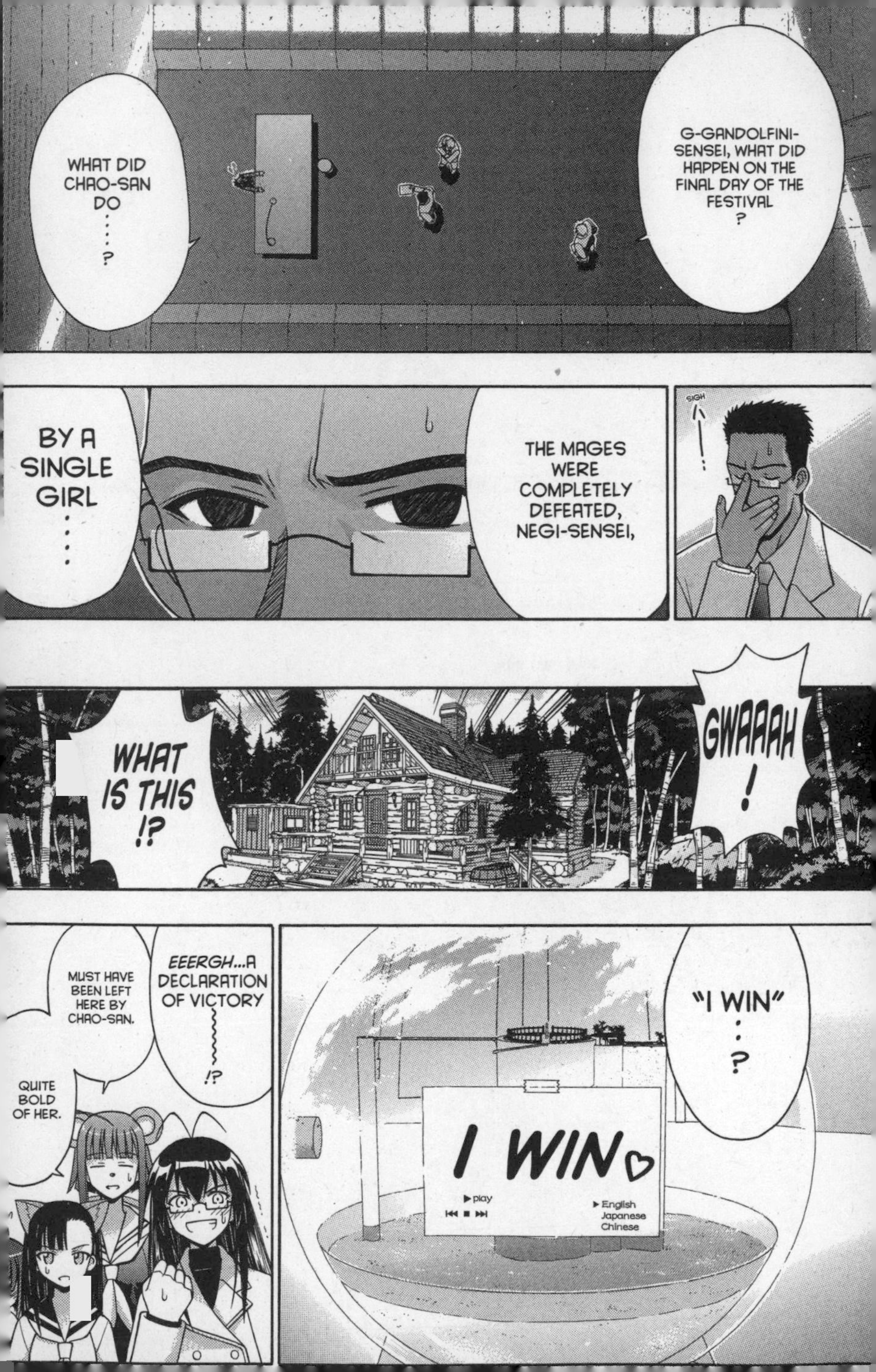
G-GANDOLFINI-SENSEI, WHAT DID HAPPEN ON THE FINAL DAY OF THE FESTIVAL?
WHAT DID CHAO-SAN DO.....?
SIGH
THE MAGES WERE COMPLETELY DEFEATED, NEGI-SENSEI,
BY A SINGLE GIRL.....
GWAAAH!
WHAT IS THIS!?
"I WIN"..?
I WIN ♡
▶play
English
Japanese
Chinese
EEERGH...A DECLARATION OF VICTORY~~!?
MUST HAVE BEEN LEFT HERE BY CHAO-SAN.
QUITE BOLD OF HER.

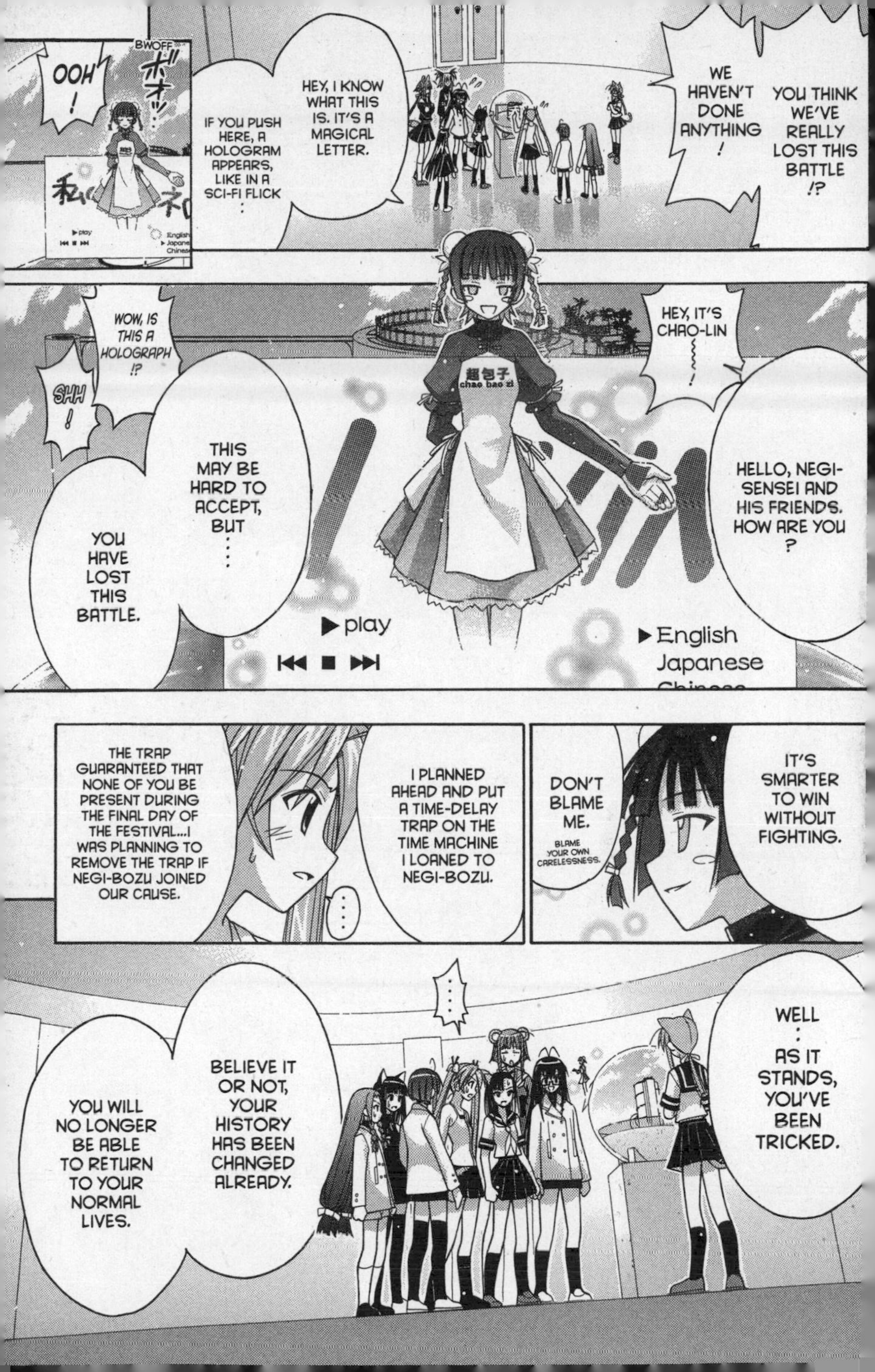
YOU THINK WE'VE REALLY LOST THIS BATTLE!?
WE HAVEN'T DONE ANYTHING!
HEY, I KNOW WHAT THIS IS. IT'S A MAGICAL LETTER.
IF YOU PUSH HERE, A HOLOGRAM APPEARS, LIKE IN A SCI-FI FLICK...
BWOFF
OOH!
HEY, IT'S CHAO-LIN~!
HELLO, NEGI-SENSEI AND HIS FRIENDS. HOW ARE YOU?
WOW, IS THIS A HOLOGRAPH!?
SHH!
THIS MAY BE HARD TO ACCEPT, BUT....
YOU HAVE LOST THIS BATTLE.
超包子 chao bao zi
▶play
▶English
Japanese
IT'S SMARTER TO WIN WITHOUT FIGHTING.
DON'T BLAME ME.
BLAME YOUR OWN CARELESSNESS.
I PLANNED AHEAD AND PUT A TIME-DELAY TRAP ON THE TIME MACHINE I LOANED TO NEGI-BOZU.
THE TRAP GUARANTEED THAT NONE OF YOU BE PRESENT DURING THE FINAL DAY OF THE FESTIVAL...I WAS PLANNING TO REMOVE THE TRAP IF NEGI-BOZU JOINED OUR CAUSE.
....
WELL: AS IT STANDS, YOU'VE BEEN TRICKED.
....
BELIEVE IT OR NOT, YOUR HISTORY HAS BEEN CHANGED ALREADY.
YOU WILL NO LONGER BE ABLE TO RETURN TO YOUR NORMAL LIVES.

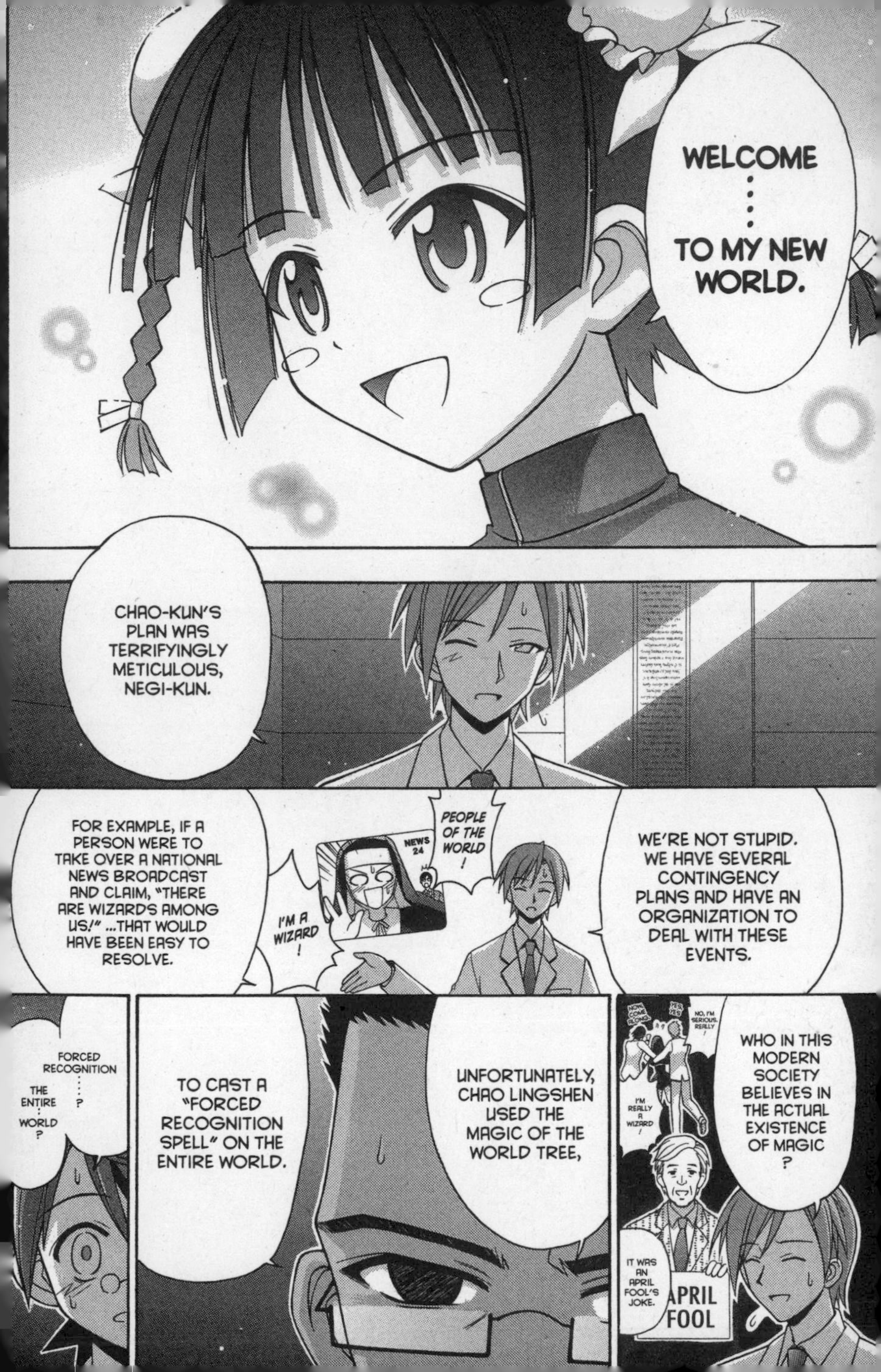
WELCOME . . . . TO MY NEW WORLD.
CHAO-KUN'S PLAN WAS TERRIFYINGLY METICULOUS, NEGI-KUN.
WE'RE NOT STUPID. WE HAVE SEVERAL CONTINGENCY PLANS AND HAVE AN ORGANIZATION TO DEAL WITH THESE EVENTS.
PEOPLE OF THE WORLD!
NEWS 24
I'M A WIZARD!
FOR EXAMPLE, IF A PERSON WERE TO TAKE OVER A NATIONAL NEWS BROADCAST AND CLAIM, "THERE ARE WIZARDS AMONG US!" ...THAT WOULD HAVE BEEN EASY TO RESOLVE.
WHO IN THIS MODERN SOCIETY BELIEVES IN THE ACTUAL EXISTENCE OF MAGIC?
NO, I'M SERIOUS. REALLY!
YES, YES.
NOW, COME ALONG.
I'M REALLY A WIZARD!
IT WAS AN APRIL FOOL'S JOKE.
APRIL FOOL
UNFORTUNATELY, CHAO LINGSHEN USED THE MAGIC OF THE WORLD TREE,
TO CAST A "FORCED RECOGNITION SPELL" ON THE ENTIRE WORLD.
FORCED RECOGNITION . . . ?
THE ENTIRE . . WORLD?

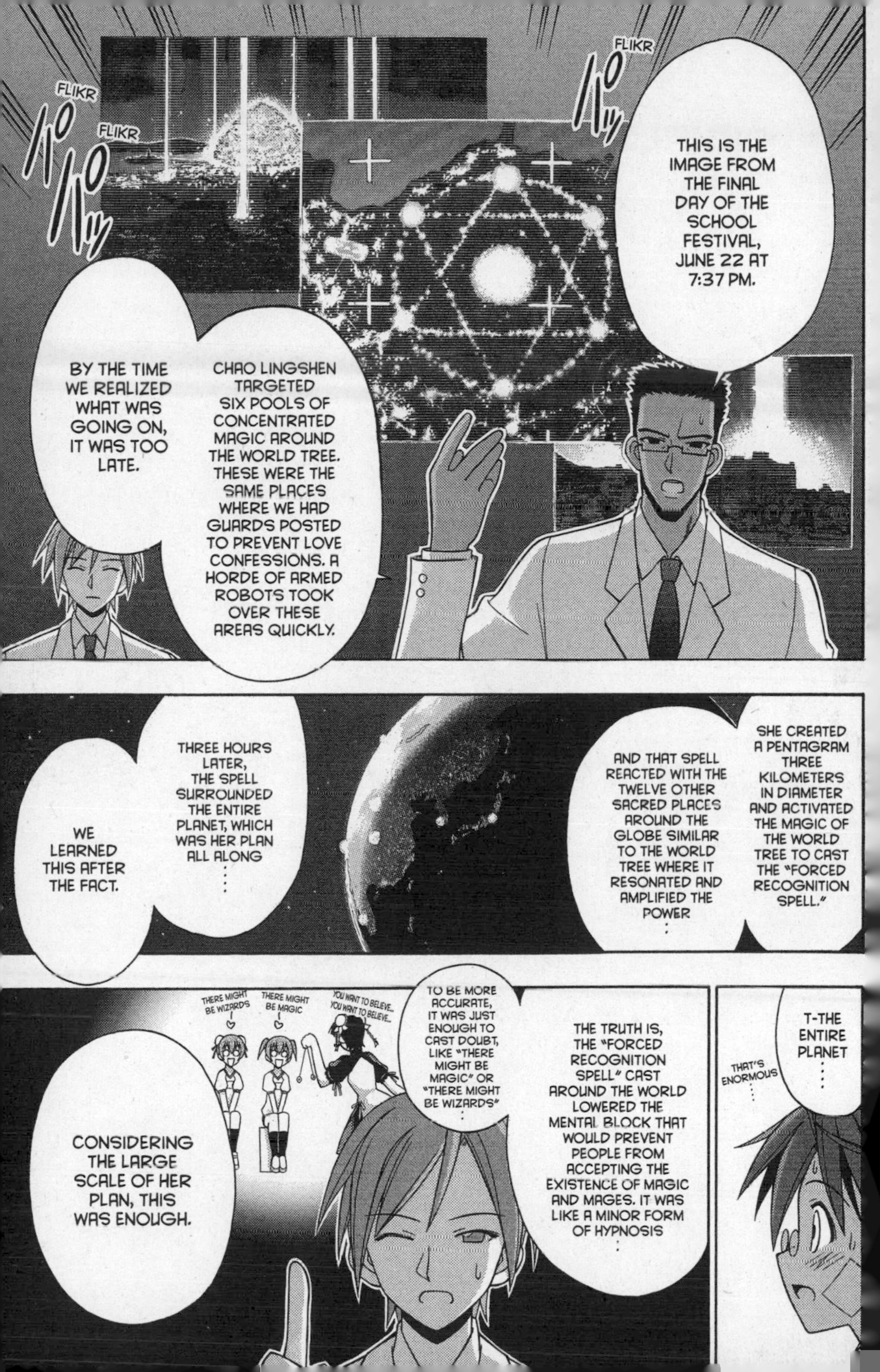
FLIKR
THIS IS THE IMAGE FROM THE FINAL DAY OF THE SCHOOL FESTIVAL, JUNE 22 AT 7:37 PM.
FLIKR
FLIKR
CHAO LINGSHEN TARGETED SIX POOLS OF CONCENTRATED MAGIC AROUND THE WORLD TREE. THESE WERE THE SAME PLACES WHERE WE HAD GUARDS POSTED TO PREVENT LOVE CONFESSIONS. A HORDE OF ARMED ROBOTS TOOK OVER THESE AREAS QUICKLY.
BY THE TIME WE REALIZED WHAT WAS GOING ON, IT WAS TOO LATE.
SHE CREATED A PENTAGRAM THREE KILOMETERS IN DIAMETER AND ACTIVATED THE MAGIC OF THE WORLD TREE TO CAST THE "FORCED RECOGNITION SPELL."
AND THAT SPELL REACTED WITH THE TWELVE OTHER SACRED PLACES AROUND THE GLOBE SIMILAR TO THE WORLD TREE WHERE IT RESONATED AND AMPLIFIED THE POWER ...
THREE HOURS LATER, THE SPELL SURROUNDED THE ENTIRE PLANET, WHICH WAS HER PLAN ALL ALONG ...
WE LEARNED THIS AFTER THE FACT.
T-THE ENTIRE PLANET ...
THAT'S ENORMOUS ...
THE TRUTH IS, THE "FORCED RECOGNITION SPELL" CAST AROUND THE WORLD LOWERED THE MENTAL BLOCK THAT WOULD PREVENT PEOPLE FROM ACCEPTING THE EXISTENCE OF MAGIC AND MAGES. IT WAS LIKE A MINOR FORM OF HYPNOSIS ...
TO BE MORE ACCURATE, IT WAS JUST ENOUGH TO CAST DOUBT, LIKE "THERE MIGHT BE MAGIC" OR "THERE MIGHT BE WIZARDS" ...
YOU WANT TO BELIEVE... YOU WANT TO BELIEVE...
THERE MIGHT BE MAGIC
THERE MIGHT BE WIZARDS
CONSIDERING THE LARGE SCALE OF HER PLAN, THIS WAS ENOUGH.

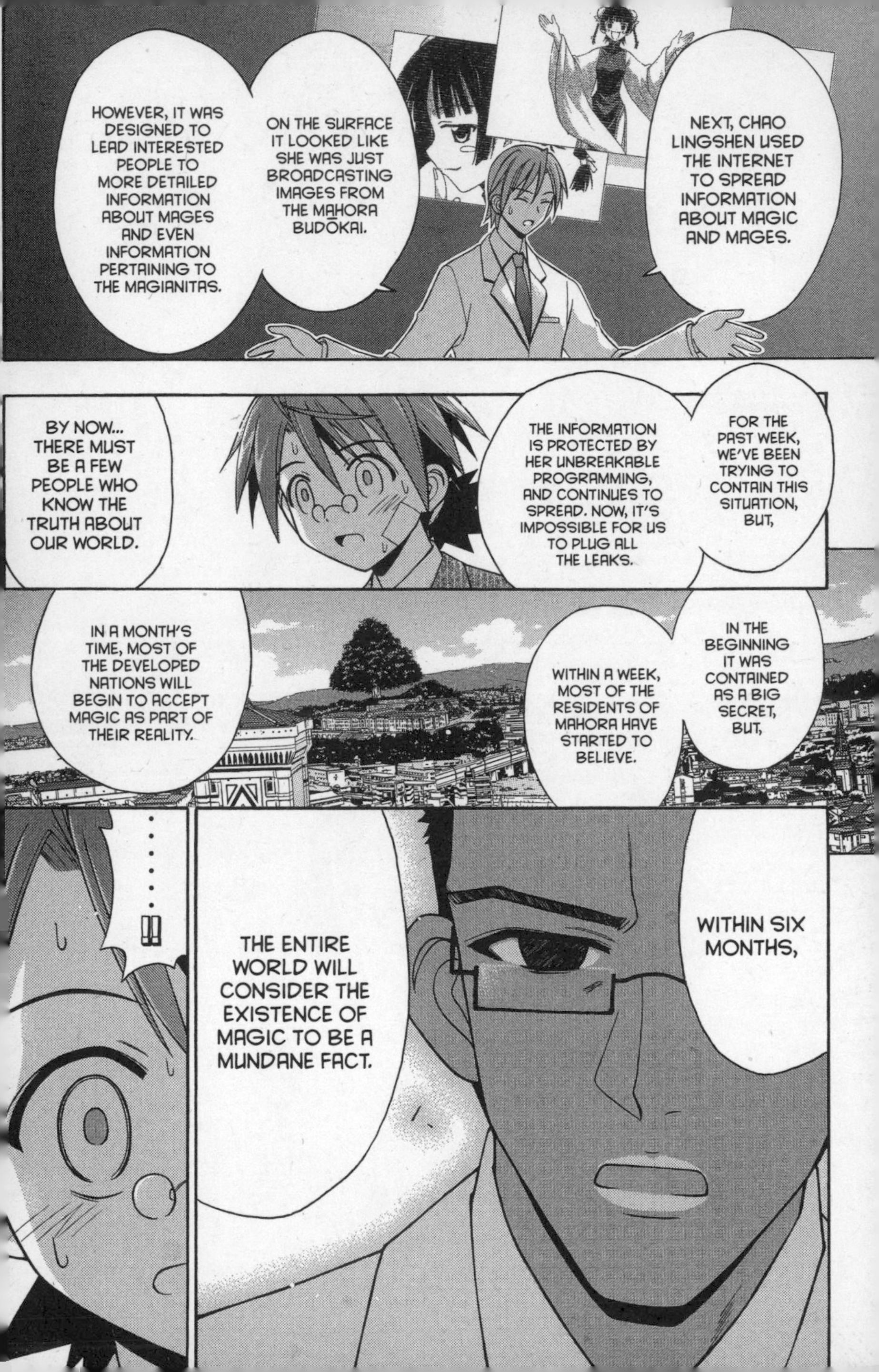
NEXT, CHAO LINGSHEN USED THE INTERNET TO SPREAD INFORMATION ABOUT MAGIC AND MAGES.
ON THE SURFACE IT LOOKED LIKE SHE WAS JUST BROADCASTING IMAGES FROM THE MAHORA BUDŌKAI.
HOWEVER, IT WAS DESIGNED TO LEAD INTERESTED PEOPLE TO MORE DETAILED INFORMATION ABOUT MAGES AND EVEN INFORMATION PERTAINING TO THE MAGIANITAS.
FOR THE PAST WEEK, WE'VE BEEN TRYING TO CONTAIN THIS SITUATION, BUT,
THE INFORMATION IS PROTECTED BY HER UNBREAKABLE PROGRAMMING, AND CONTINUES TO SPREAD. NOW, IT'S IMPOSSIBLE FOR US TO PLUG ALL THE LEAKS.
BY NOW... THERE MUST BE A FEW PEOPLE WHO KNOW THE TRUTH ABOUT OUR WORLD.
IN THE BEGINNING IT WAS CONTAINED AS A BIG SECRET, BUT,
WITHIN A WEEK, MOST OF THE RESIDENTS OF MAHORA HAVE STARTED TO BELIEVE.
IN A MONTH'S TIME, MOST OF THE DEVELOPED NATIONS WILL BEGIN TO ACCEPT MAGIC AS PART OF THEIR REALITY.
WITHIN SIX MONTHS,
THE ENTIRE WORLD WILL CONSIDER THE EXISTENCE OF MAGIC TO BE A MUNDANE FACT.
......!!

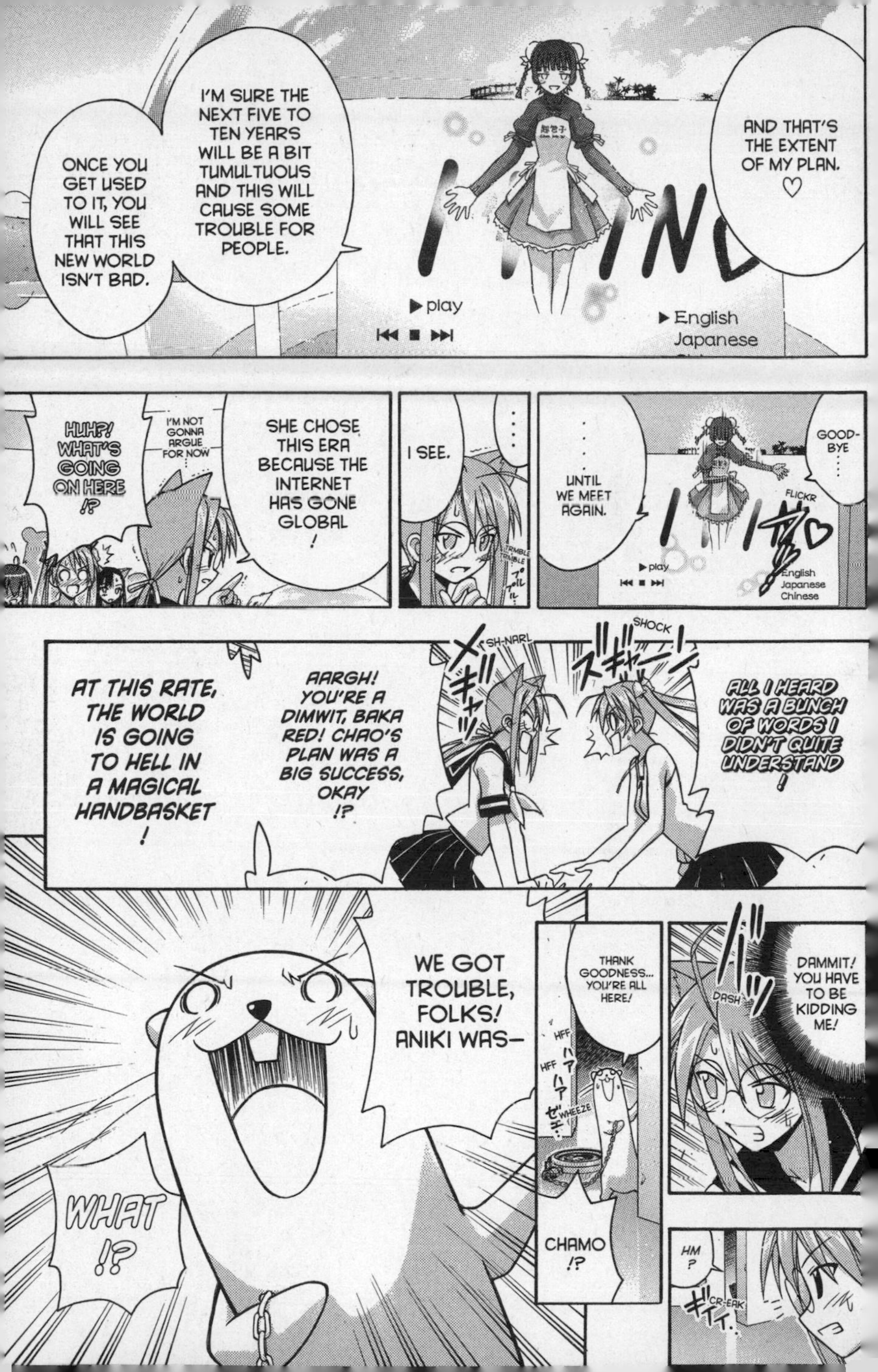
AND THAT'S THE EXTENT OF MY PLAN. ♡
I'M SURE THE NEXT FIVE TO TEN YEARS WILL BE A BIT TUMULTUOUS AND THIS WILL CAUSE SOME TROUBLE FOR PEOPLE.
ONCE YOU GET USED TO IT, YOU WILL SEE THAT THIS NEW WORLD ISN'T BAD.
▶ English
Japanese
▶ play
GOOD-BYE ...
FLICKR
... UNTIL WE MEET AGAIN.
▶ play
English
Japanese
Chinese
...
I SEE.
TRMBLE TRMBLE
SHE CHOSE THIS ERA BECAUSE THE INTERNET HAS GONE GLOBAL !
I'M NOT GONNA ARGUE FOR NOW
HUH?! WHAT'S GOING ON HERE !?
ALL I HEARD WAS A BUNCH OF WORDS I DIDN'T QUITE UNDERSTAND !
SHOCK
SH-NARL
AARGH! YOU'RE A DIMWIT, BAKA RED! CHAO'S PLAN WAS A BIG SUCCESS, OKAY !?
AT THIS RATE, THE WORLD IS GOING TO HELL IN A MAGICAL HANDBASKET !
DASH
DAMMIT! YOU HAVE TO BE KIDDING ME!
HM ?
CR-EAK
THANK GOODNESS... YOU'RE ALL HERE!
HFF
HFF
WHEEZE
CHAMO !?
WE GOT TROUBLE, FOLKS! ANIKI WAS—
WHAT !?

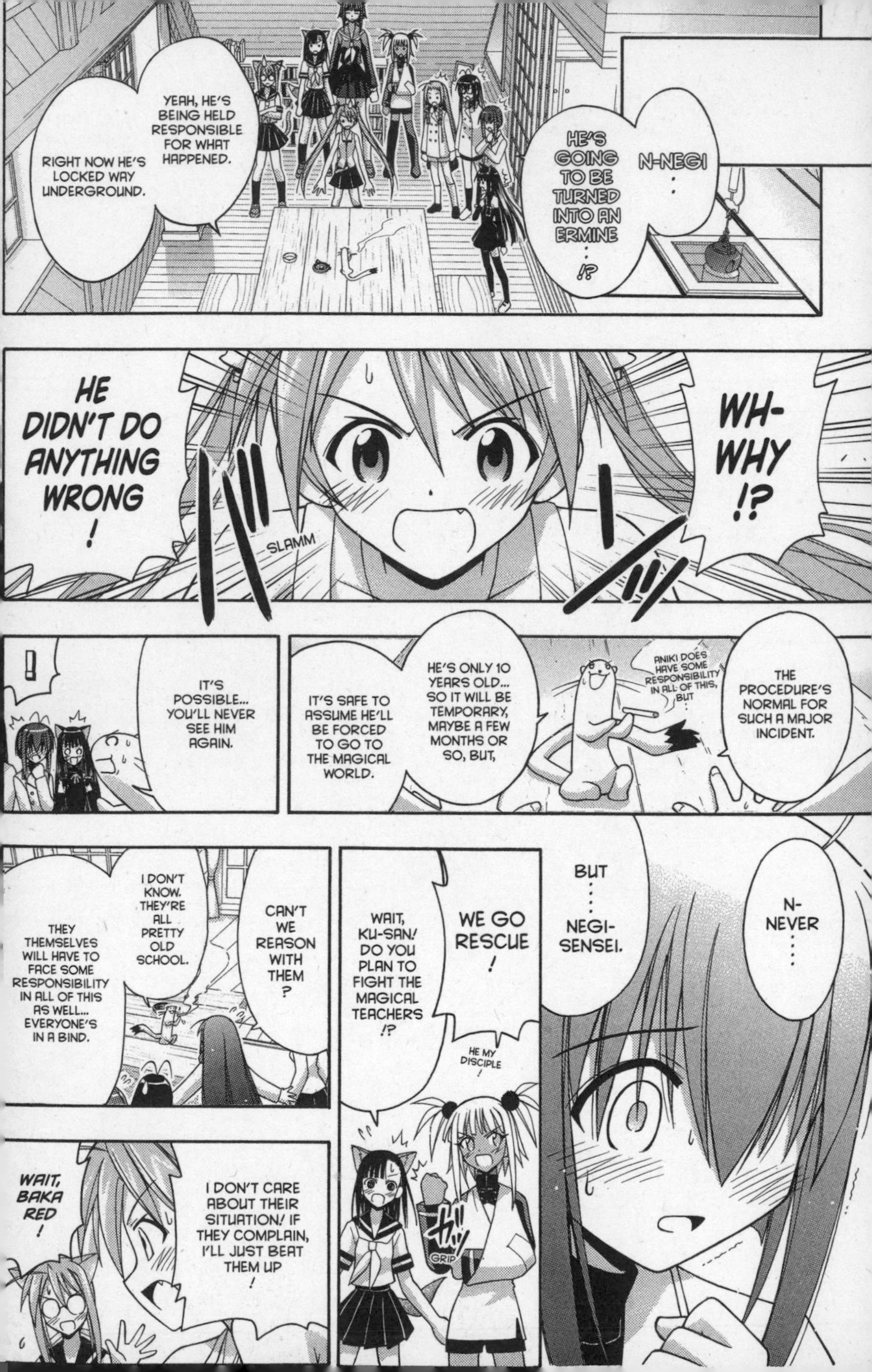
N-NEGI...
HE'S GOING TO BE TURNED INTO AN ERMINE...!?
YEAH, HE'S BEING HELD RESPONSIBLE FOR WHAT HAPPENED.
RIGHT NOW HE'S LOCKED WAY UNDERGROUND.
WH-WHY!?
HE DIDN'T DO ANYTHING WRONG!
SLAMM
THE PROCEDURE'S NORMAL FOR SUCH A MAJOR INCIDENT.
ANIKI DOES HAVE SOME RESPONSIBILITY IN ALL OF THIS, BUT...
HE'S ONLY 10 YEARS OLD... SO IT WILL BE TEMPORARY, MAYBE A FEW MONTHS OR SO, BUT,
IT'S SAFE TO ASSUME HE'LL BE FORCED TO GO TO THE MAGICAL WORLD.
IT'S POSSIBLE... YOU'LL NEVER SEE HIM AGAIN.
!
N-NEVER....
BUT... NEGI-SENSEI.
WE GO RESCUE!
WAIT, KU-SAN! DO YOU PLAN TO FIGHT THE MAGICAL TEACHERS!?
HE MY DISCIPLE!
GRIP
CAN'T WE REASON WITH THEM?
I DON'T KNOW. THEY'RE ALL PRETTY OLD SCHOOL.
THEY THEMSELVES WILL HAVE TO FACE SOME RESPONSIBILITY IN ALL OF THIS AS WELL... EVERYONE'S IN A BIND.
I DON'T CARE ABOUT THEIR SITUATION! IF THEY COMPLAIN, I'LL JUST BEAT THEM UP!
WAIT, BAKA RED

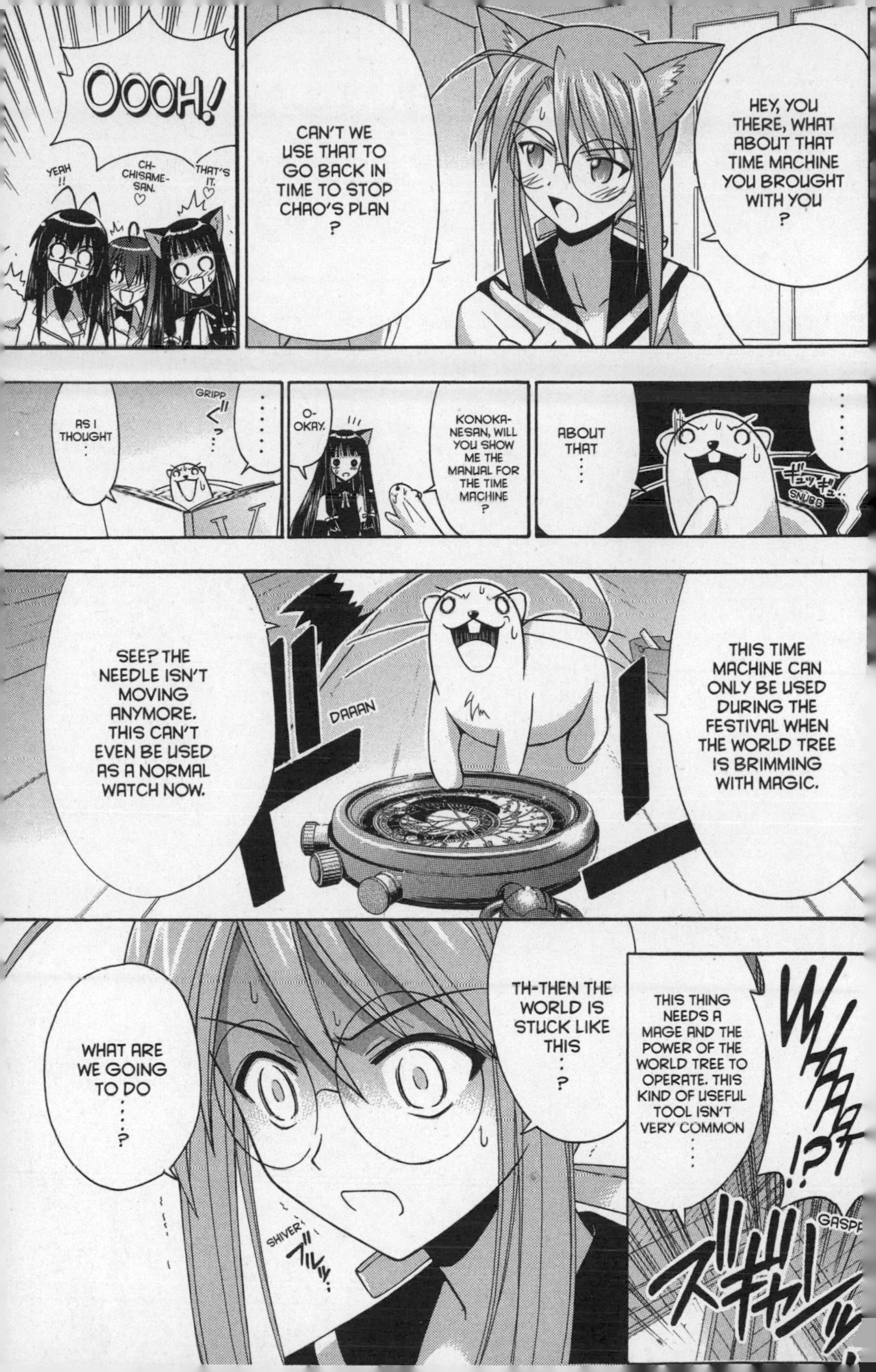
HEY, YOU THERE, WHAT ABOUT THAT TIME MACHINE YOU BROUGHT WITH YOU ?
CAN'T WE USE THAT TO GO BACK IN TIME TO STOP CHAO'S PLAN ?
OOOH!
THAT'S IT.
CH-CHISAME-SAN.
YEAH !!
....
ABOUT THAT ....
SNUBB
KONOKA-NESAN, WILL YOU SHOW ME THE MANUAL FOR THE TIME MACHINE ?
O-OKAY.
....
GRIPP
AS I THOUGHT ..
THIS TIME MACHINE CAN ONLY BE USED DURING THE FESTIVAL WHEN THE WORLD TREE IS BRIMMING WITH MAGIC.
DAAAN
SEE? THE NEEDLE ISN'T MOVING ANYMORE. THIS CAN'T EVEN BE USED AS A NORMAL WATCH NOW.
!?
GASPP
THIS THING NEEDS A MAGE AND THE POWER OF THE WORLD TREE TO OPERATE. THIS KIND OF USEFUL TOOL ISN'T VERY COMMON ....
TH-THEN THE WORLD IS STUCK LIKE THIS ..?
WHAT ARE WE GOING TO DO ....?
SHIVER

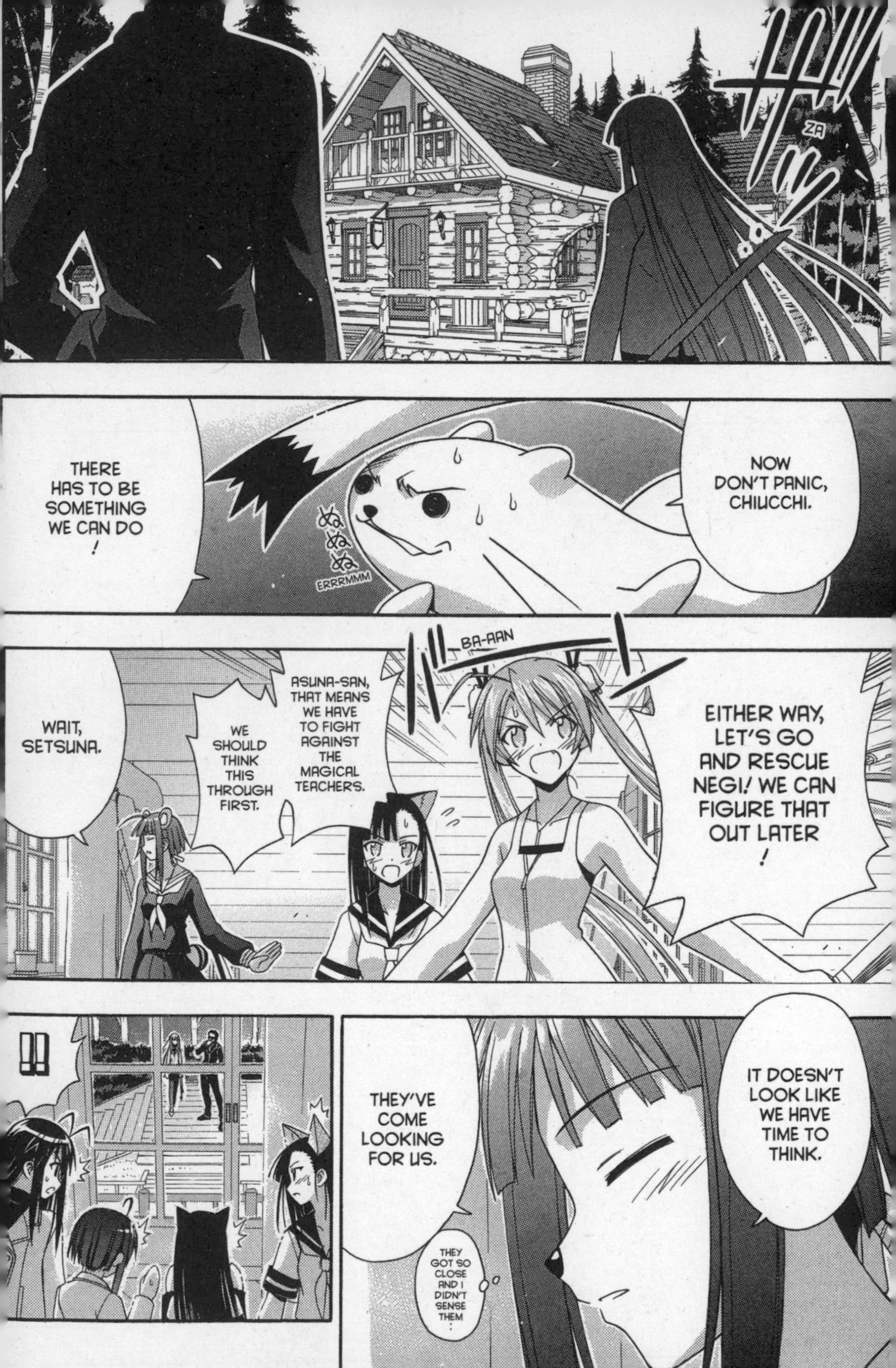
ZA
NOW DON'T PANIC, CHIUCCHI.
ぬぬぬ
ERRRMMM
THERE HAS TO BE SOMETHING WE CAN DO!
BA-AAN
EITHER WAY, LET'S GO AND RESCUE NEGI! WE CAN FIGURE THAT OUT LATER!
ASUNA-SAN, THAT MEANS WE HAVE TO FIGHT AGAINST THE MAGICAL TEACHERS.
WE SHOULD THINK THIS THROUGH FIRST.
WAIT, SETSUNA.
IT DOESN'T LOOK LIKE WE HAVE TIME TO THINK.
THEY'VE COME LOOKING FOR US.
THEY GOT SO CLOSE AND I DIDN'T SENSE THEM...
!!

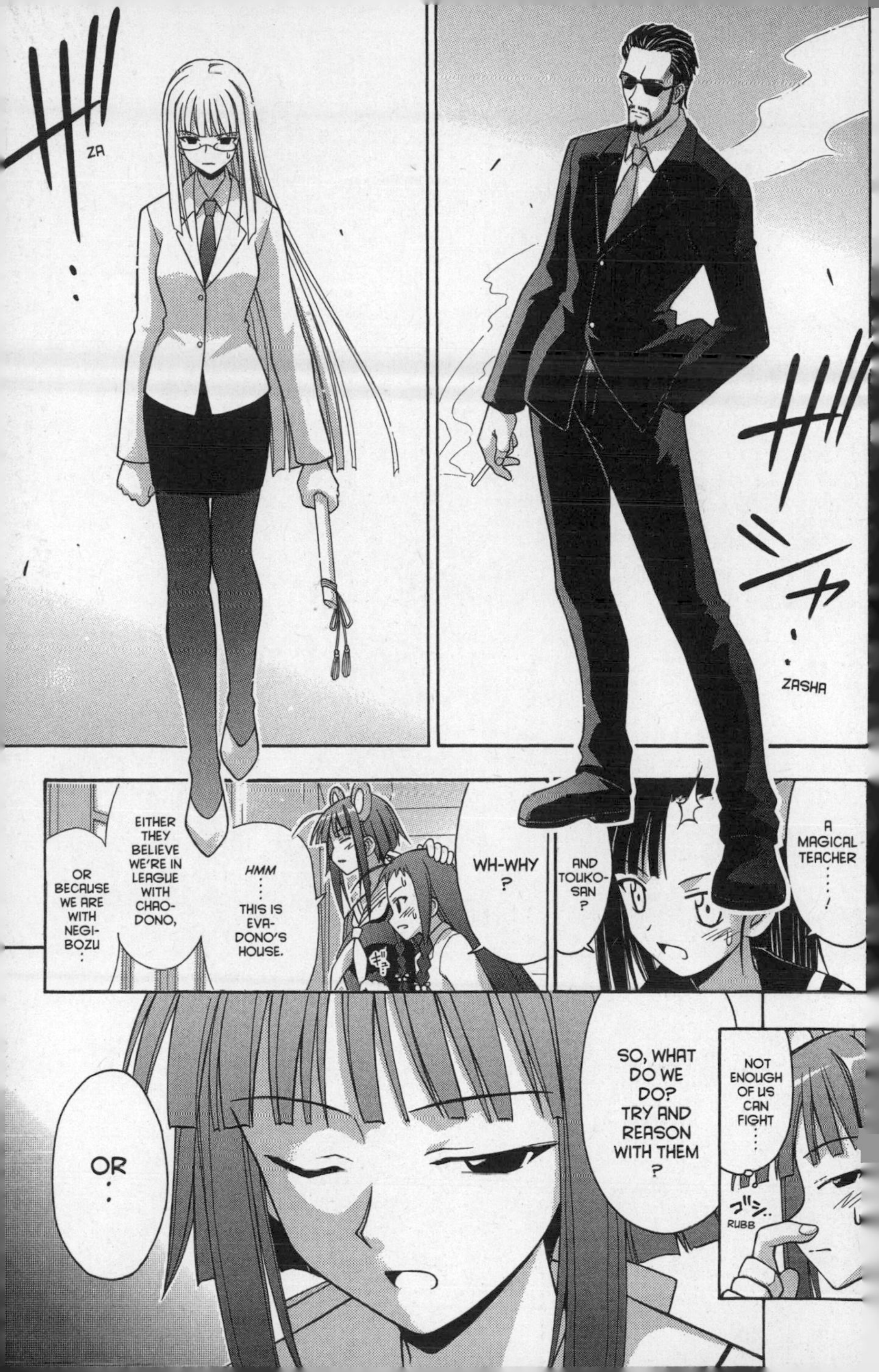
ZASHA
ZA
A MAGICAL TEACHER ......!
AND TOUKO-SAN?
WH-WHY?
HMM... THIS IS EVA-DONO'S HOUSE.
EITHER THEY BELIEVE WE'RE IN LEAGUE WITH CHAO-DONO,
OR BECAUSE WE ARE WITH NEGI-BOZU...
NOT ENOUGH OF US CAN FIGHT....
RUBB
SO, WHAT DO WE DO? TRY AND REASON WITH THEM?
OR...

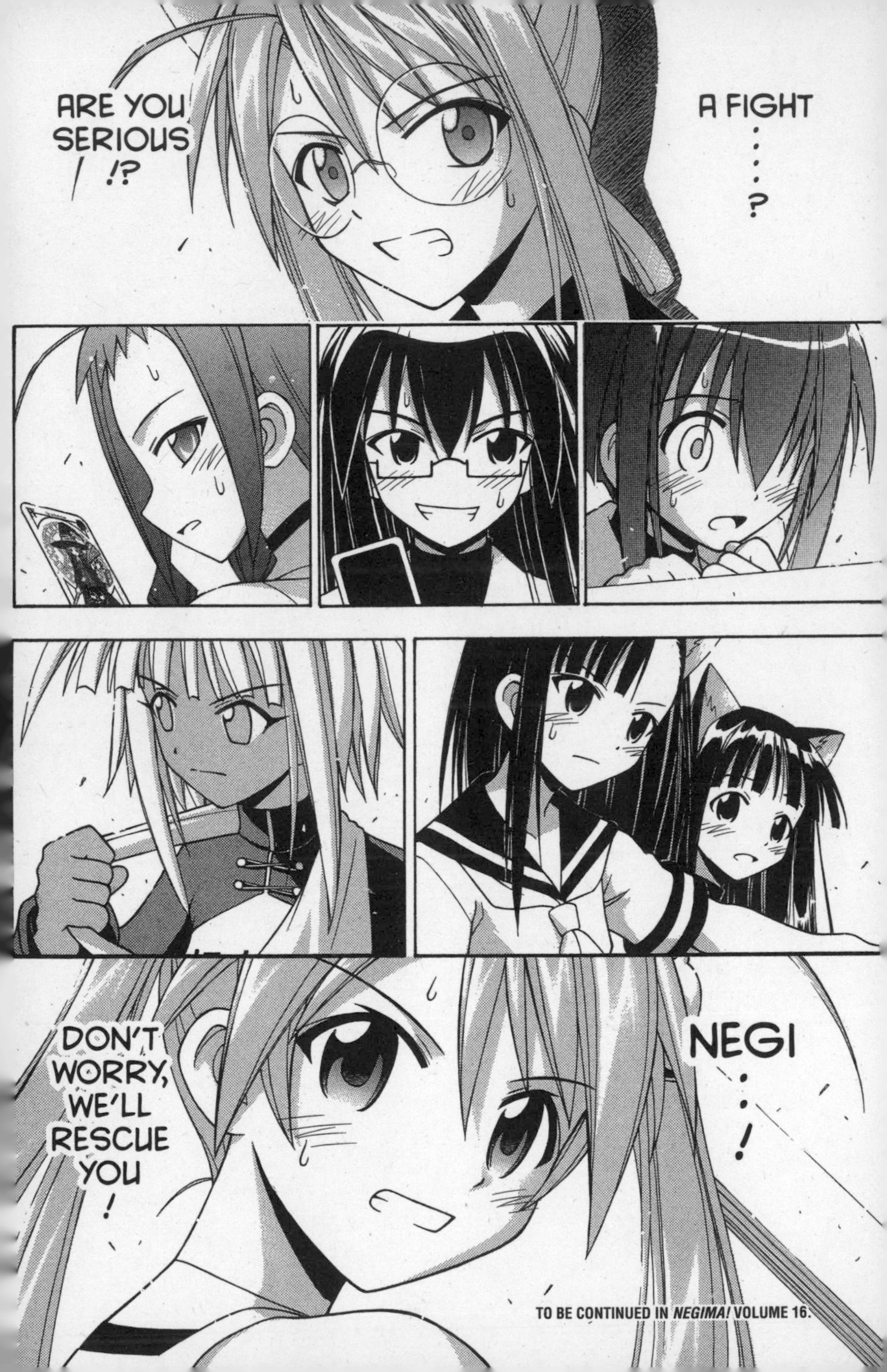
A FIGHT ...?
ARE YOU SERIOUS!?
NEGI...!
DON'T WORRY, WE'LL RESCUE YOU!

TO BE CONTINUED IN *NEGIMA!* VOLUME 16.

-STAFF-

Ken Akamatsu
Takashi Takemoto
Kenichi Nakamura
Masaki Ohyama
Keiichi Yamashita
Tadashi Maki
Tohru Mitsuhashi

Thanks to
Ran Ayanaga

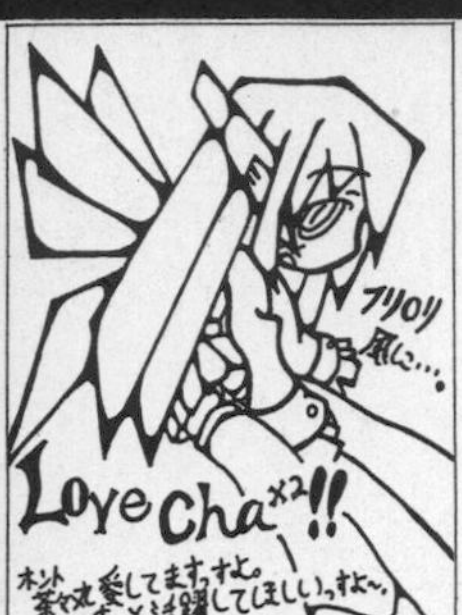
フリフリ風に…。
Love Cha×2!!
ホント茶々丸愛してますっすよ。もっと活躍してほしいっすよ～。
先生ファイトッすよ～!!

▲ DEFINITELY A "CHACHAMARU," DONE IN THE "FLOL" STYLE (HEH).

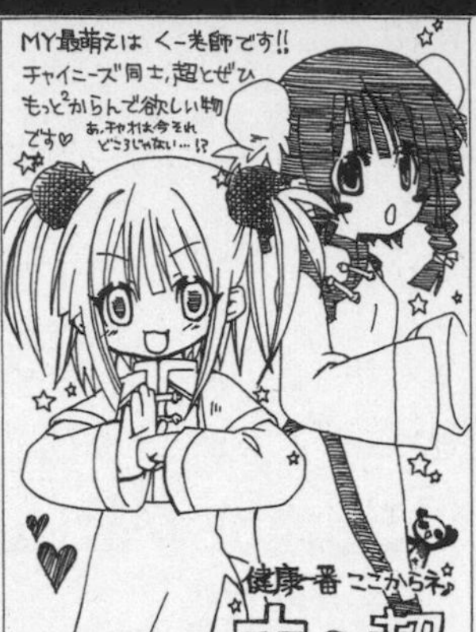
MY最萌えは くー老師です!!
チャイニーズ同士, 超とぜひもっと²からんで欲しい物です♡
あ, チャオは今それどころじゃない…!?
古&超

▲ VERY NICE...AND CUTE, TOO! WE'D LIKE TO SEE MORE FROM YOU!

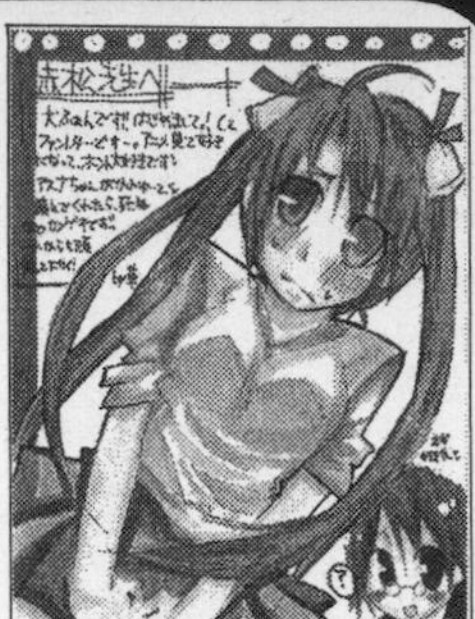

▲ THE COLOR ON THIS IS GORGEOUS. WE LOVE THE EMBARRASSED EXPRESSION ON ASUNA!

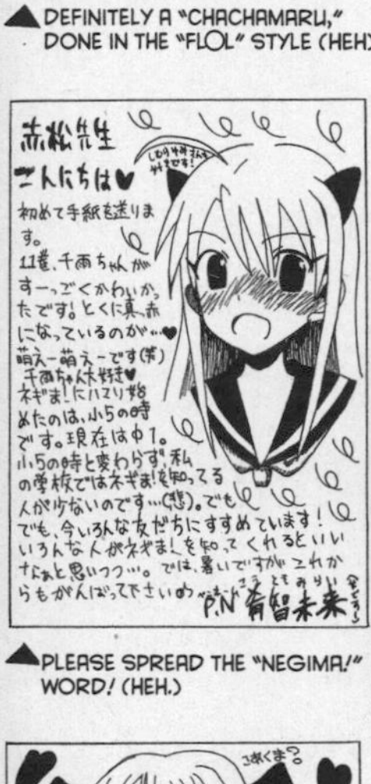
赤松先生
こんにちは♥
初めて手紙を送ります。
11巻, 千雨ちゃんがすーっごくかわいかったです。とくに真っ赤になっているのが…♥

▲ PLEASE SPREAD THE "NEGIMA!" WORD! (HEH.)

NEGIMA!
FAN ART CORNER

THANKS TO ALL OF YOU, THE POPULARITY OF THE "FAN ART CORNER" IS ON THE RISE, WITH EXTRA THANKS GOING TO THOSE WHO SENT IN PICTURES! (^^) SURE, WITH MORE POPULARITY IT'S ALSO BECOME MORE DIFFICULT TO SEE YOUR WORK MAKE IT INTO PRINT, BUT DON'T GIVE UP—KEEP SENDING IT IN! IT WOULD SEEM THAT, JUDGING FROM ARTWORK RECEIVED RECENTLY, CHISAME AND MEI'S STARS ARE REALLY ON THE RISE. THERE SEEM TO BE SOME DIE-HARD TANAKA FANS OUT THERE, TOO (HEH). NONE OF US HERE CAN WAIT FOR YOU TO SEND IN YOUR ILLUSTRATIONS OF FAVORITE CHARACTERS.

TEXT: ASS'T MAX

▼ IT'D BE INTERESTING TO SEE MEI AND KOTARŌ FORM A COUPLE.

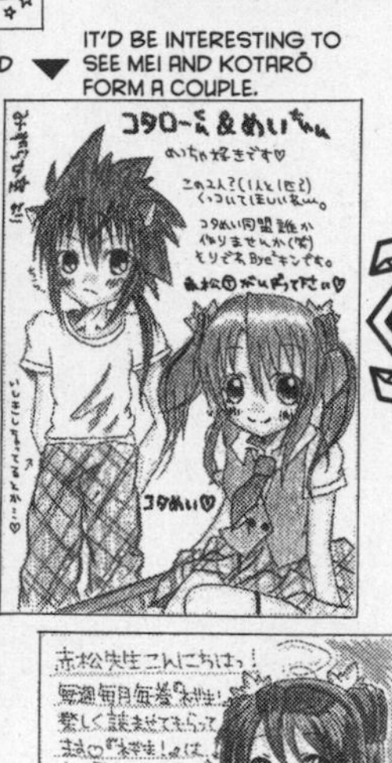
コタロ～くん&めいちゃん
めっちゃ好きです♡
コタめい♡

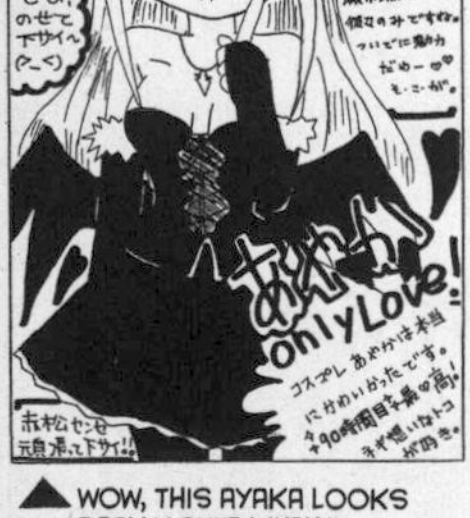
ぜひ, のせて下サイ～ (^-^)
あやか only Love!

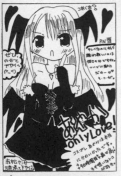

▲ WOW, THIS AYAKA LOOKS REALLY CUTE! (HEH.)

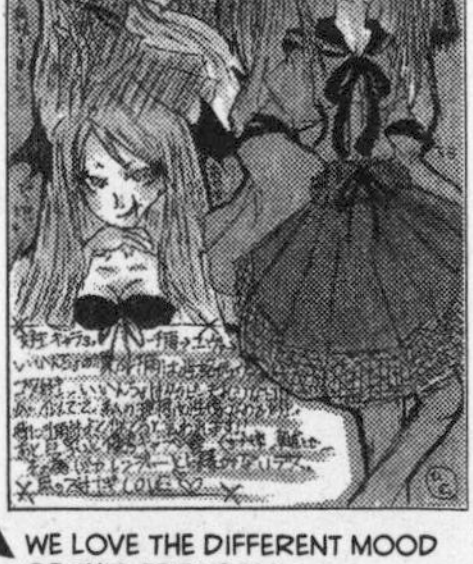

◀ WE LOVE THE DIFFERENT MOOD OF THIS ARTWORK.

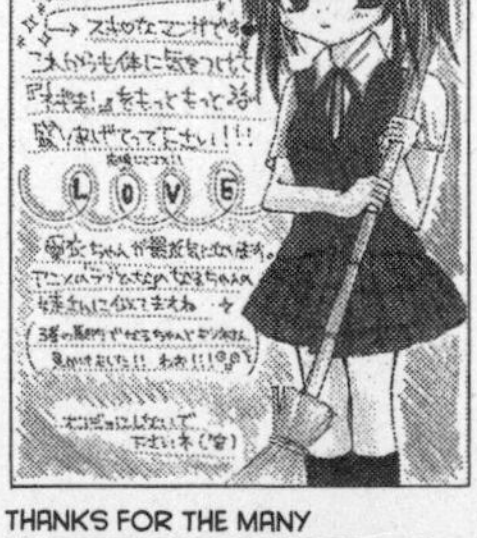
赤松先生こんにちはっ!
LOVE

◀ THANKS FOR THE MANY ILLUSTRATIONS YOU'VE SENT IN.

NEGI MA!

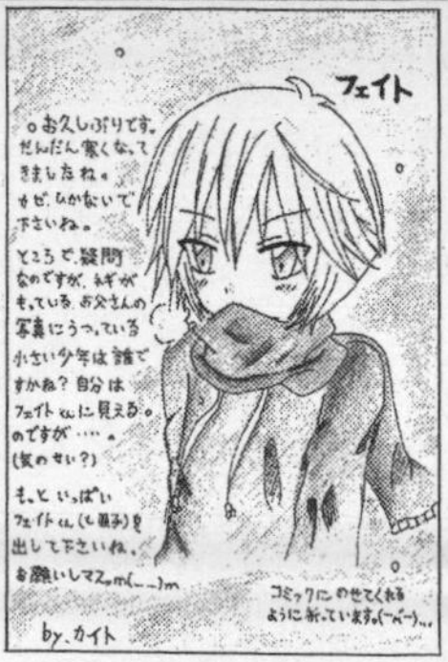
フェイト
お久しぶりです。だんだん寒くなってきましたね。
by.カイト

A NICE SURPRISE, SEEING A PICTURE OF FATE. THE LOOK IN HIS EYE IS QUITE DISTINCTIVE.

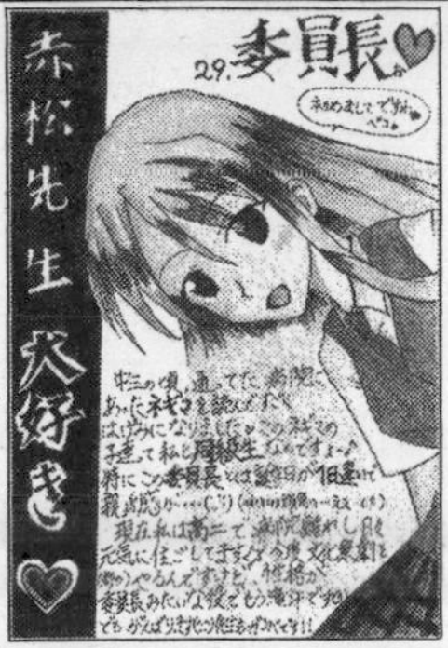
赤松先生大好き♡
29.委員長♡

A VERY LOVELY LOOKING CLASS REP!

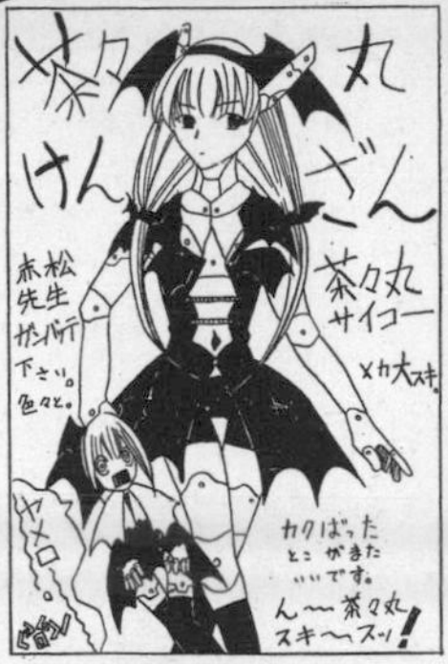
茶々丸けんざん
赤松先生ガンバテ下さい。色々と。
茶々丸サイコー
メカ大スキ。
カクばったとこがまたいいです。
ん~~茶々丸スキ~~ッ!

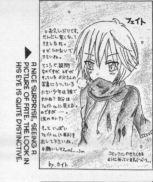

WE LOVE THE "ROBOTIC FEEL" OF THIS PICTURE. (HEH.)

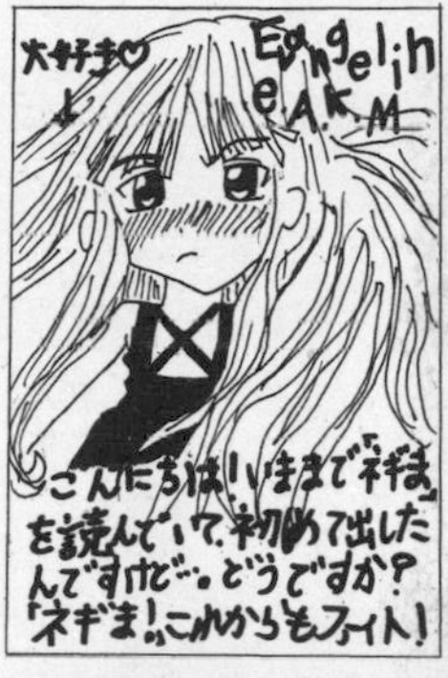
大好き♡
Evangeline A.K.M
こんにちは!いままで「ネギま」を読んでいて、初めて出したんですけど…。どうですか?
「ネギま!」これからもファイト!

YOUR LOVE FOR EVA REALLY COMES THROUGH IN THIS ONE.

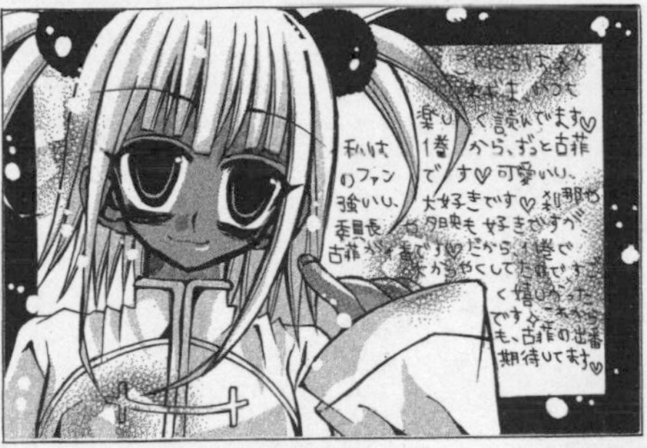
楽しく読んでます♡
私は1巻から、ずっと古菲のファンです♡

A UNIQUE STYLE FOR YOUR KŪ FEI ILLUSTRATION—WE LIKE IT!

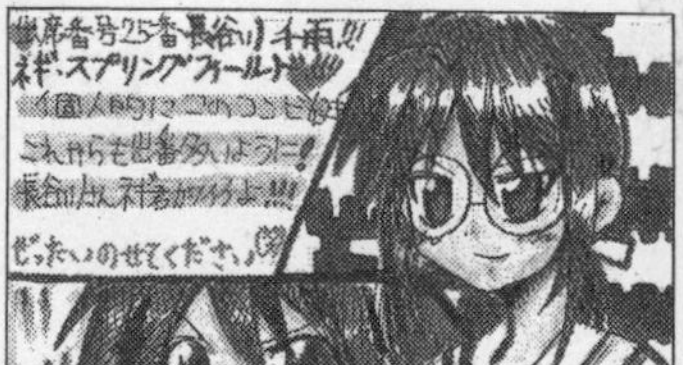
ネギ・スプリングフィールド
これからも出番多いように!

CHISAME SURE IS POPULAR LATELY. WE LIKE YOUR USE OF THE THICK LINES.

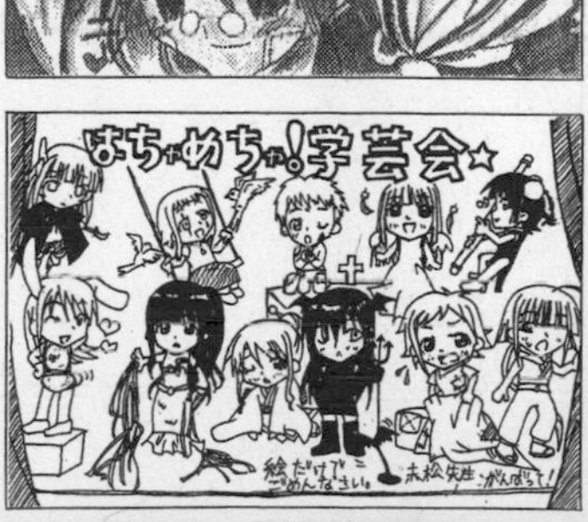
はちゃめちゃ!学芸会☆
絵だけでごめんなさい。

LOOKS LIKE QUITE AN ENTERTAINING TALENT SHOW. ZAZIE LOOKS LIKE SHE'S HAVING FUN (HEH).

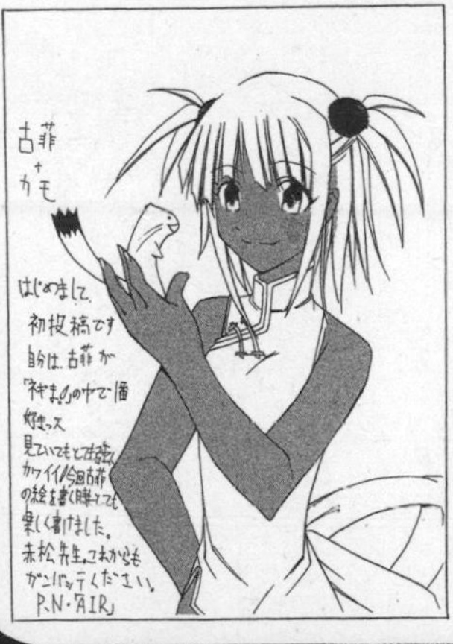
古菲
+
カモ
はじめまして、
初投稿です
赤松先生、これからも
ガンバッテください。
P.N・AIR

WE LOVE THE "CLEAN" LOOK OF YOUR KŪ FEI. VERY PRETTY.

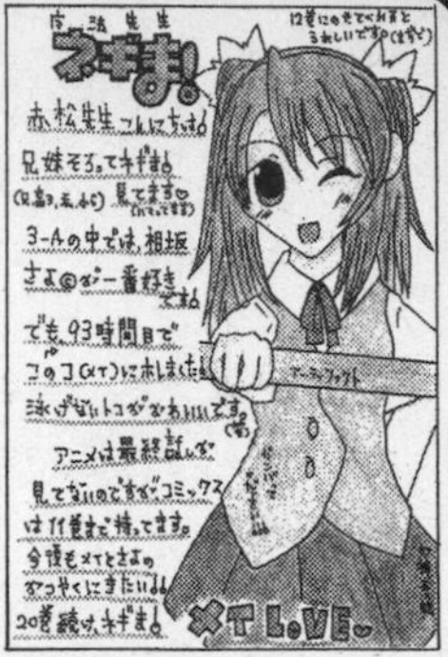
ネギま!
赤松先生こんにちわ!

MEI'S POPULARITY IS RIGHT UP THERE!

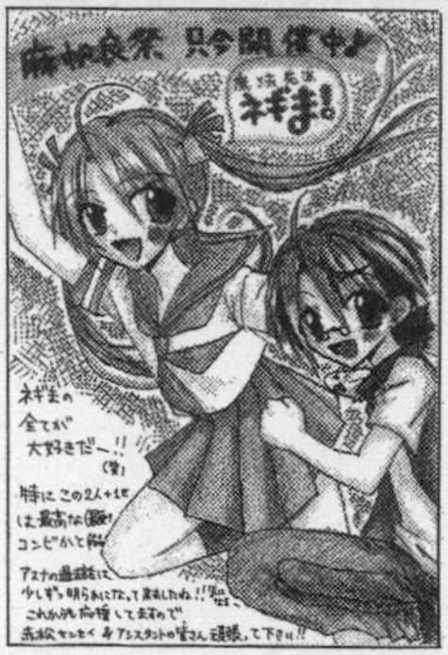
ネギま!

BACK-TO-BASICS WITH AN ASUNA AND NEGI PICTURE!

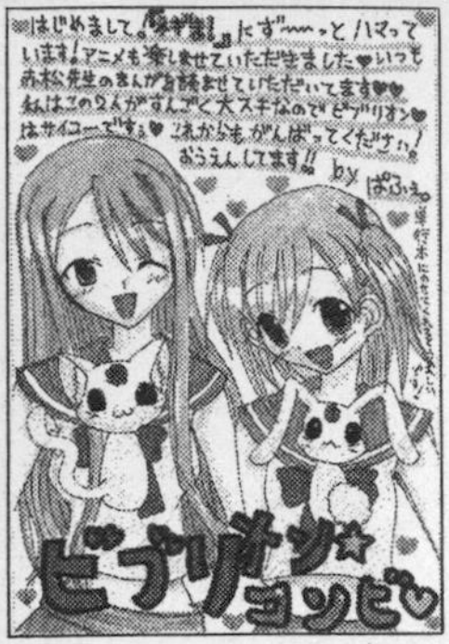
ビブリオン☆コンビ♡

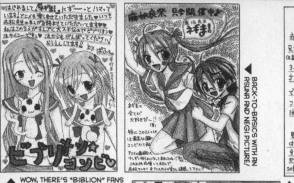

WOW, THERE'S "BIBLION" FANS OUT THERE...! (HEH.)

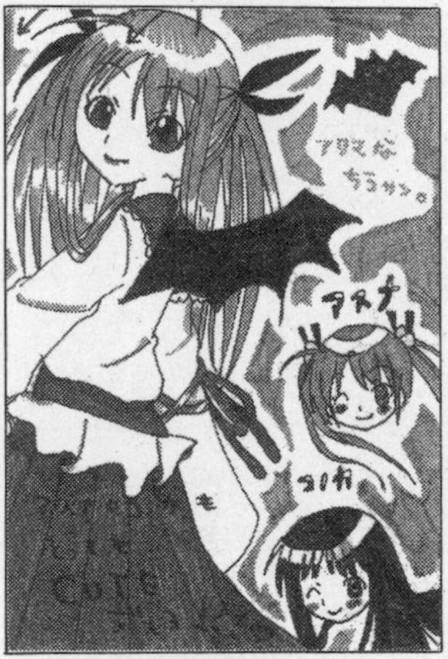
アスナ

IT'S CUTE...AND WELL-EXECUTED!

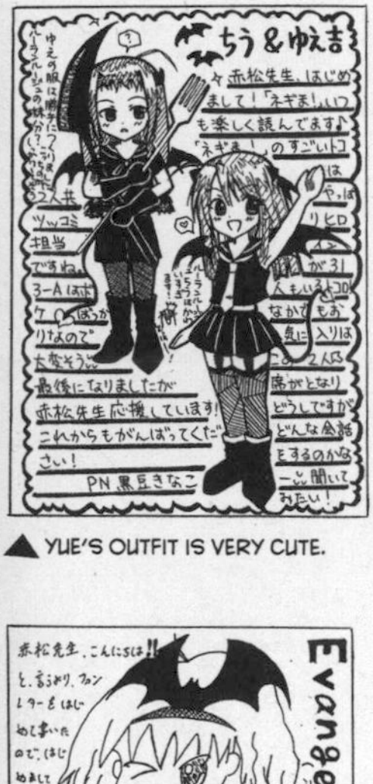
ちう＆ゆえ吉
赤松先生、はじめまして!
PN 黒豆きなこ

YUE'S OUTFIT IS VERY CUTE.

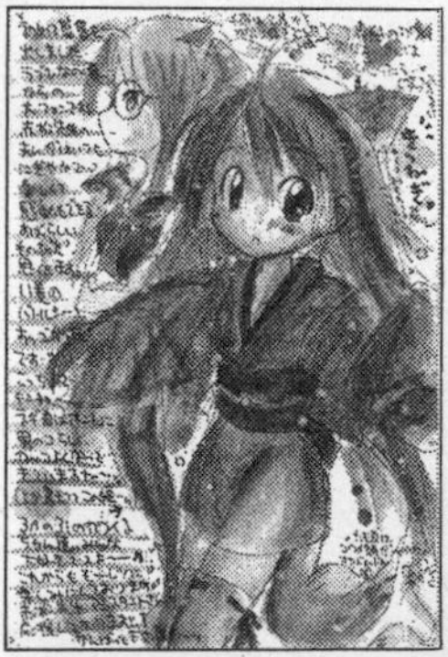

THE USE OF COLOR HERE IS WONDERFUL. (^^)

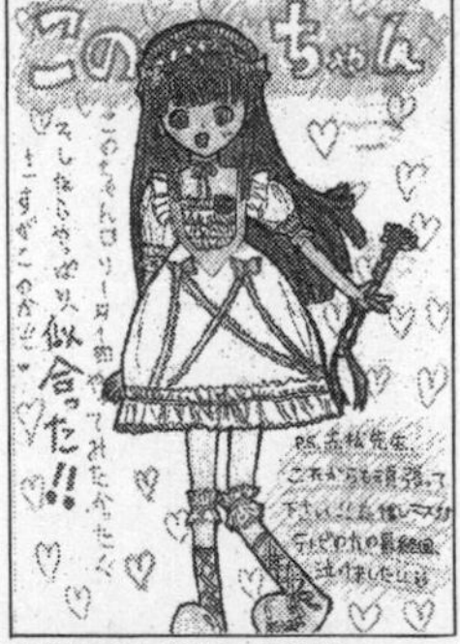
このちゃん

KONOKA LOOKS REALLY GOOD IN "LOLITA" FASHIONS, I MUST SAY.

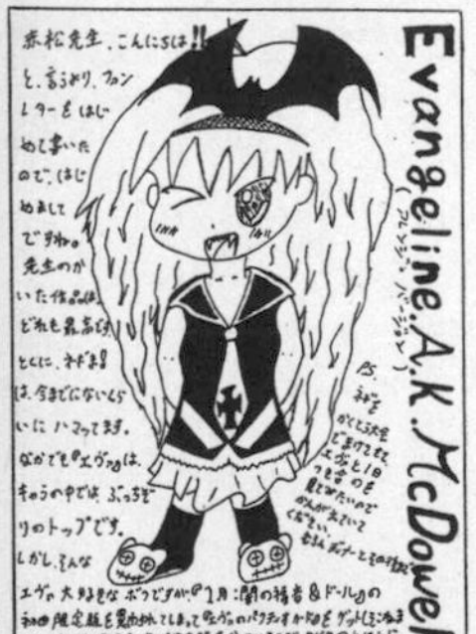
Evangeline.A.K.McDowell
赤松先生、こんにちは!!

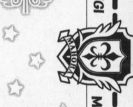

THIS EVA SEEMS RARIN' TO GET INTO TROUBLE! (^^)

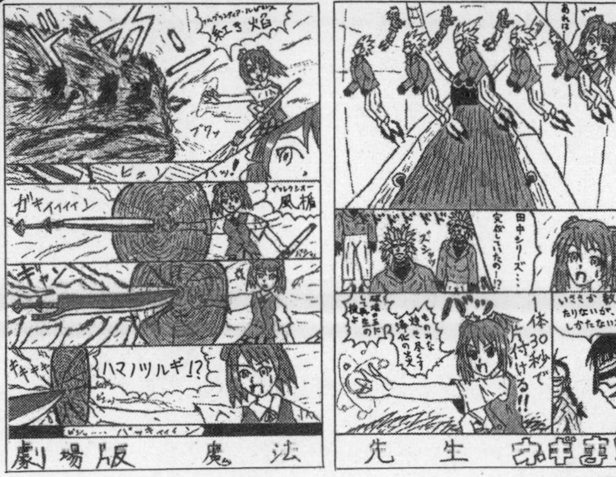
紅き焔
風楯
ハマノツルギ!?
田中シリーズ…
1体30秒で付ける!!
いささか 数が たりないが、しかたないネ…。
劇場版 魔法 先生 ネギま!

THIS COMIC STRIP HAD THE ENTIRE STAFF IN STITCHES. IT'S FABULOUS!

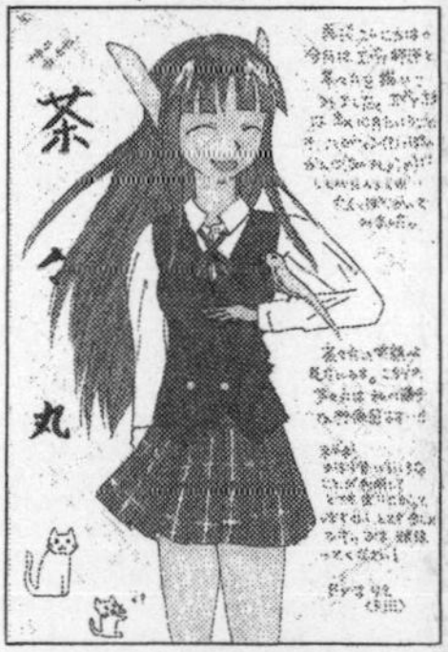
茶
丸

CHACHAMARU LOOKS HAPPY, HERE.

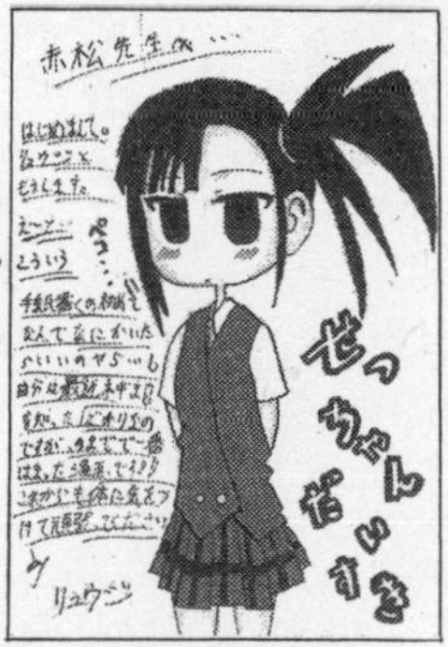
赤松先生へ
せっちゃんだいすき

WE LIKE THE SEMI-SUPER-DEFORMED SETSUNA HERE... SHE'S EVEN BOWING! (HEH.)

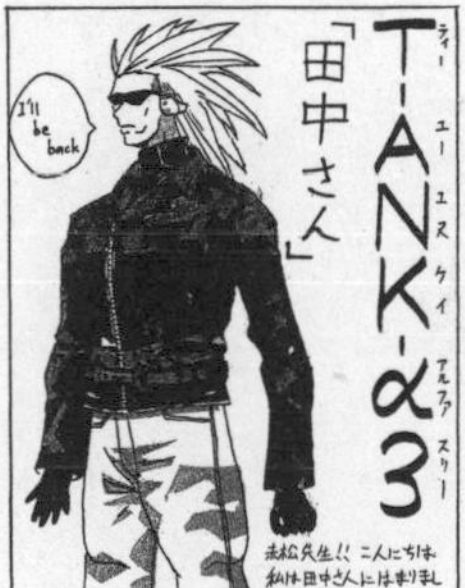
I'll be back
T-ANK-α3
「田中さん」

TANAKA-*SAN*... (HEH.)

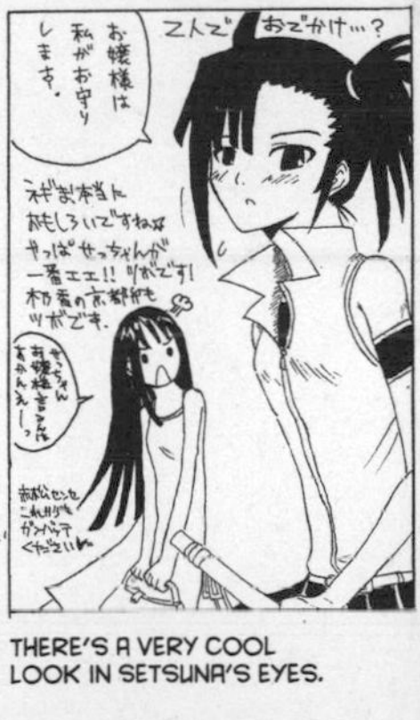
お嬢様は私がお守りします。

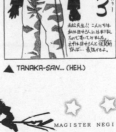

THERE'S A VERY COOL LOOK IN SETSUNA'S EYES.

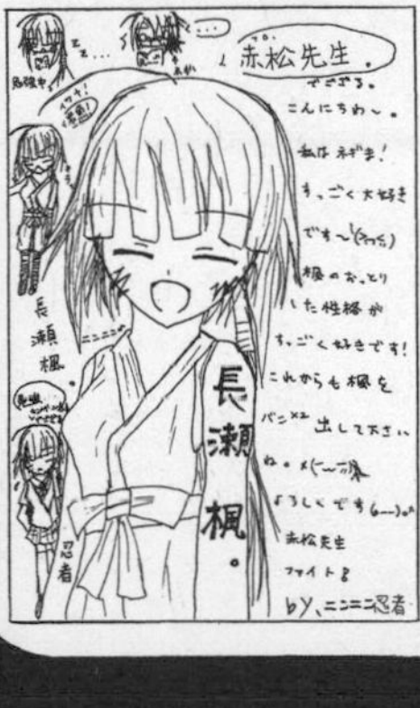
赤松先生。
長瀬楓。

THE SMILE ON KAEDE IS VERY NICE.

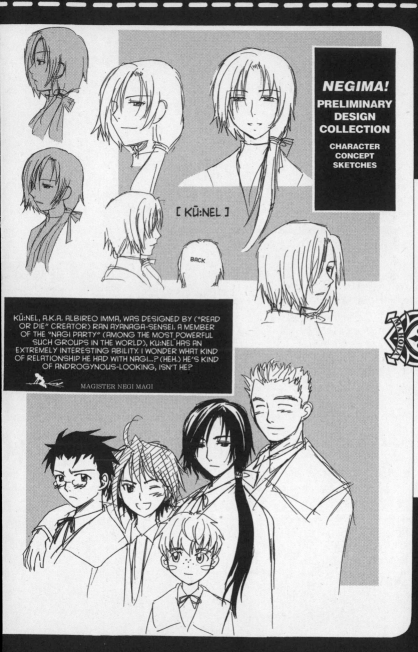

NEGIMA!

PRELIMINARY DESIGN COLLECTION

CHARACTER CONCEPT SKETCHES

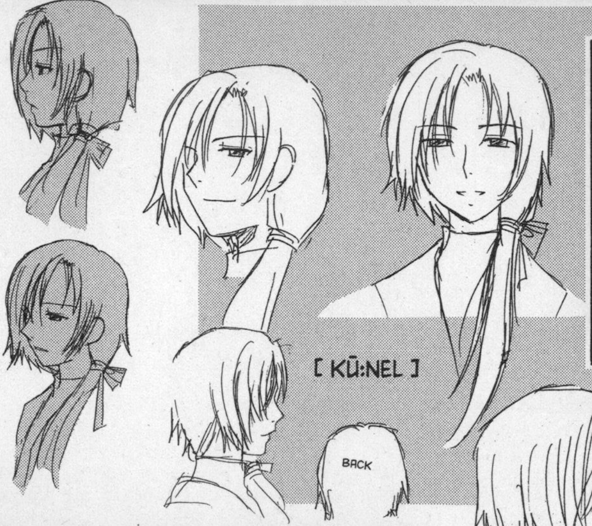

[KŪ:NEL]
BACK

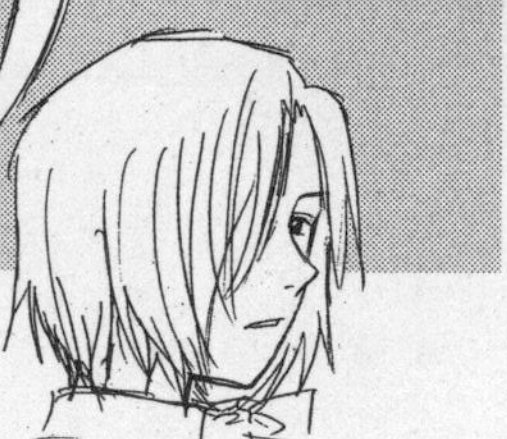

KŪ:NEL, A.K.A. ALBIREO IMMA, WAS DESIGNED BY ("READ OR DIE" CREATOR) RAN AYANAGA-SENSEI. A MEMBER OF THE "NAGI PARTY" (AMONG THE MOST POWERFUL SUCH GROUPS IN THE WORLD), KŪ:NEL HAS AN EXTREMELY INTERESTING ABILITY. I WONDER WHAT KIND OF RELATIONSHIP HE HAD WITH NAGI...? (HEH.) HE'S KIND OF ANDROGYNOUS-LOOKING, ISN'T HE?

MAGISTER NEGI MAGI

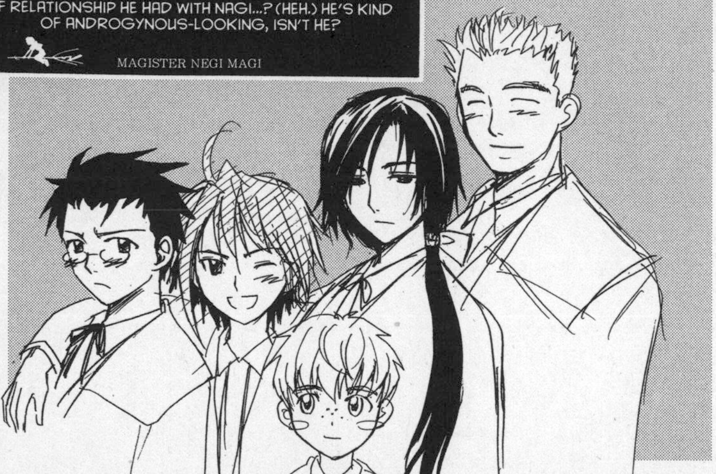

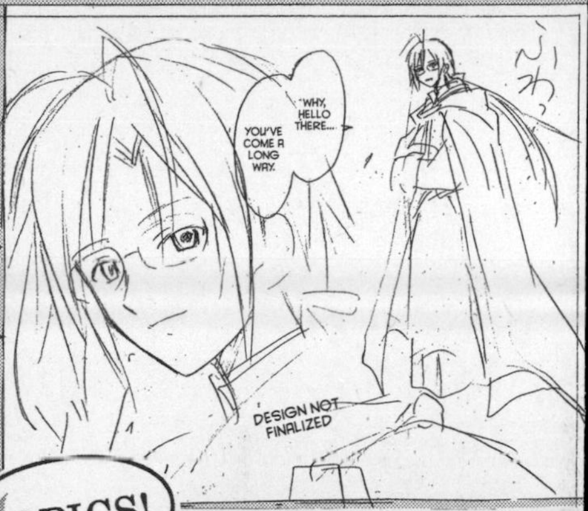
"WHY, HELLO THERE...
YOU'VE COME A LONG WAY.
DESIGN NOT FINALIZED

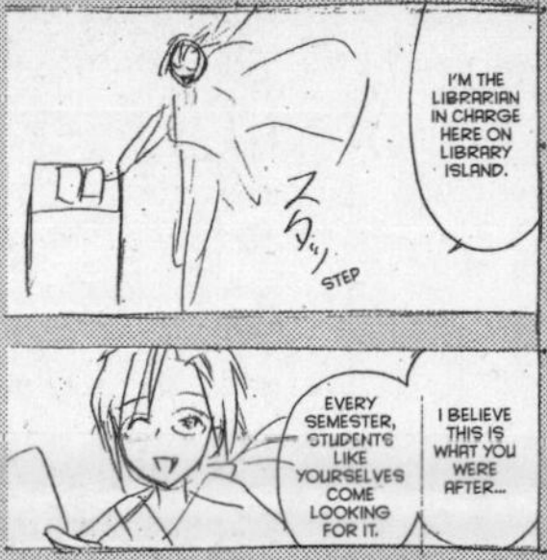
I'M THE LIBRARIAN IN CHARGE HERE ON LIBRARY ISLAND.
STEP
I BELIEVE THIS IS WHAT YOU WERE AFTER...
EVERY SEMESTER, STUDENTS LIKE YOURSELVES COME LOOKING FOR IT.

TOPICS!

DID YOU KNOW? KŪ:NEL WAS ORIGINALLY SUPPOSED TO MAKE AN APPEARANCE IN VOL. 2 DURING THE "LIBRARY ISLAND EXPLORATION" ARC...!

THIS WAS THE PROPOSED PAGE DESIGN FROM WHERE "KŪ:NEL AS LIBRARIAN" WAS TO SHOW UP ORIGINALLY DURING THE "BAKA-RANGER AND THE SECRET LIBRARY" STORY ARC. FROM A SERIES COORDINATION STANDPOINT, THOUGH, IT WORKED BETTER AT THE END OF THE SCHOOL TRIP ARC TO MERELY HINT AT HIM, NOT HAVING HIM ACTUALLY APPEAR UNTIL THE MAHORA FESTIVAL.

MAGISTER NEGI MAGI

KOKONE'S VARIOUS HAIRSTYLES

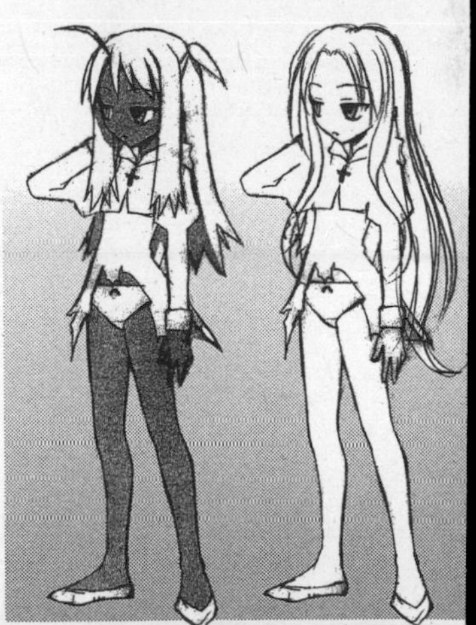

FINAL VERSION

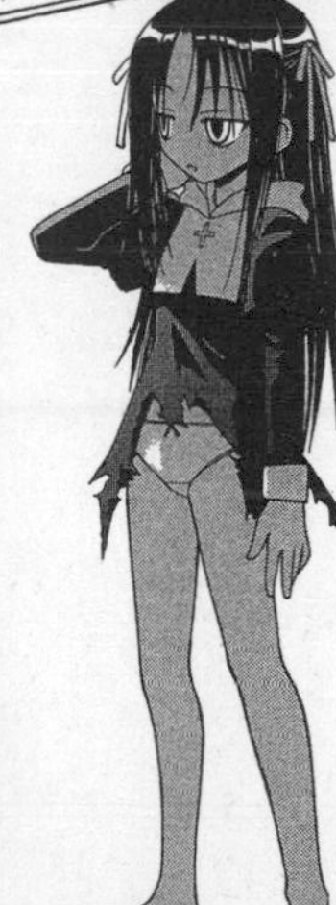

※ VARIOUS HAIR HIGHLIGHTS

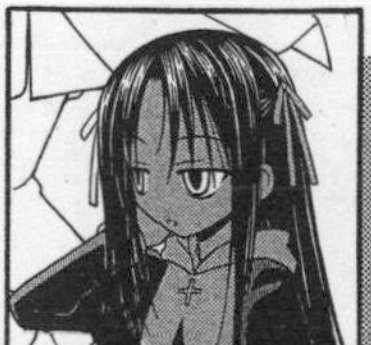

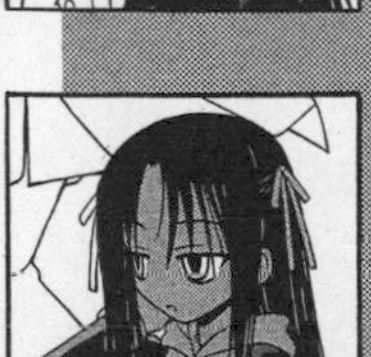

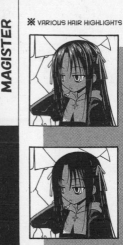

3-D BACKGROUNDS EXPLANATION CORNER

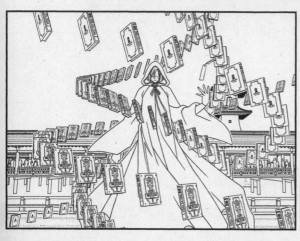

άι βυβλοι άι βιογραφικαί

SCENE NAME: ALBIREO'S BOOKS

POLYGON COUNT: 7,688

ALTHOUGH THIS IS BEING PRINTED UNDER THE TITLE "3-D BACKGROUNDS EXPLANATION CORNER," THIS TIME WE FOCUS NOT ON BACKGROUNDS, BUT ON BOOKS.

KŪ:NEL'S ARTIFACT, "άι βυβλοι άι βιογραφικαί," IS A SWIRLING COLLECTION OF BOOKS WHICH SPIRAL ALL AROUND HIM. IT WOULD BE ALMOST IMPOSSIBLE TO DRAW EACH AND EVERY ONE...AND THAT'S WHY WE DECIDED TO USE OUR SPACE THIS TIME TO DETAIL HOW IT WAS DONE. TO BEST SHOW HOW THE ENTIRE SCENE WAS MADE, LET'S START WITH HOW THE BOOKS WERE CREATED.

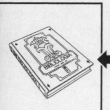

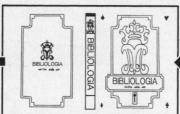

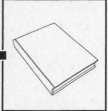

WE STARTED BY MAKING A 3-D BOOK MODEL. WITHOUT ANYTHING WRITTEN ON IT, IT DOESN'T MUCH LOOK LIKE A BOOK, DOES IT?

BIBLIOLOGIA
BIBLIOLOGIA
BIBLIOLOGIA

FOR THAT REASON, WE MADE A HAND-DRAWN TEXTURE MAP AND PLACED IT UPON THE MODEL. *BIBLIOLOGICA*, BY THE WAY, IS LATIN FOR "BIBLIOGRAPHY."

BIBLIOLOGIA

BOOK WITH TEXTURE MAP APPLIED. NOW IT REALLY *DOES* LOOK LIKE A BOOK.

LET'S TAKE THE BOOK WE'VE CREATED THUS FAR AND PUT IT INTO A COOL, SPIRAL FORMATION. BECAUSE IT WAS A BUILT-IN FUNCTION OF THE 3-D SOFTWARE WE USE, IT WAS A FAIRLY SIMPLE OPERATION. FIRST WE HAD TO DECIDE WHAT THE RADIUS OF THE SPIRAL WOULD BE, THEN WE ENTERED A FIGURE FOR THE NUMBER OF BOOKS, THEN THE ANGLE OF ROTATION, THEN THE DISTANCE BETWEEN THE TOP AND BOTTOM BOOKS, THEN....

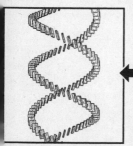

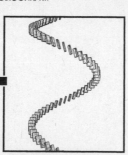

VOILA! SEE?! BY REPLICATING THIS SPIRAL ONE MORE TIME...

...WE NOW HAVE A TWIN SPIRAL OF BOOKS.

IT STILL SEEMS LACKING WITH JUST THE TWO BOOK SPIRALS, SO LET'S ADD ON ANOTHER SPIRAL. AGAIN, AS WE HAD ONLY TO PLUG IN A DIFFERENT SET OF PARAMETERS THAN BEFORE, THIS PART WAS RELATIVELY SIMPLE.

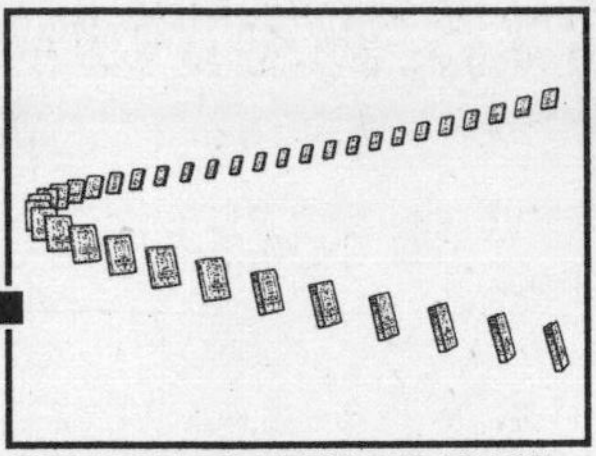

FIRST ROW OF THE SECOND SET OF BOOKS WE CREATED. BY REPLICATING AND FLIPPING THE DIRECTION FOR A SECOND SET...

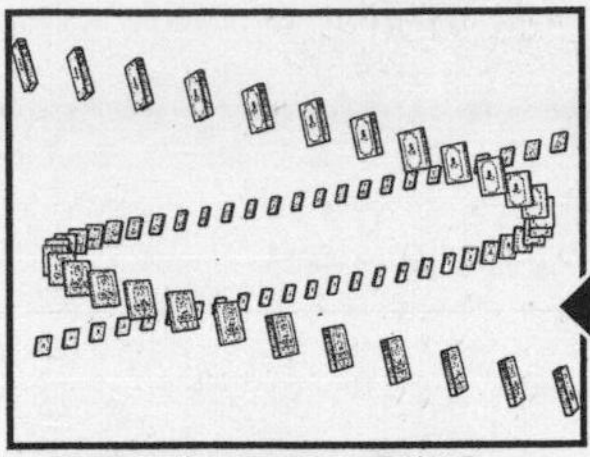

...WE GET THIS. FINALLY, WE HAVE ENOUGH BOOKS. NOW, BY COMBINING THIS WITH THE PREVIOUS SPIRALS WE CREATED...

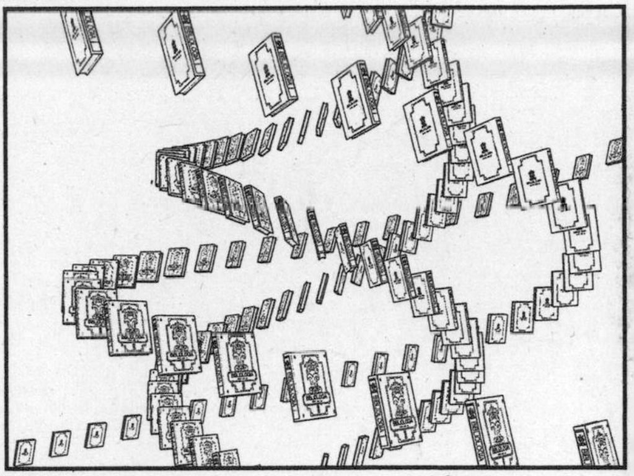

...WE HAVE QUITE AN IMPRESSIVE COLLECTION OF VOLUMES. (^^;) AS MANY AS THERE ARE, IT STILL HAS A NICE SENSE OF MOTION, SO IT WORKS. WITH THIS PART DONE, WE'RE ALMOST FINISHED.

IF YOU WERE TO LOOK DOWN AT IT FROM ABOVE, INCIDENTALLY, THIS IS WHAT YOU'D SEE.

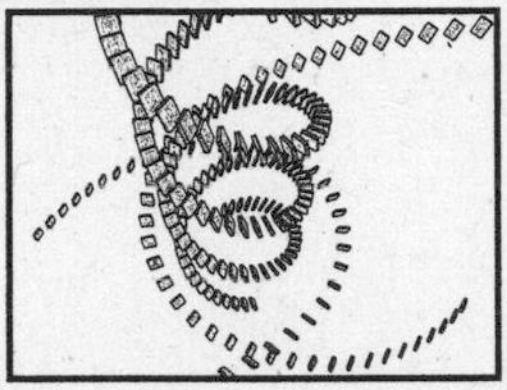

ALL THAT'S LEFT IS TO MERGE THE DRAWING OF KŪ:NEL WITH THE BACKGROUND IMAGES ON THE PC, AND THE PANEL IS COMPLETE. THE FIRST ILLUSTRATION ON THE PREVIOUS PAGE IS THE MERGED ARTWORK. BY ADDING TONE AND FINISHING THE DETAILS, WE HAVE THE COMPLETED PANEL, BELOW.

+

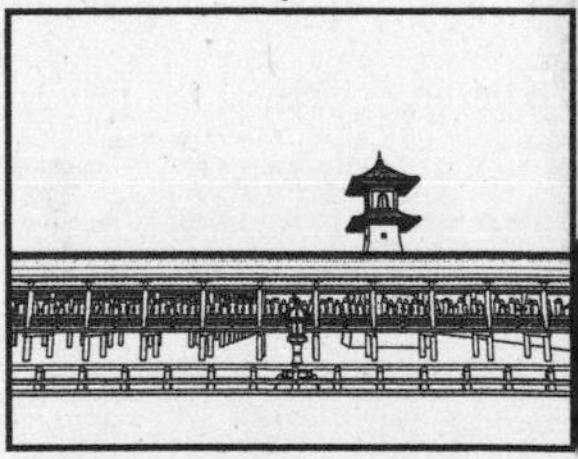

SEPARATELY CREATED BACKGROUND

+

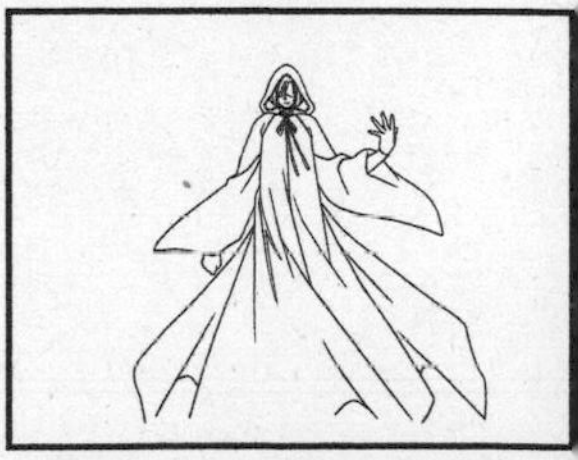

SCANNED LINE-DRAWING OF KŪ:NEL

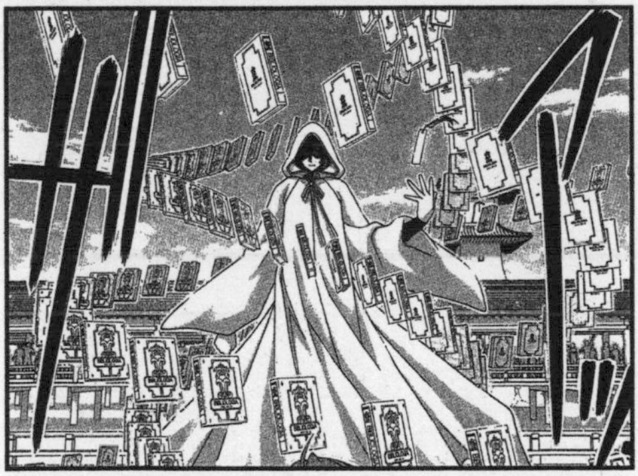

TO DO IT IN 3-D, THE CREATION OF THE PANEL TOOK SOME WORK, BUT THAT'S NOTHING COMPARED TO HOW MUCH WORK IT WOULD BE IF WE HAD TO DO THE PANEL BY HAND EVERY TIME IT SHOWED UP IN THE STORY. IN ONE SENSE, WITHOUT 3-D ARTWORK, KŪ:NEL'S ARTIFACT WOULDN'T EVEN BE POSSIBLE.

BONUS 3-D BACKGROUNDS CORNER

THERE WEREN'T TOO MANY 3-D BACKGROUNDS THAT REALLY STOOD OUT IN THE VOLUME,
BUT THERE WERE A FEW SECTIONS WHERE 3-D TECHNOLOGY WAS USED. LET'S GO OVER SOME OF
THE OTHER PLACES IT WAS IMPLEMENTED.

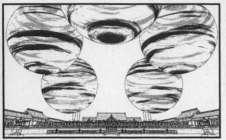

KŪ:NEL'S GRAVITATIONAL MAGIC
SCENE NAME: GRAVITY BALL
POLYGON COUNT: 14,400 X 5

THE GRAVITATIONAL MAGIC KŪ:NEL USED IN THE
MATCH AGAINST KAEDE WAS ONE OF THE TIMES IN
THE SERIES MAGICAL EFFECTS WERE DONE IN 3-D.
WE CREATED A 3-D SPHERE, ADDED A TEXTURE
OF CLOUD-LIKE LINES TO CREATE THE EFFECT
AND, AFTERWARD, USED PHOTOSHOP TO PUT IN
ADDITIONAL EFFECTS SUCH AS TONE AND LINE
REDUCTIONS FOR PRE-PRESS. IT TOOK SOME
WORK, GETTING IT ALL TO LOOK RIGHT.

VERTICAL SEWER SHAFT
SCENE NAME: SEWER BLOW
POLYGON COUNT: 279,198

THE SECTION OF THE SEWER THAT MISORA
RAN INTO, TRYING TO ESCAPE THE ROBOTS. IT
DIDN'T SHOW UP MUCH IN THE ACTUAL COMIC,
BUT THIS IS HOW THE ENTIRE SHAFT LOOKS. THEN
AGAIN, THIS IS THE KIND OF THING THAT WOULD
HAVE REQUIRED LOTS OF HAND-DRAWN DETAIL;
MOSTLY, IT WAS USED AS A REFERENCE FOR THE
COMIC PAGES.

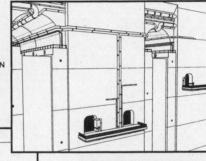

SEWER BOTTOM BRIDGE
SCENE NAME: SEWER BRIDGE
POLYGON COUNT: 197,295

BRIDGE AT THE BOTTOM OF THE VERTICAL SEWER
SHAFT. THE DESIGN IS INTERESTING IN THAT IT
SORT OF LOOKS LIKE AN ANCIENT RUIN, BUT AT
THE SAME TIME, IT HAS A FUTURISTIC FEEL TO IT.
AS YOU CAN TELL BY COMPARING IT TO THE ONE
USED IN THE COMIC, ONLY THE BRIDGE AND WALLS
ARE 3-D. THE TREES, THE DOOR, AND THE BENT
HANDRAIL WERE ALL DRAWN BY HAND. THIS IS A
GOOD EXAMPLE OF CASUALLY MERGING 2-D AND
3-D ARTWORK.

UNDERGROUND HANGAR
SCENE NAME: HANGAR
POLYGON COUNT: 15,665

HERE, THE CEILING AND THE STAIRS ARE 3-D...
BECAUSE IT'S A PAIN TO HAVE TO DRAW AN
ARCHED CEILING BY HAND. (^_^;) BY THE WAY, THE
TANAKA-SAN WAS HAND-DRAWN EXACTLY ONCE,
AND THEN JUST COPIED MANY TIMES AND LINED UP.

魔法先生ネギま! MAGISTER NEGI MAGI

赤松健 SHONEN MAGAZINE COMICS KEN AKAMATSU

13

THE GREAT MAHORA FESTIVAL OF DECEMBER 10, 2005 WAS AMAZING~~! BIG THANKS TO ALL THE VOICE ACTORS PORTRAYING THE CLASSMATES FOR ALL THEIR HARD WORK—I'M REALLY LOOKING FORWARD TO THE DVD RELEASE!

2005/12/10の大麻帆良祭、すごかった〜〜っ
クラスメート声優の皆様、おつかれさまでした!
早くDVDほしいぜ!

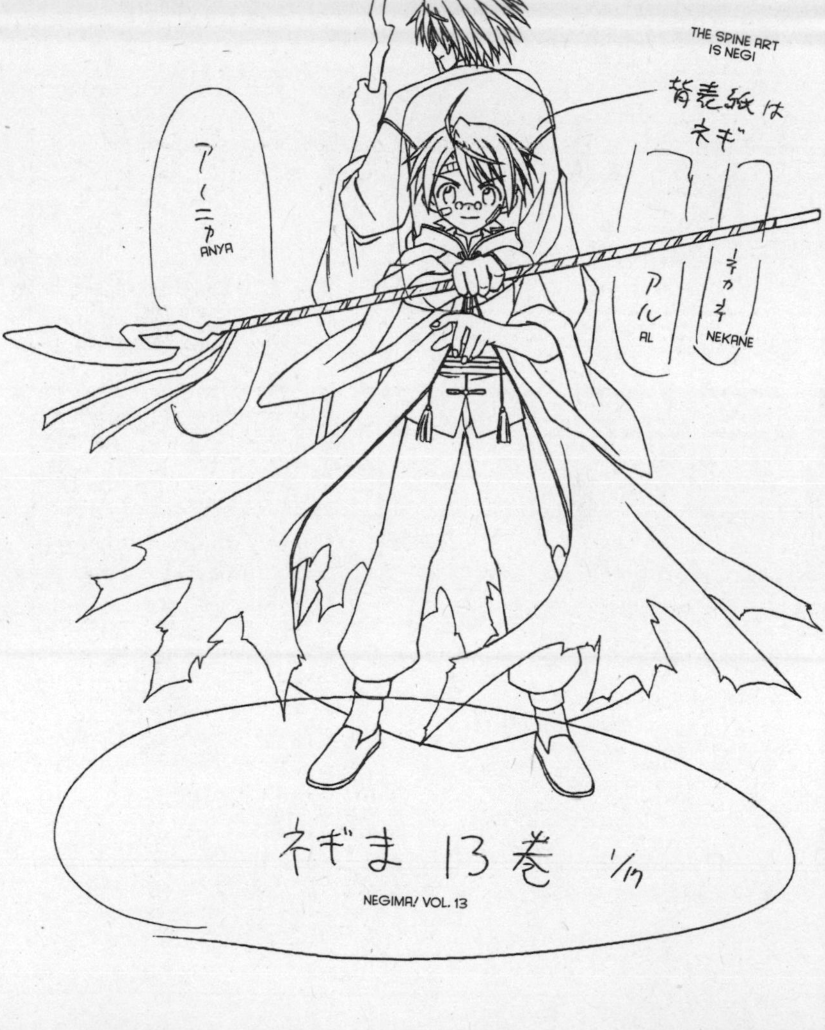
THE SPINE ART IS NEGI
背表紙はネギ
アーニャ
ANYA
アル
AL
ネカネ
NEKANE
ネギま 13巻 1/17
NEGIMA! VOL. 13

キャラ解説

CHARACTER
PROFILE

⑨ 春日美空

⑨ KASUGA, MISORA

いよいよ その本性をあらわした

MISORA'S SHOWN HER TRUE COLORS

美空です。(笑)

AT LAST (HEH).

アーティファクトは、陸上部らしく

IN KEEPING WITH HER "TRACK" BACKGROUND, HER ARTIFACT

速く走れるスニーカー。

IS A PAIR OF SNEAKERS WHICH ALLOW HER

相棒のココネと共に、

TO RUN VERY, VERY FAST. HER PAL KOKONE

一体どんな活躍を

IS NEVER VERY FAR FROM HER SIDE. WHAT

見せてくれるので

SORTS OF THINGS SHOULD WE BE

しょうか?!

EXPECTING FROM MISORA IN THE FUTURE...?!

(もう、しばらく出ない。

(SO MEAL TICKETS SAYS SHE WON'T BE

食券50枚)

SHOWING UP AGAIN FOR A WHILE).

声優は板東愛さん。

HER VOICE ACTOR IN THE ANIME IS BANDŌ AI-SAN.

アニメでも マンガでも 全然

I'M SO SORRY YOU NEVER HAD MUCH OF A ROLE IN THE

出番が無くて ゴメン!!(^^;)

ANIME OR THE MANGA!! (^^;)

あとゲーム版と 全然 性格 違っちゃって

WHILE I'M AT IT, I ALSO APOLOGIZE FOR THE FACT THAT MISORA'S

申し訳ない! 混乱したでしょ(笑)

PERSONALITY IS SO DIFFERENT FROM THE VIDEO-GAME VERSION... I HOPE YOU WEREN'T

CONFUSED TOO MUCH (HEH).

赤松

(AKAMATSU)

MAGISTER NEGI MAGI

LIBRARY EXPLORATION CLUB

EXPEDITION EVENT

magister negi magi

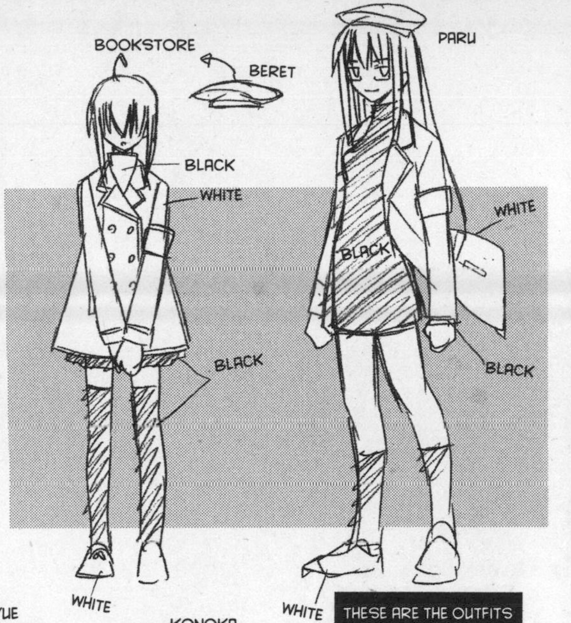

BOOKSTORE
BERET
BLACK
WHITE
BLACK
WHITE
PARU
WHITE
BLACK
BLACK
WHITE

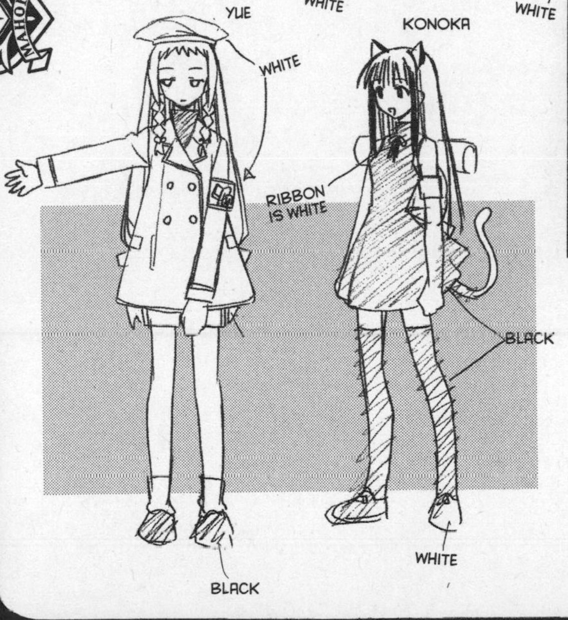

YUE
WHITE
BLACK
KONOKA
RIBBON IS WHITE
BLACK
WHITE

THESE ARE THE OUTFITS FOR THE LIBRARY EXPLORATION CLUB'S EVENT. THE SHIRTS ARE BLACK SLEEVELESS TURTLENECKS DEPENDING ON THE PERSON; THERE IS A BLAZER ON TOP. THE FINAL TOUCH IS THE ARMBAND. IF YOU LOOK CAREFULLY, THE OTHER MEMBERS OF THE CLUB ARE WEARING THE SAME OUTFIT.

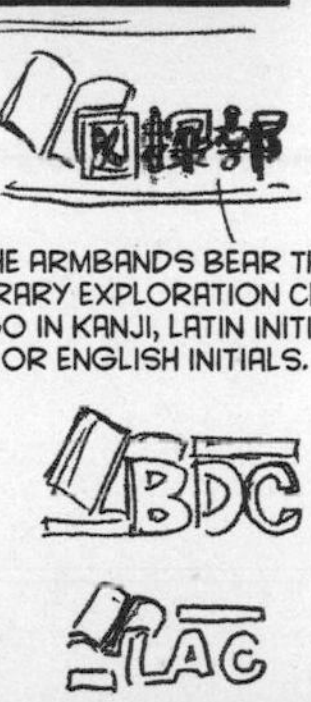

BDC
LAC

THE ARMBANDS BEAR THE LIBRARY EXPLORATION CLUB LOGO IN KANJI, LATIN INITIALS, OR ENGLISH INITIALS.

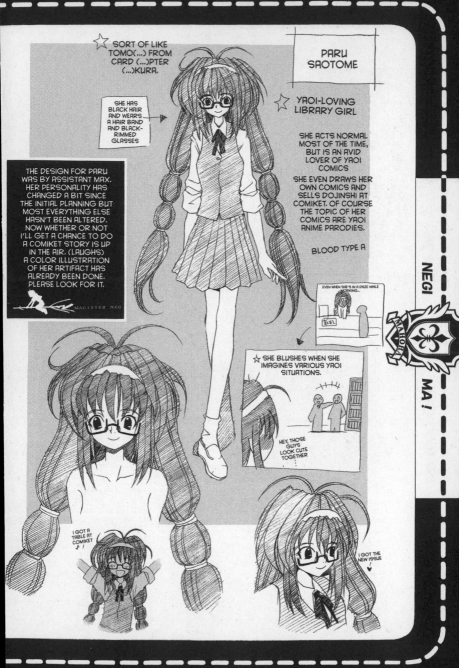

☆ SORT OF LIKE TOMOC(...) FROM CARD (...)PTER (...)KURA.

PARU SAOTOME

☆ YAOI-LOVING LIBRARY GIRL

SHE HAS BLACK HAIR AND WEARS A HAIR BAND AND BLACK-RIMMED GLASSES

SHE ACTS NORMAL MOST OF THE TIME, BUT IS AN AVID LOVER OF YAOI COMICS

SHE EVEN DRAWS HER OWN COMICS AND SELLS DOJINSHI AT COMIKET. OF COURSE THE TOPIC OF HER COMICS ARE YAOI ANIME PARODIES.

BLOOD TYPE A

THE DESIGN FOR PARU WAS BY ASSISTANT MAX. HER PERSONALITY HAS CHANGED A BIT SINCE THE INITIAL PLANNING BUT MOST EVERYTHING ELSE HASN'T BEEN ALTERED. NOW WHETHER OR NOT I'LL GET A CHANCE TO DO A COMIKET STORY IS UP IN THE AIR. (LAUGHS) A COLOR ILLUSTRATION OF HER ARTIFACT HAS ALREADY BEEN DONE. PLEASE LOOK FOR IT.

MAGISTER NEG

EVEN WHEN SHE'S IN A DAZE WHILE WORKING...

☆ SHE BLUSHES WHEN SHE IMAGINES VARIOUS YAOI SITUATIONS.

HEY, THOSE GUYS LOOK CUTE TOGETHER

I GOT A TABLE AT COMIKET ♪!

I GOT THE NEW ISSUE ♥

NEGI MA!

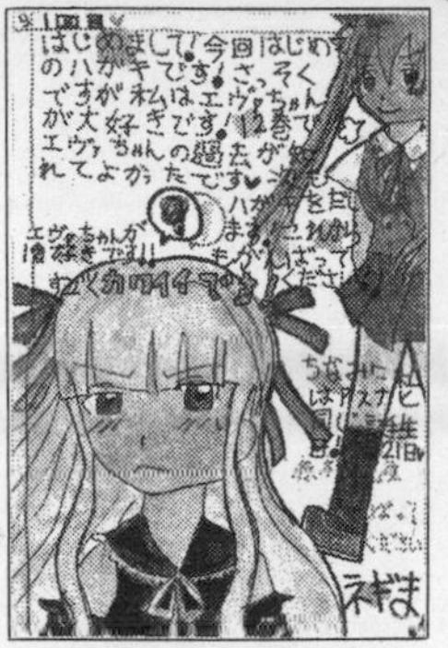
はじめまして!今回はじめてのハガキです!さっそくですが私はエヴァちゃんが大好きです!
ネギま

▲ IS EVA TROUBLED BY SOMETHING HERE? (^^)

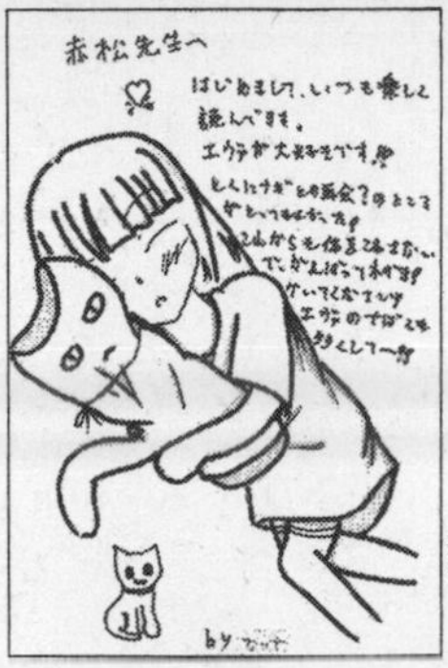
赤松先生へ
はじめまして、いつも楽しく読んでます。
エヴァが大好きです!!

▲ EVA LOOKS VERY CUTE HERE ☆

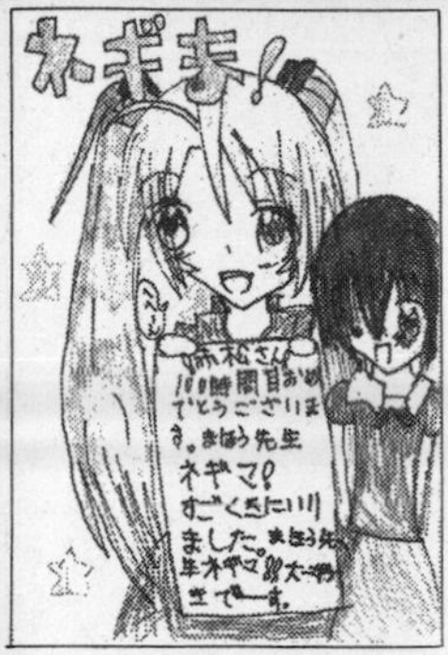
ネギま!
赤松さん100時間目おめでとうございます。

▲ THANK YOU FOR ALL YOUR SUPPORT! (^^)

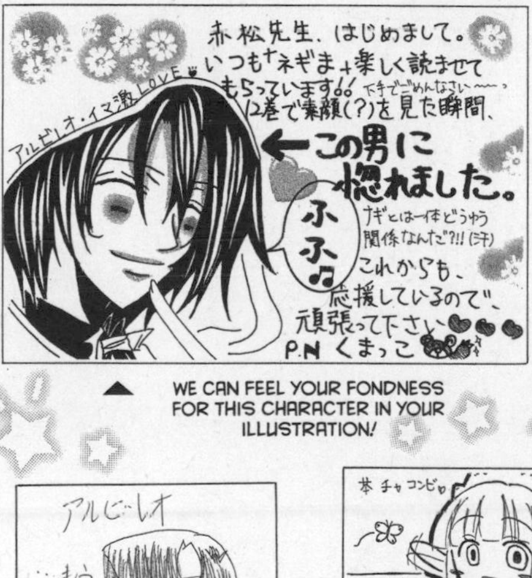
赤松先生、はじめまして。
いつも「ネギま」楽しく読ませてもらっています!! 下手でごめんなさい〜。
12巻で素顔(?)を見た瞬間、
アルビレオ・イマ激LOVE
←この男に惚れました。
ふふ♪
ナギとは一体どうゆう関係なんだ?!!(汗)
これからも、応援しているので、頑張って下さい
P.N くまっこ

▲ WE CAN FEEL YOUR FONDNESS FOR THIS CHARACTER IN YOUR ILLUSTRATION!

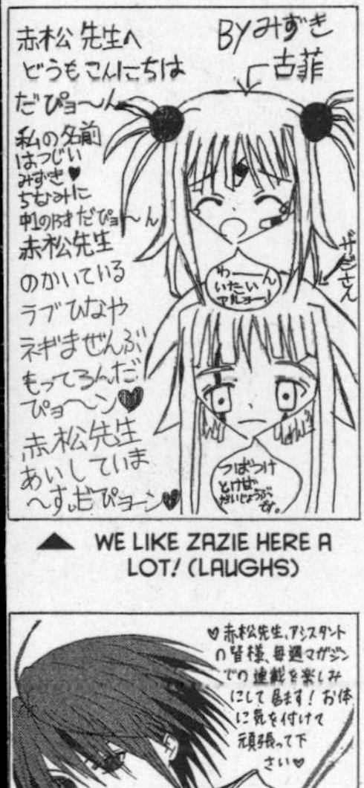
赤松先生へ
どうもこんにちはだぴョ〜ん
BYみずき
古菲
赤松先生あいしていま〜すだぴョーン

▲ WE LIKE ZAZIE HERE A LOT! (LAUGHS)

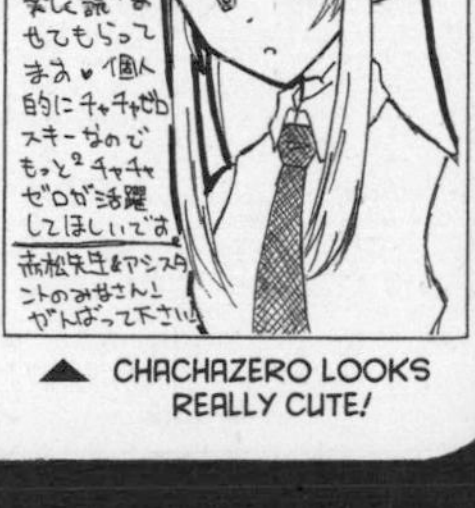
赤松先生
こんにちは!! いつも「ネギま!」楽しく読ませてもらってます♡
赤松先生&アシスタントのみなさん!がんばって下さい!!

▲ CHACHAZERO LOOKS REALLY CUTE!

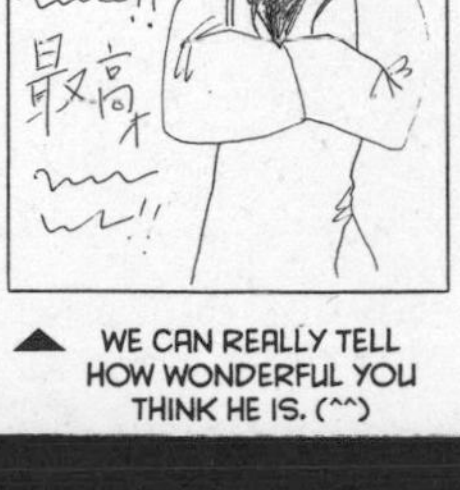
アルビレオ
…もう最高ですぅ〜
最高ォ

▲ WE CAN REALLY TELL HOW WONDERFUL YOU THINK HE IS. (^^)

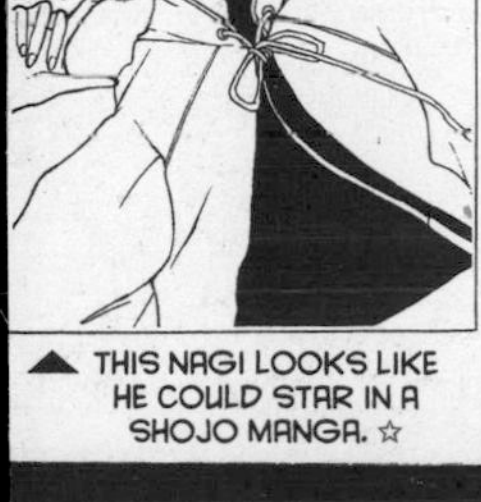
赤松先生、アシスタントの皆様、毎週マガジンでの連載を楽しみにして居ます! お体に気を付けて頑張って下さい♡
NAGI

▲ THIS NAGI LOOKS LIKE HE COULD STAR IN A SHOJO MANGA. ☆

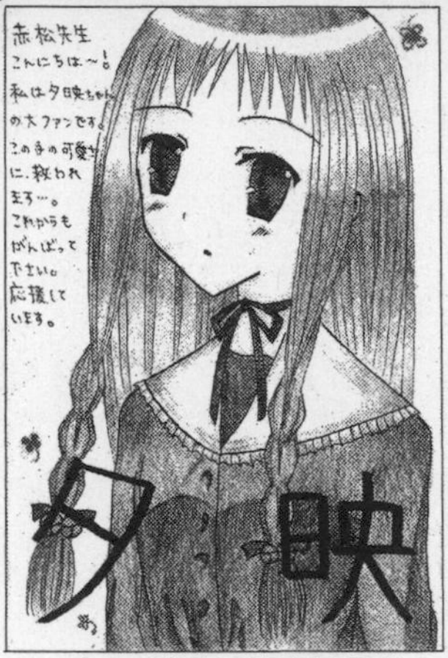
夕映

▲ THIS IS A VERY PRETTY PICTURE OF YUE! ☆

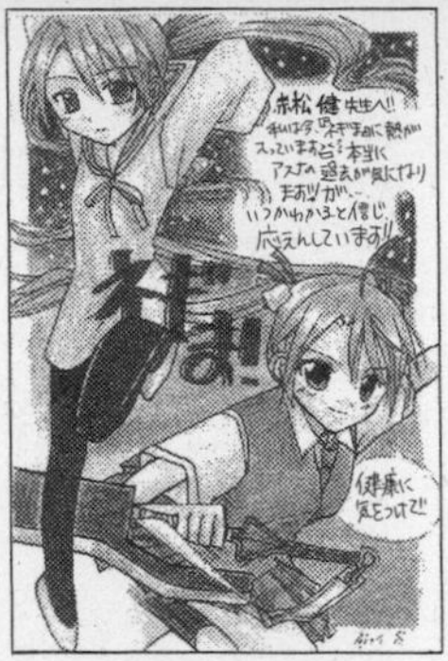

▲ HER PAST MAKES YOU WONDER, DOESN'T IT?

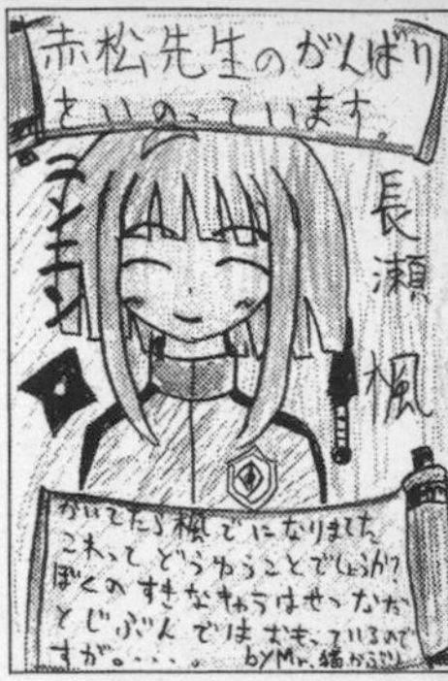
赤松先生のがんばりをいのっています。
長瀬楓

▲ NIN NIN ♪

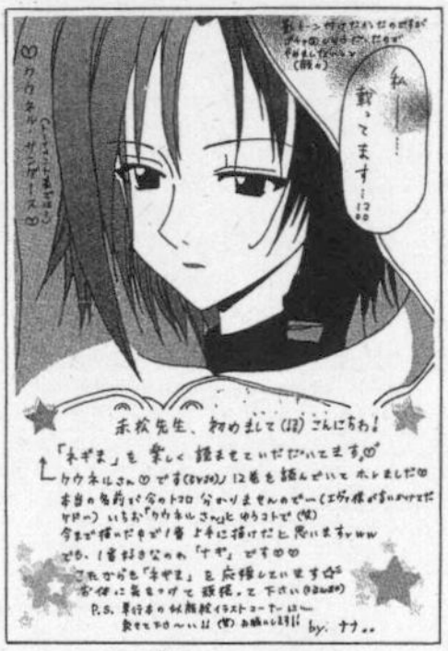

▲ KŪ:NEL IS SURE GETTING POPULAR THESE DAYS! (^^)

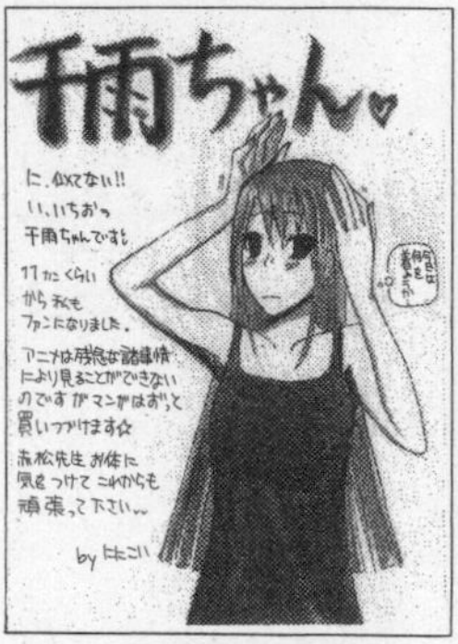
千雨ちゃん♡

▲ WE LIKE THIS UPDATED LOOK OF CHISAME HERE.

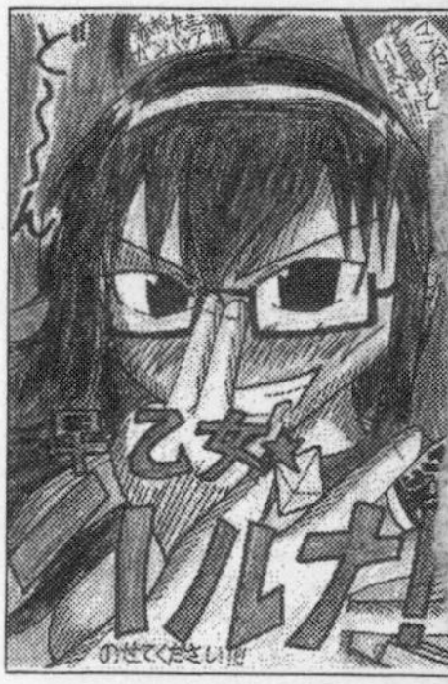

▲ WE LIKE THE INTENSITY OF HARUNA IN THIS PICTURE!

MAGISTER NE

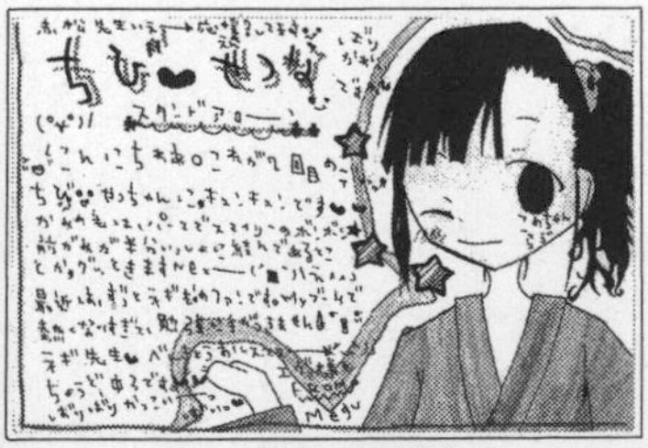

▲ CHIBI-SETSUNA IS A GOOD THING! (LAUGHS)

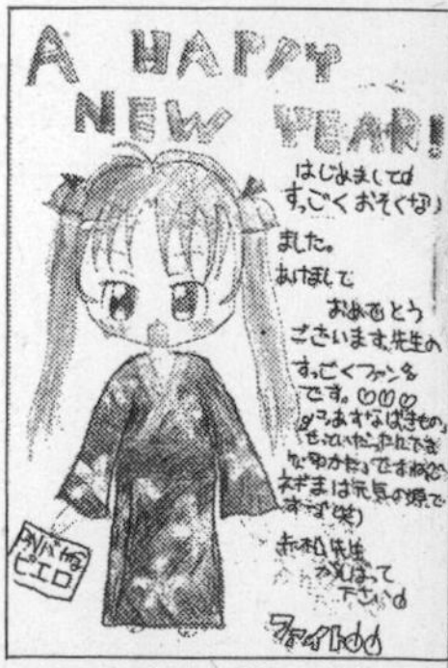
A HAPPY NEW YEAR!

▲ WE THINK THAT YUKATA LOOKS VERY CUTE! (^^)

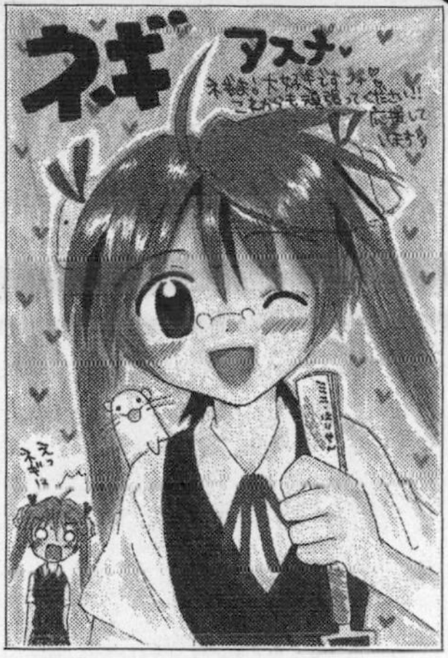
ネギ
アスナ

A CUTE NEGI-SENSEI? (LAUGHS)

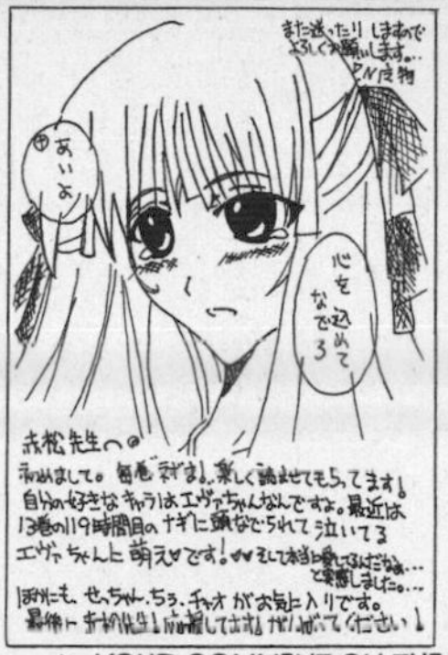
心を込めてなでろ

▲ YOUR COMMENT ON THE CHARACTERS MAKES US HAPPY.

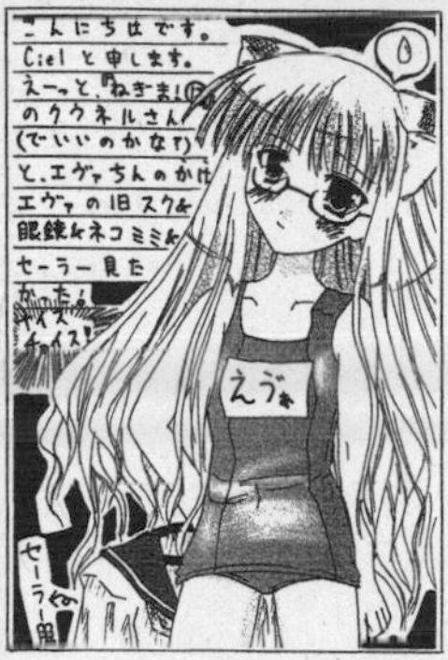

▲ THANKS FOR THE CAT-EARED ASUNA.

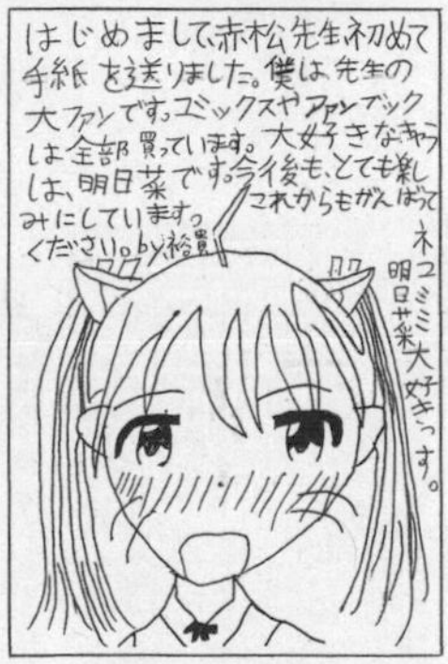
はじめまして赤松先生初めて手紙を送りました。僕は先生のファンです。コミックスやファンブックは全部買っています。大好きなキャラは、明日菜です。今後もとても楽しみにしています。これからもがんばってください。

A CUTE NEGI-SENSEI!? (LAUGHS)

NEGIMA!
FAN ART CORNER

THANKS TO ALL OF YOU, FOR ALL THE FANTASTIC ILLUSTRATIONS YOU'VE BEEN SENDING IN! (^^) TRUTHFULLY, WE WISH WE COULD SHOW YOU EVERYTHING WE RECEIVED!

LOOKING AT THE RECENT SUBMISSIONS, THERE'S BEEN A RISE IN THE NUMBER OF KU:NEL ILLUSTRATIONS. (^O^) SO LET'S SEE WHAT WE HAVE TO PRESENT THIS TIME AROUND! ALSO, WHEN SENDING SUBMISSIONS IN, REMEMBER TO NOT MAKE THEM TOO BIG SO THAT THE ARTWORK WON'T SUFFER WHEN WE SHRINK THEM DOWN FOR THIS SECTION. ABOUT A SIZE OF A POST CARD WOULD BE THE BEST. YOU CAN SEND YOUR ILLUSTRATIONS TO THE EDITORIAL OFFICES OF "KODANSHA COMICS."

– ASS'T MAX

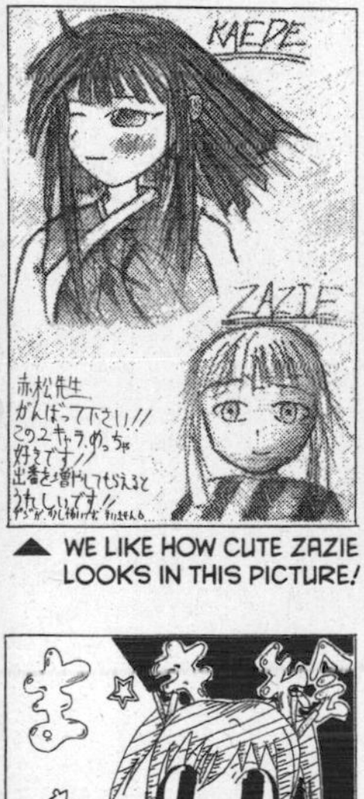
KAEDE
ZAZIE

▲ WE LIKE HOW CUTE ZAZIE LOOKS IN THIS PICTURE!

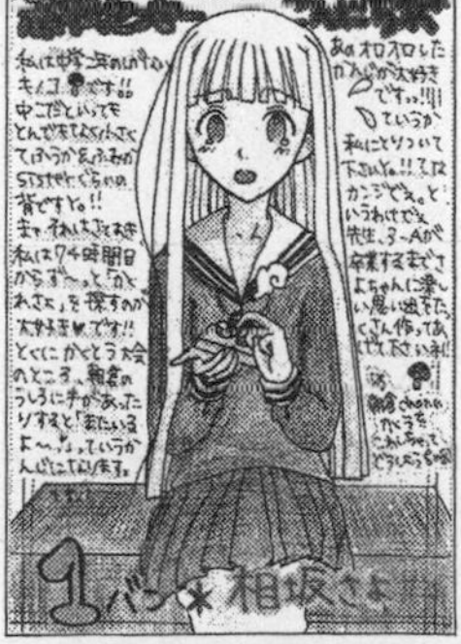
1バン★相坂さよ

▲ PLAYING HIDE AND GO SEEK WITH SAYO SOUNDS LIKE FUN! (^^)

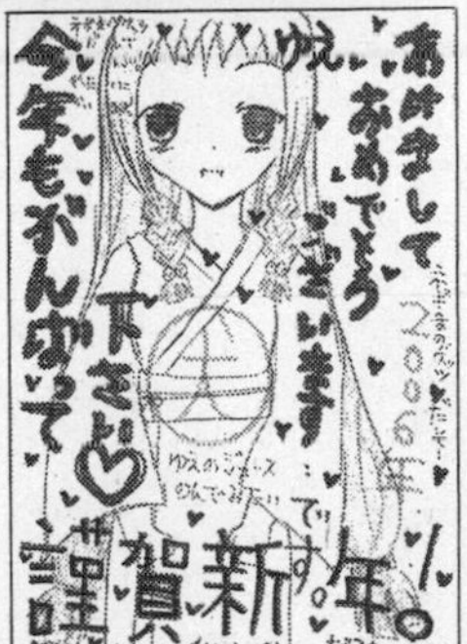
あけましておめでとうございます
今年もがんばって下さい♡
2006年
謹賀新年。

▲ THANK YOU FOR THIS NICE NEW YEAR'S GREETING! ☆

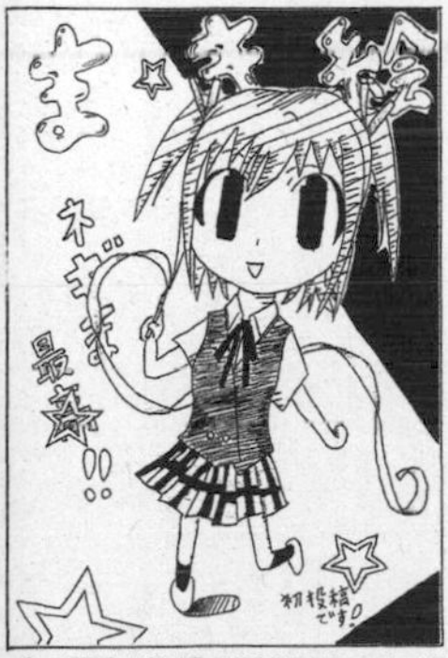

▲ ARE MAKIE PICTURES ON THE DECLINE LATELY?

NEGIMA!

PRELIMINARY DESIGN COLLECTION

CHARACTER CONCEPT SKETCHES

AKO IZUMI
HAIR IS SHORT AND PRECISE. KINDA LIKE ← THIS.
BUT WITH SO MANY CHARACTERS WE MAY NEED TO ↗ CHANGE SOME ASPECTS TO DIFFERENTIATE FROM THE OTHERS.
SHE IS THE CLASS LIAISON FOR THE NURSE'S OFFICE. HER FUTURE ASPIRATION IS TO BECOME A NURSE. ALTHOUGH, WHEN SHE SEES THE SIGHT OF BLOOD, SHE HAS A TENDENCY TO FAINT.

MAGISTER NEGI MAGI

ASSISTANT MINORU DID THE DESIGN OF AKO. SHE IS A CHARACTER WITH A FEW MORE SECRETS YET TO BE REVEALED. (PROBABLY...)

NOW IN VOL. 15, THE CLASSMATES ARE GOING TO GET INTO SOME ACTION! PLEASE LOOK FORWARD TO IT!

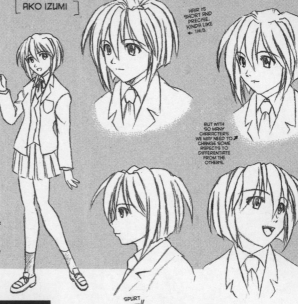

HUH? WHERE
OH, YOU'RE AWAKE.
AAH! I CUT MYSELF
SPURT
K-KURA

SENSEI, DID YOU HURT YOURSELF? CAN I DISINFECT THAT FOR YOU?
NO, I'M FINE. AND BESIDES, I'M YOUR TEACHER SO

NURSE'S ASSISTANT GIRL

NAME: AYU IZUMI
PERSONALITY: WORRYWART, EASY GOING, SERIOUS
AFFILIATIONS: NURSE'S OFFICE AIDE

SHE'S IN CHARGE OF TAKING CARE OF PEOPLE WHO NEED TO GO TO THE NURSE'S OFFICE. SINCE THERE ISN'T A MALE STUDENT WHO HAS THE SAME DUTY, SHE MAY HAVE A SITUATION WHEN SHE HAS TO TAKE CARE OF THE MAIN CHARACTER. SHE TENDS TO WORRY A LOT AND IN CASES SHE MAY GO OUT OF HER WAY TO TAKE CARE OF SOMEONE IN NEED. ALTHOUGH IF SHE WERE TO SEE A SERIOUS INJURY, SHE HAS A TENDENCY TO FAINT WHICH MAKES YOU WONDER IF SHE'S REALLY SUITED FOR THIS DUTY.

SHE HAD SOME SORT OF MAJOR ACCIDENT IN ELEMENTARY SCHOOL, WHICH LEFT HER WITH A LARGE SCAR ON HER CHEST. TOUCHED BY THE TENDERNESS OF THE NURSE WHO TOOK CARE OF HER, SHE DECIDED TO BECOME A NURSE IN THE FUTURE.

PERHAPS SHE SHOULD HAVE SOME KIND OF LINK TO THE SECRET OF THE ACADEMY?

I'M NOT SURE IF A GIRL WITH A SCAR CAN REALLY BE CUTE OR NOT... SHOULD THE SCAR BE DRAWN AS A LINE OR JUST AS A GRADATION?

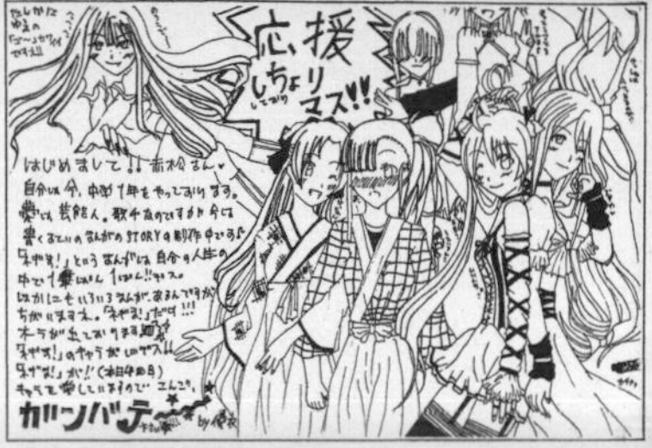
応援しちょりマス!!

THANK YOUR FOR YOUR SUPPORT!

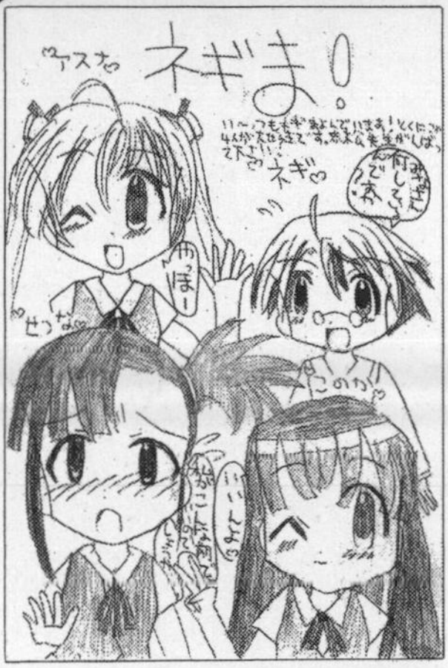
アスナ
ネギま!
ネギ
せつな
このか

WE LOVE THE TROUBLED EXPRESSION ON SETSUNA.

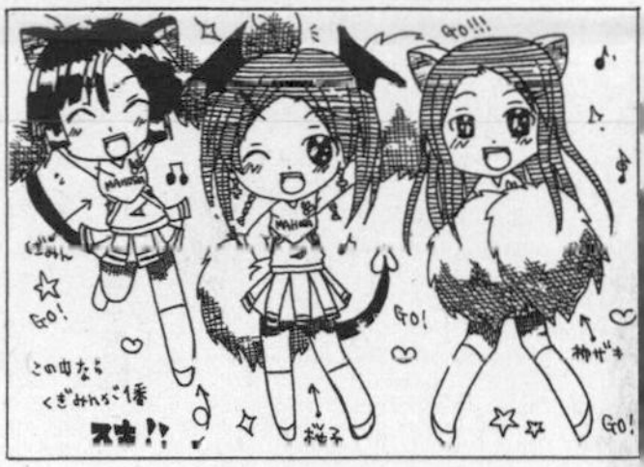
GO!!!
GO!
桜子

THE TAIL ON SAKURAKO IS REALLY CUTE! (LAUGHS)

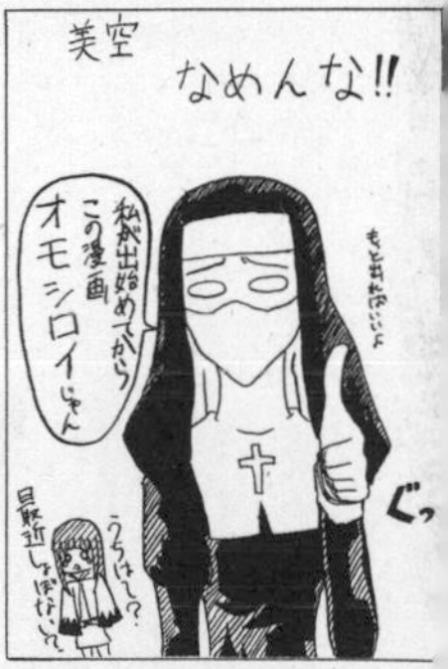
美空
なめんな!!
私が出始めてから この漫画 オモシロイじゃん

I HOPE MISORA MAKES MORE APPEARANCES FOR YOU.

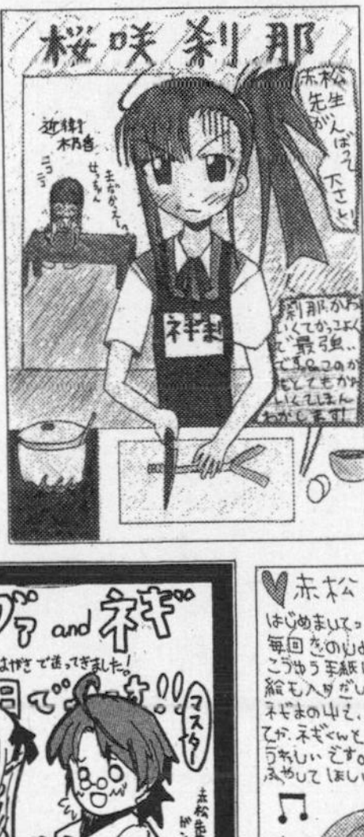
桜咲刹那
赤松先生がんばって下さい
ネギま

SEEING SETSUNA COOKING IS A GOOD THING.

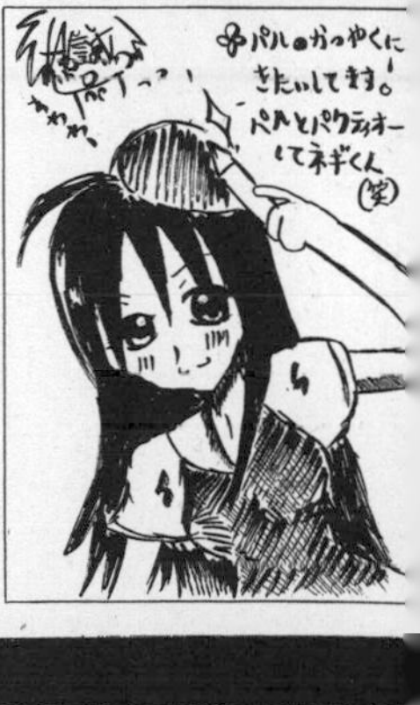
パルのかつやくにきたいしてます。

NOW DID HARUNA MAKE A CONTRACT OR NOT? (LAUGHS)

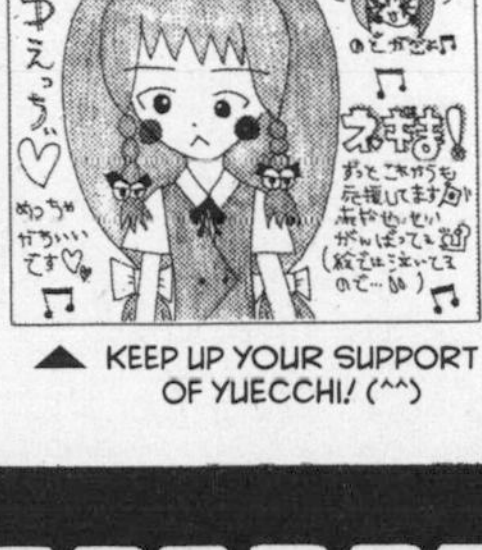
赤松健せんせい
ネギま!

KEEP UP YOUR SUPPORT OF YUECCHI! (^^)

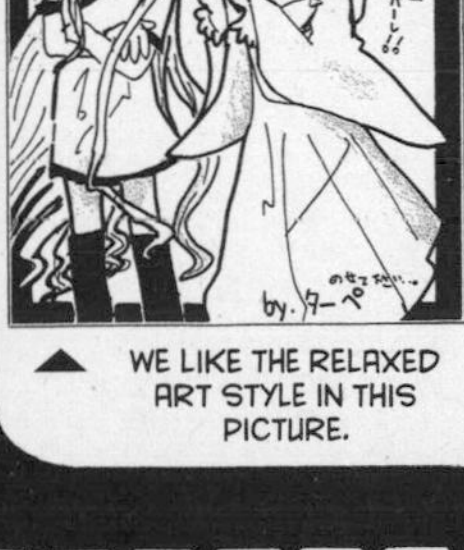
エヴァ and ネギ

WE LIKE THE RELAXED ART STYLE IN THIS PICTURE.

3-D BACKGROUNDS EXPLANATION CORNER

YES, ONCE AGAIN IT'S THE 3-D BACKGROUND EXPLANATIONS YOU'VE COME TO
LOVE AND EXPECT! AND IN THIS VOLUME, THE NUMBER OF 3-D BACKGROUNDS HAS
REALLY INCREASED! LET'S TAKE A LOOK AT SOME OF THEM.

~ PARKS SECTION ~

● JAPANESE GARDEN
SCENE NAME: J-GARDEN
POLYGON COUNT: 97,204

THIS IS THE JAPANESE-STYLE
GARDEN USED FOR THE TEA
CEREMONY CLUB'S *NODATE*.
MAHORA ACADEMY SURE HAS A
LOT OF NICE PLACES, DOESN'T IT?
(LAUGHS)
BY THE WAY, THE ONLY NEW THING
WE CREATED FOR THIS SCENE WAS
THE BRIDGE AND THE TEA ROOM
AND THE REST WE ADAPTED FROM
ALREADY EXISTING 3-D ITEMS.
I GUESS BEING ABLE TO
REUSE ITEMS IS ANOTHER
BENEFIT OF WORKING WITH 3-D
BACKGROUNDS.
UNUSUALLY, EVEN THE TREES WERE
CREATED AS 3-D ITEMS.

**● BRIDGE AND
TEA HOUSE**

● TEA ROOM
SCENE NAME: TEA ROOM
POLYGON COUNT: 8,459

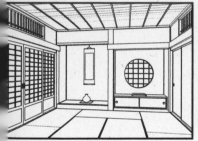

THE EXTERIOR WAS HAND-DRAWN BUT THE INTERIOR
IS MADE UP COMPLETELY OF 3-D ITEMS. THIS TEA ROOM
IS DIFFERENT FROM THE ONE THE TEA CEREMONY CLUB
NORMALLY USES.
BY THE WAY, IF YOU RECOGNIZED THIS ROOM FROM
BEFORE, YOU ARE REALLY SHARP! THIS WAS ADAPTED FROM
THE "TEMPORARY DRESSING ROOM" FROM VOL. 12. IT MIGHT
BE FUN TO SEE IF YOU CAN SPOT ALL THE CHANGES WE MADE.
(LAUGHS)

● FOUNTAIN PARK
SCENE NAME: FOUNTAIN PARK
POLYGON COUNT: 29,927

THIS IS THE PARK WITH
THE FOUNTAIN WHERE AKO
FAINTED.
IT'S LOCATED ATOP A HILL
AND SAID TO BE A BEAUTIFUL
PLACE TO WATCH THE
NIGHTSCAPE.
THE TREES IN THIS PARK
WERE HAND-DRAWN SO
WITHOUT THEM, IT LOOKS
KIND OF LONELY. (^^;)

THIS IS THE CLOCK IN
THE PARK. ON A SIDE
NOTE, THE HANDS OF
THE CLOCK CAN BE
MOVED FREELY.

~ AMUSEMENT SECTION ~

• MAHORA GREAT FERRIS WHEEL

SCENE NAME: FERRIS WHEEL

POLYGON COUNT: 281,162

THIS IS THE GREAT FERRIS WHEEL THAT STANDS 90 M TALL. IT'S AMAZING TO THINK THAT THIS STRUCTURE WAS BUILT JUST FOR THE MAHORA FESTIVAL! (LAUGHS)

BY THE WAY, THE "MAHORA FESTIVAL" ON THE WHEEL ROTATES SO IF YOU LOOK AT THE COMIC CAREFULLY, YOU'LL SEE IT IN DIFFERENT POSITIONS. (LAUGHS)

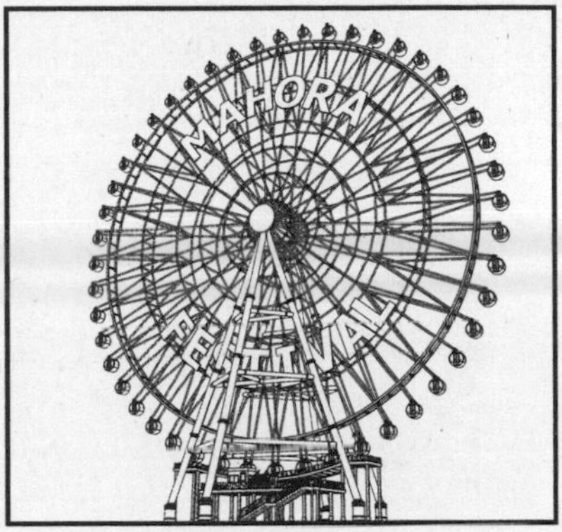
MAHORA
FESTIVAL

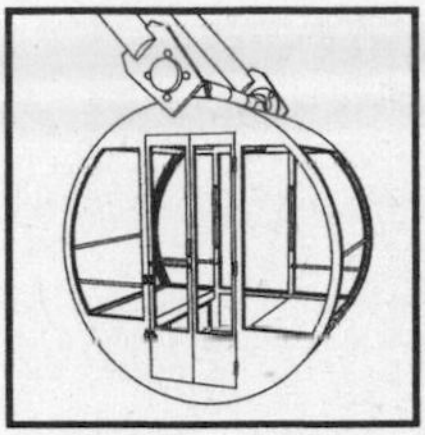

• GONDOLA

WE EVEN CREATED THE INTERIORS OF THE GONDOLA AS WELL.

• CONCERT STAGE

SCENE NAME: CONCERT STAGE

POLYGON COUNT: 3,007,607

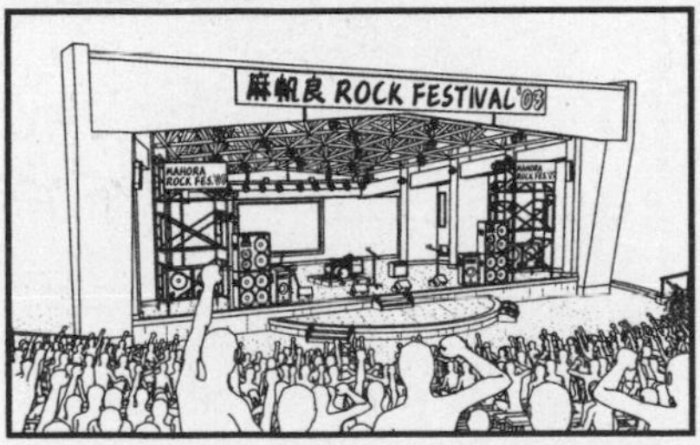
麻帆良 ROCK FESTIVAL'03

THIS STAGE FIRST MADE AN APPEARANCE IN VOL. 8. WE'D PLANNED TO USE IT FOR THE FESTIVAL WHEN WE CREATED IT, BUT WE'RE HAPPY TO FINALLY BE ABLE TO USE IT IN THIS VOLUME. (LAUGHS)

SO, IN ORDER TO MAKE TO MORE LIKE A CONCERT STAGE, WE ADDED A FEW MORE ELEMENTS. THE HARDEST TO CREATE WAS THIS DRUM SET. YOU CAN'T REALLY SEE IT VERY WELL IN THE COMIC, BUT WE SPENT A LOT OF TIME CREATING IT. (^^;)

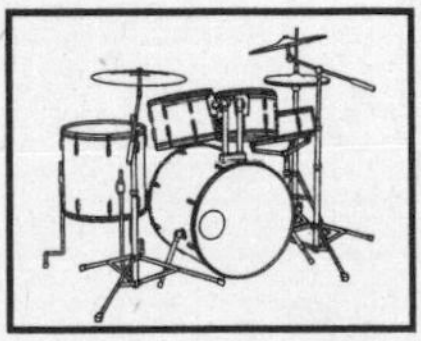

• EVENT STAGE

SCENE NAME: SMALL STAGE

POLYGON COUNT:462,377

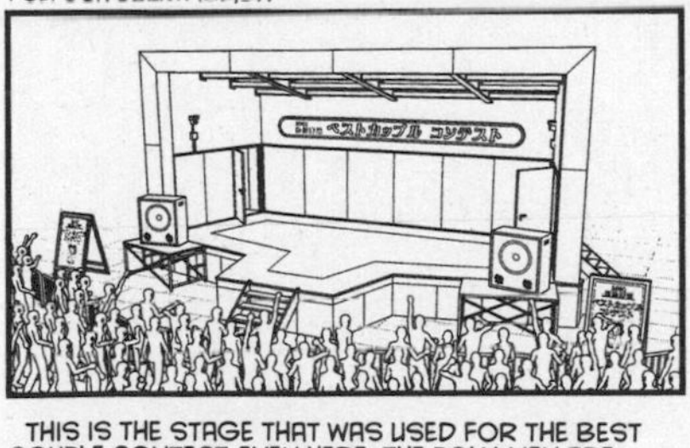

THIS IS THE STAGE THAT WAS USED FOR THE BEST COUPLE CONTEST. EVEN HERE, THE POLY-MEN ARE OUT IN FULL FORCE. (LAUGHS)

• CONCERT DRESSING ROOM

SCENE NAME: DRESSING ROOM

POLYGON COUNT: 8,962

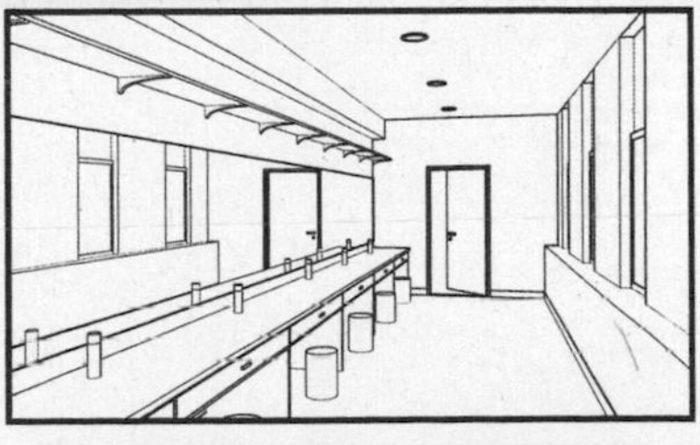

THIS IS THE DRESSING ROOM WHERE AKO WAS CHANGING. WE HAD A HARD TIME GETTING HER REFLECTION IN THE MIRROR TO LOOK RIGHT. (^_^;)

~ LIBRARY SECTION ~

• EXPEDITION DEPARTURE HALL
SCENE NAME: CHAPEL
POLYGON COUNT: 554,812

THIS IS WHERE THE PEOPLE GATHERED TO LEAVE ON THE EXPEDITION TOUR OF THE LIBRARY. IN A PREVIOUS VOLUME, IT WAS USED FOR THE COSPLAY CONTEST. THE ROOMS ON THE SECOND LEVEL WERE NEWLY CREATED FOR THIS VOLUME.

• GREAT NORTHERN CLIFF
SCENE NAME: BOOKWALL
POLYGON COUNT: 389,202

WHY WOULD SOMETHING LIKE THIS EVEN BE IN HERE? (LAUGHS)

• WORLD TREE MODEL REST AREA
SCENE NAME: LIBRARY REST AREA
POLYGON COUNT: 371,676

IT WAS HARD TO TELL IN THE ACTUAL STORY, BUT THIS ROOM CONTAINS A MINIATURE VERSION OF THE WORLD TREE. THE TREE WAS HAND-DRAWN IN THIS CASE AND MERGED WITH THE 3-D IMAGE.

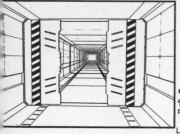

• PASSAGEWAY WITH FIREPROOF DOORS
SCENE NAME: PASSAGE
POLYGON COUNT: 27,094

THIS IS AN AWFULLY MODERN-LOOKING PASSAGEWAY FOR THE LIBRARY. THIS PLACE SURE HAS A LOT OF MYSTERIES ABOUT IT. (LAUGHS)

• BALCONY
SCENE NAME: LIBRARY BALCONY
POLYGON COUNT: 260,397

IT'S REASSURING TO SEE THAT EVEN A STRANGE LIBRARY SUCH AS THIS CAN HAVE A NORMAL-LOOKING AND FABULOUS BALCONY ONCE YOU GET OUTSIDE. (LAUGHS)

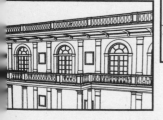

• WATERFALL OBSERVATION DECK
SCENE NAME: LIBRARY FALL
POLYGON COUNT: 266,714

YET ANOTHER LOCATION THAT'S HARD TO EXPLAIN. (LAUGHS) ON A SIDE NOTE, EVEN THE BLURRED EFFECTS OF THE MIST WERE DONE IN 3-D.

~ CITYSCAPE SECTION ~

• STONE BRIDGE WITH GATE

SCENE NAME: STONE BRIDGE

POLYGON COUNT: 1,333,776

THIS IS ONE OF THE GREAT STONE BRIDGES THAT SPANS OVER ONE OF THE RIVERS IN MAHORA CITY. IT DEFINITELY HAS AN AIR OF IMPORTANCE ABOUT IT, DOESN'T IT?

IT SEEMS THAT THIS IS A VERY POPULAR PLACE ON A NORMAL DAY.

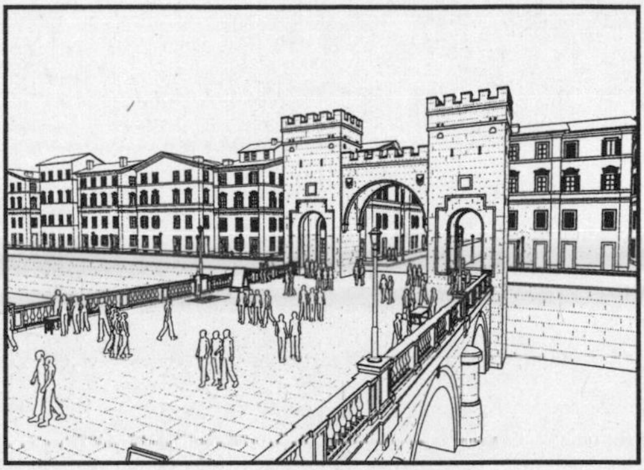

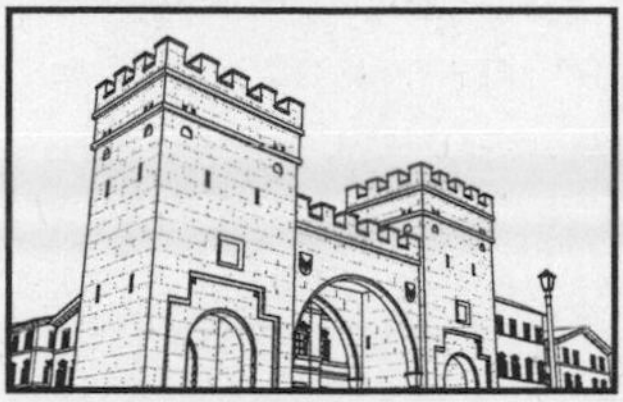

· GATE TOWER

HOW KOTARO AND THE OTHERS GOT UP THERE IS A MYSTERY. (LAUGHS)

• MAHORA'S CAFÉ

SCENE NAME: MAHORA'S CAFÉ POLYGON COUNT: 8,962

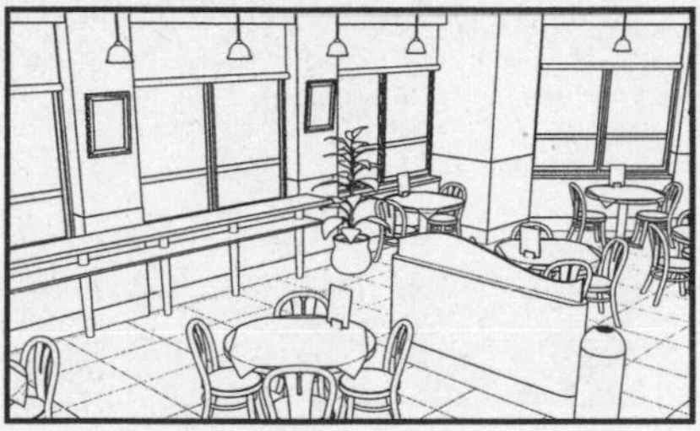

THIS IS THE PLACE WHERE ASUNA AND THE OTHERS WERE MAKING THE BATTLE PLANS (?) FOR HER DATE. THE PLACE LOOKS VERY FASHIONABLE WITH ITS COUNTERS ALONG THE WINDOWS.

WE HAVE TO ADMIT HERE THAT THE CAFE DOESN'T HAVE ANYTHING CREATED ON THE OTHER SIDE OF THE WINDOWS. (^^;)

• LIBRARY OUTDOOR CAFÉ

SCENE NAME: BRIDGE CAFÉ

POLYGON COUNT: 8,962

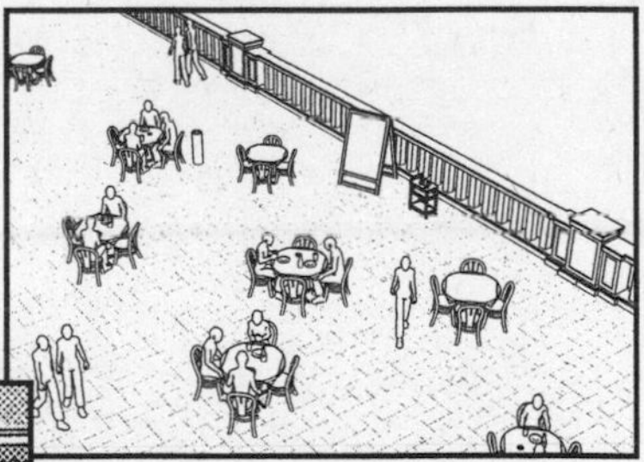

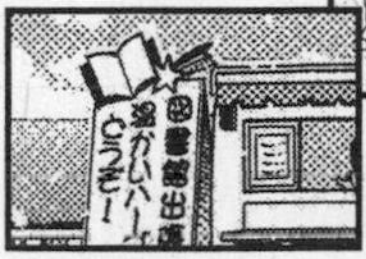

SEE? RIGHT HERE! (LAUGHS)

THIS IS THE CAFÉ THAT'S BEEN SET UP ON THE BRIDGE TO LIBRARY ISLAND. LOOKING AT THE LOGO ON TOP OF THE SIGN, YOU CAN SEE THAT IT'S AFFILIATED WITH THE EVER-POPULAR STARBOOKS CAFÉ. THEIR NAME BEING WHAT IT IS, SETTING UP RIGHT OUTSIDE THE LIBRARY IS PROBABLY A PERFECT PLACEMENT. (LAUGHS)

- BONUS -

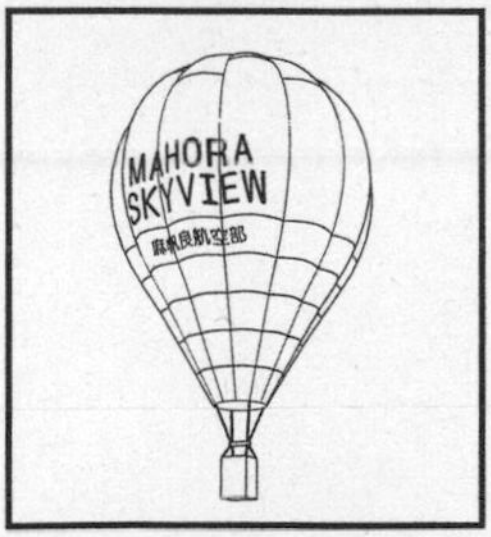
MAHORA
SKYVIEW

· HOT AIR BALLOONS OF THE MAHORA FLYING CLUB

YOU SEE THESE FLYING ALL OVER THE PLACE. IT MIGHT BE FUN TO SEE HOW MANY YOU CAN SPOT! (LAUGHS)

魔法先生 ネギま!
MAGISTER NEGI MAGI

赤松 健 SHONEN MAGAZINE COMICS
KEN AKAMATSU

14

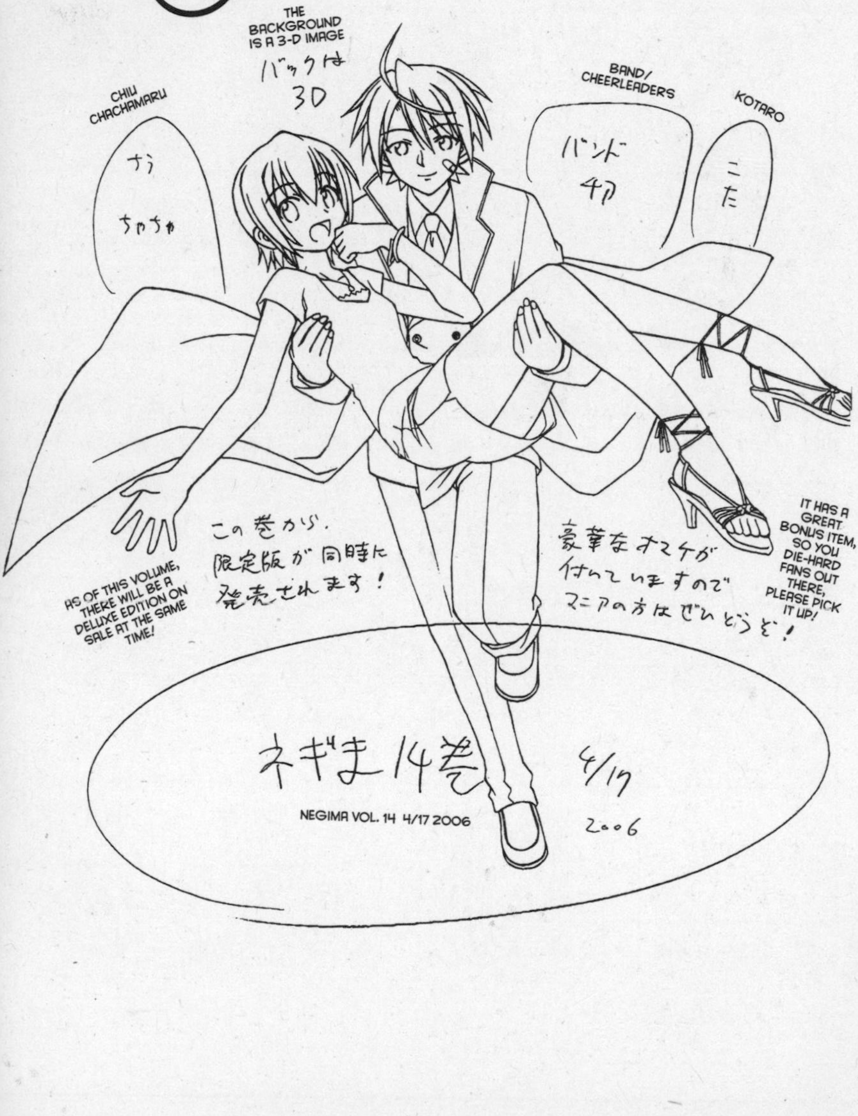

KOTARO
こた
BAND/ CHEERLEADERS
バンド
チア
THE BACKGROUND IS A 3-D IMAGE
バックは
3D
CHIU CHACHAMARU
チウ
ちゃちゃ
豪華なオマケが
付いていますので
マニアの方はぜひどうぞ！
IT HAS A GREAT BONUS ITEM, SO YOU DIE-HARD FANS OUT THERE, PLEASE PICK IT UP!
この巻から.
限定版が同時に
発売されます！
AS OF THIS VOLUME, THERE WILL BE A DELUXE EDITION ON SALE AT THE SAME TIME!
ネギま14巻
4/17
2006
NEGIMA VOL. 14 4/17 2006

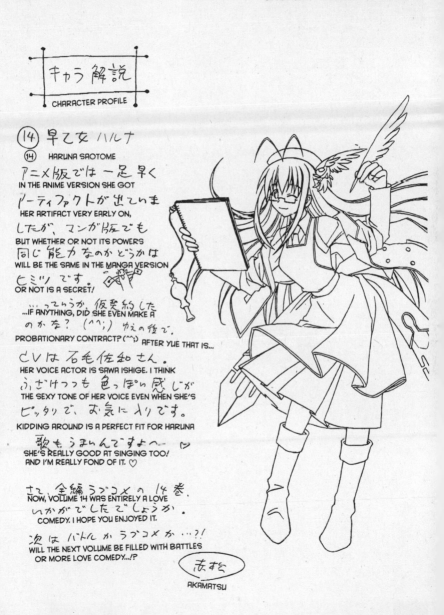

キャラ解説

CHARACTER PROFILE

⑭ 早乙女ハルナ

⑭ HARUNA SAOTOME

アニメ版では一足早く
IN THE ANIME VERSION SHE GOT
アーティファクトが出ていま
HER ARTIFACT VERY EARLY ON,
したが、マンガ版でも
BUT WHETHER OR NOT ITS POWERS
同じ能力なのかどうかは
WILL BE THE SAME IN THE MANGA VERSION
ヒミツです。
OR NOT IS A SECRET!

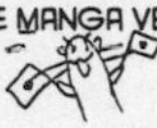

…っていうか、仮契約した
...IF ANYTHING, DID SHE EVEN MAKE A
のかな？（^^;） ゆえの後で。
PROBATIONARY CONTRACT? (^^;) AFTER YUE THAT IS...

CVは石毛佐和さん。
HER VOICE ACTOR IS SAWA ISHIGE. I THINK
ふざけつつも色っぽい感じが
THE SEXY TONE OF HER VOICE EVEN WHEN SHE'S
ピッタリで、お気に入りです。
KIDDING AROUND IS A PERFECT FIT FOR HARUNA
歌もうまいんですよ〜♡
SHE'S REALLY GOOD AT SINGING TOO!
AND I'M REALLY FOND OF IT. ♡

さて、全編ラブコメの14巻。
NOW, VOLUME 14 WAS ENTIRELY A LOVE
いかがでしたでしょうか。
COMEDY. I HOPE YOU ENJOYED IT.

次はバトルかラブコメか…?!
WILL THE NEXT VOLUME BE FILLED WITH BATTLES
OR MORE LOVE COMEDY...!?

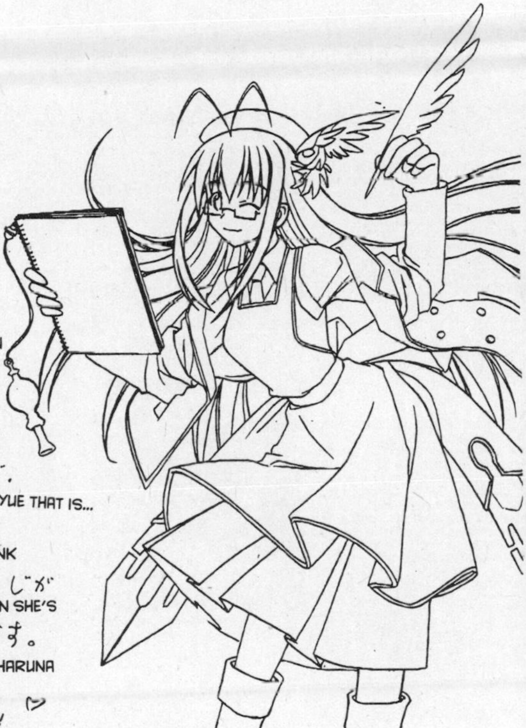

赤松
AKAMATSU

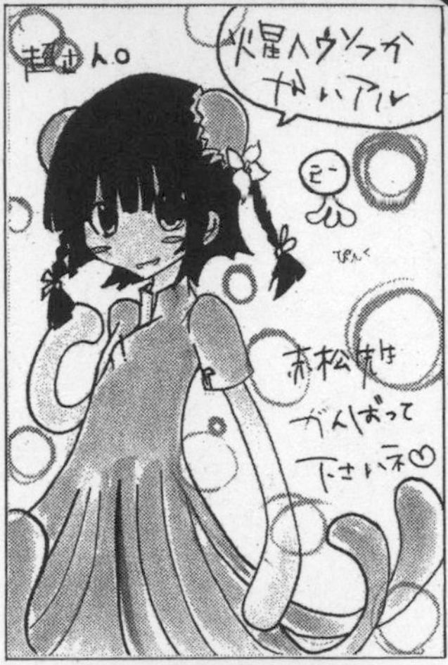
赤松先生はガんばって下さいネ♡

MARTIAN = OCTOPUS? (LAUGHS)

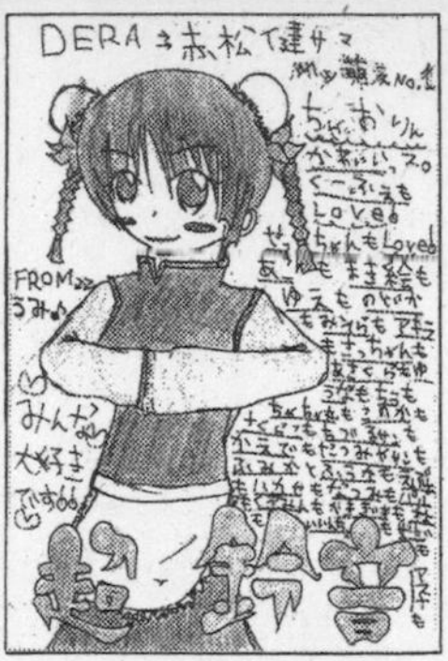

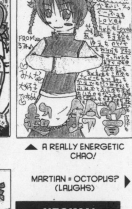

A REALLY ENERGETIC CHAO!

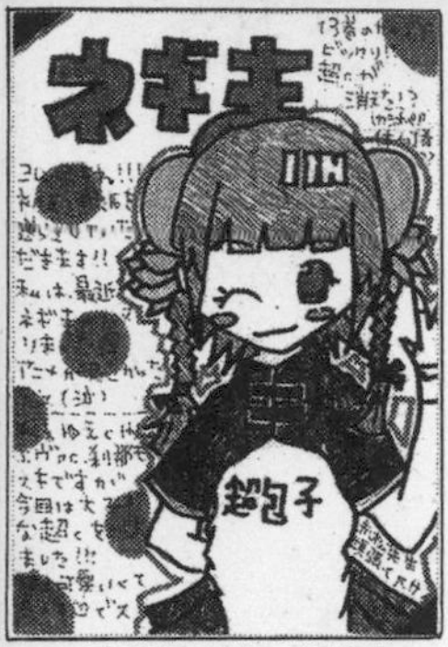

THIS IS A VERY CUTE-LOOKING CHAO.

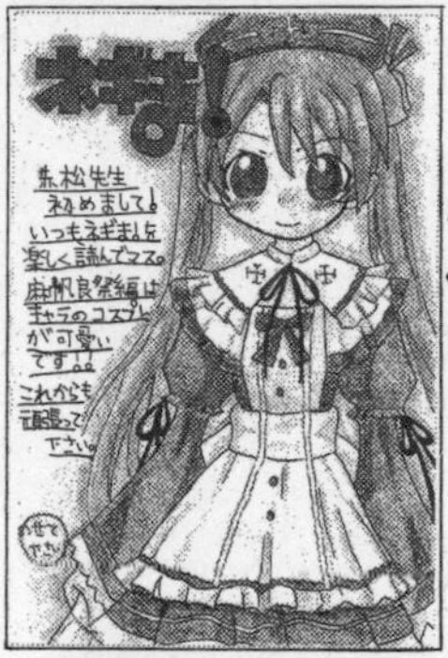

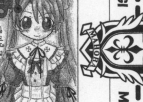

A VERY ROUND-FACED ASUNA

NEGIMA!
FAN ART CORNER

AS USUAL, WE WELCOME ALL ILLUSTRATIONS SENT IN BY THE FANS! IT'S NICE TO SEE MORE PICTURES OF CHAO COMING IN AS HER STORYLINE UNFOLDS. ★

SETSUNA PICTURES HAVE MAINTAINED THEIR POPULARITY. ★

IF YOU SEND IN PICTURES OF MINOR CHARACTERS TO GIVE THEM EXPOSURE, MAYBE THEY'LL GET THEIR OWN STORY LINE! WE LOOK FORWARD TO SEEING MORE OF YOUR ILLUSTRATIONS!

YOU CAN SEND YOUR ILLUSTRATIONS TO THE EDITORIAL OFFICES OF "KODANSHA COMICS."

TEXT: ASS'T MAX

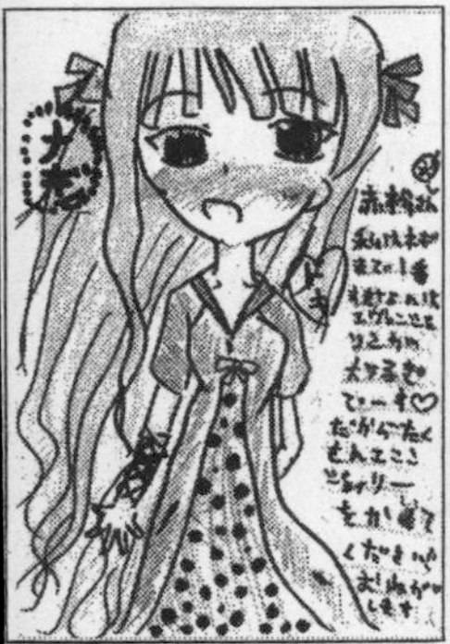

WE CAN FEEL THE ANTICIPATION IN HER EXPRESSION!

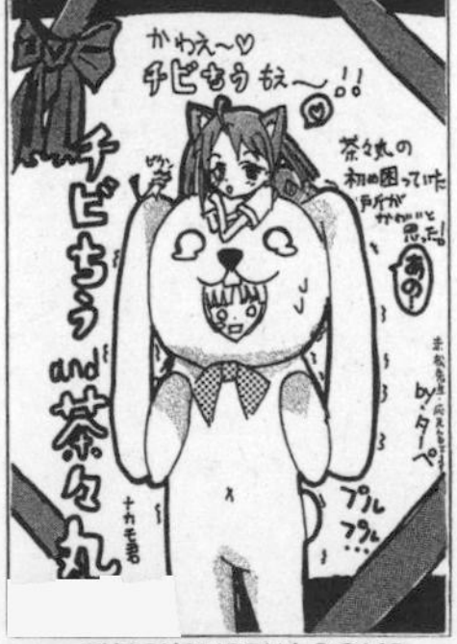

CHACHAMARU LOOKS CUTE IN HER COSTUME!

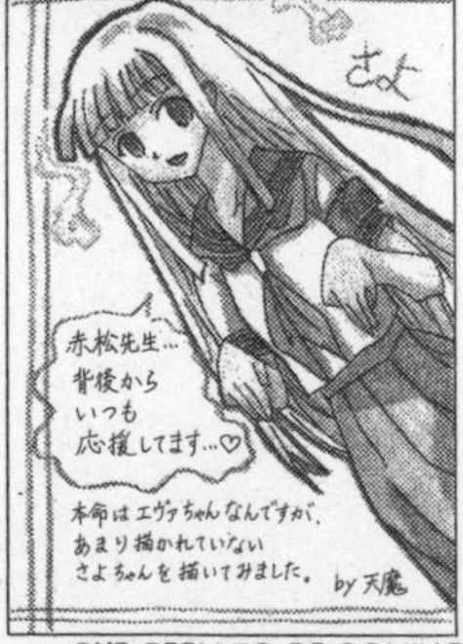
赤松先生…
背後から
いつも
応援してます…♡
本命はエヴァちゃんなんですが、
あまり描かれていない
さよちゃんを描いてみました。 by 天魔

SHE SEEM TO BE COMING OUT OF THE PAPER. I LIKE IT! (LAUGHS)

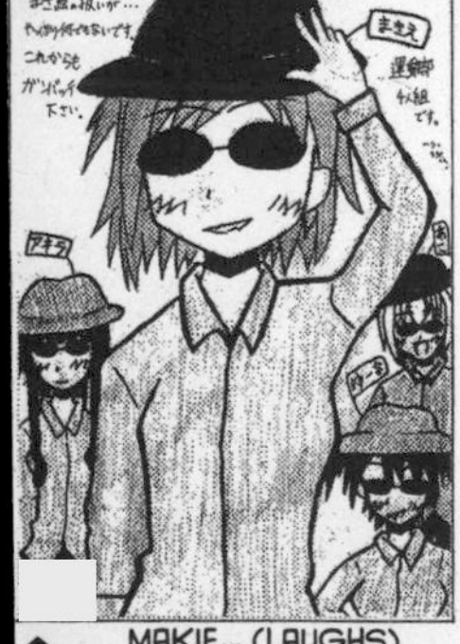

MAKIE... (LAUGHS)

[NOTE: THIS ONE IS A PUN ON HER NAME. THE "E" HERE IS THE KANJI FOR PICTURE, SO IT'S LITERALLY, "MAKI-PICTURE"]

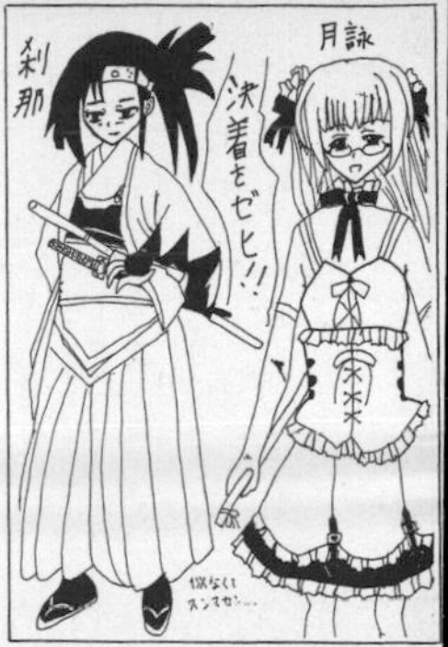
刹那
月詠
決着をゼヒ!!
▲ WE'D ALSO LOVE TO SEE A REMATCH.

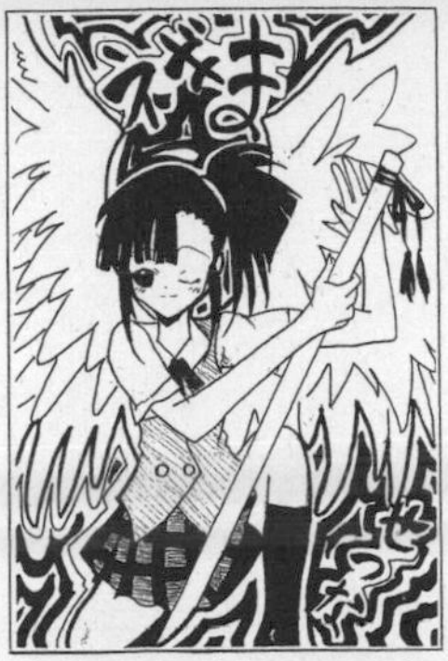
ネギま
▲ THE PICTURE GIVES OFF A VERY WONDERFUL FEELING.

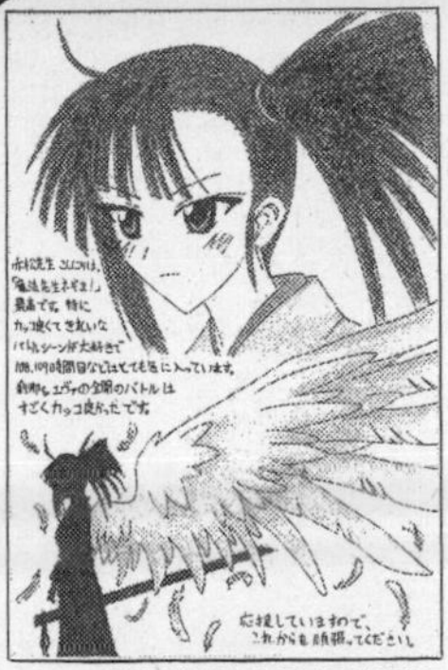
▲ SETSUNA LOOKS VERY SHARP!

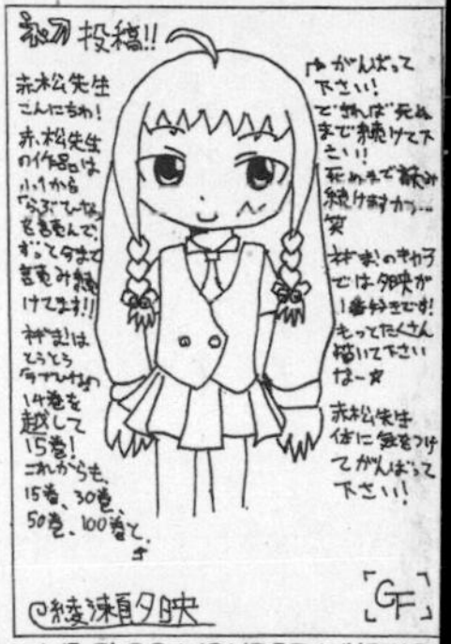
初投稿!!
▲ WE ALSO WONDER WHAT'S GOING TO HAPPEN WITH YUE...

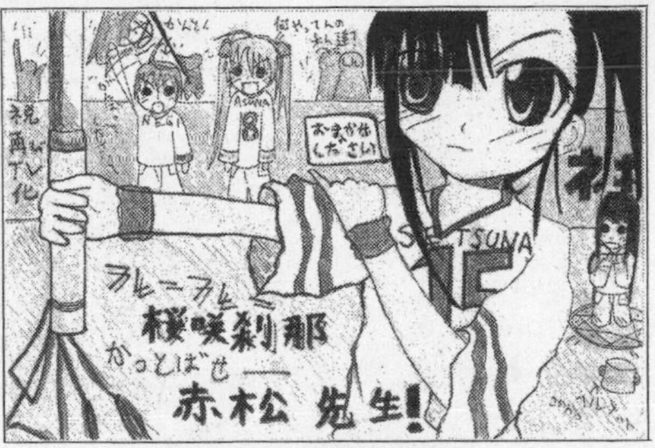
ASUNA
SETSUNA
桜咲刹那
かっとばせー
赤松 先生!
▲ SETSUNA LOOKS VERY STRONG AND DEPENDABLE.

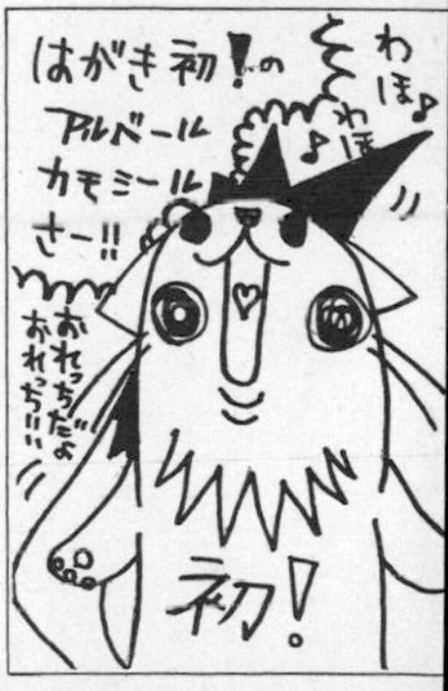
はがき初!の
アルベール
カモミール
さー!!
初!
▲ HE'S PUTTING UP A VERY TOUGH FRONT. (LAUGHS)

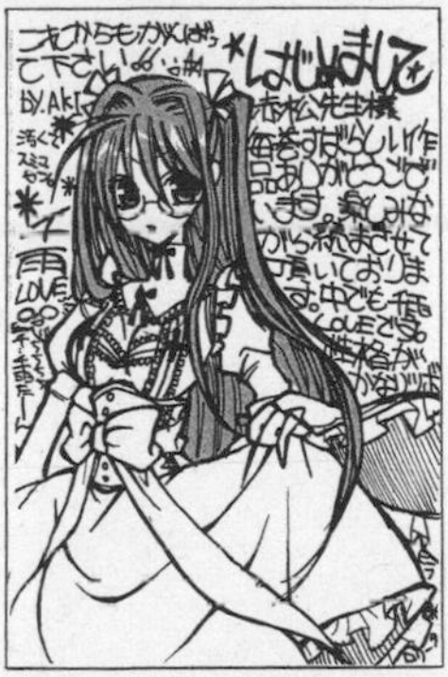
はじめまして
▲ WHAT A VERY PRETTY CHIU!

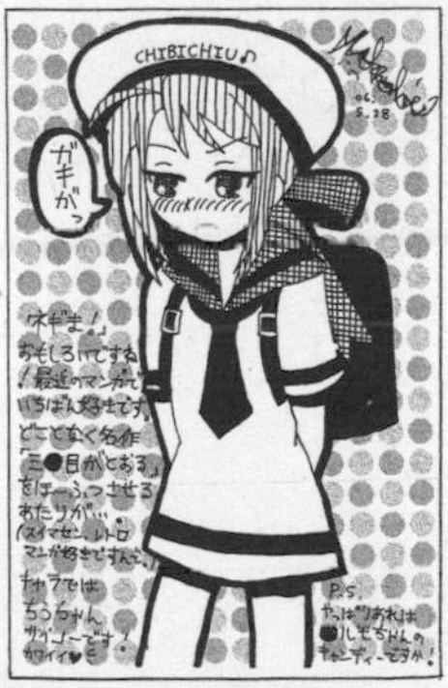
CHIBICHIU♪
ガキがっ
▲ CHIBI-CHIU IS SO POPULAR!

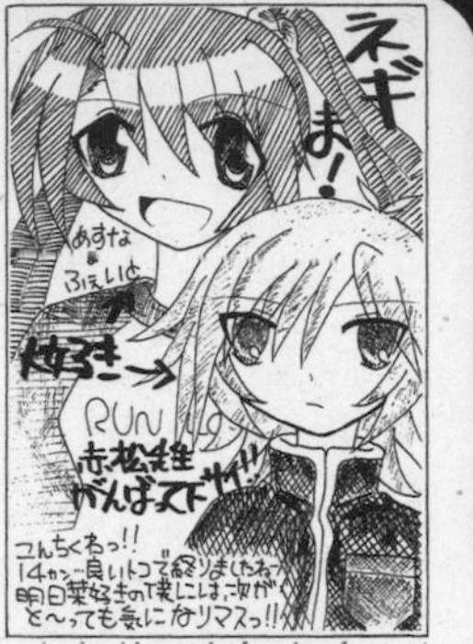
ネギま!
RUN

▲ ASUNA LOOKS ENERGETIC!

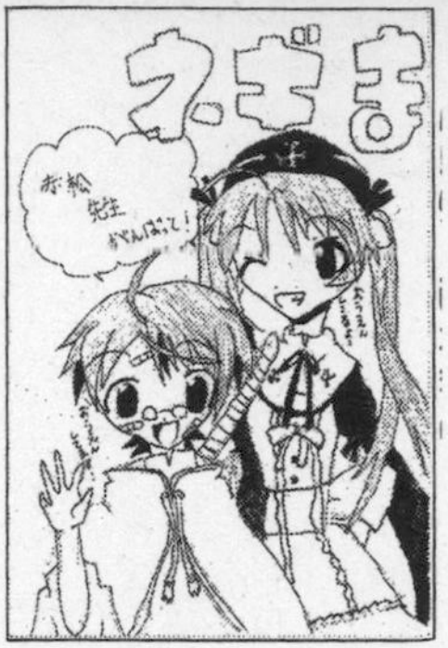
ネギま

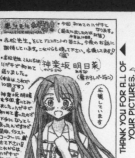

◀ THEY LOOK VERY CLOSE!

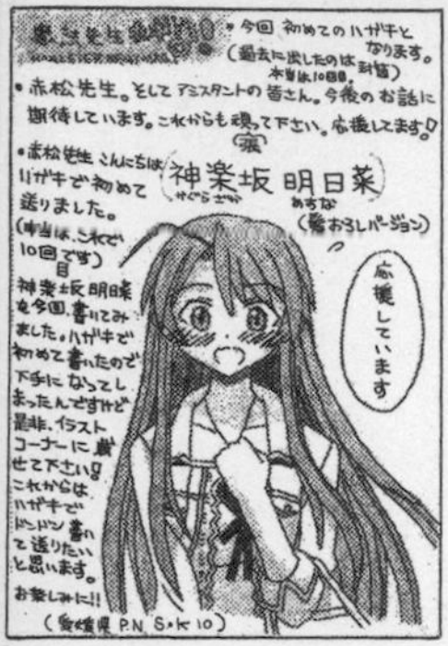
神楽坂明日菜

◀ THANK YOU FOR ALL OF YOUR PICTURES.♪

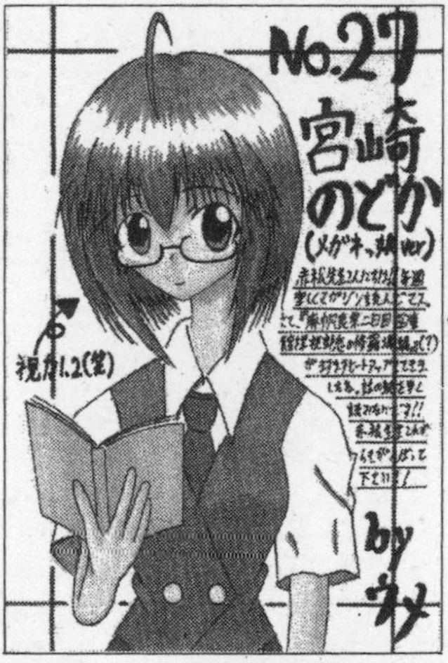
No.27
宮崎のどか

▶ THE BOOKSTORE GIRL LOOKS SMART HERE.

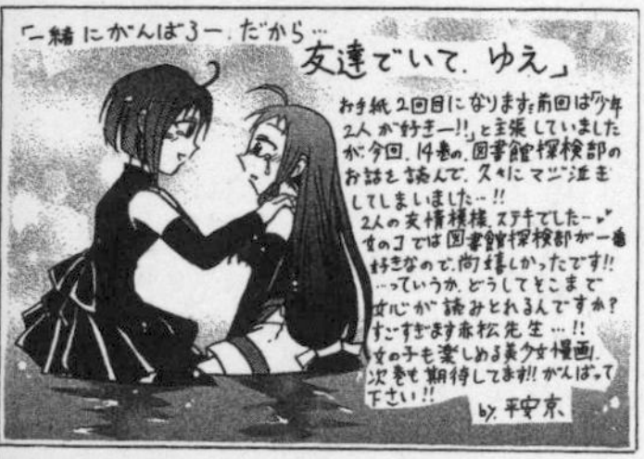
「一緒にがんばろー。だから…
友達でいて、ゆえ」

◀ THANK YOU SO MUCH.♪

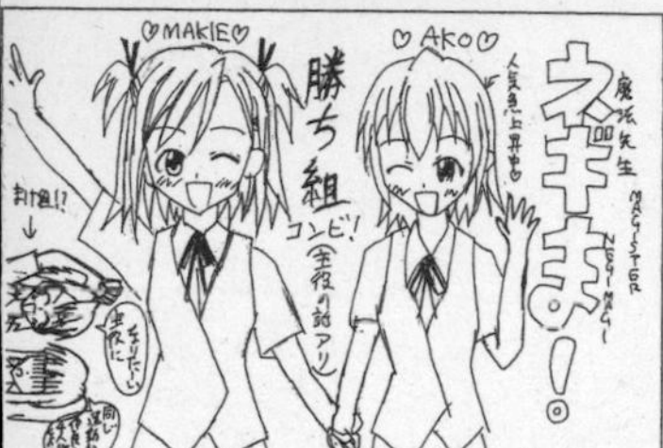
♡MAKIE♡
♡AKO♡
勝ち組コンビ!
ネギま!

◀ SO THEY'RE THE WINNING GROUP, HUH? (LAUGHS)

WHOA! WE CAN FEEL YOUR LOVE FOR HIM! ▼

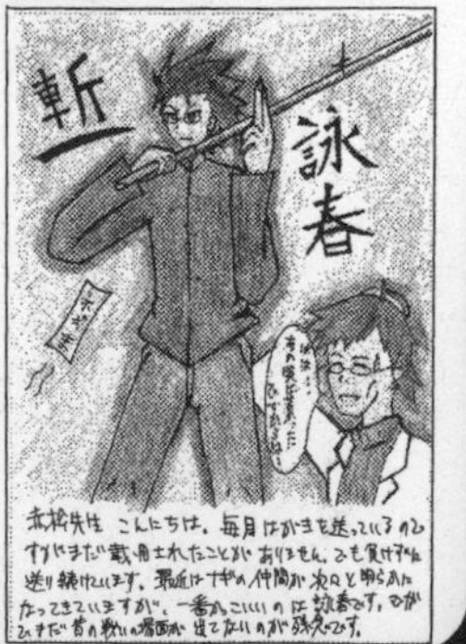
斬
詠春

▶ EISHUN! VERY NICE.

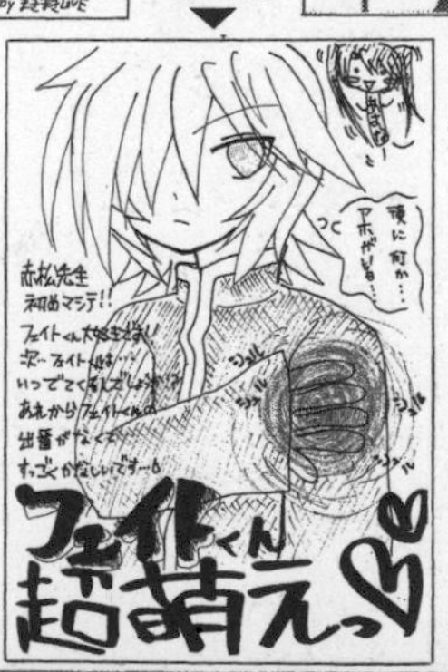
フェイトくん
超萌えっ♡

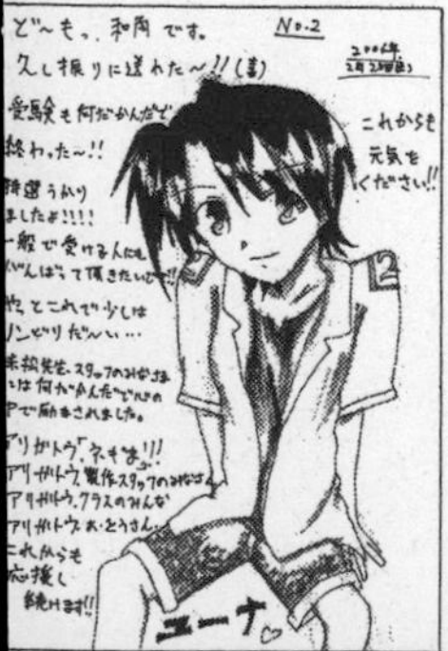
ユーナ

◀ WE WANT TO SAY THANK YOU, TOO!

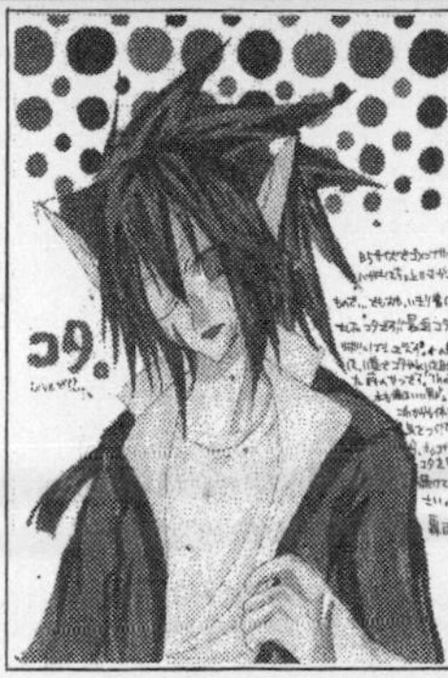
コタ.

▲ KOTARO LOOKS VERY SEXY!

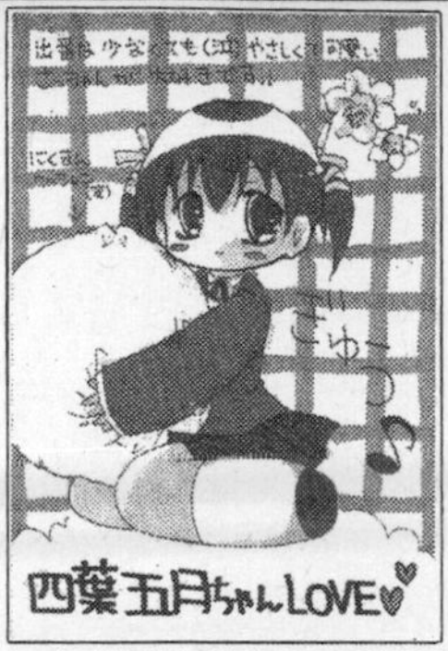
四葉五月ちゃんLOVE

▲ A SUPER-CUTE SAT-CHAN! (LAUGHS)

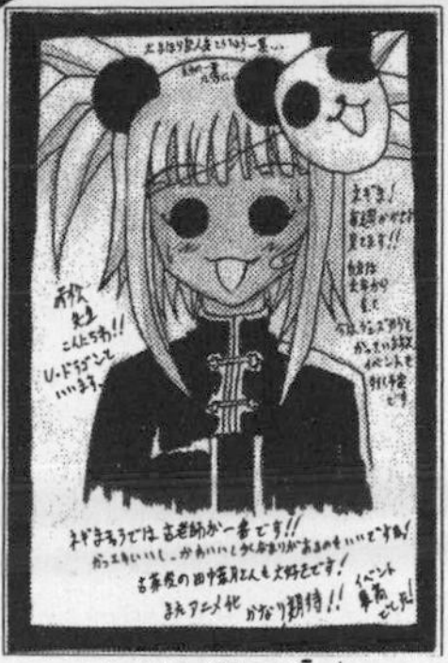

▲ MASTER KŪ.♪

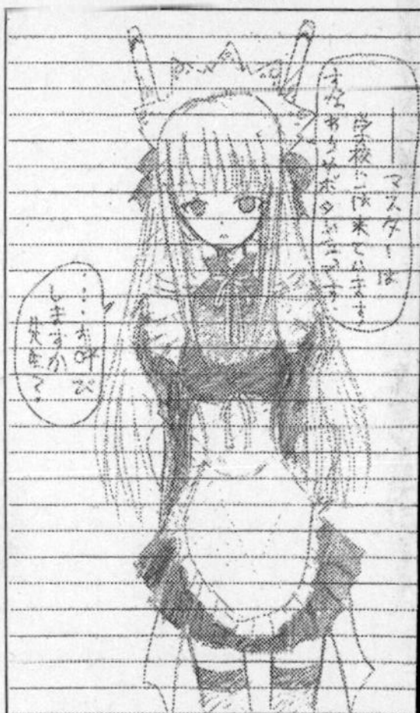

▶ CHACHAMARU LOOKING CUTE AND CASUAL.

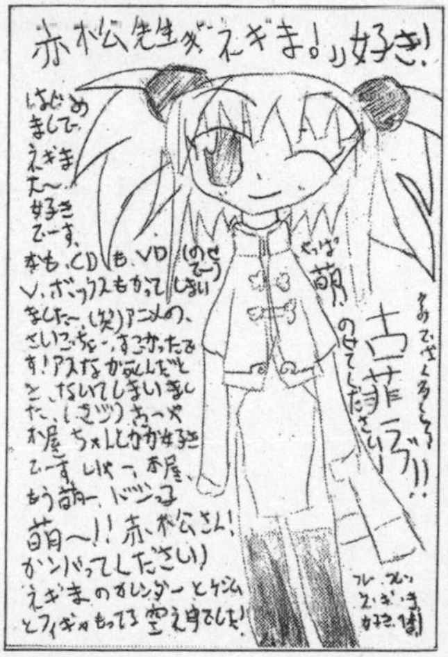
赤松公先生のネギま!!好き!

◀ YOU'RE TOTALLY DIGGING KŪ FEI.♪

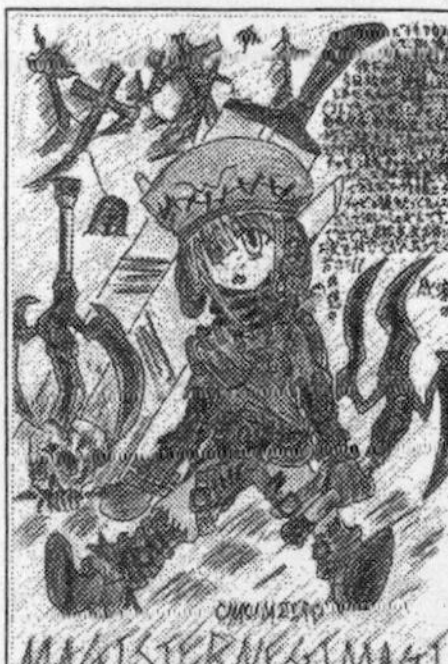
MAGISTERNEGIMAGI

▶ A VERY COOL-LOOKING CHACHAZERO.

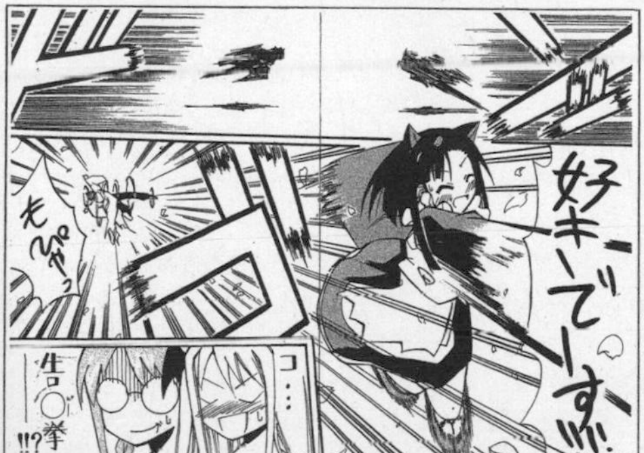
好キーでーすー!!!

◀ THE PIC HAS A GREAT, NOSTALGIC FEEL. (LAUGHS)

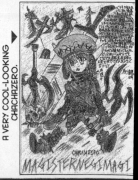

LEXICON NEGIMARUIM
DE ARTIFACTO

■匕首 十六串呂
(Sica Sisicusiro)

Setsuna Sakurazaki is awarded this tool for her use by the power of the Pactio with Negi. *Sica* is Latin for "short sword," but *sisicusiro* is Japanese. In traditional Japanese songs and poems, *shishikushiro* is a *makura kotoba* ("pillow word," a fixed epithet in poems). It means "meat on a skewer." There are several *kake kotobas* (words which have the same sound but different meanings that are used in traditional Japanese songs and poetry) for this word. *Shishi* can mean skewered meat, but it can also stand for "beast," signifying an attack. It can also mean "four by four," which works out to the number sixteen (this is the kanji character used for this artifact). The number represents the fact that this weapon can split into sixteen separate blades that can each be controlled individually. (In the third volume of the *Manyoushu* [*Collection of Ten Thousand Leaves*], there is a an example of the Japanese characters for sixteen being read as *shishi*.) The fact that the name of this artifact is not Latin denotes the special Japanese connotation that comes from the name.

Several unadorned blades appear when the blade is activated. The one with the decorative tassel is the original.

■コチノヒオウギ／ハエノスエヒロ
KOCHI NO HIOUGI / HAE NO SUEHIRO
(Flabellum Euri / Flabellum Australe)

Through the power of the Pactio with Negi, Konoka Konoe is awarded this tool for her use. The artifact materializes along with a priest's robe with magical defense properties.

Kochi and Hae refer to an easterly wind and a southerly wind. *Hiougi* is a type of fan that can be seen starting with the Middle Ages and continuing to the Modern Era as a formal wear accessory. *Suehiro* is a type of fan that folds. The priest's robe is styled after the aristocratic robes of the Heian Period.

Flabellum means "small wind" in Latin and represents the "fan." *Euri* means "easterly wind" and comes from the ancient Greek word Ευρος. *Ausutorale* comes from the name of the southerly wind of the Mediterranean.

Konoka claims that she can cure any wounds within three minutes (126th Period), but she can't cure a crushed head (136th Period), which is the ability of the Kochi no Hiougi. The Hae no Suehiro, on the other hand, can cure conditions like putrifaction and other ailments that are considered "status anomalies" in RPG games (52nd Period) within thirty minutes. However, it would be absurd to differentiate injuries to the body and "status anomalies," as explained by French philosopher and historian Michel Foucault (1926–1984) in *La Naissance de la clinique* (*The Birth of the Clinic*). He writes, "It was given the splendid task of establishing in men's lives the positive role of health, virtue, and happiness...Medicine must no longer be confined to a body of techniques for curing ills and of the knowledge that they require; it will also embrace a knowledge of healthy man, that is, a study of non-sick man and a definition of the model man. In the ordering of human existence it assumes a normative posture" (chapter 2). According to him, a "status anomaly" is an "injury" if it causes interference with social participation. The person is not considered healthy until such conditions can be resolved or cured.

Trying to differentiate the healing capacities of Kochi no Hiougi and Hae no Suehiro to heal "injuries" and "status anomalies" is rather silly when viewed in this manner. Foucault wrote, "The clinic is both a new 'carving up' of things and principles of their verbalization in a form which we have been accustomed to recognizing as the language of a 'positive science'" (preface). Maladies such as injuries and diseases are differentiated only through language. An "anomaly" is an "anomaly," but differences arise through the use of different words. Therefore, Kochi no Hiougi and Hae no Suehiro have different healing attributes, but their words and their meaning reflect the language that the magical artifacts are based on.

[Note: English Translation of *The Birth of the Clinic* is from the 1994 Vintage publication of the 1973 translation from the French by A. M. Sheridan Smith.]

■落書帝国
IMPERIUM GRAPHICES

By the power of the Pactio with Negi, Haruna Saotome is awarded this tool for her use. A magical quill, ink well, croquis tablet, and beret appear, along with an artist's apron with ties embellished with a unique design element: pen tips on the ends. It is an extremely useful artifact with the special ability to summon simple golems from anything drawn on the tablet. *Imperuim* can be translated as "empire" in English; however, it can also mean "to command or control" or even "army." *Graphices* is, of course, "graphics" in English, which is derived from the Latin word *grafice*, meaning "the ability to draw." So, *Imperium Graphices* can be translated as "army of drawings." By putting the *ministra* to the rear in battle, a golem can be created to defend the *ministra* as well as the mage. However, the golem is not controlled by the mage, so a certain level of skill is required of the *ministra* in order to properly control the creature.

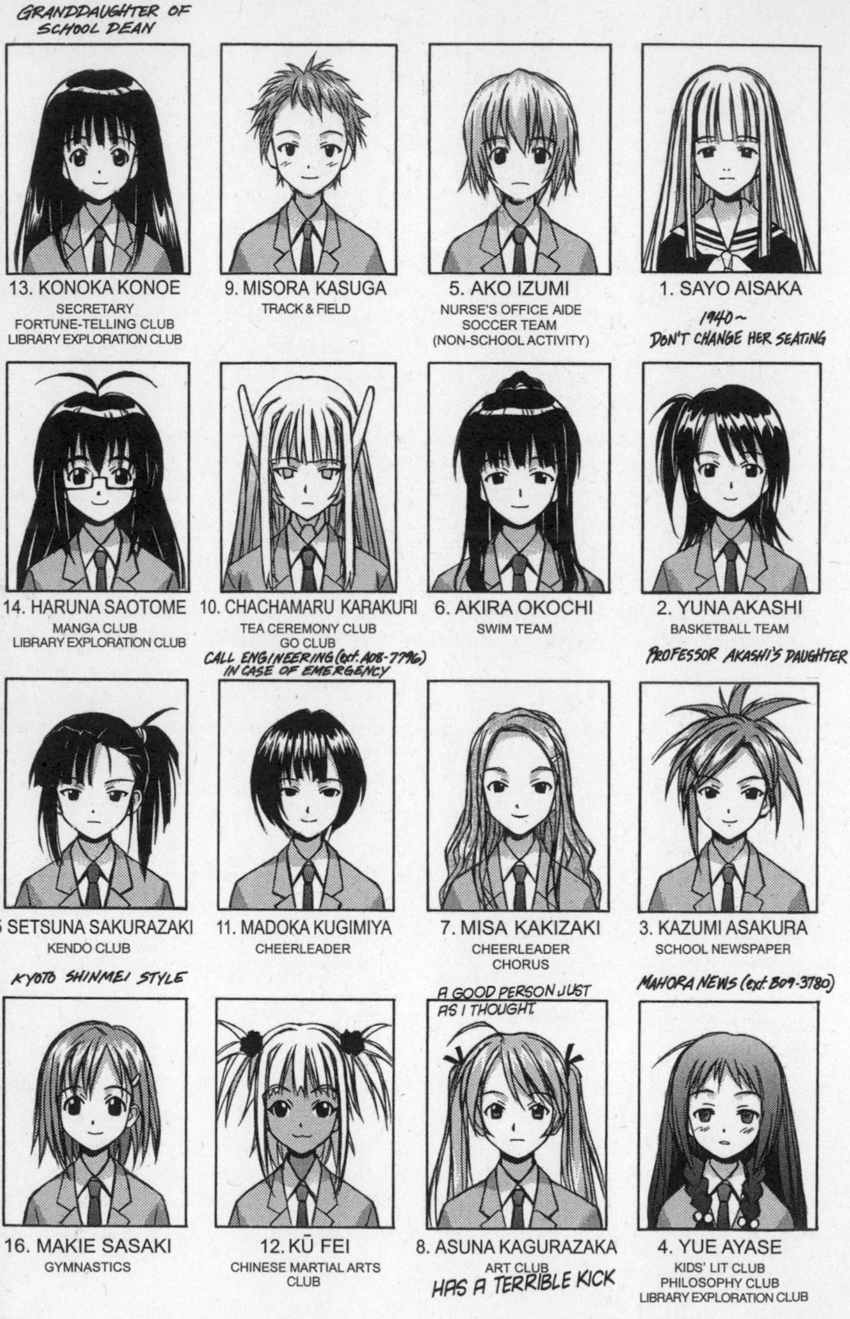
1. SAYO AISAKA
1940~
DON'T CHANGE HER SEATING
5. AKO IZUMI
NURSE'S OFFICE AIDE
SOCCER TEAM
(NON-SCHOOL ACTIVITY)
9. MISORA KASUGA
TRACK & FIELD
GRANDDAUGHTER OF SCHOOL DEAN
13. KONOKA KONOE
SECRETARY
FORTUNE-TELLING CLUB
LIBRARY EXPLORATION CLUB
2. YUNA AKASHI
BASKETBALL TEAM
PROFESSOR AKASHI'S DAUGHTER
6. AKIRA OKOCHI
SWIM TEAM
10. CHACHAMARU KARAKURI
TEA CEREMONY CLUB
GO CLUB
CALL ENGINEERING (ext. AD8-7796) IN CASE OF EMERGENCY
14. HARUNA SAOTOME
MANGA CLUB
LIBRARY EXPLORATION CLUB
3. KAZUMI ASAKURA
SCHOOL NEWSPAPER
MAHORA NEWS (ext. 809-3780)
7. MISA KAKIZAKI
CHEERLEADER
CHORUS
11. MADOKA KUGIMIYA
CHEERLEADER
15 SETSUNA SAKURAZAKI
KENDO CLUB
KYOTO SHINMEI STYLE
4. YUE AYASE
KIDS' LIT CLUB
PHILOSOPHY CLUB
LIBRARY EXPLORATION CLUB
A GOOD PERSON JUST AS I THOUGHT.
8. ASUNA KAGURAZAKA
ART CLUB
HAS A TERRIBLE KICK
12. KŪ FEI
CHINESE MARTIAL ARTS CLUB
16. MAKIE SASAKI
GYMNASTICS

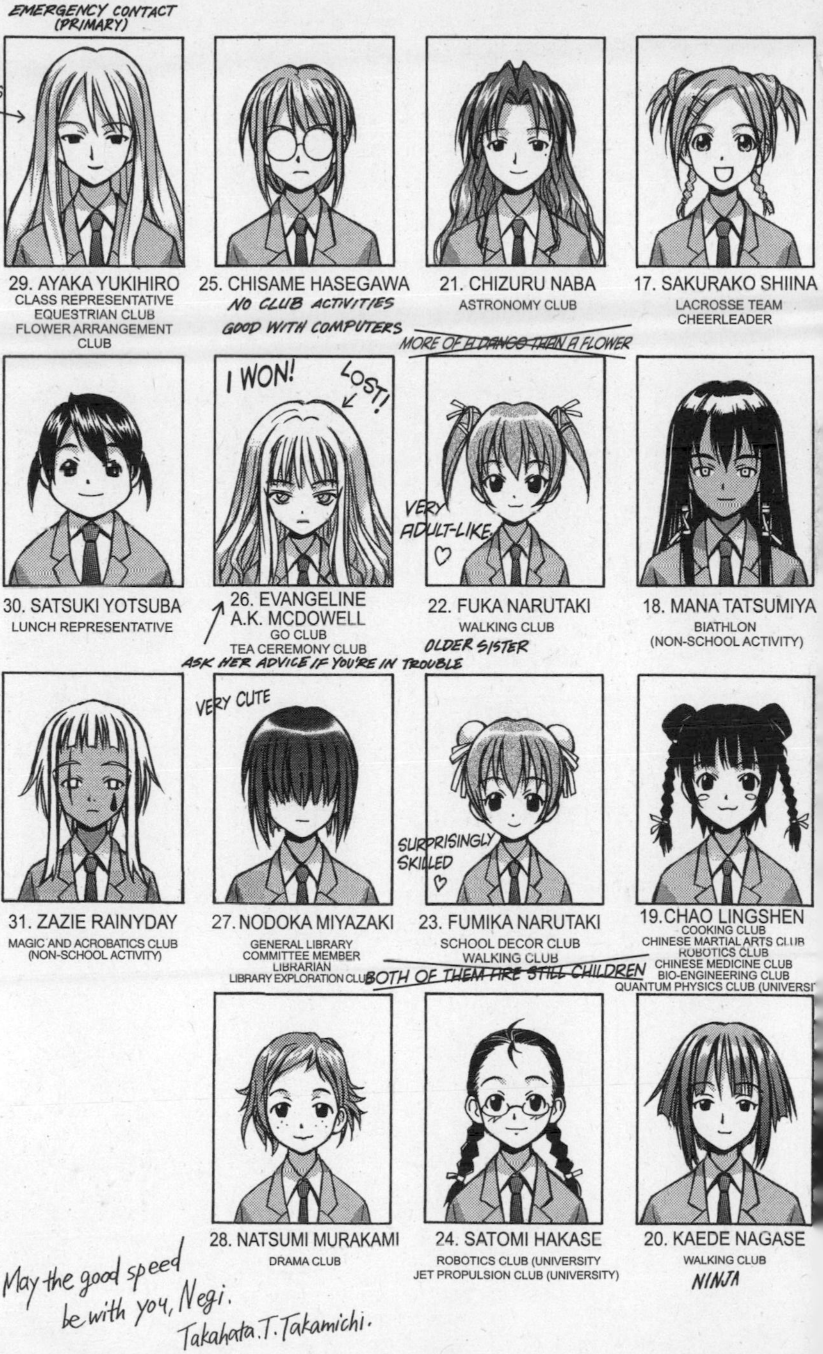
17. SAKURAKO SHIINA
LACROSSE TEAM
CHEERLEADER
21. CHIZURU NABA
ASTRONOMY CLUB
MORE OF A DANGO THAN A FLOWER
25. CHISAME HASEGAWA
NO CLUB ACTIVITIES
GOOD WITH COMPUTERS
EMERGENCY CONTACT (PRIMARY)
ASUNA'S CLOSE FRIEND.
29. AYAKA YUKIHIRO
CLASS REPRESENTATIVE
EQUESTRIAN CLUB
FLOWER ARRANGEMENT CLUB
18. MANA TATSUMIYA
BIATHLON
(NON-SCHOOL ACTIVITY)
VERY ADULT-LIKE ♡
22. FUKA NARUTAKI
WALKING CLUB
OLDER SISTER
I WON!
LOST!
26. EVANGELINE A.K. MCDOWELL
GO CLUB
TEA CEREMONY CLUB
ASK HER ADVICE IF YOU'RE IN TROUBLE
30. SATSUKI YOTSUBA
LUNCH REPRESENTATIVE
19. CHAO LINGSHEN
COOKING CLUB
CHINESE MARTIAL ARTS CLUB
ROBOTICS CLUB
CHINESE MEDICINE CLUB
BIO-ENGINEERING CLUB
QUANTUM PHYSICS CLUB (UNIVERSI
SURPRISINGLY SKILLED ♡
23. FUMIKA NARUTAKI
SCHOOL DECOR CLUB
WALKING CLUB
BOTH OF THEM ARE STILL CHILDREN
VERY CUTE
27. NODOKA MIYAZAKI
GENERAL LIBRARY COMMITTEE MEMBER
LIBRARIAN
LIBRARY EXPLORATION CLUB
31. ZAZIE RAINYDAY
MAGIC AND ACROBATICS CLUB
(NON-SCHOOL ACTIVITY)
20. KAEDE NAGASE
WALKING CLUB
NINJA
24. SATOMI HAKASE
ROBOTICS CLUB (UNIVERSITY
JET PROPULSION CLUB (UNIVERSITY)
28. NATSUMI MURAKAMI
DRAMA CLUB
May the good speed be with you, Negi.
Takahata.T.Takamichi.

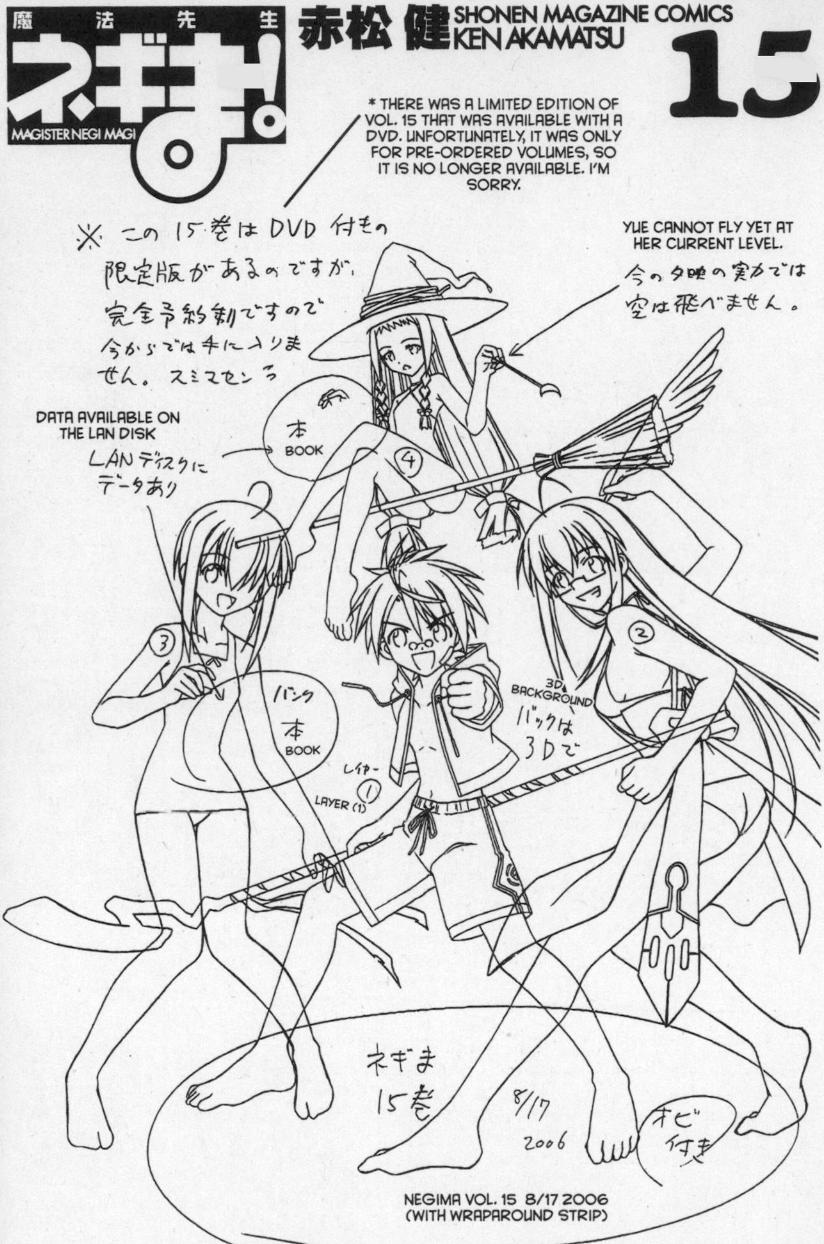
魔法先生
ネギま!
MAGISTER NEGI MAGI
赤松 健
SHONEN MAGAZINE COMICS
KEN AKAMATSU
15
* THERE WAS A LIMITED EDITION OF VOL. 15 THAT WAS AVAILABLE WITH A DVD. UNFORTUNATELY, IT WAS ONLY FOR PRE-ORDERED VOLUMES, SO IT IS NO LONGER AVAILABLE. I'M SORRY.
※ この15巻はDVD付きの
限定版があるのですが、
完全予約制ですので
今からでは手に入りま
せん。スミマセン
YUE CANNOT FLY YET AT HER CURRENT LEVEL.
今の夕映の実力では
空は飛べません。
DATA AVAILABLE ON THE LAN DISK
LANディスクに
データあり
本
BOOK
④
③
②
バック
本
BOOK
3D BACKGROUND
バックは
3Dで
レイヤー
①
LAYER (1)
ネギま
15巻
8/17
2006
オビ
付き
NEGIMA VOL. 15 8/17 2006
(WITH WRAPAROUND STRIP)

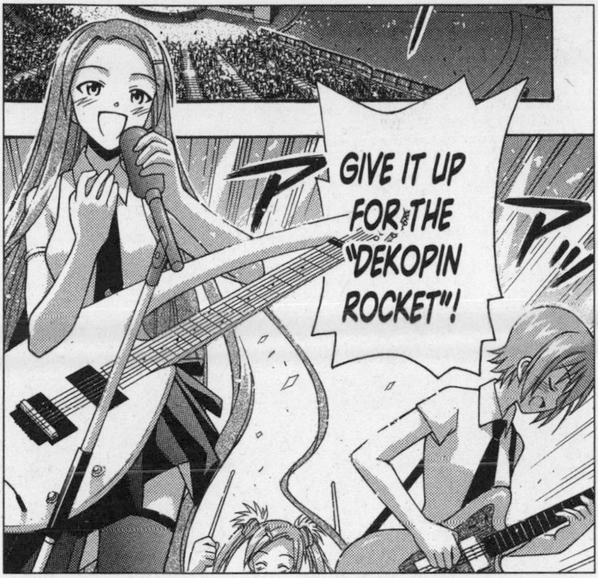
GIVE IT UP FOR THE "DEKOPIN ROCKET"!

Dekopin, page 291

The four girls in Classroom 3-A have named their band Dekopin Rocket. *Dekopin* is slang for the act of flicking one's finger at the forehead of another. *Deko* is short for *odeko*, meaning "forehead," and *pin* is onomatopoeia for the sound of the finger impacting on the head. You can see an example of this in vol. 2, page 32, panel 1.

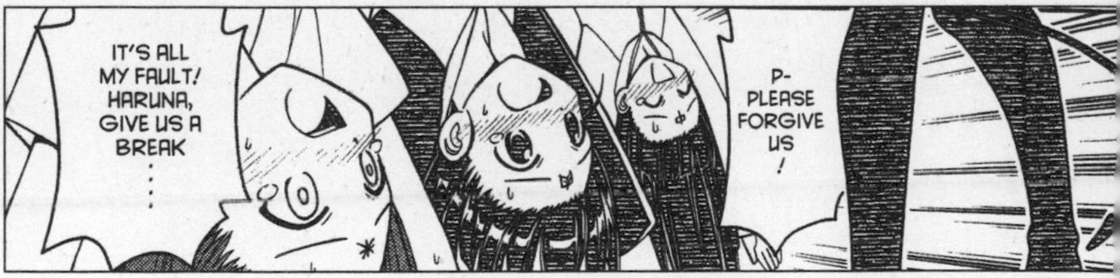
P-PLEASE FORGIVE US!
IT'S ALL MY FAULT! HARUNA, GIVE US A BREAK...

Kinnikuman homage, page 297

In Haruna's manga page, there are kanji characters for *niku* (meat) on Nodoka, *chu* (middle, or the first character in the kanji for China) on Konoka, and *kome* (rice, or the first character in the kanji characters for the United States) on Yue. This is an homage to the manga *Kinnukuman* (known as *Ultimate Muscle* in the U.S.) by Yudetamgo. The main character, Kinnikuman, has the kanji character *niku* on his forehead, the character Ramenman from China has the character *chu* on his forehead, and Terryman (an homage himself to American wrestler Terry Funk) from the U.S. has the character *kome* on his forehead. It's a throwaway gag, but people who know will recognize it.

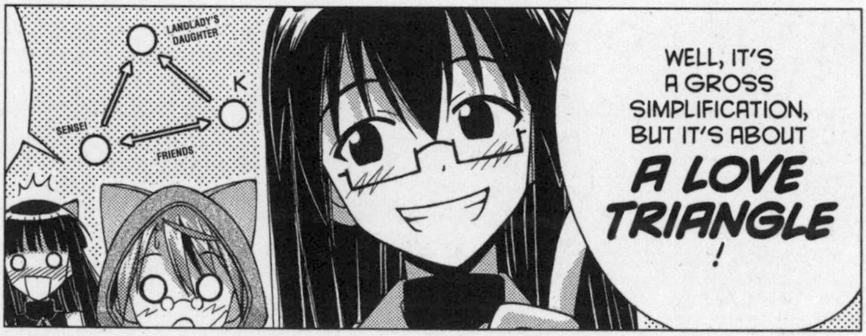
WELL, IT'S A GROSS SIMPLIFICATION, BUT IT'S ABOUT A LOVE TRIANGLE!
LANDLADY'S DAUGHTER
K
SENSEI
FRIENDS

Love triangle, pages 319-320

Soseki Natsume's novel *Kokoro* is featured. The quote on panel 6, "Anyone who has no spiritual aspirations is an idiot," is a key line that causes K severe psychological damage, driving him to slit his carotid artery with a knife.

One of the other books that Haruna shows Negi is Dostoyevsky's *The Idiot*. In this book, the love triangle is between Myshkin and his friend Rogozhin for the love of the beautiful Nastasya. This tale ends tragically: one person dies, one is sent to Siberia, and the other becomes an idiot over the loss of his love.

Volume 15

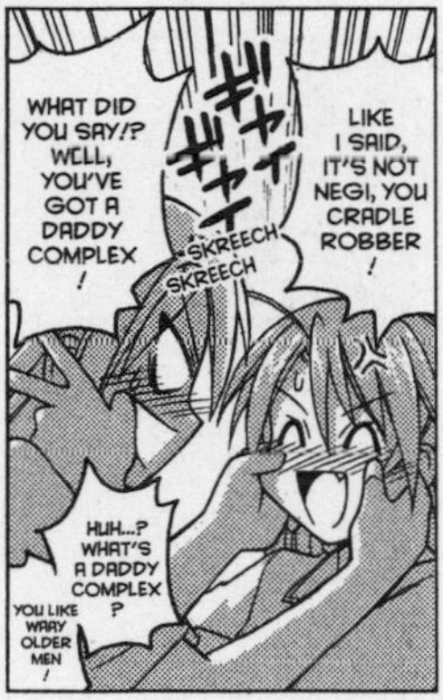
LIKE I SAID, IT'S NOT NEGI, YOU CRADLE ROBBER!
ギャーギャー
WHAT DID YOU SAY!? WELL, YOU'VE GOT A DADDY COMPLEX!
SKREECH SKREECH
HUH...? WHAT'S A DADDY COMPLEX?
YOU LIKE WAAY OLDER MEN!

Craddle robber and daddy complex, page 391

The phrases originally used were *shotacon* and *ojicon. Shotacon* is short for Shotaro complex, which occurs when a girl has a fondness for younger boys. It was made up as a counterpart to Lolicon, short for Lolita complex, which, as in the novel by Vladimir Nabokov, is when a male has a fondness for young girls. It's called a Shotaro complex after Shotaro, the main character in the series *Tetsujin 28-Go* (*Gigantor* in the U.S.), who usually wore a suit and tie with shorts and became the embodiment of the pretty young boy. *Ojicon* in this case is *ojin* complex. *Ojin* is slang for "an older man," hence the title of this chapter.

Married up, page 402

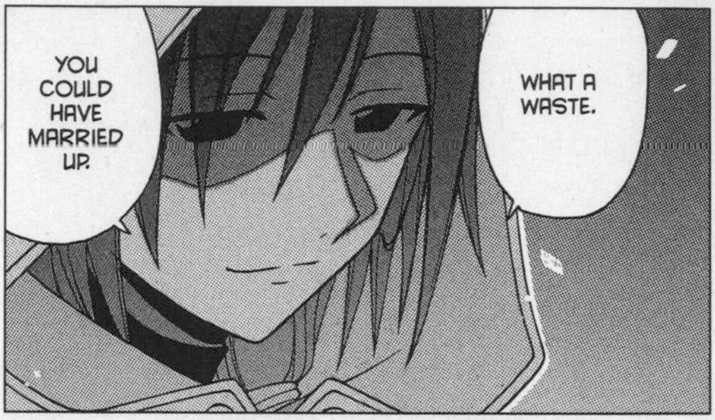
WHAT A WASTE.
YOU COULD HAVE MARRIED UP.

In panel 5, when Al says to Takahata that he could have "married up," the original Japanese used was *Gyaku Tama*. These are the characters for "reverse" and "ball," but the phrase is based on the Japanese term *Tama no Koshi,* which means "to marry into wealth." This term is usually applied to a woman looking to marry a rich or famous man. *Gyaku Tama* is used when it's a man looking to do the same. This would imply that Asuna might be someone of importance.

Cat robot and Se(xx)shi-kun, page 472

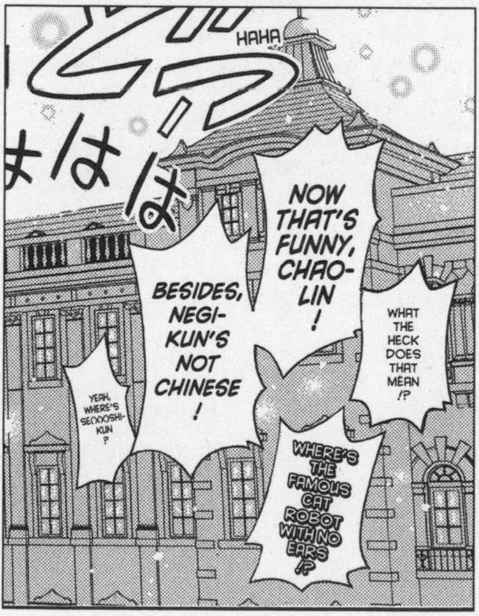
HAHA
NOW THAT'S FUNNY, CHAO-LIN!
WHAT THE HECK DOES THAT MEAN!?
BESIDES, NEGI-KUN'S NOT CHINESE!
WHERE'S THE FAMOUS CAT ROBOT WITH NO EARS!?
YEAH, WHERE'S SE(XX)SHI-KUN?

The cat robot mentioned in the second panel is, of course, Doraemon, of the famous manga, and the name with the middle letters missing is Sewashi, a descendant of Nobita, the kid who Doreamon comes to help in the present in order to make Sewashi's life better in the future. The names had to be obscured and referred to only obliquely since *Doraemon* is published by Shogakukan and *Negima!* by Kodansha.

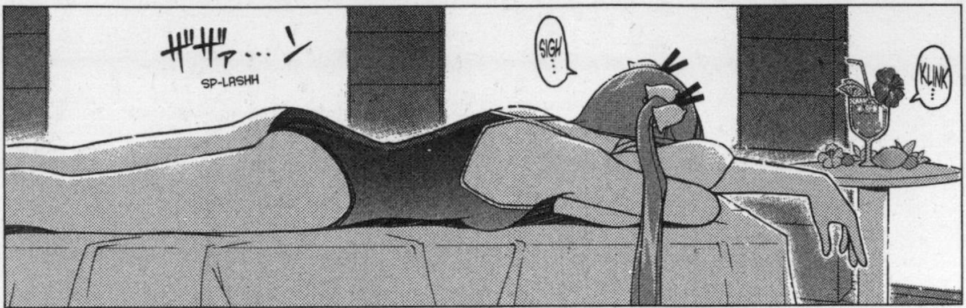
KLINK...
SIGH...
ザザァ…ン
SP-LASHH

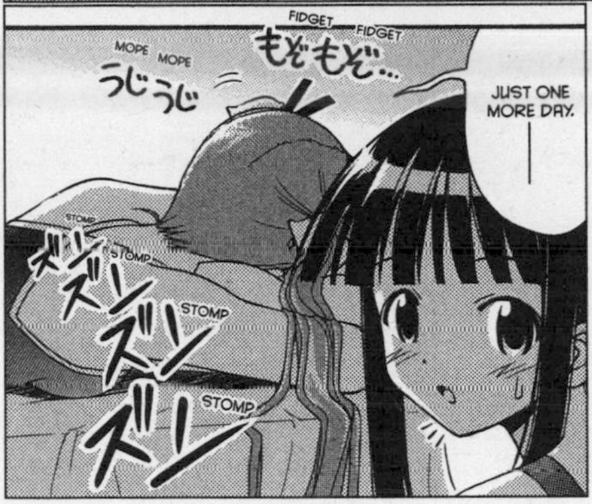
JUST ONE MORE DAY.
もぞもぞ…
FIDGET FIDGET
うじうじ
MOPE MOPE
ズン
STOMP
ズン
STOMP
ズン
STOMP
ズン
STOMP

Voice actors turned manga assistants, page 475

During a visit by some of the *Negima!* anime voice actors to get material for the web radio show, the voice actor for Negi (Rina Sato) drew the sound effect of the crashing wave in panel 2. The voice actor for Setsuna (Yu Kobayashi) did the sound effects for Asuna's fidgeting in panel 7.

Red Moon Night, Blue Moon Morning, page 484

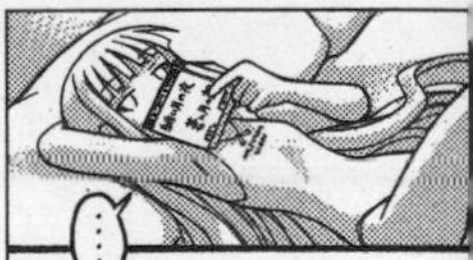

In panel 6, Eva can be seen reading a book. The title is *Akai Tsuki no Yoru, Aoi Tsuki no Asa*. This is not the title of a real book, as is often the case with books seen in *Negima!* In this case, it's a shout out by Akamatsu to the Animate TV show that the anime voice actors for Evangeline (Yuki Matsuoka) and Kazumi (Ayana Sasgawa) host.

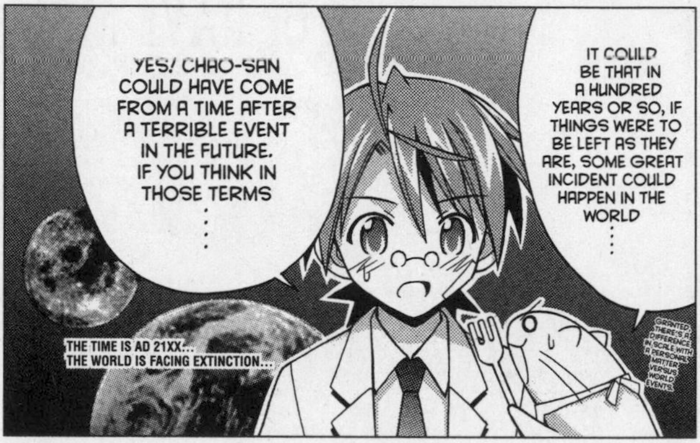
IT COULD BE THAT IN A HUNDRED YEARS OR SO, IF THINGS WERE TO BE LEFT AS THEY ARE, SOME GREAT INCIDENT COULD HAPPEN IN THE WORLD ....
GRANTED, THERE'S A DIFFERENCE IN SCALE WITH A PERSONAL MATTER VERSUS WORLD EVENTS.
YES! CHAO-SAN COULD HAVE COME FROM A TIME AFTER A TERRIBLE EVENT IN THE FUTURE. IF YOU THINK IN THOSE TERMS ....
THE TIME IS AD 21XX... THE WORLD IS FACING EXTINCTION...

The time is, page 503

Akamatsu uses this term a lot in referring to events in the future. This is most likely a homage to the TV show *Space Cruiser Yamato*. The translation really can't do this line justice, but the line is recognizable to many people. The narration that's at the start of all the movies begins with "The time is AD XXXX..." Both of the captions are actual lines from the show's narration.

TOMARE!

[STOP!]

You're going the wrong way!

Manga is a completely different type of reading experience.

To start at the *beginning*, go to the *end*!

That's right! Authentic manga is read the traditional Japanese way—from right to left, exactly the *opposite* of how American books are read. It's easy to follow: Just go to the other end of the book, and read each page—and each panel—from right side to left side, starting at the top right. Now you're experiencing manga as it was meant to be.

キャラ解説
CHARACTER PROFILE

⑲ 超 鈴音
⑲ CHAO LINGSHEN

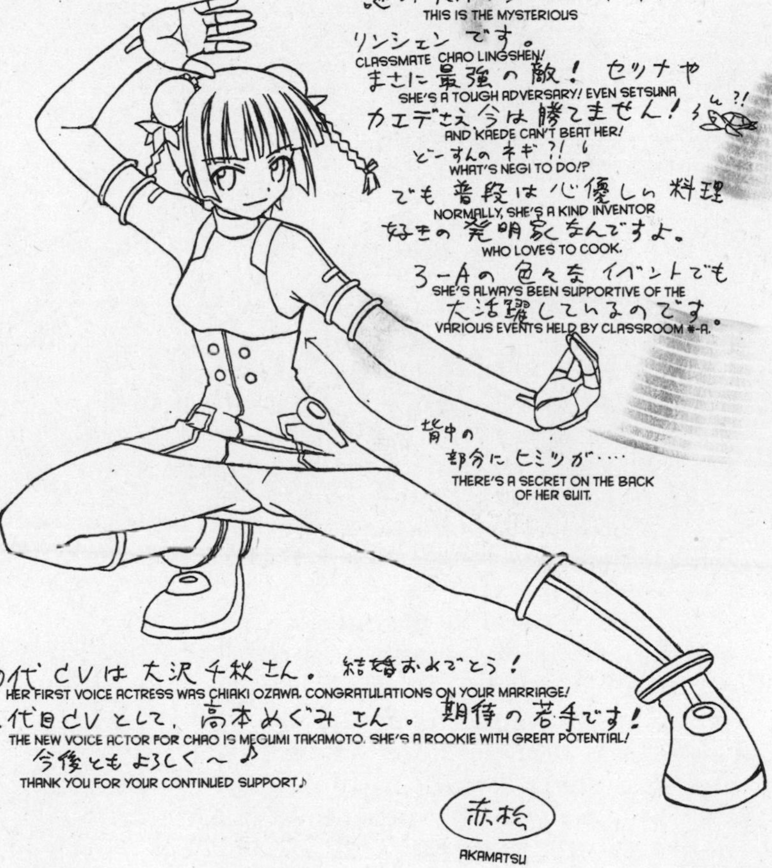

謎の天才クラスメート、チャオ
THIS IS THE MYSTERIOUS
リンシェンです。
CLASSMATE CHAO LINGSHEN!
まさに最強の敵！ セツナや
SHE'S A TOUGH ADVERSARY! EVEN SETSUNA
カエデさえ今は勝てません！
AND KAEDE CAN'T BEAT HER!
どーすんのネギ？！
WHAT'S NEGI TO DO!?
でも普段は心優しい料理
NORMALLY, SHE'S A KIND INVENTOR
好きの発明家さんですよ。
WHO LOVES TO COOK.
3-Aの色々なイベントでも
SHE'S ALWAYS BEEN SUPPORTIVE OF THE
大活躍しているのです。
VARIOUS EVENTS HELD BY CLASSROOM 3-A.

背中の部分にヒミツが…
THERE'S A SECRET ON THE BACK OF HER SUIT.

初代CVは大沢千秋さん。結婚おめでとう！
HER FIRST VOICE ACTRESS WAS CHIAKI OZAWA. CONGRATULATIONS ON YOUR MARRIAGE!
二代目CVとして、高本めぐみさん。期待の若手です！
THE NEW VOICE ACTOR FOR CHAO IS MEGUMI TAKAMOTO. SHE'S A ROOKIE WITH GREAT POTENTIAL!
今後ともよろしく～♪
THANK YOU FOR YOUR CONTINUED SUPPORT♪

赤松
AKAMATSU

Translation Notes

Japanese is a tricky language for most westerners, and translation is often more art than science. For your edification and reading pleasure, here are notes on some of the places where we could have gone in a different direction in our translation of the work, or where a Japanese cultural reference is used.

Volume 13

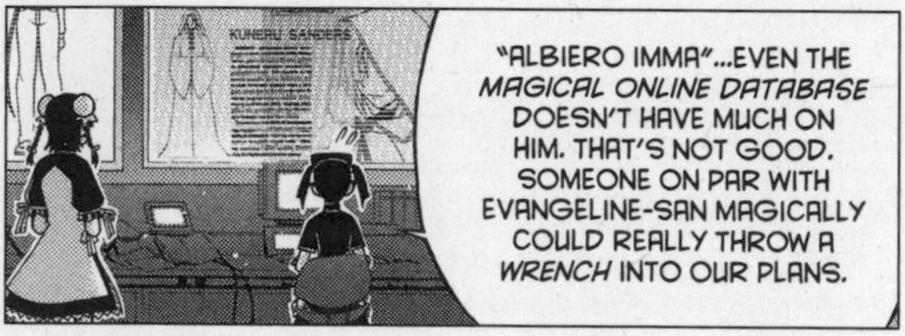
KUNERU SANDERS
"ALBIERO IMMA"...EVEN THE *MAGICAL ONLINE DATABASE* DOESN'T HAVE MUCH ON HIM. THAT'S NOT GOOD. SOMEONE ON PAR WITH EVANGELINE-SAN MAGICALLY COULD REALLY THROW A *WRENCH* INTO OUR PLANS.

Albireo Imma, page 4

In this period, the real name of the mysterious Kū:nel Sanders is at last revealed. The Beta star of the Cygnus constellation, Albireo is a double star (two stars bound gravitationally to each other), and is said to be a breathtaking sight. It's visible in the northern hemisphere in the summer and early fall.

Bu○jutsu, page 37

A Japanese typographical convention indicating something that's universally understood but, for various reasons, deliberately left unsaid, the "circle" dingbat in the word above should nevertheless be obvious to manga fans—representing as it does a martial-arts technique from a certain lo-o-ong running manga series published by a publisher other than that of *Negima!*, featuring seemingly never-ending combat as well as a search for magical spheres which allow the user to summon a certain mythical creature capable of granting wishes.

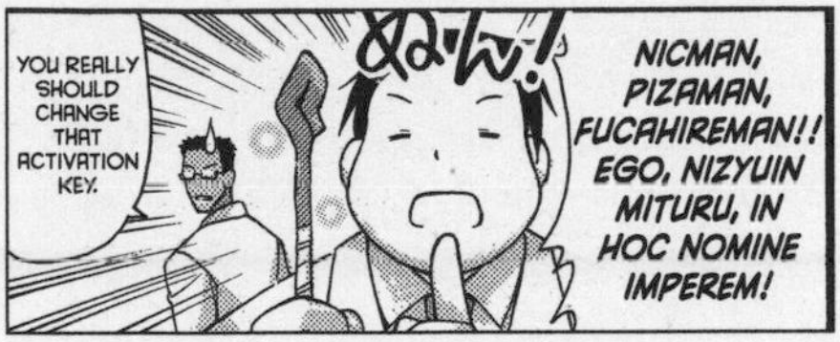
NICMAN, PIZAMAN, FUCAHIREMAN!! EGO, NIZYUIN MITURU, IN HOC NOMINE IMPEREM!
YOU REALLY SHOULD CHANGE THAT ACTIVATION KEY.

Nijūin-sensei's Activation Key, page 52

Transliterated in Latin as "Nicman/Pizaman/Fucahireman," the three are popular and delicious food items better known in Japanese as *nikuman* (steamed meat—usually pork—bun), *pizaman* (pizza-like steamed bun), and *fukahireman* (steamed shark-fin bun—a Chinese delicacy usually found in soups). In that all three *are* food items—and that Nijūin-sensei is not exactly the most slender of the Academy's instructors—Gandolfini-kun's suggestion that he "ought to change that activation key" should probably be taken as a hint for Nijūin-sensei to lay off the Japanese junk food, however tasty it may be.

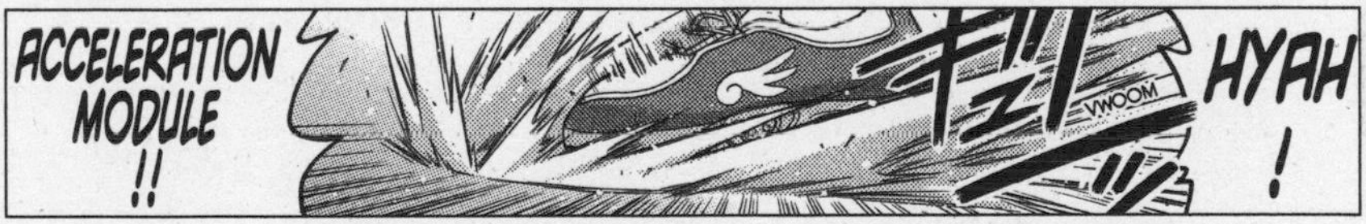
HYAH!
VWOOM
ACCELERATION MODULE!!

Acceleration Module, page 63

Acceleration device best known to anime and manga fans as that which allows Joe Shimamura (009) of creator Shōtarō Ishinomori's *Cyborg 009* to move at super speed by activating a switch on this teeth. In *Negima!*, Misora's yelling this ("*Kasoku Sochi!*") as she runs quickly away is an obvious homage.

God of the Spear, page 77

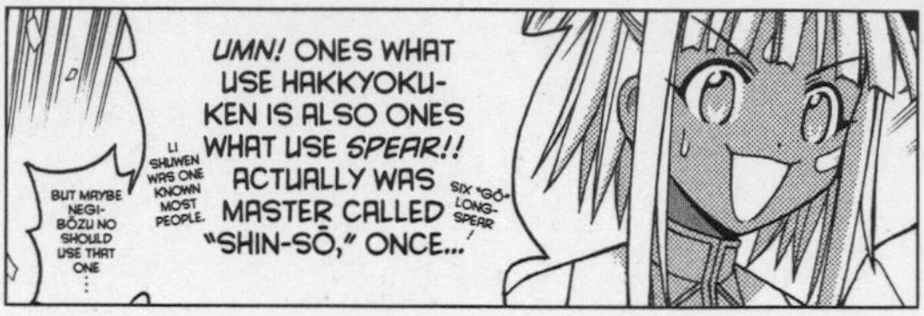
UMN! ONES WHAT USE HAKKYOKU-KEN IS ALSO ONES WHAT USE *SPEAR!!* ACTUALLY WAS MASTER CALLED "SHIN-SŌ," ONCE...
SIX "GŌ" LONG-SPEAR
LI SHUWEN WAS ONE KNOWN MOST PEOPLE.
BUT MAYBE NEGI-BŌZU NO SHOULD USE THAT ONE ...

A real-life martial artist really known as the "God of the Spear," Li Shuwen (1864–1934) was according to one account a "notorious fighter" known mostly for the sheer ruthlessness of his matches. "According to oral tradition," the account goes, "almost everyone who challenged him ended up dead. His reputation was built upon his extreme striking power and his practice of telling opponents exactly what technique would be employed to bring about their demise.... Unfortunately, these exploits eventually brought about Li Shuwen's own downfall. At the request of others, one of his students murdered him by serving him poisoned tea."

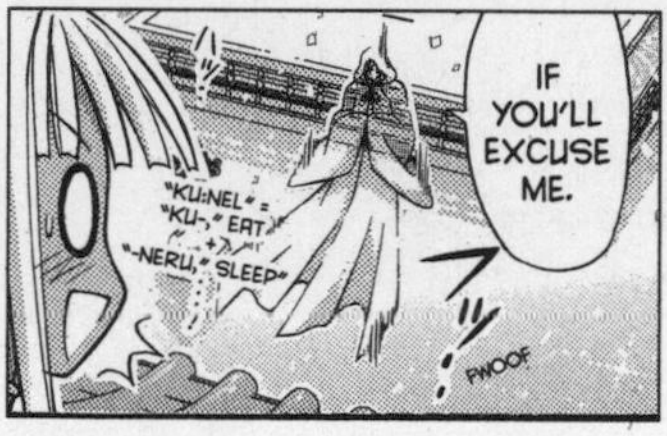
IF YOU'LL EXCUSE ME.
"KU:NEL" = "KU-," EAT + "-NERU," SLEEP
PWOOF

Kū:nel/Kūneru, page 112

In Japanese, *kū-neru* is a combination word formed from the infinitive ("to do" form) of verbs for "eat" and "sleep." Although one way to look at it is a kind of stripped-down life that doesn't include much outside eating and sleeping (thus, "*kūneru*"), another way is to see it as two of the truly essential, fundamental parts of existence—thus, *Kū:nel*, the title of a Japanese lifestyle magazine. Of course, "*kūneru*" is also punningly similar to the first part of a name for a certain fast food magnate... not that adding "Sanders" at the end cinches that or anything.

Volume 14

Nodate, page 195

Nodate is a traditional Japanese tea ceremony. It is held outdoors, usually in the autumn or spring, when the ambience and scenery can be enjoyed along with the traditional tea service.

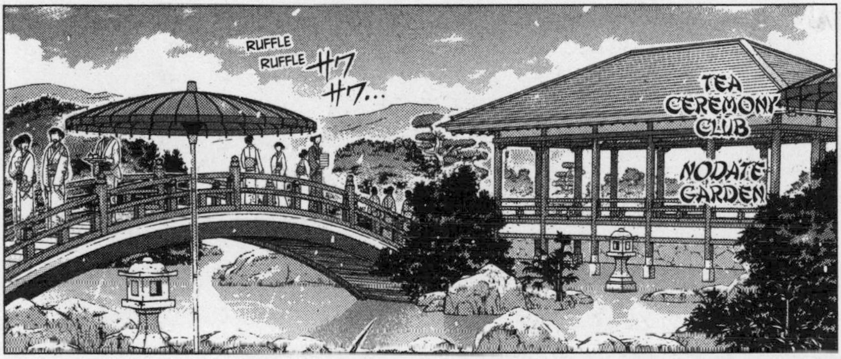
TEA CEREMONY CLUB
NODATE GARDEN
RUFFLE
RUFFLE
サワ
サワ...

On page 13, panel 2, note that Negi is drinking his tea as one should during a tea ceremony: with the thumb of his right hand resting on top of the tea cup, and the fingers and thumb of his left hand resting on the side of the cup and pointing away.

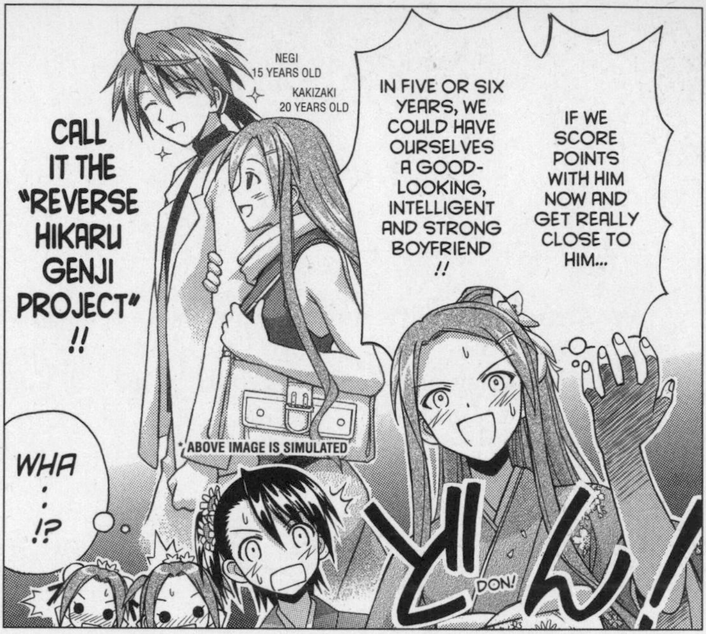
IF WE SCORE POINTS WITH HIM NOW AND GET REALLY CLOSE TO HIM...
IN FIVE OR SIX YEARS, WE COULD HAVE OURSELVES A GOOD-LOOKING, INTELLIGENT AND STRONG BOYFRIEND !!
NEGI 15 YEARS OLD
KAKIZAKI 20 YEARS OLD
CALL IT THE "REVERSE HIKARU GENJI PROJECT" !!
*ABOVE IMAGE IS SIMULATED
WHA . . !?
どん!
DON!

Reverse Hikaru Genji Project, page 202

Kakizaki's plan is inspired by a famous episode in the classic Japanese novel *The Tale of Genji* by Murasaki Shikibu. In the book, Genji takes in a young girl named Wakamurasaki so that he can raise her to become his ideal woman.

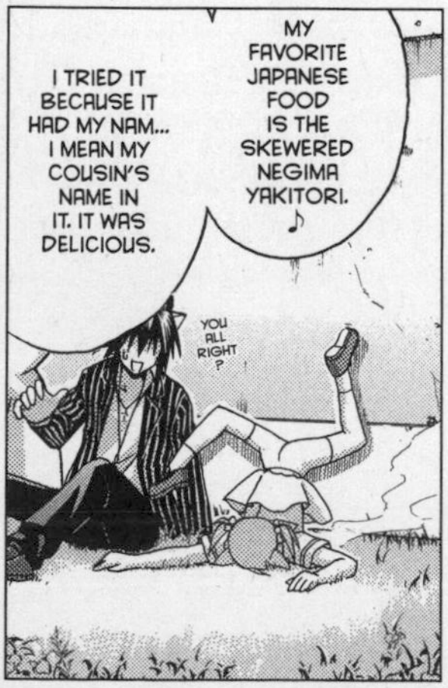
MY FAVORITE JAPANESE FOOD IS THE SKEWERED NEGIMA YAKITORI. ♪
I TRIED IT BECAUSE IT HAD MY NAM... I MEAN MY COUSIN'S NAME IN IT. IT WAS DELICIOUS.
YOU ALL RIGHT ?

Negima, page 279

When, in her failed attempt to confess her love, Ako asks Negi whether he likes dried squid, Negi replies that he likes the *yakitori* skewer called *negima*. *Negima* literally means "*negi* (green onion) in between." So the dish consists of pieces of chicken alternating on a skewer with pieces of green onion.